LEXIKON

SECOND EDITION

Dictionary of
Health Care Terms,
Organizations,
and Acronyms

JOINT COMMISSION

Joint Commission Mission

The mission of the Joint Commission on Accreditation of Healthcare Organizations is to improve the quality of care provided to the public through the provision of health care accreditation and related services that support performance improvement in health care organizations.

Joint Commission educational programs and publications support, but are separate from, the accreditation activities of the Joint Commission. Attendees at Joint Commission educational programs and purchasers of Joint Commission publications receive no special consideration or treatment in, or confidential information about, the accreditation process.

Printed in the U.S.A. 5 4 3 2 1

Requests for permission to reprint or make copies of any part of this book should be addressed to:

Permissions Editor
Joint Commission on Accreditation of Healthcare Organizations
One Renaissance Boulevard
Oakbrook Terrace, IL 60181

ISBN: 0-86688-549-8

Library of Congress Catalog Number: 97-80664

For more information about the Joint Commission, please visit our Web site at http://www.jcaho.org

CONTENTS

CONTENTS

INTRODUCTION

Nothing endures but change.
—Heraclitus

Few service fields in the United States can boast (or bemoan) the rapid, widespread rate of change experienced by all areas of health care. The explosive growth of managed care, the multiplicity of delivery models, shifting political opinions on health care reform, and constant advances in technology and practice have immeasurably expanded the language of the health care field from what it was even five years ago. It has left people from every discipline scrambling to keep up with the latest acronyms, the newest organization structures, and the most recent innovations in the quality and performance arenas.

Just as health care itself has grown and changed, so too has the Joint Commission, its accreditation and survey process, and—necessarily—its *Lexikon*. The emphasis of the current standards is on the performance of important patient care and organization functions. Like those in the health care field, we are interested in the outcomes of care and how process improvement ensures high-quality care and services for patients.

In revising the *Lexikon*, we have followed the principles of continuously improving our products based on our customers' needs. The body of the book contains the words and phrases you will encounter in reading about and discussing nearly every aspect of health care, including business and organization terms, important legal cases and legislation, and quality terminology. In keeping with the overwhelming shift toward performance measurement, we have expanded the listings pertaining to performance indicators.

Given this expansion, we looked for ways to give you the information you need and to make it even easier to find what you're looking for. To this end, we have streamlined cross-references and placed acronyms and organizations in separate appendixes. To illustrate topics and terms that involve myriad components (for example, the various Short-Form tests), we have inserted concise listings of the components to avoid making the definitions unwieldy or difficult to follow. All of the terms have been reviewed for currency to make sure you have the most up-to-date information available. We have even noted terms that, although still in general use, are moving toward obsolescence. For instance, although the term *adult-onset diabetes* is often seen and heard, the correct classification is *type 2 diabetes mellitus*.

No resource can be all things to all users, so we set concrete parameters for words and phrases to be included. For the most part, the *Lexikon* does not include definitions that may be found in any general or medical dictionary, as you probably already have those references at your fingertips. Exceptions to this rule are words and phrases that are related in some way to current "hot topics" or quality and outcomes research and measurement. Also, terms pertaining to economics, marketing, judicial process, and so on are included *only as they apply to health care*. For instance, terms for computer hardware and software (such as *mainframe, network,* and so on) are not included, but health care-specific national databases and technology such as *smart cards* are.

For all our changes, the purposes of the *Lexikon* are still the same:

- To document the language of health care;

- To clarify its meanings;

- To identify the key organizations that are part of, or relate to, the health care field;

- To decipher health care's profusion of acronyms and abbreviations; and

- To promote a common language that facilitates communication and consensus across health care.

In the years since the first *Lexikon* was published, we have seen a variety of proposals for health care reform come and go; we have tried to keep track of organization mergers; and we have witnessed a rapidly growing effort on the part of patients and families to be better informed about the issues that affect their health and health care. The next few years will undoubtedly bring even more types of change, possibly in areas no one has even thought about as yet. The inevitable changes in the health care environment will necessitate corresponding changes in our language—and, thus, in the *Lexikon*.

USING THE *LEXIKON*

The *Lexikon* has been designed to serve as a reference to health care language we will be using through the end of the millennium. Its content reflects the many complex, interrelated elements that comprise the field as a whole. This section explains the conventions used in presenting the information.

An Overview of the Entries

Each reference book seems to have its own style of alphabetizing, cross-referencing, and defining terms. Our methods are geared toward simplicity of use.

Alphabetization

Words and phrases are alphabetized letter by letter (disregarding spaces and hyphens) rather than by word. For example, the entry for *database* occurs before *data collection*. Multiple-word entries, such as "performance improvement," are listed under the first letter of the first word. In most cases, names of concepts, diseases, and so on that have acronyms or abbreviations are spelled out with the acronym and the definition following. Exceptions to this rule occur when a term is more commonly known under its acronym. For example, the definition for *acquired immunodeficiency syndrome* is listed under *AIDS* because the acronym is used far more often than the full term.

Cross-References

The cross-references have been streamlined, so you can find terms easily. In the preceding example, there is a cross-reference at the listing for acquired immunodeficiency syndrome telling you to *See* AIDS.

When *See also* follows a definition, it indicates that additional information related to the defined word or phrase can be found under other entries. Such information may include more specific categories for a condition, contrasting or comparable terms, and so on.

Language of the Definitions

We recognize that there are many ways of discussing patients, processes, conditions, and so on that are specific to individual fields. For example, patients are usually called *residents* in long term care, *members* in managed care, and *clients* in behavioral health care. For the sake of consistency and clarity, *patient* is used throughout the *Lexikon*, regardless of what field is discussed. Also, concepts, processes, and procedures that are not specific to a particular setting (for example, ambulatory care center, hospital, nursing home) refer to "organizations" and use the most universal language possible to encompass all settings.

In the interest of space, we have not spelled out well-known names and terms whenever they appear. For example, the following abbreviations and acronyms are used throughout the *Lexikon*:

AHCPR	Agency for Health Care Policy and Research
CLIA	Clinical Laboratory Improvement Act (or Amendments, depending on the year)
DRG	diagnosis-related group
DSM	*Diagnostic and Statistical Manual of Mental Disorders*
HCFA	Health Care Financing Administration
HMO	health maintenance organization
ICD	*International Classification of Diseases*

Joint Commission	Joint Commission on Accreditation of Healthcare Organizations
OBRA	Omnibus Budget Reconciliation Act
PPO	preferred provider organization

You will find full terms for abbreviations with which you are unfamiliar listed in Appendix B.

Accreditation-Specific Terms

Some of the words and phrases included in the *Lexikon* are unique to the Joint Commission and its standards and accreditation process. For example, you will find definitions of the various types of accreditation decisions the Joint Commission makes after surveying organizations and networks. When a term is defined differently for survey or accreditation purposes than it is for general use, the definitions are listed separately and the Joint Commission-specific definition is identified as such.

Appendixes

To make it easier for you to find acronyms and organizations, we have separated them from the main part of the text and placed them in end-of-book appendixes.

Appendix A: Associations, Organizations, and Government Agencies

There are literally hundreds of entries in this appendix, covering all fields, disciplines, and aspects of health care. The entries are limited to entities directly involved in health care, because related fields such as business and law have their own professional listings. In all cases we focused on national, rather than regional, associations. The organizations listed are the largest health care organizations and networks—especially those that are involved in widespread, well-known quality initiatives and outcomes research. The listings for government agencies have been updated according to federal restructuring, and are listed separately at the end of this appendix.

Each entry in this appendix lists the name of the association, organization, or agency, its location, the date it was founded, and a brief description of its mission or purpose. The format is designed to provide the basic information needed to understand a reference to a specific association, organization, or agency or to find the entity to obtain more detailed information.

Appendix B: Abbreviations and Acronyms

Every word or phrase in the text chapters that has an abbreviation or acronym is represented in this appendix, with few exceptions. Likewise, organizations, agencies, and so forth from Appendix B are included if they use acronyms to represent themselves. This section also includes entries for abbreviations and acronyms regularly seen in the health care literature. Such entries may not be defined in the text chapters if they refer to terms that are too clinically specific or technical to be within the scope of this book.

Revisions or Additions

We are always looking for ways to make our publications more useful to our readers. We encourage you to send suggestions for revisions or additions to Publications Department, Joint Commission on Accreditation of Healthcare Organizations, One Renaissance Boulevard, Oakbrook Terrace, IL 60181. We have included a postage-paid reader response card because we would like to hear from you. Please use it!

Acknowledgments

We have used primary sources whenever possible to check and update existing definitions and to create new ones. Our sources included statutes, policy statements, fact sheets, glossaries, dictionaries, brochures, and so on. The following is a list of the materials used in preparing this second edition of the *Lexikon*.

Books

Reference Books

American Medical Association, Department of Practice Parameters: *Directory of Clinical Practice Guidelines: Titles, Sources, and Updates.* 1997 ed. Chicago: AMA, 1997.

American Medical Association: *Manual of Style.* 8th ed. Baltimore: Williams & Wilkins, 1989.

ECRI: *1997 Healthcare Standards Directory.* Plymouth Meeting, PA, 1996.

Everitt BS: *The Cambridge Dictionary of Statistics in the Medical Sciences.* Cambridge: Cambridge University Press, 1995.

Iturralde MP: *Dictionary and Handbook of Nuclear Medicine and Clinical Imaging.* Boca Raton: CRC Press, 1990.

Jablonski S (comp & ed): *Dictionary of Medical Acronyms & Abbreviations.* 2nd ed. Philadelphia: Hanley & Belfus, 1993.

Mosby's Medical, Nursing, & Allied Health Dictionary. 4th ed. St Louis: Mosby, 1994.

Nash P (comp): *Health Care Terms Everyone Should Know.* Marblehead, MA: Opus Communications, 1996.

Office of Federal Register, National Archives and Records Administration: *The United States Government Manual 1994/1995.* Washington, DC: U.S. Government Printing Office, 1994.

Physician Payment Review Commission: *Annual Report to Congress.* Washington, DC: PPRC, 1997.

Rognehaugh R: *The Managed Health Care Dictionary.* Gaithersburg, MD: Aspen, 1996.

Segen JC: *Current Med Talk: A Dictionary of Medical Terms, Slang & Jargon.* Stanford, CT: Appleton & Lange, 1995.

Slee VN, Slee DA, Schmidt HJ (eds): *Slee's Health Care Terms. Third Comprehensive Edition.* St Paul, MN: Tringa Press, 1996.

Stedman's Medical Dictionary. 27th ed. Baltimore: Williams & Wilkins, 1997.

United HealthCare Corporation: *A Glossary of Terms: The Language of Managed Care and Organized Health Care Systems.* Minnetonka, MN: United HealthCare Corporation, 1992.

General Books

Brassard M, Ritter D: *The Memory Jogger™ II: A Pocket Guide of Tools for Continuous Improvement and Effective Planning.* Methuen, MA: GOAL/QPC, 1994.

Brennan TA, Berwick DM: *New Rules: Regulation, Markets, and the Quality of American Health Care.* San Francisco: Jossey-Bass Publishers, 1996.

Collinge W: *The American Holistic Health Association's Complete Guide to Alternative Medicine.* New York: Warner Books, 1996.

Goonan KJ: *The Juran Prescription: Clinical Quality Management.* San Francisco: Jossey-Bass Publishers, 1995.

Huber PW: *Galileo's Revenge: Junk Science in the Courtroom.* New York: Basic Books, 1991.

Joint Commission: *Framework for Improving Performance: From Principles to Practice.* Oakbrook Terrace, IL: Joint Commission, 1994.

Joint Commission: *Maintaining Your Quality Edge.* Oakbrook Terrace, IL: Joint Commission, 1997.

Joint Commission: *The Measurement Mandate: On the Road to Performance Improvement in Health Care.* Oakbrook Terrace, IL: Joint Commission, 1993.

Joint Commission: *Using Outcomes to Improve Performance in Long Term Care and Subacute Care Settings.* Oakbrook Terrace, IL: Joint Commission, 1997.

Joint Commission: *Using Performance Improvement Tools in Home Care and Hospice Organizations.* Oakbrook Terrace, IL: Joint Commission, 1996.

Kass LR: *Toward a More Natural Science: Biology and Human Affairs.* New York: Free Press, 1985.

Kevles DJ: *In the Name of Eugenics: Genetics and the Uses of Human Heredity.* New York: Knopf, 1985.

Kramer PD: *Listening to Prozac.* New York: Viking/Penguin, 1993.

Matthews J: *Beat the Nursing Home Trap: A Consumer's Guide to Choosing and Financing Long-Term Care.* Berkeley, CA: Nolo Press, 1993.

McDowell I, Newell C: *Measuring Health: A Guide to Rating Scales and Questionnaires.* 2nd ed. New York: Oxford University Press, 1996.

Phillips KM: *The Power of Health Care Teams: Strategies for Success.* Oakbrook Terrace, IL: Joint Commission, 1997.

Professional Guide to Diseases. 5th ed. Springhouse, PA: Springhouse Corporation, 1992.

Starr P: *The Social Transformation of American Medicine: The Rise of a Sovereign Profession and the Making of a Vast Industry.* New York: Basic Books, 1982.

Wilkin D, Hallam L, Doggett MA: *Measures of Need and Outcome for Primary Health Care.* New York: Oxford University Press, 1992.

Reports, Manuals, Textbooks, Sourcebooks, and Series

Agency for Health Care Policy and Research: *Using Clinical Practice Guidelines to Evaluate Quality of Care. Vol I: Issues. Vol II: Methods.* AHCPR Pub Nos. 95-0045 and 95-0046. Rockville, MD: 1995.

American Medical Association, Council on Ethical and Judicial Affairs: *Code of Medical Ethics: Current Opinions with Annotations.* 1994 ed. Chicago: AMA, 1994.

American Medical Association, Office of Quality Assurance and Medical Review: *Implementing Practice Parameters on the Local/State/Regional Level.* Chicago: AMA, 1993.

American Psychiatric Association: *Diagnostic and Statistical Manual of Mental Disorders, Fourth Edition* (DSM-IV). Washington, DC: American Psychiatric Press, 1994.

Bennett JC, Plum F (eds): *Cecil Textbook of Medicine.* 20th ed. Philadelphia: WB Saunders, 1996.

Calloway SD: *Ohio Nursing Law.* Cleveland, OH: Banks-Baldwin Law Publishing Co/West Publishers, 1991.

Calloway SD: *The Law for Nurses Who Supervise and Manage Others.* Eau Claire, WI: Professional Education Systems, Inc, 1994.

Center for Risk Analysis: *Reform of Risk Regulation: Achieving More Protection at Less Cost.* Boston: Center for Risk Analysis, 1995.

Easterling A, Avie J, Wesley ML, Chimner N: *The Case Manager's Guide: Acquiring the Skills for Success.* Chicago: American Hospital Publishing, Inc, 1995.

Eddy DM: *A Manual for Assessing Health Practices & Designing Practice Policies: The Explicit Approach.* Philadelphia: ACP Press, 1992.

Eddy DM: *The Explicit Approach and Clinical Decision Making: From Theory to Practice Series.* JAMA starting in 1990 [*JAMA* 263:287-290, 1990].

Eisenberg JM: *Doctors' Decisions and the Cost of Medical Care. The Reasons for Doctors' Practice Patterns and Ways to Change Them.* Ann Arbor, MI: Health Administration Press Perspectives, 1986.

Everything You Need to Know About Medical Treatments. Springhouse, PA: Springhouse Corporation, 1996.

Evidence-Based Medicine Working Group (Oxman AD, Sackett DL, Guyatt GH): *Evidence-Based Medicine and Users' Guidelines to the Medical Literature Series.* JAMA starting in 1992 [*JAMA* 268:2420-2425, 1992].

Ferguson T: *Health Online: How to Find Health Information, Support Groups, and Self-Help Communities in Cyberspace.* Reading, MA: Addison-Wesley, 1996.

Goldmann DR, Brown FH, Guarnieri DM: *Perioperative Medicine.* 2nd ed. New York: McGraw- Hill, 1994.

Healthy People 2000: National Health Promotion and Disease Prevention Objectives. Department of Health and Human Services, U.S. Public Health Service. Washington, DC: U.S. Government Printing Office, 1991. (Midcourse Review and 1995 Revisions, 1995.)

Institute of Medicine: *Medicare: A Strategy for Quality Assurance.* Volumes I and II. Washington, DC: National Academy Press, 1990.

Institute of Medicine: *Setting Priorities for Clinical Practice Guidelines.* Washington, DC: National Academy Press, 1995.

Institute of Medicine, Committee for the Study of Treatment and Rehabilitation Services for Alcoholism and Alcohol Abuse: *Broadening the Base of Treatment for Alcohol Problems.* Washington, DC: National Academy Press, 1990.

Institute of Medicine, Committee on Care at the End of Life: *Approaching Death: Improving Care at the End of Life.* Field MD, Cassel C (eds). Washington, DC: National Academy Press, 1997.

Institute of Medicine, Committee on Clinical Practice Guidelines: *Guidelines for Clinical Practice: From Development to Use.* Field MJ, Lohr KN (eds). Washington, DC: National Academy Press, 1992.

Institute of Medicine, Committee to Advise the Public Health Service on Clinical Practice Guidelines: *Clinical Practice Guidelines: Directions for a New Program.* Field MJ, Lohr KN (eds). Washington, DC: National Academy Press, 1990.

Institute of Medicine, Committee to Design a Strategy for Quality Review and Assurance in Medicare: *Medicare: A Strategy for Quality Assurance, vol II: Sources and Methods*. Lohr KN (eds). Washington, DC: National Academy Press, 1990.

Institute of Medicine: *Setting Priorities for Clinical Practice Guidelines*. Washington, DC: National Academy Press, 1995.

Joint Commission: *1996 Comprehensive Accreditation Manual for Ambulatory Health Care*. Oakbrook Terrace, IL: Joint Commission, 1995.

Joint Commission: 1997-98 *Comprehensive Accreditation Manual for Behavioral Health Care*. Oakbrook Terrace, IL: Joint Commission, 1996.

Joint Commission: 1996 *Comprehensive Accreditation Manual for Health Care Networks*. Oakbrook Terrace, IL: Joint Commission, 1995.

Joint Commission: 1997-98 *Comprehensive Accreditation Manual for Home Care*. Oakbrook Terrace, IL: Joint Commission, 1996.

Joint Commission: *Comprehensive Accreditation Manual for Hospitals: The Official Handbook*. Oakbrook Terrace, IL: Joint Commission, 1997.

Joint Commission: *1996 Comprehensive Accreditation Manual for Long Term Care*. Oakbrook Terrace, IL: Joint Commission, 1995.

Joint Commission: *1996 Comprehensive Accreditation Manual for Long Term Care Pharmacies*. Oakbrook Terrace, IL: Joint Commission, 1995.

Joint Commission: *1996 Comprehensive Accreditation Manual for Pathology and Clinical Laboratory Services*. Oakbrook Terrace, IL: Joint Commission, 1995.

Joint Commission: *1997 Comprehensive Accreditation Manual for Preferred Provider Organizations*. Oakbrook Terrace, IL: Joint Commission, 1996.

Joint Commission: *National Library of Healthcare Indicators™: Health Plan and Network Edition (NLHI)*. Oakbrook Terrace, IL: Joint Commission, 1997.

Office of Technology Assessment, U.S. Congress: *Identifying Health Technologies That Work: Searching for Evidence*. Washington, DC: U.S. Government Printing Office, 1994.

Pellegrino ED, Thomasa DC: *For the Patient's Good: The Restoration of Beneficence in Health Care*. New York: Oxford University Press, 1988.

Physician Payment Review Commission: *Annual Report to Congress* (1995). Washington, DC, 1995.

Rees AM (ed). *Consumer Health USA: Essential Information from the Federal Health Network*. Phoenix: Oryx Press, 1995.

Rees AM, Willey C (eds): *Personal Health Reporter: Excerpts from Current Articles on 148 Medical Conditions and Treatments and Other Health Issues*. Detroit: Gale Research Inc, 1993.

Rozovsky FA: *Consent to Treatment: A Practical Guide*. 2nd ed. Boston: Little, Brown, 1990.

Schroeder SA, et al (eds): *Current Medical Diagnosis & Treatment 1991*. 30th ed. Norwalk, CT: Appleton & Lange, 1991.

U.S. General Accounting Office: *Health Care: Employers and Individual Consumers Want Additional Information on Quality*. Washington DC: U.S. Government Printing Office, 1995.

U.S. General Accounting Office: *Health Care Reform: "Report Cards" Are Useful but Significant Issues Need to Be Addressed* (Report to the Chairman, Committee on Labor and Human Resources, U.S. Senate). Washington, DC: U.S. Government Printing Office, 1994.

U.S. Preventive Services Task Force: *Guide to Clinical Preventive Services. Report of the U.S. Preventive Services Task Force.* 2nd ed. Baltimore: Williams & Wilkins, 1996.

Wilson JD et al (eds). *Harrison's Principles of Internal Medicine.* 12th ed. New York: McGraw- Hill, 1991.

Woolf SH, Jonas S, Lawrence RS (eds): *Health Promotion and Disease Prevention in Clinical Practice.* Baltimore: Williams & Wilkins, 1996.

Guidelines, Standards, Policies, Interviews, Personal Correspondence, and Internet

Government Agencies, Commissions, Task Forces, National Programs

Agency for Health Care Policy and Research: clinical practice guidelines

National Asthma Education Program, National Heart, Lung, and Blood Institute: guidelines

Office of Medical Applications of Research (OMAR), National Institutes of Health: Consensus Development Conferences

Other National Institutes of Health programs

Foundations, Think Tanks, and Research Corporations

Maine Liability Demonstration Project

RAND

Medical Specialty Societies, Professional Associations, and Health Care Organizations

American Academy of Ophthalmology

American Academy of Pediatrics

American Association of Clinical Endocrinologists

American College of Cardiology

American College of Obstetricians and Gynecologists

American College of Physicians

American Diabetes Association

American Heart Association

American Hospital Association

American Medical Association

American Optometric Association

American Society of Anesthesiologists

American Society of Clinical Oncology

American Thyroid Association

Association for Health Services Research

Centers for Disease Control and Prevention

Institute for Clinical Systems Integration

Medical Outcomes Trust

National Association of Genetics Counselors

National Cancer Institute

National Heart, Lung, and Blood Institute

National Institutes of Health

Databases

MEDLINE (National Library of Medicine)

Journals, Magazines, and Newspapers

Abstracts of Clinical Care Guidelines

American Journal of Psychiatry

Annals of Internal Medicine

Caring

Chest

Circulation

Health Affairs

Healthcare Financial Management

Healthcare Leadership Review

The Hospice Journal™: Physical, Psychosocial, and Pastoral Care of the Dying

International Journal of Technology Assessment in Health Care

The Joint Commission Journal on Quality Improvement (formerly *Quality Review Bulletin*)

Journal of the American Association of Nurse Anesthetists

Journal of the American College of Cardiology

Journal of the American Geriatrics Society

Journal of Health Care Finance

Journal of Outcomes Management

Milbank Quarterly

Morbidity and Mortality Weekly Report (MMWR)

New England Journal of Medicine

Quality in Health Care

Quality Management in Health Care

Newsletters

American Medical News (AMA)

Business and Health (Medical Economics)

Hospital Management Review (COR Healthcare Resources)

Joint Commission Perspectives (Joint Commission)

Medical Liability Monitor (Malpractice Lifeline, Inc)

Medical Outcomes & Guidelines Alert (Faulkner & Gray)

Medical Outcomes Trust Bulletin (Medical Outcomes Trust)

Modern Healthcare (Crain Communications)

Parameters, Guidelines & Protocols (Legamed Publishing)

QRC Advisor (Aspen)

The Quality Letter for Healthcare Leaders (Capitol Publications)

Report on Medical Guidelines & Outcomes Research (Capitol Publications)

Aa

abandonment   The legal term for leaving a patient without treatment after a doctor-patient relationship has been established. A physician must provide adequate notice and ample opportunity for the patient to arrange for care from another physician to avoid a charge of abandonment.

Abbreviated Injury Scale (AIS)   In trauma care, an anatomic scoring instrument for assessing impact injury in seven regions of the body (external, head and face, neck, thorax, abdomen and pelvis, spine, and extremities). Six levels of possible severity are assigned to each anatomic injury, resulting in more than 500 separate injury descriptions. Originally designed in 1971 (and revised in 1985 and 1990) by the American Association for Automotive Medicine for rating tissue damage in automobile accident research, the AIS is used retrospectively, chiefly for Injury Severity Score (ISS) calculations. *See also* Injury Severity Score; trauma score; TRISS.

abbreviated new-drug application (ANDA)   An application filed by a pharmaceutical company requesting marketing and sales authority for a new drug for which the conditions of its use (as indicated in the labeling) were previously approved (for a different but similar drug) under the standard FDA approval process for prescription drugs, and whose active ingredients are the same as those of a drug that previously was approved by the Secretary of the Department of Health and Human Services. The Secretary is required to approve or disapprove an ANDA within 180 days of its submittal. *See also* Drug Price Competition and Patent Term Restoration Act of 1984; new-drug application.

abnormal psychology   The branch of psychology dealing with behavior disorders and emotional and psychological disturbances.

abortion   The premature expulsion from the uterus of the products of conception with the embryo or a nonviable fetus. Abortions are either *spontaneous* (occurring naturally)—popularly termed *miscarriage*—or *induced* (accomplished by artificial means). Abortion performed because of possible fetal defects is sometimes termed *eugenic abortion*. A legal, induced abortion performed for medical reasons, as when the pregnancy threatens the pregnant woman's life, is called *therapeutic abortion*. *See also* partial birth abortion; *Roe* v *Wade*.

abuse   **1.** Misuse or wrong use, particularly excessive use of anything. The term *abuse* has been replaced by *use* in the *DSM-IV* for substance-use disorders and other disorders. The potential for abuse and dependence is the defining criterion for the U.S. Drug Enforcement Agency's five schedules of controlled substances. *See also* schedule of controlled substances; substance-related disorders.

2. Intentional maltreatment of an individual which may cause injury, as in child abuse or elder abuse. *Mental abuse* includes humiliation, harassment, and threats of punishment or deprivation; *physical abuse* includes hitting, slapping, pinching, or kicking, as well as controlling behavior through corporal punishment; and *sexual abuse* includes sexual harassment, sexual coercion, and sexual assault. *See also* child abuse; elder abuse; fraud and abuse; neglect.

academic detailing   A type of social influence strategy for implementing clinical practice guidelines, protocols, or policies in which an expert or opinion leader delivers information one on one or in a very small group. The practice is modeled after drug detailing, in which representatives of pharmaceutical companies visit physicians to talk about medications in their specialty areas. The individually targeted, interpersonal detailing approach is one of several behavioral models of decision making that assume that peers' judgments and beliefs exert a strong influence on how new information is received and used. Academic detailing is labor intensive and costly on a per-target basis, but it has proved to be one of the most effective approaches for implementing guidelines and may be the only option in some situations, such as for physicians who do not get together often and cannot be addressed as a group. *See also* detailer, implementation techniques.

academic medical center   A medical system typically consisting of a university hospital and medical school, often including other associated teaching hospitals, research organizations and their laboratories, outpatient clinics, libraries, and administrative facilities. *Synonym*: academic health center.

academic medicine   The branch of medicine concerned with educating physicians, research, and providing health care services in academic settings, residing largely in medical schools and teaching hospitals. Those engaged in academic medicine may have university titles (professor, associate professor, assistant professor) and are often full-time university employees.

accelerated (drug) approval mechanism   A system instituted by the FDA allowing clinicians to use new drugs on the basis of preliminary data from clinical trials before the data have "matured," have met peer-review standards, or have been widely disseminated. This system puts a burden of responsibility on clinicians for keeping up to date, for monitoring and reporting adverse drug effects, and for ensuring careful use and compliance to avoid the development of drug resistance. Examples of drugs introduced under this mechanism are the HIV-I protease inhibitors, a new class of drugs to treat HIV infection.

acceptability   An overall assessment of the quality of care made by an individual or group. It is usually based on many dimensions of care including cost, appropriateness, availability, and effectiveness. *See also* appropriateness; availability; effectiveness.

acceptable alternative   A common and legitimate reason for failure of an organization or a practitioner to conform to practice guideline recommendations; for example, a physician recommends a vaginal delivery after a previous cesarean section and a patient refuses. Acceptable alternatives are specified explicitly when writing review criteria. They may be stated explicitly in a practice guideline or they may be implied. *See also* clinical practice guideline.

acceptable quality level (AQL)   The level at which quality is "good enough." The idea that quality is "good enough" has been challenged by those persons who believe that quality is never good enough, but must be constantly improved. *See also* continuous quality improvement.

accessibility   A Joint Commission performance dimension addressing the degree to which an individual or a defined population can approach, enter, and make use of needed health services. *See also* availability.

accountability   The state of being answerable for one's actions as a result of taking professional, legal, ethical, administrative, or personal responsibility for something. Accountability includes documentation or other evidence that duties or tasks have been adequately performed. The practice of accountability varies among health care entities. For example, health care professionals and institutions are primarily responsible to the patient and to professional principles, and health care providers are accountable to their patients, the organizations by which they are employed, and their professions.

accountability standards   Standards of performance used by the public, government agencies, or professionals to evaluate the finances, procedures, or medical outcomes of an individual provider, organization, or entity (such as a health plan). Formal accountability standards are particularly important in situations where there is a potential conflict of interest, for example, when a for-profit health care organization is responsible to both its patients and its shareholders.

accredit   To give official authorization or status, as to accredit a residency program or a health care organization.

accreditation   A determination by an accrediting body that an eligible organization, network, program, group, or individual complies with applicable standards. The Joint Commission offers accreditation options for ambulatory care, behavioral health care, home care, hospitals, health care networks, long term care, long term care pharmacies, managed behavioral health care, pathology and clinical laboratory services, and PPOs. *See also* certification; licensure.

accreditation appeal   For purposes of Joint Commission accreditation, the process through which an organization or a network that has been preliminarily denied Joint Commission accreditation exercises its right to a hearing by an Appeals Hearing Panel, followed by a review of the panel's report and recommendation by the Joint Commission's Board of Commissioners.

Accreditation Committee   The committee of the Joint Commission's Board of Commissioners responsible for oversight of its accreditation process.

accreditation cycle   The term at the conclusion of which accreditation expires unless a full survey is performed. For purposes of Joint Commission accreditation, the accreditation cycle for most organizations is three years, and for pathology and clinical laboratory services it is two years. *See also* accreditation survey.

accreditation decision   **1.** The conclusion reached by an accrediting body regarding an entity's accreditation status.   **2.** For purposes of Joint Commission accreditation, the conclusion regarding an organization's or a network's status after evaluation of the results of a Joint Commission on-site survey; recommendations of the surveyor(s); and any other relevant information, such as documentation of compliance with standards, documentation of plans to correct deficiencies, or evidence of recent improvements. *See also* type I recommendation.

accreditation decision grid   For purposes of Joint Commission accreditation, a single-page display of the performance areas that summarizes the standards in each Joint Commission accreditation manual, for example, a hospital accreditation decision grid summarizes the standards in the *Comprehensive Accreditation Manual for Hospitals.* The grid format allows for the presentation of a numerical summary of aggregated compliance scores for a number of related Joint Commission standards. Each score on the grid reflects an organization's or a network's assigned level of compliance for standards relating to a key performance area. *See also* compliance; grid element; performance area; summary grid score.

accreditation decision rules   For purposes of Joint Commission accreditation, rules based on grid element scores and specific standards compliance issues that determine the accreditation decision, as well as the scope (which and how many elements require monitoring) and type (focused survey or written progress report) of follow-up monitoring required for compliance deficiencies. *See also* accreditation; accreditation decision; aggregation rules; focused survey; written progress report.

accreditation duration   For purposes of Joint Commission accreditation, the two- or three-year time period during which an organization or a network, found to be in compliance with applicable Joint Commission standards, is awarded accreditation. *See also* accreditation cycle.

accreditation history   An account of past accreditation decisions for an organization or a network. The Joint Commission may publicly disclose the accreditation history of an accredited organization on request. *See also* early survey option I; early survey option II; track record.

accreditation manuals   The ten Joint Commission books delineating current standards for specified types of health care organizations, networks, or services. The books are designed for use in organization or network self-assessment. The ten manuals are *Accreditation Manual for Preferred Provider Organizations; Comprehensive Accreditation Manual for Ambulatory Care; Comprehensive Accreditation Manual for Behavioral Health Care; Comprehensive Accreditation Manual for Health Care Networks; Comprehensive Accreditation Manual for Home Care; Comprehensive Accreditation Manual for Hospitals; Comprehensive Accreditation Manual for Long Term Care; Comprehensive Accreditation Manual for Long Term Care Pharmacies; Comprehensive Accreditation Manual for Managed Behavioral Health Care;* and *Comprehensive Accreditation Manual for Pathology and Clinical Laboratory Services.*

JOINT COMMISSION ACCREDITATION DECISIONS

accreditation with commendation   The highest accreditation decision awarded by the Joint Commission to an organization or a network that has demonstrated exemplary performance.

accreditation (with or without type I recommendations)   A determination by an accrediting body that an eligible health care organization or network complies with applicable Joint Commission standards.

provisional accreditation   An accreditation decision that results when an organization or a network has demonstrated substantial compliance with the selected structural standards used in the first of two surveys conducted under the Joint Commission's Early Survey Policy, option 1. The second survey is conducted approximately six months after the first to allow the organization or network sufficient time to demonstrate a track record of performance. Provisional accreditation status continues until the organization or network completes a full survey.

conditional accreditation   An accreditation decision that results when an organization or a network is not in substantial compliance with Joint Commission standards but is believed to be capable of achieving acceptable compliance within a stipulated time period. Evidence of correction must be found through a short-term follow-up survey for the organization or network to be considered for full accreditation status.

preliminary nonaccreditation   An accreditation decision that is assigned to an organization when it is found to be in significant noncompliance with Joint Commission standards or when its accreditation is preliminarily withdrawn by the Joint Commission for other reasons (for example, falsification of documents) *prior* to the determination of the final accreditation decision (for example, not accredited). Preliminary nonaccreditation is an appealable accreditation decision.

not accredited   An accreditation decision that results when an organization or network has been denied accreditation, when its accreditation is withdrawn by the Joint Commission, or when it withdraws from the accreditation process. This designation also describes any organization or network that has never applied for accreditation.

accreditation survey   An evaluation of an organization or a network to assess its level of compliance with applicable standards and to make determinations regarding its accreditation status. For purposes of Joint Commission accreditation, the survey includes evaluation of documentation of compliance provided by organization or network staff; verbal information concerning the implementation of standards or examples of their implementation that will enable a determination of compliance to be made; on-site observations by surveyors; and an opportunity for education and consultation regarding standards compliance and performance improvement. *See also* conditional follow-up survey; early survey option I; early survey option II; extension survey; follow-up survey; multihospital survey option; multiorganization survey option; specialized survey; triennial survey; unannounced/unscheduled survey.

Accreditation Watch   An attribute of an organization's Joint Commission accreditation status. A health care organization is placed on Accreditation Watch when an on-site survey confirms the occurrence of a sentinel event and determines that there is reasonable potential for reducing the likelihood of such events in the future. A health care organization placed on Accreditation Watch is required to execute a thorough and credible root cause analysis of the sentinel event. Although Accreditation Watch status is not an official accreditation category, it can be publicly disclosed by the Joint Commission. *See also* sentinel event.

accreditation with commendation   *See* accreditation decision.

accuracy   *See* data accuracy; measurement accuracy.

ACE inhibitor (angiotensin-converting enzyme inhibitor)   A class of medications that lower blood pressure by blocking the hormone angiotensin, which causes vasoconstriction and increases blood pressure. ACE inhibitors have emerged as a first-line therapy for hypertension and are also used to treat heart failure.

acid fast bacilli (AFB)   Bacteria that are not readily decolorized by acid after staining, particularly *Mycobacterium tuberculosis. See also* tuberculosis isolation.

action in personam   A lawsuit against a person on the basis of personal liability. *See also* liability.

active listening   A counseling technique in which a counselor listens to both the facts and the feelings of the speaker. The listening is active because the counselor has the specific responsibilities of showing interest, of not passing judgment, and of helping the speaker to work through issues. Basic components of active listening include: not condoning, condemning, agreeing, or disagreeing; using reflective phrases, such as "in other words" or "sounds like"; using reflective rather than accusative "you" messages; asking expansion-type questions; using reflective body language, such as eye contact; and being genuine.

activities of daily living (ADLs)   The activities usually performed for oneself in the course of a normal day, such as eating, dressing, washing, combing hair, brushing teeth, and taking care of bodily functions. An ADL checklist is often used by providers to assess a patient prior to hospital discharge. If any activities cannot be adequately performed, arrangements should be made with an outside agency, such as a visiting nurse service, or with family members to provide the necessary assistance. *See also* instrumental activities of daily living; nursing care; major life activities; personal care services; physical therapy.

activity network diagram A graphic display showing total completion time, the necessary sequence of tasks, those tasks that can be done simultaneously, and the critical tasks to monitor. This tool allows a team to find both the most efficient path and realistic schedule for completion of a project.

activity services Structured activities designed to help an individual develop or maintain creative, physical, and social skills through participation in recreation, art, dance, drama, social, or other activities.

actual charge The dollar amount a physician, hospital, or other provider actually bills a patient for a particular health service, such as a procedure.

actuarial analysis Application of probability and statistical methods to calculate the risk of occurrence of events, such as illness, hospitalization, disability, or death, for a given population. A common use of actuarial analysis is the calculation of insurance premiums and, for the insurer, the necessary reserves.

acuity **1.** The degree of psychosocial risk of health treatment. **2.** The degree of dependency or functional status of the patient. *See also* level of acuity; severity.

acupressure A therapy in which symptoms are relieved by applying pressure with the thumbs or fingers to specific pressure points on the body. Types of acupressure include *shiatsu* (in Japan) and *G-Jo* (in China). *See also* acupuncture; alternative medicine.

acupuncture A technique originating in China for relieving pain or inducing regional anesthesia, in which thin needles are inserted into the body at specific points. *See also* acupressure; alternative medicine; osteopathy.

acute care Health care in which a patient is treated for a specific episode of illness, injury, or recovery from surgery. Acute care is usually delivered in the hospital setting by specialized personnel using high-tech equipment and materials. It may involve intensive and emergency care, and is often necessary for only a short time. *See also* chronic care.

acute care hospital A hospital that cares primarily for patients with acute diseases or conditions (rapid onset, with short, severe course) and whose average length of stay is less than 30 days. *See also* long term care facility; short-term hospital.

acute myocardial infarction (AMI) Death of tissue in the heart muscle which results from insufficient blood supply to the heart, sometimes leading to cardiac arrest. The decreased flow may be due to presence of a thrombus (blood clot) in one of the coronary arteries, hemorrhage within or beneath an atherosclerotic plaque, or coronary vasoconstriction or spasm. The term is usually used interchangeably with *myocardial infarction*, although some-

times the term *acute* is used to describe an undefined phase. *Synonyms:* coronary; heart attack; myocardial infarction (MI). *See also* coronary heart disease; infarction; ischemia.

ad damnum The clause in a legal complaint (the document that initiates a lawsuit) that contains a statement of the plaintiff's money loss or the damages he or she claims. Such a clause informs an adversary of the maximum amount of the claim asserted without being proof of actual injury or of liability.

addiction Dependence on a chemical substance to the extent that a physiological or psychological need is established. This may be manifested by any combination of the following symptoms: tolerance, preoccupation with obtaining and using the substance, use of the substance despite anticipation of probable adverse consequences, repeated efforts to cut down or control substance use, and withdrawal symptoms when the substance is unavailable or not used. *See also* alcoholism; dependence; narcotic; substance-related disorders.

addiction medicine The branch of medicine dealing with addiction. *See also* substance-related disorders.

addiction psychiatry The subspecialty of psychiatry concerned with the prevention and treatment of substance-related disorders. The subspecialty was established by the American Board of Psychiatry and Neurology as an added qualification in 1993. In 1996 the American Psychiatric Association released a position statement announcing its plans to strengthen training in addiction psychiatry and promote an integrated biopsychosocial approach to the patient. *See also* substance-related disorders.

addictive substance Any substance, natural or synthetic, that causes periodic or chronic intoxication through repeated consumption by most individuals exposed to it. *Synonym:* addictive drug. *See also* schedule of controlled substances.

additional drug benefit list *See* drug maintenance list.

adequacy of coverage Sufficiency of insurance protection to repay the insured in the event of loss.

ad hoc committee A committee formed to accomplish certain tasks and then disband.

adiposity *See* obesity.

adjudicate **1.** To hear and settle a case by judicial procedure. **2.** The act of determining the eligibility of health services reported on a health insurance claim for payment under a policy's benefit definitions, limitations, and exclusions. Adjudication may result in full payment, partial payment, denial of payment, or a combination of these for the services reported on a given claim. *See also* claims review.

adjusted autopsy rate The number of autopsies performed on patients over a specified period in relation to the total number of inpatient and outpatient deaths, less those bodies unavailable for autopsy. *Synonym*: net autopsy rate.

adjusted community rate (ACR)   The premium an HMO or a competitive medical plan (CMP) would charge for providing Medicare-covered benefits to its non-Medicare enrollees, adjusted to reflect the higher utilization rates of Medicare enrollees. HCFA uses this term in its Medicare risk contracts with HMOs/CMPs.

adjusted daily census   The average number of patients (inpatients plus an equivalent figure for outpatients) receiving care each day during a reporting period. *See also* average daily census.

adjustment   A procedure for correcting differences or discrepancies in the composition of two or more populations. Adjustment is frequently employed so that valid comparisons can be made between populations. For example, adjustment for age must occur to make valid comparisons between the mortality data of a nursing home and the mortality data of a freestanding ambulatory surgical center. *Synonym*: standardization. *See also* administrative adjustment; area wage adjustment; risk adjustment; severity adjustment.

adjuvant therapy   **1.** A drug that, when given in conjunction with another (main) drug, usually by incorporating the adjuvant (secondary) drug in the formulation, changes the action of the main drug in a predictable manner.   **2.** Chemotherapy, hormonal/steroid therapy, biological response modifier therapy, or other systemic agents in addition to primary treatment by surgical resection or radiation therapy for cancer.

ad lib   Abbreviation for Latin phrase *ad libitum*, meaning at pleasure, used to refer to the use of medication as required by a patient.

administration   **1.** The fiscal and general management of an organization, as distinct from the direct provision of services.   **2.** The guidance of an undertaking toward the achievement of its purpose, as in drug administration. *See also* drug administration; management; medication administration.

administrative adjustment   Bookkeeping adjustment made to (1) reflect services provided but not billed to patients because costs of billing and collection would exceed charges, or (2) to reflect partial adjustment of charges in special circumstances.

administrative agency   A governmental body charged with administering or implementing particular legislation, often including regulation of a profession or industry. Examples are workers' compensation commissions, state boards of medical examiners, and the Federal Trade Commission. *Synonym*: public agency. *See also* regulatory body.

administrative data   Data that generally reflect the content of discharge abstracts. Examples include demographic information on patients such as age, sex, zip code; information about the episode of care such as

admission source, length of stay, charges, discharge status; and diagnostic and procedural codes. The Uniform Hospital Discharge Data Set and the Uniform Bill of the Health Care Financing Administration (UB-92) are administrative data.

administrative determination of fault   A proposed method of dispute resolution in which claims would be filed with a designated agency that would determine whether negligence had occurred and, if so, whether the claimant would be paid from a compensation fund. *See also* alternative dispute resolution.

administrative law   A body of law created by administrative agencies in the form of rules, regulations, orders, and decisions to carry out the regulatory powers and duties of such agencies.

Administrative Policies and Procedures (APP)   A term used by the Joint Commission to describe its offer to provide an accreditation survey and an accreditation decision to a health care organization. Each accreditation manual published by the Joint Commission is introduced by an APP section, which embodies a comprehensive program-specific description of the accreditation process and the terms and conditions for an entity's participation in it. *See also* accreditation.

administrative process   The procedures used by administrative agencies to make decisions, such as the procedure a hospital must follow to obtain a certificate of need from an administrative agency or the means of summoning witnesses before such agencies. *See also* certificate of need.

admissible evidence   In law, evidence that is relevant (such as a medical record entry), not protected by specific laws (such as privileged information), and properly authenticated, and therefore is allowed to be presented to a judge or jury to assist in the argument of a legal case. *See also* authenticate; burden of proof; *Daubert* v *Merrell Dow* case; medical evidence; preponderance of evidence; junk science; privileged communication.

admission   The formal acceptance by a health care organization of a patient to receive health services. *See also* elective admission; urgent admission.

admission certification   *See* admission review.

admission pattern monitoring   The monitoring of the distribution of kinds of patients admitted to a health care organization.

admission review   Review of the medical necessity and appropriateness of a patient's admission to a health care organization, conducted before, at, or shortly after admission. Admission or preadmission review is performed in large part to verify the patient's eligibility for services, open the patient's claim record, and establish an expected diagnosis and length of stay. HMOs and other prepaid plans now use admission review as a cost-containment and resource-management strategy. Only patients requiring a specific type and level of care are admitted to a health care organization, and lengths of stay appropriate for the patient's admitting diagnosis are usually assigned. *Synonyms*: admission certification; preadmission certification; preadmission review. *See also* admission; DRG; prior authorization.

admission source   The point from which a patient enters a health care organization, for example, physician referral, clinic referral, HMO referral, transfer from a hospital, transfer from a skilled nursing facility, transfer from another health care facility, emergency department, or court or law enforcement admission source.

admitting privileges   Authority issued to individuals to admit patients to a health care organization. *See also* clinical privileges; privileging.

adolescence   The period of transition from childhood to adulthood, beginning with the onset of puberty to about the age of 20 years or the age of majority. *See also* adolescent medicine; age of majority; emancipated minor; gender identity; mature minor; minor.

adolescent medicine   The branch of medicine and subspecialty of pediatrics and internal medicine dealing with the care and treatment of adolescents.

adolescent psychiatry   *See* child and adolescent psychiatry.

adrenergic   **1.** Relating to nerve cells or fibers of the autonomic nervous system which employ norepinephrine as their neurotransmitter.   **2.** Relating to drugs that mimic the actions of the sympathetic nervous system. *Synonyms*: sympathomimetics; adrenergic receptors. *See also* beta blocker.

adult day care   Health, recreation, and social services offered to adults during daytime hours, generally Monday through Friday. These services can include health monitoring, occupational therapy, recreational therapy, personal care, meals, and transportation. *See also* elder care; occupational therapy services; personal care services; recreational therapy.

adult inpatient bed   A bed that is regularly maintained for adult inpatients who are receiving continuing organization services.

adult-onset cancer   Cancer that appears as a result of inherited gene mutations that predispose a person to development of cancer; such cancers may be prevented or detected early through presymptomatic genetic cancer susceptibility testing. The adult-onset cancers include breast and ovarian cancer resulting from mutations in the *BRCA1* or *BRCA2* genes and hereditary nonpolyposis colorectal cancer, also called the Lynch syndrome or the cancer family syndrome (because it is also associated with ovarian and endometrial cancer), resulting from mutations in the hMLH1, hMSH2, hPMS1, and hPMS2 genes. *See also BRCA1* and *BRCA2* genes; Gilda Radner gene; cancer susceptibility testing; genetic screening.

adult-onset diabetes   *See* diabetes mellitus.

adult protection services   Services that determine the need for protective intervention; correct hazardous living conditions or situations in which vulnerable adults are unable to care for themselves; or investigate evidence of neglect, abuse, or exploitation. *See also* child protection services.

adult respiratory distress syndrome (ARDS)   An acute severe respiratory disorder characterized by hypoxemia (insufficient oxygen in the blood) that is poorly responsive to oxygen therapy, by diffuse infiltrates in the alveolar sacs of the lungs, and by edema (collection of fluid) in the absence of left-sided congestive heart failure. The syndrome may be triggered by brain injury or other trauma, pneumonia or other respiratory infections, Gram-negative sepsis, or surgery such as coronary artery bypass grafting. ARDS usually requires mechanical ventilation. *Synonyms*: acute respiratory distress syndrome; adult hyaline membrane disease; bronchopulmonary dysplasia; congestive atelectasis; noncardiogenic pulmonary edema; posttraumatic pulmonary insufficiency; pump lung; shock lung; stiff lung syndrome; transplant lung; Vietnam lung; wet lung; white lung. *See also* mechanical ventilation.

advance directive   A document or documentation allowing a person to give directions about future medical care or to designate another person(s) to make medical decisions if the patient loses decision-making capacity. Advance directives may include living wills, durable powers of attorney, do-not-resuscitate (DNR) orders, right to die, or similar documents expressing the patient's preferences as specified in the Patient Self-Determination Act. *See also* durable power of attorney for health care; living will; Patient Self-Determination Act.

advanced cardiac life support (ACLS)   The initial assessment and management of the emergency cardiac care patient as guided by a set of national clinical protocols, standards, guidelines, and performance criteria, developed and defined by the American Heart Association. The ACLS phase of emergency cardiac care consists of basic life support; the use of adjunctive equipment and special techniques for establishing and maintaining effective ventilation and circulation; electrocardiographic monitoring and arrhythmia recognition; the establishment and maintenance of intravenous access; the employment of therapies (including drug and electrical) for stabilization in the post-cardiac or post-respiratory arrest phase; and the treatment of patients with suspected or overt acute myocardial infarction. Qualified health professionals may be trained and certified in ACLS techniques and principles. *Synonym*: advanced life support (ALS). *See also* basic cardiac life support; basic trauma life support; golden hour; mobile intensive care unit.

advanced pediatric life support (APLS)   The assessment and management of pediatric cardiorespiratory support, traumatic emergencies, environmental emergencies, neonatal emergencies, and emergencies with altered levels of consciousness, as covered in a set of national clinical protocols, standards, guidelines, and performance criteria, developed and defined by the American Academy of Pediatrics and the American College of Emergency Medicine for health care providers who care for children in emergency settings. Qualified health professionals may be trained and certified in APLS techniques and principles. *See also* basic cardiac life support; basic trauma life support.

advanced trauma life support (ATLS)　The initial assessment and management of the trauma patient guided by a set of national clinical standards and performance criteria, developed and defined by the American College of Surgeons Committee on Trauma. Physicians and other qualified health professionals may be trained and certified in ATLS techniques using a combined educational format of lecture presentation and associated skill demonstration and practicum. *See also* basic cardiac life support; basic trauma life support; golden hour; load and go; mobile intensive care unit; traumatology.

adverse drug reaction (ADR)　An undesirable response associated with use of a drug that either compromises therapeutic efficacy, enhances toxicity, or both. *See also* medication error.

adverse event　An untoward, undesirable, and usually unanticipated event, such as death of a patient, an employee, or a visitor in a health care organization. Incidents such as patient falls or improper administration of medications are also considered adverse events even if there is no permanent effect on the patient. *See also* adverse patient occurrence; adverse drug reaction; incident reporting; sentinel event.

adverse patient occurrence (APO)　An untoward patient care event which, under optimal conditions, is not a natural consequence of the patient's disease or treatment. Examples include falls, burns, drug reactions, surgical and anesthesia mishaps, misdiagnoses, and unexpected disabilities and deaths. All APOs, from the patient who falls but is uninjured to the patient who dies from an anesthesia error, are events that are not desirable outcomes of optimal medical and organizational management. An APO is not the same as a PCE (potentially compensable event) or negligence. *See also* medical injury; negligence; occurrence screening.

adverse selection　A situation in which an insurer or a benefit plan has a disproportionate enrollment of adverse risks (such as an impaired or elderly population) with the potential for higher utilization of health care services than that budgeted for an average population. Adverse selection occurs when premiums do not cover the cost of providing services.

advocacy　The act of pleading or arguing in favor of something, such as a cause, an idea, or a policy.

advocate　A person who represents the rights and interests of a patient as though they were the person's own, in order to realize the rights to which the patient is entitled, obtain needed services, and remove barriers to meeting the patient's needs.

aerosol corticosteroid　*See* asthma medications.

Aesculapius　The mythical god or deified hero of healing; also known as Asklepios. The staff of Aesculapius is the official symbol of the medical profession. *See also* caduceus; Hippocratic oath.

affective disorder　A disorder of mood, feeling, or emotion.

affidavit　A voluntary statement of facts, or a voluntary declaration in writing of facts, that a person swears to be true before an official authorized to administer an oath.

affiliated organization　An entity that is associated in some degree with another institution or program to coordinate and integrate activities without completely merging or consolidating; for example, a medical school, shared services organization, multihospital system, or religious organization.

affinity diagram　A display that allows facts, opinions, and issues to be organized into natural groupings. Often used in conjunction with brainstorming, team members list ideas or issues on a board, then rearrange them until useful groups are identified. *See also* brainstorming.

affirmative action　Steps designed to eliminate existing and continuing discrimination against minority group members, to remedy lingering effects of past discrimination, and to create systems and procedures to prevent further discrimination, especially in education and employment. Legislation is under way in several states to ban affirmative action on the grounds that it discriminates against nonminority groups. Most notably, Proposition 209 (now Section 31[a] of Article 1 in the California State Constitution) prohibits the state from discriminating against or granting preferential treatment to anyone on the basis of race and gender in the operation of public education, employment, and contracting.

affirmative defense　A response to allegations in a complaint that constitutes a defense even if the allegations being pressed are true. In effect, an affirmative defense avoids all or part of the liability by presenting new evidence to avoid judgment, rather than by denying the facts alleged in the complaint. Common examples include the statute of limitations and the contributory negligence of the opposing party. In connection with clinical practice guidelines, the affirmative defense allows adherence to the guideline to be used as a defense but does not allow failure to adhere to the guideline to be used against a defendant. *See also* Maine Medical Liability Demonstration project; statute of limitations.

aftercare　Postdischarge care and services designed to help a patient maintain and improve on the gains made during treatment; for example, a support group or counseling for chemically dependent or mentally ill persons following formal inpatient treatment.

after death care　The last stage in hospice care in which the organization helps a patient's survivors with bereavement and activities such as organ donation, autopsy, and burial and memorial services. *See also* bereavement counseling.

against medical advice (AMA) A type of discharge disposition that is patient-initiated and that is contrary to the advice of a treating physician; for example, a patient leaving an emergency department contrary to the recommendation of the staff. Related concepts are against clinical advice (ACA) and against staff advice (ASA). *Synonyms*: discharge against medical advice; elopement; non-return; patient dropout; run away; signing out AMA. *See also* discharge.

age- and sex-specific capitation Capitation payments that have been adjusted per the demographics (age and sex) of the primary care physician's practice. The age and sex of the physician's overall practice determines the types and frequency of services required most often.

aged person Any person aged 65 years or older. The aged are sometimes classified as *young old* (65–74), *old* (76–84), and *very old* or *old old* (> 85). Aged person, older adult, and elderly are overlapping terms for the same period of life.

age of majority The age when an individual is considered legally capable of being responsible for all his or her actions, such as entering into contracts, and becomes legally entitled to the rights generally held by citizens, such as voting. Generally, a person must be past the age of majority to legally consent or deny treatment or research studies. In most states, the age of majority was traditionally 21 years but is now generally 18 years, due at least in part to the enactment in 1972 of the 26th Amendment of the U.S. Constitution, allowing 18-year-olds to vote in federal elections. *Synonym*: legal majority. *See also* addensence; emancipated minor; legal age; mature minor; minor.

Agenda for Change The research and development initiatives of the Joint Commission designed to make continuous improvement in patient outcomes and organization performance the central and explicit objective of Joint Commission accreditation activities. The agenda was initiated in 1987 and encompassed the recasting of Joint Commission standards to emphasize performance of important functions, improvements in survey and decision-making processes, and creation of a national accreditation reference data system based on well-tested indicators of organization performance.

agent A chemical or biological substance or an organism capable of producing an effect. *See also* change agent.

age-specific competency A health care practitioner's knowledge, skills, and capabilities in relation to a patient population of a specific age. For example, practitioners treating patients with diabetes need to be aware of the different needs of pediatric and geriatric patients.

aggregate **1.** To combine standardized data and information. **2.** Pertaining to an entire number or quantity of something; the total amount or complete whole. Aggregate survey data include the collection of data from all surveyed health care organizations during a specified time interval.

aggregate data indicator A performance measure based on collection and aggregation of data about many events or phenomena. The events or phenomena may be desirable or undesirable and the data may be reported as a continuous variable or a discrete variable. The two major types of aggregate data indicators are rate-based indicators (also called discrete variable indicators) and continuous variable indicators. *See also* continuous variable measure; performance measure; rate-based measure; sentinel event indicator.

aggregated measurement data Measurement data collected and reported by organizations as a sum or total over a given time period, for example, monthly or quarterly.

aggregate survey data For purposes of Joint Commission accreditation, information on key organization or network performance areas and standards collected from organizations and networks surveyed by the Joint Commission. This information is combined to produce a database concerning the performance of the organizations and networks during a specified time interval. *See also* performance area.

aggregation For purposes of Joint Commission accreditation, the process by which the scores of individual standards are consolidated into a single grid element score. *See also* aggregation rules; aggregate survey data; grid element score; type I recommendation.

aggregation rules For purposes of Joint Commission accreditation, the specific rules, listed by grid element, used to incorporate all survey findings into grid element scores. The format of the rules is commonly referred to as the algorithm. Aggregation rules are reviewed and approved by the Joint Commission Board of Commissioner's Accreditation Committee. *See also* algorithm.

aide An unlicensed assistant (eg, home health aide, nurse's aide, psychiatric aide) with less training than the person being assisted (eg, registered nurse, physician assistant). Aides in health care may perform tasks such as changing clothes, diapers, and beds; assisting patients to perform exercises or personal hygiene tasks; and supporting communication or social interaction. Specific credentials and education are typically not required for this work. *See also* home health aide.

AIDS (acquired immunodeficiency syndrome) A transmissible retroviral disease caused by infection with HIV (the "AIDS virus") and involving a defect in cell-mediated immunity, manifested by various opportunistic diseases and a protracted debilitating course; requires reporting by all states according to CDC case definition criteria. The CDC's 1993 Expanded Case Definition for AIDS Among Adolescents and Adults adds three new AIDS-defining clinical conditions to the 23 clinical conditions in the former surveillance case definition (1987) and adds CD4+ T lymphocyte counts as an alternative. The current criteria for a diagnosis of AIDS are in addition to laboratory-confirmed HIV infection: either (1) the presence of any of the reliably diagnosed AIDS-defining opportunistic infections and cancers, or (2) the presence of a laboratory-confirmed CD4+ T lymphocyte count of less than 200/lmL or a CD4+ T lymphocyte percentage of less than 14%. The expanded definition, which was designed to simplify case-reporting for outpatient clinics with limited staff for surveillance and to accommodate shifts in the pattern of opportunistic diseases, has led to a significant increase in the number of reported AIDS cases. *See also* HIV; hypothermia; immunodeficiency; opportunistic infection.

CONDITIONS INCLUDED IN THE 1993 AIDS EXPANDED SURVEILLANCE CASE DEFINITION

Candidiasis of bronchi, trachea, or lungs
Candidiasis, esophageal
Cervical cancer, invasive*
Coccidioidomycosis, disseminated or extrapulmonary
Cryptococcosis, extrapulmonary
Cryptosporidiosis, chronic intestinal (> 1 month's duration)
Cytomegalovirus disease (other than liver, spleen, or nodes)
Cytomegalovirus retinitis (with loss of vision)
Encephalopathy, HIV-related
Herpes simplex: chronic ulcer(s) (> 1 month's duration); or bronchitis pneumonitis, or esophagitis
Histoplasmosis, disseminated or extrapulmonary
Isosporiasis, chronic intestinal (> 1 month's duration)
Kaposi's sarcoma
Lymphoma, Burkitt's (or equivalent term)
Lymphoma, immunoblastic (or equivalent term)
Lymphoma, primary, of brain
Mycobacterium avium complex or *M. kansasii,* disseminated or extrapulmonary
Mycobacterium tuberculosis, any site (pulmonary* or extrapulmonary)
Mycobacterium, other species or unidentified species, disseminated or extrapulmonary
Pneumocystis carinii pneumonia
Pneumonia, recurrent*
Progressive multifocal leukoencephalopathy
Salmonella septicemia, recurrent
Toxoplasmosis of brain
Wasting syndrome due to HIV

*Added in the 1993 expansion of the AIDS surveillance case definition.

Source: Centers for Disease Control and Prevention: 1993 Revised classification system for HIV infection and expanded surveillance case definition for AIDS among adolescents and adults. *MMWR* 41 (No. RR-17), 1993.

AIDS Clinical Trial Group (ACTG) An NIH-sponsored project under which 50 medical centers nationwide are participating in the evaluation of treatments for HIV-related infections, such as the new protease inhibitors and combination therapy.

AIDS Drug Assistance Program (ADAP) A federal program, originally conceived as a gap-filling program, that has become a major funder of care for uninsured HIV patients with modest incomes.

AIDS-related complex (ARC) A pre-AIDS condition in which many symptoms and signs of AIDS are present but which does not yet meet all the case definition criteria of AIDS. ARC is usually a wasting syndrome that may

include weight loss, fever, fatigue, lymph node enlargement, minor opportunistic infections, cytopenia, and T cell abnormalities associated with AIDS. *See also* HIV.

AIDS risk groups Groups at greater risk for developing AIDS because of exposure to the body fluids of infected persons, including homosexual or bisexual males, intravenous drug abusers, hemophiliacs and other blood transfusion recipients, sexual contacts of individuals infected with HIV, and newborn infants of mothers infected with the virus. Health care workers also are at risk if precautions against blood-borne pathogens are not observed. *See also* blood-borne pathogens.

AIDS virus *See* HIV.

airborne infection A transmission mechanism of an infectious agent by particles, dust, or droplet nuclei suspended in the air.

air contrast barium enema (ACBE) *See* cancer screening tests and procedures.

air fluidized bed Class of support devices to prevent pressure ulcers which uses a high flow rate of air to fluidize a fine particulate material such as sand to produce a support medium that has characteristics very similar to a liquid.

airway **1.** A route for passage of atmospheric air into and out of the lungs, formed by the oral and nasal cavities, the pharynx, larynx, trachea, and bronchi. **2.** A tubular device for securing an unobstructed passageway to the lungs to ventilate the lungs, administer anesthesia, prevent aspiration of secretions, and/or prevent entrance of foreign material, such as stomach contents, from spilling into the lungs. *See also* endotracheal intubation.

albumin The major protein in blood plasma, produced by the liver, which functions as a stabilizer and as a transport protein. Low levels of albumin occur in protein malnutrition, active inflammation, and serious liver and kidney disease.

alcohol and other drug (AOD) dependence *See* dependence; substance-related disorders.

alcoholism Defined in 1992 by the Joint Committee of the National Council on Alcoholism and Drug Dependence and the American Society of Addiction Medicine to Study the Definition and Criteria for the Diagnosis of Alcoholism as a primary, chronic disease with genetic, psychosocial, and environmental factors influencing its development and manifestations. The disease is often progressive and fatal. It is characterized by impaired control over drinking, preoccupation with the drug alcohol, use of alcohol despite adverse consequences, and distortions in thinking, most notably denial. Each of these symptoms may be continuous or periodic. This definition replaces the joint committee's 1976 definition. DSM-IV offers a different definition under the rubric of "substance use disorders," with a distinction between *substance dependence* and *substance abuse* and with application to cocaine and opioids as well as alcohol; the ICD-10 definition parallels the DSM-IV criteria. NIH's National Institute on Alcohol Abuse and Alcoholism similarly distinguishes between *alcoholism* (*alcohol dependence*) and *alcohol abuse*. For treatment purposes, the Institute of Medicine offers the broader definition *alcohol problems*, which includes *alcoholism* or *alcohol dependence syndrome*. The U.S. Preventive Services Task Force similarly defines alcoholism as alcohol dependence and as only one end of the spectrum of *problem drinking*. The definition per se of alcoholism, including several proposed typologies, continues to attract study and debate, with implications for treatment and handling in managed care. *Synonym:* alcohol dependence syndrome. *See also* addiction; CAGE; dependence; problem drinking; substance-related disorders.

alcoholism rehabilitation center   A facility with an organized professionally trained staff that provides rehabilitative services to alcoholic patients.

alcoholism treatment service   An organizational unit or service for the diagnosis and treatment of alcoholism that does not offer rehabilitation services. *See also* addiction psychiatry.

alcohol-problem screening   Identification of persons dependent on alcohol or at risk for alcohol problems by means of mnemonics (short, acronym-based list of questions), interviews and questionnaires, biochemical markers, or combined methods. The CAGE self-report mnemonic is most widely used, with variants designed for screening pregnant women (T-ACE, TWEAK). The Michigan Alcoholism Screening Test (MAST, with shorter and longer variants) is also frequently used. Some personality tests, such as the Health Screening Survey (HSS) and the Minnesota Multiphasic Personality Inventory (MMPI), are used for indirect screening by focusing on alcohol-related questions. Two biological markers in use for some time are the liver function test GGT (gamma-glutamyl transpeptidase) and the red blood cell index MCV (mean corpuscular volume). The Alcohol Clinical Index (ACI) and the Alcohol Use Disorders Identification Test (AUDIT) combine a brief interview, a clinical examination, and a biochemical test. *See also* CAGE; dependence; Minnesota Multiphasic Personality Inventory; problem drinking; substance-related disorders.

aleatory contract   A contract with effects and results that depend on uncertain events; for example, life and fire insurance are aleatory contracts.

algorithm   **1.** For purposes of Joint Commission accreditation, a series of steps for determining grid element scores addressing a specific issue. *See also* computer algorithm; decision tree; flow chart.   **2.** A format for presenting recommended patient management strategies or clinical practice guidelines which consists of a structured flowchart of decision steps and preferred clinical management pathways. An algorithm prescribes the sequence of steps to take given particular circumstances or characteristics (eg, a particular laboratory test result). In health care, algorithms are often called *clinical algorithms* to distinguish them from the widely used computer flowcharts that solve various kinds of problems through conditional

logic (if/then statements). In preparation for guideline development under its sponsorship, the AHCPR in 1992 elaborated the *annotated algorithm*. The annotated algorithm adds the capability of applying an algorithm on a case-by-case basis by using systematic annotation (narrative keyed to numbered decision nodes), which explicitly links the algorithm recommendations to the literature, as well as patient counseling and decision nodes to depict the major preference-dependent decision or branch points in the algorithm. In a similar effort, the Society for Medical Decision Making Committee on Standardization of Clinical Algorithms proposed a standard format containing the following components: four "box" shapes (rounded rectangle = clinical state box; hexagon = decision box; rectangle = action box; small oval = link box); arrows flowing from top to bottom and labeled "yes" or "no"; numbering scheme; consolidation on one page (when possible) for all-at-once viewing; a title defining the clinical topic and intended users; abbreviations only for units of measurement (other abbreviations discouraged); annotations in the body of the algorithm; and annotations written in narrative text format, separated from the algorithm. With the exception of avoidance of abbreviations, this general format has been widely adopted for published national guidelines. *See also* aggregation rules; flow chart; grid element score.

alimentation   The act or process of giving or receiving nourishment.

allergen skin tests   Widely used epicutaneous (prick/puncture) or intradermal (injection) techniques for detecting immunoglobulin E (IgE) antibodies responsible for IgE-mediated reactions in allergic rhinitis, asthma, stinging-insect hypersensitivity, food and medication, atopic dermatitis, urticaria, or anaphylaxis. The tests can be used to help establish an allergic basis for a patient's symptoms, identify specific allergens responsible for the symptoms, or provide information on the degree of sensitivity to specific allergens. *Synonym:* hypersensitivity skin tests.

allergy   A state of hypersensitivity induced by exposure to a particular antigen (allergen) resulting in harmful immunologic reactions on subsequent exposures. The term is usually used to refer to hypersensitivity to an environmental antigen (atopic allergy or contact dermatitis) or to drug allergy. *See also* allergy and immunology; desensitization; drug allergy.

allergy and immunology   The branch of medicine and medical specialty dealing with the evaluation, physical and laboratory diagnosis, and management of disorders potentially involving the immune system. Examples of such conditions include asthma; anaphylaxis; rhinitis; eczema; urticaria; adverse reactions to drugs, foods, and insect stings; immune deficiency diseases (both acquired and congenital); defects in host defense; and problems related to autoimmune disease, organ transplantation, or malignancies of the immune system. *See also* allergy; anaphylaxis; asthma; immunology; transplantation services.

TYPES OF ALLIED HEALTH PROFESSIONALS

accredited record technician (ART)	emergency medical technician (EMT)	occupational therapy assistant
advanced practice nurse	emergency medical technician–paramedic	ophthalmic laboratory technician
anesthesiologist's assistant (AA)	(EMT-P)	ophthalmic medical technician
anesthetist	fireservice paramedics	ophthalmic medical technologist
athletic trainer	hematology technologist	paramedic
audiologist	histologic technician	parophthalmic
biblio-poetry therapist	histologic technologist	perfusionist
cardiopulmonary specialist	industrial audiometric technician	perfusion technologist
certified medical assistant (CMA)	licensed clinical social worker	physical therapist (PT)
certified registered nurse anesthetist	licensed practical nurse (LPN)	physical therapist assistant
(CRNA)	licensed vocational nurse (LVN)	physician assistant (PA)
certified safety professional (CSP)	medical assistant	physician extender
circulation technologist	medical illustrator	practical nurse (PN)
clinical psychologist	medical laboratory technician	profusionist
coding specialist	medical record administrator (MRA)	psychologist
consultant dietitian	medical record technician (MRT)	radiographer
cytotechnologist	medical technologist (MT)	radiologic technologist
dental hygenist	midwife	registered record administrator (RRA)
dental laboratory technician	nuclear medicine technologist	research dietitian
diagnostic medical sonographer	nurse anesthetist	respiratory therapist
dietetic technician	nurse midwife	speech-language pathologist
dietitian	nurse practitioner	surgical technician
electroneurodiagnostic technologist	nursing assistant	surgical technologist
emergency medical care specialist	occupational therapist (OT)	vocational nurse

alliance building An approach to privatization in which public agencies develop collaborative structures with private providers for the joint delivery of services.

allied health professional A health professional qualified by training and frequently by licensure to assist, facilitate, or complement the work of physicians, dentists, podiatrists, nurses, pharmacists, and other specialists in the health care system. For example, a specialist in blood bank technology and an emergency medical technician (EMT) are allied health professionals. *Synonyms:* allied health personnel; allied health specialist; paramedical personnel.

allocation *See* cost allocation; resource allocation.

allograft An organ or tissue that is transplanted or grafted from one individual to another (formerly termed *homograft*). Most organ transplants today, such as kidney and liver transplants, are allografts. *Synonyms:* allogeneic graft; homograft. *See also* transplantation services.

allopathy A system of medicine based on the theory that successful therapy, either medical or surgical, depends on actively creating a condition antagonistic to or incompatible with the condition to be treated. For example, drugs, such as antibiotics, are given to combat diseases caused by the microorganisms to which the antibiotics are antagonistic. *See also* homeopathy; naprapathy; naturopathy; osteopathy.

allowable cost A cost incurred by a health care provider during the course of providing services that is recognized as payable by a third-party payer. *See also* ancillary charge.

all-payer system A system in which prices for health services and payment methods are the same, regardless of who is paying. For instance, in an all-payer system, the government, a private insurer, a large company, an individual, or any other payer, pays the same rates, usually set by a government agency, for specific health services. The uniform fee bars health care providers from shifting costs from one payer to another (eg, those more able to pay). *See also* cost shifting; single-payer system.

alpha-fetoprotein (AFP) A plasma protein produced by the fetal liver, yolk sac, and gastrointestinal tract and measured in the serum to screen for disorders or monitor responses to cancer therapy. Serum levels normally decline markedly by the age of one year. Elevated levels in serum may indicate the presence of liver cancers or benign liver disease (such as cirrhosis and viral hepatitis), and in amniotic fluid they may indicate neural tube defects in a fetus. *See also* prenatal screening tests and procedures.

alpha-1 antitrypsin (AAT) A plasma protein produced in the liver which inhibits the activity of trypsin and other proteolytic enzymes. Deficiency of this protein is associated with development of emphysema. *Synonym:* alpha-proteinase inhibitor.

ALS (advanced life support) unit An emergency ground vehicle (ambulance) usually staffed by two emergency medical technician-paramedics and stocked with intravenous fluids, cardiac monitor, defibrillation equipment, certain medications, and system-approved telecommunication. *See also* advanced cardiac life support; mobile intensive care unit.

alternate site testing *See* point-of-care laboratory testing.

alternative delivery system (ADS) Any system that delivers health care on a basis other than fee-for-service by integrating financing issues with patient care issues. *See also* fee for service.

alternative dental delivery system (ADDS) A dental care delivery and financing approach distinguishable from payment of fees and charges to independent and unselected dental providers.

alternative dispute resolution A method of settling claims other than through a lawsuit. *See also* administrative determination of fault; arbitration; compensation fund; early offer.

alternative financing system (AFS) A structured health care financing mode that is distinguishable from the traditional fee-for-service approach. Capitation through an HMO, for example, is an alternative financing system to fee for service. *See also* alternative delivery system; fee for service.

alternative hypothesis In statistical testing, the hypothesis accepted if a sample contains sufficient evidence to reject the null hypothesis. In most cases, the alternative hypothesis is the expected conclusion, that is, why the test was completed in the first place. *See also* null hypothesis.

alternative level of care Care provided to patients who are no longer in the acute phase of care but who require restorative services. *See also* levels of care.

alternative medicine Those treatments and health care practices not taught widely in medical schools, not generally used in health care organizations, and not usually reimbursed by insurance companies. Such treatments may be used alone or in conjunction with other interventions, including traditional medicine. The NIH Office of Alternative Medicine classifies alternative medicines into seven categories: alternative systems of medical practice; bioelectromagnetic applications; diet/nutrition/lifestyle changes; herbal medicine; manual healing; mind/body control; and pharmacological and biological treatments. *Synonym*: complementary medicine. *See also* acupuncture; acupressure; allopathy; herbal medicine; holism; holistic medicine; homeopathy; hypnotherapy; massage therapy; naprapathy; naturopathy; New Age movement; osteopathy.

altruism The act of generosity and unselfishness in which a duty is not involved. The donation of blood or a kidney is an example of altruism, not duty.

Alzheimer's disease (AD) A progressive degenerative disease of the brain, usually defined along with "other" or "related" dementias associated with aging (eg, vascular dementia, Parkinson's disease, Lewy body disease, Pick's and other frontal lobe dementias), marked by relentless erosion of intellectual abilities, causing cognitive and functional deterioration leading to impairment of social and occupational functioning, decline to a vegetative state, and ultimately death. The AHCPR, the American Psychiatric Association (APA), and the U.S. Department of Veterans Affairs with the University HealthSystem Consortium have recently (1996–1997) developed national guidelines for the early identification and/or treatment of AD, generally building on the DSM-IV criteria for dementia of the Alzheimer's type, which require evidence of decline from previous levels of functioning and impairment in multiple cognitive domains and differentiation from depression and delirium (both of which may coexist with AD but also are often misdiagnosed in

---

EXAMPLES OF COMPLEMENTARY AND ALTERNATIVE MEDICAL PRACTICES

Alternative Systems of Medical Practice
Acupuncture
Ayurveda
Environmental medicine
Homeopathic medicine
Naturopathic medicine

Bioelectromagnetic Applications
Blue light treatment and artificial lighting
Electroacupuncture
Electromagnetic fields
Electrostimulation and neuromagnetic stimulation
Magnetoresonance spectroscopy

Diet/Nutrition/Lifestyle Changes
Changes in lifestyle
Diet
Macrobiotics
Megavitamins
Nutritional supplements

Herbal Medicine
Ginkgo biloba extract
Ginseng root
Wild chrysanthemum flower
Witch hazel
Yellowdock

Manual Healing
Acupressure
Aromatherapy
Chiropractic medicine
Massage therapy
Osteopathy

Mind/Body Control
Biofeedback
Hypnotherapy
Meditation
Psychotherapy
Yoga

Pharmacological and Biological Treatments
Anti-oxidizing agents
Cell treatment
Chelation therapy
Metabolic therapy
Oxidizing agents (ozone, hydrogen peroxide)

Source: NIH Office of Alternative Medicine Clearinghouse, March 1997.

confusion with it). Clinicians are advised to regard difficulty with any of the following activities as "triggers" to undertake an initial assessment for dementia: learning and retaining new information; handling complex tasks; reasoning ability; spatial ability and orientation; language; behavior; discussion of current events in an area of interest. Two cholinesterase inhibitors—tacrine and donepezil—may be offered to patients with mild to moderate AD. A trial reported early in 1997 announced that the monoamine oxidase B inhibitor selegiline and the antioxidant alpha-tocopherol (vitamin E) may prevent further decline of moderate AD and possibly may be beneficial both earlier and later. Management is directed to treating underlying reversible conditions and alleviating a variety of associated conditions or problem behaviors such as agitation. *Synonym:* dementia of the Alzheimer's type. *See also* dementia; depressive disorders; vascular dementia.

amblyopia   Dimness of vision in one eye which is not caused by a pathologic lesion in the eye but results from an optical, physical, or ocular alignment defect during early childhood.

ambulance   An emergency vehicle used for transporting patients to a health care facility after injury or illness. Types of ambulances used in the United States include ground (surface) ambulance, rotor-wing (helicopter), and fixed-wing aircraft (airplane). *See also* ALS unit; BLS unit; emergency medical services system; emergency medical technician; emergency medical technician-paramedic; emergency services; load and go; medevac; medicar; mobile intensive care unit.

ambulance chaser   **1.** A person who solicits negligence cases for an attorney for a fee or in consideration of a percentage of the recovery.   **2.** An attorney who, on hearing of a personal injury that may have been caused by the negligence or wrongful act of another, at once seeks out the injured person with a view to securing authority to bring action on behalf of the injured.

ambulatory electrocardiography   A noninvasive testing procedure in which prolonged ECG recordings are made on a portable tape recorder (Holter monitor) or solid-state device ("real-time" system), while the patient undergoes normal daily activities. It is useful in the diagnosis and management of intermittent cardiac arrhythmias and transient myocardial ischemia. The Holter monitor is used particularly to evaluate the efficacy of antiarrhythmic drugs in patients with sustained ventricular tachyarrhythmias. *Synonym:* Holter monitoring device. *See also* ECG; monitor.

ambulatory health care   All types of health services provided to patients who are not confined to an institutional bed as inpatients during the time services are rendered. Ambulatory care services are provided in many settings, ranging from freestanding ambulatory surgical facilities to cardiac catheterization centers. *Synonym:* ambulatory care.

ambulatory health care occupancy   An occupancy used to provide services or treatment to four or more patients at the same time that either (1) render them incapable of taking their own means for self-preservation in an emergency or (2) provide outpatient surgical treatment requiring general anesthesia. *See also* occupancy.

ambulatory infusion center   A site—usually a room, an office, or a clinic—where patients are administered medications by infusion and receive related care under the supervision of a licensed health care practitioner.

ambulatory patient group (APG)   System of classification for outpatient hospital services based on payment of facility costs per visit and not including physician services, telephone contacts, home visits, long-term care, or acute inpatient care. This system, similar to DRGs, is used as a financing mechanism to reimburse hospitals for services rendered. *See also* DRG.

ambulatory surgery   Surgical services provided for patients who are admitted and discharged on the day of surgery. Examples of ambulatory surgery procedures include arthroscopy and hernia repair. *Synonyms:* in-and-out surgery; outpatient surgery; same-day surgery. *See also* ambulatory health care.

ambulatory surgical facility   A freestanding or hospital-based facility, with an organized professional staff, that provides surgical services to patients who do not require an inpatient bed. *Synonyms:* ambulatory surgery center; surgical center; surgicenter. *See also* freestanding ambulatory surgical facility.

ambulatory visit group (AVG)   A counterpart of the DRG classification but designed for use in ambulatory care settings, rather than hospital settings. *See also* DRG.

American Joint Committee on Cancer (AJCC) pathologic stage classification system   *See* cancer staging system.

American Medical Accreditation Program (AMAP)   A national, uniform, and voluntary accreditation program developed by the American Medical Association (AMA) as a "seal of approval" for physicians who successfully meet performance standards in five areas (credentials, personal qualifications such as adherence to the AMA's *Code of Medical Ethics*, environment of care, clinical performance, and patient care results and satisfaction).

American Standard Code for Information Interchange (ASCII)   A common code for the computer representation of letters, numbers, and function symbols used for data communications. The code employs eight computer bits in various combinations to handle all 128 standard characters.

Americans with Disabilities Act of 1990   (Pub L No 101-336) Legislation enacted to provide a clear and comprehensive national mandate for the elimination of discrimination against individuals with disabilities; to provide clear, strong, consistent, enforceable standards addressing discrimination against individuals with disabilities; and to ensure that the federal government plays a central role in enforcing the standards established in the act.

American Urological Association Symptom Index   A five-point scale with a series of seven questions about symptoms of benign prostatic hyperplasia (enlarged prostate gland). The index is used in planning the diagnosis and treatment of the condition. *See also* benign prostatic hyperplasia.

amniocentesis   *See* prenatal screening tests and procedures.

amnioscopy   Direct observation of the fetus and the color and amount of the amniotic fluid by means of an endoscope inserted through the vagina and the uterine cervix. *See also* amniocentesis.

anabolic steroids   Synthetic derivatives of testosterone, the male sex hormone that helps the human body build muscle and synthesize proteins. Anabolic steroids may be prescribed for certain anemias and leukemias and for lessening the pain or severity of breast cancer in women. They are taken illegally by some individuals to enhance muscle size and strength. Anabolic steroids are classified as a schedule III controlled substance. *See also* schedule of controlled substances.

anaerobic   Without oxygen, as in anaerobic bacteria, which thrive in the absence of oxygen.

analgesic   An agent that removes or diminishes sensibility to pain.

analgesic drug ladder   *See* WHO analgesic drug ladder.

analog data   Data that are represented by an infinite number of variable measurable quantities along a continuum. An example of analog data is the infinite number of measurements of body temperature that occur along a continuum, such as 98.600°F, 98.601°F, 98.602°F, and so forth. Digital data, by contrast, are data expressed in discrete numbers (eg, 0 to 9 in the decimal system, or 1 and 0 in the binary system), especially by a computer.

analyte   The substance or constituent on which testing is conducted.

analytical sensitivity   The lowest concentration or amount of an analyte or substance that can be measured.

analytical specificity   The extent to which a method responds only to the analyte or substance to be measured; interfering substances are eliminated or accounted for.

anaphylaxis   An immediate and exaggerated hypersensitivity reaction to a previously encountered outside antigen, such as penicillin. *See also* allergy; antigen.

anatomical gift   Testamentary donation of a vital organ(s) generally for the purpose of medical research or transplantation. Most states have adopted the Uniform Anatomical Gift Act of 1969, which authorizes the gift of all or part of a human body after death for specified purposes. *See also* organ procurement; Uniform Anatomical Gift Act.

anatomic pathology   **1.** The branch of medicine relating to the gross and microscopic study of organs and tissues removed for biopsy, for surgical procedures, or during postmortem examinations (autopsies).   **2.** Services relating to surgical pathology, autopsy, and cytology.

ancillary charge   **1.** The dollar amount associated with additional service performed prior to or secondary to a procedure, such as pathology, radiology, and anesthesia services.   **2.** A charge in addition to a copayment that a member of a health plan is required to pay to a participating pharmacy for a prescription that, through the request of the member or participating prescriber, has been dispensed in nonconformance with the health plan's maximum allowable cost list. *See also* allowable cost; health plan; prescription.

ancillary services   Health care organization services other than room and board and professional services. Examples of ancillary services are diagnostic imaging, pharmacy, laboratory, and therapy services not separately itemized. *See also* environmental services; support services.

andropause   A change of life for men frequently expressed as a career change, divorce, or reordering of one's life. It is associated with a decline in androgen (masculine steroid hormone) levels that occurs in many men during their late forties or early fifties. *See also* menopause.

anemia   A deficiency in the number or volume of red blood cells or hemoglobin. Anemia may result from decreased red cell production (eg, iron-deficiency anemia), increased red cell destruction (eg, hemolytic anemia), or blood loss (eg, a ruptured abdominal aortic aneurysm, traumatic hemorrhage from a wound). *See also* sickle cell anemia.

anencephaly   Congenital defective development of the brain, with absence of the bones of the cranial vault and absent or rudimental cerebral and cerebellar hemispheres, brain stem, and basal ganglia. The anencephalic infant usually has a rudimental brain stem, which regulates the lungs and heart, but the child is not conscious and rarely lives beyond a few days. Controversy arises when the infant has transplantable organs. Technically, the anencephalic infant is not dead under the Uniform Determination of Death Act, but to wait for actual brain death would cause the viable organs to no longer be suitable for transplanting. Some states allow a parent to terminate life support for the infant, others do not. Some argue for an extension of the Uniform Determination of Death Act to include these infants, while others are wary of extending the definition of death to meet various societal needs. *See also* Baby Doe regulations; brain death; neural tube defect.

anergy   State of being unable to react immunologically to an antigenic stimulus. Usually used to denote lack of response to specific antigens injected into the skin of the forearm.

anesthesia   1. Loss of feeling or sensation, especially loss of the sensation of pain. In medicine, anesthesia is induced to permit performance of surgery or other painful procedures.   **2.** For purposes of Joint Commission accreditation, the administration to a patient, in any setting, for any purpose, by any route (general, spinal, or other) of major regional anesthesia or sedation (with or without analgesia) for which there is a reasonable expectation that, in the manner used, the analgesia or sedation will result in the loss of protective reflexes.

anesthesiology   The branch of medicine and medical specialty dealing with providing pain relief and maintenance, or restoration, of a stable condition during and immediately following an operation or an obstetric or diagnostic procedure. Two subspecialties of anesthesiology are critical care medicine and pain management. *See also* anesthesia; critical care medicine; pain management.

anesthetic   A drug or agent that is used to abolish or decrease the sensation of pain or feeling. Such agents may be administered generally, through inhalation, intravenously, locally, or topically.

angina   Spasmodic, choking, or suffocating pain; now used almost exclusively to denote angina pectoris. *See also* stable angina; unstable angina.

angina pectoris   A paroxysmal thoracic pain, often radiating to the arms, particularly the left, sometimes accompanied by a feeling of suffocation and impending death. It is most often due to ischemia of the myocardium, precipitated by effort or excitement, and relieved promptly by rest or placement of nitroglycerin under the tongue. The discomfort of angina is often hard for patients to describe, and many patients do not consider it to be "pain." *See also* atherosclerosis; ischemia.

angina severity and functional classifications
Schemas for categorizing the condition of cardiac patients for the purposes of prescribing physical activity. The New York Heart Association (NYHA) and the Canadian Cardiovascular Society (CCS) have produced similar classifications, both of which are used widely. Patients are commonly described in terms of either NYHA class or CCS class by number without the description.

angiography   A procedure in which substances opaque to radiation are injected into blood vessels so that diagnostic x-rays of those blood vessels may be made. *Synonym*: arteriography. *See also* nephrography.

angiology   The branch of medicine dealing with the blood vessels of the body.

angioplasty   A procedure for eliminating areas of narrowing or blockages in blood vessels, as in coronary artery angioplasty. *See also* percutaneous transluminal coronary angioplasty.

angiotensin converting enzyme inhibitor   *See* ACE inhibitor.

NEW YORK HEART ASSOCIATION (NYHA)* AND CANADIAN CARDIOVASCULAR SOCIETY (CCS)† HEART DISEASE CLASSIFICATIONS

NYHA	CCS
Class I: No limitation of physical activity. Ordinary physical activity does not cause undue fatigue, palpitation, dyspnea, or anginal pain.	**Class I:** Ordinary physical activity–walking and climbing stairs–does not cause angina. Angina with strenuous, rapid, or prolonged exertion at work.
Class II: Slight limitation of physical activity. Comfortable at rest, but ordinary physical activity results in fatigue, palpitation, dyspnea, or anginal pain.	**Class II:** Slight limitation of ordinary activity–walking or climbing stairs rapidly; walking uphill; walking or climbing stairs after meals; in cold, in wind, under emotional stress, or during the few hours after awakening. Walking more than 2 blocks on the level and climbing more than one flight of ordinary stairs at a normal pace under normal conditions.
Class III: Marked limitation of physical activity. Comfortable at rest, but less than ordinary activity causes fatigue, palpitation, dyspnea, or anginal pain.	**Class III:** Marked limitation of ordinary physical activity–walking 1 or 2 blocks on the level or climbing one flight of stairs at a normal pace under normal conditions.
Class IV: Unable to carry on any physical activity without discomfort. Symptoms of cardiac insufficiency or of the anginal syndrome may be present even at rest. If any physical activity is undertaken, discomfort is increased.	**Class IV:** Inability to carry out any physical activity without discomfort. Anginal syndrome may be present at rest.

*The NYHA classes, which embrace heart disease in general, are often subdivided into classes II a (patient can keep up with others walking on the flat but has limitation on more severe exercise such as climbing stairs) and II b (patient has slight limitation on all forms of physical activity).

†The CCS classes are designed for angina pain.

Sources: New York Heart Association, Inc: Diseases of the Heart and Blood Vessels, 8th ed. Boston: Little Brown, 1964.

Campeau L: Grading of angina pectoris. *Circ* 54:522-23, 1976.

---

anorexia nervosa   *See* eating disorders.

antiarrhythmia devices   *See* cardiac pacemaker.

antibiotic   1. Having the ability to destroy or interfere with the development of a living organism.   **2.** An antimicrobial agent, derived from cultures of a microorganism or produced synthetically, which is used to treat infections. Examples include penicillin, streptomycin, cephalosporin, or aminoglycoside.

antibiotic resistance   *See* microbial drug resistance.

antibodies   Proteins in the blood or secretory fluids that tag and help remove or neutralize bacteria, viruses, and other harmful toxins. Antibodies are members of a class of proteins known as immunoglobulins, which are produced and secreted by B-lymphocytes in response to stimulation by antigens. Antibodies are specific for antigens and work by attaching to invading organisms or foreign substances to help defend the body. *See also* antigen; immunoglobulin.

anticoagulation Administration of a clot-inhibiting substance, such as streptokinase, warfarin, or heparin, either therapeutically for conditions in which there is undesirable clotting (eg, pulmonary embolism) or prophylactically in circumstances in which there is an increased risk of such clotting, for example, during certain surgical operations (eg, insertion of a prosthetic heart valve, total hip replacement). *See also* heparin.

antidepressant drug A class of medication used in the treatment of depressive disorders, including monoamine oxidase (MAO) inhibitors, tricyclics, heterocyclics, tetracyclics, and selective serotonin reuptake inhibitors (SSRI).

antidumping law *See* COBRA.

antiduplication clause *See* coordination of benefits.

antigen Any foreign substance that evokes an immune response when introduced into the body and reacts with the products of that response. *See also* anaphylaxis; antibodies; CD4+ T lymphocyte; histocompatibility leukocyte antigen; immunoassay.

antihemophilic factor *See* clotting factor.

antihypertensive A medication counteracting high blood pressure, such as ACE inhibitors, beta blockers, calcium channel blockers, and diuretics.

antikickback laws (1972) Legislation making it illegal for anyone to receive or offer a bribe (kickback) in exchange for a referral from another provider participating in Medicare, Medicaid, or any federally financed state health care program. The purpose of this legislation was to stop providers who received compensation for referrals from over-referring patients and thus driving up Medicare and Medicaid costs. *See also* safe harbor regulations.

antioxidants Enzymes or other organic substances, such as vitamin E or beta-carotene, that are capable of counteracting the damaging effects of oxidation in human tissue.

antiretroviral drug A drug that reduces the replication rate of HIV and is used to treat HIV- infected persons. The most commonly used are zidovudine, didanosine, and zalcitabine. *See also* AIDS; HIV.

antisepsis Destruction of pathogenic microorganisms to prevent infection. *See also* disinfect; infection; microorganism.

antisocial personality disorder *See* personality disorders.

antisubstitution laws State laws that require pharmacists to dispense a drug precisely as written in a prescription issued by a physician, dentist, or other authorized health professional. The effect is to prohibit pharmacists from substituting a different brand name of the drug or a generic equivalent of the drug that is prescribed, even in instances when the substitute drug is acknowledged to be therapeutically equivalent to the drug prescribed and perhaps less expensive. *See also* generic equivalents.

antithrombotic therapy Use of drugs to prevent or interfere with the formation of thrombi (clots). Examples of antithrombotic agents are aspirin, heparin, streptokinase, tPA (tissue plasminogen activator), and warfarin.

antitrust laws Federal and state statutes to protect trade and commerce from unlawful restraints, price discriminations, price fixing, and monopolies, and aimed at promoting free competition in the marketplace. Any agreement or cooperative effort or intent by two or more entities that affects or restrains, or is likely to affect or restrain their competitors, is illegal under these statutes. In health care, antitrust claims often concern arrangements between physicians (such as radiologists, anesthesiologists, pathologists, and sometimes cardiologists and emergency physicians) involved in exclusive service contracts with their hospitals. Plaintiffs, such as a physician or physician group excluded from the hospital as a result of the contract, have alleged that these contracts violate the Sherman Antitrust Act. The principal federal antitrust acts are the Sherman Antitrust Act (1890), Clayton Act (1914), Federal Trade Commission Act (1914), and Robinson-Patman Act (1936). *See also* monopoly.

anxiety disorders Disorders characterized by persistent feelings of apprehension, tension, or uneasiness.

APACHE (Acute Physiology and Chronic Health Evaluation) system A system that classifies patients as to severity of illness using objective, routinely collected data, such as physiological values and age. The system is not disease-dependent and consists of a physiology score representing the degree of acute illness and a preadmission health evaluation indicating health status before acute illness. Originally developed in 1978 under a HCFA research grant, the system was revised and streamlined to create APACHE II. The 12 physiological variables were later amplified to become APACHE III.

Apgar score A method of quantifying the condition of a newborn infant, developed by Virginia Apgar (1909–1974), an anesthesiologist. The Apgar score is usually determined at one minute, and again at five minutes, after birth and is the sum of points, to a maximum of 10, gained on assessment of heart rate, respiratory effort, muscle tone, reflex irritability, and color. A score of 0 to 3 represents severe distress, a score of 4 to 7 indicates moderate distress, and a score of 7 to 10 indicates an absence of difficulty in adjusting to extrauterine life. The five-minute score is normally higher than the one-minute score. *See also* neonate.

aphasia Partial or total loss of the faculty or power to articulate ideas or comprehend spoken or written language, resulting from damage to the cerebral cortex caused by injury or disease. *See also* Alzheimer's disease; stroke.

apheresis   A procedure in which blood is drawn from a donor and separated into its components, some of which are retained, such as plasma or platelets, with the remainder returned by transfusion to the donor. *Synonym:* hemapheresis.

apnea monitoring   The close observation of respiratory activity, especially in infants. Electronic apnea monitors detect changes in thoracic or abdominal movements and heart rate, and they may include an alarm that sounds if breathing stops. *See also* monitor.

appointment   The process whereby a health care organization authorizes a health care practitioner to provide patient care services in or for the organization.

apportionment of damages   The allocation of an award determined by verdict among those entitled to receive its benefit or against those obligated to pay. *See also* apportionment of fault; damages.

apportionment of fault   The allocation of responsibility for damages among those whose acts contributed to the injuries or loss. For example, a plaintiff may be partially responsible for his or her own injury or loss and may be apportioned a percentage of fault that may reduce or bar his or her recovery. Additionally, when multiple defendants have contributed to an injury or loss, they may each be assigned a percentage of fault. Depending on the rules of that jurisdiction, such an apportionment may form the basis for determining the amount of the total verdict for which each party is responsible. *See also* apportionment of damages; damages.

appropriateness   A Joint Commission performance dimension addressing the degree to which the care and services provided are relevant to an individual's clinical needs, given the current state of knowledge. *See also* dimensions of performance.

appropriateness criteria   Ratings, developed by RAND, of the appropriateness of up to several thousand separate indications for a given diagnosis or therapeutic procedure. *Appropriate* is defined as care for which the expected health benefit exceeds the expected negative consequences by a sufficient margin that the care is worth providing. Appropriateness criteria are distinguished from guidelines in that they are designed to help evaluate the appropriateness of decisions (and thus may be used retrospectively in utilization review) rather than to assist clinician and patient decision making. *See also* intervention.

appropriateness research   A line of health services research that attempts to define the appropriate uses of particular medical technologies or practices. *See also* intervention.

appropriation   A legislative act authorizing the expenditure of a designated amount of public funds for a specific purpose. *See also* backdoor authority.

arbitration   The process of dispute resolution in which a neutral third party (arbitrator) renders a decision after a hearing at which both parties have an opportunity to testify. Arbitration is one arrangement for taking and abiding by the judgment of selected persons in some disputed matter and is intended to avoid the formalities, delay, expense, and vexation of ordinary litigation. *See also* mediation.

area wage adjustment   The differences in DRG payment rates that reflect variations in area hospital wage levels based on Bureau of Labor Statistics data. *See also* DRG.

Arizona Board of Medical Examiners v Blue Cross and Blue Shield of Arizona (1992)   A landmark case involving an adverse licensure action against a managed care organization's (MCO) medical director for a decision made during routine utilization review activities. The medical director of Blue Cross and Blue Shield of Arizona requested that a plan attending physician obtain a second opinion before approval of gallbladder surgery. The physician refused on the grounds that a delay might result in a worsening of the patient's condition. He performed the surgery and filed a complaint with the state medical board alleging that the medical director exercised reckless disregard for the patient's safety. The board concurred, and a state supreme court judge found that the board had jurisdiction to review medical decisions made by MCO medical directors.

aromatherapy   A form of alternative medicine that uses natural oils from flowers, fruits, and other parts of plants to improve physical and mental well-being.

arrhythmia   An irregularity of heart rhythm, for example, atrial fibrillation or ventricular tachycardia. *Synonym:* dysrhythmia.

arterial blood gas (ABG)   *See* blood gas determination.

arteriography   *See* angiography.

arteriosclerosis   A group of diseases characterized by hardening and thickening of the walls of arteries. This condition may cause insufficient blood circulation to the area supplied by the artery or arteries, as in coronary arteriosclerosis. *Synonym:* arteriosclerosis obliterans. *See also* coronary artery disease.

arthroscopy   Examination of the interior of a joint with an arthroscope. The surgeon can either look directly into the arthroscope or observe on a screen the view projected by the arthroscope. The surgeon can diagnose a condition using only a small incision for insertion of the arthroscope and can use a tool in conjunction with the arthroscope to perform certain surgical procedures within viewing range of the scope. *See also* orthopedic surgery.

articles of incorporation   The creating document for an organization, such as the articles of incorporation for a corporation or a constitution for an unincorporated entity. *Synonym:* articles of organization.

artificial cardiac pacemaker   *See* cardiac pacemaker.

artificial insemination   The deposit of semen into a woman's genital tract by artificial means. *Artificial insemination by a donor* refers to fertilization in which sperm from an anonymous donor is injected (inseminated) into the vagina of a consenting woman (recipient). This technique may be indicated when the husband is sterile or has a genetic disorder. *Artificial insemination by a husband (AIH)* refers to fertilization in which a husband's sperm is injected into his wife's vagina, cervix, or uterus in order to bring about conception.

art therapy   The use of art and artistic processes specifically selected and administered by a qualified art therapist to restore, maintain, or improve an individual's mental, emotional, or social functioning. Therapeutic goals include symptom relief, emotional integration, and recovery from or adjustment to illness or disability. *See also* creative arts therapy; manual arts therapy; recreational therapy.

ASA-PSS (American Society of Anesthesiologists' Physical Status Score)   *See* operative risk (and accompanying table).

ASA-SCORE index   A severity-of-illness classification system based on five factors: age of patient, physiological systems involved in illness, stage of disease, complications, and patient's response to therapy. *See also* severity of illness.

ascorbic acid   *See* vitamin.

aspiration biopsy   A biopsy in which tissue is obtained by the application of suction through a needle attached to a syringe.

assessment   **1.** For purposes of performance improvement, the systematic collection and review of patient-specific data.   **2.** For purposes of patient assessment, the process established by an organization for obtaining appropriate and necessary information about each patient seeking entry into a health care setting or service. The information is used to match a patient's need with the appropriate setting, care level, and intervention.

assignment   **1.** An agreement in which a patient assigns to a health care provider the right to reserve payment from a third-party payer for the service the patient has received. *See also* third-party payer.   **2.** The acceptance by a physician of Medicare payment as full payment for services rendered. *Synonym:* assignment of benefits. *See also* Medicare.

assisted living   A broad range of residential care services that includes some assistance with activities of daily living but does not include nursing services, such as administration of medication. Assisted living stresses encouragement of residents' independence and provides less intensive care than that found in traditional nursing homes and other types of long term care facilities. *Synonym:* sheltered care.   *See also* continuing care retirement community; life care; residential treatment facility.

assisted suicide   Deliberate acceleration of death of a competent patient with an incurable disease or in the extremes of suffering. The patient seeking assistance in taking his or her own life may ask the help of a physician or other health professional, a family member, or a friend. The milieu may be a hospital, nursing home, or private residence. Assistance to the person in dire physical or psychological distress may take the form of lethal doses of medications or chemicals to be taken orally or by injection through human intervention or with a so-called suicide machine. *See also* Death with Dignity Act; physician-assisted suicide; obitiatrist; obitorium.

assumption of risk   In torts, an affirmative defense used by a defendant to a negligence suit claiming that the plaintiff had knowledge of a condition or situation obviously dangerous to himself or herself and yet voluntarily exposed himself or herself to the hazard created by the defendant, thereby relieving him or her of legal responsibility for any resulting injury. When a plaintiff knowingly and voluntarily exposes himself or herself to a risk of harm, he or she is said to "assume the risk." *See also* risk.

asthma   Now defined, in 1997 guidelines from the National Asthma Education and Prevention Program of the National Heart, Lung, and Blood Institute, as a chronic inflammatory disorder of the airways in which many cells and cellular elements play a role, in particular, mast cells, eosinophils, T lymphocytes, neutrophils, and epithelial cells. In susceptible individuals, this inflammation causes recurrent episodes of wheezing, breathlessness, chest tightness, and cough, particularly at night and in the early morning. These episodes are usually associated with widespread but variable airflow obstruction that is often reversible either spontaneously or with treatment. The inflammation also causes an associated increase in the existing bronchial hyperresponsiveness to a variety of stimuli. This definition is still in process, with recent evidence indicating that subbasement membrane fibrosis may occur in some patients with asthma and that these changes contribute to persistent abnormalities in lung function. The definition underscores the anti-inflammatory nature of the disease established in the program's first guidelines in 1991, at which time it was removed as one of the conditions classified under *chronic obstructive pulmonary disease*. The 1997 definition has redefined the asthma severity levels from the former three classes of mild, moderate, and severe to four classes: mild intermittent, mild persistent, moderate persistent, and severe persistent. Asthma stands alone as a unique mixture of conditions, requiring carefully tailored treatment strategies at home and in a health care organizations established on the basis of an accurate determination of severity. *See also* chronic obstructive pulmonary disease; forced expiratory volume; peak flow meter.

asthma guidelines and outcomes programs Numerous guidelines in a variety of settings building on key recommendations of the National Asthma Education and Prevention Program (NAEPP) of the National Heart, Lung, and Blood Institute (NHLBI) and used to measure performance. The widely disseminated 1991 *Guidelines* *for the Diagnosis and Management of Asthma* were revised in 1997 and disseminated in prepublication form to sites with ongoing asthma initiatives. The NAEPP guidelines, which are directed chiefly to primary care, require compliance in four areas to achieve control of asthma: (1) use of objective measures of lung function; (2) elimination of environmental "triggers"; (3) comprehensive drug therapy; and (4) patient education fostering a partnership with the family and clinicians. Although their formats vary considerably, guidelines developed locally invariably base their performance measures on some part of these four components of effective management of asthma. Excessive emergency room admissions and hospitalization for asthma, commonly used as an undesirable event indicator, have been labeled a *primary care sentinel event* by some health care organizations because they signal a failure of the provider-patient partnership for preventive self-management. *See also* asthma medications; forced expiratory volume; peak flow meters; pulmonary function tests.

PHARMACOLOGICAL THERAPY FOR ASTHMA: OVERVIEW MEDICATIONS

Long-Term-Control Medications

Corticosteroids: Most potent and effective anti-inflammatory medication currently available; inhaled form used in long-term control; systemic form often used to gain prompt control of the disease when initiating long-term therapy.

Cromolyn sodium and medocromil: Mild-to moderate anti-inflammatory medications; may be used as initial choice for long-term control for children; can also be used as preventive prior to exercise or unavoidable exposure to known allergens.

Long-acting beta$_2$-agonists: Bronchodilator used concomitantly with anti-inflammatory medications for long-term control of symptoms, especially nocturnal symptoms; used to prevent exercise-induced bronchospasm.

Methylxanthines: Sustained-release theophylline and mild-to-moderate bronchodilator used principal as adjuvant to inhaled corticosteroids for prevention of nocturnal asthma symptoms; may have mild anti-inflammatory effect.

Leukotriene modifiers: Zafirlukast (leukotriene receptor antagonist) or zileuton (5-lipoxygenase inhibitor) considered as alternative therapy to low doses of inhaled corticosteroids or cromolyn or nedocromil for patients ≥ 12 years of age with mild persistent asthma (further clinical experience and study needed to establish their roles).

Quick-Relief Medications

Short-acting beta$_2$-agonists: Therapy of choice for relief of acute symptoms and prevention of exercise-induced bronchospasm.

Anticholinergics: Ipratropium bromide may provide some additive benefit to inhaled beta$_2$-agonists in severe exacerbations; may be an alternative bronchodilator for patients who do not tolerate inhaled beta$_2$-agonists.

Systemic corticosteroids: Used for moderate-to-severe exacerbations to speed recovery and prevent recurrence of exacerbations.

Source: National Asthma Education and Prevention Program, National Heart, Lung, and Blood Institute: *Guidelines for the Diagnosis and Management of Asthma. Expert Panel Report II.* Pub No. 97-4051 Bethesda, MD: National Institutes of Health, July 1997.

---

asthma medications   A group of pharmacologic therapies, including single drugs and combinations, that must be selected and titrated precisely to maintain control of asthma at all levels of severity and chronicity. The 1997 new national asthma guidelines of the National Asthma Education and Prevention Program update the 1991 guidelines on the safety and efficacy of beta$_2$-agonists and inhaled corticosteroids.

atherosclerosis   A common form of arteriosclerosis in which, in addition to a hardening of the walls of the arteries, lipid (fatty) deposits build up on the inner arterial walls and interfere with blood flow. *See also* acute myocardial infarction; angina pectoris; arteriosclerosis; coronary artery disease; coronary heart disease; hypercholesterolemia.

atrial fibrillation   A rapid, irregular contraction of the atria of the heart, producing an irregular quiver instead of consistent, organized pumping. The slowed flow increases the risk of clot formation. Diseases or situations commonly involving atrial fibrillation include heart failure, heart surgery, mitral stenosis, and rheumatic fever.

at risk   The state of being subject to some uncertain event that can cause loss or difficulty, for example, a person who smokes cigarettes is at risk of developing lung cancer, or an insurance company is at risk of incurring a financial loss by agreeing to provide or pay for more services than are paid for through premiums or per capita payments.

attending physician   A member of a health care organization's medical staff who is legally responsible for the care and treatment provided a given patient.

attention-deficit/hyperactivity disorder (ADHD)   A controversial childhood mental disorder with onset before age seven, characterized by inattention and hyperactivity-impulsivity that are inconsistent with the child's developmental level and severe enough to impair social or academic functioning. Symptoms tend to be either predominantly of the inattention type or predominantly of the hyperactive-impulsive type. *Synonym (formerly):* attention deficit disorder (ADD). *See also* learning disability.

attorney-client privilege   The legally established policy that communication is confidential between an attorney and a client in the course of the professional relationship and that it cannot be disclosed without the consent of the client. This privilege covers oral or written statements, actions, and gestures. Its purpose is to encourage full and frank communication between attorneys and their clients and thereby promote broader public interest in the observance of law and administration of justice. *See also* physician-patient privilege; privileged communication; psychotherapist-patient privilege.

attribute data   Data that arise from the classification of items into categories, from counts of the number of items in a given category or the proportion in a given category, and from counts of the number of occurrences per unit. For instance, data indicating an organization's compliance *or* noncompliance with a standard would be attribute data.

attributes to guide the development of practice parameters *See* guideline attributes.

atypical connective tissue disease A term that has been used by plaintiffs in breast implant medical malpractice suits to describe harmful systemic effects of ruptures of silicone breast implants. The concept does not appear in standard medical terminology.

audiological assessment A process to delineate the site and degree of auditory dysfunction using audiological tests such as pure tone air-conduction thresholds, speech reception thresholds, speech discrimination measurements, impedance measurements, and others.

audiology The study of hearing, especially hearing defects and their treatment.

audiology services Services provided by a qualified audiologist to assist individuals in hearing and balance and their underlying processes.

audiometric screening A process to screen hearing that may include such tests as pure tone air-conduction thresholds, pure tone air-conduction suprathreshold screenings, impedance measurements, or observations of reactions to auditory stimuli. Audiometric screening is used to detect impairment in children who are unlikely to complain of a problem and who may suffer from secondary language disorders and poor school performance. Opinion is divided on the quality of evidence and justification for universal versus selective screening of high-risk newborns and infants up to age three months.

audit **1.** A systematic inspection of records or accounts to verify their accuracy and completeness. **2.** In performance measurement, regular focused inspections by the measurement system of a sample of participating organization level records and processes to ensure the accuracy and completeness of measurement data on performance.

AUDIT (Alcohol Clinical Index and Alcohol Use Disorders Identification Test) *See* alcohol-problem screening.

auscultation In physical diagnosis, the act of hearing to obtain physical signs, such as cardiac murmurs, pericardial rubs and knocks, or a noise over an arteriovenous fistula. A stethoscope is an instrument often used in auscultating the human body. *See also* physical examination.

authenticate To verify that an entry is complete, accurate, and final.

authorship Source or origin, as in authorship of an entry made in a patient's medical record.

autistic disorder A developmental disorder consisting of gross and sustained impairment in social interaction and communication; restricted and stereotyped patterns of behavior, interest, and activities; and abnormal development up to age three.

autointoxication A form of self-poisoning in which toxins are produced by the body but not eliminated, settling into different (usually the weakest) organs.

autologous blood transfusion A transfusion of an individual using his or her own blood, which usually has been drawn previously and stored for later use, typically in elective surgery. *Synonym:* autotransfusion.

autologous bone marrow transplant (ABMT) A therapy for a cancer patient (usually leukemia) for whom a suitable bone marrow donor cannot be found. The marrow is removed and the patient treated to remove cancer cells; the patient receives high-dose chemoradiation therapy and then is reinfused with the extracted bone marrow.

automated ambulatory blood pressure monitoring devices Machines that use either auscultatory or oscillometric techniques to measure blood pressure at frequent intervals during a 24-hour period and record the results for subsequent analysis. These devices were developed to avoid the phenomenon of "white coat hypertension," but they have given rise to concerns about accuracy, patient acceptability, and mechanical reliability. *See also* blood pressure; hypertension; monitor; white coat hypertension.

automated database A computerized system that processes data electronically and provides for data storage and access through electronic interface.

autonomy The condition of having one's life under one's control and making decisions or plans and acting on them. Autonomy also dictates the duty of individuals not to interfere either intentionally or negligently in another person's making of decisions or plans or acting on them. Autonomy forms the ethical basis for patient's right of autonomy, which includes, among other rights, the right to informed consent, the right to refuse treatment, and the right to die. *See also* genetic counseling; informed consent.

autopsy Dissection of a dead body, including the internal organs and structures, to determine the cause of death or the nature of pathological changes. An autopsy is normally required by statute for deaths by violent, unexplained, or unnatural means. *Synonyms:* necropsy; post-mortem.

autotransfusion *See* autologous blood transfusion.

auxiliary A self-governing membership organization founded by individuals from the community to assist a health care organization in promoting the health and welfare of the community.

availability **1.** A Joint Commission performance dimension addressing the degree to which appropriate care is available to meet an individual's needs. **2.** A measure of the supply of health resources and services relative to the needs or demands of an individual or a community. Availability is a function of the distribution of appropriate resources and services and the willingness of the provider to render services to particular patients in need. *See also* dimensions of performance.

average   *See* mean; measure of central tendency; median; mode.

average daily census   The average number of inpatients, excluding newborns, receiving care each day in a health care organization during a reporting period. *See also* census.

average length of stay (ALOS)   A measure of the average stay, counted by days of all or a class of inpatients discharged over a given period, calculated by dividing the number of inpatient days by the number of discharges. *See also* length of stay.

average payment rate (APR)   The limit that HCFA may pay an HMO or a competitive medical plan (CMP) for Medicare services under a risk contract. The rate is calculated for a specific geographic area, then adjusted according to the projected makeup of the enrollment of the HMO or CMP.

axis   **1.** One of the dimensions of a graph. A two-dimension graph has two axes, the horizontal (x axis) and the vertical (y axis). Mathematically there may be more than two axes, and graphs are sometimes drawn with a third dimension. *See also* graph.   **2.** In psychiatry, a domain of information and inquiry in the American Psychiatric Association's DSM. The DSM multiaxial classification consists of five axes, designated by Roman numerals: (I) clinical disorders and other conditions that may be a focus of clinical attention; (II) personality disorders and mental retardation; (III) general medical conditions; (IV) psychosocial and environmental problems; (V) global assessment of functioning. Use of these multiple axes is thought to facilitate comprehensive and systematic evaluation as well as to capture the diversity of individuals presenting with the same diagnosis. *See also* DSM.

ayurvedic medicine   The traditional Hindu science of medicine based on maintaining the balance of humours (wind, bile, phlegm, and blood) in the body. *See also* alternative medicine.

Bb

Baby Doe case (*Indiana ex rel. Infant Doe v Monroe Cir. Ct.*, No. 482S140 [Ind. Sup. Ct. Apr. 16, 1982]) A legal case in which hospital administration applied for a court order to override the decision of parents of an infant born with Down syndrome and esophageal atresia (blockage) to withhold consent for corrective surgery and intravenous feeding. The court ruled in favor of the parents, and the baby died before an appeal could be processed. *See also* Child Abuse Amendments.

Baby Doe regulations Federal regulations in 1985 following the Baby Doe case which were intended to prevent the withholding of medically indicated treatment from a seriously ill infant with a life-threatening condition (except under certain specific circumstances in which treatment would be futile). These regulations were ruled invalid, but the federal Child Abuse Amendments of 1984 made such withholding of treatment a form of child neglect and thus provided an avenue of legal recourse for health professionals or other interested persons. *See also* Baby Doe case; Child Abuse Amendments.

baby shots *See* immunization schedule.

backdoor authority Legislative authority for the obligation of funds outside the normal appropriation process. Some forms of backdoor authority are borrowing authority, contract authority, entitlement authority, the Environmental Protection Agency's construction grant program, and the Social Security Administration's trust funds. *Synonym:* backdoor spending. *See also* appropriation.

back school A structured educational program, usually in a group setting, designed to inform patients about low back problems and ultimately to increase functional work capacity. According to the AHCPR-sponsored guideline *Acute Low Back Problems in Adults* (December 1994), evidence on the efficacy of back schools is limited in quantity and shows contradictory results. However, schools in the workplace with worksite-specific education may be effective adjuncts to individual education efforts by the clinician in the treatment of patients with acute low back problems.

back-up hospital A hospital that provides specialized services and inpatient care for patients receiving services in ambulatory care centers, such as a freestanding ambulatory care center or a freestanding ambulatory surgical facility, should the patients require these services, especially on an emergency basis. *See also* freestanding ambulatory care center; freestanding ambulatory surgical facility; hospital-based ambulatory care center.

bacteria Unicellular microorganisms that commonly multiply by cell division and are typically contained within cell walls. They may be aerobic or anaerobic, motile or nonmotile, and may be free-living, saprophytic, parasitic, or even pathogenic, the last causing disease in humans. *See also* Gram's stain.

bacteriology The study of bacteria, especially in relation to medicine and agriculture. Bacteriology is part of the more general science of microorganisms known as microbiology. *See also* clinical laboratory; microbiology.

bad apples A term used in quality inspection to denote practitioners who do not perform up to specific standards. Early quality assurance efforts focused on finding problems in the people who implemented processes rather than problems in the processes, which is the current focus of quality improvement initiatives. *See also* quality assurance.

balance billing The practice of independent practitioners to seek payment from the patient of that portion of a patient's bill not covered by the government or other third-party payers. OBRA (1989) limits balance billing to a percentage of the amount Medicare reimburses (115% of the allowable nonparticipating provider fee).

balance sheet In health care policy and decision making, a table displaying the benefits, harms, and costs of proposed interventions and strategies. Balance sheets can be used by individual clinicians and patients to organize thinking and structure a discussion, particularly in a situation requiring a tough choice with trade-offs (eg, choosing between a mastectomy or lumpectomy for breast cancer or between a prostatectomy and "watchful waiting" for early localized prostate cancer). Balance sheets help policymakers and administrators understand the important consequences of alternative options, such as mounting a massive screening program for different age groups at different intervals with different screening modalities. Such balance sheets have been published, for example, comparing the consequences of screening for colorectal cancer with fecal occult blood tests, flexible sigmoidoscopy, or double contrast barium enema (or combinations of them).

Baldrige Award *See* Malcolm Baldrige National Quality Award.

balloon angioplasty *See* percutaneous transluminal coronary angioplasty.

bar chart *See* bar graph.

bar code Computer-readable labels used to identify many materials coming into or generated within health care organizations, such as laboratory specimens and x-rays. Bar codes containing clinical histories, prescribed interventions, and so on are sometimes used in place of written medical records.

bar graph A pictorial display of sets of rectangles, each rectangle being identified with a particular classification of data and the height of the rectangle representing a data value for that classification. *Synonym:* bar chart. *See also* graph; histogram.

bariatrics   The branch of medicine dealing with the causes, prevention, and treatment of obesity. *See also* obesity.

barium enema (BaE, BE)   A suspension of barium sulphate retained in the intestines during x-ray examination to screen for filling defects or deformities of the intestine produced by cancer or other abnormalities. *Double-contrast barium enema* (DCBE; *synonym*: air contrast barium enema), in which air is added to push the barium through and permit examination of the double contrast, has emerged as a major screening procedure for colorectal cancer. *See also* cancer screening tests and procedures; fluoroscopy.

baromedicine   *See* hyperbaric oxygen therapy.

Barton, Clara (Clarissa Harlowe 1821–1912)   A civic leader and organizer, philanthropist, volunteer nurse, and founder and first president of the American Red Cross. Barton distributed supplies for the relief of the wounded during the U.S. Civil War and later organized a bureau of records for missing men. After the Franco-Prussian War broke out in 1870, she worked with European military hospitals in developing the International Red Cross and took the idea back to the United States in 1873 to establish the American Red Cross Society.

basal metabolic rate (BMR)   The minimum rate of energy expenditure required by the body under resting (basal) conditions in order to maintain essential functions, such as circulation, respiration, and thermogenesis.

base capitation   The stipulated dollar amount to cover the cost of health services, less mental health and substance abuse services, pharmacy, and administrative charges.

baseline   An observation or value that represents the current background level of a measurable quantity, as in baseline mammography or a baseline rate for performance of ultrasonography during pregnancy (expressed as number of procedures per patient per pregnancy). The baseline rate is used for comparison with values representing responses to experimental intervention or an environmental stimulus, usually implying that the baseline and response values refer to the same individual or system.

base year Medicare costs   A health care organization's costs for the base year from which computations are made in the Medicare payment formula. The base year is, by definition, always several years behind the present. *See also* Forms 1007 and 1008.

basic benefit package   A minimum set of health services that should be generally and uniformly available in order to provide adequate health protection of the population from disease or to meet some other criteria or standards. For example, a basic benefit package might include physician visits, drugs, hospital expenses, dental services, and mental health care. There is much debate on what services should be included in a basic package and how to ensure availability of those services. *See also* availability;

comprehensive benefit package; health services; optional services.

basic cardiac life support (BCLS)   The phase of emergency cardiac care that either prevents circulatory or respiratory arrest or insufficiency through prompt recognition and intervention or externally supports the circulation and ventilation of a victim of cardiac or respiratory arrest through cardiopulmonary resuscitation (CPR). Health professionals and the public may be trained and certified in basic life support techniques and principles. *See also* advanced cardiac life support; cardiopulmonary resuscitation.

basic life support (BLS) unit   An emergency ground vehicle usually staffed with two emergency medical technicians or an emergency medical technician and an emergency medical technician-paramedic capable of providing basic cardiac life support to patients in the prehospital phase of emergency care. A BLS unit is not stocked with intravenous fluids, cardiac monitor, defibrillation equipment, or certain medications. *See also* ALS unit; ambulance; mobile intensive care unit.

basic trauma life support (BTLS)   A training course developed in 1982 for emergency medical technicians to improve the prehospital management of trauma patients. Modern trauma training teaches rapid primary assessment, extrication, packaging, and immediate transport of the critical trauma patient. *See also* advanced trauma life support; golden hour; load and go.

batch processing   The manual or computerized grouping and processing of similar data in a single operational sequence, as in batch processing of health insurance claims.

Bayesian analysis   An alternative to traditional statistics and probability theory, widely used in health care forecasting and clinical decision analysis, which permits calculating probabilities of different occurrences on the basis of prior beliefs and then adding new evidence to refine the model. Bayesian analysis may be used, for example, to estimate and compare the likelihood of survival from cancer given different single and adjunctive therapies at different stages of cancer for different age groups. Computer algorithms are available to help reduce the burden of complex computations. The method is named after the British mathematician Thomas Bayes (1702–1761) and the theorem that bears his name (Bayes' theorem).

bed conversion   The conversion of a bed allocated for one type of care to a bed allocated for another type of care, as in converting an acute-care bed to a long term care bed. *See also* swing bed.

bed count   The total number of beds regularly maintained by a health care organization for specific inpatient populations. *Synonym*: bed size. *See also* licensed beds; occupancy.

bedside diagnosis   Making a determination of a patient's disease or condition by taking a medical history and performing physical examination in the patient's presence and yielding immediate conclusions. *Synonym*: office diagnosis. *See also* medical history; physical examination.

bedside manner The degree of compassion, courtesy, and sympathy displayed by a physician toward a patient in a clinical setting. Bedside manner includes establishing rapport, explaining conditions, holding hands, or the lack thereof.

bedside rationing A physician's withholding of a medically beneficial service because of that service's cost to someone other than the patient.

bed sore *See* pressure ulcer.

bed turnover rate The average number of times over a given period that there is a change of occupant of a bed regularly maintained by a health care organization.

behavioral health For purposes of Joint Commission accreditation, a broad array of mental health, chemical dependency, forensic, mental retardation, developmental disabilities, and cognitive rehabilitation services provided in settings such as acute, long term, and ambulatory care.

Behavioral Health Care Accreditation Program The survey and accreditation program of the Joint Commission for eligible mental health care organizations, including the following types: alcohol and substance abuse organizations; community mental health centers; forensic psychiatric services; organizations serving persons with mental retardation and/or other developmental disabilities; and general psychiatric/mental health centers.

behavioral medicine *See* mind/body medicine.

behavioral science A scientific discipline, such as sociology, anthropology, or psychology, in which the actions and reactions of human beings and animals are studied through observational and experimental methods.

behavior management The use of basic learning techniques, such as biofeedback, conditioning, reinforcement, or aversion therapy, to manage and improve human behavior. *Synonym*: behavior modification. *See also* biofeedback; mind/body medicine.

behavior therapy A form of psychotherapy that uses basic learning techniques to modify maladaptive behavior patterns by substituting new responses to given stimuli for undesirable ones. *See also* psychotherapy.

Behringer case (*Estate of Behringer v Medical Center at Princeton, 592 A.2d 1251* [N.J. Super. 1991]) A 1991 case in which the estate of a New Jersey physician who died of AIDS in 1989 sued the Medical Center at Princeton, alleging that the hospital violated New Jersey's law against discrimination when it restricted Behringer's privileges to practice surgery and required him to obtain informed consent before performing invasive procedures. *See also* discrimination.

bell-shaped curve *See* normal distribution.

benchmark A point of reference or standard by which something can be measured, compared, or judged, as in benchmarks of performance. *See also* criterion standard; gold standard; measure.

benchmarking Continuous measurement of a process, product, or service to those of the toughest competitor, to those considered industry leaders, or to similar activities in the organization in order to find and implement ways to improve it. This is one of the foundations of both total quality management and continuous quality improvement. *Internal benchmarking* occurs when similar processes within the same organization are compared. *Competitive benchmarking* occurs when an organization's processes are compared with best practices within the industry. *Functional benchmarking* refers to benchmarking a similar function or process, such as scheduling, in another industry. *See also* measurement; standard.

bench to bedside Colloquial description of application of findings from clinical trial research (*bench* scientist) to clinical practice (*bedside* in clinical setting).

benefit-cost ratio The ratio of net present value of measurable benefits to costs. Calculation of a benefit-cost ratio is used, for example, to determine the economic feasibility of success of a program.

beneficence The state or quality of being charitable or producing favorable effects. For example, beneficence towards patients can be defined as preventing harm to them, benefiting them, and, if harm is unavoidable, to make certain the harm is substantially outweighed by the benefit. *See also* implied consent; paternalism.

benefits *See* balance sheet; basic benefit package; comprehensive benefit package; maternity benefits.

benign prostatic hyperplasia (BPH) A noncancerous enlargement of the prostate gland which is the most common benign tumor in aging men (approximately 95% by the age of 85). Symptoms of prostatism, scored on the self-administered American Urological Association (AUA) Symptom Index, are related to mechanical obstruction. Because of its nature as a "quality of life" disease and the great variation in individuals' perceptions of the bothersomeness of the symptoms and of possible side effects of treatments, BPH was one of the first conditions chosen for piloting of interactive physician-patient shared decision-making programs on CD-ROM. BPH was targeted for development of a clinical practice guideline by the AHCPR (1994). *Synonym*: benign prostatic hypertrophy.

bereavement counseling Counseling that helps survivors of a deceased meet their physical, emotional, spiritual, psychological, social, financial, and legal needs. *Synonym*: bereavement care. *See also* after death care.

Bernoulli distribution *See* binomial distribution.

best-before date A date marked on drug packaging to show the latest time by which the contents can be used without risk of deterioration.

best interest Regard for one's own benefit or advantage, or regard for the welfare of a patient, as in surrogate decision making when factors such as the quality of life and the extent of life sustained are taken into consideration in the patient's best interest.

beta₂-agonist A sympathomimetic bronchodilator that relaxes bronchial airway smooth muscle (bronchodilation) by stimulating $beta_2$-receptors, which increases cyclic amphetamine and produces functional antagonism to bronchoconstriction. These medications may be short or long acting, and they may be administered by inhaled or systemic (oral or parenteral) routes. *Synonyms:* adrenergic beta-agonist; $beta_2$-adrenergic agonist; $beta_2$-adrenoceptor agonist; $beta_2$-agonist-induced bronchodilator; sympathomimetic (agent). *See also* asthma.

beta blocker A drug that blocks the effect of the sympathetic nervous system (the catecholamines: dopamine, epinephrine, norepinephrine), producing a decrease in heart rate and amount of blood pumped by the heart and thus reducing oxygen demand in the myocardium (thick muscle wall of the heart) and lowering blood pressure. Beta blockers are used for treatment of anxiety, angina pectoris, cardiac arrythmias, glaucoma, hypertension, and migraine headaches. *Synonyms:* adrenergic beta-antagonists; antiadrenergi; beta-adrenergic blockers; sympatholytic (agent).

Bethesda system *See* cancer staging system.

bias **1.** An influence on results that causes them to routinely depart from the true value. **2.** In any measurement process, systematic errors in data or deviation from the truth, resulting from the methods, tools, or environment of the data collection and processing. Bias is distinguished from random error. *See also* double-blind technique; placebo effect; random error; selection bias; single-blind technique; triple-blind study.

bid Abbreviation for Latin phrase *bis in die*, meaning twice a day.

billing cycle The interval between periodic billings for goods sold or services rendered, normally one month, or a system whereby bills or statements are mailed at periodic intervals in the course of a month in order to distribute the clerical work load evenly.

bill of patient rights A statement of ethical and legal principles adopted by a health care organization to regulate its operational policies and procedures, operations staff, professional staff, and volunteers in a manner that recognizes and obligates the organization to protect and promote the human dignity and rights of patients. *Synonym:* patient bill of rights. *See also* genetic counseling; patient rights.

bimodal distribution A distribution with two regions of high frequency separated by a region of low frequency of observations; a two-peak distribution.

binomial distribution A probability distribution associated with two mutually exclusive outcomes, for example, death and survival. The binomial distribution is used to model prevalence rates and cumulative incidence rates. *Synonym:* Bernoulli distribution. *See also* probability distribution.

bioassay The measurement of the strength or concentration of a drug or other biologically active substance by comparing its effect on an organism, organ, or tissue with that of a standard preparation. *Synonym:* biological assay.

bioavailability The relative amount of and rate at which a medication dosage reaches the systemic circulation in a therapeutically active form after administration. *See also* bioequivalence.

biochemistry The study in living organisms of chemical substances and vital processes including metabolism, biological oxidation and bioenergetics, enzymes, proteins, nucleic acids, and protein biosynthesis.

bioengineering The application of engineering principles to the fields of biology and medicine, for example, the development of replacements for defective or missing body organs, or genetic engineering. *Synonym:* biomedical engineering.

bioequivalence The degree to which two formulations of the same medication have equal bioavailability. *See also* bioavailability; chemical equivalence; pharmaceutical equivalence.

bioethics A variously defined term for a multidisciplinary field concerned with the ethical and moral dimensions of the clinical and policy application of research findings in the life sciences and of biomedical research using human subjects. The matter of whether bioethics is a separate discipline as well as the definition of its principles are under debate. "Strangers at the bedside" was the description in the first formal history of the field (1992) to distinguish it from medical ethics. *Clinical ethics* is the term used for bioethics based on real individual cases in the clinical setting. Bioethicists and bioethics centers or commissions draw on traditional ethics, medical ethics, moral philosophy, social science, and theology to confront issues posed by genetic engineering, genetic testing, fetal tissue and embryo research, surrogate reproduction, organ transplantation, abortion, assisted suicide, euthanasia, human experimentation, and other interventions to fulfill the requirements of informed consent. *Synonym:* biomedical ethics. *See also* code of ethics; futility; institutional review board; medical ethics; professional ethics.

biofeedback The use of auditory or visual signals reflecting the state of a physiological function (eg, heart rate) or the position of a part of the body (eg, the arm) to help an individual gain better control of the function or positioning. For example, biofeedback may be used to treat certain conditions, such as hypertension, migraine headaches, and low back pain, by alerting the patient to areas where muscle tension should be reduced. *See also* hypnotherapy; mind/body medicine.

biohazard A biological agent (eg, an infectious microorganism) or a condition that constitutes a threat to human beings, especially in biological research or experimentation.

bioinstrumentation   Instruments, such as a thermometer, for the measurement, recording, and transmission of physiological information, such as body temperature.

biological   Any medicine made from living organisms and their products, including serums, vaccines, antigens, and antitoxins. Biologicals are regulated by the Bureau of Biologics, a division of the FDA. They differ from drugs in that biologicals are derived from living microorganisms and cannot be synthesized or readily standardized by chemical or physical means. They tend to be chemically less stable than drugs, their safety cannot be as easily assured, and they are never as chemically pure as drugs. *Synonyms*: biologic; biological product. *See also* medication.

biological markers   Measurable and quantifiable biological parameters (eg, specific enzyme concentration, specific hormone concentration, specific gene phenotype distribution in a population, presence of biological substances) that serve as indices for health- and physiology-related assessments, such as disease risk, psychiatric disorders, environmental exposure and its effects, disease diagnosis, metabolic processes, substance abuse, pregnancy, cell line development, and epidemiological studies.

biological response modifier (BRM)   Natural or synthetic substances that help control the immune system in its fight against cancer and that ultimately lead to an improvement in a patient's overall health. Examples of BRMs are interferon, interleukins, and colony-stimulating factors. Some BRMs produced by recombinant DNA technology are commercially available, such as alpha-interferon for treatment of leukemia.

biological waste   *See* hazardous waste.

biomechanics   The study of the mechanics of a living body, especially of the forces exerted by muscles and gravity on the skeletal structure.

biomedical engineering   *See* bioengineering.

biomedical ethics   *See* bioethics.

biomedicine   **1.** The field of medical science dealing with the ability of human beings to tolerate environmental stresses and variations.   **2.** The application of the principles of the natural sciences, especially biology and physiology, to clinical medicine.

biometrics   **1.** The science of the application of statistical methods to the analysis of biological data.   **2.** The quantitative measurement of biological facts, especially with respect to variation. *Synonym*: biometry.

biomonitoring   The direct measurement of toxicants in people, performed to identify individuals and population groups at greatest risk, to assess internal dose levels for health studies of exposed populations, and to assess

effectiveness of public health interventions in preventing excessive exposures. NIH's National Center for Environmental Health (NCEH) is a premier biomonitoring laboratory. Toxicants recently under study include PCBs (polychlorinated biphenyls), environmental tobacco smoke, uranium, and methyl parathion (insecticide). *See also* monitor.

biostatistics   The branch of science which applies statistical methods to the analysis of biological and medical problems.

biotechnology   The branch of technology concerned with the use of living organisms (usually microorganisms) in industrial, medical, and other scientific processes. Applications include the production of certain drugs, synthetic hormones, and bulk foodstuffs as well as the bioconversion of organic waste and the use of genetically altered bacteria in the cleanup of oil spills. *See also* recombinant DNA.

biotelemetry   The monitoring, recording, and measuring of a living organism's basic physiological functions, such as heart rate, muscle activity, and body temperature, and transmitting data without wires to a point remote from the subject (telemetry).

bipolar disorder   A major, long-term mood disorder characterized by episodes of major depression and mania or hypomania (less serious than mania); formerly called manic-depressive psychosis, circular type. According to the American Psychiatric Association's *DSM-IV*, the diagnosis of bipolar I disorder requires one or more episodes of mania (a distinct period of abnormally and persistently elevated, expansive, or irritable mood, lasting at least one week or of any duration if hospitalization is required). It is distinguished from bipolar II disorder, which is characterized by recurrent major depressive episodes with hypomanic episodes. *See also* depressive disorders.

birth certificate   A legal document recording details of a live birth, usually comprising name, date, place, identity of parents, and sometimes additional information, such as birthweight. It provides the basis for vital statistics of birth and birthrates in a political or administrative jurisdiction and for the denominator for infant mortality and certain other vital rates. *See also* fetal death certificate.

birthing center   A freestanding or hospital-based facility that provides prenatal, childbirth, and postnatal care, often incorporating family-centered maternity care concepts and practices. *Synonym*: childbirth center.

birth mother   Biological mother. *See also* parent.

birth rate   A summary rate based on the number of live births in a population over a given period, usually a year; for example, the number of live births per 1,000 persons per year.

birthweight   Infant's weight recorded at the time of birth. Certain variants of birthweight are precisely defined: *low birthweight (LBW)* less than 2,500 grams; *very low LBW*, less than 1,500 grams; *ultralow birthweight*, less than 1,000 grams. *Large for gestational age* is birthweight above the 90th percentile; *average weight for gestational age* (also called *appropriate for gestational age*) is birthweight between 10th and 90th percentiles; and *small for gestational age (SGA)* is a birthweight below 10th percentile. LBW and SGA are used as risk indicators of future developmental disability that may be reversed or diminished by early interventions such as well-baby care, home visits, and child-health centers.

black box method A method of reasoning or studying a problem in which the methods or procedures are not described, explained, or even understood. Nothing is stated or inferred about the method; discussion and conclusions relate solely to the empirical relationships observed.

blacklisting An insurer's refusal to insure high-risk industries, professions, or individuals (especially those who might inherit diseases). Most states have passed legislation prohibiting this practice. *Synonym:* industry screening. *See also* redlining.

black lung disease Common name for anthracosis (a form of pneumoconiosis), a chronic lung disease caused by inhaling coal dust and found among coal miners. Certain medical benefits for victims of the disease are available under Title IV of the Federal Coal Mine Health and Safety Act of 1969. *See also* disease.

blinded study A study in which observers or subjects are kept ignorant of some aspect of the study so observations and behaviors are not influenced. For example, clinicians or patients may be unaware of the treatments patients are receiving, or observers may not share assessments. *See also* double-blind technique; single-blind technique; triple-blind study.

block grant Federal funds allotted to state governments or agencies (such as health and education) that may be passed on to local agencies. States determine the mix of services provided and the population served and are accountable to the federal government for spending the funds in accordance with program requirements.

blood banking The branch of medicine and medical specialty dealing with the maintenance of an adequate blood supply, blood donor and patient-recipient safety, and appropriate utilization of blood components. Blood banking specifically involves pretransfusion compatibility testing, highly specialized testing procedures for antibodies, and the preparation and safe use of specially prepared blood components, including red blood cells, white blood cells, platelets, and plasma constituents. Facilities providing such services are classified as either commercial or community blood banks.

blood-body fluid precautions A category of patient isolation that involves prevention of direct or indirect contact with infected blood or body fluids. A private room is indicated if the patient's hygiene is poor. Masks are not indicated, but gowns should be used if soiling of clothing with blood or body fluids is likely. Gloves should be used for touching blood or body fluids. *See also* HIV transmission; isolation; standard precautions.

blood-borne pathogens Infectious organisms that can be transmitted from one person to another by exposure to the infected person's blood, including hepatitis B virus, hepatitis C virus, HIV, and syphilis. In the health care setting, these pathogens pose a greater risk of exposure for health care workers, who are required to observe precautions recommended by the CDC and mandated by OSHA in the handling of blood-soiled linens and bandages, needles and other sharp objects, and medical and dental waste. Body substances specifically designated by the CDC and OSHA which may transmit blood-borne pathogens include semen, vaginal secretions, cerebrospinal fluid, synovial fluid, pleural fluid, amniotic fluid, saliva in dental procedures, any body substance that is visibly contaminated with blood, and all body substances in situations for which it is difficult or impossible to determine whether blood is present. The concept of the blood-borne pathogen is differentiated from the clinical conditions of bacteremia, viremia, and fungemia, in which the organism is present in the blood of a patient as the result of a natural infectious process. *See also* standard precautions.

blood component A fraction of separated whole blood, for example, red blood cell, plasma, platelets, and granulocytes.

blood count The number of red blood cells (erythrocytes), white blood cells (leukocytes), and platelets (thrombocytes) in a definite volume of blood. *Synonym:* complete blood count. *See also* hematocrit.

blood derivative A pooled blood product, such as albumin, gamma globulin, or Rh immune globulin, whose use is considered significantly lower in risk than that of blood or blood components.

blood gas determination An analysis of the pH and the concentration and pressure of oxygen, carbon dioxide, and hydrogen ions in the blood. It is used to assess acid-base balance and ventilatory status in a wide range of conditions, including cardiac failure, respiratory failure, and diabetic ketoacidosis. A blood gas determination may be performed on arterial or venous blood. *Synonym:* arterial blood gas (ABG).

blood glucose The concentration of glucose in the blood, measured in milligrams of glucose per deciliter of blood. *Synonym:* blood sugar. *See also* diabetes mellitus.

blood groups The classification of blood on the presence or absence of genetically determined antigens on the surface of the red blood cell. There are many grouping systems, including ABO, Duffy, Kell, and Rh. Their importance derives from their clinical significance in transfusion therapy, organ transplantation, disputed paternity cases, maternal-fetal compatibility, and genetic studies. ABO blood grouping, the most important system for classifying blood, is identified by the presence or absence of two different antigens, A or B. The four blood types in this grouping are A, B, AB (both antigens are present), and O (neither is present). *See also* blood transfusion services; Rh factor.

blood pressure (BP) The pressure exerted by the blood against blood vessel walls, especially arteries, as it circulates. *Systolic pressure* reflects the maximum force (with the heart muscle contracted) and *diastolic pressure* reflects the minimum force (with the heart muscle relaxed). Blood pressure has been classified by the National High Blood Pressure Education Program of the National Heart, Lung, and Blood Institute as normal, high normal, and hypertension. Normal blood pressure for adults is less than 130 mm Hg systolic and less than 85 mm Hg diastolic. *See also* automated ambulatory blood pressure monitoring devices; hypertension; self-measured blood pressure monitoring device; vital signs; white coat hypertension.

blood sugar *See* blood glucose.

blood thinners *See* anticoagulation.

blood transfusion services Services relating to transfusing and infusing patients with blood, blood components, or blood products. *See also* histocompatability; histocompatability leukocyte antigen.

blood usage review An activity that entails measuring, assessing, and improving the ordering, distributing, handling, dispensing, administering, and monitoring of blood and blood components performance relating to blood usage in health care organizations.

Blue Cross and Blue Shield (BC/BS) plan A nonprofit health care prepayment insurance plan originating with hospitals (Blue Cross) and physicians (Blue Shield). Blue Cross and Blue Shield plans in the United States are linked by a national association known as the Blue Cross and Blue Shield Association (BCBSA). There are approximately 77 autonomous plans of each type (BC and BS) in the United States, which are typically governed by state statutes. Although plans are similar in principle, each one is autonomous; there are differences in policies, benefit structure, and administration from plan to plan. Most subscribers enroll at their place of employment in group plans. *See also* home plan; host plan; national account; nonprofit carrier.

blue dog Colloquial term for fiscally conservative Democrats in the U.S. House of Representatives, particularly with respect to health care spending. A proposal to reduce Medicare spending has been termed the *Blue Dog Bill.*

Blue Indigo A concept originated by the National Council of Community Hospitals and the Estes Park Institute maintaining that a population's health is primarily its own responsibility, and that health care reform and improvement of individual health can only be accomplished by making use of local resources under community leadership. The Indigo Institute has been established to undertake further research, to develop the concept, and to help local communities adopt it.

Blue Indigo corporation A nonprofit, health-related corporation formed by a community to implement the Blue Indigo concept. The corporation must meet specific criteria before it may be termed a Blue Indigo corporation.

board eligible Description of a physician or other health professional who is eligible for specialty board examination. Each of the specialty boards has requirements that must be met before the examination for specialty board certification can be taken. *Synonym:* board prepared. *See also* medical specialty boards.

board of health A public body with oversight and governing responsibility for a local public health department and its community health programs. Members of a board of health usually are appointed by an elected official or governing body, such as a mayor or county commission. *See also* public health.

board prepared *See* board eligible.

body mass index (BMI) A measure used to express desirable weight and obesity. The index is calculated by dividing the patient's weight (in kilograms) by the square of his or her height (in meters). According to the National Center for Health Statistics, overweight for men is ≥ 27.8 kg/m and for women is ≥ 27.3 kg/m.

body parts legislation Colloquial term for state- and federal-legislated health care mandates for specific controversial clinical procedures, medical devices, and pharmaceuticals that have been denied by managed care organizations. *Synonym:* disease-of-the-month legislation. *See also* mandated controversial medical treatments.

borderline personality disorder *See* personality disorder.

bougie A slender, flexible, hollow or solid, cylindrical instrument for introduction into the urethra or other tubular organ, usually to measure, dilate, or medicate constricted passages.

box plot A five-number summary of a set of data. A box encloses the space between the first and third quartiles. The median is indicated by a line dividing the box. The highest and lowest values are shown as the ends of lines extending from the box. *See also* schematic box plot.

Braden Scale A tool for assessing the risk of developing a pressure ulcer, considering sensory perception, moisture, activity, mobility, nutrition, and friction and shear. The scale has been tested extensively in a variety of settings and was reprinted in the AHCPR guideline *Pressure Ulcers in Adults: Prediction and Prevention* (1992). *See also* pressure ulcer.

brain attack Synonym for *stroke* used by the National Stroke Association. The term is sometimes used in quotation marks in the clinical literature (particularly nursing literature) to stress the emergency nature of stroke and the potential for diminishing brain damage through immediate intervention. The term has been promoted in connection with the federal campaign, Decade of the Brain. *See also* Decade of the Brain; stroke.

brain death   A clinical state marked by the absence of neurologic function. Declaration of brain death is based on the clinical criteria of irreversible brainstem damage and the inability of an individual to maintain functions vital to life, such as heart beat, respiration, and blood pressure, without external mechanical support or medication. The exact criteria vary among institutions. Brain death differs from a persistent vegetative state. *See also* anencephaly; death; Uniform Determination of Death Act.

brainstorming   A process used to elicit a high volume of ideas from a group of people who are encouraged to use their collective thinking power to generate ideas in a relatively short period of time in a process that is free of criticism and judgment. *Structured brainstorming* allows individuals to give ideas in turn; *unstructured brainstorming* allows individuals to give ideas as they come to mind. *See also* nominal group technique; STP brainstorming.

***BRCA1* and *BRCA2* (breast cancer) genes**   Genes in which a mutation significantly increases the risk of breast and ovarian cancer. These tumor suppressor genes are screened for germline mutations, accounting for an estimated 80% of hereditary breast cancers, 5% to 6% of all breast cancers, and in Ashkenazi (Eastern European) Jewish women, 62% of ovarian cancers and 30% of early-onset (before age of 40) breast cancers. As a result of publicity, demand is high for testing even among women with low to moderate risk, and testing is now commercially available. This recent trend has prompted surveys by MCOs to probe the extent of interest and initiatives among clinical specialty groups to develop genetic counseling services to advise women of the limits and risks of testing. *Synonyms:* breast and ovarian cancer susceptibility gene; breast cancer gene; breast-ovarian cancer syndrome; familial breast cancer gene; inherited breast-ovarian cancer gene; mastectomy. *See also* cancer susceptibility testing.

breach of duty   A failure to perform a duty owed to another human being or to society; a failure to exercise that care which a reasonable person would exercise under similar circumstances.

break-even analysis   A technique used to determine the total number of services or products that must be sold at a specified price in order to generate revenue to cover total costs.

Breakthrough Series   A series of national collaboratives, launched in 1995 by the Institute for Healthcare Improvement. Each collaborative focuses on a single area of improvement in a key clinical or operational area. Participants from 20 to 40 health care organizations work together with a panel of subject-matter experts to identify major, rapid changes designed to achieve improvement in the area addressed. The series model, which is based on the plan-do-study-act improvement cycle, emphasizes testing on a small scale, using "just enough" measurement, and building into each stage of activity a basis for

further action and improvement. As of early 1997, the collaboratives had targeted seven topics: cesarean section rates, adult intensive care, adult cardiac surgery, asthma care, low back pain, adverse drug events, and reducing delays and wait times.

breast cancer   Carcinoma of the ducts or the lobes of the breast, constituting the most common malignancy in women in the United States. Breast cancer was traditionally subdivided into three general stages (early localized disease, spread to regional lymph nodes, and distant metastasis), that have been refined into six stages according to the internationally recognized TNM (tumor node metastasis) staging system (clinical stages I, IIA, IIB, IIIA, IIIB, IV). The great increase in the awareness of breast cancer in earlier stages (due in part to better methods of and greater use of detection efforts such as mammography) and wide variations in treatment methods and results have generated intense research efforts to determine prognostic factors, efficacy of different treatment combinations, and the reasons for choice of different therapies in health care systems and by women. Current terms for general groups of breast cancer vary and are overlapping. Among several prognostic indicators indentified for breast cancer, combined criteria such as tumor estrogen receptor content, cell proliferative index, and lymph node status are frequently used for identifying subsets of patients that may require different therapeutic modalities. *See also* adult-onset cancer; adjuvant therapy; *BRCA1* and *BRCA2* genes; cancer screening tests and procedures; cancer staging system; cancer susceptibility testing; mammography; mastectomy.

breast cancer protocols   Brief documents designed to guide general practice physicians through the appropriate steps of diagnosis and referral for patients reporting or presenting with possible cancer symptoms and to thereby prevent malpractice suits over failures or delays in detecting breast cancer. The protocols are usually developed at the state level by physicians in state medical societies working together with consultants and malpractice insurance carriers. Florida and California spearheaded the movement by developing the first models.

breast-conservation treatment   Breast-conserving surgery followed by irradiation, intended to combine the dual objectives of local tumor control and cosmetic preservation of appearance. Standards of care for this treatment were jointly developed in 1992 by the American Colege of Radiology, American College of Surgeons, the College of American Pathologists, and the Society of Surgical Oncology. *See also* breast cancer; breast-conserving surgery; mastectomy.

breast-conserving surgery   Excision of the primary cancerous breast tumor and adjacent breast tissue while leaving the rest of the breast tissue in place, generally performed for stage I and II breast cancers. *Synonyms:* lumpectomy; partial mastectomy; segmental mastectomy. *See also* breast cancer; breast-conservation treatment; cancer staging systems; mastectomy.

breast examination   Systematic and regular inspection and palpation of the breast, either in *breast self-examination (BSE)* by the woman herself or in the *clinical breast examination (CBE)* in a clinical setting by a health care professional, with a complete examination of the breasts and axilla (underarm area containing lymph nodes and channels). The efficacy of BSE and CBE are usually studied both singly and in combination with each other and with mammography. While some states have mandated breast examination education, the U.S. Preventive Services Task Force reports in its 1996 screening guideline that there is insufficient evidence to recommend for or against the use of screening CBE alone or the teaching of BSE. *See also* cancer screening tests and procedures; mammography.

breech presentation   Postioning of the buttocks first in the advance of the fetus in the birth canal. Breech presentation is recorded as one of the major reasons for performing cesarean sections and is listed as an indication for them in ICD-9. However, routine C-section for breech has recently come under scrutiny with evidence that vaginal delivery (either breech delivery or following external repositioning of the fetus) is appropriate for selected candidates and that legal considerations have driven the routine resort to C-section. Several recent C-section rate reduction initiatives have targeted breech presentation as a source for potential diminution of adverse events associated with C-sections, not to mention cost savings. *See also* cesarean section; external cephalic version; Maine Medical Liability Demonstration project.

brittle diabetes   *See* diabetes mellitus.

Broders' index   *See* cancer staging system.

brokered partnership   A legal relationship between health care providers and purchasers of health care in a self-regulating organization that acts as a broker by matching providers and employers through negotiating price, use, and health services from a competitive position, with both buyers and sellers participating in the decision making.

bronchodilator   *See* asthma.

bronchoscopy   The process of visualizing the tracheo-bronchial tree using a bronchoscope, a tube that contains light-carrying fibers that project an enlarged image to the viewer. Bronchoscopy enables the practitioner to examine the bronchi, obtain a specimen for biopsy or culture, or remove a foreign body from the respiratory tract.

brown lung disease   The common name for byssinosis, a chronic lung disease among textile workers, caused by the inhalation of cotton dust.

building codes   Standards or regulations for construction that are developed to provide an environment that is safe for patient care. *See also Life Safety Code®*.

bulimia nervosa   *See* eating disorders.

burden of suffering   A concept used by the U.S. Preventive Services Task Force to examine conditions that are relatively common in the United States and are of major clinical significance, considering both the prevalence (proportion of the population affected) and the incidence (number of new cases per year) of the condition. The burden of suffering is reported for each of the 70 targeted conditions in the task force's guidelines for clinical preventive services (1996). *Synonym:* burden of illness.

Bureau of Narcotics and Dangerous Drugs (BNDD) number   An outmoded term for the registration number assigned by the U.S. Drug Enforcement Administration (DEA) to a physician, health care organization, pharmacy, or other qualified "business activity." The BNDD number is now called the *DEA registration number* and authorizes the recipient to prescribe or dispense controlled substances. *See also* DEA registration number; schedule of controlled substances.

burn severity   Degree to which severe burns are assessed. Severely burned patients may include those with the following injuries: second-degree burns of more than 25% total body surface area for adults or 20% total body surface area for children; third-degree burns of more than 10% total body surface area; any severe burns on the hands, face, eyes, ears, or feet; and all inhalation injuries, electrical burns, complicated burn injuries involving fractures, and other major traumas.

burn unit   An intensive (special) care unit for treatment of inpatients with severe burns.

business health care coalition   A voluntary organization of employers formed to monitor and communicate information on a wide range of health care issues affecting employees of the individual companies. Such coalitions consist largely of employers who purchase group health insurance coverage and strive to improve their capacity to plan and manage health care benefits and expenditures.

business occupancy   An occupancy used to provide outpatient services or treatment that does not meet the criteria in the ambulatory health care occupancy definition (eg, three or fewer patients at the same time who are rendered incapable of self-preservation in an emergency or are undergoing general anesthesia).

buyers group   Any group—corporations, businesses of any size, HMOs and other managed care organizations, or individuals—that comes together to purchase health insurance, health services, or products (eg, home medical equipment, pharmaceuticals) at lower prices.

bylaws   A governance framework that establishes the roles and responsibilities of a body and its members. Bylaws define the rights and obligations of various officers, persons, or groups within the corporate structure and provide rules for routine matters, such as calling meetings.

bypass   *See* coronary artery bypass graft surgery.

byssinosis   *See* brown lung disease.

Cc

CA-125 A cell surface glycoprotein widely used to monitor residual disease in patients undergoing chemotherapy for ovarian cancer and proposed by some as a screening tool for detecting ovarian cancer. Rising serum levels of the antigen suggest a poor prognosis, but low levels are of little clinical utility. CA-125 is normally expressed on the cell membrane of normal ovarian tissue and 80% or more of nonmucinous (usually serous type) epithelial ovarian cancers. CA-125 levels may also be rising in nongynecological cancers, liver disease, acute pancreatitis, renal failure, lymphoma, and occasionally in normal female organs. Consumer interest in the marker, which came to be known popularly as the "Gilda Radner gene," has grown, but its efficacy as a screener for ovarian cancer remains uncertain and controversial. *See also* Gilda Radner gene; ovarian cancer; tumor markers.

CABG procedure *See* coronary artery bypass graft surgery.

caduceus The wand with two snakes winding around it, carried by Hermes (or Mercury), the messenger of the gods. The official symbol of the medical profession is the staff carried by Aesculapius. The expert system CADUCEUS has taken its name from this emblem. *See also* Aesculapius.

cafeteria plan A benefit plan in which employees may choose from a "menu" of different health care coverage and provider options and pay for them with before-tax dollars. Such plans are designed to save costs for both employees and employers (who pay lower taxes).

CAGE A simple four-question screening test that has been found to predict alcoholism or problem drinking. The name is a mnemonic for words in the four questions: Have you ever felt you should *cut* down on your drinking? Have people *annoyed* you by criticizing your drinking? Have you ever felt bad or *guilty* about your drinking? Have you ever had a drink first thing in the morning to steady your nerves or to get rid of a hangover (an *eye-opener*)? *See also* alcoholism; alcohol-problem screening; dependence; problem drinking; substance-related disorders.

calcium channel blocker A drug that blocks entry of calcium into cells and inhibits the contractility of smooth muscle and as a result dilates the blood vessels and reduces blood pressure. The drug is recommended for lowering blood pressure, but there is disagreement over its best use in managing different heart disorders, such as heart failure. Controversy in the popular press has generated considerable debate over its safety. *Synonyms:* calcium antagonist; calcium entry-blocking agent.

calibration The process or act of determining the accuracy of an instrument, usually by measurement of its variation from a standard, to ascertain necessary correction factors. *See also* measure; measurement; instrument; standard; variation.

calibration material A solution that has a known amount of analyte weighed in or has a value determined by repetitive testing using a reference or definitive test method. Calibration material, also referred to as *standard*, may be traceable to a National Institute of Standards and Technology (NIST) standard.

calibration verification The process used to verify a laboratory's reportable range of individual results based on manufacturers' recommendations or instrument history, and whenever a major change in the reagents or equipment or instrument could affect the calibration. Federal regulations require that calibration verification be performed at least once every six months. *See also* reportable range.

California Medical Insurance Feasibility Study A study (1976) sponsored by the California Medical Association and the California Hospital Association in which researchers used occurrence criteria to review more than 20,000 patient charts from 23 hospitals to identify the presence of adverse events that might result in litigation for malpractice compensation. These events were termed "potentially compensable events" (PCEs). The study determined that 17% of PCEs involved negligence that would justify a verdict for the patient if the claim were brought to litigation. *See also* occurrence criteria; occurrence screening; potentially compensable event.

calorie The gram or small calorie is the amount of heat required to raise one gram of water one degree Celsius at atmospheric pressure. A large calorie (also called great calorie, kilocalorie, kilogram calorie) is the quantity of heat equal to 1,000 small calories. A unit equal to the large calorie is often used to denote the heat expenditure of an organism and the fuel or energy value of food.

Canadian Cardiovascular Society (CCS) angina class *See* angina severity and functional classifications.

Canadian Task Force on the Periodic Health Examination An advisory panel established in 1976 by the Conference of Deputy Ministers of Health of the ten Canadian provinces to determine how the periodic health examination might enhance or protect the health of Canadians and to recommend a plan for a lifetime program of periodic health assessments for all persons living in Canada. The Task Force pioneered the evidence-based approach adopted by the U.S. Preventive Services Task Force, and the two panels continue to work closely together. Guidelines are published in *The Canadian Guide to Clinical Preventive Health Care. See also* evidence-based medicine.

Cancer Genetics Studies Consortium (CGSE) A group founded in 1994 by NIH to address the issues raised by genetic research and its application in clinical settings. The group has established a Task Force on Informed Consent to address issues in cancer susceptibility testing, directed particularly to clinicians whose

AVAILABLE SCREENING TESTS AND PROCEDURES, AND GROUP RECOMMENDATIONS

Type of Cancer	Test for Cancer	American Cancer Society Recommendations	Other Guideline Sources*
Bladder	Urine dipstick Microscopic hematuria Urine cytology		USPSTF CTFPHE
Breast	Self-examination Clinical examination Mammography	F 20 and over, every month F 20-40 , every 3 years F over 40, every year F 40-49, every 1-2 years F 50 and over, every year	AAFP, ACOG, ACP, ACR, AMA, Bright Futures, CTFPHE, HP 2000, NCI, NIH, USPSTF
Cervical	PAP (Papanicolaou) test Pelvic examination HPV (Human papilloma virus)	F 18 and over or sexually active, annual Pap test and pelvic examination—after 3 or consecutive satisfactory normal annual examinations, the Pap test may be performed less frequently at the physician's discretion	AAFP, ACOG, ACP, AMA (GAPS), Bright Futures, CTFPHE, HP 2000, USPSTF
Colorectal	Digital rectal examination Fecal occult blood test Sigmoidoscopy (flexible) Double contrast air enema	M & F, 40 and over M & F, 50 and over M & F, 50 and over	AAFP, AAP, ACOG, ACP, ACR, AGA, AHCPR, HP 2000, ASGE, CTFPHE, USPSTF, WHO
Endometrial	Pelvic examination Endometrial tissue sample	F 18-40, every 1-3 years with Pap test	
Head and Neck Oral	Oral self-examination Clinical examination		CTFPHE, NCI, NIDR
Lung	Chest x-ray Sputum cytology		USPSTF
Ovarian	CA-125 (serum tumor marker) Pelvic examination		AAFP, ACOG, ACP, AMA, AMWA, ANA, CTFPHE, NCI, NIH, USPSTF
Pancreatic	CA19-9, other serologic markers		CTFPHE, USPSTF
Prostate	Digital rectal examination PSA (prostate-specific antigen: serum tumor) TRUS (transurethral ultrasound)	M 50 and over, every year M 50 and over, every year More evaluation if either is abnormal	AAFP, ACP, ACR, AUA, CTFPHE, OTA, Prostate PORT, USPSTF
Skin	Physical examination Self-examination	M & F, every year M & F, every month	AAD, AAFP, ACR, AMA, CTFPHE, NIH, USPSTF
Testicle	Physical examination Palpation Self-examination	M, every year	AAFP, ACS, CTFPHE, USPSTF
Thyroid	Neck palpation Ultrasonography Genetic testing (MEN-2)	M & F, 21-40, every 3 years M & F over 40, once every year	AAFP, CTFPHE, USPSTF

*These groups have made a recommendation for or against, are reviewing the issue and will issue a recommendation, or have found evidence insufficient to support any recommendation on screening for this cancer. The groups' positions on the particular screening or testing options for the condition vary.

AAD = American Academy of Dermatology; AAFP = American Academy of Family Physicians; AAP = American Academy of Pediatrics; ACOG = American College of Obstetricians and Gynecologists; ACP = American College of Physicians; ACR = American College of Radiology; AGA = American Gastroenterological Association; AHCPR = Agency for Health Care Policy and Research; AMA (GAPS) = American Medical Association, Guidelines for Adolescent Preventive Services; AMWA = American Medical Women's Association; ANA = American Nurses Association; ASGE = American Society for Gastrointestinal Endoscopy; Bright Futures = *Guidelines for Health Supervision of Infants, Children, and Adolescents* (1994); CTFPHE = Canadian Task Force on the Periodic Health Examination; HP 2000 = Healthy People 2000; NCI = National Cancer Institute; NIDR = National Institute of Dental Research; NIH = National Institutes of Health, Consensus Conference; OTA = Office of Technology Assessment; PORT = Patient Outcomes Research Team; USPSTF = U.S. Preventive Services Task Force; WHO = World Health Organization

Sources:

American Cancer Society: Cancer Facts and Figures–1994. Atlanta, 1994.

Bennett JC, Plum R (eds.). *Cecil Textbook of Medicine.* Philadelphia: WB Saunders Company, 1996.

U.S. Preventive Services Task Force: *Guide to Clinical Preventive Services.* Second Edition. Baltimore: Williams & Wilkins, 1996.

testing protocols do not have the benefit of institutional review board evaluations. *See also* adult onset cancer; cancer susceptibility testing; genetic counseling.

cancer predisposition   *See* adult-onset cancer; cancer susceptibility testing.

cancer screening tests and procedures   The full battery of techniques ranging from simple self-examination to molecular analysis for detecting early cancer, potential cancer, or genetic susceptibility to cancer of various types in presymptomatic patients. The tests and procedures may be used for mass screening, routine screening (begun at a given age for everyone), or case finding (performed when patients present with some noncancer-related reason). Some screening tests have clearly reduced cancer death rates (Pap smear for cervical cancer, fecal occult blood test for colorectal cancer); others are generally believed to be, or have been, ineffective (chest x-ray or sputum cytologic examinations for lung cancer); and a very large group of procedures for several types of cancer remains a matter of controversy. Major authorities may disagree on choice of screening modality (eg, fecal occult blood test versus double contrast barium enema) or on age of first initiation and screening intervals for different patient populations (eg, mammograms). *See also* laboratory screening tests; mammography.

cancer's seven warning signals   An educational aid developed by the American Cancer Society and expressed by the mnemonic CAUTION: *change* in bowel or bladder habits; *a sore* that does not heal; *unusual* bleeding or discharge; *thickening* or lump in breast or elsewhere; *indigestion* or difficulty in swallowing; *obvious* change in wart or mole; *nagging* cough or hoarseness.

cancer staging system   A system for describing in replicable terms the size and extent of spread of a malignant tumor, used to plan treatment and predict prognosis. Two commonly used systems are the TNM (tumor node metastasis) staging system (recommended by the American Joint Committee for Cancer Staging and End Results), and the Dukes' system, both of which can be adapted to describe stages specific to particular kinds of cancer, such as colorectal cancer or breast cancer. These systems can be shown side by side to permit use of both or "translation" from one to another system (see accompanying table). Another system is the FIGO group, named for any of the classification systems established by the International Federation of Gynecology and Obstetrics for the staging of gynecological cancers. For some cancer types,

---

CANCER STAGING AND TUMOR GRADING SYSTEMS
Comparison of TNM and Dukes' Staging Systems for Colorectal Cancer

Stage	TNM Designation			Dukes' Designation
	Tumor	Node	Metastasis	
0	Tis	N0	M0	—
I	T1	N0	M0	A
	T2	N	M0	
II	T3	N0	M0	B
	T4	N0	M0	
III	Any T	N1	M0	C
	Any T	N2, N3	M0	
IV	Any T	Any N	M1	D

Key: Tis = in situ; T1 = tumor invades submucosa; T2 = tumor invades muscularis propria; T3 = tumor invades through muscularis propria; T4 = tumor invades serosa, nodes, and adjacent organs; N0 = negative lymph nodes; N1 = 1-3 positive nodes; N2 = more than 3 positive nodes; N3 = positive nodes on vascular trunk; M0 = no distant metastases; M1 = distant metastases

Source: Winawer SJ, Fletcher RH, et al for the Independent Expert Guidelines Panel: Colorectal cancer screening and surveillance: Clinical guidelines and rationale. *Gastroenterology* 112:594-642, 1997. Philadelphia: W.B. Saunders

Broders' Index for Grade of Tumor*

Grade	Degree of Differentiation
1	One-fourth undifferentiated cells
2	One-half undifferentiated cells
3	Three-fourths undifferentiated cells
4	All cells undifferentiated

*An index of malignancy based on the fact that the more undifferentiated or embryonic the cells of tumor, the more malignant the tumor.

Source: *Dorland's Illustrated Medical Dictionary*, 28th Edition. Philadelphia: W.B. Saunders, 1994.

Staging of Carcinoma of the Breast

Stage 1	Tumor ≤2 cm without skin or chest wall involvement and without regional lymph node metastases
Stage II	Tumor < 2 cm without nodal metastases; tumor ≤5 cm with metastasis to moveable ipsilateral axillary nodes
Stage III	Tumor > 5 cm with regional lymph node metastases; skin involvement or chest wall attachment; any size tumor with metastases to fixed ipsilateral axillary nodes or ipsilateral internal mammary nodes
Stage IV	Distant metastases

Source: Bennett JC, Plum F (eds). *Cecil Textbook of Medicine*. Philadelphia, PA: W.B. Saunders, 1996.

such as cervical cancer (the 1991 Bethesda system has replaced the old Papanicolaou system) and lymphoma (the newest is the 1994 REAL [Revised European-American Lymphoma] system), there have been successive changing of staging categories as new discoveries are made and better ways are found to express the cancer pattern. A related concept is *grade*, which describes the degree of differentiation (well differentiated or poorly differentiated).

cancer susceptibility testing Use of molecular analysis and other genetic testing techniques to detect presence of inherited cancer susceptibility genes in presymptomatic persons. Among the many inherited cancer-predisposing genes that have been identified, those for breast or ovarian cancer, colorectal cancer, and the Lynch syndromes (multiple cancers along with breast and ovarian cancer) have received the most public attention. Although the testing has for the most part been recommended only for research settings, demand is high for its use, which is emerging in clinical practice and is the subject of surveys by managed care organizations. Out of concern about risks and the need to guarantee informed consent, the American Society of Clinical Oncology has issued a statement on genetic testing for cancer susceptibility, recommending that testing be offered only when (1) the person has a strong family history of cancer or very early age of onset of disease, (2) the test can be adequately interpreted, and (3) the results will influence the medical management of the patient or family member. *See also* adult-onset cancer; *BRCA1* and *BRCA2* genes; genetic counseling; genetic discrimination; genetic risk assessment; genetic testing; Gilda Radner gene; Human Genome Project; mastectomy.

cannabis *See* medical marijuana.

capital cost The cost of investing in the development of new facilities, services, or equipment, excluding operational costs.

capital expenditure review Prospective review by a designated state regulatory agency of the need to expend capital on specific organization proposals.

capital improvement A modification, addition, restoration, or other improvement that increases the usefulness, productivity, or serviceable life of an existing building, structure, or major item of equipment, and that increases the recorded worth of the item or entity.

capitation A method of payment for health services in which a health care provider is paid a fixed, per capita amount for each person served without regard to the actual number or nature of services provided to each person. Under this system, a managed care plan, such as an HMO, pays a physician or a hospital a fixed amount to care for a patient over a given time. Health care providers do not receive extra money even if the costs of care exceed the fixed amount. *See also* age- and sex-specific capitation; base capitation; capitation grant; fee for service; full-risk capitation; global capitation.

capitation grant A method of federal support for health professional schools, such as medical schools, in which an eligible school receives a fixed capitation payment, called a capitation grant, from the federal government for each student enrolled.

captain of the ship doctrine The principle that the person in charge of a group, such as a surgeon in charge of a surgical team, is responsible and liable for the actions of every member under his or her supervision, such as all of the members of a surgical team. The trend is to abolish this doctrine and to impose liability on the party who has actual control over the employee who performed negligently.

captive insurance company An insurance company formed to insure the risks of its owner(s), such as a hospital(s) or physicians.

carcinoembryonic antigen (CEA) An antigen existing in small amounts in adult tissue, often used as a tumor marker. An elevated amount is suggestive of cancers of the colon and rectum, pancreas, stomach, lung, and breast, although CEA levels may also be elevated in patients with alcoholic cirrhosis, pancreatitis, and inflammatory bowel disease, as well as patients who smoke.

carcinogen Any cancer-producing substance. Carcinogens in food are defined and identified under the Delaney clause of the U.S. Federal Food, Drug, and Cosmetic Act, which states that no cancer-causing agent, as demonstrated in humans or animals, shall be deliberately added to or found as a contaminant in food.

cardiac arrhythmia Irregular or abnormally slow or rapid beating of the heart.

Cardiac Arrhythmia PORT *See* Patient Outcomes Research Teams.

cardiac care unit (CCU) An intensive (special) care unit for treatment and continuous monitoring of inpatients with cardiac disorders. *Synonyms*: cardiac intensive care unit; cardiovascular care unit; coronary intensive care unit; coronary care unit.

cardiac catheterization An invasive procedure consisting of the passage of a radiopaque catheter into a peripheral vein (or an artery when the left side of the heart is being catheterized), followed by its advancement under fluoroscopic control until the tip lies in one of the chambers of the heart. The procedure is used to measure intracardiac pressure abnormalities, obtain cardiac blood samples, or image cardiac structures by injection of radiopaque dye.

cardiac electrophysiology (EP) study An invasive test using the cardiac catheter electrode system to measure the electrical conduction system of the heart. The electrode catheters are usually advanced through veins into the right atrium and right ventricle of the heart. The test can detect cardiac arrhythmias or induce a patient's arrhythmias to test antiarrhythmic drugs as therapy. Cardiac EP studies are also used as part of the diagnostic workup for syncope (fainting). *Synonyms:* electrocardiography; EP test; EP study; HIS bundle procedure.

cardiac pacemaker   A battery-driven electrical device that regulates the heartbeat by electrically stimulating the heart muscle, used to manage arrhythmias when the heart's natural pacemaker is not working properly or its electrical pathway is blocked. It may be connected from the outside (temporary transvenous or transthoracic pacemaker) or implanted under the skin (permanent cardiac pacemaker). The main types are the *fixed-rate pacemaker,* in which the generator stimulates the heart at a predetermined rate regardless of the heart's rhythm, and the *demand cardiac pacemaker*, in which the generator stimulus is inhibited for a set interval by a signal, thus minimizing the risk of pacemaker-induced ventricular fibrillation. Under an international shorthand code describing pacemaker function, pacemaker types are identified by letters or combinations of letters, appearing in a given order to identify the chamber that is paced and the chamber that is sensed for intrinsic activity (A = atrium, V = ventricle, D = dual [A & V]) and also to show the type of response to sensing (I = inhibited, T = triggered) and programmability (R = rate modulation). The most common type is a *ventricular demand pacemaker* (VVI), indicating that the ventricle is paced, that the device is sensing intrinsic activity, and that it will be inhibited when it senses an event. Other types of pacemakers are the *rate-responsive* (or *rate-adaptive*) devices (VVIR), which contain a sensor to detect physical activity and adjust the rate accordingly, and *dual-chamber pacemakers* (DDD), which can be either inhibited or triggered. The choice of pacemakers is governed by the severity and specific features of the cardiac disorder, the presence of comorbidities, and costs. Controversy over the volume and appropriate use of pacemaker technology, reflecting concern over costs and the degree of risk, has prompted the development and revision of clinical practice guidelines and consensus recommendations. *Synonym:* antiarrhythmia device. *See also* arrhythmia; cardiac arrhythmia; pacemaker syndrome.

cardiac rehabilitation program   Restorative services used after open heart surgery, angioplasty, and acute myocardial infarction and for patients identified as being at high risk for undesirable cardiovascular events. Through such programs, patients are reconditioned from a state of cardiac injury or high risk to resume activities of daily living (ADL) at an optimal level. Programs often include counseling, education, and exercise and may be structured (traditional form) or home based. AHCPR targeted cardiac rehabilitation for development of a clinical practice guideline (1995). *See also* activities of daily living; acute myocardial infarction; physical fitness program.

cardiology   *See* cardiovascular medicine.

cardiopulmonary resuscitation (CPR)   The administration of artificial heart and lung action in the event of cardiac and/or respiratory arrest. The two major components of cardiopulmonary resuscitation are artificial ventilation and closed-chest cardiac massage. *See also*

basic cardiac life support; code blue; crash cart; slow code.

cardiorespiratory fitness   The body's ability to perform high-intensity activity for a prolonged period of time without undue stress or fatigue. *Synonym:* aerobic capacity.

cardiovascular medicine   The branch of medicine and subspecialty of internal medicine dealing with diseases of the heart and blood vessels and management of complex cardiac conditions, such as heart attacks and life-threatening abnormal heart rhythms. *Synonym:* cardiology. *See also* internal medicine.

cardiovascular surgery   *See* thoracic surgery.

cardioversion   The restoration or attempt at restoration of a normal rhythm of the heart by electrical shock or administration of certain medications.

care   The provision of accommodations, comfort, and treatment to an individual, implying responsibility for safety, including care, treatment, services, habilitation, rehabilitation, or other programs instituted by the organization or network for the individual.

care and service provider organization   For purposes of Joint Commission accreditation, an organized site of service in a managed health care delivery system for which the Joint Commission has relevant standards (eg, partial hospitalization, residential treatment center, outpatient mental health clinic, community mental health center, therapeutic foster care) or other entities with which the delivery system contracts for specific services. The care and service provider organization performs the important functions of a health care organization and may also be known as a program.

care coordination   *See* coordination of care and services.

caregiver   A family member, a significant other, a friend, a volunteer, or an individual employed by an organization or the patient to provide services in the home.

care management   Coordination of care within a specific unit or area, focusing on effectively managing patient care during the time a patient is located within a specific geographic area (eg, hospital unit, home health program).

care path   *See* critical pathway.

care plan   *See* plan of care.

care planning   A process that identifies individual needs of, treatment goals for, and resulting plans of action for patients receiving home care or other health services. Care planning includes activities designed to reduce the risk of illness, injury, or a disabling condition or the provision of equipment necessary to treatment.

carotid endarterectomy   Surgical removal of the inner layer of the carotid artery (a major blood vessel leading to the head) when it is thickened and obstructed.

Carotid endarterectomy is sometimes performed for asymptomatic patients to lower the risk of a future stroke after discovery of a bruit (murmur, abnormal sound) through screening auscultation of the carotid arteries. Asymptomatic patients found to have high-grade stenosis or total occlusion are often advised to undergo the procedure. However, controversy remains after many comparative efficacy studies with conflicting results over how to define the candidate for the invasive procedure and how to calculate the benefit-harm ratio (with harms such as perioperative complications including stroke or death).

carrier **1.** An individual who harbors the specific organisms of a disease without manifesting symptoms and who is capable of transmitting the infection. **2.** An individual who bears a recessive gene that can be transmitted to offspring. **3.** An insurance company (a commercial health insurer, a government agency, an insurance plan, a service plan, or a prepaid plan) that underwrites or administers programs that pay for insured health services. *See also* Medicare locality; nonprofit carrier; third-party payer.

carve out **1.** The largely prohibited practice of denying coverage or arranging alternative coverage for potentially costly services or individuals. This technique, which is prohibited in 40 states, is used to avoid adverse selection. *See also* adverse selection. **2.** A method used to identify which benefits are paid by an employer's program (private insurer) and which are paid by Medicare. **3.** A cost-saving practice among large corporations that eliminates a specific set of services from a health plan and contracts with a separate provider for those services. For example, mental health services may be "carved out" from health insurance and provided through employee assistance programs. *See also* employee assistance program.

cascade iatrogenesis A sequence of two or more serious undesirable occurrences resulting from a diagnostic, prophylactic, or therapeutic intervention; an error of omission involving a reasonable clinical standard; or an accidental injury occurring in a health care setting.

case abstract A group of data elements summarizing information in a medical record and used for billing, performance review, and research.

case-based review An approach to quality-of-care evaluation based on review of individual medical records by health professionals who make judgments as to whether the care delivered was of acceptable quality.

case conference *See* morbidity and mortality conference.

case-control study An inquiry in which groups of individuals are selected because they do (the cases) or do not (the controls) have the disease whose cause and other attributes are being studied. The groups are then compared with respect to their past, existing, or future characteristics judged likely to be relevant to the disease to see which of the characteristics differ, and how, in the cases as compared to the controls. For example, persons with hepatic cancer (cases) are compared with persons without hepatic cancer (controls), and history of hepatitis B is determined for the two groups. A case-control study is a type of retrospective study. *Synonyms*: case-comparison study; case-referent study. *See also* retrospective study.

case finding Clinicians' search for disease by screening their own patients when they visit the office or clinic for reasons other than the screened-for condition. Case finding is contrasted with screening of unselected populations. Case finding may be used, for instance, to check for hypertension, depression, or problem drinking. *See also* laboratory screening tests.

case history The collected data concerning an individual, his or her family, and environment, including his or her medical history and any other information that may be useful in analyzing and diagnosing his or her condition for instructional purposes.

case management A process to manage and coordinate health care resource use in the provision of care and services. Its goals are to coordinate patient or group patient care across an episode or continuum; ensure and facilitate achievement of quality and clinical cost outcomes; negotiate, procure, and coordinate services and resources needed by patients and their families; intervene at key points or significant variances for individual patients; address and resolve patterns in aggregate variances that have a negative quality-cost impact; and create opportunities and systems to enhance outcomes.

case mix The relative frequency of patients classified into categories by disease, procedure, method of payment, and other characteristics. *See also* DRG; patient mix.

case-mix index In prospective payment systems, the comparison of a hospital's cost for its case mix to the national or regional average hospital cost for a similar case mix. *See also* prospective payment system.

case-mix management information system (CMMIS) A computerized data system in which elements from case abstracts and patient bills are analyzed for costs and charges by DRGs in relation to hospital and physician fees for those DRGs.

case-mix severity Level of severity of illness or disability within a particular case-mix grouping.

case series In research, a series of patients with a defined disorder, as in series of patients with false aneurysms of the femoral artery. The term usually describes a study reporting on a consecutive collection of patients treated in a similar manner, without a concurrent control group. For example, a surgeon might describe the characteristics of and outcomes for 30 consecutive patients with a femoral artery false aneurysm who received a revascularization procedure.

case severity A measure of the intensity or gravity of a patient's illness for a specified condition or diagnosis. Also, the average severity of illnesses for all patients of a health care organization during a given period. Case severity is often indirectly measured by the average length of stay, implying that "sicker" patients require longer periods of hospitalization. The direct measurement of case severity has become increasingly important with the use of DRGs to determine hospital reimbursements by Medicare and other third-party payers. Many view case severity as a needed modifier for DRG-based reimbursement.

casework   Social work devoted to the needs of individual clients or cases.

cataract   An opacity, partial or complete, of one or both eyes, on or in the lens or capsule, especially an opacity impairing vision or causing blindness.

cataract surgery   Removal of an opacified lens (cataract) from the eye to restore sight.

catastrophic illness   An illness that incurs great costs beyond the average person's ability to pay and is usually life threatening or results in disability.

catastrophic insurance   Insurance intended to protect against the cost of a catastrophic illness, with catastrophic defined as greater than a predetermined cost. *See also* insurance.

catchment area   A geographic region defined and served by a health program or organization. *Synonym:* service area. *See also* health service area; Medicare locality; patient origin study.

categorically needy   Individuals who are members of certain categories or groups eligible to receive public assistance and who are economically needy (eg, the aged, the blind, the disabled, a member of a family with children under age 18 or 21 years, if in school). These individuals generally are receiving cash assistance under the Aid to Families with Dependent Children (AFDC) or Supplemental Security Income programs. States must cover all recipients of AFDC payments under Medicaid. The categorically needy must meet state income and resource requirements. *See also* Medicaid; medically indigent; supplemental security income.

catheterization   The process of passing a catheter into a cavity or organ of the body, as in urinary catheterization or cardiac catheterization.

catheter-related infection (CRI)   Infection at the site of catheter insertion, frequently occurring in central venous catheters in critically ill infants and children. CRIs are major problems for health care organizations because of their harm to the patient, prolongation of hospitalization, and increased costs for therapy. Antimicrobial silver coating of intravascular catheters may be effective, according to preliminary studies. *See also* central venous catheterization.

CAT scan   *See* computed axial tomography.

cauda equina syndrome   Compression (usually due to the extrinsic pressure of a massive, centrally herniated disk) on a sheaf of nerve roots from the lower cord seg-

ments (resembling the tail of a horse), often resulting in bilateral motor weakness of the lower extremities, saddle anesthesia, and urine retention or incontinence from loss of sphincter function. The symptoms are a red flag in managing low back pain and require immediate attention. *See also* low back pain.

causation   The act by which an effect is produced. In epidemiology, the doctrine of causation is used to relate certain factors (predisposing, enabling, precipitating, and/or reinforcing factors) to disease occurrence. The doctrine of causation is also important in the fields of negligence and criminal law. *Synonym:* causality.

cause-and-effect diagram   A pictorial display drawn to represent the causal relationship between outcomes and factors in those outcomes. The causes, or "bones," increase in detail and branch off from the main horizontal line, or "backbone," towards the effect or outcome. Common causal categories include work methods, people, materials, and equipment.

cause of action   The fact(s) that gives a person a right to judicial redress against another. *See also* malpractice.

causes-of-death rankings   Lists of leading causes of death and preventable causes of death issued by the Centers for Disease Control and Prevention and used for education and advocacy by various other groups. Top causes of death in the United States include heart disease and cancer. Actual cause of death—major external (nongenetic) factors that contribute to death—include pollutants, firearms, motor vehicles, and sexual behavior.

CD4+ T lymphocyte   *See* HIV infection.

center of excellence   A tertiary care facility that has established a reputation for superior quality in one or more areas. Its reputation tends to draw patients from extended geographical areas, thereby lowering the cost of providing care through economies of scale. *See also* catchment area; economies of scale.

central line   *See* central venous catheterization.

central operations   A centralized structure that coordinates services provided by care and service provider organizations and practitioners participating in the delivery system.

central processing   The receiving, decontaminating, cleaning, preparing, disinfecting, and sterilizing of reusable items. Central processing is the function of the central service unit of a health care organization.

central tendency   A property of the distribution of a variable, usually measured by statistics such as the mean, median, and mode.

central venous catheterization   Placement of an intravascular catheter in the subclavian, jugular, or other central vein for central venous pressure determination, chemotherapy, hemodialysis, or hyperalimentation. *Synonym:* central line. *See also* catheter-related infection.

central venous pressure (CVP) Blood pressure measured within the main veins of the body, usually with a specially designed catheter called a central venous pressure catheter.

cephalosporin A broad-spectrum antibiotic closely related to penicillin and originally derived from the fungus *Cephalosporium*. Cephalosporins are commonly referred to as first-generation, second-generation, or third-generation cephalosporins.

cerebral death *See* persistent vegetative state.

cerebrovascular accident (CVA) *See* stroke.

certificate of compliance A document signed by an authorized party affirming that the supplier of a service or product has met the requirements of the relevant specifications, contract, or regulation. *Synonyms*: certificate of conformance; certificate of conformity.

certificate of insurance (COI) A certificate issued by an insurance company to verify that an individual (such as a physician) or an institution is insured for a certain type of risk during a specific period.

certificate of need (CON) A certificate issued by a governmental body, such as a state health planning and development agency, to an individual or a health care organization proposing to construct or modify a facility, incur a major capital expenditure, or offer a new or different health service. When a certificate is required (eg, for proposals that change bed capacity), it is a condition of licensure of the organization or service and is intended to control expansion of health care organizations and services in the public interest by preventing excessive or duplicate development of organizations and services.

certification The procedure and action by which a duly authorized body evaluates and recognizes (certifies) an individual, institution, or educational program as meeting predetermined requirements, such as standards. Certification differs from accreditation in that certification can be applied to individuals (eg, a medical specialist), whereas accreditation is applied to institutions or programs (eg, a hospital or a residency program). Certification programs are generally nongovernmental and do not exclude the uncertified from practice as do licensure programs. While licensure is meant to establish the minimum competence required to protect the public health, safety, and welfare, certification enables the public to identify those practitioners who have met a standard of training and experience set above the level required for licensure. *Synonym*: occupational certification. *See also* accreditation; labor certification; licensure.

certified hospital A hospital recognized by the U.S. Department of Health and Human Services as meeting its standards for participation as a provider in the Medicare program. *See also* Medicare.

cervical cancer screening *See* cancer screening tests and procedures; Pap smear.

cesarean section (C-section) Surgical delivery of a fetus through incisions in the abdominal wall (laparotomy) and the uterine wall (hysterotomy), usually designated in hospital policies or protocols as the procedure of choosing certain defined circumstances, such as fetal distress or failure to progress. This definition does not include removal of the fetus from the abdominal cavity in case of rupture of the uterus or abdominal pregnancy. Hospitals' C-section rates are widely used as a quality indicator or benchmark (especially as an indicator of overuse of a procedure), and the patterns of use are studied closely for adherence to guidelines or policies on appropriate indications for choosing of the procedure over vaginal delivery. A recent initiative at one hospital, for example, states an objective of reducing a total C-section rate by 30% over a 12-month period with no increase in adverse outcomes for mothers or infants (which is determined by tracking perinatal mortalities, Apgar scores, and transfers to the neonatal intensive care unit). *Synonyms*: abdominal delivery; cesarean delivery; C-section. *See also* dystocia; fetal distress; Patient Outcomes Research Teams; Maine Medical Liability Demonstration project.

chairside The dentistry equivalent of *bedside* in medicine, meaning the clinical setting. *See also* dentistry.

change agent An individual whose efforts facilitate change in a group or organization.

HEALTH CARE WORKERS WHO MAY BE CERTIFIED

Individual	Certifying Institution
Certified coding specialist (CCS)	American Health Information Management Association
Certified counselor	National Board for Certified Counselors
Certified critical care nurse (CCRN)	American Association of Critical-Care Nurses
Certified medical assistant (CMA)	American Association of Medical Assistants
Certified medical representative	Certified Medical Representatives Institute
Certified nurse	American Nurses Association
Certified nurse-midwife (CNM)	American College of Nurse-Midwives
Certified patient account manager (CPAM)	American Guild of Patient Account Managers
Certified professional bureau executive (CPBE)	Medical-Dental-Hospital Bureaus of America
Certified professional in quality assurance (CPQA)	National Association of Quality Assurance Professionals
Certified registered nurse anesthetist (CRNA)	Council on Certification of Nurse Anesthetists
Certified safety professional (CSP)	Board of Certified Safety Professionals

channeling In long term care, directing patients to community-based long term care services in an effort to avoid institutionalization.

chaplaincy service *See* pastoral care.

charitable immunity A now largely discarded doctrine under which charitable enterprises, such as a hospital, were held blameless for their negligent actions. *See also* immunity.

charitable organization An organization whose revenues are generated in whole or in substantial part from charitable donations and that specializes in inpatient services for the indigent. Many children's hospitals are charitable organizations.

charity allowance A reduced charge for health care services for indigent or medically indigent patients. *See also* medically indigent.

charity care Free or reduced-fee care provided to patients with financial constraints.

Charlson Index A method of classifying prognostic comorbidity in longitudinal studies.

chart *See* medical record.

charter statement In quality improvement, a list of the duties and responsibilities of a quality improvement project team. *See also* quality improvement team.

chart review A form of medical record review that may be carried out routinely or in a focused review aimed at a particular topic or practitioner. As routine medical record review, it may cover such matters as admission history, operative notes, or discharge diagnosis for DRG assignment to determine the timeliness of completion of various elements of care. A focused chart review may be conducted when occurrence screening or clinical indicators warrant further evaluation. For example, a hospital may conduct a chart review of all patient deaths within 24 hours of death or after autopsy. *See also* medical record; sentinel event.

checklist A list of actions or items to be reviewed or completed during a process, such as a performance improvement project. The tasks or items are checked off as they are completed or identified.

check sheet A data-collection form that helps to summarize data based on sample observations and to identify patterns and trends. Check sheets are a basic statistical tool, used to record data that answer objective questions requiring a simple "yes" or "no" response using agreed-upon operational definitions. The check sheet starts the process of translating opinions into facts. The completed form displays the data in a simple graphic summary and includes source information (name of project, location of data collection, date, other important identifiers) and content information (event name, collection dates, totals). *Synonym*: checksheet.

chelation therapy An alternative therapy for heavy metal poisoning using agents that remove the metal from organs or tissues and bind it firmly within the ring structure of a new compound that can be eliminated from the body.

chem 6, chem 12 Basic blood chemistry laboratory tests, performed together in a test battery.

chemical abuse *See* substance-related disorders.

chemical equivalence The degree to which drug products contain identical amounts of the same active ingredients in the same dosage forms, meet existing physicochemical standards in official compendia, and are chemically indistinguishable. *See also* bioequivalence; pharmaceutical equivalence.

chemical pathology The branch of medicine and subspecialty of pathology dealing with the application of biochemical data to the detection, confirmation, or monitoring of disease.

chemosurgery A surgical technique in which skin cancer is microscopically excised.

chest pain observation unit (CPOU) A section of, or a center based in, an emergency department (ED), where patients can be admitted for a 12-hour stay or otherwise sufficient time in order to perform tests to establish or rule out heart attack. The component is designed to avoid unnecessary hospitalization. ED-based CPOUs are growing rapidly in urban areas and are undergoing comparative patient satisfaction and cost-effectiveness study.

chest surgery *See* thoracic surgery.

child A person between birth and 13 years of age.

child abuse Physical, emotional, or sexual maltreatment of children, usually by parents, relatives, or caretakers. *See also* abuse; child protection services; medical neglect.

Child Abuse Amendments (1985) Regulations intended to prevent the withholding of medically indicated treatment from a seriously ill infant with a life-threatening condition, except under certain specific circumstances where treatment would be futile. These regulations were ruled invalid, but the federal Child Abuse Amendments of 1984 made such withholding of treatment a form of child neglect, and thus provided an avenue of legal recourse for health professionals or other interested persons.

child and adolescent psychiatry The branch and subspecialty of psychiatry dealing with the diagnosis and treatment of mental, addictive, and emotional disorders of childhood and adolescence. *See also* adolescence; child protection services; play therapy.

childbirth center *See* birthing center.

child death rate The number of deaths of children aged 1 to 4 years in a given year per 1,000 children in this age group. This rate is a useful measure of the burden of preventable communicable diseases in the child population.

Child Health Act of 1967   A part of the federal Social Security Act that authorizes funds for maternal and infant care and care for preschool and school-age children. Dental care, crippled children's services, family planning services, and training and research funding are covered under this act. *See also* Social Security Act.

child health insurance coverage acts   Policy options introduced by members of the U.S. Congress, state legislatures, and the Clinton administration, starting in the 1997 legislative sessions, to address the gap between Medicaid and current private insurance coverage. The proposals are a response to growing public interest and support following release of government reports showing that children comprise the largest group of Americans without health insurance (1 out of 4 uninsured persons). The acts include the Children's Health Coverage Act of 1997, the Healthy Children's Pilot Program Act of 1997, the Children's Health Insurance Act of 1997, the Child Health Insurance and Lower Deficit (CHILD) Act, and the Children's Health Insurance Provides Security (CHIPS) Act of 1997. Most of the proposals use income-adjusted approaches, and several include mechanisms to prevent further deterioration in employer-based coverage.

childhood immunization   *See* immunization schedules.

child life specialist   A specialist who works to reduce the stress of hospitalization for children, adolescents, and their families.

child protection services   Services that help families recognize the causes of any problems and strengthen parental ability to provide acceptable care. *See also* adult protection services; child abuse.

chiropody   *See* podiatry.

chiropractic   A system of medicine, founded in 1895 by D.D. Palmer, based on the principles that the nervous system largely determines the state of health and that disease results from nervous system malfunctioning. Treatment consists primarily of adjusting or manipulating parts of the body, especially the spinal column, and radiography is used only for diagnosis. Operations, drugs, and immunizations are usually rejected as violations of the human body. *Straight chiropractic* adheres strictly to the original Palmer principles and objects to any departures in terminology and scope of practice. It is in contention with the rest of the profession, sometimes called *mixing* or *mixed chiropractic* because of the cooperation with traditional medical doctors and use of some medical principles of diagnosis and referral. The World Chiropractic Alliance (mixed) and the Congress of Chiropractic State Associations (straight) both published practice guidelines in 1993.

chi-square distribution   In statistics, a variable with K degrees of freedom that is distributed like the sum of the squares of K independent random variables, each of which has a normal distribution with mean zero and variance one. *See also* goodness-of-fit test.

chi-squared test   The probability distribution of the sum of the squares of two or more variables, each of which has a normal distribution with mean zero and variance one. It is best used with nominal data. *Synonym*: chi-square test. *See also* goodness-of-fit test .

chlamydia   *See* sexually transmitted disease.

cholecystectomy   Surgical removal of the gallbladder, which may be performed through traditional open surgery or through laparoscopic (keyhole) surgery. *See also* laparoscopic cholecystectomy.

cholesterol   A fat-like substance (lipid) present in cell membranes and a precursor of bile acids and steroid hormones; it travels in the blood in distinct particles containing both lipid and proteins (lipoproteins). It is the most abundant steroid in animal tissues, especially in bile and gallstones, and is present in food, especially animal fats. The level of cholesterol in the blood is determined partly by inheritance and partly by acquired factors such as diet, calorie balance, and level of physical activity. It is essential in moderate amounts and harmful in excess (associated with development of coronary heart disease), especially with too much "bad" cholesterol (low-density lipoprotein) in proportion to "good" cholesterol (high-density lipoprotein) in the total cholesterol. *See also* the following cholesterol terms, as well as atherosclerosis; coronary heart disease; high-density lipoprotein; hypercholesterolemia.

cholesterol-lowering drugs   Medications given singly or in combination to lower the level of LDL-C. Drug therapy may be given as primary prevention of CHD for patients without evidence of CHD whose high LDL-C levels cannot be reduced by dietary therapy and counseling; it is given as secondary prevention for most patients with CHD. Available drug therapies are bile acid sequestrants, nicotinic acid, the HMGCoA reductase inhibitors (statins), fibric acid derivatives, and probucol. *See also* coronary heart disease; atherosclerosis.

cholesterol profile   The total cholesterol (C), high-density and low-density lipoprotein (HDL-C; LDL-C) levels and their ratio. A *lipid* profile includes these cholesterol values and triglycerides. Expert panels have defined *high* (more than 240 mg/dL) and *borderline high* (200 to 239 mg/dL) total C, but the association with coronary heart disease is multifactorial. Risk is due primarily to high levels of LDL-C, and there is an independent inverse association between high HDL-C and CHD risk. A single measurement may not reflect a patient's true or average cholesterol, which may vary as much as 14% from an individual's average under acceptable laboratory conditions. For this reason, advising patients of their range rather than a single value is recommended. *See also* lipid profile.

cholesterol screening   Measurement of cholesterol in asymptomatic or high-risk adults and children to identify hypercholesterolemia (elevated blood cholesterol) and related lipid disorders and to aid in preventing coronary heart disease (CHD). The question of who to screen has generated sharp debate among experts, who do not agree. Most professional groups support screening patients who are at high risk for CHD, but they are divided into "universal" screening and "at risk" screening camps in their recommendations for everyone else. The National Heart, Lung, and Blood Institute (NHLBI) of the National Cholesterol Education Program (NCEP) *Second Report of the Expert Panel on Detection, Evaluation, and Treatment of High Blood Cholesterol in Adults* (1993) recommends wide screening, reaffirmed in 1996 by the American Heart Association's endorsement. The American College of Physicians, in its 1996 updated revision of their guidelines, and the U.S. Preventive Services Task Force recommend more targeted screening. Difficulties in reaching agreement on specific risk factors and populations in order to formulate public health screening policies have been compounded by the appearance of home cholesterol testing kits (approved by the FDA). *See also* coronary heart disease; evangelists and snails; hypercholesterolemia.

Christian Science A religion that prohibits all forms of medical care and relies solely on spiritual healing. Adherents' belief that disease and sin are caused by mental error and may be eliminated through spiritual treatment without medical intervention is protected by the principle of autonomy. If, however, a child of a Christian Scientist family is ill and these beliefs would seriously jeopardize the child's health, the parents would have limited power in decision making. The services of Christian Science sanatoria are covered under some health insurance programs including Medicare and, in some states, Medicaid. *Synonyms*: Christian Science Church; Church of Christ, Scientist; Churches of Christ Scientist.

chronic care Care provided to patients on a long-term basis. *See also* acute care.

chronic disease A disease with one or more of the following characteristics: it is permanent; it leaves residual disability; it is caused by nonreversible pathological alteration; it requires special rehabilitative training for the patient; and it may be expected to require a long period of supervision, observation, or care. *Synonym*: chronic illness.

chronic disease facility A facility that provides medical and skilled nursing services to patients with long-term illnesses who are not in an acute phase but who require an intensity of services not available in nursing homes.

chronic obstructive pulmonary disease (COPD) A disease state characterized by the presence of air-flow obstruction due to chronic bronchitis or emphysema; the obstruction is generally progressive and may be partially reversible. Under a new classification and a proposed staging system in comprehensive guidelines (November 1995) from the American Thoracic Society (ATS), asthma is no longer subsumed under COPD and is treated as a separate condition—with the exception of an unremitting asthma, which remains classified as COPD because of the difficulty in differentiating between the two. The ATS proposes a staging based on FEV1 (forced expiratory volume in one second) to gauge the prognosis, the impact on health-related quality of life (HRQOL), and the most appropriate care setting. The primary cause (80%–90% of risk) of COPD is exposure to tobacco smoke. In 1997 NIH announced the formation of a new program to implement a national strategy on COPD, the National Lung Health Education Program (LHEP), which will function much like NIH's National Asthma Education Prevention Program. *See also* asthma; forced expiratory volume; lung volume reduction surgery.

chronic vegetative state *See* persistent vegetative state.

chronobiology The scientific study of the effect of time on living systems. *See also* circadian rhythm.

chronological age A person's age expressed as the period of time that has elapsed since birth. This may not be the same as the person's developmental age. *See also* developmental age; functional age; mental age.

chronotherapeutics A branch of therapeutic medicine in which the administration of drugs is synchronized with circadian (natural daily) rhythms. The concept is based on the response of biological functions to time-related events, such as the low point in epinephrine levels between 10 pm and 4 am or the elevated histamine levels

Chronic Obstructive Pulmonary Disease (COPD) Classification and Staging System		
Stage	**Pulmonary Function**	**Health Care Impact and Setting**
I	$FEV_1 \geqq 50\%$ predicted	These patients (great majority of COPD) usually do not have severe hypoxemia (deficient oxygenation of blood), and arterial blood gas measurements are not required. They will usually be cared for on a continuing basis by a generalist (the presence of severe dyspnea warrants additional studies and evaluation by a respiratory specialist). COPD has minimal impact on health-related quality of life and results in only modest per capita health expenditure.
II	FEV_1 35%-49% predicted	COPD has a significant impact on health-related quality of life and results in large per capita health care expenditure. Patients usually merit evaluation by a respiratory specialist and may receive continuing care by such a specialist.
III	$FEV_1 < 35\%$ predicted	COPD has a profound impact on health-related quality of life and results in large per capita health care expenditure. Patients will usually be under the care of a respiratory specialist.

*forced expiratory volume in one second

Source: Standards for the diagnosis and care of patients with chronic obstructive pulmonary disease. Official Statement of the American Thoracic Society. *American Journal of Respiratory and Critical Care Medicine* 152:S77-121, 1995.

between midnight and 4 am. The treatment is aimed at supporting normal rhythms or modifying therapy based on known variations in body rhythms. Chronotherapy is commonly used in cancer chemotherapy.

churning **1.** The practice of repeatedly discharging and readmitting a patient during the same episode of care to qualify for time-limited insurance coverage. From a medical standpoint, only the last discharge is "real." **2.** In insurance, the practice of offering extremely low rates to healthy people to encourage enrollment, then raising rates substantially when enrollees become ill and use their insurance. This results in a constant turnover of enrollees. *See also* predatory pricing.

circadian rhythm The rhythmic repetition of certain phenomena in living organisms at about the same time each day. Without cues provided by light, the human circadian cycle lasts 25.9 hours. *See also* chronobiology.

circuit testing The periodic testing, in terms of conductivity, of all alarm-initiating and notification appliance wiring circuits that are connected to the main fire-alarm system control panel.

city hospital *See* municipal hospital.

civil commitment A type of confinement order used in the civil context for mentally ill, incompetent, alcoholic, and drug-addicted individuals, as contrasted with criminal commitment.

claim **1.** A request to an insurer by an insured person (or, on his behalf, by the provider of a service or good) for payment of benefits under an insurance policy. *See also* adjudicate; uniform claim form. **2.** A demand for money or other property due, or believed to be due, such as a medical malpractice claim. *See also* counterclaim.

claims data **1.** Data derived from providers' claims to third-party payers. **2.** Data derived from liability claims.

claims-incurred coverage Insurance that covers the insured, such as a physician, for any claims arising from an event that occurred or is alleged to have occurred during the policy period, regardless of when the claim is made.

claims-made coverage Insurance that covers the insured (such as a physician) for any claim made, rather than any injury occurring, while the policy is in effect. Claims made after the insurance policy lapses are not covered as they are by claims-incurred coverage. *See also* occurrence policy; tail coverage.

claims reserve In insurance, funds put aside to pay for anticipated future claims. *See also* prospective payment.

claims review A retrospective review by government agencies, medical foundations, insurers, or other organizations responsible for payment to determine the financial liability of the payer, eligibility of the beneficiary and the provider, appropriateness of the service provided, amount requested under an insurance or prepayment contract, and utilization rates for specific plans. *See also* adjudicate.

class In insurance, a grouping of people with similar characteristics or risks. Such groupings are used to set insurance rates.

Clayton Act *See* antitrust laws.

Clean Air Act A federal statute passed in 1963 and amended since, to protect public health and welfare from the effects of air pollution. The act establishes national air quality standards and specific automobile emission standards to achieve these goals.

clean room A room with environmental controls that prevent bacteria and dirt from entering or leaving. A filtered air supply and methods for manipulating patients without direct contact are used. *See also* isolation.

clear and convincing evidence In legal terms, a burden of proof that falls between preponderance (one thing is more likely than another) and beyond a reasonable doubt. *See also* Cruzan case.

clearing and staging unit (CSU) A component of the U.S. National Disaster Medical System that provides several disaster medical assistance teams and bed facilities for casualties.

CLIA '67 (Clinical Laboratory Improvement Act of 1967) An amendment to the Public Health Service Act requiring federal licensure of clinical laboratories operating as interstate commerce. *See also* CLIA '88; Public Health Service Act.

CLIA '88 (Clinical Laboratory Improvement Amendments of 1988) A federal law stating standards for laboratory personnel, quality control, and quality assurance based on the complexity of a laboratory test, set by Congress to improve the quality of clinical laboratory testing in all laboratories in the United States. These regulations, which became effective September 1, 1992, expand government oversight from 12,000 previously regulated Medicare, Medicaid, and interstate laboratories to more than 150,000 laboratories, primarily physician office laboratories. *See also* CLIA '67; moderate-complexity test; waived testing.

client **1.** An entity or individual to whom an organization provides services or that it considers a customer. Clients may include administrative or caregiving staff, physicians, or patients. This term is usually employed by health professionals educated in the social sciences (such as psychologists and counselors), while the term "patient" is more typically used by health professionals educated in the medical sciences. *See also* patient. **2.** An insurance carrier, employer, or other health care purchaser who uses the PPO's panel as the source of providers for the delivery of health care services to enrollees, employees, and others.

clinic A facility, or part of one, for diagnosis and treatment of outpatients. *See also* free clinic; outpatient services.

clinical Involving or based on direct observation of a patient, originally meaning at the patient's bedside, as distinguished from theoretical or basic sciences.

clinical algorithm *See* algorithm.

clinical care guideline *See* clinical practice guidelines.

clinical criteria *See* appropriateness; medical review criteria.

clinical data Data derived from clinical examinations, as by a physician or other health professional, and tests, such as diagnostic laboratory tests, x-rays, and electrocardiograms.

clinical data-based severity adjustment methods Methods that quantify risks of short-term outcomes based on clinical data.

clinical decision analysis The application of decision analysis in a clinical setting with the aim of applying epidemiological and other data in calculating probability of outcomes when alternative decisions can be made about diagnostic procedures, therapeutic regimens, prognostic expectations, and other important aspects of patient care. *See also* decision analysis; decision tree.

clinical decision support models and tools *See* decision support system.

clinical depression *See* depressive disorders.

Clinical Efficacy Assessment Project *See* health care technology assessment programs.

clinical engineering The management, maintenance, service, and, in some cases, design and development, of an organization's medical equipment and instrumentation. *Synonym*: biomedical engineering.

clinical ethics *See* bioethics.

clinical genetics The branch of medical genetics dealing with health and disease in individuals and their families or the science and practice of diagnosis, prevention, and management of genetic disorders, such as inborn errors of metabolism, hemoglobinopathies, chromosome abnormalities, and neural tube defects. *See also* genetics; human genetics.

clinical information system (CIS) An information system that collects, stores, and transmits information that is used to support clinical applications (eg, pharmacy, laboratory, radiology, nursing, performance measurement). Billing systems and other financial systems would not be considered clinical information systems. *See also* hospital information system; management information system.

clinical integration The extent to which patient care is coordinated across the functions and operating units of an organized delivery system. The demand for such integration is largely determined by the nature of patient illnesses or needs and the decisions of physicians. Clinical integration includes both horizontal and vertical integration. *See also* continuum of care; integration.

clinical laboratory A facility that is equipped to examine material derived from the human body to provide information for use in diagnosing, preventing, or treating disease. *Synonyms*: laboratory; medical laboratory. *See also* hematology laboratory; histopathology laboratory; laboratory; pathology and clinical laboratory services.

clinical measures Quantitative tools that are designed to evaluate the processes or outcomes of care associated with the delivery of clinical services; allow for intra- and interorganizational comparisons to be used to continuously improve patient health outcomes; may focus on the appropriateness of clinical decision making and implementation of these decisions; and may be condition specific, procedure specific, or address important functions of patient care, for example, medication use, infection control, patient assessment, and so forth. Utilization measures are not clinical measures unless the rates are compared to a standard of quality.

clinical monitoring The ongoing review and evaluation of patient data to determine the patient's clinical status and response to care or services and the need for further action. *See also* monitor.

clinical pathology Services relating to solving clinical problems, especially using laboratory methods in clinical diagnosis. Includes clinical chemistry, bacteriology and mycology, parasitology, virology, clinical microscopy, hematology, coagulation immunohematology, immunology, serology, and radiobioassay.

clinical pathway A treatment regime, agreed upon by consensus, that includes all the elements of care, regardless of the effect on patient outcomes. It is a broader look at care and may include tests and x-rays that do not affect patient recovery. *Synonym*: clinical path. *See also* critical pathway; practice parameters.

clinical performance indicators Performance measures that address the care processes and outcomes for specified conditions and procedures.

clinical pharmacology The branch of pharmacology that deals with the actions and uses of drugs in patients.

clinical practice guidelines (CPGs) Defined by the Institute of Medicine (in developing definitions for the legislation establishing the AHCPR) as systematically developed statements to assist practitioners and patients in choosing appropriate health care for specific clinical conditions. The term *clinical practice guideline* is generally accepted as an umbrella term by organizations that might name and describe their own guidelines differently, such as practice parameters, clinical care guidelines, practice policies, and protocols. Many medical specialty organizations have adopted the American Medical Association's original term *practice parameter* for their own guidelines (although the AMA in 1997 shifted to use of *clinical practice guideline*). Guidelines reflect current scientific knowl-

---

CLINICAL PRACTICE GUIDELINES DEVELOPED WITH THE SUPPORT OF THE AGENCY FOR HEALTH CARE POLICY AND RESEARCH

CPG Number	Title (Date of Release and Publication)
1.	*Acute Pain Management: Operative or Medical Procedures and Trauma* (February 1992)
2.	*Urinary Incontinence in Adults* (March 1992)
3.	*Pressure Ulcers in Adults: Prediction and Prevention* (May 1992)
4.	*Cataract in Adults: Management of Functional Impairment* (February 1993)
5.	*Depression in Primary Care: vol 1: Detection and Diagnosis; vol 2: Treatment of Major Depression* (April 1993)
6.	*Sickle Cell Disease: Screening, Diagnosis, Management, and Counseling in Newborns and Infants* (April 1993)
7.	*Evaluation and Management of Early HIV Infection* (January 1994)
8.	*Benign Prostatic Hyperplasia* (February 1994)
9.	*Management of Cancer Pain* (March 1994)
10.	*Unstable Angina: Diagnosis and Management* (March 1994)
11.	*Heart Failure: Evaluation and Care of Patients with Left-Ventricular Systolic Dysfunction* (June 1994)
12.	*Otitis Media with Effusion in Young Children* (July 1994)
13.	*Quality Determinants of Mammography* (October 1994)
14.	*Acute Low Back Problems in Adults: Assessment and Treatment* (December 1994)
15.	*Treatment of Pressure Ulcers* (December 1994)
16.	*Post-Stroke Rehabilitation* (May 1995)
17.	*Cardiac Rehabilitation* (October 1995)
18.	*Smoking Cessation* (April 1996)
19.	*Recognition and Initial Assessment of Alzheimer's Disease and Related Dementias* (November 1996)

Source: Office of the Forum for Quality and Effectiveness in Health Care, Agency for Health Care Policy and Research, Rockville, Md, 1997.

edge of practices and expert clinical judgment on the best ways to prevent, diagnose, treat, or manage diseases and disorders. Guidelines may appear in different formats, such as critical pathways, clinical pathways, flowcharts, or narratives. *Synonyms:* clinical care guidelines; guidelines. *See also* clinical pathway; guideline attributes; health care technology assessment; medical review criteria; practice parameters; practice policies.

clinical practice plan   *See* medical practice plan.

clinical preventive services   *See* preventive services.

clinical privileges   Authorization granted by the appropriate authority (eg, a governing body) to a practitioner to provide specific care services in a health care organization or network within well-defined limits, based on the following factors, as applicable: license, education, training, experience, competence, health status, and judgment. *Synonym:* medical staff privileges; privileging. *See also* admitting privileges; delineation of clinical privileges; emergency privileges; temporary privileges.

clinical protocol   Precise and detailed plans for the study of a medical or biomedical problem or plans for a regimen of therapy.

clinical psychology   The branch of psychology in which psychological principles and methods derived from developmental and abnormal psychology are applied to the diagnosis and treatment of mental and behavioral disorders.

clinical record   The account, compiled by health care professionals, of an individual's history, present illness, findings on examination, details of care and services, and progress notes. *See also* medical record.

clinical respiratory services   Services provided for the treatment of patients with disorders of the cardiopulmonary system, including diagnostic testing, therapeutics (administration of gases, such as oxygen), monitoring, education, and rehabilitation.

clinical résumé   A component of a medical record consisting of a concise recapitulation of the reasons for admittance, the significant findings, the procedures performed, the treatment rendered, the patient's condition on discharge, and any specific instructions given to the patient or family. *Synonym:* discharge summary. *See also* medical record.

clinical toxicology   The branch of medicine and subspecialty of emergency medicine, pediatrics, and preventive medicine dealing with the evaluation and management of patients with accidental or intentional poisoning through exposure to prescription and nonprescription medications, drugs of abuse, household or industrial toxins, and environmental toxins. *Synonym:* medical toxicology. *See also* poison control center.

clinical trial phases   Classification of therapy-testing clinical trials in three or sometimes four stages on the basis of purpose, size, and scope. *Phase I* studies are performed to evaluate the safety of diagnostic, therapeutic, or prophylactic drugs, devices, or techniques in healthy subjects and to determine the safe dosage range (if appropriate). They involve a small number of persons and usually last about one year. *Phase II* trials are usually controlled to assess the effectiveness and dosage (if appropriate) of the drugs, devices, or techniques. These studies are performed on several hundred volunteers, including a limited number of patients with the target disease or disorder, and last about two years. *Phase III* trials are comparative studies to verify the effectiveness of the drugs, devices, or techniques determined in Phase II studies by monitoring patients to identify any adverse reactions from long-term use. These studies are performed on groups of patients large enough to identify clinically significant responses and usually last about three years. *Phase IV* trials are planned, postmarketing studies of the drugs, devices, or techniques that have been approved for general sale. These studies are often conducted to obtain additional data about the safety and efficacy of a product.

clinician A practitioner, such as a physician, psychologist, or nurse clinician, who is involved in clinical practice or clinical studies.

clinicopathologic conference A case conference at which presentation and discussion of the clinical features and diagnosis precede exposition of the pathological findings, the latter being presented usually on the basis of autopsy examination. *See also* autopsy.

Clinton health plan *See* Health Security Act.

clone 1. A group of genetically identical cells descended from a single common ancestor, such as a bacterial colony whose members arose from a single original cell as a result of binary fission. **2.** A replica of a DNA sequence, such as a gene, produced by genetic engineering. *See also* DNA; genetic engineering.

closed access *See* closed panel group practice.

closed date A production code that manufacturers stamp on a drug product to ensure quality and monitor distribution.

closed panel group practice A health plan that contracts or employs providers who exclusively or primarily see only the patients enrolled in that plan. Services provided in a group practice facility and prepaid by some agency are more precisely called *prepaid group practice*. *Synonyms*: closed access; closed panel group plan; gatekeeper model. *See also* corporate dentistry; group practice; open panel group practice; prepaid group practice.

closed staff 1. An arrangement wherein no new applicants are accepted to a health care organization's medical staff unless a vacancy exists or is anticipated. **2.** Organization-physician contracts in which a physician or physician group provides administrative and clinical services required for operating a department on an exclusive basis. Other physicians are excluded from practicing that specialty in that institution for the period of the contract. *See also* exclusive contract; medical staff; open staff.

clot buster *See* thrombolytic therapy.

CLOTTING FACTORS

International Nomenclature	Synonym
Factor I	Fibrinogen
Factor II	Prothrombin
Factor III	Thromboplastin
Factor V	Proaccelerin Labile factor AC globulin
Factor VII	Serum prothrombin conversion accelerator (SPCA) Convertin Stable factor
Factor VIII	Antihemophilic globulin (AHG) Antihemophilic factor A
Factor IX	Plasma thromboplastin component (PTC) Antihemophilic factor B
Factor X	Stuart factor (Stuart-Prower)
Factor XI	Plasma thromboplastin antecedent (PTA) Antihemophilic factor C
Factor XII	Hageman factor Antihemophilic factor D
Factor XIII	Fibrin stabilizing factor (FSF) Laki-Lorand factor

clotting factor A substance that interacts in the blood to cause coagulation, or formation of clots. Factors are always identified by Roman numeral as well as name and may also have synonyms, for example, factor VIII, the antihemophilic factor (AHF), which is also known as platelet cofactor 1 and thromboplastinogen. *Synonym*: coagulation factor.

coach In quality improvement, a key resource person from within an organization who supports the organization's leadership in quality and performance improvement activities. A coach is knowledgeable about quality improvement, respected, enthusiastic, eager to learn, and eager to help other persons learn. *See also* continuous quality improvement.

coagulation *See* clotting factor.

COBRA (Consolidated Omnibus Budget Reconciliation Act of 1985) Legislation that includes protection of patients against hospital "dumping" because of suspicion that hospitals with emergency services were limiting access to save money (enacted April 7, 1986). COBRA also mandated the 1½-year window in which employers must continue to carry former employees on group health insurance plans. *See also* patient dumping.

Coburn bill *See* HIV Prevention Act of 1997.

cocaine A narcotic schedule II drug. *See* schedule of controlled substances.

cochlear implant An electronic prosthetic device designed to replace the acoustic functions of the cochlea (inner ear) of a profoundly sensorineural deaf patient by translating sound waves into electrochemical signals, which stimulate any remaining neuronal elements in the inner ear. A 1995 NIH Consensus Development Conference and Consensus Statement reported on the state of the technology and the best candidates for implants, stressing the importance of ensuring auxiliary education and rehabilitation services (especially for children) to maximize the benefits. The informed consent procedure for persons considering an implant must contain information about the incompatibility of some devices with the high magnetic fields of a magnetic resonance image scanner.

Cochrane Collaborative and Centres   An initiative with several program components founded in the 1970s by British physician and health sciences reformer Archie Cochrane, who criticized the medical profession for its failure to systematically collect and evaluate treatment effectiveness data from clinical trials. The program, with its review centers and the Cochrane Database of Systematic Reviews (and Database of Abstracts of Effectiveness [DARE]), disseminated as an electronic journal, has expanded to the United States and elsewhere outside the United Kingdom.

cocktail   A mixture of drugs taken together for therapeutic effect, such as the *Brompton cocktail* (containing an opioid and other drugs in an alcoholic solution) to treat terminal cancer pain. The term *cocktail* refers to the fact of mixing, not to the mode of administration; cocktails can be given orally or parenterally. A related term is *cocktail medium*, describing the mixture in which cells are cultured. The cocktail mode can pose problems in monitoring for side effects and harmful drug-drug interactions because of individual drugs' different mechanisms of action and toxicity profiles. Most recently the term has been used to describe combination therapy with protease inhibitors and other antiviral drugs to treat AIDS. *Synonym*: cocktail therapy.

code blue   A term assigned to a patient in cardiopulmonary arrest who requires the immediate care of a designated team of health professionals who may be dispersed throughout an organization. "Code blue" is announced over the organization's communications system to summon providers to the scene of the emergency. *See also* cardiac arrest; cardiopulmonary resuscitation; do-not-resuscitate order; slow code.

code creep   The practice of fitting patient diagnoses into categories of illness that receive the highest reimbursement, based on their code or DRG, to maximize reimbursement from payers.

code of ethics   A statement of principles and standards concerning the conduct of those who subscribe to the code, as in a code of ethics that defines proper professional behavior and practices. Codes of ethics are distinguished from licensure laws or practice acts in that they are a form of collective self-regulation rather than of regulation by external bodies. *See also* Hippocratic oath; medical ethics.

Code of Hammurabi   The legal code laid down by Hammurabi, the founder of the first Babylonian empire (circa 2100 BC), which was discovered in Susa (now western Iran) in 1902. Clauses 215–223 relate to medicine, laying down the fees appropriate to various services and setting penalties for unsuccessful outcomes. *See also* Hippocratic oath.

coding   The process by which a number or other symbol is substituted for a more extensive item of information, such as a description of a disease entity or diagnosis. *See also* decoding; ICD-9; ICD-10; medical record coding; procedure-coding manual.

Codman, Ernest Amory (1869–1940)   A surgeon who practiced in Boston at the Massachusetts General Medical School, where he developed the concept of the end-results system, and who helped found the College of Surgeons and its Hospital Standardization Program, a forerunner of the Joint Commission. He was an ardent and outspoken advocate for the need for surgeons and hospitals to collect performance and outcomes data and make these data available to the public.

coefficient   *See* coefficient of determination; coefficient of variation; confidence coefficient; correlation coefficient; interobserver reliability coefficient.

coefficient of determination   A statistic that shows the proportion of variability in a dependent variable explained by the regression model's independent variable(s). It is denoted by r to the second power and ranges from 0 to 1. If 0, there is no explanation of the dependent variable at all; if 1, the independent variables explain all the variability of the dependent variable. *See also* coefficient of variation; confidence coefficient; correlation coefficient; dependent variable; independent variable.

coefficient of variation (CV)   In statistics, the standard deviation divided by the mean, sometimes multiplied by 100. It indicates the amount of variability relative to the size of the mean. *See also* coefficient of determination; confidence coefficient; correlation coefficient mean; standard deviation.

cognition   The mental process or faculty of knowing, including aspects such as awareness, perception, reasoning, and judgment. *See also* judgment.

cognitive-behavioral psychotherapy   A short-term psychotherapy directed at specific target conditions or symptoms and directed toward revising a person's maladaptive processes of thinking, perceptions, attitudes, and beliefs. In the initial phase, the patient is taught to recognize the negative cognitions that contribute significantly to the development or maintenance of symptoms and to evaluate and modify such thinking patterns. The underlying problem is addressed in the second phase. *Synonym*: cognitive therapy.

cohort   Any defined group of persons sharing a common characteristic, such as members of the same age or the same sex, who are followed or traced over a period of time to determine the incidence of a disorder or complications of an established disorder. *See also* cohort study; comparison group; inception cohort.

cohort study   In the field of epidemiology, a prospective investigation of the factors that might cause a disorder in which a cohort of individuals who do not have evidence of an outcome of interest but who are exposed to the putative cause are compared with a concurrent cohort who are also free of the outcome but not exposed to the putative cause. Both cohorts are then followed to compare the incidence of the outcome under study. *Synonym:* prospective study. *See also* longitudinal study.

coinsurance   In a health insurance policy, a form of cost sharing in which the insured pays a set portion or percentage of the cost of each health service provided. *See also* copayment; cost sharing.

collaborative culture   An organization culture characterized by a shared vision, shared leadership, empowered workers, cooperation among organizational units as they work to improve processes, a high degree of openness to feedback and data, and optimization of the organization whole versus its many parts.

collaborative practice   A model of patient care delivery in which each discipline's approved practices for patient care are woven into an integrated plan. Accountability for care, its timing, and its sequencing are shared among the disciplines.

collection cycle   The time interval between the rendering of a service or a bill and payment of the bill in full.

collective bargaining   Negotiation between the representatives of organized workers and representatives of their employer or employers to determine wages, hours, rules, and working conditions.

colonoscopy   A procedure that uses a colonoscope (a long, flexible, fiber-optic instrument) to visualize the large intestine to detect signs of colon cancer or other abnormalities; a biopsy (tissue sample) can be taken as part of the same procedure.

colorectal cancer   Carcinoma of the colon or rectum, which is believed to develop from precancerous adenomatous polyps in a progression that appears to be associated with an accumulation of genetic alterations acquired after birth. Although not known precisely, the average "polyp dwell time" for a small (less than 1 cm) adenomatous polyp to transform into invasive cancer is thought to be ten years. It is one of the most preventable cancers, but the precise mode and intervals of screening remain under debate and policies vary in the major managed care organizations. *See also* adult-onset cancer; cancer-screening tests and procedures; cancer staging system; cancer susceptibility testing.

colposcopy   Examination of the vagina and cervix with a colposcope.

coma   A state of unconsciousness (Glasgow coma score of 8 or less) from which an individual cannot be aroused, even by powerful stimulation. *See also* Glasgow Coma Scale.

comfort care   *See* palliative care.

commercial health insurance   Any health insurance for medical care other than that written by Blue Cross and Blue Shield, which are considered to be noncommercial because they are nonprofit organizations.

commitment   The proceedings directing confinement of a mentally ill or an incompetent person for treatment. Commitment proceedings may be either civil or criminal and voluntary or involuntary. Due process protections are afforded to persons involuntarily committed, for example, periodic judicial review of continued confinement. *See also* civil commitment; involuntary commitment; medical hold.

common-cause variation   Variation in a process that is due to the process itself and is produced by interactions of variables of that process. Common-cause variation is inherent in all processes; it is not a disturbance in the process. It can be removed only by making basic changes in the process. *Synonyms:* endogenous cause variation; systemic cause variation. *See also* process variation; tampering.

communicable disease   A disease, such as chicken pox, caused by a defined infectious agent or its toxic products that arises through transmission of that agent or its products from an infected person, animal, or reservoir to a susceptible host, either directly or indirectly through an intermediate plant or animal host, vector, or the inanimate environment. *See also* child death rate; infectious diseases; notifiable disease.

community-based planning   Health services planning that emphasizes local efforts to stimulate, support, and improve health care quality in communities.

community care plan (CCP)   An alternative to the accountable health plan, proposed and developed by the Eutaw Group, which takes a proactive approach toward equal health status for a community. The plan comprises gatekeeper services—handled by a physician or an allied health professional with physician oversight—for the "assessment of health needs via surveillance, outreach, and screening," as well as referral services for hospital, home care, long term care, and rehabilitation services. *See also* gatekeeper mechanism; Health Security Act.

community health care   Activities and programs intended to improve the general health status of a community.

community health care system (CHCS)   Integrated system for delivering and financing comprehensive health care organized within a local community or service area. Essential elements of the CHCS include disease prevention, wellness, and health promotion; an ambulatory delivery network; traditional services (acute care, subacute care, mental health services, substance abuse treatment, rehabilitation services, outpatient care); services for the aging; home care; and alternative financing.

community health center (CHC) A health care organization established in a residential community that generally has scarce or nonexistent health services. *Synonym*: neighborhood health center.

community health information network (CHIN) A network of computer and communication systems that link all health care–related components in a community (including hospitals, pharmacies, physicians, schools, employers, and others) to facilitate the exchange of clinical, financial, and management information. All components of the system have access to information at all times, lowering the costs of care and information management by minimizing delays and eliminating duplicate record keeping. *Synonym*: community health integrated management information system (CHIMIS).

Community Health Intervention Partnerships (CHIPs) Projects designed to help hospitals and health systems work with community development corporations to assess local health needs, identify major community health problems, and develop plans to address them. The projects were instituted in 1995 by the Hospital Research and Educational Trust of the American Hospital Association under a grant from the Robert Wood Johnson Foundation.

community health network (CHN) A state, county, or city health system for delivering health care to the poor. *Synonym*: community network. *See also* health care network.

community hospital A hospital established to meet the medical needs of the residents of the community in which the hospital is located. Generally, community hospitals are short-term, general, not-for-profit hospitals, but they may be proprietary or governmental hospitals.

community living facility *See* halfway house.

community mental health center (CMHC) A health care organization capable of providing comprehensive, principally ambulatory, mental health services to individuals residing or employed in a defined catchment area. Patients develop skills for daily living and prevent or minimize the need for hospitalization through vocational rehabilitation, counseling, and short-term stabilization services.

community rating A method of determining premiums for health insurance in which a premium is based on the average cost of the actual or anticipated health services used by all subscribers in a specific geographic area or industry. The premium does not vary for different groups of subscribers or with the group's claims experience, age, sex, or health status. The intent of community rating is to spread the cost of illness evenly over all subscribers to an insurance plan, rather than charging the sick more than the healthy for health insurance. *See also* experience rating.

community residential facility A facility that provides living accommodations and guidance with activities of daily living principally to persons with mental retardation. *See also* intermediate care facility; residential care facility.

comorbidity A disease or condition present at the same time as the principal disease or condition of a patient. Comorbidities may cause an increase in hospital length of stay and are used in third-party payer reimbursement methodologies for inpatient stays. *See also* severity of illness; third-party payer.

comparative measure-related feedback Information comparing the performance of organizations in a measurement system to each other (interorganizational) based on measure-related data (eg, indicator rates, ratios, indices, percentages), according to pre-defined, standardized parameters.

comparison group The group to which a health care organization compares itself when multiple comparison groups exist. *See also* cohort.

ELEMENTS OF QUALITY CARE FOR PATIENTS IN THE LAST PHASE OF LIFE

Every patient should be able to expect

- The opportunity to discuss and plan for end-of-life care with his or her health care provider.
- Assurance that physical and mental suffering will be carefully attended to and comfort measures intently secured.
- Assurance that preferences for withholding or withdrawing life-sustaining interventions will be honored.
- Assurance that there will be no abandonment by the physician.
- Assurance that dignity will be a priority.
- Assurance that the burden to family and others will be minimized through community support networks, palliative care, hospice, or home care.
- Assurance that attention and priority will be given to personal goals such as the need to communicate with family and friends, attend to spiritual needs, or die at home.
- Assurance that care providers will assist the bereaved through the early stages of mourning and adjustment.

Source: From the Compassionate, Competent Care Initiative, a program of the American Medical Association under a grant from the Robert Wood Johnson Foundation, 1997.

Compassionate, Competent Care Initiative An American Medical Association (AMA) program funded by the Robert Wood Johnson Foundation in 1997 to teach physicians how to recognize the needs of dying patients and how to talk with them about dying and advanced care planning. Physicians will also be trained to recognize and treat pain, shortness of breath, incontinence, depression, paranoia, and hallucinations and to recognize when patients should be referred to palliative care specialists. A palliative care curriculum is being prepared for medical schools as well as nationwide education initiatives for practicing physicians and medical directors. In June 1997 the AMA issued under this program eight principles called Elements of Quality Care for Patients in the Last Phase of Life, representing what any patient facing death should be able to expect from physicians, health care institutions, and the community.

compensable injury In workers' compensation law, an injury caused by an accident arising out of and in the course of employment and for which the affected employee is entitled to receive compensation. *See also* workers' compensation.

compensation **1.** Direct and indirect monetary and nonmonetary rewards given to employees on the basis of the value of the job, their personal contributions, and their performance. **2.** Payment of damages; indemnification. Usually the equivalent in money for a loss sustained. *See also* workers' compensation.

compensation fund A fund into which insurers, practitioners, and health care organizations deposit money to be used to compensate anyone injured in the course of receiving health care services, regardless of whether the provider or professional was negligent. *See also* administrative determination of fault; alternative dispute resolution; early offer.

compensatory damages Damages that are awarded in court as the measure of actual loss suffered. The doctrine is designed to place the injured party in the same position he or she occupied prior to the injury and to provide nothing in addition. *See also* damages.

competence **1.** A determination of an individual's capability to perform up to defined expectations. *Synonym:* competency. *See also* credentialing; cultural competency. **2.** In behavioral health, sufficient mental ability to understand the nature and consequence of one's actions and make a rational decision. A competent patient possesses the ability to understand and communicate information, reason and deliberate about his or her choices, and choose in the light of some goals and values. Legally, all adults are competent until proven incompetent. Competence is defined by state statute. *See also* decisional capacity; incompetent; license; *non compos mentis*.

competitive medical plan (CMP) **1.** A state-licensed health care plan that provides health care services to enrolled members on a prepaid, capitated basis. **2.** An HMO or a CMP that has met federal requirements and is eligible for a risk contract with HCFA to provide Medicare services to Medicare beneficiaries.

complete blood count (CBC) *See* blood count.

compliance **1.** To act in accordance with stated requirements, such as standards. For purposes of Joint Commission accreditation, levels of compliance include noncompliance, minimal compliance, partial compliance, significant compliance, and substantial compliance. **2.** Adherence to a prescribed course of treatment or action, such as patient compliance with a treatment regimen or physician compliance with generally accepted medical practice. *See also* focused survey; type I recommendation.

complication A detrimental patient condition that arises during the process of providing health care, regardless of the setting in which the care is provided. For instance, perforation, hemorrhage, bacteremia, and adverse reactions to medication (particularly in the elderly) are four complications of colonoscopy and the associated anesthesia and sedation. A complication may prolong an inpatient's length of stay or lead to other undesirable outcomes. *See also* morbidity.

component For purposes of Joint Commission accreditation, an organized site of service in a health care network, PPO, or MCO for which the Joint Commission has relevant standards (eg, hospital, ambulatory surgical center, long term care organization) or other entities with which a network, PPO, or MCO contracts for specific services (eg, mental health). *See also* health care network.

composite score A weighted average calculated by (weight × frequency)/number of respondents and used to express results of a survey or study. Because it takes the weight of each component or response into account, composite score is often the preferred method for presenting results used in prioritization of action (such as patient satisfaction data). *See also* percentage format; top-box score format.

comprehensive benefit package A package proposed in the Health Security Act (1993) that would have provided benefits consisting of hospital services; services of health professionals; emergency and ambulatory medical and surgical services; clinical preventive services; mental illness and substance abuse services; family planning services and services for pregnant women; hospice care; home health care; extended care services; ambulance services; outpatient laboratory, radiology, and diagnostic services; outpatient prescription drugs and biologicals; outpatient rehabilitation services; durable medical equipment and prosthetic and orthotic devices; vision care; dental care; health education classes; and investigational treatments. *See also* health plan.

Comprehensive Drug Abuse Prevention and Control Act (1970) A federal act regulating access to controlled substances—narcotics and other drugs that can be legally obtained only by licensed individuals or institutions or by prescription.

comprehensive health care Services that meet the total health care needs of a patient, including outpatient, inpatient, and home care. *See also* health care.

Comprehensive Health Enhancement Support System™ (CHESS™) An interactive computer system, developed at the University of Wisconsin, that allows individuals with a personal computer and a modem to access current information about health topics such as breast cancer, HIV/AIDS, and stress management.

comprehensive health insurance Insurance that provides broad coverage, including most medical and surgical services in both inpatient and outpatient settings. *See also* insurance.

Comprehensive Health Insurance Plan (CHIP) A national health insurance proposal submitted to Congress in 1974. The plan would have given all U.S. citizens identical benefits under three separate plans that had different administrative, financing, and cost-sharing arrangements. Each plan would have covered a segment of the population according in part to income and in part to employment status. CHIP and other national health insurance proposals failed to obtain a national consensus.

comprehensive health planning (CHP) A health planning initiative—initiated by the Comprehensive Health Planning and Public Health Services Amendment of 1966 and replaced by the National Health Planning and Resources Development Act of 1974—that was intended to encompass all factors and programs affecting the health of the American people. CHP was meant to be conducted by areawide and state agencies that had the authority to intervene in matters of environmental and occupational health, health education, and health behaviors, as well as medical resources and services. A council guided the planning in CHP and was composed of a majority of health services consumers, not providers. Federal support for CHP was completely eliminated in 1986.

comprehensive health planning agency (CHPA) A type of agency originally established under the Comprehensive Health Planning and Public Health Services Amendment of 1966 to perform specified health care planning functions. These agencies were superseded by Health Systems Agencies, state health planning and development agencies, and statewide health coordination councils established by the Health Planning and Resources Development Act of 1974.

comprehensive major medical insurance Insurance that includes both basic and major medical health coverage. It is characterized by a relatively small deductible sum, a coinsurance provision, and maximum benefits of $250,000 or more. *See also* catastrophic insurance; insurance.

Comprehensive Smoking Education Act (1984) A federal law providing for research, education, and communication of information about the effects and dangers to human health presented by cigarette smoking. The law also provides for cigarette packages and advertising to carry one of four specified warnings from the Surgeon General. *See also* secondhand smoke; smoking cessation counseling and therapy.

computed axial tomography (CAT) The recording of internal body images at a predetermined plane by means of an emergent x-ray beam that is measured by a scintillation counter. The electronic impulses are recorded on a magnetic disk and then are processed by a minicomputer for reconstruction display of the body in cross-section on a cathode ray tube. *Synonyms:* CAT scan; computed tomography; computerized axial tomography. *See also* imaging; nephrography.

computer-based patient record (CPR) A computerized record of all data and images collected over the course of a patient's health history, and is part of a larger computer system. *See also* electronic medical record.

computer-based patient record system A record system that captures, stores, retrieves, and transmits patient-specific health care-related data, including clinical, administrative, and payment data.

Computerized Needs-Oriented Quality Measurement Evaluation System *See* CONQUEST.

computerized severity index (CSI) *See* severity measurement system.

computer modeling Use of computers to simulate real-world operating environments so that the outcome of proposed changes can be estimated before implemented. Computer modeling is used extensively in systems analysis and systems thinking. *See also* systems analysis; systems thinking.

conciliation *See* mediation.

concurrent data collection In health care performance measurement, the process of gathering data on how a process works or is working while a patient is in active treatment. *See also* data collection.

concurrent review Evaluative activities conducted while a patient is in active treatment. *See also* continued-stay review.

conditional accreditation *See* accreditation decision.

conditional follow-up survey A survey of a health care organization conditionally accredited by the Joint Commission, conducted within six months following Joint Commission staff approval of findings of correction to determine the degree to which deficiencies have been corrected and whether full accreditation should be awarded. *See also* accreditation survey.

conditions of enrollment Rules that determine eligibility for health insurance enrollment. *See also* insurance.

conditions of participation The various conditions that a health care provider (eg, hospital, home health agency, skilled nursing facility) desiring to participate in a health care or insurance program (eg, Medicare) is required to meet before participation is permitted. Investigations to determine whether health care providers meet or continue to meet conditions of participation are made by an appropriate state health agency, which is responsible for certifying that the conditions have been met and that the provider is eligible to participate. *See also* deemed status; HCFA certification; Medicare Conditions of Participation.

conductivity testing Measurement of the conductive properties (capacity to conduct a current of electricity) of floors in areas where inhalation anesthetics are used.

confidence coefficient   The probability that a confidence interval will contain the true value of the population parameter (eg, the population mean). For example, if the confidence coefficient is .95, 95% of the confidence intervals so calculated for each of a large number of random samples will contain the parameter and 5% will not. *Synonym*: coefficient of confidence. *See also* coefficient of determination; coefficient of variation; confidence interval; correlation coefficient.

confidence interval (CI)   In statistics, an interval or a range of values based on a random sample for which there is a stated probability (eg, 90%, 95%, or 99%) that the population parameter (eg, the population mean) is contained within this interval. The endpoints of the confidence interval are called confidence limits. *See also* confidence coefficient.

confidentiality   **1.** Restriction of access to data and information to individuals who have a need, a reason, and permission for such access.   **2.** An individual's right, within the law, to personal and informational privacy, including his or her health care records. *See also* Freedom of Information Act; medical record; bill of patient rights.

confidentiality and disclosure policy   *See* Public Information Policy.

conflict of interest   A situation in which regard for one duty leads to disregard of another, or might reasonably be expected to do so. For example, when a family of an incompetent patient has wishes that are not in the patient's best interest; when more profit may be achieved by less health care given to a patient by physicians in prepaid health plans; when a government employee's personal or financial interest conflicts or appears to conflict with his or her official responsibilities; or when a fiduciary of an organization votes on a matter that may affect his or her own personal or financial affairs.

confounding factor   An intervening variable that distorts the true relationship between or among the variables of interest. Confounding factors are related to the outcome of interest but extraneous to the study question and are nonrandomly distributed among the groups being compared. They can hide a true correlation or give the appearance of a correlation when none actually exists. *See also* scatter diagram; variable.

congestive heart failure (CHF)   *See* heart failure.

CONQUEST (Computerized Needs-Oriented Quality Measurement Evaluation System)   A publicly available tool, maintained by AHCPR, containing 1,200 clinical performance measures that can be used to assess quality of care for 52 clinical conditions. The system includes information on the ways the measures were constructed and tested and on whether they were validated, which enables health plans, practitioners, employers, and other users to identify and compare alternative quality of care measures in a meaningful way. CONQUEST is the framework for QMNET (Quality Measurement Network), an initiative under development by AHCPR in collaboration with the Joint Commission, the

National Committee on Quality Assurance, and the Foundation for Accountability. *See also* QMNET.

conscience clause   A law or clause allowing individuals or institutions the right to refuse to perform an activity that is contrary to their moral or religious beliefs.

consciousness   The state of being aware of one's own existence, sensations, thoughts, surroundings, and other phenomena; fully alert, awake, and oriented. Levels of consciousness refer to clinically differentiated degrees of awareness and alertness, variably classified and defined. Classifications include *alert* (the state of wakefulness, oriented to people, place, and time); *confused* (the state of being awake but disoriented to people, place, and time); *somnolent* (the state of being drowsy and frequently falling asleep when alone); *stuporous* (the state of partial or nearly complete unconsciousness, manifested by response only to vigorous stimulation); and *comatose* (a state of unconsciousness from which an individual cannot be aroused, even by powerful stimulation). *See also* coma; Glasgow Coma Scale.

conscious sedation   For purposes of Joint Commission accreditation, a medically controlled state of depressed consciousness that (1) allows protective reflexes to be maintained; (2) retains the patient's ability to maintain an airway independently and continuously; and (3) permits appropriate response by the patient to physical stimulation or verbal command, for example, "open your eyes." *See also* loss of protective reflexes.

consecutive sample   A sample in which the units are chosen on a strict "first come, first chosen" basis. For example, all individuals eligible for a clinical study in which consecutive sampling is employed should be included as they are seen. *Synonym*: sequential sample. *See also* sample.

consensus   **1.** In quality terms, working agreement among all team members concerning an issue.   **2.** In social science and health science decision making, the culmination of a structured process to reach general agreement. In the levels of evidence to support a finding or recommendation (as in a clinical practice guideline), consensus along with expert opinion is on the lowest rung and should be deferred to only when better forms of evidence are lacking. *See also* Delphi technique; group judgment methods.

consensus statement   *See* NIH Consensus Development Conferences and Consensus Statements.

consent   *See* implied consent; informed consent; medicolegal; presumed consent.

consequential damages   Losses or injuries that are the consequence of some act but are not the direct and immediate result of that act. *Synonym*: special damages. *See also* damages.

conservative care   The management of a condition with the least invasive or aggressive modality available or the exercise of caution in starting a therapy before all the evidence is in on a diagnosis. The term is used to contrast approaches taken to conditions such as low back pain, for which exercise (the conservative option) is prescribed before conducting imaging tests or considering surgery. *See also* evangelists and snails.

Consolidated Omnibus Budget Reconciliation Act of 1985 *See* COBRA.

consortium A formal voluntary alliance of individuals or organizations (such as hospitals, associations, or societies), usually from the same geographic area, for a specific purpose, usually to promote a common objective or engage in a project of benefit to all members. A consortium functions under a set of bylaws or other written rules to which each member agrees to abide, may or may not be incorporated and in which control of assets resides with each member, except as prescribed in the bylaws.

conspiracy of silence An alleged unspoken agreement between physicians or other health care professionals not to testify against each other in malpractice lawsuits.

constancy of purpose *See* Deming's Fourteen Points.

constructed beds The total number of beds that a health care organization is constructed to accommodate.

construct validity The degree to which a study measures or manipulates what a researcher claims it does. For instance, if, on theoretical grounds, an occurrence rate for some phenomenon should change with increasing age, a measurement with construct validity would reflect this change. If construct validity has been established for a measure, it may be used as a criterion standard (gold standard) against which other measures (tests, indicators) are evaluated. *See also* external validity.

consultation 1. Provision of professional advice or services. *See also* referral. 2. For purposes of Joint Commission accreditation, advice that is given to staff members of surveyed organizations relating to compliance with standards that are the subject of the survey. 3. A review of an individual's problem by a second practitioner, such as a physician or other health care provider, and the rendering of an opinion and advice to the referring practitioner. In most instances, the review involves the independent examination of the individual by the consultant. The opinion and advice are not usually binding on the referring individual. *See also* referral.

consultation report 1. A potential component of the medical record consisting of a written opinion by a consultant that reflects, when appropriate, an examination of the individual and the individual's medical record(s). *See also* medical record. 2. Information given verbally by a consultant to a care provider that reflects, when appropriate, an examination of the patient. The patient's care provider usually documents those opinions in the patient's record.

consumer In the provision of health care, one who may or does receive health services, including patients and enrollees in health plans. In health legislation and programs, a person who is not involved or associated (directly or indirectly) with the provision of health services (a provider) or in paying for health care for another (a purchaser). The definition of consumer is important in public health programs, in which a majority of consumer seats may be required on a governing body. *See also* health care consumer.

consumer health informatics (CHI) The study of consumer interfaces in health care systems, recently recognized officially as a subspecialty by the American Medical Informatics Association. The field includes community (lay) resources accessible to anyone through a home computer and clinical resources developed by clinicians or health organizations for selected groups of members or patients.

contact isolation A category of patient isolation, intended for less transmissible or serious infections, to prevent the spread of diseases or conditions that disseminate primarily by close or direct contact. A private room is indicated but patients infected with the same pathogen may share a room. Masks are indicated for those who come close to the patient, gowns are indicated if soiling is likely, and gloves are indicated for touching infectious material. *See also* isolation.

contact tracing The public health practice of identifying individuals who have been exposed to a communicable disease through person-to-person contact in order to identify and treat new cases of the disease and prevent it from spreading.

content validity The degree to which a sample of items represents the universe it was intended to represent. *See also* validity.

contingency fund A sum of money set aside or budgeted for an organization to cover possible unknown future expenses.

contingency planning The process of developing alternative plans for achieving an objective.

continued-stay review Periodic evaluation throughout a patient's hospitalization to determine the medical necessity and appropriateness of continued inpatient treatment. A continued-stay review may be conducted by the health care team providing the patient's care, the hospital utilization review committee, a third-party payer, or an external utilization review organization. *See also* concurrent review.

continuing care Matching a patient's ongoing needs to the appropriate level and type of medical, psychological, health, or social service within an organization or across multiple organizations.

continuing care retirement community (CCRC) A community that provides services and housing options to meet the elderly's needs. A CCRC provides independent and congregate living and personal, intermediate, and skilled nursing care and attempts to create an environment that allows each resident to participate in the community's life to whatever degree desired. *See also* life care; retirement center.

continuing education Education beyond initial professional preparation that is relevant to the type of care delivered in an organization or a network, that provides current knowledge relevant to an individual's field of practice or service responsibilities, and that may be related to findings from performance-improvement activities. *See also* graduate medical education; in-service; license.

continuing medical education (CME) Continuing education as it applies to physicians. CME may be gained via formal coursework, medical journals and texts, teaching programs, and self-study courses. CME programs are provided by organizations including medical schools, professional organizations, and hospitals. *See also* graduate medical education; implementation techniques; mandatory CME.

continuity A Joint Commission performance dimension addressing the degree to which the care of patients is coordinated among practitioners, among organizations, and over time. *See also* dimensions of performance.

continuous data Data with a potentially infinite number of possible values along a continuum. Examples of continuous data are the weight over time of a patient who is receiving total parenteral nutrition, or the number of minutes spent by prehospital personnel at a prehospital trauma scene. *See also* data.

continuous quality improvement (CQI) In health care, a management approach to the continuous study and improvement of the processes of providing health care services to meet the needs of patients and other persons. Continuous quality improvement focuses on making an entire system's outcomes better by constantly adjusting and improving the system itself, instead of searching out and getting rid of "bad apples" (outliers). *Synonyms:* continuous improvement (CI); quality improvement (QI); total quality management (TQM). *See also* acceptable quality level; facilitator; FADE process; FOCUS-PDCA; future state; outlier; plan-do-check-act cycle; process improvement; quality improvement; total quality management.

continuous variable A measurement in which the value of each measurement can fall anywhere along a scale, for example, the time (in minutes) from emergency department arrival to administration of thrombolysis. *See also* rated-based measure.

continuous variable measure An indicator in which the value of each measurement can fall anywhere along a continuous scale (eg, patient length of stay following inpatient surgery). *See also* aggregate data indicator; indicator; rate-based measure.

continuum of care Care of all levels and intensity (eg, skilled nursing care, intermediate care) provided to patients in various settings (such as hospitals or nursing homes) over an extended period of time. *Synonym:* cross-continuum care. *See also* clinical integration; levels of care; nursing care.

contract A formal agreement for health care or services with any organization, agency, or individual that specifies the services, personnel, products, or space provided by, to, or on behalf of the applicant organization and specifies the fees or other compensation to be paid in exchange. *See also* aleatory contract; direct contract model; exclusive contract; group contract; independent contractor; rescission; risk contract; risk management contract; terminable-at-will.

contracted services Services provided through a written agreement with another organization, agency, or individual. The agreement specifies the services or staff to be provided on behalf of the applicant organization and the fees to provide these services or staff. Examples include laundry services, laboratory services, and emergency services. *Synonym:* contract services.

contract practice Individual health care provider, such as a physician or dentist, under contract to an employer group or other organization for the provision of services to its members and dependents.

contractual adjustment Accounting adjustment made by a health care provider to reflect uncollectible differences between established charges for services rendered to insured persons and rates payable for those services under contracts with third-party payers. *See also* third-party payer.

contraindication A factor or condition that renders the administration of a drug or agent or the performance of a procedure or other practice inadvisable, improper, and/or undesirable. *See also* package insert.

contrast medium A substance used to improve the visibility of structures during radiologic imaging such as angiography or computed tomography. A positive contrast medium absorbs x-rays more strongly than the tissue of the structure being examined, and a negative contrast, or *radiopaque*, medium (such as barium in examination of the colon) does so less strongly.

contributory insurance Group health insurance in which the employee pays part or all of the premium and the employer or union pays the remaining part. *See also* insurance.

contributory negligence In law, a portion of the responsibility for a compensable injury or loss ascribed to the plaintiff due to his or her own fault.

control chart A graphic display of data in the order they occur with statistically determined upper and lower limits of expected common-cause variation. A control chart is used to identify special causes of variation, to monitor a process for maintenance, and to determine if process changes have had the desired effect. *See also* special-cause variation.

control group   A group used as a standard of comparison in a control experiment. This group does not receive the experimental treatment and is compared to the treatment group to determine whether the treatment had an effect. *See also* historical control.

controlled decentralization   Distribution among specific individuals or groups of the authority, responsibility, and accountability for clinical, professional, and administrative decisions. Such distribution is based primarily on the individual's or group's areas of expertise and is in keeping with the organization's mission, philosophy, goals, and budget.

controlled substances   Drugs whose general availability is restricted in the United States under jurisdiction of the Controlled Substances Act of 1970 because of their potential for abuse or addiction. *See also* schedule of controlled substances.

Controlled Substances Act of 1970   A federal law establishing controls over drugs of abuse and narcotics and providing financing for program development for the treatment and rehabilitation of addicted persons, study of the causes and effects of addiction, and health education related to drugs and their effects. *See also* addiction; schedule of controlled substances; drug.

control limit   A statistically determined limit on a control chart used to ascertain whether a process is in control. Control limits are usually set three standard deviation units above and below the mean. Variation beyond a control limit is evidence that special causes are affecting a process. Control limits are calculated from process data and are not to be confused with engineering specifications or tolerance limits. *See also* control chart.

control plan   A Blue Cross or Blue Shield plan that sells a health plan to a local company with employees in other states or areas and arranges for other Blue Cross and Blue Shield plans in those locations to provide the same benefits. The other plans function as subcontractors to the control plan. *See also* host plan; participating plan.

convalescent center   A skilled nursing facility or an intermediate care facility providing health services to patients recovering from severe or debilitating illnesses or injuries. *See also* intermediate care facility; skilled nursing facility.

convenience sample   Individuals or groups selected at the convenience of an investigator or primarily because they were available at a convenient time or place.

convergent validity   Evidence of the validity of a construct from different sources gathered in different ways, all indicating the same or similar meaning of the construct. *See also* criterion standard.

conversion factor   The dollar amount for one base unit in the relative value scale. The price paid to the provider for a given service equals the relative value of the service multiplied by the conversion factor. *See also* relative value scale.

conversion of coverage   The process of maintaining continuous health insurance during a change of employers without the need for reevaluation for insurability. Under most circumstances, this is guaranteed under COBRA.

cookbook medicine   Pejorative slang for clinical practice guidelines and related tools arising out of fear of oversimplification of clinical decision making or abridgment of individual clinical judgment. *See also* clinical practice guidelines.

Cooperative Health Statistics System (CHSS)   A program of the National Center for Health Statistics in which federal, state, and local governments cooperated in collecting health statistics. The CHSS collected data in seven areas, including health manpower, health facilities, hospital care, and long term care. The program was terminated in 1981. The Vital Statistics Cooperative Program, a former component of CHSS, continues to collect information on births, deaths, causes of death, marriages, divorces, abortions, and other events. *See also* health statistics; vital statistics.

cooperative service organization   *See* shared service organization.

Coordinated Transfer Application System (COTRANS)   A system begun in 1979 by the Association of American Medical Colleges to evaluate U.S. citizens receiving undergraduate medical education outside of the United States and to sponsor those it deems qualified for Part I of the national medical board examinations. Students who take and pass the national board examinations with COTRANS sponsorship may then apply to U.S. medical schools for completion of their training with advanced standing. Some students obtain sponsorship for the board examinations from a medical school without using COTRANS. *See also* national board examination.

coordination of benefits (COB)   Provisions and procedures used by insurers to avoid duplicate payment for losses insured under more than one insurance policy. Some people, for instance, have a duplication of benefits (in their automobile and health insurance policies) for their medical costs arising from an automobile accident. A coordination of benefits, or *antiduplication clause*, in one or the other policy will prevent double payment for the expenses by making one of the insurers the primary payer and ensuring that no more than 100% of the costs are covered. *See also* benefits; duplication of benefits; primary payer.

coordination of care and services   The process of coordinating care or services provided by a health care organization, including referrals to appropriate community resources and liaison with others (such as the patient's physician, other health care organizations, or community services involved in patient care) to meet patients' ongoing identified needs, to ensure implementation of the plan of care, and to avoid unnecessary duplication of services. *Synonym:* care coordination. *See also* care planning; case management.

copayment In a health insurance policy, a form of cost sharing in which the insured individual pays a specified amount for a specified service, while the insurer pays the remaining cost. Unlike coinsurance, the amount paid by the insured individual does not vary with the cost of the service. *See also* coinsurance; cost sharing; deductible; insurance.

coronary angiography An invasive procedure in which a contrast medium (radiopaque) is injected into the coronary arteries to determine coronary artery anatomy, including the presence, severity, and location of any obstruction.

coronary arteriography *See* angiography.

coronary artery bypass graft (CABG) surgery A surgical procedure in which a graft of a vein or an artery is attached to the internal mammary arteries to bypass a portion of a coronary artery that is constricted by atherosclerosis. *Synonym*: coronary bypass procedure.

coronary artery disease (CAD) Any of several abnormal conditions that may affect the arteries of the heart, such as narrowing or blockage, which may lead to coronary heart disease, myocardial infarction, or sudden death. Both inherited and preventable risk factors contribute to the disease, including smoking, diabetes mellitus, hypertension, hypercholesterolemia, or low levels of high-density lipoproteins. *See also* left main disease.

coronary care unit (CCU) *See* cardiac care unit.

coronary heart disease (CHD) Deterioration of the heart caused by narrowing or clogging of arteries supplying the heart muscles, with resulting chest pain, heart attacks, and damage to the heart.

coronary thrombosis A blood clot (thrombosis) blocking a coronary artery and causing a heart attack (myocardial infarction).

coroner An elected or appointed public official responsible for investigating and providing official opinions about the causes and circumstances of deaths that occur in selected circumstances. *See also* medical examiner.

coroner's jury A panel of citizens that officially reviews the circumstances, manner, and evidence in a death that appears to be due to natural causes.

corporate dentistry Company-owned and -operated facilities providing dental services to employees and sometimes to their dependents. This approach to dental services delivery involves a closed panel arrangement in which the beneficiaries must use the specified dentists and facilities. *See also* closed panel group practice; dentistry.

corporate diversification The process by which an organization, such as a health care organization, broadens the sources of revenue-generating activities and services through the establishment of corporations, limited partnerships, foundations, and joint ventures to provide services, such as home care, primary care, and long term care.

corporate liability Legal responsibility of a corporation, as opposed to individual or professional liability. In health care, this phrase often denotes a specific responsibility, such as the responsibility of an institution to exercise reasonable care in carrying out processes of credentialing and privilege delineation of its medical staff members. A hospital may be liable to a patient injured by a physician, for example, if the hospital knew or should have known that the physician was not competent to perform the procedure involved or otherwise treat the patient, and did not reasonably act to protect the patient by, for instance, restricting the physician's privileges or by requiring supervision.

corporate medicine The business of an entity other than a practitioner that defines itself as a provider of health care.

corporate planning A management process that involves determining an organization's basic immediate and long-term objectives and adopting specific action plans for attaining these objectives. *See also* management.

corporate structure The setup of an organization (eg, departments, agencies, other units) and the distribution and delegation of functional responsibilities throughout an organization.

corporate veil The assumption in law that a corporation as a whole, rather than particular individuals or entities, is responsible for acts executed by, or on behalf of its, owners during normal corporate performance.

corporation A legal entity, chartered by a state or the federal government, separate and distinct from the persons who own it, and regarded by the courts as an "artificial person." It may own property, incur debts, sue, or be sued. Its three chief distinguishing features are limited liability (owners can lose only when they invest); easy transfer of ownership through the sale of shares of stock; and continuity of existence.

corporatization of health care The trend in which community hospitals in the United States are restructuring themselves into new corporate forms, typically consisting of a holding company and several subsidiaries. Renal dialysis, home health care, rehabilitation, ambulatory surgery, and health promotion activities are increasingly being provided by large, corporately owned organizations. *See also* health care network.

correlation A relationship between statistical variables that tend to vary, be associated, or occur together in a way that is not expected on the basis of chance alone. *See also* correlation coefficient; negative correlation; positive correlation.

correlation coefficient A statistical measure of the relationship between two sets of data. This coefficient, represented by the letter r, can vary between +1 and -1. *Synonym*: coefficient of correlation. *See also* interobserver reliability coefficient; measure of association; negative correlation; positive correlation.

corticosteroids *See* asthma medications.

cost allocation The assignment, to each of several organization units, of an equitable proportion of the costs of activities that serve all of them and that cannot be assigned to any specific cost center. *See also* cost center.

cost-based reimbursement Payment based on the costs of health care delivery in which all allowable costs (as determined by the insurer) incurred by a health care organization in providing services are covered by the plan or program. This method is still used by some insurers to pay health care providers; increasingly, however, cost-based reimbursement is being replaced by prospective payment. *See also* prospective payment; prospective payment system; reimbursement.

cost-benefit analysis A method of measuring the benefits expected from a decision, calculating the costs of the decision, then determining whether the benefits outweigh the costs. In health care, cost-benefit analysis involves comparing the costs of medical care with the economic benefits of the care, with both costs and benefits expressed in units of currency. The benefits typically include reductions in future health care costs and increased earnings due to the improved health of those receiving the care. *See also* cost-effectiveness analysis.

cost center An accounting device whereby all related costs attributable to some center within an organization, such as an activity, department, or program, are segregated for accounting or reimbursement purposes. *See also* cost allocation.

cost containment The process of maintaining organization costs within a specified budget or restraining expenditures to meet organizational or project financial targets.

cost control Regulation and limitation of costs, such as price.

cost-effectiveness analysis (CEA) A form of analysis that seeks to determine the costs and effectiveness of an activity, or to compare similar alternative activities to determine the relative degree to which they will obtain the desired objectives or outcomes. For example, health care CEA might compare alternative programs, services, or interventions in terms of the cost per unit clinical effect (cost per life saved, cost per millimeter of mercury of blood pressure lowered, or cost per quality-adjusted life-year gained). *See also* cost-benefit analysis; cost-utility analysis.

cost outlier In prospective payment systems of reimbursement for health care services, a patient whose cost of treatment exceeds greater than 200% of the federal rate for the DRG into which the patient is assigned, or $15,000. *See also* DRG; prospective payment system.

cost sharing Provision of a health insurance policy that requires the insured or otherwise covered individual to pay some portion of his or her covered medical expenses. Several forms of cost sharing are used, including deductibles, copayments, and coinsurance. *See also* copayment; coinsurance; deductible; health insurance; premium.

cost shifting **1.** The practice of charging certain patients or groups or classes of patients higher rates to recoup losses sustained when a health care organization receives inadequate reimbursement for other patients or groups of patients. **2.** A financial management strategy used by governments or employers in which payment methods are established that do not meet the full cost of care delivered by a provider, thus forcing the provider to cover these costs through higher charges to other patients.

cost-utility analysis A form of cost-effectiveness analysis in which values are assigned to different kinds of health outcomes, reflecting the relative importance of the different outcomes to people, with the results expressed in units such as cost per quality-adjusted life year. Expressing results in this way facilitates comparisons across health care interventions with very different effects (eg, saving lives versus reducing disability). These analyses are often used to guide choice of therapies (or no therapy) in shared physician-patient decision making programs for early local prostate cancer, angina, or the like. *See also* cost-effectiveness analysis; patient utilities measurement.

counseling psychology The branch of psychology dealing with the study of people as individuals to help them develop as fully and effectively as possible. A counseling psychologist may use the interview technique with high school and college students, employees, persons needing vocational rehabilitation, and people in general who have problems concerning personal, social, educational, and vocational development and adjustment. In addition to the interview technique, counseling psychologists may use tests and observational methods to collect additional information about their clients as individuals, in groups, and in the environments in which they live and work.

counseling services Professional services for individuals, groups, or families dealing with problems due to personal relationships or stress. *See also* psychotherapy; stress.

counterclaim A claim brought by a defendant against a plaintiff in the same suit, and which asserts an independent cause of action. The claim may be based on the same transaction or any other occurrence giving rise to a right of recovery by the defendant against the plaintiff. For example, a physician sued for malpractice may counterclaim for payment of his or her bill. *See also* claim.

county hospital A hospital controlled by an agency of county government.

court-ordered emancipation *See* emancipated minor.

covariance   A statistical term that expresses the measure of association between two variables; the expected value of the product of the deviation of corresponding values of two variables from their respective mean values. A positive covariance indicates that the two variables tend to move up and down together; a negative covariance indicates that when one moves higher, the other tends to go lower. *See also* standard deviation; variable.

coverage   The guarantee against specific losses provided under the terms of an insurance policy. Coverage is sometimes used interchangeably with *benefits* or *protection*, and is also used to mean insurance or an insurance contract. *See also* adequacy of coverage; claims-incurred coverage; claims-made coverage; first-dollar coverage; full coverage; insurance; limits on liability; occurrence-based coverage; occurrence policy; out-of-area coverage; tail coverage; umbrella coverage.

covered charge   A charge for services provided to an insured patient that is recognized as payable by a third-party payer. *See also* third-party payer.

covered services   Services provided by a physician to a member of a health plan at no charge other than the applicable copayment or deductible. *See also* copayment; deductible; health plan.

crash cart   A wheeled vehicle containing supplies, such as medications, and equipment, such as laryngoscopes and syringes, that may be necessary for cardiopulmonary resuscitation of patients. *Synonym*: resuscitation cart. *See also* cardiopulmonary resuscitation.

creatinine clearance test   A measurement of the rate at which kidneys clear creatinine from the blood, used to evaluate renal function, follow the treatment response and progression of renal disease, and adjust medication dosage.

creative arts therapy   Therapy that uses creative arts modalities and creative processes during intentional intervention in a therapeutic, rehabilitative, community, or educational setting to foster communication and expression; promote integration of physical, emotional, and cognitive states; enhance self-awareness; facilitate change; and maintain social well-being. Examples of creative arts therapies include art, dance and movement, music, poetry, drama, and psychodrama therapies. *See also* manual arts therapy; recreational therapy.

credentialing   The process of obtaining, verifying, and assessing the qualifications of a health care practitioner to provide patient care services in or for a health care organization or network. The process of periodically checking the status of staff qualifications is called *recredentialing*. *See also* clinical privileges; credentials; economic credentialing; primary source.

credentialing agency   Any entity used by a health care organization to obtain information, including from primary sources, for the purpose of verifying an individual's credentials. *See also* credentials; credentialing; primary source.

credentials   Evidence of current competence, current and relevant licensure, education, training, and experience. Other criteria or requirements may be added by a health care organization. *See also* competence; credentialing; credentials verification process.

credentials verification process   For purposes of Joint Commission accreditation, verification with the primary sources of information provided by an applicant about his or her core credentials. This verification can be done through one or a combination of the following pathways: directly with the primary source or a designated equivalent source; through the verification process of a component's credentialing process or the component's appointment and reappointment decisions; or from a credentials verification organization (CVO). *See also* credentialing; primary source.

crisis management   A reactive method of management whereby strategies are formulated as events occur. This shortsighted approach frequently leads to organizational confusion reflected in lowered levels of both performance and the achievement of desired outcomes. *Synonyms*: management by crisis; "putting out fires" approach. *See also* management; management by objectives.

criteria of survey eligibility   For purposes of Joint Commission accreditation, conditions necessary for health care organizations to be surveyed. The criteria address the structure, functions, and services of health care organizations.

criteria set   A series of related criteria addressing the same patient sample; for example, a criteria set applied to patients presenting to the emergency department with chest pain or a different set applied to patients undergoing a cesarean section for failure to progress in labor.

criterion standard   A method having established or widely accepted accuracy for determining a diagnosis, providing a standard to which a new screening or diagnostic test can be compared. Criterion standards can also be used in studies of the quality of care to indicate a level of performance, agreed to by experts or peers, to which individual practitioners or organizations can be compared. *See also* benchmark; construct validity; convergent validity; gold standard; standard.

critical appraisal   *See* evidence-based medicine.

critical care medicine   A medical subspecialty primarily involved with all aspects of management of the critically ill patient in an intensive (special) care unit. The medical specialties of anesthesiology, internal medicine, neurological surgery, obstetrics and gynecology, pediatrics, and surgery currently offer subspecialty certificates in critical care medicine. *See also* pediatrics; surgical critical care.

critical pathway   **1.** The longest sequential series of tasks in a project.   **2.** Minimum necessary tasks to accomplish an objective or meet a goal.   **3.** In health care, a tool that helps practitioners manage an episode of care for a patient population or condition by providing a sequence of steps of the expected course of care with expected patient outcomes in specified time lines. The critical pathway is designed to improve the quality of patient care and promote the efficient utilization of resources. *Synonyms:* care path; critical path. *See also* clinical pathway; critical pathway method; practice parameters.

critical pathway method   A planning and control technique that reduces variation and cost by optimizing the order of steps in a process. Manufacturing industries use this method to plan and control the complete process of material deliveries, paperwork, inspections, and production. *Synonym:* critical path method. *See also* critical pathway; Program Evaluation and Review Technique.

cromolyn sodium   *See* asthma medications.

cross-continuum   *See* continuum of care.

crossfunctional   Pertaining to processes or groups that are organized along system or process lines, rather than along department lines. For example, the process of distributing laboratory results might be addressed by a crossfunctional team involving clinical laboratory staff, information management staff, nursing staff, and medical staff. *See also* interdisciplinary; multidisciplinary.

crossover trial   In research, a method of comparing two or more treatments or interventions in which subjects or patients, on completion of the course of one treatment, are switched to another. Typically, allocation to the first treatment is by random process. Participants' performance in one period is used to judge their performance in other periods, usually reducing variability. *See also* clinical trial phases.

cross-sectional study   A study that examines the relationship between diseases (or other health-related characteristics) and other variables of interest as they exist in a defined population at one particular time. *See also* cohort study.

crude death rate   *See* mortality rate.

Cruzan case   (*Cruzan v Director, Missouri Dept. of Health* [U.S., 110 S.Ct. 2841, 1990]) This case, involving a young woman left in a persistent vegetative state following an automobile accident, was the first right-to-die case to reach the U.S. Supreme Court. The patient's parents petitioned the court to terminate artificial nutrition and hydration; the patient was not sustained by any life-support machinery. A trial court granted the request; the state supreme court reversed it; and the parents appealed to the U.S. Supreme Court, which upheld the state's requirement of "clear and convincing evidence" that an incompetent patient would wish to have life-sustaining treatment withdrawn before permitting the cessation of such treatment. Additional testimony was supplied to the trial court, which then granted authorization to terminate artificial nutrition and hydration. *See also* clear and convincing evidence; persistent vegetative state.

cryosurgery   Application of extreme cold to tissues, often via a probe containing liquid nitrogen or carbon dioxide, to destroy or eliminate abnormal cells.

cryotherapy   The local or general use of low temperatures in medical therapy, as in cryosurgery.

cued speech   Use of hand shapes and placements to clarify lipreading and aid hearing-impaired persons in visually perceiving spoken language. It is used by families and professionals working with hearing-impaired persons. Speech pathologists also use cued speech with hearing persons in teaching phonetics, phonics, the sounds of second languages, and in therapy for articulation and language disorders. *See also* speech pathology.

culdoscopy   The inspection of the female pelvic organs by means of an endoscope (an illuminated tube with a viewing instrument) introduced into the pelvic cavity.

cultural competency   Possessing the attributes of relevance and sensitivity to the cultural background or setting of patients in any component of service delivery, including patient education materials, questionnaires, office or health care organization setting, bedside manner, and public health campaigns.

culture   *See* team culture.

culture-bound syndrome   According to the DSM-IV, a recurrent, locality-specific pattern of aberrant behavior and troubling experience, which may or may not be linked to a particular DSM-IV diagnostic category. Many of these patterns are considered illnesses or afflictions within the culture in which they appear, and most have local names. Some conditions may be conceptualized as culture-bound syndromes specific to industrialized culture rather than to an ethnic or distinctive geographic group (eg, anorexia nervosa). Examples of ethnic-specific culture-bound syndromes are *ataque de nervios*, in Latin American and Latin Mediterranean groups (following a stressful event); *falling-out* or *blacking out*, in southern U.S. and Caribbean groups; *ghost sickness*, in many native American tribes; and *mal de ojo* (evil eye), in Mediterranean cultures, often applied to ailments of children. *See also* eating disorders.

curative   Tending to overcome disease and promote recovery. Curative therapy or management is distinguished from palliative care, which affords relief but not cure. *See also* palliative care.

curettage   The removal of growths or other material from the wall of a cavity or other surface by scraping with a curette. *See also* dilation and curettage.

current procedural terminology (CPT)   *See* Physicians' Current Procedural Terminology.

custodial care   Care in which board, room, and other nonmedical personal assistance are provided, generally on a long-term basis to, for example, mentally retarded individuals. *See also* residential care.

customary, prevailing, and reasonable charge
The dollar amount a physician or other practitioner normally or usually charges the majority of his or her patients. Such fees vary by specialty, geographic area, and physicians, and they are under the scrutiny of many third-party payers, including Medicare. Under Medicare, a customary charge is the median charge used by a particular physician for a specified type of service during the calendar year preceding the fiscal year in which a claim is processed. There is, therefore, an average delay of a year and a half in recognizing any increase in actual charges. Customary charges, in addition to actual and prevailing charges, are taken into account in determining reasonable charges under Medicare. *See also* Medicare; third-party payer; usual, customary, and reasonable charge.

customer In health care, a person who initiates use of a service, decides which provider to use, arranges for usage, and pays for it. Several people may share in these customer activities. Refers to both external customers (patients, families, other health care facilities, government agencies) and internal customers (nursing staff, physicians, technicians, administrators). *See also* consumer.

customer-supplier sundial A graphic representation of an organization or a component of an organization and those served by it. Within such a graphic, the supplier is in the middle, and each customer is at the end of a spoke projecting outward.

cybernetics The theoretical study of communication and control processes in biological, mechanical, and electronic systems, especially the comparison of these processes in biological and artificial systems.

cystoscopy The process of visualizing the urinary tract by means of a cystoscope inserted in the urethra. Cystoscopy is also used for obtaining biopsies of tumors and for the removal of polyps.

cytogenetics The branch of biology that deals with the study of heredity and variation by the methods of both cytology and genetics; the study of chromosomes.

cytology The branch of biology dealing with the formation, structure, and function of cells. *See also* cytopathology.

cytomegalovirus (CMV) *See* HIV; opportunistic infection.

cytopathology The branch of medicine and subspecialty of pathology dealing with the diagnosis of human disease by means of the study of cells. The cells are obtained from body secretions and fluids by scraping, washing, or sponging the surface of a lesion, or aspirating a tumor mass or body organ with a fine needle. The cells are studied using special stains and chemical analyses. *See also* cytology; Gram's stain.

Dd

daily service charge The dollar amount charged by a health care organization for a day's stay in an inpatient care unit.

damages In law, pecuniary compensation or indemnity that may be recovered in the courts by any person who has suffered loss, detriment, or injury, whether to his or her person, property, or rights, through the unlawful act or commission of negligence of another individual. *See also* apportionment of damages; apportionment of fault; compensation; compensatory damages; consequential damages; foreseeability; future damages; general damages; life table; lost chance of cure; lost chance of survival; measure of damages; nominal damages; noneconomic damages; recovery; tort.

dance and movement therapy The use of psychotherapeutic movement, facilitated by a qualified therapist, to further a patient's emotional, cognitive, social, and physical integration. *See also* creative arts therapy; manual arts therapy; recreational therapy.

Darling case (*Darling v Charleston Community Hospital*, 211 NE 2nd 53, Illinois [1965]) A landmark decision that was the first to admit state department of public health regulations, hospital bylaws and rules, and standards for hospital accreditation of the Joint Commission as evidence of the standards for health care services and their delivery. This evidence was used to establish the standard of care that the hospital and physician should have delivered (but failed to). The case established the responsibility of hospitals for the care they provide to patients and the accountability of the medical staff for care provided by its members. *See also* accountability; standard of care.

data Facts, clinical observations, or measurements collected during an assessment activity. The initial data a researcher has before beginning analysis is called *raw data*. *See also* analog data; attribute data; clinical data; continuous data; data element; discrete data; information; measurement data; operational data; performance database; primary data; process data; qualitative data; quantitative data.

data accuracy The extent to which data are free of identifiable errors. *See also* measurement accuracy.

data analysis The process of interpreting data and drawing valid conclusions leading to a decision or judgment. *See also* data dredging; tampering.

database An organized, comprehensive collection of data elements (variables), and their values, typically stored in a computer system so that any particular item or set of items can be extracted or organized as needed. Databases may vary in content, type of information contained, and design. *Synonym:* data bank. *See also* database management; data set; performance database; registry.

database management A methodology of storing, manipulating, and retrieving data in a database. Aspects of database management may include entering, classifying, modifying, and updating data and presenting output reports.

database management system A computer software package that manages, updates, secures, and gains computer access to databases; for example, ORACLE, ACCESS, APPROACH.

data capture **1.** The acquisition or recording of data and information. **2.** The process of transferring information from a written, paper format to machine-readable form on a computer.

data collection The act or process of capturing raw or primary data from a single or a number of sources. *Synonym:* data gathering. *See also* concurrent data collection; prospective data collection.

data connectivity The ability to link data from different sources or systems.

data definition The identification of the data to be used in analysis.

data dictionary A list of the specifications (eg, name of patient, name of test, test result) and locations of all data contained in a given information system.

data disclosure acts or initiatives *See* state data initiatives.

data dredging Analysis of previously collected data which is undertaken without a prestated hypothesis. This approach is sometimes employed when data have been collected on a large number of variables and hypotheses are suggested by study of the data. The validity of data dredging is usually unacceptable. *See also* data analysis.

data editing The process of correcting erroneous or incomplete existing data, exclusive of data entry input edits.

data element A discrete piece of data, such as patient birth date or principal diagnosis. Data elements may be aggregated with other data elements to identify occurrences of an indicator event targeted for measurement. *See also* indicator; valid value.

data integrity The accuracy, consistency, and completeness of data.

data noise Irrelevant or meaningless data generated by extraneous variables or measurement errors in a study. Noise may make it difficult or impossible to accurately determine the relationships between the variables being studied. *See also* variable.

data parity The degree to which data are equivalent.

data pattern An identifiable arrangement of data that suggests a systematic design or orderly formation relative to a data set. *See also* data set.

data processing Conversion of data into a usable form, usually by means of a computer and a computer program.

data quality The accuracy and completeness of performance measure data, in the context of the analytic purposes for which they will be used.

data reliability The stability, repeatability, and precision of data. *See also* data validity; indicator reliability.

data security The protection of data from intentional or unintentional destruction, modification, or disclosure.

data set An aggregation of uniformly defined and classified data or items of information that describe an element, episode, or aspect of health care, as in the Uniform Hospital Discharge Data Set. *See also* data pattern; discharge abstract; minimum data set; ordered data set; Uniform Clinical Data Set; Uniform Hospital Discharge Data Set.

data transformation The process of changing the form of data representation, for example, changing data into information using decision-analysis tools.

data transmission The sending of data or information from one location to another.

data trend A statistical pattern in a set of data reflecting a general direction; for example, a trend on a run chart or control chart is the continued rise or fall of a series of points. *See also* data pattern; trending.

data validity The degree to which data are a reasonable representation of the construct they are collected to measure. *See also* data reliability; indicator validity; validity.

data verification process A process in which data are checked for accuracy and completeness.

DATTA *See* Diagnostic and Therapeutic Technology Assessment.

Daubert v Merrell Dow case (*Daubert v Merrell Dow Pharmaceuticals, Inc*, 113 S Ct 2786 [1993]) A U.S. Supreme Court decision on the admissibility of novel scientific evidence in a case involving the pregnancy anti-nausea drug Bendectin and evidence about birth defects taken from animal research. The court ruled that "general acceptance" is not a necessary precondition to the admissibility of scientific evidence under the Federal Rules of Evidence, but that those rules (especially Rule 702) do assign to the trial judge the task of ensuring that an expert's testimony both rests on a reliable foundation and is relevant to the task at hand. *See also* expert witness; junk science.

day bed A bed regularly maintained by a health care organization for use during the day by patients who require partial hospitalization. *See also* night bed; partial hospitalization.

day care center A facility offering services in a group setting ranging from active rehabilitation to social and health care. *See also* adult day care.

day hospital A facility or dedicated part of a facility providing a full range of hospital services, except that its patients return home or to alternative living arrangements in the evening. *See also* hospital; night hospital.

day hospitalization *See* partial hospitalization.

days per thousand A standard unit of measurement of utilization, referring to the annualized use of a health care organization; the number of organization days that are used in a year for each thousand covered lives.

day treatment Structured services for individuals with mental health problems. Treatment may be devoted to teaching of living skills, or rehabilitation, therapy, and social skills.

DEA registration number A number assigned to an individual or entity (a physician, a pharmacist, a hospital, a pharmacy, or some other qualified business activity) by the federal Drug Enforcement Agency (DEA) showing that the individual or entity is authorized to dispense controlled substances. The Bureau of Narcotics and Dangerous Drugs (BNDD), the DEA's precursor agency, formerly issued a BNDD number (now called the DEA number). *See also* Bureau of Narcotics and Dangerous Drugs number; schedule of controlled substances.

death A permanent cessation of all vital functions; the end of life; expiration. Death is variously defined in precise terms according to three types of criteria: the *nonbrain* or *heart-lung criterion,* the permanent cessation of the flow of vital bodily fluids; the *whole-brain criterion,* the permanent cessation of the integrated functioning of the organism as a whole; and the *higher-brain criterion,* the permanent loss of what is essential to the nature of human beings—consciousness. Most states in the United States use the Uniform Determination of Death definition, based on whole-brain death. The definition remains controversial and is engaged in policies on transplantation of organs and tissues. *See also* anencephaly; brain death; death certificate; death with dignity; euthanasia; hospice; natural death acts; Uniform Determination of Death Act; wrongful death.

death certificate A vital record signed by a licensed physician that includes immediate and underlying causes of death in addition to the decedent's name, sex, birthdate, and place of residence and of death. *Causes of death* are diseases, morbid conditions, or injuries that either resulted in or contributed to death. *Underlying cause of death* is the disease or injury that initiated the chain of events leading to death or the circumstances of the accident or violence that produced the fatal injury. *See also* birth certificate; fetal death certificate; vital records.

death-prolonging procedure Any procedure or intervention, such as artificial ventilation, that prolongs the dying process when death will occur within a short time. *Synonym*: death-delaying procedure. *See also* life-sustaining procedure; living will.

death rate *See* mortality rate.

death spiral The practice of substantially increasing health insurance premiums for individuals or small groups as the beneficiary becomes sicker and incurs more health care costs, eventually making the insurance unaffordable. *See also* insurance.

death with dignity **1.** The obligation to care for the dying patient sensitively, compassionately, and ethically, including respect for the dying patient's wishes to refuse further medical care when therapy becomes futile. *See also* futility; informed refusal. **2.** The slogan used in the unsuccessful campaign to pass a bill permitting euthanasia in the state of Washington (Initiative 119, 1991). *See also* assisted suicide; euthanasia.

Death with Dignity Act An initiative permitting physician-assisted suicide passed by referendum in Oregon (Ballot Measure 16, 1994).

Decade of the Brain A campaign undertaken by NIH to promote and fund vigorous research efforts in neuroscience in the 1990s to prevent and treat neurological disease, signed into law by the U.S. Congress and recognized by presidential proclamation on July 25, 1989. *See also* brain attack.

decentralization The distribution of administrative functions or powers of a central authority among several local authorities, as in distributing decision-making powers and policy formulation to several locations throughout an organization. The objective is to give decision-making authority to those most directly responsible for the outcome of those decisions who have first-hand experience and knowledge about the issues involved. *See also* distributed leadership.

decentralized laboratory testing *See* point-of-care laboratory testing.

decentralized pharmaceutical services The storage, preparation, and dispensing of drugs at organization sites physically located outside the organization's central pharmacy. *Synonym*: satellite pharmacy. *See also* drug dispensing.

decisional capacity The capacity of an individual to understand the ramifications of a decision that must be made, consider the benefits and burdens of various choices, and communicate his or her choices either verbally or nonverbally. In general, individuals with decisional capacity are regarded as capable of providing informed consent to medical treatment. *See also* competence; informed consent.

decision analysis A process for identifying all available choices and potential outcomes of each choice in a series of decisions. The choices are often plotted on a

decision tree and at each branch, or decision node, the probabilities of each outcome that can be predicted are displayed. The decision tree shows the choices available to those responsible for patient care and the probabilities of each outcome that will follow the choice of a particular action or strategy in patient care. *See also* clinical decision analysis; decision tree; utility.

decision grid *See* accreditation decision grid.

decision node *See* algorithm; decision analysis; decision tree.

decision rules *See* accreditation decision rules.

decision support software (DSS) Computer software designed to give decision makers access to relevant information. There are three classes of health care DSS: *reference*, giving physicians and other professionals access to the published literature; *lay education*, giving consumers access to health care information through a variety of informal networks; and *guidance*, giving professionals and patients access to the same current information presented in understandable language.

decision support system (DSS) A system that integrates and synthesizes data into information. Such systems depend on large databases of patient records that allow practitioners to examine important trends in outcomes and processes of care to find opportunities for improvement. They include cost accounting, market research, executive information, and ad hoc query systems.

decision theory A unified approach to all problems of estimation prediction and hypothesis testing.

decision tree A graphical representation of alternatives, developed to express alternative choices in quantitative terms that can be made in a decision-making problem. A series of decision options are represented as branches, and subsequent possible outcomes are represented as further branches. The junction where a decision must be made is called a *decision node*. *See also* decision analysis.

decoding The process of translating a code (usually a number) back into the term (such as a diagnosis) that the code represents. *See also* coding; encoding.

decubitus ulcer *See* pressure ulcer.

deductible In a health insurance policy, a form of cost sharing in which a set amount must be paid by the insured before any payment of benefits occurs. It is often a feature of traditional indemnity insurance plans in order to reduce premiums. *See also* coinsurance; copayment; cost sharing; premium.

deemed status Status conferred by HCFA on a health care provider when that provider is judged or determined to be in compliance with relevant Medicare Conditions of Participation because it has been accredited by a voluntary organization whose standards and survey process are determined by HCFA to be equivalent to those of the Medicare program or other federal laws, such as CLIA '88.

For purposes of Joint Commission accreditation, organizations accredited under the Hospital Accreditation Program, Home Care Accreditation Program, and Pathology and Clinical Laboratory Accreditation Program may be "deemed" to meet most of the health and safety requirements for participation in Medicare. *See also* conditions of participation; HCFA certification; Medicare.

deep venous thrombosis (DVT)   The clotting of blood in the deep veins of the leg or the arm. The condition occurs most frequently in the leg following hip replacements or other lower limb surgery without preventive anticoagulation therapy. DVT can produce an embolus (broken off piece of clot) resulting in fatal pulmonary thromboembolism.

defamation   An intentional false communication, either published or publicly spoken, which injures another's reputation or good name. Written defamation is called libel; oral defamation, slander. Both libel and slander are torts for which the defamer may face liability. *See also* liability.

defendant   In a civil proceeding, the party responding to the complaint, that is, the one who is sued and called upon to make satisfaction for a wrong complained of by another party, known as the plaintiff. In criminal proceedings, the defendant is also called the *accused*.

defensive medicine   A popular notion describing what is perceived to be physicians' tendency to alter their medical practice, particularly in the direction of overusing tests and procedures, in order to avoid the risk of malpractice suits or to provide a defense in the event that such suits occur. The precise nature of the phenomenon and its dimensions have not been defined. *See also* Maine Medical Liability Demonstration Project; malpractice; professional liability.

deferred care   Needed medical care that is delayed, usually because the patient does not have health insurance or cannot afford to pay for services.

defibrillator   Implantable device that continuously monitors the electrical activity of the heart and automatically detects and terminates ventricular tachycardia and ventricular fibrillation. Consists of an impulse generator, batteries, and electrodes. *See also* cardiac pacemaker.

Deficit Reduction Act of 1984   A complex federal law containing a large number of cost-containment and reimbursement-reform provisions for Medicare and Medicaid. Examples include development of a prospective payment hospital wage index, changes in payment for skilled nursing facilities, payment for clinical psychologist services, expansion of Medicaid coverage to qualified pregnant women and children, establishment of selective waivers of requirement for HMOs, and provisions leading to the development of different payment allowances for participating versus nonparticipating physicians. *See also* Medicaid; Medicare; prospective payment.

defined contribution plan   A health care plan in which the employer's contribution is fixed.

defined measure   A structured measure used in defined populations to measure specific events; such measures may have numerators and denominators, take the form of a continuous variable, or result from survey questions. *See also* measure.

defined population   A set of individuals (and their dependents, as appropriate) who choose or are enrolled (by choice or assignment) to receive specified health care services from a specific network or managed care component or group of health practitioners for a specified period of time.

deinstitutionalization   The removal of individuals from institutional settings and returning them to community life, as in the discharge of mental patients from mental health care organizations, with continued care provided in the community. The movement of mental patients back into the community was made possible in part by the development of psychotropic drugs capable of positively modifying patients' behavior so that they can function in the community. *See also* psychotropic medication.

delineation of clinical privileges   The listing of the specific clinical privileges an organization's staff member is permitted to perform in the organization. *See also* clinical privileges.

Delphi technique   A procedure for forecasting events or selecting organizational or program goals, developed by RAND. Experts are asked to write their best judgments about the probability of a specific event and implications of its occurrence or nonoccurrence. The results are collated and then returned to the original experts for their interpretation, along with an opportunity to revise their own predictions. Revisions with supporting arguments are then recirculated. In theory, this feedback, which is repeated, continues to narrow the range of predictions and, in the end, a group judgment will have been reached while minimizing the possibility of distortion. *Synonyms*: Delphi method; Delphi study. *See also* consensus; group judgment methods; nominal group technique.

Delta Dental plan   The franchise name for any one of the statewide prepaid dental service plans that were developed through sponsorship by dental professional societies and use principles similar to those in Blue Shield medical and surgical plans. The plans are nonprofit service corporations established under state law. *See also* Blue Cross and Blue Shield plan; dentistry; nonprofit carrier.

demand for health services   Willingness or ability to seek, use, and, in some settings, pay for health services. Expressed demand is equated with use, and potential demand with need. *See also* needs assessment.

demand management   In managed care, a technique for influencing (lowering) consumers' demands for health care services, resulting in lower costs of care. Demand management supports individuals in making informed health and medical decisions on the basis of consideration of benefits and risk.

demand pacemaker *See* cardiac pacemaker.

dementia A syndrome of progressive decline that relentlessly erodes intellectual abilities, causing cognitive and functional deterioration, which leads to impairment of social and occupational function. Its diagnosis requires differentiation from delirium or depression and documentation of decline from a previous baseline or normal level of cognitive functioning, either by an informant close to the patient or by serial tests over time. The major types are Alzheimer's disease (most common) and vascular (multi-infarct) dementia, together accounting for 85% of cases out of approximately 70 different dementias. The American Psychiatric Association's DSM-IV recognizes five forms of dementia: (1) dementia due to a general medical condition; (2) substance-induced persisting dementia (alcohol, inhalants, sedatives/hypnotics/anxiolytics); (3) dementia due to multiple etiologies; (4) dementia of unknown etiology; and (5) dementia not otherwise specified. Recent guidelines containing diagnostic criteria for dementia are available from the AHCPR (1996), the American Academy of Neurology (1995), the American Psychiatric Association (1997), the U.S. Department of Veterans Affairs and University HealthSystem Consortium (1997), and the American Association on Mental Retardation and the International Association for the Scientific Study of Intellectual Disability (1995). *See also* Alzheimer's disease; Mini-Mental State Examination; vascular dementia.

DEMING'S FOURTEEN POINTS

1. Create consistency of purpose toward improvement of products and services.
2. Adopt the philosophy embedded in these 14 points.
3. Cease dependence on mass inspection to achieve quality.
4. End the practice of awarding business on the basis of price tag alone. Instead, minimize total cost by working with a single supplier.
5. Improve constantly and forever every process for planning, production, and service.
6. Institute training on the job.
7. Adopt and institute leadership.
8. Drive out fear.
9. Break down barriers between departments.
10. Eliminate slogans, exhortations, and targets for the work force.
11. Eliminate numerical quotas for the work force and numerical goals for management.
12. Remove barriers that rob people of pride of workmanship. Eliminate the annual rating system.
13. Institute a vigorous program of education and self-improvement for everyone.
14. Put everyone in the organization to work to accomplish the transformation.

Deming cycle *See* plan-do-check-act cycle.

Deming's Fourteen Points The Fourteen Points are the foundation of W. Edwards Deming's message to man-

agement. They include a blend of leadership, management theory, and statistical concepts that highlight the responsibilities of management while enhancing the capacities of employees, as together they seek to build the knowledge and application of the knowledge for improvement. *See also* Deming, W. Edwards; leadership; management.

Deming, W. Edwards (1900-1993) A statistics educator, consultant, and patriarch of total quality management who was responsible for the first sampling program in the United States used on the 1940 census. Deming taught statistical quality control to engineers and inspectors during World War II and then took the methods to Japan, where they were in part responsible for the post-World War II revitalization of Japanese industry. *See also* acceptable quality level; Deming's Fourteen Points; red bead experiment; statistical quality control; total quality management.

demonstration project An experimental health care program, system, or organization that measures important data, such as costs per unit of service, rates of use by patients or clients, and clinical outcomes of encounters between providers and users. The aim of using a demonstration project is to determine and, when necessary, improve on the efficiency, effectiveness, and other dimensions of performance and quality before a system, program, or organization is broadly implemented. *Synonym:* demonstration model. *See also* dimensions of performance.

DEMPAQ (Develop and Evaluate Methods for Promoting Ambulatory Care Quality) A joint research project of Harvard University, HCFA, and the State of Maryland's and District of Columbia's Peer Review Organization covering performance measures for ambulatory care. DEMPAQ is an accountability model developed for Medicare, and collects data both from claims records and from office medical records.

denial of accreditation *See* accreditation decision.

denominator The lower portion of a fraction used to calculate a rate, proportion, or ratio. The denominator statement of a clinical indicator is the population (or population experience) at risk in the calculation of a rate. *See also* numerator; rate; ratio.

dentacare A group dental plan similar to an HMO in which a fixed monthly payment (capitation) made to a group of dentists ensures needed dental care to enrolled members. Traditional dental insurance processes and pays dental claims on the basis of fees charged for services (fee for service). *See also* capitation; fee for service.

dental audit A qualitative or quantitative evaluative review of dental services rendered or proposed by a dentist. *See also* audit; medical audit.

dental hygiene *See* oral hygiene.

dental implantology *See* implant dentistry.

dental insurance Insurance that covers the costs of specified aspects of dental care, ranging from coverage of basic diagnostic, preventive, and restorative services to coverage that includes oral surgery and orthodontics. *Synonym:* dental plan. *See also* insurance.

dental jurisprudence   *See* forensic dentistry.

dental laboratory technology accreditation   An accreditation process in which the Commission on Dental Accreditation evaluates and, when appropriate, accredits dental laboratory technology programs.

dental plan   *See* dental insurance.

dental practice act   A state, commonwealth, or territorial statute or law delineating the legal scope of the practice of dentistry within the geographic boundaries of the jurisdiction. *See also* medical practice act; nurse practice act.

dental service   An organization unit that provides ambulatory or inpatient dental services including preventive care, diagnosis, and treatment.

dental service corporation   A nonprofit corporation organized by the dental profession to provide prepaid dental care coverage to the public on a group basis.

dental services   Services, provided by a dentist or a qualified individual under the supervision of a dentist, to improve or maintain the health of an individual's teeth, oral cavity, and associated structures.

dental specialties   Eight areas of expertise in dentistry recognized by the American Dental Association: endodontics, oral and maxillofacial surgery, oral pathology, orthodontics, pediatric dentistry (pedodontics), periodontics, prosthodontics, and public health dentistry.

dentistry   The branch of the healing arts and sciences devoted to maintaining the health of the teeth, gums, and other hard and soft tissues of the oral cavity. *Synonyms:* dental medicine; dental surgery. *See also* chairside; corporate dentistry; forensic dentistry; implant dentistry; oral medicine.

denturism   The practice of making and fitting of dentures by dental technologists without benefit of a dentist's expertise.

deontological ethics   An ethical theory or system that holds that right or wrong is not determined by assessment of consequences, which distinguishes it from utilitarian ethics. Deontological ethics is based on the assumption that value is inherent in the principle or duty. *See also* ethics; utilitarianism.

deoxyribonucleic acid   *See* DNA.

dependence   In psychiatry, the need for protection, security, food, and so forth, as in a child's dependence on a parent or an elderly person's dependence on a caregiver. It also refers to a substance abuser's need to continue using a drug. *See also* alcoholism; substance-related disorders.

dependent personality disorder   *See* personality disorder.

dependent variable   A variable whose value is dependent on the effect of independent variable(s) in the relationship under study. In statistics, the dependent variable is the one predicted by a regression equation. *See also* coefficient of determination; independent variable; regression analysis; variable.

deposition   A method of pretrial discovery consisting of a statement of a witness under oath, taken in question-and-answer form, as it would be in court, with opportunity given to the adversary to be present and cross-examine, with all proceedings reported and transcribed stenographically. The information is obtained for preparation prior to trial; part or all of it may itself be admissible (allowed as evidence) at the trial, depending on the jurisdiction. *See also* discovery; interrogatory.

depressant   **1.** Any agent tending to decrease the function or activity of a body or a body system.   **2.** A class of controlled substances, including barbiturates and tranquilizers. These drugs are used to produce sedation, to induce sleep, to combat anxiety, and to treat epilepsy.

depression   A mental state of depressed mood characterized by feelings of sadness, despair, and discouragement. As such, depression may be a normal feeling. Depression may be a symptom, a syndrome, or a mental disorder. *See also* bipolar disorder; depressive disorders.

depressive disorders   According to the DSM-IV, a group of mood disorders classified by the depression's severity, recurrence, and association with hypomania or mania. The diagnosis of *major depressive disorder* can be made in the presence of at least five of the following symptoms during the same period, with at least one of the first two symptoms also present (the symptoms must be present most of the day, nearly daily, for at least two weeks): depressed mood, markedly diminished interest or pleasure in virtually all activities, significant weight gain or loss, insomnia or hypersomnia, psychomotor agitation or retardation, fatigue or loss of energy, feelings of guilt or worthlessness, indecisiveness or impaired ability to concentrate, and recurrent thoughts of death or suicide. *Dysthmic disorder* is a chronically depressed mood that occurs for most of the day more days than not for at least two years. The required minimum duration in children to make this diagnosis is one year. During periods of depressed mood, at least two of the following additional symptoms are present: poor appetite or overeating, insomnia or hypersomnia, low energy or fatigue, low self-esteem, poor concentration or difficulty making decisions, and feelings of hopelessness. *See also* antidepressant drug; bipolar disorder; electroconvulsive therapy.

dermatology   The branch of medicine and medical specialty dealing with the diagnosis and treatment of pediatric and adult patients with benign and malignant disorders of the skin, mouth, external genitalia, hair, and nails. Dermatopathology and immunodermatology are two subspecialties of dermatology.

descriptive statistics A branch of statistics that quantifies or summarizes data without implying or inferring anything beyond the sample. *See also* data; inferential statistics; statistics.

descriptive study A study concerned with and designed only to describe the existing distribution of variables. With no attempt to make causal or other hypotheses. One example is a survey used to determine practitioner practice patterns relating to use of a certain technology.

desensitization A treatment of allergy by the injection of gradually increasing amounts of the allergen responsible for the allergy. *See also* allergy.

designer drug A drug deliberately synthesized to circumvent antidrug regulations, using a structure that is not yet illegal but which mimics the chemistry and effects of an existing, banned drug; hence, any recreational drug with an altered structure. For example, China White, popular in the 1970s and 1980s, is an example of designer "look-alikes" of heroin. *See also* drug; generally recognized as safe; generally recognized as effective; "me too" drug.

detailer A sales representative of a pharmaceutical manufacturer or medical supply company who promotes prescription drugs and medical supplies for use by physicians, dentists, and pharmacists. Detailing includes personally presenting products, advertising, and providing drug samples, supplies, and educational materials (prepared by the manufacturer) to professionals in their offices or places of work. *Synonyms*: detail person; drug rep; drug sales representative; medical representative; pharmaceutical representative. *See also* academic detailing.

detection A past-oriented strategy that attempts to identify unacceptable output after it has been produced and separate it from the acceptable output. *See also* inspection; prevention.

detoxification **1.** The systematic reduction of the amount of a toxic agent in the body or the elimination of a toxic agent from the body. **2.** The treatment of a person for alcohol or drug dependence, such as under a medically supervised program. *See also* medical detoxification; social detoxification.

developmental age A measure of a child's developmental progression, for example, body size, motor skills, or psychological functioning, expressed as an age. *See also* chronological age; functional age; mental age.

developmental disability A mental or physical limitation affecting major life activities, arising before adulthood and usually lasting throughout life. Developmental disabilities can be grouped into four major categories: autism, cerebral palsy, epilepsy, and mental retardation. *See also* autistic disorder; disability; major life activities; mental retardation.

developmental psychology The branch of psychology dealing with the emotional, intellectual, and social changes that occur across the life span of human beings. Many developmental psychologists specialize in the study of children or adolescents.

deviation In statistics, the difference, especially the absolute difference, between one number in a set and the mean of the set. *See also* standard deviation.

device A nondrug item or apparatus, ranging from cotton swabs to artificial heart valves, used for diagnosing, treating, or preventing disease. A device specifically does not achieve its purpose through chemical action on or within the body, as compared to drugs. Devices are regulated by the FDA. *See also* medical device; Safe Medical Devices Act of 1990.

diabetes care provider A provider recognized in the American Diabetes Association's disease-specific provider recognition program for fulfilling the 11 measures of essential diabetes care.

MEASURES OF ESSENTIAL DIABETES CARE

- Blood pressure measurement
- Eye exams
- Foot exams
- Glycosylated hemoglobin tests
- Identification of tobacco use and referral for counseling
- Lipid profiles
- Medical nutrition therapy
- Patient satisfaction
- Self-management education
- Self-monitoring of blood glucose
- Urinary protein measurement

Diabetes Control and Complications Trial (DCCT) A multi-institutional, randomized, controlled 6½-year clinical trial (1983-1989), supported by several institutes of the NIH and corporate sponsors, that demonstrated that intensive therapy effectively delayed the onset and slowed the progression of the chief long-term complications of type 1 diabetes mellitus (then called insulin-dependent diabetes mellitus)—diabetic retinopathy, nephropathy, and neuropathy. The intensive therapy involved insulin administered by either pump or injection and frequent self-monitoring of blood glucose to maintain near-normal levels (glycemic regulation). Implementations of the recommendations have been widely studied in a variety of settings and for different populations. Applicability of the findings to type 2 diabetes mellitus, which is sometimes controlled by diet and lifestyle modifications and thus entails a different risk-benefit ratio, remains a matter of speculation. *See also* diabetes mellitus; diabetic retinopathy.

diabetes mellitus A group of metabolic diseases characterized by hyperglycemia (greater than normal level of blood glucose) resulting from defects in insulin secretion, insulin action, or both. The chronic hyperglycemia of diabetes is associated with long-term damage, dysfunction, and failure of various organs, especially the eyes, kidneys, nerves, heart, and blood vessels. The long-term complications of diabetes include retinopathy with potential loss of vision; nephropathy leading to renal failure;

CLASSIFICATION OF DIABETES MELLITUS AND OTHER CATEGORIES OF GLUCOSE REGULATION

Category Name	Causation/Test Value/Characteristics
Diabetes	Fasting plasma glucose (FPG) ≥ 126 mg/dL
Type 1 diabetes	Absolute deficiency of insulin secretion and proneness to ketoacidosis
Immune-mediated	Autoimmune destruction of the beta cells; typically children or young adults who are slim (but found in adults of any age)
Idiopathic type 1	Rare forms of the disease which have no known cause (non- autoimmune-specific causes, eg, cystic fibrosis)
Type 2 diabetes	Combination of resistance to insulin action and an inadequate compensatory insulin secretory response; typically adults older than 45 years, overweight, and sedentary, with a family history of diabetes.
Gestational diabetes mellitus (GBM)	Oral glucose tolerance test (50 g) followed by FPG 1 hour later ≥ 140 mg/dL*; any degree of glucose intolerance with onset or first recognition during pregnancy
Impaired glucose homeostasis	At high risk for developing diabetes and macrovascular complications (eg, heart attacks, strokes)
Impaired fasting glucose (IFG)†	FPG ≥ 110 but < 126 mg/dL
Impaired glucose tolerance (IGT)	Oral glucose tolerance test ≥ 140 but < 200 mg/dL (in 2-hour sample)
Normal blood glucose	FPG < 110 mg/dL

*This is the screening test used by most U.S. obstetricians, but there is disagreement over the criteria between different authorities.

†New category established in 1997, between "normal" and "diabetes."

Source: Expert Committee on the Diagnosis and Classification of Diabetes Mellitus, American Diabetes Association: *Diabetes Care* 20:1183, 1997.

peripheral neuropathy with risk of foot ulcers, amputation, and Charcot joints (degenerative disease of the joints); and autonomic neuropathy causing gastrointestinal, genitourinary, and cardiovascular symptoms and sexual dysfunction. A new diagnosis and classification of diabetes was published in July 1997 by the Expert Committee on the Diagnosis and Classification of Diabetes Mellitus and replaces the definition established by the National Diabetes Data Group (NDDG) in 1979. The defining cutpoint for diabetes has been lowered, which means that more patients will be diagnosed with diabetes. The old categories of *insulin-dependent diabetes mellitus* (IDDM) and *non-insulin-dependent diabetes mellitus* (NIDDM) have been eliminated, and Arabic numerals have replaced the Roman numerals for the two broad types of diabetes, now called *type 1 diabetes* (formerly IDDM or juvenile onset diabetes) and *type 2 diabetes* (formerly NIDDM or adult onset diabetes). Malnutrition-related diabetes mellitus has been eliminated as a class. Another category, *gestational diabetes mellitus* (GDM), is defined as any degree of glucose intolerance with onset or first recognition during pregnancy (with disagreement over the precise test values); the former recommendation to screen all pregnant women has been dropped. The 1997 redefinition was motivated by consensus within the diabetes community that classification should be based on etiology rather than type of pharmacologic treatment. *See also* the surrounding diabetes terms, as well as blood glucose; Diabetes Control and Complications Trial; gestational diabetes; ketosis.

Diabetes PORT *See* Patient Outcomes Research Team.

Diabetes Prevention Program A multicenter clinical trial launched in 1997 by the National Institute of Diabetes and Digestive and Kidney Diseases to determine whether early treatment can prevent or delay the development of diabetes in people with impaired glucose homeostasis.

diabetes test The fasting plasma glucose (FPG) test, with a value of 126 mg/dL, confirmed by repeat testing on a different day, as diagnostic of the presence of diabetes. Although other tests for diabetes exist, this test was officially identified as the preferred test, and its diagnostic cutpoint for diabetes was lowered by the Expert Committee on the Diagnosis and Classification of Diabetes Mellitus (July 1997). Other tests are the casual plasma glucose plus symptoms test, the oral glucose tolerance test (OGTT), and the hemoglobin A1c test (HbA1$_c$, or glycosylated hemoglobin; not recommended at this time). The FPG test was recommended for universal use for testing and diagnosis because of its ease of administration, convenience, acceptability to patients, and lower cost (compared with the OGTT). According to the Expert Committee, the finger-prick test used for monitoring blood glucose levels and sometimes used at health fairs is not considered a diagnostic procedure.

diabetic ketoacidosis (DKA) An acute, life-threatening complication of uncontrolled diabetes mellitus in which urinary loss of water and electrolytes results in abnormally low circulating blood volume, electrolyte imbalance, elevated blood glucose levels, and breakdown of free fatty acids causing acidosis, often with coma (diabetic coma). *See also* blood gas determination; ketosis.

diabetic retinopathy   A vascular complication of both type 1 and type 2 diabetes mellitus directly related to the duration of the diabetes, and a major cause of blindness, in which the blood vessels of the retina exhibit microaneurysms, hemorrhage, exudates, and the formation of new vessels and fibrous tissue. Guidelines for screening and intervention may be tailored to levels of the disorder: diabetic macular edema, high-risk proliferative diabetic retinopathy (PDR), and lower-risk PDR and non-proliferative diabetic retinopathy. A series of diabetic retinopathy trials and published guidelines have documented that proper preventive management depends on a dilated-eye exam (funduscopy) each year starting five years after diagnosis of type 1, at the time of diagnosis of type 2, and during the first trimester for any pregnant woman with diabetes. Despite these well-established guidelines, many patients with diabetes do not receive annual eye exams. *See also* Diabetes Control and Complications Trial.

diagnosis (dx)   A scientifically or medically acceptable term given to a complex of symptoms (disturbances of function or sensation of which the individual is aware), signs (disturbances the physician or another individual can detect), and findings (detected by laboratory, x-ray, or other diagnostic procedures, or by responses to therapy). *See also* physical examination.

TYPES OF DIAGNOSES

Admitting	The diagnosis made at the time of the patient's admission to a health care organization or program; includes the reason for admission; may or may not be codable.
Bedside	A diagnosis made by taking a medical history and performing physical examination in the patient's presence and yielding immediate conclusions. *Synonym:* office diagnosis.
Clinical	A diagnosis made on the basis of knowledge obtained from the medical history and physical examination, usually without the benefit of laboratory tests, x-rays, or other ancillary diagnostic modalities.
Codable	A diagnosis expressed in terminology that permits classification by numeric code from the ICD-9-CM.
Differential	Diagnosis to determine which of two or more diseases or conditions is present by systematically comparing and contrasting results of diagnostic measures.
Discharge	The diagnosis made at the time of the patient's discharge from care or services; codable and more exact than admitting diagnosis.
Principal	The diagnosis established, after study of the patient, to be chiefly responsible for his or her need for treatment.
Secondary	Any diagnosis other than the principal diagnosis. *Synonym:* other diagnosis.

Diagnostic and Statistical Manual of Mental Disorders   *See* DSM; DSM-IV; DSM-IV-PC.

Diagnostic and Therapeutic Technology Assessment (DATTA)   A project initiated by the American Medical Association in 1982 to evaluate the safety and effectiveness of drugs, devices, and procedures used in medical practice. Evaluations integrate opinions of expert panels of physicians with systematic reviews of the scientific literature. DATTA evaluations are disseminated in report form through a subscription series and may be published in the *Journal of the American Medical Association. See also* group judgment methods; health care technology assessment programs.

diagnostic cost group (DCG)   A proposed alternative payment system being tested by HCFA for reimbursing Medicare HMOs. The DCG model uses both demographic and diagnostic information to predict total plan payments for health care. There are eight DCGs, ranked by cost of services linked to the patient's age, sex, and welfare status. A formula is then used to set the HMO's capitation rate.

diagnostic imaging   Any visual display of structural or functional patterns of organs or tissues for diagnostic evaluation. It includes measuring physiologic and metabolic responses to physical and chemical stimuli, as well as ultramicroscopy. The appropriateness of use of diagnostic imaging has come under scrutiny with concern over avoiding unnecessary procedures, outcomes measurement, and cost cutting. Frameworks developed for assessing the efficacy of specific modalities or of diagnostic testing in general include concepts such as sensitivity and specificity (diagnostic accuracy), diagnostic yield, incremental value, impact on diagnostic or prognostic thinking, and impact on outcomes. *See also* computed axial tomography; echocardiography; magnetic resonance imaging; radiography; radionuclide imaging; ultrasonography.

diagnostic journey   The sequence of problem-solving steps in which an individual or a team moves from the symptoms of a problem to the root causes of the problem. *See also* diagnosis.

diagnostic profile   A physician, health care organization, or population profile subcategorized by specific condition or diagnosis.

diagnostic radiology   The branch of radiology that deals with the utilization of all modalities of radiant energy in medical diagnoses and therapeutic procedures using radiologic guidance. This includes, but is not restricted to, imaging techniques and methodologies utilizing radiation emitted by x-ray tubes, radionuclides, and ultrasonographic devices and the radio-frequency electromagnetic radiation emitted by atoms.

diagnostic testing   Laboratory and other invasive, diagnostic, and imaging procedures.

diagnostic yield   A measure of the value of a diagnostic test performed for a particular population, usually computed by dividing the number of patients with positive diagnostic test results by the number of tested patients. For some tests, the absolute value of the diagnostic yield may not be as important as the ability of the test to exclude a serious diagnosis. Another important consideration is how much information a test adds that cannot be obtained by less invasive or less costly alternative means. The concept is used by health care organization policy makers and guideline developers to establish clinical policies, patient care recommendations, or reimbursement policies on use of specific tests and procedures in defined circumstances. *See also* incremental benefit.

diathermy Heat treatment in body tissues by high-frequency currents that are insufficiently intense to destroy tissues or to impair their vitality. Diathermy is used in treating chronic arthritis, bursitis, fractures, and other conditions. *See also* cryotherapy; hyperthermia.

Dietary Reference Intake (DRI) A standard for expressing upper reference levels of nutrients, proposed by the Institute of Medicine's Food and Nutrition Board to replace the current dietary standards (Recommended Dietary Allowance [RDA]). A project to develop and evaluate new standards was launched at the end of 1996 with establishment of the Panel on Risk Assessment in Establishing Upper Reference Levels of Nutrients. The maximum levels will indicate thresholds of risk of adverse effects. *See also* Food Guide Pyramid.

dietary risk factors Diet patterns (such as overeating, lack of adequate fluid intake, or high-fat diets) that increase a person's likelihood of developing diseases or other adverse health effects. Dietary risk differs from nutritional risk in that the former involves the food itself while the latter involves an anatomic process (eg, ulcer, cancer).

dietetics The science dealing with the relationships of foods and nutrition to human health. *See also* nutrition.

dietetic services The delivery of care pertaining to the provision of optimal nutrition and quality food service for individuals.

differential cost *See* marginal cost.

dilation and curettage (D&C) A surgical procedure in which the cervix is expanded using a dilator and the uterine lining is scraped with a curette, performed for diagnosing and treating various uterine conditions. *See also* curettage; gynecology.

dimensions of performance For purposes of Joint Commission accreditation, nine definable, measurable, and improvable attributes of organization performance that are related to "doing the right things" and "doing things well". *Dimensions* of performance differ from *domains* of performance in the absence of a tenth attribute of prevention/early detection, which was added for purposes of performance measurement. *See also* domains of performance.

direct cause A cause that sets in motion a chain of events that brings about a result without the intervention of any other independent source. *See also* causation; immediate cause; proximate cause; root cause analysis; special cause.

JOINT COMMISSION DIMENSIONS OF PERFORMANCE

Doing the Right Thing
- Appropriateness
- Availability
- Continuity

Doing Things Well*
- Effectiveness
- Efficacy
- Efficiency
- Respect and caring
- Safety
- Timeliness

*A tenth attribute of prevention/early detection is added to the dimensions of performance to create the *domains* of performance for purposes of performance measurement.

---

direct contact A mode of transmission of infection between an infected host and a susceptible host. It occurs when skin or mucous surfaces touch, as in shaking hands, kissing, and sexual intercourse. *See also* indirect contact; infection.

direct contract model A health plan, such as an open panel HMO, that contracts directly with private practice physicians.

direct cost The cost that is directly identifiable with a particular service or area.

directive to physicians *See* living will.

directly observed therapy (DOT) Provision of a health care professional to watch a patient take a medication in compliance with a regimen—(particularly in the case of multidrug regimens to treat tuberculosis)—to prevent development of a primary drug resistance. *See also* antimicrobial drug resistance.

directors' and officers' (D&O) liability insurance Insurance for corporate directors and officers against claims based on negligence and failure to disclose. Such insurance provides coverage against expenses, and to a limited extent, fines, judgments, and amounts paid in settlement. *See also* insurance.

direct provider agreement (DPA) An agreement between an employer, an HMO or other health care plan, and a health care provider to provide health care services to enrollees.

disability Any restriction or limitation resulting from an impairment of ability to perform an activity in a manner or with the range, considered normal for a human being, according to the *International Classification of Impairments, Disabilities, and Handicaps* (1980) published by the World Health Organization (WHO). The term *disability* reflects the consequences of impairment. In 1997 revision by a WHO working group was under way to change terminology, clarify concepts, and provide an integrated framework for developing ways of measuring disabilities. *See also* developmental disability; handicap;

impairment; learning disability; nonservice-connected disability; service-connected disability; unemployment compensation—disability.

disability insurance   Insurance designed to compensate individuals who lose wages because of illness or injury. *See also* workers' compensation insurance; insurance; unemployment compensation—disability.

LEVELS OF DISABILITY

occupational disability   A condition in which an employee is unable to perform the functions required to complete a job satisfactorily because of an occupational disease or an occupational accident.

partial disability   An illness or injury that prevents a person from performing one or more functions of his or her occupation or profession.

permanent disability   A continuous condition resulting from illness or injury that prevents an individual from performing some or all of the functions of his or her occupation.

temporary disability   An illness or injury that prevents an insured individual from performing functions of his or her usual occupation or profession for an interim period of time.

total disability   An illness or injury that prevents an individual from performing any duty pertaining to his or her occupation or profession or from engaging in any other type of work for remuneration.

---

disability plan for home care benefits   A type of insurance policy that pays home care benefits directly to an insured individual who has been confirmed to have a disability (usually meaning that he or she cannot perform a certain number of activities of daily living without assistance) through medical record review and receipt of a certificate from the patient's physician. *See also* insurance.

disabled veteran   A veteran of the armed services who has a service-connected disability and is considered to be disabled to an extent of 10 percent or greater by the Veterans Administration. *See also* Americans with Disabilities Act of 1990; Department of Veterans Affairs.

disaster   For purposes of Joint Commission accreditation, a natural or man-made event that significantly disrupts the environment of care, such as damage to an organization's buildings and grounds due to severe windstorms, tornadoes, hurricanes, or earthquakes. Also, an event that disrupts patient care and treatment, such as loss of utilities (power, water, telephones) due to floods, riots, accidents, or emergencies within the organization or in the surrounding community. *See also* emergency-preparedness plan.

disaster drill   A simulation of a disaster to assess and improve the effectiveness of a health care organization's or system's emergency-preparedness plan. *See also* emergency-preparedness plan.

disaster medical assistance team (DMAT)   A team that stabilizes casualties in a clearing and staging unit in the event of a disaster. Such teams use advanced trauma life-support methods, sorting (triage), and evacuation. *See also* clearing and staging unit.

disaster plan   *See* emergency-preparedness plan.

discharge   The point at which a patient's active involvement with an organization or program is terminated and the organization or program no longer maintains active responsibility for the care of the patient. Types of discharge are discharge by death, discharge by transfer, and discharge to home.

discharge abstract   A summary description of data abstracted from a hospitalized patient's medical record that usually includes specific clinical data, such as diagnostic and procedural codes, as well as other information about the patient, the physician, and insurance and financial status. An example of a discharge abstract is the Uniform Hospital Discharge Abstract. *See also* data set; hospital discharge abstract system; Uniform Hospital Discharge Data Set.

discharge against medical advice   *See* against medical advice.

discharge instructions   The list of instructions given to a patient on discharge, as in how to take medications and when and from whom to obtain continuing care.

discharge planning   A formalized process in a health care organization through which a program of continuing and follow-up care is planned and carried out for each patient. Discharge planning encompasses a documented sequence of tasks and activities designed to achieve, within projected time frames, stated goals that lead to the timely release of patients to either their homes or to facilities or programs with a lower level of care. Discharge planning is undertaken to ensure that patients remain in a health care organization only for as long as medically needed.

discharge summary   *See* clinical résumé.

disclaimer   *See* guideline disclaimer.

discovery   In legal practice, the pretrial devices that can be used by one party to obtain facts and information about the case from the other party to assist in preparation for trial.

discrete data   Data that can be arranged into naturally occurring or arbitrarily selected groups or sets of values, as opposed to continuous data, which have no naturally occurring breaks. An example of discrete data is the number of medical records that are complete and incomplete per given measurement period. *See also* continuous data; probability distribution; rate-based measure.

discrete variable   *See* rate-based measure.

discriminant validity   A demonstration of the validity of a measure by the lack of correlation among two or more supposedly unrelated measures of a concept. *See also* validity.

discrimination   The effect of statute or established practice which confers particular privileges on a class arbitrarily selected from a large number of persons, all of whom stand in the same relation to the privileges granted and where no reasonable distinction can be found between those favored and those not favored. *See also* Behringer case; genetic discrimination; Pregnancy Discrimination Act.

disease control   Defined by the World Health Organization as a variety of basic public health measures designed to prevent disease or reduce the likelihood of it occurring in a population, including control of factors contributing to disease, immunization, and curative care.

disease notification   Notification or reporting by a physician or other health care provider of the occurrence of specified contagious diseases such as HIV and hepatitis to public health agencies. Each state has its own list of notifiable diseases and system for reporting. For some diseases, such as HIV infection and AIDS, surveillance case definitions are provided by the CDC for the terminology and values to be used in reporting. *See also* mandatory reporting; notifiable disease.

disease state management (DSM)   The continuous process of identifying and delivering, within selected patient populations, the most efficient combination of resources for the treatment or prevention of the disease.

disk herniation   *See* herniated disk.

diskography   Radiography of the spine for visualization of an intervertebral disk, after injection of an absorbable contrast medium into the disk itself. *Synonym:* discography.

dispense   The provision of drugs and medical devices, in accordance with applicable state and federal regulations, to a patient or a patient's authorized representative. *See also* drug dispensing.

dispensing fee   One of two ways in which pharmacists charge for preparing and filling prescriptions, the other being a standard percentage markup on the acquisition cost of drugs. The dispensing fee reflects the fixed cost of the pharmacist's service in handling, preparing, compounding, and dispensing the drug, independent of the cost of the drug being dispensed. *See also* drug dispensing.

disposable medical equipment   Devices and equipment used for short-term use by a single patient, including syringes, plastic bedpans, and paper gowns. Many disposables have replaced previously durable or reusable items. *See also* durable medical equipment.

disproportionate share hospital (DSH)   A Medicare term for a hospital that serves a higher-than-average proportion of low-income patients.

distributed leadership   The division of traditional leadership responsibilities, such as scheduling, among team members, particularly in the context of self-directed teams. *See also* self-directed team.

distributed site testing   *See* point-of-care laboratory testing.

distribution   In statistics, the complete summary of the frequencies of the values or categories of measurement made on a group of persons or other entities. The distribution determines either how many or what proportion of a group was found to have each value (or each range of values) out of all possible values that the quantitative measure can have. A bell-shaped curve or normal distribution is an example of a distribution in which the greatest number of observations falls in the center with fewer and fewer observations falling evenly on either side of the average. *See also* bimodal distribution; frequency distribution; median; normal distribution; probability distribution; *t*-distribution.

district hospital   A type of hospital controlled by a political subdivision of a state; this subdivision is created solely for establishing and maintaining health care organizations.

diversification   The trend of health care organizations to enter different business areas in an effort to obtain revenue from a variety of sources and remain solvent. For example, a long term care provider that specializes in geriatric populations might merge with nearby organizations that provide subacute, hospice, and home care services. *See also* corporatization of health care; restructuring.

Dix, Dorothea Lynde (1802-1887)   A social reformer who campaigned for the improvement of insane asylums and prisons and worked to advance the idea of communal responsibility for the welfare of the mentally disabled. A Massachusetts schoolteacher and Superintendent of Female Nurses for the Union forces during the Civil War, she organized the first nurse corps of the U.S. Army and led the founding of many mental hospitals in the United States, Europe, and Japan.

DNA (deoxyribonucleic acid)   Chemical substance found in the chromosomes in the nucleus of a cell whose molecular structure contains the organism's genetic information. The DNA is altered directly or indirectly in gene therapy and genetic engineering. *See also* recombinant DNA technology; genetic engineering; genetic fingerprinting.

DNR (do-not-resuscitate) order   An order placed in a patient's medical record by an attending physician, with patient or surrogate consent, that directs hospital personnel not to revive the patient if cardiopulmonary arrest occurs. The decision is based on the patient's overall condition and values. *Synonym:* no code. *See also* cardiopulmonary resuscitation; code blue.

doctor   A physician, dentist, podiatrist, chiropractor, scientist, administrator, or other person holding a doctoral degree awarded by a recognized academic or professional school.

TYPES OF DOCTORATE DEGREES

Doctor of Business Administration (DBA)

Doctor of Chiropractic (DC)

Doctor of Dental Surgery (DDS)

Doctor of Dental Medicine (DMD)

Doctor of Osteopathy (DO)

Doctor of Public Administration (DPA)

Doctor of Public Health (DPH, DrPH)

Doctor of Podiatric Medicine (DPM)

Doctor of Education (EdD)

Doctor of Medicine (MD)

Doctor of Naturopathy (ND)

Doctor of Optometry (OD)

Doctor of Pharmacy (PharD, PharmD)

Doctor of Philosophy (PhD)

Doctor of Psychology (PsyD)

Doctor of Science (ScD)

doctor-patient privilege *See* physician-patient privilege.

doctor-patient relationship *See* patient-provider relationship.

documentation The process of recording information in the patient's medical, home care, or other health record and other source documents. *See also* medical record; source document.

domains of performance For purposes of Joint Commission accreditation, ten definable, measurable, and improvable attributes of organization performance that are related to "doing the right things" (appropriateness, availability, and efficacy) and "doing things well" (timeliness, effectiveness, continuity, safety, efficiency, respect and caring, and prevention/early detection). *Domains* of performance add a tenth attribute (prevention/early detection) to the *dimensions* of performance for purposes of performance measurement. *See also* dimensions of performance.

domicile Legal home or permanent residence. An individual can have many transient residences where he or she may temporarily be found, but only one legal domicile, which is the residence to which he or she always intends to return and to remain indefinitely.

domiciliary care Residential care including those services necessary for maintaining a secure homelike environment, given a patient's condition. The services may be provided either in a care facility, such as a nursing home, in an alternative living residence, such as a rest home or retirement center, or in a patient's home. Board, lodging, supervision, personal care, and home leisure activities are included. Health services are excluded. *See also* residential care.

do no harm *See* Hippocratic oath.

do-not-resuscitate order *See* DNR order.

Doppler color flow imaging *See* echocardiography.

Doppler effect The change in frequency of sound and light waves emitted by a source as it moves away from or toward the observer. The principle, named after the Austrian physicist and mathematician Christian J. Doppler (1803-1853), is applied in Doppler imaging technology to measure the speed of blood flow as well as the shape and functioning of internal bodily structures. *Synonyms*: Doppler phenomenon; Doppler principle; Doppler shift. *See also* echocardiography.

dosage The regulated administration of doses of therapeutic agents, expressed as amounts of drug per units of time. *See also* dose.

dose A specified amount of a therapeutic agent, such as a drug or radiation, prescribed to be taken at one time or at stated intervals. *See also* dosage; unit-dose system.

dosimetrist The person on the cancer treatment radiation team who calculates the number of treatments and the duration of each one.

double-blind technique A method of studying a drug, device, or procedure in which both subjects and investigators are kept unaware of (blind to) who is actually getting which specific treatment. This is done to reduce both subject and researcher biases. In a triple-blind study, data analyzers are also kept unaware of the treatment used. *Synonyms*: double-blind study; double-mask study; double-mask technique. *See also* clinical trial phases; triple-blind study.

double-contrast barium enema (DCBE) *See* barium enema.

double-effect principle An action that may have both a positive and a negative effect. The negative effect may be tolerated if the negative was not intended but is simply a by-product of the good, or positive, effect. The positive effect must outweigh the negative effect.

drainage/secretion precautions A category of patient isolation intended to prevent infections transmitted by direct or indirect contact with purulent material or drainage from an infected body site. A private room and masking are not indicated. Gowns should be used if soiling is likely and gloves used for touching contaminated materials. *See also* direct contact; indirect contact; infection; isolation.

drama therapy Intentional use of drama and theater processes, facilitated by a qualified therapist, to achieve the therapeutic goals of symptom relief, emotional and physical integration, and personal growth. It is used with individuals, groups, and families to maintain health and to treat emotional disorders, learning difficulties, geriatric problems, and social maladjustments. *See also* creative arts therapy; manual arts therapy; recreational therapy.

DRG (diagnosis-related group) A classification for a health care service mandated for Medicare's prospective payment system by the Social Security Amendments of 1983. Classifications are based on principal diagnosis, secondary diagnosis, surgical procedures (if any), age, sex, and presence of complications. Groupings of diagnostic categories are drawn from the ICD-9-CM. The DRG system is used as a financing mechanism to reimburse hospitals and other providers for services rendered. The amount paid under the system is based on the average cost of treating a particular condition and DRG into which a discharge is classified, regardless of the number of services received or the length of the patient's stay in the organization. *See also* ambulatory visit group; case mix; complication; comorbidity; GROUPER software; ICD-9; ICD-10; major diagnostic category; Medicare; pediatric-modified DRGs; Social Security Amendments of 1983; uniform capital factor.

DRG creep The phenomenon in which the distribution of patients among DRGs changes without a real change in the distribution of patients treated in the organization. This results when organizations and physicians alter their record keeping and reporting so that more patients appear in higher-priced DRGs, resulting in increased income without a corresponding increase in cost. DRG creep is often inappropriately used to refer to natural growth in case-mix severity and efforts to provide more accurate and descriptive coding.

DRG outlier In health care reimbursement (especially in prospective payment systems), a patient who requires an unusually long stay in a health care organization and whose stay generates unusually high costs.

DRG weight Index number that reflects the relative resource consumption associated with each diagnosis-related group.

drive out fear *See* Deming's Fourteen Points.

drive-through delivery *See* length-of-stay mandates.

drug **1.** Any substance, other than food or devices, that may be used on or administered to persons as an aid in the diagnosis, treatment, or prevention of disease or other abnormal condition. *Synonym:* medication. **2.** A general term for any substance, stimulating or depressing, that can be habituating or addictive, especially a narcotic. Under the jurisdiction of the Controlled Substances Act of 1970, administered by the DEA within the U.S. Department of Justice, drugs are divided into five categories according to potential for abuse and physical and psychological dependence. *See also* designer drug; generally recognized as safe; generally recognized as effective; "me too" drug; schedule of controlled substances.

drug abuse Persistent or sporadic drug use inconsistent with or unrelated to acceptable medical or cultural practice. *See also* impaired health care provider; substance-related disorders.

drug addiction *See* substance-related disorders.

drug administration The act of giving a prescribed and prepared dose of an identified drug to a patient. *Synonym:* medication administration.

drug allergy A state of hypersensitivity induced by exposure to a particular drug antigen resulting in harmful immunologic reactions on subsequent drug exposures, such as a penicillin drug allergy.

drug dispensing The issuance of one or more doses of a prescribed and prepared drug by a pharmacist or other authorized staff member to another person responsible for administering it. Drug dispensing includes the preparation, compounding, packaging, and labeling necessary for delivery of the drugs. *See also* dispensing fee; drug.

Drug Efficacy Study A study undertaken in 1966 by the National Research Council of the National Academy of Sciences to evaluate all the drugs the FDA had approved as safe before 1962, when Congress first required that drugs had to be proved effective before they could be marketed. The Drug Efficacy Study Group evaluated nearly 4,000 individual drug products, finding many ineffective or of only possible or probable effectiveness. The vast majority of the study's recommendations have been implemented.

drug error *See* medication error.

drug formulary A list of drugs, usually by their generic names, and indications for their use. A formulary is intended to include a sufficient range of medicines to enable physicians, dentists, and, as appropriate, other practitioners to prescribe all medically appropriate treatment for all reasonably common illnesses.

drug history A delineation of the drugs used by a patient, including prescribed and unprescribed drugs and alcohol. A drug history includes, but is not necessarily limited to, the following: drugs used in the past; drugs used recently, especially within the preceding 48 hours; drugs of preference; frequency with which each drug has been used; route of administration of each drug; drugs used in combination; dosages used; year of first use of each drug; previous occurrences of overdose, withdrawal, or adverse drug reactions; and history of previous treatment for alcohol or drug abuse. *See also* drug profile.

drug holiday Slang for failure to comply with drug regimens, usually discontinuance of a therapeutic drug for a limited period of time. Disrupting a dosing schedule can contribute to development of drug resistance or accelerate the process. *See also* drug resistance.

drug maintenance list A list of a limited number of prescription medications, as designated by a health plan, commonly prescribed by physicians for long-term patient use. The list is subject to periodic review and modification by the health plan. *Synonym:* additional drug benefit list.

drug monograph A document specifying the types and amounts of ingredients a drug or class of related drugs may contain, the conditions for which the drug may be given or prescribed, the directions for its use, and warnings and other information that must appear on labels for the drug's containers. Drug monographs established by the FDA state the conditions under which specific drugs may be marketed as safe and effective. Once a monograph is promulgated, anyone who meets its requirements can market the drug without seeking approval from the FDA. *See also* new drug application.

Drug Price Competition and Patent Term Restoration Act of 1984   The act that amended the Federal Food, Drug and Cosmetic Act to provide additional patent protection and patent extensions for prescription drugs and eased the requirements and procedures for making generic, equivalent drugs available when the patents on a drug run out. The act also establishes requirements for abbreviated new-drug applications and their approval. *See also* abbreviated new-drug application; generic drug law; generic equivalents; new-drug application.

drug profile   **1.** A written or computer listing (kept in one location) of all medications a patient is receiving, such that the total medication therapy can be reviewed as a whole. *See also* drug history.   **2.** A pharmacist's database of patient clinical information and medication use as required by law and regulation.

drug resistance   Diminished or failed response of a human, animal, disease, or tissue to the intended effectiveness of a chemical or drug. In technical discourse, this does not include the resistance of microorganisms to drugs, for which the term *antimicrobial drug resistance* is preferred. It should be differentiated from *drug tolerance*, which is the progressive diminution of the susceptibility of a human or animal to the effects of a drug, as a result of continued administration. *See also* antimicrobial drug resistance; microbial drug resistance.

drug sales representative   *See* detailer.

drug screening   Testing used to determine the presence of drugs or to measure the amount of drugs in an individual.

drug therapy monitoring   The ongoing review and evaluation of patient data for medication effectiveness and actual or potential medication-related problems. *See also* monitor.

drug usage evaluation   A health care organization's medical staff responsibility in cooperation with other relevant departments/services of the organization that entails measuring, assessing, and improving the appropriate and effective use of drugs. Drug usage evaluation may be performed retrospectively, prospectively, or concurrently and can either address a process, such as adhering to a protocol, or an outcome, such as determining the effectiveness of parenteral nutritional support for patients.

drug utilization review (DUR)   Formal programs for assessing drug prescription against some standard. Pharmacists performing DURs must review past patterns of drug misuse, monitor current therapy, and offer patient counseling. The review may also consider clinical appropriateness, cost effectiveness, and outcomes. Review is usually retrospective, but some analysis may be done before drugs are dispensed (as in computer systems that advise physicians when prescriptions are entered). DURs were established by OBRA in 1990 and mandated for Medicaid programs beginning in 1993. *See also* OBRA '90.

DSM (*Diagnostic and Statistical Manual of Mental Disorders*)   The American Psychiatric Association's classification of mental disorders providing a multiaxial system for evaluation, diagnostic criteria, and official nomenclature. The DSM is accepted as the international standard for psychiatric research and clinical care and is coordinated with the ICD system. A diagnosis for an individual will reflect consideration of five axes, or domains of inquiry. *See also* axis; DSM-IV; DSM-IV-PC; ICD-9-CM; ICD-10.

DSM-IV (*Diagnostic and Statistical Manual of Mental Disorders, Fourth Edition—Primary Care*)   The fourth edition (1994) of the DSM, which sets out widely revised and redefined criteria, based on a substantial increase in research on diagnosis generated by DSM-III (1981) and DSM-III-R in the first complete change of the manual in 13 years. DSM codes and terms are compatible with both ICD-9-CM and ICD-10. *See also* mental disorder; mood disorders; personality disorder.

DSM-IV-PC (*Diagnostic and Statistical Manual of Mental Disorders, Fourth Edition—Primary Care*)   A primary care version of the DSM- IV designed in collaboration with primary care clinicians and formatted specifically for use in primary care settings.

dual choice   The practice of giving persons a choice of more than one health insurance to pay for or to provide their health services. *See also* insurance.

dual coverage   *See* duplication of benefits.

due care   That degree of care which an ordinarily prudent person would have exercised under the same or similar circumstances. Usually used in cases centering on a defendant's negligence, this term implies both that a party has not been negligent or careless and that he or she has not violated the law relating to the subject matter or transaction that constitutes the basis of the case.

due process   The right of fundamental fairness in proceedings that are judicial in nature. *Substantive due process* implies that all legislation should (or must) be in furtherance of a legitimate governmental objective, and *procedural due process* guarantees procedural fairness when the government would deprive an individual of his or her property or liberty. This requires that notice and right to a fair hearing be accorded before a deprivation. One requirement for granting of immunity to a health care entity is that the peer review action is justified by the facts after satisfying due process of law.

Duke Activity Status Index   A measure of functional class for patients with diseases or conditions such as angina.

Dukes' classification   *See* cancer staging system.

Duke Treadmill Score   *See* exercise test.

dumping   *See* patient dumping.

duplication of benefits   The situation in which a person covered under more than one health or accident insurance policy collects, or may collect, payments for the same hospital or medical expenses from more than one insurer. *Synonym*: dual coverage. *See also* benefits; insurance.

durable medical equipment (DME) Medical equipment—such as a ventilator, wheelchair, hospital bed, oxygen system, or home dialysis system—that may be prescribed by a physician for a patient's use for an extended period of time. *See also* disposable medical equipment; medical equipment.

durable power of attorney for health care An advance directive wider in scope than a living will which designates a family member or friend to make decisions about a patient's care should the patient become unable to do so. This type of power of attorney, in contrast to ordinary power of attorney, remains or becomes effective when the principal becomes incompetent to act for herself or himself. *Synonym*: health care proxy. *See also* advance directive; living will; natural death acts; Patient Self Determination Act; power of attorney.

Dutch cure Euphemism for aggressively advocated physician-assisted suicide, named after abuses of the Netherlands euthanasia reporting law and after a book about physician-assisted suicide in the United States. The term was heard in testimony before U.S. Congress on assisted-suicide bills. *See also* physician-assisted suicide.

duty to warn The legal, moral, or ethical responsibility of a health professional to warn an intended victim of specific threats of harm or to warn a person of potential risk for acquiring a disease as the result of a relationship to a patient. This obligation was established in the Tarasoff rule (1976) and has since expanded to cover a wide range of threats or harms. *See also Tarasoff* v *The Regents of the University of California.*

dysthymic disorder *See* depressive disorders.

dystocia Abnormally slow progress of labor during the process of childbirth. *Synonym*: failure to progress. *See also* cesarean section.

Ee

80/20 rule *See* Pareto principle.

Early and Periodic Screening Diagnosis and Treatment Program (EPSDT)   A program mandated by Medicaid for eligible people under 21 years of age to assess the presence of physical or mental defects and ensure treatment for them. *See also* Medicaid.

early offer   A dispute resolution in which the practitioner or provider, in cases of injury, makes an offer of prompt payment for costs (excluding pain and suffering) to the claimant, who agrees not to take further legal action. *See also* administrative determination of fault; alternative dispute resolution; arbitration.

early survey option I (ESO I)   A two-part survey by the Joint Commission conducted for health care organizations in operation less than six months. The initial survey assesses only organization structure. A mandatory follow-up survey is conducted six months from the date of the initial survey to assess the process of care or service delivery through review of established performance records and implementation of policies and procedures. *See also* accreditation decision; accreditation survey.

early survey option II (ESO II)   A two-part survey by the Joint Commission conducted for health care organizations in operation for at least one month. The initial survey is a full accreditation survey, as opposed to ESO I which assesses only organization structure. If the organization demonstrates satisfactory standards compliance, it will be granted Accreditation with type I recommendations to reflect the preliminary nature of the assessed performance. A mandatory follow-up survey is conducted four months from the date of the initial survey to address track record requirements not assessed in the first survey due to the limited time of operation. Other follow-up activities may be required on the basis of survey findings from either of the two surveys. *See also* accreditation survey.

eating disorders   A group of disorders characterized by physiological and psychological disturbances in appetite or food intake, of which the most common types are anorexia and bulimia; other types are hyperphagia, pica, and rumination. According to the DSM-IV, *anorexia nervosa* is characterized by a refusal to maintain a minimally normal body weight, and *bulimia nervosa* is characterized by repeated episodes of binge eating followed by inappropriate compensatory behaviors such as self-induced vomiting; misuse of laxatives, diuretics, or other medications; fasting; or excessive exercise. A disturbance in perception of body shape and weight is an essential feature of both disorders. The term *anorexia*, which means loss of appetite, is a misnomer because it is rare. Unlike individuals with anorexia nervosa, individuals with bulimia nervosa are able to maintain body weight at or above a minimally normal level. Both disorders are found disproportionately in industrialized cultures and in girls or young women, and as a result may be conceptualized as a culture-bound syndrome.

ECG (electrocardiography)   The graphic recording of the variations in electrical potential caused by electrical activity of the heart muscle and detected at the body surface through the placement of numbered electrodes (leads) on the chest wall over the heart (leads V1-V6) and on the extremities (leads I-III). The ECG alone is called a *resting ECG* to distinguish it from an *exercise ECG* (ECG plus exercise test) or *ambulatory ECG* (also called Holter monitoring). The graphic record produced in electrocardiography is an electrocardiogram (ECG or EKG), or cardiogram. *See also* ambulatory electrocardiography; exercise test; Holter monitor.

echocardiography   A special application of diagnostic ultrasound focused on the heart, in which a microphone-like transducer sends out sound waves and detects the echoes bouncing back from the surfaces of internal structures, such as the heart muscle and heart valves. The transducer is placed on the body or even in the body to take soundings from as close as possible to the area of the heart under study. A computer reconstructs the shape of the heart through calculations of the time it takes the sound waves to travel to and from the heart. This information, which can be displayed on a video screen or printed on paper, permits observation of various dimensions of the health of the heart, including size, pumping strength, location and extent of damaged heart muscle, severity and type of heart valve problems, site and degrees of abnormal blood flow patterns, structural abnormalities, and pulmonary blood pressure. Revised guidelines from the American College of Cardiology and the American Heart Association in collaboration with the American Society of Echocardiography (1997) warn that since the procedure is noninvasive and has no known complications, has led to overuse, including unnecessary repeat echocardiograms and inappropriate choices of patients for undergoing the procedure. This not only adds unnecessary costs but also can generate unnecessary further testing or inappropriate and potentially detrimental therapy when the echocardiogram "finds" conditions that do not need fixing. *Synonym*: ultrasonic cardiography. *See also* diagnostic imaging; Doppler effect; exercise test; imaging; ultrasonic diagnostic service.

TYPES OF ECHOCARDIOGRAPHY

M-mode echocardiography
2-dimensional (2-D) transthoracic echocardiography (TTE)
3-dimensional (3-D) echocardiography*
Doppler echocardiography
Color Doppler echocardiography
Transesophageal echocardiography (TEE)

*A new mode, adding depth, which is still under development

---

eclampsia   The onset of convulsions or coma in a previously diagnosed patient with pregnancy-induced hypertension (PIH; previously termed pre-eclampsia and toxemia), a condition of late pregnancy (after the 24th week) characterized by hypertension, swelling of the extremities, and protein in the blood. The PIH is classified as *mild* or *severe* depending on the extent of elevated blood pressure, but if grand mal convulsions and coma occur, it is classified as *eclampsia*. *See also* pregnancy-induced hypertension.

economic credentialing   The use of economic performance data and information in determining a practitioner's qualifications for membership and privileges on a hospital medical staff or in establishing eligibility to participate in a health care network or managed care plan. *See also* credentialing; medical staff; practice pattern analysis.

economic indicator   **1.** A quantitative measure used to monitor performance and change in the economy. **2.** A statistical value that provides an indication of the condition or change in direction over time of the state of the economy.

Economic Stabilization Program (ESP)   A federal program established by law to control wages and prices. On August 15, 1971, all wages and prices in the United States were frozen for 90 days during which time a system of wage and price controls, administered through a Cost of Living Council, was implemented. The controls continued until April 1974 when the legislative authority for them expired. Wages and prices in the health care industry were controlled through a specialized series of regulations. The 32-month period during which the controls were in effect was the only period before 1984 in which increases in U.S. medical care fees slowed markedly since the enactment of Medicare and Medicaid.

economies of scale   Cost savings resulting from the aggregation of resources or mass production. *See also* center of excellence.

ectopic pregnancy   The implantation and subsequent development of a fertilized ovum outside the uterus, almost always in a fallopian tube but rarely in the abdominal cavity, an ovary, or the cervix. Usually, the embryo grows until it bursts the tube, which is an emergency requiring immediate surgery to remove the tube with the fetus and to stop the bleeding.

educational psychology   The branch of psychology that attempts to improve teaching methods and materials, solve learning problems, and measure learning ability and educational progress. Researchers in this field may devise achievement tests, develop and evaluate teaching methods, or investigate how children learn at different ages. *See also* learning; psychology; learning psychology.

Education for All Handicapped Children Act of 1975 (EAHCA)   A federal law mandating that all physically and mentally handicapped children, ages 3 to 21, be given a free, appropriate education and related services necessary to obtain an education. Following litigation over the meaning of the term *appropriate*, the U.S. Supreme Court in *Board of Education* v *Rowley* (458 U.S. 176 [1982]) determined that a "free appropriate public education" consists of educational instruction specially designed to meet the unique needs of the handicapped child, supported by such services as are necessary to permit the child to benefit from the instruction.

effectiveness   A Joint Commission performance dimension addressing the degree to which care is provided in the correct manner, given the current state of knowledge, to achieve the desired or projected outcome(s) for the patient. *See also* dimensions of performance; efficacy; efficiency; intervention.

efficacy   **1.** A Joint Commission performance dimension addressing the degree to which the care of the patient has been shown to accomplish the desired or projected outcome(s). *See also* dimensions of performance; intervention.   **2.** The extent to which a specific intervention, procedure, regimen, or service produces a beneficial result under ideal conditions. Efficacy is often used (incorrectly) as a synonym for effectiveness in health care delivery; it is distinguished from effectiveness, which concerns conditions that exist in reality—usual or normal circumstances—not ideal conditions. *See also* effectiveness.

efficiency   A Joint Commission performance dimension addressing the relationship between the outcomes (results of care) and the resources used to deliver care. The ultimate measure of efficiency is the cost of achieving a goal to the benefit achieved by the goal. *See also* dimensions of performance; effectiveness; efficacy; intervention; outcome; patient health outcome.

ejection fraction (EF)   The percentage of blood emptied from the heart ventricle by the end of a contraction. The EF is a threshold measure for heart failure (35%, compared with normal left ventricular function at 65%).

elder abuse   Mistreatment of the elderly involving direct acts of commission such as physical violence, emotional harm, or financial exploitation.

elder care   Any care of any older adult by relatives or friends. *See also* aged person.

elderly   *See* aged person.

elder neglect   Failure of a caregiver to provide needed services to a dependent elderly person.

elective admission   The formal acceptance by a health care organization of a patient whose condition permits adequate time to schedule the availability of a suitable accommodation. *See also* admission.

elective surgery   Surgery that does not have to be performed immediately to prevent death or serious disability. If surgery can be scheduled at some future date, it is, by definition, elective. Elective surgery may result in correction of a medical problem, such as inguinal hernia repair or removal of a bunion, or it may be performed in response to patient desires, for example, cosmetic surgery. *See also* emergency surgery; surgery.

electroacupuncture A form of acupuncture using low-frequency electrically stimulated needles to produce analgesia and anesthesia and to treat disease. *See also* alternative medicine.

electrocardiogram *See* ECG.

electrocardiography *See* ECG.

electroconvulsive therapy (ECT) A form of somatic treatment that uses electricity to evoke a convulsive response; used as a treatment for mental disorders, primarily depression, in which convulsions and loss of consciousness are induced by application of low-voltage alternating current to the brain via scalp electrodes for a fraction of second. ECT produces a therapeutic response in a majority of cases of major depression. *Synonyms:* electric convulsive therapy; electric shock therapy; electroshock therapy; shock therapy. *See also* depressive disorders.

electrodiagnosis Any diagnostic method employing an electrical or electronic apparatus. *See also* physical medicine and rehabilitation.

electroencephalography (EEG) The recording of the electric currents in the brain by means of electrodes applied to the scalp or the surface of the brain or placed within the substance of the brain. Electroencephalography is a method for making neurological diagnoses based on data obtained from the electroencephalogram. *See also* brain death.

electrolytes Substances that, when dissolved, separate into ions capable of conducting electricity. Sodium, potassium, magnesium, and chloride are electrolytes in the body that are instrumental in transmitting nerve impulses, contracting muscles, and maintaining a proper fluid level and acid-base balance.

electronic data interchange (EDI) The process whereby orders, invoices, and sometimes money are transferred electronically between customers' and vendors' computers, replacing traditional paper, mail, and phone transmission of these items.

electronic medical record (EMR) A medical record that is created in an electronic format, such as with digital dictation or automated speech recognition, so that it can be stored, transmitted, referenced, and audited electronically. *See also* computer-based patient record; medical record; voice input/output technology.

electronic surrogate patient record (ESPR) A proposed adjunct to the computer-based patient record (CPR) that would be created automatically at the same time as the CPR. The ESPR would contain a standard, coded data set filtered from the CPR's original data and would be used for two primary purposes: (1) To construct a security system to ensure that the original CPR remains intact and is safe from external tampering or intrusion; (2) To provide an electronic data source for external users who require clinical data for research. *See also* coding; computer-based patient record.

electrostimulation *See* transcutaneous electric nerve stimulation.

eligible In insurance, whether an individual is entitled to benefits under a specified insurance plan, governmental program, or other health care plan. *See also* insurance.

emancipated minor **1.** In general, a person under 18 years of age who is totally self-supporting. **2.** In health care, a minor who has sole authority to make personal health care decisions. *See also* age of majority; legal age. **3.** In law, there are three general-ly recognized categories of emancipated minors: *court-ordered emancipation* (eg, minors living separately from parent(s) who petition the court to be treated as though they have reached legal majority); *statutorily-defined emancipation* (eg, married minors, minors who are parents, minors who are in the military); or *medical emancipation* granted by a particular state (eg, minors seeking treatment for certain medical conditions, such as sexually transmitted diseases, pregnancy, and drug or alcohol abuse). The situations in which minors are deemed to be totally or partially emancipated are defined by statute and case law and vary among states. *See also* mature minor; minor.

embolism A blockage of a blood vessel, especially an artery, by a thrombus (clot), embolus (piece of clot that has broken off) air bubble, fat globule, or other material that has traveled through the blood vessel to the point of blockage from elsewhere. *See also* deep venous thrombosis; ischemia; thromboembolism; thrombolytic therapy.

emergency *See* disaster.

emergency care Immediate evaluation of and intervention in illnesses or injuries that may be life-threatening or limb-threatening. *See also* emergency services.

emergency medical responder (EMR) A trained individual who arrives on the scene of a medical emergency and administers assistance prior to the arrival of emergency medical technicians or paramedics. *Synonym:* first responder.

emergency medical services system (EMSS) An integrated system of health human resources, facilities, and equipment that provides all necessary emergency care in a defined geographic area. *See also* Emergency Medical Services System Act of 1973.

Emergency Medical Services System (EMSS) Act of 1973 A federal law that established funding and systematic requirements for emergency medical services systems, including sufficient trained personnel to ensure the availability of care at all times, regional training programs for all levels of personnel, emergency medical communications systems, specialized facilities, transportation, disaster plans, integration with public safety agencies, regional and interregional mutual assistance pacts, critical care units, patient transfer continuity, consumer participation, consumer education, standard medical records, care accessibility and availability, and ongoing review and evaluation. Federal funding for the EMSS program has been eliminated.

Emergency Medical Treatment and Active Labor Act (EMTALA) (42 U.S.C.A. § 1395dd [1985]) A federal law, passed as part of COBRA, that requires participating Medicare hospitals to provide a medical screening to any patient who comes to their emergency departments. *See also* COBRA.

emergency medicine The branch of medicine and medical specialty that deals with the recognition, stabilization, evaluation, treatment, and disposition of an undifferentiated population of patients with acute illness or injury. Emergency care is episodic and handles a full spectrum of physical and behavioral conditions. Pediatric emergency medicine, sports medicine, and medical toxicology are three subspecialties of emergency medicine. *See also* medical toxicology; medicine; sports medicine; triage.

emergency patient An outpatient with a potentially disabling or life-threatening condition who receives initial evaluation and medical, dental, or other health-related services in an emergency department or a freestanding emergency center. *See also* freestanding emergency center.

emergency-preparedness plan A component of a health care organization's or network's environment of care program designed to manage the consequences of natural disasters or other emergencies that disrupt the organization's or network's ability to provide care and treatment. *Synonyms:* disaster plan; disaster-preparedness plan. *See also* disaster; disaster drill.

emergency privileges Temporary authorization granted by the governing body of a health care organization to a licensed practitioner to provide patient care services in the organization in an emergency situation, within limits based on the individual's professional license and without regard to regular service assignment or staff status. *See also* clinical privileges; temporary privileges.

emergency services 1. Health services that are provided after the onset of a medical condition that manifests itself by symptoms of sufficient severity, including severe pain, that the absence of immediate medical attention could reasonably be expected by a prudent layperson, who possesses an average knowledge of health and medicine, to result in placing the patient's health in serious jeopardy, serious impairment to bodily functions, or serious dysfunction of any bodily organ or part. **2.** The component of a health care organization responsible for delivery of emergency services, as in the emergency department or emergency service(s) of a hospital. *See also* emergency care; out-of-area coverage.

emergency services levels of care (I-IV) A classification, based on specific and general requirements, that describes the capability of a health care organization to provide a range of emergency services for patients who need them. For example, a hospital with Level I emergency services offers the most comprehensive emergency care services, while a hospital with Level IV emergency services provides the least comprehensive care. *See also* levels of care.

emergency surgery Surgery that a physician has determined must be performed without delay to prevent death or serious disability. Trauma surgery is a good example of emergency surgery. *See also* elective surgery; surgery.

emergicenter *See* freestanding emergency center.

EMI scan An outdated term for CAT scan. The first computerized axial tomography (CAT) scanners were made by the British firm EMI. *See also* CAT scan.

emphysema *See* chronic obstructive pulmonary disease.

Empirics The second of the post-Hippocratic schools of medicine (2nd century BC), under the leadership of Philinos of Cos and Serapion of Alexandria. As opposed to the Dogmatists, the Empirics declared that the search for the ultimate causes of phenomena was vain and instead tried to discover the immediate causes. In choosing a treatment to benefit a particular set of symptoms, they used the "tripod of the Empirics," after which their mode of discovery is named—their own observations and experience, the experience of others, and application of their observations, by analogy, to new diseases. *See also* Hippocrates of Cos.

empiric therapy Treatment based on the clinician's judgment and the patient's symptoms and signs and offered before a diagnosis has been confirmed.

employee assistance program (EAP) A formal occupational health service program designed to assist employees with personal problems through internal counseling and referral to outside counseling or treatment resources. *See also* impaired health care provider.

employee development plan A process standard that outlines a critical area for development, desired outcomes, required activities, and a timeline for completion directed at improving an individual staff member's performance. *See also* in-service.

employee exclusion cap A limitation on the amount of employer-provided health benefits an employee may receive tax-free.

employee health benefit plan An organization's insurance plan for health benefits for its employees and their dependents, provided by the employer as a benefit not included in the employees' gross salaries. The benefit plan usually requires employees to pay a percentage of the premium and to share in the cost of services covered under the plan through payment of a deductible and a percentage of the charges for at least some of the services. *See also* insurance.

employee health service A service providing pre-employment medical screening and health care services to employees.

Employee Retirement Income Security Act (ERISA) (29 U.S.C.A. §§ 1001-1461 [1974]) Federal legislation that exempts self-insured health plans from state insurance regulations and insurance taxes. Thus, self-insured companies that meet the requirements of the act are exempt from state laws prohibiting discrimination against insuring people with certain diseases, mandatory contributions to state risk pools, and state mandates requiring all health plans to include certain benefits. *See also* self-insurance.

KEY POINTS OF HEALTH PLANS' AND ENROLLEES' RESPONSIBILITIES UNDER ERISA

1. Health care plans and agents must act solely in the interest of plan participants and beneficiaries.

2. The plan's sole purpose is providing benefits and defraying expenses.

3. Plan agents and enrollees must act with the care, skill, prudence, and diligence that a similar person in a like capacity would act in similar circumstances.

4. The plan and its agents must function according to written plan documents.

Source: Lehman LB. Precedent-setting legal cases in managed care. *The Journal of Outcomes Management* 3(1):15, May 1996.

---

employer deduction cap   A proposed limitation on employers' tax deduction for employee health care benefits to no more than a predetermined per capita cost. *See also* Health Security Act.

empower   In total quality management, to encourage employees to participate in analyzing and improving processes that directly or indirectly affect their work. This is accomplished through changes in organization design and culture that encourage information and resource sharing, participative management, and improvement of communication and collaboration among departments and employees. *See also* total quality management.

encoding   Converting information into a code. *See also* coding; decoding.

encounter   *See* health care encounter.

endarterectomy   *See* carotid endarterectomy.

endemic infection   **1.** The habitual presence of an infection within a geographic area, as in diseases endemic to the tropics.   **2.** The usual prevalence of a given disease within such an area. *See also* epidemic infection; infectious diseases; pandemic.

endocrinology   The branch of medicine and subspecialty of internal medicine dealing with disorders of the internal (endocrine) glands, such as the thyroid and adrenal glands; disorders, such as diabetes and metabolic and nutritional disorders; pituitary diseases; and menstrual and sexual problems. *See also* internal medicine; reproductive endocrinology.

endodontics   The branch of dentistry and dental specialty dealing with the causes, diagnosis, prevention, and treatment of diseases of the pulp and other dental tissues that affect the vitality of the teeth. *See also* dental specialties.

endogenous infection   Infection due to reactivation of previously dormant organisms, as occurs in tuberculosis, histoplasmosis, and other diseases. *See also* infection.

endorsement   The recognition by one jurisdiction of a license given by another jurisdiction, when the qualifications and standards required by the licensing jurisdiction are equivalent to or higher than those of the endorsing jurisdiction. Endorsement relieves licensees of the burden of obtaining a second license in the endorsing jurisdiction. Endorsement does not necessarily require reciprocity between the two jurisdictions. *See also* license; licensure.

endoscopy   Visual inspection of a body cavity by means of an endoscope (an illuminated tube with a viewing instrument). *See also* amnioscopy; arthroscopy; bronchoscopy; colonoscopy; colposcopy; culdoscopy; cystoscopy; fluoroscopy; gastroscopy; keyhole surgery; laparoscopy; opthalmascopy; othalmoscopy; otoscopy; proctoscopy; proctosigmoidoscopy; sigmoidoscopy.

endotracheal intubation   The process of inserting an endotracheal tube into the trachea through the mouth or nose to maintain an airway, administer anesthesia, ventilate the lungs, or prevent entrance of foreign material, such as stomach contents, into the tracheobronchial tree.

end point   A point of termination; for example, a health event that leads to completion or termination of follow-up of an individual in a clinical trial or study, such as death or major morbidity, particularly related to the study question. *See also* outcome.

end-result system   A system of hospital organization—first recommended by the Committee on Standardization of Hospitals of the Clinical Congress of Surgeons and made popular by Ernest A. Codman—mandating a hospital's management should see that an effort is made to follow up each patient treated, long enough to determine whether the treatment given has permanently relieved the condition or symptoms for which it was implemented. *See also* outcome.

End Stage Renal Disease Program   A Medicare program, first enacted in 1972, that covers treatment of patients with kidney failure, including long-term hemodialysis in the hospital or in the home. Congressional amendments in 1981, 1990, and 1993 specified the length of time an employer-paid plan would be accountable as the primary payer for such services before Medicare took over. *See also* Medicare.

enhancement   *See* genetic engineering.

enrollment   **1.** The total number of individuals enrolled with an insurance company or HMO.   **2.** The process by which a health plan signs up groups and individuals for membership, or the number of enrollees who sign up in any one group. *See also* conditions of enrollment; enrollment period; open enrollment.

enrollment period   The period during which individuals may enroll for insurance or HMO benefits.

enteral nutrition   Nutrition provided via the gastrointestinal tract. Enteral nutrition encompasses both oral (delivered through the mouth) and tube (provided through a tube or catheter that delivers nutrients distal to the mouth) routes. *See also* nutrition.

enteric precautions   A category of patient isolation intended for infections transmitted by direct or indirect contact with feces. Specifications include use of a private room if patient hygiene is poor. Masks are not indicated, but gowns are used if soiling is likely. Gloves are used for touching contaminated materials. *See also* isolation.

enterostomy   A surgical procedure that produces a permanent opening into the intestines through the abdominal wall, as in a colostomy or ileostomy.

enterprise liability   **1.** A plan relating to tort reform in which medical liability is shifted from physicians to health plans (eg, HMOs). Patients would sue the health plans rather than physicians, thereby providing physicians immunity from medical liability. Some observers contend that this approach could further erode physician autonomy by giving nonphysicians more reasons to dictate how physicians perform services. In theory, these nonphysicians would be closely examining the care provided by physicians to prevent lawsuits. *See also* professional liability.   **2.** In law, a ruling of liability on each member of an industry that manufactures a product that causes injury or harm to a consumer; for example, in the case action against manufacturers of intrauterine devices. The distribution of liability is based on each industry member's market share. *See also* damages.

entitlement   An individual's right to benefits, income, or property, such as veterans' pensions and civil-service retirement pay, which may not be reduced without due process. The legislation for some health programs, such as Medicare and Civilian Health and Medical Program of the Uniformed Services (CHAMPUS), establishes health benefits as entitlements, rendering such programs uncontrollable without changing laws.

entitlement program   A government program, such as Social Security or Medicare, that guarantees and provides benefits to a particular group of people, such as individuals over the age of 65 years. *See also* backdoor authority; Medicare.

entrusted lives   Individuals "entrusted" to an integrated delivery system through a managed care product so that their health care needs can be met.

entry   The process by which an individual is screened or assessed by the organization or the practitioner in order to determine the capabilities of the organization or practitioner to provide the care of services required to meet the individual's needs.

environmental assessment   A listing of all influences and events outside an organization that may lead to potential problems or opportunities. This technique is used in organizational planning.

environmental carcinogens   Any of the natural or synthetic substances that can cause cancer, such as chemical agents, physical agents, hormones, or viruses. Examples are asbestos, uranium, vinyl chloride, ultraviolet rays, x-rays, and coal tar derivatives. Most are unreactive or secondary carcinogens but are converted to primary carcinogens in the body. Numerous factors, such as heredity, affect the susceptibilities of different individuals to cancer-causing agents.

environmental health   The health profession dealing with detecting, identifying, controlling, and managing physical and social conditions affecting the health of populations, such as workers in factories or residents of communities. Practitioners of environmental health include, among others, sanitarians, inspectors, and environmentalists. *Synonym:* industrial health. *See also* health; occupational health; sanitation.

environmental medicine   A medical specialty concerned with environmental factors that may impinge on human disease and with the development of methods for the detection, prevention, and control of environmentally related disease.

environmental services   Ancillary services, such as housekeeping, laundry, maintenance, and liquid and solid waste control, performed to improve safety, sanitation, and efficiency of the operation of a health care organization. *See also* ancillary services.

environment of care   For purposes of Joint Commission accreditation, a variety of sites where patients are treated, including inpatient settings (such as acute care hospitals, psychiatric hospitals, hospice facilities, subacute care facilities, or nursing homes) and outpatient settings (such as patient homes, clinics, counseling centers, preadmission testing offices, infirmaries, same-day surgery centers, dialysis centers, or imaging centers). All environments are made up of three components: buildings (including the home), equipment (including delivery vehicles), and people. *See also* disaster drill; emergency-preparedness plan; interim life safety measures; *Life Safety Code*®; life safety management program; utilities management.

epidemic infection   An outbreak in a community or region of a group of infections of similar nature, clearly in excess of normal expectancy and derived from a common or propagated source. *Epidemic* applies especially to infectious diseases, as in an epidemic of cholera, but is also applied to any disease, injury, or other health-related event occurring in outbreaks, as in an epidemic of teenage suicide. *See also* endemic infection; epidemiologically significant infection; infectious diseases; pandemic.

epidemiologically significant infection   An outbreak in a community or region of a group of similar illnesses that is statistically in excess of normal expectations.

epidemiology   Field of medicine concerned with the determination of causes, incidence, and characteristic behavior of disease outbreaks affecting human populations. It includes the interrelationships of host, agent, and environment as related to the distribution and control of disease. *Clinical epidemiology* is a decision-making process applied by an individual practicing physician, where decisions are based on the likelihood of a patient having a given disease process, given a patient's age, previous state of health, family history, the season, the previous appearance of similar diseases in the community, and other factors.

episode   An occurrence or incident that is part of a progression or a larger sequence, as in a period in which a disease or other health problem exists, measured from its onset to its resolution; for example, a major depressive episode. *See also* incident.

episode of care (EOC)   A term coined by Lovelace Health Systems meaning all services provided to a patient with a particular medical problem within a specified period of time. The Lovelace Episodes of Care™ Program was initiated in 1993 to improve the treatment of complex, high-cost, and chronic diseases, thus enhancing cost-effectiveness and patient satisfaction. *See also* continuum of care.

eponym   The name of a person or place used as part of the name of a disease, syndrome, finding, anatomical feature, device, procedure, or scale, such as Alzheimer's disease, Down syndrome, Babinski's reflex, Dupuytren's contracture, Holter monitoring, Ilizarof device, Heimlich maneuver, Apgar score, or Likert scale.

equipment maintenance, preventive   The planned or scheduled evaluation—visual, mechanical, engineering, or functional—of equipment conducted before its initial use and at specified intervals throughout its lifetime. The purpose is to maintain equipment performance within manufacturers' guidelines and specifications and to help ensure accurate patient diagnosis, treatment, or monitoring. It includes measuring performance specifications and evaluating specific safety factors.

equipment maintenance, routine   The performance of basic safety checks, that is, the visual, technical, and functional evaluations of equipment, to identify obvious deficiencies before they have a negative impact on a patient. It normally includes inspections of the case, power cord, structural frame, enclosure, wheels, controls, indicators, and so on, as appropriate. It must be performed after equipment is reprocessed and before use by another patient, and also may be performed during its use on or by a patient.

equivalency   For purposes of Joint Commission accreditation, evidence that an organization has complied with the intent of a standard in a manner other than that described in the standard. The concept is employed, for example, in the selection of pharmaceuticals and in the determination of qualifications in educational, professional, and organizational certifications. *See also* compliance; standard.

ergonomics   The study of humans in their working environment, particularly in relation to the principles

governing the efficient use of human energy. *See also* euthenics.

essential access community hospital (EACH)   A type of rural hospital, an EACH is a facility with at least 75 beds and provides backup services to rural primary care hospitals as part of a patient referral network. This designation was created by Congress in 1989 (Public Law 101-239) and is limited to hospitals in only a few states.

established name   The name given to a drug or pharmaceutical product by the United States Adopted Names Council, as required by the federal Food, Drug and Cosmetic Act. Established names are usually shorter and simpler than chemical names and are most commonly used in the scientific literature, for example, penicillin. Most physicians and pharmacists learn about drug products using the products' established names.

established patient   A patient for whom a physician or other provider has a medical record. *See also* medical history.

estimate   In quality measurement, an approximation of a single value (point) or interval (range) of an unknown population parameter based on a sample statistic.

estrogen replacement therapy (ERT)   The use of estrogenic hormonal substances in postmenopausal or other estrogen-deficient women to alleviate the effects of hormone deficiency, such as vasomotor symptoms and progressive development of osteoporosis. Use of estrogen alone (unopposed estrogen; without progesterone) is associated with greater risks of developing cancer. *See also* hormone replacement therapy.

ethics   The branch of philosophy that deals with systematic approaches to moral issues, such as the distinction between right and wrong and the moral consequences of human actions. Ethics involves a system of behaviors, expectations, and morals composing standards of conduct for a population or a profession. *See also* bioethics; code of ethics; deontological ethics; ethics committee; ethics consultation; futile care; futility; Helsinki Declaration; Hippocratic oath; institutional review board; medical ethics; normative ethics; Nuremberg Code; situation ethics; Tuskegee experiments; utilitarianism.

ethics committee   A multidisciplinary committee of a health care organization that provides case consultation designed to help resolve moral conflicts that arise in difficult medical cases; educates institutional personnel in the ways in which ethics affects their job responsibilities; and develops institutional policies on various ethical issues. *See also* euthanasia; institutional review board.

etiology   The science of causes; causality, as in the etiology of coma.

eugenics   Founded by anthropologist and biologist Sir Francis Galton (1822-1911), a science for improving a population by selecting its best specimens for breeding. Galton defined *national eugenics* as the study of agencies under social control that may improve or impair the racial qualities of future generations either physically or mentally. *Negative eugenics* is concerned with prevention of reproduction (procreation) by individuals with inferior or undesirable traits (synonym: eugenic sterilization) and *positive eugenics* with promotion of optimal reproduction by individuals with superior or desirable traits. *Eugenic abortion* is performed because of possible fetal defects. Eugenics was discredited as a science when discoveries were made about mutations, and popular eugenics movements in the United States lost favor after the exposure of the Nazis' eugenics program. Old controversies over eugenics are sometimes evoked in debate over emerging new technologies in genetics and biological engineering, sometimes termed the *new eugenics. Synonym:* orthogenics. *See also* gene therapy; genetic counseling; genetic engineering.

euthanasia   The act or practice of administering a lethal agent or instituting a lethal procedure for the purpose of terminating the life of a person who is undergoing intolerable suffering. Euthanasia has been discussed in terms of a distinction between *active euthanasia*, which involves an intervention with the intention of causing death, and *passive euthanasia*, which involves permitting death by withdrawing or withholding extraordinary treatment that prolongs life. Although controversy over the practice exists within the health professions, the American Medical Association *Code of Medical Ethics* (1994) and position statements issued in connection with the debate over physician-assisted suicide place the medical profession against the practice of euthanasia. *Synonym:* mercy killing. *See also* assisted suicide; death with dignity; Dutch cure; obitiatrist; obitorium; physician-assisted suicide.

euthenics   The study of the improvement of human functioning and well-being by improvement of living conditions. *See also* ergonomics.

evaluation   1. The process or act of determining significance or worth by careful appraisal or study, as in the measurement and assessment of the performance of a health care organization, practitioner, or program. *See also* APACHE; CONQUEST; drug usage evaluation; external review; monitoring and evaluation; performance-based quality-of-care evaluation; Program Evaluation and Review Technique; standards-based evaluation.   **2.** In mathematics, the calculation of the numerical value of something.   **3.** For purposes of Joint Commission accreditation, an assessment of the performance of a network, PPO, or a managed care organization based on Joint Commission standards without rendering an accreditation decision. The results of the assessment are made available to the requesting network or organization, which can draw its own conclusions regarding performance. The evaluation may be identical to an accreditation survey (without the rendering of a decision) or may be customized to meet the requestor's needs. *See also* accreditation.

evangelists and snails   A sobriquet revived from ideological debate between advocates and methodologists over use of a therapy or other intervention in current controversies, such as recommendations for cholesterol screening. *Evangelists* call for immediate massive or routine screening or some other intervention, on the basis of minimal evidence plus common sense without waiting for sound evidence of efficacy, in the hopes of forestalling development of a serious disorder. *Snails,* on the other hand, maintain that any untested health maneuver may do more harm than good and must meet scientific as well as political criteria before it is implemented. *See also* cholesterol screening; conservative care; intervention; laboratory screening tests.

evidence-based medicine   An evolving science and movement in medicine defined by the Evidence-Based Medicine Working Group as making medical decisions by combining the best external evidence with the physician's clinical expertise and the patient's desires. Evidence-based care extends to managerial and policy decision making and to teaching. The approach calls for understanding conflicting results and assessing the quality and strength of evidence and its applicability to patients and health care policy. The AHCPR and many medical societies in the United States and the United Kingdom's National Health Service have adopted this approach for developing clinical practice policies and guidelines. *Synonyms:* critical appraisal; evidence-based practice. *See also* Canadian Task Force on the Periodic Health Examination; Cochrane Collaborative and Centres; explicit approach; guideline attributes; strength of evidence; U.S. Preventive Services Task Force.

Evidence-Based Medicine Working Group   Founders of the evidence- based medicine approach at the Faculty of Health Sciences at McMaster University (Hamilton, Ontario, Canada) in the 1980s and producers of the series "Users' Guides to the Medical Literature" designed to help clinicians translate the results of medical research into clinical practice. The first article in the series in 1992, "Evidence-Based Medicine: A New Approach to Teaching the Practice of Medicine," gave the movement its name.

Evidence-Based Practice Centers (EPCs)   Program launched by AHCPR at the end of 1996 to replace its clinical practice guideline development program. The EPCs are designed as public-and private-sector partnerships to produce evidence reports and technology assessments for use by health care systems, professional societies, purchasers, and others to develop and tailor their own guidelines, performance measures, and other quality improvements and clinical assessments.

evoked potentials (EP)   In electroneurodiagnostic testing, the electric response evoked in the central nervous system by stimulating sensory receptors or some point on the sensory pathway leading from the receptor to the cortex. The evoked stimulus can be auditory or acoustic, somatosensory, or visual, although other modalities have been reported. *Event-related potentials* is sometimes used synonymously with evoked potentials, but is often associated with the execution of a motor, cognitive, or psychophysiological task, as well as with the response to a stimulus.

exacerbation   An increase in the seriousness of a disease or disorder as marked by greater intensity in signs or symptoms. It may be only a temporary increase, particularly in pulmonary disease such as asthma, in which it refers to what is popularly called an asthma attack. *See also* asthma medications; peak flow meter.

excess billing   Overcharging for services by physicians. Federal legislation (OBRA) stipulates the amount physicians can bill Medicare patients for charges not covered by Medicare. As of October 1994, HCFA has been required to monitor excess billing by nonparticipating physicians and can obtain refunds or credits from those who overbill. *See also* balance billing; nonparticipating provider; participating physician.

exclusions   In insurance, specific hazards, perils, or conditions listed in an insurance or medical-care-coverage policy for which the policy does not provide benefit payments. Preexisting conditions are usually exclusions, including heart disease, diabetes, hypertension, and pregnancies that existed before a policy was in effect. Exclusions often prevent persons who have a serious condition or disease from securing insurance coverage, either for the particular disease or in general. *See also* general exclusion; preexisting condition; waiver.

exclusive contract   An agreement that gives a physician or group of physicians the right to provide all administrative and clinical services required for the operation of a hospital department and precludes other physicians from practicing that specialty in that institution for the period of the contract. *See also* closed staff; contract; open staff.

exclusive dealing arrangement   An arrangement in which a buyer agrees to purchase certain goods or services only from a particular seller during a given period.

exclusive provider organization (EPO)   A health plan that combines features of HMOs and PPOs. Providers are paid on a fee-for-service basis and assume little to no risk. Employers agree not to contract with any other insurer or plan. Enrollees cannot choose health care providers outside the system without paying out-of-pocket. *See also* PPO.

executive committee   A standing committee of the governing body of an organization, the functions and authority of which vary among organizations. For instance, an executive committee may function as the governing body between board meetings and have full authority to make binding decisions for the governing body on a broad range of issues. Alternatively, the executive committee may be restricted to routine functions, such as creating meeting agendas and recommending committee appointments.

executive information system   A computer system process developed to give top and middle management information they need for decision making. *See also* information system.

executive oversight   The sum of the processes by which an executive attempts to exercise control and direction of an organization and to hold individual managers responsible for the implementation of their programs.

exercise test   Controlled physical activity, usually on a bicycle or treadmill, which is more strenuous than at rest, performed along with ECG and blood pressure monitoring to assess cardiovascular and pulmonary functions. Maximal (most intense) exercise is usually required but submaximal exercise is also used. The intensity of exercise is often graded, using criteria such as rate of work done, oxygen consumption, and heart rate. Physiological data obtained from a test may be used for diagnosis, prognosis, and evaluation of disease severity; to assess suitability for cardiac transplantation; or to evaluate therapy. Imaging techniques, particularly echocardiography (called *stress echocardiography* when it is used as an exercise test) and thallium-201 scintigraphy, may be added to increase the accuracy of the test. The *Duke Treadmill Score* is well validated and clinically useful for risk assessment in patients with either established or suspected coronary artery disease for whom the desirability of additional invasive testing must be determined. Despite published recommendations from authorities (the American College of Cardiology, the American Heart Association, and the U.S. Preventive Services Task Force) against routine use of exercise testing to screen for coronary artery disease in healthy asymptomatic persons, the practice remains widespread. Such screening rarely identifies patients with severe heart disease, and false-positive results may cause unnecessary anxiety, loss of time from work, and increased insurance costs. *Synonyms:* conventional exercise testing; exercise ECG; standard exercise test; stress test; treadmill test. *See also* ECG.

exercise thallium-201 scintigraphy   Intravenous administration of the isotope as an adjunct to conventional exercise electrocardiography to aid in the diagnosis, prognosis, and functional evaluation of patients with known or suspected coronary artery disease. The thallium produces a homogeneous image of a normal heart during early recovery from exercise, showing uniform perfusion of the heart, but it produces defects in the images of ischemic or infarcted regions of myocardium (middle layer of the wall of the heart), showing underperfusion of areas of the heart. *See also* exercise test.

exercise tolerance   The exercise capacity of an individual as measured by endurance (maximal exercise duration and/or maximal attained work load) during an exercise test. Test results may be used to develop an exercise program for individual fitness improvement or in cardiac rehabilitation. *Synonym:* exertion tolerance.

exogenous cause   *See* special cause.

exogenous infection   Infection caused by organisms not normally present in the body but which have gained entrance from the environment, as in meningococcal meningitis.

expected morbidity The predicted incidence of illness or injury in a defined population over a defined time interval. *See also* expected mortality; morbidity; morbidity rate.

expected mortality The predicted incidence of death in a defined population over a defined time interval. *See also* expected morbidity; mortality; mortality rate.

expeditious evacuation *See* load and go.

experience rating In insurance, the process of setting rates based partly or wholly on the previous claims experience of various groups and subgroups of subscribers, members, or beneficiaries, and then projecting required revenues for a future policy year for a specific group or pool of groups. Premiums vary with the health experience of different groups and subgroups or with such variables as age, sex, and health status. Experience rating is the most common method of determining premiums for health insurance in private programs. *See also* community rating; group insurance; insurance; premium; rating.

experimental A classification of a therapy or technology made by different factors for different purposes with varying meanings, as in technology assessments, utilization review, and coverage and reimbursement decisions. *See also* health care technology assessment.

experimental medical care review organization (EMCRO) The forerunner of the professional services review organization (PSRO) program; the PSRO was, in turn, a forerunner of the peer review organization (PRO). The use of explicit criteria and standard definitions was required of all EMCROs, but particular approaches to organizing reviews were determined by individual organizations. *See also* peer review organization; professional standards review organization.

experimental method An approach to a question in which an investigator intentionally alters one or more factors under controlled conditions to study the effects of so doing. *See also* scientific method.

experimental psychology The branch of psychology dealing with the processes of sensation, perception, learning, and motivation. The work of experimental psychologists may involve studying how people attend to and use different kinds of visual and auditory information and how this processing of information is affected by what they are looking or listening for. *See also* psychology.

expert panel **1.** A group of people who are able to render judgment on an issue based on their knowledge and experience. **2.** Common term for groups that develop clinical practice guidelines and are formerly recorded as authors of such. For example, the expert panels that authored the AHCPR guidelines and the recommendations from national programs, such as the National Asthma Education and Prevention Program. *See also* clinical practice guidelines.

expert system A type of artificial intelligence in which the decision practices and principles of well-regarded specialists in a field are built into the computer program. The program then guides users to sound conclusions in situations similar to those covered by the system, such as in medical diagnosis or treatment.

expert task force for indicator development A group of experts in specific fields (eg, perioperative care, obstetrics care, trauma care, cardiovascular care, oncology care, infection surveillance and control, medication usage) convened by the Joint Commission to draft indicator sets as part of the Agenda for Change. *See also* Agenda for Change.

expert witness An individual who has special knowledge of the subject about which he or she is to testify, and whose input is obtained by a plaintiff who is trying to demonstrate that he or she has been injured. *See also* Daubert v Merrell Dow case; medical evidence.

explanation of benefits (EOB) A notice describing the actions relating to payment (or nonpayment) of an insurance claim, issued by the insurance company to the beneficiary after each claim has been processed. *See also* benefits; Explanation of Medicare Benefits.

Explanation of Medicare Benefits (EOMB) A notice printed by a Medicare carrier or fiscal intermediary that identifies what services were actually covered, what charges were actually approved, how much of the allowed charges were credited toward the yearly deductible, and the amount Medicare actually paid. Each Medicare beneficiary receives this notice after each Medicare claim has been processed. *See also* benefits; explanation of benefits; Medicare.

explicit approach A formally recorded (written down) systematic analysis of evidence, estimation of outcomes, calculation of costs, and assessment of preferences in the development of practice policies. This explicit approach is contrasted with an *implicit* approach, which is based on seeking consensus. Key principles, developed in a manual by David M. Eddy in collaboration with the Council of Medical Specialty Societies Task Force on Practice Policies, have been widely adopted in both public- and private-sector efforts to develop clinical practice guidelines. These include identifying the degree of flexibility (guideline, standard, or option) and the "balance sheet" of benefits and harms. *Synonym:* explicit criteria. *See also* evidence-based medicine; explicit review; guideline attributes; implicit criteria.

explicit review Review of the processes and outcomes of patient care using explicit criteria specified in advance. *See also* explicit approach; implicit review.

exploratory panel *See* screening panel.

exposure-prone procedures As defined by the Centers for Disease Control and Prevention, procedures during which a health care worker's fingers and a needle or other sharp object are both in a poorly visualized or highly confined anatomic site.

extended benefits   Supplemental insurance coverage for services, such as mental health services. *See also* benefits.

extended care   Care provided in a skilled treatment facility rather than a hospital when acute care is not required but skilled nursing care is necessary. *See also* extended care facility; extended care services; skilled nursing care.

extended care facility (ECF)   An outdated term (since 1972 when the Social Security statute was amended) for skilled nursing facility. *See also* extended care; skilled nursing facility.

extended care services   Under Medicare, carefully delineated services provided in a skilled nursing facility for a limited time after a hospital stay and for the same condition as the hospital stay. *See also* extended care.

extension survey   A survey of limited scope conducted by the Joint Commission to ensure that a previously demonstrated level of compliance is being maintained following an organizational change. *See also* accreditation survey.

external cephalic version   The rotating of a fetus presenting feet first (breech), through external manipulation, for delivery in a head-first position. The practice has been pulled into the debate over how much can be done to safely reduce cesarean section deliveries, and it has come under scrutiny for its safety, efficacy, and cost-effectiveness in comparison with a vaginal breech delivery or with a cesarean section. *See also* breech presentation; cesarean section; Maine Medical Liability Demonstration Project.

external customer   A customer who buys a product or a service but who is not a member of the organization that produces the product or service; for example, a patient and a third-party payer are external customers of a health care organization or a physician. *See also* customer; customer-supplier sundial; internal customer.

external environmental factor   An environment-related variable, such as the number of nursing beds available in a community or payer reimbursement policies, that may influence a health care organization's performance data. These factors are often not within an organization's or practitioner's control but can affect organizational performance and outcomes achieved. *See also* organization factor; patient factor; practitioner factor.

external review   Review in which criteria and standards are set or ratified by persons or organizations other than the individuals or organizations undergoing evaluation. *See also* evaluation; internal review; medical review; utilization review.

external validity   The extent to which an experimental finding can be projected to a population at large; the extent to which the results of a study may be generalized beyond the subjects of a study to other settings, providers, procedures, and diagnoses. An experiment has high external validity when the sample is representative of the population and simulates real-life conditions. *See also* construct validity; content validity; face validity; predictive validity; validity.

extraordinary care   **1.** Use of advanced technology in medical treatment to keep a patient alive, for example, mechanical ventilation. *See also* advance directive; life-support care; living will.   **2.** Care that involves life-supporting medical interventions that offer no significant health improvement or that cannot be administered without excessive pain. *See also* futile care; ordinary care.

extrasystemic cause   *See* special cause.

face validity   The degree to which a method or process appears to measure what it claims to measure. Face validity is the most superficial type of validity; nevertheless, it often contributes to the presumed legitimacy of a test and is, therefore, an important consideration in gaining acceptance of a measure or test. *Synonym*: faith validity. *See also* validity.

facilitator   In quality improvement, a person who has developed special expertise in the quality improvement process. He or she is not a member of a quality improvement team but helps it achieve results by helping to focus its efforts, teaching quality improvement methods, consulting to the team leader, and helping connect the work to the knowledge necessary for improvement. *See also* continuous quality improvement; quality improvement team.

facility-based hospice   A setting of care provided to terminally ill patients in a facility or institution rather than the patient's place of residence. The facility promotes a hospice philosophy of care. *See also* hospice inpatient care; living-in-unit.

factitious disorder   *See* Munchausen's syndrome.

factor   **1.** Something that produces or influences a result. *See also* clotting factors; confounding factor; dietary risk factor; Rh factor.   **2.** In statistics, an independent variable used to identify membership of qualitatively different groups. A causal role may be implied; for instance, a faulty medical staff credentialing process may be a factor in a malpractice case. *See also* conversion factor; external environmental factor; factor analysis; independent variable; indicator underlying factors; occupancy factor; organization factor; patient factor; practitioner factor; risk factor modification; uniform capitol factor; variable.

factor analysis   A variety of statistical techniques and methods whose common objective is to represent a set of variables in terms of a smaller number of hypothetical variables. *See also* factor.

factor VIII   *See* clotting factors.

fact sheet   A document used in media relations and development that provides a concise statement about an organization or a program.

faculty practice plan   *See* medical practice plan.

FADE process   A quality improvement process composed of *focus, analyze, develop,* and *execute* steps, developed by Organizational Dynamics, Inc. *See also* continuous quality improvement; FOCUS-PDCA; plan-do-check-act cycle.

failure desensitization   A situation in which individuals have worked with a flawed system for so long that they come to believe failures of the system are normal.

failure to progress   *See* dystocia.

faith healer   One who treats disease with prayer.

faith validity   *See* face validity.

false negative   A negative result in a person or a case that actually has the condition or characteristic for which the test was conducted. A false negative occurs, for example, when a pregnancy test is negative for a woman who is pregnant. *See also* false positive; sensitivity; specificity; true negative.

false positive   A positive result in a person or a case that does not have the condition or characteristic for which the test was conducted. A false positive occurs, for example, when a pregnancy test is positive for a nonpregnant woman. *See also* false negative; HCFA generic quality screens; sensitivity; specificity; true positive.

falsification of information   For purposes of Joint Commission accreditation, the fabrication, in whole or in part, of any information provided by an applicant or accredited organization to the Joint Commission. This includes, but is not limited to, any redrafting, reformatting, or content deletion of documents.

familial colon cancer syndrome   *See* adult-onset cancer; cancer susceptibility testing.

family   For purposes of Joint Commission accreditation, the person(s) who plays a significant role in the patient's life. This may include a person(s) not legally related to the patient. This person(s) is often referred to as a surrogate decision maker if authorized to make care decisions for a patient should the patient lose decision-making capacity. *See also* guardian; significant other; surrogate decision maker.

Family and Medical Leave Act (1993)   Legislation mandating that employers provide, among other requirements, the same health benefits during an employee's unpaid leave as when he or she was working.

family ganging   The practice of requiring or encouraging a patient to return for care to a health program with his or her entire family, even when the rest of the family does not need care, so that the program or provider can charge the patient's third-party payer for care given to each member of the family. The practice and the term originated and is most common in Medicaid mills, which frequently have the mother of a sick child bring in all her other children for care whether or not they need it. *See also* Medicaid mill.

family history   Part of a patient's medical history in which questions are asked about the incidence and prevalence of specific diseases and disorders in his or her family in an attempt to determine whether the patient has a hereditary or familial tendency toward a particular disease or condition for example, a family history of heart disease. *See also* medical history.

family planning   Social, educational, or medical services and supplies to help individuals determine family size or prevent unplanned pregnancies. This may include birth control counseling and referral, pregnancy testing, sterilization counseling, venereal disease referrals, public education service, and infertility counseling and referrals.

family practice (FP)   The branch of medicine and medical specialty dealing with the prevention, diagnosis, and treatment of a wide variety of ailments in patients of all ages. Geriatric medicine and sports medicine are two subspecialties of family practice.

family therapy   A form of psychotherapy that focuses on the individual as a family member. It involves examination of the interrelationships of family members while all members are together in group sessions, in order to identify and alleviate the problems of one or more members of the family. *See also* group therapy; psychotherapy.

fatality rate   The number of deaths during a given period for a stipulated population, for example, the percentage of people in the United States who die of lung cancer or trauma in one year. *See also* mortality rate.

favorable selection   *See* skimming.

feasibility   In the context of evaluations of performance indicators, whether use of a certain indicator to convey information to the public about performance is reasonable or practical. *See also* feasibility study.

feasibility study   A preliminary study to determine practicability of a proposed program or process and to appraise the factors, such as cost, that may influence its practicability. *See also* feasibility; pilot study.

fecal occult blood test (FOBT)   *See* cancer screening tests and procedures.

federal assistance programs   Programs available to state and local governments including county, city, metropolitan, and regional governments; schools, colleges, and universities; health care organizations; nonprofit and profit-making organizations; and individuals and families. Current federal assistance programs are listed in the *Catalogue of Federal Domestic Assistance*, published annually.

federal component   Under Medicare, the applicable federal rate, based on regional and national rates published in the *Federal Register* and dependent on the health care organization's location, as part of the prospective payment system.

Federal Employee Health Benefits Program (FEHBP or FEP)   A voluntary health insurance subsidy program, administered by the Office of Personnel Management, for civilian employees (including retirees and dependents) of the federal government. Enrollees select from a number of approved plans, the costs of which are primarily borne by the government.

federal government hospital   A hospital that is managed by an agency or department of the federal government, such as the Department of Defense, the Department of Veterans Affairs, or the Indian Health Service. *See also* government hospital.

Federal Register   A daily publication that makes federal agency regulations and other legal documents of the executive branch available to the public. These documents cover a wide range of federal government activities. An important function of the *Federal Register* is its inclusion of proposed changes (eg, rules, regulations, standards) of all governmental agencies.

Federal Trade Commission Act   *See* antitrust laws.

feedback   The return of a portion of the output of a process or system to the input, especially when used to maintain performance or to control a system or process. *See also* biofeedback; implementation techniques; measure-related feedback.

fee for service (FFS)   An arrangement under which patients pay for each encounter or service rendered (the payment does not exceed their billed charge), as contrasted with salary, per capita, or prepayment systems in which the payment is not changed with the number of services actually used or if no services are used. *See also* alternative delivery system; capitation; dentacare; prepayment plan; private practice.

fee maximum   In health insurance, the maximum amount a participating health care provider may be paid for a specific service provided to plan members under a specific contract. *See also* fee schedule.

fee schedule   A comprehensive list of (maximum) charges or allowances for health services used to reimburse physicians or other providers on a fee-for-service basis. *See also* fee maximum.

fee splitting   An unethical practice by a health care specialist or consultant involving the return of part of his or her fee to another health professional who referred the patient in the first place.

fellow   **1.** An individual who has been granted status or fellowship higher than that of membership by an association, usually after meeting additional requirements for education and performance. *See also* graduate medical education; medical subspecialty. **2.** An individual whose position is supported by special stipends for advanced study and research, as in a "fellow in toxicology."

Fellowship and Residency Electronic Interactive Data Access (FREIDA)   An electronic database sponsored by the American Medical Association with information about each residency program. The database is made available to medical schools and certain health care organizations.

fertility rate   A measure of human reproduction calculated as the number of live births per 1,000 women aged 15 through 44 years.

TYPES OF FELLOWS			
Acronym	**Fellow**	**Acronym**	**Fellow**
FAAFP	Fellow of the American Academy of Family Physicians	FACMGA	Fellow of the American College of Medical Group Administrators
FAAN	Fellow of the American Academy of Nursing	FACOG	Fellow of the American College of Obstetricians and Gynecologists
FAAOS	Fellow of the American Academy of Orthopaedic Surgeons		
		FACP	Fellow of the American College of Physicians
FAAO–HNS	Fellow of the American Academy of Otolaryngology–Head and Neck Surgery	FACPE	Fellow of the American College of Physician Executives
FAAP	Fellow of the American Academy of Pediatrics	FACPM	Fellow of the American College of Preventive Medicine
FACA	Fellow of the American College of Angiology		
FACC	Fellow of the American College of Cardiology	FACR	Fellow of the American College of Radiology
FACCP	Fellow of the American College of Chest Physicians	FACS	Fellow of the American College of Surgeons
		FACSM	Fellow of the American College of Sports Medicine
FACD	Fellow of the American College of Dentists	FAOTA	Fellow of the American Occupational Therapy Association
FACEP	Fellow of the American College of Emergency Physicians		
		FAPA	Fellow of the American Psychiatric Association; Fellow of the American Psychological Association
FACFS	Fellow of the American College of Foot Surgeons		
		FAPHA	Fellow of the American Public Health Association
FACHE	Fellow of the American College of Healthcare Executives	FCAP	Fellow of the College of American Pathologists

fetal death certificate   A legal record registering a fetal death or stillbirth. Some health jurisdictions require the use of a fetal death certificate for all products of conception, whereas other jurisdictions require its use only in cases in which gestation has reached a particular duration, usually the 20th or the 28th week. *See also* birth certificate; death; death certificate.

fetal death rate   The number of fetal deaths in relation to total births, that is, live births and fetal deaths combined, usually expressed as the number of fetal deaths per 1,000 total births. *See also* infant mortality rate; mortality rate; neonatal death rate.

fetal distress   Compromised or abnormal condition of the fetus, usually characterized by abnormal heart rhythm and discovered during pregnancy or labor, sometimes through the use of a fetal monitor. Fetal distress may necessitate emergency cesarean delivery. *See also* cesarean section; dystocia; fetal monitor.

fetal monitor   An electronic device that measures and records the vital signs of a fetus during pregnancy, labor, and childbirth, producing a tracing tape that can be retained as a record. Originally intended primarily for high-risk pregnancies, it is now used for most pregnancies in the United States, and its use has been pressed by lawyers as a way to reduce malpractice exposure risk. Studies of patterns of use of the fetal monitor (as opposed to manual auscultation) show that it contributes to increased numbers of diagnoses of fetal distress, which in turn leads to a greater number of cesarean sections. This makes the device a player in the "defensive medicine" phenomenon and rising health care costs but also credits it with saving more lives. The U.S. Preventive Services Task Force (1996) recommends against routine electronic fetal monitoring for low-risk women in labor and maintains that there is insufficient evidence to recommend for or against monitoring for high-risk pregnant women. The matter of whether fetal monitors are overused remains under debate. *See also* dystocia; fetal distress; home uterine activity monitoring; monitor.

fever   Elevation in the temperature of the body above normal (98.4°F) caused by severe stress, strenuous exercise, dehydration, or infection or other disease.

fibrillation   Uncoordinated tremors or twitching of cardiac muscle resulting in an irregular pulse.

fiduciary   **1.** Relating to or founded upon trust, confidence, responsibility, or obligation. A physician has a fiduciary relationship with a patient, and a hospital trustee with a hospital.   **2.** A person having a legal duty, created by his or her understanding, to act primarily for the benefit of another in matters connected with his or her undertaking. *See also* privileged communication.

field theory of motivation   A theory explaining how motivation depends on the organization environment because human behavior is based not only on the unique personality of the employee but also on organization forces in the midst of which he or she operates. *See also* motivation psychology.

fifth pathway   One way in which an individual with all or part of his or her undergraduate medical education abroad can enter graduate medical education in the United States. The fifth pathway consists of a period of supervised clinical training sponsored by a U.S. medical school for such students who, on successful completion of the training, then become eligible for an approved internship or residency. *See also* foreign medical graduate; graduate medical education; labor certification.

FIGO (Federation of Gynecology and Obstetrics) staging   *See* cancer staging system.

financing   The process of acquiring money for a purpose. Most health care financing uses debt financing (borrowing money), donations (charitable contributions), equity financing (selling ownership), or tax financing (the use of tax revenues).

fine-needle biopsy   *See* needle biopsy.

finding   In clinical care, a discrete piece of information about a patient that can be elicited during patient assessment, such as a physical finding (eg, a heart murmur or an enlarged spleen) or a laboratory finding (eg, a high hemoglobin level or a negative test for the AIDS virus). Findings include both signs and symptoms. *See also* sign; symptom.

first-dollar coverage   Insurance or prepayment coverage under which the third-party payer assumes liability for covered services as soon as the first dollar or expense for such services is incurred, without requiring the insured to pay a deductible. *See also* coverage; full coverage.

first responder   *See* emergency medical responder.

fiscal intermediary (FI)   A person or an organization that serves as another's financial agent. A fiscal intermediary processes claims, provides services, and issues payments on behalf of certain private, federal, and state health benefit programs or other insurance organizations. For instance, providers of health care select public or private fiscal intermediaries, which enter into an agreement with the secretary of the Department of Health and Human Services under Part A of Medicare, to pay claims and perform other functions. Blue Cross or private insurance companies are usually, but not always, the intermediaries in these arrangements. *Synonym:* fiscal agent. *See also* GROUPER software; third-party administrator.

fiscal year (FY)   Any 12-month period for which an organization plans the use of its funds. The fiscal year of the federal government is from October 1 to September 30.

fishbone diagram   *See* cause-and-effect diagram.

fitness   *See* physical fitness program; wellness program.

fixed charge   A charge that remains the same regardless of the extent of use. For example, rent and property insurance are often fixed charges that are unaffected by the production level of a health care organization or professional practice.

fixed cost   A cost that remains the same regardless of sales volume. Fixed costs include, for example, executives' salaries, interest expense, rent, depreciation, and insurance expenses. They contrast with variable costs, such as the cost of supplies, which vary, but not necessarily in direct relation to sales.

fixed fee   A set price for the completion of a project. For a contractor, setting a fixed fee entails the risk of absorbing higher than anticipated costs before a project is completed, but for the customer a fixed fee is more easily budgeted.

fixed-wing aircraft   *See* ambulance.

flesh-eating bug   Layperson's and popular media's term for necrotizing fasciitis, a rapidly spreading bacterial infection that can destroy skin and facial structures under the skin.

Flexner Report   An inquiry and report commissioned by the Carnegie Foundation for the Advancement of Teaching and the American Medical Association in 1910 out of concern over the quality of medical education. Basing his highly critical report on visits to all 163 medical schools in the United States, Abraham Flexner, a young educator, called for consolidation or elimination of schools of poorer quality and for reorientation of medical schools from the guild-apprenticeship and practice approach to the academic university-hospital exemplified by his alma mater, Johns Hopkins University. Publication of the report coincided with economic changes that led to closing of many proprietary medical schools and a reduction in the number of physicians. The Flexner Report set the pattern for foundation support of medical education for years to come.

flow chart   A pictorial summary that shows with symbols and words the steps, sequence, and relationship of the various operations involved in the performance of a function or a process. A flowchart completely describes an algorithm. *Synonym:* flow diagram. *See also* algorithm; matrix flow chart.

fluoroscopy   Production of an image by a fluoroscope, a screen device for use with an x-ray generator to visualize an x-ray shadowgraphy similar to that obtained by photography. Fluoroscopy is used to examine the position, contour, movement time, and patency of the colon during the double contrast barium enema. *See also* barium enema; radiology.

fluoxetine   *See* Prozac.

focused survey   A survey conducted during the Joint Commission accreditation cycle to assess the degree to which an organization has improved its level of compliance relating to specific type I recommendations. The subject matter of the survey is typically an area(s) of identified deficiency in compliance; however, other performance areas may also be assessed by a surveyor(s), even though they may not have been previously identified as deficiencies. *See also* accreditation survey; compliance; type I recommendation.

focus group   Individuals gathered to express their opinions on a specific subject(s). Focus groups are often used in market research, as well as in quality projects as an informal data source.

FOCUS-PDCA   A quality improvement strategy that helps build knowledge of process, customer, and small-scale improvement using the scientific method. The acronym stands for *find* a process to improve; *organize* a team that knows the process; *clarify* current knowledge of the process; *understand* sources or process variation; *select* the process improvement; *plan* the improvement and continued data collection; *do* the improvement, data collection, and analysis; *check* and study the results; and *act* to hold the gain and to continue improving the process. *See also* continuous quality improvement; FADE process; plan-do-check-act cycle.

folk medicine   The use of home remedies and procedures handed down by tradition.

follow-up survey   *See* conditional follow-up survey.

Food Guide Pyramid   A graphic aid in the shape of a pyramid, designed by the U.S. Department of Agriculture to help individuals choose healthy diets by taking specified numbers of servings from different groups. The pyramid, sometimes referred to as the Pyramid guidelines, replaces the seven food-group wheel or pie chart used previously by health educators. The base of the pyramid frames pictures of the most important food types—bread, cereals, pasta, and rice (8-11 servings); the next level shows vegetables (3-5 servings) and fruits (2-4 servings); the third level from the bottom shows milk, yogurt, and cheese (2-3 servings) and meat, poultry, fish, dry beans, eggs, and nuts (2-3 servings); and the top mentions fats, oils, and sweets (to be used sparingly). *See also* Dietary Reference Intake.

food supplement   A concentrate of one or more nutrient substances, used to supplement a nutritionally inadequate diet. Some food supplements are, in fact, unsafe food additives, by definition of U.S. law.

for-cause unannounced survey   *See* unannounced/unscheduled survey.

forced expiratory volume (FEV)   Measure of the maximum amount of air during a forced vital capacity determination that can be expelled in a given number of seconds. It is usually written as *FEV* followed by a subscript indicating the number of seconds over which the measurement is made, although it is sometimes presented as a percentage of forced vital capacity. As National Heart, Lung, and Blood Institutes representatives noted in a January 1997 workshop report on setting up a national chronic obstructive pulmonary disease (COPD) education and prevention program, the FEV_1 rate of decline is a powerful prognostic indicator in COPD, lung cancer, and cardiovascular disease, yet few primary care physicians screen for it or consider it in designing a preventive health plan. Showing patients their rate of decline on FEV_1 has been found to be an effective motivator to stop smoking. *See also* asthma; chronic obstructive pulmonary disease; peak flow meter; pulmonary function tests.

force-field analysis   A method for understanding competing forces that increase or decrease the likelihood of successfully implementing change. *See also* force-field theory.

force-field theory   A theory maintaining that creative problem solving can best be accomplished by a group working with objective data rather than relying on intuition. Such groups require a leader to keep them from straying from the topic and to limit discussion to a reasonable amount of time. *See also* force-field analysis.

forecasting   The process of estimating future trends that relies on extrapolating existing trends. An example of forecasting is extrapolation of mortality trends in 1990-1991 for coronary artery disease in women, suggesting that mortality rates will continue to rise in the future. *See also* scenario building.

foreign medical graduate (FMG)   A physician who graduated from a medical school outside the United States or Canada. To practice in the United States, an FMG must meet certain requirements, such as certification by the Educational Commission for Foreign Medical Graduates (ECFMG). An American citizen who graduated from a medical school outside the United States is called a *United States foreign medical graduate* or USFMG. A citizen of another nation who is a graduate of a foreign medical school is called an *alien foreign medical graduate* or alien FMG. *See also* certification; fifth pathway; labor certification; limited licensure.

forensic dentistry   The branch and specialty of dentistry dealing with investigating, preparing, preserving, and presenting dental evidence and opinion in courts and other legal, correctional, and law-enforcement settings. *Synonyms*: dental jurisprudence; forensic odontology.

forensic medicine   The branch of medicine that interprets or establishes the medical facts in civil or criminal law cases. Subspecialties of forensic medicine include forensic pathology, forensic psychiatry, forensic toxicology, and forensic biochemistry. *Synonym*: medical jurisprudence. *See also* medical-legal analysis; medicolegal.

forensic mental health services   Psychiatric services provided to patients diagnosed with mental illness and hospitalized on an order issued by a criminal or juvenile justice system. *See also* mental illness.

forensic odontology   *See* forensic dentistry.

forensic pathology   The branch of medicine and subspecialty of pathology dealing with the investigation and evaluation of specific classes of death defined by law, such as cases of sudden, unexpected, suspicious, or violent death. *See also* pathology.

forensic program or service   For purposes of Joint Commission accreditation, an identified program or service (eg, jail or prison mental health services, court evaluation centers, outpatient probation, parole services) that provides diagnosis, evaluation, or services mandated by the legal/corrections system.

forensic psychiatry   The branch and subspecialty of psychiatry dealing with the legal evaluation of patients with sexual disorders, antisocial personality disorders, paranoid disorders, and addictive disorders. Forensic psychiatry also may involve observing persons for malingering, using ancillary information (such as police reports), interviewing relatives and witnesses, reviewing prior medical records, and testifying in court. *See also* psychiatry.

foreseeability   The ability to see or know in advance; for example, the reasonable anticipation that harm or injury is a likely result of certain acts or omissions. Used in law to measure the extent of damages for which one may be responsible. *See also* damages.

Forms 1007 and 1008   Forms used in the Medicare prospective payment system to calculate a hospital's adjustments to its base year Medicare costs. *See also* base year Medicare costs; prospective payment system.

formulary   *See* drug formulary; hospital formulary; National Formulary.

for profit   A designation that indicates whether an organization is liable for federal income taxes as a result of profits earned in conducting business.

foster care services for adults   Twenty-four-hour supervised living arrangements for adults in a family setting with access to social services and community resources. *See also* foster care services for children.

foster care services for children   Twenty-four-hour substitute family or group home care for a planned period of time. This home provides experiences and conditions that promote normal growth. The child, his or her family, and the foster parents are provided with casework services and other treatment or community services. *See also* foster care services for adults.

foundation   The establishment of an institution with provisions for continuing existence; for example, a non-profit organization with private funds (usually from a single source, either an individual, a family, or a corporation) whose program is managed by its own trustees or directors, established to maintain or aid social, educational, charitable, religious, or other activities serving the common welfare primarily through making grants. *See also* grant; medical foundation.

fourth party   Business and industry purchasers of health care services (eg, employers and business coalitions) who are interested in managing health care costs. The first party is the patient, the second party is the health care provider, and the third party is the third-party payer. The fourth party as a purchaser of health care services may contract with a third party. *See also* health care provider; patient; third-party payer.

fractionation   The act or process of charging separately for several services or component services that were previously subject to a single charge or not billed at all, usually resulting in an increase in the total charge. Fractionation is often a response by health care providers to limitations made by third-party payers on increases in specific charges, changed medical practices, or advances in medical technology. *See also* unbundling.

Frailty and Injuries: Cooperative Studies of Intervention Techniques (FIC-SIT)   A study sponsored by the National Institute on Aging and the National Institute of Nursing Research to understand and reduce injuries and frailty in the elderly by the year 2000. The study includes eight independent clinical trials that assess the efficacy and feasibility of various interventions, such as exercise, in reducing falls and/or frailty.

Framingham Heart Study   A longitudinal cohort study begun in the Boston suburb of Framingham (Mass.) in 1948 with an enrollment of 5,209 men and women aged 28 to 62 years, who have been examined every two years since, with morbidity and mortality continuously monitored by hospital surveillance and by communication with personal physicians and relatives. Each examination includes an extensive cardiovascular history and examination with measurement of many physiological variables (including bone mass density) and with documentation of drugs taken, illnesses, diet, health habits (such as smoking), and so forth. The data are made available for each biennial examination cycle. A Framingham Offspring cohort has been added. The major cardiovascular risk factors identified in the study were high blood pressure, cigarette smoking, high blood cholesterol, type A personality, environmental stress, obesity, diabetes, and sedentary lifestyle. Additional studies have been conducted on the basis of Framingham data for all of these as well as other conditions (such as osteoporosis and arthritis), and criteria and indexes have been developed, such as the Framingham Physical Activity Index. A 30-year follow-up was published by the National Heart, Lung, and Blood Association in 1987.

franchise dentistry   A system for marketing dental practice, usually under a trade name, where permitted by state law and regulations. Participating dentists receive the benefits of media advertising, a national referral system, and financial and management consultation support in return for financial investment or other consideration.

fraternal insurance   A cooperative insurance plan provided by an organization to its members. *See also* insurance.

fraud and abuse   A criminal (felony) misuse of the Medicare system. *Fraud* is a false statement, willfully made, for material gain and with the intent to deceive; for example, acts, such as misrepresenting eligibility or need for health services, claiming reimbursement for services not rendered or for nonexistent patients. *Abuse* is an exaggerated statement, willfully made, for material gain and with the intent to confuse. *See also* Health Insurance Portability and Accountability Act of 1996; kiting; medical review agency; safe harbor regulations.

free choice of provider   The view that any health care financing mechanism should preserve the ability of a patient or client to choose any care provider in the marketplace without being restrained by economic sanctions of insurers and other third-party payers. *See also* health care provider.

free clinic   A neighborhood clinic or health program that provides health services in a relatively informal setting to students, transient youth, and minority groups. Care is provided free or for a nominal charge by staff members who are predominantly volunteers. *See also* clinic.

Freedom of Information Act   Enacted by Congress in 1966, the act requires federal agencies to make certain information available to the public. Medical records are exempt. *See also* confidentiality; medical record.

freestanding   Refers to a health care facility that is separate from a health care organization. "Freestanding" does not necessarily indicate separate ownership.

freestanding ambulatory care center   A facility with an organized professional staff that provides various health treatments on an outpatient basis only and that may be, depending on the level of care it is equipped to provide, a freestanding emergency center, freestanding urgent care center, or primary care center. *See also* freestanding emergency center; freestanding urgent care center; hospital-based ambulatory care center; primary care center.

freestanding ambulatory surgical facility   A health care facility, physically or geographically separate from a hospital, that provides surgical services to outpatients who do not require hospitalization. Offices of private physicians or dentists are not included in this category unless the offices have a distinct area that is used solely for outpatient surgical treatment on a routine, organized basis. *Synonyms:* freestanding surgicenter; surgical center; surgicenter. *See also* ambulatory surgical facility.

freestanding emergency center (FEC)   A facility that is designed, organized, equipped, and staffed to provide health care on a 24-hour-per-day basis for injuries and illness (including those that are life-threatening); that provides laboratory and radiologic services and has established arrangements for transporting critical patients or patients requiring hospitalization once stabilized; and that does not provide continuity of care but treats episodic, emergency, and primary care cases. *Synonym:* emergicenter. *See also* emergency patient; freestanding ambulatory care center.

freestanding laboratory   A clinical pathology laboratory that is not a part of another health care organization. *Synonym:* independent laboratory.

freestanding urgent care center   A facility that provides primary and urgent care treatment on a less than 24-hour-per-day basis and that is supported by laboratory and radiology services but does not receive patients transported by ambulance, is not equipped to treat true medical emergencies, such as heart attack or stroke victims, and does not provide continuity of care. *Synonyms:* urgent care center; urgicenter. *See also* freestanding ambulatory care center.

frequency distribution   The division of a sample of observations into a number of classes, together with the number of observations in each class. *See also* histogram.

friendly visit   Regular visits to isolated, homebound, or institutionalized elderly people to reduce their isolation and loneliness.

full coverage   Insurance that pays for every dollar of a loss with no maximum and no deductible amount. *See also* coverage; first-dollar coverage.

full-risk capitation   Capitation accepted by a delivery system that agrees to provide all health care services, including outpatient care, hospitalization, preventive care, prescription drugs, home care, dental care, mental health services, and substance-abuse treatment, to a specific enrolled population. *See also* capitation; risk-adjusted capitation.

full survey   The accreditation survey conducted by the Joint Commission every three years (two years for pathology and clinical laboratories) by a full complement of surveyors. *See also* accreditation survey; triennial survey.

full-time equivalent (FTE)   A work force equivalent of one individual working full time for a specific period, which may be made up of several part-time individuals or one full-time individual. For example, three part-time nurses working a combined total of 60 hours equals 1.5 FTEs when the normal full-time work week for a single individual is 40 hours. *See also* staffing ratio.

function   1. A goal-directed, interrelated series of processes, such as the continuum of care or management of information. *See also* high-risk function; high-volume function; important function; line function.   **2.** A quality, trait, or fact that is so related to another as to be dependent on and to vary with this other, as when the success of the endeavor is a function of the commitment of management and employees to continuously improving performance and the quality of services. *See also* angina severity and functional classifications; pulmonary function tests; liver function tests; quality function deployment.

functional age   Age defined by ability and performance rather than chronologically. *See also* chronological age; developmental age; mental age.

functional illiterate   A person whose reading and writing skills are so poor that he or she cannot function effectively in the most basic business, office, or factory employment. Such individuals may have earned a high school diploma, making that credential less valid as a predictor of performance.

functional integration   The state in which two entities share common management, support, and clinical services. *See also* integration.

functional status   The ability of individuals to perform age-appropriate tasks of self-care and self-fulfillment. Functional status may be broken down into *social*, *physical*, and *psychological* functions. Functional status may be assessed routinely through questioning in the periodic health examination or through use of formal screening instruments. *See also* measure.

functional team   A group of people addressing an issue in which any recommended changes would not be likely to affect people outside the specific area. *See also* crossfunctional; interdisciplinary; multidisciplinary.

fundoscopy   *See* ophthalmoscopy.

futile care   According to the American Medical Association *Code of Medical Ethics* (1994), care that in the physician's judgment will not have a reasonable chance of benefiting the patient. The *code* asserts that physicians are not ethically obligated to deliver such care and should not provide treatment simply because patients demand it. *See also* medical ethics; palliative care.

futility   According to many of those who use the concept, the absence of a useful purpose or useful result in a diagnostic procedure or therapeutic intervention, in a situation in which a patient's condition will not be improved by treatment or in which treatment preserves permanent unconsciousness or cannot end dependence on intensive medical care. The concept is controversial and, according to the American Medical Association *Code of Medical Ethics* (1994), should not be used to justify denial of treatment because it cannot be meaningfully defined. Originally approached to develop a project on "futile" treatments, the Institute of Medicine instead refocused its work (*Approaching Death*, 1997) on care because of a deficient evidence base for making judgments about futility and a lack of operational definitions of the concept. *Synonym:* medically futile. *See also* bioethics; death with dignity; medical ethics; withdrawing treatment.

future damages   The loss or injury expected to occur in the future for which the law allows recovery. In most jurisdictions, with the exception of noneconomic damages, such as future pain and suffering, the amount awarded is reduced to its present monetary value. *See also* damages; noneconomic damages.

future state   In an organization transformation, the vision of where the organization will be after it is transformed. For the transformation to continuous quality improvement, the future state includes constancy of purpose, leaders who model the new way, collaboration, customer-mindedness, and a process focus. *See also* continuous quality improvement.

Gg

gag clause   A controversial clause in contracts between physicians and HMOs or other health plans that restricts the type of information the physician can provide to patients. Physicians and other health care professionals contend that such clauses are aimed at cutting costs by denying patients knowledge of possible health care options and that it precludes the patient's ability to give informed consent. *See also* gag rule.

gag rule   **1.** Any regulation that prohibits public discussion of a specific topic.   **2.** A regulation first drafted during the Reagan administration and enacted during the Bush administration which prohibited federally funded family planning clinics from discussing abortion with patients. The rule was challenged and upheld in 1991 (*Rust* v *Sullivan*), but abolished by executive order in the Clinton administration. *See also* gag clause.

gaming   The unethical or illegal manipulation of a process or system for the purpose of unwarranted gain or advantage, as in gaming the DRG reimbursement system.

Gantt chart   A schedule-monitoring tool that uses horizontal bars to show which tasks can be performed simultaneously over the life of a project. Its primary disadvantage is that it cannot show which tasks are dependent on each other.

gastroenterology   The branch of medicine and subspecialty of internal medicine dealing with the digestive organs, including the stomach, bowel, liver, and gallbladder, and disorders, such as abdominal pain, ulcers, diarrhea, cancer, and jaundice. *See also* alimentation; hepatology; internal medicine.

gastroscopy   The process of visualizing the interior of the stomach by means of an endoscope (gastroscope) inserted through the esophagus.

gastrostomy   A surgical procedure in which a tube is placed through the abdominal wall directly into the stomach for feeding. *See also* nutritional support.

gatekeeper   An individual who monitors or oversees the actions of other persons, as in a physician who determines health services to be provided to a patient and coordinates provision of the services by other persons. *See also* gatekeeper mechanism.

gatekeeper mechanism   An arrangement whereby a patient is assigned to or chooses from a selected group of primary care physicians, and the primary care physician assumes responsibility for, reviews, and approves all health services the patient receives, including care from specialists. *See also* gatekeeper; health services; open access; primary care physician.

gatekeeper model   *See* closed panel group practice.

gateway drug   In prevention theory, particularly regarding teenagers' risky behavior, any drug or addictive substance that may lead to abuse of additional drugs, especially more serious ones. For example, smoking cigarettes may be an entry point for teenagers to experiment with marijuana, and marijuana may lead to use of heroin or cocaine.

Gaussian distribution   *See* normal distribution.

gender identity   Awareness of knowing to which sex (female or male) one belongs; this awareness normally begins in infancy, continues through childhood, and is reinforced during adolescence.

general damages   The compensatory damages that one would reasonably expect to result from an act; for example, pain and suffering and disfigurement could all reasonably be expected to result from unnecessary surgery. General damages are distinguishable from consequential (special) damages, which do not necessarily result from such an act. *See also* damages.

general exclusion   A provision in a health insurance contract or health service plan that stipulates a type of specific service that is not covered as a benefit. *See also* exclusions.

general fund   Unrestricted monies and other liquid assets that are available for an organization's general use.

general hospital   A hospital whose primary functions are to provide diagnostic and therapeutic services to patients for short-term, acute surgical and medical conditions. Some specialized treatment and some longer-term chronic care may also be provided.

general liability insurance   Insurance covering the risk of loss for most accidents and injuries to third parties (the insured and its employees are not covered), which arise from the actions or negligence of the insured and for which the insured may have legal liability, except those injuries directly related to the provision of professional health services, which are usually separately covered by professional liability insurance. One situation in which general liability insurance would pay, for instance, is if a hospital visitor slips and falls on a wet floor. *Synonym:* liability insurance. *See also* insurance; liability.

generally recognized as effective (GRAE)   A condition that a drug must fulfill if it is not to be considered a new drug and thus not be the subject of premarket approval requirements of the federal Food, Drug, and Cosmetic Act. To qualify as GRAE, a drug must be so considered by experts qualified by scientific training and experience to evaluate the safety and effectiveness of drugs and must have been used to material extent or for a material time. *See also* generally recognized as safe; new drug.

generally recognized as safe (GRAS)   A condition that a drug must fulfill if it is not to be considered a new drug, or a food must fulfill if it is not to be considered a food additive. A drug that is GRAS and GRAE (generally recognized as effective) does not require the premarket approval prescribed for new drugs in the Food, Drug, and Cosmetic Act. Safety is determined by experts qualified by scientific training and experience to evaluate the safety and effectiveness of drugs. *See also* generally recognized as effective; new drug.

general practice (GP)   A medical practice that is not oriented to a specific medical specialty and in which a physician covers a variety of medical problems in patients of all ages. *See also* medical specialty.

general surgery   The branch of medicine and medical specialty dealing with the management of a broad spectrum of surgical conditions affecting almost any area of the body. Management includes diagnosis and provision of preoperative, operative, and postoperative care to surgical patients. Surgery also involves management of trauma and critically ill patients. Four subspecialties of surgery are general vascular surgery, pediatric surgery, surgical critical care, and surgery of the hand. *See also* surgery; surgical critical care; vascular surgery.

generic drug law   Modern statutes enacted by many states that permit or require pharmacists in certain circumstances to substitute a drug with the same active ingredients and of the same generic type for the drug prescribed by the physician. *See also* Drug Price Competition and Patent Term Restoration Act of 1984; generic equivalents.

generic equivalents   Drugs not protected by a trademark and sold under generic names with the same active chemical ingredients as those sold under proprietary brand names. Generic equivalents are not necessarily therapeutic equivalents. *See also* antisubstitution laws; Drug Price Competition and Patent Term Restoration Act of 1984; generic drug law; generic name; therapeutic equivalents.

generic name   The descriptive or nonproprietary (nontrade) name of a drug or other product; for example, acetaminophen is the generic name for *Tylenol*. Each drug is licensed under a generic name and also may be given a brand name by its manufacturer.

generic screen   *See* HCFA generic quality screens; screening.

gene splicing   *See* genetic engineering; recombinant DNA technology.

gene therapy   The replacement or modification of missing or defective genes to restore or enhance cellular function. Two types are *somatic cell gene therapy*, which alters human body cells but leaves the germ cells unaltered, and *germ line gene therapy*, in which a replacement gene is integrated into a person's reproductive cells and thus passed on to the individual's offspring and subsequent generations. The techniques include injection of new genes into the nuclei of single-cell embryos and use of recombinant DNA technology and vectors (altered carrier organisms). Rapidly expanding knowledge and accompanying technologies are raising issues for clinical practice and clinical policies in health care organizations, particularly with respect to biosafety, therapeutic monitoring, laboratory quality assurance, patient selection, appropriateness, informed consent, access and affordability, and the ethics of use in embryos, infants, and children. Initial clinical trials of gene therapy are regulated for public safety by the NIH Recombinant DNA Advisory Committee and the FDA. Diseases and applications undergoing trial in several hundred protocols in the 1990s include cystic fibrosis, enzyme deficiency disease (eg, Gaucher disease, severe combined immunodeficiencies), cardiovascular disease (eg, vascular thrombotic disease, high cholesterol levels), hemoglobinopathies (disorders of red blood cells as in sickle cell and other anemias), neurodegenerative disease (eg, Huntington's disease, Parkinson's disease), leukemias and other cancers (eg, p53 gene), and drug sensitivity, particularly for leukemia. A temporary moratorium has been placed on protocols for modifying germ line cells. *Synonym*: molecular therapy. *See also* eugenics; genetic counseling; human body shop; Human Genome Project; institutional review board; recombinant DNA technology.

genetic counseling   The provision of information and support to patients and their families concerning identified or potential risks of disease in themselves or their offspring. In the past, genetic counseling usually involved advising families of the risks pertaining to birth defects to inform their decisions about current or future pregnancies. But the advent of the ability to test for hereditary and acquired genetic mutations associated with a variety of diseases, the prospect of more opportunities for intervention upon completion of the Human Genome Project, the ambiguity of many tests' results, the absence of effective treatments for many of the diseases, the commercial availability of tests without standards governing their administration, popular misunderstandings about the level of risk and the burdens of testing, and the real and perceived threats of genetic discrimination by employers and long-term insurance companies have greatly expanded the scope and complexity of genetic counseling. Counseling is urged before making a decision to be tested as well as to deal with the results of testing. In its Code of Ethics, the National Society of Genetic Counselors defines the counselor-client relationship as based on values of care and respect for the client's autonomy, individuality, welfare, and freedom. This code states that given that the primary concern is the interests of their clients, genetic counselors strive to equally serve all who seek services; respect their clients' beliefs, cultural traditions, inclinations, circumstances, and feelings; enable their clients to make informed independent decisions, free of coercion, by providing or illuminating the necessary facts and clarifying the alternatives and anticipated consequences; refer clients to other competent professionals when they are unable to support the clients; maintain as confidential any information received from clients, unless released by the client; and avoid the exploitation of their clients for personal advantage, profit, or interest. *See also* autonomy; bill of patient rights; Cancer Genetics

Studies Consortium; cancer susceptibility testing; gene therapy; genetic screening; Human Genome Project; informed consent; institutional review board; medical ethics.

genetic discrimination   Use of information about an individual's potential genetic predisposition to disease to deny employment, to reduce or restrict employer-provided insurance or other benefits, or to deny long-term care insurance. The information may be obtained from family and individual medical histories, from results of DNA-based tests for genetic disorders, or even from the fact of undergoing genetic testing (whether or not results are available). The threat of genetic discrimination has arisen particularly for persons with high-risk profiles for development of early onset Alzheimer's disease, inherited cancer syndromes, alcoholism, and schizophrenia.

genetic engineering   Directed modification of the genetic makeup of a living organism to correct a deficiency or directed molecular evolution to produce molecules exhibiting properties that conform to the demands of the experimenter. As a broad term, it includes the work of recombinant DNA technology, gene therapy, genetic enhancement, cloning, and germ line modification. The term is sometimes used pejoratively to suggest out-of-control manipulation for social or economic purposes or experimentation without regard for individual welfare. The American Medical Association's *Code of Medical Ethics* (1994) has outlined factors to consider in the event that gene replacement with normal DNA becomes a practical reality for treating of human disorders, and it draws a clear line between what is therapeutic, the only legitimate motive for genetic manipulation, and what is enhancement or improvement for the eugenic development of offspring, which is contrary to the ethical tradition of medicine and to the egalitarian values of society. The code observes that because of the potential for abuse, genetic manipulation to affect nondisease traits may never be acceptable, but that if it is ever allowed, at least three conditions would have to be met to be ethically acceptable: (1) clear and meaningful benefit to the child, (2) no trade-off with other characteristics or traits, and (3) equal access to the technology by all citizens irrespective of income or other socioeconomic characteristics. *Synonyms*: Brave New World; designer genes; gene splicing; genetic enhancement; new eugenics; new genetics. *See also* DNA; eugenics; human body shop; Human Genome Project; medical ethics; recombinant DNA technology.

genetic enhancement   *See* genetic engineering.

genetic fingerprinting   The analysis of genetic information from a blood sample, semen sample, or other small piece of human material as an aid to identifying a person. This technique has revolutionized the forensic sciences. *Synonym*: DNA fingerprinting.

genetic parent   A parent who furnishes the sperm (the genetic father) or the ovum (the genetic mother) to an embryo. *See also* parent.

genetic risk assessment   *See* cancer susceptibility testing; genetic counseling; genetic testing.

genetics   The study of genes and their heredity. *See also* Cancer Genetics Studies Consortium; clinical genetics; cytogenetics; Dix, Dorothea Lynde; eugenics; human genetics; immunogenetics; medical genetics; molecular genetics; multiplex genetic testing.

genetic screening   A search in a population or sub-population for persons possessing certain genotypes that are already associated with disease or that predispose to disease, that may lead to disease in their descendants, or that produce other variations not known to be associated with disease. Examples are screening persons of Mediterranean background for Tay-Sachs and beta-thalassemia disease, family screening for hereditary hemochromatosis or Huntington's disease, couple screening for carriers of cystic fibrosis, prenatal screening of older pregnant women for Down syndrome, and screening of Ashkenazi Jewish women for BRCA1 susceptibility to breast cancer. *See also* adult-onset cancer; cancer susceptibility testing; genetic counseling; genetic testing; Human Genome Project; prenatal screening tests and procedures.

genetic testing   Determination of the presence, absence, or activity of genes in cells to predict an individual's lifetime course of health or status as a carrier of an inherited disease. *Predictive genetic testing,* which specifies an individual's chance of developing a certain disease because of a single-gene mutation (as in Huntington's disease), is distinguished from *genetic risk assessment,* which identifies genetic risk factors that could increase an individual's chance of developing the disease. The American Medical Association's *Code of Medical Ethics* (1994) contains several opinions with updates on genetic testing for employers, genetic testing by health insurance companies, and ethical issues in carrier screening. Physicians are advised not to participate in genetic testing by health insurance companies to predict a person's predisposition for disease. An issue of particular concern is predictive testing of children and adolescents for inherited adult-onset disease, which poses problems of informed consent and psychological harm. Several organizations have released position statements or consensus statements to serve as interim guidelines on indications for testing, performance of the testing, records management and tissue storage, and patient management after testing, especially in the areas of Alzheimer's disease and cancer susceptibility testing. Among these are the National Study Group supported by the National Institutes of Health (NIH) National Human Genome Research Institute, NIH's Cancer Genetics Studies Consortium with its Task Force on Informed Consent, the Ethics Advisory Panel established by the Alzheimer's Association, and the American Society of Clinical Oncology. *See also* cancer susceptibility testing; gene therapy; genetic counseling; genetic screening; Human Genome Project; informed consent; institutional review board; multiplex genetic testing.

geriatric dentistry   The branch of dentistry dealing with dental disorders and diseases of the aged. *See also* geriatric medicine.

geriatric medicine   The branch of medicine and subspecialty of family practice and internal medicine dealing with the prevention, diagnosis, treatment, and rehabilitation of disorders common to elderly people. *Synonym:* geriatrics. *See also* gerontology; internal medicine.

geriatric psychiatry   The branch and subspecialty of psychiatry dealing with the diagnosis and treatment of mental, addictive, and emotional disorders of the elderly. *See also* psychiatry.

gerodontics   An area of dentistry dealing with research, diagnosis, and treatment of dental diseases of the elderly. *Synonym:* gerodentistry.

gerontology   The branch of science dealing with the holistic nature of the aging process and old age. *See also* geriatric medicine.

gestalt therapy   A form of psychotherapy that emphasizes treating a person as an integrated whole by focusing on perceptual structures and patterns and interrelationships with other people and the environment. *See also* psychotherapy.

gestational diabetes   Diabetes mellitus that appears during some pregnancies, triggered by the increase in hormones during pregnancy, which partially blocks the action of insulin. *See also* diabetes mellitus.

gestational mother   The woman who bears a child. The gestational mother may also be the genetic mother, the rearing mother, or neither. *See also* parent.

Gilda Radner gene   A popular, if unscientific, term for CA-125, the antigen associated with ovarian cancer, arising during the Hollywood personality's campaign to create awareness about ovarian cancer as a result of her own experience. The campaign generated great demand for the "Gilda Radner test" and led to establishment of the Gilda Radner Familial Ovarian Cancer Registry, which has provided data for numerous studies of familial cancer syndromes. *See also* CA-125; adult-onset cancer; cancer susceptibility testing.

Glasgow Coma Scale (GCS)   A simple 15-point scoring instrument used to assess the degree of impaired consciousness, usually in patients with severe head injury, on the basis of eye opening, verbal response, and motor response. The GCS offers a standardized system for recording changes in neurological status over time following the initial assessment. Patients who cannot follow commands, do not open their eyes to a pain stimulus, and fail to utter words or comprehensible sounds are considered in coma, receiving a GCS score of 8 or less. A score of 15 indicates no impairment; a score of 3 suggests brain death. The GCS is combined with other measures to form the revised trauma score. *See also* overtriage; revised trauma score.

glaucoma   A disorder defined by slowly progressive loss of vision in association with characteristic signs of damage to the optic nerve. The death of retinal ganglion cells leads to the gradual enlargement of the optic cup and loss of vision, starting with peripheral vision. Although increased intraocular pressure (IOP) is common and may contribute to damage of the optic nerve, it is no longer considered a diagnostic criterion. To be a meaningful indicator, IOP must be monitored for an individual from a baseline. For a patient identified as a *high-risk glaucoma suspect* (ie, consistently elevated IOP, age > 50 years, African-American descent, family history of glaucoma, findings suggestive of optic nerve or nerve fiber layer damage, other ocular or systemic risk factors), treatment by medical or surgical means is usually started to lower IOP.

Gleason score   *See* cancer screening tests and procedures; cancer staging systems; PSA.

global budget   A nationwide limit or cap on categories of private and public health care spending. *See also* top-down global budgeting.

global capitation   Capitation accepted by a delivery system that agrees to provide all health care services, including outpatient care, hospitalization, preventive care, home care, dental care, mental health services, and substance-abuse treatment, to the entire (not just enrolled) population of a specific geographic area. *See also* capitation.

Global Utilization of Streptokinase and Tissue Plasminogen Activator for Occluded Coronary Arteries   *See* GUSTO.

golden hour   In trauma care, the concept that mortality rates are lowest when trauma victims are provided with definitive care within one hour after injury. *See also* advanced trauma life support; basic trauma life support; traumatology.

gold standard   A method, procedure, or measurement that is widely accepted as being the best available. It provides a reference point against which the performance of other methods, procedures, or measurements can be measured. *See also* benchmark; criterion standard.

good faith   In law, the total absence of intention to seek unfair advantage of, or to defraud, another party and the honest intention to fulfill one's obligations.

goodness-of-fit test   A statistical procedure, such as the chi-square test, that tests the hypothesis that a particular probability distribution fits an observed set of data. *See also* chi-squared test; hypothesis.

Good Samaritan laws   Statutes in most states which provide some protection from liability to a volunteer rescuer who risks his or her own life or serious injury in attempting to effect a rescue, provided the attempt is not reckless or rash. *See also* immunity.

governing body   The individual(s), group, or agency that has ultimate authority and responsibility for establishing policy, maintaining patient care quality, and providing for organization management and planning. *Synonyms*: administrative board; board; board of commissioners; board of directors; board of governors; board of trustees; governing board; partners.

government hospital   A hospital that is owned by either the local, state, or federal government. *See also* federal government hospital.

Government Performance and Results Act of 1993   Legislation that imposed requirements for strategic management, performance measurement, and accountability mechanisms—similar to those used in the private health care sector—on public-sector organizations.

grade of tumor   *See* cancer staging system.

graduate medical education (GME)   Medical education after receipt of the Doctor of Medicine (MD) or equivalent degree, including the education received as an intern, resident, or fellow, as well as continuing medical education. *See also* continuing education; continuing medical education; fellow; fifth pathway; residency.

Gram's stain   An empirical method of identifying and classifying bacteria according to color when a stain is applied to them. Red-staining or pink-staining bacteria are *gram-negative* bacteria; violet-staining or blue-staining bacteria are *gram-positive* bacteria. The method was described by the Danish physician Hans Christian Joachim Gram (1853-1938). *See also* bacteria; microbiology.

grandfather clause   A provision of policy or law that allows persons, engaged in a certain business before the passage of an act regulating that business, to receive a license or prerogative without meeting all the criteria that new entrants into the field would have to fulfill. For example, the Food, Drug, and Cosmetic Act exempts certain drugs from its premarket approval requirements on the basis of their long use.

grand rounds   A weekly meeting held in medical schools and teaching and other hospitals in which one or more important medical cases and relevant educational material are presented to health professionals, especially the members of the medical staff, as a learning experience. *See also* morbidity and mortality conference; rounds.

grant   A financial award, gift, or bestowal made by a foundation, governmental agency, or other organization to support a project, program, individual, or organization. *See also* block grant; capitation grant; foundation; matching grant.

graph   A visual display of the relationship between variables. The values of one set of variables are plotted along the horizontal *x*, axis and the values of a second variable along the vertical *y*, axis. Typical relationships between *x* and *y* are linear, exponential, or logarithmic. *See also* axis; bar graph; histogram; interrelationship digraph; line graph; variable.

grid element   A performance area that receives a discrete score on the Joint Commission accreditation decision grid. *See also* accreditation decision grid. ·

grid element score   A number representing the aggregated scores of individual Joint Commission standards in a grid element. *See also* summary grid score.

grievance process   A system for identifying adverse patient occurrences (APOs) through information from dissatisfied patients or representatives of these patients. *See also* occurrence screening.

gross and flagrant violation   A violation that presents an imminent danger to the health, safety, or well-being of a Medicare beneficiary or that unnecessarily places the beneficiary at risk of substantial and permanent harm. Utilization and quality control peer review organizations (PROs) identify potential violations and recommend sanctions, but the Office of the Inspector General of the US Department of Health and Human Services makes the final decision as to whether to impose sanctions. *See also* substantial violation.

gross negligence   The failure to use even slight care in the provision of health services or of an expected duty. In the law of torts, the degrees of negligence are, in general, *slight negligence*, which is failure to use great care; *ordinary negligence*, which is failure to use ordinary care; and *gross negligence*. Gross negligence occurs when an individual knows the harmful consequences of his or her actions and is indifferent to these consequences. *See also* negligence.

group contract   An insurance contract made with an employer or other entity that covers a group of persons identified by their employment, dependent relationship to employees, or by some other relationship to the contracting entity. *See also* contract.

GROUPER software   Computer software used to assign patient discharges to the appropriate DRGs using the following information abstracted from the inpatient financial bill: patient's age, sex, and principal diagnosis; principal procedures performed; and discharge status. The GROUPER uses the Uniform Hospital Discharge Data Set (UHDDS), with up to five diagnoses and four procedures coded by the ICD-9-CM. *See also* DRG; fiscal intermediary; Uniform Hospital Discharge Data Set.

group insurance   Any insurance plan, such as health insurance, that covers individuals by means of a single-group agreement, contract, or policy issued to an employer or association with which the insured individuals are affiliated. Group insurance is usually much lower in cost than comparable individual insurance. Group insurance is usually experience rated. *See also* experience rating; insurance.

group judgment methods   A class of techniques widely used in health care, and particularly technology assessment, to secure consensus after considering areas of uncertainty, disagreement, contradiction, or deficient research. They include formal methods, such as the Delphi technique and nominal group process, and federal and private-sector organizations' ongoing programs designed to address submitted questions about safety and efficacy. *See also* Delphi technique; Diagnostic and Therapeutic Technology Assessment; health care technology assessment programs; judgment; NIH Consensus Development Conferences and Consensus Statements; nominal group technique.

group medicine *See* group practice.

group model HMO An HMO that predominantly contracts with one independent group practice to provide health services, usually in HMO-owned or HMO-managed facilities. *See also* HMO.

group practice A formal association of three or more physicians, dentists, podiatrists, or other health professionals providing services, with income from the medical practice pooled and redistributed to the members of the group according to a prearranged plan. *Synonym:* group medicine. *See also* closed panel group practice; corporate dentistry; group practice without walls; integrated provider; management service organization; medical group practice; medical practice; multispecialty group practice; network model HMO; open panel group practice; prepaid group practice.

group practice without walls (GPWW) A network of physicians who have merged into one legal entity but maintain individual practice locations. A larger group has acquired the assets of the individual practices, but some autonomy is retained at each site. The central management owns both the facility and the equipment and provides administrative services. Links to hospitals vary widely. *Synonym:* group without walls. *See also* group practice; integrated provider; management service organization; physician-hospital organization.

group purchasing A shared service combining the purchasing power of individual organizations to obtain lower prices for equipment, supplies, and services.

group therapy A form of psychotherapy involving approximately six to eight people and a therapist. The interactions of the group members are considered an important part of the therapy. *Synonym:* group psychotherapy. *See also* family therapy; psychotherapy.

guardian A person appointed by a court and empowered by law to administer the personal affairs or property of an individual who is not capable of such duties. For purposes of Joint Commission accreditation, a guardian may be a parent, trustee, committee, conservator, or other person or agency. *Synonym:* legal guardian. *See also* family; guardian ad litem; legal age; minor; surrogate decision maker.

guardian ad litem An individual charged by a court with the authority and duty to represent the interests of an infant, a ward, an unborn person, or an incompetent adult in a particular legal action. *See also* guardian.

guideline *See* clinical practice guidelines.

guideline attributes Qualities identified as requisites for good clinical practice guidelines and used as criteria to appraise guidelines. The Institute of Medicine identified eight attributes when assisting in developing a guideline program for the federal AHCPR, and the American Medical Association has identified five attributes (labeled by Roman numerals) for practice parameters (its original term for guidelines). *See also* clinical practice guidelines; evidence-based medicine; explicit approach; medical review criteria; practice parameters.

DESIRABLE ATTRIBUTES OF CLINICAL PRACTICE GUIDELINES

The Institute of Medicine (IOM) Attributes*
Validity
  Strength of Evidence
    Estimated Outcomes
Reliability/Reproducibility
Clinical Applicability
Clinical Flexibility
Clarity
Multidisciplinary Process
Scheduled Review
Documentation

The American Medical Association (AMA) Attributes†

  I. Practice parameters should be developed by or in conjunction with physician organizations.

 II. Reliable methodologies that integrate relevant research findings and appropriate clinical expertise should be used to develop practice parameters.

III. Practice parameters should be as comprehensive and specific as possible.

IV. Practice parameters should be based on current information.

 V. Practice parameters should be widely disseminated.

*Source: Institute of Medicine, Committee on Clinical Practice Guidelines: *Guidelines for Clinical Practice: From Development to Use.* Field MJ, Lohr KN, eds. Washington, DC: National Academy Press, 1992.

†The AMA's attributes were undergoing review in 1996 and 1997 for possible expansion and refinement. In 1997, the AMA began to shift to using the term *clinical practice guideline* along with or instead of its original term, *practice parameter.* **Source:** American Medical Association, Department of Practice Parameters: *Directory of Clinical Practice Guidelines: Titles, Sources, and Updates.* Chicago, 1997. Appendix A, pp 219–22.

---

guideline disclaimer A statement designed to convey that the guideline does not purport to reflect all relevant medical considerations, usually placed in a preface or note to a guideline and sometimes used by hospitals and embedded in their policy when they take a national clinical practice guideline to develop into a care path or protocol. An example of language commonly used: "Adherence to this clinical practice guideline is voluntary. This guideline should not be considered inclusive of all proper methods of care or exclusive of other methods of care reasonably directed to obtaining the same results. The ultimate judgment regarding the propriety of any specific procedures must be made by the physician in

CRITERIA FOR CHOOSING TOPICS FOR NEW GUIDELINES AND TECHNOLOGY ASSESSMENTS

- Prevalence of the clinical problem (number of affected persons per 1,000 in the general U.S. population)
- Burden of illness imposed by the problem (individual mortality, morbidity, or functional impairment)
- Cost of managing the problem (per person)
- Variability in practice (significant differences in utilization rates for prevention, diagnosis, or treatment options)
- Potential for improving health outcomes (expected effect on health outcomes)
- Potential for reducing costs (expected effect on costs to sponsoring organization, other relevant agencies, patients and families, and/or society in general)

These recommendations, reported to the U.S. Congress in June 1995 concerning the work of the AHCPR, offer a serviceable framework to any organization willing and able to commit resources for the required data collection and analytic steps in developing clinical practice guidelines or conducting technology assessments. The Institute of Medicine incorporated criteria from the priority-setting processes of the following public and private organizations: American College of Physicians/Clinical Efficacy Assessment Program; Intermountain Health Care; Kaiser Permanente, Northern California Region; The state of Minnesota (the Minnesota Care Act of 1992 and its Practice Parameter Advisory Committee); Office of Medical Applications of Research, National Institutes of Health (Consensus Development Conferences and Technology Assessment Conferences); and U.S. Preventive Services Task Force, Department of Health and Human Services.

Source: Institute of Medicine: *Setting Priorities for Clinical Practice Guidelines.* Washington, DC: National Academy Press, 1995.

light of the individual circumstances presented by the patient."

guideline priority-setting process Preferred needs assessment and evaluation process specified by the Institute of Medicine (IOM) in its guidance of the AHCPR's Office of the Forum for Quality and Effectiveness in Health Care. In a June 1995 report to the U.S. Congress, the IOM identifies six general criteria to govern choice of topics for both guidelines and technology assessments, drawing on the priority-setting processes and criteria used by several public and private organizations. As a public agency, AHCPR must maintain a priority-setting process that is open and defensible. The recommended approach includes targeting areas in which the AHCPR is in a position to mobilize expertise around available evidence.

GUSTO (Global Utilization of Streptokinase and Tissue Plasminogen Activator for Occluded Coronary Arteries) A large, international random-ized clinical trial involving more than 41,000 patients in almost 1,100 hospitals in the United States and Canada, Europe, Israel, New Zealand, and Australia, conducted from 1989 to 1993, to evaluate and compare four strategies using thrombolytic agents in the treatment of acute myocardial infarction: two new accelerated tissue plasminogen activator(t-PA) regimens and streptokinase administered with either intravenous or subcutaneous heparin. GUSTO showed t-PA having a slight superiority in terms of both survival and overall clinical benefit, but the trial's chief message was the importance of reducing time to thrombolytic therapy in order to restore perfusion (blood flow through tissue), confirming the "open-artery" theory.

gynecology The branch of medicine and specialty dealing with the health care of women, including the function and diseases of the female genital tract. It encompasses both medical and surgical concerns and is usually practiced in combination with obstetrics.

Hh

habeas corpus An independent proceeding instituted to determine whether a defendant is being unlawfully deprived of his or her liberty. This procedure is used to challenge the legality of detention or custody.

habilitation Medical, educational, and other measures undertaken for individuals born with limited functional abilities. Rehabilitation, by contrast, refers to similar measures for individuals who have lost abilities because of injury or disease. *See also* rehabilitation; vocational habilitation.

Hahnemann, Samuel *See* homeopathy.

halfway house A residence that uses community resources to assist persons who have left highly structured institutions for treatment of mental illness or substance abuse to adjust and reenter society. The facility emphasizes emotional growth through confrontation and support. *Synonym:* community living facility. *See also* residential community-based care.

halo effect The tendency of an observer to overrate a subject's performance on a test or in an interview based on his or her perception of the subject's positive performance in an earlier exercise or interview. *See also* Hawthorne effect; placebo effect.

handicap **1**. According to the *International Classification of Impairment, Disabilities, and Handicaps*, a disadvantage for a given individual, resulting from an impairment or a disability, that limits or prevents the fulfillment of a role that is normal, depending on age, sex, and social and cultural practices, for that individual. **2**. According to the Americans with Disabilities Act (1974 Amendment, 29 USC S706), a handicap may be any one of a broad range of physical or developmental disabilities that limit one or more of a person's major life activities. *See also* disability; impairment.

Harry and Louise Names of the two characters in the Group Health Insurance Association of America's high-visibility television advertising campaign against the Clinton administration's health reform plan. Each vignette showed the couple discussing a facet of the plan that disturbed them and then ended with one of them saying, "There's got to be a better way." *See also* Health Security Act.

harvesting of organs Colloquial term, sometimes intended as a derogatory term, for practices surrounding the procuring of organs to replace diseased organs or organ tissue.

Hawthorne effect An effect that may be produced in an experiment from the subjects' awareness that they are participating in some form of scientific investigation. The name comes from classic industrial management experiments conducted at the Hawthorne (Ill.) plant of the Western Electric Company in the 1920s. *See also* halo effect; placebo effect.

hazard A situation or event that introduces or increases the probability of an adverse event arising from a danger or peril, or that increases the extent of an adverse event. Examples of hazards include infectious waste, slippery floors, and unqualified individuals providing health services. *See also* biohazard; occupational hazard; proportional hazards model; risk.

hazardous materials Substances, such as radioactive or chemical materials, that are dangerous to humans and other living organisms. *See also* safety management.

hazardous materials and wastes Materials whose handling, use, and storage are guided or defined by local, state, or federal regulation (eg, OSHA's Regulations for Bloodborne Pathogens regarding the disposal of blood and blood-soaked items; the Nuclear Regulatory Commission's regulations for the handling and disposal of radioactive waste), hazardous vapors (eg, glutaraldehyde, ethylene oxide, nitrous oxide), and hazardous energy sources (eg, ionizing or nonionizing radiation, lasers, microwave, ultrasound). Though the Joint Commission considers infectious waste as falling into this category of materials, federal regulations do not define infectious or medical waste as hazardous waste.

hazardous materials and waste management program For purposes of Joint Commission accreditation, a management process that includes all materials and waste that require special handling in order to address identified occupational and environmental hazards. Infectious waste and medical waste fall into the special handling category since there are recognized occupational exposure issues that must be dealt with properly. The program is expanded, when appropriate, to residential occupancies.

hazardous waste Waste materials—such as biologic waste that can transmit disease, radioactive materials, and toxic chemicals—that are dangerous to living organisms and require special precautions for disposal. *Synonyms:* biological waste; infectious waste. *See also* safety management.

hazard-surveillance program For purposes of Joint Commission accreditation, a program involving routine periodic surveys by personnel or staff to identify hazards or unsafe conditions or practices occurring in the buildings or on the grounds, or residential occupancies.

HCFA *See* Health Care Financing Administration (Appendix A).

HCFA 1500 A universal claims form, developed by HCFA, for health care providers to use in billing insurance carriers. By law, this form must be used for Medicare claims submitted by individual health care practitioners. *Synonym:* Universal UNIFORM Health Insurance Claim Form.

HCFA certification A statement by HCFA that a health care organization meets HCFA's conditions of participation. Certification by HCFA is required for Medicare and Medicaid reimbursement. *See also* conditions of participation; deemed status.

HCFA Common Procedure Coding System (HCPCS) A listing of health care services, procedures, and supplies with the corresponding codes providers must use in submitting Medicare claims. The HCPCS includes current procedural terminology codes, national alphanumeric codes, and local alphanumeric codes.

HCFA generic quality screens The list of occurrences that are applied by utilization and quality control peer review organizations to select medical cases that may have quality problems and that merit scrutiny. Because these screens generate a large amount of false positives, their application is only the first step in a multistage review process. *See also* occurrence criteria; occurrence reporting; occurrence screening.

health According to the World Health Organization, a state of complete physical, mental, and social well-being, and not merely the absence of disease or infirmity. *See also* the following health terms, as well as board of health; environmental health; holism; occupational health; oral suffering; public health; wellness program.

health aide program A program of the Indian Health Service in which members of a target population are trained to assist physicians, public health nurses, sanitarians, medical social workers, and other persons in clinical and field health programs.

health alliance As proposed in the Health Security Act, a regional health or corporate alliance that pools individuals for the purpose of buying health insurance at lower prices. *See also* health insurance purchasing cooperative; Health Security Act; managed competition; regional alliance.

Health and Nutrition Examination Survey (HANES) A survey conducted every four years by the National Center for Health Services Research and Health Care Technology Assessment. The survey gathers data in many areas, such as medically defined illnesses and population distributions based on blood pressure, serum cholesterol levels, and nutritional status.

health assessment questionnaire (HAQ) A multidimensional instrument developed by the Stanford Arthritis Centre that measures outcomes in terms of mortality, disability, pain, iatrogenic events, and economic impact.

health behavior Conduct or manner demonstrated by a person to maintain, attain, or regain health and to prevent illness. Health behavior often reflects a person's health beliefs. *See also* health behavior counseling; health belief model.

health behavior counseling Efforts to encourage or persuade patients to adopt healthy habits, use preventive

services, and change harmful personal practices. This type of counseling embraces a wide variety of topics, including contraception and safer sex practices, diet and weight management, hormone replacement therapy, immunizations, tobacco and other substance use, hearing and vision testing, lead exposure, oral hygiene, and cancer screening. *See also* health behavior.

health belief model A paradigm that describes a person's health behavior as an expression of health beliefs. Components of the model include the person's perception of his or her susceptibility to disease; the severity of the consequence of contracting a disease; the perceived benefits of care and barriers to preventive behavior; and the internal or external stimuli that result in health behavior by the person. *See also* health behavior.

health benefits *See* basic benefit package; comprehensive benefit package.

health card An identification card, similar to a credit card, proposed in several national health insurance bills, that would be issued to each covered individual or family unit. This card would be presented at the time of services and would be rendered in lieu of any cash payment. The individual would subsequently receive a bill for any cost-sharing not covered under the insurance plan. Health cards, some argue, would simplify eligibility determination, billing and accounting, and the study of use of services. *Synonym*: health security card. *See also* smart card in health care.

health care Care provided to individuals or communities by agents of the health services or professions for the purpose of promoting, maintaining, monitoring, or restoring health. Health care is broader than, and not limited to, medical care, which implies therapeutic action by or under the supervision of a physician. *See also* comprehensive health care; medical care and services.

health care administration The management of resources, procedures, and systems that operate to meet patients' needs and wants in the health care system. *Synonyms*: health administration; health care management.

health care coalition An organization composed of provider, business, and consumer representatives, and sometimes representatives of government, interested in health care issues, such as cost. *See also* business health care coalition.

health care consumer One who may receive or is receiving health services. While all people at times consume health services, a consumer, as the term is used in health legislation and programs, is usually someone who is never a provider, that is, not associated in any direct or indirect way with the provision of health services. The distinction has become important in programs in which a consumer majority on the governing body is required, as is the case with community health centers and health systems agencies assisted under the Public Health Service Act. *See also* consumer; health care provider.

health care encounter A contact between a patient and a health professional in which a health service is provided. In managed care, an encounter is a face-to-face meeting between a covered person and a health care provider in which services are provided.

health care informatics *See* medical informatics.

health care network An entity that provides, or provides for, integrated health care services to a defined population of individuals and that offers comprehensive or specialty services. Networks are characterized by a centralized structure that coordinates and integrates services provided by components and practitioners participating in the network. A network may take the form of an HMO, a PPO, or other cooperative system of provider organizations, practitioners, or insurers that contracts with purchasers to provide health services. *Synonyms*: health plan; health network; network. *See also* community health network; corporatization of health care; health plan; health system; multihospital system; network model HMO; primary care network.

Health Care Network Accreditation Program The survey and accreditation program of the Joint Commission for eligible health care networks.

health care occupancy An occupancy used for purposes such as medical or other treatment or care of persons suffering from physical or mental illness, disease, or infirmity; and for the care of infants, convalescents, or infirm aged persons. Health care occupancies provide sleeping facilities for four or more occupants and are occupied by persons who are mostly incapable of self-preservation because of age, physical or mental disability, or security measures not under the occupant's control. Health care occupancies include hospitals, nursing homes, and limited care facilities. *See also* occupancy.

health care organization A generic term used to describe many types of organizations that provide health care services, including ambulatory care centers, behavioral health institutions, home care organizations, hospitals, laboratories, and long term care organizations. *Synonym*: health care institution.

health care professional *See* health professional.

health care provider A health professional or health care organization, or group of health professionals or health care organizations, that provides health services to patients. Examples include an individual, such as a physician, dentist, nurse, or allied health professional, or an organization, such as a physician-hospital organization, skilled nursing facility, or home health agency. *Synonyms*: health provider; health service provider; health services provider; provider. *See also* fourth party; free choice of provider; health care consumer; impaired health care provider; integrated provider; nonparticipating provider; participating physician; primary care provider; referral provider.

Health Care Quality Improvement Act (HCQIA) of 1986 Federal legislation, which went into effect in 1990, that created the National Practitioners Data Bank. It provides immunity from liability, including antitrust liability, for peer review decisions by health facilities regarding physicians and dentists, provided requirements of the act are satisfied. *See also* National Practitioner Data Bank.

Health Care Quality Improvement Program (HCQIP) A Medicare-based national outcomes measurement system introduced by HCFA in 1994, based on recommendations from the Institute of Medicine, and implemented by the national peer review organizations (PROs). Its goal is to "move from dealing with individual clinical errors to helping providers improve the mainstream of care" and to create a situation in which "PROs will focus primarily on persistent differences between the observed and the achievable in both care and outcomes and less on occasional, unusual deficiencies in care." It has been proposed that HCQIP should serve as the foundation for all future utilization and quality control activities by PROs. *See also* outcomes measurement; utilization review.

health care record The account compiled by physicians and other health care professionals of a variety of health information, including a patient's medical history, present illness, examination findings, treatment details, and progress notes. The health care record is the legal record of care. Portions of this record may be found in components or practitioner sites where care is being rendered. However, access to needed information regarding the patient's care should be available to those providing service to the patient at any site of service. *See also* medical history; medical record; progress notes.

health care technology Drugs, devices, procedures, and the organizational and support systems within which health care is delivered. *See also* health care technology assessment; health care technology assessment programs.

health care technology assessment (TA) A structured analysis of a health care technology, a set of related technologies, or a technology-related issue, which is performed for the purpose of providing input to a policy decision, including coverage and reimbursement decisions and consideration of the technology's future impact on social, ethical, and legal systems. The principles and terminologies for structuring the TA vary among the many public- and private-sector TA programs, but generally they involve placing a technology on a continuum of appropriateness between "untested" or "experimental" and "established" or "standard" or "state of the art." *Synonyms*: health technology assessment (HTA); technology assessment (TA). *See also* clinical practice guideline; health care technology assessment programs; Human Genome Project; NIH Consensus Development Conferences and Consensus Statements.

health care technology assessment programs Scheduled and structured activities by an organization, agency, or panel to evaluate the safety, efficacy, and cost-effectiveness of a technology. The program's assessments may be triggered by a specific request to guide reimbursement decisions (as in some government programs and in

HEALTH CARE TECHNOLOGY ASSESSMENT PROGRAMS

Government
U.S. Congress
   Prospective Payment Assessment Commission
   Office of Technology Assessment*
U.S. Department of Health and Human Services
   Agency for Health Care Policy and Research: Center for
     Health Care Technology (CHCT)
   Food and Drug Administration
   Health Care Financing Administration
   National Institutes of Health: Office of Medical Applications
     of Research (NIH Consensus Development and
     Technology Assessment Programs)
U.S. Department of Veterans Affairs

Academic
Brandeis University: Health Policy Center, Organ Procurement
   Project
Duke University: Center for Health Policy Research and
   Education
Georgetown University Medical Center: Institute for Health Policy
   Analysis
Harvard University: School of Public Health, Institute for Health
   Research
Johns Hopkins University: Program for Medical Technology and
   Practice Assessment
University of California, San Francisco: Institute for Health Policy
   Studies
University HealthSystem Consortium
University of Pennsylvania: Leonard Davis Institute of Health
   Economics

Provider/Payer
American Academy of Neurology
American Academy of Ophthalmology
American Academy of Pediatrics
American College of Cardiology/American Heart Association
   Task Force on Assessment of Cardiovascular Procedures
American College of Obstetricians and Gynecologists
American College of Physicians: Clinical Efficacy Assessment
   Project (CEAP)
American College of Radiology
American Dental Association
American Diabetes Association
American Gastroenterological Association
American Hospital Association
American Medical Association: Diagnostic and Therapeutic
   Technology Assessment (DATTA)
American Society for Gastrointestinal Endoscopy
Blue Cross and Blue Shield Association: Technology Evaluation
   Center (TEC)
California Medical Association
College of American Pathologists
Group Health Cooperative (GHC) of Puget Sound
The HMO Group (THMOG): Technology Management Information
   Exchange
Institute for Clinical Systems Integration (ICSI)

Other Private
Battelle Memorial Institute
ECRI: Health Technology Assessment Information Service
   (HTAIS)
Lewin and Associates, Inc
Medical Technology and Practice Patterns Institute
Policy Analysis, Inc
Project HOPE Center for Health Affairs
RAND
U.S. Administrators. Inc

*Terminated in Fall 1995.

Source: Adapted in part from (1) Office of Technology Assessment, U.S. Congress: *Identifying Health Technologies that Work: Searching for Evidence.* Washington, DC: U.S. Government Printing Office, Sept. 1994. (2) Healthcare Information Center: *The 1997 Medical Outcomes and Guidelines Sourcebook.* New York: Faulkner & Gray, 1996.

managed care), or the program may be set-up to select technologies for review according to specified criteria, such as overuse or underuse, high variation in patterns of use, investigational or experimental status, public debate and disagreement, or new discoveries or experience that might alter the status of a technology evaluated previously. *See also* Diagnostic and Therapeutic Technology Assessment; group judgment methods; NIH Technology Assessment Conferences and Statements.

health data disclosure acts *See* state data initiatives.

health decision The actual choice made by health care practitioners or recipients of care when confronted by a defined health problem. A specific decision is a choice between a primary scenario and an alternative scenario(s).

health economics The social science dealing with the demand for and supply of health care resources and the impact of health services on the health of a population.

health education Providing information to the general public or to a special group which increases awareness and favorably influences behavior in such a way as to promote health and prevent disease. *See also* health fair; health promotion; prevention; wellness program.

health facility A health or medical institution whose primary function is to provide health services, such as a hospital, nursing home, rehabilitation center, reproductive health center, independent clinical laboratory, facility-based hospice, or ambulatory surgical center.

health fair A community health education event that focuses on prevention of disease and promotion of health through such activities as audiovisual exhibits and free screening services. *See also* health education; health promotion; patient education; prevention.

health history *See* medical history.

health identifier *See* standard unique health identifier.

health information infrastructure   A communications network consisting of computer-based patient record systems, computerized knowledge-based systems, and reference databases, all of which are connected through high-speed communications links using common definitions, codes, and forms. *See also* computer-based patient record.

health insurance claim number (HICN)   An identification number of a Medicare beneficiary (often his or her Social Security number), consisting of seven or nine digits and an alphabetical prefix or suffix. Medicare requires that the HICN number appear on all documents related to a beneficiary. *See also* Medicare.

Health Insurance for the Aged and Disabled, Title XVIII   *See* Medicare.

Health Insurance Portability and Accountability Act of 1996   Legislation that includes a major initiative to expand federal efforts to combat fraud and abuse as well as the provisions that provoked the most publicity and debate over passage, such as transfer of health insurance between employers, limits on preexisting condition exclusions, and the establishment of a medical savings account pilot project. *See also* fraud and abuse; medical savings account.

health insurance purchasing cooperative (HIPC)   A private, nonprofit organization that pools individuals in order to purchase health insurance at reduced costs. *See also* health alliance; regional alliance.

health intervention   *See* intervention.

Health Interview Survey (HIS)   A survey conducted annually by the National Center for Health Statistics to collect health-related information, such as illness and injury recall, health conditions and related disabilities, hospitalization, and physician visits, on a sampling of American households.

health maintenance   Preservation of the physical, mental, and social well-being of a person. *See also* health promotion.

health maintenance diaries   A handout form often used in patient education. The diary usually lists patient responsibilities on one side and contains a personal prevention record for the patient to fill in on the other side. *See also* patient education; prevention.

health maintenance organization   *See* HMO.

Health Maintenance Organization Act of 1973   A federal statute that sets standards of qualifications for HMOs and mandates that employers of 25 or more persons who currently offer a medical benefit plan must also offer the option of joining a qualified HMO if one exists in the area. *See also* HMO.

health maintenance schedule   A series of interventions offered to patients at defined intervals, depending on their age, sex, and risk factors, for the primary or secondary prevention of disease. These interventions include screening tests, immunizations, history taking, and counseling. Providers in a group usually meet to develop a minimum acceptable protocol rather than consensus on all preventive interventions. Most health maintenance schedules indicate the frequency or intervals of procedures as well as list them. An example is the Lifetime Health Monitoring Program of the Group Health Cooperative of Puget Sound. *See also* Lifetime Health Monitoring Program.

health network   *See* health care network.

health plan   1. In health insurance, a specific set of benefits packaged for general offering for the needs of a specific purchaser. *See also* Blue Cross and Blue Shield plan; drug maintenance list; incentive benefit plan; prepaid health plan.   **2.** According to the Health Security Act (1993), a plan that provides a comprehensive benefit package which covers specifically defined medical benefits, procedures, and services. *See also* comprehensive benefit package; health care network; Health Security Act; health system; hospital affiliation; prepayment plan; primary care network.

Health Plan Employer Data and Information Set   *See* HEDIS.

health planning   Strategizing to improve health for a whole community, a particular population, a type of health service, or a health program. Some definitions include all activities undertaken for the purpose of improving health (such as education and nutrition); other definitions are limited to including conventional health services and programs, public health, or personal health services. *See also* National Health Planning and Resources Development Act of 1974.

health professional   Any person who has completed a course of study and is skilled in a field of health, such as a nurse, occupational therapist, or osteopathic physician. Health professionals are often licensed by a government agency or certified by a professional organization. *Synonym:* health care professional. *See also* allied health professional; health care provider.

health promotion   Efforts to change people's behavior to promote healthy lives and to help prevent illnesses and accidents. *See also* health education; health maintenance; prevention; wellness program.

health record   *See* medical record.

health-related quality of life (HRQOL)   An outcomes measure of the functional effects of an illness and the chosen therapy upon a patient as perceived by the patient. HRQOL may be measured by generic instruments useful in various conditions (such as the SF-36) or by disease-specific questionnaires. The concept is used internationally with common U.S. instruments sometimes culturally modified as well as translated into the host language. One series of measures is the McMaster Health-Related Quality of Life Instruments, which covers specific chronic diseases, such as asthma, and is further broken down by population (eg, adult, pediatric, and caregiver questionnaires). *See also* health status measurement; measures (and accompanying table); patient utilities measurement.

health resources   Personnel, facilities, funds, and technology used, or that could be made available, in providing health services.

health risk appraisal (HRA)   A process of gathering, analyzing, and comparing an individual's prognostic characteristics of health with a standard age group, thereby predicting the likelihood that a person may prematurely develop a health problem associated with a high morbidity and mortality rate. One purpose of health risk appraisal is to prescribe measures and programs to counter detected risks. *Synonym*: health risk assessment. *See also* high-risk group; risk factor modification.

Health Screening Survey (HSS)   *See* alcohol-problem screening.

Health Security Act (HSA)   A health reform bill introduced by the Clinton administration in 1993 and defeated in Congress the same year. The purposes of the bill were to ensure that all Americans had health care coverage, to contain the growth in health care costs, to promote responsible health insurance practices, to encourage choice in health care, and to ensure and protect the health care of all Americans. Although the plan was defeated, many of the terms used in it have become commonplace in current health care jargon. *Synonyms*: American Health Security Act; Clinton health plan. *See also* community care plan; comprehensive benefit package; employer deduction cap; Harry and Louise; health alliance; health plan; regional alliance.

health security card   *See* health card.

health service area (HSA)   A defined geographic region designated under the National Health Planning and Resources Development Act of 1974 for the effective planning and development of health services. An HSA covers such factors as geography, political boundaries, population, and health resources. *See also* catchment area; medically underserved area; Medicare locality.

health service provider   *See* health care provider.

health services   Services that are performed by health professionals, or by other supervised persons, for the purpose of promoting, maintaining, monitoring, or restoring health. *See also* basic benefit package; community health care; demand for health services; employee health service; gatekeeper mechanism; mental health services; national health service; oral health services; occupational health services; personal health services.

health services research (HSR)   The integration of epidemiological, sociological, economic, and other analytical sciences in the study of health services. Health services research is concerned with relationships among need, demand, supply, use, cost, and outcomes of health services. *See also* health services.

health statistics   Aggregated data describing and enumerating attributes, events, occurrences, structures, processes, and outcomes relating to health, disease, and health services. The data may be derived from survey instruments, medical records, administrative documents, and other source documents. Vital statistics are a subset of health statistics. *See also* vital statistics.

health-state preferences   *See* patient utilites measurement.

health status measurement   Assessment to evaluate and relate several dimensions of patient health, both in general and in relation to specific conditions, including the functional well-being of specific populations such as overall health status and health status change over time (eg, physical functioning, bodily pain, social functioning, mental health). *See also* health-related quality of life; measures.

health status objectives   See *Healthy People 2000*.

health status questionnaire   *See* measure (and accompanying table).

health system   The network of organizations and individuals that provides health services in a defined geographic area. A health system is established, according to the American Hospital Association, when a single hospital owns, leases, or contract-manages nonhospital, preacute, or postacute health-related facilities (eg, wellness services, mental health services, outpatient services, employer health services, long term care); or two or more hospitals are owned, leased, sponsored, or contract-managed by a central organization. *Synonym*: health care system. *See also* health care network; health plan; multihospital system.

Healthy People 2000   A report published by the U.S. Public Health Service in 1990 outlining achievable health promotion and disease prevention goals for Americans for the year 2000. Fully titled *Healthy People 2000: National Health Promotion and Disease Prevention Objectives*, the report was compiled by a consortium that included nearly 300 national organizations, all of the state health departments, and the Institute of Medicine of the National Academy of Sciences. Together, the initiative and its involved networks is often referred to under the short, nonitalicized rubric Healthy People 2000. The report is intended as a statement of national opportunities; it is not intended as a statement of federal standards or requirements. Overall broad goals are to (1) increase the span of healthy life for Americans; (2) reduce health disparities among Americans; and (3) achieve access to preventive services for all Americans. Specific objectives are set forth, organized in 22 priority areas, and further broken down into Health Status Objectives, Risk Reduction Objectives, and Services and Protection. The original document has been supplemented with *Healthy People 2000: Midcourse Review and 1995 Revisions*, which reports that a network of plans for the year 2000 is in place in 41 states and 2 territories, and that 70% of local health departments are using Healthy People 2000 as a framework. The 1995 docu-

HEALTHY PEOPLE 2000: HEALTH STATUS OBJECTIVES AND THEIR CRITERIA

Health Promotion
1. Physical Activity and Fitness
2. Nutrition
3. Tobacco
4. Alcohol and Other Drugs
5. Family Planning
6. Mental Health and Mental Disorders
7. Violent and Abusive Behavior
8. Educational and Community-Based Programs

Health Protection
9. Unintentional Injuries
10. Occupational Safety and Health
11. Environmental Health
12. Food and Drug Safety
13. Oral Health

Preventive Services
14. Maternal and Infant Health
15. Heart Disease and Stroke
16. Cancer
17. Diabetes and Chronic Disabling Conditions
18. HIV Infection
19. Sexually Transmitted Diseases
20. Immunization and Infectious Diseases
21. Clinical Preventive Services

Surveillance and Data Systems
22. Surveillance and Data Systems

Age-Related Objectives
Children
Adolescents and Young Adults
Adults
Older Adults

Credibility—Objectives should be realistic and should address the issues of greatest priority.

Public comprehension—Objectives should be understandable and relevant to a broad audience, including those who plan, manage, deliver, use, and pay for health services.

Balance—Objectives should be a mixture of outcome and process measures, recommending methods tor achieving changes and setting standards for evaluating progress. Measurability—Objectives should be quantified.

Continuity—Year 2000 objectives should be linked to the 1990 objectives where possible but reflect the lessons learned in implementing them.

Compatibility—Objectives should be compatible where possible with goals already adopted by Federal agencies and health organizations.

Freedom from data constraints—The availability or form of data should not be the principal determinant of the nature of the objectives. Alternate and proxy data should be used where necessary.

Responsibility—The objectives should reflect the concerns and engage the participation of professionals, advocates, and consumers as well as State and local health departments.

ment also provides a table showing progress on 47 sentinel objectives.

heart attack Familiar term for myocardial infarction. *See* acute myocardial infarction.

heart failure A clinical syndrome or condition characterized by (1) signs and symptoms of intravascular and interstitial volume overload, including shortness of breath, rales, and edema, or (2) manifestations of inadequate tissue perfusion, such as fatigue or poor exercise tolerance. These signs and symptoms result when the heart cannot pump enough blood to meet the metabolic requirements of body tissue. The term *heart failure* is used in preference to the common *congestive heart failure* because many patients with heart failure do not manifest pulmonary or systemic congestion. The most common cause of heart failure is left-ventricular systolic dysfunction, a reduction in the pumping power to the point when the left ventricular ejection fraction is less than 35% to 40% as opposed to the normal range of 50%. Guidelines for managing heart failure have been issued by AHCPR (1994) and by the American College of Cardiology and the American Heart Association (1995).

HEDIS (Health Plan Employer Data and Information Set) A performance measurement set developed in 1989 that helps consumers, corporations, and public purchasers of health care evaluate and compare the quality of managed care plans. Measurement areas are quality, access and patient satisfaction, membership and utilization, finance, and descriptive information on health plan management. The measures have been revised twice under the sponsorship of the National Committee for Quality Assurance, producing HEDIS 2.0 in 1993 and HEDIS 2.5 in 1995. *See also* performance measure.

Helicobacter pylori (H pylori) A species of gram-negative bacteria discovered in 1983, formerly classified in the genus *Campylobacter*, which is believed to be responsible for most cases of gastritis, is highly correlated with gastric and duodenal ulcers, and is possibly implicated in gastric malignancies. The role of *H pylori* in peptic ulcers was the subject of a National Institutes of Health Consensus Development Conference in 1994. The infection is easily suppressed, but sustained cure (necessary to prevent ulcer recurrence) requires carefully selected regimens combining antimicrobials with other agents to deal with the ulcer symptoms and prevent development of resistance. *See also* peptic ulcer disease.

helper T cell *See* HIV infection.

Helsinki Declaration A document, based on the Nuremberg Code of Ethics and signed in Helsinki, Finland, which offers recommendations for conducting experiments using human subjects. The requirement of informed consent is clearly delineated between two separate categories: clinical research combined with professional care and non-therapeutic clinical research. The Helsinki Declaration offered rules for consent which more closely resembled practice in the clinical setting than did the Nuremberg Code, the founding document for informed consent. The declaration was adopted by the 18th World Medical Assembly (WMA) in Helsinki in 1964, and subsequently revised at the 19th WMA in Tokyo in 1975, the 35th WMA in Venice in 1983, and the 41st WMA in Hong Kong in 1989. In medicine it is often referred to as the founding document on ethics of clinical research, human experimentation, consent, and other questions of medical ethics. *See also* informed consent; Nuremberg Code.

hematocrit (Hct) A measure of the packed cell volume of red blood cells, expressed as a percentage of the total blood volume. The normal range is between 43% and 49% in men and between 37% and 43% in women. *See also* blood count.

hematology The branch of medicine and subspecialty of internal medicine, pathology, and pediatrics dealing with diseases of the blood, spleen, and lymph glands. The scope of hematology includes disorders such as anemia, clotting conditions, sickle cell disease, hemophilia, leukemia, and lymphoma. *See also* internal medicine; pathology.

heparin A naturally occurring ring mucopolysaccharide (complex carbohydrate) that has potent anticoagulant properties. In the form of heparin sodium (sodium salt), it is used to prevent and treat disorders in which there is excessive or undesirable clotting, such as thrombophlebitis, pulmonary embolism, and certain cardiac conditions. It is administered intravenously or subcutaneously. A variant form is the *low-molecular-weight heparin* (molecular weight usually between 4000 and 6000 kD), which is more expensive but has a higher bioavailability, a longer half-life, and does not require monitoring. These agents are administered with a reduced risk of hemorrhage, and their platelet interactions are reduced in comparison with unfractionated heparin. They also provide an effective treatment of deep venous thrombosis and prophylaxis against postoperative major pulmonary embolism. *See also* anticoagulation.

hepatitis Inflammation of the liver by various causes, including bacterial or viral infection, parasitic infestation, alcohol, drugs, toxins, or incompatible blood transfusion. It may be mild, severe, or fulminant and life threatening, and it may be acute or chronic. *Hepatitis A virus* (also known as infectious hepatitis) is found in fecal matter and is spread by improper food handling or by contaminated seafood. *Hepatitis B virus* is spread by direct blood contact, such as with blood transfusions or use of contaminated needles. *Hepatitis C* is similar to type B post-transfusion hepatitis but is caused by a virus that is serologically distinct from the agents of hepatitis A, B, and E, and may persist in the blood of chronic asymptomatic carriers. Hepatitis C is parenterally transmitted and associated with transfusions and drug abuse. Several other forms have been identified, and with each new discovery the terminology changes slightly. *See also* sexually transmitted disease.

hepatology The branch of medicine dealing with diseases of the liver. *See also* gastroenterology.

herbal medicine A type of alternative medicine that uses plants or herbs to treat disease or alleviate pain. *See also* alternative medicine; traditional medicine.

hereditary nonpolyposis colorectal cancer (HNPCC) *See* cancer susceptibility testing; colorectal cancer.

herniated disk Rupture of the fibrocartilage surrounding an intervertebral disk, which causes protrusion of the central gelatinous material (nucleus pulposus) of the disk through its fibrous outer covering (annulus fibrosis). *Synonym:* slipped disk. *See also* low back pain.

herpes simplex A group of acute and extremely contagious infections caused by a type of herpes virus, occurring as a primary infection or recurring as a result of reactivation of latent infection. Characterized by the development of one or more small fluid-filled blisters with a raised erythematous base on the skin or mucous membrane (such as "cold sores"). Most infections of the lips, mouth, pharynx, eye, and central nervous system are caused by *herpes simplex virus type 1* (HSV-1). Genital and neonatal infections are usually caused by *herpes simplex virus type 2* (HSV- 2). Neonatal herpes, caused by HSV-1 or HSV-2 infection passed from the mother to the newborn infant, varies from mild to fatal. HSV-2 is a precursor of cervical cancer. HSV is a condition included in the 1993 expanded surveillance case definition of HIV. *See also* HIV infection.

hidden time effects Effects arising in data sets that may simply be a result of the collection of observations over a period of time. *See also* historical control.

high-complexity test A test that meets CLIA '88 requirements based on: the need for personnel with scientific and technical knowledge and specialized training and substantial experience to perform the test; possibly labile reagents and materials that may require special handling to ensure reliability and reagents and materials preparation that may include manual steps; operational steps in the testing process that require close monitoring or control and may require special specimen preparation, precise temperature control or timing of procedural steps, accurate pipetting, or extensive calculations; and calibration, quality control, and proficiency testing of materials that may not be available or may be labile. In these tests, troubleshooting is not automatic and requires decision making and direct intervention to resolve most problems, and maintenance requires special knowledge, skills, and abilities. Extensive independent interpretation and judgment are required to perform preanalytic, analytic, and postanalytic processes, and resolution of problems requires extensive interpretation and judgment.

high-density lipoprotein (HDL)   The smallest and densest of the lipoproteins. The cholesterol on them is nicknamed "good cholesterol." HDLs retrieve cholesterol from the body's tissues and transport it to the liver, which excretes much of it in the bile. *See also* cholesterol; lipoprotein.

high-mortality outlier   A health care provider, such as an individual hospital, with mortality rates that are higher than expected after adjustment for patient-based factors, such as age, comorbidities, and severity of illness. *See also* low-mortality outlier.

high-risk function   **1**. An important function that exposes individual patients to a greater chance of undesirable occurrences if not carried out effectively and appropriately.   **2**. Services that are inherently risky, even when effectively and appropriately performed, because of certain patient attributes or newness of the service.

high-risk group   Categorization of a subpopulation for special consideration in recommendations for screening, diagnosis, therapy, and management. For example, in tables of recommendations on the periodic health examination for the birth-to-10-years age range in the U.S. Preventive Services Task Force *Guide to Clinical Preventive Services*, blood-lead-level testing is recommended only for HR7, described as children about 12 months of age who live in houses or communities known for hazardous lead levels, live in dilapidated houses built before 1950, who are in contact with persons who have elevated lead levels, or who have other sources of exposure to lead. *See also* health risk appraisal; risk factor modification.

high-risk nursery   *See* neonatal intensive care unit.

high-risk pool   A fund set up by an organization or agency to offer health insurance to small groups and individuals who have been denied coverage or whose medical history makes rates too high. *See also* insurance; risk pool.

high-risk procedure   **1.** A procedure that exposes individual patients to a greater chance of undesirable outcomes if not carried out effectively and appropriately, for example chronic dialysis, radiation oncology services, or emergency or urgent care.   **2.** Procedures that are inherently risky, even when effectively and appropriately performed, because of certain patient attributes or the newness of the procedure.

high-volume function   A function that is performed frequently or affects large numbers of patients, for example, discharge planning.

high-volume procedure or condition   A procedure (such as coronary artery graft bypass procedure) that is performed or condition (such as congestive heart failure) that is treated frequently or affects large numbers of patients. A high-volume procedure or condition often

provides the basis for an organization's performance measurement, assessment, and improvement activities.

Hill-Burton Act   Legislation, and the programs under that legislation, for federal assistance in construction and modernization of health facilities, beginning with the Hospital Survey and Construction Act of 1946.

Hippocrates of Cos (460-375 BC)   A Greek physician who is generally regarded as the father of medicine. An oath that appears in the body of work attributed to Hippocrates and his school, known as the *Hippocratic oath*, has served as an ethical foundation of the medical profession. *See also* Hippocratic oath.

Hippocratic oath   A statement, attributed to the ancient Greek physician Hippocrates, that serves as an ethical guide for physicians and is incorporated into the graduation ceremonies at many medical schools. The duty to do no harm and the ethic of confidentiality are based in the Hippocratic oath. *See also* Aesculapius; code of ethics; code of Hammurabi; ethics.

THE HIPPOCRATIC OATH

I swear by Apollo the physician, by Aesculapius, Hygeia, and Panacea, and I take to witness all the gods, and all the goddesses, to keep according to my ability and my judgment the following Oath: To consider dear to me as my parents him who taught me this art; to live in common with him and if necessary to share my goods with him; to look upon his children as my own brothers, to teach them this art if they so desire without fee or written promise; to impart to my sons and the sons of the master who taught me and disciples who have enrolled themselves and have agreed to the rules of the profession, but to these alone, the precepts and the instruction. I will prescribe regimen for the good of my patients according to my ability and my judgment and never do harm to anyone. To please no one will I prescribe a deadly drug, nor give advice which may cause his death. Nor will I give a woman a pessary to procure abortion. But I will preserve the purity of my life and my art. I will not cut for stone, even for patients in whom the disease is manifest; I will leave this operation to be performed by practitioners (specialists in this art). In every house where I come I will enter only for the good of my patients, keeping myself far from all intentional ill-doing and all seduction, and especially from the pleasures of love with women or with men, be they free or slaves. All that may come to my knowledge in the exercise of my profession or outside of my profession or in daily commerce with men, which ought not to be spread abroad, I will keep secret and will never reveal. If I keep this oath faithfully, may I enjoy my life and practice my art, respected by all men and in all times; but if I swerve from it or violate it, may the reverse be my lot.

---

histochemistry   An extension of microscopic staining techniques whereby known chemical reactions are used in order to identify particular compounds or types of compounds in the tissues and structures under examination. *See also* histology; pathology; Gram's stain.

histocompatibility   A state of mutual tolerance that allows some tissues to be grafted effectively to other tissues or blood to be transfused without rejection by a recipient. *See also* blood transfusion services; histocompatibility leukocyte antigen; transplantation.

histocompatibility leukocyte antigen (HLA) Any of various antigens on the surface of cell membranes that serve to identify a cell as self or nonself. These antigens determine whether a tissue graft or blood transfusion will be accepted or rejected by a recipient. *See also* blood transfusion services; histocompatibility; transplantation.

histogram A graphic display, using a bar graph, of the frequency distribution of a variable. Rectangles are drawn so that their bases lie on a linear scale representing different intervals, and their heights are proportional to the frequencies of the values within each of the intervals. *See also* bar graph; frequency distribution.

histology The branch of biology dealing with the microscopic identification of cells and tissue and the organization of cells into various body tissues. *See also* histochemistry; histopathology.

histopathology The branch of pathology addressing the changes in diseased tissues. *See also* histology; pathology.

histopathology laboratory A laboratory in which tissues are microscopically examined. *See also* clinical laboratory.

historical control In a research study, a group of patients treated in the past with a standard therapy and used as the control group for evaluating a new treatment or therapy on current patients. This approach is commonly used in clinical investigations but is not recommended because possible biases, due to other factors that might have changed over time, can never be satisfactorily eliminated. *See also* control group; hidden time effects.

HIV (human immunodeficiency virus) The organism isolated and recognized as the etiologic agent of AIDS. HIV is classified as a lentivirus in a subgroup of the retroviruses. It infects and destroys a class of lymphocytes, CD4+ cells, thereby causing progressive damage to the immune system. This family of retroviruses has RNA as its genetic material and makes an enzyme, reverse transcriptase, that converts viral RNA into viral DNA, then is incorporated into the host cell's DNA and is replicated along with it. There are two known types of HIV: HIV-1 is the most common in the United States; HIV-2 causes a milder immune suppression and is found primarily in West Africa. *See also* the following HIV-related terms, as well as AIDS; immunodeficiency; opportunistic infection.

HIV antibody (HIV-ab) The antibody to HIV, which usually appears within six weeks after infection. Antibody testing early in the infection process may not produce accurate results, since some recently infected people have not yet begun producing antibodies and may test negative even though they are infected. Thus, a single negative antibody test result is not a guarantee that a person is free from infection. The change from HIV-negative to HIV-positive status is called seroconversion. *See also* the surrounding HIV-related terms, as well as AIDS; immunodeficiency; opportunistic infection.

HIV counseling Information provided to an individual before and after HIV testing (pretest and posttest counseling) regarding the implications and impact of testing, HIV infection care, and prevention of HIV transmission.

HIV infection Harboring the retrovirus that produces a wide spectrum of disease manifestations, ranging from asymptomatic infection to the life-threatening conditions of AIDS, characterized by severe immunodeficiency, serious opportunistic infections, and cancers. In 1993 the Centers for Disease Control and Prevention replaced its 1986 classification system with a revised classification system for HIV infection based on the CD4+ T-lymphocyte count (or an equivalent in percentage of total lymphocytes) and clinical conditions associated with the infection. That definition is intended for use in public health practice. *See also* the surrounding HIV-related terms, as well as AIDS; herpes simplex; immunodeficiency; opportunistic infection; nucleoside analogue; partner notification.

REVISED 1993 HIV DEFINITION*

Category	Definition
CD4+ T-lymphocyte	
Category 1	≥ 500 cells/μL
Category 2	200–499 cells/μL
Category 3	≤ 200 cells/μL

Clinical	
Category A	One or more of asymptomatic HIV infection, persistent generalized lymphadenopathy, or acute (primary) HIV infection with accompanying illness or history of acute HIV infection.
Category B	Conditions not listed in the AIDS-defining Category C—these include but are not limited to bacillary angiomatosis; candidiasis (oropharyngeal [thrush] or vulvovaginal and persistent, frequent, or poorly responsive to therapy; cervical dysplasia/cervical carcinoma in situ; constitutional symptoms (fever 38.5°C or diarrhea lasting longer than one month; oral hairy leukoplakia; herpes zoster (shingles); idiopathic thrombocytopenic purpura; listeriosis; pelvic inflammatory disease; and peripheral neuropathy.
Category C	Conditions listed in the expanded AIDS surveillance case definition.

*The CDC's new system of HIV infection in adolescents or adults defines three CD4+ T-lymphocyte and three clinical categories intended for use in public health practice.

Source: Centers for Disease Control and Prevention

HIV Prevention Act of 1997 Legislation, introduced by Rep Tom Coburn, MD (R-Okla), mandating the confidential report of HIV infection to state health departments and the CDC and mandating contact tracing. *Synonym:* Coburn bill.

HIV transmission Infection of another person through the blood and body fluids of an HIV- infected individual. Infection is possible if the infected individual's blood or secretions come in contact with another person's blood (sharing needles, needle stick accidents, blood transfusions), cavity linings (vagina, rectum), or broken skin (cuts, abrasions). *See also* blood-body fluid precautions; safe sex; safer sex; perinatal transmission.

HMO (health maintenance organization) A health care organization that, in return for prospective per capita (capitation) payments, acts as both insurer and provider of comprehensive but specified medical services. Under an HMO, a defined set of physicians provides services to a voluntarily enrolled population. *See also* group model HMO; Health Maintenance Organization Act of 1973; independent practice association model HMO; network model HMO; staff model HMO.

hold harmless clause **1.** A clause often used in managed care contracts stating that if either the HMO or a participating physician is held liable for corporate malfeasance or malpractice, the other party is not. **2.** A clause in a managed care contract that prohibits a provider from billing patients if its managed care organization becomes insolvent. State and federal regulations may require this language.

hold the gains The monitoring and maintenance phase in many quality improvement project models, particularly those based on the Juran Institute's model. *See also* quality improvement.

holism The belief that the body is a network of systems (physical, mental, and emotional) that are all interconnected and that influence each other. Thus, to maintain optimum health, all systems must be addressed and treated in both preventive and curative measures. *See also* alternative medicine; health; mind/body medicine; osteopathy, preventive medicine.

holistic medicine A doctrine of preventive and therapeutic medicine that emphasizes the importance of regarding a patient as a whole person, giving equal attention to physical, intellectual, and emotional needs, and taking into consideration his or her social, cultural, and environmental context rather than treating him or her as merely a physical body with an isolated malfunction of a particular system or organ. *See also* alternative medicine; kinesiology; New Age movement; osteopathy, preventive medicine.

Holter monitoring device *See* ambulatory electrocardiography.

homebound person Any individual who is unable to leave home without exceptional effort and support. Patients in this condition are provided with or are eligible for home care services, including medical treatment and personal care. Persons are considered homebound even if they may be infrequently and briefly absent from home if these absences do not indicate an ability to receive health care in a professional's office or health care facility. *See also* home health services; homemaker services; home management services.

home care Any care or services provided in a patient's place of residence. This includes care and services such as home health, home medical equipment services, and infusion therapy services.

Home Care Accreditation Program The survey and accreditation program of the Joint Commission for eligible home care organizations.

home care record The centralized location for documenting data and information about the patient as well as the care and services provided to a patient by an organization. *See also* medical record.

home equipment management services Services to meet a patient's needs in his or her place of residence, and the education of patients in using such equipment. These services include the selection, delivery, setup, and maintenance of equipment. *See also* home health services; home infusion services; home medical equipment.

home for the aged A residential care facility that provides health-related, personal, social, and recreational services to elderly persons. *See also* nursing home; residential care facility.

home health agency (HHA) A public or private organization that provides home health care. A designation of Medicare certification in which an agency must provide skilled nursing services and at least one additional therapeutic service (physical therapy, speech therapy, occupational therapy, medical social services, or home health aide services) in the home, under a plan established and periodically reviewed by a physician. *See also* home health services; visiting nurse association.

home health services Services provided by health care professionals in a patient's place of residence on a per-visit or per-hour basis to patients who have, or are at risk of, an injury, an illness, or a disabling condition or who are terminally ill and require short- or long-term intervention by health professionals. These services may include dental, medical, nursing, occupational therapy, pediatric, physical therapy, speech-language pathology, audiology, social work, and nutrition counseling services. *See also* homebound person; home equipment management services; home infusion services; home management services; home pharmaceutical services; hospital-based home care program; intermittent care; maintenance home health care; nursing care; personal care services.

home infusion services Home health services, home pharmaceutical services, and home equipment management services directly related to the administration of drug therapy by continuous or intermittent infusion to patients or clients in their place of residence. *See also* home equipment management services; home health services; home pharmaceutical services.

Homemade Cereal Based Oral Rehydration Theory PORT *See* Patient Outcomes Research Team.

homemaker services   Nonmedical support services given as a part of care and services to homebound individuals who are unable to perform various tasks. These services are provided by a *homemaker,* an aide who performs mainly housekeeping duties, shops for groceries and household supplies, plans and makes meals, changes bed linens, and does laundry. Homemaker services are intended to preserve independent living and normal family life for the aged, disabled, sick, or convalescent. *See also* homebound person.

home management services   Chore services, such as routine housekeeping tasks, minor household repairs, shopping, lawn care, and snow shoveling; homemaking services, which provide for and teach child care, personal care, and home management to individuals and families; housing services, which help individuals get, keep, and improve housing and modify existing housing; and money management services, which help set up workable budgets and deal with debts. *See also* homebound person; home health services.

home medical equipment   Items necessary to facilitate independence and improve the patient's ability to function outside the hospital environment, for example, mobility aids (eg, canes, walkers and wheelchairs); beds and patient lifts; respiratory equipment, supplies and services; apnea monitors; continuous passive motion (CPM); orthotic and prosthetic devices; disposable supplies; and safety devices, such as bath/tub rails, elevated commode seats, and bath transfer equipment. *See also* durable medical equipment; medical equipment.

Homeopathic Pharmacopeia of the United States   One of three official compendia of drugs and medications in the United States recognized in the federal Food, Drug, and Cosmetic Act. The other two are the *United States Pharmacopeia* and the *National Formulary.*

homeopathy   A system of medicine founded by Samuel Hahnemann (1755–1843) based on the law of similars (like cures like); that is, remedies made from plants, animals, and minerals, when administered in minute doses, could cure the same symptoms they would normally cause in massive doses. *See also* allopathy; naprapathy; naturopathy; osteopathy.

home pharmaceutical services   Services that procure, prepare, preserve, compound, dispense, or distribute pharmaceutical products to meet a patient's needs in his or her place of residence, and that monitor a patient's clinical status while in his or her place of residence. *See also* home health services; home infusion services.

home plan   In Blue Cross and Blue Shield reciprocity programs, the particular Blue Cross organization that provides a subscriber's coverage. *See also* Blue Cross and Blue Shield plan; host plan; reciprocity.

home uterine activity monitoring (HUAM)   Use of external tocodynamometers in the home setting to measure increased uterine contractile activity that may be associated with preterm labor. These devices provide estimates of the frequency and duration of contractions as well as some indication of intensity. The clinical utility of HUAM is controversial, and there is evidence of wide variation in interpretation of the devices. A Health Technology Review from AHCPR's Office of Technology Assessment in 1992 and the U.S. Preventive Services Task Force in 1996 reported that good evidence could not be found to recommend its widespread use. *See also* fetal distress; fetal monitor; monitor.

horizontal integration   1. The formation of entities that include multiple groupings of similar care components along the continuum of care for purposes of mutual financial benefit.   **2.** Within a health care organization, coordination of activities across operating units that are all involved in the same stage of care, for example, acute care. *See also* integration; vertical integration.

hormone replacement therapy (HRT)   The administration of estrogen, or estrogen combined with progestin, to women to alleviate the symptoms produced by waning ovarian hormones during menopause (eg, hot flashes, urogenital problems), to prevent or delay osteoporosis, or to prevent cardiovascular disease. Guidelines call for counseling of all perimenopausal women to help them weigh the benefits (proven efficacy against osteoporosis and coronary heart disease) and risks (which include an increased lifetime probability of developing endometrial cancer or breast cancer) along with individual history and preference to make a decision. *See also* estrogen replacement therapy; menopause; osteoporosis; progestin.

Hoshin planning   A planning and management technique with seven specific tools designed to help an organization target one or two breakthrough goals, rather than trying to accomplish too many things at once. *Hoshin* is a Japanese word meaning "focus like the arrow on a compass." *See also* kaizen.

hospice   1. A concept, originated in England, of caring for the terminally ill and their families in a manner that enables the patient to live as fully as possible, makes the entire family the unit of care, and centers the caring process in the home whenever appropriate. Inpatient facilities are available for patients unable to be cared for at home. The hospice team includes nurses, social workers, chaplains, and volunteers, as well as physicians.   **2.** For purposes of Joint Commission accreditation, an organized program that consists of services provided and coordinated by an interdisciplinary team at a frequency appropriate to meet the needs of patients who are diagnosed with terminal illnesses and have limited life spans. The hospice specializes in palliative management of pain and other physical symptoms, meeting the psychosocial and spiritual needs of the patient and the patient's family or other primary care person(s). The program also includes a continuum of interdisciplinary team services across all settings where hospice care is provided, the availability of 24-hour access to care, utilization of volunteers, and bereavement care to the survivors, as needed, for an appropriate period of time. *See also* bereavement counseling; palliative care.

hospice benefit   A Medicare benefit that pays for hospice care for beneficiaries with a life expectancy of six months or less. Hospices authorized under Medicare must provide nursing care, social services, physician care, and counseling services.

hospice inpatient care   Hospice services provided in freestanding facilities or in dedicated units or contracted beds within other health care facilities. A facility, unit, or area providing hospice care is designed to create a home-like atmosphere conducive to achieving patients' care goals. *See also* facility-based hospice.

hospital   A health care organization that has a governing body, an organized medical staff and professional staff, and inpatient facilities and provides medical, nursing, and related services for ill and injured patients 24 hours per day, 7 days per week. For licensing purposes, each state has its own definition of hospital. *See also* Hill-Burton Act; medical staff.

Hospital Accreditation Program (HAP)   The survey and accreditation program of the Joint Commission for eligible hospitals.

hospital acquired infection   *See* nosocomial infection.

hospital affiliation   A contractual agreement between a health plan and one or more hospitals whereby the hospital provides the inpatient benefits offered by the health plan. *See also* health plan.

hospital-based ambulatory care center   An organized hospital facility providing nonemergency medical or dental services to patients who are not assigned to a bed as inpatients during the time services are rendered. An emergency department in which services are provided to nonemergency patients does not constitute an organized ambulatory care center. *See also* freestanding ambulatory care center.

hospital-based home care program   A home care program sponsored by a hospital. *See also* home health services.

hospital-based skilled nursing facility (HBSNF)   A skilled nursing facility eligible for skilled nursing facility benefits under third-party payer contracts. *See also* skilled nursing facility.

hospital bed   In census activities, an accommodation including lodging, food, and routine medical and nursing services provided in a hospital.

hospital chain   *See* multihospital system.

hospital component   In Medicare, the hospital-specific target rate per discharge, reflecting the hospital's average base-year experience in treating patients under the cost-based reimbursement methodology used prior to prospective pricing.

hospital discharge abstract system   A system for abstracting a minimum data set from hospital medical records for the purpose of producing summary statistics about hospitalized patients, for example, the hospital inpatient enquiry (HIPE) and professional activity study (PAS). The statistical tabulations commonly include length of stay by final diagnosis, surgical operations, and specified hospital services, and also give outcomes, such as "death" and "discharged alive from hospital." *See also* discharge abstract.

Hospital Discharge Survey (HDS)   Since 1965 an annual national survey conducted by the National Center for Health Statistics, monitoring admissions and discharges of patients to and from a sample of short-stay general and specialty hospitals. Data are collected on, for example, diagnoses, procedures, and lengths of stay.

hospital hospitality house   A temporary residential facility for patients and their families.

hospital indemnity   A form of insurance that provides a stated weekly or monthly payment while the insured is hospitalized regardless of expenses incurred or other insurance. *See also* indemnity.

hospital infection   *See* nosocomial infection.

hospital information system (HIS)   An integrated, computer-assisted system designed to store, manipulate, and retrieve information dealing with administrative and clinical aspects of providing health services within the hospital. *See also* clinical information system; information system; management information system.

Hospital Insurance Program   *See* Medicare, Part A.

hospitalism   The effects of lengthy or repeated hospitalization or institutionalization on patients, especially infants and children (in whom the condition may be characterized by social regression, personality disorders, and stunted growth) and the elderly (in whom the condition may be characterized by disorientation).

hospital-physician independent contractor relationship   As applied to a hospital-physician contract, the relationship in which a hospital is presumed to control only the result to be accomplished by a physician under contract, not the methods by which a physician exercises professional judgment in fulfillment of contractual obligations. *See also* independent contractor.

Hospital Survey and Construction Act   *See* Hill-Burton Act.

host plan   A Blue Cross reciprocity program in which one Blue Cross plan pays the claims of an individual who is a subscriber to a different Blue Cross plan. *See also* Blue Cross and Blue Shield plan; control plan; home plan; reciprocity.

housestaff   Individuals, licensed as appropriate, who are graduates of medical, dental, osteopathic, or podiatric schools; who are appointed to a health care organization professional graduate training program that is approved by a nationally recognized accrediting body approved by the U.S. Department of Education; and who participate in patient care under the direction of licensed independent practitioners of the pertinent clinical disciplines who have clinical privileges in the organization and are members of, or are affiliated with, the medical staff. *Synonyms:* house officer; housestaff. *See also* medical staff; teaching hospital.

human body shop   Colloquial and derogatory term for the activities and policies of biotechnology and genetic engineering, particularly in connection with debate over the Human Genome Project. *See also* gene therapy; genetic engineering; Human Genome Project; recombinant DNA technology.

human capital model   A model for evaluating the economic implications of a disease in terms of the economic loss of a person succumbing to morbidity or morality at a specified age. This model usually has two components: (1) the direct cost of disease, such as the cost of treatment; and (2) the indirect cost of disease, meaning the loss of economic productivity from the loss of a member of the workforce.

human genetics   The science of biological variation in humans. *See also* clinical genetics; genetics; medical genetics.

Human Genome Project (HGP)   An international research program, begun in the 1980s initially under the Department of Energy and the National Institutes of Health (NIH), which was designed to construct detailed genetic and physical maps of the human genome, to determine the complete nucleotide sequence of human DNA, to localize the estimated 50,000 to 100,000 genes within the human genome, and to perform similar analyses on the genomes of several other organisms used extensively in research laboratories as model systems. In 1989 the National Human Genome Research Institute (NHGRI) was established to spearhead NIH's role in the project. The scientific products of the HGP will comprise a resource of genomic maps and DNA sequence information that will provide detailed information about the structure, organization and characteristics of human DNA, information that constitutes the basic set of inherited "instructions" for the development and functioning of a human being. Significantly improved technology for biomedical research is an important product of the HGP, which has momentous implications for both individuals and society and poses a number of consequential choices for public and professional deliberation. Analysis of the ethical, legal, and social implications of the availability of genetic information about individuals, and the development of policy options for public consideration, are therefore yet other major components of the human genome research effort. For this work the Ethical, Legal, and Social Implications (ELSI) Branch has been set up. It in turn has established a National Study Group to help ensure responsible use of the genetic information and provide guidance to providers, health care administrators, institutional review boards, and other groups. *See also* cancer susceptibility testing; gene therapy; genetic counseling; genetic engineering; genetic screening; genetic testing; health care technology assessment; human body

shop; institutional review board; recombinant DNA technology.

human immunodeficiency virus   *See* HIV.

human papillomavirus (HPV)   A group of viruses, including several types that cause genital warts and sexually transmitted disease and several other types strongly implicated in the development of cervical cancer. Use of HPV DNA testing to guide therapy for women with atypical, borderline, or cancerous lesions was regarded as an investigational technology in evaluation by the American Medical Association Diagnostic and Therapeutic Technology Assessment panel (1993). *See also* sexually transmitted disease.

human resources management   The field of managing people in work organizations.

human subject research   The use of individuals in the systematic study, observation, or evaluation of factors in preventing, assessing, treating, and understanding an illness. The term applies to all behavioral and medical experimental research that involves human beings as experimental subjects.

human T lymphotropic virus, type III (HTLV III)   The former name for the human immunodeficiency virus (HIV). *See* HIV.

humoralism   The ancient theory that health and illness result from a balance or imbalance of bodily liquids called humors (phlegm, blood, black bile or gall, yellow bile or choler). *Synonyms:* humoral theory; humorism.

hydrotherapy   The use of water to treat disorders. Hydrotherapy is mostly limited to exercises in special pools for rehabilitation of paralyzed patients. *See also* physical therapy.

hygiene   **1.** The science dealing with the promotion and preservation of health.   **2.** Conditions and practices that serve to promote or preserve health, as in personal hygiene. *Synonym:* cleanliness. *See also* oral hygiene.

hyperbaric oxygen therapy   The treatment of disease in an environment of atmospheric pressure with higher than normal oxygen applied either to the whole patient inside a pressurized chamber or to a localized area (such as an arm or leg) inside a smaller chamber. It is used to treat carbon monoxide poisoning, decompression sickness, gangrene, and other disorders and to hasten wound healing. It has also been offered by some alternative health care providers as a form of oxidative therapy. *Synonym:* baromedicine.

hypercholesterolemia   A metabolic condition, usually inherited, which is characterized by excessive amounts of cholesterol in the blood. High levels of cholesterol and other lipids may lead to the development of atherosclerosis (fatty deposits on the arteries' inner walls). *See also* atherosclerosis; cholesterol; lipoprotein.

hyperglycemia   *See* diabetes mellitus.

hypergeometric distribution *See* probability distribution.

hypertension Elevated blood pressure persistently 140 mm Hg or greater systolic and 90 mm Hg or greater diastolic. The National High Blood Pressure Education Program of the National Heart, Lung, and Blood Institute in its 1993 report (JNC-V) established a new classification of adult blood pressure on the basis of impact on risk. Hypertension should not be diagnosed on the basis of a single measurement. *See also* automated ambulatory blood pressure monitoring devices; hypertensive crises; JNC-V; self-measured blood pressure monitoring device; white coat hypertension.

hypertensive crises Especially risky levels of high blood pressure calling for special handling of patients. *Hypertensive emergencies* require immediate blood pressure reduction (not necessarily to normal ranges) to prevent or limit target-organ disease (eg, hypertensive encephalopathy, intracranial hemorrhage, acute left ventricular failure with pulmonary edema, dissecting aortic aneurysm, eclampsia or severe hypertension associated with pregnancy, unstable angina pectoris, acute myocardial infarction). *Hypertensive urgencies* are situations in which it is desirable to reduce blood pressure within 24 hours (eg, accelerated or malignant hypertension without severe symptoms or progressive target-organ complications, severe perioperative hypertension). *See also* hypertension.

CLASSIFICATION OF ADULT BLOOD PRESSURE

Classification	Blood Pressure
Normal	< 130/< 85
High normal	130–139/85–89
Hypertension	
Stage 1 (mild)	140–159/90–99
Stage 2 (moderate)	160–179/100–109
Stage 3 (severe)	180–209/110–119
Stage 4 (very severe)	≥ 210/≥ 120

Source: National High Blood Pressure Program of the National Institute of Health's National Heart, Lung, and Blood Institute: The Fifth Report of the Joint National Committee on Detection, Evaluation, and Treatment of High Blood Pressure (JNC-V), 1993.

hyperthermia Controversial treatment for AIDS, approved for expanded clinical trial in 1996, which involves draining the patient's blood, heating it to 114° F, and steaming it back in, while keeping the blood circulating during the process. The procedure causes the overall body temperature to rise to around 108°F, which early trials demonstrated could be done safely without incurring brain damage or other harm. The new trial will test the theory that using the heat to kill some of the HIV will give an exhausted immune system the chance to fight back. *Synonym:* blood scalding. *See also* AIDS.

hypnotherapy Therapy based on or using hypnosis—a state of increased receptivity to suggestion and direction, initially induced by the influence of another person. Hypnotherapy is used in psychotherapy and in medicine to induce relaxation and relieve anxiety and chronic pain. One subtype of hypnotherapy, sometimes called *self-hypnosis,* uses relaxation/mental imagery (RMI) techniques. A recent innovative use of RMI is teaching asthma self-management, including breathing exercises and symptom recognition, to young children. *See also* alternative medicine; biofeedback; mind/body medicine; psychotherapy.

hypomania *See* bipolar disorder.

hypothesis **1.** A supposition or conjecture, arrived at from observation or reflection, that leads to predictions that can be proved or refuted. **2.** Any conjectured case in a form that will allow it to be tested and proved or refuted. *See also* alternative hypothesis; goodness-of-fit test; hypothesis testing; null hypothesis.

hypothesis testing A statistical procedure that involves stating something to be tested, collecting evidence, and then making a decision as to whether the statement should be accepted as true or rejected. *See also* hypothesis.

hysterectomy The surgical removal of the uterus, performed either through the abdominal wall (abdominal hysterectomy) or through the vagina (vaginal hysterectomy). Types of hysterectomy, referring to the scope of the surgery, are *partial hysterectomy* in which the cervix is left in place (synonyms: subtotal hysterectomy; supracervical hysterectomy; supravaginal hysterectomy); *radical hysterectomy,* in which the lymph nodes are removed along with a wide lateral excision of parametrial and paravaginal supporting structures; and *total hysterectomy,* in which the uterus and cervix are completely removed. Wide variations in rates of use of this procedure within the United States and in comparison with other countries have prompted several studies, which show several contributing factors including physician attributes, patient preferences, and uncertainty in knowledge about appropriate indications for use of the procedure. These studies have targeted hysterectomies as an area needing practice guidelines.

iamatology   The study or science of remedies.

iatrogenic   **1.** Resulting from the professional activities of physicians, or, more broadly, from the activities of health professionals. Originally applied to disorders induced in the patient by autosuggestion based on a physician's examination, manner, or discussion, the term is currently applied to any undesirable condition in a patient occurring as the result of treatment by a physician (or other health professional), especially to infections acquired by the patient during the course of treatment. **2.** Pertaining to an illness or injury resulting from a procedure, therapy, or other element of care. *See also* cascade iatrogenesis; nosocomial infection.

iatrology   Rarely used term for the science of medicine. *See* medicine.

ICD-9-CM (*International Classification of Diseases, Ninth Revision, Clinical Modification***)**   The two-part classification system still in widespread use for coding patient medical information used in abstracting systems and for classifying patients into DRGs for Medicare and other third-party payers. The first part is a comprehensive list of diseases with corresponding codes compatible with the World Health Organization's list of disease codes. The second part contains procedure codes independent of the disease codes. *See also* coding; DRG; ICD-10; *International Classification of Health Problems in Primary Care.*

ICD-10 (*International Statistical Classification of Diseases and Related Health Problems***)**   The tenth revision of the International Classification of Diseases to be published in 1998 by the World Health Organization (the psychiatric section is currently available). The ICD-10 lists more than 10,000 medical and surgical diagnoses and conditions with corresponding codes to be used in coding patient medical information. Substantial changes have been made from the ninth revision: (1) use of alphanumeric, rather than numeric, codes; (2) inclusion of categories of additional factors, such as loss of a loved one, that can influence health; (3) changes in the details of the categories throughout the classification; (4) changes in chapters and chapter headings; and (5) insertion of previous supplementary classifications as chapters within the classifications. Although the title has changed from that of the ninth revision (ICD-9-CM), the shortened title ICD-10 is used. *See also* coding; DRG; ICD-9.

imaging   Use of technologies to produce pictures or images of body structures and functions, especially in radiologic and ultrasound images. *See also* computed axial tomography; echocardiography; interventional imaging; low osmolality contrast medium; magnetic resonance imaging; myocardial perfusion imaging; radiography; ultrasonography.

immediate cause   The last of a series or chain of causes tending to a given result and, without the intervention of any further cause, subsequently producing the result or event. It is not necessarily the direct or proximate cause. *See also* direct cause; proximate cause; root cause; root cause analysis.

immunity   **1.** The condition of being protected against infectious disease conferred either by the immune response generated by immunization or previous infection or by other nonimmunologic factors. *See also* immunogenetics; isolation bed.   **2.** In law, exemption from normal legal prosecution; for example, an organization and its medical staff are granted immunity from civil damage actions related to performing formal peer review if certain minimum due process rights are afforded the physician being reviewed as part of a disciplinary hearing process. *See also* charitable immunity; Good Samaritan laws.

immunization schedules   A list of vaccinations with indications and contraindications, dose or route of administration, and timetable (age or intervals). Such a list is issued by national groups, chiefly the Advisory Committee on Immunization Practices (ACIP) of the Centers for Disease Control and Prevention, the American Academy of Pediatrics, the American College of Physicians, the American Academy of Family Physicians, and the U.S. Preventive Services Task Force. These authorities do not agree on all particulars. For childhood immunizations, the ACIP has added to the traditional "baby shots" (diphtheria-tetanus-pertussin; polio; measles-mumps-rubella) Hemophilus influenza type b and hepatitis B virus. Immunization schedules for adults usually include vaccines for missed childhood immunization or disease for which incidence of immunity may be lacking (tetanus-diphtheria, measles, mumps, rubella, inactivated polio), hepatitis B, and (for adults age 65 and older) influenza and pneumococcal polysaccharide. Adaptations are suggested for special patient groups such as pregnant women, immunocompromised persons, and other persons at high risk, and for special circumstances such as exposure during travel or in the workplace. *See also* National Childhood Vaccine Injury Act of 1986 and National Vaccine Injury Compensation Program; OBRA '93; Vaccines for Children program.

immunoassay   Any of several methods for the quantitative determination of chemical substances that use the highly specific binding between an antigen or hapten and homologous antibodies, including radioimmunoassay, enzyme immunoassay, and fluoroimmunoassay. An *enzyme immunoassay* is any of several immunoassay methods that use an enzyme covalently linked to an antigen or antibody as a label, the two most common being ELISA (enzyme-linked immunosorbent assay) and EMIT (enzyme multiplied immunoassay technique).

immunocompromised   Unable to develop a normal immune response, as in the case of persons with AIDS. *See also* AIDS; HIV infection; opportunistic infection.

immunodeficiency Absence or depression of the immune response as a result of increased susceptibility to infection. The deficiency may be primary, with a defect involving T cells, B cells, or lymphoid tissues, or it may be secondary, stemming from an underlying disease or factor that depresses or blocks the immune response. The most common forms are caused by viral infection (such as AIDS) or are iatrogenic in origin. *See also* AIDS; HIV and related terms; opportunistic infection.

immunogenetics **1.** The study of genetic control of immunity. *See also* immunity. **2.** The branch of immunology dealing with the molecular and genetic bases of the immune response. *See also* immunology.

immunoglobulin (Ig) Any of the structurally related glycoproteins that function as antibodies, divided into five classes on the basis of structure and biologic activity: IgA, IgD, IgE, IgG, and IgM. IgE has the unique function of mediating immediate hypersensitivity reactions. *See also* antibodies; immunology.

immunology The branch of biomedical science dealing with the response of an organism to antigenic challenge, the recognition of self and nonself, and all the biological (in vivo), serological (in vitro), and physical chemical aspects of immune phenomena. *See also* antibodies; immunogenetics; immunoglobulin; immunopathology.

immunopathology The branch of medical science and subspecialty of pathology dealing with the causes, diagnoses, and prognoses of disease by applying immunological principles to the analyses of tissues, cells, and body fluids. *See also* immunology; pathology.

immunosuppressive Drugs such as corticosteroids, biological agents, or procedures such as irradiation, which depress all or part of the immune system.

immunotherapy The treatment of disease by administering the patient an antibody raised in another individual or another species (*passive immunotherapy*) or by immunizing the patient with antigens appropriate to the disease (*active immunotherapy*). *See also* antibodies.

impaired health care provider A health care provider, such as a physician or nurse, who is unable to provide services with reasonable skill and safety to patients because of physical or mental illness, including alcoholism or substance dependence. *See also* drug abuse; employee assistance program; health care provider; impairment; physician impairment.

impairment Any loss or abnormality of psychological, physiological, or anatomical structure or function, according to the *International Classification of Impairments, Disabilities, and Handicaps* first published in 1980 by the World Health Organization. *See also* disability; handicap; *International Classification of Impairments, Disabilities, and Handicaps*; physician impairment.

implant dentistry The field of dentistry dealing with surgically inserting dental transplants and designing and inserting prosthodontic devices to replace missing teeth. *Synonym:* dental implantology; implant prosthodontics. *See also* dentistry; prosthodontics.

implementation The process of putting policies, procedures, goals, objectives, and tasks into action. This is the step in quality and performance improvement when actions based on design, measurement, and assessment are put into effect and the process begins again.

implementation techniques The full battery of planned activities and strategies to get individuals, groups, or organizations to adopt and maintain a policy, guideline, action, or behavior change. *See also* academic detailing; continuing medical education; feedback; opinion leader; reminder system.

MENU OF GUIDELINE IMPLEMENTATION TECHNIQUES

Concurrent feedback
Retrospective feedback
Academic detailing
Opinion leaders
Case management
Disease management clinic
Incentives, removal of disincentives
Information technology (reminders and warnings)

Source: Weingarten S: Measuring and improving physicians' compliance with practice guidelines: Check out implementability first. *Joint Commission Journal on Quality Improvement* 22:560-63, 1996.

---

implicit criteria Criteria that are subjective and not specified in advance of a medical review process. *See also* explicit approach; implicit review.

implicit review Review of processes or outcomes of care using subjective or implied criteria. *See also* explicit review; implicit criteria.

implied consent The apparent acceptance of a proposed course of action or promise of outcome; for example, in life-threatening situations, a physician may undertake life-saving treatment without the patient's expressed consent when he or she is unable to provide consent. Most states have a statute implying the consent of individuals who drive upon their highways to submit to some type of scientific test or tests measuring the alcoholic content of the driver's blood. Implied consent is based on the principle of beneficence, which prescribes that a person in serious need must be helped by one who can do so without harm or great inconvenience. *See also* informed consent.

important aspects of care Care activities or processes that (1) occur frequently or affect large numbers of patients; (2) place patients at risk of serious consequences if not provided correctly; or (3) tend to produce problems for patients or staff. Such activities or processes are important for purposes of continuous measurement and improvement.

important function For purposes of Joint Commission accreditation, an organization function believed, on the basis of evidence or expert consensus, to increase the probability of achieving desired patient outcomes, such as patient assessment or nutritional care.

imprinting   Rapid learning of species-specific behavioral patterns that occurs with exposure to the proper stimulus at a sensitive period in early life.

improvement   *See* continuous quality improvement; FADE process; FOCUS-PDCA; performance improvement; plan-do-check-act cycle; plan for improvement; process improvement; quality improvement; quality trilogy.

IMSystem™ (Indicator Measurement System™)
A performance measurement system developed by the Joint Commission in conjunction with accredited health care organizations. It is designed to (1) continuously collect objective performance data that are derived from the application of aggregate data indicators by health care organizations; (2) aggregate, risk-adjust as necessary, and analyze the performance data on a national level; (3) provide comparative data to participating organizations for use in their internal performance-improvement efforts; (4) identify patterns that may call for more focused attention by the Joint Commission at the organization level; and (5) provide a national performance database that can serve as a resource for health services research. Formerly (1992) referred to as the Indicator Monitoring System. *See also* expert task force for indicator development; performance assessment; performance database; performance measurement.

incentive   An expectation of a reward or the fear of punishment that induces action or motivates effort. For example, the requirement that a patient pay the first dollars for a health service (a deductible) is a *negative incentive* (also called *disincentive*). A monetary reward to a health care organization or practitioner for decreasing hospital and practitioner costs is a *positive incentive*. *See also* implementation techniques; incentive benefit plan; incentive pay plan.

incentive benefit plan   A health plan that rewards beneficiaries for lowering their consumption of health services. *See also* health plan; incentive.

incentive pay plan   A compensation program whereby wages increase as productivity increases above a set standard or base. *See also* incentive.

inception cohort   A group of persons, assembled at a common time early in the development of a specific clinical disorder (eg, at the time of first exposure to a reputed cause of a disorder, at the time of initial diagnosis), who are followed thereafter in a study. *See also* cohort.

incidence   In epidemiology, the frequency of new occurrences of a condition or disease within a defined time interval, as in the number of times a disease occurs during a year. *Synonym:* occurrence. *See also* incidence rate.

incidence rate   The number of new events or cases of a specified disease or condition divided by the number of people in a population at risk for the disease or condition

during a specified period time, usually one year. *See also* incidence; prevalence rate; morbidity rate.

incident   An event or an occurrence that is usually unexpected and undesirable. An incident in a health care organization, for example, is generally an event resulting in injury or the immediate threat of injury to a patient or other persons and for which the organization may be liable. When an incident is unexpected and occurs because of chance, it is often called an accident rather than an incident. *See also* adverse patient occurrence; incident report; incident reporting.

incident report   The documentation for any unusual problem, incident, or other situation that is likely to lead to undesirable effects or that varies from established policies and procedures or practices. *Synonym:* occurrence report. *See also* incident; incident reporting.

incident reporting   A system in many health care organizations for collecting and reporting adverse patient occurrences (APOs), such as medication errors and equipment failures. It is based on individual incident reports. For several reasons, including fear of punitive action, reluctance of nonphysicians to report incidents involving physicians, lack of understanding of what a reportable incident is, and lack of time for paperwork, the effectiveness of incident reporting is limited. *See also* adverse patient occurrence; occurrence reporting; occurrence screening; risk management.

incompetent   **1.** Pertaining to a person who is legally incapable of understanding the nature and consequence of his or her actions and incapable of making a rational decision, for example, the mentally ill and minors. *See also* commitment; minor; *non compos mentis*; substituted judgment doctrine; surrogate decision maker; ward. **2.** Lack of the capacity to understand the nature of, or assess adequately, or to manage effectively a specified transaction or situation that the ordinary person could reasonably be expected to handle. As used in the law, the term refers primarily to cognitive defects that interfere with judgment.

incremental benefit   The value contributed uniquely by a single diagnostic or therapeutic procedure or other modality after taking into account all the options used to manage a patient. For instance, considered alone, high-power imaging technology may provide copious information about a patient, but after a good history and physical examination with common laboratory tests it may not provide additional information relevant to the patient's problem. The concept is often used to compare complex management strategies, such as coronary artery bypass graft surgery versus medical treatment for patients with one-, two-, or three-vessel disease. *Synonyms:* comparative benefit; incremental value.

incremental cost   *See* marginal cost.

incubation period   The time period between exposure to a disease-causing organism, such as chicken pox, and the appearance of the symptoms and signs of the disease.

incubator bed   An administrative term for a bed regularly maintained for premature and other infants who require special environmental conditions. *See also* neonatal intensive care unit.

indemnity   **1.** Reimbursement.   **2.** A contractual or equitable right under which the entire loss is shifted from a person who is only technically or passively at fault to another who is primarily or actively responsible.   **3.** A benefit payable under an insurance policy.   **4.** Compensation given to make a person whole from a loss already sustained. *See also* hospital indemnity; indemnity plan; managed indemnity plan.

indemnity plan   A health benefit plan that provides for reimbursement of some portion of incurred medical expenses. Employees are usually responsible for submitting claims and may seek care from any health care provider, who bills for eligible expenses on a fee-for-service basis. Payments may be made to the individual submitting the claim or directly to the provider. *Synonyms*: indemnity benefits; indemnity insurance. *See also* indemnity; managed indemnity plan.

independent contractor   An individual who is self-employed and who contracts to perform a piece of work according to his or her own methods. An independent contractor is subject to his or her employer's control only as to the end product or final result of his or her work. *See also* contract; contracted services; hospital-physician independent contractor relationship.

independent practice association (IPA)   A partnership, corporation, association, or other legal entity that enters into an arrangement for the provision of services with persons who are licensed to practice medicine, osteopathic medicine, and dentistry, and with other care personnel. IPAs are one source of professional services for HMOs and are modeled after medical foundations. IPAs may also be the primary management and financial bases for some HMOs. *Synonyms*: independent physician association; individual practice association. *See also* individual practice association

independent practice association model HMO   An HMO that contracts directly with physicians in independent practices, with one or more associations of physicians in independent practices, or with one or more multispecialty group practices. The plan is predominantly organized around solo/single specialty practices. *See also* HMO; independent practice association.

independent practitioner   *See* licensed independent practitioner.

independent variable   The characteristic being observed or measured that is thought to influence an event or manifestation (the dependent variable) within the defined area of the relationships under study. The independent variable is not influenced by the event or manifestation but may cause it or contribute to its variation. In statistics, an independent variable is one of several variables that appear as arguments in a regression equation. *See also* dependent variable; factor; regression; regression analysis; variable.

index   A nonweighted type of composite measure that sums individual scores on several items and divides this sum by the number of items scored (eg, the SF-36 provides an index of health status for a group of patients putting that condition into context). Indexes are often used to make adjustments in rates, such as wage rates and pension benefits, set by long-term contracts. *See also* American Urological Association Symptom Index; ASA-SCORE index; case-mix index; Charlson Index; Duke Activity Status Index; medical consumer price index; performance index; risk-adjusted mortality index; severity measurement system; therapeutic index.

index case   The first case, or model case, of a disease, as contrasted with subsequent cases.

Index Medicus   A monthly subject-author print catalog of the world's biomedical journal literature, a component of the National Library of Medicine's MEDLARS® appearing online as MEDLINE. As of October 1995 the publication indexed 3,147 journals. *See also* MEDLARS; MEDLINE.

indicated   A course of action that is warranted, given a certain set of circumstances; for example, an electrocardiogram is indicated for an adult patient complaining of crushing substernal chest pain. *See also* indication.

indication   A guideline, recommendation, or rule that specifies when certain courses of action are necessary, expedient, advisable, or otherwise appropriate for a specific disease or condition and a specific patient type. Some specialty societies, such as the American College of Cardiology, have a regular classification system for indications which they apply in their guidelines on the use of given procedures and technologies. *See also* appropriateness criteria; clinical practice guideline; evidence-based medicine; explicit approach; indicated.

AMERICAN COLLEGE OF CARDIOLOGY/AMERICAN HEART ASSOCIATION CLASSIFICATION OF INDICATIONS

Class I: Conditions for which there is evidence and/or general agreement that a given procedure or treatment is useful and effective

Class II: Conditions for which there is conflicting evidence and/or a divergence of opinion about the usefulness/efficacy of a procedure or treatment
  IIa: Weight of evidence /Opinion is in favor of usefulness/ efficacy
  IIb: Usefulness/efficacy is less well established by evidence/opinion

Class III: Conditions for which there is evidence and/or general agreement that the procedure/treatment is not useful/effective and in some cases may be harmful

---

indicator   **1.** A measure used to determine, over time, performance of functions, processes, and outcomes. *See also* the following indicator terms, as well as aggregate data indicator; continuous variable measure; outcomes indicator; performance indicator; process indicator; rate-based measure; reliability testing; sentinel event indicator. **2.** A statistical value that provides an indication of the condition or direction over time of performance of a defined process or achievement of a defined outcome. *See also* clinical performance indicators; data element; economic indicator.

indicator development form A form used to describe and record the development process for an individual indicator. *See also* indicator; indicator information set.

indicator information set Indicator-specific information typically composed of an indicator statement, definition of terms, indicator type, rationale, description of indicator population, indicator data collection logic, and underlying factors that may explain variations in data. *See also* the surrounding indicator terms.

Indicator Measurement System™ *See* IMSystem™.

indicator population A statement that describes an indicator's numerator and denominator; populations may be subcategorized to provide more homogeneous populations for subsequent data assessment. *See also* indicator information set.

indicator rationale A statement that explains why an indicator is useful in specifying and assessing the process or outcome of care measured by the indicator. *See also* indicator information set.

indicator reliability The degree to which an indicator accurately and consistently identifies occurrences from among all cases at risk of being indicator occurrences. *See also* data reliability; indicator validity; reliability.

indicator statement A description of the function, process, or outcome being measured; for example, "patients for whom percutaneous transluminal coronary angioplasty has succeeded." *See also* indicator information set.

indicator threshold The level, value, or point at which indicator data signal the need for more in-depth review of the process or outcome measured by the indicator. *See also* threshold.

indicator underlying factors Indicator information set component that delineates patient, practitioner, organization, and community systems' characteristics that may explain variations in performance data and thereby direct performance-improvement activities and efforts. *See also* factor; indicator information set; variation.

indicator validity The degree to which an indicator identifies events that merit further review by various individuals or groups providing, or in some way influencing, the process or outcome defined by the indicator. *See also* data validity; indicator reliability; validity.

indigent A needy or poor person or one who does not have sufficient property or income to furnish a living nor anyone able or willing to provide support. *See also* medical indigence.

indigent medical care *See* medical indigence.

indirect contact A mode of transmission of infection between an infected host organism and a susceptible host organism via fomites (contaminated articles or objects) or vectors (organisms that transmit diseases). Vectors may be mechanical (eg, flies) or biological (eg, the disease agent undergoes part of its life cycle in the vector species). *Compare* direct contact. *See also* contact; fomite; infection; vector.

indirect cost A cost that cannot be easily seen in the product or service. The costs of electricity and hazard insurance on buildings are examples of indirect costs. *See also* cost.

individual A person who receives treatment services. The term is synonymous with patient, client, resident, consumer, individual served, and recipient of treatment services.

individual health care account (IHCA) *See* medical savings account.

individual health insurance Coverage of a single life, in contrast to group health insurance, which covers many lives. Individual health insurance is usually considerably more costly than group health insurance. *See also* group insurance; health insurance; insurance.

individual insured A person (ie, employee, enrollee) who receives health care services from a provider panel. *See also* named insured.

individual practice *See* solo practice.

individual practice association *See* independent practice association.

individual practice plan A health plan offered by a medical foundation, PPO, or HMO, which obtains its professional services by agreement with a network of individual practitioners from an individual practice association. Originally synonymous with medical foundation. *See also* HMO; individual practice association; medical foundation; solo practice.

induced labor Labor brought on by mechanical or other extraneous means, usually by the intravenous infusion of oxytocin (a hormone that stimulates uterine contractions).

inductive reasoning Adjusting a course of action based on a limited amount of information gathered. It is a process in which one starts from a specific experience and draws inferences (generalizations) from it. For example, a physician, by observing a patient's reaction to a therapeutic maneuver (eg, palpating the abdomen), may induce a patient's diagnosis (appendicitis) and what should be done to meet those needs (laparotomy). *See also* inductive statistics.

inductive statistics The branch of statistics that deals with generalizations, predictions, estimations, and decisions from data initially presented. *See also* inductive reasoning; statistics.

industrial disease *See* occupational disease.

industrial engineering The use of human and material resources management techniques to manage a health care organization's resources. Industrial engineering works toward an integrated system of workers, materials, and equipment. *See also* human resources management.

industrial health services *See* occupational health services.

industry screening *See* blacklisting.

infant A child from age one month to two years. *See also* infant mortality; infant mortality death rate; neonate; term infant; Women, Infants, and Children's Program.

infant mortality Death of live-born children less than one year old. *Synonym:* infant death. *See also* infant; infant mortality rate; neonatal death rate.

infant mortality rate A measure of the annual rate of deaths of live-born children less than one year old. The denominator is the number of live births in the same year. This is a common measure of health status in a community. *See also* infant; infant mortality; neonatal death rate.

infarction The process of tissue dying as a result of diminished or stopped blood flow to the tissue, as in myocardial infarction or cerebral infarction (stroke). *See also* acute myocardial infarction.

infection *See* endemic infection; epidemic infection; nosocomial infection.

infection-control program An organizationwide program, including policies and procedures, for the surveillance, prevention, control, and reporting of infection. Examples of infection-control methods include hand washing, protective clothing, isolation procedures, and ongoing measurement of performance. *See also* isolation.

infectious diseases The branch of medicine and subspecialty of internal medicine dealing with the diagnosis and management of patients with infectious diseases. Types of infectious disease include, for example, chicken pox, cholera, rabies, rubella, smallpox, and syphilis. *See also* antibiotic; communicable disease; epidemic infection; internal medicine; notifiable disease; respiratory isolation; tropical medicine.

infectious waste *See* hazardous waste.

inference In statistics, the development of a generalization from sample data, usually with calculated degrees of uncertainty. *See also* inferential statistics; statistical inference.

inferential statistics The branch of statistics dealing with the process of drawing information from samples of observations of a population and making conclusions about the population. Sampling must be conducted to be representative of the underlying population, and procedures must be capable of drawing correct conclusions about the population. *See also* descriptive statistics; inference.

infirmary A place for care of sick or injured people, especially a small hospital or dispensary in an institution.

informal leader A leader whose power and authority over a group are derived from his or her acceptance by the group rather from his or her office, position, status, or rank in the chain of command in the formal organization. An informal leader has earned a group leadership role by the group's acceptance. *See also* leader.

informatics The whole of information technology and its applications. *See also* the following information terms, as well as medical informatics.

information Interpreted set(s) of data that can assist in decision making. *See also* data.

information management The interdisciplinary field concerning the creation, use, sharing, and disposition of data or information critical to the effective and efficient operation of organization activities. This includes the structuring of management improvement processes to produce and control the use of data and information in functional activities; information resources management; and supporting information technology, and information services. *See also* management information system.

information question The precise question that a team of people (such as a quality-improvement project team) is trying to answer by collecting and analyzing data.

information resource dictionary system (IRDS) A software tool for controlling, describing, protecting, and accessing an organization's information resources. The IRDS is usually built by combining an organization's various data dictionaries. *See also* data dictionary.

information system Equipment and procedures for collecting, recording, processing, storing, retrieving, and displaying information to make decisions. Information systems include information-processing methodologies, such as telecommunications and records management. *See also* case-mix management information system; clinical information system; executive information system; hospital information system; management information system.

informed consent In law, the principle that a physician has a duty to disclose what a reasonably prudent physician in the medical community, in the exercise of reasonable care, would disclose to his or her patients about whatever risks of injury might be incurred from a proposed course of treatment, testing, or research. A patient, exercising ordinary care for his or her own welfare, and faced with a choice of undergoing the proposed or alternate treatment, testing , or research, or none at all, may then intelligently exercise judgement by reasonably balancing the probable risks against the probable benefits.

Synonym: patient consent. *See also* autonomy; decisional capacity; genetic counseling; genetic testing; Helsinki Declaration; implied consent; informed refusal; institutional review board; multiplex genetic testing; Nuremberg Code; organ procurement; patient participation; presumed consent; right of privacy; therapeutic privilege; Tuskagee experiments.

BASIC ELEMENTS OF INFORMED CONSENT

Information on the specific test, procedure, or research being performed
Implications of a result
Possibility that the test will not be informative
Options for risk estimation without testing
Risk of passing a mutation to children
Technical accuracy
Fees involved
Risks of psychological distress
Risks of insurance or employer discrimination
Confidentiality issues
Options and limitations of follow-up medical surveillance and screening

Source: American Society of Clinical Oncology: Genetic testing for cancer susceptibility. *J Clin Oncol* 14:1730-36, 1996.

---

informed refusal   Rejection of treatment by a patient or his or her representatives after receiving full information on the treatment's benefits and risks. *See also* autonomy; death with dignity; informed consent.

infrastructure   An underlying base or foundation, especially for an organization or a system; for example, the infrastructure of a health care organization consists of the basic facilities, equipment, services, and human resources needed for the organization to function. *See also* health information infrastructure.

infusion therapy services   Services for providing therapeutic agents or nutritional products to patients by intravascular infusion to improve or sustain an individual's health condition. *See also* enteral nutrition; parenteral nutrition.

VEHICLES FOR INFUSION THERAPY

intra-arterial	Involving entry by way of an artery
intra-articular	Involving entry by way of a joint
intradermal	Involving entry within or between the layers of the skin
intramuscular	Involving entry by way of a muscle
intravascular	Involving entry by way of a blood vessel
intravenous	Involving entry by way of a vein

---

inhalation therapy   A method of administering gases or drugs in gaseous, vapor, or aerosol form by drawing them into the lungs along with inhaled air. Inhalation is used with gaseous and volatile anesthetics; volatile substances, such as amyl nitrite; and drugs in aqueous solution, which can be atomized to form a finely dispersed mist. *See also* anesthetic.

initial survey   An accreditation survey of a health care organization not previously accredited by the Joint Com-

mission, or an accreditation survey of an organization performed without reference to any prior survey findings. *See also* accreditation survey.

injury-prevention counseling   A component required in all trauma center programs by the American College of Surgeons and the American College of Emergency Physicians to address personal behaviors that contribute to the problems seen in emergency services (eg, drinking and driving, motorcycling without a helmet). *See also* prevention.

Injury Severity Score (ISS)   In trauma care, the sum of the squares of the highest Abbreviated Injury Scale (AIS) score for three body areas. The ISS has a high correlation with mortality and length of hospital stay and a low correlation with morbidity and disability prediction. Because of the mortality correlation, the ISS has become the gold standard for comparing the quality of care - between hospitals or emergency medical services systems or following quality of care in the same institution over time. The ISS has limited utility in the field and emergency departments because it is calculated retrospectively. *See also* Abbreviated Injury Scale; Revised Trauma Score; Trauma Score; trauma severity indices; TRISS; quality of care.

inlier   A patient who is included within the trim points, or expected length-of-stay boundaries, of a DRG. *See also* DRG; outlier.

in loco parentis   Latin phrase meaning in place of parents. A legal doctrine that allows a legal representative to exercise the legal rights, duties, and responsibilities a parent possesses toward a child.

in-network services   Health care services provided by a contracted network provider. Under point-of-service managed care programs, employees receive more toward expenses incurred for in-network services than for services received outside the network.

inpatient   An individual who receives health services while lodged in a health care organization at least overnight. *See also* outpatient; patient.

inpatient census   The number of inpatients in a health care organization at a given time. *See also* average daily census; adjusted daily census.

input measure   A measure of the quality of services based on structural components of an organization, such as the number and type of resources used to provide services, the number of board-certified medical specialists, or ownership of certain technologies. Input measures provide a measure of what an organization puts into a system or expends in its operation to achieve certain results, but do not provide information about an organization's actual level of performance (output, outcomes, or results) in providing the services it is capable of providing. *See also* outcome measure; process measure.

in-service   Organized education designed to enhance the skills of staff members or teach them new skills relevant to their responsibilities and disciplines. *See also* learning; on-the-job training.

in situ   Confined to site of origin, not having invaded adjoining tissues or metastasized to other parts of the body, for example, ductal cancer *in situ*.

inspection   A reactive strategy associated with quality control that attempts to identify unacceptable outcomes and separate them from acceptable outcomes. *See also* detection; prevention; quality control; quality inspection.

institutional review board (IRB)   An organizational committee, mandated in 1981 and since governed by the U.S. Department of Health and Human Services, designated to review and approve biomedical research involving humans as subjects. IRBs provide certain protections for human subjects of research and research proposals only if conditions established by federal regulations are met. Example conditions are minimized risks to which subjects are exposed; reasonable risks to subjects in relation to the anticipated benefits, if any; and the informed consent of all participants is sought and appropriately documented. *See also* bioethics; gene therapy; genetic counseling; genetic testing; Human Genome Project; informed consent; medical ethics.

institution for mental disease (IMD)   A type of health care organization primarily engaged in diagnosing, treating, and caring for persons with mental diseases.

instrument   A tool used to perform a task, such as a measurement; for example, a clinical indicator is an instrument to measure the level of performance in carrying out an important clinical process or achieving an important clinical outcome. *See also* bioinstrumentation; bougie; calibration; survey instrument.

instrumental activities of daily living (IADL) Complex activities required for independent living, such as using a telephone, managing a home or finances, cooking, or using public transportation. *See also* activities of daily living.

insulin-dependent diabetes mellitus (IDDM) Former terminology, eliminated in 1997. *See* diabetes mellitus.

insurance   The contractual relationship and benefit that exist when one party, for a consideration, agrees to reimburse another for loss to a person or thing caused by designated contingencies. The first party is the insurer; the second, the insured; the contract, the insurance policy; the consideration, the premium; the person or thing, the risk; and the contingency, the hazard or peril. Insurance is a formal social device for reducing the risk of losses for individuals by spreading the risk over groups. *See also* actuarial analysis; adequacy of coverage; catastrophic insurance; certificate of insurance; child health insurance coverage acts; coinsurance; commercial health insurance; comprehensive health insurance; comprehensive major medical insurance; conditions of enrollment; contributory insurance; coverage; dental insurance; directors' and officers' liability insurance; disability insurance;

dual choice; duplication of benefits; eligible; experience rating; fraternal insurance; general liability insurance; group insurance; health insurance claim number; health insurance purchasing cooperative; high-risk pool; indemnity plan; individual health insurance; mandated employer insurance; medical malpractice insurance; Medicare; medigap policy; national health insurance; noncontributory insurance; Old Age, Survivors, and Disability Insurance Program; Old Age, Survivors, Disability and Health Insurance Program; out-of-pocket payments; patient service representative; portability; professional liability insurance; recurring clause; reinsurance; self-insurance; social insurance; specified disease insurance; sponsored malpractice insurance; subrogation; supplemental health insurance; tail coverage; trolley car policy; umbrella coverage; underinsured; underwriting; unemployment compensation—disability; waiting period; workers' compensation insurance.

insurance pool   An organization of insurers through which particular types of risks are shared or pooled. The risk of high loss by any particular insurance company is thus transferred to the group as a whole (the insurance pool) with premiums, losses, and expenses shared in agreed amounts. The advantage of a pool is that the size of expected losses can be predicted for the pool with much more certainty than for any individual party to it. Pooling arrangements are often used for catastrophic coverage or for certain high-risk populations such as the disabled. *See also* catastrophic illness; insurance.

integrated delivery system (IDS)   A network of health care organizations that delivers a coordinated continuum of services to a specific population. The network is fiscally and clinically accountable for that population's health status. An IDS either owns or has a close relationship with an insurance product. *Synonyms*: integrated delivery network; integrated health delivery network.

integrated provider   A health care provider that offers a comprehensive corporate umbrella for the management of a diversified health care delivery system. The system typically includes one or more hospitals, a large group practice, a health plan, and other health care operations. Physicians practice as employees of the system or in a tightly affiliated physician group. The system can provide several levels of health care to patients in geographically contiguous areas. *See also* corporate diversification; group practice; group practice without walls; health care provider; management service organization; physician-hospital organization.

integration   The linking together of components of a health care system. *See also* clinical integration; functional integration; horizontal integration; vertical integration.

integrity of data   *See* data integrity.

intense rehabilitation   Rehabilitation involving three or more hours of acute physical, occupational, psychological, or speech and language therapy per day, five or more days per week. *See also* rehabilitation.

intensity of service The amount or degree of service provided to a patient or a group of similar patients in a health care organization, such as the average number of laboratory tests or x-rays provided per emergency department patient or per hospitalized patient per day, subcategorized by attending physician. *See also* level of service.

intensive care Continuous health services provided to critically ill patients with life-threatening conditions, usually in an organization setting where professional and supportive services are concentrated for that purpose. *See also* level of care; neonatal intensive care unit.

interactive software A computer program that requires or allows the user to determine how the program will proceed by responding to onscreen prompts. Interactive programs are becoming increasingly popular for educating patients (and the public) as well as staff.

interdisciplinary Relating to, or involving, two or more clinical disciplines that are usually considered distinct, as in medicine and nursing. *See also* crossfunctional; multidisciplinary.

interdisciplinary patient care plan A plan required by federal regulations for patients in long term care and rehabilitation facilities. The plan defines the patient's problems and needs and sets measurable goals, approaches to the care, and the profession responsible for the care. *Synonyms:* care plan; patient care plan. *See also* long term care; plan of care.

interface pressure A measure of prevention or treatment of pressure ulcers, specifically the force per unit area that acts perpendicularly between the body and the support surface. Interface pressure is measured in terms of pounds per square inch (psi), which is the pressure exerted by a stream of fluid against one square inch of skin or wound surface. This parameter is affected by the stiffness of the support surface, the composition of the body tissue, and the geometry interface pressure of the body being supported. *See also* pressure ulcer.

interim life safety measures (ILSM) A series of 11 administrative actions required to temporarily compensate for significant hazards posed by existing National Fire Protection Association 101® 1997 *Life Safety Code*® (*LSC*®) deficiencies or construction activities. ILSM apply to appropriate staff (including construction workers), must be implemented upon project development, and must be continuously enforced through project completion. Implementation of ILSM is required in or adjacent to all construction areas and throughout buildings with existing LSC® deficiencies. ILSM are intended to provide a level of life safety comparable to that described in chapters 1 through 7, 31, and the applicable occupancy chapters of the *LSC*®. Each ILSM action must be documented through written policies and procedures. Frequencies for inspection, testing, training, and monitoring and evaluation must be established by the organization. *See also Life Safety Code*®; life safety management program.

interim rate An amount of money periodically paid to a health care provider by a third-party payer under a ret-

rospective reimbursement arrangement until a more accurate rate can be determined. The final payment is then established by adjustments to the total of the interim payments based on the determined rate. *See also* retrospective reimbursement; third-party payer.

interjudge reliability *See* interobserver reliability.

intermediate care *See* nursing care.

intermediate care facility (ICF) A health care organization recognized under the Medicaid program and licensed under state law to provide, on a regular basis, health services to individuals who do not require hospital or skilled nursing facility care, but who, because of their mental or physical condition, require institutional care above that provided by assisted living. *See also* assisted living; intermediate care facility for the mentally retarded; nursing care; nursing home.

intermediate care facility for the mentally retarded A public institution for care of the mentally retarded or people with related conditions. *See also* intermediate care facility.

intermediate service *See* level of service.

intermittent care Home care provided on a visit or hourly basis, typically not exceeding four hours per day. *See also* home health services.

internal audit An audit performed by staff of an organization to determine the degree to which internal procedures, operations, and accounting practices are in proper order.

internal consistency The extent to which all items in a particular scale measure the same dimension.

internal customer A member of an organization who receives products and services supplied by other individuals within an organization with the intent of supporting the organization's mission or business objectives. For example, a medical technologist (as supplier) working in a clinical laboratory provides certain services in response to a request for a laboratory test made by a physician, who is, in this scenario, the medical technologist's internal customer. *See also* customer.

internal medicine The branch and specialty of medicine dealing with the long-term, comprehensive management of both common and complex medical illnesses of adolescents, adults, and the elderly. Adolescent medicine, cardiovascular medicine, clinical cardiac electrophysiology, critical care medicine, diagnostic laboratory immunology, endocrinology, gastroenterology, geriatric medicine, hematology, infectious diseases, medical oncology, nephrology, pulmonary diseases, rheumatology, sports medicine, and allergy and immunology are subspecialty areas of internal medicine. *Synonym:* general internal medicine. *See also* hematology; nephrology.

internal review Review in which practitioners are involved in setting or adopting the criteria and standards by which they evaluate themselves. *See also* external review; medical review; utilization review.

internal validity   The extent to which the design of a study contributes to the confidence that can be placed in the study's results. Internal validity is relevant to both measurement studies and studies of causal relationships; it is the extent to which the detected relationships are most likely due to factors accounted for in the study, rather than other factors. *See also* validity.

International Classification of Health Problems in Primary Care   A classification of diseases, conditions, and other reasons for providing primary care. This classification may be used for labeling conditions in problem-oriented records as used by primary care health professionals. It is an adaptation of the ICD-9-CM but makes more allowance for the diagnostic uncertainty that characterizes primary care. *See also* ICD-9-CM.

International Classification of Impairments, Disabilities, and Handicaps   A classification that attempts to produce a systematic taxonomy of the consequences of injury and disease; first published by the World Health Organization in 1980. *See also* disability; handicap; impairment.

interobserver reliability   The degree to which different observers give similar ratings. *Synonyms:* conspect reliability; interjudge reliability; interrater reliability; scorer reliability. *See also* interobserver reliability coefficient; intrarater reliability; reliability; reliability testing.

interobserver reliability coefficient   A correlation coefficient that expresses the degree to which raters agree or disagree. *See also* correlation coefficient; interobserver reliability.

interpolation   The prediction or estimation of the value of variables within a range of observations.

interpretation   1. The act or process of interpreting, for example, translating or explaining.   **2.** The result of interpreting, as in differing interpretations of the data.

interrater reliability   *See* interobserver reliability.

interrelationship digraph   A planning and problem-solving tool that starts with a central idea, issue, or problem, then maps out logical or sequential links among related items. It is a creative process that allows for multidirectional rather than linear thinking. *See also* graph.

interrogatory   In civil actions, such as a malpractice lawsuit, a pretrial discovery tool in which written questions put forth for consideration by one party are served on the adversary, who must answer by written replies made under oath. Although an interrogatory is not as flexible an instrument as a deposition, which includes the opportunity to cross-examine, an interrogatory is regarded as an effective and efficient means of establishing important facts held by the adversary. *See also* deposition.

interval scale   A type of ordinal scale in which values have a natural equal distance between them and in which

a particular distance (interval) between two values in one region of the scale meaningfully represents the same distance between two values in another region of the scale (eg, Celsius and Fahrenheit temperature scales). The zero point is arbitrary. Addition and subtraction are permissible, but multiplication and division of such scales are not. Statistical analyses, such as the Pearson correlation, factor analysis, or discriminant analysis, may be used with interval scales. *See also* nominal scale; ordinal scale; ratio scale.

intervening cause   An act of an independent agency which destroys the causal connection between the negligent act of a defendant and the wrongful injury. The independent act serves as the immediate cause, and thus damages are not recoverable because the original wrongful act is not the proximate cause. However, the original wrongful act may still be deemed the proximate cause where the independent act is foreseeable. For example, if a physician commits a negligent act that will ultimately result in a patient's injury and a different physician commits a later negligent act that triggers the injury, the original physician may still be held liable, as most courts hold the actions of the second physician to have been foreseeable by the first. *Synonym:* supervening cause. *See also* foreseeability.

intervention   In the broadest sense, the act or fact of interfering so as to favorably modify a condition. *Crisis intervention*, used chiefly in contexts such as emergency rooms of psychiatric or general hospitals or in the home or place of crisis occurrence, is a brief therapeutic approach that ameliorates rather than cures acute psychiatric emergencies and focuses on interpersonal and intrapsychic factors and environmental modification. This approach has been extended to a modality called *intervention* in the recovery movement and some substance-abuse organizations. An intervention is an organized and carefully planned effort by family and friends to confront a person with a substance-abuse problem with evidence of the problem and its consequences and to get the person to immediately agree to take action, such as entering a treatment program. The concept *early intervention* has two senses: (1) procedures and programs that facilitate the development of skill acquisition in infants and young children who have disabilities, who are at risk for developing disabilities, or who are gifted; it includes programs designed to prevent handicapping conditions in infants and young children and family-centered programs designed to affect the functioning of infants and children with special needs; and (2) activities that are designed to detect and reverse the early stages of dysfunctional drinking of either groups or individuals; these activities are a kind of secondary prevention. *Synonym:* health intervention.

interventional imaging   Diagnostic and therapeutic imaging procedures that are invasive or surgical and require special training and expertise; in general, they are more invasive than diagnostic imaging but less invasive than major surgery. Interventional radiography, for example, may involve catheterization, fluoroscopy, or computed tomography for applications such as balloon angioplasty and arterial embolization, combining organ system radiography, catheter techniques, and sectional imaging. *See also* imaging.

intervention studies Investigations designed to test a hypothesis about a cause-effect relationship by modifying the supposed causal factor or factors in the study population. The factor that is modified may be specific to patients, therapy, diagnostic tools, setting, providers, and so forth.

intra-arterial *See* infusion therapy services.

intractable pain A pain state in which the cause of the pain can not be eliminated or otherwise treated and which in the generally accepted course of medical practice no relief or cure of the cause of the pain is possible or none has been found after reasonable efforts have been documented in the patient's medical records. *See also* pain management.

intractable pain treatment acts Legislation on using opioids to alleviate pain, introduced in several states in connection with the debate over physician-assisted suicide and evidence that pain was not being managed properly. These acts may describe reasonable standards of care, such as producing a treatment plan. The acts are intended to remove restrictions on physicians' use of pain medicine but, in some cases, have led to more restrictions by requiring steps that were not necessary previously, such as signing an informed-consent document or consulting with a medical specialist. *See also* pain management; palliative care; physician-assisted suicide.

intradermal *See* infusion therapy services.

intramuscular *See* infusion therapy services.

intraorganization transfer A transfer of a patient within the same health care organization, as from one patient care unit to another, from one clinical service to another, or from one practitioner to another. *See also* transfer.

intrarater reliability Consistency of judgments by a single observer. *See also* interobserver reliability; reliability.

intravascular (IV) *See* infusion therapy services.

intravenous (IV) *See* infusion therapy services.

intubation Placement and maintenance of a tube in an opening, especially passage of a breathing tube into the trachea to allow passage of oxygen or anesthetic gas. *See also* airway; endotracheal intubation; nasogastric intubation.

invasive procedure A procedure involving puncture or incision of the skin, or insertion of an instrument or foreign material into the body. Examples of invasive procedures include percutaneous aspirations, biopsies, cardiac and vascular catheterizations, endoscopies, angioplasties, and implantations, and excluding venipuncture and intravenous therapy.

investigational new drug (IND) A drug available solely for experimental use to determine its safety and effectiveness. An IND is not yet approved by the FDA for marketing to the general public, and only experts qualified by training and experience to investigate the drug's safety and effectiveness may prescribe it. Use of the drug in humans requires FDA approval of an IND application, which includes reports of animal toxicity tests with the drug, a description of proposed clinical trials, and a list of the names and qualifications of the investigators conducting these studies. *See also* new drug; new drug application.

in vitro Latin phrase meaning "in glass," that is, outside of the living organism and in an artificial environment, such as a test tube.

in vivo Latin phrase meaning "in the living organism."

involuntary commitment A court-directed admission of a patient to a behavioral health care facility against the patient's will. In most jurisdictions, the individual with mental illness must be incapable of taking care of himself or herself, likely to injure himself or herself, or likely to injure another person. *See also* civil commitment; commitment.

involuntary seclusion A patient's separation from other individuals or from the patient's room against his or her will or the will of his or her legal representative.

involuntary smoking *See* secondhand smoke.

iridology The study of the pigment and structure of the iris to identify the condition of tissues in the human body. Although this practice cannot identify diseases, practitioners use it in conjunction with other diagnostic activities to determine toxins and their location(s), stages of inflammation, inherent weakness or strength, constitution, and general health level.

ischemia Decreased supply of oxygenated blood to a body organ or part, which may cause pain and dysfunction, as in ischemic heart disease or ischemic pain in the extremities from obstructed blood flow.

Ischemic Heart Disease PORT *See* Patient Outcomes Research Teams.

Ishikawa diagram *See* cause-and-effect diagram.

ISO 9000 A set of standards for quality management and quality assurance first published by the International Organization for Standardization in 1987. The series, which has been adopted in more than 80 countries, represents an international consensus on the essential features of a quality system. Organizations use such standards to ensure effective operation.

isolated systolic hypertension (ISH) Systolic blood pressure consistently 160 mm Hg or greater with diastolic blood pressure less than 90 mm Hg. ISH frequently occurs in older people. *See also* hypertension.

isolation The separation of infected persons or animals from other persons or animals to prevent or limit the direct or indirect transmission of the infectious agent from those infected to those who are susceptible or who may spread the agent to others. *Synonym*: patient isolation. *See also* blood-body fluid precautions; contact isolation; drainage/secretion precautions; enteric precautions; infection-control program; isolation bed; respiratory isolation; strict isolation; tuberculous isolation.

isolation bed A bed regularly maintained by a health care organization for inpatients who require isolation. *See also* immunity; isolation.

Jj

Jackson Hole approach   An approach to managed competition that advocates three major changes in the U.S. health insurance system. Regional health insurance purchasing cooperatives (HIPCs) are formed to manage the marketplace for health care coverage, especially for small firms and individuals. Employers and HIPCs contribute the same amount of money for coverage regardless of which plan a consumer chooses. New rules are created, making it more difficult for plans to avoid enrolling high-risk individuals. This approach was proposed by the Jackson Hole group, an informal think tank on health care reform headed by Paul Ellwood, Jr, and including people interested in health care reform from academic institutions, private business, publishing, and the health care industry. The group was named for Jackson Hole (Wyo.), where meetings were held at a participant's home. *See also* managed competition.

Jehovah's Witnesses   A religious denomination founded in Pittsburgh whose members practice evangelism. A Jehovah's Witness will undergo needed surgery but will not accept any blood transfusions even in the event of an emergency.

JNC-V (The Fifth Report of the Joint National Committee on Detection, Evaluation, and Treatment of High Blood Pressure)   A report published in 1993 by the National High Blood Pressure Program of the National Institute of Health's National Heart, Lung, and Blood Institute. The JNC-V established a revised classification of hypertension. *See also* hypertension.

job description   Definition of an employment position or a task including duties, responsibilities, and conditions required to perform the job.

job sharing   A situation in which the responsibilities, hours, and pay of one position are divided between two or more people.

job specification   Requirements for a particular position or task including the skills, education, and experience needed.

joint and several liability   A rule of law that allows an individual who has suffered loss or injury as a result of the acts of more than one person to collect the entire compensation from any one of the wrongdoers without regard to his or her individual fault or contribution. *See also* liability.

Joint Commission survey   *See* accreditation survey; conditional follow-up survey; criteria of survey eligibility; early survey option I; early survey option II; extension survey; focused survey; full survey; initial survey; multihospital survey option; multiorganization survey option; special survey; specialized survey; survey team; tailored survey; triennial survey; unannounced/unscheduled survey.

joint enterprise   Joint undertaking of common purpose under such circumstances that each party has authority, expressed or implied, to act for all in respect to the control, means, or agencies employed to execute such common purpose.

joint probability   The probability that two or more specific outcomes or results will occur in an event. *See also* probability.

joint venture   A legal entity in the nature of a partnership engaged in the joint undertaking of a particular transaction for mutual profit. For example, a hospital and members of its medical staff may create a formalized cooperative effort (such as setting up a diagnostic imaging facility). *See also* corporate diversification; partnership; safe harbor regulations.

judgment   A sense of knowledge sufficient to comprehend the nature of a transaction. *See also* case-based review; cognition; group judgment methods; substituted judgment doctrine.

junk science   An epithet from Peter W. Huber's *Galileo's Revenge: Junk Science in the Courtroom* (1991) leveled at courts that are perceived to be permissive in their admission of scientific evidence in medical liability cases. *See also* admissible evidence; *Daubert v Merrell Dow case*.

Juran trilogy   *See* quality trilogy.

just in time (JIT)   **1.** A supply system organized so that the right amount of supplies is always available. **2.** In total quality management, training in specific tools and techniques that is delivered to an improvement team just in time to be used. This avoids providing team members with large amounts of pretraining, much of which may be forgotten before it is actually used. *See also* total quality management.

juvenile-onset diabetes   *See* diabetes mellitus.

Kk

kaizen Japanese word meaning gradual, unending improvement. *See also* Hoshin planning.

Kerr-Mills A popular name for the Social Security Amendments of 1960, which expanded and modified the federal government's responsibility for helping states to pay for medical care for the aged poor. *Synonym*: Medical Assistance for the Aged. *See also* Social Security.

ketosis A condition caused by deficiency or inadequate utilization of carbohydrates, in which ketones accumulate in the blood rendering it acidic. Ketosis is seen most frequently in diabetes mellitus and starvation. Untreated, it may progress to ketoacidosis, coma, and death. *See also* diabetes mellitus; diabetic ketoacidosis.

keyhole surgery Minimally invasive surgery, carried out through a very small incision using fiber- optic instruments, for example, laparoscopic cholecystectomy. *See also* endoscopy.

key process variable A component of a process that has a cause-effect relationship of sufficient magnitude with the key quality characteristic such that manipulation and control of the key process variable will reduce variation of the key quality characteristic or change its level. *See also* key quality characteristic; operational definition; variable.

key quality characteristic (KQC) The most important quality characteristic of a service or product. KQCs must be operationally defined by combining knowledge of the customer with knowledge of the process. KQCs are measured to understand the actual performance of a process. *See also* key process variable; operational definition; quality characteristics.

kinesiology The study of muscles and the movement of the human body. In holistic medicine, it is the balance of movement and the interaction of a person's energy systems. *Applied kinesiology* is the name given to the system of applying muscle testing diagnostically and therapeutically to different aspects of health care.

kinetics The study of the rates at which chemical reactions and biological processes proceed, as in cell kinetics. *See also* pharmacokinetics.

kiting Increasing the quantity of a drug ordered by a prescription. A pharmacist, patient, or other individual may kite the quantity of the original prescription, for example, by adding zeros to the number shown on a prescription. When done by a pharmacist, he or she may then provide the patient with the quantity originally prescribed but bill a third party, such as Medicaid, for the larger quantity. A patient who kites is often dependent on the drug. *See also* fraud and abuse; shorting.

knowledge base The database of facts, inferences, and procedures needed for problem solving on a particular subject.

knowledge-based information A collection of stored facts, models, and information found in the clinical, scientific, and management literature that can be used for designing and redesigning processes and for problem solving.

knowledge-based system A system that combines access to data and systematic use of logic rules and probability statements intended to help health care providers make better clinical decisions; for example, by recognizing out-of-range laboratory values or undesirable trends, associating symptoms with the correct diagnosis, or selecting the optimal treatment approach.

L1

labeling **1.** Written, printed, or graphic matter displayed on or accompanying a food, drug, device, or cosmetic, or on any of their containers or wrappers, according to the federal Food, Drug, and Cosmetic Act, for example, a package insert for a prescription drug product. Labeling is regulated by the FDA. A label cannot contain any false or misleading statements and must include adequate instructions for use, unless a product is exempt by regulation. *See also* package insert. **2.** The potentially stigmatizing effect that the results of screening (eg, blood pressure, cholesterol) or the attribution of high-risk behavior or lifestyle (eg, smoking, obesity) can have on a patient, which may, as a result, make some patients reluctant to seek health care.

laboratory **1.** A place for observation, practice, or testing, as in a cardiac catheterization laboratory. *See also* pulmonary function laboratory. **2.** A facility in which materials from the human body are examined to provide information about the state of health of human beings. *See also* CLIA '67; CLIA '88; clinical laboratory; freestanding laboratory; histopathology laboratory; pathology and clinical laboratory services; point-of-care laboratory testing; special-function laboratory.

laboratory screening tests Blood tests, tests performed at the bedside, imaging studies, and other laboratory tests performed on asymptomatic persons for the early detection of risk factors and preclinical disease. Wide disagreement prevails in practice and theory over the routine provision of individual tests or panels (groups of tests bundled together). The Canadian Task Force on the Periodic Health Examination (1994) and the U.S. Preventive Services Task Force (1996), which have developed evidence-based formal criteria, maintain that, in general, screening tests are not recommended unless (1) scientific evidence shows that the test can detect early-stage disease accurately (few false-positive results), and (2) early detection improves clinical outcome. *See also* cancer screening tests and procedures; case finding; evangelists and snails; prevention; preventive services; pulmonary function tests; screening.

labor certification Certification required and provided by the U.S. Department of Labor for certain aliens, such as foreign medical graduates. The certification may be considered for individuals with occupations for which a shortage exists in the United States (eg, physicians, nurses). *See also* certification; fifth pathway; foreign medical graduate; limited licensure.

labor intensive Requiring a high proportion of human effort relative to capital investment, for example, health services. Labor costs are more important than capital costs in labor-intensive activities.

labor relations The manner of conducting operations between management and labor, especially on the part of a business organization with respect to the demands of its labor force.

labor union An organization of wage earners formed to serve members' interests with respect to wages and working conditions.

laparoscopic cholecystectomy An abdominal surgical procedure, often done under local anesthesia, in which the gallbladder is removed by inserting through a

---

COMMONLY USED LABORATORY SCREENING TESTS FOR ASYMPTOMATIC PERSONS

Tests Recommended for Routine Use*
T_4/TSH (free thyroxine/thyroid-stimulating hormone)
Phenylalanine (for newborns)
Total cholesterol (M 35-65, F 45-65)
Fecal occult blood test (> 50)
Sigmoidoscopy (> 50)
Papanicolaou smear (F > 18, sexually active F)
Mammography (F 40-79)*

Tests Recommended for Persons with Risk Factors†
Hemoglobin/hematocrit
Hemoglobin electrophoresis
Blood glucose
VDRL/RPR (Venereal Disease Research Laboratory/rapid plasma reagin—syphilis test)
Gonorrhea culture
Chlamydia test
Lead
ECG (electrocardiogram)
Otacoustic emissions (hearing, BAER)
Mantoux PPD (purified protein derivative—tuberculosis test)
Colonoscopy

Tests Lacking Consensus on Routine Use‡
Blood chemistry panels
Complete blood counts
Routine screening urinalyses
Prostate-specific antigen (PSA)
Other serum tumor markers (eg, CA125)
Illicit-drug screening
Chest radiography
Abdominal ultrasound
Peripheral artery examination
Bone density measurement
Pulmonary function testing
Colposcopy
Endometrial biopsy
Tonometry for glaucoma

* These tests have been demonstrated to improve health outcomes (morbidity or mortality) or have other scientific support. Currently there is controversy over whether to start mammography screening at age 40 or age 50 and whether to discontinue at age 70, 75, or 79 years.

† Only specified risk factors (eg, age, ethnic background, family history, comorbidity, lifestyle, physical residential and community environment, HIV infection) warrant use of any of these tests.

‡ The existing evidence (or absence of evidence) does not support routine use of any of these tests.

Sources: U.S. Preventive Services Task Force: *Guide to Clinical Preventive Services.* Second Edition. Baltimore: Williams & Wilkins, 1996. Woolf SH, Jonas S, Lawrence RS: *Health Promotion and Disease Prevention in Clinical Practice.* Baltimore: Williams & Wilkins, 1996.

small incision instruments for visualizing inside the abdomen and instruments for manipulating (such as cutting), applying lasers, and sewing. *Lap cholys* is the slang term for the procedure. *See also* cholecystectomy; laparoscopy.

laparoscopy The process of examining the interior of the abdomen (peritoneal cavity) by means of a laparoscope (endoscope) inserted through the abdominal wall, as for examining the liver or for surgically treating endometriosis. *Synonym:* peritoneoscopy. *See also* endoscopy; laparoscopic cholecystectomy; peritoneal cavity.

lap cholys *See* laparoscopic cholecystectomy.

laryngology The branch of medicine dealing with the throat, pharynx, larynx, nasopharynx, and tracheobronchial tree. *See also* otolaryngology.

laryngoscopy Examination of the interior of the larynx with a specially designed illuminated instrument (laryngoscope) before intubating a patient.

laser (light amplification by stimulated emission of radiation) An instrument that produces a thin beam of light by converting electromagnetic radiation of mixed frequencies to one or more discrete frequencies of highly amplified and coherent ultraviolet, visible, or infrared radiation. Laser is used surgically to destroy tissue or to separate parts.

latex-free environment A health care work setting devoid of latex-glove use by any personnel and with no direct or patient contact with other latex devices. This environment is recommended particularly when procedures are performed on children with spina bifida and on patients with positive skin test results. *See also* latex rubber allergy.

latex rubber allergy A hypersensitivity, including systemic reactions that are type I immunologic responses mediated by immunoglobulin E (IgE) antibody as well as less serious immunologic responses, reported by health care workers regularly exposed to latex in the workplace. Sensitized patients who become re-exposed may develop contact urticaria, allergic rhinoconjunctivitis, asthma, or anaphylaxis. In vitro testing for latex protein-specific IgE antibodies using radioallergosorbent tests (RAST), enzyme-linked immunosorbent assays, and Western blots may identify most persons with IgE sensitivity. Guidelines for preventing latex allergy or managing it in a latex-free environment were issued by the American Academy of Allergy and Immunology in 1993. *Synonym:* latex allergy. *See also* latex-free environment; RAST.

layoff The removal, either temporarily or permanently, of an employee from a payroll, not because of poor performance, but because of an economic slowdown or a production cutback. *See also* job sharing.

lazaretto A hospital treating contagious diseases, especially a leprosarium, or a quarantine station.

leader An individual who sets expectations, develops plans, and implements procedures to assess and improve the quality of an organization's governance, management, and clinical and support functions and processes. Leaders include, when applicable to the organization's structure, the owners, members of the governing body, the chief executive officer and other senior managers, nursing executive and other senior nurses, and the leaders of the licensed independent practitioners. *See also* informal leader; leadership; network leader; opinion leader; team leader.

leadership The capacity or ability to lead. *See also* distributed leadership; leader; management style; participative leadership.

learning A relatively permanent change in behavior that is the result of past experience or practice. Identifying the ways people learn most effectively (through demonstration, lectures, written materials, etc.) and providing for these differences are crucial when developing both patient and staff education programs. *See also* educational psychology; health education; health maintenance diaries; implementation techniques; inservice; learning disability; learning psychology; multimedia education; patient education.

learning disability An abnormal condition in understanding or using spoken or written language, affecting a person of normal intelligence and not arising from emotional disturbance or impairment of sight or hearing. *See also* attention-deficit/hyperactivity disorder; disability; learning.

learning organization An organization that practices creative learning by using certain basic principles relating to total quality management. *See also* learning; total quality management.

learning psychology The branch of psychology that examines how experience, practice, or training cause lasting changes in behavior; for example, the importance of rewards and punishment in the learning process, the different ways individuals and species learn, and the factors that influence memory. *See also* educational psychology.

leased line A private communications channel leased from a common carrier, such as AT&T. Leased lines are commonly used to connect distant terminals to a central computer system or a private communication network. For example, leased lines might connect the main computer system of an area hospital to the computer systems in local physician offices, as well as to its subsidiary ambulatory clinic, long term care facility, and home health agency.

left main disease Stenosis of the left main coronary artery. *See also* coronary artery disease.

legal age The age at which a person may enter into binding contracts or commit other legal acts. In most states a minor reaches legal age or majority (ie, becomes of age) at age 18, though for certain acts (eg, drinking) it may be higher and for others (eg, driving) it may be lower. *See also* age of majority; guardian; minor.

legal guardian   *See* guardian.

legal injury   A violation or invasion of a legal right, for example, an antitrust injury.

legal majority   *See* age of majority.

legal malpractice   Failure of an attorney to use such skill, prudence, and diligence as lawyers of ordinary skill and capacity commonly possess and exercise in performing tasks that they undertake, and when such failure proximately causes damage, giving rise to an action in tort. *See also* malpractice; medical malpractice.

legend drug   A prescription drug that carries the labeling, "Caution: Federal law prohibits dispensing without prescription." *See also* over-the-counter drug; prescription drug.

legibility   Capable of being deciphered, as in handwriting that is legible.

legislative history   The background and events, including committee reports, hearings, and floor debates, leading up to enactment of a law. Such history assists courts in determining the legislative intent of a particular statute. Legislative histories of major statutes are published in the *U.S. Code, Congressional and Administrative News. See also* legislative intent.

legislative intent   Interpretation of the meaning of a law, usually provided by regulators and the courts, but also by a legislative history and other means. *See also* legislative history.

length of stay (LOS)   The number of calendar days that elapse between an inpatient's admission and discharge in a health care organization, used as a measure of the use of health facilities. It is typically reported as an average number of days spent in a facility per admission or discharge, calculated as follows: total number of days in the facility for all discharges and deaths occurring during a period divided by the number of discharges and deaths during the same period. In concurrent review, an appropriate length of stay may be assigned each patient on admission. Average lengths of stay vary and are measured for people with various ages, specific diagnoses, or sources of payment. *See also* average length of stay; comorbidity; length of stay mandates; outlier threshold.

length of stay (LOS) mandates   Acts introduced in several states to counter managed care's efforts to set same-day or 24-hour limits on length of stay (length-of-stay caps) for given procedures, such as childbirth and mastectomies, referred to variously in public debate as early newborn discharge, drive-by delivery, ambulatory mastectomy, outpatient mastectomy. The state mandates may specify 48 hours instead of 24 hours. Such efforts have become controversial for lack of proof that the limited LOS is harmful or counter to actual patients' wishes. *See also* length of stay.

level of acuity   The degree or state of disease or injury existing in a patient prior to treatment. The greater the level of acuity, the greater the number of health care resources (eg, health professionals, laboratory services, operating rooms, special care units) required to treat the patient. *See also* acuity; emergency care; severity of illness; Snellen visual acuity test; urgent.

level of service   A relative intensity of services provided for a patient, for example, minimal, brief, limited, intermediate, extended, comprehensive, or unusually complex designations when a physician provides one-on-one services for a patient, or various levels of service provided by a health care organization, such as partial hospitalization, ambulatory surgery, or tertiary services. *See also* levels of care.

level of significance   The probability (*p*) of a false rejection of the null hypothesis in a statistical test. *Synonym*: significance level. *See also* null hypothesis; *p* value; statistical significance.

levels of care   A classification of health care service levels by the kind of care given, the number of people served, and the people providing the care. The main levels of care are primary, secondary, and tertiary. *See also* alternative level of care; continuum of care; emergency services levels of care; level of service; national standard rule; nursing care; primary care; referred care; secondary care; tertiary care.

liability   A broad legal term encompassing almost every responsibility (absolute, contingent, or likely). *See* action in personam; affirmative defense; corporate liability; defamation; defensive medicine; enterprise liability; general liability insurance; joint and several liability; limits on liability; Maine Medical Liability Demonstration project; no-fault medical practice liability; occurrence policy; patient compensation fund; product liability; professional liability; tort liability; vicarious liability.

liability insurance   *See* general liability insurance; professional liability insurance.

libel   *See* defamation.

license   An official or a legal permission, granted by competent authority, usually public, to an individual or organization to engage in a practice, an occupation, or an activity otherwise unlawful, for example, a license to practice medicine and surgery. A license is usually needed to begin lawful practice; thus, it is usually granted on the basis of examination and proof of education rather than on measurement of actual performance. A license is usually permanent but may be conditioned on annual payment of a fee, proof of continuing education, or proof of competence. Grounds for revoking a license include incompetence, commission of a crime (whether or not related to the licensed practice), or moral turpitude (an instance of baseness or depravity). There is no national licensure system for health professionals, although requirements are often so nearly standardized as to constitute a national system. *See also* competence; continuing education; endorsement; licensure; state board of medical examiners.

licensed beds   The total number of beds that a state licensing agency authorizes a health care organization to operate on a regular basis. *See also* adult inpatient bed; air fluidized bed; bed conversion; bed count; constructed beds; day bed; hospital bed; incubator bed; inpatient census; isolation bed; night bed; occupancy; outpatient bed; regularly maintained beds; occupancy; resident bed; specialty bed; swing bed; temporary bed.

licensed independent practitioner (LIP)   Any individual permitted by law and by an organization to provide patient care services without direction or supervision, within the scope of his or her license and consistent with individually granted clinical privileges. *See also* medical staff; organized professional staff; physician; practitioner; privileging.

licensure   A legal right that is granted by a government agency in compliance with a statute governing an occupation (eg, medicine, dentistry, or nursing) or the operation of an activity (eg, acute care in a hospital). Licensure of a physician is the legal permission granted by a state government to take personal and unsupervised responsibility for diagnosing and treating patients in the practice of medicine. *See also* accreditation; allied health professional; certificate of need; certification; endorsement; license; limited licensure; mandatory licensure; medical licensure; national board examination; National Council Licensure Examinations; National Practitioner Data Bank; practitioner; reappointment of physicians; reciprocity; state board of medical examiners.

life care   Long-term, continuing care offered by retirement communities to their residents on a contract basis through provision of services ranging from independent living to skilled nursing care. *See also* assisted living; continuing care retirement community.

life events   Changes or disturbances in the pattern of living that may be associated with or cause changes in health. Examples include death of a spouse or other close relative, loss of a regular job, relocation, marriage, having and raising children, and divorce.

life expectancy   The number of years a person is expected to live based on present age and sex. The figure is most often used by actuaries to determine insurance premiums. *See also* actuarial analysis.

Life Safety Code® (LSC®)   A set of standards for the construction and operation of buildings, intended to provide a reasonable degree of safety to life during fires. The *LSC®* is prepared, published, and periodically revised by the National Fire Protection Association (NFPA) and is adopted by the Joint Commission to evaluate health care organizations or networks under its life safety management program. *Life Safety Code®* is a registered trademark of the National Fire Protection Association (Quincy, Mass.). *See also* building codes; interim life safety measures; life safety management program; occupancy.

life safety management program   A health care organization's documented management plan describing the processes for protecting patients, staff members, visitors, and property from fire and the products of combustion (smoke). *See also* environment of care; interim life safety measures; *Life Safety Code®*.

life signs   *See* vital signs.

lifestyle   **1.** The set of attitudes, behaviors, beliefs, and values that is influenced by the process of socialization, including, for instance, use of substances such as alcohol, tobacco, and coffee; exercise; dress; recreation; and dietary habits. Lifestyle often affects health. *See also* risk factor modification.   **2.** In marketing, the sum total of the likes and dislikes of particular customers or a section of the market, as expressed in the products they buy to fit their self-image and way of life. *See also* value system.

lifestyle modifications   *See* risk factor modification.

life-support care   Health services provided for patients requiring extraordinary measures in order to sustain and prolong life. *See also* extraordinary care; life-support system.

life-support system   Equipment (eg, a respirator), medications, and services (eg, nursing care) that create a viable environment for patients who otherwise might not survive. The phrase "termination of life-support systems" refers to discontinuing products and services that support the life of a patient who is completely dependent on artificial means for survival. *See also* life-support care; life-sustaining procedure; withdrawing treatment.

life-sustaining procedure   Any intervention that is judged likely to be effective in prolonging a patient's life or that is being used to sustain a patient's life. In law, a life-sustaining procedure is one that may be suspended on a court order or pursuant to a living will in the case of, for example, a comatose and terminally ill person. Life-sustaining procedures include mechanical or other artificial means to sustain, restore, or supplant some vital function, such as breathing, which serve to prolong the moment of death when, in the judgment of attending and consulting physicians (as reflected in the patient's medical records), death is imminent if such procedures are not used. *See also* death-prolonging procedure; living will.

life table   A statistical table exhibiting mortality and survivor characteristics of a given population. A life table may be used, for example, to compute damages resulting from injuries that destroy a person's earning capacity. *See also* damages.

Lifetime Health Monitoring Program   The name that Group Health Cooperative of Puget Sound applies to a schedule of recommended health maintenance, including recommended physical examination visits and the preventive services delivered at those visits. *See also* health maintenance schedule; monitor; prevention.

lifetime reserve   A Medicare term referring to the pool of 60 days of hospital care upon which a patient may draw after he or she has used up the maximum Medicare benefit for a single illness. *See also* Medicare.

likelihood ratio   A ratio for a screening or diagnostic test (including clinical signs or symptoms) that expresses the relative odds that a given test result would be expected in a patient with (as opposed to one without) the disorder or condition of interest. *See also* ratio.

Likert scale   A five-point measure of preference that asks a respondent to rank likes and dislikes or indicate agreement or disagreement with statements.

limitations period   *See* statute of limitations.

limited code   *See* slow code.

limited licensure   Licensure restricting a physician's practice to a single health care organization, such as a mental hospital, designated by the state. Physicians with limited licenses are often foreign medical graduates. *See also* foreign medical graduate; labor certification; licensure.

limited partnership   A partnership consisting of one or more general partners, jointly and severally responsible as ordinary partners, who conduct the business. One or more special partners contribute in cash payment a specific sum as capital to the common stock and are not liable for the debts of the partnership beyond the funds contributed. *See also* corporate diversification; partnership.

limits on liability   **1.** In insurance, limits on dollar coverage contained in an insurance policy. Malpractice insurance, for instance, generally contains such limits on the amounts payable for an individual claim or in the policy year. *Excess coverage* describes insurance with limits higher than these conventional amounts. *See also* liability. **2.** State and federal statutes that limit liability for certain types of damages, such as pain and suffering; that limit the liability of certain persons or groups, for example, the liability of corporate directors for acts of the corporation; or that limit the time period in which action can be maintained, as in statute of limitations. *Synonym*: limitation of liability acts. *See also* statute of limitations.

line function   An interlinked group of activities, such as organizational operations or clinical services, that contributes directly to an organization's output. *See also* line management.

line graph   A series of line segments connecting points of paired numerical data, representing the functional relationship between two variables. *See also* graph.

line management   The administration of line functions of an organization. *See also* line function.

lipid profile   The battery of tests that shows total cholesterol, low-density lipoprotein cholesterol, high-density lipoprotein cholesterol, and triglycerides. *Lipids* are fatty substances composed of different proportions of hydrogen, carbon, and oxygen, including triglycerides, cortisol, and cholesterol. *See also* cholesterol profile.

lipoprotein   A soluble complex of a lipid (fat) and a protein. Since lipids are insoluble in water, proteins serve as the main lipid-transport mechanism in plasma. Some lipoproteins transport cholesterol in the blood. *High-density lipoproteins* (HDLs) carry so-called good cholesterol, which they retrieve from the body's tissues and transport to the liver, which secretes much of it in bile. *Low-density lipoproteins* (LDLs), the most abundant of the lipoproteins, usually carry about 65% of the circulating cholesterol (so-called bad cholesterol) to cells. Other types are *very- low-density lipoprotein* (VLDLs) and *intermediate-density lipoproteins* (IDLs). *See also* cholesterol; high-density lipoprotein; hypercholesterolemia; lipid profile.

lithotripsy   The destruction of a stone in the kidney, ureter, bladder, or gallbladder by physical forces, including crushing with a lithotritor through a catheter. Focused percutaneous ultrasound and focused hydraulic shock waves may be used without surgery. Lithotripsy does not include the dissolving of stones by acids or litholysis. *Extracorporeal shock wave lithotripsy* (ESWL) refers to the type of lithotripsy in which shock waves are generated in a water-filled bath in which the patient sits.

litigation   Contest in a court of law to enforce a right or seek a remedy.

live birth   According to the World Health Organization (1950), the complete expulsion or extraction from its mother of a product of conception, irrespective of the duration of the pregnancy, which, after such separation, breathes or shows any other evidence of life, such as beating of the heart, pulsation of the umbilical cord, or definite movement of voluntary muscles, whether or not the umbilical cord has been cut or the placenta is attached; each product of such a birth is considered live born. This definition includes no requirement that the product of conception be viable or capable of independent life and thus includes very early and patently nonviable fetuses.

liver function tests   A series of laboratory tests usually performed when liver disease is known or suspected, most of which consist of biochemical measurements made on serum or plasma. They include measurements of bilirubin, alkaline phosphatase, albumin, globulin, prothrombin, and various liver enzymes.

living-in unit   A hospital room regularly maintained for mothers to assume care of newborns or for relatives to assist in the care of a chronically ill or other type of patient, under the supervision of nursing personnel. *See also* facility-based hospice.

living will   Instructional directives in written form that indicate the author's wishes for medical treatment should he or she become incapacitated and unable to participate in medical decision making. Many states have living will legislation, for example, Kansas has the Natural Death Act and Missouri has the Death-Prolonging Procedures Act. *Natural death acts* are pieces of legislation generally enacted to codify living wills and often contain specific examples. *Synonyms*: directive to physicians; medical directive; terminal care document. *See also* advance directives; death-prolonging procedure; durable power of attorney of health care; life-sustaining procedure; natural death acts; Patient Self-Determination Act; severability clause.

load and go The management by prehospital personnel (eg, first responder, rescue worker) of trauma patients whose conditions are so critical that they may die if they do not receive definitive care within a matter of minutes. Once such a patient is recognized, he or she is immediately transported to the nearest appropriate trauma facility. *Synonym*: expeditious evacuation. *See also*: advanced trauma life support; ambulance; basic trauma life support; traumatology.

loading In insurance, the amount added to the actuarial value of the coverage (expected or average amounts payable to the insured) to cover the expense to the insurer of securing and maintaining the business. *See also* premium.

lobbying Any attempt by a person or a group of persons (lobbyists) to influence federal or state legislation or a government official for or against a specific cause by the provision of information, argument, or other means. The term derives from the frequent presence of such persons in the lobbies of congressional and other government chambers. OBRA '93 expanded the definition of lobbying to include efforts to influence actions or positions of certain high-level federal executive branch officials. *See also* advocacy; OBRA '93.

lobular carcinoma in situ (LCIS) *See* breast cancer.

locality rule A legal doctrine stating that the standard of care in a malpractice lawsuit is measured by the degree to which it adheres to standards of care exercised by similar professionals within the same or similar geographic area or locality, rather than within the world, nation, state, or profession at large. *See also* malpractice; national standard rule; standard of care.

lock-in A situation in which a health plan enrollee must use designated providers for all covered services.

longitudinal patient record A record, either paper or electronic, that details a patient's lifetime medical history, including diagnoses, treatments, pharmacologic interventions, and other health care services. *See also* medical history.

longitudinal study A study in which the same individuals or group of individuals are examined on a number of occasions over a long period of time. *See also* cohort study.

long-range planning *See* strategic planning.

long-term acute care facility A health care facility licensed as a hospital that typically treats patients with very complex diagnoses and multisystem failure. These patients are sicker than those in most acute care hospitals' intensive care units.

long term care (LTC) The health and personal care services provided to chronically ill, aged, disabled, or retarded persons in an institution or in the place of residence. These persons are not in an acute phase of illness but require convalescent, physical supportive, or restorative services on a long-term basis. LTC is sometimes used more narrowly to refer only to long-term institutional care, such as that provided in nursing homes, homes for the retarded, and mental health care organizations. Ambulatory services, such as home health care, which also can be provided on a long-term basis, are seen as alternatives to long-term institutional care.

Long Term Care Accreditation Program The survey and accreditation program of the Joint Commission for eligible hospital-based and freestanding long term care organizations.

long term care facility An organization that provides nursing care and related services for residents who require medical, nursing, rehabilitation, or subacute care services. Such a facility may be certified for participation in the Medicare or Medicaid program as a skilled nursing facility or other nursing facility. *See also* nursing home; skilled nursing facility.

Long Term Care Pharmacy Accreditation Program The survey and accreditation program of the Joint Commission for eligible long term care pharmacy organizations.

long term care pharmacy organization For purposes of Joint Commission accreditation, an organization that provides pharmaceutical services for residents of a long term care facility, including the subacute environment. These services may be provided by employees of the pharmacy organization or through a written agreement with other individuals.

long-term hospital A hospital that treats patients who are not in an acute phase of illness, but who require an intensity of medical and nursing services not available in nursing homes, such as a rehabilitation hospital. *See also* chronic disease facility.

long-term planning *See* strategic planning.

loss **1.** Any diminution of quantity, quality, or value of property, resulting from the occurrence of some undesired event. **2.** In insurance, the basis for a claim under the terms of an insurance policy.

loss of protective reflexes An inability to handle secretions without aspiration or to maintain a patient airway independently. *See also* conscious sedation.

lost chance of cure An element of damages which allows recovery if a patient's opportunity to be cured of a disease has been reduced by another's negligence. Some jurisdictions require proof that cure was probable before the negligent act but is no longer probable as a result of the negligence. *See also* damages; lost chance of survival; negligence.

lost chance of survival An element of damages which allows recovery if a patient's opportunity to survive a disease has been reduced by another's negligence. Some jurisdictions require proof that survival was probable before the negligent act but is no longer probable as a result of the negligence. *See also* damages; lost chance of cure; negligence.

low back pain A common and generally self-limiting condition for which a diseased or herniated disk is only one of many causes, for which spinal imaging and surgery have been found to be greatly overused, and for which widely varying alternative or experimental therapies have been attempted. Low back pain lasting more than three months is termed *chronic* (or *chronic pain syndrome*). The symptom complex *acute low back problems* has been defined in an AHCPR guideline (1994) as activity intolerance due to back-related symptoms including pain or discomfort primarily in the back and pain or numbness moving down the leg (sciatica). Acute low back problems are classified as *potentially serious spinal condition* (spinal tumor, infection, fracture, cauda equina syndrome), *sciatica* (back-related lower limb symptoms suggesting nerve root compromise), or *nonspecific back symptoms* (symptoms occurring primarily in the back suggesting neither nerve root compromise nor a serious underlying condition). This guideline states that the physician should first seek potentially dangerous underlying conditions and then in the absence of signs of dangerous conditions should refrain from calling for special studies since 90% of patients will recover spontaneously within four weeks. In 1995 the state of Florida enacted legislation as part of its health care and insurance reform and workers' compensation reform acts, which contained guidelines on low back pain or injury based on the AHCPR guideline (but covering chronic as well as acute conditions); it spells out exclusionary diagnoses, red flags warranting immediate lumbar spine x-ray imaging (such as cauda equina syndrome), and both recommended and nonrecommended therapies. *See also* herniated disk; pain management; radiculopathy.

low-molecular-weight heparin (LMWH) *See* heparin.

low-mortality outlier A health care provider, such as an individual hospital, with mortality rates that are lower than expected after adjustment for patient and other characteristics. *See also* high-mortality outlier; outlier.

low osmolality contrast medium (LOCM) New contrast agent that is substantially safer than the standard media used in diagnostic imaging in procedures such as angiography and myelography but is also about 15 times more expensive and is associated with a risk for clot formation. *See also* imaging.

low tech Products or services using earlier or less developed technology; for example, a gauze bandage to wrap or cover a laceration or a visit to a physician or other health professional for suture removal are considered low tech.

Luddite Derogatory term for persons harboring an extreme distrust of or antipathy toward technological

---

FEDERALLY SPONSORED GUIDELINE: ACUTE LOW BACK PROBLEMS

Treatment Recommendations

- Acetaminophen and nonsteroidal anti-inflammatory drugs (NSAIDs) such as ibuprofen, naproxen, and aspirin are safe and acceptable medications for pain control. Muscle relaxants and opioid analgesics are an option for short-term treatment but appear to be no more effective than NSAIDs and may cause drowsiness and other side effects in up to 35% of patients.
- Spinal manipulation (by qualified therapists) can be helpful when symptoms begin, but reevaluation is needed if there is no symptom improvement after 4 weeks.
- Low-stress exercise such as walking, swimming, or biking can be started during the first 2 weeks after symptoms begin, if the problems are mild or moderate.
- Conditioning exercises for trunk muscles can be started and gradually increased after the first 2 weeks of symptoms.

Reasons for Not Recommending Treatment

- Lack of sound scientific basis for effectiveness:
  - Spinal traction, biofeedback, TENS (transcutaneous electrical nerve stimulation), and acupuncture; and
  - Lumbar corsets (except perhaps when used for prevention), support belts, and back machines.
- Effectiveness insufficient to justify potential harms:
  - Extended bed rest (resting more than 4 days can weaken muscles and bones and delay recovery);
  - Oral steroids, colchicine, antidepressants, and phenylbutazone (side effects may include gastrointestinal irritation and bone marrow suppression); and
  - Injection of local anesthetics, corticosteroids, or other substances (potential harms include rare but serious problems such as nerve damage and hemorrhage).
- Insufficient evidence of benefit to justify cost of treatment:
  - Heat/diathermy, massage, ultrasound, cutaneous laser treatment, and electrical stimulation (other than TENS).

Source: Acute Low Back Problems Guideline Panel (Bigos SJ et al): *Acute Low Back Problems in Adults. Guideline No. 14.* Rockville, MD: Agency for Health Care Policy and Research, Public Health Service, U.S. Department of Health and Human Services, December 1994.

CARE EFFECTIVENESS/COST-SAVING MEASURES FOR LOW BACK PAIN OR INJURY

Nonspecific Pain With or Without Radicular Symptoms

- Activity modification
- Bed rest for limited circumstances and no more than 4 days
- Self-exercise program (low-stress aerobic exercise, aerobic exercise programs, conditioning exercises, gradually increased exercise quotas)
- Structured patient education (worksite-specific back school)
- Medications (NSAIDS, analgesics including ointments; anti-inflammatory muscle relaxants for acute spasms 7 days or less; opioid analgesics on a time-limited course; antidepressants for chronic back pain)
- Thermal modalities (self-applied ice or heat)
- Osteopathic or chiropractic manipulation therapy in limited circumstances (if function is not improved by 1 month after, therapy should be stopped and the patient reevaluated)
- Licensed professional physical therapy (maximum 12 sessions)
- Licensed professional occupational therapy (maximum 12 sessions)

Modalities and Processes Not Recommended, Not Worth the Cost, or Lacking Sufficient Supporting Evidence

- Lack of referral to neuromusculoskeletal (NMS) specialists when sciatica is severe, disabling, or persistent
- Several uses of imaging tests, such as routine x-ray within first month without a red flag or suspected exclusionary diagnosis; bone scan imaging without suspected spinal tumor, infection, or occult fracture; MRI (magnetic resonance imaging) done on non–ACR (American College of Radiology)-certified equipment; MRI, CT (computed tomography), bone scan, or discogram prescribed without prior consultation with an NMS specialist or without consideration for surgery; thermography; and ultrasound
- Several surgical procedures under particular circumstances, such as percutaneous discectomy, spinal fusion without a decompressive laminectomy, surgical treatment for elderly patients with spinal stenosis who can adequately perform activities of daily living, and surgical decisions for patients with spinal stenosis based solely on imaging tests
- Other treatment modalities, such as TENS, spinal manipulation beyond 30 days from the onset of acute pain, applied ice or heat (which the patient can do at home), massage, cutaneous laser treatment, back schools (outside an occupational setting), and use of back-specific machines

Source: Agency for Health Care Administration, State of Florida, in consultation with the Medical/Surgical Neuro-Musculo-Skeletal Guideline Committee and its Neurological Surgery Subcommittee: Universe of Florida Patients with Low Back Pain or Injury. Medical Practice Guidelines for Practitioners Licensed Under Chapter 458 (Medicine) or Chapter 459 (Osteopathy), Florida Statutes. Florida Health Care and Insurance Reform Act of 1993, Section 408.02; Florida Workers' Compensation Reform Act of 1993, Section 440.13(15). Endorsed October 6, 1995; amended February 2, 1996.

advances or technology itself. The term originated with Ned Ludd and the early nineteenth-century English workers who destroyed workplace machinery in protest against the mechanization of work.

lumbar puncture (LP) The insertion of a hollow needle beneath the spinal membrane (arachnoid) at the lumbar region (lower back) of the spinal cord to withdraw cerebrospinal fluid for diagnostic purposes, such as determining the presence of meningitis, or to administer medications. *Synonyms:* spinal puncture; spinal tap.

lumpectomy The least invasive procedure for breast cancer involving removal of the lump (tumor) and a small amount of tissue through a small incision, leaving only a slight depression in the breast. *See also* breast-conserving surgery; mastectomy.

lung age The age at which a patient's pulmonary function is normal. Lung age that is considerably older than chronological age is used as an indicator of the need to address a condition or problem behavior (such as smoking). Public health authorities have recommended establishing lung-age thresholds to be considered by managed care organizations in their screening programs.

lung volume reduction surgery (LVRS) An increasingly performed, risky, and unproven group of procedures used to lighten up emphysema-burdened lungs. A 1996 technology assessment by AHCPR's Center for Health Care Technology and a 1996 official statement of the American Thoracic Society both indicate that LVRS may be efficacious for some but not all patients with chronic obstructive pulmonary disease. Finding the evidence insufficient to permit making precise recommendations or guidelines, both groups called for a clinical trial to answer questions. In 1997 NIH announced plans for a clinical trial to test LVRS. *See also* chronic obstructive pulmonary disease.

M A computer programming language originated at Massachusetts General Hospital in the late 1960s and the 1970s. It is now used in many different industries in addition to health care. Formerly called MUMPS (Massachusetts General Hospital Utility Multiprogramming System).

macrobiotics An approach to nutrition based on whole cereal grains, beans, cooked vegetables, and the Chinese yin-yang principle. It advocates a diet consisting of organic and locally grown foods, seasonal vegetables, complex carbohydrates, and fewer fats, sugars, and chemically processed foods. *See also* nutrition.

magnetic resonance imaging (MRI) An imaging modality using a strong magnetic field and radio frequency signals to produce multiplanar images of the body. Image contrast is based on the hydrogen concentration, molecular response to radio frequency signals, and flow of structures within the part of the body being imaged. *See also* imaging.

Maimonides (1135-1204) Rabbi Moses Maimon (known as Rambam to Jewish scholars), a physician/scholar, rabbi, and Jewish philosopher born in Cordova, Spain, whose skill won him appointment to the court of Saladin, caliph of Cairo, as personal physician. He wrote many medical works in Arabic, among them a commentary on the aphorisms of Hippocrates, a letter "On the Management of Health" to the caliph's son, and treatises on asthma, diet, poisons, and hygiene. The Morning Prayer, attributed to Maimonides, is considered to rank

---

DAILY PRAYER OF A PHYSICIAN*

Almighty God, Thou has created the human body with infinite wisdom. Ten thousand times ten thousand organs hast Thou combined in it that act unceasingly and harmoniously to preserve the whole in all its beauty—the body which is the envelope of the immortal soul. They are ever acting in perfect order, agreement and accord. Yet, when the frailty of matter or the unbridling of passions deranges this order or interrupts this accord, then forces clash and the body crumbles into the primal dust from which it came. Thou sendest to man diseases as beneficent messengers to foretell approaching danger and to urge him to avert it.

Thou has blest Thine earth, Thy rivers and Thy mountains with healing substances; they enable Thy creatures to alleviate their sufferings and to heal their illnesses. Thou hast endowed man with the wisdom to relieve the suffering of his brother, to recognize his disorders, to extract the healing substances, to discover their powers and to prepare and to apply them to suit every ill. In Thine Eternal Providence Thou hast chosen me to watch over the life and health of Thy creatures. I am now about to apply myself to the duties of my profession. Support me, Almighty God, in these great labors that they may benefit mankind, for without Thy help not even the least thing will succeed.

Inspire me with love for my art and for Thy creatures. Do not allow thirst for profit, ambition for renown and admiration, to interfere with my profession, for these are the enemies of truth and of love for mankind and they can lead astray in the great task of attending to the welfare of Thy creatures. Preserve the strength of my body and of my soul that they ever be ready to cheerfully help and support rich and poor, good and bad, enemy as well as friend. In the sufferer let me see only the human being. Illumine my mind that it recognize what presents itself and that it may comprehend what is absent or hidden. Let it not fail to see what is visible, but do not permit it to arrogate to itself the power to see what cannot be seen, for delicate and indefinite are the bounds of the great art of caring for the lives and health of Thy creatures. Let me never be absent-minded. May no strange thoughts divert my attention at the bedside of the sick, or disturb my mind in its silent labors, for great and sacred are the thoughtful deliberations required to preserve the lives and health of Thy creatures.

Grant that my patients have confidence in me and my art and follow my directions and my counsel. Remove from their midst all charlatans and the whole host of officious relatives and know-all nurses, cruel people who arrogantly frustrate the wisest purposes of our art and often lead Thy creatures to their death.

Should those who are wiser than I wish to improve and instruct me, let my soul gratefully follow their guidance; for vast is the extent of our art. Should conceited fools, however, censure me, then let love for my profession steel me against them, so that I remain steadfast without regard for age, for reputation, or for honor, because surrender would bring to Thy creatures sickness and death.

Imbue my soul with gentleness and calmness when older colleagues, proud of their age, wish to displace me or to scorn me or disdainfully to teach me. May even this be of advantage to me, for they know many things of which I am ignorant, but let not their arrogance give me pain. For they are old and old age is not master of the passions. I also hope to attain old age upon this earth, before Thee, Almighty God!

Let me be contented in everything except in the great science of my profession. Never allow the thought to arise in me that I have attained to sufficient knowledge, but vouchsafe to me the strength, the leisure and the ambition ever to extend my knowledge. For art is great, but the mind of man is ever expanding.

Almighty God! Thou has chosen me in Thy mercy to watch over the life and death of Thy creatures. I now apply myself to my profession. Support me in this great task so that it may benefit mankind, for without Thy help not even the least thing will succeed.

*Although there is considerable debate about this prayer's true authorship, it was first attributed to Moses Maimonides.

Source: Reich, Warren T. (Ed.): *Encyclopedia of Bioethics,* Vol. 15. New York: Macmillan, 1995.

beside the Hippocratic oath as an ethical guide to the medical profession. *See also* Hippocrates of Cos.

Maine Medical Liability Demonstration project
A five-year experiment, supported by a coalition of Maine associations and established by state legislation in 1990 (effective in 1992), and extended to a total of eight years, to test the relationships between practice guidelines and medical liability, in particular the affirmative defense. The legislation stipulates that the project produce standards of practice designed to avoid malpractice claims and increase the defensibility of the malpractice claims that are pursued. Advisory committees developed or adopted guidelines focusing on anesthesia, obstetrics and gynecology, emergency medicine, and radiology. Defendant physicians can cite the guidelines in their defense in malpractice cases, but plaintiffs cannot use them unless they were first cited by the defense or the provisions they cited were identical to those in some other independently developed set of guidelines. Questions have been raised about the constitutionality of the "defendant use only" provision, but the legislation remains in place; however, to date, no suit has been filed to permit testing the affirmative defense. Several studies conducted to explore the impact of the legislation on practice, particularly with respect to cesarean sections, have found mixed results. *See also* affirmative defense; cesarean section; external cephalic version; vaginal birth after cesarean section.

maintenance home health care Home health care provided to persons whose primary needs are usually for personal care or other supportive environmental and social services. *See also* home health services; personal care services.

maintenance therapy The prescription of a drug(s) on a long-term basis in doses sufficient to sustain a therapeutic effect that has been established initially by a different drug or drug combination or the same drug in different dosage.

major depressive disorder *See* depressive disorders.

major diagnosis Diagnosis accounting for the greatest resource consumption during a patient's stay in a health care facility. *See also* diagnosis.

major diagnostic category (MDC) A broad classification of diagnoses, typically grouped by body system. In prospective payment systems, each patient is first classified by principal diagnosis into an MDC. He or she is then further categorized according to age, complications, and other characteristics into a DRG. *See also* DRG; prospective payment system.

major life activities The activities and conditions of self-care, language, learning, mobility, self-direction, capacity for independent living, and economic self-sufficiency. The level of these activities is used to determine eligibility for social services programs for people with handicaps, mental retardation, and developmental disabilities. *See also* activities of daily living; developmental disability; mental retardation.

major medical insurance *See* catastrophic insurance.

major surgery Surgery in which the operative procedure is extensive or hazardous, such as entering one of the body cavities (chest, head, abdomen) or amputating above the ankle or wrist; it usually requires general anesthesia or assistance in respiration. *See also* anesthesia; surgery.

Malcolm Baldrige National Quality Award A national award to recognize manufacturing firms, service firms, and small businesses that excel in quality achievement and quality management. Established in 1987 and named for a former U.S. Secretary of Commerce, the award is based on an examination of categories of organization characteristics and operations. In 1996, 45 health care organizations participated in the Baldrige Health Care Pilot Study. Criteria for the program is intended to encourage and reward performance excellence through a dual focus on ever-improving delivery of health care and customer satisfaction. The Baldrige Award is the U.S. equivalent of the Deming Award in Japan. *Synonym*: Baldrige Award.

male menopause *See* andropause.

malice The intent, without just cause or reason, to commit a wrongful act that will result in harm to another.

malingering The willful, deliberate, and fraudulent feigning or exaggeration of the symptoms of illness or injury, to achieve a consciously desired end, such as collecting insurance or avoiding work or duty.

malnutrition Any disorder of nutrition, resulting from an inadequate, excessive, or unbalanced diet or from impaired ability to absorb and assimilate foods. *See also* nutrition.

malpractice Improper or unethical conduct or unreasonable lack of skill by a holder of a professional or official position, often applied to physicians, dentists, lawyers, and public officers to denote negligent or unskillful performance of duties when professional skills are obligatory. Malpractice is a cause of action for which damages are allowed. *See also* cause of action; defensive medicine; legal malpractice; locality rule; medical malpractice; occurrence policy; professional liability; standard of care.

malpractice insurance *See* medical malpractice insurance.

maltreatment Treatment in which the practitioner lacks adequate skill or knowledge, in which he or she performs willful acts of neglect. *See also* neglect.

mammography A procedure in which the soft tissues of the breast (mammary gland) are radiographed. *Screening mammography* is an x-ray examination to detect unsuspected breast cancer at an early state in asymptomatic women. It usually consists of two views of each breast. *Diagnostic mammography* is an x-ray examination used to evaluate a patient with a breast mass or masses, other breast signs or symptoms (eg, spontaneous discharge from the nipple, skin changes), an abnormal or questionable screening mammogram, a history of breast cancer with breast conservation, or special cases such as augmented breasts. *See also* breast cancer; breast examination; cancer screening tests and procedures; Mammography Quality Standards Act of 1992; radiography; ultrasonography; xeromammography.

Mammography Quality Standards Act (MQSA) of 1992 An act requiring that, as of October 1, 1994, all mammography facilities in the United States be certified by the FDA, except for Veterans Health Administration (VHA) facilities, which have their own mammography quality process that parallels MQSA. All mammography facilities except VHA must display the FDA certificate and must be accredited by an FDA-approved accreditation body. Currently approved accreditation bodies are the American College of Radiology and the state of Iowa (for facilities located in that state). Other private, nonprofit organizations or state agencies may also become approved accreditation bodies. In addition, certification requires annual inspections of all facilities by qualified MQSA personnel. Certification lasts for three years, the time period of accreditation. Provisional certification may last for an interim six-month period while the facility is in the process of receiving accreditation. *See also* mammography.

Manacaid The provision of managed care services to Medicaid beneficiaries. This phrase was coined by investment bankers. *See also* Medicaid.

managed behavioral health care delivery system An entity that manages the provision of behavioral health care services to a defined population and that may also manage the behavioral health care benefits for that population.

managed care Organizations of health care providers, such as physicians and hospitals, formed to enhance efficiency of work performed. This is accomplished by, for example, increasing beneficiary cost sharing, controlling inpatient admissions and lengths of stay, establishing cost-sharing incentives for outpatient surgery, selectively contracting with health care providers, and directly managing high-cost health care cases. An HMO is a common form of managed care. *Synonym:* managed health care. *See also* health care encounter; HMO; managed competition; physician-hospital organization.

Managed Care Consumer Protection Act Model legislation to safeguard consumers, cooperatively developed by state lawmakers in nine states in 1997.

managed competition A proposed system for financing and delivering health care that attempts to blend employers into large purchasing networks to shop for the best health coverage at the lowest price. In this proposed system, the government would require any insurance company, HMO, or other health plan bidding for business to offer a standard core-benefits package. The thesis behind this proposal is that the large purchasing

networks' considerable buying power would generate competition among health plans, resulting in lower prices and improved quality. All employers would be required to contribute to the cost of health coverage for their employees, and the government would subsidize the cost for the low-income and unemployed populations. *See also* health alliance; Jackson Hole approach; managed care.

managed health care *See* managed care.

managed indemnity plan A traditional indemnity insurance plan that offers a variety of utilization review features. *See also* indemnity; utilization review.

management *See* the following management terms, as well as administration; behavior management; care management; case management corporate planning; crisis management; database management; demand management; disease state management; empower; hazardous materials and waste management program; health care administration; home equipment management services; home management services; human resources management; information management; life safety management program; line management; medical equipment management; open-door policy; organizational planning; outcomes management; plan management; personnel management; plant, technology, and safety management; project management; quality management; records management; risk management; safety management; theory x; theory y; theory z; top-down management; total quality management; utilities management; utilization management; vector management; vertical integration.

management by crisis *See* crisis management.

management by objectives (MBO) An approach to management in which control is exercised by results and outputs, rather than by inputs. Performance is continuously measured in an organization, objectives are stated in measurable terms, staff participate in decision making, rewards are based on performance, and specific performance standards for management and professional personnel are set and directed at attaining the organization's overall goals. *See also* crisis management.

management development Any deliberate effort by an organization to provide managers with skills they need for future duties, such as providing them with the opportunity for advanced education. A manager is usually trained so that he or she can be of greater organization value not only in present but also in future assignments.

management information system (MIS) An information system consisting of a group of computer programs designed to collect, store, and transmit data to support management in planning and directing organization operations. *See also* case-mix management information system; clinical information system; hospital information system; information system.

management science A school of management emphasizing the use of mathematics and statistics as an aid in resolving production and operations problems. A major objective is to provide management with a quantitative basis for decisions and actions.

management service organization (MSO) A legal entity that provides administrative and practice management services to physicians. For example, a physician entity owned by one or more physicians may contract with an MSO for administrative, management, and support services. An MSO is usually a direct subsidiary of a hospital, but it may also be owned by investors. *See also* group practice without walls; integrated provider; physician-hospital organization.

management style The leadership style a manager uses in administering an organization or its components. Four basic leadership styles are exploitative-authoritative, benevolent-authoritative, consultative-democratic, and participative-democratic. *See also* leadership.

mandated controversial medical treatments Legislation guaranteeing access by patients to specific controversial clinical procedures, medical devices, and pharmaceuticals that have been denied by managed care organizations. The various acts and bills have been dubbed *body parts legislation* and have raised questions for some groups about whether the technical merits of the affected technologies have been adequately considered. One technology assessment group, ECRI, has issued an Executive Briefing on Mandated Controversial Medical Treatments to guide legislators and other interested parties in evaluating such legislation. *See also* body parts legislation.

mandated employer insurance Health insurance for employees that employers are required by law to purchase. *See also* insurance.

mandatory CME Study commissioned by the state of Virginia for report back to the state on continued medical education (CME). The study explores the concept of continuing competency as a prerequisite for renewal of licensure. *See also* continuing medical education.

mandatory licensure The legal requirement by a state or other jurisdiction that professional practitioners, such as physicians, dentists, nurses, and lawyers, must be licensed. *See also* licensure.

mandatory reporting System under which a physician is required by law to inform health authorities when a specified illness is diagnosed. For example, mandatory reporting is required for AIDS in all 50 states, and it has been proposed that the requirement be extended to HIV infection. *See also* disease notification; notifiable disease.

manic-depressive Former term for a mood disorder now referred to as bipolar disorder. *See* bipolar disorder.

Mantoux test The tuberculin skin test preferred in the United States, involving injection of a known quantity of purified protein derivative (PPD) under the surface of the skin.

manual arts therapy The use of work-related skills, such as metalworking or graphic arts, to rehabilitate and restore patients' physical and emotional health. *See also* creative arts therapy; recreational therapy.

marginal analysis A method of studying the difference in costs or benefits between the status quo and the production or consumption of an additional unit of a specific good or service.

marginal benefit In health economics, the additional benefit of consuming one extra unit of a good or service.

marginal cost In health economics, the additional cost of producing one extra unit of a good or service. This cost varies with the volume of the operation. A hospital, for example, has a high cost for its first percutaneous transluminal coronary angioplasty procedure or its first meal served. Subsequent angioplasties and meals each have lower costs (marginal costs) until the volume becomes so large as to require improvements in facilities and increases in personnel. At this point, the marginal costs rise until a new output level is reached. *Synonyms*: differential cost; incremental cost. *See also* marginal revenue.

marginal revenue The extra revenue generated by producing an additional unit of a good or service. To maximize profits in a competitive health care market, an organization needs to produce additional units of service until marginal cost and marginal revenue are the same. *See also* marginal cost.

marijuana *See* medical marijuana.

market analysis The process of determining the characteristics of a market and the measurement of its capacity to contribute to or buy a service or product. *See also* market research.

market penetration **1.** A marketing strategy used by an organization to increase the sales of a good or service within an existing market through the employment of more aggressive marketing tactics, such as a health care organization that runs frequent radio and television commercials on several channels over many months. **2.** The degree to which a particular product or service is purchased in a particular market.

market power The ability to profitably maintain prices above competitive levels or restrain output for a significant period.

market research The gathering and evaluation of data regarding consumers' preferences for products and services and the moving of goods and services from the producer to the consumer. Market research typically covers three broad areas: market analysis, which yields information about the marketplace; product research, which yields information about the characteristics and desires for the product; and consumer research, which yields information about the consumers' needs and motivations. *Synonym*: marketing research. *See also* market analysis; research and development; response rate.

market share   The part of the potential market that a provider or network has captured. Market share is usually expressed as a percentage of the potential market.

marriage and family counseling   Counseling that helps with a variety of issues, including crisis situations, family violence, incest, suicide, family conflicts, parenting skills, communications, and stress management.

masked study   *See* blinded study.

Massachusetts General Hospital Utility Multi-programming System   *See* M.

massage therapy   Hands-on manipulation of the body's soft tissues to promote healing and improve overall quality of life by improving circulation of the blood and lymphatic fluid, releasing toxins and tension, increasing energy, and reducing stress. Basic principles are that the body's structure and function are interdependent, as are the body and the mind. The main varieties of massage therapy are traditional European massage, contemporary Western massage, structural/functional/movement integration, Oriental methods, and energetic methods. *See also* alternative medicine; osteopathy.

Types of Mastectomies	
lumpectomy	Removal of the tumor and a small amount of tissue through a small incision, leaving only a slight depression in the breast.
modified radical mastectomy	Removal in a single block, if possible, of the entire breast and often some of the lymph glands under the arm but leaving the chest muscles intact and the possibility of breast reconstruction later with an implant.
quadrantectomy	Removal of cancerous tissue plus a wedge of surrounding tissue, and possible removal of portions of the underarm lymph nodes, leaving the breast slightly smaller.
(Halsted) radical mastectomy	Removal of the breast, chest muscles, all of the underarm lymph nodes, and some additional fat and skin.

mastectomy   Surgical removal of one or both breasts. It and other forms of breast cancer surgery have several variants depending on the amount of tissue removed. Breast cancer surgical treatment methods used alone or in combination with other methods (chemotherapy, radiation, hormone therapy) remain a subject of debate; the choice is usually made by the woman after discussion of the options with her physician. A new application is prophylactic mastectomy for presymptomatic women with gene mutations or a family history predisposing them to the later development of breast cancer. *See also* BRCA1 and BRCA2 genes; breast cancer; breast-conservation treatment; breast-conserving surgery; cancer susceptibility testing; lumpectomy; Shared Decisionmaking Program.

master's degree   An academic degree conferred by a college or university upon those who complete at least one year of prescribed study beyond the bachelor's degree, as in a Master of Social Work. *See also* doctor and accompanying table.

Master's Degrees	
MA	Master of Arts
MBA	Master of Business Administration
MDiv	Master of Divinity
MEd	Master of Education
MHA	Master of Health Administration; Master of Hospital Administration
MHSA	Master of Health Services Administration
MPA	Master of Public Administration
MPH	Master of Public Health
MPhil	Master of Philosophy
MS	Master of Science
MSc	Master of Science
MSN	Master of Science in Nursing
MSW	Master of Social Welfare; Master of Social Work
PharM	Master of Pharmacy

matching grant   A grant made under the condition that additional funds be raised from other sources.

maternal and child health (MCH) services   Organized health and social services for pregnant women, mothers, children, and (rarely) fathers. Mothers and children are often considered vulnerable populations with special health needs, who will benefit from preventive medicine and being accorded a high public priority. *See also* preventive medicine.

maternal death   Death of a pregnant woman or of a woman within a specified postdelivery period, as in maternal death secondary to postdelivery infection or blood loss. The World Health Organization defines maternal death as the death of a woman while pregnant or within 42 days of termination of pregnancy, regardless of the duration of the pregnancy, from any cause related to or aggravated by the pregnancy or its management but not from accidental or incidental causes. Maternal deaths may be divided into direct obstetrical deaths, deaths resulting from preexisting disease, or conditions not due to direct obstetric causes. *Synonym*: maternal mortality. *See also* abruptio placenta; maternal mortality rate.

maternal deprivation   The deprivation of an infant or child of the stimulation, considered important to mental and emotional development, normally provided by mother-child interaction.

maternal-fetal medicine   A subspecialty of obstetrics and gynecology involving management of patients with complications of pregnancy.

maternal mortality rate   A rate measuring maternal death from causes associated with childbirth. Deaths used in the numerator are those arising during pregnancy or from puerperal causes (ie, deaths occurring during or due to deliveries, or due to complications of pregnancy, childbirth, and the puerperium). The denominator is the number of live births that occurred among the population of a given geographic area during the same year. *Synonym:* maternal death rate. *See also* live birth; maternal death.

maternity benefits   Insurance coverage for the costs of pregnancy, labor and delivery, postpartum care, complications of pregnancy, and in some plans, family planning. *See also* benefits.

matrix flowchart   A flowchart that places the activities in the diagram under columns representing the individual organizational units performing the work. *Synonym:* matrix flow diagram. *See also* flowchart.

matrix manager   A manager who shares with another manager formal authority over a subordinate.

matrix organization   An organization that uses a multiple command system whereby an employee may be accountable to a particular manager for overall performance as well as to one or more leaders of particular projects.

mature minor   A minor who is judged by a health care provider to have the capacity to make decisions and is allowed to authorize or consent to medical treatment. *See also* age of majority; emancipated minor; informed consent; minor.

maturity-onset diabetes   Former term for type 2 of diabetes mellitus. *See* diabetes mellitus.

maxillofacial surgery   *See also* oral and maxillofacial surgery.

maximum charge   *See* fee maximum.

maximum response time   In home care, the estimated time needed to arrive at a patient's home in the presence of obstacles (eg, blizzards, storms, heavy traffic, vehicle breakdown, off-hours). *See also* normal response time.

maximum security unit   A unit in a penal or mental health facility that provides a fully secured environment for residents considered dangerous to other persons in the facility's population. *See also* security hospital.

Meals on Wheels   A system for providing and transporting meals to the elderly and disabled at home through local authority or voluntary agencies.

mean   A measure of location or central tendency for a continuous variable. The value is the sum of the observations divided by the total number of observations. The mean is best used when the distribution of data is balanced and unimodal. If the distribution is normally distributed, the mean coincides with the median and mode. *Synonym:* average. *See also* coefficient of variation; distribution; measure of association; measure of central tendency; median; mode; normal distribution.

means testing   An investigation into the financial well-being of a person to determine the person's eligibility for financial assistance, as for government programs, such as Medicaid. Income tests are means tests based on income. Assets tests are means tests based on personal assets. *See also* Medicaid.

measurable   Possible to be quantified, as in measurable temperature or measurable performance.

measure   **1.** A quantitative tool or instrument used to make measurements, for example, an indicator. *See also* benchmark; calibration; clinical measures; continuous variable measure; defined measure; indicator; input measure; Norton Scale; outcome measure; performance measure; process measure; quality measure; rate-based measure; scale; standard; structural measure of quality. **2.** To collect quantifiable data about a function or process. *See also* benchmarking; comparative measure-related feedback; functional status; health-related quality of life; measurement; quality measure; quality of life scale; structural measure of quality.

measurement   **1.** The application of a rule or rules by which numbers are assigned to cases to represent the presence, absence, or quantity of a specified attribute possessed by each case. *See also* biometrics; calibration; performance measurement.   **2.** The number resulting from a quantification process.   **3.** For purposes of Joint Commission accreditation, the systematic process of data collection, repeated over time or at a single point in time. *See also* data collection.

measurement accuracy   The degree to which a measurement, or an estimate based on measurements, represents the true value of the attribute that is being measured. A measurement may be accurate but not express detail (ie, it may lack a degree of precision). For instance, a temperature of 98.6°F may be accurate but not precise if a newer measuring instrument measures the temperature as 98.63432°F. Measurements should have acceptable degrees of accuracy and precision. *See also* data accuracy.

measurement data   Data resulting from quantifying attributes or characteristics, as in measurement data forming an important basis for performance assessment and improvement activities.

measurement error   Variation in measurements due to causes, such as sampling error or random error, other than real differences in the attribute being measured. *See also* error; random error; sampling error; systematic error.

measurement system   *See* performance measurement system.

measure of association   A quantity that expresses the strength of statistical dependency of two or more variables. Commonly used measures of association are differences between means, proportions, or rates; the rate ratio; the odds ratio; and correlation and regression coefficients. *See also* correlation coefficient; mean; rate; variable.

COMMONLY USED HEALTH STATUS MEASURES

Measure	Purpose
Arthritis Impact Measurement Scale	To measure health status outcomes for treatment of rheumatic diseases.
Barthel Index	To assess degree of independence in patients with neuromuscular or musculoskeletal disorders before hospital admission and after discharge; to identify patients who would benefit from rehabilitation programs; to predict length of stay; to estimate progress; to anticipate outcomes; and to evaluate services.
Beck Depression Inventory (BDI)	To assess the presence and severity of depression for clinical and research purposes.
Berg Balance Scale	To assess disability based on 14 balance criteria.
Boston Diagnostic Aphasia Examination	To assess sample speech and language behavior based on fluency, naming, word finding, repetition, serial speech, auditory comprehension, reading, and writing.
Center for Epidemiologic Studies Depression (CES-D)	To measure the severity of depressive symptoms based on the patient's self-perceived mood and level of functioning.
Client Satisfaction Questionnaire (CSQ)	To measure overall patient satisfaction in a wide variety of health care settings.
Coop Function Charts	To provide primary care clinicians with a system for screening, assessing, monitoring, and maintaining patient function in routine office practice.
Disability/Distress Scale	To provide a basis for calculating quality-adjusted life years, which are applied to health service policy decisions.
Duke–UNC Functional Social Support (DUFSS) Questionnaire	To measure qualitative or functional aspects of supportive relationships (not number of relationships or size of social network).
Duke–UNC Health Profile (DUHP)	To assess the effect of primary care services on patient-reported functional status and feelings.
Evaluation Ranking Scale (ERS)	To evaluate patient satisfaction with health care delivery within practices.
Family Assessment Device (FAD)	To assess, monitor, and maintain family functioning in problem solving, communication, roles, affective responsiveness, affective involvement, behavior control, and general functioning.
Frenchay Activities Index	To measure instrumental activities of daily living (ADLs) in and outside the home based on patient and family and self-reports.
Fugl-Meyer	To measure impairment of motor function in the domains of pain, range of motion, sensation, volitional movement, and balance.
Functional Independence Measure (FIM)	To measure disability in six domains of ADLs (self-care, sphincter control, mobility, locomotion, communication, and social cognition).
Functional Limitations Profile (FLP)	British version of the Sickness Impact Profile (see below).
Functional Status Index (FSI)	To measure the degree of dependence, pain, and difficulty of movement experienced by people suffering from arthritis.
Functional Status Questionnaire (FSQ)	To provide a comprehensive assessment of physical, psychological, social, and role function in ambulatory patients.
General Health Questionnaire (GHQ)	To detect nonpsychotic psychiatric illness/affective disorder in a community setting.
Geriatric Depression Scale (GDS)	To assess the presence and severity of depression in the elderly and the cognitively impaired.
Glasgow Coma Scale	To measure a patient's level of consciousness in the acute poststroke period by scoring eye opening, motor, and verbal responses to voice commands or pain.
Hamilton Depression Scale	To rate somatic and nonsomatic symptoms of depression.
Health Perception Questionnaire (HPQ)	To measure people's perceptions of their health.
Hospital Anxiety and Depression (HAD) Scale	To detect the presence and severity of relatively mild degrees of mood disorders usually found in nonpsychiatric outpatients.
Index of Independence in Activities of Daily Living	To measure and evaluate the degree of functional incapacity or independence of people suffering from chronic diseases, especially the elderly; to predict the course of illness, care needs, and functional/sociobiological outcomes; to evaluate different treatments.
Karnofsky Performance Status Scale (KPS)	To assess the overall ability of cancer patients undergoing chemotherapy to perform normal activities.
Lambeth Disability Screening Questionnaire	To identify adults within a community who have some degree of disability.
Life Satisfaction Index (LSI)	To measure the psychological well-being of older people.
McGill Pain Questionnaire (MPQ)	To provide quantitative measures of clinical pain.
McMaster Health Index Questionnaire (MHIQ)	To measure global health status (physical, emotional, and social functioning) within a community or other specified population.

(continued on next page)

COMMONLY USED HEALTH STATUS MEASURES *(continued)*

Measure	Purpose
Medical Interview Satisfaction Scale (MISS)	To measure satisfaction with a specific provider or consultation.
Mental Health Inventory (MHI)	To measure psychological distress and well-being (not clinically defined mental illness).
Mini-Mental State Examination (MMSE)	To screen domains of mental status, including orientation to time and place, registration of words, attention, calculation, recall, language, and visual construction.
Montgomery–Asberg Depression Rating Scale (MADRAS)	To evaluate the severity of depression and changes in severity resulting from treatment.
MOS Short Form General Health Surveys (SF-12, SF-20, SF-36, etc)	To measure quality of life in the domains of physical functioning, role limitations due to physical or emotional problems, social functioning, bodily pain, mental health, vitality, and general health perceptions.
Motor Assessment Scale	To measure impairment and disability through volitional arm and hand movements, tone, and mobility.
Motricity Index	To measure impairment of motor function based on strength and trunk control.
Neurobehavioral Cognitive Status Examination (NCSE)	To screen domains of mental status, including orientation, attention, comprehension, naming, construction, memory, calculation, similarities, judgment, and repetition.
NIH Stroke Scale	To evaluate main dimensions (consciousness, vision, extraocular movement, facial palsy, etc) of stroke deficits for acute care screening, formal assessment, and monitoring purposes.
Norbeck Social Support Questionnaire (NSSQ)	To measure multiple dimensions of social support, including affect, affirmation, and aid.
Nottingham Health Profile (NHP)	To measure levels of self-reported distress, including that caused by pathological changes and that resulting from adverse social or environmental conditions.
OARS Multidimensional Functional Assessment Questionnaire (MFAQ)	To assess overall functional capacity, utilization of services, and the connection between them for people aged 55+ who live at home.
Patient Satisfaction Questionnaire (PSQ)	To measure patient satisfaction across different systems of care in different settings; to identify major sources of (dis)satisfaction within a single setting or system.
Patient Satisfaction Scale (PSS)	To assess the relative contributions of physicians' communications skills, affective behavior, and technical competence on patients' overall satisfaction.
PGC Instrumental Activities of Daily Living	To measure patients' ability to perform instrumental ADLs using the Guttman scale to evaluate use of the telephone, walking, shopping, food preparation, housekeeping, laundry, use of public transportation, and health care.
Porch Index of Communicative Ability (PICA)	To assess multidimensional speech and language functions based on auditory and visual comprehension, written and verbal expression, and pantomime.
Quality of Life Index	To measure the general well-being of cancer patients.
Quality of Well-Being Scale (QWB)	To indicate the benefits of medical care in terms of well years or quality-adjusted life years.
RAND Functional Status Indexes	To measure physical health in three broad areas of functioning: personal limitations, role limitations, and physical capacities.
Rand Social Activities Questionnaire	To examine the effects of health care on social contacts and resources for adults; to examine the relationships between social support, medical care consumption, and physical and mental health status.
Rankin Scale	To measure degrees of disability during acute hospitalization.
Rivermead Mobility Index	To measure physical mobility disability based on sitting, standing, transferring, walking, and turning over in bed.
Scale for the Measurement of Satisfaction with Medical Care	To measure patient satisfaction with medical care within a community.
Sickness Impact Profile (SIP)	To measure sickness-related behavioral dysfunction based on the patient's perception of the illness' impact on normal daily activities.
Social Relationship Scale (SRS)	To measure the role of social support in coping with life stressors and their effects on health.
Stanford Health Assessment Questionnaire (HAQ)	To assess four outcome dimensions (disability, pain, drug side effects, and costs) of medical care.
Western Aphasia Battery	To assess comprehensive speech and language functions based on spontaneous speech, repetition, comprehension, naming, reading, writing, and construction.
Zung Self-Rating Depression Scale	To provide a quantitative measurement of the subjective experience of depression as characterized by affective, cognitive, behavioral, and psychological symptoms.

measure of central tendency A statistic used to describe the typical or average score in a distribution. The principal measures of central tendency are the mean, median, and mode. *See also* mean; median; mode.

measure of damages The system of rules governing the adjustment or apportionment of damages as a compensation for injuries in actions of law.

measure-related feedback Information on performance that is available, on a timely basis, to organizations actively participating in the performance measurement system, for use in the organization's ongoing efforts to improve patient care and organization performance. Feedback can reflect information within individual organizations or across organizations.

mechanical ventilation Breathing accomplished by extrinsic means, as with a ventilator for a patient who is intubated. *See also* adult respiratory distress syndrome; ventilation; ventilator.

medevac (medical evacuation) Air transport of persons to a place where they can receive medical care, as in medevac from the island to the mainland for medical care. *See also* ambulance.

median The value in a group or set of ranked observations that divides the data into two equal-sized parts; that is, the middle number of a data set. The median is the most valid measure of central tendency whenever a distribution is skewed. *See also* average; distribution; mean; measure of central tendency; mode.

mediation In law, an attempt to bring about a peaceful settlement or compromise between disputants through the objective intervention of a neutral party who is trained in dispute resolution. *Synonym:* conciliation. *See also* arbitration.

Medicaid The medical assistance program, established in 1965 by amendment to the Social Security Act, that is jointly funded by the states and the federal government. It reimburses hospitals, physicians, long term care facilities, and some home-based services for providing care to needy and low-income people who cannot finance their own medical expenses. Medicaid eligibility includes a means test. It is the main source of public assistance for nursing home costs. *See also* the following Medicaid terms, as well as categorically needy; Deficit Reduction Act of 1984; Early and Periodic Screening Diagnosis and Treatment Program; means testing; medically needy; national health insurance; notch; open-ended program; primary payer; required services; Social Security Act; spend down; supplemental security income.

Medicaid health facility A hospital that is owned or operated by a unit of state or local government, is a public or private nonprofit corporation that is formally granted government powers by a unit of state or local government, or is a private nonprofit hospital that has a contract with a state or local government to provide health services to low-income individuals who are not entitled to benefits under Title XVIII of the Social Security Act or eligible for assistance under a state's plan under this title. *Synonym:* public hospital.

Medicaid mill A health program that primarily serves Medicaid beneficiaries, typically on an ambulatory basis. The mills, originating in the ghettos of New York City, are still found primarily in urban slums with few other medical services. They are usually organized on a for-profit basis, characterized by their great productivity, and frequently accused of a variety of abuses. *See also* family ganging; ping-ponging.

Medi-Cal California's Medicaid program. *See* Medicaid.

Medical Assistance for Aged *See* Kerr-Mills.

medical association A national, state, regional, or local voluntary membership organization for the advancement and control of a medical profession, as in the American Medical Association. *See also* medical specialty societies.

medical audit *See* medical record review.

medical boards *See* medical specialty boards; state board of medical examiners.

medical care and services The provision of health services by a physician. *See also* health services; medical indigence.

medical center A place where medical services are provided, ranging from an academic medical center encompassing several hospitals to the office of a single physician. There is no licensure requirement before the phrase may be used. *See also* academic medical center.

Medical College Admission Test (MCAT) A nationally standardized test, developed by the Association of American Medical Colleges and administered by American College Testing, which nearly all U.S. medical schools require or strongly recommend for individuals seeking admission to medical school. *See also* standardized test.

medical consult *See* consultation.

medical consumer price index (MCPI) The medical component of the consumer price index, providing specific data on hospital, dental, medical, and drug prices.

medical deduction A federal income tax deduction for expenditures on health insurance and other medical expenses in excess of 3% of a person's income, the only national health insurance program in the United States. Deductible medical expenses are broadly defined and include the services of physicians, dentists, podiatrists, chiropractors, and Christian Science practitioners, as well as equipment, drugs, supplies, and special diets prescribed by such professionals. *See also* medical expenses.

medical detoxification The process of providing medical treatment and life-support services when necessary for patients critically ill due to the presence of a toxic substance in the body or from acute withdrawal symptoms related to the substance. *See also* detoxification; social detoxification; withdrawal symptoms.

medical device An instrument, apparatus, implement, machine, contrivance, implant, in vitro reagent, or other similar or related item, including any component, part, or accessory that is recognized in the official *National Formulary*, the *United States Pharmacopoeia*, or any supplement to them. A medical device is intended for use in diagnosing disease or other conditions or in curing, mitigating, treating, or preventing disease; or intended to affect the structure or any function of the human body. A medical device does not achieve its primary intended purposes through chemical action within or on the body of humans or other animals and is not dependent on being metabolized for achieving any of its intended principal purposes. The FDA classifies all medical devices according to the level of control necessary to ensure their safety and effectiveness, in accordance with amendments to the Food, Drug, and Cosmetic Act in 1976 and the Safe Medical Devices Act of 1990. All medical devices are subject to general controls, which include formal registration and listing for marketing and labeling regulation, and may also require compliance with the Good Manufacturing Practices (GMP) regulation and submission of a premarket notification before marketing. *Special controls* for Class II and III devices may include special labeling requirements, mandatory performance standards, postmarket surveillance, and premarket approval from the FDA. The FDA may on its own or in response to an outside petition change a device's classification by regulation. *See also* antiarrythmia devices; automated ambulatory blood pressure monitoring device; device; Holter monitoring device; Medical Device Amendments of 1976; reusable medical device reprocessing; Safe Medical Devices Act of 1990; self-measured blood pressure monitoring device.

MEDICAL DEVICE REGULATORY CLASSES

Class I
Bandages
Examination gloves
Hand-held surgical instruments

Class II
Powered wheelchairs
Infusion pumps
Surgical drapes

Class III
Replacement heart valves
Silicone gel-filled breast implants
Implanted cerebellar stimulators
Implantable pacemaker pulse generators
Vascular grafts > 6 mm long
Endosseus implants

Medical Device Amendments of 1976 Legislation that expanded the basic definition of *medical device* to include devices intended for use in diagnosing conditions other than disease, such as pregnancy and in vitro diagnostic products, including those previously regulated as drugs.

medical directive *See* living will.

medical emancipation *See* emancipated minor.

medical equipment Any fixed and portable nondrug item or apparatus used for the diagnosis, treatment, monitoring, and direct care of patients. *See also* disposable medical equipment; durable medical equipment; medical supplies.

medical equipment management For purposes of Joint Commission accreditation, a component of an organization's management of the environment of care program designed to assess and control the clinical and physical risks of fixed and portable equipment used for the diagnosis, treatment, monitoring, and care of patients.

Medic Alert Organ Donor Program (MAODP) A program founded in 1968 that provides medical identification emblems to be worn at all times, identifying the wearers' wishes to donate either some or all of their organs. It encourages organ donors to make all legal and medical arrangements to facilitate a donation, provides only emergency information, and does not counsel individuals or assist in locating recipients of organs or medical schools who may use the donation in a medical research program. *See also* organ procurement.

medical ethics The principles of proper professional conduct concerning the rights and duties of physicians themselves, their patients, and their fellow practitioners, as well as their actions in the care of patients and in relations with their families. In the United States, these principles are embodied in the *Code of Medical Ethics: Current Opinions with Annotations*, maintained and periodically updated by the American Medical Association's Council on Ethical and Judicial Affairs. *See also* bioethics; code of ethics; ethics; futile care; futility; genetic counseling; genetic engineering; Hippocratic Oath; institutional review board; Tuskagee experiments.

medical evidence Evidence found in treatises on medicine or surgery or furnished by physicians, nurses, and other health professionals testifying in a professional capacity as experts. *See also* expert witness.

medical examiner (ME) **1.** A physician authorized by a government unit to ascertain causes of deaths, especially those not occurring under natural circumstances. *See also* coroner. **2.** A member of a board of medical examiners; for example, a state board of medical examiners or a national board of medical examiners. *See also* state board of medical examiners.

medical expenses Money spent by an individual on health care, including medications and health insurance premiums, which is allowed as an itemized deduction to the extent that such amounts (less insurance reimbursements) exceed a certain percentage of adjusted gross income. *See also* medical deduction.

medical foundation An independent organization of physicians, generally sponsored by a state or local medical association or society, concerned with delivering medical services at reasonable cost. Many medical foundations operate as prepaid group practices or as individual practice associations for HMOs. Although these foundations are prepaid on a capitation basis for services to some or all of their patients, they still pay their individual members on a fee-for-service basis for the services they provide. Some foundations are organized only for peer review purposes or other specific functions. *Synonym*: foundation for medical care. *See also* foundation.

AMA PRINCIPLES OF MEDICAL ETHICS

- A physician shall be dedicated to providing competent medical service with compassion and respect for human dignity.

- A physician shall deal honestly with patients and colleagues, and strive to expose those physicians deficient in character or competence, or who engage in fraud or deception.

- A physician shall respect the law and also recognize a responsibility to seek changes in those requirements that are contrary to the best interests of patients.

- A physician shall respect the rights of patients, of colleagues, and of other health professionals, and shall safeguard patient confidences within the constraints of the law.

- A physician shall continue to study, apply, and advance scientific knowledge, make relevant information available to patients, colleagues and the public, obtain consultation, and use the talents of other health professionals when indicated.

- A physician shall, in the provision of appropriate patient care, except in emergencies, be free to choose whom to serve, with whom to associate, and the environment in which to provide medical services.

- A physician shall recognize a responsibility to participate in activities contributing to an improved community.

Source: American Medical Association, Council on Ethical and Judicial Affairs: *Code of Medical Ethics: Current Opinions with Annotations.* 1994 Edition. Chicago, 1994.

---

medical genetics The branch of science and specialty of medicine dealing with biological variation as it relates to health and disease, including diagnosis and therapy for patients with genetic-linked diseases. Areas of subspecialization include clinical genetics, medical genetics, clinical cytogenetics, clinical biochemical genetics, and clinical molecular genetics. *See also* Cancer Genetics Studies Consortium; clinical genetics; cytogenetics; genetics; human genetics; immunogenetics.

medical group practice A group of at least three licensed physicians engaged in a formally organized and legally recognized entity, sharing equipment, facilities, common records, and personnel involved in both patient care and business management. *See also* group practice.

medical history **1.** A component of a medical record consisting of an account of the events in a patient's life that have relevance to his or her mental and physical health. More than the patient's unprompted narrative, it is a specialized literary form in which a physician or other qualified health professional composes and writes an account based on facts, supplied by a patient or other informants, offered spontaneously or obtained by probing. Items are accepted for the medical record only after evaluation by the physician or other health professional, who uses his or her knowledge of the natural history of diseases to secure pertinent details and establish the sequence of events. The components of a complete medical history typically include identification and vital statistics (eg, birth date, residence, occupation), source of information and the informant's relation to the patient, chief complaint(s), details of the present illness, relevant past history (eg, general health, infectious diseases, operations and injuries, previous hospitalizations, systems review), relevant inventory by body systems, social history, and family history. *Synonyms*: health history; patient history. *See also* bedside diagnosis; case history; drug history; family history; longitudinal patient record; medical record; new patient; physical examination. **2.** For purposes of Joint Commission accreditation, a component of the medical record consisting of an account of a patient's history, obtained whenever possible from the patient, and including at least the following information: chief complaint, details of the present illness or care needs, relevant past history, and relevant inventory by body systems.

medical hold The act of holding a patient for treatment against the patient's will, used in situations when people are thought to be suffering from mental disease and are considered a danger to self or other persons. *See also* commitment.

Medical Illness Severity Grouping System (MedisGroups or MEDISGRPS) A proprietary computerized data system developed by MediQual Systems, Inc, for classifying hospital patients by severity of illness using objective data specially abstracted from patients' medical records. *See also* severity adjustment; severity of illness.

Medical Impairment Bureau (MIB) A clearinghouse of information on people who have applied for life insurance. Adverse medical findings on previous medical examinations are recorded in code and sent to companies subscribing to the service.

medical indigence As defined in a statute or administrative rule, the condition of having insufficient income to pay for adequate health care without depriving oneself or one's dependents of food, clothing, shelter, and other essentials of living. Medical indigence may occur when a self-supporting individual, able under ordinary conditions to provide basic maintenance for himself or herself and his or her family, is, in times of catastrophic illness, unable to finance the total cost of medical care. *See also* charity allowance; medically needy.

medical-industrial complex Business, market, and commercial orientation of the health care system with emphasis on investor-owned health care organizations.

medical informatics The study of the management and use of biomedical information. *Synonym*: medical information science. *See also* informatics.

medical injury   An adverse patient occurrence that may or may not have been avoidable. *See also* adverse patient occurrence; negligence; potentially compensable event.

medical intensive care unit (MICU)   An intensive care unit for nonsurgical inpatients. *See also* cardiac care unit; intensive care; special care unit.

medical IRA   *See* medical savings account.

medical jurisprudence   *See* forensic medicine.

medical laboratory   *See* clinical laboratory.

medical laboratory services   Clinical laboratory tests conducted for a patient, either directly by a health care organization or as a contracted service, to gather specific information about the patient's condition. *See also* clinical laboratory; pathology and clinical laboratory services.

medical-legal analysis   A field of study dealing with forensic and jurisprudential aspects of medicine and surgery. *See also* forensic medicine.

medical liability   *See* professional liability.

medical liability insurance   *See* professional liability insurance.

medical licensure   The process by which a legal jurisdiction, such as a state, grants permission to a physician to practice medicine upon finding that she or he has met acceptable qualification standards. Medical licensure also involves ongoing state regulation of physicians, including the state's authority to revoke or otherwise restrict a license to practice. *Synonyms*: medical licensing; physician licensing; physician licensure. *See also* licensure; state board of medical examiners.

Medical Literature Analysis and Retrieval System   *See* MEDLARS®.

medically futile   *See* futility.

medically indigent   *See* medical indigence.

medically necessary   A treatment or service that is appropriate and consistent with diagnoses and which, in accordance with local accepted standards of practice, cannot be omitted without adversely affecting the patient's condition or the quality of care.

medically needy   In the Medicaid program, individuals who have enough income and resources to pay for their basic living expenses, and so do not require welfare, but who do not have enough income and resources to pay for their medical care. These individuals receive benefits if their income after deducting medical expenses is low enough to meet the eligibility standard. *See also* categorically needy; Medicaid; medical indigence; medically underserved area; medically underserved population.

medically underserved area   A geographic location, such as an urban or a rural area, that has inadequate health resources to meet the health care needs of the resident population. *Physician shortage area* applies to a medically underserved area that is particularly short of physicians. *See also* health service area; medically needy; medically underserved population; physician shortage area; scarcity area.

medically underserved population   A group of people with inadequate health services who may or may not reside in a specified area that is medically underserved. Thus, migrants, native Americans, or prison inmates may constitute such a population. The term is defined and used to give such populations priority for federal assistance. *See also* medically needy; medically underserved area.

medical malpractice   A judicial determination that there has been a negligent (or, rarely, willful) failure to adhere to current standard(s) of care, resulting in injury or loss to a patient and legal liability of the provider responsible for the negligent act. Since the judgment of malpractice is sociolegal and is made on a case-by-case rather than systematic basis, standards and processes for determining malpractice may vary by area. *See also* legal malpractice; malpractice; medical malpractice insurance; professional liability.

medical malpractice insurance   Insurance against the risk of suffering financial damage because of malpractice. *Synonym*: malpractice insurance. *See also* insurance; medical malpractice; professional liability insurance; sponsored malpractice insurance.

medical marijuana   A term for therapeutic uses or potential of the smoked drug, described primarily in anecdotal reports and debated along with proposed legislation in some states to permit legal prescription by physicians. Currently, smoked marijuana is a Schedule I drug that cannot be prescribed, although this status has been clouded by state initiatives legalizing medicinal use if "recommended" by a physician. Most controlled research has focused on the effects of oral doses of the drug's primary active ingredient, delta-9-THC, which is a legal drug. Conditions for which marijuana has been said to have a beneficial effect include chemotherapy-related nausea and vomiting, loss of appetite in the AIDS wasting syndrome, and high intraocular pressure in glaucoma. Early in 1997, the matter of smoked marijuana's therapeutic uses was placed under scrutiny by the NIH, which will design studies and clinical trials to test its efficacy and track the effects of long-term use. Following passage of voter initiatives in the fall of 1996 in California and Arizona in favor of medicinal use, officials of the Clinton administration denounced the laws as significant threats to the government's efforts to limit the traffic in illegal drugs and to dissuade younger people from using them, and the White House Office of National Drug Control Policy led the government in a public relations offensive. Law enforcement officials warned physicians that they could lose the prescription licenses they received from the Drug Enforcement Administration or could even face criminal prosecution. A group of California doctors filed suit, arguing that threats from government officials constituted a violation of the physicians' right to free speech, which prompted a restraining order issued by a federal district judge to bar the Clinton administration from taking action to punish California doctors who recommended marijuana under the state's new law. The district court also ordered both sides to meet to try to work out a settlement. In February the U.S. Department of Justice and the Department of Health and Human Services issued a clarification statement making clear that no federal "gag" rule existed to stop physicians and patients from talking about the therapeutic use of marijuana but that "physicians may not intentionally provide their patients with oral or written statements in order to enable them to obtain controlled substances in violation of federal law." In March 1997 the California Medical Association released guidelines for physicians on discussing medical marijuana. As of summer 1997, the precise boundary lines between "discussing," "recommending," "prescribing," and "obtaining" had not been established or tested in court. *See also* Proposition 215; regulation; schedule of controlled substances.

CMA GUIDELINES ON DISCUSSING MEDICAL MARIJUANA WITH PATIENTS

- Provide scientific evidence that reflects both the potential risks and benefits of marijuana for the patient's condition.

- Try to answer questions about risks and benefits while making clear that marijuana has not been fully tested in controlled clinical trials.

- Describe experiences of other similarly situated patients who have used marijuana.

- Counsel on possible ways to balance the risks and benefits, while also advising that you cannot lawfully recommend marijuana.

- Warn that regardless of the new state law, cultivation, possession, and use of marijuana for any reason is illegal under federal law.

- State that you cannot take any action to enable a patient to obtain marijuana—including cooperating with a cannabis buyers' club in issuing a written marijuana "recommendation" as a potential legal defense or offering in advance to testify for the patient in court.

Source: California Medical Association: Guidelines as reported in *American Medical News,* 40:3,42 April 7, 1997.

---

medical neglect Withholding medically indicated treatment from an individual, especially a child. Medical neglect is one form of child abuse. *See also* child abuse; neglect.

Medical Outcomes Study (MOS) RAND's large observational study of adult patients from the offices of general medical providers and mental health specialists in three U.S. urban areas (Boston, Chicago, and Los Angeles), which generated a new multiple-choice short-form health survey now widely used and adapted in many languages—the 36-item MOS Short Form General Health Survey (SF-36) and its shorter variants, the SF-20 and SF-12. *See also* measure (and accompanying table).

medical practice The professional business of a physician, as in solo practice or group practice. *See also* group practice; solo practice.

medical practice act A state, commonwealth, or territorial statute or law governing the practice of medicine. *See also* dental practice act; nurse practice act.

medical practice plan The set of policies and procedures, usually presented in a single document, that governs the manner in which patient services are rendered by medical school faculty physicians, the method of obtaining reimbursement, and the disposition of the funds obtained for such services. *Synonyms:* clinical practice plan; faculty practice plan. *See also* teaching hospital.

medical record 1. The written documentation of a patient's medical history, diagnostic and therapeutic procedures performed, and clinical status at the most recent previous visit to a practitioner. An account compiled by physicians and other health professionals of a patient's medical history; present illness; findings on physical examination; details of treatment; reports of diagnostic tests; findings and conclusions from special examinations; findings and diagnoses of consultants; diagnoses of the responsible physician; notes on treatment, including medication, surgical operations, radiation, and physical therapy; and progress notes by physicians, nurses and other health professionals. The medical record has medical and legal purposes. Medical purposes include assisting physicians and other health professionals in making diagnoses; assisting physicians, nurses, and other health professionals in the care and treatment of the patient; and serving as a record for teaching medicine, performing clinical research, and improving practitioner and organization performance. Legal purposes include documentation of insurance claims for the patient and serving as legal proof in cases of malpractice claims, injury or compensation, cases of poisoning, and cases of homicide and suicide. *Synonyms:* chart; clinical record; health record; patient chart; patient health record; patient medical record; patient record. *See also* the following medical record terms, as well as case abstract; case-based review; chart review; clinical résumé; coding; computer-based patient record; confidentiality; consultation report; documentation; electronic medical record; established patient; Freedom of Information Act; health care record; home care record; medical history; nursing record; online medical record; open charting; physical examination; problem-oriented medical record; progress notes; record; SOAP; systemized nomenclature of medicine. **2.** For purposes of Joint Commission accreditation, the account compiled by physicians and other health care professionals of a variety of patient health information, such as assessment findings, treatment details, and progress notes. A medical record is considered complete when (1) its contents reflect the diagnosis, results of diagnostic tests, therapy rendered, condition and in-house progress of the patient, and condition of the patient at discharge, and (2) its contents, including any required clinical résumé or final progress notes, are assembled and authenticated, and all final diagnoses and any complications are recorded without the use of symbols or abbreviations.

medical record abstraction The selection and separation of essential material of a medical record or other source document in order to create a summary (abstract) of that record or document. *Synonyms*: abstracting; abstraction. *See also* discharge abstract; case abstract; hospital discharge abstract system.

medical record audit *See* medical record review.

medical record coding The process of assigning and sequencing codes (eg, numbers) for terms (eg, congestive heart failure) for use in research, reimbursement, performance improvement, and health care planning. *See also* coding.

medical record entry Notes written, dated, and signed in the medical record by physicians, nurses, respiratory therapists, physical therapists, and all other health professionals permitted to do so by the organization.

medical record index A system of indexing medical records so that they can be located according to patient names, diagnoses, procedures, physicians, and other categories.

medical record progress note A component of the medical record consisting of a pertinent, chronological report of a patient's course. The SOAP format (subjective data, objective data, assessment of status, plan for care) is typically used to organize and record progress notes. *See also* problem-oriented medical record; SOAP.

medical record review For purposes of Joint Commission accreditation, the process of measuring, assessing, and improving the quality of medical record documentation—that is, the degree to which medical record documentation is accurate, complete, and performed in a timely manner. *Synonyms*: medical audit; medical record audit.

medical record services The activities designed to ensure the accuracy, completeness, timeliness, accessibility, and safe, secure, and confidential storage of patients' medical records.

medical review A quality-of-care review, including the appropriateness and effectiveness of services, conducted by physicians, nurses, and other health and social service personnel to meet external (eg, government) or self-imposed requirements. *See also* external review; internal review; medical review agency; utilization review.

medical review agency An agency established under a prospective payment system to carry out certain surveillance functions with respect to organization and physician performance and detection of fraud. *See also* fraud and abuse; medical review.

medical review criteria Defined by the Institute of Medicine (IOM), in developing definitions for the legislation establishing the AHCPR, as systematically developed statements that can be used to assess the appropriateness of specific health care decisions, services, and outcomes. The IOM identified eight desirable attributes of these criteria. *See also* guideline attributes.

medical savings account (MSA) A consumer-contributed, tax-deferred account to be used for future medical expenses. The plan encourages patients to accept more responsibility for medical expenses and use of health care resources by contributing a certain amount of money per year. Rules for proposed MSAs include: (1)

DESIRABLE ATTRIBUTES OF MEDICAL REVIEW CRITERIA: THE INSTITUTE OF MEDICINE

Attribute	Explanation
Sensitivity	Review criteria are sensitive when it is highly likely that a case will be identified as deficient given that it really is deficient. (This assumes that a guideline or other source provides a "gold standard.")
Specificity	Review criteria are specific if it is highly likely that they will identify truly good care as such.
Patient Responsiveness	Review criteria specifically identify a role for patient preferences or the process for using them allows for some consideration of patient preferences.
Readability	Review criteria are presented in language and formats that can be read and understood by nonphysician reviewers, practitioners, and patients/consumers.
Minimum Obtrusiveness	Review criteria and the process for applying them minimize inappropriate direct interaction with and burdens on the treating practitioner or patient.
Feasibility	The information required for review can be obtained easily from direct communication with providers, patients, records, and other sources, and the decision criteria are easy to apply. Review criteria are accompanied by explicit instructions for their application and scoring.
Computer Compatibility	Review criteria are straightforward enough that they can be transformed readily into the computer-based protocols and similar formats that can make the review process more efficient for all involved parties.
Appeals Criteria	Criteria provide explicit guidance about the considerations to be taken into account when adverse review decisions are appealed by professionals or patients.

Source: Institute of Medicine, Committee on Clinical Practice Guidelines: *Guidelines for Clinical Practice: From Development to Use.* Field MJ, Lohr KN, eds. Washington, DC: National Academy Press, 1992.

such accounts may be established only if the consumer has no insurance other than catastrophic coverage, usually with high deductibles; (2) there is a limit to the amount that may be contributed to an MSA and excluded or deducted from gross income; (3) funds drawn from an MSA to cover health care costs are excludable from gross income, but funds used for nonmedical purposes would be taxed as ordinary income with an additional penalty. *See also* Health Insurance Portability and Accountability Act of 1996.

medical school admission test   *See* Medical College Admission Test.

medical services   *See* medical care and services.

medical society   Any professional association of physicians.

medical specialty   An area of expertise in medicine, recognized by the American Board of Medical Specialties (ABMS). Currently the ABMS recognizes 25 medical specialty areas, which are further broken down into subspecialties in some cases. Physicians who become medical specialists must meet specific educational and other requirements to become board certified. *See also* medical subspecialty.

MEDICAL SPECIALTIES

Title	Abbreviation
Allergists and Immunologists	A&I
Anesthesiologists	Anes
Colon and Rectal Surgeons	CRS
Dermatologists	D
Emergency Medicine Physicians	EM
Family Physicians	FP
Internists	IM
Medical Geneticists	MG
Neurological Surgeons	NS
Neurologists	N
Nuclear Medicine Specialists	NuM
Obstetricians and Gynecologists	ObG
Ophthalmologists	Oph
Orthopaedic Surgeons	OrS
Otolaryngology	Oto
Pathologists	Path
Pediatricians	Ped
PM & R Specialists (Physiatrists)	PMR
Plastic Surgeons	PlS
Preventive Medicine Specialists	PrM
Psychiatrists	Psych
Radiological and Radiological Physicists	Rad
Surgeons	S
Thoracic Surgeons	TS
Urologists	U

Source: *The Official ABMS Directory of Board Certified Medical Specialists®* 1997. 29th Edition. New Providence, NJ: Marquis Who's Who,® A Division of Reed Elsevier, Inc, 1997.

medical specialty boards   **1.** National bodies that certify physicians as diplomates of one or more specialty boards when all requirements have been met. Specialty boards influence graduate medical education through setting criteria that must be met for eligibility to take the cer-

tification examinations. Each board sets the minimum length of time for education in an accredited residency program and, in part, determines the content of the training program, since it determines the content of the certifying examination. *See also* board eligible; medical specialty.   **2.** Slang term for specialty board examinations. *See* specialty boards.

medical specialty societies   Professional associations whose members practice primarily in recognized specialties and subspecialties. *See also* listings in Appendix A.

medical staff   A body that has overall responsibility for the quality of the professional services provided by individuals with clinical privileges and also the responsibility of accounting, therefore, to the governing body. The medical staff includes fully licensed physicians and may include other licensed individuals permitted by law and by the organization to provide patient care services independently (ie, without clinical direction or supervision) within the organization. Members have delineated clinical privileges that allow them to provide patient care services independently within the scope of their clinical privileges. Members and all other persons with individual clinical privileges are subject to medical staff and departmental bylaws and are subject to review as part of the organization's performance assessment and improvement activities. *See also* attending physician; clinical privileges; closed staff; delineation of clinical privileges; hospital; housestaff; licensed independent practitioner; open staff; reappointment of physicians; self-governance.

medical staff credentialing   *See* credentialing.

medical staff privileges   *See* clinical privileges.

Medical Subject Headings   *See* MeSH.

medical subspecialty   A more specific area of a medical specialty. For example, infectious disease is a subspecialty of internal medicine, and critical care medicine is a subspecialty of anesthesiology. Physicians who wish to become medical subspecialists must complete training in a general medical specialty and then take additional training in a more specific area of that specialty. This training requires an additional one or more years of full-time education in a program called a fellowship. *See also* fellow; medical specialty.

medical supplies   Medical items, usually of a disposable nature, such as bandages, suture material, and sterile drapes. Supplies differ from permanent and durable capital goods, such as an examining or operating table whose use lasts more than a year. *See also* medical equipment.

medical technology   *See* health care technology.

medical toxicology   *See* clinical toxicology.

medicar   A vehicle that transports patients in wheelchairs between facilities or on home-to-hospital transfers. It is staffed with a driver who does not provide medical care. *See also* ambulance.

Medicare A federal program administered under HCFA that reimburses health care providers for health care provided to qualifying people aged 65 years and older, persons eligible for Social Security disability payments for at least two years, and certain workers and their dependents who need kidney transplantation or dialysis. Part A is inpatient/skilled nursing insurance that covers facility costs. Part B is supplemental medical insurance that covers physician and other qualifying outpatient services (Title XVIII). *See also* the following Medicare terms, as well as assignment; base year Medicare costs; catchment area; certified hospital; conditions of participation; customary, prevailing, and reasonable charge; deemed status; Deficit Reduction Act of 1984; DRG; End Stage Renal Disease Program; entitlement; entitlement program; Explanation of Medicare Benefits; health insurance claim number; hospice benefit; hospital component; lifetime reserve; medigap policy; national health insurance; Old Age, Survivors, Disability and Health Insurance Program; participating physician; pass-through cost; peer review organization; Physician Payment Reform; primary payer; PRO scope of work; prospective payment system; provider-based physician; prudent buyer principle; referral center; safe harbor regulations; Social Security Act; specified disease insurance; supplemental health insurance; Supplementary Medical Insurance Program (Part B); unbundling; voucher system.

Medicare Conditions of Participation (COPs) Requirements that institutional providers (eg, hospitals, skilled nursing facilities, home health agencies) must meet to be allowed to receive payments for Medicare patients; for example, hospitals must conduct utilization reviews. *See also* conditions of participation; deemed status; utilization review.

Medicare locality A geographic area in which a Medicare carrier obtains information about prevailing charges for the purpose of making reasonable charge determinations. *See also* carrier; catchment area; health service area; reasonable cost.

Medicare, Part A The hospital care portion of Medicare that automatically covers all persons aged 65 and older who are entitled to benefits under Old Age, Survivors, Disability and Health Insurance or railroad retirement plans; persons under 65 years old who have been eligible for disability for at least two years; and insured workers and their dependents needing kidney dialysis or kidney transplantation. Part A pays for inpatient care and care in skilled nursing facilities and home health agencies following a period of hospitalization, after cost-sharing requirements are met. The Part A, Hospital Insurance Program is financed from a separate trust fund whose monies come from a contributory tax (payroll tax) levied on employers, employees, and the self-employed. *Synonym:* Hospital Insurance Program.

Medicare, Part B The portion of Medicare through which individuals entitled to Medicare, Part A, may obtain assistance with payment for physicians' and qualifying outpatient services. Individuals participate volun-tarily through enrollment and the payment of a monthly fee. *See also* unbundling.

Medicare Provider Analysis and Review (MEDPAR) A database containing health care organization and physician financial claims and clinical data for Medicare beneficiaries, in which data elements are defined by Medicare billing requirements and are maintained by HCFA.

Medicare secondary payer The Medicare role in the coordination of benefits as a secondary payer to other health insurance plans, as defined in the Tax Equity and Fiscal Responsibility Act of 1982. For example, Medicare pays only the remaining part of Medicare benefits after the benefits from other insurance have been paid for persons who are eligible for health coinsurance benefits from the Veterans Administration and the Federal Employees Program. *See also* payer; TEFRA.

Medicare supplement A health insurance plan that pays all or a percentage of the deductible and coinsurance amounts not covered by Medicare. Benefits not covered by Medicare (eg, prescription drugs, nursing care) are also covered under some Medicare supplement plans. *See also* medigap policy.

medication Any substance, other than food or devices, that may be used on or administered to persons as an aid in the diagnosis, treatment, or prevention of disease or other abnormal condition. *Synonym:* drug. *See also* the following medication terms, drug and its accompanying terms, as well as asthma medications; biological; dose; medical marijuana; medicine; psychotropic medication; self-medication; significant medication errors and significant adverse drug reactions; unit-dose system.

medication administration *See* drug administration.

medication dispensing *See* drug dispensing.

medication error A discrepancy between what a physician orders and what is reported to occur. Types of medication errors include omission, unauthorized drug, extra dose, wrong dose, wrong dosage form, wrong rate, deteriorated drug, wrong administration technique, and wrong time. An omission medication error is the failure to give an ordered dose; a refused dose is not counted as an error if the nurse responsible for administering the dose tried, but failed, to persuade the patient to take it. Doses withheld according to written policies, such as for x-ray procedures, are not counted as omission errors. An *unauthorized drug* medication error is the administration of a dose of medication not authorized to be given to that patient. Instances of "brand or therapeutic substitution" are counted as unauthorized medication errors only when prohibited by organization policy. A *wrong dose* medication error occurs when a patient receives an amount of medicine that is greater than or less than the amount ordered; the range of allowable deviation is based on each organization's definition. *Synonym:* drug error. *See also* significant medication errors and significant adverse drug reactions; sentinel event.

medication order   A written order by a physician, dentist, or other designated health professional for medication to be dispensed by a pharmacy for administration to a patient. *See also* drug administration; drug dispensing; medication error; medication system; order.

medication system   A series of interlinked processes required to provide medications to patients. At a minimum, a medication system includes handling a physician's or other health professional's order, transcribing of the order by a nurse or a pharmacist, filling the medication order in the pharmacy, transferring the medication to the patient care unit, and administering the medication to the patient. *See also* drug administration; drug dispensing; medication order.

medication-use assessment   A patient-centered process used to ensure that the patient's medication regimen meets his or her needs. The initial evaluation of each new medication for a patient, regarding the medication's safety and appropriateness, is based on permanent patient data, such as medication history, pertinent physical findings, laboratory test results, and the patient's current drug regimen.

medication-use measurement   The measurement, assessment, and improvement of the prescribing or ordering, preparing and dispensing, administering, and monitoring of medications.

medication-use reassessment   The periodic reevaluation of a patient's entire medication regimen based on new or updated patient data. For compliance with Joint Commission standards, the drug-regimen review performed by a consultant pharmacist can be considered a reassessment activity.

medicine   **1.** The art and science of diagnosing, treating, or preventing disease and other damage to the body or mind. A rarely used term for the science of medicine is iatrology.   **2.** An agent, such as a drug, used to treat disease or injury. *See also* medication.

Medicine and Public Health Initiative   A multidisciplinary panel of practitioners and scholars, a series of focus groups, and a nationwide survey of medicine and public health interactions supported by the Robert Wood Johnson Foundation, the American Medical Association, and the American Public Health Association, launched late in 1996.

medicolegal   Pertaining to medicine and law, especially to topics such as malpractice, patient consent for services, and patient information. *Synonym:* medical legal. *See also* consent; forensic medicine; malpractice.

medigap policy   A health insurance policy sold by private insurance companies designed to supplement Medicare benefits by paying for health services that are not paid by Medicare. *See also* insurance; Medicare supplement.

MedisGroups   *See* Medical Illness Severity Grouping System.

meditation   A state of consciousness in which the individual eliminates environmental stimuli from awareness so that the mind can focus on a single thing, producing a state of relaxation and relief from stress. There are hundreds of varieties of meditation, and studies have shown it to be an effective adjunct to treatment of conditions such as hypertension. *See also* mind/body medicine; yoga.

medium   *See* contrast medium.

MEDLARS® (Medical Literature Analysis and Retrieval System)   The computerized system of databases and databanks offered by the National Library of Medicine (NLM), including MEDLINE and several specialized databases such as CANCERLIT and TOXLINE. MEDLARS is used worldwide by researchers, health care practitioners, educators, administrators, and students. MEDLARS began as a pioneering effort to use the emerging computer technology of the early 1960s. *See also* MEDLINE; MeSH.

MEDLINE (Medlars Online)   A computerized bibliographic database (the online counterpart to Index Medicus) produced by the National Library of Medicine (NLM), covering the fields of medicine, nursing, dentistry, veterinary medicine, the health care system, and the preclinical sciences. MEDLINE contains about 8.8 million citations dating back to 1966, 72% of them with English abstracts, from more than 3,800 biomedical journals in the United States and 70 foreign countries. MEDLINE is updated weekly from January through October and twice in December. In addition to the citations appearing in the Index Medicus, it contains citations of special list journals, including those indexed for the Index to Dental Literature and the International Nursing Index. Citations for MEDLINE are created by the National Library of Medicine, International MEDLARS partners, and cooperating professional organizations. On June 26, 1997, the NLM announced that MEDLINE would be available free on the World Wide Web. *See also* MEDLARS; MeSH.

megavitamin therapy   An alternative therapy that uses very large doses of vitamins or other naturally occurring substances normally present in the body to treat specific conditions, frequently mental disorders. *See also* orthomolecular therapy.

member   For purposes of Joint Commission accreditation, an individual who is a member of a defined population, that is, a set of individuals (and their dependents, as appropriate) who are enrolled (by choice or assignment) to receive specified care and services from a designated MCO, network, or group of practitioners for a specific period of time. *See also* individual insured; subscriber.

menopause   The cessation of ovulation and menstruation, usually between the ages of 48 and 55 years in the United States, after which time a woman is unable to become pregnant. The changes that take place with declining hormones during menopause place women at greater risk for coronary heart disease and osteoporosis. *See also* hormone replacement therapy; osteoporosis.

mental abuse   *See* abuse.

mental age   The score achieved by a person in an intelligence test, expressed in terms of the chronological age of an average individual showing the same degree of attainment. *See also* chronological age; developmental age; functional age; standardized test.

mental anguish   A compensable injury embracing all forms of mental pain, as opposed to physical pain, including deep grief, distress, anxiety, and fright. *See also* pain and suffering.

mental disorder   A clinically significant behavioral or psychological syndrome or pattern that is associated with current distress (a painful symptom) or disability (impairment in one or more important areas of functioning) or with a significantly greater risk of suffering, death, pain, disability, or an important loss of freedom. The DSM-IV stresses that whatever its original cause, this must be considered a sign of a behavioral, psychological, or biological dysfunction. *See also* DSM-IV; mental health; mental health services; mental illness; psychiatric hospital; psychiatry.

mental health   A state of complete mental well-being. *See also* mental disorder; mental illness.

mental health care   *See* behavioral health.

mental health nursing   *See* psychiatric nursing.

mental health parity acts   Legislation requiring adherence to a principle of equal treatment in health insurance coverage for mental illness. The first of these acts, passed in Texas in the early 1990s, applied only to state and local government employees and covered a narrow range of specific diseases. Broader parity laws or commissions to study the issue started appearing in the mid-1990s. Most laws and bills cover specified illnesses (usually depression, bipolar disease, schizophrenia, and paranoia), but there are broader ones that have created a parity issue debate over the impact on costs and the potential for fraudulent diagnosis of disease.

mental health services   Diagnosis, treatment, and care of patients with mental disorders. *See also* forensic mental health services; mental disorder; partial care program.

mental hospital   *See* institution for mental disease; psychiatric hospital.

mental illness   All forms of illness in which psychological, intellectual, emotional, or behavioral disturbances are the dominating feature. The term is relative and variable in different cultures, schools of thought, and definitions. *See also* forensic mental health services; institution for mental disease; mental disorder; mental health; somatotherapy.

mental retardation   Decreased mental development, adaptive skills, or cognitive functioning that is the result of congenital causes, brain injury, environmental deprivation (cultural-familial retardation), or disease, and is char-acterized by any of various difficulties, ranging from impaired learning ability to social and vocational limitations. *See also* developmental disability; major life activities.

mentoring   A career development and training technique whereby senior professionals provide guidance, direction, and support to less experienced staff who hope to improve their own performance.

mercy killing   *See* euthanasia.

merger   The combination of two or more entities into a single entity so that only one of the companies survives as a legal entity.

MeSH® (Medical Subject Headings)   The controlled-vocabulary thesaurus (a standardized list of medical terms) created by the National Library of Medicine to index articles in its MEDLINE database and to catalog publications and other materials. The thesaurus consists of subject headings arranged in both an alphabetic and a hierarchical structure, with extensive cross-references. The are more than 18,000 main headings in the primary structure of MeSH and an additional 80,000 headings within a special chemical thesaurus. *See also* MEDLARS; MEDLINE.

MET   Metabolic equivalents of oxygen consumption, used to measure the intensity of physical activity, which is defined as the ratio of the metabolic rate during exercise to the metabolic rate at rest. Activity is scored from the minimum of 1 (sleeping, watching television) to a maximum of 8 (extreme exertion such as jogging uphill or aggressive sports with no rest).

meta-analysis   A quantitative method of combining the results of independent studies (usually drawn from the published literature) and synthesizing summaries and conclusions, which may then be used to apply formal statistical methodology to evaluate a question of interest, such as therapeutic effectiveness.. The rationale behind this approach is to provide a test with more weight than is provided by the separate studies themselves. Although the procedure has become increasingly popular, it is not without its critics, particularly because of the difficulties of knowing which studies should be included and to which population final results actually apply. *See also* systemic review.

method   *See* black box method; clinical-based severity adjustment methods; critical pathway method; Delphi technique; DEMPAQ; experimental method; group judgment methods; methodology; nominal group technique; scientific method; targeted mortality method; technique.

methodology   A collection of methods, rules, and postulates employed by a discipline. *See also* method; technique.

"me too" drug   A drug that is identical, similar to, or closely related to a drug for which a new drug application has already been approved. Many "me too" drugs are copies of approved new drugs and are introduced into the market by manufacturers without FDA approval, on the belief that the original drug has become generally recognized as safe and effective. Other "me too" products are marketed with abbreviated new-drug applications, which require the submission of manufacturing, bioavailability, and labeling information, but not data relating to safety and effectiveness, which are assumed to be established. *See also* abbreviated new-drug application; generally recognized as effective; generally recognized as safe; new-drug.

metric system   *See* Système International units.

Michigan Alcoholism Screening Test (MAST)
See alcohol-problem screening.

microbial drug resistance   The ability of microorganisms, especially bacteria, to resist or to become tolerant to chemotherapeutic agents, antimicrobial agents, or antibiotics. The term is distinguished from *drug resistance*, which refers to the resistance of a human, animal, disease, or tissue to a drug. As a result of widespread antimicrobial use, the resistance of many community- and hospital-acquired pathogens to common antibiotics has emerged as a major public health challenge in both community and health care organization settings. *See also* drug resistance.

microbiology   The branch of biology dealing with microorganisms, including bacteria, viruses, Rickettsia, fungi, and protozoa, and their effects on other living organisms. *See also* bacteriology; Gram's stain; pathology; virology.

microsurgery   Surgery performed using special operating microscopes and miniaturized precision instruments to perform delicate procedures on very small structures, such as parts of the eye. *See also* surgery.

middle age   The time of human life between youth and old age, usually the years between ages 40 and 60. *Synonym:* midlife. *See also* adolescence; andropause; elderly; menopause.

middle ear infection   *See* otitis media.

midwifery   The practice of assisting women in childbirth. Some states authorize midwifery, others prohibit it as unauthorized practice of medicine, and still others license nurse-midwives.

mind/body medicine   A cross-disciplinary field of medicine based on the biopsychosocial theory, which maintains that health is the outcome of many factors (genetic vulnerabilities, environmental inputs, psychological factors, and social factors) interacting together. Practitioners help patients restore, maintain, or improve health through a variety of behavioral techniques, including relaxation training, meditation, imagery, breath therapy, lifestyle changes, and biofeedback. Mind/body therapy programs have been found effective in treating hypertension and infertility, reversing heart disease, reducing symptoms of AIDS, and increasing survival times in breast cancer. *Synonym:* behavioral medicine. *See also* allopathy; behavior management; biofeedback; holism; hypnotherapy; meditation; naturopathy.

minimax principle   A strategy in game theory that is based on reducing as much as possible the difference between possible outcomes and the best possible outcome from a decision. This principle is used to select methods that will generate the least amount of regret in case of failure.

minimum data set   **1.** A widely agreed-on set of terms and definitions constituting a core of data acquired from medical records and used for developing statistics suitable for diverse types of analyses and users. Such data sets have been developed for ambulatory care, hospital care, and long term care. *Synonym:* uniform basic data set. *See also* data set; hospital discharge abstract system; Uniform Clinical Data Set; Uniform Hospital Discharge Data Set. **2.** An agreed-on and accepted set of terms and definitions constituting a core of data; a collection of related data items.

COMPONENTS OF THE MINIMUM DATA SET

Topics Covered on All Residents
Cognitive patterns
Communication/hearing patterns
Vision patterns
Physical functioning and structural problems
Continence
Psychosocial well-being
Mood and behavior patterns
Activity pursuit patterns
Disease diagnoses
Health conditions
Oral nutritional status
Oral/dental status
Skin condition
Medication use
Special treatments and procedures

Resident Assessment Protocol Topics
Delirium
Cognitive loss/dementia
Visual function
Communication
Activities of daily living function/rehabilitation potential
Urinary incontinence/indwelling catheter
Psychosocial well-being
Mood
Behavior
Activities
Falls
Nutrition
Feeding tubes
Dehydration/fluid maintenance
Dental care
Pressure ulcers
Psychotropic drug use
Physical restraints

Source: Kane RL: Improving the quality of long-term care. *JAMA* 273: 1376, 1995.

Minimum Data Set (MDS)   A standardized, comprehensive assessment of a long term care resident's functional, medical, psychosocial, and cognitive status. Developed by HCFA in response to the OBRA '87, this tool drives the process for providing a comprehensive assessment and care plan for each resident. The first revision to the MDS was called MDS+, and the newest version (MDS 2.0) was implemented by all states in January 1996, at which time HCFA pushed for computerization and electronic transmission of all MDS records. *See also* OBRA '87; Resource Utilization Groups.

minimum standard   A statement of acceptable expectations relating to a structure, a process, or an outcome; for example, the FDA has minimum standards of quality pertaining to the color, tenderness, and allowable freedom from defects permissible for many canned fruits and vegetables.

Minimum Standard for Hospitals   A one-page document developed in 1917 by the American College of Surgeons in response to the need for a hospital standardization program.

ministroke   *See* transient ischemic attack.

Minnesota model (The Minnesota Model of Chemical and Dependence Intervention and Treatment)   A substance abuse treatment strategy blending professional concepts and practices with the 12-step approach developed by Alcoholics Anonymous. An Institute of Medicine study of alcohol-problem treatment approaches (1990) finds that the vast majority of U.S. treatment programs in both the private and public sectors are based on what is now known simply as the Minnesota model. This model has spun off several variants, all generally claiming to reflect a biopsychosocial model. *See also* substance-related disorders.

Minnesota Multiphasic Personality Inventory (MMPI)   A personality inventory consisting of 550 true-false statements, yielding patterns of response characteristic of certain personality attributes or types. The 50-plus-year-old, "classic" MMPI has undergone revision and continues to be the subject of debate over the need for further revision or for adaptation to subpopulations such as the elderly or adolescents. *See also* alcohol-problem screening.

minor   A person who has not yet attained an age required by law (usually between 18 and 21 years, depending on the state) for a particular purpose. For example, a minor is usually legally unable to give consent for medical treatment. *See also* age of majority; emancipated minor; guardian; incompetent; legal age; mature minor.

minutes   An official record of who attends and what is said and done during a committee or other group meeting.

mission statement   A written expression that sets forth the purpose of an organization or one of its components. The generation of a mission statement usually precedes the formation of goals and objectives. *See also* objective; vision statement.

mistake   In law, an act or omission arising from ignorance or misconception, which may, depending on its character or the circumstances, justify rescission of a contract or exoneration of a defendant from tort or criminal liability. *See also* rescission.

mobile health unit   A mobile facility in which preventive, diagnostic, and therapeutic ambulatory services are provided to a community.

mobile intensive care unit (MICU)   An emergency vehicle that is staffed by emergency medical technicians-paramedics and stocked with resuscitation equipment and extensive trauma supplies. *See also* advanced cardiac life support; advanced trauma life support; ALS unit; ambulance; intensive care.

mode   In statistics, a measure of central tendency of a collection of data consisting of the measurement of the data set that occurs most *often*. *See also* average; mean; measure of central tendency; median; normal distribution.

moderate-complexity test   A test that meets CLIA '88 requirements based on knowledge required to perform the test; minimal training and limited experience required to perform the test; reagents and materials that are generally stable and reliable, and reagents and materials that are prepackaged, premeasured, or require no special handling, precautions, or storage conditions; operational steps that are either automatically executed or are easily controlled; and stable and readily available calibration, quality control, and proficiency testing materials. Test-system troubleshooting is automatic or self-correcting, or is clearly described or requires minimal judgment. Equipment maintenance provided by the manufacturer is seldom needed, or can easily be performed. Minimal interpretation and judgment are required to perform preanalytic, analytic, and postanalytic processes, and resolution of problems requires limited independent interpretation and judgment. *See also* CLIA '88.

molecular biology   The study of chemical structures and events underlying biological processes, including the relation between genes and the functional characteristics they determine. *See also* biology.

molecular genetics   The branch of genetics dealing with the chemical structure, functions, and replications of the molecules (DNA and RNA) involved in the transmission of hereditary information. *See also* clinical genetics; cytogenetics; genetics.

monitor   To systematically keep track, with a view to collecting information and keeping a close watch over something. *See also* admission pattern monitoring; ambulatory electrocardiography; apnea monitoring; automated ambulatory blood pressure monitoring devices; biomonitoring; clinical monitoring; drug therapy monitoring; fetal monitor; home uterine activity monitoring; Lifetime Health Monitoring Program; monitoring and evaluation; patient monitor; self-measured blood pressure monitoring device.

monitoring and evaluation A process designed to help health care organizations effectively use their performance measurement, assessment, and improvement resources by focusing on high-priority performance issues. The process includes identifying the most important aspects of the care the organization or its component provides, using indicators to systematically monitor these aspects of care, evaluating the care when thresholds are approached or reached to identify opportunities for improvement or problems, taking action(s) to improve care or solve problems, evaluating the effectiveness of the action(s), and communicating findings through established channels. *See also* evaluation; monitor; surveillance; watchful waiting.

monopoly Exclusive control of the production and distribution of a product or service by one organization or a group of organizations acting together. Monopoly is characterized by an absence of competition and often leads to high prices and a general lack of responsiveness to the needs and desires of consumers. The most flagrant monopolistic practices in the United States were outlawed by antitrust laws. *See also* antitrust laws.

mood disorders In psychiatry the DSM-IV class containing the disorders that have a disturbance in mood as the predominant feature; these include the depressive disorders (unipolar), bipolar disorder (I and II), mood disorder due to a general medical condition, and substance-induced mood disorder. *See also* DSM-IV.

moral hazard A risk to an insurance company resulting from uncertainty about the honesty of the insured, as in the tendency of the insured to spend the insurer's money more readily than he or she would spend his or her own money. For example, extra insurance provided by an employer decreases an employee's motivation to seek out lower-cost health care providers. Similarly, supplemental insurance plans defeat the incentives of deductibles and coinsurance for lower utilization.

moral philosophy *See* ethics.

morbidity A term used in epidemiology to describe sickness in human populations. Morbidity is usually measured in three units: (1) persons who were ill; (2) the illnesses that those persons experienced; and (3) the duration of the illnesses. *Synonyms:* illness; morbid condition; sickness. *See also* comorbidity; complication; expected morbidity; morbidity rate.

morbidity and mortality conference A medical staff conference or meeting, often department-based, in which one or more cases are presented and reviewed because they are unusual or complex, forced difficult management choices, or resulted in unexpected outcomes. Discussions typically cover many topics, such as the value of new technologies, approaches to care that might have been used, or an ethical dilemma presented by the case. Case conferences tend to be highly valued by clinicians as an effective method of learning and are typically conducted in a nonjudgmental atmosphere. *See also* grand rounds.

morbidity rate The number of cases of a morbidity or illness in a population divided by the total population at risk for that specific morbidity or illness. *See also* incidence rate; morbidity; prevalence rate.

morbidity survey A method for estimating the prevalence or incidence of disease or diseases in a population. A morbidity survey is usually designed simply to ascertain the facts as to disease distribution, and not to test a hypothesis. *See also* morbidity.

mortality A term used in epidemiology to describe death in human populations. *See also* expected mortality; infant mortality; maternal death; morbidity; morbidity and mortality conference; mortality rate; mortality table; targeted mortality method.

mortality rate The proportion of a population that dies during a specified period in relation to the population at risk of dying. The mortality rate may be expressed as a *crude death rate* (eg, total deaths in relation to total population during a year) or as rates specific for diseases or conditions, age, sex, place of death, or other attributes (eg, number of deaths from acute myocardial infarction in relation to all deaths within an organization, subcategorized by intraorganization location of death). *Synonym:* death rate. *See also* fatality rate; fetal death rate; high-mortality outlier; infant mortality rate; low- mortality outlier; maternal mortality rate; neonatal death rate; perinatal mortality; risk-adjusted mortality index.

mortality table A chart showing the rate of death at each age in terms of number of deaths per thousand persons.

motion study The process developed by Frederick W. Taylor and Frank and Lillian Gilbreth of analyzing work to determine the cost-efficient motions for performing tasks. *Synonyms:* stopwatch study; Taylorism; time and motion study; time-motion study.

motivation psychology The branch of psychology dealing with what conscious and unconscious forces cause human beings and other animals to behave as they do. Motivational psychologists focus on bodily needs, sexual drives, aggression, and emotion. *See also* field theory of motivation.

multidisciplinary Comprising representatives of a range of professions, disciplines, or service areas.

multidrug-resistant tuberculosis (MDR-TB) Tuberculosis caused by a strain of the organism *Mycobacterium tuberculosis,* which is resistant to more than one of the major antituberculous drugs. *See also* microbial drug resistance.

multifactorial etiology *See* multiple causation.

multihospital survey option An option offered by the Joint Commission to multihospital systems that own or lease at least two hospitals. The survey includes four components: a corporate orientation, a consecutive survey of participating organizations with the same team leader, and a corporate summation. *See also* accreditation survey; multihospital system; multiorganization survey option.

multihospital system　A central association that owns, leases, or controls, by contract, two or more hospitals. Some of the benefits of such a system are improved availability of capital markets, mutual purchasing for greater economies of scale, and mutual use of technical and management personnel. There are two types of multihospital systems: nonprofit (which includes church affiliated) and investor-owned (for profit). *Synonym:* hospital chain. *See also* economies of scale; health care network; health system; regional alliance.

multi-infarct dementia　*See* vascular dementia.

multimedia education　Activities that employ any combination of methods for conveying information, including written materials, video demonstrations, audiotape instructions, cue cards, medication diaries, and so on. Patient education programs include a variety of media to meet the learning needs of specific patients and patient populations. *See also* learning; patient education.

multimedia technology　Computer hardware and software that is capable of displaying text as well as digitized voice, image, and video presentations. Many health care organizations use multimedia presentations in both patient education and staff training.

multiorganization survey option　A survey option of the Joint Commission that is available to a single corporation or governmental agency that operates or governs two or more health care organizations. The survey includes a corporate orientation; a consecutive survey of participating organizations with the same team leader; a separate survey, accreditation decision, and certificate for each member organization; and a corporate summation conference. *See also* accreditation survey; multihospital survey option.

multiple causation　The concept that a given disease, condition, or outcome may have more than one basis or explanation. *Synonym:* multifactorial etiology.

multiple drug resistance (MDR)　Simultaneous resistance to a broad spectrum of structurally and functionally distinct drugs following exposure to a single agent.

multiple organ dysfunction syndrome (MODS)　A rubric agreed on by an expert consensus group to describe the continuum of changes that occur in more than one organ system following a significant insult (eg, trauma, burns, infections, aspiration, multiple blood transfusions, pulmonary contusion, pancreatitis). The dysfunction can include the complete failure of an organ (eg, oliguric renal failure) or the chemical failure of an organ that may or may not result in clinical findings (eg, an elevated serum creatinine level). *See also* systemic inflammatory response syndrome; sepsis.

multiple voting　*See* multivoting.

multiplex genetic testing　Testing for several serious conditions at one time. Beyond the ethical and policy issues surrounding genetic testing, this technology raises the additional problems such as defining informed consent for multiple components. *See also* genetic testing; informed consent.

multispecialty group practice　A group practice of three or more practitioners in which the members specialize in a minimum of two different clinical areas. *See also* group practice.

multivariate analysis　In statistics, any method that analyzes the simultaneous relationships among several variables.

multivoting　A group decision-making technique designed to reduce a long list to a shorter one. *Synonym:* multiple voting.

MUMPS　*See* M.

Munchausen's syndrome　A pseudo-disease, factitious condition in which a person presents himself or herself repeatedly, often to multiple physicians and health care organizations, with a complex of alleged symptoms calling for numerous and complicated tests. The complaints are often realistic and somewhat dramatic in nature, but no clinical evidence of disease is ever found, and the person may perform harmful actions to simulate a symptom or induce illness. The syndrome was named after Baron Karl F. H. von Munchausen (1720-1797), a German swashbuckler renowned for his mendacious fables of his prowess as a soldier and sportsman. The syndrome is called a *factitious disorder* in the DSM-IV. A related syndrome is the Munchausen syndrome by proxy, in which a parent or caretaker presents a child with the made-up or induced ailments or symptoms. Efforts have been made to share lists of known persons with the disorder and to develop profiles to help identify persons with the syndrome. *Synonym:* factitious disorder; pathomimicry.

municipal hospital　A hospital that is controlled by an agency of municipal government. *Synonym:* city hospital.

music therapy　The use of musical or rhythmic interventions specifically selected by a qualified music therapist to restore, maintain, or improve the social or emotional functioning, mental processing, or physical health of individuals. Therapeutic goals include symptom relief, emotional integration, and recovery from or adjustment to illness or disability. *See also* creative arts therapy; manual arts therapy; recreational therapy.

mutagen　An agent, such as ultraviolet light or a radioactive element, that can induce or increase the frequency of mutation in an organism by causing changes in DNA.

mutual insurance company　An insurance company owned by its policy owners, who elect a board of directors that is responsible for its operation. Profits take the form of policy dividends, or refunds of part of premiums paid, and are distributed to policy owners. *See also* captive insurance company; stock insurance company.

***Mycobacterium avium* complex (MAC)** *See* opportunistic infection.

myelography A diagnostic imaging procedure in which the spinal cord and subarachnoid space are photographed after injection of a contrast medium. The resulting image is called a myelogram.

myocardial infarction *See* acute myocardial infarction.

myringotomy with insertion of tympanostomy tube An operation in which a small incision is made through the tympanic membrane (eardrum) for the insertion of a tube. After myringotomy and suctioning of fluid from the middle ear, a small tube (tympanostomy tube) is inserted into the eardrum. The procedure is usually performed on both ears simultaneously. The procedure is most often performed to treat otitis media with effusion in children in order to remove the effusion, provide ventilation, and restore hearing. Questions about the volume and the appropriateness of the procedures performed inspired conflicting reports in the popular press and have made tympanostomy tubes a subject of national controversy.

Nn

naive patients Patients in studies and trials who have not previously used a drug or other therapy under study, for example, antiretroviral-naive patients in studies of HIV therapies.

named insured A holder of an insurance policy whose name appears on the insurance policy. *See also* individual insured.

naprapathy A system of medicine based on the theory that many diseases result from the displacement of connective tissues, such as tendons and ligaments, and that manipulation of these tissues, as well as dietary measures, will bring relief. *See also* homeopathy.

narcissistic personality disorder *See* personality disorder.

narcoanalysis Psychoanalysis assisted by the administration of a drug (usually a short-acting barbiturate), which causes mental disinhibition and facilitates expression of thoughts, ideas, and memories. *See also* psychoanalysis.

narcotic Any drug, as set out in the Comprehensive Drug Abuse Prevention and Control Act of 1970, produced directly or indirectly by extraction from substances of vegetable origin, by means of chemical synthesis, or by a combination of extraction and chemical synthesis. *Opiates* are narcotics derived from the opium poppy plant and include opium, heroin, morphine, and codeine. Nonopiate synthetic narcotics include demerol and methadone. Narcotics are used clinically as painkillers and, outside of medicine, to produce euphoria. All narcotics are physically and psychologically addicting, with the likelihood of addiction depending on the drug, the frequency and duration of its use, and its dosage. *See also* addiction; schedule of controlled substances.

nasogastric intubation The process of inserting a tube through the nose into the esophagus and stomach to provide a passageway to the stomach for feeding, suction, or other needs. *See also* intubation; nutrition.

national account In insurance, a group of insured persons or organizations having members in localities in more than one state who are all served by the same insurance or prepayment plan.

national board examination A standardized national examination for medical students and physicians developed and administered by the National Board of Medical Examiners. It is given in three parts, which are generally taken during the second and fourth years of medical school and the internship year or first postgraduate year (PGY-1). Successful completion of the national board examination is a requirement for licensure as a physician in a number of states and, in other cases,

functions as an acceptable alternative to a state's own medical examinations. *Synonym*: national boards. *See also* licensure.

National Childhood Vaccine Injury Act of 1986 and National Vaccine Injury Compensation Program Legislation that mandates distribution of educational materials about the disease, the benefits and harms of the vaccine, the recommended immunization schedule, indications for delaying or not administering the vaccine, potential complications, and contacts for reporting adverse effects and obtaining federal compensation. The legislation requires use of the specially prepared "Vaccine Information Statements" developed by the CDC before administering measles, mumps, rubella, diphtheria, tetanus, pertussis, or polio vaccines. Use of available statements for hepatitis B and *Hemophilus influenzae* type b is optional. *See also* immunization schedules.

National Council Licensure Examinations (NCLEX) An examination, developed and administered by the National Council of State Boards of Nursing, designed to test basic competency for nursing practice. The NCLEX-RN (registered nurse) test plan has three components, including nursing behaviors, the process of decision making, and cognitive ability. *See also* nurse.

National Demonstration Project on Quality Improvement in Health Care One of the earliest efforts at moving total quality management into the health care field, organized jointly by the Harvard Community Health Plan and the Juran Institute. The study paired 21 health care organizations with industrial total quality management experts to determine if the principles of total quality management were transferrable from industry to health care. *See also* total quality management; quality improvement; quality trilogy.

National Formulary (NF) A compendium of official standards for the preparation of various pharmaceuticals not listed in the *United States Pharmacopeia*. The *National Formulary* is one of three official compendia of drugs and medications in the United States recognized by the Federal Food, Drug, and Cosmetic Act. The other two are the *Homeopathic Pharmacopeia of the United States* and the *United States Pharmacopeia*. The *National Formulary* is a publication of the United States Pharmacopeia Convention. *See also Homeopathic Pharmacopeia of the United States; United States Pharmacopeia*.

national health insurance (NHI) A federal government-regulated health insurance program for financing health services for all or most citizens. The United States does not have national health insurance, but such insurance is common in many developed countries in the world. *See also* Medicaid; Medicare; national health service; social insurance; socialized medicine; Wagner-Murray-Dingell Bill.

National Health Planning and Resources Development Act of 1974 The federal law that established health systems agencies to conduct health system planning and resource development activities in state or substate geographic areas. Federal funding of health planning ended on September 30, 1986, although many states continue planning through their health systems agencies under local funding. *See also* health planning; resource allocation.

national health service   A health program in which a national government directly operates a health system that serves some or all of its citizens. National health service and national health insurance are not synonymous; national health insurance usually refers to programs in which the government insures or otherwise arranges financing for health care without directly arranging for, owning, or operating a health care program. *See also* national health insurance; social insurance; socialized medicine.

National Organ Transplant Act (1984)   A federal law that prohibits the sale of human organs, provides grant assistance in organ procurement activities, has established a task force for organ transplantation, and provides for a demonstration bone-marrow registry and research study to ensure public equity in the availability and appropriate use of organ transplantation. *See also* organ procurement; transplantation.

National Practitioner Data Bank (NPDB)   A data bank established by the Health Care Quality Improvement Act of 1986 and brought into operation in 1990 to be the sole and central repository of information on disciplinary and malpractice actions against physicians. Hospitals must request information from the NPDB when a physician or dentist applies for medical staff membership or clinical privileges, and every two years thereafter while the practitioner is on the staff or has privileges. A practitioner may request information concerning himself or herself at any time. State licensing authorities, nonhospital health care facilities, and professional societies with formal peer review processes may also request data. Attorneys may request data only when representing a plaintiff in a professional liability claim against a hospital and only when the hospital involved has failed to make a mandatory NPDB request regarding the practitioner named in the action. *See also* clinical privileges; Health Care Quality Improvement Act of 1986; licensure; privileging.

national standard rule   A test used for measuring the required level of care for a patient. It is based on the level of care provided by similar practitioners throughout the country. *See also* levels of care; locality rule; standard of care.

natural death acts   Statutes enacted in many states that establish procedures by which a competent individual can make provision for the withholding or withdrawing of medical therapy at the time when he or she loses the capacity to make such medical decisions. Natural death acts were enacted, in large part, to codify the increasingly popular living wills. *See also* death; durable powers of attorney for health care; living will.

natural history   The patterns of the course of a disease when left untreated.

naturopathy   A holistic approach to health and healing that emphasizes the treatment of disease through the stimulation, enhancement, and support of the patient's inherent healing capacity. No drugs or artificial substances are used in naturopathy, the practice of which includes the following: botanical medicine, clinical nutrition, homeopathy, physical medicine (therapeutic manipulation of muscles, bones, and spine), oriental medicine, natural obstetrics, psychological medicine (eg, biofeedback, hypnotherapy), and minor in-office surgery (eg, stitching of minor wounds, removal of foreign bodies). *Synonyms:* natural medicine; naturopathic medicine. *See also* allopathy; homeopathy; mind/body medicine; osteopathy.

necropsy   *See* autopsy.

needle biopsy   Removal of a segment of tissue or fluid for microscopic analysis by inserting a hollow needle through the skin or external surface of an organ and twisting the needle to obtain a sample of cells. *Synonym:* fine-needle biopsy.

needs assessment   **1.** An evaluation of a population's health status.   **2.** An evaluation of the productivity and performance of a health care organization, department, program, or plan. A needs assessment is performed prior to establishing or redefining the goals, priorities, and tasks of a program or organization.

negative binomial distribution   *See* probability distribution.

negative correlation   In statistics, an inverse association between two variables, meaning that as one variable becomes larger, the other becomes smaller. Negative correlation is represented by correlation coefficients of less than zero. *See also* correlation; correlation coefficient; positive correlation.

neglect   An impaired quality of life for a patient resulting from the absence of minimal services or resources to meet basic needs. Neglect includes withholding or inadequately providing food and hydration (without physician, patient, or surrogate approval), clothing, medical care, and good hygiene. It may also include placing the patient in unsafe or unsupervised conditions. *See also* abuse; elderly neglect; maltreatment; medical neglect.

negligence   Failure to use such care as a reasonably prudent and careful person would use under similar circumstances. *See also* adverse patient occurrences; contributory negligence; gross negligence; lost chance of cure; lost change of survival; medical injury; negligence per se; potentially compensable event; professional negligence; tort; vicarious liability; wrongful death.

negligence per se   Unexcused violation of a statute that is automatic negligence in some states.

negotiated settlement   The resolution of a malpractice claim before a judicial determination.

neighborhood health center   *See* community health center.

neonatal death rate   The number of neonatal deaths in relation to all infants born in a given population over a given period, usually expressed as the number of neonatal deaths per 100 or 1,000 live births in a defined health care organization, geographic area, or period of time. *Synonym:* neonatal mortality rate.

neonatal intensive care unit (NICU)   A unit of a hospital for the treatment and continuous monitoring of infants with life-threatening conditions who are generally less than 23 days old on admission to the unit. *Synonyms:* high-risk nursery; neonatal ICU; newborn intensive care unit; premature nursery. *See also* intensive care unit; special care unit.

neonatal-perinatal medicine   The branch of medicine and subspecialty of pediatrics dealing with the care of sick newborn infants. *Synonyms:* neonatology; perinatology. *See also* pediatrics.

neonate   An infant from birth to four weeks (28 days) of life. *See also* Apgar scale; infant.

neonatology   *See* neonatal-perinatal medicine.

nephrography   Radiographic visualization of the kidneys on plain x-ray films or with the assistance of pyelography, angiography, or computed axial tomography. *See also* angiography; computed axial tomography; nephrology; x-ray.

nephrology   A subspecialty of internal medicine and pediatrics dealing with disorders of the kidney, high blood pressure, fluid and mineral balance, dialysis of body wastes when the kidneys do not function, and consultation with surgeons about kidney transplantation. *See also* internal medicine; nephrography.

nepotism   Favoritism shown or patronage granted to relatives, as in business.

network   *See* health care network.

Network Accreditation Program   The survey and accreditation program of the Joint Commission for eligible health plans, integrated delivery networks, preferred provider organizations, and provider-sponsored organizations.

networking   **1.** Making use of contacts to acquire information or some professional advantage.   **2.** A process whereby software and hardware are arranged for interaction among computers in a multiuser system. In this process, the computers can share information and programs and use the same printers and other peripheral devices.

network model HMO   A type of HMO that contracts with two or more independent group practices, possibly including a staff group, to provide health services. Although a network model HMO may contain a few solo practices, it is predominantly organized around group practices. *See also* group practice; health care network; HMO; solo practice.

neurological surgery   *See* neurosurgery.

neurology   The branch and medical specialty dealing with the diagnosis and treatment of all categories of disease or impaired function of the brain, spinal cord, peripheral nerves, muscles, and autonomic nervous system, as well as the blood vessels that relate to these structures. Clinical neurophysiology is a subspecialty of neurology. *See also* neuropsychology.

neuropathology   The branch of medicine and subspecialty of neurology dealing with structural and other aspects of disease of the nervous system. *See also* pathology.

neuropharmacology   The study of the action of drugs on the nervous system. *See also* pharmacology.

neurophysiology   The branch of physiology dealing with the functions of the nervous system. *See also* physiology.

neuroprotective agents   New classes of drugs to treat a stroke which attempt to slow down cell death from a blood clot. *See also* stroke; transient ischemic attack.

neuropsychiatry   The combined medical study of neurological and psychiatric disorders. *See also* neurology; psychiatry.

neuropsychology   The study of the psychological effects of organic brain disease. *See also* psychology.

neuroradiology   The branch of radiology dealing with the nervous system. *See also* radiology.

neuroscience   Any of the sciences, such as neuroanatomy and neurobiology, that deal with the nervous system.

neurosurgery   A specialty concerned with the treatment of diseases and disorders of the brain, spinal cord, and peripheral and sympathetic nervous systems. *Synonym:* neurological surgery. *See also* psychosurgery.

neurotology   *See* otology/neurotology.

neurotransmitters   Chemical substances released in minute amounts at the endings of nerve fibers in response to arrival of a nerve impulse, causing excitation of the adjacent nerve or effector organ. The best known neurotransmitters are epinephrine (adrenaline), norepinephrine (noradrenaline), acetylcholine, dopamine, and serotonin.

New Age movement   Spiritual and consciousness-raising cultural movement of the 1980s characterized by rejection of modern Western-style values and culture and promotion of a more integrated or holistic approach in areas such as religion, medicine, philosophy, and the environment. *See also* alternative medicine; holistic medicine.

newborn   *See* neonate.

new drug   A drug for which premarketing approval is required by the Federal Food, Drug, and Cosmetic Act. A new drug is any drug that is not generally recognized among experts qualified by scientific training and experience to evaluate the safety and effectiveness of drugs, as safe and effective under its prescribed conditions of use. Since 1962, most new prescription drugs have been subject to the new-drug application and premarket approval process for new drugs. The vast majority of drugs marketed over the counter, however, have not been through the new-drug approval process. *See also* abbreviated new-drug application; generally recognized as effective; generally recognized as safe; investigational new drug; "me too" drug; new-drug application.

new-drug application (NDA) An application, which must be approved by the FDA before any new drug is marketed to the general public, that provides information designed to demonstrate safety and effectiveness. Once the application is approved, the drug may be prescribed by any physician or other health professional authorized under state law. The new-drug application must include reports of animal and clinical investigations; a list of ingredients, including the active drug and any vehicle, excipient, binder, filler, flavoring, and coloring; a description of manufacturing methods and quality control procedures; samples of the drug; and the proposed labeling. Approval of a new-drug application must be based on valid scientific evidence that the drug is safe and adequate and well-controlled clinical studies demonstrating that it is effective for its intended (labeled) uses. *See also* abbreviated new-drug application; drug monograph; Drug Price Competition and Patent Term Restoration Act of 1984; investigational new drug; "me too" drug; new drug.

new patient A person who has not previously been seen by a particular physician, clinic, hospital, or other health professional or health care organization. A new patient generally requires new medical records and a complete medical history and physical examination. *See also* medical history; patient; physical examination.

next of kin The person or persons most closely related by blood to another person, for example, a spouse, child, parent, sibling, or other nearest relative, in genealogical order.

nicotine dependence and withdrawal In psychiatry, two degrees of tobacco use that are classified as disorders involving clinically significant psychosocial problems from tobacco use. *Nicotine abuse*, in contrast, is not classified as a disorder. The DSM-IV recommends two tests to measure dependence and withdrawal: its criteria for substance dependence and the Fagerstrom Test for Nicotine Dependence.

nicotine replacement therapy Use of nicotine-containing substances or applications to alleviate the symptoms of nicotine withdrawal for the purpose of ultimately ceasing to smoke. The three nicotine replacement therapy delivery systems currently approved for use in the United States are nicotine chewing gum (nicotine polacrilex), the nicotine patch (nicotine transdermal delivery system), and a nicotine nasal spray. *See also* smoking-cessation counseling and therapy.

FAGERSTROM TEST FOR NICOTINE DEPENDENCE

Questions

1. How soon after you wake up do you smoke your first cigarette?
2. Do you find it difficult to refrain from smoking in places where it is forbidden (eg, in church, at the library, in the cinema, etc)?
3. Which cigarette would you hate most to give up?
4. How many cigarettes per day do you smoke?
5. Do you smoke more frequently during the first hours of waking than during the rest of the day?
6. Do you smoke if you are so ill that you are in bed most of the day?

Answers (Points)*

1. Within 5 minutes (3); 6-30 minutes (2); 31-60 minutes (1); After 60 minutes (0).
2. Yes (1); No (0).
3. The first one in the morning (1); All others (0).
4. 10 or less (0); 11-20 (1); 21-30 (2); 31 or more (3).
5. Yes (1); No (2).
6. Yes (1); No (0).

*Scores greater than 7 indicate nicotine dependence.

Source: Giovino GA, Henningfield JE, Tomar SL, Escobedo LG, Slade J: Epidemiology of tobacco use and dependence. *Epidemiol Rev* 17:48-65, 1995.

DSM-IV DIAGNOSTIC CRITERIA FOR NICOTINE WITHDRAWAL

A. Daily use of nicotine for at least several weeks

B. Abrupt cessation of nicotine use, or reduction in the amount of nicotine used, followed within 24 hours by four (or more) of the following signs:

1. Dysphoric or depressed mood
2. Insomnia
3. Irritability, frustration or anger
4. Anxiety
5. Difficulty concentrating
6. Restlessness
7. Decreased heart rate
8. Increased appetite or weight gain

C. The symptoms in Criterion B cause clinically significant distress or impairment in social, occupational, or other important areas of functioning.

D. The symptoms are not due to a general medical condition and are not better accounted for by another mental disorder.

Source: *Diagnostic and Statistical Manual of Mental Disorders, Fourth Edition* (DSM-IV). Washington, DC: American Psychiatric Press, 1994.

---

night bed A bed regularly maintained by a health care organization for use during the night by patients who require partial hospitalization. *See also* day bed; partial hospitalization.

night hospitalization *See* partial hospitalization.

Nightingale, Florence (1820-1910) Widely regarded as the founder of modern nursing, she elevated nursing to a noble profession during the Crimean War, established a training school for nurses at St. Thomas' Hospital in London, and recognized the importance of statistical analysis of hospital records. *See also* nursing.

NIH Consensus Development Conferences (CDCs) and Consensus Statements   A federal program of the Office of Medical Applications of Research (OMAR; a component of the National Institutes of Health [NIH]) which brings together researchers, practicing physicians and other clinicians, representatives of public interest groups, consumers, and others to carry out scientific assessments of drugs, devices, and procedures in an effort to evaluate their safety and effectiveness. Each conference is jointly sponsored by one or more components in NIH and sometimes by other entities outside NIH. The resultant NIH Consensus Statements are intended to advance understanding of the technology or issue in question and to be useful to health professionals and the public. Over a 2½-day period, a nonadvocate nonfederal

expert panel develops the statement after expert presentations, open discussion forum, and closed deliberations. *See also* group judgment methods; health care technology assessment; health care technology assessment programs (and accompanying table); NIH Technology Assessment Conferences and Statements.

NIH Technology Assessment Conferences and Statements   A federal program of the Office of Medical Applications of Research (OMAR; a component of the National Institutes of Health) that convenes experts to evaluate available scientific information related to a biomedical technology and invites public testimony or questioning to help frame the issues. Some conferences adhere to the NIH Consensus Development Conference format, and others are organized around unique presentation formats. Statements and reports are also published in a variety of formats including articles in journals. *See also* health care technology assessment programs (and accom-

NIH CONSENSUS DEVELOPMENT AND TECHNOLOGY ASSESSMENT CONFERENCES AND STATEMENTS	
Topic (Year of Conference)	**Principal Cosponsors**
Alternative Medicine: Acupuncture (1994)*	Office of Alternative Medicine
Alternative Medicine: Examining Research Assumptions (1994)*	Office of Alternative Medicine
Bioelectrical Impedance Analysis in Body Composition Measurement (1994)*	National Institute of Diabetes and Digestive and Kidney Diseases
Cancer of the Cervix (1996)	National Cancer Institute
Cochlear Implants in Adults and Children ((1995)	National Institute on Deafness and Other Communication Disorders
Early Identification of Hearing Impairment in Infants and Young Children (1993)	National Institute on Deafness and Other Communication Disorders
Effect of Corticosteroids for Fetal Maturation on Perinatal Outcomes (1994)	National Institute of Child Health and Human Development
An Evidence-Based Health Care System: The Case for Clinical Trials Registries (1993)*	National Institute of Child Health and Human Development
Gaucher Disease: Current Issues in Diagnosis and Treatment (1995)*	National Institute of Mental Health
Helicobacter pylori in Peptic Ulcer Disease (1994)	National Institute of Diabetes and Digestive and Kidney Diseases
Infectious Disease Testing for Blood Transfusions (1995)	National Heart, Lung, and Blood Institute; National Institute of Allergy and Infectious Diseases
The Integration of Behavioral and Relaxation Approaches Into the Treatment of Chronic Pain and Insomnia (1995)*	Office of Alternative Medicine
Management of Temporomandibular Disorders (1996)	National Institute of Dental Research
Mortality and Morbidity of Dialysis (1993)	National Institute of Diabetes and Digestive and Kidney Diseases
Optimal Calcium Intake (1994)	National Institute of Arthritis and Musculoskeletal and Skin Diseases
Ovarian Cancer: Screening, Treatment, and Followup (1994)	National Cancer Institute
The Persian Gulf Experience and Health (1994)*	OMAR, Department of Defense, Department of Veterans Affairs, Department of Health and Human Services, Environmental Protection Agency
Physical Activity and Cardiovascular Health (1995)	Office of Alternative Medicine
Total Hip Replacement (1994)	National Institute of Arthritis and Musculoskeletal and Skin Diseases
Ultrasound Screening: Implications of the Radius Study (1993)	National Institute of Child Health and Human Development
*Technology Assessment Conference or Workshop.	
Source: National Institutes of Health, Office of Medical Applications of Research, 1997.	

panying table); NIH Consensus Development Conferences and Consensus Statements.

no code   *See* do-not-resuscitate order.

no-fault medical practice liability   A proposal that all people injured during medical care be automatically reimbursed, even if the care was not negligent. Patients would forfeit their right to sue and instead would be paid out of a pool funded by doctors and hospitals. Theoretically, no-fault liability would save money currently spent on lawsuits and distribute awards to a wider variety and number of injured people. *See also* liability; professional liability.

nominal group technique   A group process designed to efficiently generate a large number of ideas through input from individual group members initially working independently and concurrently without fear of criticism. The technique allows a team to prioritize a large number of issues without creating "winners" and "losers." *Synonym*: nominal group process. *See also* brainstorming; group judgment methods; technique.

nominal scale   A scale in which classification occurs according to unordered qualitative categories, such as color of eyes, race, religion, and country of birth; hence, observations are distinguished by name alone. These measurements of individual attributes are purely nominal, as there is no inherent order to their categories. This is the weakest qualitative classification of samples into separate categories. *See also* interval scale; ordinal scale; qualitative data; ratio scale.

non compos mentis   Latin phrase meaning no control over the mind or intellect; insane. In certain circumstances, it means not legally competent. *See also* competence.

noncontributory insurance   Group health insurance in which the employer pays all of the premium. *See also* contributory insurance; group insurance; insurance.

nondisease factor   A patient-based source of performance variation, such as age, sex, and refusal of consent, which has an impact on care but is not related to illness. *See also* patient factor.

noneconomic damages   Elements of injury or loss that cannot easily or accurately be calculated in terms of money damages. For example, noneconomic losses might include pain and suffering, while economic losses would include lost wages. *See also* damages; future damages.

non-insulin-dependent diabetes   Former term, eliminated in 1997. *See* diabetes mellitus.

nonlinear scale   A scale in which the divisions corresponding to the steps are unequal, for example, a scale with divisions showing logarithmic or exponential change.

nonparticipating provider   A health care organization or a health professional that has not agreed to payment schedules or charge allowances offered by a health care insurer, service plan, or prepayment plan. *See also* health care provider; participating physician.

nonprescription drug   *See* over-the-counter drug.

nonprobability sampling   A technique in which a nonrepresentative sample is used to help define a problem or its causes when only a few cases are required for analysis and controls cannot be obtained. The technique cannot be used for drawing sweeping conclusions. Subsets are convenience sampling, purposive sampling, and quota sampling. *See also* sampling.

nonprofit carrier   A health insurance, service, or prepayment organization that falls under state nonprofit statutes; for example, Delta Dental plans and many Blue Cross and Blue Shield plans are nonprofit carriers. *Synonym*: not-for-profit carrier. *See also* Blue Cross and Blue Shield plan; carrier; Delta Dental plan.

nonprofit hospital   A general acute care, nontaxable hospital that operates on a nonprofit basis under the ownership and control of a private corporation, usually a community, church, or other organization concerned with community services and resources. Profits are turned back into maintenance and improvement of the hospital's facilities and services. Donations to such hospitals are often tax-deductible. *Synonym*: not-for-profit hospital.

nonrandomized controlled trial   A study or experiment in which assignment of patients to the intervention groups is at the discretion of the investigator or according to some other method that does not guarantee assignment of patients totally according to chance. This method risks introducing selection bias into the process. *See also* randomized controlled trial.

nonservice-connected disability   In the Veterans Administration health care system, a disability that was not incurred or aggravated in the line of duty during active military service. Care is available from the program for patients with such disabilities on a bed-available basis after service-connected disability patients are cared for. *See also* disability; service-connected disability.

nonurgent   Pertaining to care that does not require the resources of an emergency department. *See also* urgent.

norm   **1.** The average or usual numerical level or pattern at which an action, event, or other measured phenomenon occurs within a defined population; for example, the norm for all surgeons in a defined geographic area in performing laparotomies for penetrating abdominal trauma.   **2.** A numerical level of a desired action, event, or other measured phenomenon, as in "performing below the (desired) norm." In this sense, *norm* is employed as a standard against which to evaluate, for example, performance or quality. *See also* standard.

normal distribution   A distribution that is continuous and symmetrical, with both tails of the distribution extending to infinity. The arithmetic mean, mode, and median are identical, and the shape of the distribution is completely determined by the mean and standard deviation. *Synonyms:* bell-shaped curve; Gaussian distribution. *See also* distribution; mean; median; mode; probability distribution.

normalization   The act or process of making available to developmentally disabled individuals and institutionally older adults patterns and conditions of everyday life similar to those of mainstream society. This process allows such individuals to enjoy a manner of living close to that considered normal within their community. The basic principle of normalization asserts is that providing the least departure from normal patterns of living can effectively meet individuals' developmental and psychosocial needs.

normal response time   In home care, the time needed to arrive at a patient's home in normal traveling conditions. *See also* maximum response time.

normative ethics   Theories that formulate and defend basic moral principles and rules that determine what is right or wrong. *See also* ethics.

normotensive   Normal blood pressure.

Norton Scale   A validated risk assessment tool for pressure ulcers, reprinted in the AHCPR guideline *Pressure Ulcers in Adults* (1993). *See also* measure; pressure ulcer.

nosocomial infection   An infection acquired by an individual while receiving care or services in a health care organization. Common nosocomial infections are urinary tract infections, surgical wound infections, pneumonia, and bloodstream infections. *Synonyms:* hospital-acquired infection; hospital infection; postoperative infection. *See also* iatrogenic; infection; nosocomial infection rate; Study on the Efficacy of Nosocomial Infection Control project; surgical-site infection.

nosocomial infection rate   The ratio describing the number of patients with nosocomial infections divided by the number of patients at risk of developing nosocomial infections. Rates may be stratified by taking into account certain factors that may predispose a specified group of patients to an increased risk of acquiring a nosocomial infection. *Synonym:* rate stratification by infection risk. *See also* infection; nosocomial infection.

nosology   The science and classification of diseases. *Synonyms:* nosonomy; nosotaxy. *See also* taxonomy.

not accredited   *See* accreditation decision.

notch   A precipitous drop in health care benefits for individuals or families despite a marginal increase in incomes, where those with earnings above the "notch" will not qualify for the benefits. For example, in Medicaid, a family just below the income eligibility standard receives full subsidized coverage, while families with only slightly more income who are just above the eligibility standard receive no benefits. Spend-down provisions, governing the expenditure of assets until income eligibility levels are met, are used to compensate for notches. *See also* Medicaid.

notifiable disease   A disease that, by statutory requirements issued by the Centers for Disease Control and Prevention, must be reported to the public health authority in the pertinent jurisdiction when the diagnosis is made by a provider. A notifiable disease is deemed of sufficient importance to the public health as to require that its occurrence be reported to health authorities. Examples include hepatitis, influenza, measles, and sexually transmitted diseases. *Synonym:* reportable disease. *See also* disease notification; mandatory reporting.

nuclear medicine   The branch and specialty of medicine dealing with the scientific and clinical delivery of diagnostic, therapeutic (exclusive of sealed radium sources), and investigative use of radionuclides for patients. *See also* nuclear radiology.

nuclear radiology   The branch of radiology that involves the analysis and imaging of radionuclides and radiolabeled substances in vitro and in vivo for diagnosis and the administration of radionuclides and radiolabeled substances for the treatment of disease. *See also* nuclear medicine; radioisotope; radiology; radionuclide imaging.

nuclear sexing   The determination of genetic sex by examining the nuclei of cells, usually in a stained smear from the buccal mucosa (inside the mouth). In normal females a large proportion of nuclei show a small stainable body (Barr body).

nucleoside analogue   A synthetic compound similar to one of the components of DNA or RNA; a general type of antiretroviral drug (eg, acyclovir, didanosine, zidovudine) widely used in combination with other drugs in preventing or treating HIV infection. *See also* HIV infection; protease inhibitor.

null hypothesis   The hypothesis or prediction that there is no relationship between two or more variables, as opposed to the experimental hypothesis, which predicts that there is a relationship between two or more variables. The null hypothesis states that the results observed in a study, experiment, or test are no different from what might have occurred as a result of the operation of chance alone. *Synonym:* test hypothesis. *See also* alternative hypothesis; hypothesis; level of significance; statistically significant; probability; test statistic; variable.

numerator   The upper portion of a fraction used to calculate a rate, proportion, or ratio. The numerator statement of a clinical indicator is the population(s) of the event being measured. For example, "Total number of cesarean sections" in the calculation of a cesarean section birth rate indicator. *See also* denominator; indicator; performance measure; rate.

Nuremberg code   The set of principles formulated to govern the ethics of research on human beings, following the Nuremberg tribunal at the end of World War II, which declared Nazi physicians guilty of crimes against humanity for experimenting on human beings without their consent. The code forms the underpinnings of the law and ethics of informed consent. *See also* ethics; Helsinki Declaration; informed consent; Tuskegee experiments.

THE NUREMBERG CODE

Permissible Medical Experiments

The great weight of evidence before us is to the effect that certain types of medical experiments on human beings, when kept within reasonably well-defined bounds, conform to the ethics of the medical profession generally. The protagonists of the practice of human experimentation justify their views on the basis that such experiments yield results for the good of society that are unprocurable by other methods or means of study. All agree, however, that certain basic principles must be observed in order to satisfy moral, ethical and legal concepts:

1. The voluntary consent of the human subject is absolutely essential. This means that the person involved should have legal capacity to give consent; should be so situated as to be able to exercise free power of choice, without the intervention of any element of force, fraud, deceit, duress, over-reaching, or other ulterior form of constant or coercion; and should have sufficient knowledge and comprehension of the elements of the subject matter involved as to enable him to make an understanding and enlightened decision. This latter element requires that before the acceptance of an affirmative decision by the experimental subject there should be made known to him the nature, duration, and purpose of the experiment; the method and means by which it is to be conducted; all inconveniences and hazards reasonably to be expected; and the effects upon his health or person which may possibly come from his participation in the experiment. The duty and responsibility for ascertaining the quality of the consent rests upon each individual who initiates, directs or engages in the experiment. It is a personal duty and responsibility which may not be delegated to another with impunity.

2. The experiment should be such as to yield fruitful results for the good of society, unprocurable by other methods or means of study, and not random and unnecessary in nature.

3. The experiment should be so designed and based on the results of animal experimentation and a knowledge of the natural history of the disease or other problem under study that the anticipated results will justify the performance of the experiment.

4. The experiment should be so conducted as to avoid all unnecessary physical and mental suffering and injury.

5. No experiment should be conducted where there is an a priori reason to believe that death or disabling injury will occur; except, perhaps, in those experiments where the experimental physicians also serve as subjects.

6. The degree of risk to be taken should never exceed that determined by the humanitarian importance of the problem to be solved by the experiment.

7. Proper preparations should be made and adequate facilities provided to protect the experimental subject against even remote possibilities of injury, disability, or death.

8. The experiment should be conducted only by scientifically qualified persons. The highest degree of skill and care should be required through all stages of the experiment of those who conduct or engage in the experiment.

9. During the course of the experiment the human subject should be at liberty to bring the experiment to an end if he has reached the physical or mental state where continuation of the experiment seems to him to be impossible.

10. During the course of the experiment the scientist in charge must be prepared to terminate the experiment at any stage, if he has probable cause to believe, in the exercise of the good faith, superior skill and careful judgment required of him that a continuation of the experiment is likely to result in injury, disability, or death to the experimental subject.

Source: *Trials of War Criminals before the Nuremberg Military Tribunals under Control Council Law No. 10*, vol 2. Washington, DC: U.S. Government Printing Office, 1949, pp 181-8.

nurse An individual qualified by education and authorized by law to practice nursing. There are many different types and specialties of nurses, the names of which are generally descriptive of their special responsibilities. *See also* National Council Licensure Examinations.

Nurse Corps The branch within each of the armed services comprised of registered nurses within that service, for example, Army Nurse Corps. The members of the Nurse Corps have the rank, title, responsibilities, and status of officers.

nurse practice act A state, commonwealth, or territorial statute or law delineating the legal scope of the practice of nursing within the geographic boundaries of the jurisdiction. *See also* dental practice act; medical practice act; practitioner.

nursing The health profession dealing with nursing care and services as defined in relevant state, commonwealth, or territorial nurse practice acts and other applicable laws and regulations, and as permitted by a health care organization in accordance with these definitions.

Synonym: nursing practice. *See also* the following nursing terms, as well as Nightingale, Florence; psychiatric nursing; team nursing.

nursing care Professional processes intended to assist an individual in the performance of those activities contributing to health or its recovery (or to peaceful death), which he or she would perform unaided if he or she had the necessary strength, will, or knowledge. This includes, but is not limited to, assisting patients in carrying out therapeutic plans and understanding the health needs of patients. The special content of nursing care varies in different countries and situations, and, as defined, is not given solely by registered nurses but also by other health care professionals. *See also* home health services; levels of care; nursing; nursing services; progressive patient care.

nursing care plan A formal plan of the nursing care activities to be conducted on behalf of a given patient and used to coordinate the activities of all nursing personnel involved in that patient's care. *See also* nursing orders; nursing record; plan of care.

LEVELS OF NURSING CARE

acute care Nursing care to treat a patient for an acute episode of illness or injury or during recovery from surgery. Care is specialized (often requiring high-tech equipment and materials) and may include intensive care and emergency care.

subacute care Nursing care that requires frequent (daily to weekly) patient assessment and review of the clinical course and treatment plan for a limited time period (several days to several months), until a condition is stabilized or a predetermined treatment course is completed.

skilled care Nursing care for patients whose professional nursing needs do not require acute nursing care, but who need inpatient supervision by an RN, either because of the nature of procedures that must be performed, the amount of care needed, or both. Some of the procedures and treatments generally included in skilled care include injections, administration of medications, changing of dressings, and observation and monitoring of a patient's condition, including taking vital signs.

intermediate care Nursing care generally requiring overall supervision by an RN at least one shift per day. Patients receiving intermediate care can typically perform some of the activities of daily living.

self-care Often the goal of preceding levels of nursing care, self-care is personal and medical care performed by a patient, usually in collaboration with and after instruction by a health professional.

nursing home A nonhospital health care organization with inpatient beds and an organized professional staff that provides continuous nursing and other health-related, psychosocial, and personal services to residents who are not in an acute phase of illness, but who require continued care on an inpatient basis. Nursing homes provide a broad range of services and levels of care, ranging from skilled nursing care to custodial care. *Synonyms:* custodial care facility; nursing care facility; nursing care institution; nursing facility. *See also* home for the aged; intermediate care facility; long term care facility; residential care facility; skilled nursing facility.

nursing home reform legislation *See* OBRA '87.

nursing orders Instructions for implementing the nursing care plan based on the assessment of patient needs that includes, but is not limited to, timing of activities, patient and family education, and discharge preparation. *See also* nursing care plan.

nursing practice *See* nursing.

nursing record The portion of the medical record completed by nurses, containing the nursing care plan, nursing orders, and nursing notes about all nursing activities on behalf of the patient. *See also* medical record; nursing care plan.

nursing services Services provided to patients by an individual who is qualified by virtue of an approved post-secondary program, baccalaureate, or higher degree in nursing and who is licensed or certified by the state to practice nursing. *See also* nursing care.

nursing specialties Areas of specialized nursing including, for example, surgical, school, or psychiatric nursing. *See also* nurse (and accompanying table).

nursing staff Registered nurses, licensed practical or vocational nurses, nursing assistants, and other nursing staff who perform nursing care in a health care organization.

CLINICAL NURSING CATEGORIES

cardiac care nurse
circulating nurse
critical care nurse
emergency nurse
enterostomal therapist
geriatric nurse
general duty nurse
hemodialysis nurse
industrial nurse
infection control nurse
nurse anesthetist
nurse epidemiologist
nurse-midwife
obstetric-gynecologic nurse practitioner
obstetric nurse
occupational health nurse
operating room (OR) nurse
pediatric nurse
pediatric nurse practitioner (PNP)
psychiatric nurse
public health nurse (PHN)
rehabilitation nurse
school nurse
scrub nurse
staff nurse
surgical nurse

nutrient A substance that must be supplied by the diet to provide for normal health of the body, energy supplies, and materials for growth. Nutrients include protein, carbohydrates, lipids, vitamins, electrolytes, minerals, and water. *See also* nutrition; nutritional support; vitamin.

nutrition **1.** Nourishment. *See also* macrobiotics; malnutrition; Meals on Wheels **2.** The sum of the processes to take in and use nutrients, including ingestion, digestion, absorption, assimilation, and excretion. *Enteral nutrition* is provided via the gastrointestinal tract and encompasses both oral and tube routes; *parenteral nutrition* is provided intravenously. *See also* the following nutrition terms as well as alimentation; enteral nutrition; infusion therapy services; nasogastric intubation; nutrient; parenteral nutrition; total parenteral nutrition. **3.** The study of food and drink as related to the needs of the body. *See also* Health and Nutrition Examination Study; nutritional support.

nutritional support Delivering food and water by artificial methods when a patient is unable to consume adequate amounts by eating, drinking, and swallowing. Tube feedings are most frequently accomplished with intravenous, nasogastric, and gastrostomy tubes. An *intravenous* tube is placed in a neck or arm vein; a *nasogastric* tube is passed through the nose and throat ending in the

TYPES OF NURSING STAFF

advanced practice nurse   A nurse who has had advanced education and has met clinical practice requirements beyond the two to four years of higher education required for all registered nurses. Advanced practice nurses include nurse practitioners, nurse-midwives, clinical nurse specialists, and nurse anesthetists.

certified nurse   An RN who has obtained a credential of certification in a nursing specialty.

charge nurse   An RN or other qualified individual who directs and supervises the provision of nursing care in a nursing unit for a given period of time, as in one shift.

chief of nursing   The individual responsible for the management of all nursing services in a health care organization.

clinical nurse specialist (CNS)   An RN who has acquired advanced knowledge, clinical skills, and competence in a specialized area of nursing and health care. CNSs hold a master's degree in nursing, preferably with an emphasis in clinical nursing. Synonym: nurse specialist.

degree nurse   A nurse whose nursing education is obtained in an educational institution that grants an academic degree.

diploma nurse   A nurse whose education was obtained in a hospital school of nursing which granted a diploma rather than an academic degree.

float nurse   A nurse who is assigned to patient care duty when needed, usually to assist in times of unusually heavy workloads or to assume the duties of absent nursing personnel.

floor nurse   A nurse working on, but not in charge of, a patient care unit.

head nurse   The clinical and administrative leader of the nurses working in a given area of a health care organization, such as a floor, ward, or unit. The head nurse is continuously responsible for the activities of the unit.

licensed practical nurse (LPN)   A nurse who has completed a practical nursing program and is licensed by a state to provide routine patient care under the direction of an RN or a physician.

licensed vocational nurse (LVN)   An LPN who is permitted by license to practice in California or Texas.

nurse coordinator   An RN who coordinates and manages the activities of nursing personnel for two or more nursing units. *Synonyms:* patient care coordinator; supervisory nurse.

nurse executive   An RN on the hospital executive management team who is responsible for the management of the nursing organization (that is, nursing department, division, or service) and for the clinical practice of nursing throughout a health care organization. *Synonyms:* director of nursing; nursing service administrator; nursing service director; vice president for nursing.

nurse intern   An individual who has completed educational preparation in nursing and who undergoes practical clinical experience, usually under the supervision of a head nurse or other qualified person in the clinical area in accordance with state nurse practice laws or statutes.

nurse manager   An RN holding 24-hour accountability for the management of a unit(s) or area(s) where nursing care is delivered within a health care institution.

nurse practitioner (NP)   An RN who has completed additional training beyond basic nursing education and who provides primary health care services in accordance with state nurse practice laws or statutes.

nurse practitioner specialist   A nurse practitioner who focuses on a particular field of care, such as family practice, gerontology, pediatrics, obstetrics-gynecology, and school practice.

nursing assistant   An individual who performs routine patient-care–related tasks under the supervision of a nurse. *Synonyms:* nurse aide; nursing aide.

nursing supervisor   A nurse whose function is the administrative and clinical leadership of the nursing service of a division of a health care organization.

office nurse   An individual employed by a physician in his or her office to perform or to assist in the performance of certain procedures. This person may be an RN, licensed practical nurse, licensed vocational nurse, or nursing assistant who provides services according to education and as authorized by state laws or statutes.

pool nurse   An RN, LPN, or LVN who is not a member of the nursing staff of a health care organization, but who is hired through an agency to provide patient care on a temporary basis when inadequate numbers of regular nursing staff are available to provide care. *Synonym:* agency nurse.

primary nurse   An RN who provides all nursing care to an assigned group of patients throughout their hospitalization.

private-duty nurse   A nurse who, as an independent contractor employed by a patient, provides direct nursing care to the patient.

registered nurse (RN)   A nurse who has passed a state registration examination and has been licensed to practice nursing. The registration license is intended to ensure minimum levels of competence and thus protect the public. General responsibilities may include nursing care of patients, teaching health care, counseling, patient assessment, analyzing laboratory reports, and operating equipment. Registered nurses may also oversee the work of other health care workers.

team nurse   A nurse who is a member of a nursing team composed of a group of registered nurses and ancillary personnel who provide nursing services under a team leader for a designated group of patients during a single nursing shift.

stomach; and a *gastrostomy* tube is passed through an artificial opening of the abdominal wall into the stomach. *See also* gastrostomy; nasogastric intubation; nutrient; total parenteral nutrition.

nutrition assessment   A comprehensive process for defining a patient's nutritional status using medical, nutrition, and medication intake histories, physical examination, anthropomorphic measurements, and laboratory data.

nutrition care   Interventions and counseling to promote appropriate nutrition intake, based on nutrition assessment and information about food, other sources of nutrients, and meal preparation consistent with the patient's cultural background and socioeconomic status. Nutrition therapy, a component of medical treatment, includes enteral and parenteral nutrition.

nutrition criteria   Characteristics known to be associated with nutrition problems. These criteria are used to pinpoint patients who are at high nutrition risk for malnourishment or are malnourished.

nutrition risk   *See* dietary risk factors.

nutrition screening   The process of using characteristics known to be associated with nutrition problems in order to determine if a patient is malnourished or is at a high nutrition risk for malnourishment. *See also* screening.

Oo

obesity   The state of having an excess accumulation of body fat, generally defined as body weight 20% above the desirable body weight for a person's age, sex, height, and body build. *Morbid obesity* is defined as weight two times greater than the ideal or standard weight and is associated with many serious and life-threatening disorders, such as diabetes mellitus, hypertension, and cardiovascular disease. Obesity is classified as *endogenous* when it is due to metabolic (endocrine) abnormalities and as *exogenous* when it is due to overeating. *Synonym:* adiposity. *See also* bariatrics.

obitiatrist   The term Jack Kevorkian has suggested for a physician who assists in the suicide of a patient. *See also* physician-assisted suicide.

obitorium   The term Jack Kevorkian has suggested for an assisted-suicide clinic. *See also* physician-assisted suicide.

objective   A quantifiable statement of a desired future state or condition with a stated deadline for achieving the objective, which must have a relationship to the attainment of a goal. *See also* management by objectives; mission statement.

OBRA '87 (Omnibus Budget Reconciliation Act of 1987)   Legislation, passed in 1987 and put into effect in 1990, aimed at improving the quality of life of long term care residents. Among the regulations were those that recognized the importance of involving residents in care decisions and defined necessary resident rights; restricted the use of psychotropic drugs (especially antipsychotics) and physical and chemical restraints; and advocated activities and services to attain or maintain the highest possible level of physical, mental, and psychosocial well-being for residents. Also, Medicare payments for 11 surgical procedures were reduced, and the regulations and interpretive guides specified the medical director's role, physician services, and resident assessments to be applied to all long term care facilities. *See also* long term care; Medicare; Minimum Data Set; Nursing Home Reform legislation.

OBRA '89 (Omnibus Budget Reconciliation Act of 1989)   A federal act that amended Title XVIII of the Social Security Act and called for significant physician payment reform and increased funding for effectiveness research. Included in the changes brought about by this act were the creation of a fee schedule for payment of provider services, the rate of increases in Medicare expenditures, and limits on the amounts that nonparticipating providers could charge Medicare beneficiaries. *See also* Medicare; Physician Payment Reform; Stark I.

OBRA '90 (Omnibus Budget Reconciliation Act of 1990)   A federal act that introduced changes in phar-maceutical services. Regulations established the drug utilization review (DUR), which was implemented by state Medicaid outpatient prescription programs in 1993. The legislation also required pharmacists to offer counseling to all patients receiving prescription drugs. *See also* drug utilization review; pharmaceutical care and services; Stark II.

OBRA '93 (Omnibus Budget Reconciliation Act of 1993)   A federal act that, among other things, created the Vaccines For Children (VFC) program, a new vaccine program implemented on October 1, 1994. OBRA '93 also amended the Social Security Act to incorporate the physician incentive plan rules as part of the physician self-referral ban. Under the provisions, compliance with the physician incentive plan rules will be necessary to meet the exemption for personal services arrangements if a personal services compensation arrangement involves compensation that varies based on the volume or value of referrals. The legislation also set provisions for lobbying and estate recovery procedures. *See also* immunization schedules; lobbying; Vaccines for Children program.

observational study   A study in which nature is allowed to take its course and observed changes are studied in relation to changes in others. The investigator(s) does not intervene in an observational study.

observation medicine   A hybrid of emergency medicine and inpatient care.

observation period   A time period following an event (eg, administration of a penicillin injection) during which a patient is watched closely for evidence that the care provided does no harm (eg, an allergic reaction to penicillin).

obsessive-compulsive disorder   A disorder described in DSM-IV as distinct from the personality disorder with the same name, characterized by recurrent obsessions or compulsions that are severe enough to be time-consuming or to cause marked distress or significant impairment. By definition, adults with the disorder have at some point recognized that the obsessions or compulsions are excessive or unreasonable. *See also* DSM-IV; personality disorder.

obsessive-compulsive personality disorder   *See* personality disorder.

obstetrics and gynecology (OB-GYN)   The branch and specialty of medicine that deals with the management of pregnancy, labor, and the postlabor recovery period (obstetrics) and diseases of the female genital tract (gynecology). *See also* gynecology; maternal-fetal medicine; reproductive endocrinology; rooming-in.

Occam's razor   *See* Ockham's razor.

occasion of service   A specific identifiable act of service provided a patient, such as performance of a test, medical examination, treatment, or procedure. *See also* services.

occupancy   In a health care organization, the ratio of average daily census to the average number of beds maintained during the reporting period. *See also* ambulatory health care occupancy; average daily census; bed count; business occupancy; health care occupancy; licensed beds; *Life Safety Code*; occupancy factor; occupancy rate; residential occupancy.

occupancy factor (*T*)   The level of occupancy of an area adjacent to a source of radiation, used to determine the amount of shielding required in the walls. *T* is rated as full, for an office or laboratory next to an x-ray facility; partial, for corridors and restrooms; and occasional, for stairways, elevators, closets, and outside areas. *See also* factor; occupancy; x-ray.

occupancy rate   A measure of inpatient health facility use, determined by dividing available bed days by patient days. It measures the average percentage of a hospital's beds occupied and may be organizationwide or specific for one department or service. *See also* occupancy; patient days.

occupational accident   An accidental injury that occurs in the workplace. *See also* occupational hazard; Occupational Safety and Health Act of 1970.

occupational disability   *See* disability.

occupational disease   A disease, such as occupational asthma, resulting from the conditions of a person's employment, usually from long-term exposure to a noxious substance or from continuous repetition of certain acts. *Synonym:* industrial disease. *See also* Safety and Health Act of 1970.

occupational exposure   Subjection to risk of infection or other disease as a result of exposure at the worksite to potentially harmful chemical, physical, or biological agents. The concept comes up most frequently in connection with HIV infection. Guidelines are available from the Centers for Disease Control and Prevention and the U.S. Public Health Service on avoiding risk of exposure and on postexposure prophylaxis against the disorder. *See also* Occupational Safety and Health Act of 1970.

occupational hazard   Any condition of a job, such as exposure to radiation or chemicals, that can result in injury or illness. *See also* disability; hazard; occupational accident; occupational health and safety; Occupational Safety and Health Act of 1970.

occupational health   The degree to which an employee is able to function at an optimum level of well-being at work as reflected by productivity, work attendance, disability compensation claims, and employment longevity. *See also* disability; environmental health; occupational health and safety; Occupational Safety and Health Act of 1970; workers' compensation claims.

occupational health and safety   The recognition, control, and prevention of health hazards and illnesses associated with occupations and the work environment. This includes promotion of the mental and physical health of employed persons. *See also* occupational hazard;

occupational health; Occupational Safety and Health Act of 1970.

occupational health services   Health services involving the physical, mental, and social well-being of individuals in relation to their work and working environment. *Synonym:* industrial health services. *See also* employee health service.

occupational medicine   The branch of medicine dealing with the prevention and treatment of disease and injuries occurring at work or in specific occupations.

Occupational Safety and Health Act of 1970   The principal federal statute providing for the health and safety of employees on the job, administered by the Occupational Safety and Health Administration and the National Institute for Occupational Safety and Health. The act created the Occupational Safety and Health Review Commission, the Occupational Safety and Health Administration, and the National Institute for Occupational Safety and Health. *Synonym:* Williams-Steiger Act. *See also* occupational accident; occupational disease; occupational exposure; occupational hazard; occupational health; occupational health and safety.

occupational therapy services   Services that provide for goal-directed, purposeful activity to aid in the development of adaptive skills and performance capacities by individuals of all ages who have physical disabilities and related psychological impairment(s). Occupational therapy focuses on the active involvement of a patient in specially designed therapeutic tasks and activities to improve function, performance capacity, and the ability to cope with demands of daily living. Such therapy is designed to maximize independence, prevent further disability, and maintain health, and is provided by a qualified individual. *See also* disability.

occurrence   The frequency of a disease or other attribute or event in a population or group without distinguishing between incidence and prevalence. *See also* episode; incident.

occurrence-based coverage   Insurance that covers claims only when the event that gives rise to the claim happens during the period of time that the policy is in effect, regardless of when the claim is made. *See also* claims-made coverage; coverage; insurance; occurrence policy.

occurrence criteria   Criteria used in occurrence reporting and occurrence screening systems to screen for and identify adverse patient occurrences. Examples of occurrence criteria include nosocomial infections and unplanned readmissions to the hospital after discharge to home or a nursing home. *Synonym:* occurrence screening criteria. *See also* adverse patient occurrence; HCFA generic quality screens; occurrence reporting; occurrence screening.

occurrence policy   A professional liability insurance policy that covers the holder during the period an alleged act of malpractice occurred. *See also* claims-made coverage; malpractice; occurrence-based coverage; professional liability.

occurrence reporting A system for identifying adverse patient occurrences (APOs) which relies on individuals to report events that correspond to objective occurrence criteria. Occurrence reporting can be organizationwide, although typically it focuses on high-risk areas within a hospital. Occurrence reporting provides data concurrently and generally outperforms incident reporting in its yield of APOs (40% to 60%). However, occurrence reporting systems are event-oriented and seldom identify misdiagnoses or inappropriate treatment patterns that would be found in a criterion-based review of a patient's chart. Occurrence reporting is also subject to personal interpretations and other impediments to individuals' filing reports. *See also* adverse patient occurrence; grievance process; HCFA generic quality screens; incident reporting; occurrence; occurrence criteria; occurrence screening.

occurrence screening A system for concurrent or retrospective identification of adverse patient occurrences (APOs) through chart-based review according to objective screening criteria. Examples of criteria include admission for adverse results of outpatient management, readmission for complications, incomplete management of problems on previous hospitalization, or unplanned removal, injury, or repair of an organ or structure during surgery. Criteria are used organizationwide or adapted for departmental or topic-specific screening. Occurrence screening identifies about 80% to 85% of APOs. It will miss APOs that are not identifiable from the medical record. *See also* adverse patient occurrence; grievance process; HCFA generic quality screens; incident reporting; occurrence; occurrence criteria; occurrence reporting; screening.

Ockham's razor A fourteenth-century dictum stating that entities should not be multiplied needlessly. This rule formulated by William of Ockham (1285-1349) has been interpreted in science and philosophy to mean that the simplest of two or more competing theories (eg, diagnoses) is preferable and that an explanation for unknown phenomena should first be attempted in terms of what is already known. *Synonyms*: law of parsimony; Occam's razor; scientific parsimony.

odontology The study of the structure, development, and abnormalities of the teeth.

office hypertension *See* white coat hypertension.

Official Accreditation Decision Report In the Joint Commission accreditation process, the report resulting from the on-site assessment of an organization that outlines the nature of the accreditation decision, including enumeration of type I recommendations, the remediation of which will be monitored by the Joint Commission through focused surveys or written progress reports.

official drug Pertaining to drugs authorized by or contained in the *United States Pharmacopoeia* or *National Formulary*.

Old Age, Survivors, and Disability Insurance (OASDI) Program A federal program created by the Social Security Act (1965), which taxes both workers and employers to pay benefits to retired and disabled persons, their dependents, widows or widowers, and the children of deceased workers. *See also* Social Security.

Old Age, Survivors, Disability and Health Insurance (OASDHI) Program A program administered by the Social Security Administration that provides monthly cash benefits to retired and disabled workers and their dependents, and to survivors of insured workers. The OASDHI also provides health insurance benefits for persons aged 65 years and older, and for disabled persons younger than age 65. The legislative authority for the OASDHI is in the Social Security Act, originally enacted in 1935. The health insurance component of OASDHI, known as Medicare, was initiated in 1965. *See also* Medicare; social insurance.

Older Americans Act of 1965 A federal statute that, as amended, attempts to provide a national policy for assisting older Americans in securing equal opportunity and an enhanced quality of life.

ombudsperson A person who investigates complaints and reports findings, especially between aggrieved parties, such as patients, and an organization, such as a hospital or a component of a hospital. *See also* patient advocate.

Omnibus Budget Reconciliation Act of 1987 *See* OBRA '87; OBRA '89; OBRA '90; OBRA '93.

oncogene A class of gene that is capable of inducing cancerous transformation in cells, including genes for growth factors, growth factor receptors, protein kinases, signal transducers, nuclear phosphoproteins, and transcription factors.

oncology The branch of medicine and subspecialty of gynecology, internal medicine, and pediatrics, dealing with the diagnosis and treatment of patients with cancer. *See also* cancer staging system; radiation oncology.

one-to-one service A method of organizing nursing services in an inpatient care unit by which one registered nurse assumes responsibility for all nursing care provided one patient for the duration of one shift.

online Connected to and communicating directly with a computer's central processing unit. It is the type of computer system in which information entered into the system is immediately reflected in the database so that inquiries will always reflect up-to-the-minute transaction status.

online database A database stored on a mainframe computer, which is transmitted by telephone, microwaves, or other means and can be accessed with a decoding device (modem) and displayed on a monitor or as a printout. *See also* database; online.

online medical record A medical record stored in a computer, with constant instantaneous access via a computer terminal. *See also* electronic medical record; medical record.

on-the-job training (OJT) Work-related training that occurs at the actual worksite while one is engaged in the occupation or profession; hands-on instruction. *See also* in-service.

open access In health care, describes a health plan member's ability to self-refer for specialty care with a participating provider without first obtaining referral from another physician. *See also* gatekeeper mechanism.

open charting A system of medical recordkeeping in which the patient has access to his or her chart. Open charting in varying degrees is authorized in some mental health institutions. *See also* medical record.

open-door policy A management policy of encouraging a relaxed environment with employees by leaving the manager's door open to encourage informal employee interaction. *See also* management.

open-ended HMO *See* point-of-service plan.

open-ended programs Entitlement programs, such as Medicaid, in the federal budget for which eligibility requirements are determined by law. Actual obligations and outlays are only limited by the number of eligible persons who apply for benefits and the actual benefits received. *See also* entitlement; entitlement program; Medicaid.

open enrollment A period of time when new subscribers may enroll in a group or individual health insurance plan or a prepaid group practice. Individuals perceived as high-risk (eg, because of a preexisting illness) may be subjected to high premiums or exclusion during open enrollment periods. *See also* enrollment; exclusions; preexisting condition.

open panel group practice A medical or dental group practice that invites all physicians or dentists who meet its membership requirements to participate in marketing, delivery, and business administration of the group's health or dental care services. *Synonym*: open panel practice. *See also* closed panel group practice; group practice.

open staff An arrangement in which a medical staff of a health care organization accepts new physician applicants to the medical staff, if the physicians are qualified and approved by the governing body of the organization. The term is also applied to organization-physician contracts in which physicians provide administrative and clinical services to an organization on a nonexclusive basis. *Synonym*: open medical staff. *See also* closed staff; exclusive contract; medical staff; organized medical staff.

operational data A form of secondary data that are collected and maintained by an organization to meet its ongoing information needs; for example, hospital medical records and hospital billing records. *See also* data.

operational definition A description in quantifiable terms of what to measure and the steps to follow to consistently measure it. A desirable operational definition includes a criterion to be applied, a way to determine whether the criterion is satisfied, and a way to interpret the results of the test. An operational definition is developed for each key quality characteristic or key process variable before data are collected. *See also* key process variable; key quality characteristic.

operative risk The probability of adverse outcome and death associated with surgery and anesthesia. Decisions to proceed with surgery are based on conceptualized risk-benefit ratios, which can be accurate only when they are applied to groups of comparable patients undergoing similar procedures. The risks can be classified as

---

THE AMERICAN SOCIETY OF ANESTHESIOLOGISTS' PHYSICAL STATUS CLASSIFICATION

Class I: No organic, physiologic, biochemical, or psychiatric disturbance. The pathologic process for which operation is to be performed is localized and does not entail a systemic disturbance. Examples: inguinal hernia in a fit patient; fibroid uterus in an otherwise healthy woman.

Class II: Mild to moderate systemic disturbance caused either by the condition to be treated surgically or by other pathophysiologic processes. Examples: non- or only slight limiting organic heart disease; mild diabetes; essential hypertension; anemia. Some might choose to list the extremes of age here, the neonate and the octogenarian, even though no discernible systemic disease is present. Extreme obesity and chronic bronchitis may be included in this category.

Class III: Severe systemic disturbance or disease from whatever cause, even though it may not be possible to define the degree of disability with finality. Examples: severely limiting organic heart disease; severe diabetes with vascular complications; moderate to severe degrees of pulmonary insufficiency; angina pectoris; healed myocardial infarction.

Class IV: Severe systemic disorders that are already life-threatening and not always correctable by operation. Examples: organic heart disease with marked signs of cardiac insufficiency, persistent anginal syndrome, or active myocarditis; advanced degrees of pulmonary, hepatic, renal, or endocrine insufficiency.

Class V: Moribundity with little chance of survival. Examples: burst abdominal aneurysm with profound shock; major cerebral trauma with rapidly increasing intracranial pressure; massive pulmonary embolus. Most patients of this class require operation as a resuscitative measure with little if any anesthesia.

Emergency Operation (E): Any patient in one of the classes listed above who is operated upon as an emergency is considered to be in poorer physical condition than normal. The letter E is placed beside the numeric classification. Thus, the patient with a hitherto uncomplicated hernia now incarcerated and associated with nausea and vomiting is classified as IE.

Source: After Hallen B: *Acta Anesthesiol Scand* (Suppl)52:5, 1973. Munksesard International Publishers Ltd, Copenhagen, Denmark.

patient related, procedure related, provider related, and anesthetic agent related. The patient's overall status may be assessed and scored by the American Society of Anesthesiologists' Physical Status Scale (ASA-PSS), which has been found to correlate with surgical outcome, although it was not originally designed as a predictor of risk. *See also* health risk appraisal.

ophthalmology The branch and specialty of medicine dealing with comprehensive eye and vision care, including diagnosis, monitoring, and medically or surgically treating all eyelid and orbital problems affecting the eye and visual pathways. Vision services, such as prescribing glasses and contact lenses, are included in the area of ophthalmology. *See also* ophthalmoscopy; optometry; orthoptics.

ophthalmoscopy The process of examining the interior of the eye with an ophthalmoscope (an instrument containing a perforated mirror and lenses), as in performing ophthalmoscopy to diagnose for signs of diabetic retinopathy or hypertensive vascular changes. *Synonym:* fundoscopy. *See also* endoscopy; ophthalmology.

opinion leader An individual whose ideas and behavior serve as a model to other persons. Opinion leaders communicate messages to a primary group, influencing the attitudes and behavioral changes of people in the group. *See also* implementation techniques; leader.

opioid abuse. *See* substance-related disorders (and accompanying table).

opioid use guidelines Consensus statement released by the American Academy of Pain Medicine and the American Pain Society in March 1997 on prescribing opioids (eg, morphine) for managing chronic pain. The guidelines address physicians' unwarranted fears about addiction, respiratory depression and other side effects, and regulatory action, and offer practical tips on history taking, development of a treatment plan, periodic review of treatment efficacy, consultation, and documentation. *See also* pain management.

opportunistic infection (OI) An infection caused by a normally harmless organism that becomes pathogenic under certain conditions, such as the immunosuppression of HIV infection or drugs given to help sustain organ transplants. Systemic fungal infections, such as aspergillosis, and systemic candidiasis, toxoplasmosis, cytomegalovirus infection, and pneumocystic pneumonia are examples. *See also* AIDS; HIV and related terms; immunocompromised; immunodeficiency; opportunistic infection.

opportunity cost The value that resources, used in a particular way, would have if used in the best possible or another specified alternative way. When opportunity costs exceed the value the resources have in the way they are being used, they represent lost opportunities to derive value from the resources. For example, the opportunity cost of devoting physician time to tertiary care is the lost value of devoting the same time to primary care.

opportunity statement A concise description of a process or an outcome in need of improvement, its boundaries, the general area of concern where a quality improvement team should begin its efforts, and why work on the improvement is a priority. *See also* problem statement.

optimum achievable standard A statement of expectation about the highest level of performance that is practically attainable.

optional services Services that may be provided or covered by a health program or provider and, if provided, will be paid for in addition to any required services that must be offered. Examples of optional services under Medicaid in many states are prescribed drugs, dental services, and skilled nursing facility services for individuals younger than 21 years.

options *See* standards, guidelines, and options.

optometry The profession dealing with problems of human vision and their correction through the prescription and adaptation of visual training (orthoptics), lenses, or other optical aids. Optometry is not a branch of medicine, but optometrists must be authorized to practice by law. They may examine the eyes and vision system for visual defects, diagnose impairments, prescribe corrective lenses, use drugs for diagnostic purposes, and (in most states) prescribe them for therapeutic purposes. *See also* ophthalmology; orthoptics.

oral and maxillofacial surgery A branch and specialty of dentistry that includes a broad scope of diagnostic, operative, and related services dealing with diseases, injuries, and defects in the jaw and associated structures. *Synonym:* oral surgery. *See also* dental specialties; dentistry.

oral health The state of normality and functional efficiency of the teeth and supporting structures, the surrounding parts of the oral cavity, and the various structures related to mastication and the maxillofacial complex. *See also* dentistry.

oral health services All services designed or intended to promote, maintain, or restore dental health, including educational, preventive, and therapeutic services; all procedures that dentists are licensed to perform. *See also* dentistry.

oral hygiene **1.** The practice of keeping the mouth, teeth, and gums clean and healthy to prevent disease, as by regular brushing and flossing and visits to a dentist. *Synonym:* dental hygiene. *See also* hygiene. **2.** The work performed by a dental hygienist.

oral hygiene accreditation An accreditation process in which the Commission on Dental Accreditation evaluates and, when appropriate, accredits oral hygiene programs.

oral medicine An aspect of dentistry dealing with hospital-based, medical diseases of the mouth.

oral pathology   A dental specialty dealing with the nature of mouth diseases through study of their causes, processes, and effects. *See also* dental specialties; pathology.

oral surgery   *See* oral and maxillofacial surgery.

order   A directive, for example, about treatment, examination, drugs, and other care to be given to a patient. *See also* code blue; DNR order; medication error; nursing orders; prescribing and ordering; standing orders; time-limited order.

ordered data set   A data set that has been arranged to show the observations from the smallest to the largest value. *See also* data set.

ordinal data   Data resulting from use of an ordinal scale. *See also* ordinal scale.

ordinal scale   A scale in which classification occurs along ordered qualitative categories where the values have a distinct order, but their categories are qualitative in that there is no natural numerical distance between the possible values. Only the relative sizes of numbers (larger than, smaller than) are important. *See also* ordinal data; qualitative data; ratio scale.

ordinary care   Care that will offer reasonable hope of benefit to a patient with less chance of creating the burdens that may be associated with extraordinary care. *See also* extraordinary care; nursing care.

Oregon right-to-die law   *See* Death with Dignity Act.

organ bank   A repository and registry service for human tissues and organs for use or implantation in patients. *See also* organ procurement; National Organ Transplant Act; tissue bank.

organizational behavior   An academic field of study, primarily taught in business schools and psychology departments, dealing with human behavior in organizations. The field deals with subject matter such as motivation, group dynamics, leadership, organization structure, decision making, careers, conflict resolution, and organizational development. *Synonym:* organizational psychology.

organizational culture   The fundamental beliefs and attitudes that powerfully affect the behavior of people in and around an organization over time. The organizational culture is transmitted to new members through socialization processes; is maintained and transmitted through a network of rituals, rites, myths, communication, and interaction patterns; and is enforced and reinforced by group norms and the organization's system of rewards and controls. Sources of organizational culture include the attitudes and behaviors of dominant, early organization "shapers" and "heroes"; the organization's nature of work, including its functions and interactions with the external environment; and new members' attitudes, values, and willingness to act. Organizational culture provides a framework for the shared understanding of events, defines behavioral expectations, provides a source of and

focus for members' commitment, and functions as an organizational control system.

organizational development   Planned, systematic processes in which behavioral-science principles and practices are used to improve an organization's functioning. *See also* organizational planning.

organizational performance   The way in which an organization, such as a hospital, carries out or accomplishes its important functions so as to increase the probability that desired outcomes will be achieved. *See also* organizational development; outcome.

organizational planning   The process of transforming organizational objectives into specific management strategies and tactics designed to achieve objectives. Organizational planning is one of the most important management responsibilities. *See also* management; strategic planning.

organizational psychology   *See* organizational behavior.

organization factor   An organization-related variable that may contribute to variation in organizational performance. An organization factor is usually controllable by the organization and is the object of performance measurement and improvement processes. *Synonym:* organization-based factor. *See also* external environmental factor; factor; patient factor; practitioner factor; variable.

organized medical staff   A formal organization of practitioners having the responsibility and authority, delegated by the governing body, to maintain proper standards of resident care and to plan for the continued improvement of that care. Long term care organizations do not necessarily have organized medical staffs. *See also* closed staff; medical staff; open staff.

organized professional staff   A formal organization of the professional personnel of a health care organization that includes one or more physicians and to whom is delegated the responsibility for maintaining standards of medical care and/or health-related care. In addition to physicians, the organized professional staff includes registered nurses, rehabilitation specialists, and other professional staff. *Synonym:* organized staff. *See also* licensed independent practitioner; medical staff.

organ procurement   The process of obtaining vital human organs, such as livers, hearts, and kidneys, for implantation in other humans who need them. Organs can be procured from cadavers or live donors, such as patients on life-support systems who are proclaimed dead. There are many ethical issues involved with organ procurement. For example, informed consent must be obtained without coercion prior to removal of an organ from a live donor, yet coercion is difficult to avoid when one family member is being asked to donate an organ for another family member. *See also* anatomical gift; informed consent; Medic Alert Organ Donor Program; National Organ Transplant Act; organ transplantation; presumed consent; required request law; Uniform Determination of Death Act.

organ transplantation   To transfer an organ from one body to another. Solid organs, such as the heart, kidney, and liver, are viable only from patients in whom an intact circulatory system can be maintained despite brain death. *See also* opportunistic infection; organ procurement; tissue transplantation.

orientation   A process to provide initial training and information and to assess staff members' competence related to their job responsibilities and the organization's mission, vision, and values.

Orion Project   An initiative, currently being tested by the Joint Commission, to test various accreditation models to support health care organizations' efforts to improve their performance. The project's continuous evaluation and improvement process is based on selected performance measures drawn from a variety of sources. It evaluates the following elements: (1) a regional service representative program in which Joint Commission representatives provide accreditation consultation and advocacy services, as well as assistance in implementing performance improvement systems, to organizations in different regions; (2) adaptation of performance measures (indicators) to organization needs; and (3) coordination of Joint Commission evaluation with that of other external review bodies.

orphan drug   A therapeutic agent that is unlikely to be manufactured by private industry unless special incentives are provided by others. An orphan drug may not be available in the United States for several reasons, including a small sales potential, failure to gain approval from the FDA's Bureau of Drugs, or inability to protect the medication against competition from a similar form (in the case of synthetics). The U.S. Orphan Drug Act of 1982 offers federal financial incentives to commercial and nonprofit organizations to develop and market drugs previously unavailable in the United States. *See also* Orphan Drug Act.

Orphan Drug Act (1982)   A federal law providing tax incentives and developmental grants for the testing of drugs designated by the secretary of health and human services as possibly effective for the treatment of many diseases and conditions that affect only small numbers of persons. *See also* orphan drug.

orthodontics   A dental specialty involving treatment of problems relating to irregular dental development, missing teeth, and other abnormalities in order to establish normal function and appearance. Orthodontists straighten teeth and correct the position of jaws by using braces and/or other appliances that affect oral growth and development. *Synonyms:* orthodontia; orthodonture. *See also* dental specialties.

orthomolecular medicine   The study of the concentrations of substances, such as vitamins, normally found in the body but appearing disproportionately in schizophrenics, alcoholics, children with learning disabilities,

and older people suffering memory loss, depression, and other senile illnesses. *See also* megavitamin therapy.

orthopedics   The branch of medicine that deals with the prevention or correction of injuries or disorders of the skeletal system and associated muscles, joints, and ligaments. *See also* orthopedic surgery; sports medicine.

orthopedic surgery   The branch and specialty of medicine dealing with the preservation, investigation, and restoration of the form and function of the extremities, spine, and associated structures by medical, surgical, and physical means. *See also* arthroscopy; orthopedics.

orthopsychiatry   The psychiatric study, treatment, and prevention of emotional and behavioral problems, especially those that arise during early development. *See also* psychiatry.

orthoptics   Practice of using nonsurgical measures, especially eye exercises, to treat abnormalities of vision and uncoordinated eye movement. *See also* ophthalmology; optometry.

orthotics   The science dealing with the use of specialized mechanical devices to support or supplement weakened or abnormal joints or limbs. *See also* prosthetics.

ORYX (ORYX Outcomes: The Next Evolution in Accreditation)   A performance measurement initiative of the Joint Commission which is intended to be a flexible and affordable approach to progressively increasing the relevance of accreditation, and an important building block for supporting quality improvement efforts in accredited organizations. The use of performance measures as an integral feature of the new accreditation process should significantly enhance its value to health care organizations and to those who rely on accreditation information. The basic ORYX implementation plan will initially apply only to hospitals and long term care organizations. A parallel group of requirements is being put in place for health care networks (eg, health plans, provider sponsored organizations). The implementation plan is to be phased-in over time to assure that its modest expectations accommodate the real-world capabilities of the full range of accredited organizations. Other types of organizations accredited by the Joint Commission—clinical laboratories and home care, behavioral health care, and ambulatory care organizations—will follow. *See also* performance measurement; performance measurement system.

OSCAR   A computer program that evaluates dose-column histograms consistently for use in three-dimensional treatment planning. Based on a dose prescription specified by a radiation oncologist, the technique provides a quantitative, easy-to-understand visual analysis of a proposed drug distribution.

osteology   The study and knowledge of the bones.

osteopathic manipulative treatment (OMT)   The diagnosis and treatment of injury and illness through manual movement and stimulation of joints and tissues.

OMT may be employed in combination with all other medical and alternative procedures. *See also* osteopathy.

osteopathy   A system of medicine based on the theory that the normal body, when in correct adjustment, is a vital mechanical organism naturally capable of making its own responses to and defenses against diseases. Osteopaths search for and, if possible, correct any peculiar position of the joints or tissue or peculiarity of diet or environment that is a factor in destroying the body's natural resistance. The measures used are physical, hygienic, medicinal, and surgical. Osteopathy is distinguished from allopathy mainly by its greater reliance on manipulation. *Synonym:* osteopathic medicine. *See also* allopathy; alternative medicine; chiropractic; holism; holistic medicine; homeopathy; massage therapy; naprapathy; naturopathy; osteopathic manipulative treatment.

osteoporosis   According to an international consensus definition developed under the leadership of the European Foundation for Osteoporosis (1993) and adopted by several groups, a systemic skeletal disease characterized by low bone mass and microarchitectural deterioration of bone tissue and consequent susceptibility to fracture. The condition results over a period of years from a complex interplay of genetic, hormonal, nutritional, and other factors, occurring most frequently in postmenopausal women, sedentary or immobilized individuals, and patients on long-term steroid therapy. Adequate dietary calcium while bone is being laid down (birth to age 35 years) delays onset. Controversy continues over use of bone densitometry to identify osteoporosis risk. *See also* hormone replacement therapy; menopause.

otitis media   Inflammation of the middle ear, with or without signs of fluid or infection. Related conditions are *otitis media with effusion* (fluid in the middle ear without signs or symptoms of ear infection), *persistent acute otitis media* (middle ear inflammation with signs of infection that does not resolve after initial treatment), and *recurrent acute otitis media* (middle ear inflammation with signs of infection that occurs shortly after resolution of an episode of acute otitis media). *See also* speech-language pathology services.

otolaryngology   The branch and specialty of medicine dealing with medical and surgical treatment of the head and neck, including the ears, nose, and throat. Head and neck oncology and facial plastic and reconstructive surgery are areas of expertise. *Synonym:* otorhinolaryngology. *See also* laryngology; otology/neurotology; rhinology.

otology/neurotology   The branch of medicine and subspecialty of otolaryngology concerned with diagnosis, management, prevention, cure, and care of patients with diseases of the ear and temporal bone, including disorders of hearing and balance. The subspecialty deals specifically with care for patients in need of cochlear implants, implantable hearing aids, and extensive reconstruction of the tympanum (eardrum) and ossicular chains (small bones of the middle ear). *Synonym:* neurotology. *See also* otolaryngology.

otorhinolaryngology   *See* otolaryngology.

otoscopy   Examination of the external ear, the tympanic membrane (eardrum), and, through the eardrum, the small bones of the middle ear using an endoscope. *See also* endoscopy.

outbreak   *See* epidemic infection.

outcome   The result of the performance (or nonperformance) of a function(s) or process(es). *See also* the following outcome terms, as well as intervention; organizational performance; patient health outcome.

outcome assessment   Evaluation based on the premise that care is delivered in order to bring about certain results; criteria are developed to measure the actual outcomes of patient care and service against the predetermined criteria. *See also* outcome; outcome criteria.

outcome criteria   Criteria against which the level of outcomes achieved may be compared. *See also* outcome; outcome assessment.

outcome(s) data   Data collected to evaluate a specified outcome, such as changes in a patient's health status attributable to care processes received by the patient. *See also* data; outcome; process data.

outcome(s) indicator   An indicator that measures what happens or does not happen after a process(es), service(s), or activity(ies) is performed or not performed. *See also* indicator; outcome measure; process indicator.

outcome measure   A measure that indicates the result of the performance (or nonperformance) of a function(s) or process(es). Outcome measures quantify an organization's, a practitioner's, or a community's actual results in providing services the organization is capable of providing. *See also* input measure; measure; outcome indicator; process measure.

outcome of care   *See* patient health outcome.

outcomes management   A proactive approach to improving health care outcomes by using information gained through monitoring activities to improve clinical decision making and care delivery. Outcomes management comprises three components: outcomes measurement, outcomes monitoring, and outcomes management.

outcomes measurement   The process of systematically tracking a patient's clinical treatment and responses to that treatment, including measures of morbidity and functional status, for the purpose of improving care. *See also* Health Care Quality Improvement Program; quality improvement.

outcomes monitoring   The ongoing measurement of outcomes indicators over time to support hypotheses regarding the causes of the outcomes.

outcomes research   Health services research that attempts to identify the clinical outcomes of the delivery of health care services. *See also* outcome.

outcome standard   A statement of expectation set by competent authority concerning a degree or level of acceptable outcome achieved by an individual, group, organization, community, or nation, according to preestablished requirements and/or specifications. *See also* outcome; process standard; standard.

outdated blood   Donated whole blood that has been stored under refrigeration in CDPA-1 anticoagulant solution for more than 35 days after phlebotomy and consequently is unusable for transfusion. *See also* blood transfusion services.

outlier   **1.** Observations differing so widely from the rest of a set of data as to lead one to suspect that a gross error may have been committed or suggest that these values come from a different population; for example, health care providers with performance or outcomes rates that are outside the range of expected rates after adjustment for patient or other characteristics.   **2.** A patient having either an extremely long length of stay (day outlier) or incurring an extraordinarily high cost (cost outlier) when compared with most patient discharges classified in the same DRG. *See also* continuous quality improvement; cost outlier; DRG outlier; high-mortality outlier; inlier; low-mortality outlier; outlier threshold.

outlier threshold   The maximum length of stay a patient can have before being labeled a day outlier. This threshold is calculated by HCFA. *See also* length of stay.

out-of-area benefits   Benefits an HMO provides to its members when they are outside the HMO's geographic area. Coverage is restricted to emergency services. *See also* benefits.

out-of-area coverage   Benefits that a health plan will provide to its members who are outside the plan's coverage area. With rare exceptions, out-of-area coverage is limited to emergency services only. *See also* coverage.

out-of-network services   Health care services received from providers who do not participate in a managed care program's contracted network. Under point-of-service managed care programs, enrollees receive less toward expenses incurred for out-of-network services than for those provided within the network. *See also* in-network services.

out-of-pocket payments   Payments or costs borne directly by a patient without benefit of insurance. *See also* insurance.

outpatient   An individual who receives health care services in a clinic, emergency department, or other health care facility without being admitted to (lodged overnight in) a health care facility as an inpatient. *See also* the following outpatient terms, as well as inpatient; outpatient bed; patient.

outpatient bed   A bed regularly maintained by a health care organization for patients who require medical services for less than 24 hours.

outpatient care   Care that is provided to patients who are not confined to an institutional bed as inpatients during the time services are rendered, such as an emergency department visit that does not result in hospitalization overnight. *Synonym*: ambulatory care. *See also* ambulatory health care.

outpatient mastectomies   *See* length of stay mandates.

outpatient program   In behavioral health, a program that provides services to persons who generally do not need the level of care associated with the more structured environment of an inpatient or a residential program.

outpatient services   **1.** Medical or other services provided to patients who do not require admission as inpatients. Such services include physical therapy or diagnostic x-ray and laboratory tests.   **2.** For purposes of Joint Commission accreditation, outpatient services refers to a patient appointment system, and all the stated requirements do not apply. *See also* clinic.

outpatient surgery   *See* ambulatory surgery.

outpatient visit   All services provided an outpatient in the course of a single appearance in an outpatient or inpatient unit. *See also* visit.

outreach program   A program sponsored and administered by an organization whose purpose is to bring a specified type of health service, such as primary care or home care, into the community the organization serves. *See also* community health care.

ovarian cancer   *See BRCA1* and *BRCA2* genes; cancer susceptibility testing.

overflow incontinence   *See* urinary incontinence.

over-the-counter (OTC) drug   A nonprescription medication that is legally sold over the counter in a retail store. Over-the-counter medicines can be purchased in any quantity without restrictions at the retail store level. *Synonyms*: nonprescription drug; over-the-counter medicine; patent medicine. *See also* drug; legend drug; prescription drug.

overtriage   The process of transporting patients to trauma centers when the patients could have received appropriate care in a nontrauma center. The use of trauma scoring instruments, such as the Glasgow coma scale, are intended to increase the probability of matching trauma patients with the appropriate level of trauma care. *See also* Glasgow Coma Scale; triage; Trauma Score; undertriage.

overuse   *See* utilization.

overweight   *See* obesity.

owner   In quality improvement, a person(s) who has or is given the responsibility and authority to lead the continuing improvement of a process. Process ownership is a designation made by leaders of organizations and depends on the boundaries of a process.

oximetry   Noninvasive measurement of patient oxygenation through either spectrophotometric evaluations of arterial blood flow or simple diffusion measurements of oxygen through capillary membranes.

Pp

pacemaker *See* cardiac pacemaker.

pacemaker syndrome A complication arising in approximately 7% of patients with implanted cardiac pacemakers, occurring as a result of the loss of the synchronized contraction of the atria and ventricles and characterized by dizziness, syncope (fainting), hypotension, dyspnea (shortness of breath), weakness and fatigue, and diminished exercise tolerance. Detection is difficult because the symptoms may mimic those that led to the implantation of a pacemaker in the first place. The complication is alleviated by switching to dual-chamber pacemakers. *See also* cardiac pacemaker.

package insert **1.** The labeling, approved by the FDA for a prescription drug product, that accompanies a product when it is shipped by a manufacturer to a pharmacist. The package insert is used by prescribing professionals, principally physicians. It states indications and contraindications of a drug, mode(s) of administration, dosage information, and warnings. **2.** The labeling manufacturers must provide for all laboratory test reagents to be used by laboratory professionals. Information required by the FDA includes the principal methodology, instructions for test performance, chemical content of the reagents, quality control processes, reference ranges, and bibliography. *See also* contraindication; labeling; *Physicians' Desk Reference*; prescription drug.

packaging laws *See* labeling.

pack year A rough measure of how much a person has smoked over a lifetime, calculated by multiplying the number of cigarette packs smoked per day by the number of years of smoking. For example, a person who has smoked two packs of cigarettes a day for 40 years would be recorded as having 80 pack years. The figure is used to calculate a patient's risk of developing lung cancer, chronic obstructive pulmonary disease, and other diseases. *See also* smoking cessation counseling and therapy.

pain and suffering In law, the term used to describe not only physical discomfort or distress but also the mental or emotional trauma which are recoverable as elements of damage in torts. Recovery for pain and suffering is restricted by statute in certain states. *See also* mental anguish.

pain drawings Drawings by patients depicting the severity, type, and location of their pain as a technique for assessing psychological involvement in the pain complaints. *See also* visual analog scale.

pain management **1.** A system to deal with patients experiencing problems with acute or chronic pain. *See also* anesthesiology; physical medicine and rehabilitation; transcutaneous electric nerve stimulation. **2.** The lessening of discomfort that accompanies chronic and acute conditioning. *See also* low back pain; opioid use guidelines; pain management program; palliative care; WHO analgesic drug ladder.

pain management program A specialized program for the management of chronic and acute pain, using a multidisciplinary approach with medical, nursing, pharmacy, and allied health professionals. *See also* pain management.

palliative care A range of treatments and support services intended to alleviate pain and suffering rather than cure terminally ill patients. Palliative therapy may include surgery or radiotherapy that is not intended to be curative but rather is undertaken to reduce or shrink tumors compressing vital structures and thereby improve the quality of life. Palliative care includes attention to the psychological and spiritual needs of the patient and support for the dying patient and the patient's family. *Synonyms:* comfort care; palliative treatment. *See also* Compassionate, Competent Care Initiative; curative; futile care; holistic medicine; hospice; pain management.

palliative care curriculum *See* Compassionate, Competent Care Initiative.

pandemic An epidemic of intercontinental or worldwide proportions, such as the malaria pandemic among early settlers until the introduction of quinine. *See also* endemic infection; epidemic infection.

Pap (Papanicolaou) smear A test, using a simple smear obtained during a routine pelvic examination, to detect cervical dysplasia (a precursor to cancer) carcinoma in situ, invasive cervical and uterine carcinoma, herpes or trichomonad infections, and human papillomavirus. The test is named after its developer, George Papanicolaou (1883-1962), an American anatomist. The accuracy and the reliability of this test depend on the skill of the examiner in obtaining a good specimen and of the cytotechnologist or cytopathologist in interpreting the smears. The cervical cancer staging-class system based on Pap findings has generally been replaced by the Bethesda System, although some physicians continue to prefer the Pap system. There is consensus among concerned specialty groups and agencies that all women who are or have been sexually active or who have reached age 18 should have annual Pap smears, although details and exceptions for different risk groups vary. *See also* Bethesda System; cancer screening tests and procedures; cervical cancer screening.

paradigm shift A time when the model, example, or pattern that underlies a science or discipline changes in such a fundamental way that the beliefs and behavior of the people involved in the science or discipline are changed.

paramedic A person who is certified by a state agency to perform advanced cardiac life support procedures and other emergency medical treatment under the direction of a physician. *See also* allied health professional; ambulance; emergency medical responder.

parametric test   A statistical test that depends on assumption(s) about the distribution of the data; for example, the assumption that the data will be normally, versus bimodally, distributed. *See also* statistical test.

paranoid disorder   Informally, any of a group of mental disorders characterized by an impaired sense of reality and persistent delusions of persecution or grandeur. In the DSM-IV, which does not use the term *paranoia* per se, the attributes of paranoia are identified in a subtype of schizophrenia and in a type of personality disorder (*paranoid personality disorder*). The paranoia may be organized into an elaborate and logical system of thinking and is often centered on a specific theme, such as a job situation or a financial matter. *See also* personality disorder; schizophrenia.

paraprofession   Occupations requiring successful completion of a training program at or above the college level or its equivalent, typically lasting one to two years; the program resembles that of the profession to which it corresponds, except that the paraprofessional program is shorter and more limited in content. Members of the occupation work under the direction and supervision of the professionals whose service capabilities they extend and to whom they are responsible. Paraprofessionals work in many fields, including law, medicine, library science, teaching, and social services. Examples of paraprofessionals in health care include physician assistants and dental hygienists. *See also* allied health professional.

parapsychology   The study of extrasensory perception and allied phenomena (eg, clairvoyance, telepathy) that appear to transcend natural laws. *See also* clairvoyance.

parasitology   The scientific discipline dealing with the study of parasites.

parens patriae   Latin phrase meaning the power of the government to protect an individual for his or her own good.

parent   A child's father or mother, who may be distinguished as genetic parents, gestational mother, and rearing parents. *See also* birth mother; genetic parent; gestational mother; rearing parent; reproductive technologies.

parenteral nutrition   The intravenous administration of nutrient fluids, amino acids, carbohydrates, fats, vitamins, or minerals to those individuals who have lost gastrointestinal function or who cannot maintain adequate nutrition care status through conventional intake of nutrients. Parenteral nutrition allows safe administration, through a variety of veins, of all daily nutrition requirements to effect protein synthesis and maintain adequate nutrition status. The essential components of parenteral nutrition are fluids, carbohydrates, electrolytes, protein, lipids, vitamins, and trace minerals. *See also* enteral nutrition; infusion therapy services; nutrition; total parenteral nutrition.

parenteral product   A sterile pharmaceutical preparation administered by injection into the vein or through subcutaneous tissues. Parenteral is derived from the Greek words *para* and *enteron*, meaning "outside the intestine."

Pareto chart   A special form of vertical bar graph that displays information in such a way that priorities for process improvement can be established. It shows the relative importance of all the data and is used to direct efforts to the largest improvement opportunity by highlighting the "vital few" in contrast to the "many others." *See also* check sheet; Pareto principle.

Pareto principle   A principle developed by Vilfredo Pareto (1848-1923), an Italian economist and sociologist, which is employed to identify the "vital few" (eg, customers, customer needs, product features, process features, inputs) to help direct resources and attention to areas where they do the most good. For example, the Pareto principle states that a few contributors to the cost of poor quality are responsible for the bulk of the cost. These vital few contributors need to be identified so that improvement resources can be concentrated in the few contributors. *Synonym:* 80/20 rule. *See also* Pareto chart; useful many; vital few.

parity check   A test performed by checking a unit of data for even or odd parity to determine whether a mistake has taken place in reading, writing, or transmitting information. For example, if data are written, the computed parity bit is compared to the parity bit already appended to the data. If these match, it indicates that the data are correct. If they do not agree, a *parity error* exists. *See also* mental health parity acts.

parity error   *See* parity check.

parity of data   *See* data parity.

parsimony   Adoption of the simplest assumption in the formulation of a theory or in the interpretation of data, especially in accordance with the rule of Ockham's razor. *See also* Ockham's razor.

partial birth abortion   Defined in legislation proposing to ban a type of abortion, known clinically as dilation and extraction, as a procedure in which the provider partially vaginally delivers a living fetus before killing the fetus and completing the delivery. The procedure usually involves moving the fetus to a breech position (feet first) and extracting it intact through the birth canal with all but the head delivered and then collapsing the head with a sharp instrument at the base of the skull to suction out the brain, which makes the head small enough to deliver through a partially delivered cervix. *See also* abortion; dilation and curettage.

partial care program   Mental health services provided to individuals who spend only part of a 24-hour period in a facility. These mental health services are provided in an environment that is more structured than that of an outpatient program, but less structured than that of either a residential treatment program or an inpatient treatment program. *See also* mental health services; partial hospitalization program; residential care facility.

partial code   *See* slow code.

partial hospitalization   A formal program of care that provides services to persons who spend only part of a 24-hour period in a facility. Two principal types are *night hospitalization*, for patients who need hospitalization but can work or attend school outside the hospital during the day, and *day hospitalization*, for people who require in-hospital diagnostic or treatment services but can safely spend nights and weekends at home. *See also* day bed; night bed; partial hospitalization program; weekend hospitalization.

partial hospitalization program   A program that provides services to persons who spend only part of a 24-hour period in a health facility, such as for psychiatric treatment or the treatment of alcohol and other drug dependencies. Partial-hospitalization programs do not provide overnight care. *See also* alcoholism treatment service; partial care program; partial hospitalization; psychiatry; substance-related disorders.

participating physician   Under Medicare, a physician who has signed a contract agreeing to refrain from charging a Medicare patient the difference between the physician's usual charge and Medicare payment allowance. *See also* health care provider; Medicare; non-participating provider.

participating plan   A Blue Cross and Blue Shield plan that agrees to process national account claims in its jurisdiction on behalf of another plan that serves as the control plan for that national account. *See also* Blue Cross and Blue Shield plan; control plan.

participative leadership   Consultative management method that encourages other individuals to participate. Leadership decisions are achieved as the end result of group participation. *See also* management.

partner notification   The process of informing sexual or needle-sharing partners of a person infected with HIV of the fact of past or current risk of contracting HIV infection. The notification may be made by the person infected with HIV, a health care provider, or a public health worker. *See also* HIV infection.

partnership   A legal relationship between two or more competent persons who have contracted to place their money, effects, labor, or skill in lawful commerce or business, with the understanding that there will be a proportionate sharing of profits and losses. *See also* brokered partnership; Community Health Intervention Partnerships; joint venture; limited partnership.

passive-aggressive personality disorder   *See* personality disorder.

passive negligence   *See* vicarious liability.

passive smoking   *See* secondhand smoke.

pass-through cost   An overhead cost, which is not incorporated in DRG prices. Medicare funds are provided to the organization directly, that is, the costs are passed through (around) the DRG mechanism.

pastoral care   A service ministering religious activities and providing pastoral counseling to patients, their families, and staff of a health care organization. Pastoral counselors are ministers who are qualified to assist patients in dealing with acute, chronic, and terminal illnesses through individual and group counseling. *Synonyms:* chaplaincy service; pastoral counseling department.

patent medicine   *See* over-the-counter drug.

paternalism   A traditional model of the physician-patient relationship in which the physician is held to know what is best for the patient and acts accordingly, sometimes by choosing among alternative treatments without consulting the patient and sometimes by withholding information from the patient, such as the diagnosis of and prognosis for a terminal illness. The concept is under challenge both within and outside the profession with a growing concern for patient autonomy and a growing trend toward patient and family participation and shared decision making. *See also* patient participation; patient-provider relationship; shared decision making; therapeutic privilege.

pathology   The branch and specialty of medicine dealing with the essential nature of disease, especially the structural and functional changes in tissues and organs of the body that cause or are caused by disease. Ten subspecialties of pathology are blood banking, chemical pathology, cytopathology, dermatopathology, forensic pathology, hematology, immunopathology, medical microbiology, neuropathology, and pediatric pathology. *See also* anatomic pathology; blood banking; chemical pathology; clinical pathology; cytopathology; forensic pathology; hematology; histochemistry; histopathology; immunopathology; microbiology; neuropathology; oral pathology; speech pathology.

pathology and clinical laboratory services   The services that provide information on diagnosis, prevention, or treatment of disease through the examination of the structural and functional changes in tissues and organs of the body that cause or are caused by disease. *Synonym:* medical laboratory services. *See also* clinical laboratory; laboratory; pathology.

pathomimicry   *See* Munchausen's syndrome.

patient   An individual who receives care or services. For hospice providers, the patient and family are considered a single unit of care. Similar terms used by various health care fields include client, resident, customer, individual served, patient and family unit, consumer, or health care consumer. *See also* the following patient terms, as well as against medical advice; bill of patient rights; client; emergency patient; established patient; fourth party; informed consent; inpatient; naive patient; new patient; outpatient; physician-patient relationship; private patient; resident; self-pay patient; ward patient.

patient abandonment   Improper withdrawal from the care of a patient after the creation of a patient relationship by any health care practitioner or organization.

patient advocate   A person who investigates and mediates patients' problems and complaints in relation to a health care organization's services. *Synonym*: patient representative. *See also* discharge planning.

patient bill of rights   *See* bill of patient rights.

patient care audit   A retrospective review of selected hospital medical records, performed by a multidisciplinary professional committee, for the purpose of comparing the quality of care provided with accepted standards. *See also* dental audit; medical audit; medical record review.

patient care committee   A committee composed of medical, nursing, and other professional staff members whose purpose is to monitor patient care practices to increase the probability that predetermined standards are met.

patient-centered standards   For purposes of Joint Commission accreditation, standards that are organized around what is done with, for, or to patients, such as assessment, treatment, and education. *See also* patient-focused care.

patient chart   *See* medical record.

patient compensation fund   A fund established by state law, most commonly financed by a surcharge on malpractice premiums of all professional liability policyholders in a state, and used to pay malpractice claims. *See also* malpractice; professional liability insurance.

patient consent   *See* implied consent; informed consent; informed refusal; presumed consent.

patient-controlled analgesia (PCA)   Self-administration of analgesics by a patient instructed in doing so; usually refers to self-dosing with intravenous opioid (eg, morphine) administered by means of programmable pump.

patient days   A measure of institutional use, usually measured as the number of inpatients at a specified time (eg, at midnight). *See also* occupancy rate.

patient dropout   *See* against medical advice.

patient dumping   The denial or limitation of the provision of medical care to, or the transfer to other institutions of, patients who are not able to pay or for whom payment methods do not pay the hospital enough to cover its costs. COBRA was passed in 1986 to protect patients against dumping because of suspicion that hospitals with emergency services were limiting access to conserve money. *See also* COBRA; transfer agreement.

patient education   Teaching and learning directed toward increasing a patient's ability to manage personal health, such as patient education for newly diagnosed diabetes. *See also* Comprehensive Smoking Education Act; health education; health maintenance diaries;

learning; multimedia education; prevention; wellness program.

patient escort service   A service often provided by organization volunteers to accompany patients who need help getting to a location or in moving about a health care facility. *See also* medicar.

patient factor   An individual, patient-related variable describing some characteristic that may influence health care related outcomes. Patient factors can include complications (conditions arising after the beginning of health care observation and treatment that modifies the course of the patient's health or illness and the intervention or care required), comorbidities (preexisting diseases or conditions), severity of illness classifications (seriousness or stage of illness at the time of the beginning of health care observation or treatment), functional status (factors related to health status including physical functioning, role disability due to physical health problems, bodily pain, general health perceptions, vitality, social functioning, role disability due to emotional problems, and general mental health), and patient demographics (age, ethnicity, gender, location, and so forth). Patient factors usually are not within practitioners' or organizations' control. *Synonym*: patient-based factor. *See also* cancer staging system; complication; external environmental factor; factor; functional status; nondisease factors; organization factor; practitioner factor.

patient-focused care   An approach to care that consciously adopts a patient's perspective. This perspective can be organized around dimensions such as respect for patient's values, preferences, and expressed needs; coordination and integration of care; information, communication, and education; physical comfort; emotional support and alleviation of fear and anxiety; involvement of family and friends; and transition and continuity. *See also* patient-centered standards.

patient health outcome   The result that happens to a patient from performance (or nonperformance) of one or more processes, services, or activities carried out by health care providers. A patient health outcome represents the cumulative effect of one or more processes at a defined time, for example, survival to discharge following a gunshot wound to the chest or an acute myocardial infarction. *Synonym*: outcome of care. *See also* efficiency; outcome; Patient Outcomes Research Teams; quality of care.

patient health record   *See* medical record.

patient history   *See* medical history.

patient identification system   An organized procedure for establishing accurate and complete patient identity.

patient mix   The numbers and types of patients served by a hospital or other health care organization or program. Patients may be classified according to socioeconomic characteristics, diagnoses, or severity of illness. Knowledge of an organization's patient mix is important

Patient Outcomes Research Teams: PORTs and PORT-IIs

Title	Site/Institution
PORTs*	
Analysis of Practices: Hip Fracture Repair and Osteoarthritis	University of Maryland, Baltimore
Assessing and Improving Outcomes: Total Knee Replacement	Indiana University, Indianapolis
Assessing Therapies for Benign Prostatic Hypertrophy and Localized Prostate Cancer	Dartmouth Medical School, Hanover, NH
Assessment of the Variation and Outcomes of Pneumonia	University of Pittsburgh
Back Pain Outcome Assessment Team	University of Washington, Seattle
The Consequences of Variation in Treatment for Acute Myocardial Infarction	Harvard Medical School, Boston
Low Birthweight in Minority and High-Risk Women	University of Alabama, Birmingham
Outcome Assessment of Patients with Biliary Tract Disease	University of Pennsylvania, Philadelphia
Outcome Assessment Program in Ischemic Heart Disease	Duke University Medical Center, Durham, NC
Schizophrenia Patient Outcomes Research Team	University of Maryland, Baltimore
Secondary and Tertiary Prevention of Stroke	Duke University, Durham, NC
Variations in Cataract Management: Patient and Economic Outcomes	Covance Health Economics and Outcomes Services, Inc, Washington, DC
Variations in Management of Childbirth and Patient Outcomes	RAND, Santa Monica, CA
Variations in the Management and Outcomes of Diabetes [Type II]	New England Medical Center, Boston
PORT-IIs**	
Cardiac Arrhythmia Management: Patient and Economic Outcomes	Stanford University, Stanford, CA
Care, Costs, and Outcomes of Local Breast Cancer	Georgetown University, Washington, DC
Dialysis Care: Choices, Outcomes, Costs, and Tradeoffs	Johns Hopkins University, Baltimore
Effectiveness of Outpatient Treatment for PID [Pelvic Inflammatory Disease]	University of Pittsburgh
Homemade Cereal Based Oral Rehydration Therapy	Boston City Hospital
Improving Cost-Effectiveness of Prepaid Depression Care	RAND, Santa Monica, CA
PORT II for Prostatic Disease	Massachusetts General Hospital, Boston
Value of Medical Testing Prior to Cataract Surgery	Johns Hopkins Hospital, Baltimore

* Under the AHCPR's MEDTEP (Medical Treatment Effectiveness Program), PORTs are focused on variations in clinical practice and outcomes for particular clinical problems. All PORTs use a similar, multimethod strategy to identify and address major questions of treatment effectiveness.

** PORT-IIs build on and retain the basic goals of the original PORTS, focusing on outstanding issues of outcomes that matter to patients and on realities of clinical practice. They use whatever individual methods and combinations of methods can most efficiently answer the question at hand.

for planning and comparison. *See also* case mix; scope of care or services.

patient monitor   A device used for continuous measurement or display of particular parameters of physiological function, such as heart rate, arterial blood pressure, and arterial oxygen tension. A patient monitor is used for constant surveillance of patients under intensive care, general anesthesia, and other relevant circumstances. *See also* automated blood pressure monitoring devices; fetal monitor; Holter monitoring device; home uterine activity monitoring; monitor; peak flow meter; self-measured blood pressure monitoring device; spirometry.

patient origin study   A study to determine the geographic distribution of the homes of patients served by health programs, used to define catchment areas and to

plan the development of health services and facilities. *See also* catchment area; needs assessment.

Patient Outcomes Research Teams (PORTs)
Large-scale, multisite, multispecialty, and multidisciplinary five-year projects established as part of AHCPR's Medical Treatment Effectiveness Program (MEDTEP) to compare outcomes of different ways of preventing, diagnosing, treating, and managing a particular condition. Studies focus on common clinical problems to clarify for consumers and clinicians which options are most effective. Some PORTs are also evaluating the effects of disseminating the findings and recommending changes in practice patterns. The program consists of the first 14 PORTs and 8 PORT-IIs.

patient participation   Patient involvement in the decision-making process in matters pertaining to his or her health. *See also* informed consent; paternalism; patient-provider relationship; Patient Self-Determination Act; respect and caring.

patient profile   A list of all health care services provided to a particular patient during a specified period of time, for example, during a hospitalization. *See also* profile; profiling; *Wickline v State of California.*

patient-provider relationship   A relationship initiated and sustained by a patient who has legal and moral authority over the relationship. An agreement is established in a relationship in which the practitioner will respond to the patient's preferences and the patient will accept the practitioner's recommendations. *See also* health care provider; paternalism; patient participation; physician-patient privilege; privileged communication; psychotherapist-patient privilege; self-efficacy.

patient record   *See* medical record.

patient representative   *See* patient advocate.

patient rights   Liberties and privileges (eg, autonomy, confidentiality, privacy) that individuals retain during their status as patients, to the extent permitted by law. *See also* bill of patient rights; confidentiality; genetic counseling; informed consent; resident bill of rights; right of privacy.

patient satisfaction   The degree to which the individual regards a health care service or product, or the manner in which it is delivered by the provider, as useful, effective, or beneficial.

Patient Self-Determination Act (PSDA)   Legislation passed in the Bush administration (1990) stating that hospitals, skilled nursing facilities, hospices, home health care agencies, and HMOs are responsible for developing patient information for distribution. The information must include patients' rights, advance directives (eg, living wills), ethics committees' consultation and education functions, limited medical treatment (supportive/comfort care only), mental health treatment, resuscitation, restraints, surrogate decision making, and transfer of care. The purpose of the act is to assure that individuals receiving health care services will be given an opportunity to participate in and direct health care decisions affecting themselves. *See also* advance directive; durable power of attorney for health care; living will; patient participation.

patient service representative   An individual trained to complete health insurance claim forms and to assist health care providers, such as physicians and health care organizations, in collecting payments for services from patients and insurers. *See also* insurance.

patient utilities measurement   Tools or methods to quantitatively present patients' preferences for health outcomes (particularly in choices of therapies that involve risks), usually expressed in terms of utilities ranging from 0 (zero), which represents the worst outcome (such as death), to 1, which represents the best possible outcome (such as normal health). *Synonyms:* health-state prefer-

ences; preference measurement methodology. *See also* cost-utility analysis; health-related quality of life; measure; standard gamble; time trade off; utility; visual analog scale.

pattern analysis   *See* practice pattern analysis.

pattern of care   The distribution of rates of performance among members of a group of practitioners, health care organizations, or communities. *See also* performance.

pattern of data   *See* data pattern.

payback period   The time necessary for a new item of equipment to produce revenues or result in savings equal to its cost.

payer   An organization (such as the federal government or a commercial insurance company) or a person who furnishes the money to pay for the provision of health care services. *See also* all-payer system; fourth party; Medicare secondary payer; primary payer; private patient; single-payer system; third-party payer.

payment   *See* average payment rate; copayment; cost-based reimbursement; fee for service; out-of-pocket payments; Physician Payment Reform; prospective payment; prospective payment system; unified payment.

PDCA cycle   *See* plan-do-check-act cycle.

peak flow meter   A small, portable, inexpensive device that is used by and for people with asthma to monitor small changes in breathing capacity. The instrument can be used at home, at work, or at school. Implementation of national asthma guidelines (the National Asthma Education Program) depends on patients' or their families' regular use of the device to identify and respond properly to exacerbations (asthma attacks). *See also* asthma; exacerbation; forced expiratory volume; patient monitor; spirometry.

pediatric immunization   *See* immunization schedules.

pediatric-modified diagnosis-related groups (PM-DRGs)   Approximately 100 DRGs developed by the National Association of Children's Hospitals and Related Institutions (with funding from HCFA) to classify pediatric medical conditions. This classification system is used when a prospective payment system is applied to pediatric patients and by hospitals for analyzing utilization management, studying pediatric case mix, and pricing services. *See also* DRG; prospective payment system.

pediatrics   The branch and specialty of medicine dealing with the physical, emotional, and social health of children from birth to young adulthood. Fourteen subspecialties of pediatrics are adolescent medicine, pediatric cardiology, pediatric critical care medicine, pediatric endocrinology, pediatric emergency medicine, pediatric gastroenterology, pediatric hematology-oncology, pediatric infectious disease, neonatal-perinatal medicine, pediatric nephrology, pediatric pulmonology, pediatric rheumatology, pediatric sports medicine, and medical toxicology. *See also* advanced pediatric life support; Standards for Pediatric Immunization Practices.

pedodontics   Pediatric dentistry.

peer   In utilization and quality-of-care reviews of health care organizations, peers are defined as professionals in the same specialty of professional practice or a related specialty as the professionals whose services are being reviewed.

peer review   In health care, concurrent or retrospective review of a health professional's performance (eg, a physician's performance) of clinical professional activities by peer(s) through formally adopted written procedures that provide for adequate notice and an opportunity for a hearing of the professional under review. Immunity from civil damage actions attaches to an organization and its medical staff members if certain rights are afforded the physician as part of the disciplinary hearing process. *See also* retrospective review.

peer review organization (PRO)   A medical review organization established by the Tax Equity and Fiscal Responsibility Act of 1982 as a part of the prospective payment system to review the appropriateness of settings of care and the quality of care provided to Medicare beneficiaries. A PRO is under contract to the U.S. Department of Health and Human Services. It replaces the professional standards review organization. *Synonym:* utilization and quality control peer review organization. *See also* experimental medical care review organization; gross and flagrant violation; Medicare; professional standards review organization; PRO scope of work; quality control; substantial violation; TEFRA; Uniform Clinical Data Set.

peptic ulcer disease   Open sores in the mucous membrane lining of the lower esophagus, stomach, or pylorus duodenum, or jejunum. It is caused by infection with *Helicobacter pylori*, use of nonsteroidal anti-inflammatory drugs, or pathologic hypersecretory states (eg, Zollinger-Ellison syndrome). *See also Helicobacter pylori*; psychosomatic disease.

perceived need   A felt need, meaning that the need is felt by an individual or group, though it may not be perceived by other individuals or groups. *See also* needs assessment.

percentage format   A method for presenting data which depicts percentages of responses within each possible rating. This format is advantageous because it preserves much of the original data and is comprehensible, but it is difficult to use when evaluating performance over time.

perception psychology   The branch of psychology that studies how an organism becomes aware of objects, events, and relationships in the outside world through its senses. Psychologists in the field of perception analyze vision, hearing, taste, smell, touch, movement, and other topics. *See also* psychology.

percutaneous transluminal coronary angioplasty (PTCA)   Dilatation of a coronary blood vessel by means of a balloon catheter inserted through the skin and through the lumen of the vessel to the site of the narrowing, where the balloon is inflated to flatten plaque against the artery wall. *Synonym:* balloon angioplasty. *See also* angioplasty.

per diem cost   Cost per day. Per diem costs are an average and do not reflect the true cost for each patient.

performance   The way in which an individual, a group, or an organization carries out or accomplishes its important functions and processes. *See also* the following performance terms, as well as clinical performance indicators; dimensions of performance; domains of performance; indicator; measure; organizational performance; pattern of care; track record; quality of care.

performance area   An element of the Joint Commission accreditation decision grid that summarizes a standard or group of related standards. The performance areas identified on the accreditation decision grid are considered to be the most critical to the final accreditation decision. *See also* accreditation decision grid.

performance assessment   An analysis and interpretation of performance measurement data to transform them into useful information. The product of assessment is information. *See also* indicator; IMSystem; information; measurement data; performance improvement; performance measurement; track record.

performance-based quality-of-care evaluation   A system of evaluation using three distinct, but interlinked, tools: (1) performance measures, such as indicators; (2) guidelines and standards; and (3) a performance database. *See also* evaluation; indicator; performance database; practice guidelines; quality of care; standard.

performance database   An organized collection of data designed primarily to provide information concerning organization or practitioner performance. *See also* database; IMSystem; performance-based quality-of-care evaluation.

performance dimensions   *See* dimensions of performance.

performance improvement   The continuous study and adaptation of a health care organization's functions and processes to increase the probability of achieving desired outcomes and to better meet the needs of patients and other users of services. *See also* IMSystem; improvement; performance assessment.

performance index   A measurement approach in which several different measures of performance are weighted as to their relative importance and then displayed simultaneously against a 100% attainment goal. *See also* index.

performance indicator   An instrument that measures performance. *See also* clinical performance indicators; indicator.

performance measure A quantitative tool (eg, rate, ratio, index, percentage) that provides an indication of an organization's performance in relation to a specified process or outcome. *See also* aggregate data indicator; denominator; HEDIS; indicator; measure; numerator; performance measurement.

EXAMPLES OF EXISTING PERFORMANCE MEASURES

Program

Computerized Needs-Oriented Quality Measurement Evaluation System (CONQUEST)
Consortium Research on Indicators of Accrediting & Regulatory Agencies, System Performance (CRISP)
Developing and Evaluating Performance Measures for Ambulatory Care Quality (DEMPAQ)
Health Plan Employer Data and Information Set (HEDIS)
HMO/Purchaser Collaborative Effort
Joint Commission IMSystem
Maryland Hospital Association's Quality Indicator Project

Targeted Users of Information

Health plans, practitioners, employers
Large purchasers, consumers, clinicians, system managers, CEOs
Physicians
Employers
Employers, state Medicaid, health plans
Purchasers, payers, patients, accreditation, professional organizations
Hospitals

Source: Adapted from Jennings BM, Staggers N: The hazards in outcomes management. *The Journal of Outcomes Management* 4(1):20, February 1997.

---

performance measurement The quantification of processes and outcomes using one or more dimensions of performance, such as timeliness or availability. *See also* dimensions of performance; IMSystem; measurement; ORYX; performance assessment; performance measure; reliability testing.

performance measurement system An interrelated set of process measures, outcome measures, or both that facilitates internal comparisons over time and external comparisons of an organization's performance. For purposes of Joint Commission accreditation, it is anticipated that performance measurement systems will meet the Joint Commission's needs by supplying comparative data that can be incorporated into the survey and accreditation process; and used to monitor an accredited organization's performance between on-site surveys. *See also* ORYX.

performance rate A measurement produced by using a performance measure, providing a quantitative evaluation of patient care events being monitored. *See also* rate.

performance standard A statement of expectation set by competent authority concerning a degree or level of requirement, excellence, or attainment in performance of a task achieved by an individual, group, organization, community, or nation, according to preestablished requirements or specifications. *See also* outcome standard; process standard; standard.

perinatal transmission Transmission of a disease from mother to infant by blood or body fluids. May occur in utero, at the time of delivery, and possibly by breast-feeding. *Synonym:* vertical transmission. *See also* communicable disease; HIV transmission.

perinatology *See* neonatal-perinatal medicine.

periodic health examination *See* Early and Periodic Screening Diagnosis and Treatment Program.

periodontics A dental specialty concerned with diseases that affect the oral mucous membranes and tissues that surround and support the teeth. *Synonyms:* periodontia; periodontology. *See also* dental specialties.

persistent vegetative state (PVS) An enduring form of the vegetative state, which was defined in a 1994 consensus statement from the Multi-Society Task Force on PVS as capable of being diagnosed according to the following criteria: (1) no evidence of awareness of self or environment and an inability to interact with others; (2) no evidence of sustained, reproducible, purposeful, or voluntary behavioral responses to visual, auditory, tactile, or noxious stimuli; (3) no evidence of language comprehension or expression; (4) intermittent wakefulness manifested by the presence of sleep-wake cycles; (5) sufficiently preserved hypothalamic and brainstem autonomic functions to permit survival with medical and nursing care; (6) bowel and bladder incontinence; and (7) variably preserved cranial-nerve reflexes (pupillary, oculocephalic, corneal, vestibulo-ocular, and gag) and spinal reflexes. The current consensus understanding of PVS and other definitions offered in surveys of health care practitioners regarding PVS and end-of-life decisions have come under challenge with recognition of disparities in definitions of the term and with some events that have challenged attempts to determine the irreversibility of apparent PVS. *Synonyms:* cerebral death; chronic vegetative state. *See also* Cruzan case; right to die; vegetative state.

personal care institution *See* residential care facility.

personal care services Services provided in the place of residence on a per-visit or per-hour basis to meet the identified needs of patients who have, or are at risk of, an injury, an illness, or a disabling condition and who require assistance in personal care, activities of daily living, or the administration of treatments. These services may include those provided by home health aides, personal care aides, or home attendants. *See also* activities of daily living; home health services; maintenance home health care.

personal effects Tangible property privately owned by a person and regularly worn or carried on one's person, for example, keys, jewelry, wallet, and clothing.

personal health services Health services provided to individuals, in contrast to health services directed at populations, such as environmental health, community health, public health, consultation, and health education. *Synonym: personal health care. See also* health services; home health services.

personal injury **1.** In law, wrongful conduct causing false arrest, invasion of privacy, libel, slander, defamation of character, or bodily injury. The injury is against a person in contrast to property damage or destruction. **2.** In workers' compensation acts, any harm or damage to the health of an employee, however caused, whether by accident, disease, or otherwise, which arises in the course of and out of his or her employment, and incapacitates him or her in whole or in part. *See also* disability; workers' compensation.

personality disorder (PD) Enduring pattern of inner experience and behavior that deviates markedly from the expectations of the individual's culture, is pervasive and inflexible, has an onset in adolescence or early adulthood, is stable over time, and leads to distress or impairment in social, occupational, or other important areas of functioning. The DSM-IV groups PDs into three clusters, based on descriptive similarities: (A) paranoid, schizoid, schizotypal; (B) antisocial, borderline, histrionic, narcissistic; and (C) avoidant, dependent, obsessive-compulsive. The DSM-IV cautions that the clustering system, while helpful in various situations, should not be applied rigidly since it has not been consistently validated and since patients can have co-occurring PDs from different clusters. Other pervasive personality patterns or combinations of patterns may be diagnosed as PDs in the DSM system under the rubric *Not Otherwise Specified*; examples are depressive personality disorder and passive-aggressive personality disorder (synonym: negativistic personality disorder). *See also* DSM-IV; obsessive-compulsive disorder; paranoid disorder; psychotic disorder; schizophrenia.

personality psychology The branch of psychology dealing with the characteristics that make individuals different from one another and account for the way they behave. Personality psychologists investigate how an individual's personality develops, the chief personality types, and the measurement of personality traits. *See also* psychology.

personnel costs Total costs to an organization of its employees' salaries, fringe benefits, and other direct and indirect components of its total employee compensation package. *See also* benefits; human resources management.

personnel management *See* human resources management.

personnel psychology The branch of psychology dealing with the study and improvement of personnel practices in industry and government. *See also* psychology.

personnel record The complete employment record of a staff member or an employee, including job application, education and employment history, job description, performance evaluation(s), and, when applicable, evidence of current licensure, certification, or registration.

pharmaceutical A medicinal drug. *See also* drug.

pharmaceutical care and services Services that include procuring, preparing, dispensing, and distributing pharmaceutical products and the ongoing monitoring of the patient to identify, prevent, and resolve drug-related problems. *See also* decentralized pharmaceutical services; home pharmaceutical services; OBRA '90.

pharmaceutical equivalence The degree to which two formulations of the same medication are identical in strength, concentration, and dosage form. *See also* bioequivalence; chemical equivalence.

pharmaceutical representative *See* detailer.

PERSONALITY DISORDERS: THE CLUSTERING SYSTEM

Type of Disorder	Associated Features
Cluster A	*Odd or eccentric*
Paranoid	A pattern of distrust and suspiciousness to the extent that other people's motives are interpreted as malevo-
Schizoid	A pattern of detachment from social relationships and a restricted range of emotional expression
Schizotypal	A pattern of acute discomfort in close relationships, cognitive or perceptual distortions, and eccentricities of behavior
Cluster B	*Dramatic, emotional, or erratic*
Antisocial	A pattern of disregard for, and violation of, the rights of others (formerly called psychopathic personality)
Borderline	A pattern of instability in interpersonal relationships, self-image, affects and control over impulses
Histrionic	A pattern of excessive emotionality and attention seeking
Narcissistic	A pattern of grandiosity, need for admiration, and lack of empathy
Cluster C	*Anxious or fearful*
Avoidant	A pattern of social inhibition, feelings of inadequacy, and hypersensitivity to negative evaluation
Dependent	A pattern of submissive and clinging behavior related to a need to be taken care of
Obsessive-Compulsive	A pattern of preoccupation with orderliness, perfectionism, and control

Source: American Psychiatric Association: *Diagnostic and Statistical Manual of Mental Disorders, Fourth Edition.* Washington, DC: APA Press, 1994.

pharmacodynamics The study of the biochemical and physiological effects of drugs and the mechanisms of their actions, including the correlation of actions and effects of drugs with their chemical structure. *See also* drug; pharmacokinetics; pharmacology.

pharmacokinetics The study of the action of drugs in the human body over a period of time, including the method and rate of absorption and excretion and the duration of effect. *See also* drug resistance; kinetics; pharmacodynamics; pharmacology.

pharmacology The science of drugs, including their composition, uses, and effects. *See also* bioavailability; bioequivalence; clinical pharmacology; neuropharmacology; pharmacodynamics; pharmacokinetics; pharmacotherapeutics; psychopharmacology.

pharmacopeia An authoritative treatise on recognized drugs used in medicine and including their preparations, formulas, doses, and standards of purity. *See also Homeopathic Pharmacopeia of the United States; National Formulary; United States Pharmacopeia.*

pharmacotherapeutics The study of drugs used in the treatment of disease. *See also* pharmacology; subtherapeutics; therapeutics.

pharmacy **1.** The branch of health sciences dealing with the preparation, preserving, compounding, dispensing, and proper use of drugs. *See also* decentralized pharmaceutical services; drug; polypharmacy. **2.** A licensed location where drugs are stored and compounded or dispensed.

pharmacy and therapeutics (P&T) committee A medical staff committee including representatives of pharmacy, nursing, management and administration, and other services and individuals of a health care organization to measure, assess, and improve the policies and procedures relating to drug and diagnostic testing material and investigational or experimental drug usage; develop and maintain a drug formulary; and review all significant untoward drug reactions. *See also* adverse drug reaction; formulary; medication error; therapeutics.

pharmacy organization *See* long term care pharmacy organization.

phases of clinical trials Common designation of type and scope of clinical trials by Roman numeral. A *phase I* clinical trial typically involves 20 to 100 patients and lasts several months. The major purpose is to determine safety and dose. Approximately 70% of drugs successfully complete phase I. A *phase II* clinical trial typically involves up to several hundred patients and usually lasts from several months to two years. The major purposes are to continue to determine short-term safety and, primarily, effectiveness. Approximately 33% of drugs successfully complete phase II. A *phase III* clinical trial typically involves from several hundred to several thousand patients and may last from one to four years. The major purposes are to study safety, effectiveness, and dosage. Approximately 25% to 30% of drugs successfully com-

plete phase III. *See also* clinical trial phases; new-drug application; randomized controlled trial.

phototherapy The treatment of disease, such as acne and hyperbilirubinemia (high levels of bilirubin in the blood) in the newborn, with exposure to light, such as ultraviolet and infrared radiation.

physiatry *See* physical medicine and rehabilitation.

PHYSICAL ACTIVITY SCALES AND MEASURES

Physical Activity Questionnaires Used in the General Population

The Aerobics Center Longitudinal Study Physical Activity Questionnaire Baecke Questionnaire of Habitual Physical Activity

Bouchard Three-Day Physical Activity Record

CARDIA Physical Activity History

Framingham Physical Activity Index

Godin Leisure-Time Exercise Questionnaire

Health Insurance Plan of New York (HIP) Activity Questionnaire

Historical Leisure Activity Questionnaire

The Physical Activity Questionnaires of the Kuopio Ischemic Heart Disease Study (KIHD)

    KIHD Seven-Day Physical Activity Recall

    KIHD 12-month Leisure-Time Physical Activity History

    KIHD 24-Hour Total Physical Activity Record

    KIHD Occupational Physical Activity Interview

Lipid Research Clinics Questionnaire

Minnesota Leisure-Time Physical Activity Questionnaire

Modifiable Activity Questionnaire

Modifiable Activity Questionnaire for Adolescents

Paffenbarger Physical Activity Questionnaire

Seven-Day Physical Activity Recall

Stanford Usual Activity Questionnaire

Tecumseh Occupational Physical Activity Questionnaire

Physical Activity Questionnaires for Older Adults

Modified Baecke Questionnaire for Older Adults

Physical Activity Scale for the Elderly

YALE Physical Activity Survey

Zutphen Physical Activity Questionnaire

Physical Activity Questionnaires Used in Major Population-Based Surveys

Behavioral Risk Factor Surveillance System

Canada Fitness Survey

The MONICA Optional Study of Physical Activity (MOSPA)

National Children and Youth Fitness Study I and II

National Health Interview Survey

National Health and Nutrition Examination Survey I, II, and III

Youth Risk Behavior Survey

Source: Marks JS, Caspersen CJ (eds): A collection of physical activity questionnaires for health-related research. *Medicine & Science in Sports & Exercise* 29(6):S1-S205, June 1997.

---

physical activity and fitness A state of well-being in which performance is optimal, often as a result of physical conditioning that may be prescribed for disease therapy. A 1995 NIH Consensus Development Conference issued a statement of definitions of the components in the activity-fitness concept. *Physical activity* is bodily movement produced by skeletal muscles which requires energy expenditure and produces healthy benefits. *Exercise*, a type of physical activity, is a planned, structured, and repetitive bodily movement done to improve or maintain one or more components of physical fitness. *Physical inactivity* denotes a level of activity less than that needed to maintain good health. It is known to be a cardiovascular risk factor, and characterizes most Americans. *Moderate-intensity physical activity*, which the NIH Consensus Statement recommends to everyone who is able bodied, is an accumulation of at least 30 minutes of such activity on most, and preferably, all days of the week. *See also* physical activity and fitness goals; preventive medicine; wellness program.

physical activity and fitness goals   Efforts to establish reasonable, doable objectives that will lead to improvement of health, such as those established through the Healthy People 2000 initiative. It is not clear what exact types and amounts of physical activity are required for precise health benefits, but several health-related dimensions of physical activity are thought to be most important. The Healthy People 2000 agenda sets out specific activity fitness targets to ensure that health-related activity engaging key physiologic and physical mechanisms becomes part of regular behavioral patterns. *See also* physical activity and fitness; physical fitness program.

Physical Activity Readiness Questionnaire (PAR-Q)   A simple seven-question pre-exercise screen for symptoms and risk factors that a patient should discuss with a physician before starting an exercise program. The screening tool is recommended by the U.S. Preventive Services Task Force. *See also* physical fitness program.

PHYSICAL ACTIVITY READINESS QUESTIONNAIRE (PAR-Q)

Has your doctor ever said you had heart trouble?

Do you frequently have pains in your heart and chest?

Do you often feel faint or have spells of severe dizziness?

Has your doctor ever said your blood pressure was too high?

Has your doctor ever told you that you have a bone or joint problem, such as arthritis, that has been aggravated by exercise or might be made worse by exercise?

Is there a good physical reason not mentioned here why you should not follow an activity program even if you wanted to?

Are you over age 65 and not accustomed to vigorous exercise?

Source: Chishold DN, Collis ML, Kulak LL: Physical activity readiness. *Br Columbia Med J* 17:375-78, 1975, as reprinted in Wheat G, et al: Addressing a neglected coronary heart disease risk factor in an HMO: Exercise counseling and fitness testing at Group Health Cooperative. *HMO Practice* 10(3)131-36, Sept 1996.

---

physical examination   An examination in which a clinician brings the five senses of sight, hearing, touch, smell, and taste to bear on the patient through inspection, palpation, percussion, and auscultation. When the clinician recognizes the abnormal in the physical examination, he or she uses the facts of pathology to make a diagnosis. *See also* auscultation; bedside diagnosis; diagnosis; medical history; medical record; new patient.

physical fitness program   A health promotion program designed to improve body performance with emphasis on cardiovascular fitness, strength, and flexibility and other motor fitness elements, such as agility and balance. Cardiopulmonary fitness is measured in terms of VO_2 max (maximal oxygen consumption) through techniques such as the One-Mile Test. *Synonym:* fitness. *See also* cardiac rehabilitation program; physical activity and fitness goals; Physical Activity Readiness Questionnaire; wellness program; worksite wellness program.

SELECTED TARGETS FOR PHYSICAL ACTIVITY AND FITNESS

To increase physical activity and fitness, by the year 2000...

1.3 Increase moderate daily physical activity to at least 30% of people

1.4 Increase to at least 20% the proportion of people aged 18 and older and to at least 75% the proportion of children and adolescents aged 6 through 17 who engage in vigorous physical activity that promotes the development and maintenance of cardiorespiratory fitness 3 or more days per week for 20 or more minutes per occasion. (Baseline: 12% for people aged 18 and older in 1985; 66% for youth aged 10 through 17 in 1984.)

1.5 Reduce sedentary lifestyles to no more than 15% of people (a 38% decrease)

Source: *Healthy People 2000: National Health Promotion and Disease Prevention Objectives.* Washington, DC: U.S. Public Health Service, 1991.

---

physical medicine and rehabilitation   The branch and specialty of medicine concerned with diagnosing and treating patients with impairments or disabilities that involve musculoskeletal, neurologic, cardiovascular, or other body systems. The primary focus is on maximal restoration of physical, psychological, social, and vocational functions and on alleviation of pain. In addition to traditional treatment modes, a physiatrist may use therapeutic exercise, prosthetics, orthotics, and mechanical and electrical devices. *Synonyms:* physiatrics; physiatry; rehabilitation medicine. *See also* electrodiagnosis; electromyography; orthotics; pain management; physical rehabilitation services; physical therapy; prosthetics; rehabilitation.

physical rehabilitation services   The professional and technical care that assists physically disabled persons and postoperative patients to attain, increase, or maintain functional capacity. *See also* disability; physical medicine and rehabilitation; rehabilitation; rehabilitation services.

Physical Status Score   *See* operative risk (and accompanying table).

physical therapy (PT)   The health care field concerned primarily with the treatment of disorders with physical agents and methods, such as massage, manipulation, therapeutic exercises, cold, heat (including shortwave, microwave, and ultrasonic diathermy), hydrotherapy, electric stimulation, and light to assist in rehabilitating patients and in restoring normal function after an illness or injury. *Synonym:* physiotherapy. *See also* activities of daily living; hydrotherapy; massage therapy; physical medicine and rehabilitation; range of motion.

GENERAL CLASSIFICATIONS OF PHYSICIAN STAFF

admitting physician   The physician responsible for admitting a patient to a health care organization.

attending physician   A medical staff member who is legally responsible for the care and treatment provided a given patient.

board-certified physician   A physician who has been certified by a specialty board as a specialist.

contract physician   A physician who, under a full- or part-time contract, provides care in an organization and whose payment as defined in the contract may be an institutional responsibility, or on a fee or another agreed-on basis.

hospital-based physician   A physician who spends the predominant part of his or her practice time within one or more hospitals instead of in an office setting, or who provides services to one or more hospitals or their patients.

medical director   A physician who directs and/or provides care in a health care facility. *Synonym:* director of medical affairs.

medical specialist   A physician who concentrates on body systems, age group, or procedures and techniques developed to diagnose and/or treat certain types of disorders.

medical subspecialist   A physician who has completed training in a general medical specialty and then takes additional training (one or more years of full-time education) in a more specific area of that specialty (a subspecialty area).

participating physician   Under Medicare, a physician who has signed a contract agreeing to refrain from charging a Medicare patient the difference between the physician's usual charge and Medicare payment allowance.

personal physician   A physician who assumes responsibility for the care of an individual on a continuing basis.

physician executive   A physician whose primary professional responsibility is management of a health care organization.

physician member of the medical staff   A physician who, by virtue of education, training, and demonstrated competence, is granted medical staff membership and clinical privileges by an organization to perform specified diagnostic or therapeutic procedures.

provider-based physician   Under Medicare, a physician who performs services in a provider setting and has a financial arrangement under which he or she is compensated through or by a provider or provider-related entity.

salaried physician   A physician who is employed as a physician by a hospital or other health care organization on a salaried basis.

physician   A doctor of medicine or doctor of osteopathy who, by virtue of education, training, and demonstrated competence, is fully licensed to practice medicine and may be granted clinical privileges by a health care organization to perform specific diagnostic or therapeutic procedures. *See also* credentialing; doctor; gatekeeper mechanism; health care provider; licensed independent practitioner; medical practice act; medical staff; medicine; participating physician; primary care physician; provider-based physician.

physician-assisted suicide   Generally, physician's provision of equipment, medication, or instructions on how to use already available means for the sole purpose of helping a patient end his or her own life. Statutory definitions opposing or supporting physician-assisted suicide vary by state, and two different constitutional interpretations in the federal district courts of appeal went before the U.S. Supreme Court in 1997. On June 26, 1997, the Court in *Vacco* v *Quill* (2nd) and *Washington* v *Glucksberg* (9th) ruled that the Constitution does not guarantee a right to commit suicide with a physician's help and that states may decide for themselves. The Court specifically sustained a critical distinction between refusing life-sustaining treatment and taking active steps to end life. The organized medical profession, with some dissent among its ranks, took the lead under the American Medical Association and 51 other medical groups in opposing physician-assisted suicide and framing the issue as signaling the need for better pain management and end-of-life care. *See also* assisted suicide; Death with Dignity Act; Dutch Cure; euthanasia; obitiatrist; obitorium; voluntary active euthanasia.

Physician-Based Assessment and Counseling for Exercise   *See* Project PACE.

Physician Data Query (PDQ)   A computerized system devised by NIH's National Cancer Institute to give cancer patients and physicians quick and easy access to descriptions of current clinical trials that are accepting patients, up-to-date information about the standard treatment for most types of cancer, and names of organizations and physicians involved in cancer care. Physicians can access PDQ by an office computer with a telephone hookup and a PDQ access code, a fax machine, or the services of a medical library with online searching capability. Cancer Information Service offices (1-800-4-CANCER) provide PDQ searches to callers and can tell physicians how to obtain regular access to the database.

physician deselection   Practice adopted by some HMOs of removing physicians from their listings of participating providers when the physicians use more resources than the HMO deems necessary. For example, an HMO may drop a physician who orders more tests for his or her patients than the average participating provider. *See also* participating physician.

physician-hospital organization (PHO)   A legal entity formed by a hospital and a group of physicians to further mutual interests and to achieve market objectives. A PHO generally combines physicians and a hospital into a single organization for the purpose of obtaining payer contracts. Doctors maintain ownership of their practices. They agree to accept managed care patients according to the terms of a professional services agreement with the PHO. The PHO serves as a collective negotiating and contracting unit. The PHO typically is owned and governed jointly by a hospital and shareholder physicians. *See also* group practice without walls; integrated provider; managed care; management service organization; medical foundation.

physician impairment   The inability of a physician to practice medicine with reasonable skill and with safety to patients due to a disability, such as alcohol or drug abuse, mental illness, handicap, or senility. *See also* disability; impaired health care provider; impairment.

physician licensure   *See* medical licensure.

CLINICAL CLASSIFICATIONS OF PHYSICIAN STAFF

addictionologist	oncologist
allergist	ophthalmologist
anesthesiologist	orthopedic surgeon
bacteriologist	osteopathic physician
chiropractor	otolaryngologist-head and neck
critical care physician	surgeon
dermatologist	otologist/neurotologist
emergency physician	pathologist
family physician	pediatric critical care specialist
general practitioner (GP)	pediatric emergency physician
general surgeon	pediatric gastroenterologist
geriatrician	pediatric hematologist-oncologist
gynecologist	pediatrician
hepatologist	pediatric infectious disease
immunologist	specialist
internist	pediatric nephrologist
medical adviser	physiatrist
medical consultant	physician director of quality
medical epidemiologist	assurance
medical examiner (ME)	primary care physician
medical geneticist	psychiatrist
medical toxicologist	public health physician
microbiologist	(administrative)
naturopath	public health physician (clinical)
neurological surgeon	radiologist
neurologist	surgeon
neuropsychiatrist	teaching physician
nuclear medicine	thoracic surgeon
physician	traumatologist
obstetrician	urologist
obstetrician-gynecologist	

physician-patient privilege   In law, a privilege protecting communications between a physician and a patient, in the course of their professional relationship, from disclosure unless consent is given by the patient. This privilege is statutory and did not exist under common law. Its purpose is to allow persons to secure medical service without the fear of betrayal or humiliation. This privilege, however, does not hold if a physician examines a patient for a purpose other than treatment, such as by court order (eg, to determine sanity or obtain a blood sample to determine intoxication). The privilege does not preclude a physician from giving expert opinion testimony in response to a hypothetical question involving the physical or mental condition of the patient when such testimony is not dependent on information protected by the privilege. In general, the privilege does not apply to a

nurse, unless acting as the doctor's assistant, medical students, dentists, pharmacists, or chiropractors. It does not extend after the death of the patient. *Synonym*: doctor-patient privilege. *See also* attorney-client privilege; patient-provider relationship; privileged communication; psychotherapist-patient privilege.

Physician Payment Reform   Legislation (OBRA '89) enacted that provides for a major change in the Medicare physician payment rules enacted in 1992 and stronger enforcement of restricting antitrust and financial relationships with clinical laboratories and equipment providers. *See also* antitrust laws; clinical laboratory; Medicare; OBRA '89.

physician profiling   A process of aggregation and analysis of physician-related health care data, often in the form of tables or graphs, giving a statistical summary of physician-specific (whether individual or group), objective health care data used to assess and improve health care delivery. *See also* profiling.

Physicians' Current Procedural Terminology (CPT)   A systematic listing and coding of procedures and services performed by physicians that is widely used for coding in billing and payment for physician services. The book is divided into five sections: medicine, anesthesiology, surgery, radiology, and pathology and laboratory. Each procedure or service is identified with a five-digit code, for example, a radiologic examination of the skull (complete, minimum of four views, with or without stereo) has the code 70260. CPT is published by the American Medical Association. *See also* coding.

***Physicians' Desk Reference* (PDR)**   A compendium of labeling information on pharmaceutical and diagnostic products, published annually by Medical Economics Company. Sections include full product information (information found in package inserts required by law) for most pharmaceuticals, both prescription and over the counter, product overviews for selected drugs, and accurate photographs of many products for identification. Information is also provided on active and inactive ingredients, educational materials, pregnancy categories used in drug labeling, poison control centers, and procedures for reporting drug and vaccine adverse events. There is a supplemental publication for nonprescription drugs, *PDR for Nonprescription Drugs. See also* package insert.

physician shortage area   A geographic area with an inadequate supply of physicians, usually defined as an area having a physician-to-population ratio of less than some defined standard, such as 1 to 4,000. *See also* medically underserved area.

physician volume   The number of a procedure performed (such as an endoscopy) or a condition treated (such as acute myocardial infarction) by individual physicians.

physiological psychology   The branch of psychology that examines the relationship between behavior and body structures or functions, particularly the workings of the nervous system. Physiological psychologists explore the functions of the brain, how hormones affect behavior, and the physical processes involved in learning and emotions. *See also* physiology; psychology.

physiology The branch of biology that deals with the functions of the living organism and its parts and of the physical and chemical factors and processes involved. *See also* APACHE system; biology; cardiac electrophysiology study; neurophysiology; physiological psychology.

physiotherapy *See* physical therapy.

pie chart A circle representing a whole amount, with wedge-shaped sectors indicating the fraction in each category.

pilot study A study designed to prove or test methods that may be used in full-scale plans. A pilot study reduces the investment risk in unproven methods. *See also* feasibility study.

ping-ponging A slang term for the process of passing a patient from one physician to another in a health program for unnecessary cursory examinations so that the program can charge the patient's third-party payer for a physician visit to each physician. The practice and term originated and is most common in Medicaid mills. *See also* family ganging; Medicaid mill.

placebo Any therapeutic procedure or chemically inert substance, such as sugar or distilled water, or less-than-effective dose of a harmless substance prescribed and administered as if it were an effective dose of a needed drug. Placebos are administered to a control group in a controlled clinical trial so that the specific and nonspecific effects of the experimental treatment can be distinguished. In such trials, the experimental treatment must produce better results than the placebo to be considered effective. A physician may deceptively, but ethically, prescribe a placebo to a patient if the condition being treated has a high response rate to placebo, if the alternative to placebo is continued illness or a drug with known toxicity, or if the patient demands a prescription to improve his or her condition. *See also* ethics; placebo effect.

placebo effect A usually beneficial change in a patient following a particular treatment that arises from the patient's expectations concerning the treatment and the power of suggestion, rather than from the treatment itself. *See also* bias; halo effect; Hawthorne effect; placebo.

plan-do-check-act (PDCA) cycle A schema for continuous quality improvement originally developed by Walter Andrew Shewhart, an engineer with Western Electric, and made popular by Deming, who ascribed inherent variation in processes to chance and intermittent variation to assignable causes. The PDCA cycle was his four-part method for discovering and correcting assignable causes to improve the quality of processes. *Synonyms:* Deming cycle; Shewhart cycle. *See also* continuous quality improvement; FADE process; FOCUS-PDCA; process decision program chart; quality improvement.

plan for improvement For purposes of Joint Commission accreditation, an organization's written statement that details the procedures to be taken to correct existing *Life Safety Code*® deficiencies and, where applicable, includes the interim life safety measures to be implemented to temporarily reduce the hazards associated with the deficiencies. *See also* interim life safety measures; *Life Safety Code*®.

plan of care A plan, based on data gathered during patient assessment, that identifies the patient's care needs, lists the strategy for providing services to meet those needs, documents treatment goals and objectives, outlines the criteria for terminating specified interventions, and documents the patient's progress in meeting specified goals and objectives. The format of the plan in some health care organizations may be guided by patient-specific policies and procedures, protocols, practice guidelines, clinical paths, care maps, or a combination of these. The plan of care may include care, treatment, habilitation, and rehabilitation. *See also* nursing care plan.

plan of correction, conditional accreditation For purposes of Joint Commission accreditation, an organization's written plan, approved by Joint Commission staff, that outlines the actions the organization will take to address compliance issues that caused the Joint Commission Accreditation Committee to make a decision of conditional accreditation. The plan is the basis for the follow-up survey at a specified time once the plan is approved. *See also* accreditation decision.

plant Assets comprising land, buildings, machinery, natural resources, furniture and fixtures, and all other equipment permanently used. In a more narrow sense, plant refers to only buildings or only land and buildings. *See also* environment of care.

plant, technology, and safety management (PTSM) Obsolete term for a facility-based environmental management program. *See* environment of care.

plastic surgery The branch and specialty of medicine dealing with the repair, reconstruction, and enhancement of the skin and its underlying musculoskeletal system. *See also* surgery.

play or pay An approach to increasing insurance coverage by requiring employers to contribute toward covering workers and their families proposed in the defeated 1993 Health Security Act. Employers could choose to "play" by buying private insurance for workers or "pay" a set amount, usually a percentage of payroll, into a government program to subsidize the cost of health coverage for all individuals without employer-sponsored coverage. *See also* coverage; insurance.

play therapy A form of psychotherapy for children in which play with games and toys is used to gain insight into the child's feelings and thoughts and to help treat conflicts and psychological problems. *See also* child and adolescent psychiatry; psychotherapy.

pleadings   The formal written documents, in legal format, filed with the court by the parties that set out the plaintiff's allegations (cause of action) and the defendant's answer to those allegations. Pleadings generally include the complaint, answer, response to affirmative defenses raised in the answer, third-party claims, counterclaims, and the answer to each. *See also* affirmative defense.

plexor   A small, rubberheaded hammer used in examination or diagnosis by percussion, as in elicitation of a knee-jerk reflex.

***Pneumocystis carinii* pneumonia (PCP)**   An opportunistic life-threatening infection striking immuno-compromised patients, such as those with AIDS, leukemia, or lymphoma and those who have received organ transplants, corticosteroids, or cancer chemotherapy. Recurrent PCP has been added as a defining criterion to the CDC's revised 1993 AIDS surveillance case definition. *See also* AIDS; opportunistic infection.

pneumothorax   Collection of air or gas in the pleural cavity of the chest, causing the lung to collapse. Symptoms include sharp chest pain and difficulty in breathing. *See also* thoracic surgery.

podiatry   The profession of the health sciences dealing with the examination, diagnosis, treatment, and prevention of diseases, conditions, and malfunctions affecting the human foot and its related or governing structures, by use of medical, surgical, or other means. Specialty areas of podiatric medicine are podiatric orthopedics, podiatric public health, and podiatric surgery. Formerly called chiropody.

poetry therapy   The initial use of literature or writing by a qualified biblio-poetry therapist for healing and personal growth in patients with mental states ranging from neurosis to acute psychosis, as well as in people with physical or learning disabilities. Methods of using poetry for therapy include reading poems and encouraging clients to write their own poetry. The purpose is to lead a person into talking or writing about himself or herself and bringing out emotions not previously shown or discussed. *See also* creative arts therapy; manual arts therapy; recreational therapy.

point-of-care laboratory testing   Analytical testing performed at sites in a health care organization and located outside the organization's central laboratory. The testing sites are either under the jurisdiction of the organized pathology and clinical laboratory or another department or service. Examples of this testing include bedside testing and on-unit testing, such as occult-blood testing, serological screens (eg, mononucleosis), urinalysis, Gram stains, and glucose meter testing. *Synonyms:* alternate site testing; decentralized laboratory testing; distributed site testing. *See also* decentralized pharmaceutical services; clinical laboratory; laboratory.

point-of-service (POS) plan   A type of health plan that allows covered individuals to choose from participating or nonparticipating providers each time they receive care (as opposed to choosing twice a year as in "lock-in" or indemnity plans). The plan encourages the use of participating providers by offering better levels of coverage for in-network services. As in traditional HMO plans, the primary care physician acts as a gatekeeper for referrals to other providers. *Synonyms:* open-ended HMO; point-of-care plan. *See also* gatekeeper; insurance; pre-paid health plan.

poison control center   A facility that provides information concerning poisons and the management of poisoning in emergency situations. *See also* clinical toxicology; medical toxicology.

Poisson distribution   A type of probability distribution typically applied to distributions that are not continuous, named after Simeon Denis Poisson (1781-1840), a French mathematician. *See also* probability distribution.

political action committee (PAC)   An organization formed by business, labor, or other special-interest groups to raise money and make contributions to the campaigns of political candidates whom they support.

polymerase chain reaction (PCR)   A laboratory, genetic engineering technique employing molecular biology technology to identify the nucleic acid sequence of HIV in the cells of an infected individual. This technique is sensitive and can detect a single copy of viral DNA in 1 cell out of 10,000. It is useful for early detection of perinatally infected infants and monitoring patients in clinical trials. *See also* genetic engineering; HIV.

polypharmacy   The administration of many drugs at the same time.

polysomnographic technology   The field dealing with the measurement and recording of multiple physiological activity, such as eye movement and heart rate, during sleep. *See also* apnea monitoring; somnology.

population profiling   A process of aggregation and analysis of population-specific health care data, often in the form of tables or graphs, giving a summary of population-specific objective health care data used to assess and improve health care delivery. *See also* profiling.

portability   The circumstance in which an individual is guaranteed health insurance coverage with a new employer, without a waiting period or having to meet additional deductible requirements, when the individual changes jobs or residence. *See also* COBRA; insurance.

positive correlation   A direct association between two variables meaning that as one variable becomes large, the other also becomes large, and vice versa. Positive correlation is represented by a correlation coefficient greater than zero. *See also* correlation; correlation coefficient; negative correlation; variable.

postmortem examination   *See* autopsy.

postoperative care   Provision of medical, nursing, and other health services for patients following surgery. *Synonym:* postsurgical care. *See also* nosocomial infection; recovery; surgical-site infection; wound infection.

postoperative infection *See* nosocomial infection.

posttraumatic stress disorder (PTSD) A psychological disorder affecting individuals who have experienced profound emotional trauma, such as torture or rape, characterized by recurrent flashbacks of the traumatic event, nightmares, eating disorders, anxiety, fatigue, forgetfulness, and social withdrawal. *Synonym:* posttraumatic stress syndrome (PSS). *See also* service-connected disability; stress.

potentially compensable event (PCE) An adverse patient care event that ultimately may be involved in a liability claim. The event involves a disability (temporary or permanent) caused by health care management (including acts of commission and omission by health care providers). This term was originally coined by researchers in the California Medical Insurance Feasibility Study (1976) sponsored by the California Medical Association and the California Hospital Association. In this study, more than 20,000 patient charts from 23 hospitals were reviewed for the presence of adverse events that might result in litigation for malpractice compensation. These adverse events were called potentially compensable events (PCEs). The 20 PCEs developed by physicians and medical audit experts during this study later became the basis for occurrence screening criteria, adapted and modified for use by individual institutions. A PCE is not the same as an adverse patient occurrence (APO) or negligence. *See also* adverse patient occurrence; California Medical Insurance Feasibility Study; medical injury; negligence; occurrence criteria; occurrence screening.

potentially ineffective care A measure for predicting which patients are unlikely to benefit from critical care. Developed at Stanford University, it is derived from a special use of APACHE III model information. *See also* APACHE system.

potential vision tests Subjective or objective tests designed to determine whether patients with obviously impaired vision have the potential to see well following cataract surgery. These tests attempt to ascertain whether the limiting factor to visual impairment is cataract rather than other pathology. *See also* cataract surgery.

potential years of life lost (PYLL) The sum of the years a group of individuals would have lived had they not died premature deaths. It is a measurement of the loss to a society due to disease, war, auto accidents, or other causes. *Synonym:* years of potential life lost. *See also* well-year.

power of attorney An instrument whereby one person, as principal, appoints, in writing, another as his or her agent and confers authority to perform certain specified acts or kinds of acts on behalf of the principal. The agent is attorney in fact, and his or her power is revoked on the death of the principal by operation of law. Such power may be either general (full) or special (limited). *See also* durable power of attorney for health care.

PPO (preferred provider organization) A prenegotiated arrangement between purchasers and providers to furnish specified health services to a group of employees/patients. An insurance company or employer negotiates discounted fees with networks of health care providers in return for guaranteeing a certain volume of patients. Providers under contract in such arrangements are called preferred providers. Enrollees in a PPO can receive treatment outside the network but must pay higher copayments or deductibles for it. PPO contracts usually have three distinguishing features: discounts from standard charges, monetary incentives for single subscribers to use contracting providers, and broad-utilization management programs. *See also* exclusive provider organization; health care network; HMO.

practice guidelines Descriptive tools or standardized specification for care of the typical patient in the typical situation, developed through a formal process that incorporates the best scientific evidence of effectiveness with expert opinion. *Synonyms:* algorithm; clinical criteria; guideline; parameter; practice parameter; preferred practice pattern; protocol; review criteria. *See also* acceptable alternative; clinical practice guidelines; guideline attributes; performance-based quality-of-care evaluation; practice parameters; protocol.

practice parameters The term the American Medical Association used up to 1997 for clinical practice guidelines, practice policies, and standards, which it defines as strategies for patient management, developed to assist physicians in clinical decision making. Many medical specialty societies have adopted this term for their guidelines and policies. In spring 1997, the AMA began using the term *clinical practice guideline* for its directory and other guideline-related products. *See also* clinical pathway; clinical practice guidelines; critical pathway; guideline attributes; practice guidelines.

practice pattern analysis A method of aggregating data by practitioner, diagnosis, DRG, or other defined category to show patterns of care or variations in care. *Synonym:* practice profiling. *See also* economic credentialing; practitioner profiling; preferred practice pattern; profiling; variation.

practice policies Preformed recommendations issued for the purpose of influencing decisions about health interventions; the term used by David M. Eddy to describe the whole guideline "family." Many medical specialty associations have adapted this term and terms for subtypes. *See also* clinical practice guidelines; standards, guidelines, and options.

practice privileges Permission to render care within well-defined limits based on an individual's professional license and his or her training, experience, competence, ability, and judgment. *See also* privileging.

practice profiling *See* practice pattern analysis.

practitioner Any individual who is qualified to practice a health care profession (eg, physician, nurse). Practitioners are often required to be licensed as defined by law. *See also* the following practitioner terms, as well as dental practice act; licensed independent practitioner; licensure;

medical practice act; Nurse Practitioner Data Bank; nurse practice act; primary care provider; private practice.

practitioner factor Individual practitioner-related variable that may contribute to variation in performance data; usually controllable and one of the objects of a thorough monitoring process. *See also* external environmental factor; factor; organization factor; patient factor.

practitioner profiling A process of aggregation and analysis of practitioner-specific health care data, often in the form of tables or graphs, representing distinctive features or characteristics of a practitioner or group of practitioners. *See also* practice pattern analysis; profile; profiling.

practitioner site The office of a clinician or licensed independent practitioner who is a member of the practitioner panel of a managed care organization or network. *See also* care and service provider organization; component; licensed independent practitioner.

preadmission certification (PAC) A process to review and approve elective care proposed for a patient before he or she is admitted to a health care organization. Under a PAC program, certification must be obtained for reimbursement. *See also* admission; admission pattern monitoring; admission review; prior authorization.

preadmission procedures An organization's process for obtaining appropriate and necessary information for each individual seeking admission into a health care setting or service. Sources for this information include the patient, his or her practitioner, or another health care organization. The information is used to match individual need with level of care required and to the appropriate setting. These procedures may also include screening for insurance eligibility. *See also* admission review; preadmission screening.

preadmission review *See* admission review.

preadmission screening (PAS) An evaluation program for applicants for admission to nursing homes under Medicare and Medicaid. Some states also require preadmission screening for private pay applicants. *See also* preadmission procedures.

predatory pricing A practice by insurers of giving a low rate on health insurance to a small low- risk group or individual, then raising the rate when the insured files claims. *Synonyms*: churning the books; price churning.

predictive validity The ability of an indicator or other measure to predict future events. *See also* external validity; validity.

predictive value of a screening test A probability determined by the sensitivity and specificity of a test, and by the prevalence of the condition for which the test is used. When the prevalence of a given condition is low in a tested population, a test with a high sensitivity functions fairly well at both ruling in the correct diagnosis and ruling out the incorrect one. But as the prevalence increases, the sensitivity of the test must also increase to maintain

the same number of false negatives. *See also* sensitivity; screening; specificity.

preeclampsia *See* pregnancy-induced hypertension.

preexisting condition In the field of health insurance, an injury occurring, a disease contracted, or a physical condition that exists prior to the issuance of a health insurance policy. It usually results in an exclusion from coverage under the policy for costs resulting from the condition. *See also* exclusions; job lock; open enrollment.

preference measurement-methodology *See* patient utilities measurement.

preferred practice pattern The term used by the American Academy of Ophthalmology for its clinical practice guideline. *See also* clinical practice guidelines; practice guidelines; practice pattern analysis.

preferred provider organization *See* PPO.

Pregnancy Discrimination Act (1978) An amendment to Title VII of the Civil Rights Act of 1964, which holds that discrimination on the basis of pregnancy, childbirth, or related medical conditions constitutes unlawful sex discrimination. *See also* discrimination.

pregnancy-induced hypertension (PIH) A condition, formerly termed preeclampsia, of late pregnancy (after the 24th week) characterized by hypertension, swelling of the extremities, and protein in the blood. PIH is classified as *mild* or *severe* depending on the extent of elevated blood pressure. If grand mal convulsions and coma occur, it is classified as *eclampsia*. *Synonyms*: preeclampsia; toxemia; toxemia of pregnancy. *See also* eclampsia.

premium The amount paid or payable, often in installments, by an insured person or policyholder to an insurer or third-party payer for insurance coverage under an insurance policy. Premium amounts are related to the actuarial value of the benefits provided by the policy, plus a "loading" to cover administrative costs and profit. Premiums are paid for coverage whether benefits are actually used or not. Premiums should not be confused with cost sharing (copayments, coinsurance, and deductives), which are paid only if benefits are actually used. Premiums can be established by either an experience rating or a community rating method. *See also* community rating; cost sharing; deductible; experience rating; loading; open enrollment; risk charge.

prenatal screening tests and procedures Techniques for determining genetic and physical abnormalities in the fetus such as Down syndrome or spina bifida. The decision to conduct prenatal screening to detect abnormalities and selection among different methods are guided by consideration of risk of fetal loss, the time period during pregnancy of performing the test, sensitivity and specificity, and personal preferences and values of the parents.

PRENATAL SCREENING AND TESTING PROCEDURES	
Test	Description (Time Administered in Gestational Weeks)
Alpha-fetoprotein (AFP)	Measurement of plasma protein produced by the fetal liver, yolk sac, and gastrointestinal tract in the maternal serum or amniotic fluid to detect neural tube defects such as spina bifida (16-18 weeks)
Amniocentesis	Percutaneous transabdominal puncture of the uterus with an ultrasonographically guided needle to obtain amniotic fluid for analysis of chromosomal abnormalities such as Down syndrome (14-20 weeks)
Chorionic villus sampling (CVS)	Sampling of the cells of the placental chorionic villi for DNA analysis, presence of bacteria, concentration of metabolites, and so forth to detect chromosomal abnormalities such as Down syndrome (9-13 weeks)
Ultrasonography	Visualization of fetal tissues through recording of the echoes of ultrasonic waves directed into the body to detect physical abnormalities such as neural tube defects (as early as 5 weeks)

prepaid group practice Group practice providing care for a defined population under a prepayment arrangement. *See also* closed panel group practice; group practice; medical foundation.

prepaid health plan A contract between an insurer and a subscriber or group of subscribers whereby the prepaid health plan provides a specified set of health benefits in return for a period premium. *See also* health plan; point-of-service plan.

prepayment plan A contractual arrangement for health services in which a prenegotiated payment is made in advance, covering a certain time period, and the health care provider agrees, for this payment, to furnish certain services to the beneficiary. *See also* fee for service; health plan; voucher.

preponderance of evidence With respect to the burden of proof in civil actions, this standard implies greater weight of evidence, or evidence that is more credible and convincing to the mind. It is in contrast to "clear and convincing evidence" and "proof beyond a reasonable doubt," which are progressively higher standards of proof. *See also* admissible evidence; clear and convincing evidence; expert witness; medical evidence.

prescriber Physicians, dentists, and others who are permitted by law and regulation to prescribe or order medications.

prescribing and ordering Directing the selection, preparation, or administration of medication(s). *See also* order; prescription.

prescription (Rx) A written direction by a physician, dentist, or other authorized health care provider for the preparation and administration of a medication, therapy, or device. A prescription consists of a heading or *superscription* (the symbol *Rx* or the word *recipe*, meaning "take"); the *inscription* (the names and quantities of ingredients); the *subscription* (directions for compounding); and the *signature* (directions for the patient that are to be marked on the receptacle). *See also* antisubstitution laws; prescribing and ordering; prescription drug.

prescription drug A drug that can be provided to a person only on the prescription of a physician, dentist, or other authorized health professional. The prescription specifies the drug to be given, the amount of the drug to be dispensed, and the directions necessary for the patient to use the drug. *Synonym:* prescription medicine. *See also* drug; legend drug; over-the-counter drug; package insert; prescription.

pressure ulcer A lesion caused by prolonged pressure on a person allowed to remain in a particular position (sitting or lying) for a long period of time or prolonged contact with equipment adjacent to the body. Pressure ulcers are graded in four stages (I-IV) on the basis of degree of tissue damage, in a schema developed by the National Pressure Ulcer Advisory Panel Consensus Development Conference (1989), adopted in the national clinical practice guidelines developed by AHCPR (1992, 1994), and widely implemented in health care organizations' protocols. *Synonyms:* bed sore; decubitus; decubitus ulcer; pressure sore. *See also* Braden Scale; clinical practice guidelines (and accompanying table); Norton Scale; shear; support surfaces.

presumed consent A policy advocated by some people that would presume that an individual would allow his or her organs to be retrieved for transplantation after death unless he or she specifically issues a directive that forbids organ harvesting or retrieval. Currently, the practice allows for cadaver donation when there is consent from living relatives of a deceased donor or when the donor has issued a directive prior to death permitting organ retrieval. *See also* consent; informed consent; organ procurement.

prevalence rate The total number of individuals who have an attribute, a condition, or a disease at a particular time or during a particular period, divided by the population at risk of having the attribute, condition, or disease at a specified time or midway through a period of time, multiplied by 100. *See also* incidence rate; morbidity rate.

prevention Action taken or services provided to avoid or delay a disease condition. *Primary prevention* is intervention to avert initial disease or injury (eg, vaccination and immunization, lead control programs, sex education and counseling, safety education, and hormone-replacement therapy to prevent coronary artery disease or osteoporosis). *Secondary prevention* is early detection and treatment of an evolving disease process or a handicapping disability (eg, screening for hypertension, avoidance of allergic triggers, use of eye drops to prevent progression of high intraocular pressure due to glaucoma, hospital safety training programs for persons injured in motorcycle accidents, use of nitrates or beta-blockers to manage angina). *Tertiary prevention* is intervention to prevent the progression of an established disease (eg, insulin injections for patients with diabetes mellitus, inhaled steroids for chronic asthma, laser therapy for a diabetic patient with proliferative diabetic retinopathy). *See also* the following prevention and preventive terms, as well as Comprehensive Drug Abuse Prevention and Control Act; detection; Diabetes Prevention Program; health education; health fair; health maintenance diaries; health maintenance schedule; *Healthy People 2000*; HIV Prevention Act of 1997; injury-prevention counseling; inspection; laboratory screening tests; Lifetime Health Monitoring Program.

prevention-early detection   A Joint Commission performance domain addressing the degree to which appropriate services are provided for promotion, preservation, and restoration of health and early detection of disease. This domain was added to the original nine *dimensions* of performance (making them all *domains*), specifically for purposes of performance measurement. *See also* domains of performance.

Preventive GAPS (Goals-Assessment Planning Starting Approach)   A four-step process developed by Group Health Cooperative of Puget Sound, a large consumer-governed HMO, to help individual practices tailor the delivery of preventive services to their patients. The model stresses the importance of a team approach, with a broad distribution of organized roles and responsibilities for staff rather than reliance solely on physicians and nurses.

preventive maintenance   *See* health maintenance schedule.

preventive medicine   The branch and specialty of medicine that focuses on the health of individuals and defined populations to protect, promote, and maintain health and well-being and to prevent disease, disability, and premature death. It includes biostatistics, epidemiology, health services administration, environmental and occupational influences on health, social and behavioral influences on health, and measures that prevent the occurrence, progression, and disabling effects of disease or injury. Medical toxicology is a subspecialty of preventive medicine. *See also* biostatistics; epidemiology; holism; holistic medicine; maternal and child health services; medical toxicology; physical activity and fitness; preventive services; public health; wellness program.

preventive services   Interventions designed to promote health and prevent disease, including identification of and counseling on modifiable risk factors (eg, smoking, lack of physical activity), screening to detect disease (eg, breast cancer, sexually transmitted diseases), immunizations, and chemoprophylaxis (eg, hormone replacement therapy). Guidelines and recommendations are regularly offered and updated by agencies of the U.S. Department of Health and Human Services, such as the Centers for Disease Control and Prevention (through the *Morbidity and Mortality Weekly Report*) and the U.S. Preventive Services Task Force (through its *Guide to Clinical Preventive*

Services, Second Edition, 1996). *Synonym:* clinical preventive services. *See also* Early and Periodic Screening Diagnostic and Treatment Program; health maintenance schedule; health services; laboratory screening tests; prevention; preventive medicine; U.S. Preventive Services Task Force.

price blending   Under the prospective pricing system in health care, a method for equitably determining prices for DRGs by comparing an individual hospital's range of cost per case for any given DRG to the national average for that DRG. *See also* DRG.

price churning.   *See* predatory pricing.

primary care   Basic health care and a branch of medicine that emphasizes the point when a patient first seeks assistance in a health care system and the care of the simpler and more common illnesses and injuries. Primary care can be provided by primary care physicians and health professionals other than physicians, notably nurse practitioners or physician assistants. Thus, primary care is typically characterized by the nature of the contact (first contact in the health care system) rather than the qualifications of the practitioners providing that care. *See also* the following primary care terms, as well as levels of care.

primary care center   A facility that provides primary care on a scheduled basis and is open approximately eight hours per day, is staffed by a physician or other qualified practitioner (eg, a physician assistant), is supported by basic laboratory and sometimes radiology services, and provides continuity of care. A primary care center typically offers first-contact health care only, and patients requiring specialized medical care are referred elsewhere. *See also* continuity; freestanding ambulatory care center.

primary care network   A group of primary care physicians who have joined together to share the financial risk of providing prepaid care to those of their patients who are members of a given health plan. *See also* health area network; health plan.

primary care physician (PCP)   A general practitioner, family practitioner, primary care internist, or primary care pediatrician who usually provides only primary care services. A person with specialty qualifications may also provide primary care, alone or in combination with referral services. *See also* gatekeeper mechanism; physician; primary care provider.

primary care provider   An individual, such as a physician or other qualified practitioner, who provides primary care services and manages routine health care needs. Care requiring certain specialized knowledge or skill is obtained by referral from the primary care provider to a specialist for consultation or continued care. *Synonym:* primary care practitioner. *See also* health care provider; primary care physician.

primary contact   A person in direct contact with a communicable disease case. *See also* contact isolation; direct contact; secondary contact.

primary data   Data collected exclusively and specifically to conduct a study. *See also* data; operational data.

primary nursing   A system of nursing care in which one nurse is responsible around the clock for planning, supervising, and, when present, giving nursing care to an assigned individual or group of patients. This approach to nursing care is replacing team nursing, in which a group of individuals of different levels of skill, rather than a given individual, carries out nursing functions. *See also* team nursing.

primary payer   The insurer obligated to pay losses before any liability of other, secondary insurers. Medicare, for instance, is a primary payer with respect to Medicaid. *See also* coordination of benefits; duplication of benefits.

primary prevention   *See* prevention.

primary source   For purposes of Joint Commission accreditation, the original source of a specific credential that can verify the accuracy of a qualification reported by an individual health care practitioner. Examples include medical schools, graduate medical education programs, and state medical boards. *See also* credentialing agency; source document.

prime-boost strategy   Use of two vaccines in sequence, designed to use each vaccine to its best advantage by stimulating the immune system to mount two different immune responses when provoked by HIV.

primum non nocere   Latin phrase meaning "above all, do no harm." *See also* Hippocratic oath.

principal diagnosis   *See* diagnosis.

prior authorization   A requirement imposed by a third-party payer, under many systems of utilization review, that a provider must justify before a peer review committee, insurance company representative, or state agent the need for delivering a particular service to a patient before actually providing the service to receive reimbursement. This generally applies to expensive non-emergency services or services that are overused or abused. *See also* admission review; preadmission certification.

prison hospital   *See* security hospital.

Privacy Act of 1974   A federal statute that reasserts the fundamental right to privacy as derived from the Constitution of the United States. It provides a series of basic safeguards for individuals so as to prevent the misuse of personal information by the federal government. Safeguards include, for example, making known to the public the existence and characteristics of all personal information systems kept by federal agencies, permitting individuals access to records containing personal information about that individual, and providing for civil remedies for individuals whose records are kept or used in contravention of the requirements of the act. *See also* right of privacy.

private health agency   *See* voluntary health agency.

private hospital   Investor-owned or not-for-profit hospital that is controlled by a legal entity other than a government agency.

private patient   A patient whose care is the responsibility of an individual physician and whose care is paid for directly by the patient or a third-party payer, as opposed to a public, service, or ward patient, whose care is the financial responsibility of a health program or institution. *See also* patient; third-party payer; ward patient.

private practice   A medical or other type of practice in which the practitioner and his or her practice are independent of any external policy control. It usually requires that the practitioner be self-employed, except when he or she is salaried by a partnership in which he or she is a partner with similar practitioners. It is not synonymous with fee-for-service practice, in which the practitioner may sell his services by another method, such as capitation; or solo practice, because group practices may be private. Regulation, which does exert external control, is not generally thought to make all practice public. *See also* fee for service; practitioner; solo practice.

privatization   The shifting of authority and financial responsibility for health care services from the public (governmental) sector to the private (for-profit) sector to improve efficiency and increase productivity. There is a rising move toward privatization throughout the health care industry due to spiraling delivery costs and inefficient use of resources.

privileged communication   A confidential communication that is legally protected from discovery in a lawsuit or use as evidence in a trial. For example, communications between a physician and patient are privileged communications and cannot be revealed without the patient's permission or a court order. Most contents of a medical record are also protected by this privilege. A patient can waive the privilege, but the privilege cannot be waived by a physician or hospital, nor can the physician invoke the privilege if the patient waives it. *See also* admissible evidence; attorney-client privilege; fiduciary; patient-provider relationship; physician-patient privilege; psychotherapist-patient privilege.

privileging   The process whereby a specific scope and content of patient care services (ie, clinical privileges) are authorized for a health care practitioner by a health care organization based on evaluation of the individual's credentials and performance. *See also* admitting privileges; clinical privileges; licensed independent practitioner; National Practitioner Data Bank; practice privileges; temporary privileges.

probability   **1.** The chance or likelihood that something will happen or has happened   **2.** The limit of the relative frequency of an event in a sequence of N random trials as N approaches infinity.   **3.** A measure, ranging from zero to one, of the degree of belief in a hypothesis or statement. *See also* actuarial analysis; joint probability; nonprobability sampling; p value.

probability distribution A mathematical formula that relates the values of a characteristic being measured with their probability of occurrence in a population. A *continuous probability distribution* occurs when the characteristic being measured can take on any value (subject to the fineness of the measuring process). For example, the probability distribution for time spent by emergency medical technicians at a trauma scene, because the characteristic being measured (time) could have any value, limited only by the fineness of the measuring instrument. Most continuous characteristics follow one of several common probability distributions: the normal distribution, the exponential distribution, and the Weibull distribution. A *discrete probability distribution* occurs when the characteristic being measured can take on only certain specific values, such as greater than 20 minutes *or* less than or equal to 20 minutes spent by emergency medical technician-paramedics at a trauma scene. Common discrete probability distributions are the Poisson, binomial, negative binomial, and hypergeometric. *See also* binomial distribution; continuous data; discrete data; discrete variable; distribution; normal distribution; parametric test; Poisson distribution; random variable; rate-based measure.

probability theory The branch of mathematics dealing with the purely logical properties of probability. Its theorems underlie most statistical methods.

probability value *See p* value.

probable error (PE) In statistics, the amount by which the arithmetic mean of a sample is expected to vary because of chance alone.

problem drinking Reformulated definition of drinking behavior that can be harmful, arising out of awareness that majority of alcohol morbidity and mortality in the general population is caused by nondependent drinkers. No single definition of hazardous drinking in asymptomatic persons has been established, but successful intervention trials have generally defined five drinks per day in men, three drinks per day in women, or frequent intoxication to identify persons at risk. Several U.S. organizations have suggested lower limits for *safe drinking*: two drinks per day in men and one drink per day in women. An Institute of Medicine report on broadening the base of treatment (1990) favored an expanded definition of treatment so that all individuals who are identified as having a problem with their use of alcohol should receive some assistance with their problems. *See also* alcoholism; alcoholism treatment service; alcohol-problem screening; CAGE; dependence; substance-related disorders.

problem-oriented medical record (POMR) A type of medical record in which a patient's history, physical findings, laboratory results, and other data and information are organized according to problems, such as chest pain or vomiting blood, instead of according to diseases, such as pneumonia or peptic ulcer, or not at all. The problem-oriented record includes subjective, objective, assessment, and diagnostic and treatment plans (SOAP) for each problem. This contrasts with a medical record in which information is recorded in a less organized manner without regard for careful documentation of subjective, objective, assessment, and planning information about individual problems. *See also* medical record; medical record progress note; SOAP.

problem-prone procedure A procedure, function, process, or service that has historically resulted in less than satisfactory outcomes for an organization, practitioners, patients, or a community. Usually applied, along with high risk and high cost, to patient populations (eg, patients with diabetes) that might be the focus of quality-improvement efforts. *See also* high-volume procedure or condition.

problem statement A description in specific and measurable terms of how a perplexing or difficult question or issue affects the performance of an organization. *See also* opportunity statement.

procedure capture Efforts to persuade a referring physician or other practitioner to refer patients to a specific health care facility or specialist physician.

process A goal-directed, interrelated series of actions, events, mechanisms, or steps. *See also* the following process terms, as well as administrative process; credentials verification process; data verification process; due process; FACE process; grievance process; guideline priority-setting process; key process variable; nominal group technique.

process capability The measured, built-in reproducibility or consistency of a product turned out by a process. Such a determination is made using statistical methods, not wishful thinking. The statistically determined pattern or distribution can only then be compared to specification limits to decide if a process can consistently deliver a product within those parameters. *See also* analysis; capability; parameter; process.

process data Data describing what is done to, for, or by patients, as in performance of a procedure. *See also* data; outcome(s) data.

process decision program chart (PDPC) A method, based on the PDCA cycle, that maps out foreseeable events and contingencies that can occur during implementation of a plan. This, in turn, allows for the identification of countermeasures to respond to the possible problems. *See also* plan-do-check-act cycle.

process improvement The continuous endeavor to learn about all aspects of a process and to use this knowledge to change the process to reduce variation and complexity and to improve the level of its performance. Process improvement begins by understanding how customers define quality, how processes work, and how understanding the variation in those processes can lead to wise management action. *See also* continuous quality improvement; improvement.

process indicator An indicator that measures a discrete process, service, or activity. The best process indicators focus on processes that are closely linked to outcomes, meaning that a scientific basis exists for believing that the process, when executed well, will increase the probability of achieving a desired outcome. *See also* indicator; outcome(s) indicator; process measure.

process measure   A measure of performance used to assess a goal-directed, interrelated series of actions, events, mechanisms, or steps, such as a performance measure that describes what is done to, for, or by patients. *See also* input measure; measure; outcome measure; process indicator.

process standard   A statement of expectation set by a competent authority concerning a degree or level of acceptable performance of a process achieved by an individual, group, organization, community, or nation, according to preestablished requirements or specifications. *See also* outcome standard; performance standard; standard.

process variation   The spread of process output over time. There is variation in every process, and all variation is caused. The causes are of two types: special or common. A process can have both types of variation at the same time or only common-cause variation. The management action necessary to improve the process is different depending on the type of variation being addressed. *See also* common-cause variation; special-cause variation; variation.

pro choice   Belief that all decisions regarding abortion and reproductive health services should remain a woman's choice. Supporters work for policies that enable women and men to make responsible, deliberate decisions about sexuality, contraception, pregnancy, childbirth and abortion. *See also* abortion; assisted suicide; right to life; *Roe* v *Wade*.

proctology   The study of disorders of the anus and rectum.

proctoscopy   Inspection of the rectum with a proctoscope. *See also* endoscopy.

proctosigmoidoscopy   Inspection of the rectum and sigmoid colon with a proctosigmoidoscope. *See also* endoscopy.

product liability   The onus on a producer or others to make restitution for loss related to personal injury, property damage, or other harm caused by a product. *See also* liability.

products of ambulatory care (PAC)   Twenty-four ambulatory care product categories into which patient visits are assigned by computer, depending on the type of problem presented and resources received. Developed by the New York State Ambulatory Care Reimbursement Demonstration Project in 1985.

Professional and Technical Advisory Committee (PTAC)   A group of public and health care professional organization representatives who provide staff of the Joint Commission with knowledge and experience and who help to establish and refine standards and strengthen the accreditation process for each specific accreditation program.

professional liability   The legal obligation of a health professional or health care organization resulting from a breach (performing or failing to perform something that was done or should have been done), for which the law provides a remedy. A physician, for example, who fails to make a diagnosis resulting in patient injury is professionally liable for the injury. Professional liability is not the same as professional negligence. *Synonym:* medical liability. *See also* defensive medicine; enterprise liability; liability; malpractice; medical malpractice; no-fault medical practice liability; occurrence policy; professional liability insurance; professional negligence; reappointment of physicians.

professional liability insurance   Insurance covering the risk of loss from patient injury or illness resulting from professional negligence or other professional liability. Professional liability insurance pays malpractice claims. Often, an organization's professional liability policy will not cover the actions of physicians on the medical staff, in which case those physicians need to obtain their own individual policies. *Synonym:* medical liability insurance. *See also* insurance; liability insurance; medical malpractice insurance; patient compensation fund; professional liability.

professional negligence   Failure of a professional, such as a physician, to exercise the degree of care considered reasonable under the circumstances, with such failure resulting in an unintended injury to another party. Professional negligence is not synonymous with professional liability. *See also* negligence; professional liability; tort.

professional standards review organization (PSRO)   A now-defunct organization of physicians in a designated area, state, or community established to monitor health care services paid for through Medicare, Medicaid, and Maternal and Child Health programs to ensure that services provided were medically necessary, met professional standards, and were provided in the most cost-effective setting. The requirement for the establishment of PSROs was added to the Social Security Act via the Social Security Amendments of 1972. PSROs were preceded by experimental medical care review organizations (EMCROs) and were replaced in 1982 by utilization and quality control peer review organizations (PROs) *See also* peer review organization; Social Security Amendments of 1972.

proficiency testing   **1.** The assessment of technical knowledge and skills relating to certain occupations.   **2.** A peer comparison program used by laboratories to assess reliability of tests performed. Samples, whose precise content is unknown, are provided to laboratories for testing periodically, the results of which are compared with other laboratories who perform the same tests. *See also* competence.

profile   A longitudinal or cross-sectional aggregation of health care data used to assess and improve some aspect of health care delivery. *See also* cholesterol profile; diagnostic profile; drug profile; lipid profile; patient profile; population profile; profile analysis; profiling.

profile analysis   Use of aggregate statistical data at the practitioner, regional, or national level to compare and assess various characteristics of practice patterns. *See also* profile.

profiling   An aggregation and analysis of health care data, often in the form of a table or graph, representing distinctive features or characteristics of the object of the data, as in profiling patients, physicians, hospitals, or populations. *See also* patient profile; physician profiling; population profiling; practice pattern analysis; practitioner profiling; profile.

progestin   Generic term for any substance, natural or synthetic, that brings about some or all of the biological changes produced by progesterone (an anti-estrogenic steroid thought to be the active principal of the corpus luteum in the ovary). Used along with estrogen in postmenopausal hormone replacement therapy to reduce the risk of endometrial cancer associated with unopposed estrogen. *See also* hormone replacement therapy.

prognosis   The forecasting or foretelling of the outcome of a disease or condition. *See also* SUPPORT Prognostic Model.

Program Evaluation and Review Technique (PERT)   A planning and control technique that minimizes interruptions and/or delays in a process with interrelated functions. PERT helps reduce the time required to complete a project. A PERT chart (also called PERT diagram) shows the sequence and interrelationships of activities from the beginning of a project to the end and uses probabilities for activity start and completion dates. *See also* critical pathway method.

Program of All-Inclusive Care for the Elderly (PACE)   A federal program begun in 1986 to study the cost-effectiveness of comprehensive long term care programs.

progressive patient care   A common method of organizing nursing services within a health care organization by which patients are grouped into levels of inpatient care units (intensive, intermediate, and self-care) according to their degree of illness. Patients are moved from one unit to another as their illness advances or their condition improves. *See also* continuum of care; intensive care; levels of care; self-care; nursing care.

progress notes   A component of the medical record consisting of a pertinent, chronological report of the patient's course. *See also* health care record; medical record.

projective technique   A kind of diagnostic or personality test that uses unstructured or ambiguous stimuli, such as inkblots, a series of pictures, abstract patterns, or incomplete sentences, to elicit responses that reflect a projection of dimensions of a person's personality. Projective techniques are used not only by behavioral health clinicians but also by career counselors, focus group facilitators, and "creatives" in advertising and public relations agencies to generate ideas for campaigns. *See also* Rorschach test; thematic apperception test.

project management   A set of principles, methods, and techniques for effective planning of objective-oriented work, thereby establishing a sound basis for effective scheduling, controlling, and replanning in the management of projects.

Project PACE (Physician-based Assessment and Counseling for Exercise)   An exercise counseling tool designed for primary care physicians, developed by Group Health Cooperative (Seattle) with support from the Centers for Disease Control and Prevention. The program matches the physician's counseling with readiness for behavioral change on the part of patients, who are identified as "precontemplators," "contemplators," or "active exercisers." The program is undergoing testing in a long-term randomized controlled trial.

project team   A crossfunctional team of workers throughout an organization assigned the responsibility of diagnosing and improving a problem. *See also* team.

proportional hazards model   *See* Cox proportional hazards model.

Proposition 215   Successful voters' initiative in California (1996) to legalize the possession or cultivation of marijuana when its use is "recommended" by a doctor. The law was attacked by officials in the Clinton administration and has been the subject of a campaign to undermine it, but it passed its first test in the courts in March 1997 when drug-possession charges were dropped against a member of a cannabis-buying club. *See also* medical marijuana laws, regulations, and guidelines.

proprietary drug   A drug manufactured and sold only by the owner of the patent, formula, brand name, or trademark associated with the drug. *See also* drug.

PRO scope of work (PRO-SOW)   A contract that details the specific obligations of a peer review organization (PRO). It defines the duties and functions of the Medicare review for a specific contract cycle. For instance, the first SOW was used during the first contract cycle (1984-1986) and emphasized the detection of inappropriate utilization and payments under the new Medicare hospital prospective payment system after October 1983. Contract activities, which concentrated on inpatient hospital care, included reducing unnecessary admissions, ensuring that payment rates matched diagnostic and procedural information contained in the patient records, and reviewing patients who were transferred or readmitted to an acute care hospital within seven days of discharge. *See also* Medicare; peer review organization.

prospective data collection   The process of data collection in anticipation of an event or occurrence, as compared with retrospective data collection, which is the process of data collection for events that have already occurred. *See also* concurrent data collection; data collection.

prospective payment   Payment for services in which the payment is set before the services are actually provided, and this payment is issued regardless of the cost incurred providing the services. This contrasts with retrospective payment, in which payment for services is based on actual costs determined after the services have been provided. *Synonym:* prospective reimbursement. *See also* cost outlier; Deficit Reduction Act of 1984; payment; prospective payment system; reasonable cost; reimbursement; retrospective reimbursement.

prospective payment system (PPS)   The method of third-party payment by which rates of payment to health care providers for services to patients are established in advance for the coming fiscal year. Providers are paid these rates for services delivered regardless of the cost actually incurred in providing these services. Prospective pricing is best exemplified by the prospective payment system for Medicare patients by DRGs established by the Tax Equity and Fiscal Responsibility Act of 1981. *Synonym:* prospective pricing system (PPS). *See also* case-mix index; cost-based reimbursement; DRG; Forms 1007 and 1008; major diagnostic category; pediatric-modified diagnosis-related groups; prospective payment; referral center; retrospective reimbursement; unbundling; uniform capitol factor.

prospective review   Review of a proposed schedule of treatment, which could include patient care or discharge plans, as well as any policies or procedures that specify how care is or will be provided. *See also* retrospective review.

prospective study   *See* cohort-study.

prostate cancer screening   *See* cancer screening tests and procedures; PSA.

prostatectomy   Surgical removal of the prostate or a part of it. There are many removal methods, including perineal prostatectomy, transurethral resection of the prostate (performed by means of a cystoscope passed through the urethra), retropubic prevesical prostatectomy, and suprapubic transvesical prostatectomy. *See also* transurethral resection of the prostate.

prosthetics   The field of knowledge relating to the design and use of prostheses, appliances used to correct extremity ailments. *See also* orthotics; physical medicine and rehabilitation.

prosthodontics   A dental specialty dealing with the restoration and maintenance of oral function, comfort, appearance, and health by replacing missing natural teeth and associated structures with fixed or removable substitutes, such as dentures and bridgework. *See also* dental specialties; implant dentistry.

prosumers   Participants in a recovery program or group who simultaneously give aid to others and receive services from others. *See also* recovery movement.

protease inhibitor (PI)   A new class of drug for treatment of HIV infection, which interrupts the growth and replication of infectious virions and which acts synergistically with other agents in combination therapy. In 1997 the National Institute of Allergy and Infectious Diseases, a component of the National Institutes of Health, terminated the trial (of which one PI was a part) when its efficacy and safety in triple therapy (used with the nucleoside analogues zidovudine or stavudine and lamivudine) and the superiority of this combination were demonstrated beyond a doubt. *See also* antiretroviral drug; nucleoside analogue.

protective services   A range of sociolegal, assistive, and remedial services that facilitate the exercise of individual rights and provide certain supportive and surrogate mechanisms. Such mechanisms are designed to help developmentally disabled individuals reach the maximum independence possible, yet protect them from exploitation, neglect, or abuse. Depending on the nature and extent of individual needs, protective services may range from counseling to full guardianship. *See also* adult protection services; child protection services.

protocol   A plan, or set of steps, to be followed in a study, an investigation, or an intervention, as in clinical protocols used in the care of trauma patients. *See also* algorithm; breast cancer protocols; clinical protocols; practice guidelines.

provider   *See* health care provider.

provider-based physician   Under Medicare, a physician who performs services in a provider setting and has a financial arrangement under which he or she is compensated through or by a provider or provider-related entity.

provider service network (PSN)   A type of health care organization proposed in the 1995 Republican House Medicare reform bill. Designed to operate like an HMO, offering HMO services and assuming risk, the PSN would be operated by providers and funded in part by member contributions. All members would be required to provide health care to Medicare beneficiaries, and compensation received would be distributed among the members. A PSN would be exempt from regulation as an insurance company and would be given some antitrust protection with regard to establishment of fee schedules and conduct of the network.

provider-sponsored organization (PSO)   A type of provider service network proposed in the 1995 Republican House Medicare reform bill. A PSO could be established and conduct business without obtaining state licensure as an insurance company (required for other types of health care plans). States could issue a certificate that the PSO met federal requirements, and the PSO would not be subject to any state law imposing capitalization or insolvency requirements preventing it from doing business.

FEDERAL PROGRAMS ESTABLISHED FOR PROTECTION AND ADVOCACY

Protection and Advocacy for Persons with Developmental Disabilities (PADD)   Created in 1975 under the Developmental Disabilities Assistance and Bill of Rights Act and administered by a branch of the Department of Health and Human Services. To receive its basic grant allotment for developmental disabilities, each state and territory was required to establish a protection and advocacy system to pursue the legal, administrative, and other appropriate remedies to protect the rights of individuals with developmental disabilities under federal and state laws.

Client Assistance Program (CAP)   Established by the 1984 amendments to the Rehabilitation Act of 1973 and administered by a branch of the Department of Education. To receive allotments under Section 110 of the act, each state and territory was required to establish a CAP to provide information and assistance to individuals seeking or receiving services under the act.

Protection and Advocacy for Individuals with Mental Illness (PAIMI)   Established by law in 1986 and administered by a branch of the Department of Health and Human Services. The PAIMI program had two fundamental purposes: to protect and advocate the rights of individuals with mental illnesses; and to investigate allegations of abuse and neglect and rights violations of patients living in residential care and treatment facilities.

Protection and Advocacy for Individual Rights (PAIR)   Authorized by Congress under the Rehabilitation Act of 1978 but not funded until 1991; administered by the Rehabilitation Services Administration. PAIR has the authority to protect and advocate for legal and human rights of all persons with disabilities.

Protection and Advocacy for Assistive Technology (PAAT) Program   Established by Congress in 1994 as an expansion of the Technology-Related Assistance for Individuals with Disability Act and administered by the National Institute on Disability and Rehabilitation Research. These programs are meant to assist individuals with disabilities and their family members, guardians, advocates, and authorized representatives in accessing technology devices and assistive technology services through case management, legal representation, and self-advocacy training.

Source: Schauer C: Special report: Protection and advocacy: What nurses need to know. *Archives of Psychiatric Nursing* IX(5):233-239, October 1995.

---

provisional accreditation   *See* accreditation decision.

provocation testing A technique for reproducing a patient's main signs or symptoms suggesting allergy by controlled exposure to a suspected substance. The test is carried out by placing an extract of the suspected allergen on the conjunctiva or nasal mucous membrane or by having the subject either inhale the extract (bronchial provocation) or swallow it (oral challenge). *See also* allergen skin tests; allergy; sensitivity.

proximate cause   In negligence law, an act or omission that naturally and directly produces a consequence. In some jurisdictions, for an act to be considered the proximate cause of a loss or injury, it must be proved that, but for the act or omission, the injury or loss would not have occurred. *See also* direct cause; immediate cause; root cause; root cause analysis.

proxy   *See* durable power of attorney for health care.

Prozac   Trade name for fluoxetine HCI, a 5-hydroxy-tryptamine (5-HT) selective serotonin reuptake inhibitor (SSRI) approved by the FDA for treating clinical depression. The drug has received much attention in the popular press as the result of several books and accounts of its use as a kind of "happiness drug" for a variety of nonapproved conditions. Reported side effects (10% to 15% of users) include anxiety, nervousness, insomnia, and weight loss in underweight individuals. It is contraindicated for patients who are also taking monoamine oxidase inhibitors for depression. Some studies have found that it may cause a small subset of patients to consider or attempt suicide, which is thought to be related to its effects on serotonin. *See also* antidepressant drug; depressive disorders; selective serotonin reuptake inhibitor.

prudent buyer principle The principle that Medicare or other third-party payers should not reimburse a provider for a cost that is not reasonable because it is more than the amount that a prudent and cost-conscious buyer would be expected to pay. *See also* third-party payer.

PSA (prostate-specific antigen) A substance secreted exclusively by the prostate epithelium, which is increased in 30% to 50% of patients with benign prostatic hypertrophy (BPH; enlarged prostate) and 25% and 92% of those with prostate cancer. Some clinicians and researchers maintain that because PSA is also elevated in acute prostatitis and in BPH, serum PSA levels are not a cost-effective screening modality for prostatic cancer. Expert opinion, however, is divided on this matter. *See also* cancer screening tests and procedures; tumor markers.

psychiatric hospital   A hospital that provides diagnostic and treatment services to patients with mental or emotional disorders. *Synonym:* mental hospital. *See also* mental disorder.

psychiatric nursing   The branch of nursing dealing with the prevention and treatment of mental or emotional disorders. *Synonym:* mental health nursing. *See also* nursing; psychiatry.

psychiatry   The branch of medicine and medical specialty dealing with the prevention, diagnosis, and treatment of mental, addictive, and emotional disorders, such as psychoses, depression, anxiety disorders, substance abuse disorders, developmental disabilities, sexual dysfunctions, and adjustment reactions. Addiction psychiatry, child and adolescent psychiatry, clinical neurophysiology, forensic psychiatry, and geriatric psychiatry are psychiatric subspecialties. *See also* addiction psychiatry;

child and adolescent psychiatry; forensic psychiatry; geriatric psychiatry; mental disorder; neuropsychology; orthopsychiatry; partial hospitalization program; social psychiatry.

psychiatric surgery *See* psychosurgery.

psychoanalysis A method of psychiatric therapy and branch of psychiatry that originated with the Austrian physician Sigmund Freud (1856-1939) during the late 1800s and early 1900s. According to Freud, mental disorders could be cured by uncovering a patient's unconscious wishes and fears. Freud believed that all behavior is influenced by instincts, fears, and unconscious mental processes not controlled by rational thought. He claimed that early childhood bodily experiences, especially sexual ones, shape individual behavior in later life. Psychoanalysts believe that unpleasant experiences, especially during childhood, may become buried in the unconscious mind and cause mental illness. Psychoanalytic treatment tries to bring these experiences out of a patient's unconscious mind and into the conscious mind through use of free association, dream interpretation, and analysis of resistance and transference. Psychoanalytic theory includes the following ideas: the mind is divided into the id, the ego, and the superego; there are five overlapping stages of psychosexual development (oral phase, anal phase, phallic stage, latency, and adolescence); and there is a strong attraction of children to the parent of the opposite sex, called the Oedipus complex. *See also* narcoanalysis.

psychodrama therapy Developed by J.L. Moreno (1889-1974), the use of action methods of enactment, sociometry, group dynamics, role theory, and social systems analysis by a qualified therapist to facilitate constructive change in individuals and groups by developing new perceptions or reorganizing old cognitive patterns and concomitant changes in behavior. *See also* creative arts therapy; manual arts therapy; recreational therapy.

psychology The branch of science that deals with mental processes and behavior, composed of the following major fields: abnormal, clinical, comparative, counseling, developmental, educational, engineering, experimental, industrial, learning, motivation, perception, personality, physiological, psychometrics, school, and social psychology. *See also* abnormal psychology; clinical psychology; counseling psychology; developmental psychology; educational psychology; experimental psychology; learning psychology; motivation psychology; neuropsychology; organizational behavior; parapsychology; perception psychology; personality psychology; personnel psychology; physiological psychology; psychometrics; reinforcement; role playing; social psychology.

psychometrics The branch of psychology that deals with the design, administration, and interpretation of quantitative tests the measuring psychological variables, such as intelligence, aptitude, and personality traits. *Synonym*: psychometry. *See also* psychology.

psychopharmacology The branch of pharmacology that deals with the study of the actions and effects of psychoactive drugs. *See also* drug; pharmacology.

psychosomatic illness A disorder having physical symptoms but originating from mental or emotional causes. For instance, disorders that are thought to be related to or exacerbated by emotional disturbances include asthma, peptic ulcer, and neurodermatitis. *Synonym*: psychosomatic disease. *See also* asthma; peptic ulcer disease.

psychosurgery A generic term for brain surgery performed to treat psychiatric disorders and alleviate symptoms that cannot be alleviated by any other means. Now uncommon, brain surgery must meet strict criteria (determination that the patient is unresponsive to all other therapy; that the condition has lasted longer than three years). The best known form—lobotomy—came in for heavy criticism and infamy in the lay press because of overuse in the late 1940s. Current techniques include radioactive 90Yt implants, cryoprobes, coagulation, proton beams, and ultrasonic waves. *Synonyms*: functional neurosurgery; psychiatric surgery. *See also* neurosurgery; somatotherapy.

psychotherapist-patient privilege A privilege, recognized by many states, for disclosures to psychologists or other general practitioners treating mental or emotional disorders, such as drug or alcohol dependence. Such a privilege arises from the special therapeutic need to assure the patient that disclosures will not be made. *See also* physician-patient privilege; privileged communication.

psychotherapy A treatment technique of alleviating or curing certain forms of mental disorders by suggestion; persuasion; encouragement; the inspiration of hope or confidence; the discouragement of morbid memories, associations, or beliefs; and other similar means. Psychotherapy relies principally on verbal communications within the relationship between a mental health professional (psychotherapist) and a patient(s). The primary treatment modalities of psychotherapy are individual, family, and group therapies. The length of the treatment may be short term or long term. *See also* behavior therapy; cognitive-behavioral psychotherapy; counseling services; family therapy; gestalt therapy; group therapy; hypnotherapy; play therapy;

psychotic disorder A generic term for a group of severe mental disorders, termed *schizophrenia and other psychotic disorders* in the DSM-IV and including schizophrenia, schizophreniform disorder, schizoaffective disorder, delusional disorder, brief psychotic disorder, shared psychotic disorder, psychotic disorder due to a general medical condition, substance-induced psychotic disorder, and psychotic disorder not otherwise specified. These disorders are characterized by behavior, such as delusions or hallucinations and disorganized speech and thought patterns, which result in impairment that grossly interferes with the capacity to meet the ordinary demands of life. *See also* personality disorder.

psychotropic medication   Any drug that alters perception or behavior. These include, but are not limited to, those drugs that produce drug dependence. *See also* alcohol and other drug dependence; deinstitutionalization; drug.

public data reporting   The gathering and sharing of health care practice information on a national level. *See also* report card.

public health   The science and practice of protecting and improving the health of a community, as by preventive medicine, health education, control of communicable diseases, application of sanitary measures, and monitoring of environmental hazards. *See also* board of health; preventive medicine; sanitation.

Public Health Service Act   [42 U.S.C. §§ 254-257 (1944)] One of the principal acts of Congress providing legislative authority for federal health activities. The act was a complete codification of all the accumulated federal public health laws. Generally, it contains authority for public health programs, biomedical research, health personnel training, family planning, emergency medical services systems, HMOs, regulation of drinking water supplies, and health planning and resources development. The act also established the National Health Service Corps and provided for a loan-repayment program and scholarship opportunities through community health centers. *See also* CLIA '67; surgeon general.

public hospital   *See* Medicaid health facility.

Public Information Policy   A Joint Commission policy governing the confidentiality or disclosure of information about the performance of a health care organization or network. This policy covers the Joint Commission's performance reports, information publicly disclosed on request, complaint information, aggregate performance data, data released to government agencies, and the Joint Commission's right to clarify information an accredited organization releases about its accreditation status.

public patient   *See* ward patient.

public welfare   The prosperity, well-being, or convenience of the public at large or of a whole community, as distinguished from the advantage of an individual or particular class. It embraces the primary social interests of order, morals, safety, economic interest, and nonmaterial and political interest.

pulmonary embolism (PE)   An obstruction of the pulmonary arterial bed by a dislodged thrombus or foreign substance, usually resulting from dislodged thrombi originating in the leg veins. More than half of such thrombi arise in the deep veins of the legs and are usually multiple. Although pulmonary infarction may be so mild as to be asymptomatic, massive embolism (more than 50% obstruction of pulmonary venous or arterial circulation) can be rapidly fatal. Risk factors for pulmonary embolism include long-term immobility, chronic pulmonary disease, congestive heart failure or atrial fibrillation, thrombophlebitis, polycythemia vera, thrombocytosis, cardiac arrest, defibrillation, cardioversion, autoimmune hemolytic anemia, sickle cell disease, varicose veins, recent surgery, advanced age, pregnancy, lower extremity fractures or surgery, burns, obesity, vascular injury, occult cancer, and oral contraceptives. *See also* embolism; thromboembolism.

pulmonary function laboratory   A laboratory for examination and evaluation of patients' respiratory functions by means of electromechanical equipment. *See also* laboratory; pulmonary medicine.

pulmonary function tests   Techniques and equipment for objectively measuring the processes of respiration, including inspiration, expiration, oxygen and carbon dioxide exchange, and lung volume and flow. The group as a whole consists of two types: one measures ventilation (lung volume and flow) through spirometry; the other measures gas exchange and lung perfusion. The most common use of the term refers to spirometry, which is appropriately used in evaluation of pulmonary dysfunction such as asthma, evaluation of cough and other symptoms, early detection of lung dysfunction, surveillance in occupational settings, follow-up of response to therapy,

PULMONARY FUNCTION TESTS	
Test Terminology	**Definition**
Static Measurements	
Tidal volume (V$_T$)	Volume of air contained in a normal breath
Functional residual capacity (FRC)	Volume of air remaining in the lungs after normal expiration
Vital capacity (VC)	Volume of air that can be exhaled after maximal inspiration
Residual volume (RV)	Air remaining in the lungs after maximal expiration
Total lung capacity (TLC)	Volume of air in the lungs after maximal inspiration
Dynamic Measurements	
Forced expiratory volume in 1 second (FEV$_1$)	Maximum volume of air that can be expired in one second from total lung capacity
Peak expiratory flow rate (PEFR)	The maximal airflow rate achieved in the FVC maneuver
Maximal voluntary ventilation (MVV)	Volume of air that can be expired in one minute with the patient's maximum voluntary effort
Forced vital capacity (FVC)	Maximal volume of air that the patient can exhale from TLC

preoperative evaluation for high-risk patients, and disability assessment. Normal values are individualized by body stature and age and are reported in percentage of the normal predicted value. Routine preoperative pulmonary function testing has come under scrutiny because of the failure to define the circumstances in which the tests are helpful in clinical decision making. Routine spirometric screening of healthy persons is not recommended without an indication or risk factor. Spirometry should be performed using equipment and techniques that meet standards developed by the American Thoracic Society (1995). *Synonym:* respiratory function tests. *See also* asthma; asthma guidelines and outcomes programs; chronic obstructive pulmonary disease; forced expiratory volume; laboratory screening tests; peak flow meter; spirometry.

pulmonary medicine A subspecialty of internal medicine and pediatrics dealing with diseases of the lungs and airways, such as pneumonia, cancer, pleurisy, asthma, occupational diseases, bronchitis, sleep disorders, emphysema, and other disorders. Pulmonology involves testing lung functions, performing endoscopy of the bronchial airways, and prescribing and monitoring mechanical assistance to ventilation. *See also* internal medicine; pulmonary function laboratory.

purchase authority model A case-management model in which public or private nonprofit organizations provide case management services to functionally impaired individuals who are eligible to receive community-based long term care under Medicaid, Medicaid waivers, or some other publicly funded program.

***p* value** The probability of concluding that a statistical association exists between, for instance, a risk factor and a health endpoint, when, in fact, there is no real association; the likelihood that an observed association in a study is due to chance alone. The letter *p*, followed by the abbreviation *n.s.* (not significant) or by the symbol < (less than) and a decimal notation, such as 0.01, 0.05, and so forth, is a statement of the probability that the difference observed could have occurred by chance, if the groups are really alike as required under the null hypothesis. Most biomedical work sets significance levels at a *p* value of less than 5% (p less than 0.05) or 1% (p less than 0.01), meaning that the test result is sufficiently unlikely to have occurred by chance to justify the designation "statistically significant". *Synonym:* probability value. *See also* level of significance; probability; statistical significance; test statistic; type I error.

Qq

QMNET (Quality Measurement Network) An initiative under development by the AHCPR in collaboration with the Joint Commission, the National Committee on Quality Assurance, and the Foundation for Accountability to provide a comprehensive, publicly accessible, self-supporting quality measurement resource. When completed, this network will have the capabilities of CONQUEST (AHCPR's computerized quality assessment system) as well as a technical assistance network to provide online help to people implementing quality measures. *See also* CONQUEST.

qualified individual An individual or staff member who is qualified to participate in one or all of the organization's provisions for care or services by virtue of the following: education, training, experience, competence, applicable licensure, law or regulation, registration, or certification.

qualitative analysis Analysis of a process or an object of interest to determine the nature of the elements or ingredients of which it is composed. *See also* quantitative analysis.

qualitative data Data characterized by measurement on a dichotomous scale or a nominal scale or, if the categories are ordered, an ordinal scale. Examples are sex, hair color, death or survival, and nationality. *See also* data; nominal scale; ordinal scale; quantitative data.

qualitative research Research that deals with the quality, type, or components of a group, substance, or mixture. For example, patient satisfaction surveys represent qualitative research. Qualitative research is exploratory in nature and uses various procedures, such as in-depth interviews and focus group interviews, to gain insights and guide subsequent decision-making processes. *See also* quantitative research.

quality-adjusted life years (QALYs) Years of life saved by a technology or service, adjusted according to the quality of those lives (as determined by some valuation process). The QALY is the most commonly used unit to express the results of cost-utility analyses. *See also* cost-utility analysis.

quality assessment The measurement and analysis of the quality of care for individuals, groups, or populations. The name of this activity was changed to "quality assurance" to reflect its intention to maintain and improve quality of care rather than simply assess it.

quality assurance (QA) Activities to determine the quality of care, develop and maintain programs to keep it at an acceptable level of quality, and institute improvements when the opportunity arises or the care does not meet the desired standard of care. This approach focuses on examining the performance of individual providers and looking for "bad apples," giving QA activities a punitive connotation and discouraging employee participation. This approach gave way to quality improvement and total quality management. *See also* quality assurance engineering; quality improvement.

quality assurance engineering The name given to Joseph M. Juran's system of total quality management. *See also* quality assurance; total quality management.

quality audit A retrospective, systematic, and independent examination and evaluation to determine whether quality activities and results comply with action plans and whether these plans have been implemented effectively and are suitable to achieve objectives. *See also* audit.

quality characteristics Characteristics of the output of a process (service or product) that are important to a customer. The identification of quality characteristics requires knowledge of customer needs and expectations. *See also* key quality characteristics.

quality circle A small group of professionals or employees of a health care organization who perform similar work and who meet regularly to learn and apply techniques for identifying, analyzing, and solving work-related problems. Quality circles originated in Japan as a total quality management technique in which groups of workers were organized and empowered to make improvements in the areas in which they worked. *See also* total quality management.

quality college A center within organizations, such as Motorola and Whirlpool, devoted to formal instruction, applied research, and pure research on quality matters. Employees typically are rotated through as students, and managers as instructors.

Quality Compass Database established by the National Committee for Quality Assurance (NCQA) that integrates provider information from NCQA's accreditation files and HEDIS. *See also* HEDIS.

quality control (QC) The performance of process(es) through which actual performance is measured and compared with goals, and the difference is acted on. *See also* Deming, W. Edwards; peer review organization; quality trilogy; statistical quality control.

quality function deployment (QFD) An approach to quality in which an organization is set up to assess the needs of external customers. The "house of quality," a set of seven matrixes, is the basic graphic used in QFD for showing customer requirements and means of meeting requirements. It often is used by service departments within organizations to survey customers' needs and assess the degree to which these needs are being met.

quality improvement (QI) The continuous study and improvement of the processes of providing health care services to meet the needs of patients and others. *See also* the surrounding quality terms, as well as continuous quality improvement; FADE process; FOCUS-PDCA; Health Care Quality Improvement Act of 1986; Health Care Quality Improvement Project; hold the gains; National Demonstration Project on Quality Improvement in Health Care; outcomes measurement; plan-do-check-act cycle; remedial journey; total quality management.

quality improvement council   A group composed of senior leadership and others in an organization which is primarily responsible for planning, strategy development, deployment, monitoring, educating, and promoting the acquisition and application of the knowledge necessary for quality improvement. *Synonym*: QI committee.

quality improvement project (QIP)   A discrete activity of continuous quality improvement consisting of a process that has been identified as needing improvement and has been given priority. A team composed of representatives from all departments and disciplines involved in the process is assigned to measure, assess, and improve the process. For the project to be successful, management must support the team. *See also* storyboard.

quality improvement team (QIT)   Groups of employees, often cross-departmental, who plan, direct, develop strategy, teach, train, assess, and provide feedback and praise in order to reach a solution to a system or process needing improvement in an organization. *See also* charter statement; coach; facilitator; quality improvement; remedial journey; storyboard; team.

quality inspection   A reactive process in which organizations sample, measure, and sort to remove defective goods or services and thereby improve quality, rather than proactively designing quality into the product or service. *See also* inspection.

quality management (QM)   Activities to determine the quality of care, to develop and maintain programs to keep it at an acceptable level of quality, to institute improvements when the opportunity arises or the care does not meet the desired standard of care, and to provide evidence that the desired level of quality is being maintained. *See also* total quality management.

quality measure   A quantitative measure of the features and characteristics of a service or product. *See also* CONQUEST; measure; QMNET.

Quality Measurement Network   *See* QMNET.

quality of care   According to the Institute of Medicine, the degree to which health care services for individuals and populations increase the likelihood of desired health outcomes and are consistent with current professional knowledge. Efforts to ensure high-quality care must prevent or detect and overcome three main problems: (1) overuse of unnecessary and inappropriate care; (2) underuse of necessary care; and (3) poor performance in both technical and interpersonal areas. *See also* dimensions of performance; patient health outcome; performance; performance-based quality-of-care evaluation.

quality of evidence   *See* strength of evidence/quality of evidence.

quality of life (QOL)   An attribute or dimension of health. The definition of this term varies depending on the individual, his or her goals, social setting and expectations, and other factors. It is difficult to measure quality of life so that improvement can be identified and QOL can be used as a factor in cost-benefit analysis. *See also* health-related quality of life.

quality of life scale   A method for measuring quality of life based on one or more aspects of an individual's life and health. More than 50 such measurement methods have been developed, including Duke Activity Status Index, Medical Outcomes Study Short Form General Health Survey, Quality of Well-Being Scale, Sickness Impact Profile, and Specific Activity Scale. *See also* measure (and accompanying table).

quality planning   According to Joseph M. Juran, the development of goods and services required to meet customer needs. This involves a series of universal steps: determining who the customers are, determining their needs, developing features of goods or services that respond to those needs, developing processes to produce these features, and transferring the resulting plans to the operating forces. *See also* quality trilogy.

quality surveillance   The continual monitoring and verification of the status of procedures, methods, conditions, products, processes, and services, in addition to the analysis of records in relation to stated references to ensure that requirements for quality are being met. *See also* surveillance.

quality trilogy   The processes of quality planning, quality control, and quality improvement. *Synonym*: Juran trilogy. *See also* National Demonstration Project on Quality Improvement in Health Care; quality control; quality improvement; quality planning; total quality management.

quantitative analysis   Analysis dealing with actual measurement of the actual amounts or proportions of the various components of an object or a process. It is distinguished from qualitative analysis, which may assess, for example, the character of management or the state of employee morale. *See also* measurement; qualitative analysis.

quantitative data   Data expressed in numerical quantities, such as continuous measurements or counts. *See also* continuous data; data; qualitative data.

quantitative research   Research that deals with the quantities of things and that involves the measurement of quantity or amount. *See also* qualitative research.

quiet room   In a mental health setting, room in which a patient may be involuntarily confined for clinical reasons. *See also* seclusion.

Quinlan case   [*In re Quinlan*, 70 N.J. 10, 355 A.2d 647 (N.J. 1976) *cert. denied*, *Garger* v *New Jersey*, 429 U.S. 922

(1976)] A landmark legal case involving Karen Quinlan, a 22-year-old who sustained severe brain damage, became comatose, and remained in a chronic vegetative state. The hospital and physicians refused her parents' request to terminate the mechanical respirator that aided her breathing. The New Jersey Supreme Court approved her father's request to be appointed his daughter's guardian and have the support systems discontinued. The patient continued to breathe on her own, receiving antibiotics and nasogastric tube feedings, until her death in 1985. This decision upheld the doctrine of *substituted judgment* under which an incompetent person's guardian makes a decision that he or she believes reflects the decision the patient would have made had he or she been capable. *See also* persistent vegetative state; substituted judgment doctrine.

Rr

radiation oncology The branch of radiology that deals with the therapeutic applications of radiant energy and its modifiers and the study and management of disease, especially malignant tumors. *Synonym:* therapeutic radiology. *See also* oncology; phototherapy; radiology.

radiation therapy The use of beam radiation, radioactive implants, or radioisotopes for cancer-directed therapeutic intent. The radiation interferes with the division of cells and the synthesis of deoxyribonucleic acid (DNA) in the cells. Many cancer cells are destroyed by radiation; the major disadvantage is possible damage to cells and tissues in adjacent areas. *Synonym:* radiotherapy. *See also* radioisotope; thermography; x-ray therapy.

radiculopathy Dysfunction of a nerve root often caused by compression of the root. Pain, sensory impairment, weakness, or depression of deep tendon reflexes may be noticed in the distribution of nerves derived from the involved nerve root. *See also* low back pain.

radioactive isotope *See* radioisotope.

radioallergosorbent test *See* RAST.

radiobiology The branch of biology concerned with the effects of radiation on living organisms and the behavior of radioactive substances in biological systems.

radiography The process by which radiographs (film records) are made of internal structures of the body by passage of x-rays or gamma rays through the body to act on specially sensitized film. *Synonym:* skiagraphy. *See also* imaging; mammography; radiology; roentgenology; roentgenography; xeroradiography; x-ray.

radioimmunoassay (RIA) A method of determining the concentration of a protein, such as a hormone, in the blood serum by monitoring any reaction produced by the injection of a radioactively labeled substance known to react in a particular way with the protein under study. *See also* immunoassay.

radioimmunology The study of immunity using radiolabeling and other radiological methods. *See also* allergy and immunology; immunology.

radioisotope A natural or artificially produced radioactive isotope of a chemical element, such as iodine-131 or phosphorus-32, given orally, into a cavity, or by intravenous injection, used in medicine for diagnosis or therapy. *Synonym:* radioactive isotope. *See also* nuclear radiology; radiation therapy; radionuclide imaging.

radiology The branch of health sciences and medical specialty dealing with radioactive substances and radiant energy and with the diagnosis and treatment of disease by means of both ionizing (eg, roentgen rays) and nonionizing (eg, ultrasound) radiations. Branches of radiology include therapeutic radiology (radiation oncology), diagnostic radiology, nuclear radiology, and radiological physics, which includes therapeutic radiological physics, diagnostic radiological physics, and medical nuclear physics. *See also* angiography; angioplasty; diagnostic radiology; fluoroscopy; imaging; nuclear radiology; neuroradiology; radiation oncology; radiography; roentgenology.

radionuclide imaging A diagnostic test in which a radioactive substance (nuclide, which is a type of atom specified by its atomic number, atomic mass, and energy state, such as carbon-14) is injected into the bloodstream and the emitted radioactivity is detected by a scanner, used to visualize the heart and vessels. *See also* diagnostic imaging; nuclear radiology; radioisotope.

radiopaque dye *See* contrast medium.

radiotherapy *See* radiation therapy.

radium therapy The use of radium (a highly radioactive metallic element) in treating cancer.

RAND criteria *See* appropriateness criteria.

random In statistics, relating to the same or equal chances or probability of occurrence for each member of a group; for example, in clinical research, the probability of assignment of a given subject to a specified treatment group is fixed and constant (typically 0.50), but the subject's actual assignment cannot be known until it occurs.

random error The portion of variation in a measurement that has no apparent connection to any other measurement or variable and that is generally regarded as due to chance. *See also* bias; measurement error; reliability.

randomization A technique for selecting or assigning cases or individuals, such that each case or individual has an equal probability of being selected or assigned. Randomization is done to stimulate change distribution, reduce the effects of confounding factors, and produce unbiased statistical data. Randomization differs from systematic allocation (eg, on even and odd days of the month) or discretionary allocation. *Synonym:* random allocation.

randomized controlled trial (RCT) An experimental study designed to test the safety, efficacy, or effectiveness of a health care intervention, in which people are randomly allocated to experimental or control groups and the outcomes are compared. *Synonyms:* random control trial; randomized clinical trial; randomized trial. *See also* nonrandomized controlled trial; phases of clinical trials.

random sampling A process in which a sample has been derived by selecting sampling units (eg, individual patients) such that each unit has an independent and fixed (generally equal) chance of selection. Whether a given unit is selected is determined by chance (eg, by a table of randomly ordered numbers). *See also* sample; simple random sampling; stratified random sampling.

random variable   In statistics, a variable whose values are distributed according to a probability distribution. *See also* probability distribution; regression; *t*-distribution; variable; variate.

range   In statistics, a measure of the variation in a set of data calculated by subtracting the lowest value in the data set from the highest value in that same set. *Synonym:* range of distribution.

range of motion (ROM)   The extent of movement of a limb or other body part, often used as a measure of rehabilitation. *See also* physical therapy.

ranking scale   A scale that arranges the members of a group from high to low according to the magnitude of the observations, assigns numbers to the ranks, and neglects distances between members of the group. *See also* causes-of-death rankings.

rank order voting   A team process for prioritizing ideas, often used in conjunction with brainstorming and multiple voting. For example, a quality-improvement team's members may come up with five opportunities for improvement and, by rank order voting on the importance of each, decide in what sequence they should be addressed.

RAST (radioallergosorbent test)   An in vitro radioisotopic method for quantifying specific allergenic IgE antibodies in serum. Although RAST is neither more sensitive nor specific than skin testing, it avoids the risk of sensitization and anaphylaxis characteristic of in vivo testing. The test is cited in the newly revised national asthma guidelines released February 1997 by the National Health, Lung, and Blood Institute's National Asthma Education and Prevention Program, which call for devoting more time to identifying individual patients' specific asthma triggers. RAST is the only available test for detecting indoor allergens. *See also* latex rubber allergy; triggers.

rate   A measure of a part with respect to a whole dividing the numerator (eg, cases that meet a criterion for good or poor care) by the denominator (eg, all cases to which the criterion applies) within a given time frame. The use of rates rather than raw numbers is essential for comparison of experiences between populations at different times, different places, or among different categories of persons. *See also* denominator; incidence rate; measure of association; numerator; performance rate; prevalence rate; ratio; underreporting.

rate-based measure   An aggregate data indicator in which the value of each measurement is expressed as a proportion or a ratio. In a proportion, the numerator and denominator express portions of the same population; in a ratio, the numerator and denominator measure different phenomena. *Synonym:* discrete variable indicator; rate-based indicator. *See also* aggregate data indicator; indicator; probability distribution; variable.

rate review   A regulatory agency's review of a health care organization's budget and financial statement to determine the reasonableness of its rates and rate changes. Rate review is also applied to certain prepayment plans, depending on state laws.

rate stratification by infection risk   *See* nosocomial infection rate.

ratio   A measure of a part with respect to a whole calculated by dividing the numerator by the denominator. Similar to a *rate*, except that the numerator is not necessarily a subset of the denominator. *See also* benefit-cost ratio; likelihood ratio; staffing ratio; ratio of cost to charge; ratio scale.

ratio of cost to charge (RCC)   Proportional relationship of total costs to total charges in a health care department or service. This is one of the simplest and most widely used methods for estimating costs in which one aggregate ratio (RCC) is calculated and applied equally to each procedure in the department or service. *See also* ratio.

ratio scale   A type of interval scale with a meaningful and true zero point; thus, products involving the data points demonstrate the relations between the data points. A ratio scale is the most powerful measurement scale, not only because the differences between observations are quantifiable, but also because the observations can themselves be expressed as a ratio. *See also* interval scale; nominal scale; ordinal scale; ratio.

readmission rate   A number showing the proportion of a health care organization's patients (or a class of patients, such as asthmatics) who reenter the organization within a specified interval after discharge with the same diagnosis (such as asthma).

real resources   All inputs, such as money, time, and other goods and services used to produce a product or service. *See also* resource allocation.

real-time imaging   Immediate (within microseconds) visualization of a dynamic process through technology such as the "B" mode ultrasound and ultrafact computers in computed tomography.

reappointment of physicians   The process of assessing a physician's current clinical competence and compliance with a medical staff's bylaws, rules, and regulations for reappointment and renewal of his or her clinical privileges. Medical staff appointments and clinical privileges are usually granted for one to two years. *See also* licensure; medical staff; professional liability.

rearing parent   A parent who actually rears a child. *See also* genetic parent; gestational mother; parent.

reasonable charge   For any specific service covered under Medicare, the lower of the customary charge by a particular physician for that service and the prevailing charge by physicians in the geographic area for that service. Generically, the term is used for any charge payable by an insurance program that is determined in a similar, but not necessarily identical, fashion. *See also* customary, prevailing, and reasonable charge; reasonable cost.

reasonable cost The amount a third-party payer using cost-related reimbursement will actually reimburse. Costs are considered reasonable if they are not unnecessary or excessive. Virtually all major purchasers of health care have already abandoned, or are planning to abandon, reasonable cost in favor of prospective payment and contracted price mechanisms, which provide greater long-term price stability for health care services. *See also* Medicare locality; prospective payment; reasonable charge; third-party payer.

reasonable person standard In law, a test often used by a fact finder (judge or jury) to measure conduct in his or her determination of negligence; the general level of care expected of individuals under the same or similar circumstances. For physicians defending themselves in a negligence suit, this generally refers to the behavior expected of a reasonable physician, familiar with the appropriate standards of practice that should be applied in certain circumstances, such as those under question in a lawsuit.

reassessment Ongoing data collection that begins on or after initial assessment, comparing the most recent data with the data collected on the previous assessment. *See also* medication-use reassessment.

recertification To renew certification, especially that given by a licensing or certification board, as in recertification of a hospital for Medicare by HCFA or recertification of a physician by a medical specialty board. *See also* certification.

reciprocity **1.** Relationship between persons, corporations, states, or countries in which privileges granted by one are returned by the other; for example; recognition by one jurisdiction of the licenses of physicians of a second jurisdiction when the second jurisdiction extends the same recognition to physician licenses of the first jurisdiction. *See also* endorsement; licensure; state board of medical examiners. **2.** A mutual agreement and business process in which Blue Cross and Blue Shield organizations process claims for services rendered by providers in their respective jurisdictions against coverage plans written by other Blue Cross and Blue Shield organizations. *See also* home plan; host plan.

recombinant DNA technology A method of replicating genes by combining segments of DNA from different sources and placing them in host cells grown in a laboratory. This type of genetic engineering has been applied to develop synthetic drugs such as human recombinant erythropoietin (used to treat the anemia resulting from depletion of the hormone in kidney failure), recombinant interferon gamma (used to treat some cancers), or recombinant insulin-like growth factor (used to treat patients with insulin-dependent diabetes). *Synonym:* gene splicing. *See also* biotechnology; DNA; gene splitting; gene therapy; genetic engineering; human body shop; Human Genome Project.

recommendation For purposes of Joint Commission accreditation, a citation requiring corrective action based on the nature, severity, or number of compliance problems, which is accompanied by appropriate follow-up monitoring. Recommendations can be either *type I* or *supplemental*. *See also* accreditation; compliance; type I recommendation; supplemental recommendation.

recommended dietary allowances (RDAs) Former standards created by nutrition experts and adopted by the Food and Nutrition Board of the National Research Council of the National Academy of Sciences for levels of average daily intake of essential nutrients. In 1996 this board proposed replacing the RDA with the Dietary Reference Intake (DRI). *See also* Dietary Reference Intake; Food Guide Pyramid; recommended dietary intakes.

recommended dietary intakes (RDIs) Standards set by the World Health Organization for the level of average daily nutrient intake to encompass the nutritional needs of essentially all healthy persons, plus some extra for storage. RDIs are international recommended dietary allowances. *See also* recommended dietary allowances.

reconstructive surgery *See* plastic surgery.

record **1.** An account set down in writing as a means of preserving information or facts, for example, a medical record. *See also* clinical record; coding; computer-based patient record; electronic medical record; health care record; home care record; medical record; nursing record; vital records. **2.** In data processing, a collection of related data items. A collection of records is called a file. *See also* personnel record; records management; track record.

records management A system used to collect, record, store, and eventually discard an organization's records. *See also* record.

recovery **1.** Return to a previous state or condition of health or function that preceded the occurrence of a disease or disability, as in patient recovery. *See also* curative; postoperative care; rehabilitation. **2.** In psychology and social work, a process that supports abstinence from alcohol or other drugs, involves changes in social, physical, and psychological functioning, and may or may not have an end. **3.** In law, the money awarded by a court to the successful plaintiff in a lawsuit. *See also* damages.

recovery movement Groups making use of self-help support-group techniques, particularly those based on the 12 steps of Alcoholics Anonymous, for assistance in overcoming addiction. *See also* prosumer; twelve-step program.

recreational therapy The use of recreational activities, such as athletics, arts and crafts, movies, and camping, to rehabilitate and restore patients' physical and emotional health. Recreational therapists or other qualified staff (such as an activity director) provide services for special populations, such as the elderly, handicapped, and mentally ill in hospitals, nursing homes, recreation centers, and long term care facilities. *Synonym:* therapeutic recreation. *See also* adult day care; creative arts therapy; manual arts therapy.

recruitment   The act of seeking prospective new employees or members for an organization. Recruitment is an important function for an organization to maintain personnel. *See also* human resources management.

recurrent brain injury   *See* second-impact syndrome.

recurring clause   A provision in some health insurance policies that specifies a time period during which the recurrence of a condition is considered a continuation of a prior period of disability or hospital confinement rather than a separate spell of illness. *See also* insurance.

red bead experiment   A simple exercise developed by W. Edwards Deming to model a production system. The exercise demonstrates that many managers hold workers to standards beyond workers' control, that variation is part of any process, and that workers work within a system beyond their control. The simulation also shows that some workers always will be above average, some average, and some below average; that the system, not the skills of individual workers, determines to a large extent how workers perform in carrying out repeating processes; and that only management can change the system or empower other persons to change it. *Synonyms:* red bead game; red bead parable. *See also* Deming, W. Edwards.

redlining   Insurers' refusal to insure high-risk industries, professions, and individuals in a given geographic area. This has been a civil rights issue. *See also* blacklisting.

reduction in force (RIF)   The elimination of specific job categories in organizations. A person who has been "riffed" has not been fired, but nevertheless is without a job.

reengineering   The fundamental rethinking and radical redesign of processes to achieve dramatic improvements in critical measures of performance, such as costs, quality, service, and speed.

reference database   An organized collection of similar aggregate data from many organizations, which can be used to compare an organization's performance to that of others. Data can be used for effectiveness research, financial analyses, and other purposes. *See also* database; reference population.

reference population   The population to which one can refer for authoritative information and against which a population being studied can be evaluated and compared. *See also* reference database.

reference range   The range of test values expected for a designated population or individuals, for example, 95% of individuals who are presumed to be healthy or normal.

referral   The sending of an individual (1) from one clinician to another clinician or specialist, (2) from one setting or service to another, or (3) by one physician (the referring physician) to another physician(s) or other resource, either for consultation or care that the referring source is not prepared or qualified to provide. *See also* the following referral terms, as well as consultation; selective referral.

referral center   Under Medicare prospective pricing, those rural hospitals that are paid the appropriate urban rate, adjusted by the rural wage index, because they meet the specified criteria as a referral center. *See also* Medicare; prospective payment system.

referral guidelines   Statements issued or published, generally by managed care organizations, to encourage or require primary care physicians to refer patients with a specified set of symptoms or characteristics to a specialist within a defined period of time. Referral guidelines are intended to improve both short-term and long-term clinical outcomes as well as prevent unnecessary referrals and contain costs. Specialty societies have started issuing their own referral guidelines or including a section of referral guidelines in their published practice guidelines to match the many commercial referral guidelines already in use. Managed care organizations' guidelines are likely to be more restrictive or involve a longer delay than specialists' guidelines.

referral provider   A provider (usually a specialty physician or other health entity) that renders a service to a patient who has been sent by a participating provider in a health plan. *See also* health care provider.

referred care   Medical care provided to a patient when referred by one health professional to another with more specialized qualifications or interests. There are two levels of referred care: secondary and tertiary. Secondary care is usually provided by a broadly skilled specialist, such as a general surgeon, a general internist, or an obstetrician. Tertiary care is provided on referral of a patient to a subspecialist, such as a neonatologist or a pediatric pulmonologist. *See also* levels of care; secondary care; tertiary care.

referred pain   Pain that is felt in a part of the body different from the injured or diseased organ or tissue causing the pain, as in angina pain (from insufficient blood supply to the heart) that is sometimes felt in the left shoulder, arm, or jaw, or in gallbladder pain felt in the right shoulder or under the shoulder blade.

regional alliance   A formal arrangement among several health care organizations or health systems from two or more states, for specific purposes, that functions under a set of bylaws or other written rules that each member agrees to follow. *See also* health alliance; health insurance purchasing cooperative; Health Security Act; health system; multihospital system.

registered hospital   A hospital recognized by the American Hospital Association as having the essential characteristics of a hospital.

registry   A database containing data pertinent to a specified topic, as in a tumor registry or a registry of clinical chemistry practitioners or emergency medical technicians. *See also* database; trauma registry; tumor registry.

regression In statistics, the relationship between the mean value of a random variable and the corresponding values of one or more independent variables. A common form of regression is a *linear regression* in which the model chosen for the analysis is a linear equation. *See also* dependent variable; independent variable; random variable; regression analysis; variable.

regression analysis A statistical procedure for determining the best approximation of the relationship between a dependent variable, such as the revenues of a health care organization, and one or more independent variables, such as gross national product or per capita income. By measuring exactly how large and significant each independent variable has historically been in its relation to the dependent variable, the future value of the dependent variable can be predicted. Regression analysis attempts to measure the degree of correlation between dependent and independent variables, thereby establishing the predictive value of the independent variable. The most common form of regression analysis is a linear regression model. Multiple regression analysis measures the effects of several factors concurrently. *See also* dependent variable; independent variable; regression; variable.

regularly maintained beds The total number of beds that a health care organization has regularly set up and staffed for use by patients. *See also* licensed beds.

regulation Rules or other directives issued by administrative agencies that are used to carry out a law. Many government agencies prepare regulations to administer a law. Regulatory programs can be described in terms of their purpose, who or what is regulated, who is the regulator, and method of regulation. *See also* Baby Doe regulations; medical marijuana law, regulations, and guidelines; safe harbor regulations.

regulatory body A government agency responsible for controlling and supervising a particular activity or area of public interest, as in regulatory affairs concerning health care products. *See also* administrative agency; Safe Medical Devices Act of 1990.

regulatory capture The ability of special interest groups within a regulated industry to influence, and sometimes dictate, the rules that industry will follow. *Synonym*: industry capture.

rehabilitation The combined and coordinated use of medical, social, educational, and vocational measures for training or retraining individuals disabled by disease or injury. The goal is enabling patients to achieve their highest possible level of functional ability. *See also* the following rehabilitation terms, as well as alcoholism rehabilitation center; cardiac rehabilitation program; habilitation; intense rehabilitation; physical medicine and rehabilitation; physical rehabilitation services; recovery; vocational rehabilitation.

Rehabilitation Act of 1973 [PL 93-112] Legislation prohibiting government agencies, certain entities contracting with the federal government, certain recipients of federal grants, and recipients of federal financial assis-

tance from discriminating against the handicapped. Section 504 of the act provides that "no otherwise qualified handicapped individual shall, solely by reason of his handicap, be excluded from the participation in, be denied the benefits of, or be subjected to discrimination under any program or activity receiving Federal Financial Assistance (FFA) including Medicare or Medicaid." Regulations implementing this legislation define "handicapped individual" very broadly (including individuals who regard themselves as being handicapped and alcoholics and drug addicts), prohibit discrimination in employment on the basis of handicap, require FFA recipients to make reasonable accommodations so that a qualified handicapped individual may be able to perform the essential elements of a job, require FFA recipients to make their services and programs accessible to the handicapped, require that all hospitals with emergency services establish procedures for effective communication with the hearing impaired, and prohibit discrimination in the treatment and admission of patients addicted to drugs and alcohol. *See also* Americans with Disabilities Act of 1990; handicap.

rehabilitation center A health care organization specializing in rehabilitation. *See also* alcoholism rehabilitation center; rehabilitation hospital.

rehabilitation hospital A hospital or facility that provides health-related, social, or vocational services to disabled persons to help them attain their maximum functional capacity. *Synonym*: rehabilitation facility. *See also* hospital; physical rehabilitation services; rehabilitation center; TEFRA.

rehabilitation medicine *See* physical medicine and rehabilitation.

reimbursement Compensation to another party for money spent or losses incurred, as in reimbursement made by an insurance company to a health care organization for services provided to patients covered by an insurance contract. *See also* cost-based reimbursement; prospective payment; retroactive reimbursement; retrospective reimbursement; Zero Balanced Reimbursement Account.

reinforcement Strengthening of a particular response or behavioral pattern by rewarding desirable behavior and punishing undesirable behavior. This is an important part of patient education and changing physician behavior. *See also* behavior management; psychology.

reinsurance Special insurance coverage obtained by a provider or health plan to protect against certain unanticipated and potentially crippling losses incurred on covered services for members. Such insurance may limit exposure on a per-case or an aggregate basis. In some cases, physicians can obtain reinsurance through the contracted health plan. *See also* insurance.

relative value scale (RVS) A numerical scale designed to permit comparisons of the resources needed for various procedures or units of service provided. *See also* conversion factor; resource-based relative value scale.

relaxation/mental imagery (RMI) *See* hypnotherapy.

release **1.** A mechanism by which an individual relinquishes a health care organization or other provider from responsibility or liability resulting from the patient's refusing treatment, cooperation, or compliance with a physician's orders. *See also* release of information. **2.** In law, a mechanism by which an individual relinquishes his or her right to maintain a claim or cause of action. *See also* cause of action.

release of information A consent form signed by a patient authorizing information to be given to a third party, such as an insurance company or lawyer. *See also* release.

reliability **1.** In performance measurement, consistency in results of a measure, including the tendency of the measure to produce the same results twice when it measures some entity or attribute believed not to have changed in the interval between measurements. *See also* data reliability; indicator reliability; interobserver reliability; intrarater reliability; reliability testing. **2.** In statistics, the degree to which scores are free from random error. *See also* random error.

reliability testing In performance measurement, quantification of the accuracy and completeness with which indicator occurrences are identified from among all cases at risk of being indicator occurrences; a component of an indicator-testing process. *See also* indicator; interobserver reliability; performance measurement; reliability; test reliability; test, retest reliability.

rem The standard unit of measurement of absorbed radiation in living tissue, usually expressed in *millirems*. There is considerable debate among scientists over the safety of repeated low doses of radiation.

remedial journey A sequence of problem-solving steps that move a quality-improvement team from the identified root cause of a problem to implementing a solution or remedy that will hold the gains the team has made. *See also* quality improvement; quality-improvement team.

reminder system A manual or computerized tool to send timely notices about specific clinical events to practitioners. Reminders, also called *feedback reports*, embrace a wide variety of techniques that vary in their intention and design as well as terminology. They have been broadly classified as concurrent reports, intervisit reminders, registry reminders, enhanced laboratory reports, and statistical summaries. *See also* implementation techniques.

reportable disease *See* notifiable disease.

reportable range The range of test values over which the relationship between the instrument, kit (packaged test), or system's measurement response is shown to be valid. *See also* calibration verification.

report card A performance statement about a health care professional and/or provider. A report card may be designed to provide internal quality-improvement information, present the benefits of a practitioner's or organization's services to an insurer or potential partner, or be released to the public. It may be issued by a health care organization, regulatory agency, managed care organization, accrediting body, or other entity to give information on outcomes, costs, charges, severity of illness of patients, intensity of services, staffing, medical staff composition, patient satisfaction, and so on. *See also* public data reporting.

reported but not incurred (RBNI) A procedure or service that is planned (and sometimes scheduled) under

CLINICAL REMINDER SYSTEM DESIGNS	
Reminder Type	**Targeted Failure Mode/Need**
Concurrent Report	Lack of knowledge of clinical guideline content or whether appropriate care has already been provided • Failure to recall agreed-upon clinical guideline • Physician or patient oversight • Inability to easily locate results of documented past care • Assurance for provider that patient has received appropriate care
Intervisit Reminder	Abnormal test result not acted upon appropriately by physician • Patient failure to follow up after notification • Physician or organizational failure to notify patient
Registry Reminder	Physician or patient oversight • Inability to easily locate results of documented past care • Routine monitoring not initiated by physician • Patient failure to follow up with recommendations for routine monitoring • Assurance for providers that patient has received appropriate care
Enhanced Lab Report	Lack of knowledge of clinical guideline content or essential information about the patient • Failure to recall agreed-upon clinical guideline • Inability to easily locate essential medical record information
Statistical Summaries	Performance monitoring and holding the gains • Reminder types can be designed to target physicians or patients

Source: Murrey KO, Gottlieb LK, Schoenbaum SC: Implementing clinical guidelines: A quality management approach to reminder systems. *QRB* 18(12): 423-33, 1992.

a managed care plan's benefit structure and has been reported to the plan, but which has not been provided to the patient.

reproductive endocrinology   A subspecialty of obstetrics and gynecology concerning management of complex problems relating to reproductive endocrinology and infertility. *See also* endocrinology; obstetrics and gynecology.

reproductive technologies   A variety of ways of achieving reproduction; for example, in-vitro fertilization, preembryo transfer, and surrogate motherhood. *See also* artificial insemination; parent.

required request law   A law that requires health care providers to develop programs for asking families of deceased patients to donate the organs of the deceased for transplantation. *Synonym:* routine inquiry law. *See also* Medic Alert Organ Donor Program; organ procurement; transplantation.

required services   Services that must be offered by a health program to meet some external standard. For example, under Title XIX of the Social Security Act, each state must offer certain basic health services before it can qualify as having a Medicaid program and thus be eligible for receiving federal matching funds. Examples of required services include hospital services, skilled nursing facility services for individuals aged 21 years and over, and home health care services for all persons eligible for skilled nursing facility services. *See also* Medicaid.

rescission   The cancellation of a contract and the return of parties to the positions they would have occupied if the contract had not been made. *See also* contract; mistake.

research and development (R&D)   Activities performed by a team of professionals working to transform a product idea into a technically sound product capable of being promoted. *See also* health services research; market research.

residency   A period of on-the-job training of variable length beginning after an individual graduates from a medical, dental, podiatric, or other professional school. The resident performs professional duties under supervision. Satisfactory completion of a residency is a requirement for credentialing in some professional fields and specialties. The first graduate year of training following completion of medical school and the awarding of the doctor of medicine (MD) degree is now generally called the PGY-1 (postgraduate year 1), although internship has been the more traditional term. Medical residencies for graduate physicians are approved by a formal review system. *See also* internship; Fellowship and Residency Electronic Interactive Data Access; graduate medical education.

resident   **1.** The recipient of care from a long term care provider. *Synonym:* long-term resident. *See also* patient; resident bill of rights.   **2.** A graduate of a medical, dental, podiatric, or other professional school receiving on-the-job training at a health care organization. *See also* fellow.

resident bed   A bed regularly maintained in a health care organization for use by persons who require custodial care and personal service but not nursing or medical services.

resident bill of rights   Federal protections for nursing home residents first provided for in OBRA '87 amendments. States are also required to have a Bill of Resident Rights which are least as protective as the federal statutes. Provisions outline the minimum standards of respect and caring, privacy, health, safety, patient autonomy, notice requirements, and fiduciary duties of facilities. Failure to comply with any federal provisions can result in a loss of Medicare or Medicaid certification for the facility. *See also* bill of patient rights; patient rights; right of privacy.

residential care   Care, including lodging and board, provided in a protective environment to patients, including the mentally retarded, those needing assisted living, the chemically dependent, the elderly, or the mentally ill, who are not in an acute phase of illness and would be capable of self-preservation during a disaster. There is minimum supervision and little or no formal program activity. Residential care can be provided within a residential facility; child-caring institutions and group homes, providing therapeutic care for emotionally handicapped children; halfway houses, providing therapeutic and supportive living arrangements to bridge the gap between residential treatment and community living; and extended care facilities, providing very long term care and treatment with 24-hour supervision and almost all services provided in the facility. This type of care does not include medical, nursing, or rehabilitative services. *Synonym:* board and lodging. *See also* assisted living; community residential facility; custodial care; domiciliary care; halfway house; residential care facility; residential program.

residential care facility   A live-in facility that provides custodial care to persons who, because of their physical, mental, or emotional condition, are not able to live independently. *Synonyms:* personal care institution; residential center; residential facility; residential treatment facility. *See also* assisted living; community residential facility; custodial care; home for the aged; nursing home; partial care program; residential care; residential program.

residential occupancy   An occupancy in which sleeping accommodations are provided for normal residential purposes and include all buildings designed to provide sleeping accommodations. *See also* occupancy.

residential program   A setting in which mental health services are provided to individuals who require an overnight but less structured environment than that of an inpatient program, but who also require more structure than that of either a partial care program or an outpatient program. *See also* residential care; residential care facility.

residential treatment facility   *See* residential care facility.

resource allocation   Societal or organizational decisions about the distribution of available health care resources involving, among other scarce resources, expensive life-saving technologies, location of physician's practices, and intensive care unit access. *See also* the following resource terms, as well as allocation; health planning; health resources; National Health Planning and Resources Development Act of 1974; Ryan White Comprehensive AIDS Resources Emergency Act of 1989.

resource-based relative value (RBRV)   The actual figure or value arrived at in relative, nonmonetary work units (relative value units) that can later be converted into dollar amounts as a means for determining reimbursement for provider services (such as physicians and hospitals). The formula for RBRV for a given service is: RBRV = $(TW) \times (1 + RPC) \times (1 + AST)$, in which TW represents total work input by the provider, RPC is an index of relative specialty practice cost, and AST is an index of amortized value for the opportunity cost of specialized training. Total work input is defined by four attributes: time, mental effort and judgment, technical skill and physical effort, and psychological stress. *See also* relative value scale; resource-based relative-value scale.

resource-based relative-value scale (RBRVS)   A method of reimbursement under Medicare that attempts to base physician reimbursement on the amount of resources, including cognitive and evaluative skills, required to diagnose and treat conditions. The approach weighs what resources, such as practice costs and the cost of specialty training, have gone into the "manufacture" of a service or procedure. Since the 1930s physicians have been paid according to the "customary, prevailing and reasonable" fee for a region of the country, and fee schedules reimbursed disproportionately for procedural services. *See also* relative value scale; resource-based relative value.

resource capacity   The number, type, and distribution of providers and facilities available for the delivery of health services for a defined population, such as people within a geographic or political area. *See also* health resources, resource allocation.

resource constraint   The maximum amount of resources available to produce a product or service.

Resource Utilization Groups (RUGs) II   A New York State case-mix payment system for long term care patients under Medicare and Medicaid. RUGs are tied to the Minimum Data Set for reimbursement of nursing facility Medicare in other states as well. *See also* Minimum Data Set.

respect and caring   A Joint Commission performance dimension addressing the degree to which those providing services do so with sensitivity for the patient's needs, expectations, and individual differences, and the degree to which a patient or a designee is involved in his or her own care decisions. *See also* dimensions of performance; patient participation.

respiratory care services   Delivery of care to provide ventilatory support and associated services for individuals. *See also* clinical respiratory services.

respiratory distress syndrome of the newborn (RDS)   An acute lung disease, especially of premature infants, characterized by inelastic lungs, difficult breathing (air hunger) with more than 60 respirations a minute and grunting on expiration, nasal flaring, cyanosis, and edema in the extremities. It is caused by a deficiency of pulmonary surfactant, which results in overdistended alveoli and, at times, formation of a hyaline membrane over the alveoli, increased pulmonary resistance, and decreased cardiac output. *Synonym*: hyaline membrane disease. *See also* adult respiratory distress syndrome.

respiratory isolation   A category of patient isolation intended to prevent transmission of infectious diseases over short distances through the air. A private room is indicated, but patients infected with the same organism may share a room. Masks are mandatory for those who come in close contact with the patient; gowns and gloves are not. *See also* infectious diseases; isolation.

respiratory function tests   *See* pulmonary function tests.

respiratory therapy (RT)   The health care field dealing with treatment of diseases or disability due to respiratory illness or injury. *See also* inhalation therapy.

respite care   Short-term care to individuals in the home or an institution to provide temporary relief to the family home caregiver. This care may be provided during the day or overnight.

response rate   In survey research, the percentage of persons given questionnaires who complete and return them. *See also* market research.

responsible party   **1.** An individual or organization responsible for placing a patient in a health care facility and ensuring that adequate care is provided; for example, a parent is usually the responsible party for a child.   **2.** The party responsible for payment of services.

restenosis   The reformation of a stenosis (narrowing) in a coronary artery following therapy, such as in a coronary artery after angioplasty.

rest home   A facility providing custodial care and, sometimes, limited nursing care, as by a visiting nurse. *See also* custodial care.

restraint   **1.** Use of a physical, chemical, or mechanical device to involuntarily restrain the movement of the whole or a portion of a patient's body as a means of controlling his or her physical activities to protect him or her or other persons from injury. Restraint differs from mechanisms usually and customarily used during medical, diagnostic, or surgical procedures that are considered a regular part of such procedures. These mechanisms include body restraint during surgery, arm restraint during intravenous administration, and temporary physical restraint before administration of electroconvulsive therapy. Devices used to protect the patient, such as bed rails, tabletop chairs, protective nets, helmets, or the temporary use of halter-type or soft-chest restraints, and mechanisms, such as orthopedic appliances, braces, wheelchairs, or other appliances or devices used to posturally support the patient or assist him or her in obtaining and maintaining normative bodily functions, are not considered restraint interventions. *See also* seclusion. **2.** For long term care organizations, any method (chemical or physical) of restricting a resident's freedom of movement, including seclusion, physical activity, or normal access to his or her body that (1) is not a usual and customary part of a medical diagnostic or treatment procedure to which the resident or his or her legal representative has consented; (2) is not indicated to treat the resident's medical condition or symptoms; or (3) does not promote the resident's independent functioning. *See also* seclusion.

restructuring   Reorganization of an organization to better deal with new functions, enterprises, and demands. *See also* diversification.

retention   *See* risk charge.

retinopathy   *See* diabetic retinopathy.

Retired Senior Volunteer Program (RSVP)   A federally funded program through which retired citizens volunteer to help other, less mobile elderly people, providing various kinds of general assistance with nonmedical daily needs.

retirement center   A facility or organized program that provides social services and activities to retired persons who generally do not require ongoing health care. *See also* adult day care.

retroactive reimbursement   Additional payment by a third-party payer to an institution for services not identified at the time of initial reimbursement. *See also* reimbursement; retrospective reimbursement.

retrospective reimbursement   A method of third-party payment in which costs incurred by a provider in providing services to covered patients are based on actual costs determined after the services have been provided, usually at the end of a fiscal period. This contrasts with prospective payment, in which rates of payments to providers for patient services are established in advance for the coming fiscal year, and providers are paid these rates for services delivered regardless of the costs actually incurred in providing these services. *See also* interim rate; prospective payment; prospective payment system; reimbursement; retroactive reimbursement; TEFRA.

retrospective review   **1.** A method of determining medical necessity and/or appropriate billing practice for services that have already been rendered. prospective review. *See also* audit; peer review; prospective payment; prospective review; retrospective study.   **2.** In behavioral health, evaluative activities conducted when an individual being served is no longer in active treatment.

retrospective study   An inquiry planned to observe and collect data for events that have already occurred, as compared with a prospective study, which is planned to observe events that have not yet occurred. A case-control study is usually retrospective. *See also* case-control study; cohort study; retrospective review.

retrovirus   A ribonucleic (RNA) virus characterized by the presence of an enzyme, reverse transcriptase, which enables transcription of RNA to deoxyribonucleic acid (DNA) inside an affected cell and replication within the cell. A well-known retrovirus is HIV, which makes copies of itself in host cells, such as T4 helper lymphocytes, leading to a disruption of normal immune responses. *See also* DNA; HIV; RNA.

reusable medical device reprocessing   Designing, cleaning, disinfecting, sterilizing, testing, and labeling activities to maintain safety of reprocessed devices and prevent outbreaks of device- associated nosocomial infections in hemodialysis centers and other facilities. *See also* medical device.

revascularization   Restoration, to the extent possible, of normal blood flow to the myocardium by surgical or percutaneous means or with removal or reduction of an obstruction as occurs when a coronary artery bypass graft surgery or a percutaneous transluminal coronary angioplasty is performed.

review criteria   *See* medical review criteria.

Revised Trauma Score (RTS)   Revision in 1989 of former (1981) trauma score including addition of Glasgow Coma Scale, systolic blood pressure, and respiratory rate and excluding capillary refill and respiratory expansion. *See also* Abbreviated Injury Scale; Glasgow Coma Scale; Injury Severity Score; trauma severity indices; Trauma Score.

rework   The act of performing a task two or more times because it was not performed correctly the first time. Continuous quality improvement identifies the many reasons rework occurs, including insufficient planning, failure of a customer to specify the needed input, and failure of a supplier to provide a consistently high-quality output.

rheumatology   The branch of medicine and subspecialty of internal medicine and pediatrics dealing with the management of diseases of joints, muscle, bones, and tendons. *See also* internal medicine.

Rh (rhesus) factor   Any of several substances on the surface of red blood cells that induce a strong response in individuals lacking the substance. Approximately 85% of people have Rh factor. It is called Rh factor because it was first identified in the blood of rhesus monkeys. *See also* blood groups.

rhinology   The branch of medicine dealing with the anatomy, physiology, and pathology of the nose. *See also* otolaryngology.

ribonucleic acid   *See* RNA.

right of privacy   The constitutional right of privacy to prohibit unwanted invasion, especially of one's own body. This right is the basis for informed consent and restriction of governmental intrusion in areas such as birth control, sterilization, abortion, and the right to refuse medical treatment. *See also* confidentiality; informed consent; patient rights; Privacy Act of 1974; resident bill of rights.

right to die   The legal right to refuse life-saving or life-sustaining (or death-prolonging) procedures. A competent adult has the legal right to refuse medical treatment, even if that treatment is essential to sustaining life. The question of a patient's right to die arises when a person has a condition that makes his or her quality of life so intolerable that he or she believes that death is preferable. Serious legal and ethical issues arise when the patient is unconscious or incompetent and the decision to withdraw or refuse treatment must be made for him or her by someone else. *See also* Cruzan case; persistent vegetative state.

right to life   Belief that life begins at conception and ends at natural death. Supporters oppose abortion, infanticide, and euthanasia. *See also* abortion, euthanasia; pro choice; *Roe* v *Wade*.

right to refuse treatment   *See* autonomy.

risk   **1.** Any measurable or predictable chance of loss, injury, disadvantage, hazard, danger, peril, or destruction. Risk to a health care organization may arise, for example, through general or professional liability or physical property damage. Insurance is purchased to cover such exigencies.   **2.** The chance of occurrence of disease, injury, or death among various groups of individuals and from different causes. An applicant for a health insurance policy whose physical condition fails to meet health status standards is referred to as an *impaired risk. See also* the following risk terms, as well as AIDS risk groups; assumption of risk; at risk; captive insurance company; dietary risk factors; full-risk capitation; genetic risk assessment; hazard; health risk appraisal; operative risk; underwriting.

risk-adjusted mortality index (RAMI)   A model for measuring the risk of death during a hospital stay for specific diagnoses and procedures. The following variables are used: the patient's age, race, sex, and DRG cluster; the presence or absence of comorbidities; the presence of any secondary diagnosis of cancer (other than skin cancer); and total number of morbidities. *See also* mortality rate.

risk adjustment   A statistical process for reducing, removing, or clarifying the influences of confounding factors that differ among comparison groups (eg, logistic regression, stratification). For example, patients with emphysema who undergo surgery requiring general anesthesia will usually have a higher risk of morbidity and mortality than a patient with normal lung function receiving the identical intervention. Risk adjustment is important so that performance and quality can be compared meaningfully across organizations, practitioners, and communities. *See also* adjustment; risk-adjustment model; severity adjustment; severity of illness.

risk-adjustment model   The statistical algorithm that specifies the numerical values and the sequence of calculations used to risk-adjust (such as reduce or remove the influence of confounding factors) performance measures. *See also* risk adjustment.

risk analysis   In health insurance, the process of evaluating the expected health care costs for a prospective group and determining what product, benefit level, and price to offer to best meet the needs of the group and carrier. *See also* carrier.

risk assessment   The qualitative or quantitative estimation of the likelihood of (adverse) effects that may result from exposure to specified events or processes or from the absence of beneficial influences. *See also* genetic risk assessment; health risk appraisal.

risk-benefit analysis   The process of analyzing and comparing on a single scale the benefits and risks of an action or failure to act.

risk charge   In insurance, the fraction of a premium that goes to generate or replenish surpluses that a carrier must develop to protect against the possibility of excessive losses under its policies. Profits, if any, on the sale of insurance are also taken from the surpluses developed using risk charges. *Synonyms:* retention; retention rate. *See also* carrier; premium.

risk contract   A legal agreement between a provider and payer that exposes the provider to uncertainty of financial loss or expense. The provider agrees to provide health care services to a population without knowing the extent or cost of the services. *See also* contract.

risk-factor modification   An approach to prevention that attempts to prioritize among strategies to reduce risk of contracting a particular disease, such as coronary artery disease. One model, developed at the American College of Cardiology 27th Bethesda Conference, identified four questions to be asked in determining the most cost-effective interventions: (1) What is the expected impact of an intervention on mortality and quality of life? (2) How high are the costs of the strategy compared with alternatives, and will these costs be offset by economic savings due to delays or prevention of adverse outcomes? (3) What is the time frame in which the costs and benefits are expected to occur? and (4) How likely is your patient to adhere to the recommended therapy? *Synonym:* lifestyle modification. *See also* health risk appraisal; high-risk group; lifestyle.

risk management   Clinical and administrative activities undertaken to identify, evaluate, and reduce the risk of injury to patients, staff, and visitors and the risk of loss to the organization itself. Three components of many risk-management programs include *risk financing,* determining the types of potential exposures to the institution and then ensuring that adequate insurance coverage is available in the event that a loss occurs; *claims management,* involving the investigation and payment of claims in such a manner as to minimize the organization's financial loss; and *loss prevention*, creating systems to identify, evaluate, and minimize or prevent potential areas of risk. *See also* incident reporting.

CARDIOVASCULAR RISK FACTORS

Category I (risk factors for which interventions have been proved to lower CVD risk)
Cigarette smoking
LDL cholesterol
High fat/cholesterol diet
Hypertension
Left ventricular hypertrophy
Thrombogenic factors (fibrinogen, aspirin, warfarin)

Category II (risk factors for which interventions are likely to lower CVD risk)
Diabetes mellitus
Physical inactivity
HDL cholesterol
Triglycerides; small, dense LDL
Obesity
Postmenopausal status (women)

Category III (risk factors associated with increased CVD risk that, if modified, might lower risk)
Psychosocial factors
Lipoprotein(a)
Homocysteine
Oxidative stress
No alcohol consumption

Category IV (risk factors associated with increased CVD risk, but which cannot be modified)
Age
Male gender
Low socioeconomic status
Family history of early-onset CVD

Key: CVD = cardiovascular disease; HDL = high-density lipoprotein; LDL = low-density lipoprotein.

Source: Adapted from summary table in American College of Cardiology (Fuster V, Pearson TA): 27th Bethesda Conference: Matching the intensity of risk factor management with the hazard for coronary disease events. *J Am Coll Cardiol* 27(5):957-1047, 1996.

---

risk-management contract   A contract between a group purchaser and an insurer, service plan, medical foundation, or other third party in which the third-party organization agrees to administer, but not underwrite, the group's health care coverage plan. The third-party organization receives an administrative fee for its services, but the payment of benefits comes from funds provided by the group. The group purchaser self-insures its employees or group members. *See also* contract.

risk pool   A financial agreement that spreads the risk of utilization and cost among the participants—generally an HMO, a hospital, and individual providers. The pool may insure against unusually high utilization and costs and may provide incentives for controlling utilization. The most common types of pools are (1) *surplus-sharing pools*, which provide incentives to participants by sharing savings when actual expenses are below budgeted expectations; (2) *loss-sharing pools*, which penalize overutilization by sharing losses when actual expenses exceed budgeted

expenses; and (3) *combined risk-sharing pools*, which provide incentives and penalties by sharing both savings and losses. *See also* high-risk pool; risk sharing.

risk sharing   The distribution of financial risk among parties furnishing a service. For example, if a health care organization and a corporate group of physicians provide health care at a fixed price, a risk-sharing arrangement would entail both the organization and the group being held liable if expenses exceed revenues. *See also* risk pool.

RNA (ribonucleic acid)   A nucleic acid that in most cells transmits genetic information from the DNA in the nucleus to the cytoplasm and functions in the synthesis of proteins. It is the genetic material of some viruses. *See also* DNA; molecular genetics; retrovirus.

Robinson-Patman Act   *See* antitrust laws.

Robinson v Magovern   [521 F.Supp. 842 (W.D.Pa. 1981), *aff'd*, 688 F.2d 824 (3d Cir. 1982), *cert. denied*, 459 U.S. 971 (1982)] An important district court case in which a physician was denied surgical privileges at a hospital that did not need additional thoracic surgeons. Dr. Robinson alleged that the hospital had violated Sections 1 and 2 of the Sherman Act because its denial was not based on competence, credentials, or character. The court upheld the hospital's decision, which was judged reasonable given the organization's goals and market position and which did not inhibit Dr. Robinson (who had privileges at other hospitals) from practicing his profession.

roentgen (R)   A unit of radiation exposure equal to the quantity of ionizing radiation that will produce one electrostatic unit of electricity in 1 cm^3 of dry air at 0°C (32% F) and standard atmospheric pressure. *See also* radiography.

roentgenology   Radiology using x-rays. *See also* radiography; radiology; x-ray.

roentgenotherapy   The treatment of disease with x-rays. *See also* radiography; x-ray therapy.

roentgen ray   Obsolete term for x-ray. *See* x-ray.

Roe v Wade   [410 U.S. 113 (1973), reh'g denied, 410 U.S. 959 (1973)] The landmark U.S. Supreme Court case that legalized abortion by striking down restrictive state abortion laws as unconstitutional, ruling that those laws violated a woman's right of privacy to make her own decisions concerning her body. The Court held that the state could regulate abortions only where necessary to serve a compelling state interest, defined as protection of the life and health of pregnant women and protecting the "potentiality of human life." The decision did not address, nor did it decide, the question of when life began or when the fetus became a "person." *See also* abortion; pro choice; right to life.

role playing   A continuous quality improvement technique designed to reduce the conflict inherent in various social situations, in which participants act out particular behavioral roles to better understand a situation by experiencing a realistic simulation. It is useful in therapeutics (psychology) and as a training exercise. *See also* psychology.

rooming-in   A method of organizing obstetric services in which mothers share accommodations with and assume the care of newborn infants with help as needed from nursing personnel. *See also* obstetrics and gynecology.

root cause   The original cause for the failure or inefficiency of a process. *See also* common-cause variation; direct cause; immediate cause; proximate cause; root cause analysis; sentinel event; special-cause variation.

root cause analysis   A process for identifying the basic or causal factor(s) that underlie variation in performance, including the occurrence or possible occurrence of a sentinel event. *See also* direct cause; immediate cause; proximate cause; root cause.

Rorschach test   A psychodiagnostic projective technique using a patient's associations from "inkblot" patterns to discover personality conflicts, ego function and structure, thought processes, and affective (emotional) integration. The test, which was designed by the Swiss psychiatrist Hermann Rorschach (1884-1922) and is still used by some psychologists for children (aged three years or older) and adults, involves presenting a series of ten cards with symmetrical patterns to the patient, who describes what he or she sees in each pattern. *Synonym:* inkblot test. *See also* projective technique; thematic apperception test.

rotor-wing   *See* ambulance.

rounds   Visits by a physician or other health professional, or a group of health professionals, to the bedsides of patients in a health care organization. The purpose of rounds is to evaluate treatment, analyze and document progress, and determine whether current care should be continued or changed. *See also* grand rounds; morbidity and mortality conference; teaching rounds.

routine inquiry law   *See* required request law.

routine services   **1.** Services that do not require specialized equipment, knowledge, or human resources, and which are inpatient services provided to most patients. **2.** Outpatient services that are usually included in an office visit or limited examination.

run chart   A display of data in which data points are plotted as they occur over time (eg, observed weights plotted over time) to detect trends or other patterns and variations occurring over time. Run charts, as opposed to tabular frequency displays, are capable of time-ordering analytic studies. *Synonym:* time plot.

Ryan White Comprehensive AIDS Resources Emergency (CARE) Act of 1990   Designed to provide services for persons infected with HIV, this act seeks "to improve the quality and availability of care for individuals and families with HIV disease." Named after an Indiana teen who died of AIDS, it directs financial assistance to metropolitan areas with the largest numbers of reported cases of AIDS for emergency services and to all states for improved care and support services and early intervention services. *See also* AIDS; resource allocation.

Ss

safe harbor regulations Regulations that describe certain acts or behaviors that are legal under a specific law, even though they might be illegal otherwise. This term has been applied to certain joint ventures and other arrangements between health care organizations and physicians or among physicians, meaning that these activities would not violate Medicare fraud and abuse laws. Such regulations can be found in the *Code of Federal Regulations* § 1001.952. *See also* antikickback laws; fraud and abuse; joint venture; Medicare; regulation.

Safe Medical Devices Act of 1990 A federal law with subsequent FDA amendments that imposes reporting requirements on the users and manufacturers of medical devices. The FDA requires medical device manufacturers, distributors, and device-user facilities (such as health care organizations) to investigate, document, and report deaths, serious illnesses, and serious injuries that have been or may have been caused by medical devices. The FDA also has the power to require facilities to track certain devices from receipt, through patient use, to disposal. Lack of compliance may carry civil and criminal penalties, affect liability and risk management, and influence accreditation. *See also* device; medical device; medical device regulatory classes.

safer sex Sexual activity conducted in such a way that transmission of a sexually transmitted disease is minimized by reducing the exchange of body fluids (eg, consistent use of condoms, avoiding unprotected anal intercourse). *See also* HIV transmission; safe sex; sexually transmitted disease.

safe sex Sexual activity conducted in such a way that there is no risk of transmission or acquisition of a sexually transmitted disease. Use of this term has been replaced by *safer sex*, as no method other than abstinence can be considered completely safe. *See also* HIV transmission; safer sex; sexually transmitted disease.

safety A Joint Commission performance dimension addressing the degree to which the risk of an intervention (use of a drug or a procedure) and risk in the care environment are reduced for a patient and other persons, including health care practitioners. *See also* dimensions of performance.

safety management A component of an organization's management of the environment of care program that maintains and improves the general safety of the care environment. *See also* environment of care; emergency-preparedness plan; hazardous materials; hazardous waste; management.

same-day surgery *See* ambulatory surgery.

sample In statistics, a sample is a selected subject of a population used to estimate the characteristics of the parent population or universe. *See also* consecutive sample; convenience sample; sampling; sequential sampling.

sampling A basic statistical technique or process consisting of drawing a limited number of measurements from a larger source (population) and then analyzing those measurements to estimate characteristics of the population from which the measurements have been drawn. *See also* nonprobability sampling; random sampling; sample; sampling error; simple random sampling; stratified random sampling; systematic sampling.

sampling error The unavoidable potential for error whenever a random sample is used rather than a whole population, due to the smaller size of the sample. *See also* measurement error; sampling.

sanitation Formulation and application of measures designed to protect public health, particularly with respect to the provision of toilet facilities, drainage, sewage disposal. *See also* public health.

satellite hospital Part of a hospital that is geographically separated from the hospital and that offers limited services to persons in its geographical area.

satellite pharmacy *See* decentralized pharmaceutical services.

saturation For insurance or HMOs, the point at which further penetration of a market is improbable or too costly.

scarcity area An area lacking an adequate supply of a particular type of health professional(s) or health service(s). *See also* medically underserved area.

scatter diagram A graphic representation of data depicting the possible relationship between two variables. A scatter diagram displays what happens to one variable when another variable changes to test a theory that the two variables are related. A scatter diagram cannot prove that one variable causes the other, but it does clarify whether a relationship exists and the strength of that relationship (positive, negative, zero). *Synonyms:* scattergram; scatterplot. *See also* confounding variable.

scenario building A method of predicting the future that relies on a series of assumptions about alternative possibilities, rather than on simple extrapolation of existing trends, as in forecasting. *See also* forecasting.

schedule of controlled substances A classification of five schedules of drugs based on their potential for abuse; established by the Controlled Substances Act of 1970 for the purpose of controlling the possession and use of certain drugs. *See also* controlled substances; drug abuse; medical marijuana; narcotic; stimulant.

schematic box plot A graphic display of the important characteristics of a set of observations. The median and quantiles have the same definitions as in a basic box plot. The lines, however, are drawn to the adjacent values.

SCHEDULES OF CONTROLLED SUBSTANCES

Substances	Description
Schedule I	Substances that have no accepted medical use and a high abuse potential. *Examples:* dihydromorphine, heroin, LSD, marijuana, mescaline, nicocodeine, nicomorphine, peyote, psilocybin.
Schedule II	Substances that have a high abuse potential with severe psychic or physical dependence liability, but have a legitimate medical use. They include certain depressants, narcotics, and stimulants. *Examples (narcotics):* anileridine, cocaine, codeine, diphenoxylate, hydromorphine, meperidine, methadone, morphine, pantopon, opium, oxycodone, oxymorphone. *Examples (nonnarcotics):* amobarbital, amphetamine, etorphine hydrochloride, glutethimide, methamphetamine, methylphenidate, pentobarbital, phencyclidine, phenmetrazine, secobarbital.
Schedule III	Substances that have less abuse potential than Schedule II substances and moderate dependence liability. They include compounds containing limited quantities of certain narcotic and nonnarcotic drugs, except those that are listed in another schedule. *Examples:* anabolic steroids, benzphetamine, chlorhexadol, chlorphentermine, clortermine, mazindol, mehyprylon, nolorphine, paregoric, phendimetrazine.
Schedule IV	Substances that have less abuse potential than Schedule III substances and limited dependence liability. *Examples:* barbital, chloral betaine, chloral hydrate, chlorodiazepoxide, clonazepam, clorazepate, dextrpropoxyphene, diazepam, diethypropion, ethchlorvynol, ethinamate, fenfluramine, flurazepam, lorazepam, mebutamate, meprobamate, methylphenobarbital, methohexital, oxazepam, paraldehyde, phenobarbital, phentermine, prazepam.
Schedule V	Substances that have limited abuse potential. This group contains preparations that have limited quantities of certain narcotic drugs, generally for antitussive and antidiarrheal purposes. *Examples:* over-the-counter cough syrups containing codeine.

Asterisks indicate outlier points lying beyond the adjacent values. *See also* box plot.

schizoid personality disorder *See* personality disorder.

schizophrenia A chronic psychotic disorder characterized, according to DSM-IV, by two or more of the following, each present for a significant portion of time during a one-month period (or less if successfully treated): delusions, hallucinations, disorganized speech (eg, frequent derailment, incoherence), grossly disorganized or catatonic behavior, and other negative symptoms (ie, affective flattening, alogia, or avolition; social or occupational dysfunction; continuous signs of the disturbance for at least six months, with an exclusion of schizoaffective and mood disorder). *See also* paranoid disorder; personality disorder.

school rule A legal doctrine stating that the standard of care in a malpractice suit will be measured by the degree of care exercised by professionals with the same specialty or school of medicine as that of the practitioner being sued.

sciatica Pain along the pathway of the sciatic nerve, radiating from the buttock down the back and outside of the thigh and lower leg. According to an AHCPR-sponsored clinical practice guideline on acute low back problems (1994), sciatica is usually related to mechanical pressure and/or inflammation of lumbosacral nerve roots. Although sciatica may suggest nerve root compromise, *limited sciatica* (during first month of appearance and not disabling) does not warrant use of special imaging tests or referral for surgery. *See also* low back pain; spinal manipulation.

scientific method The principles and empirical processes of discovery and demonstration considered characteristic of, or necessary for, scientific investigation, generally involving the observation of phenomena, the formulation of a hypothesis concerning the phenomena, experimentation to demonstrate the truth or falseness of the hypothesis, and a conclusion that validates or modifies the hypothesis. *See also* experimental method; method.

scientific parsimony *See* Ockham's razor.

scope of care or services The activities performed by governance, managerial, clinical, and support personnel. *See also* patient mix.

scope of employment Acts performed while doing one's job duties. The courts adopted the phrase to determine an employer's liability for employees' acts. The employer is said to be vicariously liable only for those torts of the employee committed within the range of his or her job duties.

scorer reliability *See* interobserver reliability.

screening 1. Use of a preliminary test, procedure, or questionnaire to detect the presence of disease. **2.** Examination of a large sample of the population to check for presence of a particular disease. A screening test is not intended to be diagnostic. Individuals, groups, organizations, or events identified by a screening process must be further assessed to establish a diagnosis. *Synonym:* mass screening. *See also* alcohol-problem screening; audiometric screening; cancer screening tests and procedures; case finding; cholesterol screening; drug screening; Early and Periodic Screening Diagnosis and Treatment Program; HCFA generic quality screens; genetic screening; laboratory screening tests; nutrition screening; occurrence screening; preadmission screening; predictive value of a screening test; screening panel; sensitivity; specificity; speech screening.

screening panel   In malpractice, a fact-finding body used in the early stages of a malpractice dispute. A defense panel seeks to develop the best possible defense for a health care professional accused of malpractice. An exploratory panel examines the facts for both the accused professional and the plaintiff and makes its determination on the merits of the case. *See also* screening.

seclusion   The involuntary confinement of a patient alone in a room, which the patient is physically prevented from leaving, for any period of time. Seclusion does not include involuntary confinement for legally mandated but nonclinical purposes, such as confining a person facing serious criminal charges, or serving a criminal sentence, to a locked room. *See also* involuntary seclusion; quiet room; restraint.

secondary care   Services provided by medical specialists (eg, general surgeon, dermatologist) who generally do not have first contact with patients. In the United States, however, patients often self-refer to specialists providing secondary care or even tertiary care, rather than being referred by a primary care provider. *Synonym:* specialized care. *See also* levels of care; referred care; tertiary care.

secondary contact   A person in contact with a primary contact. A primary contact is a person in direct contact with a communicable disease case. *See also* contact isolation; primary contact.

secondary negligence   *See* vicarious liability.

secondary payer   *See* Medicare secondary payer.

second-generation recommendation   *See* type I recommendation.

secondhand smoke   Smoke inhaled by nonsmokers through exposure to the smoke from cigarettes smoked by other people. Harmful effects include reduced exercise capability, acceleration of atherosclerotic lesions, and increased tissue damage following ischemia or myocardial infarction. OSHA includes the effects of secondhand smoke (which it terms *environmental tobacco smoke*) in its risk assessment as part of a proposed rule that workplaces be essentially smoke free. *Synonyms:* environmental tobacco smoke (ETS); involuntary smoking; passive smoking; sidestream smoke.

second-impact syndrome   Repeated mild brain injuries occurring within a short period (hours, days, or weeks) of an initial brain injury such as a sports-related concussion which can be catastrophic or fatal. The repeated injury, however mild, can cause irreversible brain swelling as a result of failure of an autoregulation of cerebral circulation that has not fully recovered from the initial injury. *Synonyms:* recurrent brain injury; recurrent traumatic brain injury. *See also* syndrome.

second-line drug   A generic term for any medication that is not the drug of choice or the first one used to treat a condition.

second-look surgery   A second surgical procedure at the same site as the first, usually performed in the abdom-inal area for patients with cancer (particularly ovarian cancer), to check the success of the first operation and the accuracy of initial staging, to identify any spread of cancer cells, and to plan the next stage of therapy.

second opinion   A consultation involving a health care provider's examination of a patient and subsequent opinion as to the need for surgery or other treatment already recommended by another provider. *See also* peer review; second-opinion program.

second-opinion program   A cost-containment and quality-control method in which health insurers, prepayment organizations, or practitioners advise or require a patient to obtain a second opinion from another qualified provider before deciding to undergo a procedure or treatment. *See also* second opinion.

security hospital   A hospital controlled by, physically located within, or attached to, and providing services to, inmates of a penal institution. *Synonym:* prison hospital. *See also* maximum security unit.

sedation   *See* anesthesia; conscious sedation.

selection bias   Apparent treatment effects due to comparing groups that differed even before the treatment was administered. *See also* bias.

selective referral   The referral or attraction of patients to physicians and health care organizations with better outcomes. *See also* referral.

selective serotonin reuptake inhibitor (SSRI)   A class of antidepressants that have increasingly been given preference over traditional antidepressants, particularly for special populations such as the elderly, because of their proven efficacy, safety, and tolerability. SSRIs have also been used to treat panic disorder, obsessive-compulsive behavior, alcoholism, obesity, and bulimia (eating disorder). *See also* antidepressant drug; Prozac.

self-care   The performance of activities or tasks traditionally performed by professional health care providers. The concept includes care of oneself or one's family and friends. *See also* levels of care; nursing care; progressive patient care.

self determination   *See* Patient Self Determination Act.

self-directed team   An integrated and interdependent small group that performs a common set of tasks within a larger organization, for example, a performance-improvement team. *See also* distributed leadership; team.

self-efficacy   A component of health belief models and a key concept in patient education and the patient-provider partnership, reflecting the patient's confidence in being able to exercise control over or have an impact on his or her health or a disease condition. *See also* health belief model; patient-provider relationship.

self-governance   A medical staff's duties, delegated by the governing body, to evaluate care or control physician practices. In an organization with a self-governing medical staff, the governing body is still ultimately responsible for the care provided. *See also* medical staff.

self-hypnosis *See* hypnotherapy.

self-insurance Payment of employees' health care expenses through a special fund established by an employer rather than by arranging for an insurer to provide such coverage. The employer directly assumes the insurer's normal functions, responsibilities, and liabilities, although the employer may arrange for any entity (insurer) to handle the administrative tasks associated with running the plan. *See also* Employee Retirement Income Security Act; insurance.

self-insured hospital A hospital that assumes the risk of loss without an insurance policy.

self-limited Pertaining to a disease or condition that tends to end or resolve without treatment.

self-measured blood pressure monitoring device A commercially available apparatus, using mercury, aneroid, or electronic systems, which allows patients to measure their own blood pressure. Many of the devices provide unsatisfactory accuracy under controlled and field conditions, and their appropriate use has also been challenged. Patients vary widely in their ability to use the devices correctly, and many may need additional training beyond the manufacturer's instructions. The devices have been offered as a way to eliminate "white coat" or "office" hypertension. *See also* automated ambulatory blood pressure monitoring devices; blood pressure; hypertension; monitor; white coat hypertension.

self-medication The self-administration of medication not prescribed by a physician or in a manner not directed by a physician.

self-pay patient A patient who pays out of personal resources for either all or part of his or her hospital and other health care provider bills, without the assistance of insurance or other third-party benefits. *Synonym:* self-responsible patient. *See also* patient; uncompensated care; underinsured.

Senior Plan Network (SPN) An alliance of HMOs offering enrollment in the network and thus its participating HMOs. Medicare prepays part or all of the cost of enrollment in an SPN.

sensitivity **1.** A measure of the ability of a diagnostic test, screening test, or other predictor to correctly identify the individuals or cases actually having (are positive for) the condition or occurrence for which the test is being conducted. Operationally, sensitivity is the number of true positive test results divided by the sum of true positives plus false negatives. *Synonym:* true positive rate. *See also* analytical sensitivity; Bayesian analysis; false negative; false positive; predictive value of a screening test; screening; specificity; true negative; true positive. **2.** The capacity to respond to stimulation. *See also* allergen skin tests; allergy; provocation testing. **3.** Awareness of the needs and emotions of others. *See also* sensitivity training.

sensitivity training Training in small groups in which people learn how to interact with each other by developing a sensitive awareness and understanding of themselves and of their relationships with other people. *See also* sensitivity.

sentinel event An unexpected occurrence or variation involving death or serious physical or psychological injury, or the risk thereof. Serious injury specifically includes loss of limb or function. The event is called "sentinel" because it sends a signal or sounds a warning that requires immediate attention. *See also* Accreditation Watch; chart review; medication error; root cause analysis; sentinel event indicator.

sentinel event indicator A performance measure that identifies an individual event or phenomenon that always triggers further analysis and investigation. *See also* aggregate data indicator; indicator; sentinel event.

sepsis The presence of various pus-forming and other pathogenic organisms or their toxins in the blood or tissues. Clinical signs of blood-borne sepsis include fever, tachycardia, hypotension, leukocytosis, and a deterioration in mental status. The same organism is often isolated in both the blood and a pressure ulcer. A 1991 consensus conference, convened to define multiple organ failure syndrome and related concepts, defined sepsis as a type of systemic inflammatory response syndrome caused by infection. It subdivided sepsis into *severe sepsis, sepsis with hypotension,* and *septic shock* on the basis of organ function, lactic acidosis, oliguria, or mental status changes and whether blood pressure is transiently below 90 mm Hg or persistently low despite fluid administration. *See also* antisepsis; multiple organ dysfunction syndrome.

Sequential Multiple Analyzer (SMA) A multiple chemistry panel, typically including more than 20 tests, which can potentially detect hundreds of medical problems but which also has unacceptably high false-positive rates. *See also* false positive.

sequential sample *See* consecutive sample.

seroreverter Describes a person whose antibody status has changed from positive to negative. The term is used to describe perinatally HIV-exposed infants who are not truly infected and become HIV antibody negative as they lose maternal HIV antibody. *See also* HIV; HIV antibody.

serology The science dealing with the properties and reactions of serums, especially blood serum. Blood serum contains antibodies, which represent the body's response to exposure to certain disease-causing agents. Detection of the presence of disease-specific antibodies with various serologic tests is helpful in making diagnoses.

service area *See* catchment area.

service-connected disability In the Department of Veterans Affairs health system, a disability incurred or aggravated in the line of duty in active military service.

See also disability; non-service-connected disability; post-traumatic stress syndrome.

service patient   *See* ward patient.

services   **1.** Structural divisions of an organization, its medical staff, or its licensed independent practitioner staff.   **2.** The delivery of health care. *See also* catchment area; occasion of service.

service shedding   An approach to privatization of health care organizations in which a given function (such as governance) is transferred completely from the public organization to a private provider.

set point   A target value of a controlled variable that is maintained by an automatic control system.

settlement   A compromise or agreement achieved by the adverse parties in a civil suit before final judgment, whereby they agree between themselves on their respective rights and obligations, thus eliminating the necessity of judicial resolution of the controversy. *See also* negotiated settlement; structured settlement.

severability clause   A legal understanding in the Missouri Living Will in which, if other specific directions are added to the sample declaration and are found to be invalid, the validity of the remainder of the declaration would not be affected. *See also* living will; Uniform Rights of the Terminally Ill Act.

severity   The degree of biomedical risk, morbidity, or mortality of medical treatment. *See also* the following severity terms, as well as acuity; burn severity; trauma severity indices.

severity adjustment   The process of classifying patients by severity-of-illness data so that performance and quality across organizations and practitioners can be more meaningfully compared. Examples of systems that classify patients in this manner include Medical Illness Severity Grouping System (MedisGroups) and APACHE. *See also* adjustment; APACHE system; clinical data-based severity adjustment methods; Medical Illness Severity Grouping System; risk adjustment; severity of illness.

severity index   *See* trauma severity indices.

severity measurement system   A method for measuring severity of illness using objective data abstracted from the patient's medical record to track the illness's progression or assess the patient's response to treatment. *See also* angina severity and functional classification (and accompanying table); severity of illness; trauma severity indices.

severity of illness   The degree or state of disease existing in a patient prior to treatment. Severity of illness is an important patient-based source of variation in organizational and practitioner performance and is an important consideration in the interpretation of performance data. For instance, a hospital that accepts the most severely injured trauma patients might be expected to have a higher trauma-related mortality rate than a hospi-

tal that does not accept this group of patients because of the severity of illness present before patients receiving treatment. *See also* ASA-SCORE index; case-mix severity; case severity; comorbidity; level of acuity; severity adjustment; severity measurement system; trauma severity indices; urgent.

severity-refined diagnosis-related groups (SRDRGs)   A modified classification system reportedly being developed by HCFA for use in the Medicare payment process for early implementation. The system is meant to address the criticism aimed at the original DRG system that the same reimbursement is given for all patients within a given category, without considering that some patients are sicker than others and require additional resources. *See also* DRG.

sexology   The study of sex and sexual relations and their evolutionary, physiological, developmental, sociological, and medical aspects.

sexual harassment   Unwanted and offensive verbal or physical sexual advances, as those made by an employer to an employee. Sexual harassment often carries with it threats of employment reprisals if such advances are refused. It has been defined by the federal government and courts as illegal employment discrimination (Civil Rights Act of 1964).

sexually transmitted disease (STD)   A class of infections and/or growths acquired through sexual intercourse or direct genital contact. Over the past 25 years, many diseases have been added to the original major STDs, syphilis and gonorrhea. *Synonyms:* social disease (declining in popular vernacular); venereal disease (VD). *See also* AIDS; hepatitis; HIV infection; human papillomavirus; safe sex; safer sex; venerology.

SEXUALLY TRANSMITTED DISEASES

AIDS
Anorectal herpes
Bacterial vaginosis
Chancroid
Chlamydia
Cytomegalovirus
Ectoparasites
Genital Candidiasis
Genital herpes
Genital warts
Gonorrhea
Granuloma inguinale
Hepatitis B
Lymphogranuloma venereum
Molluscum contagiosum
Mucopurulent cervicitis
Nongonococcal urethritis
Pediculosis
Pelvic inflammatory disease
Scabies
Syphilis
Trichomoniasis

SF-36, SF-20, SF-12   The MOS (Medical Outcomes Study) Short Form General Health Surveys. *See* measures (and accompanying table).

shaman   A member of certain tribal societies who acts as a medium between the visible world and an invisible spirit world and who practices magic for purposes of healing, divination, and control over natural events.

shared decision making   The collaboration of patients and health care providers in deciding on the diagnostic and treatment options to be used in the patient's care. Under this concept, the patient is seen as a partner in the health care experience, and providers are responsible for providing the patient with necessary, understandable information about his or her condition, options, costs, and so on. This contrasts with the traditional paternalistic attitude still held by many practitioners. *Synonym:* patient empowerment. *See also* continuous quality improvement; paternalism; team.

Shared Decisionmaking Program (SDP)   Multimedia computer- and interactive videodisc-based tool for enhancing patients' acquisition of information and treatment decisions. The program has been developed by the Foundation for Informed Medical Decisionmaking for several conditions involving difficult risk/benefit trade-offs highly dependent on individual patients' preferences, such as benign prostatic hyperplasia, PSA (prostate-specific antigen) testing, early localized prostate cancer, high blood pressure, low back pain, ischemic heart disease, early-stage breast cancer, and hormone-replacement therapy. Video programs on advance directives and the informed health care consumer are also available. The programs have prompted studies of their efficacy, impact on utilization of resources, and the quality of the decisions. Ongoing studies are attempting to pin down the extent to which observed drops in surgery rates can be attributed to the SDP.

shared service organization   An external organization that provides common administrative, clinical, or support service functions to two or more health care organizations to improve service or contain cost through economy of scale. Such an organization may be independently owned or a subsidiary of a contracting organization; it may or may not be under the contracting organizations' joint control.

shear   A concept used in evaluating risk of pressure ulcers, referring to mechanical force that acts on a unit area of skin in a direction parallel to the body's surface. Shear is affected by the amount of pressure exerted, the coefficient of friction between the materials contacting each other, and the extent to which the body makes contact with the support surface. *See also* pressure ulcer.

sheltered care   *See* assisted living.

Sherman Antitrust Act   *See* antitrust laws.

Shewhart cycle   *See* plan-do-check-act cycle.

shiatsu   *See* acupressure.

shock therapy   *See* electroconvulsive therapy.

shorting   Dispensing a quantity of a drug that is less than the quantity prescribed for the purpose of increasing profit by charging for the prescribed amount. *See also* fraud and abuse; kiting.

short-term hospital   A hospital in which the average length of stay for all patients is less than 30 days or in which more than 50% of all patients are admitted to units where the average length of stay is less than 30 days. *Synonym:* short-stay hospital. *See also* acute care hospital.

show code   *See* slow code.

sickle cell anemia   A congenital hemolytic anemia that occurs primarily in Africans and others of African descent, resulting from a defective hemoglobin molecule (hemoglobin S) that causes red blood cells to roughen and become sickle-shaped and thereby impairing circulation and causing swollen joints, pain, and tissue infarctions. *See also* anemia; hematology; sickle cell screening; sickle cell trait.

sickle cell screening   As recommended by the expert panel of the AHCPR, universal screening of all newborns, performed only in laboratories that meet appropriate standards of performance and reporting. *See also* screening.

sickle cell trait   In itself, a relatively benign condition resulting from heterozygous inheritance of the abnormal hemoglobin S-producing gene, most commonly found in Africans and persons of African descent. In carriers of this trait, 20% to 40% of total hemoglobin is hemoglobin IS, and the rest is normal. If two sickle cell carriers marry, each of their children has a 25% chance of inheriting sickle cell anemia.

side effect   Pharmacological effect of a drug other than the one(s) for which the drug is prescribed.

sidestream smoke   *See* secondhand smoke.

sigmoidoscopy   The principal screening test for detecting adenomatous (precancerous) polyps and colorectal cancer. The procedure involves use of a lighted endoscope to inspect the most distant third of the colon (where malignancies are most likely to occur). *See also* endoscopy; proctosigmoidoscopy.

sign   Objective evidence of a condition, disease, or disorder that is perceptible to an observer; for example jaundice is a sign of hepatic dysfunction. *See also* finding; symptom; vital signs.

significance level   *See* level of significance.

significant   In statistics, relating to observations or occurrences that are too closely correlated to be attributed to chance and therefore indicate some type of systematic relationship. *See also* the following significant terms, as well as statistical significance.

significant medication errors and significant adverse drug reactions   For purposes of Joint Commission accreditation, unintended, undesirable, and unexpected effects of prescribed medications or of medication errors that require discontinuing a medication or modifying the dose, require initial or prolonged hospitalization, result in disability, require treatment with a prescription medication, result in cognitive deterioration or impairment, are life threatening, result in death, or result in congenital anomalies. *See also* medication error.

significant other An individual with whom a patient has a close or formalized relationship, such as a parent, spouse, friend, caretaker, court-ordered fiduciary, or any other person so identified by the patient. *See also* family.

sign language A language that uses manual movements to convey grammatical structure and meaning.

sign out *See* discharge.

simple random sampling A process in which a predetermined number of cases from a population as a whole is selected for review. It is predicated on the idea that each case has an equal probability of being included in the sample. *Synonym:* true random sampling. *See also* random sampling; sampling; stratified random sampling..

single-blind technique A method of studying a drug, device, or procedure in which either the subject or the investigator is kept unaware of (blind to) who is receiving what level of the treatment. This is done to reduce either subject bias or researcher bias, depending on which type of bias is more likely. *See also* bias; blinded study; double-blind technique; triple-blind study.

single-payer system A centralized health care payment system in which one entity, such as the federal government, pays for all health care services. Canada has the best-known single-payer system. It is financed by taxes, and people go to the physician and health care organization of their choice and bill the government according to a standard fee schedule. *See also* all-payer system; payer.

situation ethics A system of ethics that evaluates acts in light of their situational context rather than by applying moral absolutes. *See also* ethics.

situation, target, proposal brainstorming *See* STP brainstorming.

sixth sigma In statistics, six standard deviations from the mean or average of the population. *See also* standard deviation.

skiagraphy *See* radiography.

skilled nursing care *See* nursing care.

skilled nursing facility (SNF) A facility or part of a facility that meets criteria for accreditation established by the sections of the Social Security Act that determine Medicare and Medicaid reimbursement for skilled nursing care, including rehabilitation and various medical and nursing procedures. Law requires the following: (1) Written policies designate the level of caregiver responsible for implementing each policy; (2) a physician supervises each patient's care; (3) a physician is available on an emergency basis; (4) records are kept regarding each patient's condition and care; (5) nursing services are available 24 hours a day; and (6) at least one full-time registered nurse is employed. SNFs were formerly called extended care facilities. *See also* convalescent center; hospital-based skilled nursing facility; long term care facility; nursing home.

skimming The practice in health care organizations paid on a prepayment or capitation basis, and in health insurance, of seeking to enroll only the healthiest people as a way of controlling costs (since income is constant whether services are actually used). *Synonyms:* creaming; favorable selection. *See also* adverse selection; skimping.

skimping The practice in health care organizations paid on a prepayment or capitation basis of denying or delaying the provision of services needed or demanded by enrolled members as a way of controlling costs. *See also* adverse selection; skimming.

slipped disk *See* herniated disk.

slow code An intermediate course of action between full cardiopulmonary resuscitation and do-not-resuscitate orders. This option is usually inappropriate unless sound reason is known; for example, the patient requests chest compression but no intubation. *Synonyms:* limited code; partial code; show code. *See also* cardiopulmonary resuscitation; code blue; DNR order.

smart card in health care A credit card–sized identification device containing an integrated circuit chip capable of storing or processing an individual's health insurance coverage, medical information, and demographic information, such as name, address, age, and sex. The three kinds of technology currently used for smart cards are single magnetic stripe (holds about 250 bytes of data), optical stripe (uses the same technology as a compact disc and holds about two megabytes of data), and electronic stripe (holds about 8,000 bytes of data and has a software program resident in the card). *See also* health card.

smoking-cessation counseling and therapy A collection of techniques and strategies to help every type of provider play a role in urging and supporting a patient to commit to quit smoking, to support the patient through relapses, and to maintain the patient in ultimate success. Clinical practice guidelines (eg, from the AHCPR and the American Psychiatric Association), tobacco-control ordinances regulating access in public places and to adolescents, and coordinated initiatives (American Medical Association and Robert Wood Johnson Foundation) have created the momentum of a national campaign to get Americans to stop smoking. *See also* nicotine replacement therapy; pack year; states of change.

snails *See* evangelists and snails.

Snellen visual acuity test A standard method of measuring vision, named after the Dutch ophthalmologist Hermann Snellen (1834-1908). Snellen's chart, bearing rows of block letters of standard, decreasing size, is set at a predetermined distance from the patient. One eye is covered, and the patient reads as far down the chart as possible. The procedure is repeated for the second eye. *Synonym*: eye chart. *See also* visually impaired.

SOAP   A mnemonic device for conceptualizing the data included in a problem-oriented medical record and recorded in each entry in a patient's progress notes: S—subjective data obtained from the patient or a representative of the patient; O—objective data obtained by observation, physical examination, and diagnostic studies; A—assessment of the patient's status with a summary of any new subjective and objective data; and P—plan for diagnostic or therapeutic action for patient care. *See also* medical record progress note; problem-oriented medical record.

SNOMED   *See* systematized nomenclature of medicine.

social detoxification   A period of enforced abstinence from a toxic substance to which one is habituated or addicted but not critically ill and whose treatment does not require intensive or comprehensive medical services. *See also* detoxification; medical detoxification.

social disease   *See* sexually transmitted disease.

social insurance   A mechanism for pooling risks by their transfer to an organization, usually governmental, that is required by law to provide indemnity (cash) or service benefits to, or on behalf of, covered persons upon the occurrence of certain predesignated losses. Examples include social security, railroad retirement, and workers' and unemployment compensation. Social insurance aims to provide minimum standards of living for those in lower and middle wage groups. In other countries, health insurance is often a government-sponsored social insurance program. *See also* insurance; national health insurance; national health service; Old Age, Survivors, Disability and Health Insurance Program; socialized medicine.

socialized medicine   **1.** A health care system in which the organization and provision of health care services are directly controlled by the government, and health care providers are employed by, or contracted for providing services directly with, the government.   **2.** Derogatory term for a health care system that is believed to be subject to excessive governmental control. *Synonym*: state medicine. *See also* national health insurance; national health service; social insurance.

social psychiatry   The branch of psychiatry dealing with the relationship between social environment and mental illness. *See also* psychiatry.

social psychology   The branch of psychology that studies the social behavior of individuals and groups, with special emphasis on how behavior is affected by the presence or influence of other people. Social psychology deals with such processes as communication, political behavior, learning, and the formation of attitudes. *See also* psychology.

Social Security   A government program that provides economic assistance to persons faced with unemployment, disability, or old age, financed by tax assessment of employers and employees. *See also* the following terms, as well as Kerr-Mills; Old Age, Survivors, and Disability Insurance.

Social Security Act   Federal legislation signed into law in 1935 that created the Social Security Administration. The main purpose of the law is to protect as a matter of right the American worker in retirement. Major provisions included Old Age Assistance and Old Age, Survivors, and Disability Insurance. *See also* the following terms, as well as Kerr-Mills; Social Security amendments, as well as Child Health Act; Medicaid; Medicare; Social Security; supplemental security income; Supplemental Security Medical Insurance Program.

Social Security Amendments of 1960   *See* Kerr-Mills.

Social Security Amendments of 1972   Amendments to the Social Security Act that authorized Medicare to contract with HMOs on either a cost reimbursement or risk basis, established the professional standards review organizations (PSRO) program, and defined kidney failure as a disability. *See also* professional standards review organization; Social Security Act.

Social Security Amendments of 1983   Amendments to the Social Security Act that established a comprehensive prospective payment system for hospital services provided under Medicare, using DRGs. *See also* DRG; Social Security Act.

social work discharge planning   The evaluation of a patient's needs by a social worker or other qualified individual, beginning on the day of admission to a health care facility. It involves assessing the family, extended family, and other resources to determine what resources are available to help the patient in returning home or if plans should be made for placement elsewhere. *See also* discharge planning.

social worker   An individual qualified by education and authorized by law to practice in the field of social work. Social worker definitions vary between states. The National Association of Social Workers classifies several levels of social work positions within two groups: preprofessional and professional. Social workers practice in a multitude of settings and provide a wide array of services.

social work services   Services to assist patients and their families in addressing social, emotional, and economic stresses associated with illness, injury crisis, or social condition. Such services are provided by a qualified social worker or a social worker assistant under the supervision of a qualified social worker. These services may be provided directly or through contract with another organization or individual.

solo practice   Practice of a health professional as a self-employed individual. Solo practice is by definition private practice but is not necessarily a fee-for-service

TYPES OF SOCIAL WORKERS

caseworker Works with individual cases or clients.

casework supervisor Supervises social service agency staff, volunteers, and students of schools of social work. May assign caseloads and related duties, evaluate staff performance, and recommend needed actions.

child welfare caseworker Qualified by education to perform many activities relating to child welfare including, but not limited to, the following: investigating homes to protect children from harmful environments; arranging for adoption and foster care for children; identifying evidence of abuse or neglect; advising parents on the care of severely handicapped infants; counseling children and youth with social adjustment difficulties; arranging homemaker's services during parents' illness; starting legal action to protect neglected or abused children; helping unmarried parents; counseling couples on adoption; evaluating homes and parents for possible placement of children for adoption or foster care; and consulting with parents, teachers, counselors, and other persons to help identify problems.

clinical social worker Provides psychotherapy or counseling in all types of health delivery settings.

clinical social worker, private practice Provides psychotherapy or counseling to individual families or groups in the private practice setting. Counsel families of troubled adolescents and people with marital problems and may also organize group sessions for families of people with special health problems.

eligibility worker Interviews applicants or recipients to determine eligibility for public assistance and authorizes the amount of money payment, food stamps, medical care, or other general assistance.

family counselor Works with families having problems in family relationships or other social areas. Perform counseling for married couples, parents and their children, and unwed parents and may also help in home management, work adjustment, vocational training, or the need for financial assistance. They may also help clients use agency services, such as homemaker and day care services, as well as other community resources, and help determine clients' eligibility for financial assistance.

industrial social worker Works in employee assistance programs that typically provide a social service to employees whose personal problems are interfering with their job performance. *Synonyms:* occupational social worker; personal assistance social worker.

licensed social worker Licensed in a particular state to practice (requirements for and definitions of social workers vary from state to state).

medical social worker Identifies and establishes beneficial resources to help patients and their families with social and emotional difficulties associated with illnesses or that are interfering with treatment. Discharge planning is an important area of practice, especially since the advent of prospective payment. *Synonym:* hospital social worker.

psychiatric social worker Works in a psychiatric hospital, residential treatment center, psychiatric unit of a general hospital, or a mental health center. Assists individuals and their families in dealing with social, emotional, and environmental problems resulting from mental illness or disability. Serves as a link between patient, psychiatrist or clinical psychologist, family, and community.

public health social worker Provides social work services to children and adults in public health agencies, through public health clinics, and in state facilities, such as hospitals and institutions for the developmentally disabled.

registered social worker Has a graduate degree from an accredited school of social work, has successfully completed the Academy of Certified Social Workers examination, and has met other requirements necessary for certification.

school social worker Aids children when they are having difficulties adapting to school life. May assist with vocational counseling or serve as a liaison between a school and community resources, such as family service agencies, child guidance clinics, protective services, physicians, and ministers. *Synonyms:* home and school visitor; school adjustment counselor; visiting teacher.

social group worker Works with small groups of people to promote the group work concept to help members develop their own activities. Social group workers may work in community centers, neighborhood or settlement houses, youth centers, and housing projects; organize groups, such as senior citizens; and develop recreational, physical education, or cultural programs.

social service caseworker Counsels and helps individuals and families requiring assistance from a social service agency.

social welfare administrator Directs the agency or the major function of a public or voluntary organization that provides services in the social welfare field. *Synonym:* social welfare director.

practice. Solo practitioners may be paid by capitation, although fee for service is more common. *Synonym:* individual practice. *See also* medical practice; network model HMO; private practice.

somatotherapy Treatment of mental illness by physical means, such as drugs, electroconvulsive (shock) therapy, or lobotomy. *See also* electroconvulsive therapy; mental illness; psychosurgery.

somnology The study of sleep and sleep disorders. *See also* polysomnographic technology.

sonography *See* ultrasonography.

source document An original record, usually written or typed on paper and used as a data source; for example, a medical record. *See also* documentation; primary source.

special cause A factor that intermittently and unpredictably induces variation over and above that inherent in the system. It often appears as an extreme point, such as a point beyond the control limits on a control chart, or some specific, identifiable pattern in data. *Synonyms:* assignable cause; exogenous cause; extrasystemic cause. *See also* common cause; control chart; special-cause variation; statistical control.

special-cause variation The variation in performance and data that results from special causes. Special-cause variation is intermittent, unpredictable, and unstable. It is not inherently present in a system; rather, it arises from causes that are not part of the system as designed. It tends to cluster by person, place, and time, and should be eliminated by an organization if it results in undesirable outcomes. *Synonyms:* assignable-cause variation; exogenous-cause variation; extrasystemic-cause variation. *See also* common-cause variation; control chart; control limit; process variation; special cause; tampering; variation.

special damages *See* consequential damages.

special-function laboratory A laboratory not under the jurisdiction of a main laboratory in a health care organization. Special-function laboratories are sometimes focused on a discrete testing procedure, such as blood gas determination. *See also* clinical laboratory; laboratory.

specialized care *See* secondary care.

specialized survey A survey conducted by the Joint Commission in which a surveyor with specific knowledge and experience is added to the core survey team for an accreditation survey of a health care organization; for example, adding a Mental Health Care Accreditation Program surveyor to survey a health care organization's alcohol and other drug dependence program. *See also* accreditation survey; Joint Commission survey.

special survey Any survey conducted by the Joint Commission at an accredited health care organization that is not classified as a triennial, focused, initial, follow-up, or conditional validation survey; it may be conducted anytime during the organization's accreditation cycle. *See also* accreditation survey.

specialty A particular profession or branch of study or research which is limited to a certain branch of medicine, dentistry, laboratory medicine, nursing, or other health science. Specialties frequently cover specific services or procedures provided (eg, anesthesiology, radiology, pathology), age categories of patients (eg, pediatrics), body systems (eg, gastroenterology, orthopedics, cardiology), or types of diseases (eg, allergy, periodontics). *See also* dental specialties; medical specialty; medical subspecialty; subspecialty; surgical specialties.

specialty association *See* medical specialty societies.

specialty bed A bed regularly maintained for a specific category of patients, as in an intensive care unit bed or an inpatient pediatric bed.

specialty boards Private, nongovernmental, voluntary bodies that certify physicians, nurses, dentists, pharmacists, podiatrists, and other health professionals who are specialists or subspecialists in medical, nursing, dental, pharmacy, podiatric, and other health fields. The standards for certification relate to length and type of training and experience and may include written and oral examination of applicants for certification. The boards are not educational institutions, and the certificate of a board is not considered a degree. Examples of specialty boards are the American Board of Emergency Medicine, American Board of Dental Public Health, American Board of Neuroscience Nursing, and American Board of Podiatric Orthopedics. *See also* board eligible; certification; medical specialty boards.

specialty societies *See* medical specialty societies.

specificity A measure of the ability of a diagnostic test, a screening test, or other predictor to correctly identify the individuals or cases *not* having the condition being tested for, who are correctly identified as negative by the test. Operationally, specificity is the number of negative test results divided by the number of individuals or cases who actually do not have the condition (true negatives divided by the sum of true negatives plus false positives). *Synonym:* true negative rate. *See also* analytical specificity; false negative; false positive; predictive value of a test; screening; sensitivity; true negative; true positive.

specified disease insurance Insurance that provides benefits, usually in large amounts or with high maximums, toward the expense of the treatment of a specific disease or diseases named in the policy. Coverage for diseases, such as polio and end-stage renal disease under Medicare, are examples of specified disease insurance. *See also* insurance.

speech-language pathology services Services provided to assist individuals in speech, language, oral and pharyngeal sensorimotor function, cognitive or communicative function, and their underlying processes. Such services are provided by a qualified speech-language pathologist. *See also* otitis media; speech pathology.

speech pathology The study or diagnosis and treatment of disturbances of articulation, phonation, and language function (aphasia) or speech disturbances due to psychiatric illness. *See also* audiology; cued speech; pathology; speech-language pathology services; speech screening.

speech screening A process to determine language abilities that may include such tests as articulation in connected speech and formal testing situations; voice, in terms of judgments of pitch, intensity, and quality and determinations of appropriate vocal hygiene; and fluency, usually measured in terms of frequency and severity of stuttering or dysfluency (based on evaluation of speech flow-sequence, duration, rhythm, rate, and fluency). *See also* screening; speech pathology.

spell of illness The period of time beginning when a patient enters a health care organization and ending at the conclusion of a 60-consecutive-day period during which he or she has not been an inpatient in any hospital or skilled nursing facility. Used in determining Medicare benefits.

spend down A method by which an individual establishes eligibility for a health care program, such as Medicaid, by reducing gross income through incurring medical expenses until net income after medical expenses becomes low enough to make him or her eligible for the program.

sphygmomanometer An instrument for measuring blood pressure in the arteries, especially one consisting of a pressure gauge and a rubber cuff that wraps around an extremity and is inflated to constrict the arteries. *See also* blood pressure.

spinal manipulation Manual therapy for symptomatic relief and functional improvement of the back in which loads are applied to the spine using short- or long-lever methods. The selected spinal joint is moved to its end range of voluntary motion, followed by application of an impulse load. According to an AHCPR-sponsored clinical practice guideline on acute low back problems (1994), rigorous efficacy studies have shown that spinal manipulation can be helpful for patients with acute low back problems without radiculopathy (nerve root compression) when used within the first month of symptoms, but updated reviews have found that its efficacy remains unproven for any other low back patient group and requires further study to resolve controversy and divergence in practice among clinicians. *See also* low back pain (and accompanying table); sciatica.

spinal puncture *See* lumbar puncture.

spinal tap *See* lumbar puncture.

spirometry Pulmonary function testing which measures the maximal volume of air forcibly exhaled from the point of maximal inhalation (forced vital capacity, FVC) and the volume of air exhaled during the first second of the FVC (forced expiratory volume in one second, FEV_1). Spirometry should be performed using equipment and techniques that meet standards developed by the American Thoracic Society (1995). *See also* patient monitor; peak flow meter.

sponge count A count conducted during a surgical operation and immediately before closure of the surgical incision that compares the number of sponges placed in the surgical field with the number of sponges (used and unused) remaining. *See also* surgery; wound infection.

sponsored malpractice insurance A malpractice insurance plan that involves an agreement by a professional society (such as a state medical society) to sponsor a particular insurer's medical malpractice insurance coverage and to cooperate with the insurer in administering of the coverage. The cooperation may include participation in marketing, claims review, and review of rate making. Until 1975, this was the predominant approach to coverage. Since then, sponsored malpractice insurance has been replaced by professional society-operated plans, joint underwriting associations, state insurance funds, and other arrangements. *See also* insurance; medical malpractice insurance.

sports medicine The branch of medicine and subspecialty of emergency medicine, family practice, internal medicine, and pediatrics dealing with promoting wellness and preventing injury during physical exercise, either as an individual or in team participation. *See also* emergency medicine; orthopedics.

stable angina Chest pain due to insufficient oxygen to the heart muscle, occurring in attacks of predictable frequency and duration after provocation by circumstances that increase myocardial oxygen demands, such as exercise, emotional stress, or excitement, with the precipitating circumstances tending to remain constant from episode to episode. *See also* angina; unstable angina.

staff Individuals, including employees, volunteers, contractors, or temporary agency personnel, who successfully complete a credentialing process and are granted clinical privileges by the organization. *See also* the following staff terms, as well as housestaff; medical staff.

staff-development program An ongoing educational program for improving the knowledge and skills of a health care organization's staff. It may involve in-service training of employees in specific areas, such as infection control and patient rights, and may also include cooperative education programs with colleges as well as tuition and book reimbursement for job-related training and education.

staffing The analysis and identification of a health care organization's human resource requirements, recruitment of persons to meet these requirements, and initial placement of those persons to ensure adequate numbers, knowledge, and skills to perform the organization's work. *See also* full-time equivalent; human resources management; staffing ratio.

staffing ratio The total number of full-time equivalent employees in a defined unit or facility divided by its average daily patient census. *See also* average daily census; full-time equivalent; ratio; staffing.

staff model HMO An HMO that hires its own providers. As with a group model HMO, all services except hospital care are provided under one roof, but the providers are employed directly by the HMO. *See also* HMO.

staff privileges *See* privileging.

stages of change In the current context of health care and problem behaviors, particularly smoking, the milestones in a process leading to improvement, as described in James O. Prochaska's model of five strategies to be used by a clinician or counselor to encourage a person to become totally abstinent. Based on the person's commitment and success, these stages are termed (1) *precontemplation*, (2) *contemplation*, (3) *preparation*, (4) *action*, and (5) *maintenance*. One measure of success is moving a patient to a higher stage of readiness through office interventions or during a "teachable moment" for a hospitalized patient who is aware of a need to change. *See also* addiction psychiatry; smoking cessation counseling and therapy.

staging The determination of the distinct phases or periods in the course of a disease, the life history of an organism, or any biological process; for example, the classification of cancer according to the anatomical extent of the tumor (primary neoplasm, regional lymph nodes, metastases). *Synonyms:* disease staging; staging of disease. *See also* angina severity and functional classifications (and accompanying table); cancer staging system (and accompanying table).

standard **1**. For purposes of Joint Commission accreditation, a statement that defines the performance expectations, structures, or processes that must be substantially in place in an organization to enhance the quality of care. **2**. A criterion established by authority or general consent as a rule for the measure of quality, value, or extent. *See also* the following standard terms, as well as accountability standards; benchmark; building codes; calibration; criterion standard; Darling case; equivalency; gold standard; measure; minimum standard; national standard rule; norm; optimal achievable standard; outcome standard; patient-centered performance-based quality-of-evaluation; performance standard; process standard; reasonable person standard; required services; structural standard; universal precautions.

standard deviation A measure of variability that indicates the dispersion, spread, or variation in a distribution. The Greek letter sigma (σ) is often used to indicate the estimated standard deviation. *See also* coefficient of variation; covariance; distribution; sixth sigma; standard error; variance.

standard error The standard deviations of the sample in a frequency distribution, obtained by dividing the standard deviation by the total number of cases in the frequency distribution. *See also* distribution; standard deviation.

standard exercise test *See* exercise test.

standard gamble A technique that quantifies patients' preferences for a specific health state by determining what chance of death the patient would be willing to take to be freed from symptoms. The patient imagines a treatment that will completely cure his or her symptoms but involves a risk of immediate death. The standard gamble utility is defined as one minus the risk of death at the point of indifference. *See also* patient utilities measurement.

standardized patient encounter An encounter between a health care practitioner and a "standardized patient" for purposes of teaching and/or evaluating the practitioner's performance. A *standardized patient* is a nonphysician who has been trained to simulate a patient encounter accurately and consistently.

standardized test An examination for which average levels of performance have been established and which has shown consistent results. In addition, uniform methods of administering and scoring the test must have been developed. Standardized tests are used to help measure abilities, aptitudes, interests, and personality traits. For example, most students who plan to attend medical school take a standardized test called the Medical College

Admission Test during their junior or senior year in college. This test measures some of the abilities thought to contribute to a student's success in medical school. *See also* Medical College Admission Test; mental age; national board examination.

standard of care Generally, in health care law, that degree of care which a physician, who possesses average skills and practices in the same or similar locality, should exercise in the same or similar circumstances. In cases involving specialization, however, certain courts have disregarded geographical considerations, holding that in the practice of a board-certified medical or surgical specialty, the standard should be that of a reasonable specialist practicing medicine or surgery in the same special field. If a physician's conduct falls below the standard of care, he or she may be liable for any injuries or damages resulting from that conduct. *See also* locality rule; malpractice; medical malpractice; national standard rule.

standard precautions *See* universal precautions.

standards-based evaluation Evaluative approach to quality of care that measures health care organizations' or practitioners' compliance with preestablished standards.

Standards for Pediatric Immunization Practices (SPIP) Eighteen suggestions, issued in 1993 by the National Vaccine Advisory Committee, regarding organizational practices to help providers ensure timely and comprehensive immunization of all appropriate patients. The SPIP have been endorsed by the U.S. Public Health Service and the American Academy of Pediatrics.

standards, guidelines, and options Classification of recommendations in practice policies or generic "guidelines," developed by David M. Eddy and widely used by national medical specialty societies, to reflect the degree of certainty associated with a particular recommendation. *Standards* represents accepted principles of patient management that reflect a high degree of clinical certainty. *Guidelines* represents a particular strategy or range of management strategies that reflect a moderate clinical certainty. *Options* represents strategies for patient management for which there is unclear clinical certainty. *See also* practice policies.

standards manuals *See* accreditation manuals.

standard unique health identifier A combination of digits and symbols that is required by the Health Care Portability and Accountability Act of 1996 to appear on every patient record by February 1998. The number can be used to indirectly identify the patient by name as well as to establish standards for the electronic transmission of medical records, such as claims records. The health identifier might be either a slightly modified Social Security number or a new number. The identifier concept, which is described under the rubric of "Administrative Simplification" in the act, has provoked controversy and concern over privacy and confidentiality, spelled out in a report of the National Research Council (National Academy of Sciences) in March 1997. *Synonym:* health identifier.

standing orders Instructions for patient care under specified circumstances (eg, orders for patients presenting with chest pain), which are to be followed for all patients unless the attending physician intervenes with different instructions. *See also* order.

Stark I [42 U.S.C.A. § 1395nn (1989)] Legislation introduced by U.S. Representative Pete Stark and passed as part of OBRA '93, with the intention of saving Medicare dollars by discouraging overuse of health services. The bill prohibited a physician from referring a patient to a clinical laboratory in which the physician or a member of his or her family had a financial interest, except in certain circumstances. This differed from antikickback laws because it dealt with self-referral rather than referral to another physician. *See also* OBRA '89; STARK II.

Stark II [42 U.S.C.A. § 1395nn(h)(6) (1993)] Amendment to Stark I as part of OBRA '93. This legislation prohibits a physician from referring a Medicare or Medicaid patient to a facility in which the physician has a financial interest. Instead of being limited to a laboratory, however, such a facility could include those providing physical therapy, occupational therapy, radiology and other diagnostic services, radiation therapy, durable medical equipment, parenteral and enteral nutrition, equipment and supplies, prosthetics and orthotics, home health services, outpatient prescription drugs, and inpatient or outpatient hospital services. This and similar legislation was intended to encourage physicians to form groups and join health systems as employees. *See also* OBRA '93; STARK I

stat A medical term meaning "immediately" (as in a stat laboratory test), which has come into the common vernacular.

state board of medical examiners A body, established by the laws of a state, responsible for overseeing the practice of medicine within the state. The board of medical examiners, among its other activities, reviews the credentials of physicians applying for licensure to practice within the state, administers examinations if required, investigates applicants' backgrounds, and approves or denies licensure and imposes penalties or revokes licensure for transgressions. *Synonym*: state medical board. *See also* license; licensure; medical examiner; medical licensure; reciprocity.

state data initiatives Initiatives that expand state regulatory efforts to require the public reporting and dissemination of severity-adjusted cost, quality, and utilization data by health care organizations. For example, the Health Care Cost Containment Council in Pennsylvania has implemented state reporting requirements for MedisGroups admission severity and morbidity scores. Colorado hospitals with more than 100 beds report severity-adjusted outcomes data to their state's data commission. *Synonym*: health data disclosure acts.

state disability insurance *See* unemployment compensation—disability.

state medical boards *See* state board of medical examiners.

state medicine *See* socialized medicine.

Statement of Conditions™ (SOC™) For purposes of Joint Commission accreditation, a proactive document that helps an organization do a critical self-assessment of its current level of compliance and describes how to resolve any *Life Safety Code*® (LSC®) deficiencies. *See also* *Life Safety Code*.

state of the art The highest level of development as of a device, technique, or scientific field, achieved at a particular time, as in the designation of state-of-the-art surgical procedure or device that has undergone technology assessment for safety and efficacy.

statins *See* cholesterol-lowering drugs.

statistical control The condition describing a process from which all special causes have been removed, evidenced on a control chart by the absence of points beyond the control limits and by the absence of nonrandom patterns or trends within the control limits. *See also* control chart; control limit; special cause.

statistical inference The process of using observations of a sample to estimate the properties of a population from which the sample is derived. *See also* inference; inferential statistics.

statistically significant A test statistic that is as large as, or larger than, a predetermined requirement, resulting in rejection of the null hypothesis. *See also* null hypothesis; significant; type I error.

statistical process control (SPC) The application of statistical techniques, such as control charts, to analyze a process or its output so as to take appropriate actions to achieve and maintain a state of statistical control and to improve the capability of the process. *See also* control chart; process capability; statistical quality control.

statistical quality control (SQC) The application of statistical techniques for measuring and improving the quality of processes. SQC includes statistical process control, diagnostic tools, sampling plans, and other statistical techniques. *See also* Deming, W. Edwards; quality control; statistical process control.

statistical significance The likelihood that an observed association is not due to chance. *See also* level of significance; p value; significant.

statistical test A procedure used to decide whether a hypothesis about the distribution of one or more populations or variables should be rejected or accepted. Statistical tests may be parametric or nonparametric. *See also* parametric test; variable.

statistics *See* biostatistics; Cooperative Health Statistics System; descriptive statistics; health statistics; inductive statistics; inferential statistics; management science; vital statistics.

statute of limitations A statute setting time limits on legal action in certain cases. The federal government and various states set a maximum time period during which certain actions can be brought or rights enforced. After the time period set out in the applicable statute of limitations has expired, no legal action can be brought regardless of whether any cause of action ever existed. *Synonym:* limitations period. *See also* affirmative defense; limits on liability.

statutorily defined emancipation *See* emancipated minor.

steering committee A committee that sets agendas and schedules of business, as for a health care organization or legislative body.

stenosis Abnormal narrowing of an orifice or a passage, as in aortic stenosis (narrowing of the aortic heart valve). *Synonym:* stricture. *See also* restenosis.

step-down unit A specialized intensive nursing unit capable of providing the same monitoring and patient support services as an intensive care unit but which has a higher ratio of patients to nurses. *See also* intensive care.

stepped care The practice of initiating treatment with a low-intensity intervention and then referring treatment failures to successively more intense interventions.

sterile technique A method of establishing and maintaining an environment free from pathogenic and nonpathogenic microorganisms.

steroid Any of numerous naturally occurring or synthetic compounds, including bile acids, adrenal hormones, and sex hormones, and certain drugs, such as digitalis compounds and the precursors of certain vitamins. *See also* anabolic steroids; asthma medications.

stimulant A group of controlled substances (including cocaine, a drug extracted from the leaves of the South American coca plant) and amphetamines, synthetic drugs first developed during the late 1800s. This class of drugs stimulates the central nervous system and is used medicinally to combat depression and narcolepsy. *See also* schedule of controlled substances.

stock insurance company A company owned and controlled by stockholders and operated for the purpose of making a profit. Profits take the form of stockholders' dividends, which are distributed to stockholders. *See also* captive insurance company; mutual insurance company.

stoma A surgically constructed opening, especially one in the abdominal wall, that permits the passage of waste after a colostomy (opening to the large intestine) or an ileostomy (opening to the small intestine).

stomatology The study of the mouth and its diseases.

stopwatch study *See* motion study.

storyboard A technique that uses pictures and/or diagrams and short narratives to illustrate the essential steps of a quality improvement project. Through the use of storyboards, storytelling can act to accelerate the process of organization wide quality improvement by helping quality improvement teams organize their work and their presentations so other persons can more readily learn from them. Storytelling can reduce variation in the process of quality improvement so that the focus of learning is on content, not the method of telling. *See also* quality improvement project; quality improvement team.

STP (situation, target, proposal) brainstorming A brainstorming technique that fosters collaborative problem solving. Participants' ideas are grouped under the following three headings to identify patterns and help focus on the problem under discussion: (1) *target* ideas—possible outcomes, ideals, values, and so on; (2) *situation* observations about the current status of the situation and opinions as to its cause; and (3) *proposals*—methods, actions or techniques—for moving from the current situation toward the targeted goal. *See also* brainstorming.

straitjacket Colloquial term for a type of physical restraint, formally called a *camisole*, which restricts use of the arms to prevent a patient from hurting himself or herself or others. The device consists of a jacket with extra long sleeves and straps that buckle in the back. *See also* restraint.

strategic planning The management act of planning action(s) resulting from strategy or intended to accomplish a specific goal. *Synonyms:* long-range planning; long-term planning. *See also* forecasting; organizational planning.

stratification The process of classifying data into subgroups based on one or more characteristics, variables, or other categories.

stratified random sampling A process in which a population is divided into subgroups, and cases are pulled randomly from each subgroup rather from the population as a whole. *See also* random sampling; sampling; simple random sampling.

strength of evidence/quality of evidence Key attributes of clinical practice guidelines or recommendations which rank the origin of evidence and how well it supports recommendations. *Synonym:* clinical confidence. *See also* clinical practice guideline; evidence-based medicine.

streptokinase A proteolytic (protein-dissolving) enzyme produced by hemolytic streptococci, capable of dissolving fibrin and used medically to dissolve blood clots. *See also* anticoagulation; GUSTO; thrombolytic therapy; tissue plasminogen activator.

stress Bodily or mental tension, anxiety, or emotional distress that can contribute to disease and fatigue. Stress is the totality of the physiological reaction to an adverse or threatening stimulus, such as physical, mental, or emotional trauma. The hormones of the adrenal cortex play an important role in adapting stress. *See also* counseling services; exercise test; posttraumatic stress disorder; stress echocardiography.

U.S. PREVENTIVE SERVICES TASK FORCE RATINGS SYSTEM: STRENGTH AND QUALITY

Quality of Evidence

I: Evidence obtained from at least one properly randomized controlled trial.

II-1: Evidence obtained from well-designed controlled trials without randomization.

II-2: Evidence obtained from well-designed cohort or case-control analytic studies, preferably from more than one center or research group.

II-3: Evidence obtained from multiple time series with or without the intervention. Dramatic results in uncontrolled experiments could also be regarded as this type of evidence.

III: Opinions of respected authorities, based on clinical experience; descriptive studies and case reports; or reports of expert committees.

Strength of Recommendations

A: There is good evidence to support the recommendation that the condition be specifically considered in a periodic health examination.

B: There is fair evidence to support the recommendation that the condition be specifically considered in a periodic health examination.

C: There is insufficient evidence to recommend for or against the inclusion of the condition in a periodic health examination, but recommendations may be made on other grounds.

D: There is fair evidence to support the recommendation that the condition be excluded from consideration in a periodic health examination.

E: There is good evidence to support the recommendation that the condition be excluded from consideration in a periodic health examination.

Source: U.S. Preventive Services Task Force: *Guide to Clinical Preventive Services.* Second Edition. Baltimore: Williams & Wilkins, 1996. The USPSTF adapted this rating system from the Canadian Task Force on the Periodic Health Examination: The periodic health examination. *Can Med Assoc J* 1979:1193-1254.

stress echocardiography   Use of echocardiography along with a variety of methods that induce stress by increasing cardiac workload or by causing coronary arterial or vasodilations and increased coronary blood flow; these include exercise (treadmill, upright or supine bicycle) or drugs (adrenergic-stimulating or vasodilating agents). This diagnostic imaging modality is both sensitive and specific for detecting inducible myocardial ischemia in patients with intermediate to high pretest probability of coronary artery disease and thus offers significant added clinical value over standard treadmill exercising testing for those patients. *See also* echocardiography; exercise test.

stress incontinence   *See* urinary incontinence.

stress test   *See* exercise test; stress echocardiography.

strict isolation   A category of patient isolation designed to prevent transmission of highly contagious or virulent infections that may be spread by both air and contact. The specifications include a private room and the use of masks, gowns, and gloves for all persons entering the room. Special ventilation requirements with the room at negative pressure to surrounding areas are desirable. *See also* isolation; respiratory isolation.

stroke   The sudden development of a neurological defect and loss of consciousness resulting from lack of supply of oxygen to brain tissue, caused by hemorrhage (internal bleeding) or blockage of blood vessels by a thrombus (clot) or an embolism and leading to paralysis, weakness, and speech defects. *Synonym:* cerebral vascular accident. *See also* aphasia; brain attack; cerebrovascular accident; neuroprotective agents; transient ischemic attack; vascular dementia.

structural data   Data about organizational resources in place and arranged to deliver health care. *See also* resource allocation; structural standard.

structural measure of quality   A measure of whether organizational resources and arrangements are in place to deliver health care, such as the number, type, and distribution of medical personnel, equipment, and facilities. Underlying the use of such measures to assess quality is the assumption that such characteristics increase the likelihood that providers will perform well and, in their absence, that providers will perform poorly. This assumption, in turn, raises the question whether specific structural characteristics are associated with better processes or outcomes. In many instances, this association has not been demonstrated. *See also* measure.

structural standard   A statement of expectation that defines a health care organization's structural capacity to provide quality care; pertains to characteristics of organizations' resources and form, such as the organization of the medical staff body and the numbers and qualifications of medical staff members. *See also* standard; structural data.

structured interview   An interview in which the interviewer carefully controls the subjects discussed and the nature of the question-and-answer format. *See also* unstructured interview.

structured settlement   A method of paying an agreed-upon amount that generally allows predetermined payments to be made periodically. *See also* settlement.

study arm   One segment, among two or more, to which patients in clinical trials are assigned. One arm receives a different treatment from another. Reference may be made to the treatment arm as opposed to the no treatment or placebo arm, the monotherapy arm as opposed to the combination therapy arm, and so forth.

Study on the Efficacy of Nosocomial Infection Control (SENIC) project   A ten-year study (1974-1984), conducted by the Hospital Infections Program of the National Center for Infectious Diseases, to evaluate critical elements of hospital infection control programs. The study found that to be effective programs must include: organized surveillance and control activities; a trained hospital epidemiologist; one infection control practitioner for every 250 acute care beds; and a system for reporting surgical wound infection rates back to practicing surgeons. *See also* nosocomial infection.

subacute care   Care that is rendered immediately after, or instead of, acute hospitalization to treat one or more specific, active, complex medical conditions or to administer one or more technically complex treatments in the context of a patient's underlying long-term conditions and overall situation. Subacute care requires the coordinated services of an interdisciplinary team. It is given as part of a specifically defined program, regardless of the site. Subacute care is generally more intensive than traditional nursing facility care and less intensive than acute inpatient care. It requires frequent (daily to weekly) assessment and review of the clinical course and treatment plan for a limited time period (several days to several months), until a condition is stabilized or a predetermined treatment course is completed. *See also* acute care; long term care.

subjective data   Data not readily quantified or measured, such as personal opinions, values, concepts, and social relationships. *See also* data.

subrogation   A provision of an insurance policy that requires an insured individual to turn over any rights he or she may have to recover damages from another party to the insurer, to the extent to which he or she has been reimbursed by the insurer. Some experts have argued that private health insurance, including Blue Cross or group insurance, should have subrogation rights similar to those in most property insurance policies. Having paid the hospital bill of a policyholder, the health insurance company could assume the right to sue the party whose negligence might have caused the hospitalization and be reimbursed for its outlay to the policyholder. *See also* insurance.

subscriber   An individual who has elected to contract for, or participate in (subscribe to), an insurance or HMO plan for himself or herself and dependents, if any. *See also* individual insured; member.

subspecialty   A narrow field of study within a specialty, as pediatric nephrology is a subspecialty of pediatrics (a specialty) and geriatric psychiatry is a subspecialty of psychiatry (a specialty). *See also* medical subspecialty; specialty.

substance abuse   *See* substance-related disorders.

substance abuse facility   A facility specializing in the treatment of patients suffering from alcoholism or chemical dependency. *See also* alcoholism rehabilitation center.

substance dependence   *See* substance-related disorders.

substance-related disorders   As classified in the DSM-IV, a broad class of disorders including those related to the taking of a drug of abuse (including alcohol), the side effects of a medication, or toxin exposure. *Substance*

DSM-IV SUBSTANCE-RELATED DISORDERS*	Dependence	Abuse	Intoxication	Withdrawal
Alcohol	X	X	X	X
Amphetamines	X	X	X	X
Caffeine			X	
Cannabis	X	X	X	
Cocaine	X	X	X	X
Hallucinogens	X	X	X	
Inhalants	X	X	X	
Nicotine	X			X
Opioids	X	X	X	X
Phencyclidine	X	X	X	
Sedatives, hypnotics, or anxiolytics	X	X	X	X
Polysubstance	X			
Other	X	X	X	X

*Comorbidities commonly associated with these class of substances include intoxication delirium, withdrawal delirium, diamagnet, amnestic disorder, psychotic disorders, mood disorders, anxiety disorders, sexual dysfunctions, and sleep disorders.

Source: Extracted from a table in American Psychiatric Association: *Diagnostic and Statistical Manual of Mental Disorders, Fourth Edition.* (DSM-IV). Washington, DC: APA Press, 1994, p. 177.

dependence is characterized by a cluster of cognitive, behavioral, and physiological symptoms indicating that the individual continues to use the substance despite suffering significant problems related to it; it can apply to all the 11 classified controlled substances except caffeine. The pattern usually consists of repeated self-administration resulting in tolerance, withdrawal, and compulsive drug-taking behavior. *Substance abuse* is a maladaptive pattern manifested by recurrent and significant adverse consequences related to the repeated use of substances. The use disorder does not include tolerance, withdrawal, or a pattern of compulsive use. *See also* addiction; addiction medicine; addiction psychiatry; alcohol and other drug dependence; alcoholism; CAGE; dependence; Minnesota model; partial hospitalization program; problem drinking.

substantial violation   A pattern of care over a substantial number of cases that is inappropriate, unnecessary, does not meet the recognized standards of care, or is not supported by the documentation of care required by a peer review organization (PRO). PROs identify potential violations; the Office of the Inspector General of the U.S. Department of Health and Human Services makes the final decision as to whether the violation occurred. *See also* gross and flagrant violation.

substituted judgment doctrine   A legal rule, applied by some courts, which requires a guardian or other person making treatment decisions on behalf of an incompetent person to base that decision on what the incompetent person himself or herself would want under the circumstances, as distinguished from what the decision maker believes would be in the best interest of the incompetent patient. *See also* incompetent; judgement; Quinlan case.

subtherapeutic   Below the dosage levels used to treat disease. *See also* pharmacotherapeutics.

suicide   *See* assisted suicide; physician-assisted suicide.

summary grid score   For purposes of Joint Commission accreditation, a number that indicates an organization's overall accreditation performance. The summary grid score is calculated from the grid element scores. *Synonym*: grid score. *See also* accreditation decision grid; grid element score.

sundowning   Although there is no universally held definition and no clear explanation of this phenomenon, the term commonly refers to episodes of agitated behavior and/or delirium that become more frequent or more severe in the late afternoon or at night. It is usually seen in patients with dementia and is often termed a "disruptive nocturnal behavior."

sunshine law   A state or federal law that requires most meetings of regulatory bodies to be held in public and most of their decisions and records to be disclosed.

superseding cause   In law, an intervening cause that is so substantially responsible for the ultimate injury that it acts to cut off the liability of preceding actors, regardless of whether their prior negligence was a substantial factor in bringing about the injury complained of. *See also* intervening cause.

supervening cause   *See* intervening cause.

supervised living   For purposes of Joint Commission accreditation, an environment providing 24-hour mental illness, alcohol/drug abuse, mental retardation/developmental disabilities, assisted living for the elderly, or post-acute traumatic brain injury rehabilitation services to patients who are not in an acute phase of illness, do not require 24-hour professional nursing supervision, and are capable of self-preservation in case of an internal disaster. Supervised living takes place in a dormitory or less structured setting than an inpatient environment.

supplemental health insurance   Insurance that covers medical expenses not covered by separate health insurance already held by the insured individual. For example, many insurance companies sell insurance to Medicare beneficiaries, which covers either the costs of cost sharing required by Medicare, services not covered, or both. *See also* cost sharing; insurance.

supplemental recommendation   In Joint Commission accreditation, a recommendation or group of recommendations that encompasses a standard(s) that was scored in less than substantial compliance (ie, less than a score of 1) but did not result in a type I recommendation. If not resolved, a supplemental recommendation may affect a future accreditation decision. *See also* accreditation decision; type I recommendation.

supplemental security income (SSI)   Federally sponsored supportive income for low-income aged, blind, and disabled individuals, established by Title XVI of the Social Security Act. Supplemental security income replaced state welfare programs for the aged, blind, and disabled on January 1, 1972. Receipt of federal SSI benefits or a state supplement to SSI is often used to establish Medicaid eligibility. *See also* categorically needy; Social Security Act.

Supplementary Medical Insurance Program (Part B)   The voluntary portion of Medicare in which all persons entitled to the hospital insurance program (Part A) may enroll for a monthly premium that is matched in amount from federal general revenues. Covered services include physician services, home health care services, outpatient hospital services, and laboratory, pathology, and radiological services. Part B refers to Part B of Title XVIII of the Social Security Act, the legislative authority for the program. *See also* Medicare; Social Security Act.

support care   Care provided to assist patients in activities of daily living or maintenance and management of household routines. *See also* activities of daily living; homemaker services; transitional living.

support group   A group of individuals with the same or similar problems or issues, which meet periodically to share experiences and solutions to problems and to support each other, for example, an alcoholism support group. *See also* group therapy.

supportive living *See* transitional living.

SUPPORT (Study to Understand Prognoses and Preferences for Outcomes and Risks of Treatment) Prognostic Model A system for making objective estimates of the probable survival of seriously ill, hospitalized adults over a 180-day period, using each patient's diagnosis, age, number of days in the hospital before entry into the study, presence of cancer, neurological function, and 11 physiological variables recorded on day 3 of the study. *See also* prognosis.

support services Services, exclusive of medical, nursing, and ancillary services, provided in a patient's place of residence to meet the identified needs of patients who require help in maintaining and managing household routines such as cleaning or shopping. Examples include laundry service, chore service, housekeeping, food service, purchasing, maintenance, central supply, materials management, and security. *See also* ancillary services; environmental services.

support surfaces Special beds, mattresses, mattress overlays, or seat cushions that reduce or relieve pressure while sitting or lying, used to prevent or alleviate pressure ulcers. They include such devices as air flotation beds, alternating-air mattresses or overlays, donut-type devices, dynamic devices, foam mattress overlays, static air mattresses, static devices or surfaces, and static water. *See also* pressure ulcer.

surface ambulance *See* ambulance.

Surgeon General of the United States An individual appointed by the president of the United States with the consent of the Senate, serving as the nation's chief spokesperson on public health and as an advisor both to the government and to the general population about hazards or dangers to health and about actions that can be taken to prevent disease and maintain health. Under successive government reorganizations, the surgeon general has maintained a separate office in or has been located within another office in the Department of Health and Human Services (DHHS). The position was vacant from January 1, 1995 (with national debate over the viability of the position) up to fall of 1997, when a nomination was prepared for submission. The position is now located within the Office of Public Health and Science in DHHS. *See also* Public Health Service Act, and in Appendix A, government organization section.

surgery **1.** Any operative or manual procedure undertaken for diagnosing or treating a disease, injury, or deformity. *See also* breast-conserving surgery; bypass graft surgery; cataract surgery; coronary artery surgery; elective surgery; emergency surgery; endoscopy; major surgery; mastectomy; second-look surgery; sponge count. **2.** The branch and specialty of medicine dealing with diagnosing and treating injury, deformity, and disease by manual and instrumental means. *See also* ambulatory surgery; chemosurgery; cryosurgery; general surgery;

microsurgery; neurosurgery; oral and maxillofacial surgery; orthopedic surgery; operation; plastic surgery; psychosurgery; surgical specialties; surgical team; thoracic surgery; vascular surgery.

surgical center *See* freestanding ambulatory surgical facility.

surgical critical care A branch of medicine and subspecialty of general surgery involving the management of the critically ill and postoperative patient, particularly the trauma victim, in the emergency department, intensive care unit, trauma unit, burn unit, or other similar settings. *See also* critical care medicine; general surgery.

surgical-site infection (SRI) **1.** A major type of nosocomial infection, which may be introduced preoperatively (as during hair-removal to prepare for surgery), during surgery, or postoperatively during care of the surgical wound. **2.** An infection that occurs in the surgical wound after discharge. Surveillance of SRI rates, preventable SRIs, and risk is a major task for health care organizations because of concerns about harm to the patient, prolongation of hospitalization, and increased costs for therapy. *See also* catheter-related infection; infection-control program; nosocomial infection; postoperative care; wound infection.

surgical smoke Airborne particulate matter and gases associated with smoke (plumes) from laser and electrosurgical procedures. The health hazards of exposure include mutagenic and carcinogenic potential, infection, and annoyances and disruptions (eg, visual impairment from smoke obscuring the operating site). Surgical smoke can be removed by smoke-evacuator units and smoke-evacuation pencils (catheters attached to electrocautery pencil).

surgical specialties A branch of surgery in which surgeons specialize, such as general surgery, neurological surgery, plastic surgery, and thoracic surgery. *See also* specialty; surgery.

surgical team The group of professionals including surgeons, other physicians, nurses, technicians, and other skilled personnel who work together to perform surgical procedures on patients. *See also* surgery; team.

surgicenter *See* freestanding ambulatory surgical facility.

surrogate decision maker Someone appointed to act on behalf of another. Surrogates make decisions only when an individual is without capacity or has given permission to involve others. *Synonym:* surrogate. *See also* advocate; family; guardian.

surrogate reporter A person such as a caregiver who reports symptoms, activities, and other information normally supplied by self-report for patients whose direct responses to questions may not be reliable (eg, patients with Alzheimer's or other kinds of dementia).

surrogate's court A trial court responsible for hearing proceedings regarding the estates of deceased and incompetent persons.

surveillance Ongoing monitoring using methods distinguished by their practicability, uniformity, and rapidity, rather than by complete accuracy. The purpose of surveillance is to detect changes in trend or distribution to initiate investigative or control measures. *See also* hazard-surveillance program; monitoring and evaluation; quality surveillance.

Surveillance, Epidemiology, and End Results (SEER) A national cancer registry and monitoring system maintained by the National Cancer Institute. The program collects data on incidence rates for geographical regions, different population groups, and different cancers.

survey An on-site assessment of a health care organization for purposes of accreditation, certification, or licensure. *See also* accreditation survey.

survey instrument The interview schedule, questionnaire, medical examination record form, or other instrument used in a survey.

surveyor For purposes of Joint Commission accreditation, a physician, nurse, administrator, laboratorian, or any other health care professional who meets the Joint Commission's surveyor selection criteria, evaluates standards compliance, and provides education and consultation regarding standards compliance to surveyed organizations or networks.

survey team For purposes of Joint Commission accreditation, the group of health care professionals who work together to perform an accreditation survey.

swing bed A bed regularly maintained by a health care organization for short- and long-term use, depending on need. *See also* bed conversion.

symptom An indication of disorder or disease, especially when experienced by an individual as a change from normal functions, sensation, or appearance; for example, headache is a symptom of many diseases or conditions ranging from migraine to meningitis. *See also* American Urological Association Symptom Index; finding; sign; symptomatology; syndrome; withdrawal symptoms.

symptomatology **1.** The science of symptoms. **2.** The combined symptoms of a disease or condition. *See also* symptom.

syndrome A group of symptoms that collectively indicate or characterize a disease, a psychological disorder, or another abnormal condition, as in Down syndrome. *See also* adult respiratory distress syndrome; AIDS; asthma; attention-deficit/hyperactivity disorder; cauda equina syndrome; congestive heart failure; culture-bound syndrome; familial colon cancer syndrome; multiple organ dysfunction syndrome; Munchausen's syndrome; pacemaker syndrome; posttraumatic stress disorder; respira-

tory distress syndrome of the newborn; second-impact syndrome; systemic inflammatory response syndrome; symptom; temporomandibular disorder.

systematic error **1.** Error that often has a recognizable source, such as a faulty measurement instrument or a pattern that is consistently wrong in a particular direction. *See also* bias; measurement error. **2.** Difference of results or inferences from the truth, or processes leading to such differences. **3.** The extent to which the statistical method used in a study does not estimate the quantity to be measured, or does not test the hypothesis to be tested. *See also* measurement error.

systematic review A highly structured review article that synthesizes the results of previously conducted studies on a particular health topic. A meta-analysis is one type of systematic review. *See also* meta-analysis.

systematic sampling A process in which one case is selected randomly, and the next cases are selected according to a fixed period or interval; for example, every fifth patient who arrives in a hospital unit becomes part of the random sample. *See also* sampling.

systematized nomenclature of medicine (SNOMED) A comprehensive, multiaxial nomenclature classification created by the College of American Pathologists for the indexing of the entire medical record, including signs and symptoms, diagnoses, and procedures. SNOMED is officially titled the Systematized Nomenclature of Human and Veterinary Medicine. Originally developed as a system for pathology in the 1960s, SNOMED International was introduced in 1993 and is rapidly being accepted worldwide as a standard for indexing medical record information. SNOMED modules are topography; morphology; function; living organisms; chemicals, drugs, and biological products; physical agents, activities, and forces; occupations; social context; diseases/diagnoses; procedures; and general linkages/modifiers. *See also* medical record.

Système International units (SI units) An international measurement system, commonly known as the metric system. It is based on seven base units, from which all other measurements are derived. The units are length (meter), mass (kilogram), time (second), amount of substance (mole), thermodynamic temperature (Kelvin), electric current (ampere), and luminous intensity (candela). *Synonym:* metric system.

systemic-cause variation *See* common-cause variation.

systemic inflammatory response syndrome (SIRS) Defined by a 1991 consensus conference on definitions to characterize the clinical manifestations of hypermetabolism, replacing the term *sepsis syndrome* with SIRS as the presence of two or more of the following: (1) temperature greater than 38° C or less than 36° C, (2) heart rate greater than 90 beats per minute, (3) tachypnea (> 20 respirations per minute or PCO_2 < 32 mm Hg), (4) white blood cell count greater than 12.0×10^9/L, or (5) more than 10% band forms. *See also* sepsis.

systemic problem   A problem caused not by employees but by the faulty structure of a working (or nonworking) system.

systems analysis   The analysis of the resources (human, financial, material, and so forth), organization, administration, procedures, and policies needed to carry a specific process. The analysis usually includes a list of options in each category and their relative merits. *See also* computer modeling.

systems thinking   A school of thought evolving from earlier systems analysis theory, propounding that virtually all outcomes are the result of systems rather than individuals. The theory is characterized by extensive use of computer modeling to simulate the effects or changes on existing systems. *See also* computer modeling.

Tt

tachycardia A rapid heart rate, especially one above 100 beats per minute in an adult. *See also* arrhythmia.

tail coverage Insurance purchased to protect the insured after the end of a claims-made policy and to cover events that occurred during the period of the claims-made policy, but for which a claim was not made during the period. Tail coverage protects the insured in case a claim is made after the original policy has lapsed. *See also* claims-made coverage; coverage.

tailored survey A Joint Commission survey in which standards from more than one accreditation manual are used in assessing compliance. This type of survey may include using specialist surveyors appropriate to the standards selected for survey. *See also* Joint Commission survey.

talking over testing Describes a key finding of the U.S. Preventive Services Task Force, based on review of the evidence, that clinicians are now more likely to help their patients prevent future disease by asking, educating, and counseling them about personal health behaviors than by performing physical examinations or tests. *See also* testing over talking.

tamoxifen A nonsteroidal anti-estrogen chemopreventive agent used to treat estrogen receptor-positive breast cancer and sometimes used in chemoprevention for postmenopausal women at high risk for breast cancer. As of mid-1996, a Grand Rounds report of the National Cancer Institute indicated that because precise overall risk could not be predicted, tamoxifen chemoprevention could not be recommended outside of a clinical trial.

tampering In data analysis, taking action on some signal of variation without taking into account the difference between special-cause and common-cause variation. *See also* common-cause variation; data analysis; special-cause variation.

tamper resistant A package that is constructed so as to make tampering with the product difficult or impossible.

Tanner staging A five-stage system for rating sexual physical maturity, correlating chronological age with anatomical features of development.

Tarasoff* v *The Regents of the University of California [551 P.2d 334 (Cal. 1976)] A landmark decision by the California courts holding that when a patient presents a serious danger to a foreseeable victim, the patient's psychotherapist has a duty to use reasonable care to protect the intended victim. Thirty jurisdictions have issued a ruling or statute involving some variation of this decision. *Synonym*: Tarasoff rule. *See also* duty to warn.

targeted mortality method An approach to quality assessment in which deaths in certain types of cases are targeted for review. Examples include deaths in diagnosis-related groups (DRGs) with an average death rate of more than 5%, deaths occurring within one day of any procedure, and deaths in which burns are reported as a secondary diagnosis.

target organ **1.** An organ designated to receive treatment (especially from radiation); an organ at risk of damage from a disease process (such as the kidney from high blood pressure). **2.** In nuclear medicine, an organ intended to receive the greatest concentration of a diagnostic radioactive tracer (such as the liver, when it is injected to detect hepatic lesions). **3.** In endocrinology, an organ most affected by a specific hormone (such as the thyroid gland, which is the target organ of thyroid-stimulating hormone).

task force A temporary grouping of individuals and resources assembled to accomplish a specific objective, as in a task force for developing performance measures in a specified organizational area, such as medication use. A task force actively pursues its mission, after which it is disbanded. *See also* ad hoc committee; expert task force for indicator development.

Tax Equity and Fiscal Responsibility Act *See* TEFRA of 1982.

taxonomy The science of the classification of organisms according to their resemblances and differences, with the application of names or other labels. *See also* nosology.

Taylorism *See* motion study.

T cell *See* HIV.

***t*-distribution** The distribution of a quotient of independent random variables, the numerator of which is a standardized normal variate and the denominator of which is the positive square root of the quotient of a chi-square distributed variate and its number of degrees of freedom. *See also* distribution; random variable; *t*-test.

teaching hospital A medical school-affiliated or university-owned hospital with accredited programs in medical, allied health, or nursing education. Hospitals that educate nurses and other health personnel but do not train physicians, or that have only programs of continuing education for practicing professionals, are not considered to be teaching hospitals. *See also* housestaff; medical practice plan; tertiary care center; university hospital.

teaching rounds A clinical instructional process in which a teaching physician takes his or her medical students, interns, or residents to the bedsides of patients in a teaching hospital to review the patients' course and treatment. *Synonym*: ward rounds. *See also* rounds.

team A group of people pooling their skills, talents, and knowledge. *See also* the following team terms, as well as charter statement; coach; crossfunctional; disaster medical assistance team; distributed leadership; facilitator; functional team; interdisciplinary; multidisciplinary; Patient Outcomes Research Teams; project team; quality improvement team; self-directed team; shared decision making; surgical team; survey team.

team building   An organizational development technique for improving a work group's performance and attitudes by clarifying its goals and its members' expectations of each other.

team culture   The acquired and shared beliefs, values, and attitudes of a team manifested by working collaboration and shared judgments and behavior.

team nursing   A type of organization of nursing services in which a team headed by a registered nurse, with other registered nurses and ancillary personnel, cares for a group of patients in an inpatient care unit. *See also* nursing; primary nursing; team.

technique   *See* Delphi technique; double-blind technique; Frailty and Injuries: Cooperative Studies of Intervention Techniques; implementation techniques; method; nominal group technique; Program Evaluation and Review Technique; projective technique; single-blind technique; sterile technique.

technological obsolescence   Technology becoming outdated due to technological advances. For example, respirators have made iron lungs obsolete.

technology assessment (TA)   *See* health care technology assessment; health care technology assessment programs (and accompanying table).

TEFRA (Tax Equity and Fiscal Responsibility Act of 1982)   Federal legislation passed in 1982 that raised tax revenue and established a Medicare prospective payment system for reimbursing specialty hospitals providing services to postacute patients (eg, rehabilitation and long term care hospitals). Because risk contracts with HMOs offered the potential to constrain Medicare costs, Congress modified the program's HMO provision to permit HCFA to enter risk contracts with HMOs and comprehensive medical plans, to pay for hospice care, and to extend coverage for ancillary services. It also prohibited employers from forcing employees aged 65 to 69 to use Medicare instead of participating in the employer's health plan. *See also* Medicare secondary payer; peer review organization; rehabilitation hospital; retrospective reimbursement.

telemedicine   The practice by which a registered nurse or other qualified practitioner supplies patients with information about health care and advice on nonurgent medical conditions via the telephone. For example, many insurers have set up toll-free numbers that members can call to get advice on nutrition, treating colds and flu, preventive medicine, and so forth. For serious medical conditions or urgent care, the practitioner taking the call refers the member to his or her primary care physician.

telemetry   The science and technology of automatic measurement and transmission of data by wire, radio, or other means from remote sources, as from mobile intensive care units (ambulances) to a receiving station, such as one located in a hospital emergency department, where the data may be recorded and analyzed. *See also* biotelemetry.

temporary bed   A bed provided for use by patients at times when a health care organization's patient census exceeds the number of beds regularly maintained.

temporary privileges   Temporary authorization granted by a governing body to a licensed individual to provide patient care services in the organization for a limited period or to a specific patient for that patient's hospitalization, within limits based on the individual's professional license, education, training, experience, competence, health status, and judgment. *See also* clinical privileges; emergency privileges; privileging.

temporomandibular disorder (TMD)   A group of often painful medical and dental conditions that affect the temporomandibular joint (TMJ) and chewing muscles, embracing a wide variety of symptoms and signs that are overlapping but have no common etiology or biological explanation. A 1996 NIH Technology Assessment Conference examined the controversy surrounding virtually all aspects of TMD, starting with the very term for the disorder. Depending on the practitioner and the diagnostic methodology, the term TMD has been used to characterize conditions presenting as pain in the face or jaw joint area, headaches, earaches, dizziness, masticatory musculature hypertrophy, limited mouth opening, closed or open TMJ lock, abnormal occlusal wear, clicking or popping sounds in the jaw joint, and other complaints. In the absence of a consensus on an etiological basis for a definition, the NIH Technology Assessment Statement recommends using for a temporary definition the detailed description of symptoms and underlying conditions developed by the American Association of Oral and Maxillofacial Surgeons in its 1995 Parameters of Care for Oral and Maxillofacial Surgery. Given evidence that the disorder is frequently self-limiting, a treatment plan based on self-management or conservative, noninvasive, reversible therapies is recommended. The extensive restorations carried out by some practitioners do not seem warranted to treat a disorder that may change over time. *See also* syndrome.

teratology   The branch of science dealing with the production, development, and classification of abnormal embryos and fetuses.

terminable-at-will   A contract that can be terminated at any time without cause. *See also* contract.

terminal care document   *See* living will.

term infant   Any neonate whose birth occurs from the beginning of the first day (260th day) of the 38th week, through the end of the last day (294th day) of the 42nd week following onset of the last menstrual period.

tertiary care   Health services provided by highly specialized providers, such as medical subspecialists (eg, pediatric endocrinologist, hand surgeon). These services frequently require complex technological and support facilities. *Synonym:* tertiary health care. *See also* levels of care; referred care; secondary care; tertiary care center.

tertiary care center   A medical facility that receives referrals from both primary and secondary care levels and usually offers tests, treatments, and procedures that are not available elsewhere. Most tertiary care centers offer a mixture of primary, secondary, and tertiary care services. *See also* center of excellence; teaching hospital; tertiary care.

tertiary prevention   *See* prevention.

test hypothesis   *See* null hypothesis.

testing over talking   Describes a tendency of clinicians to emphasize preventive screening approaches that use tests and procedures rather than relying on counseling, asking questions, and education approaches that encourage patients to change harmful personal behaviors. *See also* talking over testing.

test reliability   In research, the dependability of a measuring tool, as reflected in the consistency of the result it provides when repeated measurements are made of the same parameter. *See also* reliability testing; test, retest reliability.

test, retest reliability   A technique of repeating a measurement procedure on the same set of subjects to estimate reliability. The source of error assessed is that of fluctuating, temporary characteristics of the subjects. *See also* reliability testing; test reliability.

test statistic   A measure calculated from data sampled from a population, used to measure difference between the data and what is expected on the null hypothesis. Rejection of the null hypothesis will take place if either the p (probability) value is small enough or the test statistic is larger than a predetermined requirement. *See also* null hypothesis; p value; two-tailed test.

thanatology   The study of death and dying, especially in their psychological and social aspects.

thematic apperception test (TAT)   A psychodiagnostic projective technique using an adult patient's telling of "stories" about pictures to discover personality conflicts. The test involves presenting stimulus pictures to the patient, who makes up a story about the figures and objects in each picture. *See also* projective technique; Rorschach test.

theophylline   *See* asthma medications (and accompanying table).

theory x   A management theory stating that managers must coerce, cajole, threaten, and closely supervise subordinates to motivate them. It is an authoritarian supervisory approach to management. *See also* management; theory y; theory z.

theory y   A management theory stating that the right conditions and rewards will result in the average employee finding work to be a source of satisfaction,

being willing to exercise self-direction toward goals to which he or she is committed, and being creative. *See also* management; theory x; theory z.

theory z   A management theory describing the Japanese system of management characterized by workers' involvement in management, resulting in higher productivity than the U.S. management model, and a highly developed system of organizational and sociological rewards. *See also* management; theory x; theory y.

therapeutic environment   The social and physical surroundings of a health care setting that support and encourage recovery or maintenance of health. For example, a more homelike atmosphere and informative, supportive staff have in many cases been more successful at encouraging recovery in hospitals, subacute facilities, and intermediate care centers than traditional, sterile-looking surroundings and staff with paternalistic attitudes toward care delivery.

therapeutic equivalence   The degree to which two formulations of different active ingredients are judged by the clinical staff to have acceptable similar therapeutic effects.

therapeutic equivalents   Drugs that have essentially identical effects in treating a disease or condition. Therapeutic equivalents are not necessarily chemical equivalents or bioequivalents. Drugs with the same treatment effect that are not chemically equivalent are called clinically equivalent. *See also* generic equivalents.

therapeutic foster care   For purposes of Joint Commission accreditation, intensive services provided to no more than two patients in treatment in a single residence. Services are delivered primarily by treatment foster parents who bear direct responsibility for implementing the select in-home aspects of the treatment plan.

therapeutic index   The ratio between the toxic dose and the therapeutic dose of a drug, used as a measure of the relative safety of the drug for a specified treatment. *See also* therapeutic range.

therapeutic misadventure   Accidental overdose of a drug due to effects of a second drug or a special situation that makes the drug more potent or toxic; for example, the overingestion of acetaminophen by alcoholics, leading to hepatotoxicity (liver poisoning).

therapeutic nihilism   A recurring attitude of skepticism about the whole medical system and its cost-effectiveness, dating back to a nineteenth-century doctrine that existing drugs and therapies were useless. The attitude reappears under new forms with new targets.

therapeutic privilege   A legal exception to the rule that an informed consent must be obtained before therapy. It generally requires that the disclosure of information would likely worsen a patient's condition or render him or her so emotionally distraught as to hinder effective therapy. It is not an excuse to omit disclosure because of a physician's concern that a competent patient will elect to forgo the care. *See also* informed consent; paternalism.

therapeutic radiology　*See* radiation oncology.

therapeutic range　Dose of medication determined for specific patients, within a lowest and highest recommended amount, that is likely to produce a desired clinical response. *See also* dose; therapeutic index; subtherapeutic.

therapeutic recreation　*See* recreational therapy.

therapeutics　The science of the treatment of diseases and healing. *See also* chronotherapeutics; pharmacotherapeutics; pharmacy and therapeutics committee.

therapy　The treatment of a disease or condition.

thermography　The pictorial representation of an area in terms of its temperature and temperature differences. The most commonly used method detects and records infrared radiation from the body surface, as in detecting tumors of the breast.

third-party administrator　*See* fiscal intermediary.

third-party billing　The preparation of bills, statements, and related documentation by a health care provider on behalf of a patient and their submission to a third-party payer (an insurer or a third-party administrator) for payment directly to either the health care provider or to the beneficiary. *See also* third-party payer.

third-party payer　A payer (usually an insurance company, a prepayment plan, or a government agency) that pays or insures health or medical expenses on behalf of beneficiaries or recipients, but does not receive or provide health care services. The payer is the third party, and the patient and the provider are the first two parties. *See also* allowable cost; assignment; carrier; covered charge; fourth party; interim rate; payer; private patient; prudent buyer principle; reasonable cost; third party billing.

third sector　Organizations, especially nonprofit organizations, that fit neither in the public sector (government) nor the private sector (business).

thoracic surgery　The branch and specialty of medicine that encompasses the operative, perioperative, and critical care of patients with pathologic conditions within the chest. It includes both heart and lung surgery. *Synonyms:* cardiothoracic surgery; cardiovascular surgery; chest surgery. *See also* pneumothorax; surgery.

thoracotomy　Surgical incision of the chest wall.

threshold　The level or point at which a stimulus is strong enough to signal the need for organization response to indicator data and the beginning of the process for determining why the threshold has been approached or crossed. *See also* indicator threshold; outlier threshold.

thromboembolism　A condition in which a blood vessel is blocked by an embolus carried in the bloodstream from its site of formation. *See also* antithrombotic therapy; embolism; pulmonary embolism.

thrombolytic therapy　Administration of a pharmacological agent with the intention of causing thrombolysis of an abnormal blood clot, such as in the coronary (myocardial infarction) or pulmonary (pulmonary embolism) arteries. Available agents include streptokinase, urokinase, and tissue plasminogen activator. These preparations may be given either intravenously or directly into the blocked artery. *Synonym:* clotbuster. *See also* anticoagulation; embolism; GUSTO; streptokinase; TIMI studies; tissue plasminogen activator.

thrombus　An intravascular blood clot.

tilt table test　A clinical maneuver in which a patient is placed head up on a table tilted at a 40° to 80° angle from horizontal and held in a motionless upright position to provoke syncope (fainting), bradycardia, or hypotension. The tilt table can be rocked back and forth to test a patient's circulatory system's response to different gravitational forces; usually, it is used to detect neurocardiogenic syncope.

time and motion study　*See* motion study.

time-limited order　Guideline or policy on an intervention that has only provisional or temporary approval under specifically defined and documented circumstances. Often such an order is for a therapy or procedure that is generally discouraged or regarded as a last resort after ruling out alternatives. An example is orders on use of chemical (drug) or physical restraints for patients with Alzheimer's disease or other dementias.

timeliness　A Joint Commission performance dimension addressing the degree to which care is provided to a patient at the most beneficial or necessary time. *See also* intervention; dimensions of performance.

time plot　*See* run chart.

time trade-off (TTO)　Technique that quantifies preferences for a specific health state, by assessing how much time a patient would be willing to give up to be freed from a reduced health state. The time trade-off utility is defined as the number of symptom-free years divided by the number of years with symptoms, at the point of indifference. *See also* patient utilities measurement.

TIMI (Thrombolysis in Myocardial Infarction) studies　A series of long-term, multicenter, multinational, multiagent studies designed to determine which of a number of early interventions will provide the best survival for myocardial infarctions. The TIMI trials have tested early thrombolytic therapy, various combinations of tissue plasminogen activator (t-PA), heparin, and aspirin and coronary arteriography followed by prophylactic percutaneous transluminal angioplasty.

tissue bank　A facility for collecting, cataloging, storing, and distributing body tissues for use in surgery (eg, corneal tissue, bone) or tissue culture. *See also* organ bank.

tissue plasminogen activator (t-PA) An enzyme that converts plasminogen to plasmin, used to dissolve blood clots rapidly and selectively, especially in the treatment of heart attacks. *See also* GUSTO; streptokinase; thrombolytic therapy; TIMI studies.

tissue transplantation To transfer tissue from one body to another. Tissues that can be transplanted include corneas, cardiac valves, bone, tendon, arteries, veins, middle ear bones, cartilage, and skin. Tissue donation can take place following death from most causes, including brain death. Tissues can be recovered up to 24 hours after death. Tissues are transplanted far more commonly than organs. *See also* organ transplantation.

TNM (Tumor-Node-Metastasis) System *See* cancer staging system (and accompanying table).

tobacco control regulations **1.** FDA Regulations Restricting the Sale and Distribution of Cigarettes and Smokeless Tobacco Products to Protect Children and Adolescents, issued in February 1997. The FDA's advertising restrictions, which were struck down by a federal district court, are under appeal by the government, and the scope of the FDA's jurisdiction over tobacco as a drug delivery device remained unsettled as of the summer of 1997. **2.** Initiative launched in May 1994 by working group of state attorneys general to study problem of illegal tobacco sales to minors. The report and recommendations of the state attorneys general initiative has prompted action on several fronts to limit youth access to tobacco, including work with the Campaign for Tobacco-Free Kids (comprising several medical specialty societies)and antismoking groups, negotiation with the tobacco industry and trade groups, and coordination with the Clinton administration's antismoking campaign.

tolerance **1.** Physiological resistance to a drug or poison. **2.** Acceptance of a tissue graft or transplant without immunological rejection.

top-box score format A method for presenting aggregated data, which looks only at the percentage of responses in the top (most positive) category. *See also* composite score.

top-down global budgeting A total level of expenditure on health care set by government mandate. *See also* global budget.

top-down management Traditional management system in which top management plans and institutes organizationwide processes without the input of frontline workers. This system is contrary to the bottom-up empowerment model advocated under quality improvement. *See also* management.

tort In law, a private or civil (not criminal) wrongful act that is neither a crime nor a breach of contract, but that renders the perpetrator liable to the victim for damages, as in trespassing or negligence. The essential elements of a tort are the existence of a legal duty owed by a defendant to a plaintiff, breach of that duty, and a causal relation between a defendant's conduct and the resulting damage

to a plaintiff. Torts generally involve personal injuries. *See also* damages, medical injury; negligence; professional negligence; tort liability.

tort liability Liability imposed by a court for breach of a duty implied by law, contrasted with contractual liability, which is breach of duty arising from an agreement. The tort liability system determines fault and awards compensation for civil wrongs, including medical malpractice. *See also* liability; tort.

total hip Slang for total hip replacement, as in "16 total hips were done during that period."

total parenteral nutrition (TPN) The process of giving *all* nutriment within a vein (directly into the bloodstream) and not through the alimentary tract. TPN involves the continuous infusion of a hyperosmolar solution containing carbohydrates, amino acids, fats, vitamins, and other necessary nutrients through an indwelling catheter (tubing) inserted into the superior vena cava. The principle indications for TPN are found in seriously ill patients suffering from malnutrition, sepsis (blood poisoning), or surgical or accidental trauma when use of the gastrointestinal tract for feeding is not possible. *Synonym:* total parenteral alimentation. *See also* enteral nutrition; infusion therapy services; nutrition; nutritional support; parenteral nutrition.

total quality management (TQM) A structured, systematic process for creating organizationwide participation in planning and implementing continuous quality improvement (CQI) programs. TQM embodies a set of principles that includes customer focus, prioritizing quality over cost, understanding and improving processes, employee involvement, cross-functional management, continuous improvement, and standardization. *See also* just in time; learning organization; National Demonstration Project on Quality Improvement in Health Care; quality assurance engineering; quality circle; quality management; quality trilogy; zero defects.

toxemia *See* pregnancy-induced hypertension.

toxicology The quantitative study of the nature, effects, and detection of materials that may or may not adversely affect the health of humans or animals. *See also* clinical toxicology; medical toxicology.

tracer A condition or disease chosen for appraisal in programs and organizations that seek to measure and assess performance and quality of care. The assumption is that performance and quality of care relating to the tracer condition or disease is typical or representative of the performance and quality of care provided in general.

track record A record of actual performance or accomplishment, as in a health care organization with an excellent track record in improving the quality of care provided to patients. *See also* performance; performance assessment.

traditional medicine Systems of medicine based on cultural beliefs and practices handed down from generation to generation. The concept includes herbal therapy, mystical/spiritual rituals, and other treatments that may not be explained by modern Western medicine. *See also* alternative medicine; herbal medicine.

tranquilizer A traditional grouping of drugs said to have a soothing or calming effect on mood, thought, or behavior, including anti-anxiety agents (minor tranquilizers), antimanic agents, and antipsychotic agents (major tranquilizers). These drugs act by different mechanisms and are used for different therapeutic purposes.

transcutaneous electric nerve stimulation (TENS) A noninvasive, nonaddictive method of pain control involving electrical stimulation of nerves or muscles. Electrodes are placed on the skin and attached to a stimulator by wires. (The optimal placement of electrodes—trigger points—may correspond with acupuncture analgesia points.) The electric impulses generated block transmission of pain signals to the brain. *Synonym:* electrostimulation. *See also* pain management.

transdermal nicotine *See* nicotine therapy replacement.

transfer The formal shifting of responsibility for the care of a patient from (1) one care unit to another, (2) one clinical service to another, (3) the care of one licensed independent practitioner to another, or (4) one organization to another organization. *See also* discharge; intraorganization transfer; transfer agreement.

transfer agreement A written understanding that provides for the reciprocal transfer of individuals between health care organizations. A formal agreement between two health care organizations indicating the conditions under which there can be transfer of patients and exchange of clinical information between them. *See also* intraorganization transfer; patient dumping; transfer.

transfusion reaction A response by the body to the administration of incompatible blood. Causes may include red cell incompatibility or allergic sensitivity to leukocytes, platelets, or plasma protein components of the transfused blood or to the potassium or citrate preservatives in the banked blood. Transfusion reactions are variable in severity, ranging from isolated fever to severe vascular collapse and death. *See also* autologous blood transfusion; histocompatibility.

transient ischemic attack (TIA) An episode of temporary blockage of the blood supply to the brain (cerebrovascular insufficiency), usually associated with a partial blockage of an artery by atherosclerotic plaque or an embolism. Symptoms vary with the site and the degree of blockage. and may include weakness, inability to speak normally (dysphasia), numbness, and other manifestations. *Synonym:* ministroke. *See also* embolism; neuroprotective agents; stroke.

transitional living **1.** For purposes of Joint Commission accreditation, 24-hour-a-day living arrangements provided to individuals in need of a supportive environment but who are not a significant clinical risk. This level

of care is typically provided as a community reentry phase within the care continuum. **2.** When applied to networks, postacute convalescence, rehabilitation, and psychiatric care, whether provided within acute or long term care facilities or in separate programs or facilities. *Synonym:* supportive living. *See also* support care.

transition period In total quality management, a description of the time when an organization is visibly moving from an old way toward a new way. During this time, employee attitudes and behaviors range from being excited and busy to being confused and resistant. When the support for change is building, new leaders emerge, champions of the change come forward, and, with proper leadership, confusion over roles begins to clear. *See also* total quality management.

transplantation *See* histocompatibility; National Organ Transplantation Act; organ procurement; organ transplantation; required request law; tissue transplantation.

transplantation services Delivery of care pertaining to grafting tissues or organs taken from the patient's own body or from another person's.

transportation services Services relating to carrying a patient from one place to another.

transurethral resection of the prostate (TURP) A surgical technique involving the insertion of an instrument through the urethra (urinary conduit) to remove tissue from the prostate gland. *See also* prostatectomy.

trauma center A service providing emergency and specialized intensive care to critically ill and injured patients. *Synonym:* trauma unit. *See also* advanced trauma life support; traumatology.

trauma registry A repository of data on trauma patients, including causes of trauma, diagnoses, treatment, and outcome. *See also* registry.

Trauma Score (TS) A physiologic measure of injury severity developed in 1981, providing a mechanism for predicting outcomes, allocating resources, and evaluating the quality of trauma care. It evaluates respiratory, cardiovascular, and neurological characteristics of trauma patients' conditions and assigns weighted point values. The TS was revised in 1989. *See also* Abbreviated Injury Scale; Glasgow Coma Scale; overtriage; Revised Trauma Score; TRISS.

trauma severity indices Systems for assessing, classifying, and coding injuries. These systems are used in medical records, surveillance systems, and state and national registries to aid in the collecting and reporting of trauma. *See also* Abbreviated Injury Scale; Glasgow Coma Scale; Injury Severity Score; Revised Trauma Score; severity; severity measurement system; severity of illness; Trauma Score; TRISS.

traumatology The branch of medicine that deals with the treatment of serious wounds, injuries, and disabilities. *Synonym:* trauma surgery. *See also* the previous trauma terms, as well as advanced trauma life support; basic trauma life support; golden hour; load and go.

treadmill test *See* stress test.

treatment plan *See* plan of care.

tree diagram A tool that systematically maps out, in detail, the full range of paths and tasks that need to be accomplished to achieve a specific goal.

trending The process of recording and analyzing general directions of indicator rates over time. By showing both desirable and undesirable trends, trending serves as a powerful tool in monitoring and evaluating the quality of care. *See also* data trend.

triage Sorting out or screening patients seeking care to determine which service is required, with what priority, and where the service is best provided. Originally developed in military medicine and used to describe the sorting-out of battle casualties into groups of individuals who could wait for care, would benefit from immediate care, and were beyond care. Triage is used today on the battlefield, at disaster sites, in prehospital care of patients, in hospital emergency departments, and in any other situation when limited medical resources must be allocated. *See also* emergency medicine; overtriage; undertriage.

triennial survey An accreditation survey of the Joint Commission conducted every three years. *See also* accreditation survey; full survey; Joint Commission survey.

trigger point A well-localized point of tenderness. In low back problems, these points are usually located in the paravertebral areas. *See also* low back pain.

triggers In asthma, the immediate cause of allergic reaction (eg, dust mites, pets, mold). *See also* asthma; RAST.

triple-blind study A study in which subjects, investigators, and data analyzers are kept unaware of what treatment was used on which groups of individuals. *See also* bias; blinded study; double-blind technique; single-blind technique.

triple combination therapy *See* protease inhibitor.

TRISS (Trauma and Injury Severity Score) A combination of the Revised Trauma Score and the Injury Severity Score used to assess and compare different population groups. *See also* Injury Severity Score; Revised Trauma Score; trauma severity indices.

trolley car policy A facetious name for an insurance policy for which benefits are so hard to collect that it is as though the policy provided benefits only for injuries resulting from being hit by a trolley car. *See also* insurance.

tropical medicine The branch of medicine concerned with diagnosing and treating diseases, such as schistosomiasis, malaria, and yellow fever, found most commonly in tropical regions of the world. *See also* infectious diseases.

true negative A negative result in a case that does not have the condition or characteristic for which a test is conducted; for example, a true negative result occurs when a pregnancy test is negative for a nonpregnant woman. *See also* false positive; sensitivity; specificity; true positive.

true negative rate *See* specificity.

true positive A positive result in a case that has the condition or characteristic for which a test is conducted; for example, a true positive result occurs when a pregnancy test is positive for a woman who is actually pregnant. *See also* false negative; sensitivity; specificity; true negative.

true random sampling *See* simple random sampling.

t-test A significance test for assessing a hypothesis about population means. Different versions test whether the means of a population takes a particular value or tests the equality of the means of two populations. *See also* t-distribution.

tube feeding *See* nutritional support.

tuberculosis isolation A category of isolation for patients with pulmonary tuberculosis who have a positive sputum smear or chest x-ray that strongly suggests active tuberculosis. Specifications include use of a private room with special ventilation and a closed door. Gowns are used to prevent gross contamination of clothing; gloves are not indicated. *Synonym*: AFB (acid fast bacilli) isolation. *See also* acid fast bacilli; isolation.

tumor debulking Removal by surgery of as much of a cancer as possible.

tumor markers Chemical substances in the blood or other body fluids that suggest the presence of cancer. Tests to measure these substances may be used to screen people with no symptoms of the disease, to diagnose cancer in someone suspected of having it, or to monitor the course of the illness. Examples of pancreatic tumor markers are carcinoembryonic antigen (CEA), CA 19-9, pancreatic oncofetal antigen (POA), alpha-fetoprotein (AFP), neuron-specific enolase (NSE), and CA-195. *See also* alpha-fetoprotein; CA-125; cancer screening tests and procedures; PSA.

tumor-node-metastasis (TNM) *See* cancer staging system.

tumor registry A repository of data drawn from medical records and other sources on the incidence of cancer and the personal characteristics, treatment, and treatment outcomes of cancer patients. *Synonym*: cancer registry.

tumor staging *See* cancer staging system.

Tuskegee experiments [The Tuskegee Study of Untreated Syphilis in the Negro Male] A prospective study undertaken by the U.S. Public Health Service in 1932 (and later the Centers for Disease Control [CDC]), to follow 400 black men with syphilis without treating them to understand the natural course of the disease.

Both the standard syphilis treatments at the start of the study (mercury and arsenic compounds) and penicillin when it was discovered in 1947 were withheld, and federal researchers approached local physicians asking them not to provide antibiotics. The study was terminated in 1972 when it got media attention and left an enduring legacy of distrust of public health workers and the government among rural blacks in the South. This distrust surfaced in the 1980s with rumors of genocide when public health workers tried to establish AIDS education projects. President Clinton issued a formal apology for the Tuskegee medical experiment in a public ceremony on May 16, 1997, to survivors of the experiment and participants' families. At that time, the director of the CDC identified several transgressions of ethical principles related to informed consent: the participants had never been informed about the purpose of the study, had never been asked to give their informed consent, and had been intentionally misled about receiving treatment. Tuskegee University is to receive a grant from the U.S. Department of Health and Human Services to establish a Center for Bioethics in Research and Health Care to serve as a memorial to the study's legacy. *See also* ethics; informed consent; medical ethics; Nuremberg Code.

twelve-step program   A support-group approach to assist recovery from addiction or other compulsive or dysfunctional behaviors, based on the twelve steps of Alcoholics Anonymous (AA). These programs may be entirely self-help and self-governed groups or they may be guided by professionals, and they may comprise the only therapy or they may be used in conjunction with traditional psychotherapy and/or medication. Since publication of the twelve steps in 1939, AA has given permission for many self-help groups to use these steps in their own recovery programs (eg, Narcotics Anonymous, Gamblers Anonymous, Overeaters Anonymous). The central con-

cept of twelve-step programs is the devastating takeover by an addictive substance or process that makes one's life unmanageable and requires placing oneself under the direction of a higher power. In the place of words related to alcoholism, these groups may substitute "addiction," "codependency" (dysfunctional contribution to or response to the target behavior), or other terms. They may also secularize some or all of the many references to God in the original AA twelve steps. *See also* prosumer; recovery movement.

two-tailed test   A test in which the alternative hypothesis is not directional. The hypothesis examines whether two estimates of parameters are equal, without caring which one is smaller or larger. The tested hypothesis is rejected if the test statistic is an extremely small or a large value. *See also* hypothesis; test statistic.

tympanostomy tube   *See* myringotomy with insertion of tympanostomy tube.

type 1 diabetes mellitus   *See* diabetes mellitus.

type 2 diabetes mellitus   *See* diabetes mellitus.

type I error   In research and statistics, a conclusion error in which the null hypothesis is rejected when it is in fact true. A conclusion is reached that there are effects (or relationships) when there are none. *Synonym:* alpha error. *See also* error; *p* value; statistically significant.

type II error   In research and statistics, a conclusion error in which there is failure to reject the null hypothesis when it is false. In other words, a conclusion is reached that there are no effects (or relationships) when these effects (or relationships) do exist. *Synonym:* beta error. *See also* statistically significant.

type I recommendation   For purposes of Joint Commission accreditation, recommendation or group of rec-

---

THE TWELVE STEPS OF ALCOHOLICS ANONYMOUS (AA)*

1. We admitted we were powerless over alcohol—that our lives had become unmanageable.

2. Came to believe that a Power greater than ourselves could restore us to sanity.

3. Made a decision to turn our will and our lives over to the care of God as we understood Him.

4. Made a searching and fearless moral inventory of ourselves.

5. Admitted to God, to ourselves, and to another human being the exact nature of our wrongs.

6. We're entirely ready to have God remove all these defects of character.

7. Humbly asked Him to remove our shortcomings.

8. Made a list of all persons we had harmed, and became willing to make amends to them all.

9. Made direct amends to such people wherever possible, except when to do so would injure them or others.

10. Continued to take personal inventory and when we were wrong promptly admitted it.

11. Sought through prayer and meditation to improve our conscious contact with God as we understood Him, praying only for knowledge of His will for us and the power to carry that out.

12. Having had a spiritual awakening as the result of these steps, we tried to carry this message to alcoholics and to practice these principles in all our affairs.

*These steps, which describe the experience of the earliest members of the society, comprise the heart of AA's suggested program of personal recovery. Newcomers are not asked to accept or follow these steps in their entirety if they feel unwilling or unable to do so. They will usually be asked to keep an open mind, to attend meetings at which recovered alcoholics describe their personal experiences in achieving sobriety, and to read AA literature describing and interpreting the AA program.

Source: Official description on the Internet home page of Alcoholics Anonymous as of September 1997.

ommendations that addresses insufficient or unsatisfactory standards compliance in a specific performance area. Resolution of type I recommendations must be achieved within stipulated time frames for an organization to maintain its accreditation. *See also* accreditation decision; aggregation; compliance; focused survey; recommendations; supplemental recommendation.

type II recommendation   An outdated term for a supplemental recommendation resulting from a Joint Commission survey. *See* supplemental recommendation.

Uu

ultrasonic diagnostic service   A department of a health care organization providing ultrasound imaging services. *See also* echocardiography.

ultrasonography   An imaging technique, usually applied noninvasively, which uses high-frequency sound to produce an image of internal structures by the differing reflection signals produced when a beam of sound waves is projected into the body and bounces back at interfaces between those structures. Types of *noninvasive ultrasonography* include Doppler color ultrasonography, echocardiography, echoencephalography, endosonography, mammography (mammary ultrasonography), and prenatal ultrasonography. *Interventional ultrasonography* uses invasive or surgical procedures along with the ultrasound, particularly for intravascular imaging and for urological and intra-abdominal conditions. *Synonyms:* sonography; ultrasonics; ultrasound imaging. *See also* diagnostic imaging; echocardiography; imaging; mammography.

umbrella coverage   Insurance coverage relating to a broad high-limit liability policy, usually requiring underlying insurance. For instance, a health care organization may be insured for $1 million for general liability, $3 million for professional liability, and $10 million for umbrella coverage. This additional $10 million is the umbrella that picks up excess liability (not in excess of $10 million) over and above the other two policies. *Synonym:* umbrella liability insurance. *See also* coverage.

unannounced or unscheduled survey   A survey that is conducted without prior notification by the Joint Commission to a health care organization. It may occur *for cause*, meaning that the Joint Commission becomes aware of circumstances in an accredited organization that suggest a potentially serious standards-compliance problem (eg, when there is reason to believe that an immediate threat to patient health or safety exists). Alternatively, an unannounced survey may occur at *random*. Beginning July 1, 1993, approximately 5% of all institutions accredited by the Joint Commission are surveyed by one surveyor for one day at the approximate mid-accreditation point. *See also* accreditation survey; Joint Commission survey.

unbundling   **1.** The practice of separate pricing of goods and services that are normally billed under a single charge, resulting in a higher overall cost. *See also* fractionation.   **2.** Under Medicare, Part B, for nonphysician services, services that are provided to hospital inpatients and furnished to the hospital by an outside supplier or another provider. Unbundling is prohibited under the Medicare prospective payment system, and all nonphysician services provided in an inpatient setting are paid as hospital services. *See also* Medicare, Part B; prospective payment system.

uncompensated care   Care for which no payment is expected or no charge is made. It is the sum of bad debts and charity care absorbed by a health care organization in providing medical care for patients who are uninsured or are unable to pay. *See also* self-pay patient; underinsured.

underinsured   Pertains to people who do not have sufficient insurance coverage to compensate in the event of loss of life or property. *See also* adequacy of coverage; insurance; individual insured; self-pay patient; uncompensated care.

underlying cause of death   *See* death certificate.

underreporting   Failure to identify and/or count all cases, leading to reduction of the numerator of a rate, as in a (falsely) low mortality rate due to underreporting of deaths resulting from some condition. *See also* rate; report.

undertriage   The transportation of a patient who should have been cared for in a trauma center to a nontrauma center. This may result in increased patient morbidity or mortality. *See also* overtriage; triage.

underuse   *See* utilization.

underwriting   In insurance, the process of selecting, classifying, evaluating, and assuming risks according to their insurability. Its purpose is to make sure that the group insured has the same probability of loss and probable amount of loss, within reasonable limits, as the universe on which premium rates were based. Since premium rates are based on an expectation of loss, the underwriting process must classify risks into classes with about the same expectation of loss. *See also* insurance; risk.

unemployment compensation—disability   Insurance that protects people against loss due to off-the-job injury or illness. Unemployment compensation is funded by payroll deductions and is administered by a state agency. *Synonym:* state disability insurance. *See also* compensation; disability; workers' compensation.

Unified Medical Language System (UMLS)   A research and development project of the National Library of Medicine begun in 1986 to aid the development of information retrieval systems for health professionals and researchers and to make it easy for users to link disparate information systems, including computer-based patient records, bibliographic databases, factual databases, and expert systems. The project develops machine-readable "Knowledge Sources" for use by a wide variety of applications programs to overcome retrieval problems caused by differences in terminology and by the scattering of relevant information across many databases. *See also* computer-based medical record.

unified payment   A payment method in which a health care organization and a physician or other health professional are paid a single, fixed amount for each service, day, or patient case. This method usually is applied to services performed by a facility and by a physician in the facility setting. *See also* payment.

Uniform Anatomical Gift Act (1969) A statute adopted by every state that makes it legally possible for individuals to make known their intentions, while living, to donate their organs after death. *See also* anatomical gift.

uniform basic data set *See* minimum data set.

Uniform Bill of 1992 (UB-92) A revision of UB-82, a federal directive requiring hospitals to follow specific billing procedures, itemizing all services included and billed for each invoice.

uniform capital factor A uniform percentage added onto all DRG prices to cover an organization's capital costs for pricing in prospective payment systems. *See also* DRG; prospective payment system.

uniform claim form A standardized claim form and a standardized format for electronic claims, which would reduce administrative costs. *See also* claim.

Uniform Clinical Data Set (UCDS) A HCFA initiative and part of the Peer Review Organization Fourth Scope of Work that involves collection from the medical records of Medicare beneficiaries of approximately 1,800 data elements that describe patient demographic characteristics, clinical history, clinical findings, and therapeutic interventions. This database assists HCFA in defining Medicare research and review samples. For instance, the UCDS will allow longitudinal analyses of large beneficiary cohorts and the identification of regional, interhospital, and intrahospital practice variations. *See also* clinical data; data set; minimum data set; peer review organization.

Uniform Determination of Death Act This act, adopted by 26 states and used as a model in others, provides a legal definition of death: An individual who has sustained either (1) irreversible cessation of circulatory and respiratory functions, or (2) irreversible cessation of all functions of the entire brain, including the brainstem, is dead. A determination of death must be made in accordance with accepted medical standards. The determination of death is critical in cases of organ donation where time is critical to the viability of transplantation. *See also* brain death; organ transplantation.

Uniform Health Insurance Claim Form *See* HCFA 1500.

Uniform Hospital Discharge Data Set (UHDDS) The data element set required by the federal government as the medical content of a patient's bill under Medicare and Medicaid. Assignment to a DRG is made from this data set by a fiscal intermediary. UHDDS contains, for instance, patient age, sex, and diagnoses and procedures expressed in the category codes of *International Classification of Diseases, Ninth Revision, Clinical Modification* (ICD-9-CM). The Uniform Hospital Discharge Abstract used to collect the Uniform Hospital Discharge Data Set is an example of a discharge abstract. *See also* data set; discharge abstract; DRG; fiscal intermediary; GROUPER software; ICD-9-CM; minimum data set.

uniform reporting Reporting of financial and service data in conformance with prescribed standardized definitions to permit accurate and meaningful comparisons among providers, such as physicians and health care organizations.

Uniform Rights of the Terminally Ill Act A model act designed to provide various means by which a patient's preferences can be carried out with regard to the administration of life-sustaining treatment. The act permits an individual to execute a declaration that instructs a physician to withhold or withdraw life-sustaining treatment in the event the individual is in a terminal condition and is unable to participate in medical treatment decisions or, in the alternative, designates another individual to make decisions regarding the withholding or withdrawal of life-sustaining treatment. Further, the act authorizes an attending physician to withhold or withdraw life-sustaining treatment in the absence of a declaration upon the consent of a close relative if the action would not conflict with the individual's known intentions. A number of states have adopted the act. *See also* severability clause; withdrawing treatment.

uniform standard precautions *See* universal precautions.

unit-dose system A method of providing medications to patients whereby all medications to be given a particular patient at a specific time are packaged together in the exact dosage required for that time. *See also* dose; drug administration.

United States Adopted Names (USAN) A nonproprietary designation for any compound used as a drug, established by negotiation between the manufacturer of the compound used as a drug and a nomenclature committee known as the USAN Council, which is sponsored jointly by the American Medical Association, the American Pharmaceutical Association, and the United States Pharmacopeial Convention.

United States medical graduate (USMG) A graduate of a medical school in the United States, Puerto Rico, or Canada. *See also* foreign medical graduate.

United States Pharmacopeia (USP) A compendium of standards for drugs published by the United States Pharmacopeial Convention and revised periodically; it includes essays and tests for determining drug strength, quality, and purity. One of the three official compendia of drugs and medications in the United States recognized in the federal Food, Drug, and Cosmetic Act. The other two are the *Homeopathic Pharmacopeia of the United States* and the *National Formulary. See also Homeopathic Pharmacopeia of the United States; National Formulary;* pharmacopeia.

universal precautions An approach to infection control designed to prevent transmission of blood-borne diseases such as AIDS and hepatitis B in health care settings. Originally developed by the Centers for Disease Control and Prevention, the guidelines include specific recommendations for use of personal protective equipment, including gloves, masks, and protective eyewear. *Synonyms:* infection precautions; standard precautions; uniform standard precautions. *See also* blood-body fluid precautions; blood-borne pathogens; infection-control program; standard.

university hospital A hospital that is owned by or affiliated with a medical school and functions in the education of physicians.

unstable angina Broadly defined in the 1994 clinical practice guideline of the Agency for Health Care Policy and Research as a clinical syndrome falling between stable angina and acute myocardial infarction. It has three possible presentations, in most cases caused by significant coronary artery disease: (1) *rest angina*—chest pain that occurs at rest (usually prolonged more than 20 minutes), (2) *new onset angina*—chest pain with exertion of at least Canadian Cardiovascular Society Classification (CCSC) class III in severity occurring within two months of initial presentation, or (3) *increasing angina*—previously diagnosed angina pain that is distinctly more frequent, longer in duration, or lower in threshold, increased by at least one CCSC class within two months of initial presentation to at least CCSC III severity. *See also* angina; stable angina.

unstable medical condition A fluctuating and unpredictable condition that may warrant imminent intervention based on observable signs and symptoms.

unstructured interview An interview in which the interviewer does not determine the format or subject to be discussed. Rather, the interviewee has major control of the conversation. *See also* structured interview.

upper control limit *See* control limit.

urge incontinence *See* urinary incontinence.

urgent A degree of severity of illness or injury that is less severe than immediately life-threatening (emergency), but requiring care more quickly than elective care. *See also* level of acuity; nonurgent; severity of illness.

urgent admission The formal acceptance by a health care organization of a patient who requires immediate attention for the care and treatment of a physical or mental disorder. Generally, such a patient is admitted to the first available and suitable accommodation. *See also* admission; elective admission.

urgent care center *See* freestanding urgent care center.

urgicenter *See* freestanding urgent care center.

urinary incontinence (UI) Involuntary loss of urine, which has several possible causes that may be temporary (urinary tract infection, vaginal infection or irritation, constipation, effects of medicine) or permanent (weakness of muscles holding the bladder in place, weakness of the bladder itself, weakness of the urethral sphincter mus-

cles, overactive bladder muscles, blocked urethra as from prostate enlargement, hormone imbalance in women, neurologic disorders, immobility and consequent inability to make it to the bathroom in time). Types of UI are *stress incontinence* (due to anatomic displacement, which exerts an opening pull on the bladder orifice, as in straining or coughing (leakage may occur after laughing, getting up from a chair or bed, bending over or kneeling to pick something up); *urge incontinence* (immediate loss of urine upon feeling the need to urinate (leakage due to the inability to get to the bathroom in time; the "key in the lock" syndrome); and *overflow incontinence* (loss of small amounts of urine day and night; passing only a small amount of urine but feeling as though the bladder were still full). A wide array of techniques is available to treat UI, including behavioral techniques (bladder training, pelvic muscle exercises), medication, abstinence from caffeine (in coffee or cola drinks), and surgery. Clinical practice guidelines from AHCPR have made it clear that catheters and pads are not the first line of treatments and should be used only to make other treatments more effective or when other treatments have failed.

urology The branch and specialty of medicine dealing with the management of benign and malignant medical and surgical disorders of the adrenal gland and of the reproductive and urinary systems and their adjoining structures. *See also* bougie.

use-by date A date marked on a drug package or other perishable goods to show the latest time by which the contents should be used to avoid risk of deterioration. *See also* best-before date.

useful many The remaining factors in Pareto analysis after the vital few have been identified; the relatively large set of factors that account for only a small minority of any problem. *See also* Pareto principle; vital few.

U.S. Preventive Services Task Force (USPSTF) Established by the U.S. Public Health Service in 1984 (and currently located in AHCPR) as an independent panel of nonfederal experts that uses a systematic methodology to review the evidence of effectiveness for clinical preventive services and issues clinical practice recommendations reflecting the strength of the supporting evidence (published in the *Guide to Clinical Preventive Services,* 1996). The USPSTF works in close collaboration with primary care medical specialty societies and federal government health agencies, and it collaborates with a similar panel in Canada (Canadian Task Force on the Periodic Health Examination), which developed the methodology used by the USPSTF. *See also* Canadian Task Force on the Periodic Health Examination; evidence-based medicine.

usual, customary, and reasonable (UCR) charge A method used by health insurance plans for determining payment for services and procedures rendered by an individual health care provider. A reimbursement is based on allowing the provider's full charge if it does not exceed his or her usual charge, if it does not exceed the amount customarily charged for the service by other physicians in the area, or if it is justified in the specific circumstances of a given patient (otherwise reasonable). *See also* customary, prevailing, and reasonable charge; reasonable charge.

uterine activity monitoring *See* home uterine activity monitoring.

utilitarianism An ethical theory stating that an action is judged in terms of its consequences, that the value of an action is determined by its utility, and that all action should be directed toward achieving the greatest happiness for the greatest number of people. *Synonyms*: axiological ethics; consequential ethics. *See also* deontological ethics; ethics.

utility A term borrowed from economics and theories of rational choice to permit quantification of patients' preferences for states of health, health care options, and satisfaction with alternative outcomes. *See also* decision analysis; patient utilities measurement.

utilities management A component of an organization's management of the environment of care program designed to ensure the operational reliability, assess the special risks, and respond to failures of utility systems that support the patient care environment. *See also* environment of care.

utilities measurement *See* patient utilities measurement.

utility systems Organization systems for life support; surveillance, prevention, and control of infection; environment support; and equipment support. May include electrical distribution; emergency power; vertical and horizontal transport; heating, ventilating, and air conditioning; plumbing, boiler, and steam; piped gases; vacuum systems; or communication systems, including data-exchange systems. *See also* life-support system.

utilization The use, patterns of use, or rates of use of a specified health care service. *Overuse* is the excessive use of unnecessary services; *underuse* is the failure to use necessary heath care services. Both equally reflect a problem in quality of health care and impose a burden of increased mortality risk and diminished quality of life. Underuse is particularly evident in the area of preventive services (eg, flu shots, follow-up monitoring of high blood pressure). The case is increasingly being made to implement "underuse prevention" programs that measure underuse and address its causes. *See also* the following utilization terms.

utilization and quality control peer review organization *See* peer review organization.

utilization management The planning, organization, direction, and control of resource use relating to patient care by a health care organization. Utilization management programs are generally required by third-party payers, such as Medicare and Blue Cross, who may deny payment for services deemed inappropriate. *See also* utilization review.

utilization review (UR) The examination and evaluation of the necessity, appropriateness, and efficiency of the use of health care services, procedures, and facilities. This includes review of the appropriateness of admissions, services ordered and provided, length of stay, and discharge practices, both on a concurrent and retrospective basis. Utilization review is typically performed by a utilization review committee, peer review group, or public agency. *See also* drug utilization review; external review; Health Care Quality Improvement Program; internal review; managed indemnity plan; medical review; Medicare Conditions of Participation; utilization management.

Vv

Vaccines for Children (VFC) program A federal program created by OBRA '93 and implemented on October 1, 1994. The VFC program provides vaccines at no cost for children 0 to 18 years of age who are Medicaid-enrolled, have no health insurance, or are American Indian/Alaskan Native. In addition, children who have health insurance that does not cover immunizations are eligible if they receive vaccines at a Federally Qualified Health Center (FQHC) or a Rural Health Clinic (RHC). VFC removes vaccine cost as a barrier to immunization eligible children, reduces referrals of children to public clinics for immunization, and facilitates their return to their private medical home for comprehensive care. *See also* immunization schedules; OBRA '93.

vaginal birth after cesarean section (VBAC) A trial of labor in a patient with a history of cesarean section or uterine scar from previous surgery as documented in the medical record, resulting in vaginal delivery. An *attempted vaginal birth after cesarean section* is a trial of labor in a patient with a history of cesarean section or uterine scar from previous surgery as documented in the medical record. A *failed vaginal birth after cesarean section* is a trial of labor in a patient with a history of cesarean section or uterine scar from previous surgery as documented in the medical record, resulting in delivery by repeat cesarean section. *See also* birth; cesarean section; labor; Maine Medical Liability Demonstration project.

validation The process of establishing that a given method is sound; for example, that proper procedures are used to collect data and that the data are a reasonable representation of the phenomenon they are collected to measure. *See also* validity; validity study.

validity **1.** The degree to which an observed situation reflects the true situation. **2.** In performance measurement, the degree to which an indicator or other measure identifies opportunities for improvement in the quality of care, and the demonstration that the use of the indicator results in improvements in outcomes or quality of care. *See also* construct validity; content validity; convergent validity; data validity; discriminant validity; external validity; face validity; indicator validity; internal validity; predictive validity; validation; validity study.

validity study The degree to which an inference drawn from an inquiry, especially generalizations extending beyond the study sample, is warranted when account is taken of the study methods, the representativeness of the study sample, and the nature of the population from which it is drawn. There are two varieties of study validity: internal validity and external validity. *See also* external validity; internal validity; validation; validity.

valid value All of the possible data elements that could be assigned to a particular category of information; for instance, if the category is "month," the valid values would be January through December. *See also* data element; value.

value A judgment based on the inverse relationship between the perceived quality of an organization's service and the cost of that service. *See also* cost; *p* value; predictive value of a screening test; relative value; resource-based relative value; valid value; value-added; value system.

value-added Relating to the estimated value that is added to a product or material at each stage of its manufacture or distribution. *See also* value.

value system A set of beliefs or principles prized by an individual. The most commonly cited are life, happiness, pursuit of beauty, excellence, wealth, power, and opportunities. *See also* lifestyle; value.

variable Any item, such as a quantity, attribute, phenomenon, or event, that can have different values. Examples are length in millimeters, time in minutes, and temperature in degrees. *See also* attribute; confounding factor; continuous variable; continuous variable measure; covariance; data; dependent variable; discrete variable; factor; graph; independent variable; key process variable; measure of association; multivariate analysis; negative correlation; null hypothesis; organization factor; positive correlation; random variable; rate-based measure; regression analysis; statistical test; unit of measure; variable cost; variate.

variable cost A cost that changes directly with the amount of production or use, such as direct labor needed to provide a service. *See also* variable.

variance **1.** A measure of the differences in a set of observations. *See also* covariance. **2.** In statistics, equal to the square of the standard deviation. *See also* occurrence; standard deviation.

variate A variable that may assume any of a set of values, each with a preassigned probability (known as its distribution). *See also* multivariate analysis; random variable; variable.

variation The differences in results obtained in measuring the same phenomenon more than once. The sources of variation in a process over time can be grouped into two major classes: common causes and special causes. Excessive variation frequently leads to waste and loss, such as the occurrence of undesirable patient health outcomes and increased cost of health services. *See also* calibration; coefficient of variation; common-cause variation; indicator underlying factors; medical genetics; practice pattern analysis; process variation; special-cause variation.

vascular dementia An organic mental disorder caused by systemic vascular disease (eg, arteriosclerotic changes in the vessels, valvular heart disease, high blood pressure) and resulting in cerebral vascular disease with dementia. Vascular dementia caused by repetitive cerebral infarcts ("ministrokes") acting cumulatively to produce dementia is called *multiple-infarct dementia*. *See also* dementia; infarction; stroke; transient ischemic attack.

vascular surgery   The branch of medicine and subspecialty of general surgery dealing with the management of surgical disorders of the blood vessels, excluding those immediately adjacent to the heart, lungs, or brain. *Synonym*: general vascular surgery. *See also* general surgery; revascularization.

vegetative state   A condition in a patient in which there is no evidence of cortical (cerebral) functioning, but the patient continues to have sustained capacity for spontaneous breathing and heartbeat. A patient in a vegetative state specifically shows no evidence of verbal or nonverbal communication, demonstrates no purposeful movement or motor ability, is unable to interact purposefully with stimulation provided by his or her environment, is unable to provide for his or her basic needs, and demonstrates all these findings for longer than three months. *Synonym*: cerebral death. *See also* brain death; persistent vegetative state.

venereal disease   *See* sexually transmitted disease.

Venereal Disease Research Laboratories (VDRL) test   A screening test for syphilis developed at the Venereal Disease Research Laboratories.

venereology   The study of sexually transmitted diseases. *See also* sexually transmitted disease.

ventilation   The process of exchange of air between the lungs and the ambient air. *See also* mechanical ventilation; ventilator.

ventilator   An apparatus designed to assist or control pulmonary ventilation, either intermittently or continuously. *See also* mechanical ventilation; ventilation.

verification   The act of reviewing, inspecting, testing, checking, auditing, or otherwise establishing and documenting whether items, processes, services, or documents conform to specified requirements. *See also* calibration verification; credentials verification process; data verification process.

vertical integration   Coordinating, linking, or incorporating the processes at all stages of health care delivery within a single organization to increase efficiency and profitability; for example, the establishment of a system of health care facilities ranging from nursing homes to clinics to hospitals under one management. *See also* clinical integration; horizontal integration; integration; management.

vertical transmission   *See* perinatal transmission.

vicarious liability   One person's liability due to another's actions; for example, an employer's liability for an employee's negligence while the employee is performing work at the place of employment. In tort law, if an employee, such as a nurse, while in the scope of his or her employment for his or her employer, injures a patient, the organization may be vicariously liable for the injuries sustained by the patient, under the doctrine of respondeat superior. *Synonyms*: passive negligence; secondary negligence. *See also* liability; negligence.

viral hepatitis   *See* hepatitis.

virology   The branch of microbiology that deals with viruses. *See also* microbiology.

virtual organization   A network or program of organizations and individuals that carries out functions as one entity, although the network or program is not a separate organization. For example, some communities establish programs to combat teen substance abuse with the coordinated participation of physicians, the local hospital, the local health department, schools, churches, and social welfare agencies.

virtual reality (VR) program   A high-tech computer simulation setting that allows users to interact with graphic images and "practice" using clinical processes and techniques. Virtual reality computer models have been found particularly useful for training in use of procedures requiring hand-eye coordination skills, such as laparoscopic surgery, angioplasty, or finding a vein. VR programs have given rise to several "virtual" products, such as Yellow Man—a virtual patient used to teach diagnosis of jaundice and related disorders.

vision statement   A written description, developed by an organization's leaders, of what the organization wishes to be, what it hopes to achieve, and its relationship to those it serves. *See also* mission statement.

visit   An encounter between a patient or client and a health professional. *See also* friendly visit; outpatient visit.

visiting nurse association (VNA)   A private, nonprofit health care agency that provides nursing services in the home. Visiting nurse associations employ nurses and other personnel, such as home health aides, who are trained to perform specific tasks of personal bedside care. *Synonym*: visiting nurse service. *See also* home health agency.

visual acuity   *See* Snellen visual acuity test.

visual analog scale   A visual means by which a patient can quantify pain. The patient marks a point corresponding to the intensity of his pain on a line, one end of which represents no pain and the other end, severe, incapacitating pain. *See also* pain drawings; patient utilities measurement.

visually impaired   Pertaining to a diminished or defective sense of sight, although not blind from birth, to such an extent as to have to rely on aids. *See also* Snellen visual acuity test.

vital few   The very limited set of factors identified by a Pareto analysis as being associated with the great majority of a problem. *See also* Pareto principle; useful many.

vital records Certificates of birth, death, marriage, and divorce required for legal and demographic purposes. *See also* birth certificate; death certificate.

vital signs Signs that show the overall condition of a person, changes in which are often clues to disease or signs of alteration in a person's health. Vital signs typically include temperature, pulse, respiration, and blood pressure. *Synonym:* life signs. *See also* blood pressure; hypertension; sign.

vital statistics Tabulated data concerning births, marriages, divorces, separations, diseases, and deaths based on registrations of these vital events in vital records. *See also* Cooperative Health Statistics System; epidemiology; health statistics.

vitamin Any of various fat-soluble or water-soluble organic substances essential in minute amounts for normal growth and activity of the body and obtained naturally from plant and animal foods. *See also* megavitamin therapy; nutrient; nutrition.

vocational assessment The process of evaluating a patient's work experiences and attitudes toward work, current motivations and areas of interest, and possibilities for future training, education, and employment.

vocational habilitation The development of persons born with limited functional capability to the fullest physical, mental, social, vocational, and economic usefulness of which they are capable. *See also* habilitation; vocational rehabilitation.

vocational rehabilitation The restoration of persons with limited functioning to the fullest physical, mental, social, vocational, and economic usefulness of which they are capable. *See also* rehabilitation; vocational habilitation.

voice input/output technology Applications of voice recognition and synthesis with and through computers. *Synonyms:* automated speech technology; voice technology. *See also* electronic medical record; voice recognition.

voice recognition Direct conversion of spoken data into computer language. *See also* voice input/output technology.

voluntary active euthanasia *See* euthanasia; physician-assisted suicide.

voluntary health agency Any nonprofit, nongovernmental agency, governed by lay and/or professional individuals, whose primary purpose relates to health care; for example, the American Cancer Society. *Synonyms:* private health agency; voluntary organization.

voluntary hospital A private, nonprofit hospital that is autonomous, self-established, and self-supported, as in a facility owned and operated by a fraternal, religious, or nonprofit community organization.

volunteer services Services provided by people who donate their time and energy to providing nonmedical assistance in support of a health care organization's operations. Volunteers, for example, may operate a gift shop, escort and transport family members and patients, deliver flowers, or staff clerical desks. *See also* Retired Senior Volunteer Program.

voucher A certificate that may be exchanged for a contract for services for a given period of time under a prepayment plan. *See also* prepayment plan; voucher system.

voucher system A system in which Medicare beneficiaries use vouchers issued by the federal government to enroll in health care plans of their choice. Under the voucher system, the beneficiary enrolls in a federally

---

VITAMINS

Fat-soluble

Vitamin A Necessary for vision, reproduction, and the formation and maintenance of skin, mucous membranes, bones, and teeth. Megadoses can produce birth defects. Good sources include liver, eggs, and butter. A precursor, beta carotene, is found in yellow, orange, and dark green vegetables and fruit.

Vitamin D Necessary for the body's absorption and metabolism of calcium and phosphorus and important for the maintenance of teeth and bones. Good sources include egg yolks, fish, cod liver oil, fortified milk, and butter. The body can also derive it from exposure to sunlight. Megadoses are toxic.

Vitamin E Used to treat sterility and various abnormalities of the muscles, red blood cells, liver, and brain. It is found chiefly in plant leaves, wheat germ oil, and milk.

Vitamin K Enables the liver to manufacture prothrombin and other proteins that bind calcium and are necessary for normal blood clotting and bone crystal formation. Intestinal bacteria manufacture it to provide part of the body's requirement. Dietary sources, such as spinach and other green leafy vegetables, milk products, meats, eggs, cereals, fruits, and vegetables, provide the remainder.

Water-soluble

Vitamin B complex A group of vitamins including thiamine, riboflavin, niacin, pantothenic acid, biotin, pyridoxine, folic acid, inositol, and vitamin B_{12} and occurring in yeast, liver, eggs, and some vegetables. *Synonym:* B complex.

Vitamin C Important in the production of collagen and the maintenance of capillaries, cartilage, bones, and teeth. It promotes healing and helps the body fight infection. Good sources include citrus fruits and juices, green or leafy vegetables, potatoes, cabbage, and cauliflower. *Synonym:* ascorbic acid.

Vitamin P Promotes capillary resistance to hemorrhaging. It is found in citrus juices.

qualified health care plan, and payment is made directly to the care-providing organization in a predetermined, fixed amount in exchange for the beneficiary's voucher. *See also* voucher.

Wagner-Murray-Dingell Bill   One of the original national health insurance proposals first introduced by three U.S. Representatives in the 1940s. It is still updated and introduced in each session of Congress by U.S. Representative John Dingell of Michigan, who succeeded his father, and original sponsor, in office. *See also* national health insurance.

waiting period   In health insurance, a period of time an individual must wait either to become eligible for insurance coverage or to become eligible for a given benefit after overall coverage has commenced. Some insurance policies, for instance, will not pay maternity benefits until nine months after the policy has been in force, and insurance coverage under other policies may not begin until an employee has been with an organization more than 30 days. *See also* eligible; insurance.

waived testing   Tests that meet the CLIA '88 requirements for waived tests, are cleared by the FDA for home use, employ methodologies that are so simple and accurate as to render the likelihood of erroneous results negligible, or pose no risk of harm to the patient if the test is performed incorrectly. *See also* CLIA '88.

waiver   An agreement attached to an insurance policy that exempts from coverage certain disabilities or injuries normally covered by the policy. *See also* coverage; exclusions.

wandering   A behavior often exhibited by patients with dementia in which the patient moves—seemingly aimlessly—around his or her environment. There are different types of wandering patterns, as well as different etiologies, including both emotional and psychological origins. Wandering may have beneficial effects for the patient, such as satisfying emotional needs and improving physical limitations. *See also* dementia.

ward   **1.** A hospital room set up to accommodate more than four patients.   **2.** An individual for whom a guardian or conservator has been appointed by a court, to care for and make decisions concerning the ward's person, property, or both. A ward is legally incompetent to act on his or her behalf, usually because of immaturity or lack of mental capacity. *See also* incompetent; ward patient.

ward patient   A patient whose care is the financial responsibility of a health program or institution. *Synonyms*: public patient; service patient. *See also* patient; private patient; ward.

ward rounds   *See* teaching rounds.

warfarin   An oral anticoagulant used chiefly to prevent and treat deep venous thrombosis (clots in the leg veins) and pulmonary embolism (clots broken off and traveling to the lungs). Hemorrhage or known hypersensitivity to the drug contraindicate its use. *Synonym*: blood thinner. *See also* anticoagulation; clotting factor.

watchful waiting   A strategy of regular monitoring, in the place of therapeutic intervention, of the status of a pathological or troublesome condition, such as benign prostatic hyperplasia (BPH; enlarged prostate). The strategy is used in situations in which the alternative therapies have risks (such as impotence resulting from prostate surgery) that are regarded by the patient as worse than the current symptoms. The options need to be reevaluated each time symptoms worsen. *See also* monitoring and evaluation.

Webster v Reproductive Services   [492 U.S. 490 (1989)] The first major U.S. Supreme Court abortion decision since *Roe v Wade*. Although the opinion of the justices was divided, the court upheld two items of a Missouri statute that (1) prohibited the use of public facilities and employees for abortions not necessary to save the mother's life; and (2) required physicians to test for viability of the fetus prior to performing an abortion after 20 weeks of gestation. Based on this decision, many states are expected to pass increasingly strict legislation on abortion. *See also* abortion.

weekend hospitalization   A type of partial hospitalization in which a patient spends weekends in a health care facility and functions in the community during the rest of each week. *See also* partial hospitalization.

Weibull distribution   *See* probability distribution.

weight   In statistics, a factor assigned to a number in a computation, as in determining a mean, to make the number's effect on the computation reflect its importance; for example, DRG weight. A *weighted index* is derived when the individual items that comprise an index have been assigned different values or "weights" in computing the index in order to reflect their differential importance relative to other values. *See also* DRG weight; index; statistics.

weight management   Counseling, preventive measures, therapies, or monitoring to control weight. Methods for achieving voluntary weight loss and control have been evaluated in a National Institutes of Health Technology Assessment Conference statement (1993), which stresses the multifactorial causes and associated psychological dimensions seen in two groups of patients with weight problems: those who do not need to lose weight but are trying to do so and those who do need to lose weight but are not trying to do so or are not succeeding. *See also* bariatrics; eating disorders; obesity.

well-baby care   Proactive health care provided to normal babies for early detection of problems and for delivery of preventive advice to parents. This is a counterpart of prenatal care for women.

wellness program   A program that encourages improved health status and a healthful life-style through health education, exercise, nutrition, and health promotion. A wellness program may focus on, for example, weight reduction, smoking cessation, cholesterol reduction, and stress reduction. *See also* health education; health promotion; physical activity and fitness; physical fitness program; preventive medicine; worksite wellness program.

well-year A measure, equivalent to one completely well year of life, designed to assess health program benefits and used in a general health policy model (GHPM). The value of a well-year is derived from measures of life expectancy and health-related quality of life during the years before death. *See also* potential years of lost life.

Western blot A test for the presence of antibodies to multiple antigens of HIV; used to confirm HIV infection following a positive ELISA test. The Western blot displays antibodies to specific HIV viral proteins in a separate, well-defined band. A positive result shows stripes at the locations for two or more viral proteins. A negative result is blank at these locations. *See also* antibodies; HIV infection.

white coat hypertension The phenomenon of consistently registering higher blood pressure levels in an office setting when measured by a physician as opposed to a nonphysician, or when measured by a physician in the office as opposed to outside the office. This phenomenon has prompted many efforts to find alternative ways of monitoring blood pressure and underscores the importance of establishing averages or ranges, rather than single readings, of blood pressure. *Synonym:* office hypertension. *See also* automated ambulatory blood pressure monitoring devices; blood pressure; hypertension; self-measured blood pressure monitoring device.

WHO analgesic drug ladder An algorithm developed by the World Health Organization to display the levels of intensity of medications to manage cancer pain from mild to moderate to severe. The first step includes non-opioids with or without adjuvants; the second step includes weak opioids, with or without non-opioids and/or adjuvants; the third step includes strong opioids, with or without non-opioids and/or adjuvants. *See also* pain management.

Wickline v State of California (1986) [192 Cal. App. 3d 1630, 239 1986 Cal. App. Rptr. 810; rev'd and dis'd July 30, 1987] A case defining the relationship between the physician and patient in the managed care environment. A physician utilization review consultant denied authorization for continued hospitalization of a patient who was then forced to undergo a limb amputation (allegedly resulting from the premature discharge). The treating attending physician was found totally responsible for this action and negligent in his use of judgment and responsibility. The HMO was not found liable. *See also* patient-provider relationship.

Williams-Steiger Act *See* Occupational Safety and Health Act of 1970.

withdrawal symptoms Symptoms experienced by drug and alcohol addicts during the early stages of abstinence from the addictive substance. *See also* detoxification; medical detoxification; nicotine dependence and withdrawal; symptom.

withdrawing treatment Termination or removal of a particular treatment without termination of care. There is no necessary difference (moral or legal) between withdrawing or withholding the same treatment, for example, stopping mechanical ventilation versus not starting mechanical ventilation. *See also* futility; life-support system; Uniform Rights of the Terminally Ill Act.

Women's Health Initiative (WHI) A massive, multi-component, 15-year prevention study launched by NIH in 1991 (with continuing recruitment into 1997) to explore and test interventions that may prevent or forestall the most common causes of death, disability, and impaired quality of life in postmenopausal women. The main components of the WHI are a randomized, controlled trial of promising but unproven approaches to prevention, a long-term observational study to identify predictors of disease (new risk factors and biological markers), and a study of community approaches to developing healthful behaviors. WHI is a component of NIH's Office of Disease Prevention but operates centers on many campuses.

workers' compensation A system, required by law, of compensating workers injured or disabled in connection with work. Formerly called workmen's compensation. *Synonym:* workers' comp. *See also* compensable injury; compensation; workers' compensation insurance; workers' compensation programs.

workers' compensation insurance Insurance contract paid by an employer for all employees and providing protection against loss due to injury or illness at the workplace. *See also* disability insurance; insurance; workers' compensation.

workers' compensation programs State social insurance programs that provide cash benefits to workers or their dependents injured, disabled, or deceased in the course, and as a result, of employment. The employee is also entitled to benefits for some or all of the health services necessary for treatment and restoration to a useful life and, possibly, a productive job. These programs are mandatory under state laws in all states. *See also* workers' compensation.

worksite wellness programs Prevention programs funded by employers hoping to improve the quality of care for their employees by decreasing morbidity and ultimately decreasing cost and resource consumption. The programs vary widely in what they cover and in the depth of services provided. Some structured programs introduced at the worksite have been favorably recognized in clinical practice guidelines, such as worksite "back schools" for low back pain. *Synonym:* worksite health promotion activities. *See also* physical fitness program; wellness program.

worried well Colloquial expression used with varying nuances within the health care community for persons who are excessively (and unnecessarily) concerned with the state of their health; who seek services and procedures not indicated for them; or who have vague, poorly defined conditions. Health insurers objecting to the expansion of coverage for certain problems have applied this term to persons with chronic mental disorders or emotional problems such as anxiety and to persons who obtain fraudulent diagnoses of nonexistent disorders. *See also* Munchausen's syndrome.

EXAMPLE WORKSITE WELLNESS PROGRAMS: CALIFORNIA'S PACIFIC BELL

Health Information Program
Health Promotion Video Library
Step in Time (Pregnancy) Prenatal Program
Body Fat/Blood Pressure Screening Program
VDT/Ergonomic Hotline
Breast Health Screening
A la Carte Weight Management
Blood Pressure Machines/Weight Scale (for self-testing)
Smoking Cessation Program
Employee Assistance Program
Good Morning Sleep Program
Return to Work
Coronary Risk Modifications Program
Fitworks: Work Site Fitness Facilities
Osteoporosis Risk Profile Program
Back to Health: "Back" Prevention Injury Program
Home Equipment Purchase Program
Wellness Walker Club and Work Hardening Program
Source: Employers cardiovascular management program cuts risk 20%. *Cardiovascular Disease Management Newsletter, Cor Healthcare Resources,* 2, 6-9, 1996.

---

wound healing   A dynamic process in which anatomical and functional integrity is restored. This process can be monitored and measured. For wounds of the skin, such as pressure ulcers, it involves repair of the dermis (granulation tissue formation) and epidermis (epithelialization). Healed wounds represent a spectrum of repair: they can be *ideally* healed (tissue regeneration), *minimally* healed (temporary return of anatomical continuity), or *acceptably* healed (sustained functional and anatomical result). The acceptably healed wound is the ultimate outcome of wound healing but not necessarily the appropriate outcome for all patients.

wound infection   A postoperative infection that varies in incidence and type with the nature of a surgical procedure, degree of surgical skill, and adequacy of aseptic technique before, during, and after an operation. *See also* nosocomial infection; postoperative care; surgery; surgical-site infection.

writ   In law, a written order issued by a court, commanding the party to whom it is addressed to perform or cease performing a specified act.

written progress report (WPR)   For purposes of Joint Commission accreditation, a postsurvey activity that involves preparing a report documenting evidence that correction of a compliance problem(s) is complete. Preparing a WPR involves summarizing, documenting, and collecting facts and other evidence that prove an organization's current compliance with the standards that caused the type I recommendation. *See also* accreditation decision rules.

wrongful birth   A tort action concerning a child who would not have been born but for legally liable contraceptive failure, unsuccessful sterilization, failure to diagnose a pregnancy, unsuccessful abortion, failure to warn the parent(s) of genetic risks, or failure to timely diagnose (or inform the parents about) a birth defect or disease of the fetus. A wrongful birth action is brought by the parents on their own behalf, as opposed to a wrongful life action. *See also* wrongful life.

wrongful death   A tort action concerning a death for which there is legal liability; for example, a death caused by professional negligence. Deaths are treated differently than injuries in the legal system. For example, a different statute of limitations may apply to a wrongful death action than to a negligence action, even though negligence may have been the cause of the wrongful death, and the amount of recovery for wrongful death may be limited to a specific dollar amount. Wrongful death actions are ordinarily governed by state statutes. *See also* negligence.

wrongful life   A tort action brought by (ie, on behalf of) a child born with birth or genetic defect(s), alleging that the child would not have been born but for negligent advice to, or treatment of, the parents. These cases may involve failure to warn the parents of genetic risks, contraception or sterilization, unsuccessful abortion, or failure to diagnose and inform the parents of a birth defect or disease of the fetus. *See also* wrongful birth.

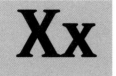

xenograph Animal-organ transplant used in the treatment of humans, which may involve whole organs (such as hearts from baboons) or parts of organs (such as heart valves from pigs). *See also* organ transplantation.

xeromammography X-ray imaging of the breast that uses (instead of x-ray film) a uniformly charged photoconductive plate held in a light-proof cassette. *See also* mammography.

xeroradiography A form of x-ray imaging that records the image on paper rather than film, using the technique described under xeromammography. *See also* radiography.

x-ray **1.** A relatively high-energy photon with a wavelength in the approximate range from 0.01 to 10 nanometers, used in a stream for its penetrating power in radiology, radiotherapy, and scientific research. *Synonym:* roentgen ray. *See also* occupancy factor; radiation; ray. **2.** The process of exposing a person or an object to x-rays for the purpose of making an image on a sensitized surface, as in x-raying a patient. *See also* nephrography; radiography; x-ray therapy. **3.** An image created by the transmission of x-rays through a person or object onto a sensitized surface.

x-ray therapy Medical therapy using controlled doses of x-ray radiation. *See also* radiation therapy; roentgenotherapy; x-ray.

YAG (yttrium aluminum garnet) capsulotomy
The usual term for the most commonly used technique for treating posterior capsular opacification. According to the clinical practice guideline *Cataract in Adults: Management of Functional Impairment* (1993), the procedure can improve vision in 65% of cases, but the evidence of wide variations in rates and timing of the cataract surgery suggests that there may be inappropriate use of the procedure. *See also* cataract surgery.

Year 2000 issue   Problems anticipated in the information technology industry as a result of computer programs making use of dates represented by only two digits (eg, 95 instead of 1995). The CDC has noted in a White Paper (May 1996) that public health information and surveillance systems at all levels of local, state, federal, and international public health are especially sensitive to and dependent upon dates for epidemiological and health statistics reasons (for core requirements such as age, duration, and so forth). Moreover, public health authorities usually depend on primary data providers such as physician practices, laboratories, hospitals, and managed care organizations as sources of their data. Several government organizations are supplying information on their Internet home pages on how to deal with the problem (eg, the National Institute for Standards and Technology, U.S. Department of Commerce; U.S. General Services Administration; Social Security Administration).

years of potential life lost   *See* potential years of life lost.

yoga   A system of mental concentration, abstract meditation, asceticism, and physical discipline derived from Hindu philosophy and practices. It includes a system of exercises for attaining bodily or mental control and well-being with liberation of the self and union with the universal spirit. *See also* alternative medicine; meditation.

Zz

Zero Balanced Reimbursement Account (ZEBRA)

A type of health care benefit plan provided by self-insured employers, who pay for care as it is provided. Beneficiaries (employees) must pay tax on any payments made for them under such a plan, and the employer must withhold income tax on benefits, except for those deemed nontaxable under federal statutes. *See also* reimbursement.

zero defects   A key goal of total quality management, meaning that everyone should do things right the first time to ensure total quality. The phrase was coined by Philip B. Crosby in his 14-step quality improvement program. *See also* total quality management.

zygote banking   Storing a cell formed by the union of an ovum and a sperm for future use in producing a child.

APPENDIX A

ASSOCIATIONS, ORGANIZATIONS, AND GOVERNMENT AGENCIES

This Appendix was developed to ease your use of the *Lexikon* and shorten the time it takes to find the information you need. Each entry in this appendix lists the name of the association, organization, or agency, its location, the date it was founded, and a brief description of its mission or purpose, including relevant products and services. The format is designed to provide the basic information needed to understand a reference to a specific association, organization, or agency or to facilitate any further searching you may want to do on your own. If you start your pursuit of an association, organization, or agency with only an abbreviation or acronym at hand, you may want to first check Appendix B (acronyms and abbreviations) to get the full title.

The appendix is limited to organizations or components of organizations that you or your colleagues may encounter in carrying out your professional health care and quality management responsibilities. The listings for government agencies have been updated according to federal restructuring, and are listed separately at the end of this appendix, beginning on page 404.

If there is something we have missed, or if you have comments on this format, let us hear from you! Your suggestions may help shape a third edition of the *Lexikon*—in the next millennium.

Academy of Ambulatory Foot Surgery (AAFS)
Founded: 1972. *Headquarters:* Tuscaloosa, AL. *Purpose:* To promote the advancement of podiatric surgical procedures that can eliminate the necessity of hospital admission, thereby keeping patients ambulatory and able to function normally, and lowering the patients' medical costs.

Academy of Behavioral Medicine Research (ABMR)
Founded: 1979. *Headquarters:* Pittsburgh, PA. *Purpose:* To foster the integration of research in biomedical and behavioral science and serve as a technical and educational resource. It serves individuals who are actively involved in more than one aspect of biobehavioral science research and who have been published in peer-reviewed journals relevant to the field.

Academy of Certified Social Workers (ACSW)
Founded: 1982. *Headquarters:* Washington, DC. *Purpose:* To provide certification through the National Association of Social Workers. Social workers certified by the ACSW are called registered social workers.

Academy of Dentistry for the Handicapped (ADH)
Founded: 1952. *Headquarters:* Chicago, IL. *Purpose:* To promote dental education research and legislation to improve the health and sensitivity of parents, advocates, and related professional groups. Members include dentists, dental hygienists, dental assistants, and allied health professionals specializing in improving the oral health of persons with special dental needs.

Academy of General Dentistry (AGD) *Founded:* 1952. *Headquarters:* Chicago, IL. *Purpose:* To serve the needs and to represent the interests of general dentists and to foster their continued proficiency through quality continuing dental education in order to better serve the public.

Academy for Health Services Marketing *See* Alliance for Healthcare Strategy and Marketing.

Academy of Hospice Physicians (AHP) *See* American Academy of Hospice and Palliative Medicine.

Academy for Implants and Transplants (AIT)
Founded: 1972. *Headquarters:* Springfield, VA. *Purpose:* To encourage and promote the art and science of implant and transplant dentistry. It serves dentists who assist generalist dentists in the field of implants and transplants.

Academy of Operative Dentistry (AOD) *Founded:* 1972. *Headquarters:* Menomonie, WI. *Purpose:* To ensure quality education in operative dentistry. Members include dentists and persons in allied industries interested in quality education in operative dentistry.

Academy of Pharmacy and Practice Management *See* American Pharmaceutical Association-Academy of Pharmacy Practice and Management.

Academy of Psychosomatic Medicine (APM)
Founded: 1952. *Headquarters:* Chicago, IL. *Purpose:* To advance scientific knowledge and practice of medicine relating to interaction of the mind, body and environment.

Academy of Rehabilitative Audiology (ARA)
Founded: 1966. *Headquarters:* Minneapolis, MN. *Purpose:* To provide a forum for the exchange of ideas in audiology and foster professional education, research, and interest in programs for the hearing impaired. It serves individuals holding graduate degrees in audiology, language or speech pathology, education of the deaf, or allied fields, and having at least two years of post-degree involvement in rehabilitative or educational programs for the hearing impaired.

Academy for Sports Dentistry (ASD) *Founded:* 1983. *Headquarters:* Iowa City, IA. *Purpose:* To foster research, development, and education in all sciences related to sports dentistry and its relationship to the body as a whole. Its membership comprises dentists, physicians, and athletic trainers.

Accreditation Association for Ambulatory Health Care (AAAHC) *Founded:* 1979. *Headquarters:* Skokie, IL. *Purpose:* To assist ambulatory health care organizations in efficiently providing a high level of care for patients by operating a voluntary, peer-based accreditation and consulting program.

Accreditation Council for Continuing Medical Education (ACCME) *Founded:* 1981. *Headquarters:* Chicago, IL. *Purpose:* To accredit sponsoring continuing medical education for physicians. Sponsoring participants are: American Board of Medical Specialties, American Hospital Association, Association for Hospital Medical Education, Federation of State Medical Boards of the United States, American Medical Association, Council of Medical Specialty Societies, and Association of American Medical Colleges.

Accreditation Council for Graduate Medical Education (ACGME) *Founded:* 1974. *Headquarters:* Chicago, IL. *Purpose:* Accredits residency training programs judged to be in substantial compliance with the *Essentials of Accredited Residencies.* The accrediting process involves a review of certain written information, a site visit to the training program, and consideration of the information by a Residency Review Committee (RRC). The 24 RRCs process the actual accreditation of residency programs, but the ACGME approves standards and processes appeals and other administrative issues. ACGME is a subgroup of the Council for Medical Affairs and oversees the accreditation of training in all specialties, approving or disapproving the recommendations of the RRCs.

Accreditation Council on Services for People with Disabilities (ACDD) *Founded:* 1969. *Headquarters:* Towson, MD. *Purpose:* Develops, reviews, and revises standards for services provided to people with disabilities, assesses agency compliance with standards on request, and awards accreditation to agencies found to be in compliance with the council's standards.

Accreditation Review Committee on Education for Physician Assistants (ARC-PA) *Founded:* 1971. *Headquarters:* Marshfield, WI. *Purpose:* Acts as an accrediting body for physician assistant education. It makes recommendations to the American Medical Association's Committee on Allied Health Education and Accreditation.

Accreditation Review Committee for Educational Programs in Surgical Technology (ARC-ST) *Founded:* 1974. *Headquarters:* Englewood, CO. *Purpose:* Reviews accreditation applications of surgical technology programs in hospitals, community colleges, technical schools, and universities and makes recommendations to the American Medical Association's Committee on Allied Health Education and Accreditation.

Accrediting Bureau of Health Education Schools (ABHES) *Founded:* 1964. *Headquarters:* Elkhart, IN. *Purpose:* Accredits health education institutions and schools conducting medical laboratory technician and medical assistant education programs. Schools apply voluntarily for accreditation and, once accredited, must report to the bureau annually and be reexamined at least every six years.

Accrediting Commission on Education for Health Services Administration (ACEHSA) *Founded:* 1968. *Headquarters:* Arlington, VA. *Purpose:* Accredits graduate education programs in health services administration, health planning, and health policy.

Action on Smoking and Health (ASH) *Founded:* 1967. *Headquarters:* Washington, DC. *Purpose:* To fight for the rights of nonsmokers to be protected from the many problems of smoking, through legal action, education, research, testimony, monitoring of developments in the tobacco industry and of legislative activity, and publications. Services and products include an airline complaint kit, a model clear indoor air act, a cost analysis of workplace smoking, and information on smoking addiction and cessation.

Administration on Aging *See* Government Organizations (Department of Health and Human Services).

Administration for Children and Families *See* Government Organizations (Department of Health and Human Services).

Administration on Children, Youth, and Families *See* Government Organizations (Department of Health and Human Services).

Administration on Developmental Disabilities *See* Government Organizations (Department of Health and Human Services).

Administration for Native Americans *See* Government Organizations (Department of Health and Human Services).

Advocate Health Care (AHC) *Founded:* 1995. *Headquarters:* Oak Brook, IL. *Purpose:* To promote the philosophy that good health care involves an understanding of human ecology and must meet the emotional and spiritual, as well as physical, needs of patients. *Formed by merger of:* Lutheran General Health Systems and EHS Health Care.

Aetna/U.S. Healthcare *Founded:* 1996. *Headquarters:* Hartford, CT, and Bluebell, PA. *Purpose:* To provide the full services of a national managed health care company, including employee benefits with indemnity and managed health care plans, dental and pharmacy benefits, and group insurance and disability products. The company has established primary operations centers and medical management centers in six geographical service regions, several of which will be supported by satellite and back-up centers. The company continues to use the expertise of its quality improvement and outcomes measurement subsidiary U.S. Quality Algorithms® Inc. (USQA®,) which offers products such as the diabetic reminder program and diabetic-specific report card. *Formed by merger of:* Aetna and U.S. Healthcare.

Agency for Health Care Policy and Research (AHCPR) *See* Government Organizations (Department of Health and Human Services).

Agency for Toxic Substances and Disease Registry
See Government Organizations (Department of Health and Human Services).

AirLifeLine (ALL) *Founded:* 1979. *Headquarters:* Sacramento, CA. *Purpose:* To provide immediate transport for medical cargo, such as blood, platelets, corneas, and human organs for transplantation, or for needy patients who require specialized treatment at medical facilities far from their homes. It serves pilots who donate their time, skills, fuel, and aircraft to fly medical missions.

Alcoholics Anonymous World Services (AA)
Founded: 1935. *Headquarters:* New York, NY. *Purpose:* Provides supportive rehabilitation for persons with alcoholism.

Alliance for Aging Research (AAR) *Founded:* 1986.
Headquarters: Washington, DC. *Purpose:* To promote research on human aging and the independence of older Americans and to advocate for a greater federal investment into scientific research that could lead to a healthy and productive old age. The Alliance is sponsored by a variety of corporate and nonprofit organizations, and advised by a bipartisan committee of members of Congress and by a board of prominent scientific advisors.

Alliance for Alternatives in Healthcare (AAH)
Founded: 1983. *Headquarters:* Thousand Oaks, CA. *Purpose:* To enhance public recognition of holistic, homeopathic, naturopathic, chiropractic, and acupuncture treatments. It serves holistic physicians, corporations, and other individuals interested in alternative health care.

Alliance for Cannabis Therapeutics (ACT) *Founded:* 1980. *Headquarters:* Washington, DC. *Purpose:* To end federal prohibition of cannabis in medicine and to construct a medically meaningful, ethically correct, and compassionate system of regulation which permits the seriously ill to legally obtain cannabis. Members include medical professionals, policymakers, and lay persons.

Alliance to End Childhood Lead Poisoning *Founded:* 1990. *Headquarters:* Washington, DC. *Purpose:* Seeks to eliminate childhood lead poisoning by raising awareness of and changing preconceptions about the causes and widespread occurrence of childhood lead poisoning. It serves as a nonmembership public interest organization.

Alliance of Genetic Support Groups (AGSG)
Founded: 1985. *Headquarters:* Chevy Chase, MD. *Purpose:* To foster a partnership among consumers and professionals to enhance education and service for, and represent the needs of, individuals affected by genetic disorders. It serves genetic organizations and professional and other individuals interested in promoting the health and well-

being of individuals and families affected by genetic disorders.

Alliance for Healthcare Strategy and Marketing
Founded: 1980. *Headquarters:* Chicago, IL. *Purpose:* To sponsor continuing education for and professional development of its members, who include marketing professionals in the health care field, and vice presidents and directors of hospitals, HMOs, nursing homes, and other health care organizations who are interested in the marketing of health services. *Formerly:* Academy for Health Services Marketing (1994).

The Alzheimer's Association *Founded:* 1980. *Headquarters:* Chicago, IL. *Purpose:* To foster research for the prevention, cure, and treatment of Alzheimer's disease and related disorders; to advocate for improved public policy and legislation at federal, state, and local levels; and to provide support and assistance to afflicted persons and their families. The association convenes a national Ethics Advisory Panel established in 1994 and encompasses the Ronald and Nancy Reagan Research Institute, created in 1995 to shorten the time of suffering and cut the financial, physical, and emotional cost of care.

Ambulatory Pediatric Association (APA) *Founded:* 1960. *Headquarters:* McLean, VA. *Purpose:* To improve methods of care for children in ambulatory care facilities. Members include health care providers, including those in outpatient departments in private university and other teaching hospitals and those engaged in public health work or private practice.

Ambulatory Sentinel Practice Network (ASPN)
Founded: 1982. *Headquarters:* Denver, CO. *Purpose:* To increase and refine the primary health care knowledge base by studying the problems that occur in primary care in the United States and Canada, through a research consortium that networks academic primary care physicians, private practice physicians, and allied health professionals. Data from practice-based research are collected through reporting cards sent weekly to ASPN, and information is disseminated through journal articles and seminars. The ASPN is funded through grants from the National Institutes of Health and collaboration with other agencies and foundations.

American Academy of Allergy, Asthma and Immunology (AAAAI) *Founded:* 1943. *Headquarters:* Milwaukee, WI. *Purpose:* To improve care and knowledge of allergies; to represent allergists, clinical immunologists, allied health professionals, and other physicians with special interest in allergy; and to educate the public about allergies and allergic-immunological diseases. Published products include a quarterly patient education newsletter, a journal, Practice Parameters and Position Statements, and the *Tips to Remember* brochures.

American Academy of Ambulatory Care Nursing (AAACN) *Founded:* 1978. *Headquarters:* Pitman, NJ. *Purpose:* To improve quality and efficiency of ambulatory care through continuing education. It serves nurses with

administrative or management responsibilities in ambulatory care.

American Academy for Cerebral Palsy and Developmental Medicine (AACPDM) *Founded:* 1947. *Headquarters:* Rosemont, IL. *Purpose:* To improve diagnosis, care, treatment, and research of cerebral palsy and developmental disabilities and acceptance of the challenges caused by these conditions. It serves physicians, researchers, and health professionals. Associate members include occupational, physical, and speech therapists.

American Academy of Child and Adolescent Psychiatry (AACAP) *Founded:* 1953. *Headquarters:* Washington, DC. *Purpose:* Establishes and supports ethical and professional standards of clinical practice; advocates for the mental health and public health needs of children, adolescents and families; promotes research, scholarship, training and continued expansion of the scientific base of the profession; maintains liaisons with other physicians and health care providers; and collaborates with others who share common goals. In keeping with the initiative to promote excellence in the practice of child and adolescent psychiatry, the Work Group on Quality Issues develops and issues a series of Practice Parameters.

American Academy of Audiology (AAA) *Founded:* 1988. *Headquarters:* McLean, VA. *Purpose:* To uphold professional excellence and to represent all audiologists and provide equal opportunities for under-represented specializations and special interest groups. The AAA offers fellow, affiliate, and candidate categories of membership and both consumer and professional resources. Federal advocacy efforts have recently concentrated on providing consumers with direct access to audiologists for hearing care without requiring physician supervision for diagnostic testing in independent diagnostic testing facilities (IDTFs) under new Medicare regulations.

American Academy of Clinical Psychiatrists (AACP) *Founded:* 1975. *Headquarters:* San Diego, CA. *Purpose:* To promote the scientific practice of psychiatric medicine. Membership is composed of practicing board-prepared or board-certified psychiatrists.

American Academy of Clinical Toxicology (AACT) *Founded:* 1968. *Headquarters:* Louisville, KY. *Purpose:* To encourage development of therapeutic methods and technology and to provide clinical certification of medical scientists in clinical technology. It serves physicians, veterinarians, pharmacists, research scientists, and analytical chemists.

American Academy of Cosmetic Surgery (AACS) *Founded:* 1985. *Headquarters:* Chicago, IL. *Purpose:* To encourage high-quality cosmetic medical and dental care and to provide continuing education for cosmetic surgeons. It operates the American Board of Cosmetic Surgery and serves cosmetic surgeons.

American Academy of Dental Group Practice (AADGP) *Founded:* 1973. *Headquarters:* Palatine, IL.

Purpose: To improve level of service provided by members through exchange and expansion of ideas and techniques for patient treatment. It serves dentists and dental group practices interested in practice management and treatment in group practice settings.

American Academy of Dental Practice Administration (AADPA) *Founded:* 1958. *Headquarters:* Palatine, IL. *Purpose:* To promote the efficient administration of dental practice.

American Academy of Dermatology (AAD) *Founded:* 1938. *Headquarters:* Schaumburg, IL. *Purpose:* To promote and advance the science and art of medicine and surgery related to the skin; to promote the highest possible standards in clinical practice, education and research in dermatology and related disciplines and to support and enhance patient care and promote the public interest relating to dermatology. The AAD's first priority is continuing medical education, supported by an annual meeting and publications, including a journal. It also serves as a source of information about dermatology for both the public and the news media and monitors and analyzes legislative developments. The AAD sponsors the National Melanoma/Skin Cancer Detection and Prevention Month each May.

American Academy of Environmental Engineers (AAEE) *Founded:* 1955. *Headquarters:* Annapolis, MD. *Purpose:* To improve standards of environmental engineering in the following areas of specialization: air pollution control, hazardous waste management, industrial hygiene, radiation protection, solid waste management, water supply, and waste water. It serves environmentally oriented registered engineers certified by examination as diplomates of the academy.

American Academy of Environmental Medicine (AAEM) *Founded:* 1965. *Headquarters:* Prairie Village, KS. *Purpose:* To promote better understanding and stimulate methods of controlling ecologic illness. Membership consists of physicians, engineers, and others interested in the clinical aspects of environmental medicine.

American Academy of Facial Plastic and Reconstructive Surgery (AAFPRS) *Founded:* 1964. *Headquarters:* Washington, DC. *Purpose:* To improve standards of facial plastic surgery. It is the world's largest association of facial plastic surgeons. The Academy has publications that describe the different types of facial plastic surgery and also maintains a toll-free telephone information service for persons contemplating surgery.

American Academy of Family Physicians (AAFP) *Founded:* 1947. *Headquarters:* Kansas City, MO. *Purpose:* To promote and maintain high-quality standards for family doctors who are providing continuing comprehensive health care to the public; to provide responsible advocacy for and education of patients and the public in all health-related matters; to preserve and promote quality cost-effective health care; to promote the science and art of family medicine and to ensure an optimal supply of well-trained family physicians; to promote and maintain high standards among physicians who practice family medicine; to preserve the right of family physicians to engage in medical and surgical procedures for which they are qualified by training and experience; to provide advocacy, representation, and leadership for the specialty of family practice; to maintain and provide an organization with high standards to fulfill these purposes; and to represent the needs of its members. The AAFP collaborates with other medical specialty societies and with other organizations in advocacy on health issues (such as tobacco control). AAFP programs and products include patient information handouts, age charts for the periodic health examination, and the "Tar Wars" antismoking program for children.

American Academy of Forensic Psychology (AAFP)
Founded: 1980. *Headquarters:* Columbia, MO. *Purpose:* To promote forensic psychology, to conduct continuing education, and to provide standards for the provision of forensic psychological services. It serves individuals who have met requirements, including passing an examination, set by the American Board of Professional Psychology.

American Academy of Forensic Sciences (AAFS)
Founded: 1948. *Headquarters:* Colorado Springs, CO. *Purpose:* To improve the practice and elevate the standards of forensic sciences. Membership includes criminalists, scientists, members of the bench and bar, pathologists, biologists, psychiatrists, examiners of questioned documents, toxicologists, odontologists, anthropologists, and engineers.

American Academy of Gnathologic Orthopedics (AAGO) *Founded:* 1970. *Headquarters:* Richmond, TX. *Purpose:* Conducts activities in fields of maxillofacial orthopedics/orthodontics and preventive and corrective orthodontics. It serves dentists dealing with the prevention or correction of malocclusion and bony malformation of the jaw and face.

American Academy of Healthcare Attorneys *See* National Health Lawyers Association/American Academy of Healthcare Attorneys.

American Academy of Hospice and Palliative Medicine (AAHPM) *Founded:* 1988. *Headquarters:* Gainesville, FL. *Purpose:* To support and represent U.S. physicians dedicated to the advancement of hospice/palliative medicine, its practice, research, and education; to promote the development of an organized discipline in the United States devoted to the special areas of palliative care and the management of terminal illness; and to serve as ombudsman in protecting the rights and personal autonomy of dying patients and their families. Services and products include hospice physician credentialing, the UNIPAC series of self-training modules, and the *Primer of Palliative Care*. *Formerly:* Academy of Hospice Physicians (1996).

American Academy of Hospital Attorneys *See* National Health Lawyers Association/American Academy of Healthcare Attorneys.

American Academy of Industrial Hygiene (AAIH)
Founded: 1960. *Headquarters:* Lansing, MI. *Purpose:* To monitor the professional aspects of industrial hygienists who have passed board examinations and have become certified members.

American Academy of Maxillofacial Prosthetics (AAMP) *Founded:* 1953. *Headquarters:* Indianapolis, IN. *Purpose:* Dedicated to the prosthetic correction and management of maxillofacial defects acquired from surgical ablation of cancer or traumatic injuries, congenital birth defects, and alterations in growth and development.

American Academy of Medical-Legal Analysis (AAMLA) *Founded:* 1981. *Headquarters:* Las Vegas, NV. *Purpose:* To disseminate information and promote research about the relationship between medical and legal services. It serves physicians and attorneys certified as diplomates of the American Board for Medical-Legal Analysis in Medicine and Surgery and other individuals interested in the field.

American Academy on Mental Retardation (AAMR)
Founded: 1960. *Headquarters:* Washington, DC. *Purpose:* To encourage investigative work in the clinical and experimental fields of mental retardation. It serves scientists actively engaged in research in any discipline relating to mental retardation.

American Academy of Natural Family Planning (AANFP) *Founded:* 1982. *Headquarters:* St. Louis, MO. *Purpose:* To improve the quality of natural family planning services by establishing specific certification and accreditation requirements for teachers and educational programs. It serves individuals who participate in natural family planning instruction.

American Academy of Neurological and Orthopaedic Surgeons (FAANaOS) *Founded:* 1977. *Headquarters:* Las Vegas, NV. *Purpose:* To provide information and understanding of neurological and orthopedic medicine and surgery. It maintains the American Board of Neurological and Orthopaedic Medicine and Surgery and the American Board for Medical-Legal Analysis in Medicine and Surgery. It serves neurological and orthopedic surgeons, neurologists, physiatrists, and professionals in allied medical or surgical specialities.

American Academy of Neurological Surgery
Founded: 1938. *Headquarters:* Ann Arbor, MI. *Purpose:* To serve leaders in the field of neurological surgery who are interested in neurosurgical education.

American Academy of Neurology (AAN) *Founded:* 1948. *Headquarters:* Minneapolis, MN. *Purpose:* To promote the best possible care for patients with neurological disorders by providing excellence in education through diverse programs in both the clinical aspects of neurology and basic neuroscience areas; to support the development of a practice environment that provides ethical, high-quality care for patients with neurological disorders; and to support clinical and basic research. Members are primarily neurologists or neuroscientists. Professional resources include a journal, regularly updated Practice

Parameters and Technology Assessments, and an annual meeting. The AAN advocates on behalf of neurologists and their patients suffering from neurological diseases by monitoring legislative and policy developments in Congress and in other specialty societies and government agencies.

American Academy of Nurse Practitioners (AANP) *Founded:* 1985. *Headquarters:* Austin, TX. *Purpose:* To provide a forum to enhance the identity and continuity of nurse practitioners and address national and state legislative issues that affect members. Its members include groups and individuals promoting high standards of health care delivered by nurse practitioners.

American Academy of Nursing (AAN) *Founded:* 1973. *Headquarters:* Washington, DC (American Nurses Association). *Purpose:* To provide the nursing profession with visionary leadership, focus the contributions of nursing leaders, advance scientific knowledge, and influence the development of effective health care policies and practices. Members of the AAN are Fellows of the American Academy of Nursing (FAAN).

American Academy of Ophthalmology *Founded:* 1896. *Headquarters:* San Francisco, CA. *Purpose:* To achieve accessible, appropriate, and affordable eye care for the public by serving the educational and professional needs of ophthalmologists. Ongoing activities include helping members prepare for credentialing through Lifelong Education for the Ophthalmologist (LEO) and developing and disseminating clinical practice guidelines through the Preferred Practice Pattern series. Advocacy efforts are focused on establishing the Academy as the most respected and effective advocate for quality eye care with federal and state governments, positioning ophthalmologists as the preferred providers of comprehensive eye care with the public and health care decision makers, and establishing the Academy as the leading source of information about eye care with the public and the media.

American Academy of Optometry (AAO) *Founded:* 1921. *Headquarters:* Bethesda, MD. *Purpose:* To develop and provide financial support for optometric research and education, conduct postgraduate education for optometrists and physicians, and confer diplomate status in five fields of optometric practice. It serves optometrists, educators, and scientists interested in clinical practice standards, optometric education, and experimental research in visual problems.

American Academy of Oral and Maxillofacial Pathology (AAOMP) *Founded:* 1946. *Headquarters:* Naperville, IL. *Purpose:* To serve oral pathologists who study and treat diseases of the mouth and oral cavity. *Formerly:* American Academy of Oral Pathology (1994).

American Academy of Oral and Maxillofacial Radiology (AAOMR) *Founded:* 1949. *Headquarters:* Jackson, MS. *Purpose:* To promote and advance the art and science of oral and maxillofacial radiology, to provide the opportunity for professionals in oral and maxillofacial radiology to communicate and achieve recognition of their work, and to seek mutual understanding and appreciation of radiology among the medical and dental professions.

American Academy of Oral Medicine (AAOM) *Founded:* 1946. *Headquarters:* Arlington, VA. *Purpose:* To promote the study of the cause, prevention, and control of diseases of the teeth and to foster better scientific understanding between the fields of dentistry and medicine. Members include dental educators, specialists, general dentists, and physicians interested in the study of diseases of the mouth.

American Academy of Oral Pathology *See* American Academy of Oral and Maxillofacial Pathology.

American Academy of Orthopaedic Surgeons (AAOS) *Founded:* 1975. *Headquarters:* Rosemont, IL. *Purpose:* To provide education and practice management services for orthopedic surgeons and allied health professionals and to serve as an advocate for improved patient care and inform the public about the science of orthopedics. The AAOS has recently released its new software program MODEMS (Musculoskeletal Outcomes Data Evaluation Management System) for collecting in-office data. Other services and products include AAOS Clinical Policies (clinical practice guidelines) and brochures for patient education and on health issues. Members of the AAOS, called fellows, are orthopedists concerned with the diagnosis, care, and treatment of musculoskeletal disorders.

American Academy of Orthotists and Prosthetists (AAOP) *Founded:* 1970. *Headquarters:* Alexandria, VA. *Purpose:* To improve patient care, to advance the profession, and to provide continuing education. It is composed of certified professional practitioners in orthotics and prosthetics.

American Academy of Osteopathy (AAO) *Founded:* 1937. *Headquarters:* Indianapolis, IN. *Purpose:* To develop and teach the science and art of osteopathic manipulative therapy and to encourage greater proficiency in the use of osteopathic structural diagnostic and therapeutic procedures.

American Academy of Otolaryngic Allergy (AAOA) *Founded:* 1941. *Headquarters:* Silver Spring, MD. *Purpose:* To sponsor scientific meetings and continuing education programs. It serves otolaryngologists who are interested in the treatment of otolaryngic allergy.

American Academy of Otolaryngology–Head and Neck Surgery (AAO-HNS) *Founded:* 1982. *Headquarters:* Alexandria, VA. *Purpose:* Represents otolaryngology in governmental and socioeconomic arenas and provides education for otolaryngologists. It serves physicians who treat disorders of the ear, nose, throat and related disorders of the head and neck.

American Academy of Pain Medicine (AAPM) *Founded:* 1983. *Headquarters:* Glenview, IL. *Purpose:* To enhance the practice of pain medicine in the United States by working to promote a socioeconomic and political climate conducive to the effective and efficient practice of pain medicine and by ensuring comprehensive quality medical care by physicians specializing in pain medicine for patients in need of such services. Activities include an annual meeting with a review course, professional and consumer publications, and collaboration with other specialty societies on policy issues, such as the consensus statement on use of opioids for treatment of chronic pain jointly issued with the American Pain Society. The AAPM serves anesthesiologists, internists, neurologists, and psychiatrists.

American Academy of Pediatric Dentistry (AAPD)
Founded: 1947. *Headquarters:* Chicago, IL. *Purpose:* To advance pediatric dentistry through practice, education, and research. It serves teachers and researchers in pediatric dentistry and dentists whose practice is limited to children.

American Academy of Pediatrics (AAP)
Founded: 1930. *Headquarters:* Elk Grove Village, IL. *Purpose:* To attain the optimal physical, mental, and social health, safety, and well-being of infants, children, adolescents, and young adults and to provide an independent pediatric forum to address children's needs. Activities include advocacy for children and youth, public education, research, professional education, and membership service and advocacy for pediatricians. AAP recommendations on the full range of pediatric health care are published in Policy Statements, Practice Parameters, and Model Bills. Under a grant from the Maternal and Child Health Bureau of the Health Resources and Services Administration, the AAP operates the Pediatric Research in Office Settings (PROS) network, which conducts national collaborative practice-based research addressing primary care issues.

American Academy of Periodontology (AAP)
Founded: 1914. *Headquarters:* Chicago, IL. *Purpose:* To advance the art and science of periodontics, improve the periodontal health of the public, and serve the interests of the members of the academy. Membership mainly consists of dental professionals, the majority of whom are periodontists—a dental specialist who is an expert in the prevention, diagnosis, and treatment of diseases affecting the gums and supporting structures of the teeth and in the placement and maintenance of dental implants.

American Academy of Physical Medicine and Rehabilitation (AAPM&R)
Founded: 1938. *Headquarters:* Chicago, IL. *Purpose:* To maximize quality of life, to minimize incidence of impairments and disability, and to enhance development of physiatry as a practice area. It serves diplomates of the American Board of Physical Medicine and Rehabilitation.

American Academy of Physician Assistants (AAPA)
Founded: 1968. *Headquarters:* Alexandria, VA. *Purpose:* To educate the public about physician assistant programs and represent the interests of physician assistants before Congress, government agencies, and health care organizations. It is comprised of physician assistants who have graduated from an American Medical Association-accredited program or are certified by the National Commission on Certification of Physician Assistants, and individuals who are enrolled in an accredited physician assistant educational program.

American Academy of Podiatric Administration (AAPA)
Founded: 1961. *Headquarters:* West Hartford, CT. *Purpose:* Works to standardize office management procedures to create more efficient podiatry practices and develops formalized procedures for obtaining and training podiatry office assistants. Serves doctors of podiatric medicine interested in practice administration.

American Academy of Podiatric Sports Medicine (AAPSM)
Founded: 1970. *Headquarters:* Potomac, MD. *Purpose:* To provide and stimulate programs for research and education; to promote and encourage publication of research findings and other literature pertaining to podiatric sports medicine; to provide a consultative service for those persons engaged in sports medicine; to increase awareness of the medical profession, sports population, and general public to the profession of podiatric sports medicine and modalities available to those who participate in sports; and to coordinate student chapters to acquaint the podiatric medical student with the needs and demands placed upon athletes. It serves podiatrists, physicians, and athletic trainers.

American Academy of Psychiatrists in Alcoholism and Addictions (AAPAA)
Founded: 1985. *Headquarters:* Greenbelt, MD. *Purpose:* To provide a forum for discussion of issues related to substance abuse. It is composed of psychiatrists and psychiatric residents interested in substance abuse.

American Academy of Psychiatry and the Law (AAPL)
Founded: 1969. *Headquarters:* Bloomfield, CT. *Purpose:* Promotes scientific and educational activities in forensic psychiatry by facilitating the exchange of ideas and practical clinical experience through publications and regularly scheduled national and regional meetings; sponsoring continuing education programs for both forensic and general psychiatrist and other mental health and legal professionals; developing ethical guidelines for forensic psychiatry; stimulating research in forensic psychiatry and providing a forum for the presentation of the results of such research; developing guidelines for education and training in forensic psychiatry for both general psychiatry residents and post-residency fellows; and providing information to the public through a speaker's bureau and published literature.

American Academy of Psychoanalysis (AAP)
Founded: 1956. *Headquarters:* New York, NY. *Purpose:* To provide an open forum for psychoanalysts to discuss relevant and responsible views of human behavior and to exchange ideas with psychiatric colleagues and other social and behavioral scientists.

American Academy of Psychotherapists (AAP)
Founded: 1955. *Headquarters:* Decatur, GA. *Purpose:* To provide a meeting ground for psychotherapists of differing backgrounds and orientations and to facilitate cross-discipline thinking, planning, and research in psy-

chotherapy. It serves psychologists, psychiatrists, clergy, and social workers engaged in the practice of psychotherapy.

American Academy of Restorative Dentistry (AARD) *Founded:* 1928. *Headquarters:* Colorado Springs, CO. *Purpose:* To research application of treatment of the natural teeth to restore and maintain a healthy functioning mouth as part of a healthy body. It serves dentists practicing restorative dentistry and educators.

American Academy of Somnology (AAS) *Founded:* 1986. *Headquarters:* Las Vegas, NV. *Purpose:* To promote somnology and the study of sleep disorders as a health care science. Membership consists of clinicians, researchers, and students interested in promoting the field of somnology.

American Academy of Spinal Surgeons (AASS) *Founded:* 1982. *Headquarters:* Las Vegas, NV. *Purpose:* To promote scientific and educational advancement in the field of spinal surgery. It serves physicians specializing in spinal surgery.

American Academy of Sports Physicians (AASP) *Founded:* 1979. *Headquarters:* Encino, CA. *Purpose:* To educate and inform physicians whose practices comprise mainly sports medicine and to register and recognize physicians who have expertise in sports medicine.

American Academy of Thermology (AAT) *Founded:* 1968. *Headquarters:* Vienna, VA. *Purpose:* Disseminates knowledge concerning the application of thermography to various medical specialties and promotes technical advancement in the field. It serves physicians, physicists, and technicians interested in the field of thermography.

American Academy of Tropical Medicine (AATM) *Founded:* 1984. *Headquarters:* Detroit, MI. *Purpose:* To provide postgraduate continuing medical education in tropical medicine. It is composed of physicians and allied health professionals interested in tropical medicine.

American Acupuncture Association (AAA) *Founded:* 1972. *Headquarters:* Flushing, NY. *Purpose:* To promote acceptance of acupuncture as a viable medical method. It works to legalize acupuncture at the state level and serves physicians, nurses, acupuncturists, physical therapists, and herbologists.

American Ambulance Association (AAA) *Founded:* 1977. *Headquarters:* Sacramento, CA. *Purpose:* To aid in development of private enterprise, pre-hospital, emergency medical treatment. It is composed of private suppliers of ambulance services.

American Art Therapy Association (AATA) *Founded:* 1969. *Headquarters:* Mundelein, IL. *Purpose:* To inform art therapists about legislative activities and issues affecting the practice of art therapy on the federal level and in each state. It serves art therapists, students, and individuals in related fields interested in the progressive development of therapeutic uses of art.

American Assembly for Men in Nursing (AAMN) *Founded:* 1971. *Headquarters:* Pensacola, FL. *Purpose:* To eliminate prejudice in nursing, draw men to the nursing profession, and promote the principles and practices of positive health care. It acts as a clearinghouse for information on men in nursing. Composed of registered nurses.

American Association for Accreditation of Ambulatory Surgery Facilities (AAAASF) *Founded:* 1981. *Headquarters:* Mundelein, IL. *Purpose:* To maintain high standards through adherence to a voluntary program of inspection and accreditation of ambulatory plastic surgery facilities.

American Association for Acupuncture and Oriental Medicine (AAAOM) *Founded:* 1981. *Headquarters:* Catasauqua, PA. *Purpose:* To elevate the standards, education, and practice of acupuncture and oriental medicine. It serves professional acupuncturists and other individuals interested in acupuncture and oriental medicine.

American Association of Anatomists (AAA) *Founded:* 1888. *Headquarters:* New Orleans, LA. *Purpose:* To foster teaching and research in the full range of morphological fields in the United States and Canada, including the medical fields of gross, microscopic, neuroanatomical, and developmental human anatomy and the biological fields of comparative anatomy, paleontology, physical anthropology, embryology, cytology, genetics, cell biology, neurobiology, and endocrinology.

American Association of Behavioral Therapists (BT) *Founded:* 1987. *Headquarters:* Ormond Beach, FL. *Purpose:* To promote the profession and the role of the behavioral therapist. It serves professionals from many fields—including mental health counseling, biofeedback therapy, hypnotherapy, and medicine—who share a common interest in the use of the behavioral sciences.

American Association of Bioanalysts (AAB) *Founded:* 1956. *Headquarters:* St. Louis, MO. *Purpose:* To sponsor a Proficiency Testing Service open to individuals engaged in the clinical laboratory field. Composed of directors, owners, managers, and supervisors of bioanalytical clinical laboratories interested in clinical laboratory procedures and testing.

American Association of Blood Banks (AABB) *Founded:* 1947. *Headquarters:* Bethesda, MD. *Purpose:* To make whole blood or its components available through blood banks, to operate a clearinghouse for exchange of blood and blood credits, and to encourage development of blood banks. Conducts educational programs for blood bank personnel, trains and certifies blood bank technologists, maintains a rare donor file and Reference Laboratory System, and sponsors workshops. Sets standards and inspects and accredits blood banks through a nationwide program. It serves community and hospital blood banks and transfusion services, physicians, nurses, technologists, administrators, and others interested in blood banking and transfusion medicine.

American Association for Cancer Education (AACE) *Founded:* 1966. *Headquarters:* Houston, TX. *Purpose:* To

provide a forum for improvement of cancer education that focuses on prevention, early detection, treatment, and rehabilitation. Its committees include Basic Science, Dental, Education Evaluation, Medical, Nursing, and Radiation. It serves physicians, dentists, nurses, health educators, social workers, and occupational therapists interested in cancer education.

American Association for Cancer Research (AACR) *Founded:* 1907. *Headquarters:* Philadelphia, PA. *Purpose:* To facilitate communication and dissemination of knowledge among scientists and others dedicated to the cancer problem; to foster research in cancer and related biomedical sciences; to encourage presentation and discussion of new and important observations in the field; to foster public education, science education, and training; and to advance the understanding of cancer etiology, prevention, diagnosis, and treatment throughout the world. The AACR publishes four journals; convenes an annual meeting; organizes several highly focused scientific conferences each year; offers educational workshops and grants to young investigators; maintains an active public education program; and interacts frequently with cancer survivors, lay advocates, and the general public in support of its mission.

American Association of Cardiovascular and Pulmonary Rehabilitation (AACVPR) *Founded:* 1985. *Headquarters:* Middleton, WI. *Purpose:* To foster the improvement of clinical practice in cardiovascular and pulmonary rehabilitation. It consists of allied health professionals involved in the field of cardiovascular and pulmonary rehabilitation.

American Association of Certified Allergists (AACA) *Founded:* 1968. *Headquarters:* Arlington Heights, IL. *Purpose:* To improve expertise in allergy treatment and promote improved standards for the practice and teaching of allergy. It consists of physicians specializing in allergy and clinical immunology.

American Association of Certified Orthoptists (AACO) *Founded:* 1940. *Headquarters:* Houston, TX. *Purpose:* To assist in postgraduate education training and to operate placement service. It serves orthoptists certified by the American Orthoptic Council and publishes a journal.

American Association of Children's Residential Centers (AACRC) *Founded:* 1956. *Headquarters:* Alexandria, VA. *Purpose:* Promotes high standards and advances the concepts and methods of residential treatment; represents children and families before standard- and rate-setting bodies; and participates in education, training, and research in the field of residential treatment. It is composed of multidisciplinary mental health professionals involved in treatment services for emotionally disturbed children.

American Association of Clinical Endocrinologists (AACE) *Founded:* 1991. *Headquarters:* Jacksonville, FL. *Purpose:* To improve the public's understanding of the function of a clinical endocrinologist, to heighten aware-

ness of underlying endocrine disease, to demonstrate the added value of the clinical endocrinologist in the treatment of endocrine disease; and to make available to patients the choice of care by a specialist trained in the treatment of endocrine disorders, all with the ultimate goal of improving the quality of care available to patients with endocrine disease. Activities include the development and dissemination of clinical practice guidelines.

American Association of Clinical Urologists (AACU) *Founded:* 1969. *Headquarters:* Schaumburg, IL. *Purpose:* To stimulate interest in the science and practice of urology and to promote understanding of socioeconomic and political affairs affecting medical practice among clinical urologists who are members of the American Urological Association and the American Medical Association.

American Association of Colleges of Nursing (AACN) *Founded:* 1969. *Headquarters:* Washington, DC. *Purpose:* To establish quality standards for bachelor's- and graduate-degree nursing education; to assist deans and directors to implement those standards; to influence the nursing profession to improve health care; and to promote public support of baccalaureate and graduate education, research, and practice in nursing.

American Association of Colleges of Osteopathic Medicine (AACOM) *Founded:* 1898. *Headquarters:* Rockville, MD. *Purpose:* To operate a centralized application service for osteopathic medical colleges. It monitors and works with the U.S. Congress and government agencies in the planning of health care programs and gathers statistics on osteopathic medical students, faculty, and diplomates.

American Association of Colleges of Podiatric Medicine (AACPM) *Founded:* 1932. *Headquarters:* Rockville, MD. *Purpose:* Provides vocational material for secondary schools and colleges and conducts public affairs activities and legislative advocacy. It serves administrators, faculty, practitioners, students, and other individuals associated with podiatric medical education.

American Association of Community Psychiatrists (AACP) *Founded:* 1984. *Headquarters:* Clackamas, OR. *Purpose:* To increase the number of psychiatrists who choose community health as a career, to inform and educate the public about the psychiatrist's role in treatment, and to provide continuing education. It serves psychiatrists practicing in community mental health centers or similar programs that provide care to populations of the mentally ill regardless of their ability to pay.

American Association for Continuity of Care (AACC) *Founded:* 1982. *Headquarters:* Hartford, CT. *Purpose:* To propose and support legislation concerning Medicare changes and home health care. It is composed of health professionals involved in discharge planning, social work, hospital administration, home health care, long term care, home health agencies, and continuity of care.

American Association for Correctional Psychology (AACP) *Founded:* 1953. *Headquarters:* South Charleston, VA. *Purpose:* To improve correctional psychological care in community and institutional programs for juvenile and adult offenders and their victims. It consists of practitioners, academicians, and researchers from such programs.

American Association of Critical-Care Nurses (AACN) *Founded:* 1969. *Headquarters:* Aliso Viejo, CA. *Purpose:* To provide certification, education and training, standards, and other services to its members, who include registered nurses specializing in critical care.

American Association of Dental Consultants (AADC) *Founded:* 1977. *Headquarters:* Lawrence, KS. *Purpose:* To operate a certification program. It serves dental insurance consultants and others interested in dental insurance plans from administrative and design perspectives.

American Association of Dental Examiners (AADE) *Founded:* 1883. *Headquarters:* Chicago, IL. *Purpose:* To assist member agencies with problems relating to state dental board examinations and licensure, and enforcement of the state dental practice act. It serves present and past members of state dental examining boards and board administrators.

American Association for Dental Research (AADR) *Founded:* 1972. *Headquarters:* Washington, DC. *Purpose:* To promote better dental health and research activities. It is composed of dentists, researchers, dental schools, and dental products-manufacturing companies.

American Association of Dental Schools (AADS) *Founded:* 1923. *Headquarters:* Washington, DC. *Purpose:* To lead the dental education community in addressing the contemporary issues influencing education, research, and the health of the public. Its members include all U.S. and Canadian dental schools, advanced dental education programs, hospital dental education programs, allied dental education programs, corporations, faculty, and students.

American Association of Diabetes Educators (AADE) *Founded:* 1974. *Headquarters:* Chicago, IL. *Purpose:* To provide diabetes education and care. It serves nurses, dietitians, social workers, physicians, pharmacists, podiatrists, and others involved in teaching diabetes management to diabetics.

American Association of Electrodiagnostic Medicine (AAEM) *Founded:* 1953. *Headquarters:* Rochester, MN. *Purpose:* To increase knowledge of electromyography and electrodiagnostic medicine and to improve patient care. It serves practicing physicians who are active in electromyography and electrodiagnosis and who have made contributions to this field.

American Association of Endodontists (AAE) *Founded:* 1943. *Headquarters:* Chicago, IL. *Purpose:* Promotes the exchange of ideas on the scope of the specialty of endodontics; stimulates endodontic research studies among its members; and encourages the highest standard of care in the practice of endodontics. It serves dentists engaged in clinical practice, teaching, and research in endodontics.

American Association of Entrepreneurial Dentists (AAED) *Founded:* 1983. *Headquarters:* Tupelo, MS. *Purpose:* To inform the public, dentists, educators, and manufacturing companies of new and beneficial techniques, products, and services; coordinates the review of specifications for dental materials and products by regulatory agencies; evaluates and represents new ideas and products to manufacturing companies at convention trade expositions; and provides lists of foreign dental dealers and buyers. It is composed of dentists and other dental professionals involved in research, industry, manufacturing, marketing, publication, and other entrepreneurial activities.

American Association of Functional Orthodontics (AAFO) *Founded:* 1982. *Headquarters:* Winchester, VA. *Purpose:* To serve its membership by being a source of the latest and best information available anywhere on the subject of functional appliance therapy and temporomandibular joint therapy through exclusive original articles published in its journal. It serves orthodontists, pediatric dentists and general practitioners from throughout the United States, Canada, and over 20 other foreign countries.

American Association for Geriatric Psychiatry (AAGP) *Founded:* 1978. *Headquarters:* Bethesda, MD. *Purpose:* To improve the quality of life for older people with mental disorders through educating physicians and the public, enhancing standards of practice, and supporting research efforts.

American Association of Gynecological Laparoscopists (AAGL) *Founded:* 1972. *Headquarters:* Santa Fe Springs, CA. *Purpose:* To improve the quality of health care for women by advancing the practice of endoscopic surgery in the treatment of gynecologic conditions and disorders. It serves physicians who specialize in obstetrics and gynecology and who are interested in gynecological endoscopic procedures.

American Association for Hand Surgery (AAHS) *Founded:* 1970. *Headquarters:* Arlington Heights, IL. *Purpose:* To conduct symposia and offer specialized education. Membership consists of plastic, orthopedic, and general surgeons and other individuals having a specific interest in hand surgery.

American Association of Healthcare Consultants (AAHC) *Founded:* 1949. *Headquarters:* Fairfax, VA. *Purpose:* To improve quality of consultation to health care organizations in such areas as strategic planning and marketing, organization and management, human resource management, and other areas. It serves individuals exclusively devoted to hospital and health care consultation.

American Association of Health Plans (AAHP) *Founded:* 1995. *Headquarters:* Washington, DC. *Purpose:* To emphasize active partnerships between patients and their physicians and to foster the belief that health care is best provided by networks of health care professionals who are willing to be held accountable for the quality of their services and the satisfaction of their patients. New initiatives include the Patients First Initiative and (in collaboration with the American Medical Association and AHCPR) the establishment of the National Guideline Clearinghouse, a comprehensive Internet-based source for clinical practice guidelines which is planned to become operative in 1998. *Formed by merger of:* American Managed Care and Review Association and Group Health Association of America.

American Association for the History of Medicine (AAHM) *Founded:* 1925. *Headquarters:* Boston, MA. *Purpose:* To promote research, study, interest, and writing in the history of medicine, including public health, dentistry, pharmacy, nursing, medical social work, and allied sciences and professions. It serves physicians and other individuals with professional or vocational interest in the history of medicine.

American Association for the History of Nursing (AAHN) *Founded:* 1978. *Headquarters:* Washington, DC. *Purpose:* To foster the importance of history in understanding the present and guiding the future of nursing by educating the public and the profession about nursing's history and heritage, encouraging research and recognizing outstanding scholarly achievement in nursing research, and serving as a resource for information about nursing history.

American Association of Homeopathic Pharmacists (AAHP) *Founded:* 1922. *Headquarters:* Albuquerque, NM (c/o Doug Campbell). *Purpose:* To work for the preservation and promotion of the use of homeotherapeutics. It serves manufacturing pharmacists of homeopathic preparations and associate members (distributors).

American Association of Homes and Services for the Aging (AAHSA) *Founded:* 1961. *Headquarters:* Washington, DC. *Purpose:* To provide a unified means of identifying and solving problems in order to protect and advance the interests of elderly persons. It serves voluntary nonprofit and governmental nursing homes, housing, and health-related facilities and services for the elderly; state associations; and other interested persons.

American Association of Hospital Dentists (AAHD) *Founded:* 1927. *Headquarters:* Chicago. *Purpose:* To promote dental education programs in hospitals.

American Association of Hospital Podiatrists (AAHP) *Founded:* 1950. *Headquarters:* Brooklyn, NY. *Purpose:* Elevate the standards of podiatry practices in hospitals and health institutions; to standardize hospital podiatry procedures; to promote understanding among personnel in podiatry, medicine, and allied health professions; and to assist in educational and teaching programs.

American Association of Immunologists (AAI) *Founded:* 1913. *Headquarters:* Bethesda, MD. *Purpose:* To promote interaction between laboratory investigators and clinicians; conducts training courses, symposia, workshops, and lectures. It serves scientists engaged in immunological research in virology, bacteriology, biochemistry, and related areas.

American Association of Legal Nurse Consultants (AALNC) *Founded:* 1989. *Headquarters:* Glenview, IL. *Purpose:* To promote registered nurses practicing in a consulting capacity in the legal field. It serves registered nurses providing medical consultation to the legal profession and conducts annual education promotion.

American Association of Medical Assistants (AAMA) *Founded:* 1956. *Headquarters:* Chicago, IL. *Purpose:* To conduct a certification program, the passage of which entitles the individual to certification as a certified medical assistant (CMA) and to conduct accreditation of one- and two-year programs in medical assisting in conjunction with the Committee on Allied Health Education and Accreditation. It is composed of assistants, receptionists, secretaries, bookkeepers, nurses, and laboratory personnel employed in the offices of physicians and other medical facilities.

American Association of Medical Society Executives (AAMSE) *Founded:* 1946. *Headquarters:* Chicago, IL. *Purpose:* Supports and enhances the profession of medical society management. AAMSE's membership comprises CEOs and staff specialists from county, state, national, and specialty medical societies; consultants to medical societies, and multiple management staff who work with medical societies.

American Association for Medical Transcription (AAMT) *Founded:* 1978. *Headquarters:* Modesto, CA. *Purpose:* To advance medical transcription and the education and development of medical transcriptionists as medical language specialists. It serves medical transcriptionists, their supervisors, teachers and students of medical transcription, owners and managers of medical transcription services, and other interested health personnel.

American Association of Medico-Legal Consultants (AAMC) *Founded:* 1972. *Headquarters:* Philadelphia, PA. *Purpose:* To perform medical malpractice screening, peer review, medical and hospital risk management, and medical audits; offers seminars for physicians and attorneys in the field of medical-legal problems. It serves physicians and physician-attorneys.

American Association of Mental Health Professionals in Corrections (AAMHPC) *Founded:* 1940. *Headquarters:* Sacramento, CA. *Purpose:* To improve the treatment, rehabilitation, and care of persons with mental illness, mental retardation, and emotional disturbances. It serves psychiatrists, psychologists, social workers, nurses, and other mental health professionals working in correctional settings.

American Association on Mental Retardation (AAMR) *Founded:* 1876. *Headquarters:* Washington, DC. *Purpose:* To improve the general welfare of persons with mental retardation and the study of the cause, treatment, and prevention of mental retardation. It serves physicians, educators, administrators, social workers, psychologists, psychiatrists, students, and others.

American Association for Music Therapy (AAMT)
Founded: 1971. *Headquarters:* Valley Forge, PA. *Purpose:* Promotes the exchange of information and certifies music therapists, approves music therapy training programs, and offers placement services. It serves certified music therapists, students, and colleges and universities offering music therapy programs.

American Association of Naturopathic Physicians (AANP) *Founded:* 1985. *Headquarters:* Seattle, WA. *Purpose:* To promote high educational standards and uniform criteria for licensing naturopathic physicians.

American Association of Neurological Surgeons (AANS) *Founded:* 1931. *Headquarters:* Park Ridge, IL. *Purpose:* To advance the specialty of neurological surgery in order to provide the highest quality care to patients. All active members are certified by the American Board of Neurosurgery.

American Association of Neuropathologists (AANP) *Founded:* 1924. *Headquarters:* Salt Lake City, UT. *Purpose:* To advance research and training in neuropathology. It serves physicians specializing in neuropathology.

American Association of Neuroscience Nurses (AANN) *Founded:* 1968. *Headquarters:* Chicago, IL. *Purpose:* To be instrumental in advancing the career growth of members, improving the quality of neuroscience patient care, educating the general public about neuroscience patient care, and promoting neuroscience nursing care and related fields. It serves registered nurses engaged in or primarily interested in neurosurgical or neurological nursing.

American Association of Nurse Anesthetists (AANA) *Founded:* 1931. *Headquarters:* Park Ridge, IL. *Purpose:* Promulgates education, and practice standards and guidelines, and affords consultation to both private and governmental entities regarding nurse anesthetists and their practice. The AANA Foundation supports the profession through award of education and research grants to students, faculty, and practicing certified registered nurse anesthetists.

The American Association of Nurse Attorneys (TAANA) *Founded:* 1982. *Headquarters:* Ellicott City, MD. *Purpose:* To provide practice tools and educational material, establish a leadership role in health care policy making, and influence the social policy, social legislation, and nursing practice acts. Serves nurse attorneys, nurses in law school, and attorneys in nursing schools.

American Academy of Nurse Practitioners (AANP) *Founded:* 1985. *Headquarters:* Austin, TX. *Purpose:* To promote the high standards of health care delivered by nurse practitioners and to act as a forum to enhance the identity and continuity of all nurse practitioner specialties.

American Association of Nutritional Consultants (AANC) *Founded:* 1948. *Headquarters:* Chula Vista, CA. *Purpose:* To create a forum for the exchange of nutritional information. Its members include nutritional consultants.

American Association of Occupational Health Nurses (AAOHN) *Founded:* 1988. *Headquarters:* Atlanta, GA. *Purpose:* To promote and set standards for the profession of occupational health nursing. It serves registered nurses employed by business and industry, nurse educators, nurse editors, nurse writers, and others interested in occupational health nursing.

American Association of Oral and Maxillofacial Surgeons (AAOMS) *Founded:* 1918. *Headquarters:* Rosemont, IL. *Purpose:* To promote the highest quality of patient care and education, to maintain high professional standards of practice through continuing education, and to foster and support specialty research. It serves dentists specializing in disease diagnosis and surgical and adjunctive treatment of diseases, injuries, and defects of the oral and maxillofacial region.

American Association of Orthodontists (AAO) *Founded:* 1901. *Headquarters:* St. Louis, MO. *Purpose:* To advance the art and science of orthodontics through continuing education, encouragement of research, provision of information to the public, and cooperation with other health groups. Members include orthodontists.

American Association of Orthopaedic Medicine (AAOM) *Founded:* 1982. *Headquarters:* Atlanta, GA. *Purpose:* To advance knowledge, diagnosis, and nonsurgical treatment of musculoskeletal and related disorders. Serves physicians and allied health professionals.

American Association of Osteopathic Examiners (AAOE) *Founded:* 1935. *Headquarters:* Washington, DC. *Purpose:* To conduct examinations and to offer certification of osteopathic physicians. It serves private physicians and state medical boards working for adequate osteopathic representation on all physician-licensing boards.

American Association for Partial Hospitalization (AAPH) *See* Association for Ambulatory Behavioral Health Care.

American Association of Pastoral Counselors (AAPC) *Founded:* 1963. *Headquarters:* Fairfax, VA. *Purpose:* To set standards and establish criteria for the operation of church-related counseling programs and to provide certification for religious professionals engaged in specialized ministries of counseling. It also approves church-related counseling centers, clergy, and other religious professionals of all faiths with special training in counseling.

American Association of Pathologists' Assistants (AAPA) *Founded:* 1972. *Headquarters:* Minneapolis, MN. *Purpose:* To promote the mutual association of trained pathologists' assistants. It serves pathologists' assistants and other qualified individuals who provide services in anatomic pathology under the direction of a qualified pathologist.

American Association for Pediatric Ophthalmology and Strabismus *Founded:* 1974. *Headquarters:* San Francisco, CA. *Purpose:* To encourage the quality of eye care for children by establishing high ethical standards of practice, supporting educational training programs for pediatric ophthalmologists, and promoting basic research in children's eye diseases. It serves ophthalmologists who limit their practice to children.

American Association of Physician-Hospital Organizations (AAPHO) *Founded:* 1993. *Headquarters:* Glen Allen, VA. *Purpose:* To help individual physician-hospital organizations (PHOs) and integrated delivery systems (IDSs), their executive staff, and member physicians to be successful in their local managed care marketplace through member services, including education, communication, and research and development. Serves PHO/IDS executives, and medical directors, physicians, health care executives, and board members and other associated professionals.

American Association of Physician Specialists (AAOS) *Founded:* 1952. *Headquarters:* Washington, DC. *Purpose:* To maintain continuing education programs and certification in 26 areas of specialization for the following members: American Academy of Osteopathic Anesthesiologists, American Academy of Osteopathic Family Practitioners, American Academy of Osteopathic Internists, American Academy of Osteopathic Neurologists and Psychiatrists, and the American Academy of Osteopathic Orthopedic Surgeons.

American Association of Physicists in Medicine (AAPM) *Founded:* 1958. *Headquarters:* College Park, MD. *Purpose:* To promote the application of physics to medicine and biology, to encourage interest and training in medical physics and related fields, and to prepare and disseminate technical information in medical physics and related fields. The AAPM is monitoring the quality of new graduate and clinical residency programs and participates as a sponsor of the Commission on the Accreditation of Medical Physics Education Programs (CAMPEP).

American Association of Plastic and Reconstructive Surgeons (AAPRS) *Founded:* 1921. *Headquarters:* Bryn Mawr, PA. *Purpose:* To support its members in their efforts to provide the highest quality patient care and maintain professional and ethical standards through education, research, and advocacy of socioeconomic and other professional activities. The Plastic Surgery Educational Foundation (PSEF) was founded in 1948 to support the education, research and domestic and international services programs of ASPRS members. *Formerly:* American Association of Plastic Surgeons (1994).

American Association of Plastic Surgeons *See* American Association of Plastic and Reconstructive Surgeons.

American Association of Podiatric Physicians and Surgeons (AAPPS) *Founded:* 1979. *Headquarters:* Washington, DC. *Purpose:* To provide training and certification for podiatry and podiatric surgery and offers accreditation to agencies providing podiatric services and podiatric peer review. It serves podiatrists.

American Association of Poison Control Centers (AAPCC) *Founded:* 1958. *Headquarters:* Washington, DC. *Purpose:* To aid in the procurement of information on the ingredients and potential acute toxicity of substances that may cause poisonings and on the management of such poisonings. Establishes standards for poison information and control centers. It serves individuals and organizations engaged in the operation of poison control centers.

American Association of Preferred Provider Organizations (AAPPO) *Founded:* 1983. *Headquarters:* Washington, DC. *Purpose:* To foster the development and promotion of PPOs and to provide educational and legislative support to organizations and individuals involved with the development of PPOs, and conducts educational seminars, consulting services, and accreditation services for PPOs. Members include health care executives, health care consultants, corporations, and PPOs.

American Association of Professional Hypnotherapists (AAPH) *Founded:* 1980. *Headquarters:* Boones Mill, VA. *Purpose:* To promote public awareness of hypnosis as applied to personal motivation and improvement, habit control, mental health services, and assistance in the healing process. Membership consists of hypnotherapists, marriage and family therapists, psychologists, clinical social workers, physicians, pastoral counselors, and others trained in hypnosis therapy.

American Association of Psychiatric Administrators (AAPA) *Founded:* 1960. *Headquarters:* Atlanta, GA. *Purpose:* To promote efficient consolidation and dissemination of information concerning treatment, care, and rehabilitation of mentally ill or handicapped persons and to conduct educational programs. It serves psychiatrists who occupy the position of chief administrative or clinical officer of a public or private neuropsychiatric hospital or clinic.

American Association of Psychiatric Services for Children (AAPSC) *Founded:* 1948. *Headquarters:* Rochester, NY. *Purpose:* To act as an information clearinghouse and to provide accreditation services. It serves members interested in the prevention and treatment of mental and emotional disorders of the young.

American Association of Psychiatric Technicians *Founded:* 1991. *Headquarters:* West Chicago, IL. *Purpose:* To promote professionalism in the mental health industry, to encourage further education of mental health workers, to provide national certification of mental health workers, and to award accreditation to mental health workers.

American Association of Public Health Dentistry (AAPHD) *Founded:* 1937. *Headquarters:* Richmond, VA. *Purpose:* To improve total health for all citizens through the development and support of effective programs of oral health promotion and disease prevention through the promotion of effective efforts in disease prevention, health promotion and service delivery; education of the public, health professionals and decision makers regarding the importance of oral health to total well-being; and expansion of the knowledge base of dental public health and fostering competency in its practice. AAPHD membership is open to all individuals concerned with improving the oral health of the public.

American Association of Public Health Physicians (AAPHP) *Founded:* 1954. *Headquarters:* Madison, WI. *Purpose:* To promote leadership in the public health field. It serves physicians actively engaged in public health.

American Association for Respiratory Care (AARC) *Founded:* 1947. *Headquarters:* Dallas, TX. *Purpose:* To encourage, develop, and provide educational programs concerning respiratory care. It serves respiratory care technicians and therapists employed by hospitals, group practices, educational institutions, and municipal organizations.

American Association of Retired Persons (AARP) *Founded:* 1958. *Headquarters:* Washington, DC. *Purpose:* To help older Americans achieve lives of independence, dignity, and purpose by improving every aspect of living for older people. Health care is an area of immediate concern. AARP is active in health legislation, health care financing, access, and quality issues. AARP maintains regional and state offices, and members are working or retired persons 50 years of age or older. Affiliates include the National Retired Teachers Association. AARP's two Advocacy Centers (for Medicare and for Social Security) support work in health and long-term care.

American Association for Social Psychiatry (AASP) *Founded:* 1971. *Headquarters:* Washington, DC. *Purpose:* To study, prevent, and treat mental illness, behavioral disorders, and human vicissitudes. It serves social psychiatry professionals and trainees interested in such fields.

American Association of Spinal Cord Injury Nurses (AASCIN) *Founded:* 1983. *Headquarters:* Jackson Heights, NY. *Purpose:* To promote and improve nursing care to the spinal cord injury patient. It serves nurses who care for patients with spinal cord injuries, nurses interested in the field of spinal cord injury, and persons who have provided extraordinary service to improve the quality of life for spinal cord injury patients.

American Association of Spinal Cord Injury Psychologists and Social Workers (AASCIPSW) *Founded:* 1986. *Headquarters:* Jackson Heights, NY. *Purpose:* To promote improvement of psychological care of spinal cord injury patients, focusing on topics such as sexuality and alcohol and drug dependence among spinal cord injury patients. It serves psychologists and social workers who treat patients with spinal cord injuries.

American Association of State Social Work Boards (AASSWB) *Founded:* 1979. *Headquarters:* Culpeper, VA. *Purpose:* To protect the recipient of social work service and promote confidence in and accountability of the social work profession by establishing national regulatory standards for the practice of professional social work. It supports state boards and authorities empowered to regulate the practice of social work within their own jurisdictions.

American Association of Stomatologists (AAS) *Founded:* 1985. *Headquarters:* Freehold, NJ. *Purpose:* To establish oral diagnosis, radiology, and medicine as recognized specialties in dentistry. It serves coordinating organizations representing the American Academy of Oral Medicine and the Organization of Teachers of Oral Diagnosis.

American Association for the Study of Headache (AASH) *Founded:* 1959. *Headquarters:* Woodbury, NJ. *Purpose:* To bring together practitioners in different areas to discuss ideas and beliefs about headaches. It serves physicians, dentists, and scientists interested in the study of headaches.

American Association for the Study of Liver Diseases (AASLD) *Founded:* 1950. *Headquarters:* Thorofare, NJ. *Purpose:* To promote the exchange of scientific information about liver disease and liver research. It serves physicians interested in such information.

American Association of Suicidology (AAS) *Foundation:* 1967. *Headquarters:* Washington, DC. *Purpose:* To advance studies of suicide prevention and life-threatening behavior. It serves psychologists, psychiatrists, social workers, nurses, health educators, physicians, directors of suicide prevention centers, clergy, and others sharing a common interest in suicide prevention.

American Association of Surgeon Assistants (AASA) *Founded:* 1973. *Headquarters:* Arlington, VA. *Purpose:* To promote academic and clinical excellence among members including surgeon assistants, surgical physician assistants, students, physicians, surgeons, and allied health professionals.

American Association for the Surgery of Trauma (AAST) *Founded:* 1938. *Headquarters:* Seattle, WA. *Purpose:* To serve surgeons interested in the cultivation and improvement of the science and art of the surgery of trauma and allied sciences.

American Association of Therapeutic Humor (AATH) *Founded:* 1987. *Headquarters:* St. Louis, MO. *Purpose:* To promote use of humor as a therapeutic technique. It serves health care providers, clergy, and educators.

American Association for Thoracic Surgery (AATS) *Founded:* 1917. *Headquarters:* Manchester, MA. *Purpose:* To encourage investigation and study of intrathoracic physiology, pathology and therapy. It serves specialists in surgery of the chest region, including cardiovascular surgeons.

American Association of Tissue Banks (AATB) *Founded:* 1976. *Headquarters:* McLean, VA. *Purpose:* To encourage the development of regional tissue banks and the establishment of guidelines and standards for the retrieval, preservation, distribution, and use of tissues for transplantation.

American Association of Women Dentists (AAWD) *Founded:* 1921. *Headquarters:* Chicago, IL. *Purpose:* To encourage women to pursue an academic degree in dentistry and to advance the status of women in the dental profession. It serves women dentists and dental students.

American Association for Women Radiologists (AAWR) *Founded:* 1980. *Headquarters:* Reston, VA. *Purpose:* To facilitate exchange of knowledge and information as it relates to women in radiology, to encourage publication of materials on radiology and medicine by members, to support women who are training in the field, and to encourage women radiologists to participate in radiological societies. It is composed of women physicians involved in diagnostic or therapeutic radiology, nuclear medicine, or radiologic physics.

American Association for World Health (AAWH) *Founded:* 1953. *Headquarters:* Washington, DC. *Purpose:* Informs Americans about world health problems and projects and acts as an advocate to support programs of the World Health Organization (WHO) and the Pan American Health Organization (PAHO). AAWH sponsors World Health Day, World AIDS Day, and World No-Tobacco Day and answers requests for information on international health. *Also known as:* U.S. Committee for the World Health Organization.

American Athletic Trainers Association and Certification Board (AATA) *Founded:* 1978. *Headquarters:* Arcadia, CA. *Purpose:* Qualify and certify active athletic trainers, to establish minimum competence standards for individuals participating in the prevention and care of athletic injuries, and to inform the public of the importance of having competent leadership in the area of athletic training.

American Auditory Society (AAS) *Founded:* 1973. *Headquarters:* Phoenix, AZ. *Purpose:* To increase knowledge of the ear, hearing and balance, disorders of the ear, and prevention of those disorders. It assists audiologists, otolaryngologists, scientists, hearing aid industry professionals, educators of hearing impaired people, and individuals involved in industries serving hearing impaired people, including the amplification system industry.

American Black Chiropractors Association (ABCA) *Founded:* 1980. *Headquarters:* St. Louis, MO. *Purpose:* To educate the public, health care organizations, and health care providers about chiropractic and promoting black chiropractic practitioners in the community. It serves individuals who have earned a recognized doctorate degree in chiropractic and students who are enrolled in a chiropractic college.

American Board of Abdominal Surgery (ABAS) *Founded:* 1957. *Headquarters:* Annapolis, MD. *Purpose:* Certifies as diplomates specialists in abdominal surgery, establishes minimum educational and training standards for the specialty and determines whether candidates have received adequate preparation as defined by the board, and provides comprehensive oral and written examinations to determine the ability and fitness of candidates.

American Board of Allergy and Immunology (ABAI) *Founded:* 1972. *Headquarters:* Philadelphia, PA. *Purpose:* To establish and examine physician candidates for certification as specialists in allergy and immunology. It serves as a joint medical specialty board of the American Board of Internal Medicine and the American Board of Pediatrics.

American Board of Anesthesiology (ABA) *Founded:* 1938. *Headquarters:* Raleigh, NC. *Purpose:* To improve standards of the practice of anesthesiology; to establish criteria of fitness for the designation of a specialist in the field; to advise the Accreditation Council for Graduate Medical Education of the American Medical Association concerning training of individuals seeking certification; to arrange and conduct examinations to determine the competence of physicians who apply; and to issue certificates to individuals meeting the required standards.

American Board of Bionic Rehabilitative Psychology (ABBRP) *Founded:* 1983. *Headquarters:* Las Vegas, NV. *Purpose:* To advance scientific knowledge and provide educational opportunities in the field of bionic rehabilitative psychology. It serves physicians specializing in bionic rehabilitative psychology.

American Board of Cardiovascular Perfusion (ABCP) *Founded:* 1975. *Headquarters:* Hattiesburg, MS. *Purpose:* To protect the public through the establishment and maintenance of standards in the field. It establishes qualifications for examination and recertification and administers annual board examinations. Members include certified clinical perfusionists.

American Board for Certification in Orthotics and Prosthetics (ABC) *Founded:* 1948. *Headquarters:* Alexandria, VA. *Purpose:* To establish qualifications, conduct examinations, and certify individuals and facilities whom the board finds qualified to practice orthotics and prosthetics.

American Board of Certified and Registered Encephalographic Technicians and Technologists (ABCRETT) *Founded:* 1980. *Headquarters:* San Diego, CA. *Purpose:* Serves certified encephalography (EEG) technologists that conduct educational and certification programs for EEG technologists.

American Board of Chelation Therapy (ABCT) *Founded:* 1982. *Headquarters:* Chicago, IL. *Purpose:* To define and establish qualifications required of licensed physicians for certification in the field of chelation therapy.

American Board of Clinical Chemistry (ABCC) *Founded:* 1950. *Headquarters:* Washington, DC. *Purpose:* To establish and enhance the standards of competence for the practice of clinical chemistry, including toxicological chemistry, and to certify qualified specialists; conducts examinations annually for certification in clinical chemistry and clinical toxicology. It is sponsored by the American Association for Clinical Chemistry, American Chemical Society, American Institute of Chemists, American Society for Biochemistry and Molecular Biology, and other organizations.

American Board of Colon and Rectal Surgery (ABCRS) *Founded:* 1934. *Headquarters:* Taylor, MI. *Purpose:* To investigate qualifications, administer examinations, and provide certification as diplomates for physicians specializing in colon and rectal surgery.

American Board of Dental Public Health (ABDPH) *Founded:* 1950. *Headquarters:* Gainesville, FL. *Purpose:* To investigate the qualifications of, administer examinations to, and certify as diplomates dentists specializing in dental public health. Sponsored by the American Association of Public Health.

American Board of Dermatology (ABD) *Founded:* 1932. *Headquarters:* Detroit, MI. *Purpose:* To ensure provision of competent care for patients with cutaneous diseases by establishing requirements of postdoctoral training and creating and conducting annual comprehensive examinations to determine the competence of physicians who meet the requirements for examination by the board; issues certificates to those who satisfactorily complete the examination.

American Board of Emergency Medicine (ABEM) *Founded:* 1976. *Headquarters:* East Lansing, MI. *Purpose:* To advance emergency medical care by designing and administering an annual two-part examination (written and oral) to evaluate physicians seeking certification as specialists in emergency medicine. Recertification is required every ten years.

American Board of Endodontics (ABE) *Founded:* 1964. *Headquarters:* Chicago, IL. *Purpose:* Certifies dentists who have successfully completed study and training in an advanced endodontics education program accredited by the Commission on Dental Accreditation of the American Dental Association and who have successfully completed the examinations administered by the board.

American Board of Environmental Medicine (ABEM) *Founded:* 1988. *Headquarters:* Prairie Village, KS. *Purpose:* To examine, evaluate, and certify physicians, training programs, and hospital units, environmental control and biodetoxification units, and rehabilitation centers.

American Board of Examiners of Pastoral Counseling (ABEPC) *Founded:* 1921. *Headquarters:* Tampa, FL. *Purpose:* To provide certification in pastoral counseling to individuals, centers, and institutions and to conduct certification testing in chaplaincy and pastoral counseling and annual reviews.

American Board of Examiners of Psychodrama, Sociometry, and Group Psychotherapy (ABEPSGP) *Founded:* 1975. *Headquarters:* Washington, DC. *Purpose:* To establish and maintain national standards for certification in the field of group psychotherapy, psychodrama, and sociometry.

American Board of Family Practice (ABFP) *Founded:* 1969. *Headquarters:* Lexington, KY. *Purpose:* Conducts certification exams and acts as a specialty board of physicians certified in family practice.

American Board of Health Physics (ABHP) *Founded:* 1960. *Headquarters:* McLean, VA. *Purpose:* To promote the health physics profession by establishing standards and procedures for certification and conducting certification examinations.

American Board of Industrial Medicine and Surgery (ABIMS) *Founded:* 1984. *Headquarters:* Las Vegas, NV. *Purpose:* To promote scientific advancement and provide educational courses in the fields of industrial medicine and surgery, serving physicians specializing in both fields.

American Board of Internal Medicine (ABIM) *Founded:* 1936. *Headquarters:* Philadelphia, PA. *Purpose:* To determine the qualifications of, administer examinations to, and certify as specialists in internal medicine those physicians meeting its standards of clinical competence. Board members are elected from certified leaders in internal medicine.

American Board of Medical Genetics (ABMG) *Founded:* 1979. *Headquarters:* Bethesda, MD. *Purpose:* To certify individuals for the delivery of medical genetics services and accredit medical geneticist training programs. Members consist of those who receive the board's certification.

American Board of Medical-Legal Analysis in Medicine and Surgery (ABMLAMS) *Founded:* 1981. *Headquarters:* Las Vegas, NV. *Purpose:* To improve patient care and further science of medical-legal analysis. It serves physicians and attorneys who are candidates for certification in the field of medical-legal analysis, which deals with forensic and jurisprudential aspects of medicine and surgery. It is maintained by the American Academy of Neurological and Orthopaedic Surgeons.

American Board of Medical Psychotherapists and Psychodiagnosticians (ABMPP) *Founded:* 1982. *Headquarters:* Nashville, TN. *Purpose:* To offer certification review and continuing education programs. It serves psychiatrists, psychologists, social workers, and psychiatric nurses interested in psychotherapy.

American Board of Medical Specialties (ABMS) *Founded:* 1970. *Headquarters:* Evanston, IL. *Purpose:* To act for approved medical specialty boards as a group. Medical specialty boards of the ABMS currently include allergy and immunology, anesthesiology, colon and rectal surgery, dermatology, emergency medicine, family practice, internal medicine, medical genetics, neurological surgery, nuclear medicine, obstetrics and gynecology, ophthalmology, orthopedic surgery, otolaryngology, pathology, pediatrics, physical medicine and rehabilitation, plastic surgery, preventive medicine, psychiatry and neurology, radiology, surgery, thoracic surgery, and urology. It serves primary medical specialty boards and joint boards; organizations with related interests are associate members.

American Board of Neurological and Orthopaedic Medicine and Surgery (ABNOMS) *Founded:* 1977. *Headquarters:* Las Vegas, NV. *Purpose:* To demonstrate expertise and capability in neurological and orthopedic surgery. It consists of individuals proficient in neurological and orthopedic medicine and surgery who have previous board certification and proper preceptorship and have made significant contributions to the field of neurological and orthopedic medicine and surgery.

American Board of Neurological Surgery (ABNS)
Founded: 1940. *Headquarters:* Houston, TX. *Purpose:* To investigate qualifications of, administer examinations to, and certify as diplomates physicians specializing in neurological surgery. It serves physicians specializing in neurological surgery.

American Board of Neuroscience Nursing (ABNN)
Founded: 1978. *Headquarters:* Chicago, IL. *Purpose:* To promote excellence by encouraging professional study; grants certification. It serves registered nurses who have passed a written examination demonstrating achievement in neuroscience nursing.

American Board of Nuclear Medicine (ABNM)
Founded: 1971. *Headquarters:* Los Angeles, CA. *Purpose:* To certify as diplomates physicians specializing in nuclear medicine. It is sponsored by the American Boards of Internal Medicine, Pathology, and Radiology and the Society of Nuclear Medicine.

American Board of Nutrition (ABN) *Founded:* 1948. *Headquarters:* Birmingham, AL. *Purpose:* To establish standards for qualification of persons as specialists in the field of human nutrition, holds examinations, and certifies as diplomates those who meet its qualifications. It serves physicians qualified to treat nutritional and metabolic disorders and doctoral recipients working on problems of human nutrition and nutrient requirements.

American Board of Obstetrics and Gynecology (ABOG) *Founded:* 1927. *Headquarters:* Dallas, TX. *Purpose:* To establish qualifications, conduct examinations, and certify as diplomates those physicians qualified to specialize in obstetrics and gynecology.

American Board for Occupational Health Nurses (ABOHN) *Founded:* 1972. *Headquarters:* Palos Hills, IL. *Purpose:* To establish standards and confer initial and ongoing certification in occupational health nursing.

American Board of Ophthalmology (ABO) *Founded:* 1916. *Headquarters:* Bala Cynwyd, PA. *Purpose:* To determine the adequacy of training, the professional preparation, and ophthalmic knowledge of ophthalmologists who wish to be certified and to certify as diplomates physicians specializing in ophthalmology.

American Board of Opticianry (ABO) *Founded:* 1947. *Headquarters:* Fairfax, VA. *Purpose:* To provide uniform standards for certifying dispensing opticians by administering the National Opticianry Competency Examination and issues certified optician certificates to those passing the examination.

American Board of Oral and Maxillofacial Surgery (ABOMS) *Founded:* 1946. *Headquarters:* Chicago, IL.

Purpose: Certifies as diplomates dentists specializing in oral and maxillofacial surgery.

American Board of Oral Pathology (ABOP)
Founded: 1948. *Headquarters:* Tampa, FL. *Purpose:* To arrange, conduct, and control examinations to determine the competence of applicants wishing to be certified in oral pathology.

American Board of Orthodontics (ABO) *Founded:* 1929. *Headquarters:* St. Louis, MO. *Purpose:* Investigates the qualifications of, administers examinations to, and certifies as diplomates dentists specializing in orthodontics.

American Board of Orthopedic Surgery (ABOS)
Founded: 1934. *Headquarters:* Chapel Hill, NC. *Purpose:* To establish qualifications, conduct annual examinations, and certify as diplomates those physicians qualified to practice orthopedic surgery.

American Board of Otolaryngology (ABO) *Founded:* 1924. *Headquarters:* Houston, TX. *Purpose:* A nonmembership board that holds examinations and certifies as diplomates qualified physicians specializing in otolaryngology.

American Board of Pathology (ABP) *Founded:* 1936. *Headquarters:* Tampa, FL. *Purpose:* Maintains a registry of certified pathologists, participates in the evaluation and review of graduate medical school pathology programs, and examines and certifies as specialists in pathology doctors of medicine or osteopathic medicine who have had three to five years postgraduate training in laboratory medicine and pathology.

American Board of Pediatric Dentistry (ABPD)
Founded: 1940. *Headquarters:* Carmel, IN. *Purpose:* Investigate the qualifications of, administer examinations to, and certify as diplomates dentists specializing in the care of children.

American Board of Pediatrics (ABP) *Founded:* 1933. *Headquarters:* Chapel Hill, NC. *Purpose:* To establish qualifications, conduct examinations, and certify as diplomates physicians qualified as specialists in pediatrics.

American Board of Periodontology (ABP) *Founded:* 1939. *Headquarters:* Baltimore, MD. *Purpose:* Conducts examinations to determine the qualifications and competence of dentists who voluntarily apply for certification as diplomates in the field of periodontology (periodontics).

American Board of Physical Medicine and Rehabilitation (ABPMR) *Founded:* 1947. *Headquarters:* Rochester, MN. *Purpose:* To establish qualifications, conduct examinations, and certify physicians qualified to specialize in physical medicine and rehabilitation.

American Board of Plastic Surgery (ABPS)
Founded: 1937. *Headquarters:* Philadelphia, PA. *Purpose:* To investigate the qualifications of, administer examinations to, and certify as diplomates physicians specializing in plastic surgery.

American Board of Podiatric Orthopedics and Podiatric Primary Medicine (ABPOPPM) *Founded:* 1975. *Headquarters:* Chicago, IL. *Purpose:* To offer a certifying examination in foot orthopedics for podiatrists. It serves podiatrists who have taken a competency examination prepared by the board.

American Board of Podiatric Surgery (ABPS) *Founded:* 1975. *Headquarters:* San Francisco, CA. *Purpose:* Certify the competence of legally licensed podiatrists.

American Board of Post Anesthesia Nursing Certification (ABPANC) *Founded:* 1985. *Headquarters:* Richmond, VA. *Purpose:* To provide a nonmembership board that administers examinations to individuals wishing to attain post-anesthesia nursing certification.

American Board of Preventive Medicine (ABPM) *Founded:* 1948. *Headquarters:* Schiller Park, IL. *Purpose:* To determine eligibility requirements, administer examinations, and certify physicians in the specialized fields of public health, aerospace medicine, occupational medicine, and preventive medicine.

American Board of Professional Disability Consultants (ABPDC) *Founded:* 1988. *Headquarters:* McLean, VA. *Purpose:* To identify and award diplomate standing to specialists in disability and personal injury. A for-profit board, it members include physicians, psychologists, counselors, and attorneys.

American Board of Professional Psychology (ABPP) *Founded:* 1947. *Headquarters:* Columbia, MO. *Purpose:* Serves members who have successfully passed oral examinations administered in eight specialties: clinical psychology, industrial and organizational psychology, forensic psychology, counseling psychology, clinical neuropsychology, family psychology, health psychology, and school psychology. Candidates must have five years of qualifying experience in psychological practice.

American Board of Psychiatry and Neurology (ABPN) *Founded:* 1934. *Headquarters:* Deerfield, IL. *Purpose:* To determine eligibility requirements, administer examinations, and certify physicians with specialized training in psychiatry, neurology, child neurology, child adolescent psychiatry, clinical neurophysiology, and geriatric psychiatry.

American Board of Psychological Hypnosis (ABPH) *Founded:* 1959. *Headquarters:* Beverly, MA. *Purpose:* To award specialty diplomas to psychologists meeting requirements in experimental and clinical hypnosis; raise the standards of individuals conducting research in hypnosis and using it in clinical practice by requiring specialized training and experience as evidenced by advanced credentials in psychology, published research, written and oral examinations, and recommendations of colleagues.

American Board of Quality Assurance and Utilization Review Physicians (ABQAURP) *Founded:* 1977. *Headquarters:* Tampa, FL. *Purpose:* To certify as diplomates physicians and other qualified individuals specializing in quality assurance and utilization review. It serves physicians and coordinators involved in quality assurance and utilization review.

American Board of Radiology (ABR) *Founded:* 1934. *Headquarters:* Tucson, AZ. *Purpose:* To establish qualifications, conduct examinations, and certify physicians in the specialty of radiology and physicists in radiological physics and related branches (sciences dealing with x-rays or rays from radioactive substances for medical use).

American Board of Registration of EEG and EP Technologists (ABRET) *Founded:* 1961. *Headquarters:* Longwood, FL. *Purpose:* To determine the competency of electroencephalography technologists through administration of written and oral examinations.

American Board of Spinal Surgery (ABSS) *Founded:* 1977. *Headquarters:* Las Vegas, NV. *Purpose:* To advance knowledge and provide education in the field of spinal surgery.

American Board of Surgery (ABS) *Founded:* 1937. *Headquarters:* Philadelphia, PA. *Purpose:* To certify as diplomates physicians specializing in surgery and to certify special qualifications in pediatric surgery and general vascular surgery and added qualifications in general vascular surgery, surgical critical care, and hand surgery. It currently offers recertification in general surgery and pediatric surgery.

American Board of Thoracic Surgery (ABTS) *Founded:* 1948. *Headquarters:* Evanston, IL. *Purpose:* To investigate the qualifications of, administer examinations to, and certify physicians specializing in thoracic surgery.

American Board of Toxicology (ABT) *Founded:* 1979. *Headquarters:* Raleigh, NC. *Purpose:* To conduct a certification program in toxicology and administer annual certification and recertification examinations.

American Board of Tropical Medicine (ABTM) *Founded:* 1980. *Headquarters:* Toledo, OH. *Purpose:* To investigate the qualifications and determine the competency of candidates applying for membership and to provide continuing medical education to specialists in tropical medicine.

American Board of Urologic Allied Health Professionals (ABUAHP) *Founded:* 1972. *Headquarters:* Stamford, CT. *Purpose:* To conduct an annual certification examination for urological professionals. Its parent organization is American Urological Association Allied. It serves physicians including dermatologists, surgeons, pediatricians, and other professionals of public health and preventive medicine and pathology.

American Board of Urology (ABU) *Founded:* 1935. *Headquarters:* Bingham Farms, MI. *Purpose:* To conduct examinations and certify physicians in the specialty of urology.

American Broncho-Esophagological Association (ABEA) *Founded:* 1917. *Headquarters:* St. Louis, MO. *Purpose:* A professional organization composed of otolaryngologists, chest specialists, thoracic surgeons, and gastroenterologists engaged in the practice of broncho-esophagology (diseases and injuries of the respiratory system and upper digestive tract).

American Burn Association (ABA) *Founded:* 1967. *Headquarters:* New York, NY. *Purpose:* To improve the care and treatment of burns, including a program to prevent burn injuries. It serves physicians, nurses, physical therapists, occupational therapists, dietitians, biomedical engineers, social workers, and researchers interested in the care of burn patients.

American Cancer Society (ACS) *Founded:* 1913. *Headquarters:* Atlanta, GA. *Purpose:* To eliminate cancer as a major health problem by preventing cancer, saving lives, and diminishing suffering from cancer, through research, education, advocacy, and service. The ACS issues regular cancer screening updates and new diagnostic and treatment recommendations through its journal *CA*. Public campaigns and support services include Reach to Recovery (breast cancer), Man to Man (prostate cancer), Can Surmount, I Can Cope, and the Great American Smokeout. The ACS has many state and local affiliates. Members include volunteers supporting education and research in cancer prevention, diagnosis, detection, and treatment.

American Celiac Society/Dietary Support Coalition (ACS/DSC) *Founded:* 1970. *Headquarters:* West Orange, NJ. *Purpose:* To provide information on following a gluten-free diet; to assist members in locating specialty foods that are gluten free; and to encourage retailers to make gluten-free products available. It serves physicians who diagnose and care for individuals with gluten-sensitive intestinal disease, dietitians, nutritionists, agencies that serve individuals with gluten-sensitive intestinal disease, and other individuals interested in a gluten-free diet.

American Center for Chinese Medical Sciences (ACCMS) *Founded:* 1974. *Headquarters:* Bethesda, MD. *Purpose:* To develop medical contacts, share experiences, and promote the exchange of scientific information between the United States and China. It sponsors meetings and tours to China, promotes joint research, and conducts lectures. It serves medical and scientific professionals from the United States and China.

American Chiropractic Association (ACA) *Founded:* 1930. *Headquarters:* Arlington, VA. *Purpose:* To promote legislation defining chiropractic care, serving chiropractors with specialties including chiropractic orthopedics, diagnosis and internal disorders, diagnostic imaging, mental health, neurology, nutrition, physiological therapeutics, sports injuries and physical fitness, and technical.

American Chiropractic Registry of Radiologic Technologists (ACRRT) *Founded:* 1982. *Headquarters:* Kalamazoo, MI. *Purpose:* To serve as a certifying agency for individuals in the field and maintains a registry of certified chiropractic radiologic technologists. It serves chiropractic assistants and radiologic technologists employed in chiropractic offices.

American Cleft Palate-Craniofacial Association (ACPA) *Founded:* 1943. *Headquarters:* Pittsburgh, PA. *Purpose:* To improve the understanding of scientific and clinical problems in habilitation of patients with cleft lip or palate. It serves physicians, dentists, speech pathologists, audiologists, psychologists, nurses, and other individuals engaged in the care of individuals with cleft lip and palate and associated craniofacial deformities.

American Clinical Laboratory Association (ACLA) *Founded:* 1971. *Headquarters:* Washington, DC. *Purpose:* To foster the elimination of inequalities in the standards applied to different segments of the clinical laboratory market and the discouragement of the enactment of restrictive legislative or regulatory policies. The ACLA is composed of corporations, partnerships, and individuals owning or controlling one or more independent clinical laboratory facilities operating for a profit and licensed under the Clinical Laboratories Improvement Act of 1967 or the Clinical Laboratories Improvement Amendment of 1988 or accredited by the Medicare program.

American Clinical Neurophysiology Society (ASET) *Founded:* 1959. *Headquarters:* Carroll, IA. *Purpose:* To advance electroneurodiagnostic technology and to develop and maintain high standards of training and practice in this field.

American College of Addiction Treatment Administrators (ACATA) *Founded:* 1984. *Headquarters:* Washington, DC. *Purpose:* To improve educational and professional standards in the field of addiction treatment administration. It serves administrators of addiction treatment facilities.

American College for Advancement in Medicine (ACAM) *Founded:* 1973. *Headquarters:* Laguna Hills, CA. *Purpose:* To promote preventive medicine throughout the world; conducts research programs in the fields of chelation therapy, nutritional medicine, and other preventive modalities. It serves physicians.

American College of Allergy, Asthma and Immunology (ACAAI) *Founded:* 1942. *Headquarters:* Arlington Heights, IL. *Purpose:* To encourage the study, improve the practice, and advance the cause of clinical immunology and allergy. It serves practicing allergists, educators, researchers, and clinical immunologists.

American College of Angiology (ACA) *Founded:* 1954. *Headquarters:* Roslyn, NY. *Purpose:* To foster the advancement of the study and research of vascular diseases. It serves physicians and basic scientists in health care industries.

American College of Apothecaries (ACA) *Founded:* 1940. *Headquarters:* Memphis, TN. *Purpose:* Translation, transformation, and dissemination of knowledge, research data, and recent developments in the pharmaceutical industry and public health; sponsors the Community Pharmacy Residency Program and offers continuing education courses. It serves pharmacists who own and operate prescription pharmacies, including hospital pharmacists, pharmacy students, and faculties of colleges of pharmacy.

American College of Cardiology (ACC) *Founded:* 1949. *Headquarters:* Bethesda, MD. *Purpose:* To foster optimal cardiovascular care and disease prevention through professional education, promotion of research, leadership in the development of standards and guidelines, and formulation of health care policy. ACC represents the majority of board-certified U.S. cardiovascular physicians, including adult cardiologists, cardiovascular surgeons, and pediatric cardiologists. ACC's primary focus is professional education, including its flagship educational activity, its annual convention or Annual Scientific Session, four clinical periodicals, and an extensive library. Standards and guidelines efforts include ACC/AHA (American Heart Association) Guidelines (related to the diagnosis and management of cardiovascular disease), ACP (American College of Physicians)/ACC/AHA Clinical Competence Statements, ACC Position Statements and Expert Consensus Documents, and Bethesda Conference Reports (providing recommendations to practitioners related to important questions in cardiology). ACC also collects, analyzes, and reports on cardiovascular data through its National Cardiovascular Data Registry. ACC actively participates in the health care policy debate, both through independent activities on the federal and state level and through a variety of coalitions.

American College of Cardiovascular Administrators (ACCA) *Founded:* 1986. *Headquarters:* Southfield, MI. *Purpose:* To represent members of the medical industry and provide credentialing of cardiology administrators. It consists of upper-level and middle-level managers in the cardiovascular health care field.

American College of Chest Physicians (ACCP) *Founded:* 1935. *Headquarters:* Northbrook, IL. *Purpose:* To promote undergraduate and postgraduate medical education and research in the field. It serves physicians and surgeons specializing in diseases of the chest (diseases of the heart and lungs).

American College of Chiropractic Orthopedists (ACCO) *Founded:* 1964. *Headquarters:* El Centro, CA. *Purpose:* To establish and maintain optimal educational and clinical standards in the field; it serves certified and noncertified chiropractic orthopedists and students enrolled in a postgraduate chiropractic orthopedic program.

American College of Clinical Pharmacology (ACCP) *Founded:* 1969. *Headquarters:* New Hartford, NY. *Purpose:* To promote the science of clinical pharmacology including excellence in the investigational and clinical testing of drugs. It serves individuals who have earned the degree of doctor of medicine or a doctorate in any one of the biomedical sciences and individuals who have had at least three years of training or the equivalent in basic science, internal medicine, or an allied field.

American College of Clinical Pharmacy (ACCP) *Founded:* 1979. *Headquarters:* Kansas City, MO. *Purpose:*

To advance the practice of clinical pharmacy and interdisciplinary health care. It serves clinical pharmacists dedicated to promoting the rational use of drugs in society.

American College of Counselors (ACC) *Founded:* 1972. *Headquarters:* Indianapolis, IN. *Purpose:* To accredit clinicians and family life educators. Serves psychologists, physicians, lawyers, counselors, psychiatrists, teachers, clergy, and social workers interested in strengthening family life through competent family counseling, family life education, and legislative activity for the good of the family unit.

American College of Cryosurgery (ACCRYO) *Founded:* 1977. *Headquarters:* Schaumburg, IL. *Purpose:* Serves, among other activities, as a national faculty to educate members and teach at university training centers. Members are physicians, general surgeons, scientists, and other individuals involved in the clinical application of cryosurgery.

American College of Dentists (ACD) *Founded:* 1920. *Headquarters:* Gaithersburg, MD. *Purpose:* To conduct educational and research programs. Members include dentists and other individuals interested in advancing the standards of the profession of dentistry.

American College of Emergency Physicians (ACEP) *Founded:* 1968. *Headquarters:* Dallas, TX. *Purpose:* To support quality emergency medical care and to promote the interests of emergency physicians, on a foundation of five value statements: (1) quality emergency care is a fundamental individual right and should be available to all who seek it; (2) there is a body of knowledge unique to emergency medicine that requires continuing refinement and development; (3) quality emergency medicine is best practiced by qualified, credentialed emergency physicians; (4) the best interests of the patient are served when emergency physicians practice in a fair, equitable and supportive environment; and (5) the emergency physician has the responsibility to play the lead role in the definition, evaluation, and improvement of quality emergency care. ACEP publishes patient care recommendations in the form of Clinical Policies. It contains the Emergency Medicine Residents' Association (EMRA) for interns, residents, and fellows.

American College of Epidemiology (ACE) *Founded:* 1979. *Headquarters:* Rockville, MD. *Purpose:* To promote education in the practice of epidemiology and maintain professional standards in the field. It serves medical professionals involved in the field of epidemiology.

American College of Foot and Ankle Orthopedic Medicine (ACFO) *Founded:* 1949. *Headquarters:* Cocolalla, ID. *Purpose:* Serves podiatrists sanctioned as specialists to practice foot orthopedics.

American College of Foot and Ankle Pediatrics (ACFAP) *Founded:* 1977. *Headquarters:* Philadelphia, PA. *Purpose:* It serves podiatric physicians and surgeons, general physicians and surgeons, psychologists, and physical therapists interested in children's foot health.

American College of Foot and Ankle Surgeons (ACFAS) *Founded:* 1940. *Headquarters:* Park Ridge, IL. *Purpose:* To promote and disseminate information on podiatric surgery among the public, podiatric surgeons, and other health professionals. It serves podiatric surgeons.

American College of Gastroenterology (ACG) *Founded:* 1932. *Headquarters:* Arlington, VA. *Purpose:* To advance the study and medical treatment of disorders of the gastrointestinal tract; to promote the highest standards in medical education; and to meet the needs of clinical gastroenterology practitioners. It carries out its mission through activities to advance knowledge of gastrointestinal disease, educate specialists in gastrointestinal disease, represent the interests of the clinician practicing in the field of gastroenterology, ensure quality in patient care, and promote patient education on gastrointestinal conditions and digestive health. ACG components and products include the Institute for Clinical Research and Education, several publications and patient education programs, and ACG Practice Guidelines and Algorithms supported by a GI Practice Guidelines Library. It serves physicians and surgeons specializing in diseases and disorders of the gastrointestinal tract and accessory organs of digestion, including disorders due to nutrition.

American College Health Association (ACHA) *Founded:* 1920. *Headquarters:* Baltimore, MD. *Purpose:* Serves institutions and individuals interested in promoting health for students and all other members of the college community.

American College of Health Care Administrators (ACHCA) *Founded:* 1962. *Headquarters:* Alexandria, VA. *Purpose:* To promote the administration of long-term care institutions, including medical administration and activities designed to improve the quality of nursing home administration. It certifies members' competence in nursing home and long term care administration.

American College of Healthcare Executives (ACHE) *Founded:* 1933. *Headquarters:* Chicago, IL. *Purpose:* To be the professional membership society for health care executives; to meet its members' professional, educational, and leadership needs; to promote high ethical standards and conduct; and to advance health care management excellence. It maintains numerous committees and task forces and collaborates with other organizations to achieve common objectives. ACHE operates the Health Administration Press, publishes a journal and a magazine, conducts research and compiles statistics; provides career development and public policy programs; and carries out activities to strengthen credentialing programs.

American College of International Physicians (ACIP) *Founded:* 1975. *Headquarters:* Washington, DC. *Purpose:* To foster initiatives to promote national efforts in international health, education, research, training, and welfare; to promote the betterment of health of all peoples; and to advance the art and science of medicine.

American College of Legal Medicine (ACLM) *Founded:* 1955. *Headquarters:* Milwaukee, WI. *Purpose:* To promote and advance the field of legal medicine or medical jurisprudence and arrange for meetings with medical, legal, and professional groups and legislative, judicial, and enforcement bodies interested in any province where law and medicine are contiguous; to make available postgraduate training in legal medicine and/or medical jurisprudence. It serves individuals who hold degrees in medicine and law.

American College of Medical Genetics (ACMG) *Founded:* 1991. *Headquarters:* Bethesda, MD. *Purpose:* To ensure the availability of genetic services without regard to considerations of race, gender, sex orientation, disability, or ability to pay. To promote and support genetic research and effective and fair health policies.

American College of Medical Physics *Founded:* 1982. *Headquarters:* Reston, VA. *Purpose:* To serve the professional needs of clinical medical physicists and address issues related to patient safety and accuracy and quality of the patient's diagnostic and therapeutic radiological procedures.

American College of Medical Practice Executives (ACMPE) *Founded:* 1956. *Headquarters:* Englewood, CO. *Purpose:* To encourage medical group practice administrators to improve and maintain their proficiency and to establish a program with uniform standards of admission, advancement, and certification in order to achieve the highest possible standards in the profession of medical group practice administration. It serves members drawn from the Medical Group Management Association.

American College of Medical Quality (ACMQ) *Founded:* 1973. *Headquarters:* Potomac, MD. *Purpose:* To conduct educational seminars and workshops in quality assurance and utilization review and to compile statistics on numbers of physicians and allied health personnel working in quality assurance and utilization review. Members include physicians, affiliates, and institutions seeking to set standards of competence in the field of quality assurance and utilization review.

American College of Medical Toxicology (ACMT) *Founded:* 1968. *Headquarters:* Harrisburg, PA. *Purpose:* To evaluate and certify physicians in medical toxicology.

American College of Medicine (ACM) *See* American Society of Contemporary Medicine, Surgery, and Opthalmalogy.

American College of Mental Health Administration (ACMHA) *Founded:* 1980. *Headquarters:* Pittsburgh, PA. *Purpose:* Serves mental health clinicians and administrators.

American College of Mohs Micrographic Surgery and Cutaneous Oncology (ACMMSCO) *Founded:* 1967. *Headquarters:* Schaumburg, IL. *Purpose:* To provide accreditation of physicians who have become proficient in the method and strives to facilitate education and the exchange of ideas. It is composed of physicians, including dermatologists, surgeons, plastic surgeons, and other specialists, who have had a minimum of one year of training in chemosurgery at an approved institution.

American College of Neuropsychiatrists (ACN)
Founded: 1937. *Headquarters:* Farmington Hills, MI. *Purpose:* To promote study and research in neurology and psychiatry in the osteopathic profession. It serves psychiatrists and neurologists.

American College of Neuropsychopharmacology (ACNP) *Founded:* 1961. *Headquarters:* Nashville, TN. *Purpose:* To promote the scientific study and application of neuropsychopharmacology and conduct study groups and plenary sessions. It serves investigators whose work is related to neuropsychopharmacology.

American College of Nuclear Medicine (ACNM)
Founded: 1972. *Headquarters:* Landisville, PA. *Purpose:* To advance the science of nuclear medicine, study the socioeconomic aspects of the practice of nuclear medicine, and encourage improved and continuing education for practitioners in the field. It serves physicians and medical scientists in nuclear medicine.

American College of Nuclear Physicians (ACNP)
Founded: 1974. *Headquarters:* Washington, DC. *Purpose:* To foster high standards of nuclear medicine service and to promote the continuing competence of practitioners of nuclear medicine. Problem-solving areas include unnecessary and costly regulations and restrictions; public fear, lack of understanding, and misinformation; complex state and federal legislation; transportation difficulties involving nuclear medicine supplies; and previous lack of cohesive efforts in addressing such problems. It serves nuclear medicine physicians, scientists, and corporations interested in nuclear medicine.

American College of Nurse-Midwives (ACNM)
Founded: 1955. *Headquarters:* Washington, DC. *Purpose:* To study and evaluate activities of nurse-midwives in order to establish qualifications; compiles statistics. It is composed of registered nurses certified to extend their practice into providing gynecological services and care of mothers and babies throughout the maternity cycle. Members have completed an ACNM-accredited program of study and clinical experience in midwifery and passed a national certification examination.

American College of Nutrition (ACN) *Founded:* 1959. *Headquarters:* New York, NY. *Purpose:* To provide education on clinical and experimental developments in the field of nutrition and to provide continuing education of physicians and other scientists on nutritional subjects. It serves physicians, research scientists, nutritionists, dietitians, allied health personnel, and post-baccalaureate students and trainees in these fields.

American College of Obstetricians and Gynecologists (ACOG) *Founded:* 1951. *Headquarters:* Washington, DC. *Purpose:* To serve as a strong advocate for quality health care for women; to maintain the highest standards of clinical practice and continuing education of its members; to promote patient education and stimulate patient understanding of, and involvement in, medical care; and to increase awareness among its members and the public of the changing issues facing women's health care. ACOG services and products include guidelines and recommendations published in ACOG Technical Bulletins, ACOG Committee Opinions, and ACOG's Patient Education Pamphlets. ACOG serves physicians specializing in childbirth and the diseases of women.

American College of Occupational and Environmental Medicine (ACOEM) *Founded:* 1988. *Headquarters:* Arlington Heights, IL. *Purpose:* To promote and protect the health of workers through preventive services, clinical care, research, and educational programs. The ACOEM provides courses and conferences; publishes newsletters, a journal, guidelines, and position statements; has developed a Code of Ethical Conduct; and offers its members the Occupational Medicine Self-Assessment Program (OMSAP III).

American College of Oral and Maxillofacial Surgeons (ACOMS) *Founded:* 1975. *Headquarters:* San Antonio, TX. *Purpose:* To enhance the level of patient care through the furthering of research and education in OMS surgery and to preserve and promote the integrity of the specialty and its advancement. The ACOMS sponsors educational programs, research activities, and fellowships as a service both to members and to the profession at large. As a multidisciplinary group, it stresses seeking input from other disciplines.

American College of Osteopathic Emergency Physicians (ACOEP) *Founded:* 1975. *Headquarters:* Chicago, IL. *Purpose:* To provide and evaluate postdoctoral and continuing education for osteopathic emergency physicians; encourage and implement the training of emergency physicians; and promote the coordination of community emergency care facilities and personnel. It maintains the American Osteopathic Board of Emergency Medicine; sponsors the Emergency Medicine Continuing Medical Education Program for Accreditation; and serves as the evaluating body for Osteopathic Emergency Medicine Residency Programs.

American College of Osteopathic Family Physicians (ACOFP) *Founded:* 1950. *Headquarters:* Arlington Heights, IL. *Purpose:* To award the degree of fellow for outstanding contributions in education to the college and to advance the standards of general practice through increasing educational opportunities and establishing a department of general practice in hospitals. It serves osteopathic physicians in general practice.

American College of Osteopathic Internists (ACOI) *Founded:* 1943. *Headquarters:* Washington, DC. *Purpose:* To provide educational programs and improve educational standards. It serves osteopathic physicians who limit their practice to internal medicine and various subspecialties and who intend, through postdoctoral education, to qualify as certified specialists in the field and osteopathic emergency physicians.

American College of Osteopathic Obstetricians and Gynecologists (ACOOG) *Founded:* 1934. *Headquarters:* Pontiac, MI. *Purpose:* To conduct educational programs and review osteopathic obstetric and gynecologic residency training programs. It serves osteopathic physicians and surgeons specializing in obstetrics and gynecology.

American College of Osteopathic Pediatricians (ACOP) *Founded:* 1940. *Headquarters:* Washington, DC. *Purpose:* To serve osteopathic physicians who have received or are receiving advanced training in pediatrics and who are specializing in pediatric practice.

American College of Osteopathic Surgeons (ACOS) *Founded:* 1927. *Headquarters:* Alexandria, VA. *Purpose:* To maintain placement service and conduct postgraduate courses. It serves osteopathic physicians specializing in surgery and surgical specialties, including general surgery, neurological surgery, orthopedic surgery, plastic surgery, thoracic-cardiovascular surgery, and urological surgery.

American College of Physician Executives (ACPE) *Founded:* 1974. *Headquarters:* Tampa, FL. *Purpose:* Among other activities, certifies physician executives as diplomates. It serves physicians whose primary professional responsibility is the management of health care organizations.

American College of Physicians (ACP) *Founded:* 1915. *Headquarters:* Philadelphia, PA. *Purpose:* To enhance the quality and effectiveness of health care by fostering excellence and professionalism in the practice of medicine through education, continuing education and self-assessment programs, publications, research and development of policy statements and legislative advocacy, and development of clinical practice guidelines. ACP programs include the Clinical Efficacy Assessment Project (CEAP) and the Medical Knowledge Self-Assessment Program (MPSAP). Members include physicians specializing in internal medicine and related subspecialties and medical students. In August 1996 the ACP issued a joint announcement with the American Society of Internal Medicine (ASIM) that the two internal medicine organizations were completing negotiations to merge and that the new organization, tentatively named the American College of Physicians-American Society of Internal Medicine (ACP-ASIM), would be established in the latter half of 1998. The ACP is a member organization of the Joint Commission.

American College of Preventive Medicine (ACPM) *Founded:* 1954. *Headquarters:* Washington, DC. *Purpose:* Sponsors special education programs. It serves physicians specializing in preventive medicine, public health, occupational medicine, or aerospace medicine.

American College of Prosthodontists (ACP) *Founded:* 1970. *Headquarters:* Chicago, IL. *Purpose:* To encourage educational activities. It serves dentists specializing in prosthetics who are either board certified, board prepared, or under training in an approved graduate or residency program.

American College of Psychiatrists (ACP) *Founded:* 1963. *Headquarters:* Greenbelt, MD. *Purpose:* An honor society of individuals who have made a significant contribution to psychiatry.

American College of Psychoanalysts (ACPA) *Founded:* 1969. *Headquarters:* Benicia, CA. *Purpose:* Contribute to the development of psychoanalysis. It serves physician psychoanalysts.

American College of Radiology (ACR) *Founded:* 1923. *Headquarters:* Reston, VA. *Purpose:* To advance the science of radiology, improve service to the patient, study the socioeconomic aspects of the practice of radiology, and encourage continuing education for radiologists, radiation oncologists, medical physicists, and persons practicing in allied professional fields. The ACR periodically defines new standards for radiologic practice to help advance the science of radiology and to improve the quality of service to patients throughout the United States, and it reviews existing standards for revision or renewal as appropriate on their fourth anniversary or sooner, if needed. Members are primarily radiologists, radiation oncologists, and clinical medical physicists in the United States.

American College of Rheumatology (ACR) *Founded:* 1934. *Headquarters:* Atlanta, GA. *Purpose:* To foster excellence in the care of people with arthritis and rheumatic and musculoskeletal diseases through programs of education, research, and advocacy. The Association of Rheumatology Health Professionals (ARHP), a professional membership society established as a division within the ACR in 1965, serves individuals from a variety of disciplines sharing an interest in rheumatology-related issues of practice, education, and research and works to establish and disseminate scientific knowledge relevant to issues of access, quality, and provision of appropriate arthritis care.

American College of Sports Medicine (ACSM) *Founded:* 1954. *Headquarters:* Indianapolis, IN. *Purpose:* To promote and integrate scientific research, education, and practical applications of sports medicine and exercise science, to maintain and enhance physical performance, fitness, health, and quality of life. A large part of ACSM's mission is devoted to public awareness and education of the positive aspects of exercise for people of all ages, from all walks of life. ACSM maintains a governmental affairs program that functions both independently and within coalitions to complement the research and education mission of ACSM in advancing sports medicine, exercise science, physical activity, and health, worldwide. ACSM is a leader in numerous coalitions, focusing on issues such as health care, biomedical research funding, health promotion, and disease prevention and working with government and private organizations. The ACSM is a leading participant in the National Coalition for Promoting Physical Activity. The ACSM also publishes a scholarly journal.

American College of Surgeons (ACS) *Founded:* 1913. *Headquarters:* Chicago, IL. *Purpose:* To improve the quality of care for the surgical patient by setting high standards for surgical education and practice. Major activities include continuing medical education programs including the Surgical Education and Self-Assessment Program (SESAP), nationwide programs to improve emergency medical services and hospital cancer programs; monitoring of socioeconomic, legislative, and regulatory issues affecting the field of surgery; sponsorship of residency reviews and postdoctoral education; publications; and public education. Twelve advisory councils, representing surgical subspecialties, advise the board and serve as liaisons with Fellows of the ACS. The ACS's Commission on Cancer serves as the executive office of the American Joint Committee on Cancer (AJCC), of which the ACS is administrative sponsor. The ACS is a member organization of the Joint Commission.

American College of Toxicology (ACT) *Founded:* 1977. *Headquarters:* Bethesda, MD. *Purpose:* To address toxicological issues and to disseminate information. It serves individuals interested in toxicology and related disciplines, such as analytical chemistry, biology, pathology, teratology, and immunology.

American Congress of Rehabilitation Medicine (ACRM) *Founded:* 1921. *Headquarters:* Glenview, IL. *Purpose:* To advance the field of rehabilitation medicine. It serves physicians and allied health specialists active in rehabilitation medicine.

American Correctional Health Services Association (ACHSA) *Founded:* 1975. *Headquarters:* Dayton, OH. *Purpose:* To improve the quality of correctional health services; aims to provide acceptable health services to incarcerated persons; conducts conferences on correctional health care management, nursing, mental health, juvenile corrections, and dentistry. Members are health care providers.

American Council on Alcoholism (ACA) *Founded:* 1953. *Headquarters:* Baltimore, MD. *Purpose:* To work to end alcohol abuse and alcoholism. Members include local, state, regional, and national groups and individuals.

American Council on Alcohol Problems (ACAP) *Founded:* 1895. *Headquarters:* Bridgeton, MO. *Purpose:* To seek long-range solutions to the problems posed by alcohol. Membership includes state affiliates, denominational judicatories, and associate members.

American Council of Applied Clinical Nutrition (ACACN) *Founded:* 1974. *Headquarters:* Florissant, MO. *Purpose:* To offer structured academic courses and certification. Members include clinical nutrition specialists.

American Council for Drug Education (ACDE) *Founded:* 1977. *Headquarters:* New York, NY. *Purpose:* To disseminate information and research on marijuana, cocaine, and other psychoactive drugs. It serves doctors, mental health counselors, teachers, clergy, school librarians, parent groups, industry leaders, and individuals.

American Council of Hypnotist Examiners (ACHE) *Founded:* 1980. *Headquarters:* Glendale, CA. *Purpose:* To educate, examine, and award certification in the field of hypnotherapy. It serves individuals certified in the field of hypnotherapy.

American Council on Pharmaceutical Education (ACPE) *Founded:* 1932. *Headquarters:* Chicago, IL. *Purpose:* To accredit professional programs of colleges and schools of pharmacy and approval of providers of continuing pharmaceutical education.

American Council on Science and Health (ACSH) *Founded:* 1978. *Headquarters:* New York, NY. *Purpose:* To provide a scientifically based and balanced consumer education consortium concerned with issues related to food, nutrition, chemicals, pharmaceuticals, lifestyle, the environment, and health. Council representatives participate in government regulatory proceedings, congressional hearings, radio and television programs, and public debates and other forums and write for professional and scientific journals, popular magazines, and newspaper columns. Recent strong positions taken by ASCH on public health policy are its warnings about cigarette smoking, alcohol abuse, neglect of preventive care, and promiscuous sexual behavior.

American Dance Therapy Association (ADTA) *Founded:* 1966. *Headquarters:* Columbia, MO. *Purpose:* To establish and maintain high standards of professional education and competence in dance therapy. Members include individuals professionally practicing dance therapy, students interested in becoming dance therapists, university departments with dance therapy programs, and individuals in related therapeutic fields.

American Deafness and Rehabilitation Association (ADARA) *Founded:* 1966. *Headquarters:* Little Rock, AR. *Purpose:* To promote definition and expansion of quality services to the deaf. It serves psychiatrists, mental health counselors, teachers, students, researchers, rehabilitation facility personnel, interpreters, speech therapists, social workers, physicians, and other individuals who serve persons with hearing and/or visual impairments.

American Dental Assistants Association (ADAA) *Founded:* 1923. *Headquarters:* Chicago, IL. *Purpose:* Sponsors workshops and seminars for individuals employed as dental assistants in dental offices, clinics, hospitals, or institutions; instructors of dental assistants; and dental students.

American Dental Association (ADA) *Founded:* 1859. *Headquarters:* Chicago, IL. *Purpose:* To promote the public's health through commitment of member dentists to provide quality oral health care accessible to everyone and to promote the profession of dentistry by enhancing the integrity and ethics of the profession, strengthening the patient-dentist relationship, and making membership the foundation of successful practice. The ADA fulfills its public and professional mission by providing services and through its initiatives in education, research, advocacy, and the development of standards. ADA programs and products include the Survey Center (SC), which monitors trends; the ADA Seal of Acceptance, which indicates a dental product's safety and effectiveness; and a direct reimbursement dental benefits plan kit. The ADA is a member organization of the Joint Commission.

American Dental Hygienists' Association (ADHA)
Founded: 1923. *Headquarters:* Chicago, IL. *Purpose:* To maintain an accrediting service through the American Dental Association's Commission on Dental Accreditation. It serves licensed dental hygienists possessing a degree or certificate in dental hygiene granted by an accredited school of dental hygiene.

American Dental Society of Anesthesiology (ADSA)
Founded: 1953. *Headquarters:* Chicago, IL. *Purpose:* To encourage study and progress in dental anesthesiology. It serves dentists and physicians.

American Dental Trade Association (ADTA)
Founded: 1882. *Headquarters:* Alexandria, VA. *Purpose:* To conduct sales and training programs. It serves dental laboratories and manufacturers and distributors of dental instruments, supplies, and equipment.

American Dermatological Association (ADA)
Founded: 1876. *Headquarters:* Augusta, GA. *Purpose:* To promote teaching, practice, and research in dermatology. It serves physicians specializing in dermatology.

American Diabetes Association (ADA) *Founded:* 1940. *Headquarters:* Alexandria, VA. *Purpose:* To promote the free exchange of information about diabetes mellitus by educating the public in the early recognition of the disease, the importance of medical supervision in its treatment, and the development of educational methods designed for people with diabetes. Members include health professionals and laypersons interested in diabetes mellitus. New initiatives include the Diabetes Quality Improvement Project (in coalition with the Foundation for Accountability, HCFA, and the National Committee for Quality Assurance).

American Dietetic Association (ADA) *Founded:* 1917. *Headquarters:* Chicago, IL. *Purpose:* To set and approve standards of education and practice. It serves dietetic professionals and registered dietitians in hospitals, colleges, universities, school food services, day care centers, research, business, and industry, and dietetic technicians who meet ADA requirements.

American Electroencephalographic Society (AEEGS) *Founded:* 1946. *Headquarters:* Bloomfield, CT. *Purpose:* A professional society for electroencephalographers and neurophysiologists.

American Endodontic Society (AES) *Founded:* 1969. *Headquarters:* Fullerton, CA. *Purpose:* To promote and provide educational and scientific information on simplified root canal therapy for the generalist dentist. It serves dentists.

American Epilepsy Society (AES) *Founded:* 1946. *Headquarters:* Hartford, CT. *Purpose:* To foster treatment of epilepsy in its biological, clinical, and social phases and promote better care and treatment of persons subject to convulsions (seizures). It serves physicians and researchers engaged in practice and research in epilepsy or closely related fields, such as electroencephalography.

American Equilibration Society (AES) *Founded:* 1955. *Headquarters:* Morton Grove, IL. *Purpose:* Increase study and proficiency in the diagnosis and treatment of occlusive and temporomandibular joint disorders. It serves 1,500 dentists, orthodontists, oral surgeons, and physicians.

American Federation for Aging Research (AFAR)
Founded: 1979. *Headquarters:* New York, NY. *Purpose:* To stimulate and fund research on aging. It serves physicians, scientists, and other individuals involved or interested in research in aging and associated diseases.

American Federation of Home Health Agencies (AFHHA) *Founded:* 1980. *Headquarters:* Silver Spring, MD. *Purpose:* To promote home health by influencing public policy. Members include agencies providing therapeutic services, such as nursing, speech therapy, and physical therapy, in the home.

American Federation of Medical Accreditation (AFMA) *Founded:* 1979. *Headquarters:* Las Vegas, NV. *Purpose:* To accredit medical and scientific organizations and continuing medical education for member organizations. It serves scientific organizations and medical associations that have primary certifying boards.

American Fertility Society *See* American Society for Reproductive Medicine.

American Fitness Association (AFA) *Founded:* 1981. *Headquarters:* Durango, CO. *Purpose:* To conduct research and educational activities in the field of aerobic exercise; disseminate information on research findings, such as the effects of stress on muscles, joints, and tendons; and to monitor the aerobics industry. Tests exercise products, such as shoes, mats, and weights; and conducts surveys on injury rates. This organization is unrelated to another group of the same name (see next entry).

American Fitness Association (AFA) *Founded:* 1986. *Headquarters:* Long Beach, CA. *Purpose:* To promote involvement and education in health and fitness and to influence legislative action and sponsor seminars, sports clinics, and competitions. It serves physicians, psychologists, exercise physiologists, and other health and fitness professionals. This organization is unrelated to another group of the same name (see previous entry).

American Fracture Association (AFA) *Founded:* 1938. *Headquarters:* Bloomington, IL. *Purpose:* To further and create interest in the study of the various accepted types of bone fracture therapy. It serves orthopedic, general, industrial, plastic, traumatic, and dental surgeons and physicians interested in the care and treatment of fractures.

American Gastroenterological Association (AGA)
Founded: 1897. *Headquarters:* Bethesda, MD. *Purpose:* To serve as an advocate for its members and their patients,

support members' practices and scientific needs, and facilitate the discovery, dissemination, and application of new knowledge leading to the prevention, treatment, and cure of digestive diseases. Membership is limited to physicians, researchers, and educators whose primary practice, research, or teaching involves the functions and disorders of the digestive system. The AGA issues policy and position statements on clinical practice. The AGA is a member of the Federated Societies of Gastroenterology and Hepatology (FSGH), established jointly in 1995 with the American Association for the Study of Liver Diseases (AASLD) and the American Society for Gastrointestinal Endoscopy (ASGE). The AGA and the ASGE jointly established the American Digestive Health Foundation (ADHF), which is currently conducting the Digestive Health Initiative (DHI), consisting of national education campaigns on ulcers, colorectal cancer, and viral hepatitis.

American Geriatrics Society (AGS) *Founded:* 1942. *Headquarters:* New York, NY. *Purpose:* To ensure the provision of quality health care to older persons by developing, implementing, and supporting programs in patient care, research, professional education, public policy, and public education. To accomplish its mission, the AGS works to promote and encourage the clinical practice of geriatrics and support practitioners providing such care; increase the number of health care professionals knowledgeable about geriatrics and committed to the clinical care of older people; promote effective, high-quality research; expand knowledge of the aging process; conduct education programs for health care professionals to promote better understanding of the aging process and its unique clinical challenges; provide public education and information that addresses the health care concerns and needs of older people, their families and other caregivers; engage in public policy efforts focused on the improvement and study of health care for older people; and develop and maintain productive and collaborative relationships with other organizations concerned with the health care of older persons. With foundation and corporate support, the AGS sponsors a Congress of Clinical Societies focusing on transdisciplinary issues in medical ethics that cut across the life span.

American Group Practice Association *See* American Medical Group Association.

American Group Psychotherapy Association (AGPA) *Founded:* 1942. *Headquarters:* New York, NY. *Purpose:* To provide a forum for the exchange of ideas among approximately 3,500 psychiatrists, psychologists, psychiatric nurses, social workers, and other mental health professionals in group psychotherapy practice meeting membership requirements.

American Gynecological and Obstetrical Society (AGOS) *Founded:* 1981. *Headquarters:* Charlottesville, VA. *Purpose:* To cultivate and promote knowledge of obstetrics and gynecology.

American Health Care Association (AHCA) *Founded:* 1949. *Headquarters:* Washington, DC. *Purpose:*

To promote standards for professionals in long-term health care delivery and to promote quality care for patients and residents in a safe environment. It focuses on issues of availability, quality, affordability, and fair payment and maintains liaisons with governmental agencies, Congress, and professional associations. It serves long term care facilities.

American Healthcare Radiology Administrators (AHRA) *Founded:* 1973. *Headquarters:* Sudbury, MA. *Purpose:* To improve management of radiology departments in hospitals and other health care organizations and to provide liaisons between related organizations, such as radiology, health care, and management groups, and government agencies. It serves radiology managers.

American Health Decisions (AHD) *Founded:* 1989. *Headquarters:* Denver, CO. *Purpose:* To assist in establishing public education programs about health care and policy and to promote personal autonomy on ethical issues, such as a patient's decision to refuse or accept treatment.

American Health Information Management Association (AHIMA) *Founded:* 1928. *Headquarters:* Chicago, IL. *Purpose:* To conduct annual qualification examinations to certify medical record personnel as registered record administrators (RRA) and accredited record technicians (ART). It serves registered record administrators and accredited record technicians with expertise in health information management, biostatistics, classification systems, and systems analysis. *Formerly:* American Medical Records Association (1991).

American Health Planning Association (AHPA) *Founded:* 1970. *Headquarters:* Falls Church, VA. *Purpose:* To conduct research, disseminate information, and perform clearinghouse functions and activities in health planning tasks and concepts. It serves state and local development agencies, health planning agencies, university health science centers, insurance and industry organizations, and affiliated organizations and individuals.

American Hearing Research Foundation *Founded:* 1956. *Headquarters:* Chicago, IL. *Purpose:* To encourage and support medical research, education, and public information concerning deafness and other hearing disorders.

American Heart Association (AHA) *Founded:* 1924. *Headquarters:* Dallas, TX. *Purpose:* To reduce premature death and disability from cardiovascular diseases and stroke through support of research, education, and community service programs serving physicians, scientists, and laypersons. The AHA, also sometimes called the Heart Fund, is a community-based organization with state and metropolitan affiliates. It is financed entirely by voluntary contributions from the public, principally during the Heart Campaign held each year in February. Professional and scientific activities include development of clinical practice guidelines and provision of training systems to teach emergency care procedures.

American Holistic Medical Association (AHMA) *Founded:* 1978. *Headquarters:* Raleigh, NC. *Purpose:* To provide medical education. It serves medical doctors, osteopathic physicians, and students who are interested in furthering the practice of holistic health care.

American Holistic Nurses Association (AHNA)
Founded: 1981. *Headquarters:* Raleigh, NC. *Purpose:* To promote education of nurses and the public on holistic care. It serves registered, licensed practical, vocational, and student nurses promoting education for nurses and the public on the concept of holistic health care.

American Horticultural Therapy Association (AHTA)
Founded: 1973. *Headquarters:* Gaithersburg, MD. *Purpose:* To foster the development of horticulture and related activities as a therapeutic and rehabilitative medium. Horticultural therapy is considered particularly useful in the fields of geriatrics and developmental disabilities. It serves professional horticultural therapists, rehabilitation specialists, institutions, and interested commercial organizations.

American Hospital Association (AHA) *Founded:* 1898. *Headquarters:* Chicago, IL. *Purpose:* To advance the health of individuals and communities through leading, representing, and serving health care provider organizations that are accountable to the community and committed to health improvement. The AHA sponsors research and education projects in health care administration, hospital economics, and community relations; represents hospitals in national legislation; offers programs for institutional effectiveness review, technology assessment, and hospital administrative services; collects and analyzes data; and maintains a health care administration library and biographical archive. Some of these activities are carried out through its professional organization Health Technology Assessment, its affiliate the Hospital Research and Education Trust (HRET), and its subsidiary American Publishing, Inc. A new joint initiative with the state associations is the "Campaign for Coverage . . . A Community Health Challenge," which aims to expand health care coverage to 4 million more by the end of 1998. The AHA is a member organization of the Joint Commission.

American Indian Health Care Association (AIHCA)
Founded: 1975. *Headquarters:* Denver, CO. *Purpose:* To provide training, technical assistance, health care delivery management, research, and evaluation for Indian health programs and organizations. It serves Native American Indian health programs.

American Industrial Health Council (AIHC)
Founded: 1977. *Headquarters:* Washington, DC. *Purpose:* To advocate and promote the implementation of scientific methods to identify potential industrial carcinogens (cancer-inducing substances) and other health hazards, such as mutagens (agents that induce mutation) and teratogens (agents that cause developmental malformations); seeks to develop a basis for the review, risk assessment, and regulation of substances that may pose significant chronic health risks. Members include industrial and commercial firms and trade associations.

American Industrial Hygiene Association (AIHA)
Founded: 1939. *Headquarters:* Fairfax, VA. *Purpose:* To promote the study and control of environmental factors affecting the health of workers; accredits laboratories and maintains 35 technical committees. It serves industrial hygienists.

American Institute of the History of Pharmacy (AIHP) *Founded:* 1941. *Headquarters:* Madison, WI. *Purpose:* To maintain pharmaceutical Americana collection and conduct research. It serves pharmacists, and organizations interested in historical and social aspects of the pharmaceutical field.

American Institute of Homeopathy (AIH) *Founded:* 1844. *Headquarters:* Denver, CO. *Purpose:* To promote research and quality homeopathic health care. It serves physicians and dentists practicing homeotherapeutics according to the three natural laws of cure proposed by Samuel Hahnemann.

American Institute of Life Threatening Illness and Loss *Founded:* 1967. *Headquarters:* New York, NY. *Purpose:* To promote improved psychosocial and medical care for critically ill and dying patients, and assistance for their families; stimulates and coordinates professional, educational, and research programs concerned with mortality and the management of grief. Members include health, theology, psychology, and social science professionals devoted to scientific and humanistic inquiries into death, loss, grief, and bereavement. It is a division of Foundation of Thanatology.

American Institute of Nutrition (AIN) *Founded:* 1928. *Headquarters:* Bethesda, MD. *Purpose:* Serves nutrition research scientists from universities, government, and industry. American Society for Clinical Nutrition is a division.

American Institute of Oral Biology (AIOB) *Founded:* 1943. *Headquarters:* Loma Linda, CA. *Purpose:* To promote and provide continuing education in the field of oral biology. It serves dental, and medical health professionals.

American Institute of Stress (AIS) *Founded:* 1979. *Headquarters:* Yonkers, NY. *Purpose:* To compile research data on topics such as relationships between emotional factors and cardiovascular disease; stress and the immune system with specific emphasis on cancer; and stress reduction programs for industry. Seeks a definition of health that recognizes the need for harmony between the individual and the physical and social environments as well as the effects of positive emotions, such as creativity, faith, and humor on health. Members include physicians, health professionals, scholars, and other individuals from varied disciplines interested in the personal and social consequences of stress.

American Institute of Ultrasound in Medicine (AIUM) *Founded:* 1951. *Headquarters:* Laurel, MD. *Purpose:* To promote the application of ultrasound in clinical medicine and in research; studies its effects on tissue; and recommends standards for its use. It serves physicians, engineers, scientists, sonographers, and other professionals using diagnostic medical ultrasound.

American In-Vitro Allergy/Immunology Society
Founded: 1988. *Headquarters:* Englewood, NJ. *Purpose:* To promote the appropriate use of in-vitro procedures in allergy and immunology and to offer services in third-party payer negotiation and in-vitro testing standardization. It serves physicians, scientists, and other professionals who study or use in-vitro technology in the diagnosis and treatment of allergic and immunologic disorders.

American Joint Committee on Cancer (AJCC)
Founded: 1959. *Headquarters:* Chicago, IL (Commission on Cancer, American College of Surgeons). *Purpose:* To uphold the ideal that all cases of patients with cancer should be staged. The AJCC formulates and publishes systems of classification and staging of cancer and reports of end results for the purpose of selecting the most effective treatment, determining prognosis, and continuing evaluation of cancer control measures. The AJCC supports the TNM (Tumor-Node-Metastasis) System for various cancer sites until technical innovations or new data necessitate changes. The *AJCC Cancer Staging Manual, 5th edition*, is scheduled to start use with 1998 cancer cases. Founding organizations of the AJCC are the American College of Surgeons (the AJCC's administrative sponsor), the American Cancer Society, the American College of Physicians, the American College of Radiology, the College of American Pathologists, and NIH's National Cancer Institute (NCI), and other organizations maintain liaison with the AJCC. Members include surgeons, physicians, radiologists, and pathologists.

American Kinesiotherapy Association (AKA)
Founded: 1946. *Headquarters:* Wheeling, IL. *Purpose:* To provide continuing education and a forum for exchange of ideas for kinesiotherapists, exercise therapists, and other individuals interested in physical and mental rehabilitation.

American Laryngological Association (ALA)
Founded: 1879. *Headquarters:* Boston, MA. *Purpose:* To advance research in medicine and surgery with emphasis on the upper aerodigestive tract.

American Laryngological, Rhinological and Otological Society (ALROS) *Founded:* 1895. *Headquarters:* St. Louis, MO. *Purpose:* To provide a professional society for medical specialists dealing with the ear, nose, and throat. *Also known as:* Triological Society.

American Leprosy Missions (ALMI) *Founded:* 1906. *Headquarters:* Greensville, SC. *Purpose:* To provide medical, rehabilitative, and social care for individuals with leprosy in 30 countries. Activities include conducting specialized training for medical workers and providing personnel and resources to conduct training programs at National Hansen's Disease Center in Carville, Louisiana.

American Licensed Practical Nurses Association (ALPNA) *Founded:* 1984. *Headquarters:* Washington, DC. *Purpose:* Lobbies and maintains relations with the government on issues and legislation that may have an

impact on licensed practical nurses and conducts continuing education classes. Serves licensed practical nurses.

American Lung Association (ALA) *Founded:* 1904. *Headquarters:* New York, NY. *Purpose:* To prevent lung disease and promote lung health. The ALA works with other organizations in planning and conducting programs in community services; public, professional and patient education; and research. Its work is supported through the annual Christmas Seal Campaign and other fundraising activities. The ALA maintains the American Thoracic Society as its medical section. Members include physicians, nurses, and laypersons interested in the prevention and control of lung disease.

American Managed Behavioral Healthcare Association (AMBHA) *Founded:* 1994. *Headquarters:* Washington, DC. *Purpose:* To serve its membership of national behavioral health managed care firms and to develop a standardized "report card" of the overall performance of managed behavioral health care delivery systems. AMBHA's first set of measures is known as PERMS.1.0 (Performance Measures for Managed Behavioral Healthcare Programs).

American Managed Care and Review Association (AMCRA) *See* American Association of Health Plans.

American Managed Care Pharmacy Association (AMCPA) *Founded:* 1975. *Headquarters:* Arlington, VA. *Purpose:* To promote managed care prescription services as suppliers of medicine to home-delivery pharmacy services and seeks to assist health plan officers and consumers in obtaining maximum value from prescription services. Members are preferred provider organizations that specialize in maintenance drug therapy in managed care environments and make available home-delivery pharmacy services.

American Massage Therapy Association (AMTA)
Founded: 1943. *Headquarters:* Evanston, IL. *Purpose:* To provide referrals to area therapists and certified schools; to accredit massage training programs; and to offer a national certification program for massage therapists. It serves massage therapists or technicians.

American Medical Association (AMA) *Founded:* 1847. *Headquarters:* Chicago, IL. *Purpose:* To serve as the voice of the American medical profession; to offer the partnership of physicians and their professional associations dedicated to promoting the art and science of medicine and the betterment of public health; and to serve the physicians and their patients by establishing and promoting ethical, educational, and clinical standards for the medical profession and by advocating for the highest principle of all—the integrity of the physician-patient relationship. The AMA is governed by a board of trustees and a house of delegates representing various state and local medical associations and government agencies. Members include physicians, county medical societies, and medical students. The AMA's political action committee is the American Medical Political Action Committee (AMPAC; Washington, DC). Ongoing AMA publications include several peer-reviewed journals, the *Code of Medical Ethics: Current Opinions with Annotations* (Council on Ethical and Judicial Affairs), and the *Physicians' Current Procedural Terminology—CPT 1998*. The AMA has established several new components and programs. A new academically independent research and educational component, the Institute for Ethics, has four sections focusing on end of life care and a curriculum (Robert Wood Johnson Foundation grant), managed care and ethics, professionalism and ethics, and genetics and ethics. Another new component is the American Medical Accreditation Program (AMAP), a voluntary comprehensive accreditation program that measures and evaluates individual physicians against national standards. The National Patient Safety Foundation (NPSF), with grants from several corporate founding sponsors announced in 1997, will fund research into ways to reduce avoidable error. The AMA is a leading participant in a broad-based multicomponent collaboration to combat smoking, including the ENACT (Effective National Action to Control Tobacco) coalition, the AMA Coalition for Tobacco-Free Investments, and a new AMA superhero in "The Extinguisher" antismoking cartoon series. The AMA is a member organization of the Joint Commission.

American Medical Directors Association (AMDA)

Founded: 1975. *Headquarters:* Columbia, MD. *Purpose:* To work for the continuous improvement of the quality of patient care by providing education, advocacy, information, and professional development for medical directors and other physicians who serve as attending physicians in the long-term care continuum. In 1996 AMDA initiated a project to develop and publish adaptations of national clinical practice guidelines for the long-term care setting.

American Medical Electroencephalographic Association (AMEEGA)

Founded: 1964. *Headquarters:* Elm Grove, WI. *Purpose:* To promote advances in clinical electroencephalography and to provide training programs for its members.

American Medical Group Association

Founded: 1996. *Headquarters:* Alexandria, VA (West Coast office: Seal Beach, CA). *Purpose:* To promote the concept of group practice and assist physician-led groups in developing and maintaining successful group practices and high standards of health care through extensive educational, informational, and support services. Its primary service areas are reimbursement practices, legislative advocacy at the national and selected state levels, and advancement of quality patient care. A major program is the Outcomes Management Consortia (OMC). Membership is open to qualified group practices and independent practice associations and also includes a Corporate Partners section for companies with an interest in health care quality and group practice medicine. *Formed by merger of:* American Group Practice Association and Unified Medical Group Association.

American Medical Informatics Association (AMIA)

Founded: 1981. *Headquarters:* Bethesda, MD. *Purpose:* To foster the application of advanced systems and information technologies to scientific, literary, and educational activities. It serves medical personnel, physicians, physical scientists, engineers, data processors, researchers, educators, hospital administrators, nurses, medical record administrators, and computer professionals.

American Medical Peer Review Association (AMPRA)

Founded: 1973. *Headquarters:* Washington, DC. *Purpose:* To develop communications programs for physicians, institutions, and other individuals interested in peer review organizations (PROs). Conducts on-site assistance programs to increase physicians' involvement and leadership in peer review organizations, improve practice patterns through review, and understand and use PRO data to improve service delivery. Members include institutions and individuals.

American Medical Political Action Committee (AMPAC)

See American Medical Association.

American Medical Publishers' Association (AMPA)

Founded: 1961. *Headquarters:* Washington, DC. *Purpose:* To provide an exchange of information among members; improve the creation, distribution, and sale of medical books and journals; and facilitate communication with medical organizations, schools, and the medical community. Members are U.S. medical publishing companies.

American Medical Records Association

See American Health Information Management Association.

American Medical Review Research Center (AMRRC)

See Center for Clinical Quality Evaluation.

American Medical Students Association

Founded: 1950. *Headquarters:* Reston, VA. *Purpose:* To improve medical education by making it relevant to today's needs and by making the process by which physicians are trained more humanistic. Serves medical students; local, state, and national organizations and pre-med students, interns and residents.

American Medical Technologists (AMT)

Founded: 1939. *Headquarters:* Park Ridge, IL. *Purpose:* Professional registry for medical laboratory technologists, technicians, medical assistants, and dental assistants.

American Medical Women's Association (AMWA)

Founded: 1915. *Headquarters:* Alexandria, VA. *Purpose:* To find solutions to problems common to women studying or practicing medicine, such as career advancement and the integration of professional and family responsibilities. It serves women holding a Doctor of Medicine (MD) or a Doctor of Osteopathy (DO) degree from approved medical colleges, and women interns, residents, and medical students.

American Mental Health Counselors Association (AMHCA)

Founded: 1976. *Headquarters:* Alexandria, VA. *Purpose:* To aim for members to deliver quality mental health services to all age groups and to establish certification and licensure procedures. It serves professional counselors employed in mental health services.

American Naprapathic Association (ANA) *Founded:* 1909. *Headquarters:* Chicago, IL. *Purpose:* To promote and publish the principles of natural healing and seek to further legislation and recognition of the naprapathic system of treatment. Members include naprapathic physicians.

American National Standards Institute (ANSI) *Founded:* 1918. *Headquarters:* New York, NY. *Purpose:* To provide a clearinghouse for nationally coordinated voluntary standards for fields ranging from information technology to building construction; to give status as American National Standards to standards developed by agreement from all groups interested in various areas; and to provide information on foreign standards and represent U.S. interests in international standardization work. It serves industrial firms, trade associations, technical societies, labor organizations, consumer organizations, and government agencies.

American Natural Hygiene Society (ANHS) *Founded:* 1948. *Headquarters:* Tampa, FL. *Purpose:* To promote health maintenance through natural means, such as natural foods, fresh air, pure water, sunshine, fasting, exercise, and rest. It emphasizes a life-style that encourages people to maximize their health by living in harmony with their physiological needs.

American Nephrology Nurses' Association (ANNA) *Founded:* 1969. *Headquarters:* Pitman, NJ. *Purpose:* To promote continuing education among members who include registered nurses, physicians, dietitians, social workers, and technicians interested in care of patients with kidney disorders.

American Network of Community Options and Resources (ANCOR) *Founded:* 1970. *Headquarters:* Annandale, VA. *Purpose:* To enhance the quality of life for persons with disabilities, with a direct concern for all living situations and to support each individual need to enhance his/her independence and chosen life-style.

American Neurological Association (ANA) *Founded:* 1875. *Headquarters:* Minneapolis, MN. *Purpose:* To advance the goals of academic neurology; to train and educate neurologists and other physicians in the neurologic sciences; and to expand both understanding of diseases of the nervous system and the ability to treat them. The ANA disseminates knowledge through an annual meeting, a scientific journal, formulation and promotion of high standards of neurologic practice, and efforts to raise the standard of neurologic training of all physicians.

American Neurotology Society (ANS) *Founded:* 1965. *Headquarters:* Hinsdale, IL. *Purpose:* To improve diagnosis and treatment of hearing and balance disorders and to promote education and research in the field of neurotology. It serves physicians and audiologists.

American Nurses Association (ANA) *Founded:* 1896. *Headquarters:* Washington, DC. *Purpose:* To advance the nursing profession by fostering high standards of nursing practice, promoting the economic and general welfare of nurses in the workplace, projecting a positive and realistic view of nursing, and by lobbying the Congress and regulatory agencies on health care issues affecting nurses and the public. It offers a full-service professional organization representing the nation's Registered Nurses through its constituent state associations and thirteen organizational affiliate members. It sponsors the American Nurses Foundation (for research), American Academy of Nursing, Center for Ethics and Human Rights, International Nursing Center, and American Nurses Credentialing Center. It develops and publishes ANA Nursing Standards, NIDSEC (Nursing Information and Data Set Evaluation Center) Standards and Scoring Guidelines, other quality improvement and measurement materials, and a journal.

American Nursing Assistant's Association (ANAA) *Founded:* 1981. *Headquarters:* Farmington Hills, MI. *Purpose:* To upgrade nursing standards, improve the image of nursing assistants, and inform the public of their contribution to health care. The ANAA conducts studies on nursing assistants' influence and image and develops educational programs.

American Occupational Therapy Association (AOTA) *Founded:* 1917. *Headquarters:* Bethesda, MD. *Purpose:* To provide services to people whose lives have been disrupted by physical injury or illness, developmental problems, the aging process, or social or psychological difficulties. It serves registered occupational therapists and certified occupational therapy assistants.

American Occupational Therapy Certification Board (AOTCB) *Founded:* 1986. *Headquarters:* Gaithersburg, MD. *Purpose:* To operate a certification program for occupational therapists and occupational therapy assistants. It also operates disciplinary mechanisms.

American Optometric Association (AOA) *Founded:* 1898. *Headquarters:* St. Louis, MO. *Purpose:* To improve the quality, availability, and accessibility of eye and vision care; to represent the optometric profession; to help members conduct their practices; to promote high standards of patient care; and to monitor and promote legislation concerning the scope of optometric practice, alternate health care delivery systems, health care cost containment, Medicare, and other issues relevant to eye/vision care. Members include optometrists, students of optometry, and paraoptometric assistants and technicians.

American Organization of Nurse Executives (AONE) *Founded:* 1967. *Headquarters:* Chicago, IL. *Purpose:* To advance nursing practice and patient care, promote nursing leadership and excellence, and shape health care public policy. AONE member services support and enhance the management, leadership, educational, and professional development of nursing leaders, and they facilitate and support research and development efforts.

American Oriental Bodywork Therapy Association (AOBTA) *Founded:* 1984. *Headquarters:* Syosset, NY. *Purpose:* To identify qualified practitioners and serve as a legal entity representing members when dealing with the government, especially in establishing professional status.

Sets teaching standards for all styles of oriental bodywork, including acupressure, five-element shiatsu, macrobiotic shiatsu, nippon, and Zen. Members include professional oriental bodyworkers and teachers.

American Orthodontic Society (AOS) *Founded:* 1974. *Headquarters:* Dallas, TX. *Purpose:* To render orthodontic information readily available to ethical dentists and monitoring third-party services and government programs and to offer courses in orthodontic techniques. It serves general and pediatric dentists.

American Orthopaedic Association (AOA) *Founded:* 1887. *Headquarters:* Rosemont, IL. *Purpose:* To further knowledge in the diagnosis and treatment of crippling diseases. Members are bone and joint surgeons.

American Orthopaedic Foot and Ankle Society (AOFAS) *Founded:* 1969. *Headquarters:* Seattle, WA. *Purpose:* To promote research on education in and care of the foot and ankle. Sponsors continuing medical education courses. It serves members of the American Academy of Orthopaedic Surgeons.

American Orthopaedic Society for Sports Medicine (AOSSM) *Founded:* 1972. *Headquarters:* Rosemont, IL. *Purpose:* To provide orthopaedic surgeons with special training in sports-related medical and surgical techniques; to offer education and research programs that benefit athletes and persons concerned with physical fitness; to support scientific research in sports medicine; to develop methods for safer, more productive and enjoyable fitness programs; to publish educational materials for medical professionals as well as for professional and amateur athletes; and to promote education and research in the prevention, recognition, treatment, and rehabilitation of sports injuries.

American Orthopsychiatric Association (ORTHO) *Founded:* 1923. *Headquarters:* New York, NY. *Purpose:* To provide a forum for those engaged in the study and treatment of human behavior. Members include psychiatrists, psychologists, social workers, educators, psychiatric nurses, lawyers, and other individuals in related fields, including anthropology, sociology, and economics.

American Osteopathic Academy of Orthopedics (AOAO) *Founded:* 1941. *Headquarters:* Hollywood, FL. *Purpose:* To provide a professional society for osteopathic orthopedic surgeons. The AOAO is affiliated with the American Osteopathic Association.

American Osteopathic Academy of Sclerotherapy (AOAS) *Founded:* 1954. *Headquarters:* Wilmington, DE. *Purpose:* To promote studies involving the treatment of unstable joints, venous abnormalities, and tendon-bone points of hyperirritability. Members include osteopathic physicians interested in sclerotherapy, a treatment involving stimulation of the formation of fibrous connective tissues by the body, in a specific location, by the application of a sclerosing agent, typically the injection of certain medications known as sclerosants.

American Osteopathic Academy of Sports Medicine (AOASM) *Founded:* 1975. *Headquarters:* Middleton, WI. *Purpose:* To promote education and development of sports medicine. Members include members of the American Osteopathic Association and other individuals interested in standards development, education, and research in the field of sports medicine.

American Osteopathic Association (AOA) *Founded:* 1897. *Headquarters:* Chicago, IL. *Purpose:* To inspect and accredit colleges and hospitals; to conduct a specialty certification program; to sponsor a national examining board satisfactory to state licensing agencies; to maintain a mandatory program of continuing medical education for members; and to conduct other activities. It is composed of osteopathic physicians, surgeons, and graduates of approved colleges of osteopathic medicine.

American Osteopathic Board of Emergency Medicine (AOBEM) *Founded:* 1980. *Headquarters:* Chicago, IL. *Purpose:* To administer examinations and certify osteopathic physicians in the specialty of emergency medicine. Sets eligibility standards for osteopathic emergency physicians and offers annual certification examinations in emergency medicine.

American Osteopathic Board of Family Practice Physicians (AOBFP) *Founded:* 1972. *Headquarters:* Arlington Heights, IL. *Purpose:* To prepare and administer semiannual certification and recertification examinations. It serves osteopathic physicians.

American Osteopathic Board of Pediatrics (AOBP) *Founded:* 1940. *Headquarters:* Chicago, IL. *Purpose:* Prepares and administers a certification examination for osteopathic pediatricians. Standards are formulated by the American Osteopathic Association, and certification is conducted by annual examination.

American Osteopathic College of Allergy and Immunology (AOCAI) *Founded:* 1974. *Headquarters:* Scottsdale, AZ. *Purpose:* Serving osteopathic physicians interested in allergies and immunology, it works to improve education in the field.

American Osteopathic College of Anesthesiologists (AOCA) *Founded:* 1952. *Headquarters:* Independence, MO. *Purpose:* To provide a professional society of members of the American Osteopathic Association who are engaged in the practice of anesthesiology.

American Osteopathic College of Dermatology (AOCD) *Founded:* 1955. *Headquarters:* Kirksville, MO. *Purpose:* To conduct specialized education programs for members of the osteopathic profession certified or involved in dermatology.

American Osteopathic College of Pathologists (AOCP) *Founded:* 1954. *Headquarters:* Pembroke Pines, FL. *Purpose:* To establish guidelines for training programs in pathology and clinical pathology for osteopathic physicians and to maintain standards in residency training programs. It serves osteopathic physicians who have completed residency training programs in pathology and clinical pathology; candidate members are in residency training in pathology.

American Osteopathic College of Preventive Medicine (AOCPM) *Founded:* 1982. *Headquarters:* Atlanta, GA. *Purpose:* To prepare and educate osteopathic doctors interested in aerospace, occupational, or public health medicine.

American Osteopathic College of Radiology (AOCR) *Founded:* 1940. *Headquarters:* Milan, MO. *Purpose:* To promote education of certified radiologists, residents-in-training, and other osteopathic physicians involved in radiology.

American Osteopathic College of Rehabilitation Medicine (AOCRM) *Founded:* 1954. *Headquarters:* Des Plaines, IL. *Purpose:* To stimulate the study and improve the practice of physical rehabilitation as a specialty. Active members are certified in the specialty by the American Osteopathic Board of Rehabilitation Medicine of the American Osteopathic Association.

American Osteopathic Healthcare Association (AOHA) *Founded:* 1934. *Headquarters:* Washington, DC. *Purpose:* To hold educational institutes on health care management and to conduct research programs and compile statistics, among other activities. It serves osteopathic hospitals.

American Otological Society (AOS) *Founded:* 1868. *Headquarters:* Maywood, IL. *Purpose:* To encourage study and research in otology. It serves otologists and contributors to the advancement of disorders of the ear and temporal bone.

American Pain Society (APS) *Founded:* 1977. *Headquarters:* Glenview, IL. *Purpose:* To promote control, management, and understanding of pain through scientific meetings and research activities. It develops standards for training and ethical management of pain patients. The APS collaborates with other associations on policy issues, such as with the American Academy of Pain Medicine in jointly issuing a consensus statement on use of opioids for treatment of chronic pain. It serves physicians, dentists, psychologists, nurses, and other health professionals interested in the study of pain.

American Paraplegia Society (APS) *Founded:* 1954. *Headquarters:* Jackson Heights, NY. *Purpose:* To advance and foster improved health care of spinal cord injury patients and to promote education and research in the neuroscience fields. It serves physicians and researchers in the spinal cord injury field.

American Pathology Foundation (APF) *Founded:* 1959. *Headquarters:* Mundelein, IL. *Purpose:* To promote the practice of pathology in private laboratories and the exchange of information that will improve anatomic and clinical pathology. Conducts seminars on direct billing and management. Members include board-certified pathologists.

American Pediatric Society (APS) *Founded:* 1888. *Headquarters:* Elk Grove Village, IL. *Purpose:* To study children and their diseases, prevention of illness, and promotion of health in childhood. Members include physician educators and researchers.

American Pediatric Surgical Association (APSA) *Founded:* 1970. *Headquarters:* Philadelphia, PA. *Purpose:* To promote competent medical care for children. It serves pediatric surgeons certified by the American Board of Surgery for competence in dealing with surgical problems of infancy and childhood.

American Pharmaceutical Association-Academy of Pharmacy Practice and Management (APhA) *Founded:* 1852. *Headquarters:* Washington, DC. *Purpose:* To ensure the quality of drug products to represent the interests of the profession before governmental bodies; and to interpret and disseminate information on developments in health care. Maintains a headquarters building in Washington, DC, called the American Institute of Pharmacy. Members include pharmacists, educators, students, researchers, editors and publishers of pharmaceutical literature, pharmaceutical chemists and scientists, food and drug officials, hospital pharmacists, and pharmacists in government service. *Formerly:* Academy of Pharmacy and Practice Management (1995).

American Physical Therapy Association (APTA) *Founded:* 1921. *Headquarters:* Alexandria, VA. *Purpose:* To act as an accrediting body for educational programs in physical therapy and is responsible for establishing standards, among other activities. It serves physical therapists, physical therapy assistants, and students.

American Physicians Association of Computer Medicine (APACM) *Founded:* 1984. *Headquarters:* Pittsford, NY. *Purpose:* To foster the development of a database of programs and a certifying board of computer medicine. It serves physicians, interns, and medical students interested in the use of computers in patient care, education, and research.

American Podiatric Medical Association (APMA) *Founded:* 1912. *Headquarters:* Bethesda, MD. *Purpose:* To serve podiatrists through committees including: Appeals and Control, Hospitals, Podiatric Therapeutics, Podiatry Political Action, and Public Health and Preventive Podiatric Medicine.

American Productivity and Quality Center (APQC) *Founded:* 1977. *Headquarters:* Houston, TX. *Purpose:* To work with businesses, unions, academic institutions, and government agencies to find ways to improve productivity and quality. It serves major corporations, foundations, and individuals interested in improving productivity and the quality of work life in the United States.

American Professional Practice Association (APPA) *Founded:* 1959. *Headquarters:* New York, NY. *Purpose:* To serve physicians and dentists by providing information on economic benefits and services, such as unsecured loan plans; equipment, furniture, and automobile leasing;

estate planning services; group insurance; and leisure and personal service programs.

American Prosthodontic Society (APS) *Founded:* 1928. *Headquarters:* Chicago, IL. *Purpose:* A professional society of dentists interested in prosthodontics.

American Psychiatric Association (APA) *Founded:* 1844. *Headquarters:* Washington, DC. *Purpose:* To further the study of the nature, treatment, and prevention of mental disorders and to support the work of physician members specializing in the diagnosis and treatment of mental and emotional illnesses and substance use disorders. Support services and benefits include legislative presence and other advocacy, clinical and research updates, educational assistance, patient and public education, practice management and reimbursement, employment assistance, insurance, and member benefit programs. The APA develops and updates the *Diagnostic and Statistical Manual of Mental Disorders (DSM)* and develops and disseminates clinical practice guidelines through its peer-reviewed journal. The APA's own publishing house, the American Psychiatric Press, Inc (APPI), publishes professional books, books for the general public, journals, CD-ROM multimedia products, electronic products, and audiotapes and videotapes.

American Psychiatric Nurses Association (APNA) *Founded:* 1987. *Headquarters:* Washington, DC. *Purpose:* To provide leadership to advance psychiatric-mental health nursing practice; improve mental health care for individuals, families, groups, and communities; and shape health policy for the delivery of mental health services. APNA is committed to the vision that all people will have accessible, effective, and efficient psychiatric-mental health care in delivery systems that fully utilize the skills and expertise of psychiatric nurses. Activities include programs and services related to the creation, exchange, and engineering of new knowledge and skills; promotion of established standards of clinical practice and professional performance; participation as partners and leaders in the formulation of policies and the design, implementation and evaluation of delivery systems in psychiatric-mental health care; and representation of psychiatric-mental health nursing as a collective and integrated specialty in the professional and public forum of the health care community. The association's government affairs office works directly with key legislators and maintains on-going contact with a number of federal agencies as well.

American Psychoanalytic Association (APsaA) *Founded:* 1911. *Headquarters:* New York, NY. *Purpose:* To foster the integration of psychoanalysis with other branches of medicine and to encourage research. It serves psychoanalysts who have graduated from or are currently attending an accredited institute and who are interested in establishing and maintaining standards for the training of psychoanalysts and for the practice of psychoanalysis.

American Psychological Association (APA) *Founded:* 1892. *Headquarters:* Washington, DC. *Purpose:* To work to advance psychology as a science, profession, and means of promoting human welfare. APA's member-

ship includes researchers, educators, clinicians, consultants, and students in the United States and around the world. APA has specialized divisions in dozens of areas of psychology and affiliations with U.S. state, territorial, and Canadian provincial psychological associations. The APA's chief activities are organized under the directorates of Education, Practice, Public Interest, and Science. The national public education campaign, Talk to Someone Who Can Help, is intended to shape evolving trends in health care, to educate and inform the American public on when and how to seek help for emotional problems, and to remove the information gap that inhibits access to appropriate care and treatment.

American Psychopathological Association (APPA) *Founded:* 1912. *Headquarters:* St. Louis, MO. *Purpose:* To serve physicians and scientists interested in the field of psychopathology and to investigate scientific problems of abnormal psychology. The scope of inquiry includes the study of phenomena arising from abnormal mental processes, organic pathological conditions directly connected with abnormal mental processes, means that may remove or modify social or individual factors operating in the production of mental diseases, and the relationship between psychopathological and social or cultural problems.

American Psychosomatic Society (APS) *Founded:* 1943. *Headquarters:* McLean, VA. *Purpose:* To conduct educational programs; maintains a speaker's bureau. Members include specialists from all medical disciplines, social scientists, and psychologists interested in scientific research and clinical practice in the field of psychosomatic medicine.

American Public Health Association (APHA) *Founded:* 1872. *Headquarters:* Washington, DC. *Purpose:* To protect and promote personal, mental, and environmental health; promulgates standards, establishes uniform practices and procedures, develops the etiology of communicable diseases, and explores medical care programs and their relationship to public health. Special interest groups of the APHA include Alternative and Complimentary Health Practice, Forum on Bioethics, Disability Forum, Health Law Forum, New Professional, and Veterinary Public Health. Members include physicians, nurses, educators, nutritionists, dentists, other health specialists, and members of the public interested in public health issues.

American Public Welfare Association (APWA) *Founded:* 1930. *Headquarters:* Washington, DC. *Purpose:* To develop, promote, and implement public human service policies that improve the health and well-being of families, children, and adults.

American Radiological Nurses Association (ARNA) *Founded:* 1981. *Headquarters:* Oak Brook, IL. *Purpose:* To conduct educational programs. Members include radiological nurses interested in sharing professional experiences and concerns.

American Radium Society (ARS) *Founded:* 1916. *Headquarters:* Philadelphia, PA. *Purpose:* To encourage liaison among medical specialties concerned with cancer treatment. It serves medical specialists and allied scientists interested in cancer treatment.

American Red Cross National Headquarters (ARC) *Founded:* 1881. *Headquarters:* Washington, DC. *Purpose:* To provide care for the wounded, sick, and homeless in wartime, according to the terms of the Geneva Convention of 1864, and now also during and following natural disasters; to conduct research programs; and to maintain local chapters that provide speakers. The emblem of the organization is a Geneva cross or a red Greek cross on a white background.

American Registry of Diagnostic Medical Sonographers (ARDMS) *Founded:* 1975. *Headquarters:* Rockville, MD. *Purpose:* To develop and administer examinations in diagnostic medical sonography and vascular technology and register successful candidates.

American Registry of Medical Assistants (ARMA) *Founded:* 1950. *Headquarters:* Westfield, MA. *Purpose:* To promote high training standards for medical assistants. Serves medical assistants who have completed an accredited medical assistant training course or who have trained with a physician.

American Registry of Pathology (ARP) *Founded:* 1976. *Headquarters:* Washington, DC. *Purpose:* To serve as a fiscal agent in the management of research grants and monies derived from tuition fees and contributions and as a link between the military and civilian medical, dental, and veterinary communities for the mutual benefit of military and civilian medicine. It serves national medical professional societies engaging in cooperative enterprises in medical research and education with the Armed Forces Institute of Pathology.

American Registry of Radiologic Technologists (ARRT) *Founded:* 1922. *Headquarters:* St. Paul, MN. *Purpose:* To provide a certification board for radiographers, nuclear medicine technologists, and radiation therapy technologists. The board is governed by trustees appointed by the American College of Radiology and the American Society of Radiologic Technologists.

American Rehabilitation Association (NARF) *Founded:* 1969. *Headquarters:* Reston, VA. *Purpose:* To promote the expansion and improvement of rehabilitation services and to provide educational seminars and workshops. NARF represents the concerns of rehabilitation providers before Congress and governmental agencies, serving rehabilitation facilities in the United States and Canada. *Formerly:* National Association of Rehabilitation Facilities (1994).

American Rehabilitation Counseling Association (ARCA) *Founded:* 1958. *Headquarters:* Alexandria, VA. *Purpose:* To promote the rehabilitation counseling profession and its services to individuals with disabilities. A division of the American Association for Counseling and Development composed of rehabilitation counselors and professionals.

American Rhinologic Society (ARS) *Founded:* 1954. *Headquarters:* Brooklyn, NY. *Purpose:* To advance the study of rhinology. Members include physicians who are diplomates of the American Board of Otolaryngology, the American Board of Plastic Surgery, and other boards and those who have additional training and interest in the study of medical and surgical rhinology.

American Roentgen Ray Society (ARRS) *Founded:* 1900. *Headquarters:* Reston, VA. *Purpose:* To conduct regional and educational programs. It serves specialists in diagnostic and/or therapeutic radiology.

American School Health Association (ASHA) *Founded:* 1927. *Headquarters:* Kent, OH. *Purpose:* To promote comprehensive school health programs. Members include school physicians, school nurses, dentists, nutritionists, health educators, dental hygienists, and public health workers interested in the development and advancement of school health programs.

American Sleep Disorders Association (ASDA) *Founded:* 1975. *Headquarters:* Rochester, MN. *Purpose:* To foster educational activities at medical schools and in continuing medical education programs and conduct site visits to ensure minimum standards at member centers. ASDA trains and evaluates the competence of individuals who care for patients with sleep disorders. Members include sleep disorders centers and individuals interested in providing full diagnostic and treatment services for patients with all types of sleep disorders.

American Social Health Association (ASHA) *Founded:* 1912. *Headquarters:* Research Triangle Park, NC. *Purpose:* To prevent control, and eventually eliminate the consequences of sexually transmitted diseases as a social health problem. It operates Herpes Resource Center, a national program for sufferers of incurable genital herpes.

American Society of Abdominal Surgery (ASAS) *Founded:* 1959. *Headquarters:* Melrose, MA. *Purpose:* To sponsor an extensive program of surgical education including study courses, postgraduate programs, lectures, and demonstrations. It serves physicians specializing in abdominal surgery.

American Society of Addiction Medicine (ASAM) *Founded:* 1954. *Headquarters:* Chevy Chase, MD. *Purpose:* To educate physicians; to improve the treatment of individuals suffering from alcoholism or other addictions; and to improve access to care as well as to increase its quality and effectiveness for patients and their families. ASAM's long-term objective is to establish a Board of Addiction Medicine recognized by the American Board of Medical Specialties; currently it is promoting the development of joint Certificates of Special Qualifications (CSDQ) to be offered by the primary care specialties. Individual members work through ASAM's twelve treatment and clinical issues committees and through activities including the development of treatment guidelines and practice parameters, publication of the ASAM Patient Placement

Criteria, and participation in national and state coalitions. ASAM collaborates with or provides representation in several other health-related organizations.

American Society for Adolescent Psychiatry (ASAP) *Founded:* 1967. *Headquarters:* Bethesda, MD. *Purpose:* To provide for the exchange of psychiatric knowledge and encourage the development of adequate standards and training facilities for treatment of adolescents. It serves psychiatrists interested in the behavior of adolescents.

American Society for Advancement of Anesthesia in Dentistry (ASAAD) *Founded:* 1929. *Headquarters:* Coral Springs, FL. *Purpose:* To sponsor continuing education seminars, symposia, and scientific sessions. Studies new anesthetics and chemicals and researches pain control methods. Members include dentists and physicians interested in dental anesthesia.

American Society for Aesthetic Plastic Surgery (ASAPS) *Founded:* 1967. *Headquarters:* Long Beach, CA. *Purpose:* To provide continuing education to members through presentation of papers, study sessions, and scientific associations. It serves board-certified plastic surgeons.

American Society on Aging (ASA) *Founded:* 1954. *Headquarters:* San Francisco, CA. *Purpose:* To offer 25 continuing education programs for professionals in aging-related fields. It serves health care and social service professionals, educators, researchers, administrators, business persons, students, and senior citizens.

American Society of Anesthesiologists (ASA) *Founded:* 1905. *Headquarters:* Park Ridge, IL. *Purpose:* To raise and maintain the standards of the medical practice of anesthesiology and improve the care of the patient by serving as the foremost advocate for all patients who require anesthesia or relief from pain. ASA publishes statements, guidelines, standards, and practice parameters focusing on ways of improving the practice of anesthesiology, and it publishes a journal and other materials to provide information on aspects of anesthetic care for both medical personnel and the lay public. ASA offers its members a special self-assessment tool, the Self-Education and Evaluation Program (SEE). The ASA maintains the Wood Library-Museum of Anesthesiology to serve not only the medical profession but also historians and interested members of the public.

American Society for Apheresis (ASFA) *Founded:* 1981. *Headquarters:* Tucson, AZ. *Purpose:* To assist in forming standards and regulations in the field of apheresis and promotes training and research in apheresis therapy for patients. It serves physicians, nurses, technologists, and other individuals active in the field of apheresis.

American Society for Artificial Internal Organs (ASAIO) *Founded:* 1955. *Headquarters:* Boca Raton, FL. *Purpose:* To promote the development, application, and awareness of organ technologies that enhance the quality and duration of life by providing education in the fields of artificial organs, organ transplantation, donors, prosthetics, and biomedical engineering.

American Society of Bariatric Physicians (ASBP) *Founded:* 1950. *Headquarters:* Englewood, CO. *Purpose:* To establish standards of bariatric practice; to foster the exchange of information; and to sponsor research and continuing education to encourage excellence in the practice of bariatric medicine. The ASBP serves physicians with an interest in the study and treatment of obesity and associated conditions.

American Society for Bone and Mineral Research (ASBMR) *Founded:* 1977. *Headquarters:* Washington, DC. *Purpose:* To develop guidelines to aid in preventing osteoporosis. Members include physicians, dentists, veterinarians, and other doctors interested in research in bone and mineral diseases.

American Society of Breast Disease (ASBD) *Founded:* 1976. *Headquarters:* Dallas, TX. *Purpose:* To further the study of diseases of the breast and to inform physicians and other health professionals of developments in the diagnosis and treatment of breast cancer and benign diseases of the breast. Serves physicians and nurses primarily engaged in the fields of obstetrics and gynecology, surgery, radiology, family practice, and medical and radiation oncology. *Formerly:* Society for the Study of Breast Disease (1994).

American Society of Cardiovascular Professionals/ Society for Cardiovascular Management (ASCP/SCM) *Founded:* 1967. *Headquarters:* Fredericksburg, VA. *Purpose:* To determine educational needs; to develop programs; to provide a structure to offer cardiovascular and pulmonary technical professionals a key to the future as a valuable member of the medical team. Serves health professionals involved in cardiology technology and pulmonary technology who are employed under the direction of a physician.

American Society of Cataract and Refractive Surgery (ASCRS) *Founded:* 1974. *Headquarters:* Fairfax, VA. *Purpose:* To offer continuing medical education to ophthalmologists, to provide public education of eye care, and to conduct research. Members include ophthalmologists interested in surgery of the anterior segment of the eye, including intraocular lens implant surgery and refractive corneal surgery.

American Society of Childbirth Educators (ASCE) *Founded:* 1972. *Headquarters:* Sedona, AZ. *Purpose:* To exchange and disseminate information relating to prepared childbirth as a shared family experience and to disseminate information to qualified professionals regarding standards and techniques relevant to prepared childbirth.

American Society for Clinical Evoked Potentials (ASCEP) *Founded:* 1981. *Headquarters:* White Plains, NY. *Purpose:* To serve physicians in physical medicine and rehabilitation, neurology, neurosurgery, ophthalmology, and anesthesiology interested in studying the central nervous system's transmissions and to teach electrodiagnostic reading of evoked potentials.

American Society of Clinical Hypnosis (ASCH) *Founded:* 1957. *Headquarters:* Des Plaines, IL. *Purpose:*

Sets standards of training and conducts teaching sessions at basic and advanced levels. Members include physicians, dentists, and psychologists with doctoral degrees interested in the field of hypnosis.

American Society for Clinical Investigation (ASCI)
Founded: 1909. *Headquarters:* Thorofare, NJ. *Purpose:* To promote cultivation of clinical research by methods of natural science. It serves physicians who have accomplished meritorious original investigations in the clinical or allied sciences of medicine. Active members are physicians under age 48 years; emeritus members are those over age 48 years.

American Society for Clinical Laboratory Science (ASCLS)
Founded: 1932. *Headquarters:* Bethesda, MD. *Purpose:* To promote and maintain high standards in clinical laboratory methods and to research and advance standards of education and training of personnel; to conduct educational programs; and to sponsor award competition to encourage the writing of scientific papers.

American Society for Clinical Nutrition (ASCN)
Founded: 1959. *Headquarters:* Bethesda, MD. *Purpose:* As a division of the American Institute of Nutrition, it promotes teaching, research, and reporting of progress in clinical nutrition. It serves physicians and scientists actively engaged in clinical nutrition research.

American Society of Clinical Oncology (ASCO)
Founded: 1964. *Headquarters:* Chicago, IL. *Purpose:* To serve the needs of the oncology community through a broad range of programs and services, including committees on cancer education, clinical practice, continuing medical education, and health services research; a cancer genetics education task force; a Congressional and Regulatory Watch; and an online resource for cancer patients, physicians, and researchers. ASCO publishes its recommendations as approved ASCO Policy Statements and ASCO Guidelines. ASCO has state and regional affiliates.

American Society of Consultant Pharmacists (ASCP)
Founded: 1969. *Headquarters:* Alexandria, VA. *Purpose:* To represent the interests of its members and promote safe and effective medication therapy for the nation's long-term care residents. Members are pharmacists who provide consultancy services on a contractual basis across the full spectrum of long-term care settings, including subacute care and assisted living facilities, psychiatric hospitals, facilities for the mentally retarded, correctional facilities, adult day care centers, hospices, alcohol and drug rehabilitation centers, ambulatory and surgical care centers, and individuals' own homes. ASCP released Long-Term Care Pharmacy Practice Standards in 1997. Advocacy is currently focused on Medicaid reform to retain federal laws governing the provision of consultant pharmacy services that protect and improve nursing home patient health and to extend ASCP's presence in state-level Medicaid initiatives. Projects of ASCP's Research and Education Foundation include the Automation in Pharmacy Initiative and the Fleetwood Project Research Initiative on The Impact of Consultant

Pharmacist Services on Patient Outcomes and Costs in Long-Term Care, which is comparing outcomes of different drug-regimen review models and developing impact measurement tools.

American Society for Clinical Pharmacology and Therapeutics (ASCPT)
Founded: 1900. *Headquarters:* Norristown, PA. *Purpose:* To provide a continuing medical education program for practicing physicians. It serves physician members interested in the promotion and advancement of the science of human pharmacology and therapeutics.

American Society of Colon and Rectal Surgeons (ASCRS)
Founded: 1899. *Headquarters:* Washington, DC. *Purpose:* To advance and promote the science and practice of the treatment of patients with diseases and disorders affecting the colon, rectum, and anus. It conducts research programs and offers placement service.

American Society for Colposcopy and Cervical Pathology (ASCCP)
Founded: 1964. *Headquarters:* Washington, DC. *Purpose:* To organize and approve training programs and to conduct research and postgraduate courses. A division of the American College of Obstetricians and Gynecologists serving obstetricians, gynecologists, and other individuals interested in the accurate and ethical application of colposcopy.

American Society of Consultant Pharmacists (ASCP)
Founded: 1969. *Headquarters:* Alexandria, VA. *Purpose:* To improve consultant pharmacist services to nursing homes and long term care facilities. It serves registered pharmacists and educators who are interested in pharmaceutical procedures within nursing homes and related health facilities.

American Society of Contemporary Medicine, Surgery, and Ophthalmology (ASCMSO)
Founded: 1981. *Headquarters:* Skokie, IL. *Purpose:* To promote the specific needs of general practitioners and to provide continuing medical education programs for maintaining competence in the practice of medicine. Divisions of ASCMSO are the American College of Medicine, American Society of Contemporary Ophthalmology, and International Society of Ocular Surgeons.

American Society of Contemporary Ophthalmology (ASCO)
Founded: 1966. *Headquarters:* Skokie, IL. *Purpose:* To offer continuing medical education on ophthalmic developments. It serves ophthalmologists interested in the advancement of clinical research and the availability of continuing education in ophthalmology.

American Society of Cytopathology (ASC)
Founded: 1951. *Headquarters:* Wilmington, DE. *Purpose:* To serve cytologists, pathologists, clinicians, researchers, and cytotechnologists interested in making the cytological method of early cancer detection universally available to the public.

American Society for Cytotechnology (ASCT)
Founded: 1979. *Headquarters:* Raleigh, NC. *Purpose:* To enhance the role of cytotechnologists in health care sys-

tems. Members include cytotechnologists, physicians, and other individuals in the field of cytopathology.

American Society of Dentistry for Children (ASDC)
Founded: 1927. *Headquarters:* Chicago, IL. *Purpose:* To conduct specialized education and research programs and provide placement service for graduates in dentistry. It serves general practitioners and specialists interested in dentistry for children.

American Society for Dermatologic Surgery (ASDS)
Founded: 1970. *Headquarters:* Schaumburg, IL. *Purpose:* To maintain the highest possible standards in medical education, clinical practice, and patient care. It serves physicians specializing in dermatologic surgery.

American Society of Directors of Volunteer Services (ASDVS) *Founded:* 1968. *Headquarters:* Chicago, IL. *Purpose:* To develop the knowledge and increase the competence of individual members and to provide a means of communication for directors of volunteer services and health care organizations. Members include those who are employed or recognized by the administration of a health care organization as having major or continuing responsibility for managing and coordinating its volunteer services program and who are eligible for personal membership in the American Hospital Association.

American Society of Echocardiography (ASE)
Founded: 1976. *Headquarters:* Raleigh, NC. *Purpose:* To promote excellence in ultrasonic examination of the heart. It serves physicians and technicians specializing in ultrasound heart imaging and diagnosis.

American Society of Extra-Corporeal Technology (AmSECT) *Founded:* 1964. *Headquarters:* Reston, VA. *Purpose:* To disseminate information necessary to proper practice of extracorporeal technology. It serves perfusionists, technologists, physicians, nurses, and other individuals interested in the practice of extracorporeal technology (involving heart-lung machines).

American Society of Forensic Odontology (ASFO)
Founded: 1966. *Headquarters:* Chicago, IL. *Purpose:* To conduct research and specialized education programs. It serves individuals interested in the field of forensic dentistry.

American Society for Gastrointestinal Endoscopy (ASGE) *Founded:* 1941. *Headquarters:* Manchester, MA. *Purpose:* To aim to further the knowledge of digestive diseases by endoscopic methods. It serves gastroenterologists, internists, and surgeons who perform gastroscopic, esophagoscopic, coloscopic, and perineoscopic examinations.

American Society for Geriatric Dentistry (ASGD)
Founded: 1965. *Headquarters:* Chicago, IL. *Purpose:* To promote continuing education of the practitioner of geriatric dentistry; nursing home administrators and personnel; and dental hygienists, nurses, and students. It serves dentists, dental hygienists, and dental students interested in oral health care for older adults in all health care set-

tings (acute care, ambulatory care, home care, and long term care).

American Society of Group Psychotherapy and Psychodrama (ASGPP) *Founded:* 1942. *Headquarters:* McLean, VA. *Purpose:* To serve social workers, psychologists, psychiatrists, clergy members, nurses, and other individuals interested in group psychotherapy, psychodrama, and sociometry.

American Society of Hand Therapists (ASHT)
Founded: 1977. *Headquarters:* Chicago, IL. *Purpose:* To promote research, publish information, and improve treatment techniques in hand therapy. Members are registered and licensed occupational and physical therapists specializing in hand therapy and hand rehabilitation.

American Society of Handicapped Physicians (ASHP) *Founded:* 1981. *Headquarters:* Pittsburgh, PA. *Purpose:* To provide a forum to address the needs of physically disabled physicians and to work against discrimination of the handicapped. It serves handicapped physicians and other individuals interested in the problems faced by handicapped physicians.

American Society for Head and Neck Surgery (ASHNS) *Founded:* 1959. *Headquarters:* Pittsburgh, PA. *Purpose:* To advance knowledge of surgical treatment of diseases of the head and neck. It serves otolaryngologists and other individuals of the American College of Surgeons whose primary interest is head and neck surgery.

American Society for Healthcare Central Service Professional (ASHCSP) *Founded:* 1967. *Headquarters:* Chicago, IL. *Purpose:* To provide education programs to individuals interested in central services in health care organizations.

American Society for Healthcare Education and Training of the American Hospital Association (ASHET) *Founded:* 1970. *Headquarters:* Chicago, IL. *Purpose:* To demonstrate the value of comprehensive education as a management strategy and to promote continuing education among all health care personnel. Members include education personnel and trainers from hospitals and other health care organizations involved in staff development and patient and community education.

American Society for Healthcare Engineering (ASHE) *Founded:* 1962. *Headquarters:* Chicago, IL. *Purpose:* To promote better patient care by encouraging and helping members to develop their knowledge and increase their competence in the field of facilities management. ASHE is a division of the American Hospital Association. Members include hospital engineers, facilities managers, directors of buildings and grounds, assistant administrators, directors of maintenance, directors of clinical engineering, design and construction professionals, and safety officers. *Formerly:* American Society for Hospital Engineering (1994).

American Society for Healthcare Environmental Services of the American Hospital Association

(ASHES) *Founded:* 1986. *Headquarters:* Chicago, IL. *Purpose:* To provide a discussion forum among members including educational opportunities. It serves managers and directors of hospital environmental services, laundry and linen services, housekeeping departments, and long term care units.

American Society for Healthcare Food Service Administrators (ASHFSA) *Founded:* 1967. *Headquarters:* Chicago, IL. *Purpose:* To promote improved administration of food service departments through continuing education and development of management skills. It serves directors and assistant directors of food service departments in health care organizations who are eligible for personal membership in the American Hospital Association.

American Society for Healthcare Human Resources Administration (ASHHRA) *Founded:* 1964. *Headquarters:* Chicago, IL. *Purpose:* To serve individuals interested in providing effective and continuous leadership in the field of health care human resources administration.

American Society for Health Care Marketing and Public Relations (ASHCMPR) *Founded:* 1964. *Headquarters:* Chicago, IL. *Purpose:* To provide a forum for its members, including persons in hospitals, hospital councils or associations, hospital-related schools, and health care organizations who are responsible for marketing and public relations.

American Society for Healthcare Risk Management (ASHRM) *Founded:* 1980. *Headquarters:* Chicago, IL. *Purpose:* To promote professional development of hospital risk managers and addresses risk management issues affecting the health care industry. It serves employees actively involved in the risk management functions of hospitals or other health care providers.

American Society of Health-System Pharmacists (ASHP) *Founded:* 1942. *Headquarters:* Bethesda, MD. *Purpose:* To represent its members and to provide leadership that will enable pharmacists in organized health care settings to extend pharmaceutical care focused on achieving positive patient outcomes through drug therapy; provide services that foster the efficacy, safety, and cost-effectiveness of drug use; contribute to programs and services that emphasize the health needs of the public and the prevention of disease; and promote pharmacy as an essential component of the health care team. ASHP aims to be the leading advocate within health systems for achieving optimum outcomes from medication use through the services of pharmacists. *Formerly:* American Society for Hospital Pharmacists (1996).

American Society of Hematology (ASH) *Founded:* 1957. *Headquarters:* Washington, DC. *Purpose:* To promote exchange of information and ideas related to blood and blood-forming tissues and investigation of hematologic problems. It serves hematologists and other individuals holding doctorate degrees with an interest in the field.

American Society for Histocompatibility and Immunogenetics (ASHI) *Founded:* 1968. *Headquarters:* Lenexa, KS. *Purpose:* To conduct proficiency testing and educational programs. Members include scientists, physicians, and technologists involved in research and clinical activities related to histocompatibility testing.

American Society for Hospital Engineering *See* American Society for Healthcare Engineering.

American Society of Hospital Pharmacists (ASHP) *See* American Society of Health-System Pharmacists.

American Society of Human Genetics (ASHG) *Founded:* 1948. *Headquarters:* Bethesda, MD. *Purpose:* To serve physicians, researchers, genetic counselors, and other individuals interested in human genetics by offering conferences, a journal, and other forums for exchange and dissemination of information.

American Society of Hypertension (ASH) *Founded:* 1985. *Headquarters:* New York, NY. *Purpose:* To promote development, advancement, and the exchange of information on the diagnosis and treatment of hypertension. It serves medical professionals, paraprofessionals, and postgraduate students interested in hypertension and related cardiovascular diseases.

American Society for Information Science (ASIS) *Founded:* 1937. *Headquarters:* Silver Spring, MD. *Purpose:* To serve information specialists, scientists, administrators, and other individuals interested in the use, organization, storage, retrieval, evaluation, and dissemination of recorded specialized information. Members are engaged in activities and specialties including classification and coding systems, automatic and associative indexing, machine translation of languages, and copyright issues.

American Society of Internal Medicine (ASIM) *Founded:* 1956. *Headquarters:* Washington, DC. *Purpose:* To address the concerns of practicing internists in the areas of quality, availability, environment, and cost of internal medical services by providing collective advocacy as well as individualized assistance, developing special tools and programs, and communicating practical and relevant information. ASIM programs include IMCARE (Internal Medicine Center to Advance Research) and the ASIM Center for Competitive Advantage. In August 1996 the ACIP issued a joint announcement with the American College of Physicians that the two internal medicine organizations were completing negotiations to merge and that the new organization, tentatively named the American College of Physicians-American Society of Internal Medicine (ACP-ASIM), would be established in the latter half of 1998.

American Society for Investigative Pathology (ASIP) *Founded:* 1976. *Headquarters:* Bethesda, MD. *Purpose:* A professional organization for experimental research pathologists who have made significant contributions to the knowledge of disease.

American Society for Laser Medicine and Surgery (ASLMS) *Founded:* 1980. *Headquarters:* Wausaw, WI.

Purpose: To facilitate the exchange of information regarding laser medicine and surgery. It serves physicians, physicists, nurses, dentists, podiatrists, technicians, and commercial representatives interested in the medical applications of lasers.

American Society of Law, Medicine and Ethics (ASLM) *Founded:* 1972. *Headquarters:* Boston, MA. *Purpose:* To provide opportunities for continuing education through publications, conferences, and information clearinghouse services. Members include physicians, attorneys, health care management executives, nurses, insurance company personnel, members of the judiciary, and other individuals interested in medicolegal relations and health law.

American Society of Lipo-Suction Surgery (ASLSS) *Founded:* 1982. *Headquarters:* Chicago, IL. *Purpose:* Serves surgeons specializing in dermatology, general surgery, gynecology, otolaryngology, plastic and reconstructive surgery, and cosmetics surgery who are interested in the art and methods of liposuction surgery. Provides training in methods of liposuction surgery.

American Society of Maxillofacial Surgeons (ASMS) *Founded:* 1947. *Headquarters:* Arlington Heights, IL. *Purpose:* To stimulate and advance knowledge of the science and art of maxillofacial surgery and improve and elevate the standard of practice. Members include physicians and dentists who have at least five years of recognized graduate training and experience in maxillofacial surgery.

American Society of Nephrology (ASN) *Founded:* 1966. *Headquarters:* Washington, DC. *Purpose:* Serves nephrologists interested in education and improving the quality of patient care.

American Society of Neuroimaging (ASN) *Founded:* 1977. *Headquarters:* Minneapolis, MN. *Purpose:* To encourage collaboration of members and improvement of neuroimaging techniques. It serves neurologists, neurosurgeons, neuroradiologists, and scientists interested in the development of computerized axial tomography, magnetic resonance imaging, and other neurodiagnostic techniques for clinical service, teaching, and research.

American Society of Neuroradiology (ASNR) *Founded:* 1962. *Headquarters:* Oak Brook, IL. *Purpose:* To foster education, basic science research, and communication in radiology. Members include radiologists who spend at least half their time practicing neuroradiology.

American Society of Nuclear Cardiology (ASNC) *Founded:* 1991. *Headquarters:* Bethesda, MD. *Purpose:* To foster optimal delivery of nuclear cardiology services; to promote research; to provide continuing medical education opportunities; to establish guidelines and standards for training and practice; and to provide information on licensure requirements.

American Society of Ophthalmic Administrators (ASOA) *Founded:* 1986. *Headquarters:* Fairfax, VA. *Purpose:* ASOA is a division of the American Society of Cataract and Refractive Surgery. Facilitates the exchange of ideas among persons involved with the administration of an ophthalmic office or clinic.

American Society of Ophthalmic Registered Nurses (ASORN) *Founded:* 1976. *Headquarters:* San Francisco, CA. *Purpose:* Serving registered nurses specializing in the field of ophthalmology, it facilitates continuing education of its members and represents members' interests before governmental agencies, hospitals, industries, research organizations, technical societies, universities, and other professional associations.

American Society of Outpatient Surgeons (ASOS) *Founded:* 1978. *Headquarters:* Chicago, IL. *Purpose:* To provide improved surgical care at lower costs. Members include anesthesiologists and surgeons in various specialties who practice surgery in an office-based setting. It is affiliated with the Accreditation Association for Ambulatory Health Care.

American Society of Parasitologists (ASP) *Founded:* 1924. *Headquarters:* Toronto, ON, Canada. *Purpose:* To improve the teaching and promote the study of parasites. Its committees include nomenclature and terminology and techniques in clinical laboratory medicine.

American Society for Parenteral and Enteral Nutrition (ASPEN) *Founded:* 1975. *Headquarters:* Silver Spring, MD. *Purpose:* To promote quality patient care. Serves physicians, dietitians, nurses, pharmacists, and other health specialists interested in nutritional support for patients during hospitalization and rehabilitation.

American Society of Pediatric Hematology/ Oncology (ASPHO) *Founded:* 1981. *Headquarters:* Glenview, IL. *Purpose:* To promote knowledge, understanding, and management of disorders of the blood and cancer in children. Members include physicians who have served residencies in pediatrics and fellowships in pediatric hematology-oncology; specialists in allied disciplines including surgery, pathology, radiology, pedodontics, and psychiatry; physicians trained in hematology or oncology of adults who are interested in the treatment of blood diseases and cancer in children; and individuals holding doctoral degrees who are involved in research relevant to the field. Affiliated members include nurses and physician assistants working with children with cancer, sickle cell disease, thalassemia, hemophilia, and other hematological disorders, and psychologists, social workers, and research scientists.

American Society for Pediatric Neurosurgery (ASPN) *Founded:* 1978. *Headquarters:* Salt Lake City, UT. *Purpose:* To represent the interests of pediatric neurosurgery as they relate to government, the public, universities, and professional societies; to support basic and clinical research in pediatric neurosurgery; and to provide leadership in undergraduate, graduate, and continuing education in pediatric neurosurgery.

American Society for Pharmacology and Experimental Therapeutics (ASPET) *Founded:* 1908. *Headquarters:* Bethesda, MD. *Purpose:* To promote pharmacological knowledge. It serves investigators in pharmacology and toxicology. Its committees cover topics such as substance abuse and public information, and its divisions include Clinical Pharmacology, Drug Metabolism, and Neuropharmacology.

American Society for Pharmacy Law (ASPL) *Founded:* 1974. *Headquarters:* Vienna, VA. *Purpose:* To further legal knowledge, to communicate accurate legal information to pharmacists, and to foster knowledge and education pertaining to the rights and duties of pharmacists. It serves pharmacists, lawyers, and students.

American Society of Plastic and Reconstructive Surgeons (ASPRS) *Founded:* 1931. *Headquarters:* Arlington Heights, IL. *Purpose:* To sponsor patient education programs, to hold clinical symposia, and to act as a liaison between members and government and medical education. It serves plastic surgeons interested in promoting care for plastic surgery patients through research, service, and education.

American Society of Plastic and Reconstructive Surgical Nurses (ASPRSN) *Founded:* 1975. *Headquarters:* Pitman, NJ. *Purpose:* To enhance leadership qualities of nurses in the field of plastic surgery and increase the skills, knowledge, and understanding of personnel in plastic surgery nursing through continuing education. It is affiliated with the American Society of Plastic and Reconstructive Surgeons. Members include registered nurses, licensed practical nurses, and licensed vocational nurses working with plastic surgeons or interested in plastic and reconstructive nursing.

American Society of Podiatric Dermatology (ASPD) *Founded:* 1914. *Headquarters:* Baltimore, MD. *Purpose:* To foster and conduct research; to conduct continuing education; and to maintain speakers' bureau. Members include doctors of podiatric medicine with expertise in foot dermatology and candidates for the Doctor of Podiatric Medicine (DPM) degree in colleges of podiatric medicine who are interested in the field of podiatric dermatology.

American Society of Podiatric Medical Assistants (ASPMA) *Founded:* 1964. *Headquarters:* Cicero, IL. *Purpose:* To administer certification examinations. It serves podiatric assistants interested in educational seminars.

American Society of Podiatric Medicine (ASPM) *Founded:* 1944. *Headquarters:* Miami Beach, FL. *Purpose:* To focus on aging and diabetes. It serves podiatrists interested in research in podiatry, postgraduate courses, and scientific programs at annual meetings.

American Society of Preventive Oncology (ASPO) *Founded:* 1977. *Headquarters:* Madison, WI. *Purpose:* To promote the exchange of information, including environmental exposures and life-styles, and works to implement programs for the prevention and early detection of cancer. It serves professionals in clinical, educational, or research disciplines interested in the area of cancer prevention.

American Society of Psychoanalytic Physicians (ASPP) *Founded:* 1985. *Headquarters:* Rockville, MD. *Purpose:* To foster a wider understanding and utilization of psychoanalytic concepts and provide an opportunity to study psychoanalytic theory from all schools of thought. Offers lectures on therapy that combine a psychoanalytic orientation with other disciplines. Members include psychiatrists, psychoanalysts, and other individuals interested in psychoanalytic concepts.

American Society of Psychopathology of Expression (ASPE) *Founded:* 1964. *Headquarters:* Brookline, MA. *Purpose:* To disseminate information about research and clinical applications in the field of psychopathology of expression. It serves physicians, psychologists, art therapists, artists, social workers, criminologists, writers, and other individuals interested in the problems of expression and the artistic activities connected with psychiatric, sociological, and psychological research.

American Society for Psychoprophylaxis in Obstetrics (ASPO/LAMAZE) *Founded:* 1960. *Headquarters:* Washington, DC. *Purpose:* To disseminate information about the theory and practical application of psychoprophylaxis in obstetrics; to administer teacher training courses; and to certify qualified Lamaze teachers. Sponsors prenatal classes in the Lamaze method for expectant parents. Composed of physicians, nurses, nurse-midwives, certified teachers of the psychoprophylactic (Lamaze) method of childbirth, and other individuals interested in Lamaze childbirth preparation and family-centered maternity care.

American Society for Quality Control (ASQC) *Founded:* 1946. *Headquarters:* Milwaukee, WI. *Purpose:* To offer courses in quality engineering, reliability engineering, managing for quality, management of quality costs, quality audit-development and administration, management of the inspection function, probability and statistics for engineers and scientists, and product liability and prevention. It serves professionals interested in the advancement of quality.

American Society of Radiologic Technologists (ASRT) *Founded:* 1920. *Headquarters:* Albuquerque, NM. *Purpose:* To advance the science of radiologic technology and establish and maintain high standards of education and training in the field. It serves diagnostic radiography, radiation therapy, ultrasound, and nuclear medicine technologists.

American Society of Regional Anesthesia (ASRA) *Founded:* 1974. *Headquarters:* Richmond, VA. *Purpose:* To conduct education workshops for physicians and researchers involved with the study and clinical use of regional anesthesia.

American Society for Reproductive Medicine (ASRM) *Founded:* 1944. *Headquarters:* Birmingham, AL. *Purpose:* To extend knowledge of all aspects of fertility and problems of infertility and mammalian reproduction. It serves gynecologists, obstetricians, urologists, reproductive endocrinologists, veterinarians, research workers, and other individuals interested in reproductive health in humans and animals. *Formerly:* American Fertility Society (1994).

American Society for Stereotactic and Functional Neurosurgery (ASSFN) *Founded:* 1968. *Headquarters:* Houston, TX. *Purpose:* To compile statistics. It serves neurosurgeons practicing stereotactic surgery and interested in promoting communication in the field.

American Society for Surgery of the Hand (ASSH) *Founded:* 1946. *Headquarters:* Englewood, CO. *Purpose:* To promote research and worthwhile contributions to the field of hand surgery. It serves surgeons specializing in surgery of the hand.

American Society for Testing and Materials (ASTM) *Founded:* 1898. *Headquarters:* Conshohocken, PA. *Purpose:* To establish standards of materials, products, systems, and services. Serves engineers, scientists, professionals, technicians, governmental agencies, educational institutions, and laboratories. Has developed 9,000 standard test methods and recommended practices now in use.

American Society for Therapeutic Radiology and Oncology (ASTRO) *Founded:* 1955. *Headquarters:* Reston, VA. *Purpose:* To extend benefits of radiation therapy to cancer patients and provide education to members. Members include physicians who limit their practice to radiation therapy.

American Society of Transplant Surgeons (ASTS) *Founded:* 1975. *Headquarters:* Des Plaines, IL. *Purpose:* To promote education and research and participate in developing programs that will benefit organ recipients. Its committees deal with topics such as heart transplantation and ethics. Members include surgeons specializing in transplantation.

American Society of Tropical Medicine and Hygiene (ASTMH) *Founded:* 1952. *Headquarters:* Northbrook, IL. *Purpose:* To provide information to physicians and scientists interested in tropical medicine and hygiene, including the areas of arborvirology, entomology, medicine, nursing, and parasitology.

Americans for Nonsmokers' Rights *Founded:* 1976. *Headquarters:* Berkeley, CA. *Purpose:* To confront and monitor the tobacco industry at all levels of government in order to protect nonsmokers from secondhand smoke and youth from tobacco addiction. The national lobbying organization has an educational nonprofit organization, the American Nonsmokers' Rights Foundation, which creates comprehensive programs for school-age youth on issues of smoking prevention and their right to breathe smokefree air and which provides educational materials to aid adults seeking a smokefree environment.

Americans for a Sound AIDS/HIV Policy (ASAP) *Founded:* 1987. *Headquarters:* Washington, DC. *Purpose:* To assist in the formulation of a workable public policy on AIDS that will be understood and accepted by the public.

Advocates early diagnosis and promotes reducing transmission of the virus through public health intervention strategies, such as confidential and voluntary partner notification. It serves physicians, public health professionals, legislators, and businesspersons.

American Speech-Language-Hearing Association (ASHA) *Founded:* 1925. *Headquarters:* Rockville, MD. *Purpose:* To act as an accrediting body for college and university graduate school programs, clinics, and hospital programs and as a certifying body for professionals providing speech, language, and hearing therapy to the public. It serves speech-language pathologists and audiologists.

American Spinal Injury Association (ASIA) *Founded:* 1973. *Headquarters:* Chicago, IL. *Purpose:* To develop knowledge and treatment of spinal injury. Members include physicians who have been trained in the care of spinal paralytic patients and who are either actively engaged in the field and acknowledged to be competent by their peers or who have made a significant contribution to the advancement of the basic sciences or one of the clinical fields of practice relating to treatment of the spine.

American Statistical Association (ASA) *Founded:* 1839. *Headquarters:* Alexandria, VA. *Purpose:* A professional society of persons interested in the theory, methodology, and application of statistics to all fields of human endeavor. Sections include Biometrics, Biopharmaceutical, and Quality and Productivity.

Americans United for Life (AUL) *Founded:* 1971. *Headquarters:* Chicago, IL. *Purpose:* To protect human life at all stages of development through legal, legislative, and educational activities, including briefs submitted to the U.S. Supreme Court opposing abortion, euthanasia, and physician-assisted suicide.

American Surgical Association (ASA) *Founded:* 1880. *Headquarters:* Manchester, MA. *Purpose:* To promote the science and art of surgery. The ASA publishes a journal and holds an annual scientific meeting.

American Therapeutic Recreation Association (ATRA) *Founded:* 1984. *Headquarters:* Hattiesburg, MS. *Purpose:* To promote the use of therapeutic recreation in hospitals, mental rehabilitation facilities, and the like. It serves therapeutic recreation professionals and students who use sports, handicrafts, and other recreational activities to improve the physical, mental, and emotional functions of persons with illnesses or disabling conditions in hospitals, mental rehabilitation centers, physical rehabilitation centers, senior citizen treatment centers, and public health facilities.

American Thoracic Society (ATS) *Founded:* 1905. *Headquarters:* New York, NY. *Purpose:* To prevent and fight respiratory diseases through research, education, and advocacy. As the medical section of the American Lung Association, it serves specialists in pulmonary diseases, physicians in the public health field interested in tuberculosis control, thoracic surgeons, and research workers in lung disease. It acts as adviser in scientific matters.

American Thyroid Association (ATA) *Founded:* 1932. *Headquarters:* Bronx, NY (Montefiore Medical Center). *Purpose:* To convene physicians and scientists dedicated to research and treatment of thyroid pathophysiology. The ATA issues guidelines for physicians, publishes a journal, and offers patient education brochures, books, and support sources.

American Transplant Association (ATA) *Founded:* 1985. *Headquarters:* Washington, DC. *Purpose:* A non-membership organization that acts as an informational referral network for transplant patients and offers support for financial expenses and emergency transportation. It provides public education on organ and tissue donation awareness.

American Trauma Society (ATS) *Founded:* 1968. *Headquarters:* Upper Marlboro, MD. *Purpose:* To prevent trauma situations, improve trauma care through professional and paraprofessional education, and educate the public through campaigns and dissemination of information. Members are physicians, nurses, emergency medical services personnel, other health professionals, institutions, and corporations.

American Urological Association (AUA) *Founded:* 1902. *Headquarters:* Baltimore, MD. *Purpose:* To promote the highest standards of urological clinical care through education, research and the formulation of health care policy. The AUA aims to be the premier professional association for the advancement of urologic patient care.

American Urological Association Allied (AUAA) *Founded:* 1972. *Headquarters:* Richmond, VA. *Purpose:* To provide continuing education to registered and licensed practical nurses, technicians, physician assistants, persons working in urology-related industries, and secretarial employees in urology offices. It supersedes the Urological Nurses Association.

Americans United for Life (AUL) *Founded:* 1971. *Headquarters:* Chicago, IL. *Purpose:* To protect human life at all stages of development and to conduct legal and legislative activities including provision of testimony, model abortion statutes, and legal briefs in cases involving abortion and euthanasia.

AMHS Institute *Founded:* 1984. *Headquarters:* Washington, DC. *Purpose:* Serving nonprofit multihospital systems, it sponsors educational programs for corporate officers and trustees of multihospital systems and monitors, investigates, and develops policy positions on developments in the field.

Anesthesia Patient Safety Foundation (APSF) *Founded:* 1985. *Headquarters:* Pittsburgh, PA. *Purpose:* To assure that no patient shall be harmed by the effects of anesthesia by fostering investigations that will provide a better understanding of preventable anesthetic injuries encouraging programs that will reduce the number of anesthetic injuries and promoting national and interna-

tional communication of information and ideas about the causes and prevention of anesthetic morbidity and mortality.

The Angel Planes (TAP) *Founded:* 1985. *Headquarters:* Las Vegas, NV. *Purpose:* A national organization founded in 1985 composed of 500 volunteer pilots who fly blood to central blood banks; make emergency flights to rural hospitals to deliver special types of blood; pick up blood from mobile blood drives so that the blood can be prepared for transfusion within six hours of its donation; transport critical care (but not trauma) patients; and transport donated organs.

The Arc of the United States *Founded:* 1950. *Headquarters:* Arlington, TX. *Purpose:* To organize volunteers committed to the welfare of all children and adults with mental retardation and their families and to promote services, research, public understanding, and legislation. The Arc provides organizational support for local and state affiliated chapters and represents the membership on advocacy and programmatic issues pertaining to mental retardation, including membership in the United States International Council on Mental Retardation and Developmental Disabilities.

Arthritis Health Professions Association (AHPA) *Founded:* 1965. *Headquarters:* Atlanta, GA. *Purpose:* To advance knowledge and improve care of health services to those with rheumatic diseases. It serves nurses, occupational and physical therapists, social workers, psychologists, vocational counselors, physicians, pharmacists, and other health professionals interested in the practice, education, and research of rheumatic disease.

Arthroscopy Association of North America (AANA) *Founded:* 1982. *Headquarters:* Rosemont, IL. *Purpose:* To advance orthopedic surgeons who perform arthroscopy and to sponsor research and continuing education.

Assembly of Episcopal Hospitals and Chaplains *Founded:* 1950. *Headquarters:* Houston, TX. *Purpose:* To foster chaplaincy as an essential expression of the church's healing ministry in response to the gospel imperative.

Associated Bodywork and Massage Professionals (ABMP) *Founded:* 1986. *Headquarters:* Evergreen, CO. *Purpose:* To promote massage therapy and bodywork and to encourage ethical therapy practices. It serves professional massage therapists and bodyworkers; polarity, movement, and sports massage therapists; Shiatsu and Trager practitioners, reflexologists, orthobionomists, and infant massage instructors; and massage therapy schools.

Association of Academic Health Centers (AHC) *Founded:* 1969. *Headquarters:* Washington, DC. *Purpose:* Focusing on total health personnel education, it serves chief executive officers of university-based health centers in the United States.

Association of Academic Health Sciences Library Directors (AAHSLD) *Founded:* 1978. *Headquarters:* Seattle, WA. *Purpose:* To promote and seek to improve academic health science libraries. It serves academic medical and allied health science school libraries, represented by their directors.

Association of Academic Physiatrists (AAP)
Founded: 1967. *Headquarters:* Indianapolis, IN. *Purpose:* To advance teaching and research of physician medicine and rehabilitation. Members are academic physicians practicing physical medicine and rehabilitation and certified by the American Board of Physical Medicine and Rehabilitation.

Association for Academic Surgery (AAS) *Founded:* 1966. *Headquarters:* Minneapolis, MN. *Purpose:* To encourage new surgeons to pursue careers in academic surgery and support them in establishing themselves as investigators and educators by providing a forum. It serves surgeons with backgrounds in all surgical specialties in academic surgical centers at chief resident level or above.

Association for Adult Development and Aging (AADA) *Founded:* 1986. *Headquarters:* Alexandria, VA. *Purpose:* A division of the American Association for Counseling and Development that seeks to improve the competence and skills of members, promote the development of guidelines for professional preparation of counselors, and provide leadership and information to families, legislators, community service agencies, counselors, and other service providers or professionals related to adult development and aging. Members are individuals holding a master's degree or its equivalent in adult counseling or a related field.

Association to Advance Ethical Hypnosis (AAEH) *Founded:* 1955. *Headquarters:* Cuyahoga Falls, OH. *Purpose:* To establish a code of ethics in the practice of hypnosis; to conduct a three-phase examination (written, oral, and practical); and to certify members as hypnotechnicians. It serves practitioners of all the healing arts, educators, police officers, attorneys, and lay technicians.

Association for the Advancement of Automotive Medicine (AAAM) *Founded:* 1957. *Headquarters:* Des Plaines, IL. *Purpose:* To reduce the number of injuries and fatalities on the nation's highways by encouraging research on the effects of diseases, disabilities, and environmental factors on driver capabilities. Supports laws and regulations to upgrade the standards for licensing drivers and the use of appropriate protective devices. Members are physicians and other professionals interested in motor vehicle safety, design, and road engineering.

Association for Advancement of Behavior Therapy (AABT) *Founded:* 1966. *Headquarters:* New York, NY. *Purpose:* To sponsor training programs and lectures and to provide referrals to the public. Members are psychologists, psychiatrists, social workers, dentists, nurses, physiotherapists, and other professionals interested in the field of behavior modification, with special emphasis on clinical applications.

Association for Advancement of Blind and Retarded (AABR) *Founded:* 1955. *Headquarters:* Jamaica, NY. *Purpose:* To operate ten group residences providing intermediate care facilities for blind and retarded adults; two-day to six-day treatment centers for blind, multihandicapped, and severely retarded adults; and a summer camp for blind and multihandicapped people. Provides information and referral services. Members include community groups and individuals interested in multihandicapped blind and adults with severe mental retardation.

Association for the Advancement of Health Education (AAHE) *Founded:* 1937. *Headquarters:* Reston, VA. *Purpose:* To advance health education through program activities and federal legislation and encourages close working relationships between all health education and health service organizations. It serves professionals who have responsibility for health education in schools, colleges, communities, hospitals and clinics, and industries.

Association for the Advancement of Medical Instrumentation (AAMI) *Founded:* 1965. *Headquarters:* Arlington, VA. *Purpose:* To improve medical care through application, development, and management of technology. It serves clinical engineers, biomedical equipment technologists, hospital administrators, physicians, consultants, engineers, and manufacturers of medical devices interested in the advancement of health care through effective application and management of health care technology.

Association for the Advancement of Psychoanalysis (AAP) *Founded:* 1941. *Headquarters:* New York, NY. *Purpose:* To encourage training in psychoanalysis; to disseminate psychoanalytic principles to the medical-psychiatric profession and the general community; to support research programs; and to sponsor public education. The AAP is a division of the Karen Horney Psychoanalytic Institute and Center.

Association for Advancement of Psychology (AAP) *Founded:* 1974. *Headquarters:* Colorado Springs, CO. *Purpose:* To advance psychology and represent the interests of psychologists in the public policy arena. It serves members of the American Psychological Association or other national psychological associations, students of psychology, and organizations with a primarily psychological focus.

Association for the Advancement of Psychotherapy (AAP) *Founded:* 1939. *Headquarters:* Bronx, NY. *Purpose:* To provide a forum where all concepts of psychotherapeutic thought can be aired for the advancement of psychotherapy in practice, research, and training. It serves physicians who are psychiatrists or in psychiatric training.

Association of Air Medical Services (AAMS) *Founded:* 1980. *Headquarters:* Pasadena, CA. *Purpose:* To provide quality medical care during rapid air transport. Seeks to develop standards for aircraft configuration, minimum professional and educational requirements for personnel on board, operations, and communications equipment. It serves air medical transport providers and manufacturers and distributors of air medical transport equipment.

Association for Ambulatory Behavioral Health Care (AABHC) *Founded:* 1965. *Headquarters:* Alexandria, VA. *Purpose:* To develop and improve partial hospitalization within the continuum of psychiatric treatment and to support, encourage, and stimulate the expansion of partial hospitalization services. Activities include educational discussions, consultation services, collaboration to establish standards, and monitoring of legislative developments. The AABHC has developed an Outcomes Measurement Protocol (1994) and an Implementing Outcomes Measurement in Behavioral Healthcare Manual (1995). *Formerly:* American Association for Partial Hospitalization (1995).

Association of American Cancer Institutes (AACI) *Founded:* 1959. *Headquarters:* Buffalo, NY. *Purpose:* To inform members of important legislative and program developments in the field and promote discussion among cancer center leadership throughout the world. Members are directors of cancer centers.

Association of American Indian Physicians (AAIP) *Founded:* 1971. *Headquarters:* Oklahoma City, OK. *Purpose:* To encourage American Indians to enter the health professions; to establish contracts with government agencies to provide consultation and other expert opinion regarding health care of American Indians and Alaskan Natives; and to receive contracts and grant monies and other forms of assistance from these sources. It serves physicians (medical doctors or doctors of osteopathy) of American Indian descent.

Association of American Medical Colleges (AAMC) *Founded:* 1876. *Headquarters:* Washington, DC. *Purpose:* To provide a centralized application service and offer management education programs for medical school deans, teaching hospital directors, department chairs, and service chiefs of affiliated hospitals. Develops and administers the Medical College Admissions Test (MCAT). Members include medical schools, graduate affiliate medical colleges, academic societies, teaching hospitals, and individuals interested in the advancement of medical education, biomedical research, and health care.

Association of American Physicians (AAP) *Founded:* 1886. *Headquarters:* Princeton, NJ. *Purpose:* A professional society of medical school faculty and clinical investigators.

Association of American Physicians and Surgeons (AAPS) *Founded:* 1943. *Headquarters:* Tucson, AZ. *Purpose:* To conduct an expert witness program and make available legal consultation services. It serves physicians interested in the socioeconomic and legal aspects of medical practice, such as medical economics, public relations, and legislation.

Association for Applied Psychoanalysis (AAP) *Founded:* 1952. *Headquarters:* Royal Palm Beach, FL. *Purpose:* To facilitate and promote training and research in applied psychoanalysis. It serves practicing and research psychoanalysts who have undergone at least 300 hours of personal psychoanalysis.

Association for Applied Psychophysiology and Biofeedback (AAPB) *Founded:* 1969. *Headquarters:* Wheat Ridge, CO. *Purpose:* To promote rapid exchange of ideas; offers continuing education. Members include persons interested in the interrelationship of external feedback systems, states of consciousness, and the physiological mechanisms involved.

Association for Assessment in Counseling (AAC) *Founded:* 1965. *Headquarters:* Alexandria, VA. *Purpose:* To support increasing competency in assessment, testing, measurement, and evaluation of professional counselors. Members are persons who plan, administer, and conduct testing programs, provide test scoring services, interpret and use test results, and develop evaluation instruments.

Association for the Behavioral Sciences and Medical Education (ABSAME) *Founded:* 1970. *Headquarters:* Phoenix, AZ. *Purpose:* To improve effectiveness, efficiency, and quality of health care through the application of social and behavioral science knowledge; to aid in continuing education; and to conduct programs for teachers, clinicians, researchers, and administrators in behavioral sciences. Serves as a member society of the Council of Academic Societies of the Association of American Medical Colleges for physicians and behavioral scientists committed to developing and advancing the teachings of behavioral science.

Association for Behavior Analysis (ABA) *Founded:* 1974. *Headquarters:* Kalamazoo, MI. *Purpose:* To conduct workshops and seminars in 16 areas including, for example, behavioral pharmacology and toxicology and developmental disabilities. Members are professionals, such as psychologists interested in the applied, experimental, and theoretical analysis of behavior.

Association for Birth Psychology (ABP) *Founded:* 1978. *Headquarters:* New York, NY. *Purpose:* To promote communication among professionals in the field. It serves obstetricians, pediatricians, midwives, nurses, psychotherapists, psychologists, counselors, social workers, sociologists, and other individuals interested in birth psychology, a developing discipline interested in the experience of birth and the correlation between the birth process and personality development.

Association of Black Cardiologists (ABC) *Founded:* 1974. *Headquarters:* Atlanta, GA. *Purpose:* To improve prevention and treatment of cardiovascular diseases. It serves physicians and other health professionals interested in lowering mortality and morbidity resulting from cardiovascular diseases.

Association of Black Nursing Faculty (ABNF) *Founded:* 1987. *Headquarters:* Lisle, IL. *Purpose:* To promote health-related issues and educational concerns of interest to the black community and the ABNF. Assists members in professional development; develops and sponsors continuing education activities; fosters networking and guidance in employment and recruitment activities; and promotes health-related issues of legislation, government programs, and community activities. Members are black nursing faculty teaching in baccalaureate and higher degree programs accredited by the National League for Nursing.

Association of Black Psychologists (ABPsi)
Founded: 1968. *Headquarters:* Washington, DC. *Purpose:* Serves psychologists and other persons interested in enhancing the psychological well-being of black people in America; defining mental health in consonance with newly established psychological concepts and standards; and developing policies for local, state, and national decision making that have impact on the mental health of the black community.

Association of Bone and Joint Surgeons (ABJS)
Founded: 1947. *Headquarters:* Rosemont, IL. *Purpose:* Serves orthopedic surgeons with information on clinical aspects of orthopedics and in training leaders in the specialty.

Association for the Care of Children's Health (ACCH)
Founded: 1965. *Headquarters:* Bethesda, MD. *Purpose:* To seek a better understanding of psychosocial needs of children in health care settings. It serves child life specialists, nurses, pediatricians, parents, child psychiatrists, psychologists, and social workers who are interested in the emotional, psychological, or social needs of children in pediatric health care settings, such as hospitals.

Association for Chemoreception Sciences (AChemS)
Founded: 1979. *Headquarters:* Tallahassee, FL. *Purpose:* To conduct research on the differences in human and animal perception of chemical stimuli in taste and smell. Members include research scientists, experimental psychologists, and industrial researchers interested in studying chemoreception (the physiological reception of chemical stimuli) by the senses of taste and smell.

Association for Child Psychoanalysis (ACP)
Founded: 1965. *Headquarters:* Ramsey, NJ. *Purpose:* To conduct national and international scientific meetings. Members are child psychoanalysts interested in discussion and dissemination of information in their field.

Association of Children's Prosthetic-Orthotic Clinics (ACPOC)
Founded: 1980. *Headquarters:* Rosemont, IL. *Purpose:* To promote the exchange of information concerning children's prosthetic-orthotic devices. Members are prosthetic-orthotic clinics for children.

Association of Chiropractic Colleges (ACC)
Founded: 1977. *Headquarters:* San Lorenzo, CA. *Purpose:* To serve as a clearinghouse of information for presidents of chiropractic colleges that are members of the Council on Chiropractic Education.

Association for Clinical Pastoral Education (ACPE)
Founded: 1967. *Headquarters:* Decatur, GA. *Purpose:* To accredit institutions, agencies, and parishes that offer clin-

ical pastoral education to theological students, ordained clergy, members of religious orders, and laypersons. It certifies ministers as supervisors of clinical pastoral education. Clinical pastoral education programs are offered as part of theological degree and graduate degree programs, as continuing education for the ministry, as training for chaplaincy and pastoral counseling, and as training for certification as supervisor of clinical pastoral education. Composed of certified clinical pastoral education supervisors, theological schools and seminaries, and denominational agencies.

Association of Community Cancer Centers (ACCC)
Founded: 1974. *Headquarters:* Rockville, MD. *Purpose:* To improve communication among providers of community cancer care and encourage clinical research using the community as a setting. Composed of institutions and individuals involved in the provision of community cancer care.

Association for Continuing Education (ACE)
Founded: 1982. *Headquarters:* Steamboat Springs, CO. *Purpose:* To conduct a weekly educational program for physicians, dentists, and allied health professionals pursuing continuing education credit in their fields. It conducts a weekly educational program.

Association for Death Education and Counseling (ADEC)
Founded: 1976. *Headquarters:* Hartford, CT. *Purpose:* To upgrade the quality of death education and patient care in hospitals, residential care facilities, and other organizations. Formulates and enforces codes of ethics and certifies death educators and counselors. Members are individuals and institutions interested in responsible and effective death education and counseling.

Association of Environmental Engineering Professors (AEEP)
Founded: 1963. *Headquarters:* Champaign, IL. *Purpose:* To study graduate curricula, entrance requirements, enrollment, and physical facilities at universities to establish criteria and improve education in environmental engineering. It serves college and university professors in the fields of environmental engineering; air, land, and water resources; pollution control; environmental health engineering; and related programs.

Association for Faculty in the Medical Humanities (AFMH)
Founded: 1983. *Headquarters:* McLean, VA. *Purpose:* To promote teaching and research in the humanities in the context of medical education and closer links among scholars in the humanities who work in medical education. Members are faculty in the humanities at medical schools.

Association of Food and Drug Officials (AFDO)
Founded: 1897. *Headquarters:* York, PA. *Purpose:* To prevent fraud in production, manufacture, distribution, and sale of food, drugs, cosmetics, and consumer product safety; to promote uniform laws and administrative procedure; and to disseminate information concerning law enforcement. Members are officials who enforce federal, state, district, county, and municipal laws and regulations

relating to food, drugs, cosmetics, and consumer product safety.

Association of Freestanding Radiation Oncology Centers (AFROC) *Founded:* 1986. *Headquarters:* Costa Mesa, CA. *Purpose:* To promote interests of freestanding radiation oncology centers to ensure high standards. It serves freestanding radiation oncology center employees, radiologists, oncologists, physicists, radiation therapists, and laboratory clinicians.

Association for Gay, Lesbian, and Bisexual Issues in Counseling (AGLBIC) *Founded:* 1974. *Headquarters:* Jenkintown, PA. *Purpose:* To educate heterosexual counselors on how to overcome homophobia and best help homosexual clients. Members are counselors and personnel and guidance workers interested in lesbian and gay issues.

Association of Gay and Lesbian Psychiatrists (AGLP) *Founded:* 1975. *Headquarters:* Jamaica Plain, MA. *Purpose:* To provide support for gay and lesbian psychiatrists; to further the understanding of members, colleagues, and the public on matters relating to homosexuality; and to promote improved mental health services for gays and lesbians. Members are gay, lesbian, and bisexual members of the American Psychiatric Association and other psychiatrists.

Association of Halfway House Alcoholism Programs of North America (AHHAP) *Founded:* 1966. *Headquarters:* Hopatcony, NJ. *Purpose:* Educating and serving halfway house programs through technical assistance, consultant services, workshops, and related services. Members are halfway house corporations, staff, board members, and individuals closely related to the halfway house movement.

Association of Healthcare Internal Auditors (AHIA) *Founded:* 1981. *Headquarters:* Washington, DC. *Purpose:* To promote cost containment and increased productivity in health care organizations through internal auditing. Members are health care internal auditors.

Association for Healthcare Philanthropy (AHP) *Founded:* 1967. *Headquarters:* Falls Church, VA. *Purpose:* To create cohesive body of healthcare fund development. It serves persons employed by health care organizations in the field of health care resource development and fundraising; hospital administrators and trustees; and hospitals.

Association of Health Facility Survey Agencies (AHFSA) *Founded:* 1968. *Headquarters:* Jefferson City, MO. *Purpose:* To exchange information between members and the Association of State and Territorial Health Officials (ASTHO); to constitute a reservoir of expertise to aid in the guidance of ASTHO; to improve the quality of health facility licensure and certification programs; and to provide a forum for state and territorial issues at the national level.

Association for Health Services Research (AHSR) *Founded:* 1981. *Headquarters:* Washington, DC. *Purpose:* To foster productive cooperation among researchers, public and private funding agencies, health professionals, policymakers, and the public; representing the views of members in the development and implementation of national legislative and administrative policies concerning health services research; and educating the public concerning the need for and contribution of health services research in improving health care in the United States. Members are individuals and organizations interested in health services research.

Association of Hospital-Based Nursing Facilities (AHBNF) *Founded:* 1991. *Headquarters:* Huntington Valley, PA. *Purpose:* To serve as a source of information for individuals involved with the provision of care in hospital-based nursing facilities; to work to ensure adequate reimbursement and shape national policies for hospital-based nursing facility care; and to organize the national network of hospital-based nursing care facility care providers.

Association for Hospital Medical Education (AHME) *Founded:* 1954. *Headquarters:* Washington, DC. *Purpose:* To conduct educational programs and workshops for members and other individuals in the area of graduate and continuing medical education. Members are physician directors of medical education in hospitals and clinics and other health profession educators.

Association for Humanistic Psychology (AHP) *Founded:* 1962. *Headquarters:* San Francisco, CA. *Purpose:* To provide a worldwide network for development of human sciences. Members are psychologists, social workers, clergy, educators, psychiatrists, and laypersons interested in the development of human sciences in ways that recognize distinctive human qualities and working toward fulfilling the innate capacities of people.

Association for Information Management (AIM) *Founded:* 1978. *Headquarters:* Silver Spring, MD. *Purpose:* Serves the management and career needs of information executives and managers and promotes information management as a management function. Members are information managers and chief information officers in corporations, government agencies, and nonprofit organizations.

Association of Maternal and Child Health Programs (AMCHP) *Founded:* 1944. *Headquarters:* Washington, DC. *Purpose:* To inform public and private sector decision makers of the health care needs of mothers and children; develop and recommend maternal and child health policies and programs; and develop coalitions with other organizations. Members are individuals responsible for or involved in the administration of state and territorial maternal and child health care programs and programs for children with special health care needs.

Association for Media Psychology (AMP) *Founded:* 1982. *Headquarters:* Washington, DC. *Purpose:* To publicize scientific psychology and promote research on the influence of the media on attitude, behavior, and well-being. Encourages innovative use of the media in the prevention of physical and mental disorders and assists mental health professionals in developing program ideas and ways of effectively communicating to the public through the media. Members include psychologists, psychiatrists, social workers, psychiatric nurses, and members of the communications media.

Association of Medical Education and Research in Substance Abuse (AMERSA) *Founded:* 1976. *Headquarters:* Providence, RI. *Purpose:* To provide general medical education to those who are involved with providing information on alcohol and other drug-related topics to medical professionals and students. Members are medical school faculty members and other persons interested in such topics.

Association of Medical School Pediatric Department Chairmen (AMSPDC) *Founded:* 1961. *Headquarters:* Chapel Hill, NC. *Purpose:* To foster education and research in the field of child health and human development. Members are chairs of the department of pediatrics of each accredited medical school in the United States and Canada.

Association of Mental Health Administrators (AMHA) *Founded:* 1959. *Headquarters:* Northbrook, IL. *Purpose:* Furthers education of administrators of services for persons with emotional disturbances, mental illness, mental retardation, developmental disabilities, and problems of alcohol and substance abuse.

Association of Mental Health Clergy (AMHC) *Founded:* 1948. *Headquarters:* Knoxville, TN. *Purpose:* To establish standards for clergy in psychiatric and mental health facilities. Members are clergy of all faiths (including pastors, priests, sisters, and rabbis) who minister to the religious needs of the mentally and emotionally troubled.

Association of Microbiological Diagnostic Manufacturers (AMDM) *Founded:* 1976. *Headquarters:* Washington, DC. *Purpose:* To inform members of regulatory policies and government legislation affecting the microbiological diagnostic equipment manufacturing industry. Members are medical device manufacturers, distributors, and users.

Association of Military Surgeons of the United States (AMSUS) *Founded:* 1891. *Headquarters:* Bethesda, MD. *Purpose:* To advance federal medicine and allied medical sciences in the federal medical services. Members include physicians, dentists, veterinarians, pharmacists, nurses, dietitians, physiotherapists, and other persons of commissioned rank or equivalent in the Army, Navy, Air Force, Public Health Service, Veterans Administration, Medical Reserve, and National Guard.

Association of Minority Health Professions Schools (AMHPS) *Founded:* 1978. *Headquarters:* Washington, DC. *Purpose:* To increase the number of minorities in health professions; improve the health of blacks in the United States; and increase the federal resources available to minority schools and students. Members are predominantly black health professional schools.

Association of Nurses in AIDS Care (ANAC) *Founded:* 1987. *Headquarters:* Reston, VA. *Purpose:* To foster the individual and collective professional development of nurses involved in the delivery of health care to persons infected or affected by HIV and to promote the health, welfare, and rights of all HIV infected persons.

Association of Oncology Social Workers (AOSW) *Founded:* 1984. *Headquarters:* Baltimore, MD. *Purpose:* To enable social workers in oncology to better serve the needs of clients, practitioners, managers, educators, and researchers. Serves accredited oncology social workers; associate members are professionals functioning as social workers without the professional degree and students in an accredited social work degree program.

Association of Operating Room Nurses (AORN) *Founded:* 1949. *Headquarters:* Denver, CO. *Purpose:* Studies existing practices and new developments in operating room nursing and education and sponsors national and regional institutes and scholarships. Members include registered nurses engaged in perioperative nursing on supervisory, teaching, or staff levels.

Association of Optometric Educators (AOE) *Founded:* 1972. *Headquarters:* Tahlequah, OK. *Purpose:* Concerned with faculty welfare, faculty-administration relations, faculty-student relations, and faculty-professional relations. Members are teachers in schools and colleges of optometry who are interested in enhancing the professional and academic status and conditions of services of optometric educators and in promoting communication among members.

Association of Osteopathic State Executive Directors (AOSED) *Founded:* 1918. *Headquarters:* Sacramento, CA. *Purpose:* To promote association procedures among members who are executives of divisional and affiliated societies of the American Osteopathic Association.

Association of Otolaryngology Administrators (AOA) *Founded:* 1983. *Headquarters:* Augusta, GA. *Purpose:* To provide a forum for interaction and exchange of information among otolaryngological managers and present educational programs. Members are composed of 360 persons employed in a managerial capacity for private or academic group medical practices specializing in otolaryngology.

Association of Pathology Chairs (APC) *Founded:* 1967. *Headquarters:* Bethesda, MD. *Purpose:* Acts as a communications center for exchange of information and for workshops on innovations for teaching and resident training, department administration, and relationships with governmental and other non-university agencies. Members are chairs of medical school departments of pathology.

Association of Pediatric Oncology Nurses (APON) *Founded:* 1973. *Headquarters:* Glenview, IL. *Purpose:* To encourage updating of literature, development of standards, and improved communication among nurses caring for children with cancer.

Association of Pediatric Oncology Social Workers (APOSW) *Founded:* 1977. *Headquarters:* St. Petersburg, FL. *Purpose:* Activities include advancing the practice of pediatric oncology social work and formulating and recording local and federal legislation relating to pediatric oncology. Members are social workers involved with pediatric cancer patients in medical settings.

The Association for Persons with Severe Handicaps (TASH) *Founded:* 1973. *Headquarters:* Baltimore, MD. *Purpose:* To ensure an autonomous, dignified lifestyle for all people with severe disabilities; to advocate quality education, from birth through adulthood; and to disseminate updated information on solutions to problems, research findings, trends, and practices relevant to people with severe disabilities.

Association for Pharmacoeconomics and Outcomes Research (APOR) *Founded:* 1995. *Headquarters:* Princeton, NJ. *Purpose:* To promote the science of pharmacoeconomics and health outcomes research and to act as a scientific leader relevant to research in the field.

Association of Physician Assistant Programs (APAP) *Founded:* 1972. *Headquarters:* Alexandria, VA. *Purpose:* To assist in the development and organization of educational curricula for physician assistant programs and contribute to defining the roles of physician assistants in the field of medicine. Sponsors the Annual Survey of Physician Assistant Educational Programs in the United States. Members consist of educational institutions with training programs for assistants to primary care and surgical physicians.

Association of Physician's Assistants in Cardio-Vascular Surgery (APACVS) *Founded:* 1981. *Headquarters:* Reston, VA. *Purpose:* To assist in defining the role of physician assistants in the field of cardiovascular surgery through educational forums. Offers a placement service and compiles statistics. Members are physician assistants who work with cardiovascular surgeons.

Association for Politics and the Life Sciences (APLS) *Founded:* 1980. *Headquarters:* DeKalb, IL. *Purpose:* To emphasize study of behavioral biology as it relates to political science and the legal and public policy implications of advances in biotechnology and biomedical technology. Members are individuals and libraries interested in the interaction of human biology and public policy.

Association of Polysomnographic Technologists (APT) *Founded:* 1978. *Headquarters:* Lenexa, KS. *Purpose:* To establish standards for polysomnographic technology. Members are individuals who practice polysomnography in research or clinical settings.

Association for Practitioners in Infection Control and Epidemiology *See* Association for Professionals in Infection Control.

Association of Professional Baseball Physicians (APBP) *Founded:* 1970. *Headquarters:* Edina, MN. *Purpose:* To provide the best possible medical care to all players and associated personnel. Conducts drug abuse seminars on topics such as amphetamine, steroid, and cocaine use by athletes. It serves physicians and surgeons of the professional baseball teams in the United States.

Association of Professional Sleep Societies (APSS) *Founded:* 1985. *Headquarters:* Rochester, MN. *Purpose:* Composed of the Sleep Research Society, American Sleep Disorders Association, and Association of Polysomnographic Technologists, it works to facilitate sleep research and development of sleep disorders medicine by encouraging cooperation and exchange of information among its members.

Association for Professionals in Infection Control (APIC) *Founded:* 1972. *Headquarters:* Washington, DC. *Purpose:* To promote quality research and standardization of practices and procedures; to develop communications among members; and to assess and influence legislation related to the field. Members include physicians, nurses, epidemiologists, microbiologists, medical technicians, pharmacists, and sanitarians interested in infection control. *Formerly:* Association for Practitioners in Infection Control and Epidemiology (1994).

Association of Professors of Gynecology and Obstetrics (APGO) *Founded:* 1962. *Headquarters:* Washington, DC. *Purpose:* To improve the study of gynecology and obstetrics and provide a means of exchanging information relating to the programs of study, teaching methods, and research activities of such departments. Members include departments of obstetrics and gynecology in approved medical schools in the United States and Canada.

Association of Professors of Medicine (APM) *Founded:* 1954. *Headquarters:* Washington, DC. *Purpose:* To conduct educational programs for 125 heads of departments of medicine (internal medicine) in U.S. medical schools.

Association of Program Directors in Internal Medicine (APDIM) *Founded:* 1977. *Headquarters:* Washington, DC. *Purpose:* To advance medical education through assisting accredited hospital internal medicine residency training programs in the United States and Puerto Rico. Conducts annual courses for chief residents and program directors. Members are physicians in internal medicine, including departmental chairs and directors of internal medicine, directors of residency-training programs, associate program directors, medical education directors, and chiefs of medical services.

Association for Psychoanalytic Medicine (APM) *Founded:* 1945. *Headquarters:* Bronx, NY. *Purpose:* To provide a forum on psychoanalytic developments for its membership and the community and to conduct postgraduate seminars. Members include physicians who are psychoanalysts.

Association for Psychological Type (APT) *Founded:* 1979. *Headquarters:* Kansas City, MO. *Purpose:* To bring together individuals interested in organizational development, religious communities, management, education, and counseling, and who are interested in psychological type, the Myers-Briggs Type Indicator, and the works of Carl G. Jung, the Swiss psychologist and founder of analytical psychology.

Association of Psychology Postdoctoral and Internship Centers (APPIC) *Founded:* 1968. *Headquarters:* Washington, DC. *Purpose:* Serves as a clearinghouse to provide college students with internship placement assistance at member facilities. Members are Veterans Administration hospitals, medical centers, state hospitals, university counseling centers, and other facilities that provide internship and postdoctoral programs in professional psychology.

Association for Quality and Participation (AQP) *Founded:* 1977. *Headquarters:* Cincinnati, OH. *Purpose:* To promote quality and participation in the workplace by providing education, conferences, and training. Members include quality managers, manufacturing executives, professionals in personnel relations, organization presidents, and employee involvement professionals, such as training directors, facilitators, and coordinators.

Association of Rehabilitation Nurses (ARN) *Founded:* 1974. *Headquarters:* Glenview, IL. *Purpose:* Committees involve members in issues of organizational, local, and national importance and provide an avenue to effect change. Members are registered nurses interested in or actively engaged in the practice of rehabilitation nursing.

Association of Reproductive Health Professionals (ARHP) *Founded:* 1963. *Headquarters:* Washington, DC. *Purpose:* To support the right of women to decide to sustain or terminate their pregnancies. Members are physicians, scientists, educators, and reproductive health professionals interested in educating the public and health professionals on matters pertaining to reproductive health, including sexuality, contraception, prevention of sexually transmitted disease, family planning, and abortion.

Association for Research in Nervous and Mental Disease (ARNMD) *Founded:* 1920. *Headquarters:* New York, NY. *Purpose:* To provide forum for exchange of ideas among members, who are individuals engaged in the practice or research of neurology, neurosurgery, or psychiatry or who are members of neurologic or psychiatric societies.

Association for Research in Vision and Ophthalmology (ARVO) *Founded:* 1928. *Headquarters:* Bethesda, MD. *Purpose:* To encourage and assist research, training, publication, and dissemination of knowledge in vision and ophthalmology.

Association of Retired Americans (ARA) *Founded:* 1973. *Headquarters:* Indianapolis, IN. *Purpose:* To offer a program of high-quality, low-cost benefits and services to members, such as discounts on prescriptions, eyeglasses, and hearing aids, and insurance benefits including emergency air medical transportation. Assists governmental bodies and agencies with the development of programs

and legislation that benefit and promote the well-being of retired Americans. Members are senior Americans interested in group benefits.

Association of Rheumatology Health Professionals (ARHP) *See* American College of Rheumatology.

Association of Schools of Allied Health Professions (ASAHP) *Founded:* 1967. *Headquarters:* unknown. *Purpose:* To enhance the effectiveness of education for the allied health professions. Provides a forum which links leaders in allied health education with state and national policy makers in government, business, and industry in efforts to effect relevant and appropriate changes in health care policy. Members include administrators, educators, and others who are concerned with critical issues affecting allied health education.

Association of Schools and Colleges of Optometry (ASCO) *Founded:* 1941. *Headquarters:* Rockville, MD. *Purpose:* To encourage optometric education and to foster optometric and visual research. Members are colleges of optometry in the United States and two in Canada.

Association of Schools of Public Health (ASPH) *Founded:* 1941. *Headquarters:* Washington, DC. *Purpose:* To serve as an information center for governmental and private groups. Members are accredited graduate schools of public health interested in the advancement of academic public health programs.

Association of State Drinking Water Administrators (ASDWA) *Founded:* 1984. *Headquarters:* Washington, DC. *Purpose:* To meet the communication and coordination needs of state drinking water program managers and facilitate the exchange of information and experience among state drinking water agencies. Acts as a collective voice for the protection of public health through assurance of high-quality drinking water overseeing the implementation of the Safe Drinking Water Act and acting as a liaison with Congress and the Environmental Protection Agency. It serves managers of state and territorial drinking water programs and state regulatory personnel.

Association of State and Territorial Dental Directors (ASTDD) *Founded:* unknown. *Headquarters:* Minneapolis, MN. *Purpose:* To provide a forum for consideration of dental health administrative problems for directors of state and territorial dental programs.

Association of State and Territorial Directors of Nursing (ASTDN) *Founded:* 1935. *Headquarters:* Phoenix, AZ. *Purpose:* To serve as a channel for sharing methods and disseminate information to increase the effectiveness of public health nursing services. Members are directors of nursing in the states and territories.

Association of State and Territorial Directors of Public Health Education (ASTDPHE) *Founded:* 1946. *Headquarters:* Santa Fe, NM. *Purpose:* To develop, among other activities, practice guidelines and support collection and dissemination of data and information relevant to public health education. As a division of the Association of State and Territorial Health Officials, membership is composed of directors of public health education in state and territorial departments of health and Native American health service areas.

Association of State and Territorial Health Officials (ASTHO) *Founded:* 1942. *Headquarters:* Washington, DC. *Purpose:* To represent state and territorial health officers on matters of federal health, legislation, and policies and aid public or private agencies dealing with human health, especially in interstate and federal relationships. Members are executive officers of state and territorial health departments.

Association for the Study of Dreams (ASD) *Founded:* 1984. *Headquarters:* Vienna, VA. *Purpose:* To provide an interdisciplinary forum for the promotion and public dissemination of information regarding research into the physiological and therapeutic aspects of dreams and their interpretation. Members are medical professionals, sociologists, counselors, educators, researchers, and other individuals whose disciplines are related to the study of dreams and dreaming.

Association for Surgical Education (ASE) *Founded:* 1980. *Headquarters:* Salt Lake City, UT. *Purpose:* To develop and disseminate information on motivation, techniques, research, and applications for presenting curricula in undergraduate surgical education. Serves surgeons and individuals involved in undergraduate surgical education.

Association of Surgical Technologists (AST) *Founded:* 1969. *Headquarters:* Englewood, CO. *Purpose:* To bring together surgical technologists and other health professionals and organizations and to promote quality patient care by developing educational programs, promoting professional standards and credentials, providing a forum for exchanging ideas, monitoring the changing health care environment, fostering other opportunities for personal and professional growth, and achieving significant internal and external support for AST's goals and objectives.

Association for Systems Management (ASM) *Founded:* 1947. *Headquarters:* Cleveland, OH. *Purpose:* To offer seminars, conferences, and courses in all phases of information systems and management. Members are executives and specialists in management information systems serving business, commerce, education, government, and the military.

Association of Teachers of Maternal and Child Health (ATMCH) *Founded:* 1968. *Headquarters:* Arlington, VA. *Purpose:* To promote the teaching and research of maternal and child health programs in public health schools and professional schools in the United States and to participate in the development and support of policy initiatives related to the field. Members are faculty and graduate students in maternal and child health.

Association of Teachers of Preventive Medicine (ATPM) *Founded:* 1942 . *Headquarters:* Washington, DC. *Purpose:* To advance prevention and public health in the education of physicians and other health profession-

als. The projects which ATPM is currently coordinating, include: Preventive Curriculum Assistance Program (PCAP); ATPM's Immunization Initiatives; Physicians' HIV Prevention Education Project; Partners in Promoting Collaborative Research; and ATPM Preventive Medicine and Public Health Fellowship program. ATPM's projects are made possible through the support of the Centers for Disease Control and Prevention (CDC), the Health Care Financing Administration, the Health Resources and Services Administration, and the Office of Disease Prevention and Health Promotion. ATPM regularly provides Congressional testimony supporting funding for preventive medicine and public health education, practice and research.

Association of Technical Personnel in Ophthalmology (ATPO) *Founded:* 1969. *Headquarters:* San Francisco, CA. *Purpose:* To advance and preserve vision and health through improved medical eye care. Members are certified and noncertified allied health personnel in ophthalmology.

Association for the Treatment of Sexual Abusers (ABTSA) *Founded:* 1985. *Headquarters:* Beaverton, OR. *Purpose:* To provide training to professionals on the treatment of sex offenders and offers instruction in the operation of penile plethysmography, a device used to determine and record variations in the size of the penis due to the amount of blood present in it. Members include professionals working with sex offenders or victims of sexual assault.

Association of University Anesthesiologists (AUA) *Founded:* 1953. *Headquarters:* Seattle, WA. *Purpose:* To encourage members to pursue original investigations in the clinic and the laboratory and develop methods of teaching anesthesiology. Members are academic anesthesiologists from medical school faculties.

Association of University Environmental Health Sciences Centers (AUEHSC) *Founded:* 1980. *Headquarters:* New York, NY. *Purpose:* To provide a focused research effort on a particular environmental health problem, to bring together many scientific disciplines to solve an environmental problem, to attract and train young investigators to the field, to answer questions from the public on environmental problems, and to help the National Institute of Environmental Health Sciences (NIEHS) identify emerging problems in the environmental health field. AUEHSC is an independent consortium of research institutions supported by grants from NIEHS.

Association of University Professors of Ophthalmology (AUPO) *Founded:* 1966. *Headquarters:* San Francisco, CA. *Purpose:* To facilitate exchange of ideas among members who are heads of departments or divisions of ophthalmology in accredited medical schools in the United States, and directors of ophthalmology residency programs in institutions not connected to medical schools.

Association of University Programs in Health Administration (AUPHA) *Founded:* 1948. *Head-*

quarters: Arlington, VA. *Purpose:* To improve the quality of education in health services administration. Members are universities offering graduate and undergraduate study in health services and hospital administration.

Association of University Programs in Occupational Health and Safety (AUPOHS) *Founded:* 1977. *Headquarters:* Atlanta, GA. *Purpose:* To provide a forum for the exchange of information among members on graduate training in occupational medicine, occupational health nursing, industrial hygiene, and industrial safety engineering. Works in conjunction with the National Institute for Occupational Safety and Health to facilitate the operation of training programs. Members are universities offering graduate training and continuing education for occupational health safety professionals.

Association of University Radiologists (AUR) *Founded:* 1953. *Headquarters:* Reston, VA. *Purpose:* To provide a forum for university-based radiologists to present and discuss results of research, teaching, and administrative issues. It serves physicians and scientists who have been appointed to a university faculty.

Association for Vital Records and Health Statistics (AVRHS) *Founded:* 1933. *Headquarters:* Atlanta, GA. *Purpose:* Serves officials of state and local health agencies responsible for registration, tabulation, and analysis of births, deaths, fetal deaths, marriages, divorces, and other health statistics.

Association for Women in Psychology (AWP) *Founded:* 1969. *Headquarters:* Los Angeles, CA. *Purpose:* To end the role that the association feels psychology has had in perpetuating unscientific and unquestioned assumptions about the "natures" of women and men, and encouraging unbiased psychological research on sex and gender in order to establish facts and expose myths. Members are psychologists.

Association of Women's Health, Obstetric, and Neonatal Nurses (AWHONN) *Founded:* 1969. *Headquarters:* Washington, DC. *Purpose:* To sponsor educational meetings and stimulate interest in obstetric, gynecologic, and neonatal nursing. Members are registered nurses and allied health workers with an interest in obstetric, gynecologic, and neonatal nursing.

Association for Worksite Health Promotion (AWHP) *Founded:* 1974. *Headquarters:* Northbrook, IL. *Purpose:* To recommend adherence to American College of Sports Medicine qualifications and professional standards for fitness directors and stimulate active research in, and serves as a clearinghouse on, employee health and fitness. Sponsors seminars and an educational committee that studies effectiveness of preparation, training programs, and certification. Members include health and fitness professionals employed by major companies to conduct fitness programs for employees; interested persons in personnel and sales for fitness facilities; health educators and other health professionals; and students interested in the field.

AVSC International (AVSC) *Founded:* 1943. *Headquarters:* New York, NY. *Purpose:* To disseminate information on voluntary surgical contraception, to promote safer, simpler techniques in surgical contraception, and to foster, stimulate, and support voluntary surgical contraception activities in various types of health programs throughout the world by providing local medical groups with training equipment and technical assistance.

Bb

Baromedical Nurses Association (BNA) *Founded:* 1985. *Headquarters:* Palm Desert, CA. *Purpose:* To define, develop, and promote the standards of baromedical nursing. It serves registered nurses practicing baromedicine (hyperbaric medicine), involved in research relating to baromedical nursing, completing basic orientation in baromedicine, or contributing to literature on baromedicine or baromedical nursing.

Bay Area Physicians for Human Rights (BAPHR) *Founded:* 1977. *Headquarters:* San Francisco, CA. *Purpose:* To maintain liaison with public officials about gay and lesbian health concerns and to offer support to gay and lesbian physicians through social functions and consciousness-raising groups. Members include graduates of and students in approved schools of medicine and osteopathic medicine, dentistry, and podiatry interested in improving the quality of medical care for gay and lesbian patients and educating the public about health care needs of the homosexual.

Bayer Institute for Health Care Communication *Founded:* 1987. *Headquarters:* West Haven, CT. *Purpose:* To improve communication between physicians and patients, promote research directly related to provider-patient communication in health-care settings, and conduct workshops on the health care communication process for hospitals, medical societies, HMOs, and medical schools.

Judge David L. Bazelon Center for Mental Health Law *Founded:* 1972. *Headquarters:* Washington, DC. *Purpose:* To clarify, establish, and enforce the legal rights of people with mental retardation and developmental disabilities. It provides technical assistance and training to lawyers, consumers, providers of mental health and special education services, and policymakers at federal, state, and local levels. Staff attorneys have represented individual plaintiffs and leading national consumer and professional associations in landmark lawsuits that have established many rights of people with mental retardation and developmental disabilities.

Behavior Genetics Association (BGA) *Founded:* 1971. *Headquarters:* St. Louis, MO. *Purpose:* To encourage and aid the education and training of research workers in the field of behavior genetics and the aiding in public dissemination and interpretation of information concerning the interrelationship of genetics and behavior and its implications for health, human development, and education. Members are individuals engaged in teaching or research in some area of behavior genetics.

Behavioral Pharmacology Society (BPS) *Founded:* 1957. *Headquarters:* Atlanta, GA. *Purpose:* Serves professional psychologists and pharmacologists interested in behavioral pharmacology and psychopharmacology or the connection between drugs and behavior.

Better Vision Institute (BVI) *See* Vision Council of America.

Bio-Electro-Magnetics Institute (BEMI) *Founded:* 1986. *Headquarters:* Reno, NV. *Purpose:* To promote the fields of energy field medicine and bioenergetics. Members are medical professionals, alternative health practitioners, and other individuals interested in the study of the relationship between living organisms and electromagnetic fields and radiation.

Bioelectromagnetics Society (BEMS) *Founded:* 1978. *Headquarters:* Frederick, MD. *Purpose:* To encourage clinical study in the bioelectromagnetics field and disseminate information. Members are scientists, engineers, and other individuals who conduct research in or are interested in the interaction of electromagnetic energy and acoustic energy with biological systems.

Biological Photographic Association (BPA) *Founded:* 1931. *Headquarters:* Atlanta, GA. *Purpose:* To advance the techniques of biophotography and biomedical communications through meetings, seminars, and workshops. It has established a board of registry to offer qualifying examinations for registered biological photographers. Members are photographers, technicians, doctors, scientists, educators, and other individuals interested in photography in the health sciences and related fields.

Biological Stain Commission (BSC) *Founded:* 1922. *Headquarters:* Rochester, NY. *Purpose:* To conduct a program of stain certification, in cooperation with manufacturers and distributors. Members are scientists in biology, medicine, and related fields working for the establishment of standards for the identification, purity, performance, and labeling of the more important biological stains, in order to improve their reliability as tools in biological research.

Biomedical Engineering Society (BMES) *Founded:* 1968. *Headquarters:* Culver City, CA. *Purpose:* To encourage development, dissemination, integration, and utilization of knowledge in biomedical engineering fields. Members are engineers, physicians, managers, and university professors representing all fields of biomedical engineering.

Birth Support Providers, International (BSPI) *Founded:* 1985. *Headquarters:* Novato, CA. *Purpose:* To provide information, resources, and referrals to childbearing families; conduct training workshops; and award childbirth assistant certification.

Black Psychiatrists of America (BPA) *Founded:* 1968. *Headquarters:* Oakland, CA. *Purpose:* To provide a resource for information, education and training on the special mental health needs of the black population. It provides a network mechanism for member psychiatrists and other national mental health organizations.

Blue Cross and Blue Shield Association (BCBSA) *Founded:* 1982. *Headquarters:* Chicago, IL. *Purpose:* To promote betterment of public health and security, secure widest acceptance of voluntary nonprofit prepayment of health services. Contracts with government for administration of federal health programs. It is a federation of nonprofit health care prepayment insurance plans, developed and sponsored by hospitals and physicians, called Blue Cross (BC) and Blue Shield (BS) plans, respectively.

Board of Certification in Pedorthics (BCP) *Founded:* 1958. *Headquarters:* Columbia, MD. *Purpose:* To sponsor a mandatory certification program and seek to maintain high standards of practice in pedorthics and facilitate continuing education of members who are pedorthists.

Board of Certified Hazard Control Management (BCHCM) *Founded:* 1976. *Headquarters:* Bethesda, MD. *Purpose:* To evaluate and certify individuals involved primarily in the administration of safety and health programs. Establishes curricula in conjunction with colleges, universities, and other training institutions to better prepare hazard control managers for their duties. Members are safety managers interested in the establishment of professional standards and refinement in the industry.

Board of Certified Safety Professionals (BCSP) *Founded:* 1969. *Headquarters:* Savoy, IL. *Purpose:* Grants the designation of certified safety professional (CSP) to safety engineers, industrial hygienists, safety managers, fire protection engineers, and other persons who have passed the two written examinations administered by the board and who have met other established criteria.

Board of Nephrology Examiners, Nursing and Technology (BONENT) *Founded:* 1974. *Headquarters:* Lenexa, KS. *Purpose:* To administer certification examinations for specific specialties in nephrology, to ensure quality care through the establishment of professional certification standards, and to encourage continuing education and communication among nephrology professionals. It serves registered nurses, licensed practical nurses, licensed vocational nurses, and dialysis technicians.

Brain Injury Association (BIA) *Founded:* 1980. *Headquarters:* Washington, DC. *Purpose:* To increase public awareness of brain injury; to provide education and information about brain injury; and to promote linkage to support groups and local resources through a toll-free family helpline. The national association has state affiliates. *Formerly:* National Head Injury Foundation (NHIF).

Bright Futures projects *See* National Center for Education in Maternal and Child Health.

Bureau of Health Professions *See* Government Organizations (Department of Health and Human Services, HRSA).

Bureau of Health Resources Development *See* Government Organizations (Department of Health and Human Services, HRSA).

Bureau of Primary Health Care *See* Government Organizations (Department of Health and Human Services, HRSA).

American Osteopathic Association (AOA) *Founded:* 1897. *Headquarters:* Chicago, IL. *Purpose:* To promote and preserve the practice rights of osteopathic doctors; to educate key decision makers in government, managed care plans, and third party payers about the benefits of osteopathic care; and to work to guarantee visibility for the profession with government policy makers. Administers programs for certification of both hospitals and physicians.

Business Roundtable (BR) *Founded:* 1972. *Headquarters:* Washington, DC. *Purpose:* An influential lobbying force representing American business, members examine public issues that affect the economy and develop positions that seek to reflect sound economic and social principles. Twelve task forces conduct extensive research, often drawing on the staffs of member companies for talent and expertise. Members are major U.S. corporations represented by their chief executive officers.

Cardiovascular Credentialing International (CCI) *Founded:* 1988. *Headquarters:* Virginia Beach, VA. *Purpose:* To conduct testing of allied health professionals throughout the United States and Canada and provide study guides and reliability and validity testing. It serves cardiovascular and cardiopulmonary technicians involved in the allied health professions. Formed by merger of National Board of Cardiovascular Technology and Cardiovascular Credentialing International.

Catecholamine Club (CC) *Founded:* 1969. *Headquarters:* Lawrence, KS. *Purpose:* To provide a forum for discussion for neuroscience researchers interested in catecholamines.

Catholic Health Association of the United States (CHA) *Founded:* 1915. *Headquarters:* St. Louis, MO. *Purpose:* To participate in the life of the Church by advancing health care ministry. Members are Catholic hospitals, health care facilities, religious orders, health care systems, and extended care facilities.

Catholic Medical Association *Founded:* 1932. *Headquarters:* Elm Grove, WI. *Purpose:* To provide a forum for doctors who wish to practice medicine and comment on medical issues in accordance with the teachings of the Catholic Church. Products include a scholarly medical review and a national convention which issues position papers and resolutions on a variety of medical-moral issues. *Formerly:* National Federation of Catholic Physicians Guilds (1996).

Catholic Medical Mission Board (CMMB) *Founded:* 1928. *Headquarters:* New York, NY. *Purpose:* To provide medical supplies and lay personnel to assist the staffs of Catholic medical institutions in all areas of the world.

CDC National AIDS Clearinghouse (NAC) *Founded:* 1987. *Headquarters:* Rockville, MD. *Purpose:* A service of the Centers for Disease Control and Prevention that collects, analyzes, and disseminates information on acquired immunodeficiency syndrome (AIDS), primarily for health professionals, educators, social service workers, attorneys, employers and human resource professionals, state HIV/AIDS programs, community organizations, and service associations.

Center for Attitudinal Healing (CAH) *Founded:* 1975. *Headquarters:* Sausalito, CA. *Purpose:* To offer support groups and arrange hospital and home visits for children, youth, and adults. Supplements traditional health care by offering free services in attitudinal healing for children and adults with life-threatening illnesses or other crises.

Center for Biologics Evaluation and Research *See* Government Organizations (Department of Health and Human Services, CDC).

Center for Clinical Effectiveness (CCE) *See* Henry Ford Health System.

Center for Clinical Quality Evaluation (CCQE) *Founded:* 1986. *Headquarters:* Washington, DC. *Purpose:* To develop, apply, and evaluate review criteria and outreach based on AHCPR guidelines. *Formerly:* American Medical Review Research Center (1995).

Center for Cost and Financing Studies *See* Government Organizations (Department of Health and Human Services, AHCPR).

Center for Dance Medicine (CDM) *Founded:* 1978. *Headquarters:* New York, NY. *Purpose:* To educate dancers about their bodies and preventive medicine in order to help them avoid injuries. Conducts workshops and seminars.

Center for Death Education and Research (CDER) *Founded:* 1969. *Headquarters:* Minneapolis, MN. *Purpose:* To sponsor research into grief and bereavement and to study attitudes and responses to death and dying.

Center for Devices and Radiological Health *See* Government Organizations (Department of Health and Human Services, CDC).

Center for Early Adolescence (CEA) *Founded:* 1978. *Headquarters:* Carrsboro, NC. *Purpose:* To provide training, technical assistance, and information services to agencies and individuals, such as teachers, social service personnel, physicians, and clergy, who work with youth aged 10 to 15 years.

Center for Ethics in Managed Care   *See* Harvard Pilgrim Health Care.

Center for Food Safety and Applied Nutrition   *See* Government Organizations (Department of Health and Human Services, CDC).

Center for Hazardous Materials Research (CHMR)   *Founded:* 1985. *Headquarters:* Pittsburgh, PA. *Purpose:* A nonmembership organization that conducts applied research programs on the use and disposal of hazardous materials and wastes. It offers many services, such as technical assistance to industry and government in the areas of pollution prevention, recycling, and waste minimization and management; technical services to communities relating to hazardous waste site cleanup; and educational and training programs in health and safety, emergency response, and hazardous materials handling.

Center for Healthcare Environmental Management (CHEM)   *See* ECRI.

Center for Health Care Rights (CHCR)   *Founded:* 1984. *Headquarters:* Los Angeles, CA. *Purpose:* To assure that consumers receive the health care benefits to which they are entitled and to increase consumer protections in the health care system.

Center for Health Care Technology   *See* Government Organizations (Department of Health and Human Services, AHCPR).

Center for Health Information Dissemination   *See* Government Organizations (Department of Health and Human Services, AHCPR).

Center for Humane Options in Childbirth Experiences (CHOICE)   *Founded:* 1977. *Headquarters:* Columbus, OH. *Purpose:* Trains and certifies attendants to attend or coach births and acts as a consumer advocate for hospital births. Members are medical professionals, paraprofessionals, and other individuals who teach and encourage parents, parents-to-be groups, and other persons working in family-oriented hospital birth centers and out-of-hospital situations.

Center to Improve Care of the Dying (CICD)   *Founded:* 1986. *Headquarters:* Washington, DC (George Washington University Medical Center). *Purpose:* To offer an interdisciplinary service of committed individuals, engaged in research, public advocacy, and education activities to improve the care of the dying and their families. Key projects and activities of CICD are SUPPORT (Study to Understand Prognoses and Preferences for Outcomes and Risks of Treatment), TIME (Toolkit of Instruments to Measure End of life care), advocacy and testimony to oppose physician-assisted suicide, advocacy for the Compassionate Care Bill (1997), and Handbook for Mortals (forthcoming 1998) for dying patients and their families.

Center for Information Technology   *See* Government Organizations (Department of Health and Human Services, AHCPR).

Center for Medical Consumers and Health Care Information (CMC)   *Founded:* 1976. *Headquarters:* New York, NY. *Purpose:* To encourage individuals to make a critical evaluation of all information received from health professionals, to use medical services more selectively, and to understand the limitations of modern medicine. Promotes awareness that life-style choices, such as smoking, exercise habits, and nutritional practices, have more effect on health than access to medical care.

Center for Mental Health Services   *See* Government Organizations (Department of Health and Human Services, SAMHSA).

Center for Organization and Delivery Studies   *See* Government Organizations (Department of Health and Human Services, AHCPR).

Center for Outcomes and Effectiveness Research   *See* Government Organizations (Department of Health and Human Services, AHCPR).

Center for Quality Measurement and Improvement   *See* Government Organizations (Department of Health and Human Services, AHCPR).

Center for Research in Ambulatory Health Care Administration (CRAHCA)   *Founded:* 1973. *Headquarters:* Englewood, CO. *Purpose:* To assist in upgrading the quality of medical care through innovative education programs and research on management systems, cost, and productivity. Works with administrators of medical group practices in the United States, Canada, Mexico, and Europe.

Center for the Rights of the Terminally Ill (CRTI)   *Founded:* 1986. *Headquarters:* Hurst, TX. *Purpose:* To oppose euthanasia, assisted suicide, and abortion; to oppose "living will" legislation as unnecessary and dangerous; and to promote a federal conscience clause law that would allow health professionals to decline to perform any act of omission or commission that would cause or hasten the death of a patient. Members are physicians, nurses, attorneys, pro-life organizations, and disability rights groups seeking to secure for the elderly, the handicapped, and the sick and dying the right to competent, compassionate, and ethical health care.

Center for Science in the Public Interest (CSPI)   *Founded:* 1971. *Headquarters:* Washington, DC. *Purpose:* To monitor current research and federal agencies that oversee food safety, trade, and nutrition. It serves scientists, nutrition educators, journalists, and lawyers interested in the effects of science and technology on society.

Center for the Study of Aging (CSA)   *Founded:* 1957. *Headquarters:* Washington, DC. *Purpose:* To promote education, research, and training, and provide leadership in the field of health and fitness for older people. Its services include programs for volunteers and professionals in aging, gerontology, geriatrics, wellness, fitness and health, and consultant services, including adult day care, nutrition, nursing homes, and retirement.

Center for the Study of Pharmacy and Therapeutics for the Elderly (CSPTE) *Founded:* 1978. *Headquarters:* Baltimore, MD. *Purpose:* To conduct research in pharmacotherapeutic and pharmacodynamic geriatrics and gerontology.

Center for Substance Abuse Prevention *See* Government Organizations (Department of Health and Human Services, SAMHSA).

Center for Substance Abuse Treatment *See* Government Organizations (Department of Health and Human Services, SAMHSA).

Center for the Well-Being of Health Professionals (CWBHP) *Founded:* 1979. *Headquarters:* Durham, NC. *Purpose:* To promote the well-being of health professionals and their families through preventive education on manifestations of disabilities, increased awareness about the stresses inherent in the system of providing health services, and efforts to improve and maintain effectiveness. Conducts research and supports efforts to study the incidence and causes of professional impairment, with prevention as a goal. It serves health and other professional associations.

Centers for Disease Control and Prevention (CDC) *See* Government Organizations (Department of Health and Human Services).

Central Neuropsychiatric Association (CNPA) *Founded:* 1922. *Headquarters:* Prairie Village, KS. *Purpose:* To promote neuropsychiatry and related fields through presentations on theoretical and chemical topics. Fosters friendly interaction and sociability among neurologists, psychiatrists, and neurosurgeons. It serves neurologists, neurosurgeons, and psychiatrists.

Central Society for Clinical Research (CSCR) *Founded:* 1928. *Headquarters:* Chicago, IL. *Purpose:* To foster the advancement of medical science; cultivation of clinical research; sponsorship of scientific meetings. Composed of individuals who have accomplished a meritorious original investigation in the clinical or allied sciences of medicine and who enjoy unimpeachable moral standing in the profession.

Certification Board for Music Therapists (CBMT) *Founded:* 1982. *Headquarters:* Midlothian, VA. *Purpose:* Certifies and recertifies (every five years) professional music therapists.

Chain Drug Marketing Associates (CDMA) *Founded:* 1988. *Headquarters:* Deerfield, IL. *Purpose:* To represent members in the market for merchandise. Members are drug store chains located in the United States, Puerto Rico, and Canada.

Child Abuse Institute of Research (CAIR) *Founded:* 1988. *Headquarters:* Cincinnati, OH. *Purpose:* To promote education and research into the cause and prevention of child abuse. Members are individuals interested in improving the quality of life for children by focusing on the problems of child abuse.

Child Abuse Listening and Mediation (CALM) *Founded:* 1970. *Headquarters:* Santa Barbara, CA. *Purpose:* To provide emergency child care for parents under stress; conducts a program of public information and education and an in-school education program for students, parents, and teachers on prevention and recognition of child maltreatment. Conducts a social service program to prevent and treat sexual, physical, and emotional abuse of children, and offers early intervention for stressed families.

Child Life Council (CLC) *Founded:* 1982. *Headquarters:* Rockville, MD. *Purpose:* To promote psychological well-being and optimum development of children, adolescents, and their families in the health care setting. It serves child life personnel, patient activities specialists, and students in the field.

Child Neurology Society (CNS) *Founded:* 1971. *Headquarters:* St. Paul, MN. *Purpose:* To foster the discipline of child neurology and the welfare of children with neurological disorders.. It serves neurologists certified by the American Board of Psychiatry and Neurology and other individuals specializing in child neurology.

Child Nutrition Forum (CNF) *Founded:* 1981. *Headquarters:* Washington, DC. *Purpose:* To provide a liaison among diverse organizations that support adequately funded and effective food programs for children. Members are organizations involved in agriculture, civil rights, education, and nutrition advocacy, as well as consumer and religious groups, unions, and elected officials.

Child Welfare Institute (CWI) *Founded:* 1984. *Headquarters:* Atlanta, GA. *Purpose:* Supports programs promoting foster parenting, minor emancipation (endowing minors with legal rights of adults), adoption, reunification of foster children with their birth parents, child abuse and neglect, and other issues. Composed of individuals interested in child welfare issues.

Child Welfare League of America (CWLA) *Founded:* 1920. *Headquarters:* Washington, DC. *Purpose:* Provides consultation, conducts research, conducts agency and community surveys, develops standards for services, and administers special projects. It serves members working to improve care and services for abused, dependent, or neglected children, youth, and their families.

Children in Hospitals (CIH) *Founded:* 1971. *Headquarters:* Boston, MA. *Purpose:* To encourage hospitals to adopt flexible visiting policies and to provide live-in accommodations for parents with hospitalized children. It serves educators, health professionals, and parents seeking to minimize the trauma of a child's hospitalization by supporting and educating parents and medical personnel regarding the need for children to have parents present whenever possible.

Children's Healthcare Is a Legal Duty (CHILD) *Founded:* 1983. *Headquarters:* Sioux City, IA. *Purpose:* Opposes religion-based denial of medical care to children; child discipline through physical abuse that is sanctioned by religious beliefs; and the exemption of religious day care centers from state licensing because they are religious bodies. Collects and disseminates information regarding state laws and court cases dealing with the legal rights of children to receive medical care regardless of religious convictions. Members are physicians, lawyers, and individuals interested in promoting the legal rights of children in obtaining medical care.

Chinese American Medical Society (CAMS)
Founded: 1962. *Headquarters:* Teaneck, NJ. *Purpose:* To advance medical knowledge and research among members, establish scholarships, and hold meetings for professional purposes. Maintains a placement service and bestows a Scientific Award annually to the member with the highest scholastic achievements. It serves physicians of Chinese origin residing in the United States and Canada.

Choice in Dying (CID) *Founded:* 1991. *Headquarters:* New York, NY. *Purpose:* Fosters communication about complex end-of-life decisions, provides advance directives, counsels patients and families, trains professionals, advocates for improved laws, and offers a range of publications and services. In 1997 the organization launched a national educational campaign, Break the Silence. *Formed by merger of:* Concern for Dying and Society of Right to Die.

Christian Association for Psychological Studies (CAPS) *Founded:* 1956. *Headquarters:* New Braunfels, TX. *Purpose:* Helps members as Christians to explore the fields of psychology, pastoral counseling, and psychotherapy for a better insight into personality and interpersonal relations. Members are psychologists, marriage and family therapists, social workers, educators, physicians, nurses, ministers, pastoral counselors, and rehabilitation workers engaged in the fields of psychology, counseling, psychiatry, pastoral counseling, and related areas.

Christian Doctors Sodality (CDS) *Founded:* 1924. *Headquarters:* unknown. *Purpose:* To conduct research and compile statistics on the importance of religious faith combined with traditional health care in healing. It serves licensed chiropractors and physicians who are also ordained ministers, elders, or deacons.

Civil Aviation Medical Association (CAMA)
Founded: 1948. *Headquarters:* Oklahoma City, OK. *Purpose:* Establishes the basic mental and physical requirements of civil air personnel and the proper methods for the physical assessment of air personnel engaged in civil aviation. It serves aviation medical examiners, physicians who are pilots, aviation medical educators, flight instructors, airline medical department physicians, NASA physicians, and fixed base operators.

Civil Rights Division *See* Government Organizations (Department of Justice).

Clearinghouse on Disability Information (CDI)
Founded: 1973. *Headquarters:* Washington, DC. *Purpose:* Responds to inquiries on topics concerning federally funded programs serving disabled persons and federal legislation affecting the disabled community.

Cleveland Health Quality Choice (CHQC) *Founded:* 1989. *Headquarters:* Cleveland, OH. *Purpose:* To work collaboratively to measure and compare the quality of selected services at Cleveland hospitals, including surgery, general medicine, intensive care, and obstetrics/gynecology; to make reports available to the public; and to evolve a world-class, comprehensive community database of health care information that serves as the underpinnings and benchmark to support a world-class community health care system. It is sponsored by The Greater Cleveland Health Quality Choice Coalition, which includes Cleveland Tomorrow, the Greater Cleveland Hospital Association, the Health Action Council of Northeast Ohio, the Academy of Medicine of Cleveland, and the Council of Small Enterprises. The program aspires to support other community, regional, state, and national efforts that share similar values and missions by providing them with technology and knowledge developed through the efforts of the CHQC program.

Clinical Efficacy Assessment Project (CEAP) *See* American College of Physicians.

Clinical Immunology Society (CIS) *Founded:* 1986. *Headquarters:* Thorofare, NJ. *Purpose:* To promote research on the causes and mechanisms of immunologic diseases and improved treatment, evaluation, and prevention of diseases related to immunity. Members are investigators and clinicians interested in immunologic diseases.

Clinical Laboratory Management Association (CLMA) *Founded:* 1971. *Headquarters:* Malvern, PA. *Purpose:* To enhance management skills and promote more efficient and productive department operations. Members are individuals holding managerial or supervisory positions with clinical laboratories, persons engaged in education of these individuals, and manufacturers or distributors of equipment or services to clinical laboratories.

Clinical Ligand Assay Society (CLAS) *Founded:* 1976. *Headquarters:* Wayne, MI. *Purpose:* To advance standards of ligand assay practice as applied to physiology in the prevention, diagnosis, and treatment of disease. It serves clinical laboratory directors and doctors, hospital technologists, private laboratories, and representatives of industry interested in ligand assays.

Clinical Practice Enhancement Project *See* Guidelines Appraisal Project.

Coalition on Sexuality and Disability (CSD)
Founded: 1978. *Headquarters:* New York, NY. *Purpose:* To educate health professionals and disabled people and to promote research in the area of sexuality and disability. It serves members interested in promoting sexual health care services through education, training, and advocacy for people with disabilities.

Coalition on Smoking or Health (CSH) *Founded:* 1982. *Headquarters:* Washington, DC. *Purpose:* Formed by the American Lung Association, American Heart Association, and American Cancer Society to more effectively bring tobacco use prevention and education issues to the attention of federal legislators and policymakers. It has supported an increase in cigarette excise tax; replacement of current health warnings on cigarette packages and advertisements with more specific and effective warnings concerning tobacco use and its effects on health; a smoking ban on all domestic and international passenger airline flights and in federal buildings; restriction of U.S. exports of tobacco products; elimination of federal support for the tobacco industry; and regulation by the Food and Drug Administration of tobacco and tobacco products.

Cognitive Science Society (CSS) *Founded:* 1979. *Headquarters:* Pittsburgh, PA. *Purpose:* To promote the dissemination of research in cognitive science and allied sciences. It serves researchers in the fields of psychology, artificial intelligence, and cognitive science.

College of American Pathologists (CAP) *Founded:* 1947. *Headquarters:* Northfield, IL. *Purpose:* To foster improvement of education, research, and medical laboratory service to physicians, hospitals, and the public. It provides placement information for members and conducts a laboratory accreditation program and laboratory proficiency testing surveys. Members are physicians practicing pathology.

College of Chaplains (COC) *Founded:* 1946. *Headquarters:* Schaumburg, IL. *Purpose:* To advocate for the provision of quality spiritual care of all persons in healthcare, corrections, long term care, rehabilitation centers, hospice, and other specialized settings and to promote excellence in pastoral care and a concern for human and spiritual values in specialized ministry settings. All members are endorsed as chaplains by their faith group.

College of Diplomates of the American Board of Orthodontics (CDABO) *Founded:* Atlanta, GA (c/o John K. Ottley, Jr). *Headquarters:* San Francisco, CA. *Purpose:* Promotes self- evaluation and ongoing professional improvement among orthodontists and conducts seminars. Members are diplomates of the American Board of Orthodontics who qualify by passing extra examinations.

College of Optometrists in Vision Development (COVD) *Founded:* 1970. *Headquarters:* Chula Vista, CA. *Purpose:* To establish a body of practitioners who are knowledgeable in functional and developmental concepts of vision, and to ensure that the public will receive continuously improving vision care. Members are optometrists involved in orthoptics and optometric vision therapy with emphasis on visual information processing in visually related learning problems.

College of Osteopathic Healthcare Executives (COHE) *Founded:* 1954. *Headquarters:* Washington, DC. *Purpose:* Encourages the development of hospital administration; establishes criteria of competency and sets standards to ensure that hospital executives continue to progress and develop skills by participating in educational programs; helps hospital executives serve their communities by efficient and responsible professional practice; conducts educational programs; and contributes to the advancement of efficient hospital administration. COHE members, who constitute the American Osteopathic Healthcare Associations individual membership section, include osteopathic hospital CEOs, administrators and senior managers, and others interested in health care management.

Commission on Accreditation of Allied Health Education Programs (CAAHEP) *Founded:* 1976. *Headquarters:* Chicago, IL. *Purpose:* Accredits educational programs in 18 allied health disciplines nationwide. CAAHEP accredits some 1,700 allied health education programs in approximately 1,000 institutions across the nation, including universities, medical health centers, junior and community colleges, hospitals, clinics, blood banks, vocational-technical schools, proprietary institutions, and United States governmental institutions and agencies. *Formerly:* Committee on Allied Health Education and Accreditation (1994).

Commission on Accreditation of Rehabilitation Facilities (CARF) *Founded:* 1966. *Headquarters:* Tucson, AZ. *Purpose:* Sponsored by rehabilitation/habilitation organizations, it is the standard-setting and accrediting authority for rehabilitation/habilitation organizations providing services to people with disabilities.

Commission on Graduates of Foreign Nursing Schools (CGFNS) *Founded:* 1977. *Headquarters:* Philadelphia, PA. *Purpose:* To help ensure safe nursing care for the American public and to protect graduates of foreign nursing schools from employment exploitation. Administers a nursing and English-language-proficiency examination to foreign-educated nurses who wish to practice as registered nurses in the United States. Identifies those foreign-educated nurses qualified to become registered nurses in the United States.

Commission on Mental and Physical Disability Law (CMPDL) *Founded:* 1976. *Headquarters:* Washington, DC. *Purpose:* To gather and disseminate information on court decisions, legislation, and administrative developments affecting people with mental and physical disabilities. Topics covered include the insanity defense, civil commitment, institutional rights, rights in the community, education of children with disabilities, discrimination against people with disabilities, and environmental barriers.

Commission on Office Laboratory Assessment (COLA) *Founded:* 1993. *Headquarters:* Kansas City, MO. *Purpose:* Sponsored by the American Academy of Family Physicians, the American Society of Internal Medicine, the College of American Pathologists, and the American Medical Association, for the purpose of accrediting office laboratories.

Commission on Opticianry Accreditation (COA) *Founded:* 1979. *Headquarters:* Bowie, MD. *Purpose:* To conduct an evaluator's workshop to train on-site evaluators. Established for ophthalmic dispensing and ophthalmic laboratory technology programs in postsecondary institutions.

Commission on Pastoral Research *Founded:* 1972. *Headquarters:* Columbia, MD. *Purpose:* To disseminate information on research in the field. Members are pastoral care and counseling organizations.

Commission on Professional and Hospital Activities (CPHA) *Founded:* 1953. *Headquarters:* Chicago, IL. *Purpose:* Offers data collection and research assistance to health personnel and institutions. The Commission operates various departments of study, including management of emergency, outpatient, and inpatient care, and collates data on length of patient stay and other variables for assessing institutions' efficiency. Maintains the Professional Activity Study, a microcomputer database which indexes patient histories and hospital utilization data for hospital planning and professional review.

Commissioned Officers Association of the US Public Health Service (COA) *Founded:* 1910. *Headquarters:* Washington, DC. *Purpose:* A national organization composed of 7,300 commissioned officers of the U.S. Public Health Service, including career active duty, retired, and inactive reserve officers who are physicians, dentists, scientists, engineers, pharmacists, nurses, and other types of professional personnel.

Committee on Allied Health Education and Accreditation *See* Commission on Accreditation of Allied Health Education Programs.

Committee for Freedom of Choice in Medicine (CFCM) *Founded:* 1972. *Headquarters:* Chula Vista, CA. *Purpose:* To conduct symposia on alternative therapies in order to educate the public and the medical profession about new discoveries in the treatment of degenerative diseases, and to direct people with questions concerning alternative therapies to physicians in their areas. Maintains databases, conducts research, and compiles statistics on people with degenerative diseases.

Committee of Interns and Residents (CIR) *Founded:* 1957. *Headquarters:* New York, NY. *Purpose:* To represent house staff in matters pertaining to compensation, benefits, hours, working conditions, and other issues affecting their employment, education, training, and the quality of health services and patient care. It serves medical and dental interns, residents, chief residents, and fellows at 50 member hospitals located in New York, New Jersey, and Washington, DC.

Committee for National Health Insurance (CNHI) *Founded:* 1969. *Headquarters:* Washington, DC. *Purpose:* Conducts research and education on the health care system in the United States, including its problems and the ways in which to bring about reform through enactment of a comprehensive national health insurance program. Members are citizen's organizations and individuals from health care fields, government, labor, academic endeavors, business, and economics.

Committee for the Scientific Investigation of Claims of the Paranormal (CSICOP) *Founded:* 1976. *Headquarters:* Amherst, NY. *Purpose:* Concerned about biased, pseudoscientific media presentations of claims of paranormal occurrences, fearing that the ready acceptance of such claims erodes the spirit of scientific skepticism and opens the public to gullibility in other areas. Its subcommittees focus on areas such as paranormal health claims and parapsychology. Members are psychologists, philosophers, astronomers, science writers, and other individuals interested in the field of the paranormal, including unidentified flying objects, astrology, and psychic phenomena.

Commonwealth Fund *Founded:* 1918. *Headquarters:* New York, NY. *Purpose:* To enhance the common good through efforts to help Americans live healthy and productive lives and to assist specific groups with serious and neglected problems. In 1986 the Fund was given the assets of the James Picker Foundation in support of Picker programs to advance the Fund's mission, now called Picker/Commonwealth Programs. Its current four national program areas are improving health care services (eg, Picker/Commonwealth Program on Health Care Quality and Managed Care; Women's Health Program; Task Force on Academic Health Canters), bettering the health of minority Americans, advancing the well-being of elderly people (eg, Picker/Commonwealth Program on Frail Elders; Quality of Life at the End of Life), and developing the capacities of children (eg, Healthy Steps for Young Children). The Fund also administers the Harkness Fellowships programs.

Community Nutrition Institute (CNI) *Founded:* 1970. *Headquarters:* Washington, DC. *Purpose:* Secure a food system that provides access to a diet that sustains cultural and social values and maintains human health. It develops standards for food products. Members are citizen advocates specializing in food and nutrition issues, which include hunger, food quality and safety, nutrition research, food programs, education, and food labeling and marketing.

Computer Users in Speech and Hearing (CUSH) *Founded:* 1981. *Headquarters:* Hudson, OH. *Purpose:* To maintain a software lending library. Members are professionals involved in communication sciences and communication disorders; companies that develop products for remediation and treatment of communication disorders; and individuals and family members who are experiencing communication disorders.

Computerized Medical Imaging Society (CMIS) *Founded:* 1976. *Headquarters:* Washington, DC. *Purpose:* To provide a forum for exchange of information about the medical use of computerized axial tomography in radiological diagnosis. Members are physicians and other medical personnel interested in computerized axial tomography and other radiological diagnostic procedures.

Concern for Dying *See* Choice in Dying.

Conference of Consulting Actuaries (CCA) *Founded:* 1950. *Headquarters:* Buffalo Grove, IL. *Purpose:* Committees focus on health issues and life issues. Members are full-time consulting actuaries or governmental actuaries.

Conference of Educational Administrators Serving the Deaf (CEASD) *Founded:* 1868. *Headquarters:* Newark, DE. *Purpose:* Coordinates research on the problems of deafness. Members are executive heads of public, private, and denominational schools for the deaf in the United States and Canada.

Conference of Podiatry Executives (COPE) *Founded:* 1960. *Headquarters:* Columbus, OH. *Purpose:* To facilitate communication among member associations and their executives and to promote the exchange of information. Members include executive directors of state podiatry associations.

Conference of Radiation Control Program Directors (CRCPD) *Founded:* 1968. *Headquarters:* Frankfort, KY. *Purpose:* To provide a forum for the interchange of experience, concerns, developments, and recommendations among radiation control programs and related agencies. Promotes radiological health and uniform radiation control laws and regulations. Members are state and local radiological program directors and individuals from related federal protection agencies.

Congress on Neurological Surgeons *Founded:* 1951. *Headquarters:* Atlanta, GA. *Purpose:* To foster discussion among neurosurgeons of views and various aspects of the principles and practice of neurological surgery; to exchange technological information and experience; and to join the study of the developments in scientific fields.

Congress Watch (CW) *Founded:* 1971. *Headquarters:* Washington, DC. *Purpose:* Represents consumer interests, specifically citizens' access to government decision making, campaign finance reform, the savings and loan crisis, consumer class actions, food and product safety, and protection of public health through environmental legislation.

Consultant Dietitians in Health Care Facilities (CDHCF) *Founded:* 1975. *Headquarters:* Chicago, IL. *Purpose:* To disseminate information to members who are dietitians employed in extended care facilities, nursing homes, and other health-care-related food service operations.

Consumer Alert (CA) *Founded:* 1977. *Headquarters:* Washington, DC. *Purpose:* To examine current and proposed regulations in terms of demonstrated need and ultimate cost in areas where it believes consumer interests are being abused. It serves those opposing excessive regulations and supporting free enterprise, consumer rights, and freedom of choice for individual consumers.

Consumer Coalition for Quality Health Care *Founded:* 1993. *Headquarters:* Washington, DC. *Purpose:* To help, educate, assist, and protect the rights of individuals under managed care plans and for quality assurance

programs that evaluate, monitor and improve these health plans. The coalition is constituted of members (consumer-based organizations such as American Association of Retired Persons and Families USA), endorsing organizations, and collaborating organizations.

Consumer Information Center (CIC) *Founded:* 1970. *Headquarters:* Washington, DC. *Purpose:* A department of the General Services Administration, established by presidential order in 1970 to assist federal agencies to develop, promote, and distribute information of interest to consumers and to increase public awareness of this information.

Consumer Product Safety Commission *See* Government Organizations.

Contact Lens Association of Ophthalmologists (CLAO) *Founded:* 1962. *Headquarters:* New Orleans, LA. *Purpose:* To disseminate scientific information on ophthalmology and provide for the sharing of techniques and expertise. Members are active and resident ophthalmologists and osteopathic physicians specializing in ophthalmology.

Contact Lens Society of America (CLSA) *Founded:* 1955. *Headquarters:* Herndon, VA. *Purpose:* Share knowledge of contact lens technology and foster the growth and ability of contact lens technicians. Members are contact lens fitters and manufacturers of products associated with contact lenses.

Corrections Program Office *See* Government Organizations (Department of Justice).

Cosmetic Ingredient Review (CIR) *Founded:* 1976. *Headquarters:* Washington, DC. *Purpose:* Sponsored by the Cosmetic, Toiletry, and Fragrance Association, seeks to ensure the safety of ingredients used in cosmetics. Reviews scientific data on the safety of ingredients used in cosmetics and documents the validity of tests used to study ingredients. Maintains a database of safety information, including information on possible effects from misuse or use by hypersensitive individuals.

Council on Accreditation of Nurse Anesthesia Educational Programs/Schools *Founded:* 1975. *Headquarters:* Park Ridge, IL. *Purpose:* To provide accreditation and evaluate nurse anesthesia programs. Conducts on-site reviews and educational workshops. It functions within the framework of the American Association of Nurse Anesthetists.

Council for Accreditation in Occupational Hearing Conservation (CAOHC) *Founded:* 1973. *Headquarters:* Milwaukee, WI. *Purpose:* To approve courses in occupational hearing conservation and certify individuals who pass these courses. Members are professional associations in the industrial health field that establish and maintain standards for the training of industrial audiometric technicians.

Council on Accreditation of Services for Families and Children (COA) *Founded:* 1977. *Headquarters:*

New York, NY. *Purpose:* An accrediting body established as independent, objective process of agency review in the field of mental health and human services. It is supported by seven national organizations representing a broad spectrum of the human service and mental health community: Association of Jewish Family and Children's Agencies, Catholic Charities USA, the Child Welfare League of America, Family Service America, Lutheran Society Ministry System, the National Council for Adoption, and the National Association of Homes and Services for Children.

Council on Anxiety Disorders (CAD) *Founded:* 1988. *Headquarters:* Clarkesville, GA. *Purpose:* Concerned with educating the public about anxiety disorders and advocating appropriate treatment. Sponsors seminars for health professionals and local support groups for persons with obsessive-compulsive and panic disorders.

Council on Arteriosclerosis of the American Heart Association (CAAHA) *Founded:* 1946. *Headquarters:* Dallas, TX. *Purpose:* To serve physicians and other individuals interested in cardiovascular diseases, especially arteriosclerosis.

Council for Behavioral Group Practices (CBGP) *Founded:* 1993. *Headquarters:* Tiburon, CA. *Purpose:* To enable group practices to track patient outcomes, measure patient satisfaction, and compare performance with other group practices nationwide.

Council for Biomedical Communications Associations *Founded:* 1970. *Headquarters:* Ann Arbor, MI. *Purpose:* Explores areas of mutual concern in the health sciences communications field. It serves the Association of Biomedical Communication Directors, Association of Medical Illustrators, Biological Photographic Association, Guild of Natural Science Illustrators, and Health Sciences Communications Association.

Council on Certification of Nurse Anesthetists (CCNA) *Founded:* 1975. *Headquarters:* Park Ridge, IL. *Purpose:* To set certification standards and policies and confer certification upon competent entry-level nurse anesthetists.

Council on Chiropractic Education (CCE) *Founded:* 1971. *Headquarters:* Scottsdale, AZ. *Purpose:* Acts as national accrediting agency for chiropractic colleges. Composed of representatives of member colleges.

Council on Chiropractic Orthopedics (CCO) *Founded:* 1967. *Headquarters:* Provo, UT. *Purpose:* To maintain the American Board of Chiropractic Orthopedists, which serves as an examining body for certification. It serves licensed chiropractic physicians.

Council on Chiropractic Physiological Therapeutics (CCPT) *Founded:* 1920. *Headquarters:* Delray Beach, FL. *Purpose:* To promote the use of physiotherapy in chiropractic practice and further the extended use of physiotherapy in the chiropractic field.

Council of Colleges of Acupuncture and Oriental Medicine (CCAOM) *Founded:* 1982. *Headquarters:* Catasauqua, PA. *Purpose:* To advance the status of acupuncture and oriental medicine through a certification program; to provide high-quality classroom and clinical instruction; and to promote the improvement of research and teaching methods. Serves schools and colleges of acupuncture that offer a minimum two-year accredited training program.

Council of Community Blood Centers (CCBC) *Founded:* 1962. *Headquarters:* Washington, DC. *Purpose:* Composed of independent, nonprofit, federally licensed blood centers serving defined geographic areas, its purpose is to provide an optimal supply of blood, blood components, and blood derivatives to people who need them.

Council on Education for Public Health (CEPH) *Founded:* 1974. *Headquarters:* Washington, DC. *Purpose:* To strengthen educational programs in schools of public health and graduate public health programs through accreditation, consultation, research, and other services. Composed of professional associations representing public health practice (American Public Health Association) and public health education (Association of Schools of Public Health).

Council on Electrolysis Education (CEE) *Founded:* 1972. *Headquarters:* Hot Springs, AR. *Purpose:* To sponsor educational programs and research in the field of electrolysis and establish criteria for accreditation and certification.

Council on Environmental Quality *See* Government Organizations (Executive Office of the President).

Council on Family Health (CFH) *Founded:* 1966. *Headquarters:* New York, NY. *Purpose:* To provide the public and interested organizations with information on proper usage of medications and other family health concerns, such as safety in the home. Members are manufacturers of prescription and over-the-counter medications.

Council for Learning Disabilities (CLD) *Founded:* 1967. *Headquarters:* Overland Park, KS. *Purpose:* To promote the education and welfare of individuals having specific learning disabilities by improving teacher preparation programs and resolving important research issues. It serves professionals interested in the study of learning disabilities.

Council on Licensure, Enforcement and Regulation (CLEAR) *Founded:* 1980. *Headquarters:* Lexington, KY. *Purpose:* To provide for the exchange of state licensing information and serve as a clearinghouse of licensing activities and programs. Works to improve management and enforcement practices of state licensure officials and trains state officials and sponsors the National Disciplinary Information System, which provides information on sanctions taken by state boards against licensed practitioners. Members are state and territorial licensing regulation officials.

Council for Medical Affairs (CFMA) *Founded:* 1980. *Headquarters:* Chicago, IL. *Purpose:* To provide a forum in which representatives can exchange information on matters relating to medical education. Member organizations include Association of American Medical Colleges, American Board of Medical Specialties, American Hospital Association, American Medical Association, and the Council of Medical Specialty Societies.

Council on Medical Education of the American Medical Association (CME-AMA) *Founded:* 1904. *Headquarters:* Chicago, IL. *Purpose:* To participate in the accreditation of and provide consultation to medical school programs, graduate medical educational programs, and educational programs for a number of allied health occupations. It provides information on medical and allied health education at all levels. It publishes the *Directory of Graduate Medical Education Programs* and *Allied Health Education Directory.*

Council of Medical Specialty Societies (CMSS) *Founded:* 1965. *Headquarters:* Lake Bluff, IL. *Purpose:* To provide a forum for discussion by specialty societies of national issues affecting the practice and teaching of medicine. Promotes communication among specialty organizations involved in the principal disciplines of medicine. Members are national medical specialty societies representing 320,000 physicians.

Council of the *National Register* of Health Service Providers in Psychology (CNRHSPP) *Founded:* 1974. *Headquarters:* Washington, DC. *Purpose:* To credential doctoral-level licensed psychologists for health care service provision. Various insurers, governmental agencies, educational institutions, managed care organizations, hospitals and employee assistance programs can then obtain verification of those credentials from the *National Register.*

Council on Optometric Education (COE) *Founded:* 1930. *Headquarters:* St. Louis, MO. *Purpose:* Accredits professional optometric degree (OD) programs, paraoptometric training programs, and optometric residency programs.

Council on Performance Measurement *Founded:* 1995. *Headquarters:* Oakbrook Terrace, IL (Joint Commission). *Purpose:* To act as an advisory body to the Joint Commission by identifying those performance measurement systems that will qualify for inclusion in the future accreditation process.

Council on Podiatric Medical Education (CPME) *Founded:* 1918. *Headquarters:* Bethesda, MD. *Purpose:* Accredits colleges of podiatric medicine, podiatric residency programs, podiatric assistant programs, and continuing education programs in podiatry.

Council on Professional Standards in Speech-Language Pathology and Audiology *Founded:* 1959. *Headquarters:* Rockville, MD. *Purpose:* To define standards for clinical certification and for the accreditation of graduate education and professional services. It monitors the interpretation and application of these standards to individuals and organizations.

Council on Resident Education in Obstetrics and Gynecology (CREOG) *Founded:* 1976. *Headquarters:* Washington, DC. *Purpose:* To promote and maintain high standards of resident training in obstetrics and gynecology. Provides consultative site visits to residency programs, a clearinghouse for residency positions, conferences, a resident data bank, and a national in-training examination.

Council for Responsible Genetics (CRG) *Founded:* 1983. *Headquarters:* Cambridge, MA. *Purpose:* Areas of interest include military uses of biological research and genetic discrimination. Members include scientists, health and medical professionals, trade unionists, feminists, and peace activists interested in monitoring and analyzing the biotechnology industry including the moral and ethical issues of genetic engineering.

Council on Social Work Education (CSWE) *Founded:* 1952. *Headquarters:* Alexandria, VA. *Purpose:* To formulate criteria and standards for all levels of social work education; accredits graduate and undergraduate social work programs; and provides consulting to social work educators on curriculum, faculty recruitment, and faculty development. It serves graduate and undergraduate programs of social work education; national, regional, and local social welfare agencies; libraries; and individuals.

Council of State Administrators of Vocational Rehabilitation (CSAVR) *Founded:* 1940. *Headquarters:* Washington, DC. *Purpose:* Serves as an advisory body to federal agencies and the public in the development of policies affecting rehabilitation of disabled persons. Members are administrators of state vocational rehabilitation agencies.

Council of Teaching Hospitals (COTH) *Founded:* 1965. *Headquarters:* Washington, DC. *Purpose:* To distribute communications analyzing congressional activities, executive branch actions, court decisions affecting teaching hospitals, and teaching-hospital reimbursement regulations. Disseminates special interest bibliographies, surveys of housestaff policies, and comparative hospital financial data. Its parent organization is the Association of American Medical Colleges and it serves medical school-affiliated or university-owned teaching hospitals.

Cranial Academy (CA) *Founded:* 1946. *Headquarters:* Indianapolis, IN. *Purpose:* Interested in study and development of osteopathic cranial concepts and the techniques of diagnosis and treatment in structural manipulation of the body. Members are osteopathic physicians who have taken a course through the academy or through Sutherland Cranial Teaching Foundation, an osteopathic college. The Cranial Academy is a society of the American Academy of Osteopathy.

Credentialing Commission (CC) *Founded:* 1962. *Headquarters:* St. Louis, MO. *Purpose:* Certifies medical technologists, laboratory technicians, and physician office laboratory technicians.

CRISP (Consortium Research on Indicators for System Performance) *Founded:* 1991. *Headquarters:* Detroit, MI. *Purpose:* To test ways to measure the performance of vertically integrated health care providers in order to coordinate care, improve health status, operate efficiently, and satisfy consumers. The consortium consists of 12 health care organizations, from regions throughout the United States. The Center coordinates the development of indicators and data collection tools and produces annual indicator reports, and participants pay an annual administrative fee to participate. It operates in the Center for Health Systems Studies at Henry Ford Health System.

Cystic Fibrosis Foundation (CFF) *Founded:* 1955. *Headquarters:* Bethesda, MD. *Purpose:* To raise money for research to find a cure for cystic fibrosis (CF) and to improve the quality of life for children and young adults with the disease. The CFF carries out its work through its nationwide CF Care Centers (patient care and clinical trials); advocacy at the federal level for more investment in basic science research and to speed drug development; medical care, public policy, and education programs with the aid of volunteers; and publications. Through its subsidiary, Cystic Fibrosis Services, Inc, it acts as a patient advocate by persuading insurance companies and managed care organizations to cover therapies for people with CF. Current major areas of concentration are gene transfer therapy (undergoing trial) and genetic discrimination (promotion of The Genetic Information Nondiscrimination in Health Insurance Act of 1997).

Dd

Delta Dental Plans Association (DDPA) *Founded:* 1954. *Headquarters:* Oak Brook, IL. *Purpose:* Carries dental, oral healthcare, and medical benefits for U.S. citizens. A new educational program, PANDA (Prevent Abuse and Neglect through Dental Awareness), teaches dental health professionals how to recognize child abuse. Members are made up of local, nonprofit Delta Dental Plans that provide groups with dental benefits coverage.

Dental Assisting National Board (DANB) *Founded:* 1948. *Headquarters:* Chicago, IL. *Purpose:* To administer examinations to and certify dental assistants.

Dental Group Management Association (DGMA) *Founded:* 1951. *Headquarters:* Glendale, WI. *Purpose:* To provide forum for exchange of ideas among members who are dental group business managers and other persons interested in group practice management.

Department of Defense (DOD) *See* Government Organizations.

Department of Education (DOE) *See* Government Organizations.

Department of Energy (DOE) *See* Government Organizations.

Department of Health and Human Services (DHHS) *See* Government Organizations.

Department of Justice (DOJ) *See* Government Organizations.

Department of Labor (DOL) *See* Government Organizations.

Department of Veterans Affairs *See* Government Organizations.

Dermatology Nurses' Association (DNA) *Founded:* 1982. *Headquarters:* Pitman, NJ. *Purpose:* Addresses professional issues involving dermatology nurses; develops standards of dermatologic nursing care; and conducts educational meetings.

Diabetes Quality Improvement Project *See* American Diabetes Association; Foundation for Accountability; HCFA; National Committee for Quality Assurance.

Dietary Managers Association (DMA) *Founded:* 1960. *Headquarters:* Itasca, IL. *Purpose:* Assists dietary managers interested in competency and quality in dietary departments and their management.

Digestive Disease National Coalition (DDNC) *Founded:* 1979. *Headquarters:* Washington, DC. *Purpose:* Informs the public and the health care community about digestive diseases and related nutrition and seek federal funding for research, education, and training. Members are professional medical and lay organizations interested in digestive diseases.

Dinshah Health Society (DHS) *Founded:* 1976. *Headquarters:* Malaga, NJ. *Purpose:* To provide for exchange of ideas among members who are health professionals and other individuals who use and promote chromotherapy.

Disability Insurance Training Council (DITC) *Founded:* 1951. *Headquarters:* Washington, DC. *Purpose:* The educational arm of the National Association of Health Underwriters, providing institutional advanced disability income and health insurance research seminars as well as marketing and underwriting clinics. It maintains the Health Insurance Training Council, Disability Training Insurance Council, and Registered Health Underwriters.

Disability Rights Section *See* Government Organizations (Department of Justice).

Doctors for Disaster Preparedness (DDP) *Founded:* 1982. *Headquarters:* Tucson, AZ. *Purpose:* Supports civil defense measures and maintains no position on specific military or foreign policy measures, weapons systems, or arms controls. Members include physicians and other health professionals interested in preparing health professionals and the public for medical response in the case of natural or human-caused disaster.

Drug and Alcohol Nursing Association (DANA)
Founded: 1979. *Headquarters:* Upper Black Eddy, PA.
Purpose: To promote and maintain the participation of the nursing profession in the treatment of addictions and to ensure that addicted patients and their families receive high-quality nursing care. Members include registered nurses, licensed practical nurses, and other health professionals involved in the treatment, prevention, and control of drug and/or alcohol addictions.

Drug, Chemical and Allied Trades Association (DCAT) *Founded:* 1890. *Headquarters:* Syosset, NJ.
Purpose: To monitor federal regulation relating to drug and chemical manufacturing. It serves manufacturers of drugs, chemicals, and related products (packaging, cosmetics, essential oils) and publications, advertising agencies, agents, brokers, and importers.

Drug Court Program Office *See* Government Organizations (Department of Justice).

Drug Enforcement Administration (DEA) *See* Government Organizations (Department of Justice).

Drug Information Association (DIA) *Founded:* 1965.
Headquarters: Maple Glen, PA. *Purpose:* To provide mutual instruction on the technology of drug information processing in all areas, including collecting, selecting, abstracting, indexing, coding, vocabulary building, terminology standardizing, computerizing data storage and retrieval, tabulating, correlating, computing, evaluating, writing, editing, reporting, and publishing. Conducts workshops and seminars. Members include persons who handle drug information in government, industry, medical and pharmaceutical professions, and allied fields.

The Duke Endowment *Founded:* 1944. *Headquarters:* Charlotte, NC. *Purpose:* To make grants to eligible universities and colleges, health care organizations, children's homes, and churches and pastors in the Carolinas.

ECRI *Founded:* 1955. *Headquarters:* Plymouth Meeting, PA. *Purpose:* To provide the health care community, both nationally and internationally, with information about the safe and efficacious use of medical technology and to support safe and cost-effective patient care. ECRI is a nonprofit, nongovernmental health services agency and a World Health Organization (WHO) Collaborating Center for Information Transfer on Medical Devices. ECRI's Center for Healthcare Environmental Management (CHEM) publishes alerts and recommendations in its *Healthcare Environmental Management System* series. Other services and products include the Universal Medical Device Nomenclature System (UMDNS) and International Medical Device Codes (IMDC), the annual Healthcare Standards Directory and Updates, other publications, laboratory services, seminars, and fellowships.

ECRI once stood for Emergency Care Research Institute, but the acronym is used alone now.

EHS Health Care *See* Advocate Health Care.

Elementary and Secondary Education *See* Government Organizations (Department of Education).

Emergency Medicine Residents' Association (EMRA) *Founded:* 1974. *Headquarters:* Irving, TX.
Purpose: To provide a unified voice for emergency medicine residents, encourage high standards in training and continuing education for emergency physicians, study socioeconomic aspects of emergency medicine, and promote education of patients and the public. Members are medical students and physicians enrolled in emergency medicine residency training programs.

Emergency Nurses Association (ENA) *Founded:* 1970. *Headquarters:* Park Ridge, IL. *Purpose:* Fosters professional and personal growth of its members; addresses current emergency nursing practice concerns by issuing position statements, providing legislatory testimony and serving as a national network mechanism; promoting emergency nursing through research and education by grant-making through the ENA Foundation; and publishes the *Journal of Emergency Nursing,* highly recognized as the only academic journal addressing the specialty of emergency nursing. Serves registered nurses, licensed practical nurses, licensed vocational nurses, emergency medical technicians, and other individuals engaged or interested in emergency patient care.

Emerging Infections Network (EIN) *See* Infectious Diseases Society of America.

Emphysema Anonymous, Inc (EAI) *Founded:* 1965.
Headquarters: Clearwater, FL. *Purpose:* To assist physicians, persons suffering from emphysema, and other individuals interested in helping people with emphysema through education, encouragement, and nonmedical counseling for patients and their families.

Employee Assistance Professionals Association (EAPA) *Founded:* 1971. *Headquarters:* Arlington, VA.
Purpose: To support EAPA programs nationwide. Maintains a library of 2,900 volumes on employee assistance program (EAP) specific concerns; members consist primarily of psychologists, counselors, and directors of EAP programs.

Employment Standards Administration (ESA) *See* Government Organizations (Department of Labor).

The Endocrine Society (ES) *Founded:* 1916. *Headquarters:* Bethesda, MD. *Purpose:* To promote excellence in research, education and the clinical practice of endocrinology. Membership represent all basic, applied, and clinical interests in endocrinology, including scientists, educators, clinicians, practicing physicians, nurses, and students.

Engineering and Analytical Center *See* Government Organizations (Department of Health and Human Services, CDC).

Engineering in Medicine and Biology Society (EMBS) *See* Institute of Electrical and Electronics Engineers.

Enteral Nutrition Council (ENC) *Founded:* 1983. *Headquarters:* Atlanta, GA. *Purpose:* To provide for communication between manufacturers and marketers of enteral nutrition products and government and regulatory bodies. Members are manufacturers and marketers of enteral formulas.

Environmental Management Association (EMA) *Founded:* 1957. *Headquarters:* Jeffersonville, PA. *Purpose:* To conduct educational programs and present awards. Subsidiaries include the Food Sanitation Institute; Buildings-Grounds; and the Health Care Institute. Members are individuals administering environmental sanitation maintenance programs in industrial plants, commercial and public buildings, institutions, and governmental agencies.

Environmental Mutagen Society (EMA) *Founded:* 1969. *Headquarters:* Reston, VA. *Purpose:* To serve bioscientists in universities, governmental agencies, and industry interested in promoting basic and applied studies of mutagenesis.

Environmental Protection Agency (EPA) *See* Government Organizations.

Epilepsy Foundation of America (EFA) *Founded:* 1967. *Headquarters:* Landover, MA. *Purpose:* To improve the lives of those who have epilepsy; to provide a federal government liaison; to sponsor research in causes, prevention, psychosocial needs, and improved methods of treatment. Provides research and training grants and fellowships to students and professionals.

Executive Office of the President *See* Government Organizations.

Exer-Safety Association (ESA) *Founded:* 1980. *Headquarters:* Orlando, FL. *Purpose:* To improve the qualifications of exercise instructors, to train instructors to develop safe exercise routines that will help people avoid injury while exercising, and to prepare instructors for national certification. Serves fitness instructors, personal trainers, health spas, YMCAs, community recreation departments, and hospital wellness programs.

Eye Bank Association of America (EBAA) *Founded:* 1961. *Headquarters:* Washington, DC. *Purpose:* To establish standards for the procurement and distribution of eyes. It serves eye banks promoting eye banking.

Eye-Bank for Sight Restoration (EBSR) *Founded:* 1944. *Headquarters:* New York, NY. *Purpose:* Collects and distributes healthy corneal tissue obtained from individuals who have arranged to donate their eyes, or whose relatives have authorized such donation, at the time of death. Provides speakers to explain the eye-bank program to hospital and professional groups.

FACCT (Foundation for Accountability) *Founded:* 1995. *Headquarters:* Portland, OR. *Purpose:* To help consumers make health care choices based on quality through developing innovative ways to measure the quality of health care, developing consumer-focused quality measures, supporting public education about health care quality, supporting efforts to gather and provide quality information, and encouraging health policy to empower and inform consumers. FACCT was created by and represents a broad group of public, private, and nonprofit organizations. In 1997 FACCT endorsed a framework to guide comparative communications about health care quality to members, employees, and enrollees in FACCT trustee organizations; the framework combines data from NCQA's HEDIS, FACCT measurement sets, AHCPR's CAHPS, the Joint Commission's ORYX, and public health databases into a concise format.

Family Therapy Network (FTN) *Founded:* 1976. *Headquarters:* Washington, DC. *Purpose:* To assist members interested in promoting the exchange of ideas and information among family therapists.

Federal Emergency Management Agency (FEMA) *See* Government Organizations.

Federal Physicians Association (FPA) *Founded:* 1978. *Headquarters:* Washington, DC. *Purpose:* Improve the health care of patients served by federal civil service physicians; to advance the practice of medicine within the federal government; and to better the working conditions and benefits of federal civil service physicians. Members include civil service physicians employed by or retired from the federal government.

Federated Ambulatory Surgery Association (FASA) *Founded:* 1974. *Headquarters:* Alexandria, VA. *Purpose:* To promote the concept of freestanding ambulatory (outpatient) surgical care. Members are physicians, nurses, health administrators, and other individuals representing more than 400 outpatient surgery facilities.

Federated Societies of Gastroenterology and Hepatology (FSGH) *See* American Gastroenterological Association.

Federation for Accessible Nursing Education and Licensure (FANEL) *Founded:* 1983. *Headquarters:* Lewisburg, WI. *Purpose:* Assists registered nurses, licensed practical nurses, educators, health care organizations, schools, and hospital administrators seeking to maintain licensure through current education programs for registered nurses and licensed practical nurses.

Federation of American Health Systems (FAHS) *Founded:* 1966. *Headquarters:* Little Rock, AR. *Purpose:* To maintain a speakers' bureau, compile statistics on the investor-owned hospitals industry, and bestow awards.

Members are private- or investor-owned (for-profit) hospitals.

Federation of American Scientists (FAS)   *Founded:* 1945. *Headquarters:* Washington, DC. *Purpose:* To provide analysis and advocacy on science, technology, and public policy for global security. Programs include Cusp Projects (eg, Drug Policy, Micronutrient Project), ProMED (Program for Monitoring Emerging Diseases)—a global communications network established in 1994 to prevent more pandemics such as AIDS— and the Chemical and Biological Weapons Program. FAS is a privately funded nonprofit policy organization.

Federation of Behavioral, Psychological and Cognitive Sciences (FBPCS)   *Founded:* 1980. *Headquarters:* Washington, DC. *Purpose:* To promote research in behavioral, psychological, and cognitive sciences, their physiological bases, and applications in health, education, and human development. Members are scientific societies representing research scientists.

Federation of Feminist Women's Health Centers (FFWHC)   *Founded:* 1975. *Headquarters:* Eugene, OR. *Purpose:* Supports women's health clinics and individuals interested in working to secure reproductive rights for women and men, educating women about the normal functions of their bodies, and improving the quality of women's health care.

Federation of Nurses and Health Professionals (FNHP)   *Founded:* 1978. *Headquarters:* Washington, DC. *Purpose:* Assists registered nurses, licensed practical nurses, and other professional and technical employees in the health field. It is a division of the American Federation of Teachers.

Federation of Podiatric Medical Boards (FPMB)   *Founded:* 1936. *Headquarters:* Potomac, MD. *Purpose:* Acts as a repository for information relating to common problems among boards of podiatry examiners and promotes competency examinations with national standards used by examining boards, among other activities. It serves state boards of podiatry examiners.

Federation of Prosthodontic Organizations (FPO)   *Founded:* 1965. *Headquarters:* Chicago, IL. *Purpose:* To improve prosthodontic service rendered to the public and to improve communication among members and other organizations. Members are organizations of dentists.

Federation of Special Care Organizations and Dentistry   *Founded:* 1965. *Headquarters:* Chicago, IL. *Purpose:* To improve the effectiveness of health care providers in providing quality patient care, especially for patients who for reasons of medical diagnosis, disabilities, or frailties prevalent in advanced age require special care and/or special settings for dental care. The group is affiliated with the Academy of Dentistry for Persons with Disabilities, American Association of Hospital Dentists, and American Society for Geriatric Dentistry.

Federation of State Medical Boards of the United States (FSMB)   *Founded:* 1912. *Headquarters:* Fort Worth, TX. *Purpose:* To be a leader in improving the quality, safety and integrity of U.S. health care by promoting high standards for physician licensure and practice, and assisting and supporting state medical boards collectively and individually in the regulation of medical practice and in their role of public protection. The Federation is composed of 68 member boards (allopathic, osteopathic and composite). In general, each state medical board has in its power the authority to license physicians, to regulate the practice of medicine, and to discipline those who violate the medical practice act.

Federation of Straight Chiropractic Organizations (FSCO)   *Founded:* 1978. *Headquarters:* Clifton, NJ. *Purpose:* Promotes the practice of straight (traditional) chiropractic medicine by conducting lobbying and educational programs.

Floating Hospital (FH)   *Founded:* 1866. *Headquarters:* New York, NY. *Purpose:* To provide medical and dental services, screening tests, social services, and health education for parents, children, and senior citizens in a recreational setting on a ship that cruises New York waters as it provides its services.

Flotation Tank Association (TANK)   *Founded:* 1982. *Headquarters:* Grass Valley, CA. *Purpose:* To provide forum for exchange among medical and other health professionals using flotation tanks in conjunction with other patient treatments; academicians and scientific researchers studying the effect of using tanks; tank manufacturers and proprietors of public tank facilities; and other individuals interested in the use of tanks for relaxation and treatment of smoking, hypertension, chronic pain, and obesity.

Flying Physicians Association   *Founded:* 1954. *Headquarters:* Orlando, FL. *Purpose:* To promote the interests of medicine in aviation safety and education. Serves doctors of medicine with a current pilot certificate.

Food and Consumer Service   *See* Government Organizations (Department of Agriculture).

Food and Drug Administration (FDA)   *See* Government Organizations (Department of Health and Human Services).

Food and Drug Law Institute (FDLI)   *Founded:* 1949. *Headquarters:* Washington, DC. *Purpose:* To provide a forum for the discussion of issues pertaining to food and drug law among members including manufacturers and distributors of food, drugs, cosmetics, and devices, and law firms interested in promoting the development of knowledge about the laws that regulate the research, production, and sale of food, drugs, medical devices, and cosmetics.

Food Safety and Inspection Service   *See* Government Organizations (Department of Agriculture).

The Ford Foundation   *Founded:* 1936 (local), 1950 (national/international). *Headquarters:* New York, NY. *Purpose:* To serve as a resource for innovative people and institutions worldwide in order to strengthen democratic values, reduce poverty and injustice, promote international cooperation, and advance human achievement. In 1996 the Foundation established a new program and organizational structure consolidating grant-making activities into three program areas: Asset Building and Community Development (including Human Development and Reproductive Health); Education, Media, Arts, and Culture; and Peace and Social Justice.

The Forum for Health Care Planning (Forum)
Founded: 1950. *Headquarters:* San Francisco, CA. *Purpose:* To plan quality health care services and facilities, and to disseminate and exchange information on hospital and health care planning.

Forum for Medical Affairs (FORUM) *Founded:* 1944. *Headquarters:* Lake Success, NY. *Purpose:* To provide for exchange of ideas among members who include presidents, presidents-elect, and past presidents of state medical associations, members of the American Medical Association (AMA) and the House of Delegates, editors of state medical association journals, executive directors of state medical associations, and representatives of AMA-recognized medical specialty societies.

Foster Family-Based Treatment Association (FFTA)
Founded: 1988. *Headquarters:* New York, NY. *Purpose:* To define and refine treatment in foster care practice; to bring experienced practitioners together to develop operating standards of treatment for foster care.

Foundation for Accountability *See* FACCT.

Foundation for Health Care Evaluation (FHCE)
Founded: 1971. *Headquarters:* Bloomington, MN. *Purpose:* To evaluate health care services at hospitals, retirement homes, and other facilities; to develop health care standards for hospitals; and to offer consultation services to operators of health care facilities to improve efficiency in service. Members include physicians interested in ensuring the availability of quality health care at reasonable costs.

Foundation for Health Care Quality (FHCQ)
Founded: 1988. *Headquarters:* Seattle, WA. *Purpose:* To support better health decision making; to improve the quality and efficiency of health services delivery; and to enhance the health status of the population. Collaborates with purchaser organizations on a Quality Measurement Advisory Service and has a separate mandate, funded by the Hartford Foundation, to assist organizations wishing to set up community networks of electronic medical information.

Foundation for Health Services Research (FHSR)
Founded: 1981. *Headquarters:* Washington, DC. *Purpose:* To conduct professional and educational activities beneficial to the field of health services research. FHSR is working with the Cecil G. Sheps Center for Health Services Research to develop and maintain HSRProj, a database of ongoing research projects in the field of health services research.

Foundation for Informed Medical Decision Making
Founded: 1989. *Headquarters:* Hanover, NH. *Purpose:* To make available the information needed to enable informed medical decision making; to provide accurate and understandable information about the nature and potential outcomes of various treatments, so that patients and physicians can work together to make informed medical decisions; to gather data on the outcomes of different treatments; and to improve the scientific basis for medical decision making.

GASP of America *See* Group Against Smokers' Pollution.

Gay and Lesbian Medical Association (LGMA)
Founded: 1981. *Headquarters:* San Francisco, CA. *Purpose:* To seek the elimination of discrimination on the basis of sexual orientation in the health professions and promote unprejudiced medical care for gay and lesbian patients; maintains a referral and support program for HIV-infected physicians. It serves physicians and medical students and their supporters.

Gay Men's Health Crisis, Inc. (GMHC) *Founded:* 1982. *Headquarters:* New York, NY. *Purpose:* To provide support and therapy groups for persons with AIDS and their families and to provide patient recreation services.

General Constituency Section for Small or Rural Hospitals (SSRH) *Founded:* 1976. *Headquarters:* Chicago, IL. *Purpose:* To provide a forum for exchange of ideas among community hospitals that have fewer than 100 acute care beds, are located outside a standard metropolitan statistical area, or admit 4,000 or fewer patients per year. The SSRH is a section of the American Hospital Association.

Generic Pharmaceutical Industry Association (GPIA) *Founded:* 1981. *Headquarters:* Washington, DC. *Purpose:* To promote the recognition, acceptance, and use of generic prescription drug products. Members include manufacturers, distributors, and retailers of generic drugs interested in increasing the availability of equivalent generic pharmaceuticals on the market.

Genetics Society of America (GSA) *Founded:* 1931. *Headquarters:* Washington, DC. *Purpose:* To provide facilities for associations and conferences of students in the field of genetics for individuals and organizations interested in the field of genetics.

Gerontological Society of America (GSA) *Founded:* 1945. *Headquarters:* Washington, DC. *Purpose:* To improve the well-being of elderly people by promoting scientific study of the aging process, publishing information for professionals about aging, and bringing together groups interested in research on aging. It sponsors fellowship programs in applied gerontology. Members include physicians, physiologists, psychologists, anatomists, biochemists, economists, sociologists, social workers, botanists, pharmacologists, nurses, and other individuals.

Group for the Advancement of Psychiatry (GAP) *Founded:* 1946. *Headquarters:* Dallas, TX. *Purpose:* To investigate topics, such as school desegregation, use of nuclear energy, religion, psychiatry in the armed forces, mental retardation, and medical uses of hypnosis. Members are psychiatrists organized in working committees interested in applying the principles of psychiatry toward the study of human relations.

Group Against Smokers' Pollution (GASP) *Founded:* 1971. *Headquarters:* College Park, MD. *Purpose:* To promote the rights of nonsmokers, educate the public about the problems of secondhand smoke, and regulate smoking in places where nonsmokers are exposed. The group has local chapters. It is also known as GASP of America.

Group Health Cooperative (Group Health) *Founded:* 1947. *Headquarters:* Seattle, WA. *Purpose:* To enhance the well-being of patients and other customers by providing quality, cost-effective, prepaid health care. Group Health includes the Northwest U.S.'s largest HMO, a point-of-service plan, self-funded health insurance options, and a research center. Group Health is a consumer-governed health care organization and an affiliate of Kaiser Permanente. Note that the acronym GHC is no longer used by the organization.

Group Health Association of America (GHAA) *See* American Association of Health Plans.

Group Practice Improvement Network (GPIN) *Founded:* 1993. *Headquarters:* Detroit, MI. *Purpose:* To improve the quality and value of medical group practices through a shared learning network focusing on better clinical outcomes, improved access to care, greater ease of consumer use, cost effectiveness, and high satisfaction for users of the health care system, their families, and the community. GPIN is a nonprofit organization sponsored by the Institute for Healthcare Improvement (IHI), the Medical Group Management Association (MGMA), and the American Medical Group Practice Association (AMGA). Members are selected from multispecialty group practices (with more than 50 full-time physicians) through an application approval process. Activities include the *Shared Learning* quarterly publication, a Leadership Information Exchange program, GPIN Intensive Studies focusing on better practices adopted by GPIN members, and the LotusNotes databases to share clinical improvement guidelines.

Guidelines Appraisal Project (GAP) *Founded:* 1991. *Headquarters:* Hamilton, Ontario, Canada. *Purpose:* To bring together health services researchers, policymakers, and practitioners in appraising, summarizing, and disseminating information about clinical practice guidelines; to study and provide what clinicians want from guidelines; to develop users guides for guidelines; and to promote a standardized approach to summarizing guidelines and maintaining guideline summary registries. The GAP

is an outgrowth of a guidelines appraisal curriculum developed at Johns Hopkins University (Baltimore) and a survey of physicians of the American College of Physicians, which has endorsed the project. An affiliated project is the Clinical Practice Enhancement Project, a nonprofit foundation created by the researchers. GAP services and products include the HIRE (Health Information Resource Executive) Internet software, a guideline abstract registry, and a guidelines glossary. GAP is located in the Health Information Research Unit at McMaster University Health Sciences Center.

Gynecologic Oncology Group (GOG) *Founded:* 1970. *Headquarters:* Philadelphia, PA. *Purpose:* To provide a forum for exchange of ideas among institutions and teaching hospitals conducting research in gynecological oncology.

Harkness Fellowships Program *See* Commonwealth Fund.

The John A. Hartford Foundation, Inc *Founded:* 1929. *Headquarters:* New York, NY. *Purpose:* To provide support through two main programs. The Aging and Health Program addresses the unique health needs of the elderly, including long term care, the use of medication in chronic health problems, increasing the nation's geriatric research and training capability, and improving hospital outcomes for frail elderly inpatients. The Health Care Cost and Quality Program is concerned with balancing the quality and cost of medical procedures, particularly by developing systems for assessing their appropriateness, quality, and value.

Harvard Community Health Plan (HCHP) *See* Harvard Pilgrim Health Care.

Harvard Pilgrim Health Care (Harvard Pilgrim) *Founded:* 1995. *Headquarters:* Quincy, MA. *Purpose:* To improve the health of the plan's members and offer unsurpassed value for customers by providing high-quality health care and excellent service through an organized system of health care delivery and financing. Harvard Pilgrim is New England's largest nonprofit managed health care organization, offering HMO, point of service, and Medicare plans. The new organization has assumed the clinical innovation and quality improvement activities and leadership role of the former organizations. Harvard Pilgrim has collaborated with Harvard Medical School to establish the Center for Ethics in Managed Care (Brookline, MA). *Formed by merger of:* Harvard Community Health Plan (HCHP) and Pilgrim Health Care.

The Hastings Center (HC) *Founded:* 1969. *Headquarters:* Briarcliff Manor, NY. *Purpose:* Sponsors education and research in bioethics. The Hastings Center has covered the broad range of problems and issues posed to our society by developments in medicine and the life sciences—from test-tube babies to genetic engineering, organ transplantation, end-of-life decisions, health care rationing, enviromental ethics, and more recently a focus on biotechnology. Research groups are composed of Hastings Center staff, Center Fellows (members of a distinguished group of national leaders in bioethics who work closely with the Center), and other individuals chosen for their expertise or experience in a particular field. The Center also publishes the *Hastings Center Report.*

Hazardous Materials Advisory Council (HMAC) *Founded:* 1978. *Headquarters:* Washington, DC. *Purpose:* To promote safe transportation of these materials, answering regulatory questions; to guide appropriate governmental resources; and to advise establishment of corporate compliance and safety programs. Members include shippers, carriers, and container manufacturers of hazardous materials, substances, and wastes.

Hazardous Materials Control Resources Institute (HMCRI) *Founded:* 1976. *Headquarters:* Rockville, MD. *Purpose:* To disseminate information about technical advances and institutional requirements in hazardous waste disposal and conduct training programs on toxic and hazardous materials control and management. It serves corporations, engineers, scientists, government and corporate administrators, and other individuals interested in the safe management of hazardous materials and waste prevention, control, and cleanup.

Health Academy (HA) *Founded:* 1989. *Headquarters:* New York, NY. *Purpose:* To assist public relations consultants and senior public relations professionals working in many health care settings including hospitals, multihospital systems, medical and dental organizations, and insurance companies and HMOs.

Healthcare Convention and Exhibitors Association (HCEA) *Founded:* 1930. *Headquarters:* Atlanta, GA. *Purpose:* To increase the efficiency and effectiveness of health care conventions and exhibits as a marketing and educational medium and provide for the professional development of convention and exhibit personnel, especially exhibit managers. It serves manufacturers and distributors of products or services used or prescribed by health professionals who exhibit at conventions. Associate members are manufacturers or other organizations that provide products or services to health care conventions.

Healthcare Financial Management Association (HFMA) *Founded:* 1946. *Headquarters:* Westchester, IL. *Purpose:* To support financial management professionals employed by hospitals and long term care facilities, public accounting and consulting firms, insurance companies, government agencies, and other organizations.

Health Care Financing Administration (HCFA) *See* Government Organizations (Department of Health and Human Services).

The Healthcare Forum (THF) *Founded:* 1927. *Headquarters:* San Francisco, CA. *Purpose:* To serve as an educational and research resource for health care executives. Members include health care executives, hospitals, and other health care providers, insurers, and industry suppliers.

Healthcare Information and Management Systems Society (HIMSS) *Founded:* 1961. *Headquarters:* Chicago, IL. *Purpose:* To provide a forum for exchange of ideas among persons engaged in the analysis, design, and operation of hospital telecommunications, management, and information systems.

Health Care Material Management Society (HCMMS) *Founded:* 1975. *Headquarters:* Cincinnati, OH. *Purpose:* To administer a certification program and develop audiovisual programs on topics such as hospital costs, distribution, logistics, life-cycle costs, and recycling management of inventory. Members are materials management personnel in health care and hospital fields concerned with advancing health care management.

Health Care Quality Alliance (HCQA) *Founded:* 1988. *Headquarters:* Washington, DC. *Purpose:* To unite national health-related organizations with a common commitment to preserving and enhancing the quality of health care made available in America.

Health Education Resource Organization (HERO) *Founded:* 1983. *Headquarters:* Baltimore, MD. *Purpose:* Provides patient services and preventive education regarding AIDS to Maryland residents and disseminates information on AIDS prevention and treatment nationwide.

Health Industry Business Communications Council (HIBCC) *Founded:* 1984. *Headquarters:* Phoenix, AZ. *Purpose:* An organization of individuals and companies in the health care industry concerned with improving the quality and economic efficiency of health care by instituting and overseeing a uniform system of computer bar coding for identification of health care equipment and by promoting the use of this and other automated technologies in the health care industry.

Health Industry Distributors Association (HIDA) *Founded:* 1902. *Headquarters:* Alexandria, VA. *Purpose:* To provide a forum to exchange ideas among distributors of medical, laboratory, surgical, and home health care equipment and supplies to hospitals, physicians, nursing homes, and industrial medical departments.

Health Industry Group Purchasing Association (HIGPA) *Founded:* 1910. *Headquarters:* Washington, DC. *Purpose:* Providing cost-containment services, such as group purchasing, to health care providers in areas such as prescription drugs, supplies, and durable medical equipment. Its membership includes for-profit and non-profit corporations, voluntary purchasing groups, trade associations, multihospital systems, and health care provider alliances.

Health Industry Manufacturers Association (HIMA) *Founded:* 1974. *Headquarters:* Washington, DC. *Purpose:* To develop programs and activities on economic, technical, medical, and scientific matters affecting the industry. Gathers and disseminates information concerning national and international developments in legislative, regulatory, scientific, or standards-making areas. It serves domestic manufacturers of medical devices, diagnostic products, and health care information systems.

Health Insurance Association of America (HIAA) *Founded:* 1956. *Headquarters:* Washington, DC. *Purpose:* To create a positive image of the health insurance industry. Members are accident and health insurance firms.

Health Physics Society (HPS) *Founded:* 1956. *Headquarters:* McLean, VA. *Purpose:* To improve public understanding of the problems and needs in radiation protection. Members are engaged in some form of activity in the field of health physics.

Health Resources and Services Administration (HRSA) *See* Government Organizations (Department of Health and Human Services).

Health Sciences Communications Association (HESCA) *Founded:* 1959. *Headquarters:* Jewett City, CT. *Purpose:* To provide a forum for the exchange information through publications, annual meetings, and workshops on the application of communications technology to health sciences education. The information exchange focuses on the design and production of media programs, such as print, television, self-instructional packages, audiovisual materials, videotapes, and films. Areas of study include medical writing, medical illustrating, medical librarianship, and medical photography. Job placement services are offered.

Health Sciences Consortium (HSC) *Founded:* 1971. *Headquarters:* Chapel Hill, NC. *Purpose:* To develop sales training and continuing education instructional materials for pharmaceutical companies. It serves health science institutions concerned with publishing effective instructional materials at a low cost.

Health Security Action Council (HSAC) *Founded:* 1969. *Headquarters:* Washington, DC. *Purpose:* To increase grassroots support for national health insurance and progressive health plans through publicity and education. Members are individuals and organizations.

Health Standards and Quality Bureau (HSQB) An organization element within the Health Care Financing Administration that is responsible for carrying out the quality assurance provisions of the Medicare and Medicaid programs, implementation of health and safety standards for providers of care in their programs, and the professional review provision of Medicare and Medicaid programs.

Hearing Industries Association (HIA) *Founded:* 1957. *Headquarters:* Alexandria, VA. *Purpose:* Cooperates in and contributes toward efforts to promote the number of hearing aid users, collects trade statistics, and conducts market research activities, investigations, and experiments with hearing aids. Members are companies engaged in the manufacture and/or sale of electronic hearing aids, their component parts, and related products and services on a national basis.

Hemlock Society U.S.A. (HSUSA) *Founded:* 1980. *Headquarters:* Denver, CO. *Purpose:* Supports the option of active voluntary euthanasia for the advanced terminally ill and seriously incurably ill. Promotes a climate of public opinion tolerant of the terminally ill individual's right to end his or her own life in a planned manner, working to improve existing laws on assisted suicide.

Healthy Steps *See* Commonwealth Fund.

Henry Ford Health System (HFHS) *Founded:* 1915. *Headquarters:* Detroit, MI. *Purpose:* To provide exceptional quality, cost-effective care, strengthened by excellence in education and research, to improve health and the quality of life in the communities of Southeastern Michigan and the neighboring regions. HFHS is nonprofit directorship corporation offering a comprehensive health system with several components including a hospital, a large group practice, ambulatory care facilities, an HMO, and several other facilities, institutes, and collaborative programs. HFHS's Center for Clinical Effectiveness (CCE) coordinates and improves the research, development, and implementation of clinical policies applicable to the health care community; its services and products include quality and outcomes measurement tools, clinical policy implementation trials (applying continuous quality improvement techniques), a practice guideline and policy library, and workgroups addressing specific clinical issues, such as the Spinal Surgery Outcomes Consortium Research (SCORE).

The Henry J. Kaiser Family Foundation *See under* Kaiser.

Histochemical Society (HS) *Founded:* 1950. *Headquarters:* Rocasset, MA. *Purpose:* A professional society of physicians and scientists who employ histochemical and cytochemical techniques in their research.

HIV/AIDS Bureau *See* Government Organizations (Department of Health and Human Services, HRSA).

Holistic Dental Association (HDA) *Founded:* 1980. *Headquarters:* Oklahoma City, OK. *Purpose:* To promote a holistic approach to better dental care for patients. To expand techniques, medications, and philosophies that pertain to extractions, anesthetics, fillings, crowns, and orthodontics. To encourage use of homeopathic medications, acupuncture, cranial osteopathy, nutritional techniques and physical therapy in addition to conventional treatments.

Karen Horney Clinic (KHC) *Founded:* 1955. *Headquarters:* New York, NY. *Purpose:* To promote the psychoanalytic and psychotherapeutic treatment of individuals and groups focusing on the special problems of children, adolescents, the developmentally disabled, victims of violent crimes, adult survivors of childhood sexual abuse, and persons with psychoneurotic and emotional problems.

Home Health Services and Staffing Association (HHSSA) *Founded:* 1982. *Headquarters:* Cherry Hill, NJ. *Purpose:* To develop, promote, encourage, and support the enactment of just and reasonable laws and regulations that affect the home health care and staffing industry; to develop, promote, encourage, and support the enactment of just and reasonable laws and regulations that establish and maintain equal status for all organizations primarily engaged in the home health care and staffing industry; and to maintain an active and informed membership of individuals and/or companies who are committed to the purpose and objectives of the association consistent with the best interests of the patient, the employee, and the provider organization.

Hospice Association of America (HAA) *Founded:* 1985. *Headquarters:* Washington, DC. *Purpose:* To heighten the public visibility of hospice services; to gather and disseminate data pertinent to the hospice industry; to foster, develop, and promote high standards of patient care in hospice services; to sponsor educational programs; and to promote research related to hospice services. The association serves hospices that are freestanding and community based, as well as those affiliated with home care agencies and hospitals. HAA is an affiliate of the National Association for Home Care (NAHC) and pubishes a monthly newsletter, magazine, and hospice newspaper.

Hospice Education Institute (HEI) *Founded:* 1985. *Headquarters:* Essex, CT. *Purpose:* A nonmembership organization providing educational and informational services to health professionals and the public on subjects such as hospice care, death and dying, and bereavement counseling.

Hospice Nurses Association (HNA) *Founded:* 1985. *Headquarters:* Pittsburgh, PA. *Purpose:* To promote high professional standards in hospice nursing among its member nurses.

Hospital Audiences, Inc (HAI) *Founded:* 1969. *Headquarters:* New York, NY. *Purpose:* To promote the cultural enrichment of mentally and physically disabled individuals, primarily in hospitals, nursing homes, mental health and retardation facilities, and shelters for the homeless by arranging for individuals to attend cultural events and bringing cultural events and art workshops into institutions for those unable to leave.

Hospitalized Veterans Writing Project (HVWP) *Founded:* 1946. *Headquarters:* Mission, KS. *Purpose:* To encourage hospitalized U.S. veterans to write for pleasure and rehabilitation during their hospital stays. Maintains speakers' bureau and conducts writing sessions in hospitals. Members are individuals and organizations.

Hospital Research and Educational Trust (HRET) *See* American Hospital Association.

Human Factors and Ergonomics Society (HFS) *Founded:* 1957. *Headquarters:* Santa Monica, CA. *Purpose:* To promote the discovery and exchange of knowledge concerning human characteristics that apply to the design of systems and devices intended for human use and operation. Members include psychologists, engineers, industrial designers, and other scientists and practitioners who

are interested in the use of human factors and ergonomics in the development of systems and devices of all kinds.

Human Genome Project *See* Department of Energy (Department of Health and Human Services, NIH).

Huntington's Disease Society of America (HDSA) *Founded:* 1986. *Headquarters:* New York, NY. *Purpose:* To promote and support research on Huntington's Disease (HD) to eradicate the disease; to assist people and families affected by HD to cope with the problems presented by the disease; and to educate the public and health professionals about HD. HDSA offers extensive resources on genetic testing, which are consulted as models by groups concerned with other genetic diseases and the potential abuses of genetic testing, and it is a member of the Alliance of Genetic Support Groups.

Impaired Physician Program (IPP) *Founded:* 1975. *Headquarters:* College Park, GA. *Purpose:* To provide assistance to physicians, other health professionals, and their spouses with problems such as alcoholism, substance abuse, or codependence. Seeks to locate and identify persons in need of help and to provide assistance. It conducts inpatient and outpatient treatment programs and assists physicians and other health professionals in re-entering their profession.

Impotence Institute of America (IIA) *Founded:* 1983. *Headquarters:* Maryville, TN. *Purpose:* To inform and educate the public on the subject of impotence and its causes and treatments. Members include urologists, psychiatrists, sex therapists and counselors, and plastic surgeons; manufacturers of penile implant devices; and hospitals and other institutions that offer assistance and meeting facilities for Impotents Anonymous and I-ANON.

Independent Hospital Workers Union (IHWU) *Founded:* 1980. *Headquarters:* Alexandria, VA. *Purpose:* To represent hospital workers and protect their rights to a fair salary and acceptable working conditions.

Indian Health Service *See* Government Organizations (Department of Health and Human Services).

Indians Into Medicine (INMED) *Founded:* 1973. *Headquarters:* Grand Forks, ND. *Purpose:* Supports American Indian students. Seeks to increase the awareness of and interest in health care professions among young American Indians; recruit and enroll American Indians in health care education programs; and place American Indian health professionals in service to American Indian communities.

Infectious Diseases Society of America (IDSA) *Founded:* 1963. *Headquarters:* Washington, DC. *Purpose:* To promote human health through excellence in research, education, prevention, and care of patients and to pursue and represent the concerns of the membership through organizational structure, journals, meetings, and other activities. Through a Cooperative Agreement Program award from the Centers for Disease Control and Prevention (CDC) in 1996, IDSA developed the Emerging Infections Network (Portland, OR), a sentinel network composed of physicians specializing in adult or pediatric infectious diseases, to function primarily as an early warning system for the CDC and other public health agencies by providing information about unusual cases encountered in clinical practice.

Injury Control Center (ICC) *Founded:* 1987. *Headquarters:* Boston, MA. *Purpose:* Support scientific research and training to improve injury control, particularly prevention activities, acute care of trauma patients, and rehabilitation of the disabled. Members include universities, medical centers, doctors, and research associates.

Institute for Advanced Research in Asian Science and Medicine (IARASM) *Founded:* 1972. *Headquarters:* Chestnut Hill, MA. *Purpose:* To advance international understanding between Asia and the West in the areas of science, medical systems, and health care delivery. Serves as a clearinghouse for international scholarly efforts in the mediation of scientific and biomedical exchange with Asian countries. Assists in generating innovative curricula in medical education, translates contemporary and classical Asian scientific and medical literature, and provides training for medical professionals in acupuncture therapeutics.

Institute for the Advancement of Human Behavior (IAHB) *Founded:* 1977. *Headquarters:* Portola Valley, CA. *Purpose:* To provide continuing education for health care professionals on behavioral topics, such as the psychology of health care, human sexuality, the healing power of laughter and play, maintaining long-term health behaviors, and the role of imagery in health care.

Institute for Aerobics Research (IAR) *Founded:* 1970. *Headquarters:* Dallas, TX. *Purpose:* To promote understanding of the relationship between living habits and health, to provide leadership in enhancing the physical and emotional well-being of individuals, and to promote participation in aerobics. Activities include sponsoring weekly training courses and certification testing of fitness leaders in education, government, human services, and corporate sectors. Divisions include behavioral sciences, computer services, continuing education, consultation, epidemiology, and exercise-physiology.

Institute for Clinical Systems Integration (ICSI) *Founded:* 1993. *Headquarters:* Minneapolis, MN. *Purpose:* To help participating organizations become living laboratories for continual improvement in the quality and value of health care they provide and in the overall health of the populations they serve. ICSI was founded by Group Health, Mayo Clinic, Park Nicollet Clinic, and Health-Partners in cooperation with the Business (now Buyers) Health Care Action Group, and is funded by HealthPartners. ICSI is designed to be an organizational bridge in a new model of integrated health care delivery

and uses continual improvement principles to standardize health care processes, improve health care outcomes, and reduce the cost of health care. Its products include ICSI Health Care Guidelines and technology assessments, which are available to other organizations and individuals outside ICSI.

Institute for Control Theory, Reality Therapy and Quality Management (ICTRTQM) *Founded:* 1967. *Headquarters:* Chatsworth, CA. *Purpose:* To assist those interested in teaching reality therapy and control theory psychology to people who are involved in the helping professions. Members are board-certified psychiatrists, psychologists, social workers, and consultants in a variety of related fields.

Institute of Electrical and Electronics Engineers (IEEE) *Founded:* 1963. *Headquarters:* New York, NY. *Purpose:* To develop devices and methods to improve the utility of electricity. Conducts lecture courses. Members include engineers and scientists in electrical engineering, electronics, and allied fields. IEEE has established the Engineering in Medicine and Biology Society (EMBS), which is concerned with application of physical and engineering sciences concepts and methods to biology and medicine, including technological developments and practical clinical applications. The institute also founded the Lasers and Electro-Optics Society (LEOS) to serve as a forum for discussion of quantum electronics, optoelectronic theory, and techniques and applications, and the design, development, and manufacture of systems and subsystems (such as lasers and fiberoptics).

Institute of Electrology Educators (IEE) *Founded:* 1979. *Headquarters:* Stow, MA. *Purpose:* To instruct teachers and standardize the curriculum and teaching of electrology. Members include electrology schools and teachers.

Institute for Gravitational Strain Pathology (IGSP) *Founded:* 1957. *Headquarters:* Rangeley, ME. *Purpose:* To study the ill effects (backaches, postural decline, aging) of terrestrial gravity on humans and to develop ways to counteract pathology of gravitational strain. Provides instruction with a tool called the "antigravity leverage technique," designed to modify and reduce the harmful consequences of gravity.

Institute for Healthcare Improvement (IHI) *Founded:* 1995. *Headquarters:* Boston, MA. *Purpose:* To engender efforts that accelerate improvement in the health care delivery systems of North America. One of IHI's mechanisms to accomplish this mission is the Breakthrough Series, which brings together groups with shared vision for making big system change happen fast. The focus of these efforts is to produce breakthrough results that simultaneously lower costs and improve outcomes. IHI's national Breakthrough Collaboratives have addressed ten areas so far (including cesarean section rates, cardiac surgery, low back pain). Other IHI products are seminars and courses in quality improvement, newsletters, and a periodical surveillance bulletin on quality improvements reported in journals.

Institute for Hospital Clinical Nursing Education (IHCNE) *Founded:* 1967. *Headquarters:* Chicago, IL. *Purpose:* To provide support for issues common to hospital schools of nursing and promote advancement of schools through educational programs and other activities. Members are hospital schools of nursing.

Institute of Mathematical Statistics (IMS) *Founded:* 1935. *Headquarters:* Hayward, CA. *Purpose:* A professional society composed of mathematicians and other individuals interested in mathematical statistics and probability theory.

Institute of Medicine (IOM) *See* Government Organizations (Boards, Commissions, etc.).

Institute for Rational-Emotive Therapy (IRET) *Founded:* 1968. *Headquarters:* New York, NY. *Purpose:* To provide professional training and moderate-cost treatment services, including individual and group psychotherapy, marriage and family counseling, and crisis intervention; consultative services for mental health professionals, corporations, and community agencies; and research programs in applied psychology.

Institute for Research in Hypnosis and Psychotherapy (IRHP) *Founded:* 1954. *Headquarters:* New York, NY. *Purpose:* Sponsors research in clinical and experimental hypnosis, offers postgraduate training in hypnosis and its applications, and develops standards and procedures for advanced education in clinical and experimental hypnosis. It serves psychologists, psychiatrists, physicians, and social workers trained in clinical hypnosis, hypnotherapy, and hypnoanalysis.

Institutes for Behavior Resources (IBR) *Founded:* 1960. *Headquarters:* Washington, DC. *Purpose:* To conduct basic and applied research in behavioral psychology; investigate human performance, law and behavior, and social problems; and work with agencies dealing with youth problems to stimulate them to seek alternatives to punishment in handling juvenile delinquent behaviors. Composed of persons with backgrounds in psychology, education, sociology, social services, and law.

Institute for Victims of Trauma (IVT) *Founded:* 1987. *Headquarters:* McLean, VA. *Purpose:* A nonpolitical group assisting victims of terrorism, accidents, and disasters, whether natural or not. It acts as a liaison between governmental and nongovernmental organizations and institutions and maintains a library on traumatic stress, victimology, and terrorism. A nonmembership organization supported by professionals specializing in post traumatic stress, crisis intervention, and the study of terrorism.

Insurance Accounting and Systems Association (IASA) *Founded:* 1928. *Headquarters:* Durham, NC. *Purpose:* Studies insurance accounting practices and their management in the insurance industry. Members are insurance companies writing all lines of insurance and independent public accountants, actuarial consultants, management consultants, statisticians, and statistical organizations.

Insurance Rehabilitation Study Group (IRSG) *Founded:* 1965. *Headquarters:* Washington, DC. *Purpose:* Created by insurance professionals closely involved in the areas of health care and rehabilitation to communicate rehabilitation principles, concepts, and techniques within the insurance industry and other businesses, including such groups as insurance executive management, claims personnel, agents and trade associations, administrators of public and private agencies and facilities, professional and paraprofessional personnel who provide rehabilitation, the legal profession, the general public, and rehabilitation associations.

Interagency Council on Information Resources for Nursing (ICIRN) *Founded:* 1960. *Headquarters:* New York, NY. *Purpose:* To promote development and improvement of library resources and services for nurses in all health science libraries. Members are representatives from agencies and organizations concerned with the library needs of nurses, including American Academy of Nursing, American Nurses' Association, Medical Library Association, American Hospital Association, American Medical Association, National League for Nursing, American Journal of Nursing Company, and U.S. Public Health Service, Nursing Division.

Interamerican College of Physicians and Surgeons (ICPS) *Founded:* 1979. *Headquarters:* New York, NY. *Purpose:* To encourage understanding and communication among members concerning all aspects of medical practice; to promote health education in Hispanic communities in the Western Hemisphere; and to maintain a library of Spanish-language medical books. Members are physicians in countries of the Americas.

Intergovernmental Health Policy Project (IHPP) *Founded:* 1979. *Headquarters:* Washington, DC. *Purpose:* To provide information on health legislation and programs to state executive officials, legislators, and legislative staff. Serves as an information clearinghouse and responds to specific information requests on state programs. Members are health policy researchers.

InterHealth *Founded:* 1984. *Headquarters:* St. Paul, MN. *Purpose:* To strengthen and preserve faith-based, values-driven health care by providing an indispensable forum for knowledge sharing and becoming the preeminent group dealing with values and innovation in health care. The values spring from religious stewardship, including caring, openness, integrity, excellence, and concern for the common good, all of which are to be upheld while confronting the hard questions in the current competitive marketplace. Member groups include Fortune 500 companies as well as religion-affiliated health care systems. The parent organization includes InterHealth Education and Research Foundation and InterHealth Ventures. The organization's activities and publications focus on leadership, the learning organization, performance management, and system improvement.

International Academy of Oral Medicine and Toxicology (IAOMT) *Founded:* 1984. *Headquarters:* Orlando, FL. *Purpose:* To encourage, sponsor, and disseminate scientific research on the biocompatibility of materials used in dentistry; to offer educational programs; and to maintain speakers' bureau.

International Anti-Euthanasia Task Force (IAETF) *Founded:* 1987. *Headquarters:* Steubenville, OH. *Purpose:* To provide information on euthanasia suicide, assisted suicide, and related issues; to resist attitudes the group feels threaten the lives and rights of those medically vulnerable, particularly the elderly and disabled.

International Association of Psychosocial Rehabilitation Services (IAPSRS) *Founded:* 1994. *Headquarters:* Columbia, MD. *Purpose:* To develop and disseminate a simple, function-oriented outcomes measurement system to assess services provided to people with serious and persistent mental illness. To focus attention on the importance of assessing changes in patients' functional status.

International Association for the Study of Pain (IASP) *Founded:* 1974. *Headquarters:* Seattle, WA. *Purpose:* To encourage research on pain mechanisms and syndromes; to improve management of patients with acute and chronic pain; to promote education and training in the field of pain; and to inform the public of results of current research. Fosters development of international data bank. Services scientists, physicians, and health professionals interested in pain research and therapy.

International Biometric Society (IBS) *Founded:* 1947. *Headquarters:* Washington, DC. *Purpose:* To advance subject-matter sciences through development, application, and dissemination of effective math and statistical techniques. Members are biologists, statisticians, and other individuals interested in applying statistical techniques to biological research data.

International Cesarean Awareness Network (ICAN) *Founded:* 1982. *Headquarters:* Redondo Beach, CA. *Purpose:* To promote vaginal births, offering encouragement, information, and support for women wanting vaginal births after cesareans (VBAC), and assisting in organizing and informing new parents and cesarean parents on preventing future cesareans by opposing unnecessary medical interventions during the birth process and by working to make hospital routines more responsive to women in labor. Offers teacher training and course materials and sponsors a childbirth education certification program. It serves those interested in the increasing rate of cesarean births.

International College of Surgeons *Founded:* 1935. *Headquarters:* Chicago, IL. *Purpose:* To promote the universal teaching and advancement of surgery and its allied sciences. Maintains library and International Museum of Surgical Sciences, and organizes postgraduate clinics around the world.

International Council of Societies of Pathology *Founded:* 1962. *Headquarters:* Chevy Chase, MD. *Purpose:* To distribute teaching sets and professional aids to pathology societies worldwide. Offers seminars and specialized education. Conducts training and research programs.

International Hearing Society (IHS) *Founded:* 1951. *Headquarters:* Livonia, MI. *Purpose:* To provide counseling for the hearing impaired and instruct them in the care and use of hearing aids; to administer a qualification program for screening persons designated as hearing instrument specialists; to administer a consumer protection program; and to establish standards of education, equipment, and techniques in the fitting of hearing aids. Serves hearing aid specialists who test hearing for the selection, adaptation, fitting, adjusting, servicing, and sale of hearing aids.

International Society for Adolescent Psychiatry *Founded:* 1985. *Headquarters:* Nashville, TN. *Purpose:* To advance treatment of psychiatric illness of adolescents. Maintains research and educational programs.

International Society for Dermatologic Surgery (ISDS) *Founded:* 1976. *Headquarters:* Schaumburg, IL. *Purpose:* To promote high standards of patient care; to provide continuing education and research in dermatologic surgery; to encourage public interest in the field; and to provide a forum for exchange of ideas.

International Society of Dermatology; Tropical, Geographic and Ecologic (ISD) *Founded:* 1957. *Headquarters:* Rochester, MN. *Purpose:* To promote interest, education, and research in dermatology.

International Society for Heart and Lung Transplantation (ISHLT) *Founded:* 1981. *Headquarters:* Dallas, TX. *Purpose:* To provide a center for discussion, exchange of information, and activities that promote the interests of heart and lung transplantation. Seeks to heighten awareness of public and governmental agencies regarding developments in the field.

International Society for Magnetic Resonance in Medicine (ISMRM) *Founded:* 1981. *Headquarters:* Berkeley, CA. *Purpose:* To further the development and application of MRI and its techniques in medicine and biology. Sponsors education and research programs. *Formerly:* Society for Magnetic Resonance Imaging (1995).

International Society of Ocular Surgeons *See* American Society of Contemporary Medicine, Surgery, and Ophthalmology.

Intersociety Committee on Pathology Information (ICPI) *Founded:* 1957. *Headquarters:* Bethesda, MD. *Purpose:* To disseminate information about the medical practice and research achievements of pathology and produce career information and supply it to schools and students. Publishes annually the *Directory of Pathology Training Programs: Anatomic, Clinical, Specialized.* Composed of one representative from each sponsoring society: American Association of Pathologists; American Society of Clinical Pathologists; Association of Pathology Chairmen; College of American Pathologists; and U.S. and Canadian Academy of Pathology.

Interstate Postgraduate Medical Association of North America (IPMANA) *Founded:* 1916. *Headquarters:* Madison, WI. *Purpose:* Presents annual four-day teaching programs in various branches of medicine and medical research, aimed at the family practitioner who must keep up with new developments in a short time away from his or her practice.

Intravenous Nurses Society (INS) *Founded:* 1973. *Headquarters:* Belmont, MA. *Purpose:* To conduct a certification program for intravenous nurses and an advanced studies program in intravenous nursing. Members are registered nurses involved in intravenous therapy, licensed practical nurses, and pharmacists.

ISA (Instrument Society of America) *Founded:* 1945. *Headquarters:* Research Triangle Park, NC. *Purpose:* To foster the advancement of knowledge and practice related to the theory, design, manufacture, and use of instruments and controls in science and industry. ISA offers a wide range of programs and activities of interest to anyone involved in measurement and control in the process and discrete manufacturing industries. Products and services include ISA Standards, Recommended Practices and Technical Reports, and the ISA Tech/Expo.

Islamic Medical Association (IMA) *Founded:* 1967. *Headquarters:* Downers Grove, IL. *Purpose:* To award scholarships to needy students and donate books, educational and research materials, and medical supplies and equipment to charity medical institutions in Muslim countries. Members are Muslim physicians and allied health professionals interested in assisting Muslim communities worldwide.

Ruth Jackson Orthopaedic Society (RJOS) *Founded:* 1983. *Headquarters:* Rosemont, IL. *Purpose:* To advance the science of orthopedic surgery; to provide support for women orthopedic surgeons; to conduct educational programs; and to operate speakers' bureau and placement services. Serves women orthopedic surgeons. Named after Dr. Ruth Jackson (b. 1902), the first woman certified by the American Board of Orthopedic Surgery and the first female member of the American Academy of Orthopedic Surgeons. Membership is composed primarily of women orthopedic surgeons, residents, those serving fellowships and medical students with an interest in orthopaedics.

Jin Shin Do Foundation for Bodymind Acupressure (JSDF) *Founded:* 1982. *Headquarters:* Palo Alto, CA. *Purpose:* A certification, referral, and educational organization composed of teachers and practitioners of the Jin Shin Do acupressure method. Jin Shin Do acupressure integrates a traditional Japanese acupressure technique with classical Chinese acu-theory, Taoist philosophy and breathing methods, and Western psychology.

The John A. Hartford Foundation *See under* Hartford.

The Robert Wood Johnson Foundation *See under* Robert Wood Johnson.

Joint Commission on Accreditation of Healthcare Organizations (Joint Commission, JCAHO) *Founded:* 1951. *Headquarters:* Oakbrook Terrace, IL. *Purpose:* To improve the quality of care provided to the public by providing health care accreditation and related services that support performance improvement in health care organizations. The Joint Commission evaluates and accredits more than 18,000 health care organizations in the United States, including hospitals, health care networks and health care organizations that provide home care, long term care, long term care pharmacy, behavioral health care, pathology and laboratory, and ambulatory care services. To support the accreditation process, the Joint Commission sponsors a variety of education programs and provides relevant publications for health care professionals on topics such as accreditation, quality improvement, and performance measurement. The Joint Commission is governed by a 28-member Board of Commissioners which includes six public members and an at-large nursing representative. Other board members are appointed by the American College of Physicians, the American College of Surgeons, the American Dental Association, the American Hospital Association, and the American Medical Association. Chief new initiatives and activities include the National Library of Healthcare Indicators (NLHI), ORYX Outcomes, the Orion Project, the Liaison Network, the Academy for Healthcare Quality, the Accreditation Watch sentinel events policy and process, and a Home Page on the Internet (http://www.jcaho.org).

Joint Commission on Allied Health Personnel in Ophthalmology (JCAHPO) *Founded:* 1969. *Headquarters:* St. Paul, MN. *Purpose:* To certify allied health personnel in ophthalmology. Encourages the establishment of medically oriented programs for training allied health personnel in ophthalmology, developing standards of education and training in the field, and examining, certifying, and recertifying ophthalmic medical personnel.

Joint Commission International (JCI) *Founded:* 1994. *Headquarters:* Oakbrook Terrace, IL. *Purpose:* Facilitates the organizational and management transitions health care organizations must make to be successful in changing environments; designs and evaluates tools to measure health care performance; evaluates a health care organization by using Joint Commission standards, adapted to local conditions; and provides consultation and education to facilitate an organization's independent application of quality improvement concepts, techniques, and leadership skills. JCI has worked for governments or organizations in such countries as Brazil, Czech Republic, France, Kazakhstan, Saudi Arabia, and the Ukraine. JCI is a partnership between the Joint Commission and its nonprofit consulting subsidiary Quality Healthcare Resources to bring education and consultation to the international health care community.

Joint Commission on Sports Medicine and Science (JCSMS) *Founded:* 1966. *Headquarters:* Stillwater, OK.

Purpose: To promote communication among organizations concerned with the health and safety of individuals engaged in athletics. Establishes guidelines and standards for athletic programs and recommends rules and administration policies for athletic programs. It serves five organizations: American College Health Association, National Association of Intercollegiate Athletics, National Athletic Trainers Association, National Federation of State High School Associations, and National Junior College Athletic Association.

Joint Council of Allergy, Asthma and Immunology (JCAI) *Founded:* 1975. *Headquarters:* Palatine, IL. *Purpose:* Serves as the political and socioeconomic arm for the American Academy of Allergy and Immunology and the American College of Allergy and Immunology. Members must belong to either organization.

Joint Review Committee on Education in Diagnostic Medical Sonography (JRCEDMS) *Founded:* 1979. *Headquarters:* Englewood, CO. *Purpose:* To evaluate, and recommend for accreditation, educational programs in the field of diagnostic medical sonography.

Joint Review Committee on Education in Radiologic Technology (JRCERT) *Founded:* 1969. *Headquarters:* Chicago, IL. *Purpose:* To evaluate, and recommend for accreditation, educational programs in the fields of radiography and radiation therapy technology. Its participants are physicians, radiographers, and radiation therapy technologists.

Joint Review Committee on Educational Programs for the EMT-Paramedic (JRCEMT-P) *Founded:* 1979. *Headquarters:* Euless, TX. *Purpose:* Cooperates with the Committee on Allied Health Education and Accreditation to accredit emergency medical technician-paramedic training programs across the United States. It establishes national education standards and programs for the EMT-paramedic.

Joint Review Committee for Respiratory Therapy Education (JRCRTE) *Founded:* 1963. *Headquarters:* Euless, TX. *Purpose:* To develop standards and requirements for accredited educational programs of respiratory therapy for recommendation to the American Medical Association (AMA); conduct evaluations of educational programs that have applied for accreditation to the AMA and make recommendations to the AMA's Committee on Allied Health Education and Accreditation; and maintain a working relationship with other organizations interested in respiratory therapy education and evaluation. Members are physicians, respiratory therapists, and public representatives.

Joseph P. Kennedy, Jr. Foundation *See under* Kennedy.

Joslin Diabetes Center (JDC) *Founded:* 1968. *Headquarters:* Boston, MA. *Purpose:* To advance knowledge and improving treatment of diabetes with the goal of discovering a means of prevention and cure. Investigates new methods in the clinical treatment of diabetes; con-

ducts research at its Elliott P. Joslin Research laboratory; and maintains a diabetes treatment unit to instruct diabetic patients in the proper management of their disease.

The Henry J. Kaiser Family Foundation *Founded:* 1948. *Headquarters:* Menlo Park, CA. *Purpose:* To support efforts in four main areas: health policy, reproductive health, HIV policy, and health and development in South Africa. The foundation also maintains a special interest in health policy and innovation in its home state of California.

Kaiser Permanente *Founded:* 1945. *Headquarters:* Oakland, CA. *Purpose:* To provide a full-service group practice prepayment program. It encompasses the Kaiser Foundation Health Plan, Inc; Kaiser Foundation Hospitals; and the Permanente Medical Groups (together serving 18 states and the District of Columbia), as well as alliances with Group Health Cooperative of Washington and Community Health Plan in New York. Its Garfield Fund supports innovations in elder care. Kaiser still follows the health care delivery model laid out by its founder, which emphasizes preventive medicine, health maintenance, and screening for early detection and treatment of ailments of all kinds.

Karen Horney Clinic *See under* Horney.

W.K. Kellogg Foundation *Founded:* 1930. *Headquarters:* Battle Creek, MI. *Purpose:* To help people help themselves through the practical application of knowledge resources to improve their quality of life and that of future generations. Since its beginning, the foundation has continuously focused on building the capacity of individuals, communities, and institutions to solve their own problems. Its current funding is in health services, health professions in education, and health support programs that help meet its goal to increase access to integrated, comprehensive health systems organized around public health, prevention, and primary care.

Joseph P. Kennedy, Jr. Foundation *Founded:* 1946. *Headquarters:* Washington, DC. *Purpose:* To identify the causes of mental retardation and to improve the means by which society deals with its mentally retarded citizens.

Kerato-Refractive Society (KRS) *Founded:* 1979. *Headquarters:* Dallas, TX. *Purpose:* To keep professionals and other persons informed of the most recent advances and developments in ophthalmologic care. Members are ophthalmologists and scientists interested in the latest advances in keratorefractive and laser techniques.

Rose Kushner Breast Cancer Advisory Center (RKBCAC) *Founded:* 1975. *Headquarters:* Kensington, MD. *Purpose:* Makes referrals and disseminates information about breast cancer.

Laser Institute of America (LIA) *Founded:* 1968. *Headquarters:* Orlando, FL. *Purpose:* To assist in the establishment of laser health and safety standards, definitions, and methods of measurements. To advance the state of laser application technology. Members are laser scientists, researchers, and manufacturers; educational and governmental institutions; and individuals and businesses.

Lasers and Electro-Optics Society (LEOS) *See* Institute of Electrical and Electronics Engineers.

Leadership Council of Aging Organizations (LCAO) *Founded:* 1978. *Headquarters:* Washington, DC. *Purpose:* Furthers the public's understanding of the potential and needs of elderly persons. It acts as a coordinating body in reviewing and acting on public policy issues. Members include professional groups serving elderly persons.

Lesbian, Gay and Bisexual People in Medicine (LGBPM) *Founded:* 1976. *Headquarters:* Reston, VA. *Purpose:* To improve the quality of health care for gay patients and improve working conditions and professional status of gay health professionals and students.

Lesbian and Gay Caucus of Public Health Workers (LGCPHW) *Founded:* 1975. *Headquarters:* Los Angeles, CA. *Purpose:* To provide a support network for gay public health workers. It serves public health workers in the fields of administration, government, nursing, direct care, and teaching, who are interested in disseminating information on the health needs of lesbians and gay men.

Liaison Committee on Medical Education (LCME) *Founded:* 1942. *Headquarters:* Chicago, IL. *Purpose:* To conduct accrediting activities in undergraduate medical education. Sponsored by the American Medical Association and the Association of American Medical Colleges, it draws membership from these groups and the Committee on Accreditation of Canadian Medical Schools.

Lifegain Institute (LI) *Founded:* 1977. *Headquarters:* Burlington, VA. *Purpose:* To promote health practices, such as exercise, nutrition, safety, and the reduction or curtailment of smoking and alcohol consumption, through health promotion programs that provide a supportive environment in which to change unhealthy practices. Members include those who work with health promotion programs in hospitals, corporations, colleges, and communities.

Long Term Acute Care Hospital Association of America *Founded:* 1996. *Headquarters:* Washington, DC. *Purpose:* To promote the best interests of long term acute care hospitals and their patients.

Long Term Care Campaign (LTCC) *Founded:* 1987. *Headquarters:* Washington, DC. *Purpose:* To promote legislation to enact social insurance, such as Social Security or Medicare, that would provide for long-term health care. It conducts lobbying on state and national levels.

Lutheran General Health Systems *See* Advocate Health Care.

Lutheran Hospitals and Homes Society (LHHS) *Founded:* 1938. *Headquarters:* Fargo, ND. *Purpose:* To operate and maintain Lutheran hospitals, nursing homes, homes for the aged, and a hospital-school for disabled children.

The John D. and Catherine T. MacArthur Foundation *Founded:* 1978. *Headquarters:* Chicago, IL. *Purpose:* To provide support through the seven major initiatives currently authorized: the MacArthur Fellow Program, for highly talented individuals in any field of endeavor who are chosen in a foundation-initiated effort; the Health Program, for research in mental health and the psychological and behavioral aspects of health and rehabilitation; the Community Initiatives Program, for support of cultural and community development in the Chicago metropolitan area; the Program on Peace and International Security; the World Environment and Resources Program, for support of conservation programs that protect the earth's biological diversity and work to protect tropical ecology; the Education Program, to focus on the promotion of literacy; and the Population Program, concerned with women's reproductive health, population, and natural resources, communications and popular education, and leadership development. Through the General Program, the foundation makes grants for a changing array of purposes.

Malignant Hyperthermia Association of the United States (MHAUS) *Founded:* 1981. *Headquarters:* Sherburne, NY. *Purpose:* To save lives by making information about MH available; to fund research on the causes, detection, and management of MH; to disseminate research information; and to provide information to MH patients and health care providers.

Maryland Hospital Association (MHA) Quality Indicator Project® (QI Project) *Founded:* 1985 (local), 1987 (national). *Headquarters:* Lutherville, MD. *Purpose:* To develop health care provider performance indicators, to determine the validity of the indicators in the field, and to educate participants as to the applications of the indicators in identifying potential opportunities for improvement. The licensed facilities participating in the project collect and submit quarterly clinical outcomes-based data according to indicator definitions and receive quarterly comparative reports. The QI Project has established inpatient, ambulatory, and psychiatric indicator sets and is currently pilot testing pediatric, long term care, and process indicators.

Maternal and Child Health Bureau *See* Government Organizations (Department of Health and Human Services, HRSA).

Maternity Center Association (MCA) *Founded:* 1918. *Headquarters:* New York, NY. *Purpose:* To maintain childbearing centers for low-risk families, sponsor research, and cosponsor the community-based nurse-midwifery education program. It serves physicians, nurses, nurse-midwives, public health workers, and laypersons interested in improvement of maternity care, maternal and infant health, and family life.

Medical Cybernetics Foundation (MCF) *Founded:* 1985. *Headquarters:* Jacksonville, FL. *Purpose:* Supports medical and medically affiliated professionals interested in researching, developing, and marketing new medical machinery, such as monitoring equipment and robotics systems.

Medical-Dental-Hospital Bureaus of America (MDHBA) *Founded:* 1938. *Headquarters:* Washington, DC. *Purpose:* To sponsor the certified professional bureau executive (CPBE) certification program. It serves business bureaus providing physicians, dentists, hospitals, and clinics with management, bookkeeping, finance, tax, and collection services.

Medic Alert Foundation International (MAFI) *Founded:* 1956. *Headquarters:* Arlington, VA. *Purpose:* To serve members who wear a descriptive warning bracelet, such as diabetics, epileptics, hemophiliacs, etc. Maintains a central database with medical information on members. Conducts continuous public and professional awareness and education programs.

Medical Group Management Association (MGMA) *Founded:* 1926. *Headquarters:* Englewood, CO. *Purpose:* To advance the art and science of medical group practice management to improve the health of communities and to be the source of excellence and innovation as the leading association in providing quality and timely services and resources for medical practice management and leadership. Serves administrators and physician leaders of medical group practices and others involved in ambulatory health care.

Medical Letter (ML) *Founded:* 1959. *Headquarters:* New Rochelle, NY. *Purpose:* To gather and publish information on the therapeutic and side effects of drugs for the use of physicians and other health professionals. The organization emphasizes new drugs.

Medical Library Association (MLA) *Founded:* 1898. *Headquarters:* Chicago, IL. *Purpose:* To foster medical and scientific libraries and to promote educational and professional growth of health and science libraries. Serves librarians and other individuals engaged in professional library or bibliographical work in medical and allied scientific libraries.

Medical Network for Missing Children (MNMC) *Founded:* 1984. *Headquarters:* Harrison, NY. *Purpose:* To identify missing children by medically identifiable char acteristics, such as dental patterns or scars. It conducts an educational program to alert health care professionals to the problem of missing children, provides a medical-dental questionnaire to health professionals and parents of missing children, offers medical profiles of known missing children to health care professionals, and maintains archives of medical and dental profiles of missing children.

Medical Outcomes Trust (the Trust) *Founded:* 1993. *Headquarters:* Boston, MA. *Purpose:* To advance the science and use of instruments for measuring health and the outcomes of health care from the patient's perspective by promoting the use of standardized questionnaires completed by patients to report on one's health status, satisfaction with health care, and health-related quality of life. The Trust hopes to foster widespread adoption of health outcomes assessment in health care to improve the value of health care services. The Trust assesses and then distributes instruments that meet its established instrument review criteria. Professional, student, and institutional membership is available to academic institutions, health care provider organizations, government agencies, other nonprofit organizations, and professional associations.

Medical Records Institute (MRI) *Founded:* 1979. *Headquarters:* Newton, MA. *Purpose:* To conduct research and education in the fields of medical documentation and computerization of patient information. Serves medical record and computer professionals, physicians, nurses, and other individuals involved in health care.

Medical Research Modernization Committee (MRMC) *Founded:* 1978. *Headquarters:* New York, NY. *Purpose:* Members evaluate the medical and/or scientific merit of research modalities in an effort to identify outdated research methods and to promote sensible, reliable, and efficient methods.

Medical Society Credentials Verification Organizations of America (MSCVOA) *Founded:* 1996. *Headquarters:* Colorado Springs, CO. *Purpose:* To distinguish medical credentials verification organizations by encouraging the highest quality standards and providing an efficient and cost-effective verification process.

Medical Society of the United States and Mexico (MSUSM) *Founded:* 1954. *Headquarters:* Los Angeles, CA. *Purpose:* To promote scientific and international goodwill, sponsor research and educational programs, and foster interchange of physicians.

Medical and Sports Music Institute of America (MSMIA) *Founded:* 1985. *Headquarters:* Bloomfield, NJ. *Purpose:* To develop and manufacture audiocassettes and videocassettes for exercise, insomnia, and stress management and seek to improve and maintain fitness levels for cardiac, drug, and physical rehabilitation. It conducts research on the relationship between target heart rate during exercise and optimum exercise pace for various forms of exercise.

Medicare Payment Advisory Council *See* Government Organizations (Boards, Commissions, etc.).

Medicine in the Public Interest (MIPI) *Founded:* 1973. *Headquarters:* Boston, MA. *Purpose:* To promote and fund research into medicine and related social, legal, and ethical issues. It disseminates research findings and proposals and encourages the development of long-range public health, welfare, and social planning at the federal, state, and local levels.

Melpomene Institute for Women's Health Research (MIWHR) *Founded:* 1982. *Headquarters:* St. Paul, MN. *Purpose:* To research and disseminate information on issues such as body image, osteoporosis, athletic amenorrhea (cessation of menstruation), exercise and pregnancy, and aging. It serves individuals professionally trained in health care, physical activity, and sports for girls and women.

Mental Health Corporations of America (MHCA) *Founded:* 1984. *Headquarters:* Tallahassee, FL. *Purpose:* To strengthen the competitive position of its members within the health care industry and to enhance their financial viability. It seeks members whose mission statements support a commitment to the community mental health mission.

Mental Research Institute (MRI) *Founded:* 1959. *Headquarters:* Palo Alto, CA. *Purpose:* To promote research, training, and service programs in the field of human behavior, with emphasis on the family as a social unit, serving psychiatrists, psychologists, and other professionals skilled in the disciplines related to the behavioral sciences.

Mental Retardation Association of America (MRAA) *Founded:* 1974. *Headquarters:* Salt Lake City, UT. *Purpose:* To work for the improvement of the quality of life for persons with mental retardation, promoting research aimed at preventing mental retardation in future generations, and working for adequate national appropriations, supportive legislation, and implementation of statutes and regulations to benefit persons with mental retardation.

Mercy Medical Airlift (MMA) *Founded:* 1984. *Headquarters:* Manassas, VA. *Purpose:* To provide long-distance air ambulance service to patients whose physicians prescribe recovery or special treatment at a distant location. Beneficiaries include patients in need of medical and nursing care en route to hospitals or other places of continuing care, especially low-income and medically indigent families. It operates an information clearinghouse and air transportation referral services. It conducts an educational program on medical air transportation.

Microscopy Society of America (MSA) *Founded:* 1942. *Headquarters:* Pocasset, MA. *Purpose:* To promote, increase, and disseminate information concerning electron microscopes and related instruments and results obtained through their use. Serves persons interested in the electron microscope, including medical, biological, metallurgical, and polymer research scientists and technicians, and physicists interested in instrument design and improvement.

Midwives Alliance of North America (MANA) *Founded:* 1982. *Headquarters:* Newton, KS. *Purpose:* To promote basic competency and to develop and encourage guidelines for education as well as to expand communication and support among midwives. Serves midwives, student and apprentice midwives, and persons supportive of midwifery.

Milbank Memorial Fund *Founded:* 1905. *Headquarters:* New York, NY. *Purpose:* To collaborate with decision makers in the public and private sectors to devise and implement new or improved solutions to pressing health problems. It also disseminates ideas and information about policy to improve health care and publishes an international peer-reviewed journal of public health and health care policy.

Milliman & Robertson (M&R) *Founded:* 1947. *Headquarters:* Seattle, WA. *Purpose:* To assist health care payers and providers such as hospitals, insurance companies, HMOs, PPOs, governmental agencies, and support institutions by offering services encompassing financial analysis, risk management, product development, rate structures, organization and operations strategies, and environmental analysis. M&R focuses on helping organizations succeed in the cost-restrictive environment of managed care and health care reform. M&R's actuarial and clinical tools and services include Healthcare Management Guidelines (HMGs), the Healthcare Management University (HMU), and the Health Cost Index Report and Health Insurance Trend Model (for M&R reports). The organization is known internationally as Woodrow Milliman.

Milton Helpern Institute of Forensic Medicine (MHIFM) *Founded:* 1968. *Headquarters:* New York, NY. *Purpose:* To train postgraduate students through symposia, seminars, lectures, and courses. It conducts research projects and undertakes investigations and related studies of sudden, suspicious, and violent deaths. Serves individuals who strengthen teaching and research in forensic medicine and forensic pathology.

MTM Association for Standards and Research (MTM) *Founded:* 1951. *Headquarters:* Des Plaines, IL. *Purpose:* To enable organizations to not only understand and analyze current operational performance, but to improve and enhance the work environment as well. The Association has pioneered in the development of computerized and manual systems which recognize, classify, describe and objectively measure the performance of an organization at various levels. Membership includes major corporations, governmental agencies, management consulting firms, universities, and individuals. Also known as Methods Time Measurement Association for Standards and Research.

Multidisciplinary Institute for Neuropsychological Development (MIND) *Founded:* 1970. *Headquarters:* Cambridge, MA. *Purpose:* To provide a forum for the cooperation of the arts, sciences, and technologies with the professions of law, medicine, and education in the study of human development; to promote the research, diagnosis, and remedy of learning and other disabilities; and to encourage the dissemination of knowledge in human perception, communication, and behavior. Serves professionals from the fields of education, medicine, theology, and human services.

Muscular Dystrophy Association *Founded:* 1950. *Headquarters:* Tucson, AZ. *Purpose:* To promote a national voluntary health agency fostering research into the care and cure of neuromuscular diseases. Supports international programs of more than 400 research awards, university-based clinical centers, and outpatient hospitals in the United States and Puerto Rico. Awards grants for research. Local chapters provide services to patients including wheelchairs, physical therapy, summer camp, medical evaluations.

Nn

National Abortion and Reproductive Rights Action League (NARAL) *Founded:* 1969. *Headquarters:* Washington, DC. *Purpose:* To promote reproductive freedom and dignity for women and their families; to educate Americans on abortion and other issues of reproductive choice; and to develop and sustain a prochoice political constituency in order to maintain the U.S. Supreme Court *Roe* v *Wade* decision in 1973 legalizing abortion and to promote codification of the decision and related abortion decisions into state law. *Formerly:* National Abortion and Reproductive Action League.

National Abortion Federation (NAF) *Founded:* 1977. *Headquarters:* Washington, DC. *Purpose:* To provide continuing education, standards, and guidelines as well as to offer information on medical, legal, and social aspects of abortion and set standards for abortion care. Serves abortion service providers, including physician offices, clinics, feminist health centers, Planned Parenthood affiliates, and other individuals committed to making safe, legal abortions accessible to all women.

National Abortion and Reproductive Action League *See* National Abortion and Reproductive Rights Action League.

National Academy of Neuropsychology (NAN) *Founded:* 1975. *Headquarters:* Aurora, CO. *Purpose:* To advance the understanding, assessment and remediation of brain dysfunction and to provide leadership in the continued development of neuropsychology as a discipline. Serves clinicians, scientist-practitioners, and researchers in neuropsychology.

National Academy of Opticianry (NAO) *Founded:* 1973. *Headquarters:* Bowie, MD. *Purpose:* To offer review of courses for national certification and state licensure examinations to members.

National Academy of Sciences (NAS) *Founded:* 1976. *Headquarters:* Washington, DC. *Purpose:* To pro-mote furtherance of contributions to either science or engineering. NAS was founded by an act of Congress to serve as official adviser to the federal government on scientific and technical matters.

National Academy of Social Insurance *Founded:* 1986. *Headquarters:* Washington, DC. *Purpose:* To promote informed discussion and debate on social insurance issues. It works to increase public understanding of Social Security. Serves experts on social insurance, including Social Security, health care financing, disability, workers' compensation, and unemployment.

National Accreditation Commission for Schools and Colleges of Acupuncture and Oriental Medicine (NACSCAOM) *Founded:* 1982. *Headquarters:* Silver Spring, MD. *Purpose:* To evaluate schools and colleges of acupuncture and oriental medicine to establish and maintain high educational standards and ethical business practices. Serves the acupuncture educational and professional community and other individuals representing the public interest.

National Accreditation Council for Agencies Serving the Blind and Visually Handicapped (NAC) *Founded:* 1966. *Headquarters:* New York, NY. *Purpose:* To develop the standards and administer a voluntary system of accreditation for schools and organizations providing direct services to blind and visually disabled people.

National Accrediting Agency for Clinical Laboratory Sciences (NAACLS) *Founded:* 1973. *Headquarters:* Chicago, IL. *Purpose:* To establish standards for quality educational programs and determine if hospitals and colleges are maintaining standards through self-evaluation and on-site surveys. Accredits hospitals, colleges, and universities in the allied health professions of medical technologist, medical laboratory technician, and histologic technologist in cooperation with the Committee on Allied Health Education and Accreditation.

National Alliance of Breast Cancer Organizations (NABCO) *Founded:* 1986. *Headquarters:* New York, NY. *Purpose:* To influence public and private health policies, serving breast centers, hospitals, government health offices, and support and research organizations providing information about breast cancer and breast diseases from early detection through continuing care.

National Alliance for Infusion Therapy (NAIT) *Founded:* 1991. *Headquarters:* Washington, DC. *Purpose:* Committed to the growth and acceptance of appropriate use of home and alternative site infusion therapies that benefit patients and payers by providing for cost-effective, technology-advanced care. Committed to the establishment and dissemination of guidelines for quality patient care; promotion of an adherence to ethical business practices; pursuit of research and educational activities to improve knowledge and acceptance of infusion therapies; pursuit of public policy and private payer advocacy to advance the interests of the association's members and their patients; and development of programs to enhance public confidence in this field of health care.

National Alliance for the Mentally Ill (NAMI)
Founded: 1979. *Headquarters:* Arlington, VA. *Purpose:* To create a common set of outcomes measures for mental health care and substance abuse treatment using input from consumers, payers, researchers, employers, and providers. Sponsors Outcomes Roundtable, which is made up of consumers of mental health and addictive disorder services, their families, insurers, employers, public and private providers, researchers, and government agencies who are all working in equal collaboration toward their common goal: to develop outcomes measures that will truly improve the quality of care for the estimated 52 million people who suffer from mental and addictive disorders.

National Assembly of National Voluntary Health and Social Welfare Organizations *Founded:* 1923. *Headquarters:* Washington, DC. *Purpose:* To serve national voluntary health and social welfare agencies interested in increasing the impact of the individual agencies and of volunteerism on human needs.

National Association of Activity Professionals (NAAP) *Founded:* 1981. *Headquarters:* Washington, DC. *Purpose:* To promote quality care and services to the elderly and handicapped and to foster research and production of relevant literature and to upgrade education programs. It has set standards and established a certification process. Serves therapists, activity directors, and activity consultants in nursing homes, senior centers, retirement housing, or adult day care programs.

National Association of Addiction Treatment Providers (NAATP) *Founded:* 1978. *Headquarters:* Washington, DC. *Purpose:* To raise public awareness of addiction as a treatable disease; to promote the very highest standards of addiction treatment; to secure adequate reimbursement for treatment programs; and to provide member education. NAATP is the national organization that represents the National Association of Addiction Treatment Providers (NAATP), American College of Addiction Treatment Administrators (ACATA), and the National Adolescent Treatment Consortium (NATC).

National Association for the Advancement of Psychoanalysis and the American Board for Accreditation in Psychoanalysis (NAAPABAP) *Founded:* 1972. *Headquarters:* New York, NY. *Purpose:* To establish standards for training and accredits psychoanalytic training institutes that may train physicians, psychologists, social workers, counselors, and other persons. It sets standards for certification of psychoanalysts and psychoanalytic psychotherapists and certifies those who have met its standards. Serves psychoanalytic training institutes and individual psychoanalysts from many schools of psychoanalytic thought interested in the advancement of psychoanalysis as a profession.

National Association of Advisors for the Health Professions (NAAHP) *Founded:* 1974. *Headquarters:* Champaign, IL. *Purpose:* To coordinate the activities and efforts of regional associations; to preserve and improve advising at all educational levels; to foster and coordinate communication between the health professions, other associations, and advisors; and to gather and disseminate information, marshal resources, and provide services regarding health professions advising to its constituency.

National Association of Air National Guard Health Technicians (NAANGHT) *Founded:* 1974. *Headquarters:* Cicero, NY. *Purpose:* To provide more effective medical services in federal Air National Guard health facilities through interchange of ideas and dissemination of information. It provides liaison with professional groups and education and government institutions.

National Association of Alcoholism and Drug Abuse Counselors (NAADAC) *Founded:* 1972. *Headquarters:* Arlington, VA. *Purpose:* To provide leadership in the alcoholism and drug abuse counseling profession by building new visions, effecting change in public policy, promoting criteria for effective treatment, encouraging adherence to ethical standards, and ensuring professional growth for alcoholism and drug abuse counselors.

National Association for Ambulatory Care (NAFAC) *Founded:* 1981. *Headquarters:* Minneapolis, MN. *Purpose:* To promote the establishment of operating standards aimed at lower cost and more convenient outpatient medical care. Serves representatives of hospital, corporate, and independently owned ambulatory care centers.

National Association of Apnea Professionals (NAAP) *Founded:* 1987. *Headquarters:* Waianae, HI. *Purpose:* To gather scientific and clinical information about causes and treatments of apnea and related sleep disorders and compile statistics. Focuses on cases found in infants. Serves physicians, nurses, respiratory therapists, social workers, polysomnographers, and manufacturers and suppliers of apnea equipment.

National Association of Area Agencies on Aging (NAAAA) *Founded:* 1975. *Headquarters:* Washington, DC. *Purpose:* To promote and achieve a reasonable and realistic national policy on aging and to advocate for the needs of older persons at the national level. Serves Area Agencies on Aging and was established under the provision of the Older Americans Act of 1965.

National Association for Biomedical Research (NABR) *Founded:* 1985. *Headquarters:* Washington, DC. *Purpose:* To monitor and, when appropriate, attempt to influence legislation and regulations on behalf of members who are dependent on animals for biomedical research and testing. Serves universities, research institutes, professional societies, voluntary health agencies, animal breeders and suppliers, and pharmaceutical, chemical, and testing companies that use laboratory animals for biomedical research and testing.

National Association of Black Social Workers (NABSW) *Founded:* 1968. *Headquarters:* Detroit, MI. *Purpose:* Involved in making demands for change within existing welfare structures; and building an organizational network on a local and national level. NABSW has taken stands on and been concerned about such issues as transracial adoptions, welfare reform, health care, energy, prisons, the aged, and social work practice and training. The organization is comprised of African American social workers and other African Americans who have strong interest in the issues affecting the African American community.

National Association of Boards of Examiners for Nursing Home Administrators (NAB) *Founded:* 1972. *Headquarters:* Washington, DC. *Purpose:* To operate continuing education review service and to disseminate information and educational materials for nursing home administrators. It produces an examination to test the competence of nursing home administrators. Serves state boards responsible for licensing nursing homes.

National Association of Boards of Pharmacy (NABP) *Founded:* 1904. *Headquarters:* Park Ridge, IL. *Purpose:* To sponsor a uniform licensure examination, to provide for interstate reciprocity in pharmaceutic licensure based upon a uniform minimum standard of pharmaceutic education and uniform legislation, and to provide legislative information and education. Serves pharmacy boards of the 50 states; the District of Columbia; Puerto Rico; Virgin Islands; the Canadian provinces of Alberta, Ontario, and British Columbia; and the state of Victoria, Australia.

National Association of Chain Drug Stores (NACDS) *Founded:* 1933. *Headquarters:* Alexandria, VA. *Purpose:* To provide interpretations of actions by government agencies in such areas as drugs, public health, federal trade, labor, and excise taxes. Its programs include NACDS/Merck, Sharp, Dohme; Cornell Executive Management; NACDS/Johnson & Johnson Performance Analysis Report; and PHOCUST (Pharmacists' Opportunities in Compliance Using Skills Training). Serves chain drug retailers and associate members including manufacturers, suppliers, manufacturers' representatives, publishers, and advertising agencies.

National Association of Childbearing Centers (NACC) *Founded:* 1983. *Headquarters:* Perkiomenville, PA. *Purpose:* To promote quality care in freestanding birth centers through state licensure and national standard-setting mechanisms, educational workshops, and support of professional education for midwives; and to provide standards for certification of birth centers. It acts as a national information service of freestanding birth centers for state health departments, insurance companies, government agencies, consultants, hospitals, physicians, certified nurse-midwives, nurses, and families. Serves birth centers and individuals and businesses interested in childbirth centers.

National Association of Children's Hospitals and Related Institutions (NACHRI) *Founded:* 1968. *Headquarters:* Alexandria, VA. *Purpose:* To promote the quality of child health care through the dissemination of information, the promotion of research and education programs, and the participation in charitable, scientific, and educational endeavors. Serves children's hospitals and related institutions whose programs are clinical, as opposed to social or custodial.

National Association of Community Health Centers (NACHC) *Founded:* 1970. *Headquarters:* Washington, DC. *Purpose:* To foster the continuing growth and development of community-based health care delivery programs for medically underserved populations. Provides technical assistance, education, and training opportunities for health center staff and board members. Serves ambulatory health care centers, administrators, clinicians, and consumers.

National Association of Counsel for Children (NACC) *Founded:* 1977. *Headquarters:* Denver, CO. *Purpose:* To provide education, support, and training for attorneys, guardians, and other advocates for children. Serves lawyers, judges, physicians, mental health professionals, social workers, court-appointed advocates, volunteers, and other individuals interested in improving legal representation of children.

National Association of County and City Health Officials (NACCHO) *Founded:* 1965. *Headquarters:* Washington, DC. *Purpose:* To stimulate and contribute to the improvement of county health programs and public health practices throughout the United States. It operates a Primary Care Project, which helps to strengthen the link between local health departments and community health centers.

National Association of the Deaf (NAD) *Founded:* 1880. *Headquarters:* Silver Spring, MD. *Purpose:* To protect the civil rights of the deaf in the areas of employment, elimination of communication barriers, and full citizenship benefits and obligations. Another activity is screening films and recommending which films should be captioned for hearing-impaired viewers. Serves adult deaf persons, parents of deaf children, professionals and students in the field of deafness, and organizations of and for deaf people.

National Association of Dental Assistants (NADA) *Founded:* 1974. *Headquarters:* Falls Church, VA. *Purpose:* To add to the professional stature of dental assistants through continuing education and to provide its members with benefits which are normally limited to specialized professional and fraternal groups. A job exchange service for dental assistants is also provided.

National Association of Dental Laboratories (NADL) *Founded:* 1951. *Headquarters:* Alexandria, VA. *Purpose:* To provide management seminars and a basic laboratory technician's training program. Offers business and personal insurance programs, hazardous materials training program, an infectious disease prevention training program, business management and technical education programs. Serves commercial dental laboratories, industry manufacturers and suppliers, and schools of dental technology.

National Association of Developmental Disabilities Councils (NADDC) *Founded:* 1975. *Headquarters:* Washington, DC. *Purpose:* To promote cooperation and communication among federal agencies, state governments, volunteer groups and other organizations, and individual state and territorial councils. It educates and informs the public about the needs of developmentally disabled people. Serves state and territorial councils interested in improving the lives of developmentally disabled people.

National Association of Directors of Nursing Administration in Long Term Care (NADONA/LTC) *Founded:* 1986. *Headquarters:* Cincinnati, OH. *Purpose:* To create and establish an acceptable ethical standard for practices in long term care nursing administration; to develop and provide programs of education and certification for the positions of director, associate director, and assistant director; and to promote a positive image of the long term health care industry. Serves directors, assistant directors, and former directors of nursing in long term care.

National Association of Disability Evaluating Professionals (NADEP) *Founded:* 1984. *Headquarters:* Richmond, VA. *Purpose:* To provide a forum for the exchange of information and functions as the membership division of the American Disability Evaluation Research Institute. Serves lawyers, doctors, psychologists, employers, and other individuals interested or involved in disability claims process, evaluation, and case management.

National Association of Disability Examiners (NADE) *Founded:* 1963. *Headquarters:* Frankfort, KY. *Purpose:* To foster, promote, and participate in activities designed to improve the documentation of applications for insurance benefits. Serves disability claims examiners, attorneys, and physicians involved in determining the eligibility of applicants for Social Security benefits based on disability.

National Association for Drama Therapy (NADT) *Founded:* 1979. *Headquarters:* Sherman, CT. *Purpose:* To develop criteria and standards of training for drama therapists; to maintain a system of registration and peer review; to encourage research and development of professional training opportunities. Serves individuals trained in the therapeutic applications of creative drama and theater and other persons trained in psychotherapy, rehabilitation, and education.

National Association on Drug Abuse Problems (NADAP) *Founded:* 1971. *Headquarters:* New York, NY. *Purpose:* To serve as an information clearinghouse and referral bureau for corporations and local communities interested in prevention of substance abuse and treatment of substance abusers. Sponsored by business and labor organizations.

National Association of Emergency Medical Service Physicians (NAEMSP) *Founded:* 1983. *Headquarters:* Pittsburgh, PA. *Purpose:* To provide a forum for debate and discussion of issues relating to emergency medical services as an important facet of medical care and of the problems and responsibilities of emergency medical services physicians and related personnel. To support research and development in the area of prehospital emergency care. Serves physicians, medical students, and other persons in the health care profession involved in emergency medical services. *Also known as:* National Association of EMS Physicians.

National Association of Emergency Medical Technicians (NAEMT) *Founded:* 1975. *Headquarters:* Clinton, MS. *Purpose:* To foster the professional status of emergency medical technicians; to promote national acceptance of a uniform standard of recognition for their skills; and to encourage constant upgrading of these skills and qualifications and educational requirements. Serves nationally registered or state-certified emergency medical technicians (EMTs).

National Association of EMS Physicians *See* National Association of Emergency Medical Service Physicians.

National Association of First Responders (AAFAR-NAFAR) *Founded:* 1984. *Headquarters:* Orange Beach, AL. *Purpose:* To provide a national certification program for first responders and educational and research programs. Serves emergency medical responders who have had 40 hours of training.

National Association of Healthcare Access Management (NAHAM) *Founded:* 1974. *Headquarters:* Washington, DC. *Purpose:* To provide a central source of information on changes and trends in health care that affect patient access services. Serves hospital admitting managers and provides educational resources for the hospital admitting field.

National Association of Health Career Schools (NAHCS) *Founded:* 1980. *Headquarters:* Washington, DC. *Purpose:* To promote interests and general welfare of health careers through schools and students and to conduct and promote research for advancement of educational offerings. Serves private, vocational, technical, and junior colleges training allied health personnel.

National Association for Healthcare Quality (NAHQ) *Founded:* 1976. *Headquarters:* Glenview, IL. *Purpose:* To improve the quality of health care by advancing the theory and practice of quality management in health care organizations and by promoting the professional growth and development of health care professionals. NAHQ members include professionals in general, acute, managed, long term, home, rehabilitation, mental health, and ambulatory care settings as well as consultants in such areas as quality management, case management, risk management, medical records, nursing, infection control utilization, management, discharge planning/continuity of care, medical/professional staff quality management.

National Association for Healthcare Recruitment (NAHCR) *Founded:* 1975. *Headquarters:* Akron, OH. *Purpose:* Promotes sound principles of professional health care recruitment and to conduct regional seminars, symposia, and workshops. Serves individuals employed directly by hospitals and other health care organizations in recruitment of allied health professionals, home health professionals, long term care professionals, nurses, and physicians.

National Association of Health Data Organizations (NAHDO) *Founded:* 1986. *Headquarters:* Falls Church, VA. *Purpose:* To improve health care through the collection, dissemination, and application of health care data. To promote public availability of and access to health care data, and support use of health care data to guide formulating of health policy, purchasing, and establishing of needed health services. To encourage uniformity and accuracy in data collection to support the development of a national health care database. Serves state and federal health data organizations; associate and supporting members are private sector organizations, including data analysis companies, commercial insurers, health services consultants, health care researchers, third-party payers, hospital associations, and managed health care plans.

National Association of Health Services Executives (NAHSE) *Founded:* 1968. *Headquarters:* Columbia, MD. *Purpose:* Conducts National Work-Study Program, sponsors educational programs, promotes the advancement and development of African American health care leaders, and works to elevate the quality of health care service rendered to poor and disadvantaged communities. Members include health care executive managers, planners, educators, advocates, providers, organizers, researchers, and consumers.

National Association of Health Underwriters (NAHU) *Founded:* 1930. *Headquarters:* Washington, DC. *Purpose:* To serve insurance agencies and individuals engaged in the promotion, sale, and administration of disability income and health insurance.

National Association of Health Unit Coordinators (NAHUC) *Founded:* 1980. *Headquarters:* St. Paul, MN. *Purpose:* To promote the professional practice of unit coordinating and establish standards of practice defining the role and responsibilities of health unit coordinators. It works to establish certification guidelines with a goal of national certification. Serves coordinators of nonclinical nursing unit activities and other persons interested in health unit coordinating.

National Association of Hispanic Nurses (NAHN) *Founded:* 1976. *Headquarters:* Washington, DC. *Purpose:* To serve the nursing and healthcare delivery needs of the Hispanic community and to work toward providing equal access to educational, professional, and economic opportunities for Hispanic nurses.

National Association for Home Care (NAHC) *Founded:* 1982. *Headquarters:* Washington, DC. *Purpose:* To affect legislative and regulatory processes concerning home care services; to gather and disseminate home care industry data; to develop public relations strategies; and work to increase political visibility of home care services. It interprets home care services to government- and private-sector bodies affecting the delivery and financing of such services. Serves providers of home health care, hospice, and homemaker/home health aide services.

National Association of Homes and Services for Children (NAHSC) *Founded:* 1975. *Headquarters:* Washington, DC. *Purpose:* Provides advocacy, leadership development, public education, information, training, and agency support to nearly 330 member agencies working for at-risk children and families.

National Association of Hospital Hospitality Houses (NAHHH) *Founded:* 1986. *Headquarters:* Muncie, IN. *Purpose:* Promotes and assists nonprofit programs that provide lodging and supportive services in a caring environment for families of hospital patients and hospital outpatients receiving medical care away from home. To encourage the development and growth of these homes, the NAHHH offers it's membership educational opportunities, serves as a network for information exchange, and provides basic assistance to groups interested in creating similar programs.

National Association of Lesbian/Gay Alcoholism Professionals (NALGAP) *Founded:* 1979. *Headquarters:* Los Angeles, CA. *Purpose:* To provide a network for support and communication among professionals working with chemically dependent gay and lesbian people. Serves doctors, nurses, social workers, psychologists, certified counselors, and other health professionals who work with gay and lesbian alcoholics, and drug, alcohol, and gay agencies, organizations, and institutes.

National Association of Long Term Hospitals (NALTH) *Founded:* 1988. *Headquarters:* Stoughton, MA. *Purpose:* To ensure an adequate reimbursement methodology in order to serve those in need of long term care hospitals; identify all hospitals serving long-term medical or rehabilitation patients; to educate our elected representatives at the state and federal level to prevent long term hospitals from becoming victimized by Medicare cutbacks; to achieve government recognition that long term hospitals deserve special consideration due to Medicare and Medicaid status as their dominant payers.

National Association of Managed Care Physicians (NAMCP) *Founded:* 1991. *Headquarters:* Glen Allen, VA. *Purpose:* To foster physician autonomy to treat patients in a manner consistent with quality health care, stronger physician-patient relationships, patient education, and public awareness of costs and benefits of services in managed health care. Serves licensed physicians and allied health professionals working in managed health care programs, such as HMOs and PPOs, medical residents and students interested in managed health care, and corporations or agencies providing services or goods to the industry.

National Association of Manufacturing Opticians (NAMO) *Founded:* 1975. *Headquarters:* Rockwall, TX. *Purpose:* To foster the development of bar coding of optical products to facilitate the ordering and processing of eyewear within the industry and to encourage the creation of objective legislation and regulations. Serves full-service optical laboratories.

National Association of Meal Programs (NAMP) *Founded:* 1973. *Headquarters:* Alexandria, VA. *Purpose:* To provide nutritionally balanced meals to disabled and homebound elderly persons, thereby reducing or eliminating the need for institutionalization and promoting independent and community-based living arrangements. Serves agencies that provide home-delivered meals and/or meals in a congregate setting and other health and social services, such as transportation, recreation, nutrition education, information, referral, and case management.

National Association of Medical Directors for Respiratory Care (NAMDRC) *Founded:* 1977. *Headquarters:* Chevy Chase, MD. *Purpose:* To provide educational opportunities to fit the needs of medical directors of respiratory care and to represent the interests of members to regulatory agencies to ensure that the needs of respiratory patients are not overlooked.

National Association of Medical Equipment Services (NAMES) *Founded:* 1982. *Headquarters:* Alexandria, VA. *Purpose:* Provides its members with timely industry communications, legislative/regulatory advocacy, educational opportunities, Medicare reimbursement assistance, networking opportunities at national conferences, and numerous products and services. Formed by the merger of two smaller associations representing the home medical equipment services industry.

National Association of Medical Examiners (NAME) *Founded:* 1966. *Headquarters:* St. Louis, MO. *Purpose:* To establish standards for modern medico-legal investigative systems. Serves medical examiners, pathologists, and other licensed physicians who have responsibilities in connection with the official investigation of sudden, suspicious, and violent deaths.

National Association Medical Staff Services (NAMSS) *Founded:* 1978. *Headquarters:* Lombard, IL. *Purpose:* Promotes the continuous improvement of quality in health care by providing educational and professional development opportunities for its members. Products and services include networking opportunities on a national, state, and local level; education on credentialing, current legal issues, management and accreditation standards; and certification in two fields of expertise. Serves individuals involved in the management and administration of medical staff services.

National Association for Music Therapy (NAMT) *Founded:* 1950. *Headquarters:* Silver Spring, MD. *Purpose:* To perfect techniques of music programming which effectively aid treatment. Aims to establish qualifications and standards of training for music therapists. Serves music therapists, physicians, psychologists, administrators, and educators supporting the use of music in therapy.

National Association of Neonatal Nurses (NANN) *Founded:* 1984. *Headquarters:* Petaluma, CA. *Purpose:* To provide educational and networking opportunities and disseminate legislative information. Serves nurses currently working in neonatal intensive care units.

National Association of Nurse Massage Therapists *Founded:* 1987. *Headquarters:* Osprey, FL. *Purpose:* To promote the integration of massage and other therapeutic forms of bodywork into existing heath care practice and to promote nurse massage therapists as specialists within the nursing profession. Establishes standards, educates the medical community, and monitors legislation.

National Association of Nurse Practitioners in Reproductive Health (NANPRH) *Founded:* 1980. *Headquarters:* Washington, DC. *Purpose:* To foster quality reproductive health services and reproductive freedom and to support the rights of nurse practitioners to administer reproductive health services to patients. Serves nurse practitioners involved in reproductive health care.

National Association of Nutrition and Aging Services Programs (NANASP) *Founded:* 1977. *Headquarters:* Grand Rapids, MI. *Purpose:* To promote professional growth; to raise the standards of the profession among members; and to encourage communication between aging services programs and federal agencies and governmental bodies. It has developed national standards for congregate and home-delivered services programs. Serves directors and staff of congregate and home-delivered nutrition services programs for the elderly.

National Association of Optometrists and Opticians (NAOO) *Founded:* 1960. *Headquarters:* Cleveland, OH. *Purpose:* To provide public affairs programs of mutual importance to members; to serve as an organizational center for special purpose programs; and to act as a clearinghouse for information affecting the retail optical industry. Dedicated to the enhancement of psychological services to people with cancer and their families. Serves licensed optometrists, opticians, and related corporations.

National Association of Orthopaedic Nurses (NAON) *Founded:* 1980. *Headquarters:* Pitman, NJ. *Purpose:* To promote continuing education and the development of patient care plans; to maintain liaisons; and to serve as a resource to hospitals, universities, industries, and government agencies. Serves registered, licensed practical, or licensed vocational nurses interested in orthopedic nursing.

National Association of Orthopaedic Technologists (NAOT) *Founded:* 1982. *Headquarters:* Raleigh, NC. *Purpose:* To promote continuing professional education of members and other orthopedic health care providers; to administer a certification examination; and to enhance public understanding of orthopedics. Serves allied health assistants working with orthopedic patients.

National Association of Pediatric Nurse Associate & Practitioners (NAPNAP) *Founded:* 1973. *Headquarters:* Cherry Hill, NJ. *Purpose:* To improve the quality of infant, child, and adolescent health care by making health care services accessible and by providing a forum for continuing education. The association serves pediatric, school, and family nurse practitioners and other persons interested in the implementation and maintenance of certification of practitioners and associates, in cooperation with the National Certification Board of Pediatric Nurse Practitioners and Nurses, and other activities.

National Association of People with AIDS (NAPWA)
Founded: 1987. *Headquarters:* Washington, DC. *Purpose:* To improve the lives of people with HIV/AIDS at home, in the community, and in the workplace. Serves as a national information resource and voice for the needs and concerns of all Americans affected by HIV.

National Association for Perinatal Addiction Research and Education (NAPARE) *Founded:* 1987. *Headquarters:* Chicago, IL. *Purpose:* To sponsor training forums and charitable programs; to operate cocaine-baby helpline; to compile statistics; and to maintain the speakers' bureau. Serves members interested in conducting educational and research programs on substance abuse during pregnancy and the effects of substance abuse on the fetus.

National Association of Pharmaceutical Manufacturers (NAPM) *Founded:* 1954. *Headquarters:* Garden City, NY. *Purpose:* To assist with problems arising from laws and regulations and the need to establish rapport with federal and state agencies. Serves pharmaceutical manufacturers, distributors, and repackagers.

National Association of Physician Nurses (NAPN)
Founded: 1973. *Headquarters:* Falls Church, VA. *Purpose:* To bring added stature and purpose to the physician nurses' profession.

National Association of Physician Recruiters (NAPR) *Founded:* 1983. *Headquarters:* Altamonte Springs, FL. *Purpose:* To promote a positive image of physician recruiting services; to establish accreditation standards for the field; and to provide marketing services for the industry.

National Association for Poetry Therapy (NAPT)
Founded: 1981. *Headquarters:* Port Washington, NY. *Purpose:* To promote the use of poetry therapy for healing and personal growth. Serves psychiatrists, psychologists, social workers, teachers, nurses, librarians, paraprofessionals, counselors, recreation and rehabilitation specialists, and poets and professors of English and psychology.

National Association for Practical Nurse Education and Service (NAPNES) *Founded:* 1941. *Headquarters:* Silver Spring, MD. *Purpose:* To provide consultation services to advise schools wishing to develop a practical/vocational nursing program on required facilities, equipment, policies, curriculum, and staffing; to provide continuing education; and to hold national certification courses in pharmacology and other areas. Serves licensed practical/vocational nurses, registered nurses, physicians, hospitals, and nursing home administrators. *Merged with:* National Association of Licensed Practical Nurses (1985).

National Association of Professional Geriatric Care Managers (NAPGCM) *Founded:* 1985. *Headquarters:* Tucson, AZ. *Purpose:* To develop, advance, and promote the humane and dignified social, psychological, and health care for the elderly and their families through counseling, treatment, and the delivery of services by qualified, certified providers. NAPGCM works through education, advocacy, and high standards of practice.

National Association of Psychiatric Health Systems (NAPHS) *Founded:* 1933. *Headquarters:* Washington, DC. *Purpose:* To promote and represent the interests of behavioral health care systems that are committed to the delivery of high-quality, efficient, and clinically effective treatment and to foster prevention programs for people with mental and substance abuse disorders.

National Association of Psychiatric Treatment Centers for Children (NAPTCC) *Founded:* 1983. *Headquarters:* Washington, DC. *Purpose:* To promote excellence in the care, delivery, accountability, and cost-effectiveness of psychiatric services for children. These residential centers are accredited by the Joint Commission on Accreditation of Healthcare Organizations. Serves residential centers for emotionally and mentally disturbed children.

National Association of Public Child Welfare Administrators (NAPCWA) *Founded:* 1983. *Headquarters:* Washington, DC. *Purpose:* To enhance the administration of services promoting the well-being of children and support the development of public policies to prevent or alleviate family disruptions, such as child abuse and juvenile delinquency. Serves state and local child welfare administrators who belong to the American Public Welfare Association.

National Association of Public Hospitals & Health Systems (NAPH) *Founded:* 1980. *Headquarters:* Washington, DC. *Purpose:* To provide national, regional and local advocacy on behalf of public and other hospitals and health systems in metropolitan areas; to conduct analysis and research concerning matters that affect such hospitals and health systems; and to assist in the development and interpretation of laws, regulations, policies, and clinical and administrative systems and strategies that maintain and enhance organizational and financial strength.

National Association of Registered Nurses (NARN)
Founded: 1979. *Headquarters:* Richmond, VA. *Purpose:* To provide financial management programs and products, consultation, and services, including individual retirement accounts, investment services, and group life insurance for its members.

National Association of Rehabilitation Facilities (NARF) *See* American Rehabilitation Association.

National Association of Rehabilitation Professionals in the Private Sector (NARPPS) *Founded:* 1977. *Headquarters:* Newton, MA. *Purpose:* To promote the field of private rehabilitation and to provide for information exchange on rehabilitation issues and techniques. Serves

private rehabilitation companies, insurance companies, rehabilitation nurses, and rehabilitation professionals in the private sector.

National Association of Rehabilitation Secretaries (NARS) *Founded:* 1971. *Headquarters:* Little Rock, AR. *Purpose:* To promote recruitment of qualified persons for secretarial and clerical positions in the rehabilitation field; to determine and analyze the skills and knowledge needed by secretaries, stenographers, and clerical workers; and to devise appropriate training. Serves rehabilitation secretaries.

National Association of Residents and Interns (NARI) *Founded:* 1959. *Headquarters:* New York, NY. *Purpose:* To provide secured loan plans, low-cost group insurance, group purchase discounts, and other services to medical and dental students, interns, residents, and fellows.

National Association of Retail Druggists (NARD) *Founded:* 1898. *Headquarters:* Alexandria, VA. *Purpose:* Serves the needs of independent pharmacists through professional development and practice management programs and services, and by promoting the competitive position of the independent pharmacist. It maintains active liaison with state and federal governments, including the White House and the administrative agencies within the Executive Department, Department of Health and Human Services, Food and Drug Administration, and the Health Care Financing Administration. Member services include continuing education, public relations, student loans, and certification of prosthetic and orthotic services, ostomy, incontinence and wound management, and diabetes care.

National Association for Rural Mental Health (NARMH) *Founded:* 1977. *Headquarters:* Wood River, IL. *Purpose:* To enhance the delivery of mental health services to rural areas. It promotes this goal and informs the field of the unique needs of rural mental health programs. It attempts to foster communication among rural mental health professionals through dissemination of information and development of education resources. NARMH arranges educational programs, publishes a newsletter, and sponsors an annual conference.

National Association of School Nurses *Founded:* 1969. *Headquarters:* Scarborough, ME. *Purpose:* To provide national leadership in the promotion of health services for schoolchildren; to promote school health interests to the nursing and health community and the public; and to monitor legislation pertaining to school nursing. Operates the National Board for Certification of School Nurses and certifies school nurses. Serves school nurses who conduct comprehensive school health programs in public and private schools.

National Association of School Psychologists (NASP) *Founded:* 1969. *Headquarters:* Bethesda, MD. *Purpose:* To provide for the mental health and educational needs of children and youth; to encourage and provide opportunities for professional growth of members; to inform the public on the services and practice of school psychology; to advance the standards of the profession; and to operate a national school psychologist certification system. Serves school psychologists.

National Association for Search and Rescue (NASAR) *Founded:* 1974. *Headquarters:* Chantilly, VA. *Purpose:* To provide for liaison of state, federal, local, and private search and rescue groups; to conduct training programs for search and rescue professionals; to promote the standardization of procedures; and to sponsor survival education programs designed to help the public cope with disaster and emergency situations. Serves directors or coordinators of state and regional emergency rescue services; medical rescue, fire, and emergency personnel; organizations involved in search, rescue, or survival activities; and state rescue-related agencies.

National Association for Senior Living Industries (NASLI) *Founded:* 1985. *Headquarters:* Annapolis, MD. *Purpose:* To improve the quality of life for senior citizens through education and developmental programs. Serves businesses, associations, governmental agencies, and other groups and organizations.

National Association of Social Workers (NASW) *Founded:* 1955. *Headquarters:* Washington, DC. *Purpose:* To create professional standards for social work practice; to advocate sound public social work policies through political and legislative action; and to provide a wide range of membership services, including continuing education opportunities and professional programs. Serves social workers who hold a minimum of a baccalaureate degree in social work; associate members are individuals engaged in social work who have a baccalaureate degree in another field.

National Association of State Alcohol and Drug Abuse Directors (NASADAD) *Founded:* 1971. *Headquarters:* Washington, DC. *Purpose:* To represent the interests of state alcohol and drug abuse directors and their agencies before Congress and federal agencies and to foster development of comprehensive alcohol and drug abuse programs on state resources, alcohol and drug issues related to AIDS, drunk driving, and criminal justice activities in each state. Serves state alcohol and drug abuse directors and their agencies.

National Association of State EMS Directors (NASEMSD) *Founded:* 1981. *Headquarters:* Falls Church, VA. *Purpose:* To coordinate activities between states, and to serve as a liaison with other national medical organizations. Serves state emergency medical services (EMS) directors interested in refining EMS activities.

National Association of State Mental Health Program Directors (NASMHPD) *Founded:* 1963. *Headquarters:* Alexandria, VA. *Purpose:* To promote cooperation of state government agencies in delivery of services to persons with mental disabilities; to foster the exchange of scientific and programmatic information in the administration of public mental health programs; and to monitor state and federal and congressional activities.

Serves state commissioners in charge of state mental disability programs; associate members are assistant commissioners for children and youth, research, aged, legal services, forensic services, human resource development, and community programs.

National Association of State Mental Retardation Program Directors (NASMRPD) *Founded:* 1963. *Headquarters:* Alexandria, VA. *Purpose:* To monitor and report on administrative, legislative, and judicial activities and other events affecting mental retardation programs. Serves state administrative personnel working with programs in the field of mental retardation.

National Association of State Units on Aging (NASUA) *Founded:* 1964. *Headquarters:* Washington, DC. *Purpose:* To provide information, technical assistance, and professional development support to state units on aging.

National Association of Vision Professionals (NAVP) *Founded:* 1976. *Headquarters:* Washington, DC. *Purpose:* To provide a forum for ideas and programs; to promote professional standards; and to certify vision screening personnel. Serves individuals responsible for or connected with vision conservation and eye health programs in public or private agencies and institutions.

National Athletic Trainers Association (NATA) *Founded:* 1950. *Headquarters:* Dallas, TX. *Purpose:* To advance, encourage and improve the athletic training profession and to improve the health and well-being of athletes worldwide. Services and products include continuing education, governmental affairs and public relations, and a scientific journal.

National Black Alcoholism Council (NBAC) *Founded:* 1978. *Headquarters:* Washington, DC. *Purpose:* To provide support and initiate activities that will improve alcoholism treatment services and lead to the prevention of alcoholism in the black community, and to provide training on how to treat black alcoholics from a cultural perspective. Serves individuals concerned about alcoholism among black Americans.

National Black Nurses Association (NBNA) *Founded:* 1971. *Headquarters:* Washington, DC. *Purpose:* To provide scholarships to student nurses; to foster interest in providing improved health care for the black community; and to support the professional advancement of its members. Serves black registered nurses, licensed practical nurses, licensed vocational nurses, and student nurses.

National Black Women's Health Project (NBWHP) *Founded:* 1981. *Headquarters:* Atlanta, GA. *Purpose:* To foster interest in encouraging mutual and self-help advocacy among women to bring about a reduction in health care problems prevalent among black women; to urge women to communicate with health care providers, seek out available health care resources, and communicate with other black women to minimize feelings of powerlessness and isolation.

National Board for Certification in Dental Laboratories (CDL) *Founded:* 1979. *Headquarters:* Alexandria, VA. *Purpose:* To provide certification and recognition of dental laboratories that demonstrate and document compliance with standards set by the industry. Serves certified dental laboratories, including commercial and private dental laboratories and dental or dental technology schools.

National Board for Certification in Dental Technology (NBC) *Founded:* 1958. *Headquarters:* Alexandria, VA. *Purpose:* To establish standards and develop and conduct examinations; to certify dental technicians with formal education in dental technology and a minimum of three years' experience.

National Board for Certification of Orthopaedic Technologists (NBCOT) *Founded:* 1983. *Headquarters:* Raleigh, NC. *Purpose:* To determine educational standards for certification of orthopedic technologists, and to provide educational programs for recertification.

National Board for Certified Counselors (NBCC) *Founded:* 1982. *Headquarters:* Greensboro, NC. *Purpose:* To establish and monitor professional credentialing standards for counselors, and to identify individuals who have obtained voluntary certification as national certified counselors.

National Board of Examiners in Optometry (NBEO) *Founded:* 1951. *Headquarters:* Bethesda, MD. *Purpose:* To administer entry-level, criterion-referenced credentialing examinations to students and graduates of accredited schools and colleges of optometry for use by individual state licensing boards.

National Board of Medical Examiners (NBME) *Founded:* 1915. *Headquarters:* Philadelphia, PA. *Purpose:* To prepare and administer qualifying examinations that, when successfully passed, certify students and graduates of U.S. and Canadian medical schools.

National Board of Osteopathic Medical Examiners (NBOME) *Founded:* 1935. *Headquarters:* Des Plaines, IL. *Purpose:* To provide osteopathic physicians, elected for three-year terms, who function as the examining and evaluating board to investigate the qualifications of, and administer examinations and grant diplomate status to, osteopathic physicians.

National Board of Podiatric Medical Examiners (NBPME) *Founded:* 1956. *Headquarters:* Princeton, NJ. *Purpose:* To prepare and administer examinations for podiatry students seeking state licensure; monitors test reliability and validity.

National Board for Respiratory Care (NBRC) *Founded:* 1960. *Headquarters:* Lenexa, KS. *Purpose:* To provide high quality voluntary credentialing examinations for practitioners of respiratory therapy and pulmonary function technology; establish standards to credential practitioners to work under medical direction; issue certificates to and prepare a directory of credentialed individuals; advance medicine by promoting use of respiratory care in treating human ailments; support ethical and educational standards of respiratory care; and cooperate with accrediting agencies to support respiratory care education, evaluate the professional competence of respiratory therapists and provide credentialing examinations.

National Cancer Institute   *See* Government Organizations (Department of Health and Human Services, NIH).

National Cancer Registrars Association (NCRA) *Founded:* 1974. *Headquarters:* Mundelein, IL. *Purpose:* To promote research and education in tumor registry administration and practice; to improve service to cancer patients; to establish standards of education; and to provide a standard course of study for tumor registrars. Serves individuals involved in central, state, regional, and hospital-based tumor registries including physicians, hospital administrators, and health care planners who maintain ongoing records of the cancer patient's history, diagnosis, therapy, and outcome.

National Catholic Council on Alcoholism and Related Drug Problems (NCCA) *Founded:* 1949. *Headquarters:* Brooklyn, NY. *Purpose:* To promote pastoral ministry to alcoholics and their families and to provide adequate treatment for all clergy and religious men and women suffering from alcoholism and drug dependency through consultation and supportive services.

National Caucus on the Black Aged   *See* National Caucus and Center on Black Aged.

National Caucus and Center on Black Aged (NCBA) *Founded:* 1970. *Headquarters:* Washington, DC. *Purpose:* To improve living conditions for low-income elderly Americans, particularly blacks. Advocates changes in federal and state laws in improving the economic, health, and social status of low-income aging population. *Formed by merger of:* National Center on Black Aged and National Caucus on the Black Aged.

National Center for the Advancement of Blacks in the Health Professions (NCABHP) *Founded:* 1988. *Headquarters:* Detroit, MI. *Purpose:* To serve as a central source of information on blacks in the health professions, to encourage black youth to seek careers in health professions, and to stimulate colleges and universities to enroll black students in health programs.

National Center for Assault Prevention *Founded:* 1985. *Headquarters:* Sewell, NJ. *Purpose:* To provide services to children and adults with mental retardation and developmental disabilities and to conduct research on the causes, consequences, and prevention of interpersonal violence. Serves individuals interested in preventing interpersonal violence against vulnerable populations through education, prevention training, and research.

National Center on Black Aged   *See* National Caucus and Center on Black Aged.

National Center for Cost Containment (NCCC) *Founded:* 1990. *Headquarters:* Milwaukee, WI. *Purpose:* To provide VA top management with comparative data

analyses on VA facilities' practice patterns; protocols and practice guidelines to improve delivery of patient care and practice patterns.

National Center for Education in Maternal and Child Health (NCEMCH)   *Founded:* 1982. *Headquarters:* Arlington, VA. *Purpose:* To provide information services to professionals and the public on maternal and child health; to collect and disseminate information on available materials, programs, and research; and to offer summer internships for graduate students in public health schools. The center is affiliated with Georgetown Public Policy Institute, Georgetown University, (Washington, DC). In partnership with the federal Maternal and Child Health Bureau and the American Academy of Pediatrics, the Bright Futures project at NCEMCH developed and disseminated national guidelines for child health supervision and is producing tools and training materials to integrate the guidelines into practice.

National Center for Health Education (NCHE) *Founded:* 1975. *Headquarters:* New York, NY. *Purpose:* To promote health education in schools, communities, and family settings, and to manage Growing Healthy, a comprehensive health education curriculum.

National Center for Homeopathy (NCH)   *Founded:* 1974. *Headquarters:* Alexandria, VA. *Purpose:* To promote the art of homeopathic healing according to the natural laws of cure from a strictly homeopathic standpoint; to facilitate the study of homeopathy by the medical and allied health professionals; and to fund scientific research in the field.

National Center on Rural Aging (NCRA)   *Founded:* 1978. *Headquarters:* Washington, DC. *Purpose:* To develop social and public policies related to the needs and interests of rural older adults; and to improve and increase services by working with national organizations. Serves planners and providers of services for the aging, academicians and students, and other persons interested in issues related to older persons living in rural areas.

National Center for Toxicological Research   *See* Government Organizations (Department of Health and Human Services).

National Certification Agency for Medical Lab Personnel (NCA)   *Founded:* 1977. *Headquarters:* Lenexa, KS. *Purpose:* To develop and administer competency-based examinations for certification of clinical laboratory personnel, and to provide for periodic recertification by examination or through documentation of continuing education. It is affiliated with the American Society for Medical Technology and the Association of Cytogenetic Technologists. Serves individuals employed as directors, educators, supervisors, or workers in clinical laboratory science.

National Certification Council for Activity Professionals (NCCAP)   *Founded:* 1989. *Headquarters:* Colorado Springs, CO. *Purpose:* To promote quality of life for persons in our care; establish national evaluative standards for the certification and recertification of individuals who attain the required competencies of the activity profession; grant certification to persons who apply and meet the standards; and monitor the adherence to the standards of the certified activity personnel.

National Child Safety Council (NCSC) *Founded:* 1949. *Headquarters:* Jackson, MI. *Purpose:* To provide complete child safety education programs through local law enforcement agencies and schools.

National Chronic Pain Outreach Association (NCPOA) *Founded:* 1976. *Headquarters:* Bethesda, MD. *Purpose:* To disseminate information about chronic pain and its management in an effort to lessen the suffering caused by chronic pain; to operate an information clearinghouse for pain sufferers, family members, and health professionals; and to provide a support group starter kit to encourage the formation of local groups.

National Citizens' Coalition for Nursing Home Reform (NCCNHR) *Founded:* 1975. *Headquarters:* Washington, DC. *Purpose:* To improve the quality of life for nursing home and boarding home residents and ensure a consumer voice in the long-term care system. Nationwide membership pursues such activities at national, state, and local levels. An information clearinghouse is available to concerned citizens working in long-term care. NCCNHR provides education and advocacy training to advocates and ombudsmen nationwide, including an Ombudsmen Resource Center.

National Clearinghouse on Marital and Date Rape (NCOMDR) *Founded:* 1980. *Headquarters:* Berkeley, CA. *Purpose:* To promote public awareness; to provide resources to battered women's shelter-crisis centers, district attorneys, and legislators; and to provide sociological and law research on court cases and legislation. Serves students, attorneys, legislators, faculty members, rape crisis centers, shelters, and other social service groups interested in educating the public about marital, cohabitant, and date rape.

National Coalition for Adult Immunization *Founded:* 1988. *Headquarters:* Bethesda, MD. *Purpose:* To promote adult immunization in high risk and other adult target groups; to promote and support National Adult Immunization Week; and to educate physicians and the public on vaccines for diphtheria, hepatitis A and B, influenza, measles, mumps, pneumococcal pneumonia, and rubella.

National Coalition Against Domestic Violence (NCADV) *Founded:* 1978. *Headquarters:* Denver, Co. *Purpose:* Represents grassroots organizations and individuals working to assist and empower battered women and their children. Current projects address teen dating violence, and helping programs provide services to women with disabilities. NCADV is also the sponsor of Domestic Violence Awareness Month, observed in October.

National Coalition Against Sexual Assault (NCASA) *Founded:* 1978. *Headquarters:* Harrisburg, PA. *Purpose:* To provide a network through which individuals and organizations working against sexual assault can share expertise, experience, and information; to act as an advocate for and on behalf of rape victims; to disseminate information on sexual assault; and to sponsor Sexual Assault Awareness Month in April.

National Coalition of Arts Therapy Associations (NCATA) *Founded:* 1979. *Headquarters:* Columbia, MD. *Purpose:* To promote the therapeutic and rehabilitative use of the arts in medicine, mental health, special education, and forensic and social services. Serves creative arts therapists representing the American Art Therapy Association, American Association for Music Therapy, American Dance Therapy Association, American Society for Group Psychotherapy and Psychodrama, National Association for Drama Therapy, National Association for Music Therapy, and National Association for Poetry Therapy.

National Coalition of Black Lung and Respiratory Disease Clinics (NCBLRDC) *Founded:* 1981. *Headquarters:* Jacksboro, TN. *Purpose:* To develop pulmonary rehabilitation programs; to provide a forum for continuing education, training, facilitation of meetings, and technical assistance; and to promote networking of federally funded projects that treat miners who have been diagnosed with black lung disease. Serves clinics receiving federal aid for research or clinic operations; allied health organizations working in conjunction with black lung clinics; and interested individuals.

National Coalition for Cancer Research (NCCR) *Founded:* 1984. *Headquarters:* Washington, DC. *Purpose:* To eradicate cancer and to educate the public and interested parties of the legislative and executive branches on the importance of cancer research and care. Serves cancer research and cancer care organizations and facilities.

National Coalition of Hispanic Health and Human Services Organizations (COSSMHO) *Founded:* 1973. *Headquarters:* Washington, DC. *Purpose:* To promote health and education; mental health, drug abuse, and alcohol abuse treatment and prevention; community health services; health careers development; and services to the elderly. Serves health, mental health, and human service agencies and organizations and professional individuals serving Hispanics. *Formerly:* National Coalition of Hispanic Mental Health and Human Services Organizations.

National Coalition of Hispanic Mental Health and Human Services Organizations *See* National Coalition of Hispanic Health and Human Services Organizations.

National Coalition of Psychiatrists Against Motorcoach Therapy (NCPAMT) *Founded:* 1985. *Headquarters:* Royal Oak, MI. *Purpose:* To abolish the practice of "motorcoach therapy," described as the "escalating and unethical practice of procuring one-way bus fares for habitual and undesirable mental health patients" upon their release from local mental health facilities. It has launched an awareness campaign targeted primarily at mental health officials. Serves psychiatrists, psychologists, social workers, counselors, and mental health officials.

National Coalition for Research in Neurological Disorders (NCR) *Founded:* 1952. *Headquarters:* Washington, DC. *Purpose:* To stimulate public information regarding the field of neurology and neurosurgery and lobby for increased funding for training and research in neurological disorders. Serves voluntary health agencies and professional societies interested in obtaining funds for neurological research.

National College of Foot Surgeons (NCFS) *Founded:* 1960. *Headquarters:* Woodland Hills, CA. *Purpose:* To provide certification to foot surgeons as fellows and associates of the college; to conduct research programs; and to maintain a speakers' bureau. Serves doctors of surgical podiatry.

National Commission for Certification of Acupuncturists (NCCA) *Founded:* 1982. *Headquarters:* Washington, DC. *Purpose:* To establish entry-level standards of competency for the safe and effective practice of acupuncture; to evaluate an applicant's qualifications by administering national board examinations in acupuncture; to certify practitioners of acupuncture who meet standards; and to act as a consultant to state agencies in development of licensure regulations and evaluation of certification mechanisms. Serves representatives of the National Council of Acupuncture Schools and Colleges and the Association of Acupuncture and Oriental Medicine.

National Commission on Certification of Physician Assistants (NCCPA) *Founded:* 1975. *Headquarters:* Atlanta, GA. *Purpose:* To certify physician assistants at the entry level and for continued competence. It has certified 19,000 physician assistants.

National Commission on Correctional Health Care (NCCHC) *Founded:* 1983. *Headquarters:* Chicago, IL. *Purpose:* To provide training programs; to conduct seminars; to organize special task forces on issues such as suicide and AIDS; and to improve the quality of and set standards for medical care in correctional institutions in the United States, including prisons, jails, and detention and juvenile facilities, and to serve as an accrediting body for these facilities. Serves professional organizations in the fields of medical and health care.

National Commission for Electrologist Certification (NCEC) *Founded:* 1982. *Headquarters:* Stow, MA. *Purpose:* To promote safety and proficiency in the practice of permanent hair removal; to conduct research in occupational credentialing; and to develop and administer credentialing examinations, seeking to enhance public confidence in electrolysis and electrolysis practitioners.

National Committee for Clinical Laboratory Standards *See* NCCLS.

National Committee for Prevention of Child Abuse (NCPCA) *Founded:* 1972. *Headquarters:* Chicago, IL. *Purpose:* To foster greater public awareness of the incidence, origins, nature, and effects of child abuse; to serve as a national advocate to prevent the neglect and physical, sexual, and emotional abuse of children; to operate the National Center on Child Abuse Prevention Research; and to conduct annual national media campaigns and child abuse prevention programs.

National Committee for Quality Assurance (NCQA) *Founded:* 1979. *Headquarters:* Washington, DC. *Purpose:* To evaluate and report on the quality of managed care plans and to provide information through accreditation and performance measurement, enabling purchasers and consumers of managed health care to distinguish among plans on the basis of quality. NCQA products include the HEDIS (Health Plan Employer Data and Information Set) standardized measures and the Quality Compass™ national database. The NCQA is collaborating (with the American Diabetes Association, FACCT, and HCFA) in the new Diabetes Quality Improvement Project.

National Committee for Quality Health Care (NCQHC) *Founded:* 1978. *Headquarters:* Washington, DC. *Purpose:* To maintain and strengthen quality health care in the United States. Serves health care professionals and organizations principally involved in the health care industry, including hospitals, physicians, HMOs, nursing homes, manufacturers of health care equipment, investment bankers, architects, contractors, and accountants.

National Committee for Radiation Victims (NCRV) *Founded:* 1979. *Headquarters:* Takoma Park, MD. *Purpose:* To serve the needs of Americans affected by exposure to human-made ionizing radiation; to offer public service information on the effects of ionizing radiation; to coordinate and encourage national action on radiation health and safety issues; and to serve as a clearinghouse for information and materials on radiation exposure, existing radiation standards and practices, radiation victims' organizations, and legislation affecting radiation victims.

National Committee on the Treatment of Intractable Pain (NCTIP) *Founded:* 1977. *Headquarters:* Washington, DC. *Purpose:* To promote education and research into more effective methods of pain prevention and control with the coordinated help of professionals in the medical, legal, bioethical, psychological, and religious fields; to endorse the hospice concept of care of the dying, which allows a dying person to remain among family, friends, community, and skilled professionals; to provide constant, effective medical and psychological support for pain control; and to advocate legalization of heroin for medical purposes.

National Community Mental Healthcare Council (NCMHC) *Founded:* 1969. *Headquarters:* Rockville, MD. *Purpose:* To improve the quality and accessibility of mental health services through developing state and national legislative policy issues, advocating for full mental health care coverage by insurance companies and federal programs, and providing workshops, technical assistance and consulting services, and publications.

National Conference of Local Environmental Health Administrators (NCLEHA) *Founded:* 1939. *Headquarters:* Cool, CA. *Purpose:* To promote improvement and greater use of science and practice of environmental health in community life. Serves environmental health personnel engaged in or officially concerned with municipal (city, county, or district) environmental health administration or teaching of environmental health.

National Conference of Standards Laboratories (NCSL) *Founded:* 1961. *Headquarters:* Boulder, CO. *Purpose:* To foster cost reduction or solution of problems, both technical and administrative, that besiege all measurement activities in the physical sciences, engineering, and technology. Its committees include biomedical and pharmaceutical metrology, measurement assurance, and recommended practices. Serves representatives of measurement standards and calibration laboratories.

National Consortium of Chemical Dependency Nurses (NCCDN) *Founded:* 1987. *Headquarters:* Eugene, OR. *Purpose:* To foster an increase in the effectiveness of nursing services for chemical dependency; to establish a professional standard in chemical dependency nursing through a system of competency-based testing and professional development; and to offer a certification examination for nurses with 4,000 hours of experience in the previous five years and 30 hours of chemical dependency coursework. Serves nurses specializing in chemical dependency treatment.

National Consortium for Child Mental Health Services (NCCMHS) *Founded:* 1971. *Headquarters:* Washington, DC. *Purpose:* To foster the exchange of information on child mental health services and to bring concerns regarding child mental health services to appropriate local, state, and federal agencies. Serves national psychiatric, psychologic, educational, social welfare, medical, parent and teacher, and consumer organizations.

National Consumers League (NCL) *Founded:* 1899. *Headquarters:* Washington, DC. *Purpose:* To identify, protect, represent, and advance the economic and social interests of consumers and workers. The NCL is a private, nonprofit advocacy group representing consumers on marketplace and workplace issues, including health care and food and drug safety.

National Contact Lens Examiners (NCLE) *Founded:* 1976. *Headquarters:* Fairfax, VA. *Purpose:* To promote continued development of opticians and technicians as contact lens fitters by formulating standards and procedures for determination of entry-level competency and to assist in the development, administration, and monitoring of a national contact lens registry examination (CLRE), which verifies entry-level competency of contact lens fitters and issues certificates.

National Coordinating Council on Emergency Management (NCCEM) *Founded:* 1952. *Headquarters:* Falls Church, VA. *Purpose:* To develop a comprehensive, workable, and effective emergency and civil defense program through coordinated action and to act as liaison among local units of government and state and federal emergency and civil defense agencies. Serves individuals responsible for preparation of emergency and civil defense plans on the city and county levels.

National Council Against Health Fraud (NCAHF) *Founded:* 1977. *Headquarters:* Loma Linda, CA. *Purpose:* To promote educating the public on fraud and quackery in health care. Its task forces address issues such as AIDS quackery, broadcast media abuse, nutrition diploma mills, and questionable methods of cancer management. Serves health and legal professionals and other interested individuals.

National Council on the Aging (NCOA) *Founded:* 1950. *Headquarters:* Washington, DC. *Purpose:* To maintain the National Association of Older Worker Employment Services, National Center on Arts and the Aging, Health Promotion Institute, National Center on Rural Aging, National Institute on Adult Daycare, National Institute of Community-Based Long-Term Care, National Institute of Senior Centers, National Institute of Senior Housing, National Interfaith Coalition on Aging, and National Voluntary Organizations for Independent Living for the Aging. Serves individuals in business and industry, organized labor, and the health professions; social workers, librarians, the clergy, and educators; housing, research, and government agencies; and state and local agencies on the aging.

National Council on Alcoholism and Drug Dependence (NCADD) *Founded:* 1944. *Headquarters:* New York, NY. *Purpose:* To foster the prevention and control of alcoholism through programs of public and professional education, medical and scientific information, and public policy advocacy and to sponsor National Alcohol Awareness Month each April and National Fetal Alcohol Syndrome Awareness Week.

National Council on Alternative Health Care Policy (NCAHCP) *Founded:* 1976. *Headquarters:* Sacramento, CA. *Purpose:* To provide policy analysis; to monitor legislative policy; to conduct education sessions in national, state, and regional health policy; and to provide technical assistance to organizations interested in developing alternative health care models, policies, and programs directed toward low-income individuals.

National Council on Child Abuse and Family Violence (NCCAFV) *Founded:* 1984. *Headquarters:* Washington, DC. *Purpose:* To foster community-based prevention and treatment programs that provide assistance to children, women, the elderly, and families who are victims of abuse and violence. It is interested in the cyclical and intergenerational nature of family violence and abuse and works to increase public awareness of family violence and to promote private sector financial support for prevention and treatment programs.

National Council of Community Hospitals (NCCH) *Founded:* 1974. *Headquarters:* Washington, DC. *Purpose:* To act as a lobbyist for legislation and federal issues affecting hospitals, physicians, and health care beneficiaries.

Serves community hospitals, hospital consultant groups, and individual health delivery representatives.

National Council on Disability (NCD) *Founded:* 1978. *Headquarters:* Washington, DC. *Purpose:* An independent council affiliated with the U.S. Department of Education and interested in research, programs, services, and resources for individuals with disabilities.

National Council on Family Relations (NCFR) *Founded:* 1938. *Headquarters:* Minneapolis, MN. *Purpose:* To provide opportunities for members to plan and act together to advance marriage and family life through consultation, conferences, and the dissemination of information and research. Serves family life professionals, including clergy, counselors, educators, home economists, lawyers, nurses, librarians, physicians, psychologists, social workers, sociologists, and researchers.

National Council Licensure Examination (NCLEX) *See* National Council of State Boards of Nursing.

National Council on Patient Information and Education (NCPIE) *Founded:* 1982. *Headquarters:* Washington, DC. *Purpose:* To increase the availability of information and improve the dialogue between consumers and health care providers about prescription medicines. It communicates, for example, with health care providers on the importance of giving consumers oral and written information on prescription medicines and encourages consumers to ask questions about medicines and explain factors that may affect their ability to follow prescriptions. Distributes public service announcements for TV and radio. Serves health care organizations, pharmaceutical manufacturing organizations, federal agencies, voluntary health agencies, and consumer groups.

National Council for Prescription Drug Programs (NCPDP) *Founded:* 1977. *Headquarters:* Phoenix, AZ. *Purpose:* To advance standardization of third-party prescription drug programs through national pharmacy listings, uniform claim forms, and standard tape format. Serves companies, organizations, agencies, and individuals with an active interest in third-party prescription drug programs.

National Council on Radiation Protection and Measurements (NCRPM) *Founded:* 1929. *Headquarters:* Bethesda, MD. *Purpose:* To foster the belief that significant advances in radiation protection and measurement can be achieved through cooperative effort; to conduct research focusing on safe occupational exposure levels; and to disseminate information.

National Council on Rehabilitation Education (NCRE) *Founded:* 1961. *Headquarters:* Logan, UT. *Purpose:* To improve services to persons with disabilities; to determine the skills and training necessary for effective rehabilitation services; and to develop standards and uniform licensure and certification requirements for rehabilitation personnel. Serves academic organizations, professional educators, researchers, and students.

National Council of State Boards of Nursing (NCSBN) *Founded:* 1978. *Headquarters:* Chicago, IL. *Purpose:* To maintain and administer the National Council Licensure Examinations (NCLEX) for registered and practical nurses to test basic competency for nursing practice; to ensure relevancy of the examinations to current nursing practice; and to aid the boards in the collection and analysis of information pertaining to the licensure and discipline of nurses. Serves state boards of nursing from the 50 states, the District of Columbia, and five U.S. territories.

National Council of State Emergency Medical Services Training Coordinators (NCSEMSTC) *Founded:* 1977. *Headquarters:* Lexington, KY. *Purpose:* To promote the responsible movement of emergency medical technicians (EMTs) throughout the nation through standardization of policies related, but not limited, to curriculum, certification, recertification, revocation, and reciprocity and to foster public recognition and trust of the emergency medical technician as a health professional. Serves individuals employed by state-level emergency medical services agencies who are responsible for coordination or supervision of emergency medical services (EMS) training programs.

National Council of State Pharmacy Association Executives (NCSPAE) *Founded:* 1927. *Headquarters:* Chapel Hill, NC. *Purpose:* To support executive officers of state pharmaceutical associations to move pharmacy forward and position it more solidly than ever before as a vital element in health care.

National Council for Therapeutic Recreation Certification (NCTRC) *Founded:* 1981. *Headquarters:* Thiells, NY. *Purpose:* To establish national standards for certification and recertification of individuals who work in the therapeutic recreation field; to grant recognition to individuals who voluntarily apply and meet established standards; and to monitor adherence to standards by certified personnel.

National Dental Assistants Association (NDAA) *Founded:* 1964. *Headquarters:* Washington, DC. *Purpose:* To encourage education and certification among dental assistants and to conduct clinics and workshops. It is an auxiliary of the National Dental Association.

National Dental Association (NDA) *Founded:* 1913. *Headquarters:* Washington, DC. *Purpose:* To foster the provision of quality dental care to the unserved and underserved public and to promote knowledge of the art and science of dentistry; to foster the integration of minority dental health care providers in the profession; to promote dentistry as a viable career for minorities through scholarship and support programs; and to advocate the inclusion of dental care services in health care programs on local, state, and national levels.

National Denturist Association (NDA) *Founded:* 1975. *Headquarters:* Portland, OR. *Purpose:* To foster the development and advancement of standards and certification of denturists; to conduct research regarding laws pertaining to the dental profession and to the profession of denturists; and to offer political action counseling and organizing assistance Serves state groups of dental laboratory technicians, denturists, and dentists.

National Digestive Diseases Information Clearinghouse (NDDIC) *Founded:* 1980. *Headquarters:* Bethesda, MD. *Purpose:* To provide a national resource to inform and educate physicians, health professionals, patients and their families, and the public on digestive health and diseases and to serve as a central information database on prevention and management of digestive diseases.

National Down Syndrome Congress (NDSC) *Founded:* 1973. *Headquarters:* Atlanta, GA. *Purpose:* To promote the welfare of persons with Down syndrome; to promote the belief that persons with DS have the right to a normal and dignified life, particularly in the areas of education, medical care, employment, and human services; and to examine issues of social policy and conditions that limit the full growth and potential of children and adults with DS.

National Drug Trade Conference (NDTC) *Founded:* 1913. *Headquarters:* Washington, DC. *Purpose:* To support associations of manufacturers, wholesalers, and boards and colleges of pharmacy.

National Easter Seal Society (NESS) *Founded:* 1919. *Headquarters:* Chicago, IL. *Purpose:* To establish and conduct programs that serve people with disabilities, including rehabilitation programs to meet the diverse needs of people with disabilities and their families, promotion of assistive technology that is leading the way to independence for people with disabilities, passage of critical legislation and programs affecting the lives of people with disabilities, and public education campaigns to encourage positive attitudes toward people with disabilities. NESS is a national federation of state and local societies that operates nearly 500 program service sites to meet the needs of more than one million people annually. *Also known as:* Easter Seals and Easter Seal Society.

National Emergency Management Association (NEMA) *Founded:* 1950. *Headquarters:* Lexington, KY. *Purpose:* To improve relations within the public safety community to provide a cohesive infrastructure for the protection of the public against natural and human-created hazards; to represent the local emergency management community before the federal government; and to produce position papers and resolutions on emergency management issues. Serves state emergency management directors, local emergency management representatives, and individuals, associations, and corporations with an interest in emergency management.

National Emergency Medicine Association (NEMA) *Founded:* 1982. *Headquarters:* Towson, MD. *Purpose:* To promote lifestyles that reduce the likelihood of trauma; to educate the public on how to help a trauma victim before emergency personnel arrive; to ensure that trained emergency personnel have necessary resources. Serves individuals interested in preventing trauma and improving emergency medical care nationwide.

National EMS Pilots Association (NEMSPA) *Founded:* 1985. *Headquarters:* Alexandria, VA. *Purpose:* To help the air medical industry prosper safely; to enhance the delivery of health care; to provide the leadership necessary to establish operation and safety standards; and to provide a forum for dissemination of knowledge and the guidance to formulate positive change in the emergency medical services (EMS) profession.

National Environmental Health Association (NEHA) *Founded:* 1937. *Headquarters:* Denver, CO. *Purpose:* To support persons engaged in environmental health and protection for governmental agencies, public health and environmental protection agencies, industry, and colleges and universities.

National Environmental Health Science and Protection Accreditation Council (EHAC) *Founded:* 1969. *Headquarters:* Rockville, MD. *Purpose:* To accredit environmental health curricula and related procedures and to carry out other responsibilities essential to the accreditation of academic programs leading to associate degrees, baccalaureate degrees, and graduate degrees in environmental health.

National Eye Institute (NEI) *See* Government Organizations (Department of Health and Human Services, NIH).

National Family Planning and Reproductive Health Association (NFPRHA) *Founded:* 1971. *Headquarters:* Washington, DC. *Purpose:* To expand and improve the delivery of family planning and reproductive health care and to establish reproductive health care as a priority preventive health care service. NFPRHA monitors legislation; holds annual meetings; offers computerized diagnostic patient flow analysis for clinic management; and provides information, resource search, and referral services to members. Membership is open to anyone concerned with accessibility and provision of quality reproductive health care.

National Federation of Catholic Physicians Guilds (NFCPG) *See* Catholic Medical Association.

National Federation of Housestaff Organizations (NFHO) *Founded:* 1984. *Headquarters:* New York, NY. *Purpose:* To provide assistance to members in collective bargaining, lobbying state and local governments, and to promote unionization among housestaff physicians.

National Federation of Licensed Practical Nurses (NFLPN) *Founded:* 1949. *Headquarters:* Garner, NC. *Purpose:* To foster and preserve the ideal of comprehensive nursing care for the ill and aged; to improve standards of practice; and to secure recognition and effective utilization of LPNs. Serves licensed practical and vocational nurses.

National Federation of Societies for Clinical Social Work (NFSCSW) *Founded:* 1971. *Headquarters:*

Arlington, VA. *Purpose:* To provide a vehicle for state and regional societies to share concerns common to clinical social work; to develop solutions to problems beyond the jurisdiction of any single society; and to carry out appropriate courses of action. Serves state societies of clinical social work.

National Federation of Specialty Nursing Organizations (NFSNO) *Founded:* 1972. *Headquarters:* Pitman, NJ. *Purpose:* To provide a forum for the discussion of issues of mutual concern to members and to gain more input in the establishment of nursing standards.

National Fire Protection Association (NFPA) *Founded:* 1896. *Headquarters:* Quincy, MA. *Purpose:* To reduce the burden of fire on the quality of life by advocating scientifically based consensus codes and standards, research, and education for fire and related safety issues. NFPA issues the *Life Safety Code*®, which the Joint Commission requires health care organizations to comply with, which contains requirements for building design, construction, operation, and maintenance to protect occupants from fire, smoke, and fumes or similar emergencies.

National Flight Nurses Association (NFNA) *Founded:* 1981. *Headquarters:* Park Ridge, IL. *Purpose:* To promote the quality of flight nursing by developing standards for the profession and exploring educational opportunities; and to provide assistance to hospitals for developing air medical services programs.

National Flight Paramedics Association (NFPA) *Founded:* 1986. *Headquarters:* Tulsa, OK. *Purpose:* To promote education, professionalism, and communication within the emergency medical services community and to maintain foundation of aeromedical research.

National Head Injury Foundation (NHIF) *See* Brain Injury Association.

National Health Law Program (NHeLP) *Founded:* 1969. *Headquarters:* Los Angeles, CA. *Purpose:* To provide information, referrals, and consultation on litigation strategy and to coordinate testimony for particular hearings. Serves attorneys and health services program attorneys and their clients in matters involving health problems of the poor.

National Health Lawyers Association/American Academy of Healthcare Attorneys (NHLA/AAHA) *Founded:* 1971/1968. *Headquarters:* Washington, DC. *Purpose:* To provide a forum for interaction and information exchange to enable its lawyer members to serve their clients more effectively; to produce the highest quality nonpartisan educational programs, products, and services concerning health law issues; and to serve as a public resource on selected health care legal issues. *Formed by merger of:* National Health Lawyers Association and American Academy of Healthcare Attorneys (1997).

National Hearing Conservation Association (NHCA) *Founded:* 1977. *Headquarters:* Milwaukee, WI. *Purpose:* To encourage education and standards development among members and industrial groups and to monitor legislation and regulatory activities relating to hearing conservation. Serves individuals holding advanced academic degrees in a discipline involving hearing and hearing loss; professional service organizations engaged in industrial hearing conservation programs; and companies that manufacture or sell occupational-noise or hearing-loss products.

National Heart, Lung, and Blood Institute *See* Government Organizations (Department of Health and Human Services, NIH).

National Heart Savers Association (NHSA) *Founded:* 1985. *Headquarters:* Omaha, NE. *Purpose:* To promote cardiac health by informing the public of the dangers of a high-cholesterol diet; to conduct public cholesterol screening programs; to influence major food-processing and fast-food restaurant companies; and to promote nutrition education in public schools.

National Home Infusion Association (NHIA) *Founded:* 1966. *Headquarters:* Alexandria, VA. *Purpose:* To lead market research efforts in the alternate-site-infusion therapy market. A current industry research project, carried out by NHIA's Home Infusion Research Center, is a survey of alternate-site-infusion provider pharmacists.

National Hormone and Pituitary Program (NHPP) *Founded:* 1963. *Headquarters:* Rockville, MD. *Purpose:* To collect human pituitary glands obtained through autopsies; to extract from them human growth hormone, human follicle stimulating hormone, human luteinizing hormone, human adrenocorticotrophic hormone, human thyroid stimulating hormone, human prolactin, and beta-lipotropin; and to distribute these to doctors in research centers for research in endocrinology.

National Hospice Organization (NHO) *Founded:* 1978. *Headquarters:* Arlington, VA. *Purpose:* To promote standards of care in program planning and implementation; to monitor health care legislation and regulation relevant to hospice care; to collect data and compile statistics; to encourage health teaching institutions to provide instruction in hospice care of terminally ill patients and their families.

National Human Genome Research Institute *See* Government Organizations (Department of Health and Human Services, NIH).

National Hypertension Association (NHA) *Founded:* 1977. *Headquarters:* New York, NY. *Purpose:* To combat hypertension by developing, directing, and implementing effective programs to educate physicians and the public about hypertension; to conduct research; and to provide school children with information on hypertension. Serves physicians, medical researchers, and business professionals interested in prevention of the complications of hypertension.

National Indian Health Board (NIHB) *Founded:* 1969. *Headquarters:* Denver, CO. *Purpose:* To foster the improvement of health conditions that directly or indirectly affect American Indians and Alaskan natives; to inform the public of the health conditions of Native Americans; and to provide technical assistance to members and Indian organizations.

National Information Center for Children and Youth with Disabilities (NICHCY) *Founded:* 1970. *Headquarters:* Washington, DC. *Purpose:* To provide personal responses to specific questions and referrals to other sources of help and to provide information concerning educational rights and special services to parents and educators of children (birth to age 22) with physical, mental, and emotional handicaps.

National Information Center on Deafness (NICD) *Founded:* 1980. *Headquarters:* Washington, DC. *Purpose:* To provide a nonmembership resource and information clearinghouse; to provide information on all aspects of deafness; to provide referrals and identify other resources for persons seeking information on deafness and hearing loss.

National Institute on Adult Daycare (NIAD) *Founded:* 1979. *Headquarters:* Washington, DC. *Purpose:* To promote and enhance adult daycare programs; to provide services and activities for disabled older persons on a long-term basis; to provide training consultation services for daycare personnel. Serves adult daycare practitioners and health and social service planners.

National Institute on Aging *See* Government Organizations (Department of Health and Human Services, NIH).

National Institute on Alcohol Abuse and Alcoholism *See* Government Organizations (Department of Health and Human Services, NIH).

National Institute of Allergy and Infectious Diseases *See* Government Organizations (Department of Health and Human Services, NIH).

National Institute of Arthritis and Musculoskeletal and Skin Diseases *See* Government Organizations (Department of Health and Human Services, NIH).

National Institute for Burn Medicine (NIBM) *Founded:* 1968. *Headquarters:* Ann Arbor, MI. *Purpose:* To provide consultation for development of specialized burn care facilities, prevention programs and materials, and education, information, and statistics in burn treatment and care; to foster a dedication to preventing burn injuries, improving the survival rate of, and developing the quality of life for, burn victims.

National Institute of Child Health and Human Development (NICHHD) *See* Government Organizations (Department of Health and Human Services, NIH).

National Institute on Community-based Long-term Care (NICLC) *Founded:* 1984. *Headquarters:* Washington, DC. *Purpose:* To promote and develop a comprehensive long term care system that will integrate home-based and community-based services enabling older adults to live in their own homes as long as possible and to provide an information clearinghouse for long term care professionals.

National Institute on Deafness and Other Common Disorders *See* Government Organizations (Department of Health and Human Services, NIH).

National Institute on Dental Research *See* Government Organizations (Department of Health and Human Services, NIH).

National Institute of Diabetes and Digestive and Kidney Diseases *See* Government Organizations (Department of Health and Human Services, NIH).

National Institute on Drug Abuse *See* Government Organizations (Department of Health and Human Services, NIH).

National Institute of Electromedical Information (NIEI) *Founded:* 1984. *Headquarters:* Bay Terrace, NY. *Purpose:* To disseminate information on research, case histories, new and proposed theories, and clinical applications of electromedicine to professionals, laypersons, and federal agencies. The NIEI serves health care practitioners, medical educators, research scientists, and electromedical device manufacturers.

National Institute of Environmental Health Sciences *See* Government Organizations (Department of Health and Human Services, NIH).

National Institute for the Family (NIF) *Founded:* 1980. *Headquarters:* Washington, DC. *Purpose:* To strengthen families in the United States; to provide educational programs to adults; to sponsor training and assessment programs; to organize workshops and seminars; and to disseminate information on family education and ministries.

National Institute of General Medical Sciences *See* Government Organizations (Department of Health and Human Services, NIH).

National Institute for Jewish Hospice (NIJH) *Founded:* 1985. *Headquarters:* Los Angeles, CA. *Purpose:* To provide a resource center to help terminal patients and their families deal with their grief and to provide information on traditional Jewish views on death, dying, and coping with the loss of a loved one. The NIJH serves individuals and organizations concerned about terminally ill Jewish people.

National Institute of Justice *See* Government Organizations (Department of Justice).

National Institute of Mental Health (NIMH) *See* Government Organizations (Department of Health and Human Services, NIH).

National Institute of Neurological Disorders and Stroke *See* Government Organizations (Department of Health and Human Services, NIH).

National Institute of Nursing Research *See* Government Organizations (Department of Health and Human Services, NIH).

National Institute for Rehabilitation Engineering (NIRE) *Founded:* 1967. *Headquarters:* Hewitt, NJ. *Purpose:* To provide custom-designed and custom-made tools and devices and intensive personal task-performance and driver training to handicapped persons. It is often the organization of last resort for permanently, severely, or multihandicapped persons. It is staffed by 400 electronics engineers, physicists, psychologists, optometrists, and other individuals who work as a team for the handicapped person.

National Institutes of Health *See* Government Organizations (Department of Health and Human Services).

National Jewish Center for Immunology and Respiratory Medicine *Founded:* 1978. *Headquarters:* Denver, CO. *Purpose:* To foster the development of treatment, research, and education in chronic respiratory diseases and immunological disorders, such as asthma, tuberculosis, cystic fibrosis, chronic bronchitis, emphysema, interstitial lung disease, and systemic lupus erythematosus.

National Kidney Foundation (NKF) *Founded:* 1950. *Headquarters:* New York, NY. *Purpose:* To improve the care and treatment of those afflicted with diseases of the kidney and urinary tract through advances in disease detection, diagnosis, and treatment. The NKF organizes activities by the government, the private sector, and lay and medical volunteers to promote research, patient services, professional and public education, organ donor programs, and community service. The NKF organized Team USA for the World Transplant Games (Sydney, Australia, October 1997).

National Kidney and Urologic Diseases Information Clearinghouse (NKUDIC) *Founded:* 1987. *Headquarters:* Bethesda, MD. *Purpose:* To disseminate educational information on kidney and urologic diseases and their causes and treatments and to develop and distribute publications about kidney and urologic organizations. It was established by the National Institutes of Health.

National Leadership Coalition on AIDS (NLCOA) *Founded:* 1987. *Headquarters:* Washington, DC. *Purpose:* To provide timely and pertinent information about AIDS to the business and labor community. Composed of 180 major corporations; labor, trade, and professional associations; and civic, voluntary, religious, gay, and ethnic groups.

National League for Nursing (NLN) *Founded:* 1952. *Headquarters:* New York, NY. *Purpose:* To provide tests used in selecting applicants for schools of nursing, to evaluate nursing student progress and nursing service and to provide national accreditations for nursing education programs, home health agencies, and other types of home care services. Serves individuals and agencies concerned with nursing education and delivery of nursing services.

National Legal Center for the Medically Dependent and Disabled (NLCMDD) *Founded:* 1984. *Headquarters:* Indianapolis, IN. *Purpose:* To defend the legal rights of indigent older and disabled persons so that such people can obtain proper medical care. Provides lawyer referral services and analysis of pertinent legislation on request of legislators and operates a speakers' bureau.

National Library of Medicine (NLM) *See* Government Organizations (Department of Health and Human Services, NIH).

National Marrow Donor Program (NMDP) *Founded:* 1986. *Headquarters:* Minneapolis, MN. *Purpose:* To provide a central registry of American bone marrow donors; to develop a large pool of potential donors; to facilitate searches and matching of donors and recipients; and to test the effectiveness of unrelated donor transplants. Serves donor and bone marrow transplant centers.

National Maternal and Child Health Clearinghouse (NMCHC) *Founded:* 1983. *Headquarters:* Vienna, VA. *Purpose:* To provide a national clearinghouse that collects and disseminates information on maternal and child health, human genetics, nutrition, and pregnancy care, primarily from materials developed by the U.S. Department of Health and Human Services.

National Medical Association (NMA) *Founded:* 1895. *Headquarters:* Washington, DC. *Purpose:* To promote the science and art of medicine and to influence society and its institutions in order to encourage, protect, and promote the betterment of the public health and the quality of life for individuals and families. While throughout its history the NMA has focused primarily on health issues related to African Americans and medically underserved populations, its principles, goals, initiatives, and philosophy encompass all sectors of the population. The NMA is composed of 24 scientific sections representing major medical specialties and maintains regional, state, and local affiliates. The NMA publishes a journal and conducts symposia and workshops.

National Medical and Dental Association (NMDA) *Founded:* 1910. *Headquarters:* Maspeth, NY. *Purpose:* To offer specialized education; to maintain a speakers' bureau and a hall of fame; and to provide a social organization for Polish-American professionals interested in preserving their heritage. Serves physicians, dentists, and lawyers of Polish extraction.

National Medical Fellowships (NMF) *Founded:* 1946. *Headquarters:* New York, NY. *Purpose:* To promote education of minority students in medicine; to conduct a financial assistance program for first-year and second-year minority medical students; and to conduct workshops in financial planning and management for medical and premedical students, administrators, and parents.

National Medic-Card Systems (NMCS) *Founded:* 1978. *Headquarters:* San Marcos, CA. *Purpose:* To produce wallet-size medical cards that have five sections, fold into the size of a credit card, and describe individuals' medical conditions in detail.

National Mental Health Association (NMHA)
Founded: 1909. *Headquarters:* Alexandria, VA. *Purpose:* To improve the mental health of all individuals and achieve victory over mental illnesses. NMHA accomplishes its mission as a force for social change through advocacy, prevention, information and referral, and public education. NMHA operates as a citizen volunteer advocacy effort through its national office and its many state and local affiliates. The current Campaign on Clinical Depression includes a national Depression Screening Day (providing anonymous screening) during Mental Illness Awareness Week in October. NMHA is a founding leader in the National Managed Care Consortium, a coalition of national mental health consumer, family and advocacy organizations, developed from a consumers' perspective.

National Minority AIDS Council (NMAC) *Founded:* 1986. *Headquarters:* Washington, DC. *Purpose:* To provide a clearinghouse of information on AIDS as it affects minority communities in the United States and to advocate funding for research to discover new and better ways to treat and prevent mental illness. Serves public health departments and AIDS service organizations.

National Minority Health Association (NMHA)
Founded: 1987. *Headquarters:* Harrisburg, PA. *Purpose:* To identify and focus attention on the health needs of minorities, serving health care providers and associations, consumers, executives and administrators, educators, pharmaceutical and health insurance companies, and other corporations with an interest in health care.

National Multiple Sclerosis Society (NMSS)
Founded: 1946. *Headquarters:* New York, NY. *Purpose:* To stimulate, support, and coordinate research into the cause, treatment, and cure of multiple sclerosis (MS); to provide services for persons with MS and related diseases and their families; and to aid in establishing MS clinics and therapy centers.

National Network for Social Work Managers
Founded: 1985. *Headquarters:* Washington, DC. *Purpose:* To enhance social work managers' careers in such areas as administration, management, planning, budgeting, economics, and legislative work. Serves individuals with degrees in social work who are engaged or interested in management within the human services field.

National Nurses in Business Association (NNBA)
Founded: 1988. *Headquarters:* Concord, CA. *Purpose:* To promote the growth of health-related businesses owned and operated by nurses. Serves nurses in all types of business, including medical and legal consulting and quality assurance.

National Nurses Society on Addictions (NNSA)
Founded: 1975. *Headquarters:* Raleigh, NC. *Purpose:* To foster continuing education and development of skills among nurses involved in the field. Serves nurses caring for persons addicted to alcohol and other drugs, and their families.

National Optometric Association (NOA) *Founded:* 1969. *Headquarters:* Bloomington, IN. *Purpose:* To conduct research programs and national recruiting programs and to maintain a speakers' bureau. Serves optometrists dedicated to increasing minority optometric manpower.

National Organization for Associate Degree Nursing (NOADN) *Founded:* 1986. *Headquarters:* Reston, VA. *Purpose:* To foster interest in retaining current competency-level examinations and endorsement of registered nurse licensure from state to state for associate degree nursing graduates and to represent and advance the status of associate degree nursing education and practice.

National Organization for Competency Assurance (NOCA) *Founded:* 1977. *Headquarters:* Washington, DC. *Purpose:* To foster public awareness and acceptance of private-sector credentialing as an alternative to licensure and to promote nonlicensed but certified practitioners as a means to achieving high quality and cost containment. Serves nonprofit organizations conducting certification programs for occupations and professionals and for trade associations representing these professionals.

National Organization on Disability (NOD)
Founded: 1982. *Headquarters:* Washington, DC. *Purpose:* To promote the full participation in all aspects of life of persons with mental and physical disabilities; and to promote for disabled persons greater educational and employment opportunities, improved access to buildings, polling places, and transportation, and increased participation in recreational, social, religious, electoral, and cultural activities.

National Organization of Gay and Lesbian Scientists and Technical Professionals (NOGLSTP)
Founded: 1983. *Headquarters:* Pasadena, CA. *Purpose:* To educate the public, especially the gay and scientific communities; to improve members' employment and professional environment; and to oppose anti-gay discrimination and stereotypes. Serves gay and lesbian individuals, and interested organizations, employed or interested in high-technology or scientific fields.

National Patient Safety Foundation (NPSF) *See* American Medical Association.

National Pediculosis Association (NPA) *Founded:* 1983. *Headquarters:* Newton, MA. *Purpose:* To eliminate the incidence, particularly among children, of pediculosis (head lice); to conduct public education campaigns to make pediculosis control a public health priority and act as a consumer advocate to ensure the quality and safety of products for treating pediculosis; and to encourage scientific research to discover methods of treatment that minimize the use of pesticides. NPA sponsors National Pediculosis Prevention Month in September and serves physicians, school nurses, individuals representing hospitals and county health departments, and parents.

National Perinatal Association (NPA) *Founded:* 1976. *Headquarters:* Tampa, FL. *Purpose:* To promote improved patient care, education, research, advocacy, and delivery systems for perinatal care.

National Pharmaceutical Association (NPhA)
Founded: 1947. *Headquarters:* Richardson, TX. *Purpose:* To provide members with a means to contribute to their common improvement as well as to the public good. The Student National Pharmaceutical Association (SNPhA), founded in 1972, is an educational and service association of students who are concerned about pharmacy issues, professional development and the lack of minority representation in pharmacy and other health related professions. Serves state and local associations of professional minority pharmacists.

National Pharmaceutical Council (NPC) *Founded:* 1953. *Headquarters:* Reston, VA. *Purpose:* To generate research; to compile statistics; and to conduct special programs. Serves pharmaceutical manufacturers that research and produce trade-name prescription medications and other pharmaceutical products.

National Phlebotomy Association (NPA) *Founded:* 1978. *Headquarters:* Hyattsville, MD. *Purpose:* To provide accreditation for phlebotomy programs and to give national certification examinations in phlebotomy at the request of approved programs.

National Podiatric Medical Association (NPMA)
Founded: 1971. *Headquarters:* Chicago, IL. *Purpose:* To foster improvement in public health, raising standards of the podiatric profession and education, and to eliminate religious and racial discrimination and segregation in American medical institutions. Serves minority podiatrists.

National Prevention Coalition (for the Prevention of Mental-Emotional Disabilities) *Founded:* 1989. *Headquarters:* Washington, DC. *Purpose:* To coordinate the efforts of many systems in a coalition to share information about current prevention efforts; to provide a forum for discussing issues relevant to prevention; to foster prevention research and seek consensus on priority needs for such research to gain acceptance of and use of prevention services as a part of the continuum of mental health services; to share information about current policies affecting prevention; and to influence those policies. Founding organizations of the coalition are the National Mental Health Association (NMHA) and NIH's National Institutes of Mental Health. The NMHA chairs and staffs the coalition, which includes 25 national organizations.

National Prevention Network (NPN) *Founded:* 1982. *Headquarters:* Washington, DC. *Purpose:* To provide a network among state agency personnel and other prevention professionals to assist in the development of effective and innovative substance abuse prevention strategies. Serves officials of state alcohol and drug agencies who work to enhance national, state, and local programs for drug and alcohol abuse prevention. Its parent organization is National Association of State Alcohol and Drug Abuse Directors.

National Psychological Association for Psychoanalysis (NPAP) *Founded:* 1946. *Headquarters:* New York, NY. *Purpose:* To conduct training programs leading to certification in psychoanalysis and to offer information and a private referral service for the public.

National Rare Blood Club (NRBC) *Founded:* 1978. *Headquarters:* New York, NY. *Purpose:* To provide a free network of persons aged 18 years to 65 years who have rare blood types and are physically able to donate blood.

National Registry in Clinical Chemistry (NRCC)
Founded: 1967. *Headquarters:* Washington, DC. *Purpose:* To evaluate the credentials of clinical chemistry practitioners; to issue certificates to those who are qualified; and to provide an annual evaluation of clinical laboratory specialists in the chemical field who voluntarily present their credentials to the registry.

National Registry of Emergency Medical Technicians (NREMT) *Founded:* 1970. *Headquarters:* Columbus, OH. *Purpose:* To foster the development and evaluation of educational programs to train emergency medical technicians; to establish qualifications for eligibility to apply for registration; to prepare and conduct examinations designed to ensure the competence of emergency medical technicians and paramedics; to establish a system for biennial registration; to establish procedures for revocation of certificates of registration for cause; and to maintain a directory of registered emergency medical technicians.

National Rehabilitation Association (NRA)
Founded: 1925. *Headquarters:* Alexandria, VA. *Purpose:* To provide opportunities through knowledge and diversity for professionals in the fields of rehabilitation by conducting legislative activities, developing accessibility guidelines, and offering education. Serves physicians, counselors, therapists, disability examiners, vocational evaluators, administrators, instructors, placement specialists, secretaries, and other persons interested in rehabilitation of persons with disabilities.

National Rehabilitation Counseling Association (NRCA) *Founded:* 1958. *Headquarters:* Manassas, VA. *Purpose:* To enhance the profession of rehabilitation counseling and to provide standards of conduct and performance among its members. As a division of the National Rehabilitation Association, it serves professional and student rehabilitation counselors.

National Rehabilitation Information Center (NARIC)
Founded: 1977. *Headquarters:* Silver Spring, MD. *Purpose:* To improve delivery of information to the rehabilitation community and to disseminate the findings of programs funded by the National Institute on Disability and Rehabilitation Research (NIDRR).

National Renal Administrators Association (NRAA)
Founded: 1977. *Headquarters:* Washington, DC. *Purpose:* To provide a vehicle for the development of educational and information services for members and to maintain contact with health care facilities and government agencies. Serves administrative personnel involved with dialysis programs for patients with kidney failure.

National Research Council (NRC) *Founded:* 1916. *Headquarters:* Washington, DC. *Purpose:* To associate the broad community of science and technology with the NRC's purposes of further knowledge and advising the federal government. It serves as an independent adviser to the federal government on scientific and technical questions and provides services to the government, the public, and the scientific and engineering communities. It is jointly administered by the National Academy of Sciences, National Academy of Engineering, and Institute of Medicine.

National Resource Center on Homelessness and Mental Illness (NRCHMI) *Founded:* 1988. *Headquarters:* Delmar, NY. *Purpose:* To provide a center for information and technical assistance on the housing and service needs of the mentally ill homeless.

National Right to Life Committee (NRLC) *Founded:* 1973. *Headquarters:* Washington, DC. *Purpose:* To protect human life from abortion, euthanasia, and infanticide, through public education, outreach, citizen action, and legislation to restore and maintain legal protection for the lives of all defenseless human beings. It monitors and conducts research on relevant social, medical, and political events and trends.

National Rural Health Association (NRHA) *Founded:* 1989. *Headquarters:* Kansas City, MO. *Purpose:* To improve the health and health care of rural Americans and to provide leadership on rural issues through advocacy, communications, education and research. NRHA provides a network for administrators, physicians, nurses, physician assistants, health planners, academicians, and other persons interested in understanding health care problems unique to rural areas.

National Safety Council (NSC) *Founded:* 1913. *Headquarters:* Itasca, IL. *Purpose:* To promote accident reduction by gathering and distributing information to the public about the causes of accidents and ways to prevent them.

National Safety Management Society (NSMS) *Founded:* 1968. *Headquarters:* Weaverville, NC. *Purpose:* To foster new concepts of accident prevention and loss control; to promote the role of safety management in the total management effort; and to advise concentration in areas where a favorable cost-benefit return can be achieved with these new concepts, while being cognizant of humanitarian considerations. Serves individuals with managerial responsibilities related to safety/loss control management, including medical, legal, and computer technology professionals.

National Society of Genetic Counselors (NSGC) *Founded:* 1979. *Headquarters:* Wallingford, PA. *Purpose:* To further the professional interests of genetic counselors, promote a network for communication within the profession, and deal with issues relevant to human genetics. The NSGC has established a code of ethics, which affirms the ethical responsibilities of its members and provides them with guidance in their relationships with self, clients, colleagues, and society.

National Society for Histotechnology (NSH) *Founded:* 1974. *Headquarters:* Bowie, MD. *Purpose:* To advance professional growth, standards, knowledge and performance of histotechnology through continuing and formal education programs. Membership is open to anyone actively engaged in or interested in histotechnology or other allied profession.

National Society of Patient Representation and Consumer Affairs (NSPRCA) *Founded:* 1972. *Headquarters:* Chicago, IL. *Purpose:* To advance the development of effective patient representative programs in health care institutions. The society conducts seminars and workshops and is affiliated with the American Hospital Association.

National Subacute Care Association (NSCA) *Founded:* 1995. *Headquarters:* Bethesda, MD. *Purpose:* To furnish subacute-care providers with a more focused presence and a unified agenda. The NSCA is dedicated to advancing the field of subacute care and to providing a national vehicle for information and education that will enable its members to better serve persons with subacute need.

National Technical Information Service (NTIS) *See* Government Organizations (Department of Commerce).

National Therapeutic Recreation Society (NTRS) *Founded:* 1966. *Headquarters:* Arlington, VA. *Purpose:* To provide therapeutic recreation services to assist individuals with disabilities achieve maximum independence and rehabilitation. Serves professionals, educators, and students whose full-time employment is to provide therapeutic recreation services for persons with disabilities in clinical facilities and in the community.

National VA Chaplain Center (NVACC) *Founded:* 1945. *Headquarters:* Hampton, VA. *Purpose:* To support a clinical chaplaincy within the Department of Veterans Affairs to provide for the constitutionally mandated free exercise of religion requirements of hospitalized veterans and support medical care by clinical pastoral interventions.

National Voluntary Health Agencies (NVHA) *Founded:* 1956. *Headquarters:* Washington, DC. *Purpose:* To receive funds generated by the Combined Federal Campaign and to distribute them to member agencies.

National Wellness Association (NWA) *Founded:* 1985. *Headquarters:* Stevens Point, WI. *Purpose:* To provide a forum for networking among health and wellness professionals. Serves health and wellness promotion professionals from corporations, universities, hospitals, community organizations, consulting firms, government organizations, and fitness clubs.

National Wellness Institute (NWI) *Founded:* 1977. *Headquarters:* Stevens Point, WI. *Purpose:* To provide national leadership in the wellness movement; to assist organizations with planning, development, implementation, and evaluation of wellness programs; and to assist in the development of high-quality wellness products and services.

National Women's Health Network (NWHN) *Founded:* 1976. *Headquarters:* Washington, DC. *Purpose:* To monitor federal health policy as it affects women; to testify before Congress and federal agencies; to support feminist health projects; and to sponsor the Women's Health Clearinghouse, a national resource file on all aspects of women's health care. Serves consumers, organizations, and health centers.

National Women's Health Resource Center (NWHRC) *Founded:* 1988. *Headquarters:* Washington, DC. *Purpose:* To foster public education and research that focuses on diseases or conditions that are unique, more prevalent, or more serious in women; and to develop and provide models for clinical services, especially those that will meet the needs of underserved women.

Natural Food Associates (NFA) *Founded:* 1952. *Headquarters:* Atlanta, TX. *Purpose:* To inform the public of the values of natural, chemical-free food grown in rich, fertile soil; to expose the dangers of chemical contamination of food, water, and land; and to offer preventive measures for metabolic disease.

NCCLS *Founded:* 1968. *Headquarters:* Wayne, PA. *Purpose:* To promote the development of national standards for clinical laboratory testing and to provide a consensus mechanism for defining and resolving problems that influence the quality and cost of laboratory work performed. Serves government agencies, professional societies, clinical laboratories, and industrial firms with interests in clinical laboratory testing. *Formerly:* National Committee for Clinical Laboratory Standards (1994).

Network for Continuing Medical Education (NCME) *Founded:* 1965. *Headquarters:* Secaucus, NJ. *Purpose:* To provide continuing medical education services for physicians, including biweekly videotapes, posters, program brochures, and workbooks covering the spectrum of medical topics.

Neuro-Developmental Treatment Association, Inc. (NDTA) *Founded:* 1967. *Headquarters:* Chicago, IL. *Purpose:* To further the unique qualities of the neuro-developmental treatment (NDT) approach by providing clinical and didactic education, clinical research, client and family advocacy and a broad range of communication services.

Neurosurgical Society of America (NSA) *Founded:* 1948. *Headquarters:* Cleveland, OH. *Purpose:* To provide a national organization composed of 162 young specialists in neurological surgery.

New York State Task Force on Life and the Law *Founded:* 1985. *Headquarters:* New York, NY. *Purpose:* To develop public policy on issues arising from medical advances, including the withholding and withdrawal of life-sustaining treatment, assisted suicide and euthanasia, assisted reproductive technologies, and organ and tissue transplantation. The interdisciplinary membership represents fields of law, medicine, nursing, philosophy, and bioethics and includes patient advocates and representatives of different religious communities. Policy recommendations are presented through proposed legislation, regulation, public education, and other measures and accompanied by reports to facilitate public discussion. A current project is the Commission on Quality of Care at the End of Life, which was established in 1997 to suggest legislation, policy, and educational activities directed to physicians and to the general public. Recommendations that have been disseminated nationally have been embraced as models for legislation in other states.

Non-Circumcision Information Center (NCIC) *Founded:* 1973. *Headquarters:* Waverly, MA. *Purpose:* To provide current, accurate, and complete information to the public regarding the safety and necessity of circumcision; to distribute information that discourages routine circumcision; and to assist in increasing the number of uncircumcised males from 40% to 90%.

Nonprescription Drug Manufacturers Association (NDMA) *Founded:* 1881. *Headquarters:* Washington, DC. *Purpose:* To act as a liaison between the industry and the Food and Drug Administration (FDA), the Federal Trade Commission (FTC), and Congress, and to conduct a voluntary labeling review service to assist members in complying with laws and regulations. Serves producers of nonprescription drugs (packaged, over-the-counter medicines), and associate members including suppliers, advertising agencies, and advertising media. *Formerly:* The Proprietory Association.

North American Clinical Dermatologic Society (NACDS) *Founded:* 1959. *Headquarters:* Jacksonville, FL. *Purpose:* To promote the exchange of information and research. Members include clinical board-certified dermatologists practicing in the United States and Canada and leaders of dermatology throughout the world.

North American Membrane Society (NAMS) *Founded:* 1985. *Headquarters:* Austin, TX. *Purpose:* To foster the advancement of membrane technology, especially synthetic membrane technology, and to provide an educational and informational center. Synthetic membranes are polymers and inorganic materials used for sterile filtration and separation processes, such as those used in gas separation, water purification, food processing, biochemistry, and the medical-pharmaceutical field. Serves academicians, graduate students, scientists, engineers, and corporate executives.

North American Menopause Society (NAMS) *Founded:* 1989. *Headquarters:* Cleveland, OH. *Purpose:* Provides a forum to promote understanding of menopause for a multitude of scientific disciplines with an interest in the human female menopause.

North American Nursing Diagnosis Association (NANDA) *Founded:* 1972. *Headquarters:* Philadelphia,

PA. *Purpose:* To develop, refine, and promote a taxonomy of diagnostic terminology for use by nurses.

North American Primary Care Research Group (NAPCRG) *Founded:* 1972. *Headquarters:* Richmond, VA. *Purpose:* To foster interest in primary care research and to maintain 11 special interest groups including ambulatory sentinel practice, clinical decision making, and health status group.

North American Society for Dialysis and Transplantation (NASDT) *Founded:* 1981. *Headquarters:* Houston, TX. *Purpose:* To promote education and research and to disseminate knowledge and technology in the fields of kidney dialysis and transplantation. Serves nephrologists, transplant surgeons and physicians, registered nurses, and transplant coordinators active in the areas of teaching, manufacturing, and administration in the fields of nephrology and transplantation.

North American Society of Pacing and Electrophysiology (NASPE) *Founded:* 1979. *Headquarters:* Natick, MA. *Purpose:* To recommend standards for electrophysiologic device testing and the training of electrophysiologists and pacemaker-implanting physicians and to inform members of new developments in the field of electrophysiology. Serves physicians, technicians, nurses, engineers, and individuals involved in pacemaker implantation and cardiac electrophysiology.

North American Society for Pediatric Gastroenterology and Nutrition (NASPGN) *Founded:* 1972. *Headquarters:* Cleveland, OH. *Purpose:* To advance the understanding of the normal development and physiology of diseases of the gastrointestinal tract and liver in infants, children, and adolescents, and to foster the dissemination of this knowledge through scientific meetings, public education, and collaboration with other organizations concerned with pediatric gastroenterology and nutrition.

North American Society for the Psychology of Sport and Physical Activity (NASPSPA) *Founded:* 1966. *Headquarters:* Greensboro, NC. *Purpose:* To promote scientific research and relations within the behavioral sciences with an application to sports psychology and motor learning, control, and development. Serves kinesiologists, psychologists, and physical educators.

North American Spine Society (NASS) *Founded:* 1985. *Headquarters:* Rosemont, IL. *Purpose:* To maintain the American Board of Neurological and Orthopaedic Medicine and Surgery and the American Board for Medical-Legal Analysis in Medicine and Surgery; to improve the quality of scientific practice in spinal disorders; and to exchange ideas. Serves physicians, osteopathic physicians, and individuals in allied medical or surgical specialties interested in neurological and orthopedic medicine and surgery.

North American Transplant Coordinators Organization (NATCO) *Founded:* 1979. *Headquarters:* Lenexa, KS. *Purpose:* To influence increased procurement and use of transplantable organs and tissues under the direction of individuals and institutions responsible for the employment of members. Serves nurses and allied health professionals working with organ recipients and those working to obtain and distribute human organs and tissues to waiting victims of end-stage organ failure.

NSF International *Founded:* 1944. *Headquarters:* Ann Arbor, MI. *Purpose:* Committed to public health safety and protection of the environment by developing standards, by providing education, and by providing third-party conformity assessment services. Products include management systems assessment and registration ISO 14000 standards for quality and for the environment. Serves representatives of the public, health professions, business, and industry.

Nuclear Medicine Technology Certification Board (NMTCB) *Founded:* 1977. *Headquarters:* Atlanta, GA. *Purpose:* To develop and administer certification examinations for nuclear medicine technologists.

Nurses' House *Founded:* 1925. *Headquarters:* New York, NY. *Purpose:* To assist registered nurses in financial and other crises by providing short-term financial aid for shelter, food, and utilities until the nurses obtain entitlements or jobs; to offer counseling on emotional problems, such as drug and alcohol dependency, and referral to those needing psychological care; and to encourage homebound or retired nurses through a volunteer corps.

Nurses Organization of Veterans Affairs (NOVA) *Founded:* 1980. *Headquarters:* Washington, DC. *Purpose:* To provide Veterans Affairs nurses with opportunities to preserve and improve quality care through legislative influence and to conduct competitions, seminars, and educational programs. Serves registered nurses of the Department of Veterans Affairs.

Nursing Home Information Service (NHIS) *Founded:* 1975. *Headquarters:* Washington, DC. *Purpose:* To provide information on nursing home standards and regulations, alternative community and health services, criteria for choosing a nursing home, and guidelines for obtaining medigap insurance (insurance covering medical expenses after Medicare's percentage is paid). Encourages consumer advocacy by persons desiring long term care for themselves or for family or friends; and to promote compliance with the Nursing Home Patients Bill of Rights, a document listing some of the requirements for a federally certified nursing home.

Nutrition Education Association (INC.) *Founded:* 1977. *Headquarters:* Houston, TX. *Purpose:* To educate the public on good nutrition as a means of acquiring and maintaining good health; to promote communication among medical investigators, researchers, and practitioners concerned with nutrition; to sponsor new nutrition study groups; and to offer home study courses in new nutrition.

Nutrition for Optimal Health Association (NOHA) *Founded:* 1972. *Headquarters:* Winnetka, IL. *Purpose:* To promote good nutrition as a means of achieving and maintaining optimal health; to conduct nutrition programs and seminars; to advance and disseminate scientifically based information on the practical applications of sound nutritional principles to daily living; to offer cooking classes and workshops; to conduct nutrition education programs and seminars; and to maintain a speakers' bureau.

Nutrition Screening Initiative (NSI) *Founded:* 1990. *Headquarters:* Washington, DC. *Purpose:* To promote routine nutrition screening and better nutrition care for older Americans throughout the continuum of care and in all practice settings through the development of checklists, screens, handbooks, and other screening tools. The NSI is a multidisciplinary coalition led by the American Dietetic Association, the American Academy of Family Physicians, and the National Council on the Aging, and comprising 32 organization representatives on its advisory board. It is partly funded through a grant from Ross Products Division, Abbott Laboratories. NSI's initial screening tool, incorporated in all its educational products, is the DETERMINE Your Nutritional Health checklist.

Occupational Safety and Health Administration (OSHA) *See* Government Organizations (Department of Labor).

Office of AIDS Research *See* Government Organizations (Department of Health and Human Services, NIH).

Office of Alternative Medicine *See* Government Organizations (Department of Health and Human Services, NIH).

Office of Behavioral and Social Sciences Research *See* Government Organizations (Department of Health and Human Services, NIH).

Office of Disease Prevention and Health Promotion *See* Government Organizations (Office of Public Health Science).

Office of the Forum for Quality and Effectiveness in Health Care *See* Government Organizations (Department of Health and Human Services, AHCPR).

Office of Justice Programs *See* Government Organizations (Department of Justice).

Office of Juvenile Justice and Delinquency Prevention *See* Government Organizations (Department of Justice).

Office of Medical Applications of Research *See* Government Organizations (Department of Health and Human Services, NIH).

Office of National Drug Control Policy *See* Government Organizations (Executive Office of the President).

Office of Prevention, Education, and Control *See* Government Organizations (Department of Health and Human Services, NIH).

Office of Public Health and Science *See* Government Organizations (Department of Health and Human Services).

Office of Research on Women's Health *See* Government Organizations (Department of Health and Human Services).

Office of the Surgeon General *See* Government Organizations (Office of Public Health and Science).

Office of Technology Assessment (OTA) *See* Government Organizations (Legislative Branch).

Office for Victims of Crime *See* Government Organizations (Department of Justice).

Office of Workers' Compensation Programs *See* Government Organizations (Department of Labor).

Oncology Nursing Society (ONS) *Founded:* 1975. *Headquarters:* Pittsburgh, PA. *Purpose:* To promote high professional standards in oncology nursing; to provide a network for the exchange of information; to encourage nurses to specialize in oncology; and to promote and develop educational programs in oncology nursing.

Ophthalmic Photographers' Society (OPS) *Founded:* 1969. *Headquarters:* Nixa, MO. *Purpose:* To encourage the highest quality of ophthalmic photography; to promote development of new and improved techniques and equipment; to provide continuing education and technical information; to provide a forum for discussion of ophthalmic photography; and to provide testing and subsequent certification. Serves ophthalmologists, pathologists, medical and ophthalmic photographers, nurses, and other persons actively involved with ophthalmology or ophthalmic photography.

Ophthalmic Research Institute (ORI) *Founded:* 1972. *Headquarters:* Bethesda, MD. *Purpose:* To conduct coordinated vision research and instrumentation and procedure evaluation needed by the ophthalmic industry. Its research programs include new examination and treatment methods.

Optical Laboratories Association (OLA) *Founded:* 1894. *Headquarters:* Merrifield, VA. *Purpose:* To provide a national organization to serve independent, wholesale ophthalmic laboratories and suppliers serving the ophthalmic field.

Opticians Association of America (OAA) *Founded:* 1926. *Headquarters:* Fairfax, VA. *Purpose:* To advance the science of optics; to conduct research and educational programs; and to maintain museum and speakers' bureau. Serves retail dispensing opticians who fill prescriptions for glasses or contact lenses written by a vision care specialist.

Optometric Extension Program Foundation (OEPF) *Founded:* 1928. *Headquarters:* Santa Ana, CA.

Purpose: To provide training seminars and graduate clinical seminars in topics related to vision. Serves registered optometrists and optometric assistants enrolled for continuing education courses.

Optometric Historical Society (OHS)
Founded: 1969. *Headquarters:* St. Louis, MO. *Purpose:* To encourage the collection and preservation of materials relating to the history of optometry and to assist in the care of archives of optometric interest. Serves optometrists and other individuals or groups interested in optometry, optics, and related disciplines.

Organization of Teachers of Oral Diagnosis (OTOD)
Founded: 1963. *Headquarters:* Indianapolis, IN. *Purpose:* To provide updated techniques, material, and knowledge in oral diagnosis education; to sponsor seminars; and to promote interests of dental educators. Serves teachers and university departments of oral diagnosis (oral medicine and oral pathology).

Osteopathic College of Ophthalmology and Otorhinolaryngology–Head and Neck Surgery (OCOO)
Founded: 1916. *Headquarters:* Dayton, OH. *Purpose:* To develop application of osteopathic concepts in this specialty; to determine minimum standards of education at undergraduate and postgraduate levels; and to sponsor research programs. Serves osteopathic physicians who have completed formal specialty training or are acquiring such training in ophthalmology, otorhinolaryngology, and orofacial plastic surgery and those who are certified specialists in one or more of these areas. *Formerly:* Osteopathic College of Ophthalmology and Otorhinolaryngology.

Outcomes Management Consortia (OMC)
See American Medical Group Association.

Outcomes Roundtable
See National Alliance for the Mentally Ill.

Outpatient Ophthalmic Surgery Society (OOSS)
Founded: 1981. *Headquarters:* San Diego, CA. *Purpose:* To promote high-quality, low-cost patient care. It serves ophthalmic surgeons interested in gathering and sharing information about outpatient eye surgery.

The David and Lucile Packard Foundation
Founded: 1964. *Headquarters:* Los Altos, CA. *Purpose:* To provide grants to organizations to strengthen them and, thereby, help people through the improvement of scientific knowledge, education, health, culture, employment, the environment, and quality of life.

Pan-American Allergy Society (PAAS)
Founded: 1956. *Headquarters:* Fredericksburg, TX. *Purpose:* To provide a means of social communication among members; to promote interspecialty cooperation; and to foster individual excellence. Serves physicians throughout the Western Hemisphere who include allergy diagnosis and management in their practices.

Pan-American Association of Ophthalmology (PAAO)
Founded: 1939. *Headquarters:* Arlington, TX. *Purpose:* To improve the treatment of eye disease and prevention of blindness in the Americas through the exchange of ideas and treatments. It serves ophthalmologists throughout the Western Hemisphere.

Pan American Health Organization (PAHO)
Founded: 1902. *Headquarters:* Washington, DC. *Purpose:* To improve physical and mental health in the Americas; to coordinate regional activities combating disease, including exchange of statistical and epidemiological information, development of local health services, and organization of disease control and eradication programs. Serves governments of Western Hemisphere nations.

Pan-American League Against Rheumatism (PANLAR)
Founded: 1942. *Headquarters:* Toronto, Ontario, Canada. *Purpose:* To conduct biomedical and epidemiological research; to provide assistance in the coordination of national, professional, and social agencies; and to educate health professionals. It serves physicians and other professionals interested in the prevention and treatment of rheumatic diseases.

Pan American Medical Association (PAMA)
Founded: 1925. *Headquarters:* New York, NY. *Purpose:* To foster the exchange of medical information and research results among physicians in Western Hemisphere countries. It has a large number of allied sections (for example, alcoholism, fundamental sciences), specialty sections (for example, anesthesiology, pathology, psychiatry, transplantation of organs), and subspecialty sections (for example, vascular surgery). *Also known as:* Associacion Medica Pan Americana.

Parapsychological Association (PA)
Founded: 1957. *Headquarters:* Fairhaven, MA. *Purpose:* To encourage parapsychological research and to disseminate information on scientific findings and to collaborate with psychical research societies. Serves persons who hold a doctorate degree or its equivalent and other individuals who are actively engaged in advancing parapsychology as a branch of science. It is affiliated with the American Association for the Advancement of Science.

Parenteral Drug Association (PDA)
Founded: 1946. *Headquarters:* Bethesda, MD. *Purpose:* To provide a liaison with pharmaceutical manufacturers, suppliers, users, academics, and government regulatory officials; to promote the advance of parenteral science and technology in the interest of public health. It serves individuals working in the research, development, or manufacture of parenteral (injectable) drugs and sterile products.

Park Ridge Center (PRC)
Founded: 1985. *Headquarters:* Chicago, IL. *Purpose:* To foster the study of religious aspects of human well-being related to prevention and treatment of disease and interpretation of illness and health and similar concerns. The PRC serves as an international forum for exchange and debate among

experts in health care, religion, law, and ethics and acts as a resource of information on religion and bioethics. It serves physicians and other health professionals, theologians, ethicists, clergy, and pastoral counselors interested in the interreligious, multidisciplinary study of health, faith, and ethics.

Patient Access to Specialty Care Coalition
Founded: 1993. *Headquarters:* Washington, DC. *Purpose:* To unite national organizations representing consumers and providers of medical services with the concern that the focus of health care must be on patients and the quality of their medical care. The coalition advocates at both the federal and state levels to ensure that people who choose managed care are guaranteed timely access to specialty care at a reasonable cost, and it also aims to educate consumers and benefits managers on how to select managed care plans that offer the highest level of medical services to their patients. Current areas of concern are physicians subjected to gag rules and patients' access to out-of-network physicians, addressed by proposed legislation such as the Senate Medicare Patient Choice and Access Act of 1997. The coalition is led by the American Academy of Orthopaedic Surgeons.

Patients First Initiative *See* American Association of Health Plans.

Pediatric Orthopaedic Society of North America (POSNA) *Founded:* 1983. *Headquarters:* Rosemont, IL. *Purpose:* To provide continuing education in the field of pediatric orthopedics and to conduct tutorial programs.

Pediatric Research in Office Settings (PROS) *See* American Academy of Pediatrics.

People's Medical Society (PMS) *Founded:* 1982. *Headquarters:* Allentown, PA. *Purpose:* To promote citizen involvement in cost, quality, and management of the American health care system; to provide training and encourage individuals to study local health care systems, practitioners, and institutions; to promote preventive health care and medical cost control by these groups; address major policy issues and control health costs; to encourage more preventive practice and research; to promote self-care and alternative health care procedures; and to launch an information campaign to assist individuals in maintaining personal health and to prepare them for appointments with health professionals.

Permanente Medical Groups *See* Kaiser Permanente.

Pension and Welfare Benefits Administration *See* Government Organizations (Department of Labor).

The Pew Charitable Trusts *Founded:* 1948. *Headquarters:* Philadelphia, PA. *Purpose:* To encourage individual growth and potential; improve the quality of people's lives; maintain and nurture democratic traditions; ensure an educated and engaged citizenry; protect religious freedom; and assist and support those in need through the action of its seven individual charitable funds. Its Health and Human Services (HHS) program generally seeks to promote the health and well-being of the American people and to strengthen disadvantaged communities but as of 1997 is very limited because the program is engaged in a planning process to develop a new structure and strategies for tackling large-scale social policy issues in a flexible and timely manner; the current focus is limited to activities designed to assess the impact of the changing health care delivery system on clinical research. New program guidelines for the HHS national program should be available by June 1998.

Pew Health Professions Commission *See* UCSF Center for the Health Professions/Pew Health Professions Commission.

Pharmaceutical Research and Manufacturers of America (PMA) *Founded:* 1958. *Headquarters:* Washington, DC. *Purpose:* To encourage high standards for quality control and good manufacturing practices; to foster research toward development of new medical products; to support enactment of uniform and reasonable drug legislation; and to disseminate information on governmental regulations and policies. It does not maintain or supply information on specific products, prices, distribution, promotion, or sales policies of its individual members. Serves research-based manufacturers of ethical pharmaceutical and biological products that are distributed under their own labels.

Pharmacists in Ophthalmic Practice (PIOP) *Founded:* 1984. *Headquarters:* Philadelphia, PA. *Purpose:* To foster an exchange of information; to conduct research and compile statistics; and to determine standards relating to ophthalmological pharmacy, pharmacology, and formulations. Serves pharmacists who serve as directors or chief pharmacists of institutions that specialize in ophthalmology or otolaryngology.

Physician Insurers Association of America (PIAA) *Founded:* 1977. *Headquarters:* Rockville, MD. *Purpose:* To further the best interests of member companies in areas related to physician liability insurance. Focuses on the availability and affordability of professional liability insurance and the effective delivery of quality health care. Conducts research and educational programs and monitors legislation.

Physicians Committee for Responsible Medicine (PCRM) *Founded:* 1985. *Headquarters:* Washington, DC. *Purpose:* To foster scientific and ethical questions about the use of humans and animals in medical research; to support research in U.S. agricultural policies; and to develop programs to encourage a shift in agricultural subsidies toward healthful crops. Serves physicians, scientists, health professionals, and other persons interested in increasing public awareness about the importance of preventive medicine and nutrition.

Physicians Education Network (PEN) *Founded:* 1977. *Headquarters:* St. Petersburg, FL. *Purpose:* To promote consumer safety legislation; to oppose legislation that could allow lower medical standards; to promote required referral legislation in each state, which would require optometrists to refer patients to ophthalmologists for any medical treatment or prescription; and to campaign against optometric drug use legislation.

Physicians Forum (PF)   *Founded:* 1939. *Headquarters:* Chicago, IL. *Purpose:* To promote development of a national health service with a single class of medical care for all, financed by a progressive income tax surcharge for health. Serves physicians, particularly those holding salaried positions, who work for health care as a human right.

Physicians for Human Rights (PHR)   *Founded:* 1986. *Headquarters:* Boston, MA. *Purpose:* To prevent the participation of doctors in torture; to defend imprisoned health professionals; to prevent physical and psychological abuse of citizens by governments; and to provide medical and humanitarian aid to victims of repression. Serves health professionals who bring the skills of the medical profession to the protection of human rights.

Physicians for a National Health Program (PNHP) *Founded:* 1987. *Headquarters:* Chicago, IL. *Purpose:* To reform health care based on social justice and medical need, specifically with a single-payer health care system. PNHP works to inform and mobilize the public, educate physicians and other health professionals, conduct and publicize research, show how the system can change, and advise Congress and the president.

Physician Payment Review Commission   *See* Government Organizations.

Physicians for Social Responsibility (PSR)   *Founded:* 1961. *Headquarters:* Washington, DC. *Purpose:* To educate the public on the medical effects of nuclear war and nuclear weapons and on the implications of national policy and legislative actions on arms control issues; to conduct media outreach and voter education programs; to encourage lobbying; to research legislative alternatives; and to disseminate legislative information. Serves medical professionals with doctoral degrees, medical students, and other persons concerned with the threat of nuclear war.

Physicians Who Care (PWC)   *Founded:* 1985. *Headquarters:* San Antonio, TX. *Purpose:* To protect traditional doctor-patient relationships; to ensure quality health care; to foster the belief that responsibility of medical care belongs to physicians, as care providers and patients, who have a choice determining the type of treatment received; and to promote communication between members and their patients on health care issues. Serves independent physicians who are interested in educating patients about making wise choices in health care between health maintenance organizations and the more traditional independent physician's practice.

Picker/Commonwealth Programs   *See* Commonwealth Fund.

The Picker Institute   *Founded:* 1994. *Headquarters:* Boston, MA. *Purpose:* To promote health care quality assessment and improvement strategies that address patients' needs and concerns as defined by patients and to help develop models of care that make the experience of illness and health care more humane. The Institute provides patient satisfaction surveys that stress incorporation of the patient's perspective into all decisions about the design and delivery of health care services at all levels of the organization. The Institute is incorporated as a nonprofit affiliate of CareGroup.

Pilgrim Health Care   *See* Harvard Pilgrim Health Care.

Planned Parenthood Federation of America *Founded:* 1916. *Headquarters:* New York, NY. *Purpose:* To provide an educational, research, and medical services organization concerned with fertility-related health topics, including abortion, contraception, family planning, and international population control; to foster relevant biomedical, social, economic, and demographic research; and to develop appropriate information, education, and training programs to increase knowledge of human reproduction and sexuality.

Plastic Surgery Research Council (PSRC)   *Founded:* 1955. *Headquarters:* Pittsburgh, PA. *Purpose:* To foster fundamental research in the fields of plastic and reconstructive surgery.

Precision Chiropractic Research Society (PCRS) *Founded:* 1976. *Headquarters:* Brea, CA. *Purpose:* To conduct research into spinal problems and treatments, such as investigating the relationship between headaches and spinal adjustments; and to document research by x-raying patients before treatment and again after treatment to determine change (if any) of spinal position. Serves doctors of chiropractic specializing in spinal stress. *Also known as:* Spinal Stress Research Society.

Precision Measurements Association (PMA) *Founded:* 1959. *Headquarters:* Los Angeles, CA. *Purpose:* To sponsor one-day courses in pressure measurement instruments; linear, optical, and electronic measurement and basic metrology; to maintain a speakers' bureau; and to provide a placement service. Serves engineers, scientists, and technically skilled persons interested in measurement science.

Presbyterian Health, Education and Welfare Association (PHEWA)   *Founded:* 1955. *Headquarters:* Louisville, KY. *Purpose:* To address issues in the health, education, and welfare fields and to establish standards for the effectiveness of services and organized social action and research. Member agencies include children's homes and services, hospitals and health services, homes and services for the aging, community centers, neighborhood houses, and programs related to the United Presbyterian Church, USA.

President's Advisory Commission on Consumer Protection and Quality in the Health Care Industry *See* Government Organizations (Boards, Commissions, etc).

Prevent Blindness America   *Founded:* 1908. *Headquarters:* Schaumburg, IL. *Purpose:* To promote and support local glaucoma screening programs, preschool vision testing, industrial eye safety, and the collection of statistical and other data. Serves professionals and laypersons interested in preventing blindness and preserving sight through a nationwide comprehensive program of public and professional education, research, and industrial and community services.

The Proprietary Association   *See* Nonprescription Drug Manufacturers Association.

Professional Aeromedical Transport Association (PATA)   *Founded:* 1986. *Headquarters:* Bonsall, CA. *Purpose:* To standardize operations and services; to improve patient care; to educate members and the public; to provide a network for locating providers of professional aeromedical services; and to conduct scientific programs. Serves firms that provide air ambulance services, primarily by means of fixed-wing aircraft, and suppliers to the industry.

Professional Standards Review Council of America (PSRCA)   *Founded:* 1977. *Headquarters:* New York, NY. *Purpose:* To monitor the quality, appropriateness, and cost of health care given to patients in hospitals, ambulatory clinics, nursing facilities, and physicians' offices. Serves physicians, nurses, health care administrators, and consumers.

ProMED (Program for Monitoring Emerging Diseases)   *See* Federation of American Scientists.

Prospective Payment Assessment Commission (ProPAC)   *See* Government Organizations (Boards, Commissions, etc).

Psychology Society (PS)   *Founded:* 1960. *Headquarters:* New York, NY. *Purpose:* To encourage use of psychology in the solving of social and political conflicts; to establish a referral service; to sponsor observation programs; to evaluate programs in use in psychology; to further the use of psychology in therapy, family and social problems, behavior modification, and treatment of drug abusers and prisoners; and to maintain a placement service.

Psychometric Society (PS)   *Founded:* 1935. *Headquarters:* Champaign, IL. *Purpose:* To develop quantitative models for psychological phenomena and quantitative methodology in the social and behavioral sciences.

Psychonomic Society (PS)   *Founded:* 1959. *Headquarters:* Houston, TX. *Purpose:* To promote communication of scientific research in psychology and allied sciences. The main function of the Society is to exchange information among scientists. To this end, it publishes six journals. Members are persons qualified to conduct and supervise scientific research in psychology or allied sciences. Members hold a doctor of philosophy (PhD) degree or its equivalent and have published significant research other than a doctoral dissertation.

Public Citizen (PC)   *Founded:* 1971. *Headquarters:* Washington, DC. *Purpose:* To support the work of citizen advocates; to focus on consumer rights in the marketplace, safe products, a healthful environment and workplace, clean and safe energy sources, corporate and government accountability, group buying to enhance marketplace clients, and citizen empowerment. In health care, its interests include hospital quality and costs, doctors' fees, physician discipline and malpractice, state administration of Medicare programs, unnecessary surgery, comprehensive health planning, dangerous drugs, carcinogens, medical devices, and overuse of medical and dental x-rays. It favors a single-payer comprehensive health care system. Its methods for change include lobbying, litigation, monitoring government agencies, research, and public education. It acquires funding primarily through direct mail and payment for publications and court awards.

Public Citizen Health Research Group (PCHRG)   *Founded:* 1971. *Headquarters:* Washington, DC. *Purpose:* To work on issues of health care delivery, workplace safety and health, drug regulation, food additives, medical device safety, and environmental influences on health; to petition or sue federal agencies on consumers' behalf and testify before Congress on health matters; to monitor the enforcement of health and safety legislation; and to publicize important health findings and make available to the public a broad spectrum of research and consumer action materials in the form of books and reports.

Public Citizen Litigation Group (PCLG)   *Founded:* 1972. *Headquarters:* Washington, DC. *Purpose:* To file consumer cases dealing with economic issues; cases involving health and safety of consumers and workers; cases compelling various federal agencies to comply with the laws they administer; cases concerning open government; and cases relating to other areas of concern to consumers and citizens.

Public Health Service (PHS)   *See* introduction to Government Organizations.

Public Responsibility in Medicine and Research (PRIM&R)   *Founded:* 1974. *Headquarters:* Boston, MA. *Purpose:* To question the development of procedures regulating research and the growth of increasingly hostile public sentiment toward the field; and to aid members in assembling data they might need for testimony before legislative and other hearings. Serves nonmembership health and legal professionals, subjects/patients, and laypersons interested in research, primarily with human subjects and animals.

Public Voice for Food and Health Policy (PVFHP)   *Founded:* 1982. *Headquarters:* Washington, DC. *Purpose:* To promote consumer interests in public and private decision making on food and health policy and to work with congressional leaders and federal officials to strengthen food safety and labeling laws, farm subsidy programs, sugar and grain price supports, school lunch nutrition, and food programs for the rural poor. Serves consumers concerned about food and health issues.

Quality Healthcare Resources (QHR)   *Founded:* 1986. *Headquarters:* Oakbrook Terrace, IL. *Purpose:* To provide knowledge that supports improvement in health related services; to provide assessment, education and consultative assistance focused on organization and patient care improvements; and to address the realistic application of performance improvement principles and established health care standards. QHR is a nonprofit subsidiary of the Joint Commission.

Quality Compass   *See* National Committee for Quality Assurance.

Quality of Life at the End of Life   *See* Commonwealth Fund.

Quality Measurement Network (QMNet)   *See* Government Organizations (Department of Health and Human Services, AHCPR).

Radiation Research Society (RRS)   *Founded:* 1952. *Headquarters:* Oak Brook, IL. *Purpose:* To promote original research in the natural sciences relating to radiation and facilitate integration of different disciplines in the study of radiation effects. Serves biologists, physicists, chemists, and physicians contributing to knowledge of radiation and its effects.

Radiation Therapy Oncology Group (RTOG)   *Founded:* 1971. *Headquarters:* Philadelphia, PA. *Purpose:* To conduct cooperative clinical trials and studies to improve the care of patients with cancer. Serves clinical radiation therapy investigative centers.

Radiological Society of North America (RSNA)   *Founded:* 1915. *Headquarters:* Oak Brook, IL. *Purpose:* To promote study and practical applications of radiology, radium, electricity, and other branches of physics related to medical science. Serves radiologists and scientists in fields closely related to radiology.

Radiology Business Management Association (RBMA)   *Founded:* 1968. *Headquarters:* Costa Mesa, CA. *Purpose:* To improve business administration of radiology practices to better serve patients and the medical profession; to provide opportunities for professional development and recognition; to offer informal placement services; and to maintain information services. Serves business managers for radiology groups and vendors of equipment, services, or supplies.

RAND   *Founded:* 1945. *Headquarters:* Santa Monica, CA. *Purpose:* To help improve public policy through research and analysis. RAND's Health Research Program was established in 1968 to improve health care delivery and policy through advancing knowledge about needs for health services and how changes in the delivery system affect cost, quality, and access to care. Funding comes from government agencies (58%), private foundations (16%), and other sources (26%). The large health policy research program includes a doctorate program in policy

analysis and embraces a wide range of disciplines. RAND's health care interest areas are quality of care (appropriateness, improvement, and assessment of care); measurement of quality of life; health research methods; health care organization, economics, and finance; HIV and AIDS; maternal, child, and adolescent health; vulnerable populations (the homeless, the elderly); alcohol, drug abuse, and mental health; military health; and international health. Research is carried out by the Center for the Study of Employee Health Benefits, Drew/RAND Center for Health and Aging, RAND/UCLA Center for Health Care Financing Policy Research (which conducted the Health Services Utilization Study [HSUS] and the Medical Outcomes Study [MOS]); and the UCLA/RAND Research Center on Managed Care for Psychiatric Disorders. The title *RAND* originally was an acronym for "Research and Development," but the full title is no longer used.

Raphael Society (RS)   *Founded:* 1966. *Headquarters:* New York, NY. *Purpose:* To study medical issues and problems as they relate to Orthodox Jewish law; to promote the welfare of Orthodox Jews in the health care field; to sponsor lectures and seminars; and to compile a listing of residency programs recommended for students. Serves Orthodox Jewish physicians, dentists, physical therapists, nurses, and other professionals in the health care field.

Registered Medical Assistants of American Medical Technologists (RMAAMT)   *Founded:* 1976. *Headquarters:* Park Ridge, IL. *Purpose:* To establish standards of training; to provide continuing education and home study programs; and to promote quality care in allied fields. Serves assistants to physicians in office practice, clinics, hospitals, and private health care facilities.

Registry of Interpreters for the Deaf (RID)   *Founded:* 1964. *Headquarters:* Silver Spring, MD. *Purpose:* To represent the needs and concern of the interpreters; to sponsor research and evaluation programs; to maintain a registry of certified interpreters and transliterators; to establish certification standards; and to offer a national certification evaluation. Serves professional interpreters and transliterators for the deaf.

Regulatory Affairs Professionals Society (RAPS)   *Founded:* 1976. *Headquarters:* Rockville, MD. *Purpose:* To identify and recognize regulatory affairs professionals and others in interacting disciplines and to offer employment advertisement. Serves professionals in the drug, medical device, biotechnology, diagnostic, cosmetic, and food industries, and lawyers, physicians, and consultants interested in advancing the regulatory affairs profession dealing with health care products.

Renal Physicians Association (RPA)   *Founded:* 1973. *Headquarters:* Washington, DC. *Purpose:* To promote optimal care and high standards of treatment for patients; to provide national representation for physicians engaged in study and management of patients with kidney and related disorders; and to express the concerns and needs of renal physicians to congressional and governmental agencies legislating, executing, and regulating the federal

End Stage Renal Disease Program. Serves physicians specializing in the treatment of renal (kidney) diseases.

Research Society on Alcoholism (RSA) *Founded:* 1976. *Headquarters:* Austin, TX. *Purpose:* To provide a forum for researchers working in the field; to aid and further application of research to problems related to alcoholism; to disseminate information; to protect the rights of researchers and human research subjects; and to enlighten the public. Serves scientists holding a doctor of medicine (MD) or doctor of philosophy (PhD) degree and other individuals actively engaged in research on alcoholism and alcohol-related problems.

Research Triangle Institute (RTI) *Founded:* 1958. *Headquarters:* Research Triangle Park, NC. *Purpose:* To improve the human condition through multidisciplinary research, development, and technical services that meet the highest standards of professional performance. RTI is an independent nonprofit organization performing research in many disciplines for government, industry and other clients throughout the United States and abroad, responding to priorities in medicine and pharmaceuticals, public health, advanced technologies, environmental protection, and public policies. A study in progress is development and testing of prototype information materials for Medicare and Medicaid beneficiaries. RTI operates as a separate affiliate of the University of North Carolina at Chapel Hill, Duke University in Durham, and North Carolina State University with its own staff and facilities.

Residency Review Committee (RRC) *See* Accreditation Council for Graduate Medical Education.

Residency Review Committee for Emergency Medicine (RRCEM) *Founded:* 1982. *Headquarters:* Chicago, IL. *Purpose:* To accredit residency training programs in emergency medicine. Serves representatives of the American College of Emergency Physicians, the American Board of Emergency Medicine, Council on Medical Education of the American Medical Association, and the Emergency Medicine Residents' Association.

Respiratory Nursing Society (RNS) *Founded:* 1990. *Headquarters:* Glenview, IL. *Purpose:* To foster the personal and professional development of respiratory nurses and quality care of their clients; to provide educational opportunities; and promote research in the field.

Retired Army Nurse Corps Association (RANCA) *Founded:* 1977. *Headquarters:* San Antonio, TX. *Purpose:* To provide educational and social opportunities for members; to disseminate information to the public; and to preserve the history of the U.S. Army Nurse Corps. Serves Army Nurse Corps officers retired from either active or reserve duty; associate members are officers with 16 or more years of service still serving on active duty and former members of the Army Nurse Corps who were honorably discharged.

Retired Persons Services (RPS) *Founded:* 1959. *Headquarters:* Alexandria, VA. *Purpose:* To provide a mail service pharmacy for members of the American Association of Retired Persons; to provide prescription and nonprescription drugs, vitamins, and other health care items through mail service and walk-in facilities in California, Texas, Missouri, Oregon, Indiana, Connecticut, Florida, Pennsylvania, Nevada, Virginia, and Washington, DC; and to encourage consumer awareness, comparison shopping, and use of generic drugs.

The Robert Wood Johnson Foundation (RWJF) *Founded:* 1936. *Headquarters:* Princeton, NJ. *Purpose:* To assure that all Americans have access to basic health care at reasonable cost; to improve the way services are organized and provided to people with chronic health conditions; and to reduce the personal, social, and economic harm caused by substance abuse—tobacco, alcohol, and illicit drugs. RWJF is the nation's largest philanthropy devoted exclusively to health and health care, and it is currently a major funder of efforts to deal with tobacco and smoking issues. RWJF's investigator-initiated, multidisciplinary Substance Abuse Policy Research Program is administered through The Bowman Gray School of Medicine, Wake Forest University (Winston-Salem, NC). RWJF is also a major funder of the Campaign for Tobacco-Free Kids through a grant to the National Center for Tobacco-Free Kids.

Ronald and Nancy Reagan Research Institute *See* The Alzheimer's Association.

Rose Kushner Breast Cancer Advisory Center *See under* Kushner.

Royal College of Physicians and Surgeons of the United States of America (RCPS) *Founded:* 1984. *Headquarters:* Bon Allie, MD. *Purpose:* To provide postgraduate continuing medical education; to confer certificates and diplomas; to maintain speakers' bureau and hall of fame; and to provide placement services. Serves physicians and allied health professionals interested in tropical medicine.

Royal Society of Medicine Foundation (RSMF) *Founded:* 1967. *Headquarters:* New York, NY. *Purpose:* To provide a forum for the discussion of topics relevant to the medical community in the United States and the United Kingdom and to sponsor conferences and exchange programs in conjunction with the Royal Society of Medicine.

Ruth Jackson Orthopaedic Society *See under* Jackson.

Ss

Scoliosis Research Society (SRS) *Founded:* 1966. *Headquarters:* Rosemont, IL. *Purpose:* To further research and education in spinal deformities, particularly scoliosis. Serves orthopedic surgeons and other physicians.

Self-Help for Hard of Hearing People, Inc (SHHH)
Founded: 1979. *Headquarters:* Bethesda, MD. *Purpose:* To provide a volunteer organization of hard-of-hearing people and their relations and friends as well as professionals working with hearing-impaired persons.

Seventh-Day Adventist Dietetic Association (SDADA) *Founded:* 1956. *Headquarters:* Loma Linda, CA. *Purpose:* Serves Seventh-Day Adventist registered dietitians and dietitians working in Seventh-Day Adventist institutions. To motivate members to attain high professional standards; to provide resources and guidance concerning vegetarian lifestyles to dietitians; and to actively promote Seventh-Day Adventist health principles.

Sex Information and Education Council of the U.S. (SIECUS) *Founded:* 1964. *Headquarters:* New York, NY. *Purpose:* To support the individual's right to acquire knowledge of sexuality and exercise nonexploitive sexual choices; to encourage the development of responsible standards of sexual behavior; and to promote and affirm the concept of human sexuality as the integration of the emotional, intellectual, physical, and social aspects of sexual being in ways that are enriching and that enhance health, personality, communication, and human caring and social justice. Serves educators, social workers, physicians, clergy, youth organizations, and parents' groups interested in human sexuality education and sexual health care.

Shock Society *Founded:* 1978. *Headquarters:* Augusta, GA. *Purpose:* To promote research into and awareness of the health importance of shock and trauma; to foster the dissemination of applications of information. Serves physicians and scientists interested in shock and trauma.

Shriners Hospitals for Crippled Children (SHCC)
Founded: 1922. *Headquarters:* Tampa, FL. *Purpose:* To provide no-cost orthopedic and burn care to children under 18 years of age. This organization is composed of 19 orthopedic hospitals and 3 burn hospitals operated by the Imperial Council of the Ancient Arabic Order of the Nobles of the Mystic Shrine for North America.

Sickle Cell Disease Association of America (SCDAA)
Founded: 1971. *Headquarters:* Culver City, CA. *Purpose:* To provide leadership on a national level to create awareness of the negative impact of sickle cell anemia on the health, economic, social, and educational well-being of individuals and families of individuals with sickle cell disease. To provide counselor training, workshops and seminars, blood banks, screening and testing, and camps for children with sickle cell disease. Serves community groups involved in sickle cell anemia programs throughout the United States.

Smart Card Industry Association (SCIA) *Founded:* 1988. *Headquarters:* Lawrenceville, NJ. *Purpose:* To stimulate the adoption, use, understanding, and innovation of smart card technology and to facilitate the adoption of industry standards, protocols, and specifications.

Smokefree Educational Services *Founded:* 1987. *Headquarters:* New York, NY. *Purpose:* To win the right to live and work in a smokefree environment and to educate youth about the unhealthy and socially undesirable consequences of tobacco addiction.

Social Security Administration (SSA) *See* Government Organizations (Independent Establishments).

Society for Academic Emergency Medicine (SAEM)
Founded: 1989. *Headquarters:* Lansing, MI. *Purpose:* To educate teachers of emergency medicine and encourage its development as an academic discipline; to apply sound educational principles, thus improving the quality of teaching; and to promote research in educational methods and clinical procedures. Members are physicians teaching emergency medicine, emergency medicine residents, and nonphysicians teaching emergency care. The society promotes improved emergency patient care through more direct involvement of teachers and consumers in the needs assessment, planning, and implementation of projects and programs.

Society for Adolescent Medicine (SAM) *Founded:* 1968. *Headquarters:* Blue Springs, MD. *Purpose:* To encourage the investigation of normal growth and development during adolescence. Serves physicians, psychologists, social workers, psychiatrists, nurses, and other health professionals interested in improving the quality of health care for adolescents.

Society of Air Force Physicians (SAFP) *Founded:* 1958. *Headquarters:* Washington, DC. *Purpose:* To foster advancement of the art and science of medicine in the U.S. Air Force. Serves air force internists, family practitioners, and specialists in emergency medicine, dermatology, allergy and immunology, and neurology.

Society for Ambulatory Care Professionals (SACP)
Founded: 1986. *Headquarters:* Chicago, IL. *Purpose:* To work to advance the development of ambulatory care and to advocate issues that enhance the value, role, delivery, and management of ambulatory care services.

Society of American Gastrointestinal Endoscopic Surgeons (SAGES) *Founded:* 1980. *Headquarters:* Santa Monica, CA. *Purpose:* To promote the concepts of gastrointestinal endoscopy as an integral part of surgery and to establish standards of training and practice and guidelines for privileging.

Society for Assisted Reproductive Technology (SART) *Founded:* 1987. *Headquarters:* Birmingham, AL. *Purpose:* To assist infertile patients in establishing pregnancy and attaining their desired families. SART has 12 member programs and is solely responsible for collecting, reporting, and validating clinic-specific outcomes data for centers offering assisted reproductive technologies. An affiliate of the American Society of Reproductive Medicine, it serves physicians, reproductive biologists, and health care professionals who apply the assisted reproductive technologies in the treatment of infertility.

Society of Behavioral Medicine (SBM) *Founded:* 1978. *Headquarters:* Rockville, MD. *Purpose:* To provide a forum of exchange of ideas and information between health care providers and basic scientists and medical researchers, and to work to integrate behavioral and biomedical research.

Society for Biomaterials (SFB) *Founded:* 1974. *Headquarters:* Minneapolis, MN. *Purpose:* To develop biomaterials as tissue replacements in patients and to promote research and development in biomaterials sciences. Serves bioengineers and materials scientists; dental, orthopedic, cardiac, and other surgeons; and scientists and corporations interested in the manufacture of biomaterials.

Society for Biomedical Equipment Technicians (SBET) *Founded:* 1976. *Headquarters:* Arlington, VA. *Purpose:* To recognize biomedical equipment technicians and engineers as a specialty group and to support certification programs including certified biomedical equipment technician, certified radiologic equipment specialist, and certified laboratory equipment specialist. Serves biomedical equipment technicians, hospital maintenance engineers, managers of hospital medical equipment departments, sales representatives, and other persons involved with the repair or installation of biomedical hospital machinery.

Society for Cardiac Angiography and Interventions (SCA&I) *Founded:* 1978. *Headquarters:* Raleigh, NC. *Purpose:* To provide a national organization for angiographers interested in the field of cardiac catheterization, especially coronary angiography and interventional angiography, and to conduct clinical research.

Society of Cardiovascular and Interventional Radiology (SCVIR) *Founded:* 1973. *Headquarters:* Fairfax, VA. *Purpose:* To facilitate exchange of new ideas and techniques and to provide education courses for physicians working in the field. Serves physicians who are leaders in the field of cardiovascular and interventional radiology.

Society for Cardiovascular Management (SCM) *See* American Society of Cardiovascular Professionals/ Society for Cardiovascular Management.

Society for Clinical and Experimental Hypnosis (SCEH) *Founded:* 1949. *Headquarters:* McLean, VA. *Purpose:* To promote educational standards; to conduct introductory and advanced workshops; and to provide continuing education seminars in therapeutic hypnosis. Serves physicians, dentists, doctoral level psychologists, and psychiatric social workers interested in research in hypnosis and its boundary areas as well as the therapeutic use of hypnosis in clinical practice.

Society for Clinical Trials (SCT) *Founded:* 1978. *Headquarters:* Baltimore, MD. *Purpose:* To promote the development and dissemination of knowledge about the design and conduct of clinical trials. Serves persons with training and expertise in behavioral science, bioethics, biostatistics, computer science, dentistry, epidemiology, law, management, medicine, nursing, and pharmacology.

Society of Critical Care Medicine (SCCM) *Founded:* 1970. *Headquarters:* Anaheim Hills, CA. *Purpose:* To improve care for acute life-threatening illnesses and injuries; to promote the development of optimal care facilities; and to foster high standards. Serves physicians, nurses, scientists, technicians, respiratory technicians, and engineers involved in the field of critical care medicine.

Society for Developmental and Behavioral Pediatrics (SDBP) *Founded:* 1982. *Headquarters:* Philadelphia, PA. *Purpose:* To improve the health care of infants, children, and adolescents by promoting research and instruction in the areas of developmental and behavioral pediatrics. Serves pediatricians, child psychiatrists and psychologists, and other health professionals.

Society for Developmental Biology (SDB) *Founded:* 1939. *Headquarters:* Bethesda, MD. *Purpose:* To provide a national organization for biologists interested in problems of development and growth of organisms.

Society of Diagnostic Medical Sonographers (SDMS) *Founded:* 1970. *Headquarters:* Dallas, TX. *Purpose:* To develop and maintain the American Registry of Diagnostic Medical Sonographers. Serves sonographers, physician sonologists, and other persons in medical specialties using high-frequency sound for diagnostic purposes.

Society for Ear, Nose, and Throat Advances in Children (SENTAC) *Founded:* 1973. *Headquarters:* Columbia, MO. *Purpose:* To improve quality of care; to promote and coordinate research; to foster scientific exchange and coordination among professionals; to sponsor lectures and symposia. Serves otolaryngologists, pediatricians, audiologists, speech pathologists, and related professionals interested in evaluating the science and practice of medicine, surgery, and rehabilitation as related to diseases and disorders of the ear, nose, and throat in infants and children.

Society for Environmental Geochemistry and Health (SEGH) *Founded:* 1971. *Headquarters:* Rolla, MO. *Purpose:* To provide a national organization for organizations, scientists, and students interested in furthering knowledge of the geochemical environment's effects on the health and diseases of plants and animals, including humans.

Society for Epidemiologic Research (SER) *Founded:* 1967. *Headquarters:* Salt Lake City, UT. *Purpose:* To stimulate scientific interest in and promote the exchange of information about epidemiologic research. Serves epidemiologists, researchers, public health administrators, educators, mathematicians, statisticians, and other persons interested in epidemiologic research.

Society of Ethnobiology (SE) *Founded:* 1978. *Headquarters:* St. Louis, MO. *Purpose:* To provide a national organization for individuals and institutions interested in ethnobiology.

Society for Experimental Biology and Medicine (SEBM) *Founded:* 1903. *Headquarters:* New York, NY. *Purpose:* To cultivate the experimental method of investigation in the sciences of biology and medicine. Serves workers engaged in research in experimental biology or experimental medicine.

Society of Experimental Psychologists (SEP) *Founded:* 1929. *Headquarters:* Princeton, NJ. *Purpose:* To provide a national organization for experimental psychologists in the United States and Canada.

Society for the Exploration of Psychotherapy Integration (SEPI) *Founded:* 1984. *Headquarters:* Great Neck, NY. *Purpose:* To encourage communication among members and to promote collaborative work among psychotherapists who adhere to different theories and methods. Serves mental health professionals interested in the integration of theories and methods of psychotherapy.

Society of Fire Protection Engineers (SFPE) *Founded:* 1950. *Headquarters:* Boston, MA. *Purpose:* To advance the art and science of fire protection engineering; to maintain a high ethical standard among members; to foster fire protection engineering education; to offer short courses; and to maintain placement service.

Society of Forensic Toxicologists (SOFT) *Founded:* 1970. *Headquarters:* Grosse Pointe Park, MI. *Purpose:* To establish uniform qualifications and requirements for certification of forensic toxicologists and to promote support mechanisms for continued certification. Serves scientists who analyze tissue and body fluids for drugs and poisons and interpret the information for judicial purposes, as well as students and other interested individuals.

Society of Gastroenterology Nurses and Associates (SGNA) *Founded:* 1974. *Headquarters:* Rochester, NY. *Purpose:* To conduct national and regional educational courses and research programs and to cooperate with other professional associations, hospitals, universities, industries, technical societies, research organizations, and governmental agencies. Serves nurses and other health professionals engaged in the field of gastroenterology and endoscopy.

Society of General Internal Medicine (SGIM) *Founded:* 1978. *Headquarters:* Washington, DC. *Purpose:* To promote improved patient care, teaching, and research in primary care and general internal medicine. Serves faculty members of medical schools in the United States and Canada interested in advancing primary care and general internal medicine through improved teaching, patient care, and research.

Society for Gynecologic Investigation (SGI) *Founded:* 1953. *Headquarters:* Washington, DC. *Purpose:* To stimulate, assist, and conduct gynecologic research. Serves present and former faculty members of institutions interested or engaged in gynecologic research.

Society of Gynecologic Oncologists (SGO) *Founded:* 1969. *Headquarters:* Chicago, IL. *Purpose:* To improve the care of patients with gynecological cancer; to encourage research in gynecologic oncology, to advance knowledge in the field, to upgrade standards of practice; and to evaluate and address trends in gynecologic oncology.

Society of Head and Neck Surgeons (SHNS) *Founded:* 1954. *Headquarters:* Arlington, VA. *Purpose:* To advance the art and science of surgery of disorders of the head and neck, particularly cancer.

Society for Health and Human Values (SHHV) *Founded:* 1969. *Headquarters:* McLean, VA. *Purpose:* To develop new understandings, concepts, and programs in the area of human values and medicine, with special emphasis on the education of health professionals; to conduct programs at national association meetings; and to act as a resource service for educational institutions. Serves educators in the health professions.

Society of Healthcare Epidemiologists of America *Founded:* 1981. *Headquarters:* Woodbury, NJ. *Purpose:* To offer educational programs; to publish *Infection Control and Hospital Epidemiology*; and to host an annual convention.

Society for Healthcare Planning and Marketing (SHPM) *Founded:* 1978. *Headquarters:* Chicago, IL. *Purpose:* To provide a national organization for employees of hospitals, allied hospital associations, multi-institutional systems, and any other direct provider of health care services; employees of consulting firms, health or hospital administration programs, government agencies, and national, state, or community health planning agencies; and other individuals interested in institutional and strategic planning and marketing policies and issues. SHPM is affiliated with the American Hospital Association.

Society for Hematopathology (SH) *Founded:* 1981. *Headquarters:* Memphis, TN. *Purpose:* To promote the exchange of information on the hematopoietic and lymphoreticular systems. Serves physicians, doctors of science, osteopathic physicians, and dental surgeons.

Society for the History of Technology (SHOT) *Founded:* 1958. *Headquarters:* Auburn, AL. *Purpose:* To cooperate with other societies and professional organizations in arranging educational programs on the history of technology. Serves academicians in science, engineering, history, sociology, economics, and anthropology interested in the study of the development of technology and its relations with society and culture.

Society for Investigative Dermatology (SID) *Founded:* 1937. *Headquarters:* Cleveland, OH. *Purpose:* To foster research in dermatology and allied subjects.

Society for In Vitro Biology (SIVB) *Founded:* 1946. *Headquarters:* Columbia, MD. *Purpose:* To foster dissemination of information concerning the maintenance and experimental use of tissue cells in vitro and to establish evaluation and development procedures. Serves individuals using mammalian, invertebrate, and plant cell tissue and organ cultures as research tools in medicine, chemistry, physics, radiation, physiology, nutrition, and cytogenetics.

Society for Leukocyte Biology (SLB) *Founded:* 1954. *Headquarters:* Bethesda, MD. *Purpose:* To foster research in the field and to sponsor workshops on macrophage methodology. Serves persons holding doctor of medicine (MD) or doctor of philosophy (PhD) degrees who conduct research with universities; private, industrial, and government institutes; hospital clinics; and members of the pharmaceutical industry who are interested in the study of the reticuloendothelial system.

Society for Life History Research (SLHR) *Founded:* 1970. *Headquarters:* Philadelphia, PA. *Purpose:* To provide representation and public research for programs carried out by individual members. Serves individuals representing the disciplines of behavioral genetics, medicine, statistics, psychology, psychiatry, and sociology who are interested in psychopathology.

Society for Magnetic Resonance Imaging (SMRI) *See* International Society for Magnetic Resonance in Medicine.

Society for Medical Anthropology (SMA) *Founded:* 1971. *Headquarters:* Arlington, VA. *Purpose:* To promote the study of anthropological aspects of health, illness, health care, and related topics and to encourage communication and utilization of the results obtained from such studies. The SMA exists as a Section of the American Anthropological Association (AAA).

Society of Medical Consultants to the Armed Forces (SMCAF) *Founded:* 1945. *Headquarters:* Kensington, MD. *Purpose:* To preserve and encourage the association of civilian consultants and military medical personnel and to assist in the development and maintenance of the high standards of medical practice in the armed forces. Serves physicians and surgeons who have been in active military service and who have acted as consultants to the surgeons general of the army, navy, or air force.

Society for Medical Decision Making *Founded:* 1979. *Headquarters:* Washington, DC. *Purpose:* To promote rational and systematic approaches to decision making that will improve the health and clinical care of individuals and assist health policy formation.

Society of Medical Friends of Wine (SMFW) *Founded:* 1939. *Headquarters:* Sausalito, CA. *Purpose:* To develop an understanding of wine's beneficial effects; to encourage an "appreciation of the conviviality and good fellowship that are part of the relaxed and deliberate manner of living that follows its proper use"; and to stimulate scientific research on wine. Serves physicians interested in the nutritional and therapeutic values of wine.

Society of Medical Jurisprudence (SMJ) *Founded:* 1883. *Headquarters:* New York, NY. *Purpose:* To promote the study and advancement of medical jurisprudence and high standards of medical expert testimony. Serves physicians, lawyers, health professionals, chemists, and law and medical school professors.

Society for Menstrual Cycle Research (SMCR) *Founded:* 1979. *Headquarters:* Scottsdale, AZ. *Purpose:* To identify research priorities, to recommend research strategies, and to promote interdisciplinary research on the menstrual cycle. It serves physicians, nurses, physiologists, psychologists, geneticists, sociologists, researchers, educators, and other individuals interested in the menstrual cycle.

Society of Military Orthopaedic Surgeons (SMOS) *Founded:* 1958. *Headquarters:* Grayslake, IL. *Purpose:* To stimulate scholarly contribution by military and medical residents; to act as a clearinghouse; and to provide opportunities for consultation with and contributions of retired military surgeons. Serves orthopedic surgeons who have served in the active or reserve military.

Society of Military Otolaryngologists–Head and Neck Surgeons (SMO–HNS) *Founded:* 1952. *Headquarters:* San Antonio, TX. *Purpose:* To further social and professional contacts of military otolaryngologists and to advance science in the field. Serves otolaryngologists and head and neck surgeons of the army, air force, and navy and former active duty members.

Society of Neurological Surgeons *Founded:* 1920. *Headquarters:* Boston, MA. *Purpose:* To provide a society for neurological surgeons interested in and contributing to education.

Society for Neuroscience *Founded:* 1969. *Headquarters:* Washington, DC. *Purpose:* To advance understanding of the nervous system, including its relation to behavior, by bringing together scientists of various backgrounds and by facilitating integration of research directed at all levels of biological organization and to maintain a central source of information on interdisciplinary curricula and training programs in the neurosciences. Serves scientists who have done research relating to the nervous system.

Society of Neurosurgical Anesthesia and Critical Care (SNACC) *Founded:* 1973. *Headquarters:* Midlothian, VA. *Purpose:* To sponsor continuing medical education and research concerning the care of neurosurgical patients. Serves neurosurgeons and anesthesiologists interested in the care of patients with neurological disorders.

Society of Nuclear Medicine (SNM) *Founded:* 1954. *Headquarters:* Reston, VA. *Purpose:* To provide a national organization for physicians, physicists, chemists, radiopharmacists, nuclear medicine technologists, and other persons interested in nuclear medicine, nuclear magnetic resonance, and the use of radioactive isotopes in clinical practice, research, and teaching.

Society for Nutrition Education (SNE) *Founded:* 1967. *Headquarters:* Minneapolis, MN. *Purpose:* To promote nutritional well-being for the public. Serves nutrition educators from the fields of dietetics, public health, home economics, medicine, industry, and education (elementary, secondary, college, university, and consumer affairs).

Society for Obstetric Anesthesia and Perinatology (SOAP) *Founded:* 1969. *Headquarters:* Richmond, VA. *Purpose:* To improve the health care of pregnant women and their unborn children and to conduct specialized education programs and compile statistics. Serves physicians and scientists interested in perinatal health care.

Society for Occupational and Environmental Health (SOEH) *Founded:* 1972. *Headquarters:* McLean, VA. *Purpose:* To focus public attention on scientific, social, and regulatory problems; to study specific categories of hazards, methods for assessment of health effects, and diseases associated with particular jobs; and to identify hazards in the occupational and general environment and propose actions to reduce their danger. Serves scientists, academicians, and industry and labor representatives.

Society of Otorhinolaryngology and Head-Neck Nurses (SOHN) *Founded:* 1976. *Headquarters:* New Smyrna Beach, FL. *Purpose:* To promote awareness of professional technology and new developments in the field; to enhance professional standards; to foster channels of ideas, concerns, and information; to develop interaction with similar groups; and to offer programs and seminars approved for continuing education credits by the American Nurses Association. Serves registered nurses specializing in otorhinolaryngology and disorders of the head and neck.

Society for Pediatric Dermatology (SPD) *Founded:* 1975. *Headquarters:* Ann Arbor, MI. *Purpose:* To provide a national organization for pediatricians, dermatologists, manufacturers of children's skin products, and researchers in biomedicine with studies in pediatric dermatology.

Society for Pediatric Psychology (SPP) *Founded:* 1968. *Headquarters:* Charleston, SC. *Purpose:* To foster the development of theory, research, training, and professional practice in pediatric psychology and the application of psychology to medical and psychological problems of children, youths, and their families and to support legislation benefiting children's health and welfare. Serves psychologists working in children's hospitals, developmental clinics, and pediatric and medical group practices.

Society for Pediatric Radiology (SPR) *Founded:* 1958. *Headquarters:* Oak Brook, IL. *Purpose:* To foster advanced knowledge in pediatric imaging and to improve medical care of infants and children. Serves physicians working in the field of pediatric radiology.

Society for Pediatric Research (SPR) *Founded:* 1929. *Headquarters:* Elk Grove Village, IL. *Purpose:* To promote research, by physicians and scientists under age 45 years, in diseases of infancy and childhood. Members over age 45 years are senior members.

Society for Pediatric Urology (SPU) *Founded:* 1941. *Headquarters:* Seattle, WA. *Purpose:* To encourage the study of pediatric urology; to improve the practice of pediatric urology; to evaluate the standards of pediatric urology; to further the advancement of pediatric urology; and to conduct educational programs. Serves physicians who are specialists in urology and who have a special interest in the field of childhood urological problems.

Society for Personality Assessment (SPA) *Founded:* 1938. *Headquarters:* Washington, DC. *Purpose:* To provide a national organization for psychologists, behavioral scientists, anthropologists, and psychiatrists interested in the study and application of personality assessment.

Society for Physical Regulation in Biology and Medicine (SPRBM) *Founded:* 1980. *Headquarters:* Dresher, PA. *Purpose:* To further research, communication, cooperation, and education in the study and clinical applications of the effects of electricity and magnetism in growth, repair, and regeneration of human cells and tissues. It serves medical professionals, engineers, biological and physical scientists, and representatives of industry.

Society of Professors of Child and Adolescent Psychiatry (SPCAP) *Founded:* 1969. *Headquarters:* Washington, DC. *Purpose:* To provide a national organization for representatives from university psychiatric departments who meet annually to discuss issues in child and adolescent psychiatry.

Society of Prospective Medicine (SPM) *Founded:* 1972. *Headquarters:* Omaha, NE. *Purpose:* To extend the useful life expectancy of persons; to develop educational programs; to supply information concerning diseases that frequently cause death and disability; to identify actual and potential health hazards; and to develop and implement risk assessment techniques and risk reduction programs. Serves physicians, allied health professionals, scientists, and other individuals.

Society for the Psychological Study of Lesbian and Gay Issues (SPSLGI) *Founded:* 1984. *Headquarters:* Washington, DC. *Purpose:* To foster interest in the psychological study of lesbian and gay issues and the delivery of mental health services to gay and lesbian individuals; to provide training to psychologists in the field; and to conduct scholarly programs. Serves psychologists, graduate students in psychology, and other individuals.

Society for the Psychological Study of Social Issues (SPSSI) *Founded:* 1936. *Headquarters:* Ann Arbor, MI. *Purpose:* To obtain and disseminate to the public scientific knowledge about social change; to promote psychological research on significant theoretical and practical quests of social life; and to encourage the application of findings to problems of society. Serves psychologists, sociologists, anthropologists, psychiatrists, political scientists, and social workers.

Society for Psychophysiological Research (SPR) *Founded:* 1960. *Headquarters:* Dallas, TX. *Purpose:* To conduct research, including the evaluation of biofeedback in the treatment of disease states; to maintain historical archives; and to conduct workshops. Serves representatives from psychology, psychiatry, physiology, medicine, and biomedical engineering interested in the interrelationship between behavioral and biological processes.

Society for Public Health Education (SOPHE)
Founded: 1950. *Headquarters:* Berkeley, CA. *Purpose:* To promote and contribute to the advancement of public health by encouraging study and elevating standards of achievement in public health education. Serves professional workers in health education.

Society for Radiation Oncology Administrators (SROA)
Founded: 1984. *Headquarters:* Oak Brook, IL. *Purpose:* To improve the administration of the business and nonmedical management aspects of therapeutic radiology. Serves individuals with managerial responsibilities in radiation oncology at the executive, divisional, or departmental level, whose functions include personnel, budget, and development of operational procedures and guidelines for therapeutic radiology departments.

Society for Research in Child Development (SRCD)
Founded: 1933. *Headquarters:* Ann Arbor, MI. *Purpose:* To provide a national organization for anthropologists, educators, nutritionists, pediatricians, physiologists, psychiatrists, psychologists, sociologists, and statisticians working to further research in child development.

Society for the Right to Die   *See* Choice in Dying.

Society for the Scientific Study of Sex (SSSS)
Founded: 1957. *Headquarters:* Mt. Vernon, IA. *Purpose:* To provide a national organization for psychiatrists, psychologists, physicians, sociologists, anthropologists, social workers, demographers, criminologists, educators, attorneys, and other persons conducting sexual research.

Society for Sex Therapy and Research (SSTAR)
Founded: 1974. *Headquarters:* New York, NY. *Purpose:* To provide a professional network for clinicians and researchers involved in the field of human sexuality and to collect and disseminate information on current basic and clinical research related to human sexual matters. Serves university-affiliated social workers, researchers, and physicians interested in sex therapy and research.

Society for Social Work Administrators in Health Care (SSWAHC)
Founded: 1966. *Headquarters:* Chicago, IL. *Purpose:* To provide a medium for the interchange of ideas; to disseminate material relative to social work administration; to promote standards and ethics for the delivery of social work in health care settings; to strengthen relationships with hospital administration; and to cooperate with allied hospital associations and professional social work organizations. Serves directors of social work departments in health care organizations.

Society for the Study of Blood (SSB)
Founded: 1945. *Headquarters:* Brooklyn, NY. *Purpose:* To further interest in hematology, blood grouping, transfusion, and the study of physiology and pathology of blood.

Society for the Study of Breast Disease   *See* American Society of Breast Disease.

Society for the Study of Male Psychology and Physiology (SSMPP)
Founded: 1975. *Headquarters:* Montpelier, OH. *Purpose:* To conduct research and examine issues of social problems (eg, crime, suicide, juvenile delinquency) and illnesses that occur at significantly higher rates among males; on factors accounting for the shorter life expectancy of males and the effects of the Y chromosome on male behavior; and on male sex roles. It serves psychologists, psychiatrists, biologists, and sociologists interested in the study of the behavior and physiology of males in isolation and in relation to women.

Society for the Study of Reproduction (SSR)
Founded: 1967. *Headquarters:* Madison, WI. *Purpose:* To promote the study of reproduction by fostering interdisciplinary communication within the science. Serves researchers in obstetrics and gynecology, urology, zoology, animal husbandry, and physiology, and clinicians in human and veterinary medicine.

Society for the Study of Social Biology (SSSB)
Founded: 1926. *Headquarters:* Oklahoma City, OK. *Purpose:* To further advance the sharing of knowledge concerning the forces affecting human populations and evolution. Serves geneticists, demographers, psychologists, physicians, psychiatrists, public health workers, educators, and sociologists interested in the study of heredity and populations.

Society for Surgery of the Alimentary Tract (SSAT)
Founded: 1960. *Headquarters:* Thorofare, NJ. *Purpose:* To stimulate, foster, and provide surgical leadership in the art and science of patient care; to teach and research the diseases and functions of the alimentary tract; to provide a forum for the presentation of such knowledge; and to encourage training opportunities, funding, and scientific publications supporting the foregoing activities.

Society of Surgical Oncology (SSO)
Founded: 1940. *Headquarters:* Arlington Heights, IL. *Purpose:* To bestow an annual award to a medical resident who is performing an original research project and to give three cash awards with medals to an outstanding cancer basic scientist, clinical scientist, and contributing layperson. Serves physicians and scientists working in the field of cancer.

Society of Teachers of Family Medicine (STFM)
Founded: 1967. *Headquarters:* Kansas City, MO. *Purpose:* To promote public welfare by improving standards and practices of medical service. Serves physicians involved in teaching or promoting family medicine and other individuals in related fields.

Society of Thoracic Radiology (STR)
Founded: 1983. *Headquarters:* Roswell, GA. *Purpose:* To train chest imagers to guide the appropriate use and study of rapidly changing technological devices. The STR intends to become a partner in this lifelong learning process by maintaining a prominent role in annual, traditional scientific sessions and refresher courses and by working to create, maintain, distribute and enhance an up-to-date database of perti-

nent information. This will be done, in part, by the creation of a chest imaging curriculum and teaching resource that will be available in multiple forms including electronic communication.

Society of Thoracic Surgeons (STS) *Founded:* 1964. *Headquarters:* Chicago, IL. *Purpose:* To improve quality and practice of thoracic and cardiovascular surgery as a specialty; to strengthen and establish basic standards and training programs; to encourage clinical and basic research; to promote professional development; and to represent and sponsor surgeons recently entering the field. Serves surgeons who confine their practice to the field of thoracic-cardiovascular surgery.

Society of Toxicologic Pathologists (STP) *Founded:* 1971. *Headquarters:* Woodbury, NJ. *Purpose:* To evaluate criteria and requirements applied to the interpretation of pathological changes produced by pharmacological, chemical, and environmental agents. Serves toxicologic pathologists, veterinarians, and physicians.

Society of Toxicology (SOT) *Founded:* 1961. *Headquarters:* Reston, VA. *Purpose:* To provide a national organization for persons who have conducted and published original investigations in some phase of toxicology and who have a continuing professional interest in this field.

Society of United States Air Force Flight Surgeons *Founded:* 1960. *Headquarters:* Brooks AFB, TX. *Purpose:* To foster advancement of aerospace medicine throughout the air force and to encourage the clinical, laboratory, flight line, and in-flight investigation of medical problems in air force flying, missile, and space operations. Serves flight surgeons who are members of the Aerospace Medical Association and who are currently serving on active duty with, or have retired from, the U.S. Air Force or are serving in the Air Force Reserve or Air National Guard.

Society of University Otolaryngologists–Head and Neck Surgeons (SUO–HNS) *Founded:* 1964. *Headquarters:* Boston, MA. *Purpose:* To encourage basic research and clinical investigation as an integral part of university training programs. Serves otolaryngologists affiliated with universities through an approved residency training program, faculty appointment, or teaching or research position.

Society of University Surgeons (SUS) *Founded:* 1938. *Headquarters:* West Haven, CT. *Purpose:* To advance the art and science of surgery by encouraging original clinical and laboratory investigations and by developing methods of graduate teaching of surgery with particular reference to the resident system. Serves surgeons connected with university teaching.

Society for Vascular Nursing (SVN) *Founded:* 1982. *Headquarters:* Norwood, MA. *Purpose:* To educate the public about peripheral vascular disease, provide educational programs, and to conduct research. Serves nurses and other health professionals providing care for persons with peripheral vascular disease.

Society for Vascular Surgery (SVS) *Founded:* 1945. *Headquarters:* Manchester, MA. *Purpose:* To promote the study of and research in the circulatory system. Serves board-certified surgeons.

Society of Vascular Technology (SVT) *Founded:* 1977. *Headquarters:* Lanham, MD. *Purpose:* To establish an information clearinghouse providing reference and assistance in matters relating to noninvasive vascular technology and to provide continuing education. Serves medical technologists and other individuals in the field of noninvasive vascular technology.

Special Constituency Section for Aging and Long Term Care Services *Founded:* 1969. *Headquarters:* Chicago, IL. *Purpose:* To promote recognition and growth and to provide support. Serves hospitals that are members of the American Hospital Association and have long term care units or community-based long term care and special services for the aging.

Special Constituency Section for Psychiatric and Substance Abuse Services (SCSMHPS) *Founded:* 1969. *Headquarters:* Chicago, IL. *Purpose:* To assist the American Hospital Association (AHA) in development and implementation of policies and programs promoting hospital-based mental health and psychiatric services. Serves as a division of the AHA for long-term and short-term care institutional members providing psychiatric, substance abuse, mental retardation, and other mental health services.

Special Education and Rehabilitative Services *See* Government Organizations (Department of Education).

Special Interest Group on Biomedical Computing (SIGBIO) *Founded:* 1967. *Headquarters:* Durham, NC. *Purpose:* To foster an understanding of the use and potential of computers in the biosciences and to encourage presentation of papers at medical and computer conferences and conventions. Serves as a special-interest group of the Association for Computing Machinery for biological, medical, behavioral, and computer scientists; hospital administrators; programmers; and other individuals interested in the application of computer methods to biological, behavioral, and medical problems.

Spina Bifida Association of America (SBAA) *Founded:* 1972. *Headquarters:* Washington, DC. *Purpose:* To develop an information service of materials relative to spina bifida; to conduct research into the causes of the birth defect; to improve vocational training of afflicted individuals, to monitor development of legislation applying to disabled persons, and to promote public awareness and action through national media.

Spinal Stress Research Society *See* Precision Chiropractic Research Society.

Statistical Process Control Society (SPCS) *Founded:* 1987. *Headquarters:* Hagerstown, MD. *Purpose:* To establish U.S. industry in competitive world markets and to enhance professionalism among members by granting certification in statistical process control. Serves individuals and companies interested in implementing statistical process control to optimize their efficiency and product quality.

Stop Teen-Age Addiction to Tobacco (STAT)
Founded: 1985. *Headquarters:* Springfield, MA. *Purpose:* To reduce the use of tobacco by children and teens through grassroots community projects, policy research, public education, advocacy, communication, and counter advertising. The group trains and educates professionals, practitioners, citizen activists, and policymakers on research and activities in tobacco addiction, youth access, and prevention. It conducts outreach through the National Tobacco Prevention Outreach Training Program.

Substance Abuse and Mental Health Services Administration *See* Government Organizations (Department of Health and Human Services).

Surgical Infection Society (SIS) *Founded:* 1981. *Headquarters:* West Haven, CT. *Purpose:* To encourage education and research in the nature, prevention, diagnosis, and treatment of surgical infections. Serves surgeons and surgical specialists engaged in laboratory or clinical research in the field of surgical infections.

Tt

Task Force on Academic Health Centers *See* Commonwealth Fund.

Technologist Section of the Society of Nuclear Medicine (TSSNM) *Founded:* 1970. *Headquarters:* Reston, VA. *Purpose:* To promote the continued development and improvement of nuclear medicine technology; to enhance the development of nuclear medicine technologists; to stimulate continuing education; and to represent the field in areas of licensure, accreditation, and certification. Serves members of the Society of Nuclear Medicine who have received formal or on-the-job training in nuclear medicine technology.

Technology Evaluation Center *Founded:* 1985. *Headquarters:* Chicago, IL. *Purpose:* To synthesize the best existing scientific evidence to determine whether these technologies improve the health outcome of the patient.

Tobacco-Free Kids *Founded:* 1996. *Headquarters:* Washington, DC. *Purpose:* Protecting children from tobacco addiction by raising awareness that tobacco use is a pediatric disease; changing public policies to limit the marketing and sales of tobacco to children; altering the environment in which tobacco use and policy decisions are made; and actively countering the tobacco industry and its special interests. The nongovernment initiative's action arm is Campaign for Tobacco-Free Kids, which disseminates information, implements media events (such as Kick Butts Day and the monthly Smoke Alarm warning program), provides outreach and assistance to state- and community-level programs, undertakes research and

analysis, and engages in advocacy with governments and policymakers. The campaign is administered with major funding from the Robert Wood Johnson Foundation and the American Cancer Society, with additional support from several health care organizations and foundations, through the National Center for Tobacco-Free Kids. The initiative is a participant in the ENACT (Effective National Action to Control Tobacco) coalition.

Transplantation Society (TS) *Founded:* 1966. *Headquarters:* Stony Brook, NY. *Purpose:* To further the information in the general area of transplantation biology and medicine. Serves physicians and scientists who have made significant contributions to the advancement of knowledge in transplantation biology and medicine.

Triological Society *See* American Laryngological, Rhinological and Otological Society.

Uu

UCSF Center for the Health Professions/Pew Health Professions Commission *Founded:* 1989. *Headquarters:* San Francisco, CA. *Purpose:* To work at the federal, state, institutional, and professional association levels to promote workforce reforms in response to regulatory and market pressures; to improve the links between health professions education and the care delivery system; to train and retrain health professionals in the competencies the commission has identified; and to expand the roles of midlevel practitioners to increase access to cost-effective primary and population-based health care. The commission is part of the center, which is affiliated with the Pew Charitable Trusts.

Undersea and Hyperbaric Medical Society (UHMS) *Founded:* 1967. *Headquarters:* Kensington, MD. *Purpose:* To develop and advance undersea and hyperbaric medicine; to provide channels of scientific communication; to disseminate information; and to conduct courses. Serves diving physiologists, physicians, biologists, and bioengineers with undersea or hyperbaric interests.

Underwriters Laboratories (UL) *Founded:* 1894. *Headquarters:* Northbrook, IL. *Purpose:* To establish and operate product safety certification programs; to ascertain that items are safeguarded against foreseeable risks; and to provide a worldwide network of field representatives who make unannounced visits to factories to check products bearing the UL mark.

Unified Medical Group Association *See* American Medical Group Association.

Uniformed Services Academy of Family Physicians (USAFP) *Founded:* 1973. *Headquarters:* Richmond, VA. *Purpose:* To sponsor continuing education programs and educational programs. Serves family physicians, teachers of family medicine, medical students, and residents in the armed services, public health service, or Indian health service.

Uniformed Services University of the Health Sciences *See* Government Organizations (Department of Defense).

Union of American Physicians and Dentists (UAPD) *Founded:* 1972. *Headquarters:* Oakland, CA. *Purpose:* To ensure reasonable compensation for physicians commensurate with their training, skill, and the responsibility they bear for their patients. Serves state federations made up of 10,000 physicians and dentists, self-employed or employed by hospitals, teaching institutions, counties, and municipalities.

United Cerebral Palsy Association (UCPA) *Founded:* 1948. *Headquarters:* Washington, DC. *Purpose:* To prevent cerebral palsy; to minimize its effects; and to involve individuals with cerebral palsy and their families in the mainstream of society. Serves state and local affiliates aiding persons with cerebral palsy.

United HealthCare Corporation (United HealthCare) *Founded:* 1992. *Headquarters:* Minnetonka, MN. *Purpose:* To develop and market successful, innovative health plan services; to provide affordable coverage which offering more choice and greater access across a diverse group of markets; and to provide specialty services and products in managed care. The research and performance evaluation of the corporation is the Center for Health Care Evaluation, which uses the company's EPIS medical management software among other tools.

United Methodist Association of Health and Welfare Ministries *Founded:* 1940. *Headquarters:* Dayton, OH. *Purpose:* To offer communications and church relations guidance; to provide leadership development training for health and welfare professionals in the United Methodist Church; to develop ethical and theological statements on institutional care; and to operate Educational Assessment Guidelines Leading Toward Excellence, a self-assessment and peer review program. Serves individual, staff, and board members of United Methodist–affiliated hospitals, retirement homes, and children's homes.

United Nations Children's Fund (UNICEF) *Founded:* 1946. *Headquarters:* New York, NY. *Purpose:* To ensure the survival, protection, and development of children. Cooperates with governments in the developing world to develop and implement low-cost, community-based programs in social service, health, nutrition, education, water and sanitation, environment, and women.

United Network for Organ Sharing (UNOS) *Founded:* 1984. *Headquarters:* Richmond, VA. *Purpose:* To provide a clearinghouse for organs used in U.S. transplant operations; to operate the Organ Center, which matches patients in need of transplants with donated organs and arranges transport of organs to transplant sites; and to formulate and implement national policies on equitable access and organ allocation, AIDS testing, and organ procurement standards. Serves transplant and organ procure-

ment centers, tissue-typing laboratories, and health care professionals engaged in organ transplant operations. Under a grant from the Human Resources and Services Administration, Office of Special Programs (in the U.S. Department of Health and Human Services), UNOS conducts tasks and projects to meet federally established goals of the Organ Procurement Transplantation Network (OPTN) and the Scientific Registry under the National Organ Transplant Act of 1984 (NOTA).

United States Conference of Local Health Officers (USCLHO) *Founded:* 1960. *Headquarters:* Washington, DC. *Purpose:* To promote cooperation and exchange of ideas to assist in the improvement of local public health administration. Serves chief health officers, commissioners, directors, and other officials representing city, county, or city-county health departments.

United States–Mexico Border Health Association (USMBHA) *Founded:* 1943. *Headquarters:* El Paso, TX. *Purpose:* To make easier and more efficient the improvement of public health along both sides of the border. Serves physicians, public health administrators, nurses, sanitary engineers, veterinarians, scientists, laboratory workers, and other health officers from the four American and six Mexican states bordering the two countries.

United States Pharmacopeial Convention (USP) *Founded:* 1820. *Headquarters:* Rockville, MD. *Purpose:* To revise and publish legally recognized compendia of drug standards (*U.S. Pharmacopeia*) and to offer continuing pharmacy education. Serves recognized authorities in medicine, pharmacy, and allied sciences.

Universities Associated for Research and Education in Pathology (UAREP) *Founded:* 1964. *Headquarters:* Bethesda, MD. *Purpose:* To provide core material in convenient form for updating and enriching teaching and researching of pathology, with special emphasis on toxicology and chemical carcinogens. Serves university pathology departments, including faculty members, residents, and research fellows.

University of California San Francisco, Center for the Health Professions *See* UCSF Center for the Health Professions/Pew Health Professions Commission.

University HealthSystem Consortium (UHC) *Founded:* 1988. *Headquarters:* Oak Brook, IL. *Purpose:* To synthesize and disseminate objective information regarding the appropriate use and efficient management of existing and emerging medical technology.

U.S. Committee for the World Health Organization *See* American Association for World Health.

U.S. Federation for Culture Collections (USFCC) *Founded:* 1970. *Headquarters:* Abbott Park, IL. *Purpose:* To encourage research in preserving collections of microorganisms; to encourage establishment of microbial strain data services; and to sponsor workshops on the preservation of microbial cultures and the operation of culture collections. Serves persons interested in culture collections, particularly those involved in collecting, maintaining, and preserving microbial cultures.

U.S. General Accounting Office (GAO)   *See* Government Organizations (Legislative Branch).

U.S. Healthcare   *See* Aetna/U.S. Healthcare.

U.S. Physical Therapy Association (USPTA)
Founded: 1970. *Headquarters:* Arlington Heights, IL. *Purpose:* To maintain the U.S. Physical Therapy Academy, which, among other activities, accredits hospital and nursing home physical therapy departments, universities and colleges of physical therapy, and certifies physical therapists through board examinations.

U.S. Preventive Services Task Force   *See* Government Organizations (Department of Health and Human Services, AHCPR).

VHA   *Founded:* 1977. *Headquarters:* Irving, TX. *Purpose:* To encourage the transfer of ideas, techniques and experiences to improve the quality and efficiency of delivering community-oriented health care. Through the Community Ownership Advocacy Initiative, VHA conducts research on the differences between nonprofit and investor-owned health care organizations, advocates the continued tax exemption of nonprofit hospitals, presents the nonprofit perspective to national and trade press, and assists members in local efforts to promote community-owned health care. *Formerly:* Voluntary Hospitals of America (1995).

Vision Council of America (VICA)   *Founded:* 1985. *Headquarters:* Arlington, VA. *Purpose:* To serve collective interests of the ophthalmic community and to encourage the public to visit eye-care practitioners regularly. Through the Better Vision Institute (BVI), its public education arm, VICA carries out public education campaigns to increase awareness of eye care and eyewear issues, including such programs as the ABC's of Eyecare, Envision Yourself, and Presbyopia.

Visiting Nurse Associations of America (VNAA)
Founded: 1982. *Headquarters:* Denver, CO. *Purpose:* To develop competitive strength among voluntary nonprofit health care agencies and to strengthen business resources and economic programs through contracting, marketing, governmental affairs, and publications. The VNAA serves voluntary, nonprofit home health care agencies.

Violence Against Women Program Office   *See* Government Organizations (Department of Justice).

Voluntary Hospitals of America   *See* VHA.

Volunteer Trustees of Not-for-Profit Hospitals
Founded: 1980. *Headquarters:* Washington, DC. *Purpose:* To provide a trustee voice in policy making and legislative activities and to develop a communications network

among trustees in order to provide the highest quality medical care at the lowest possible price. Areas of concern include Medicare, controlling hospital costs, and strategic planning for the nonprofit hospital community. Serves representatives of nonprofit hospitals and their voluntary governing boards.

Wellness Associates (WA)   *Founded:* 1975. *Headquarters:* Ukiah, CA. *Purpose:* To provide high-quality resource materials for life-style improvement integrating the major components of wellness—self-responsibility, stress management, nutrition, and physical awareness—and to provide consultation for wellness centers, individuals, universities, agencies, hospitals, and government groups.

Wellness and Health Activation Networks (WHAN)
Founded: 1980. *Headquarters:* Great Falls, VA. *Purpose:* To concentrate on programs designed to increase awareness of health rights and responsibilities; and to serve as a clearinghouse for the Wellness and Health Activation program, which designs and acts as national distributor of trainers' course guides, planning guides, program texts, home health care equipment, and other health activation materials. Serves individuals interested in health activation, that is, the process of maintaining good health and preventing illness.

Wilderness Medical Society (WMS)   *Founded:* 1983. *Headquarters:* Indianapolis, IN. *Purpose:* To promote research and educational activities that increase scientific knowledge about human activities in wilderness environments and to stimulate interest and research in health consequences of wilderness activities. Areas of interest include treatment of victims of bites and stings, exotic infectious diseases and toxic plants, desert survival, control, and search and rescue. Serves persons with advanced degrees in the biomedical or life sciences with an interest in the medical, behavioral, and life sciences aspects of wilderness environments.

William T. Grant Foundation   *See under* Grant.

W.K. Kellogg Foundation   *See under* Kellogg.

Women's Caucus of the Endocrine Society (WE)
Founded: 1975. *Headquarters:* Baltimore, MD. *Purpose:* To promote the professional advancement of women and younger members of the Endocrine Society; to maintain biographical archives; to compile statistics; and to conduct seminars and workshops.

Women's Health Initiative   *See* Government Organizations (Department of Health and Human Services, NIH).

Robert W. Woodruff Foundation, Inc   *Founded:* 1937. *Headquarters:* Macon, GA. *Purpose:* To manage the foundations' financial assets and develop grant programs in such areas as expansion and improvement of medical, nursing, and educational facilities; youth programs and child welfare; care of the aged; and cultural and civic affairs. The philosophical core of the foundations' work is based on Robert Woodruff's deep concern for the well-being of the community in which he lived and for the advancement of the basic institutions which serve the citizens of the area. It donates money primarily in Atlanta, Georgia.

Noah Worcester Dermatological Society   *See under* Noah Worcester.

World Society for Stereotactic and Functional Neurosurgery (WSSFN)   *Founded:* 1963. *Head-quarters:* Houston, TX. *Purpose:* To promote the advancement of stereotactic studies and procedures.

Wound, Ostomy, and Continence Nurses Society *Founded:* 1969. *Headquarters:* Costa Mesa, CA. *Purpose:* To support enterostomal therapy, wound, ostomy, and continence nurses by promoting education and clinical and research opportunities and to guide the delivery of expert health care to individuals with wounds, ostomies, and incontinence.

World Health Organization (WHO)   *Founded:* 1953. *Headquarters:* Geneva, Switzerland. *Purpose:* To foster the attainment by all peoples of the highest possible level of health—a state of complete physical, mental and social well-being and not merely the absence of disease or infirmity. Its functions include the following: to act as the directing and coordinating authority on international health work; to promote technical cooperation; to assist governments, on request, in strengthening health services; to furnish appropriate technical assistance and, in emergencies, necessary aid, on the request or acceptance of governments; to stimulate and advance work on the prevention and control of epidemic, endemic, and other diseases; to promote, in cooperation with other specialized agencies where necessary, the improvement of nutrition, housing, sanitation, recreation, economic or working conditions and other aspects of environmental hygiene; to promote and coordinate biomedical and health services research; to promote improved standards of teaching and training in the health, medical, and related professions; to establish and stimulate the establishment of international standards for biological, pharmaceutical, and similar products, and to standardize diagnostic procedures; and to foster activities in the field of mental health, especially those activities affecting the harmony of human relations. WHO proposes conventions, agreements, regulations and makes recommendations about international nomenclature of diseases, causes of death, and public health practices. It develops, establishes, and promotes international standards concerning foods and biological, pharmaceutical and similar substances.

Zero to Three   *Founded:* 1977. *Headquarters:* Washington, DC. *Purpose:* To help children best navigate their first three years of life in order to develop a solid intellectual, emotional, and social foundation. The organization disseminates key developmental information, trains providers, promotes model approaches and standards of practice, and works to increase public awareness about the significance of the first three years of life. Members include individuals from the fields of medicine, mental health, research science, and child development.

GOVERNMENT AGENCIES

This section of Appendix A summarizes the purpose and chief programs of federal government agencies and quasi-governmental national organizations in the United States. Its purpose is to bring you up to date on the titles and locations of agencies in the federal government structure and to facilitate any further searching you may want to do on your own. It is based primarily on *The United States Government Manual*, 1996/97 edition, but it has been supplemented and updated from material received directly from the agencies in order to incorporate changes from legislation effective late 1997 and early 1998 and to include new initiatives.

Certain recent major reorganizations merit special note. The Department of Health and Human Services (DHHS) underwent a major reorganization at the end of 1995. Under the Reinvention of Government initiative, the Office of the Assistant Secretary for Health (OASH) merged with the Office of the Secretary (OS), to create a unified corporate headquarters for the Department—the Office of Public Health and Science (OPHS)—that brings expertise in public health and science closer to the Secretary of Health and Human Services. The former Public Health Service (PHS) agencies each became full DHHS Operating Divisions, and some smaller components formerly under the PHS were moved to one of these major divisions. The figure on page 407 graphically displays the new organization of DHHS. These newly established Operating Divisions and the OPHS now constitute the Public Health Service, which does not appear by name on the chart but continues to be cited in many agencies' literature and letterheads.

With the restructuring of Medicare from the Balanced Budget Act of 1997 (effective October 1, 1997), another revision affects the Health Care Financing Administration (HCFA) and other agencies reporting on Medicare. The Physician Payment Review Commission (PPRC) and the Prospective Payment Assessment Commission (ProPAC) have been abolished with their functions consolidated within a new organization, the Medicare Payment Advisory Commission (MedPAC). Other restructuring continues.

To help you place these shifting and renamed agencies and offices at a glance, we have outlined in the table below the main divisions and subdivisions as they appear in this government section of the appendix. The agencies and offices are organized alphabetically within major headings first by the broad branch or type of government agency, and then within cabinet-level departments, and then further within divisions and offices. Acronyms or abbreviations are provided only for those agencies that are using them in their publications and external correspondence. City location is shown only for the larger entities; if the location of a subdivision is different, it is indicated in parentheses. The annotations describing the listed organizations in the text of this appendix include additional offices, programs, or special initiatives currently of concern to health care professionals.

GOVERNMENT ENTITIES INCLUDED IN APPENDIX A

EXECUTIVE BRANCH

Department of Agriculture (USDA)
Food and Consumer Service (FCS)
Food Safety and Inspection Service (FSIS)

Department of Commerce (DOC)
Technology Administration
    National Technical Information Service (NTIS)

Department of Defense (DOD)
Uniformed Services University of the Health Sciences

Department of Education (ED)
Elementary and Secondary Education
Special Education and Rehabilitative Services

Department of Energy (DOE)

Department of Health and Human Services (DHHS)
Administration on Aging
Administration for Children and Families (ACF)
    Administration on Children, Youth, and Families (ACYF)
    Administration on Developmental Disabilities (ADD)
    Administration for Native Americans (ANA)
Agency for Health Care Policy and Research (AHCPR)
    Center for Cost and Financing Studies (COFS)
    Center for Health Care Technology (CHCT)
    Center for Health Information Dissemination (CHID)
    Center for Information Technology (CIT)

    Center for Organization and Delivery Studies (CODS)
    Center for Outcomes and Effectiveness Research (COER)
    Center for Primary Care Research (CPCR)
    Center for Quality Measurement and Improvement (CQMI)
    Office of the Forum for Quality and Effectiveness in Health Care
    Office of Planning and Evaluation
    Office of Policy Analysis
    Office of Scientific Affairs
Agency for Toxic Substances and Disease Registry (ATSDR)
Centers for Disease Control and Prevention (CDC)
Food and Drug Administration (FDA)
    Center for Biologics Evaluation and Research (CBER)
    Center for Devices and Radiological Health (CDRH)
    Center for Drug Evaluation and Research (CDER)
    Center for Food Safety and Applied Nutrition (CFSAN)
    Engineering and Analytical Center
    National Center for Toxicological Research (NCTR)
Health Care Financing Administration (HCFA)
Health Resources and Services Administration (HRSA)
    Bureau of Health Professions
    Bureau of Primary Health Care
    Division of Immigration Health Services
    HIV/AIDS Bureau
    Maternal and Child Health Bureau (MCHB)
    Office of Special Programs
Indian Health Service (IHS)
National Institutes of Health (NIH)
    National Cancer Institute (NCI)   **(continued on next page)**

EXECUTIVE BRANCH

DEPARTMENT OF AGRICULTURE (USDA)

Food and Consumer Service (FCS) *Founded:* 1969. *Headquarters:* Washington, DC. *Purpose:* To ensure access to nutritious, healthful diets for all Americans through food assistance and nutrition education for consumers. The FCS works to empower consumers with knowledge of the link between diet and health by providing dietary guidance based on research. Programs, which are operated in cooperation with state and local governments, include nutrition education for families and nutrition training for health care professionals. The FCS oversees the Food Stamp Program, special nutrition programs (such as the National School Lunch Program, the School Breakfast Program, and the School Meals Initiative for Healthy Children), the Summer Food Service Program for Children, the Child and Adult Care Food Program, the Special Milk Program for Children, the Food Distribution Program (including child care centers, nutrition program for the elderly, and food banks), the Special Supplemental Food Program for Women, Infants and Children (WIC), the Commodity Supplemental Food Program (supplemental foods and nutrition education to low-income infants and children; pregnant, postpartum, and breast-feeding women; and elderly persons at risk for malnutrition), and nutrition education and training funds (including the Team Nutrition initiative in schools).

Food Safety and Inspection Service (FSIS) *Founded:* 1981. *Headquarters:* Washington, DC. *Purpose:* To regulate meat, poultry, and egg products. The FSIS tests samples of products for microbial and chemical contaminants to monitor trends for enforcement purposes. In 1996 the FSIS announced implementation of new rules for improving the safety of meat and poultry, including a Hazard Analysis and Critical Control Points (HACCP) system, a science-based strategy for protecting public health, which is to be phased in on the basis of establishment size in three increments starting in January 1998. Specific pathogen reduction performance standards have been established for *Salmonella* and *E coli* (*Escherichia coli*). In 1995 the FSIS began a multiyear, five-site collaborative project with the CDC and the FDA, known originally as the *Sentinel Site Study* and as of January 1997 as *FoodNet*, to establish and implement an active surveillance system for bacterial foodborne diseases in the United States. (The project includes a physician survey.) As of 1998, the FSIS proposes adding *Campylobacter* to the targets of surveillance and pathogen reduction standards development.

DEPARTMENT OF COMMERCE (DOC)
Technology Administration
National Technical Information Service (NTIS)
Founded: 1988. *Headquarters:* Springfield, VA. *Purpose:* To serve as a central clearinghouse for the nation and as the official resource for government-sponsored U.S. and worldwide scientific, technical, engineering, and business-related information. The NTIS is a nonappropriated, self-supporting agency within the DOC. Under the American Technology Preeminence Act (ATPA), all federal agencies are required to transfer to the NTIS all unclassified scientific, technical, and engineering information resulting from federally funded research and development activities. The NTIS maintains the FedWorld® electronic marketplace (which includes the NTIS Preview Database for titles entered within the past 30 days); the NTIS Bibliographic Database on CD-ROM or online; the *Government Reports Announcements & Index Journal*; and the Federal Research in Progress (FEDRIP) Database. It also provides numerous other information and technology transfer services and publications, including *NTIS Alerts* and *Health Care Highlights* (health care products catalog).

DEPARTMENT OF DEFENSE (DOD)
Uniformed Services University of the Health Sciences *Founded:* 1972. *Headquarters:* Bethesda, MD. *Purpose:* To educate career-oriented medical officers for the military department and the Public Health Service. It incorporates the F. Edward Hebert School of Medicine and the Graduate School of Nursing. It applies its activities to military medicine, disaster medicine, and military medical readiness.

DEPARTMENT OF EDUCATION (ED)
Elementary and Secondary Education Operates the
Safe and Drug-Free Schools (SDFS) Program, the federal government's primary vehicle for reducing drug, alcohol, and tobacco use, and violence, through education and prevention activities in schools. Many activities are coordinated with other education programs and with federal agencies. The SDFS administers both state and national grants under Title IV of the Improving America's Schools Act of 1994.

Special Education and Rehabilitative Services
Responsible for special education programs and services expressly designed to meet the needs and develop the full potential of children with disabilities and for comprehensive rehabilitation service programs specifically designed to reduce human dependency, to increase self-reliance, and to fully utilize the productive capabilities of all persons with disabilities. Programs include support for training of teachers and other personnel.

DEPARTMENT OF ENERGY (DOE) *Founded:* 1977
Headquarters: Washington, DC. *Purpose:* To contribute to the welfare of the nation, in partnership with its customers, by providing the technical information and the scientific and educational foundation for the technology, policy, and institutional leadership necessary to achieve efficiency in energy use, diversity in energy sources, a more productive and competitive economy, improved environmental quality, and a secure national defense. The Assistant Secretary for Environment, Safety, and Health provides independent oversight of departmental execution of environmental, occupational safety and health, and nuclear/nonnuclear safety and security laws, regulations, and policies. The Assistant Secretary for Environmental Management provides program policy guidance and manages the assessment and cleanup of inactive waste sites and facilities. Under its Office of Energy Research and its Office of Biological and Environmental Research, the DOE carries out work on the Human Genome Project, some of it in cooperation with the extramural division of NIH's National Human Genome Research Institute.

DEPARTMENT OF HEALTH AND HUMAN SERVICES (DHHS)
Administration on Aging *Founded:* 1965. *Headquarters:* Washington, DC. *Purpose:* To advise federal departments and officials on the characteristics, circumstances, and needs of older people and to develop policies, plans, and programs to promote their welfare under the Older Americans Act of 1965. It administers formula grants to states to establish state and community programs and administers ombudsman and legal services oversight and protective services for older adults through programs such as the Governmental Affairs, Elder Rights, and Long-Term Care Ombudsman Program, and the Office for American Indian, Alaskan Native, and Native Hawaiian Programs.

Administration for Children and Families (ACF)
Founded: 1991. *Headquarters:* Washington, DC. *Purpose:* To recommend actions and strategies to improve coordination of ACF efforts with other programs, agencies, and governmental levels or jurisdictions. It provides executive direction, leadership, and guidance to all ACF components.

Administration on Children, Youth, and Families (ACYF) Advises government officials on matters relating to the sound development of children, youth, and families and administers grant programs to assist states in providing child welfare services, foster care, and adoption assistance; to improve child abuse prevention and treatment activities; and to develop family preservation and family support services. Programs under ACYF include Head Start, Youth Gang Drug Prevention Program, and Community Schools Youth Services and Supervision Grant Program.

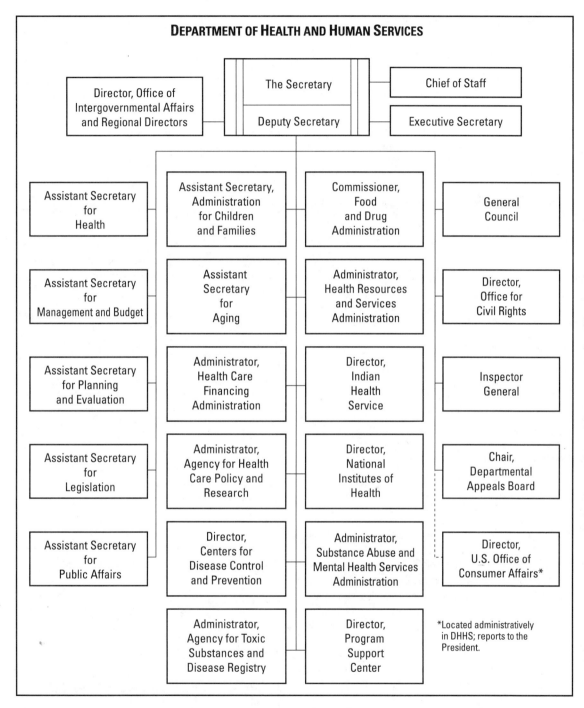

DEPARTMENT OF HEALTH AND HUMAN SERVICES

Director, Office of Intergovernmental Affairs and Regional Directors	The Secretary	Chief of Staff
	Deputy Secretary	Executive Secretary

Assistant Secretary for Health	Assistant Secretary, Administration for Children and Families	Commissioner, Food and Drug Administration	General Council
Assistant Secretary for Management and Budget	Assistant Secretary for Aging	Administrator, Health Resources and Services Administration	Director, Office for Civil Rights
Assistant Secretary for Planning and Evaluation	Administrator, Health Care Financing Administration	Director, Indian Health Service	Inspector General
Assistant Secretary for Legislation	Administrator, Agency for Health Care Policy and Research	Director, National Institutes of Health	Chair, Departmental Appeals Board
Assistant Secretary for Public Affairs	Director, Centers for Disease Control and Prevention	Administrator, Substance Abuse and Mental Health Services Administration	Director, U.S. Office of Consumer Affairs*
	Administrator, Agency for Toxic Substances and Disease Registry	Director, Program Support Center	*Located administratively in DHHS; reports to the President.

Administration on Developmental Disabilities (ADD) Advises government officials on matters relating to persons with developmental disabilities and their families. It promotes the provision of high-quality services to persons with developmental disabilities and implements research, demonstration, and evaluation strategies for improving the lives of people with disabilities.

Administration for Native Americans (ANA) Promotes the goal of social and economic self- sufficiency of American Indians, Alaskan Natives, Native Hawaiians, and other Native American Pacific Islanders. It seeks to strengthen community social and economic infrastructures with grants addressing needs in areas of social and economic development, languages, and environmental preservation. The ANA commissioner chairs the Intra-Departmental Council on Native American Affairs (IDC-

NAA), which is the focal point for all initiatives affecting Native Americans.

Agency for Health Care Policy and Research (AHCPR)

Founded: 1989. *Headquarters:* Rockville, MD. *Purpose:* To support, as the federal government's lead agency, research designed to improve the quality of health care, reduce its cost, and broaden access to essential services. It develops and disseminates research-based information to increase the scientific knowledge needed to enhance consumer and clinical decision making. Major issues covered in AHCPR's research and evaluation projects are consumer choice, including CHAPS (Consumer Assessment of Health Plans), a five-year collaborative effort with Harvard University, RAND, and Research Triangle Institute; clinical improvement; health care cost, financing, and access; health information technology; outcomes and effectiveness of health care; health care organization and delivery; quality measurement and improvement, including CONQUEST (Computerized Needs-Oriented Quality Measurement Evaluation System) and QMNET (Quality Measurement Network); and technology assessment. AHCPR comprises 14 major functional components, with the Office of the Administrator directing activities to ensure that strategic objectives are achieved.

Center for Cost and Financing Studies (COFS)

Conducts and supports studies of the cost and financing of health care and develops datasets to support policy and behavioral research and analyses.

Center for General Health Services Extramural/Intramural Research

See Center for Organization and Delivery Studies (below).

Center for Health Care Technology (CHCT)

Evaluates the risks, benefits, and clinical effectiveness of new or unestablished medical technologies. In most instances, assessments address technologies that are being reviewed for purposes of coverage by federally funded health programs. The results are published in the AHCPR series *Health Technology Assessment.*

Center for Health Information Dissemination (CHID)

Designs, develops, implements, and manages programs for disseminating the results of AHCPR activities, including public affairs, reference services, and dissemination activities.

Center for Information Technology (CIT)

Conducts and supports research on the measurement and improvement of the quality of health care, including consumer surveys and satisfaction with health care services and systems.

Center for Medical Effectiveness Research

See Center for Outcomes and Effectiveness Research (below).

Center for Organization and Delivery Studies (CODS)

Conducts and manages studies of the structure, financing, organization, behavior, and performance of the health care systems and providers within it. *Formerly:* Center for General Health Services Extramural

Research and the Center for General Health Services Intramural Research (1996).

Center for Outcomes and Effectiveness Research (COER)

Conducts and supports studies of the outcomes and effectiveness of diagnostic, therapeutic, and preventive health care services and procedures. *Formerly:* Center for Medical Effectiveness Research (1995).

Center for Primary Care Research (CPCR)

Conducts and supports studies of primary care, and clinical, preventive, and public health policies and systems.

Center for Quality Measurement and Improvement (CQMI)

Conducts and supports research on the measurement and improvement of the quality of health care, including consumer surveys and satisfaction with health care services and systems.

Office of the Forum for Quality and Effectiveness in Health Care (Office of the Forum)

Directs the Evidence-Based Practice Program, which replaced the clinical practice guideline development program with which the Office of the Forum was first charged. The program consists of (1) Evidence-Based Practice Centers (EPCs), in which AHCPR collaborates with public- and private-sector science partners; (2) the National Guideline Clearinghouse, a comprehensive, Internet-based source for clinical practice guidelines, which is being developed in collaboration with the American Medical Association and the American Association of Health Plans, scheduled to become operative in 1998; and (3) research and evaluation on translating evidence-based research into clinical practice. The U.S. Preventive Services Task Force has also been placed in this office (1995).

Office of Planning and Evaluation

Monitors and assists state-funded and -directed programs in health planning and directs selected health evaluation programs and projects.

Office of Policy Analysis

Provides support to the Administrator and technical assistance to public- and private-sector users of health services research.

Office of Scientific Affairs

Develops database programs for the AHCPR.

U.S. Preventive Services Task Force

See Office of the Forum for Quality and Effectiveness in Health Care (above).

Agency for Toxic Substances and Disease Registry (ATSDR)

Founded: 1980. *Headquarters:* Atlanta, GA. *Purpose:* To prevent exposure, adverse human health effects, and diminished quality of life associated with exposure to hazardous substances from waste sites, unplanned releases, and other sources of pollution present in the environment. It evaluates information on the release of hazardous substances into the environment to assess any current or future impact on public health and provides health-related support, including taking steps to ensure adequate response to public health emergencies.

Centers for Disease Control and Prevention (CDC)

Founded: 1973. *Headquarters:* Atlanta, GA. *Purpose:* To protect the public health of the nation by providing leadership and direction in the prevention and control of diseases and other preventable conditions and responding to public health emergencies. It administers national programs for the prevention and control of communicable and vector-borne diseases, injury, and other preventable conditions; directs and enforces foreign quarantine activities and regulations; provides consultation and assistance in upgrading the performance of public health and clinical laboratories; and organizes and implements a National Health Promotion Program. It administers the National Nosocomial Infections Surveillance (NNIS) system, the only source of national surveillance data on nosocomial infections in the United States. A new collaborative initiative begun with Glaxo Wellcome, Inc, and Merck & Co, Inc, is the HIV Postexposure Prophylaxis (PEP) Registry. The CDC is composed of 11 major operating components: Epidemiology Program Office (EPO); International Health Program Office (IHPO); National Center for Chronic Disease Prevention and Health Promotion (NCCDPHP); National Center for Environmental Health (NCEH); National Center for Health Statistics (NCHS); National Center for HIV, ST [sexually transmitted disease], and TB [tuberculosis] Prevention (NCHSTP); National Center for Infectious Diseases (NCID), which includes the Hospital Infections Program (HIP); National Center for Injury Prevention and Control (NCIPC); National Center for Prevention Services; National Immunization Program (NIP) Office, which includes the Advisory Committee on Immunization Practices (ACIP); National Institute for Occupational Safety and Health (NIOSH); and Public Health Practice Program (PHPP) Office.

Food and Drug Administration (FDA)

Founded: 1931. *Headquarters:* Washington, DC. *Purpose:* To protect the health of the nation against impure and unsafe foods, drugs, and cosmetics, and other potential hazards. It develops and administers programs concerning safety, effectiveness, and labeling of all drug, food, and cosmetic products and all medical devices for human use, and it operates MedWatch, the FDA Medical Products Reporting Program (supported by more than 120 organizations called MedWatch Partners). In February 1997, the FDA issued rules prohibiting sale and promotion of cigarettes, loose cigarette tobacco, and smokeless tobacco to anyone younger than age 18; the advertising restrictions were struck down by a federal district court, but the decision is under appeal by the government. The scope of the FDA's jurisdiction over tobacco, including regulation as a drug delivery device, remained unsettled as of the summer of 1997.

Center for Biologics Evaluation and Research (CBER)

Administers regulation of biological products under control provisions of the Public Health Service Act; works to develop an AIDS vaccine and AIDS diagnostic tests and conducts other AIDS-related activities; and plans and conducts research related to the development, manufacture, testing, and use of both new and old biological products (including blood products, insulin, and vaccines) to establish standards ensuring the safety, purity, potency, and efficacy of biological products.

Center for Devices and Radiological Health (CDRH)

Controls unnecessary exposure of humans to potentially hazardous ionizing and non-ionizing radiation. It develops programs relating to the safety, effectiveness, and labeling of medical devices for human use and develops performance standards for the proper use of radiation.

Center for Drug Evaluation and Research (CDER)

Develops policy with regard to the safety, effectiveness, and labeling of all drug products for human use and evaluates new drug applications. It coordinates with the Center for Biologics Evaluation and Research on activities for biological drug products and develops guidelines on current good manufacturing practices for use by the drug industry. It also develops and disseminates information and educational material dealing with drug products to the medical community and the public.

Center for Food Safety and Applied Nutrition (CFSAN)

Conducts research and develops standards on the composition, quality, nutrition, and safety of food and food additives, colors, and cosmetics. It also reviews industry petitions and regulates food standards to permit the safe use of color additives and food additives.

Engineering and Analytical Center

Tests medical devices, radiation-emitting products, and radioactive drugs. (*Headquarters:* Winchester, MA)

National Center for Toxicological Research (NCTR)

Conducts research programs to study the biological effects of potentially toxic chemical substances found in the environment. Develops improved methodologies and test protocols for evaluating the safety of chemical toxicants and the application of animal testing data to humans. (*Headquarters:* Jefferson, AK)

Health Care Financing Administration (HCFA)

Founded: 1977. *Headquarters:* Washington, DC. *Purpose:* To oversee the operations of the Medicare program, the federal portion of the Medicaid program (medical assistance for low-income persons), and related quality assurance activities and to regulate all laboratory testing (except research) through the Clinical Laboratory Improvement Amendments (CLIA) program. In agencywide restructuring as a beneficiary-centered purchaser of health care services (implemented in July 1997), HCFA was reorganized around three large units called *Centers* for each of its primary customers: the Center for Beneficiary Services, the Center for Health Plans and Providers, and the Center for Medicaid and State Operations. HCFA's quality assurance activities, in the Office of Clinical Standards and Quality, include developing and implementing standards, oversight of state peer review organizations (PROs) through contract, and development of conditions of participation and coverage policy. HCFA initiatives include the Children's Health Insurance Program (CHIP), the National Provider Identifier, PAYERID (a plan/employer identifier for electronic data interchange and health care administrative operations), fraud and abuse grants, the Health Care Quality Improvement Program (HCQIP), and state health reform. Medicaid covers recipients of Aid to Families with Dependent Children (AFDC); most states also cover the needy elderly, blind, and disabled who receive cash assistance under the Supplemental Security Income (SSI) Program.

Health Resources and Services Administration (HRSA) *Founded:* 1982. *Headquarters:* Rockville, MD. *Purpose:* To make essential primary care services accessible to the poor, uninsured, geographically isolated, and others who are severely underserved by the private health care system. It helps assist health providers meet the needs of the underserved by keeping pace with changes in health care, including managed care; provides primary care services to the working poor and uninsured through community and migrant health centers; and attends to the special health care needs of people with chronic health needs, minorities, and those living along the U.S. border with Mexico.

Bureau of Health Professions Provides national leadership in coordinating, evaluating, and supporting the development of the nation's health personnel. It promotes quality assurance activities, operates the National Practitioner Data Bank and the Vaccine Injury Compensation Program, funds educational services and training for health professions faculty, promotes equity in access to health services and health careers for the disadvantaged, and funds regional centers to train health professionals and faculty in the counseling, diagnosis, and management of HIV/AIDS-infected individuals.

Bureau of Health Resources Development See HIV/AIDS Bureau and Office of Special Programs (below).

Bureau of Primary Health Care Ensures the availability and delivery of health care services in health professional shortage areas, to medically underserved populations, and to those with special needs. It administers the National Health Service Corps Program, which recruits and places highly trained primary care clinicians to serve in health professional shortage areas and administers the Veterans Health Care Act of 1992, which provides that participating manufacturers sell Medicaid-covered outpatient drugs to eligible entities at discount prices.

Division of Immigration Health Services Serves as the primary focal point for planning, management, policy formulation, program coordination, direction, and liaison for all health matters pertaining to aliens detained by the Immigration and Naturalization Service.

HIV/AIDS Bureau Funds, develops, coordinates, administers, and monitors programs supporting increased access to health care and support services for people living with HIV/AIDS infections, under the expanded Ryan White Comprehensive AIDS Resources Emergency Act grant program. This bureau was established to consolidate all HRSA's AIDS-related activities into one bureau. *Formerly:* Bureau of Health Resources Development (1997).

Maternal and Child Health Bureau (MCHB) Promotes policies and programs pertaining to health and related-care systems for the nation's mothers and children. Programs address primary, secondary, and tertiary care services and related activities conducted in the public and private sector which have an impact on maternal and child health. Initiatives and projects include the Bright Futures prevention and health supervision project administered by the National Center for Education in Maternal and Child Health (Arlington, VA) through MCHB funding and the National Maternal and Child Health Clearinghouse (Vienna, VA).

Office of Special Programs Administers the national network of activities associated with organ and bone marrow donation, procurements, and transplants, including the Organ Procurement and Transplantation Network (OPTN) and the Scientific Registry through contracts to the United Network for Organ Sharing; and provides financial and oversight activities for health care facilities. These activities were assumed from the former Bureau of Health Resources Development.

Indian Health Service (IHS) *Founded:* 1955. *Headquarters:* Rockville, MD. *Purpose:* To raise the health status of American Indians and Alaskan Natives to the highest possible level. It facilitates and assists Indian tribes in coordinating health planning, in obtaining and using health resources available through federal, state, and local programs, and providing comprehensive health care services, including hospital and ambulatory medical care, preventive and rehabilitative services, and development of community sanitation facilities.

National Institutes of Health (NIH) *Founded:* 1887. *Headquarters:* Bethesda, MD. *Purpose:* To serve as the principal biomedical research agency of the federal government, with a mission to apply science in the pursuit of knowledge to improve human health conditions. NIH seeks to expand fundamental knowledge about the nature and behavior of living systems, to apply that knowledge to extend the health of human lives, and to reduce the burdens resulting from disease and disability. The NIH supports biomedical and behavioral research domestically and abroad, conducts research in its own laboratories and clinics, trains researchers, and promotes the acquisition and distribution of medical knowledge.

National Cancer Institute (NCI) Coordinates the government's cancer research program by developing programs to expand current scientific knowledge on cancer cause and prevention as well as on the diagnosis, treatment, and rehabilitation of cancer patients. The NCI maintains the Surveillance, Epidemiology, and End Results (SEER) system, supports the Cancer Information Service (CIS) public information line, and operates the PDQ (Physician's Data Query) and CANCERLIT databases and services.

National Center for Human Genome Research See National Human Genome Research Institute (next page).

National Eye Institute (NEI)   Supports research on the causes, natural history, prevention, diagnosis, and treatment of eye and visual system disorders. The NEI responds directly to requests from and the public and patients on eye diseases and vision research.

National Heart, Lung, and Blood Institute (NHLBI) Supports and conducts research to prevent, detect, diagnose, and treat cardiovascular, lung, and blood diseases and sleep disorders and to ensure the safety of the blood supply. Provides leadership for national programs and plans, conducts, fosters, and supports an integrated and coordinated program of basic research, clinical investigations and trials, and observational studies.

Office of Prevention, Education, and Control (OPEC)   Coordinates the dissemination of research findings and scientific consensus to health professionals, patients, and the public so that information can be adapted for and integrated into health care practice and individual health behavior. It oversees national health education programs and initiatives on high blood pressure, high blood cholesterol, asthma education and prevention, early warning signs of heart attack, obesity, and sleep disorders.

Women's Health Initiative (WHI)   Tests risk-factor identification, prevention, and intervention strategies to reduce coronary heart disease, breast and colorectal cancer, and osteoporotic fractures in postmenopausal women. WHI is to be conducted as a consortium effort led by NHLBI in cooperation with three other NIH institutes (National Institute of Arthritis and Musculoskeletal and Skin Diseases, National Cancer Institute, National Institute on Aging). The WHI is a large multitrial, multisite 15-year research project, launched in 1991, and was moved from the Office of Disease Prevention in October 1997.

National Human Genome Research Institute (NHGRI)   Heads up the role of NIH in the Human Genome Project, an international research program begun jointly under NIH and the Department of Energy, with expanded responsibilities to establish intramural research focusing on applying genome technologies to find human disease genes and to develop DNA-based diagnostics and gene therapies. NHGRI includes the Ethical, Legal, and Social Implications (ELSI) Branch, which explores issues in the responsible use of genetic information in clinical practice and by third parties including the study of ethical, legal, and social implications of human genome research. *Formerly:* National Center for Human Genome Research (1989).

National Institute on Aging (NIA)   Conducts and supports biomedical and behavioral research to increase knowledge of the aging process and the physical, psychological, and social factors associated with aging.

National Institute of Alcohol Abuse and Alcoholism (NIAAA)   Supports and conducts biomedical and behavioral research on the causes, consequences, treatment, and prevention of alcoholism and alcohol-related problems. NIAAA also provides leadership in the national effort to reduce these problems through promoting health services research, training, and health information distribution; through collaborating with other research institutes, programs, professional associations, and voluntary organizations; and through providing the comprehensive online database ETOH (named after the chemical name for ethyl alcohol).

National Institute of Allergy and Infectious Diseases (NIAID)   Conducts and supports broadly based research and research training on the cause, treatment, and prevention of a wide variety of infectious, allergic, and immunological diseases. Special emphasis is placed on AIDS, asthma and allergic diseases, immunologic diseases, transplantation, sexually transmitted diseases, enteric diseases (eg, hepatitis, influenza), tropical diseases, tuberculosis, and vaccine development.

National Institute of Arthritis and Musculoskeletal and Skin Diseases (NIAMS)   Conducts and supports fundamental research in the major disease categories of arthritis and musculoskeletal and skin diseases through research studies, epidemiologic studies, research grants, and cooperative agreements. It also collects and disseminates health educational materials on these diseases.

National Institute of Child Health and Human Development (NICHD)   Conducts and supports biomedical and behavioral research on child and maternal health; on problems of human development, with special reference to mental retardation; and on family structure, the dynamics of human population, and the reproductive process. NICHD recently added a National Center for Medical Rehabilitation Research, which conducts and supports research and research training related to people with physical disabilities.

National Institute on Deafness and Other Communication Disorders (NIDCD)   Conducts biomedical and behavioral research and research training on normal mechanisms as well as diseases and disorders of hearing, balance, smell, taste, voice, speech, and language.

National Institute of Dental Research (NIDR) Conducts and supports research and research training into the causes, prevention, diagnosis, and treatment of oral, dental, and craniofacial diseases and conditions.

National Institute of Diabetes and Digestive and Kidney Diseases (NIDDK)   Conducts research into the causes, prevention, diagnosis, and treatment of diabetes, endocrine and metabolic diseases, digestive diseases and nutrition, kidney and urologic diseases, and blood diseases. NIDDK also operates the Combined Health Information Database (CHID).

National Institute on Drug Abuse (NIDA)   Promotes strategic support and conducts research on the issues of drug abuse and drug addiction and uses results from research studies to develop improvements in drug-abuse and drug-addiction prevention, treatment, and policy. NIDA has developed the Web of Addictions initiative to combat pro-drug use messages and misinformation on the Internet.

National Institute of Environmental Health Sciences (NIEHS) Conducts and supports basic and applied research on how the environment interacts with genetic factors and age to cause disease and dysfunction. NIEHS supports a network of university-based environmental health science centers and operates the NIEHS Clearinghouse. (*Headquarters:* Research Triangle Park, NC)

National Institute of General Medical Sciences (NIGMS) Supports basic biomedical research that is not targeted to specific diseases but that increases understanding of life processes and lays the foundation for advances in disease diagnosis, treatment, and prevention.

National Institute of Mental Health (NIMH) Conducts a national program to increase knowledge and advance effective strategies to deal with problems and issues in the promotion of mental health and the prevention and treatment of mental illness. (*Headquarters:* Rockville, MD)

National Institute of Neurological Disorders and Stroke (NINDS) Serves as a lead agency for Congress's designated Decade of the Brain (1990s); conducts, fosters, coordinates, and guides research on causes, prevention, diagnosis, and treatment and supports basic research in related scientific areas.

National Institute of Nursing Research (NINR) Supports clinical and basic research to establish a scientific basis for the care of individuals across the life span—from management of patients during illness and recovery to the reduction of risks for disease and disability and the promotion of healthy lifestyles.

National Library of Medicine (NLM) Serves as the chief U.S. medical information source and is authorized to provide services and on-line bibliographical searching capabilities, such as MEDLINE and TOXLINE, to public and private agencies and organizations, institutions, and individuals. The NLM administers the National Center for Biotechnology Information and supports the National Network of Libraries of Medicine. An outgrowth of NLM's is the Visible Human Project, which is creating complete, anatomically detailed, 3-dimensional representations of the male and female human body, ultimately intended to link visual knowledge forms to symbolic knowledge formats (such as the names of body parts).

Office of the Director Contains several subunit offices to focus NIH-wide goals for health research and research training programs related to women and minorities, coordinates program direction, and ensures that these concerns are considered in research that NIH conducts or supports. The subunits in the Office of the Director are listed below.

Office of AIDS Research (OAR) Manages the scientific, budgetary, legislative, and policy elements of the NIH AIDS research program.

Office of Alternative Medicine (OAM) Identifies and evaluates unconventional health care practices; supports and conducts research and research training on these practices; and disseminates information.

Office of Behavioral and Social Sciences Research (OBSSR) Stimulates behavioral and social sciences research throughout NIH.

Office of Medical Applications of Research (OMAR) Serves as the focal point for health technology assessment and transfer activities at NIH; works closely with the NIH institutes and other divisions in administering the NIH Consensus Development Program, which convenes consensus development and technology assessment conferences and publishes and disseminates conference statements. OMAR also coordinates NIH responses to Medicare coverage issues.

Office for Protection from Research Risks (OPRR) Interprets and oversees implementation of the regulations regarding the Protection of Human Subjects.

Office of Research on Women's Health (ORWH) Works in collaboration and partnership with the NIH institutes and centers to establish NIH-wide goals and policies for research related to women's health and to coordinate NIH activities undertaken in performing such research. ORWH also is charged with interacting with other scientific and medical communities and organizations, Congress, and other components of government.

Women's Health Initiative *See under* National Heart, Lung, and Blood Institute (previous page).

Warren Grant Magnuson Clinical Center Serves as the research hospital for NIH and supports clinical investigations conducted by the institutes. The center was specially designed to bring patient-care facilities close to research labs so that findings of basic and clinical scientists can be moved quickly from labs to the treatment of patients.

Office of Public Health and Science (OPHS) *Founded:* 1995. *Headquarters:* Washington, DC. *Purpose:* To provide leadership and serve as the focal point for coordination across DHHS in public health and science. The office provides leadership for and management of the Office of Disease Prevention and Health Promotion (Healthy People 2000 and Healthy People 2010 work), Office of Emergency Preparedness, Office of HIV/AIDS, Office of Minority Health, Office of Population Affairs, Office of Research Integrity (ORI), Office of the Surgeon General, Office of Women's Health (OWH), and President's Council on Physical Fitness and Sports.

Substance Abuse and Mental Health Services Administration (SAMHSA) *Founded:* 1992. *Headquarters:* Rockville, MD. *Purpose:* To ensure that knowledge based on science and state-of- the-art practice is effectively used for the prevention and treatment of addictive and mental disorders. It improves access and reduces barriers to effective programs and services for individuals who are at risk, and for their families.

Center for Substance Abuse Prevention (CSAP) Promotes efforts to prevent alcohol and other drug abuse. It develops prevention and other health promotion policy; operates grant programs demonstrating prevention strategies among high-risk youth; and supports training for substance abuse practitioners and other health professionals involved in alcohol and drug abuse education.

Center for Substance Abuse Treatment (CSAT) Promotes the expansion of programs focusing on the treatment of substance abusers, as well as problems of physical illness and comorbidity. It promotes the mainstreaming of alcohol abuse, drug abuse, and mental health treatment into the health care system, and administers programs for the training of health and allied health providers. The CSAT issues a series of Treatment Improvement Protocols (TIPs).

Center for Mental Health Services (CMHS) Ensures the application of scientifically established findings and practice-based knowledge in the prevention and treatment of medical disorders. It also improves access, reduces barriers, and promotes high-quality, effective programs and services for people at risk of such disorders.

DEPARTMENT OF JUSTICE (DOJ)
Civil Rights Division *Founded:* 1957. *Headquarters:* Washington, DC. *Purpose:* To secure effective enforcement of civil rights and to serve as the primary institution within the federal government responsible for enforcing federal statutes prohibiting discrimination on the basis of race, sex, disability, religion, and national origin.

Disability Rights Section Enforces Titles I, II, and III of the Americans with Disabilities Act of 1990 (ADA) and DOJ regulations implementing these provisions, provides technical assistance to ADA-covered entities and ADA-protected persons, and coordinates the technical assistance efforts of all federal agencies with technical assistance responsibilities under the ADA. The section also certifies that state or local building codes meet or exceed ADA requirements and is also responsible for carrying out the DOJ's responsibilities under the Rehabilitation Act of 1973.

Drug Enforcement Administration (DEA) *Founded:* 1973. *Headquarters:* Arlington, VA. *Purpose:* To serve as the lead federal agency in enforcing narcotics and controlled substances laws and regulations. It enforces the provisions of the controlled substances and chemical diversion and trafficking laws and regulations of the United States.

Office of Justice Programs (OJP) *Founded:* 1984. *Headquarters:* Washington, DC. *Purpose:* To provide federal leadership, coordination, and assistance needed to make the nation's justice system more efficient and effective in preventing and controlling crime. OJP and its program bureaus are responsible for collecting and analyzing data, identifying emerging issues and testing approaches

to address them, evaluating program results, and disseminating these findings to state and local governments.

Drug Court Program Office Supports the development and implementation of effective Drug Court programming at the state, local, and tribal level, working closely with agencies and organizations involved in the areas of justice and recovery. The office administers a discretionary grant program targeting nonviolent, drug-involved offenders, and it promotes provision of continuing judicial supervision, mandatory periodic testing for substance abuse among clients, substance abuse treatment, and management and after care.

Corrections Program Office Provides leadership and assistance to state and local governments related to correctional policy and programs to reduce crime, increase public safety, and restore integrity to sentencing practices for violent offenders. Oversees the Residential Substance Abuse Treatment Program, which is designed to reduce drug and criminal activity among offenders released back into the community by expanding substance abuse treatment programs for offenders.

National Institute of Justice (NIJ) Sponsors research and development programs designed to improve and strengthen the criminal justice system and reduce or prevent crime and serves as the national and international clearinghouse of justice information for federal, state, and local governments. The NIJ evaluates innovative and promising drug control programs, including community antidrug initiatives and drug-testing programs, bootcamps, and intensive community supervision.

Office of Juvenile Justice and Delinquency Prevention (OJJDP) Oversees activities and requirements of the Juvenile Justice and Delinquency Prevention Act of 1974, administers activities under the Victims of Child Abuse Act of 1990, and funds the National Center for Missing and Exploited Children.

Office for Victims of Crime (OVC) Carries out the activities mandated by the Victims of Crime Act of 1984 (VOCA) and implements the recommendations of the President's Task Force on Victims of Crime and the Attorney General's Task Force on Family Violence.

Violence Against Women Program Office Coordinates the activities of all the OJP bureaus relating to violence against women and administers programs authorized by the Violence Against Women Act of 1994.

DEPARTMENT OF LABOR (DOL) *Founded:* 1913. *Headquarters:* Washington, DC. *Purpose:* To foster, promote, and develop the welfare of the wage earners of the United States, to improve their working conditions, and to advance their opportunities. To carry out its mission, the DOL administers a variety of federal labor laws guaranteeing workers' rights to safe and healthful working conditions, freedom from employment discrimination, workers, compensation, and other assistance.

Employment Standards Administration
Office of Workers' Compensation Programs Has responsibility for administering the federal government's three basic federal workers' compensation laws: the Federal Employees Compensation Act, the Longshore and Harbor Workers' Compensation Act; and the Black Lung Benefits Act.

Occupational Safety and Health Administration (OSHA) *Founded:* 1970. *Headquarters:* Washington, DC. *Purpose:* To develop and promulgate occupational safety and health standards; develop and issue regulations; conduct investigations and inspections to determine compliance; and to issue citations and propose penalties for noncompliance with safety and health standards. OSHA is charged with supporting the Occupational Safety and Health Act of 1970.

Pension and Welfare Benefits Administration (PWBA) Administers programs and plans required under the Employment Retirement Income Security Act of 1974 (ERISA) and is responsible for assuring responsible management of pension plans and health and welfare plans.

DEPARTMENT OF VETERANS AFFAIRS (VA)
Founded: 1930. *Headquarters:* Washington, DC. *Purpose:* To operate programs to benefit veterans and members of their families, including disability and death benefits, pensions, education, rehabilitation, and a medical care program incorporating nursing homes, clinics, and medical centers. The VA comprises three organizations that administer veterans programs: the Veterans Health Administration (VHA), the Veterans Benefits Administration (VBA), and the National Cemetery System. Each organization has a central office and field facilities. The VHA conducts both individual medical and health care delivery research projects and multihospital research programs in its VA Medical Centers (VAMCs), and it assists in the education and training of physicians and many other health care professionals. The VHA operates the Civilian Health and Medical Program (CHAMPVA), which provides dependents of certain veterans with medical care supplied by non-VA institutions and physicians. The VBA operates the Vocational Rehabilitation Service for disabled veterans and their immediate families and to certain handicapped dependents.

EXECUTIVE OFFICE OF THE PRESIDENT
Council on Environmental Quality *Founded:* 1969. *Headquarters:* Washington, DC. *Purpose:* To develop and recommend to the President national policies that further environmental quality; to perform a continuing analysis of changes or trends in the national environment; to help the President prepare the annual environmental quality report to the Congress, and to oversee implementation of the National Environmental Policy Act.

Office of National Drug Control Policy *Founded:* 1989. *Headquarters:* Washington, DC. *Purpose:* Coordinates federal, state, and local efforts to control illegal drug abuse and devises national strategies to effectively carry out antidrug activities.

LEGISLATIVE BRANCH

OFFICE OF TECHNOLOGY ASSESSMENT (OTA)
Founded: 1972. *Abolished:* 1995. *Purpose:* Was established as an organization of the U.S. Congress as a nonpartisan support agency to help Congress deal with issues of advanced technology and to anticipate and plan for the consequences of the use of technology. Some of the OTA's recent safety and efficacy studies and cost-benefit reports may still be available to purchase from the Government Printing Office or the National Technical Information Service.

U.S. GENERAL ACCOUNTING OFFICE (GAO)
Founded: 1921. *Headquarters:* Washington, DC. *Purpose:* To serve as the investigative arm of the Congress and to examine all matters relating to the receipt and disbursement of public funds. The Human Resources Division conducts health-related studies and the Audit Operations Group conducts audits on health care programs. The reports are made directly to the Congress but are often also made available to the public in published report form. The GAO announced the members of the new Medicare Payment Advisory Commission, created in the Balanced Budget Act of 1997.

INDEPENDENT ESTABLISHMENTS AND GOVERNMENT CORPORATIONS

Consumer Product Safety Commission (CPSC) *Founded:* 1973. *Headquarters:* Bethesda, MD. *Purpose:* To protect the public against unreasonable risks of injury from consumer products; to assist consumers in evaluating the comparative safety of consumer products; to develop uniform safety standards for consumer products and minimize conflicting state and local regulations; and to promote research and investigation into the causes and prevention of product-related deaths, illnesses, and injuries.

Environmental Protection Agency (EPA) *Founded:* 1970. *Headquarters:* Washington, DC. *Purpose:* To protect and enhance the environment currently and for future generations to the fullest extent possible under the laws enacted by Congress and through cooperation with state and local governments. The EPA works to control and abate pollution in the air, water, solid waste, pesticides, radiation, and toxic substances.

Federal Emergency Management Agency (FEMA) *Founded:* 1979. *Headquarters:* Washington, DC. *Purpose:* To serve as the central agency within the federal government for emergency planning, preparedness, mitigation, response, and recovery, through working closely with state and local governments. FEMA funds emergency programs, offers technical guidance and training, and deploys federal resources in times of catastrophic disaster.

Social Security Administration (SSA) *Founded:* 1946. *Headquarters:* Baltimore, MD. *Purpose:* To manage the nation's social insurance program, consisting of retirement, survivors, and disability insurance programs (Social Security) and to administer the Supplemental Security Income (SSI) program for the aged, blind, and disabled. While the administration of Medicare is HCFA's responsibility, the SSA provides Medicare assistance to the public through SSA district offices and processing centers and adjudicates requests for hearings and appeals of Medicare claims. By agreement with the Department of Labor, the SSA is involved in certain aspects of the administration of black lung benefits.

BOARDS, COMMISSIONS, COMMITTEES, AND QUASI-GOVERNMENTAL ORGANIZATIONS

Institute of Medicine (IOM) *Founded:* 1970. *Headquarters:* Washington, DC. *Purpose:* To serve as a component within the National Academy of Sciences to enlist distinguished members of the appropriate professions in the examination of policy matters pertaining to the health of the public. The IOM acts under both the academy's 1863 congressional charter responsibility to be an advisor to the federal government and its own initiative in identifying issues of medical care, research, and education. The IOM accomplishes its mission to advance scientific knowledge and health by providing objective, timely, and authoritative information to the government, the professions, and the public. Program operations in the IOM are Neuroscience and Behavioral Health; the Board on Children, Youth, and Families; Board on International Health; Food and Nutrition Board (FNB); Health Care Services; Health Promotion and Disease Prevention (includes AIDS Program); Health Sciences Policy; Medical Follow-up Agency; National Cancer Policy Board (a joint board with the Commission on Life Sciences); and Office of Health Policy Programs and Fellowships.

Medicare Payment Advisory Commission (MedPAC) *Founded:* 1997. *Headquarters:* Washington, DC. *Purpose:* Merges the functions of the Physician Payment Review Commission (PPRC) and the Prospective Payment Assessment Commission (ProPAC), both of which were abolished in the Balanced Budget Act of 1997 restructuring of Medicare payment processes. The commission is a nonpartisan congressional advisory body charged with providing policy advice and technical assistance concerning Medicare, Medicaid, and other aspects of the health system.

Physician Payment Review Commission *Founded:* 1986. *Abolished:* 1997. *See* Medicare Payment Advisory Commission (above).

President's Advisory Commission on Consumer Protection and Quality in the Health Care Industry *Founded:* 1996. *Headquarters:* Washington, DC. *Purpose:* To advise the President on changes occurring in the health care system and, where appropriate, to make recommendations on how best to promote and ensure consumer protection and health care quality. The Commission, created by executive order, is guided by regulations on the formation and use of advisory committees and is mandated to make a preliminary and a final report to the President in 1998. Subcommittees are Consumer Rights, Protections, and Responsibilities; Performance Measurement and Quality Oversight; Quality Improvement Environment; and Roles and Responsibilities of Public and Private Purchasers and Quality Oversight Organizations. The Commission is cochaired by the secretaries of DHHS and the Department of Labor.

Prospective Payment Assessment Commission *Founded:* 1983. *Abolished:* 1997. *See* Medicare Payment Advisory Commission (above).

APPENDIX B

ACRONYMS AND ABBREVIATIONS

Symbols

$24°$	24 hours
$\bar{p}$	after
H_a	alternative hypothesis
$\approx$	approximate
$\bar{\bar{X}}$	average of averages
a	before
δ	cell deviation
$\sqrt{\bar{c}}$	check with
χ^2	chi square (test)
$1-\alpha$	confidence coefficient level
$\downarrow$	decreased
$\int_a^b$	definite integral
°	degree
$\wedge$	diastolic blood pressure
$\div$	divided by
$\neq$	does not equal
$\wedge$	estimate of
$=$	equals
'	foot
#	fracture; number; pound
$\Gamma(r)$	gamma function
$>$	greater than
$\tau^{1/2}$	half-life (time)
"	inch
$\uparrow$	increased
∞	infinity
$\int$	integral
β_0	intercept in a regression equation
$<$	less than
τ	life (time)

$\times$	magnification; multiplied by
μ	mean (of population)
$\tilde{x}$	median
Π	multiply by
$-$	negative
$\emptyset$	normal
H_0	null hypothesis
$/$	per
$\%$	percent
ϕ	phi coefficient
π	ratio of circumference of a circle to its diameter (3.1416)
$+$	positive
$\pm$	positive or negative
α	probability of a type I error
β	probability of a type II error
$:$	ratio
$\sqrt{}$	root/square root
$\bar{x}$	sample mean
2d	second
$2°$	secondary
σ	1/1000 of a second; standard deviation
β_n	slope in a regression equation
Σ	sum of
$\vee$	systolic blood pressure
Δt	time interval
σ^2	variance (population)
λ	wavelength
$\bar{c}$	with
$\bar{s}$	without

Greek Alphabet

Letter	Lower Case	Capitol	Letter	Lower Case	Capitol
alpha	α	A	omega	ω	Ω
beta	β	B	omicron	o	O
chi	χ	X	phi	ϕ	Φ
delta	δ	Δ	pi	π	Π
epsilon	ϵ	E	psi	ψ	Ψ
eta	η	H	rho	ρ	P
gamma	γ	Γ	sigma	σ	Σ
iota	ι	I	tau	τ	T
kappa	κ	K	theta	θ	Θ
lambda	λ	Λ	upsilon	υ	Y
mu	μ	M	xi	ξ	Ξ
nu	ν	N	zeta	ζ	Z

4 As   Ask, Advise, Assist, Arrange

A   artery

ā   before

aa   *ana* (so much of each); arteries

AA   Alcoholics Anonymous World Services; anesthesiologist's assistant

AAA   abdominal aortic aneurysm; American Academy of Actuaries; American Academy of Audiology; American Acupuncture Association; American Ambulance Association; American Association of Anatomists

AAAAI   American Academy of Allergy, Asthma and Immunology

AAAASF   American Association for Accreditation of Ambulatory Surgery Facilities

AAACN   American Academy of Ambulatory Care Nursing

AAAHC   Accreditation Association for Ambulatory Health Care

AAAI   American Academy of Allergy and Immunology; American Association for Artificial Intelligence

AAALAC   American Association for Accreditation of Laboratory Animal Care

AAAM   Association for the Advancement of Automotive Medicine

AAANA   American Academy of Ambulatory Nursing Administration

AAAOM   American Association for Acupuncture and Oriental Medicine

AAAP   American Academy of Addiction Psychiatry

AAAS   American Association for the Advancement of Science

AAB   American Association of Bioanalysts

AABB   American Association of Blood Banks

AABHC   Association for Ambulatory Behavioral Health Care

AABR   Association for Advancement of Blind and Retarded

AABT   Association for Advancement of Behavior Therapy

AAC   Association for Assessment in Counseling

AACA   American Association of Certified Allergists

AACAP   American Academy of Child and Adolescent Psychiatry

AACBP   American Academy of Fixed Prosthodontics

AACC   American Association for Clinical Chemistry; American Association for Continuity of Care

AACCN   American Association of Critical Care Nurses

AACDP   American Association of Chairmen of Departments of Psychiatry

AACE   American Association for Cancer Education; American Association of Clinical Endocrinologists

AACI   American Academy of Crisis Interveners; Association of American Cancer Institutes

AACN   American Association of Colleges of Nursing; American Association of Critical-Care Nurses

AACO   American Association of Certified Orthoptists

AACOM   American Association of Colleges of Osteopathic Medicine

AACP   American Academy of Clinical Psychiatrists; American Association of Colleges of Pharmacy; American Association of Community Psychiatrists; American Association for Correctional Psychology

AACPDM   American Academy for Cerebral Palsy and Developmental Medicine

AACPM   American Association of Colleges of Podiatric Medicine

AACR   American Association for Cancer Research

AACRC   American Association of Children's Residential Centers

AACS   American Academy of Cosmetic Surgery

AACT   American Academy of Clinical Toxicology

AACU   American Association of Clinical Urologists

AACVPR   American Association of Cardiovascular and Pulmonary Rehabilitation

AAD   American Academy of Dermatology

AADA   Association for Adult Development and Aging

AADC   American Association of Dental Consultants

AADE   American Academy of Dental Electrosurgery; American Association of Dental Editors; American Association of Dental Examiners; American Association of Diabetes Educators

AADEP   American Academy of Disability Evaluating Physicians

AADGP   American Academy of Dental Group Practice

AADPA   American Academy of Dental Practice Administration

AADPRT   American Association of Directors of Psychiatric Residency Training

AADR   American Association for Dental Research

AADS   American Association of Dental Schools

AAE   American Association of Endodontists

AAED   American Association of Entrepreneurial Dentists

AAEE   American Academy of Environmental Engineers

AAEEH   American Association of Eye and Ear Hospitals

AAEH   Association to Advance Ethical Hypnosis

AAEM   American Academy of Environmental Medicine; American Association of Electrodiagnostic Medicine

AAFO   American Association for Functional Orthodontics

AAFP   American Academy of Family Physicians; American Academy of Forensic Psychology

AAFPRS   American Academy of Facial Plastic and Reconstructive Surgery

AAFS   Academy of Ambulatory Foot Surgery; American Academy of Forensic Sciences

AAGFO   American Academy of Gold Foil Operators

AAGL   American Association of Gynecological Laparoscopists

AAGO   American Academy of Gnathologic Orthopedics

AAGP   American Association for Geriatric Psychiatry

AAGUS   American Association of Genito-Urinary Surgeons

AAH   Alliance for Alternatives in Healthcare

AAHA   American Academy of Healthcare Attorneys (now NHLA/AAHA); American Association of Homes for the Aging

AAHC   American Association of Healthcare Consultants; Association of Academic Health Centers

AAHCC   American Academy of Husband-Coached Childbirth

AAHD   American Academy of the History of Dentistry; American Association of Hospital Dentists

AAHE   Association for the Advancement of Health Education

AAHM   American Association for the History of Medicine

AAHN   American Association for the History of Nursing

AAHP   American Association of Health Plans; American Association of Homeopathic Pharmacists; American Association of Hospital Podiatrists

AAHPM   American Academy of Hospice and Palliative Medicine

AAHS   American Association for Hand Surgery

AAHSA   American Association of Homes and Services for the Aging

AAHSLD   Association of Academic Health Sciences Library Directors

AAI   American Association of Immunologists

AAID   American Academy of Implant Dentistry

AAIH   American Academy of Industrial Hygiene

AAIM   American Academy of Insurance Medicine; American Association of Industrial Management

AAIP   American Academy of Implant Prosthodontics; Association of American Indian Physicians

AAISW   American Association of Industrial Social Workers

AALAS   American Association for Laboratory Animal Science

AALIM   American Society of Legal and Industrial Medicine

AALNC   American Association of Legal Nurse Consultants

AAM   American Academy of Microbiology

AAMA   American Academy of Medical Administrators; American Association of Medical Assistants

AAMC   American Association of Medico-Legal Consultants; Association of American Medical Colleges

AAMFT   American Association for Marriage and Family Therapy

AAMHPC   American Association of Mental Health Professionals in Corrections

AAMI   Association for the Advancement of Medical Instrumentation

AAMLA   American Academy of Medical-Legal Analysis

AAMMC   American Association of Medical Milk Commissions

AAMN   American Assembly for Men in Nursing

AAMP   American Academy of Maxillofacial Prosthetics

AAMR   American Academy on Mental Retardation; American Association on Mental Retardation

AAMS   Association of Air Medical Services

AAMSE   American Association of Medical Society Executives

AAMT   American Association for Medical Transcription; American Association for Music Therapy

AAN   American Academy of Neurology; American Academy of Nursing

AANA   American Association of Nurse Anesthetists; Arthroscopy Association of North America

AANC   American Association of Nutritional Consultants

AANFA   African-American Natural Foods Association

AANFP   American Academy of Natural Family Planning

AANN   American Association of Neuroscience Nurses

AANP   American Academy of Nurse Practitioners; American Association of Naturopathic Physicians; American Association of Neuropathologists

AANS   American Association of Neurological Surgeons

AAO   American Academy of Ophthalmology; American Academy of Optometry; American Academy of Osteopathy; American Association of Orthodontists

AAOA   American Academy of Otolaryngic Allergy

AAOE   American Association of Osteopathic Examiners

AAOGP   American Academy of Orthodontics for the General Practitioner

AAOHN   American Association of Occupational Health Nurses

AAO-HNS   American Academy of Otolaryngology–Head and Neck Surgery

AAOM   American Academy of Oral Medicine; American Association of Orthomolecular Medicine; American Association of Orthopaedic Medicine

AAOMP   American Academy of Oral and Maxillofacial Pathology

AAOMR   American Academy of Oral and Maxillofacial Radiology

AAOMS   American Association of Oral and Maxillofacial Surgeons

AAON   American Association of Office Nurses

AAOP   American Academy of Oral Pathology; American Academy of Orthotists and Prosthetists

AAOS   American Academy of Orthopaedic Surgeons

AAP   American Academy of Pediatrics; American Academy of Periodontology; American Academy of Psychoanalysis; American Academy of Psychotherapists; American Association for Parapsychology; American Association of Pathologists; American Association of Psychiatrists from India; Association of Academic Physiatrists; Association for Advancement of Psychology; Association for the Advancement of Psychotherapy; Association of American Physicians; Association for Applied Poetry; Association for Applied Psychoanalysis; Association of Aviation Psychologists

AAPA   American Academy of Physician Assistants; American Academy of Podiatric Administration; American Association of Pathologists' Assistants; American Association of Psychiatric Administrators; Asian American Psychological Association

AAPAA   American Academy of Psychiatrists in Alcoholism and Addictions

AAPB   Association for Applied Psychophysiology and Biofeedback

AAPC   American Association of Pastoral Counselors; American Association for Protecting Children

AAPCC   adjusted average per capita cost, American Association of Poison Control Centers

AAPD   American Academy of Pediatric Dentistry

AAPH   American Association for Partial Hospitalization; American Association of Professional Hypnotherapists

AAPHD   American Association of Public Health Dentistry

AAPHO   American Association of Physician-Hospital Organizations

AAPHP   American Association of Public Health Physicians

AAPHR   American Association of Physicians for Human Rights

AAPL   American Academy of Psychiatry and the Law

AAPM   American Academy of Pain Medicine; American Association of Physicists in Medicine

AAPM&R   American Academy of Physical Medicine and Rehabilitation

AAPOR   American Association for Public Opinion Research

AAPPO   American Association of Preferred Provider Organizations

AAPPS   American Association of Podiatric Physicians and Surgeons

AAPS   American Association of Pharmaceutical Scientists; American Association of Plastic Surgeons; American Association of Physician Specialists; Association of American Physicians and Surgeons

AAPSC   American Association of Psychiatric Services for Children

AAPSM   American Academy of Podiatric Sports Medicine

AAR   Alliance for Aging Research; Association for Automated Reasoning

AARC   American Association for Respiratory Care

AARD   American Academy of Restorative Dentistry

AARP   American Association of Retired Persons

AARS   American Association of Railway Surgeons

AART   American Association for Rehabilitation Therapy; American Association of Religious Therapists

AAS   American Academy of Sanitarians; American Academy of Somnology; American Apitherapy Society; American Association of Stomatologists; American Association of Suicidology; American Auditory Society; Association for Academic Surgery

AASA   American Association of Surgeon Assistants

AASCIN   American Association of Spinal Cord Injury Nurses

AASCIPSW   American Association of Spinal Cord Injury Psychologists and Social Workers

AASECT   American Association of Sex Educators, Counselors and Therapists

AASH   American Association for the Study of Headache

AASLD   American Association for the Study of Liver Diseases

AASND   American Association for the Study of Neoplastic Diseases

AASP   American Academy of Sports Physicians; American Association of Senior Physicians; American Association for Social Psychiatry

AASS   American Academy of Spinal Surgeons

AASSWB   American Association of State Social Work Boards

AAST   American Association for the Surgery of Trauma

AAT   alpha-1 antitrypsin (deficiency); American Academy of Thermology

AATA   American Art Therapy Association; American Athletic Trainers Association and Certification Board

AATB   American Association of Tissue Banks

AATH   American Association for Therapeutic Humor

AATM   American Academy of Tropical Medicine

AATP   American Association of Testifying Physicians

AATS   American Association for Thoracic Surgery

AAUAP   American Association of University Affiliated Programs for Persons with Developmental Disabilities

AAWD   American Association of Women Dentists

AAWH   American Association for World Health

AAWR   American Association for Women Radiologists

Ab   abortion; antibody

ABA   American Bar Association; American Board of Anesthesiology; American Burn Association; Association for Behavior Analysis

ABACPR   American Bar Association Center for Professional Responsibility

ABAI   American Board of Allergy and Immunology

ABAS   American Board of Abdominal Surgery

ABB   American Board of Bioanalysis

ABBRP   American Board of Bionic Rehabilitative Psychology

ABC   airway, breathing, circulation; American Blood Commission; American Board for Certification in Orthotics and Prosthetics; Association of Black Cardiologists

ABCA   American Black Chiropractors Association

ABCC   American Board of Clinical Chemistry

ABCP   American Board of Cardiovascular Perfusion

ABCRETT   American Board of Certified and Registered Encephalographic Technicians and Technologists

ABCRS   American Board of Colon and Rectal Surgery

ABCT   American Board of Chelation Therapy

ABD   abdominal; American Board of Dermatology

ABDPH   American Board of Dental Public Health

ABE   American Board of Endodontics

ABEA   American Broncho-Esophagological Association

ABEM   American Board of Emergency Medicine; American Board of Environmental Medicine

ABEPC   American Board of Examiners in Pastoral Counseling

ABEPSGP   American Board of Examiners of Psychodrama, Sociometry, and Group Psychotherapy

ABFP   American Board of Family Practice; American Board of Forensic Psychiatry

ABG   arterial blood gas

ABHES   Accrediting Bureau of Health Education Schools

ABHHA   American Baptist Homes and Hospitals Association

ABHP   American Board of Health Physics

ABHS   American Board of Hand Surgery

ABIH   American Board of Industrial Hygiene

ABIM   American Board of Internal Medicine

ABIMS   American Board of Industrial Medicine and Surgery

ABJS   Association of Bone and Joint Surgeons

ABMG   American Board of Medical Genetics

ABMLAMS   American Board of Medical-Legal Analysis in Medicine and Surgery

ABMP   Academy of Behavioral Medicine Research; American Board of Medical Psychotherapists; Associated Bodywork and Massage Professionals

ABMR   Academy of Behavioral Medicine Research

ABMS   American Board of Medical Specialties

ABMT   American Board of Medical Toxicology; autologous bone marrow transplant

ABN   abnormal; American Board of Nutrition

ABNF   Association of Black Nursing Faculty in Higher Education

ABNM   American Board of Neurological Microsurgery; American Board of Nuclear Medicine

ABNN   American Board of Neuroscience Nursing

ABNOLS   American Board of Neurological/Orthopaedic Laser Surgery

ABNOMS   American Board of Neurological and Orthopaedic Medicine and Surgery

ABNS   American Board of Neurological Surgery

ABO   American Board of Ophthalmology; American Board of Opticianry; American Board of Orthodontics; American Board of Otolaryngology

ABOG   American Board of Obstetrics and Gynecology

ABOHN   American Board for Occupational Health Nurses

ABOMS   American Board of Oral and Maxillofacial Surgery

ABOP   American Board of Oral Pathology

ABOS   American Board of Orthopaedic Surgery

ABP   American Board of Pathology; American Board of Pediatrics; American Board of Pedodontics; American

Board of Periodontology; American Board of Prosthodontics; Association for Birth Psychology

ABPANC American Board of Post Anesthesia Nursing Certification

ABPD American Board of Pediatric Dentistry

ABPDC American Board of Professional Disability Consultants

ABPH American Board of Psychological Hypnosis

ABPLA American Board of Professional Liability Attorneys

ABPM ambulatory blood pressure monitoring; American Board of Preventive Medicine

ABPMR American Board of Physical Medicine and Rehabilitation

ABPN American Board of Psychiatry and Neurology

ABPO American Board of Podiatric Orthopedics

ABPP American Board of Professional Psychology

ABPS American Board of Plastic Surgery; American Board of Podiatric Surgery

ABPsi Association of Black Psychologists

ABQAURP American Board of Quality Assurance and Utilization Review Physicians

ABR American Board of Radiology; auditory brainstem response

ABRA American Blood Resources Association

ABRET American Board of Registration of Electroencephalographic and Evoked Potentials Technologists

ABS American Board of Surgery

ABSS American Board of Spinal Surgery

ABT American Board of Toxicology

ABTA American Board of Trial Advocates

ABTM American Board of Tropical Medicine

ABTS American Board of Thoracic Surgery

ABTSA Association for the Behavioral Treatment of Sexual Abusers

ABU American Board of Urology

ABUAHP American Board of Urologic Allied Health Professionals

ac acid; *ante cibum* (before a meal)

AC (Joint Commission) Accreditation Committee

ACA against clinical advice; American Chiropractic Association; American College of Angiology; American College of Apothecaries; American Consumers Association; American Council on Alcoholism; American Counseling Association

ACACN American Council of Applied Clinical Nutrition

ACAAI American College of Allergy, Asthma and Immunology

ACAI American College of Allergy and Immunology

ACAM American College of Advancement in Medicine

ACAP American Council on Alcohol Problems

ACATA American College of Addiction Treatment Administrators

ACBE air contrast barium enema

ACC American College of Cardiology; Association of Chiropractic Colleges

ACCA American Clinical and Climatological Association; American College of Cardiovascular Administrators

ACCC Association of Community Cancer Centers

ACCE American College for Continuing Education

ACCH Association for the Care of Children's Health

ACCME Accreditation Council for Continuing Medical Education

ACCMS American Center for Chinese Medical Sciences

ACCO American College of Chiropractic Orthopedists

ACCP American College of Chest Physicians; American College of Clinical Pharmacology; American College of Clinical Pharmacy

ACCRYO American College of Cryosurgery

ACD American College of Dentists

ACDD Accreditation Council on Services for People with Disabilities

ACDE American Council for Drug Education

ACE American College of Epidemiology; angiotensin-converting enzyme (inhibitor); Association for Continuing Education

ACEHSA Accrediting Commission on Education for Health Services Administration

ACEP American College of Emergency Physicians

ACF Administration for Children and Families

ACFO American College of Foot Orthopedists

ACFS American College of Foot Surgeons

ACG American College of Gastroenterology

ACGIH American Conference of Governmental Industrial Hygienists

ACGME Accreditation Council for Graduate Medical Education

ACGPOMS American College of General Practitioners in Osteopathic Medicine and Surgery

ACHA American College Health Association

ACHCA American College of Health Care Administrators

ACHCL Academy for Catholic Healthcare Leadership

ACHE American College of Healthcare Executives; American Council of Hypnotist Examiners

AChemS   Association for Chemoreception Sciences

ACHSA   American Correctional Health Services Association

ACI   Alcohol Clinical Index

ACIP   Advisory Committee on Immunization Practices

ACI-TIPI   Acute Coronary Ischemia Time Insensitive Predictive Instrument

ACL   acceptance control limit

ACLA   American Clinical Laboratory Association

ACLAM   American College of Laboratory Animal Medicine

ACLM   American College of Legal Medicine

ACLS   advanced cardiac life support

ACM   American College of Medicine; Association for Computing Machinery

ACMGA   American College of Medical Group Administrators

ACMHA   American College of Mental Health Administration

ACMMSCO   American College of Mohs Micrographic Surgery and Cutaneous Oncology

ACN   American College of Neuropsychiatrists; American College of Nutrition

ACNM   American College of Nuclear Medicine; American College of Nurse-Midwives

ACNP   American College of Neuropsychopharmacology; American College of Nuclear Physicians

ACOEM   American College of Occupational and Environmental Medicine

ACOEP   American College of Osteopathic Emergency Physicians

ACOG   American College of Obstetricians and Gynecologists

ACOI   American College of Osteopathic Internists

ACOMS   American College of Oral and Maxillofacial Surgeons

ACOOG   American College of Osteopathic Obstetricians and Gynecologists

ACOP   American College of Osteopathic Pediatricians

ACORE   Advisory Council for Orthopedic Resident Education

ACOS   American College of Osteopathic Surgeons

ACP   American College of Physicians; American College of Podopediatrics; American College of Prosthodontists; American College of Psychiatrists; Associates of Clinical Pharmacology; Association for Child Psychoanalysis

ACPA   American Cleft Palate-Craniofacial Association; American College of Psychoanalysts

ACPE   American College of Physician Executives; American Council on Pharmaceutical Education; Association for Clinical Pastoral Education

ACPM   American College of Preventive Medicine

ACPOC   Association of Children's Prosthetic-Orthotic Clinics

ACPR   American College of Podiatric Radiologists

ACR   adjusted community rate; American College of Radiology; American College of Rheumatology

ACRM   American Congress of Rehabilitation Medicine

ACRRT   American Chiropractic Registry of Radiologic Technologists

ACS   ambulatory care sensitive (admission); American Cancer Society; American College of Surgeons; American Cryonics Society

ACS/DSC   American Celiac Society/Dietary Support Coalition

ACSH   American Council on Science and Health

ACSM   American College of Sports Medicine

ACSW   Academy of Certified Social Workers

ACT   activated clotting time; Alliance for Cannabis Therapeutics; American College Testing; American College of Toxicology; Association of Cytogenetic Technologists

ACTG   AIDS Clinical Trial Group

ACTH   adrenocorticotropin hormone

ACTL   American College of Trial Lawyers

ACT-UP   AIDS Coalition to Unleash Power

ACURP   American College of Medical Quality

ACUS   atypical cells of undetermined significance

ACYF   Administration on Children, Youth, and Families

AD   Alzheimer's disease; *aurum dextra* (right ear)

A/D   alcohol/drug

ADA   Academy of Dispensing Audiologists; American Dental Association; American Dermatological Association; American Diabetes Association; American Dietetic Association; Americans with Disabilities Act of 1990

ADAA   American Dental Assistants Association

ADAP   AIDS Drug Assistance Program

ADARA   American Deafness and Rehabilitation Center

ADD   adduction; Administration on Developmental Disabilities; attention deficit disorder

ADDS   alternative dental delivery system; American Diopter and Decibel Society

ADEC   Association for Death Education and Counseling

Adeq   adequate

ADH   Academy of Dentistry for the Handicapped; atypical ductal hyperplasia

ADHA American Dental Hygienists' Association

ADHD attention-deficit/hyperactivity disorder

ADHF American Digestive Health Foundation

ADI Adolescent Drinking Index

ADL activities of daily living

ad lib as much as needed/as desired

ADM admission; Academy of Dental Materials

ADON assistant director of nursing

ADR adverse drug reaction

ADS alternative delivery system

ADSA American Dental Society of Anesthesiology

ADT admissions, discharges, transfers; alternate day therapy

ADTA American Dance Therapy Association; American Dental Trade Association

AE above elbow

AEA American Electrology Association

AEEGS American Electroencephalographic Society

AEEP Association of Environmental Engineering Professors

AES American Endodontic Society; American Epidemiological Society; American Epilepsy Society; American Equilibration Society

AF atrial fibrillation

AFA American Fitness Association; American Fracture Association

AFAR American Federation for Aging Research

AFASAK Atrial Fibrillation, Aspirin, Anticoagulation (Study)

AFB acid fast bacilli; Association for Fitness in Business

AFCR American Federation for Clinical Research

AFDC Aid to Families with Dependent Children

AFDO Association of Food and Drug Officials

AFHHA American Federation of Home Health Agencies

AFIP Armed Forces Institute of Pathology

AFMA American Federation of Medical Accreditation

AFMH Association for Faculty in the Medical Humanities

AFOS Armed Forces Optometric Society

AFP alpha-fetoprotein

AFROC Association of Freestanding Radiation Oncology Centers

AFS alternative financing system; American Fertility Society

AFTA American Family Therapy Association

Ag antigen

AG Association for Gnotobiotics

A/G albumin/globulin ration

AGA American Gastroenterological Association; American Genetic Association

AGD Academy of General Dentistry

AGH American Guild of Hypnotherapists

agit agitate (shake)

AGLBIC Association for Gay, Lesbian, and Bisexual Issues in Counseling

AGLP Association of Gay and Lesbian Psychiatrists

AGOS American Gynecological and Obstetrical Society

AGPA American Group Practice Association; American Group Psychotherapy Association

AGS American Geriatrics Society

AGSG Alliance of Genetic Support Groups

AHA American Healing Association; American Heart Association; American Hospital Association; American Hypnosis Association; American Hypnotists' Association

AHC academic health centers; Advocate Health Care; ambulatory health care; Association for the History of Chiropractic

AHCA American Health Care Association

AHCM Academy of Hazard Control Management

AHCPR Agency for Health Care Policy and Research

AHD American Health Decisions

AHF antihemophilic factor

AHFSA Association of Health Facility Survey Agencies

AHG antihemophilic globulin

AHHAP Association of Halfway House Alcoholism Programs of North America

AHIA Association of Healthcare Internal Auditors

AHIMA American Health Information Management Association

AHLC American Hair Loss Council

AHMA American Holistic Medical Association

AHME Association of Hospital Medical Education

AHNA American Holistic Nurses Association

AHP Academy of Hospice Physicians; accountable health plan; Association for Healthcare Philanthropy; Association for Humanistic Psychology

AHPA American Health Planning Association; Arthritis Health Professions Association

AHRA American Healthcare Radiology Administrators

AHSM Academy for Health Services Marketing

AHSR Association for Health Services Research

AHTA American Horticultural Therapy Association

AI aortic insufficiency; artificial intelligence

AIBS American Institute of Biological Sciences

AICCP Association of the Institute for Certification of Computer Professionals

AICPA American Institute of Certified Public Accountants

AID artificial insemination by donor

AIDS acquired immunodeficiency syndrome

AIH American Institute of Homeopathy; artificial insemination by husband

AIHA American Industrial Hygiene Association

AIHC American Industrial Health Council

AIHCA American Indian Health Care Association

AIHP American Institute of the History of Pharmacy

AIM American Institute of Management; Association for Information Management; Automatic Identification Manufacturers

AIMS Arthritis Impact Measurement Scale

AIN American Institute of Nutrition

AIOB American Institute of Oral Biology

AIR American Institutes for Research in the Behavioral Sciences

AIRE Acute Infarction Ramipril Efficacy (study)

AIS Abbreviated Injury Scale; American Institute of Stress

AIT Academy for Implants and Transplants

AIUM American Institute of Ultrasound in Medicine

AJCC American Joint Committee on Cancer

AJDC *American Journal of Diseases of Children*

AJR *American Journal of Roentgenology*

AK above knee

AKA above knee amputation; also known as; American Kinesitherapy Association

ALA American Longevity Association; American Lung Association

alb albumin

ALD alcoholic liver disease

ALL AirLifeLine

ALMI American Leprosy Missions

ALOS average length of stay

ALPNA American Licensed Practical Nurses Association

ALROS American Laryngological, Rhinological and Otological Society

ALS advanced life support; amyotrophic lateral sclerosis

AM morning (midnight to before noon)

AMA against medical advice; Alternative Medical Association; American Management Association; American Medical Association

AMAA American Medical Athletic Association

AMAP American Medical Accreditation Program

amb ambulatory

AMBHA American Managed Behavioral Healthcare Association

AMCHP Association of Maternal and Child Health Programs

AMCPA American Managed Care Pharmacy Association

AMCRA American Managed Care and Review Association; American Medical Care Review Association

AMDA American Medical Directors Association

AMDM Association of Microbiological Diagnostic Manufacturers

AMEEGA American Medical Electroencephalographic Association

AMERSA Association of Medical Education and Research in Substance Abuse

AMGA American Medical Group Association

AMH *Accreditation Manual for Hospitals*

AMHA Association of Mental Health Administrators

AMHC *Accreditation Manual for Home Care*; Association of Mental Health Clergy

AMHCA American Mental Health Counselors Association

AMHCN *Accreditation Manual for Health Care Networks*

AMHE Association of Haitian Physicians Abroad

AMHPS Association of Minority Health Professions Schools

AMI acute myocardial infarction; Association of Medical Illustrators

AMIA American Medical Informatics Association

AMLTC *Accreditation Manual for Long Term Care*

amp amputation

AMP Association for Media Psychology

AMPA American Medical Publishers' Association

AMPAC American Medical Political Action Committee

AMPPO *Accreditation Manual for Preferred Provider Organizations*

AMPRA American Medical Peer Review Association

AMRA American Medical Records Association; Association of Medical Rehabilitation Administrators

AMRRC American Medical Review Research Center

AMS American Microscopical Society; American Motility Society

AmSECT American Society of Extra-Corporeal Technology

AMSPDC Association of Medical School Pediatric Department Chairmen

AMSUS Association of Military Surgeons of the United States

amt amount

AMT American Medical Technologists

AMTA American Massage Therapy Association

AMWA American Medical Women's Association; American Medical Writers' Association

ANA Administration for Native Americans; American Naprapathic Association; American Neurological Association; American Nurses' Association; American Nutritionists Association; antinuclear antibodies

ANAA Administration for Native Americans; American Nursing Assistant's Association

ANAC Association of Nurses in AIDS Care

ANDA abbreviated new-drug application

ANF anuric renal failure

ANHS American Natural Hygiene Society

ANNA American Nephrology Nurses' Association

ANS American Neurotology Society

ANSI American National Standards Institute

ant anterior

Anti antibody

ANR Americans for Nonsmokers' Rights

ANRF American Nonsmokers' Rights Foundation

AOA Alpha Omega Alpha; American Optometric Association; American Orthopaedic Association; American Osteopathic Association; Association of Otolaryngology Administrators

AOAO American Osteopathic Academy of Orthopedics

AOAS American Osteopathic Academy of Sclerotherapy

AOASM American Osteopathic Academy of Sports Medicine

AOBEM American Osteopathic Board of Emergency Medicine

AOBGP American Osteopathic Board of General Practice

AOBP American Osteopathic Board of Pediatrics

AOBTA American Oriental Bodywork Therapy Association

AOC American Orthoptic Council; (Joint Commission) Audit and Oversight Committee

AOCA American Osteopathic College of Anesthesiologists

AOCAI American Osteopathic College of Allergy and Immunology

AOCD American Osteopathic College of Dermatology

AOCP American Osteopathic College of Pathologists

AOCPM American Osteopathic College of Preventive Medicine

AOCPr American Osteopathic College of Proctology

AOCR American Osteopathic College of Radiology

AOCRM American Osteopathic College of Rehabilitation Medicine

AOD Academy of Operative Dentistry; alcohol and other drugs

AODM adult onset diabetes mellitus

AODME Academy of Osteopathic Directors of Medical Education

AODRM Academy of Oral Diagnosis, Radiology, and Medicine

AOE Association of Optometric Educators

AOFAS American Orthopedic Foot and Ankle Society

AOHA American Osteopathic Hospital Association

AONE American Organization of Nurse Executives; Association of Nurse Executives

AOPA American Orthotic and Prosthetic Association

AOQ average outgoing quality

AOQL average outgoing quality limit

AORN Association of Operating Room Nurses

AOS Academic Orthopaedic Society; American Ophthalmological Society; American Orthodontic Society; American Otological Society

AOSED Association of Osteopathic State Executive Directors

AOSSM American Orthopaedic Society for Sports Medicine

AOTA American Occupational Therapy Association

AOTCB American Occupational Therapy Certification Board

AP accounts payable

A/P accounts payable

A&P anterior and posterior; auscultation and percussion

APA Ambulatory Pediatric Association; American Pancreatic Society; American Psychiatric Association; American Psychological Association

APAA American Physician Art Association

APACHE Acute Physiology and Chronic Health Evaluation (system)

APACM American Physicians Association of Computer Medicine

APACVS Association of Physician's Assistants in Cardio-Vascular Surgery

APAP Association of Physician Assistant Programs

APBP   Association of Professional Baseball Physicians

APC   aspirin, phenacetin, and caffeine; Association of Pathology Chairmen

APCS   American Podiatric Circulatory Society

APDIM   Association of Program Directors in Internal Medicine

APF   American Pathology Foundation; American Physicians Fellowship for Medicine in Israel

APFC   Association of Physical Fitness Centers

APG   ambulatory patient group

APGO   Association of Professors of Gynecology and Obstetrics

APhA   American Pharmaceutical Association

APHA   American Protestant Health Association; American Public Health Association

APIC   Association for Practitioners in Infection Control

APL   acceptable process level

APLS   advanced pediatric life support; Association for Politics and the Life Sciences

AP–LS   American Psychology–Law Society

APM   Academy of Psychosomatic Medicine; Association of Professors of Medicine; Association for Psychoanalytic Medicine

APMA   American Podiatric Medical Association

APNA   American Psychiatric Nurses Association

APO   adverse patient occurrence

APON   Association of Pediatric Oncology Nurses

APOR   Association for Pharmacoeconomics and Outcomes Research

APOSW   Association of Pediatric Oncology Social Workers

APP   (Joint Commission) Administrative Policies and Procedures; Association of Pakistani Physicians

APPA   American Physicians Poetry Association; American Professional Practice Association; American Psychopathological Association; Association of Philippine Physicians in America

APPI   American Psychiatric Press, Inc

APPIC   Association of Psychology Postdoctoral and Internship Centers

APPM   Academy of Pharmacy Practice and Management

approx.   approximately

APQC   American Productivity and Quality Center

APR   average payment rate

APRS   Academy of Pharmaceutical Research and Science

APS   American Pain Society; American Paraplegia Society; American Pediatric Society; American Physiological Society; American Prosthodontic Society; American Psychosomatic Society

APSA   American Pediatric Surgical Association

APsaA   American Psychoanalytic Association

APSF   Anesthesia Patient Safety Foundation

APSS   Association of Professional Sleep Societies

APT   Association of Polysomnographic Technologists; Association for Psychological Type

APTA   American Physical Therapy Association

aPTT   activated partial thromboplastin time

APTT   activated partial thromboplastin time

APUA   Alliance for the Prudent Use of Antibiotics

APWA   American Public Welfare Association

aq   *aqua* (water)

aq dist   distilled water

AQL   acceptable quality level

AQP   Association for Quality and Participation

AR   accounts receivable

A/R   accounts receivable

ARA   Academy of Rehabilitative Audiology; Association of Retired Americans

ARC   AIDS-related complex; American Red Cross

ARCA   American Rehabilitation Counseling Association

ARC-PA   Accreditation Review Committee on Education for Physician Assistants

ARCRT   American Registry of Clinical Radiography Technologists

ARC-ST   Acreditation Review Committee for Educational Programs in Surgical Technology

ARD   acute respiratory disease; adult respiratory distress

ARDMS   American Registry of Diagnostic Medical Sonographers

ARDS   adult respiratory distress syndrome

ARF   acute renal failure

ARHP   Association of Reproductive Health Professionals; Association of Rheumatology Health Professionals

ARI   Acupuncture Research Institute

ARL   average run length

ARMA   American Registry of Medical Assistants

ARN   Association of Rehabilitation Nurses

ARNA   American Radiological Nurses Association

ARNMD   Association for Research in Nervous and Mental Disease

AROM   active range of motion

ARP   American Registry of Pathology

ARRS   American Roentgen Ray Society

ARRT   American Registry of Radiologic Technologists

ARS   American Radium Society; American Rhinologic Society

ART   accredited record technician

ARVO   Association for Research in Vision and Ophthalmology

as   *arum sinistra* (left ear)

ASA   against staff advice; American Society on Aging; American Society of Anesthesiologists; American Statistical Association; American Surgical Association; aspirin

ASAAD   American Society for Advancement of Anesthesia in Dentistry

ASAHP   American Society of Allied Health Professions

ASAIO   American Society for Artificial Internal Organs

ASAM   American Society of Addiction Medicine

ASAP   American Society for Adolescent Psychiatry; Americans for a Sound AIDS Policy; as soon as possible

ASAPS   American Society for Aesthetic Plastic Surgery

ASA-PS class   American Society of Anesthesiologists-Physical Status classification system

ASA-PSS   American Society of Anesthesiologists-Physical Status Scale

ASAS   American Society of Abdominal Surgery

ASBMB   American Society for Biochemistry and Molecular Biology

ASBMR   American Society for Bone and Mineral Research

ASBP   American Society of Bariatric Physicians

ASC   American Society for Cybernetics; American Society of Cytology

ASCB   American Society for Cell Biology

ASCCP   American Society for Colposcopy and Cervical Pathology

ASCE   American Society of Childbirth Educators

ASCEP   American Society for Clinical Evoked Potentials

ASCH   American Society of Clinical Hypnosis

ASCI   American Society for Clinical Investigation

ASCII   American Standard Code for Information Interchange

ASCMS   American Society of Contemporary Medicine and Surgery

ASCN   American Society for Clinical Nutrition

ASCO   American Society of Clinical Oncology; American Society of Contemporary Ophthalmology; Association of Schools and Colleges of Optometry

ASCP   American Society of Clinical Pathologists; American Society of Consultant Pharmacists

ASCP/SCM   American Society of Cardiovascular Professionals/Society for Cardiovascular Management

ASCPT   American Society for Clinical Pharmacology and Therapeutics

ASCR   American Society of Clinical Radiologists

ASCRS   American Society of Cataract and Refractive Surgery; American Society of Colon and Rectal Surgeons

ASCT   American Society for Cytotechnology

ASD   Academy for Sports Dentistry; aggregate survey data; ; American Society of Dermatopathology Association for the Study of Dreams

ASDA   American Sleep Disorders Association

ASDC   American Society of Dentistry for Children

ASDS   American Society for Dermatologic Surgery

ASDVS   American Society of Directors of Volunteer Services

ASDWA   Association of State Drinking Water Administrators

ASE   American Society of Echocardiography; Association for Surgical Education

ASET   American Society of Electroneurodiagnostic Technologists

ASFA   American Society for Apheresis

ASFO   American Society of Forensic Odontology

ASGD   American Society for Geriatric Dentistry

ASGE   American Society for Gastrointestinal Endoscopy

ASGPP   American Society of Group Psychotherapy and Psychodrama

ASH   Action on Smoking and Health; American Society of Hematology; American Society of Hypertension

ASHA   American School Health Association; American Social Health Association; American Speech-Language-Hearing Association

ASHCMPR   American Society for Health Care Marketing and Public Relations

ASHCSP   American Society for Healthcare Central Service Personnel

ASHE   American Society for Hospital Engineering

ASHES   American Society for Healthcare Environmental Services

ASHET   American Society for Healthcare Education and Training

ASHFSA   American Society for Hospital Food Service Administrators

ASHG   American Society of Human Genetics

ASHHRA   American Society for Healthcare Human Resources Administration

ASHI   American Society for Histocompatibility and Immunogenetics

ASHMM   American Society for Hospital Materials Management

ASHMPR   American Society for Hospital Marketing and Public Relations

ASHNS   American Society for Head and Neck Surgery

ASHP   American Society of Handicapped Physicians; American Society of Hospital Pharmacists

ASHRM   American Society for Healthcare Risk Management

ASHT   American Society of Hand Therapists

ASIA   American Spinal Injury Association

ASIM   American Society of Internal Medicine

ASIS   American Society for Information Science

ASLHA   American Speech, Language and Hearing Association

ASLM   American Society of Law and Medicine

ASLMS   American Society for Laser Medicine and Surgery

ASLSS   American Society of Lipo-Suction Surgery

ASM   American Society for Microbiology; Association for Systems Management

AsMA   Aerospace Medical Association

ASMS   American Society of Maxillofacial Surgeons

ASMT   American Society for Medical Technology

ASN   American Society of Nephrology; American Society of Neuroimaging; average sample number

ASNR   American Society of Neuroradiology

ASOA   American Society of Ophthalmic Administrators

ASORN   American Society of Ophthalmic Registered Nurses

ASOS   American Society of Outpatient Surgeons

ASP   American Society of Parasitologists; American Society of Pharmacognosy

ASPAN   American Society of Post Anesthesia Nurses

ASPD   American Society of Podiatric Dermatology

ASPE   American Society of Psychopathology of Expression

ASPECT   Anticoagulants in the Secondary Prevention of Events in Coronary Thrombosis

ASPEN   American Society for Parenteral and Enteral Nutrition

ASPET   American Society for Pharmacology and Experimental Therapeutics

ASPH   Association of Schools of Public Health

ASPHO   American Society of Pediatric Hematology/Oncology

ASPL   American Society for Pharmacy Law

ASPM   American Society of Podiatric Medicine

ASPMA   American Society of Podiatric Medical Assistants

ASPN   Ambulatory Sentinel Practice Network; American Society for Pediatric Neurosurgery

ASPO   American Society of Preventive Oncology; American Society for Psychoprophylaxis in Obstetrics

ASPP   American Society of Psychoanalytic Physicians

ASPR   American Society for Psychical Research

ASPRS   American Society of Plastic and Reconstructive Surgeons

ASPRSN   American Society of Plastic and Reconstructive Surgical Nurses

ASQC   American Society for Quality Control

ASRA   American Society of Regional Anesthesia

ASRD   American Society of Retired Dentists

ASRT   American Society of Radiologic Technologists

ASSE   American Society of Safety Engineers; American Society of Sanitary Engineering

ASSFN   American Society for Stereotactic and Functional Neurosurgery

ASSH   American Society for Surgery of the Hand

ASSO   American Society for the Study of Orthodontics

AST   Association of Surgical Technologists

ASTDD   Association of State and Territorial Dental Directors

ASTDN   Association of State and Territorial Directors of Nursing

ASTDPHE   Association of State and Territorial Directors of Public Health Education

ASTHO   Association of State and Territorial Health Officials

ASTM   American Society for Testing and Materials

ASTMH   American Society of Tropical Medicine and Hygiene

as tol   as tolerated

ASTRO   American Society for Therapeutic Radiology and Oncology

ASTS   American Society of Transplant Surgeons

ATA   American Thyroid Association; American Transplant Association

ATB   antibiotics

ATCC   American Type Culture Collection

ATD   Association of Tongue Depressors

ATLA   Association of Trial Lawyers of America

ATLS   advanced trauma life support

ATMCH   Association of Teachers of Maternal and Child Health

ATPA   American Technology Preeminence Act

ATPM Association of Teachers of Preventive Medicine

ATPO Association of Technical Personnel in Ophthalmology

ATRA American Therapeutic Recreation Association; American Tort Reform Association

ATS American Thoracic Society; American Trauma Society

ATSDR Agency for Toxic Substances and Disease Registry

AUA American Urological Association; Association of University Anesthesiologists

AUAA American Urological Association Allied

AUDIT Alcohol Use Disorders Identification Test

AUEHSC Association of University Environmental Health/Sciences Centers

AUI Alcohol Use Inventory

AUL Americans United for Life

AUPHA Association of University Programs in Health Administration

AUPO Association of University Professors of Ophthalmology

AUPOHS Association of University Programs in Occupational Health and Safety

AUR Association of University Radiologists

AV arteriovenous; atrioventricular

AVDA American Venereal Disease Association

AVG ambulatory visit group

AVRHS Association for Vital Records and Health Statistics

AVSC Association for Voluntary Surgical Contraception

A&W alive and well

AWHONN Association of Women's Health, Obstetric, and Neonatal Nurses

AWP Association for Women in Psychology

AZT azidothymidin; zidovudine

B Black

Ba Barium

BAC Blood alcohol concentration

BACOP bleomycin, Adriamycin, Cytotoxin, Oncovin, Prednisone

BAATAF Boston Area Anticoagulation Trial for Atrial Fibrillation

BaE Barium enema

BAPHR Bay Area Physicians for Human Rights

BASIC Beginner's All-Purpose Symbolic Instruction Code

BASIS Basal Antiarrhythmic Study of Infarct Survival

BBB Bundle branch block

BBT Basal body temperature

BC Blue Cross; board certified

BCAC Breast Cancer Advisory Center

BC/BS Blue Cross/Blue Shield

BCBSA Blue Cross and Blue Shield Association

BCG Bacille Calmette-Guérin (TB vaccine)

BCHCM Board of Certified Hazard Control Management

BCLS Basic cardiac life support

BCP Birth control pill; blood cell progenitors; Board of Certification in Pedorthics

BCSP Board of Certified Safety Professionals

BD Bottle drainage

BDCGS Birth Defect and Clinical Genetic Society

BDI Beck depression inventory

BE Barium enema; breast examination

BEMI Bio-Electro-Magnetics Institute

BEMS Bioelectromagnetics Society

BFP Biological false positive

BGA Behavior Genetics Association

BHA Baptist Hospital Association

BHAT Beta-Blocker Heart Attack Trial

BHI Bureau of Health Insurance

BHRD Bureau of Health Resources Development

BIA Brain Injury Association; Bureau of Indian Affairs

bid *bis in die* (twice a day)

BISH borderline isolated systolic hypertension

B&J Bone and joint

BK Below knee

BKA Below knee amputation

BLD blood

BLD/S blood sugar

BLL blood lead level

BLS basic life support

BM bowel movement

BMA Bangladesh Medical Association of North America; Biomedical Marketing Association

B-MAST Brief MAST (Michigan Alcoholism Screening Test)

BMC bone mineral content

BMD bone mass density; bone mineral density

BMES Biomedical Engineering Society

BMI body mass index

BMR basal metabolic rate

BNA Baromedical Nurses Association; Bureau of National Affairs

BNDD Bureau of Narcotics and Dangerous Drugs

BNSIG Behavioral Neuropsychology Special Interest Group

BOC board of commissioners

BONENT Board of Nephrology Examiners–Nursing and Technology

BP blood pressure; bodily pain

BPA Biological Photographic Association; Black Psychiatrists of America

BPEAOA Bureau of Professional Education of the American Osteopathic Association

BPH benign prostatic hyperplasia; benign prostatic hypertrophy

BPS Behavioral Pharmacology Society

BR bed rest; Business Roundtable

BRAGS Bioelectrical Repair and Growth Society

BRAT bananas, rice, applesauce, and toast (diet)

BRCA breast cancer (gene)

BRM biological response modifier therapy

BRP bathroom privileges

bs blood sugar

BS Bachelor of Science; Blue Shield

BSC Biological Stain Commission

BSE bovine spongiform encephalopathy (mad cow disease); breast self-examination

BSL basic life support

BSN Bachelor of Science in Nursing

BSW Bachelor of Social Work

BT American Association of Behavioral Therapists

BTLS basic trauma life support

BUA broad-band ultrasound attenuation

BUN blood urea nitrogen

BV bacterial vaginosis

BW body weight

Bx biopsy

Cc

$\bar{c}$ count

c with

C Celsius (degree or scale); centigrade; cholesterol

C1–C7 cervical vertebrae

ca coronary artery

Ca Calcium; cancer

CA cancer; carcinoma; conditional accreditation; Consumer Alert; coronary artery; Cranial Academy

CA *CA: A Cancer Journal for Clinicians*

CA125 genetic marker for risk of ovarian cancer ("Gilda Radner" gene)

C&A children and adolescents

CAAHA Council on Arteriosclerosis of the American Heart Association

CAB chest compression, airway maintenance, breathing; coronary artery bypass

CABG coronary artery bypass graft

CAC Clinical Assessment of Confusion (test)

CACF Commission on Accreditation of Correctional Facilities

CAD computer-aided design; coronary artery disease; Council on Anxiety Disorders

CAFA Canadian Atrial Fibrillation Anticoagulation (study)

CAGE cut down, annoyed by criticism, guilty about drinking, eye opener drinks (alcoholism test)

CAGE-AID CAGE Adapted to Include Drugs

CAH Center for Attitudinal Healing

CAHEA Committee on Allied Health Education and Accreditation

CAHPS Consumer Assessments of Health Plans Study (AHCPR)

CAI computer-aided instruction

CAIR Child Abuse Institute of Research

cal calorie

CALM Child Abuse Listening and Mediation

CALS consolidated accreditation of licensure survey

CAM complementary/alternative medicine; Confusion Assessment Method

CAMA Civil Aviation Medical Association

CAMAC *Comprehensive Accreditation Manual for Ambulatory Care*

CAMBHC *Comprehensive Accreditation Manual for Behavioral Health Care*

CAMH *Comprehensive Accreditation Manual for Hospitals*

CAMHC *Comprehensive Accreditation Manual for Home Care*

CAMHCN *Comprehensive Accreditation Manual for Health Care Networks*

CAMLTC *Comprehensive Accreditation Manual for Long Term Care*

CAMLTCP *Comprehensive Accreditation Manual for Long Term Care Pharmacies*

CAMMBHC *Comprehensive Accreditation Manual for Managed Behavioral Health Care*

CAMPCLS *Comprehensive Accreditation Manual for Pathology and Clinical Laboratory Services*

CAMS Chinese American Medical Society

CAN Clinical Algorithm Nosology

CAO chief administrative officer

CAOHC Council for Accreditation in Occupational Hearing Conservation

cap capsule

CAP Client Assistance Program; College of American Pathologists; community-acquired pneumonia

CAPA Clinical Algorithm Patient Abstraction

CAPD continuous ambulatory peritoneal dialysis

CAPS Christian Association for Psychological Studies

card cardiac

CARE (Ryan White) Comprehensive AIDS Resources Emergency (Act)

CARF Commission on Accreditation of Rehabilitation Facilities

CASA Clinical Algorithm Structural Analysis

CAST Children of Alcoholics Screening Test

CAST Cardiac Arrhythmia Suppression Trial

CAT computed axial tomography; computerized axial tomography

cath, CATH catheter

CAUTION change, a sore, unusual, thickening, indigestion, obvious, nagging (cancer warning signals)

CB contrast baths

CBC complete blood cell count; complete blood count

CBD cough and deep breath

CBE clinical breast examination

CBER Center for Biologics Evaluation and Research (FDA)

CBF cerebral blood flow

CBGP Council of Behavioral Group Practices

CBMT Certification Board for Music Therapists

CBO Congressional Budget Office

CBR complete bed rest

cc cubic centimeter

CC Catecholamine Club; chief complaint; Credentialing Commission

CCA Conference of Consulting Actuaries

CCAD Carnegie Council on Adolescent Development

CCBC Council of Community Blood Centers

CCBD Council for Children with Behavioral Disorders

CCC Council on Clinical Classifications

CCE Council on Chiropractic Education

CCI/NBCVT Cardiovascular Credentialing International

CCMS Congress of County Medical Societies

CCNA Council on Certification of Nurse Anesthetists

CCNCC Commission on Clinical Nomenclatures, Coding, and Classification

CCO Council on Chiropractic Orthopedics

CCOC Council on Clinical Optometric Care

CCP certified clinical perfusionist; community care plan; Cooperative Cardiovascular Project

CCPT Council on Chiropractic Physiological Therapeutics

CCQE Center for Clinical Quality Evaluation

CCR Commission on Civil Rights

CCRC continuing care retirement community

CCRN certified critical care nurse

CCS Canadian Cardiovascular Society; certified coding specialist

CCU cardiac care unit; cardiovascular care unit; coronary care unit; critical care unit

CCU nurse critical care nurse

CD compact disk

CD4 HIV helper cell count

CDABO College of Diplomates of the American Board of Orthodontics

CDBG Community Development Block Grant

CDC Centers for Disease Control and Prevention; Consensus Development Conference

CDER Center for Death Education and Research; Center for Drug Evaluation and Research (FDA)

CDF Children's Defense Fund

CDHCF Consultant Dietitians in Health Care Facilities

CDI Clearinghouse on Disability Information

CDL National Board for Certification of Dental Laboratories

CDM Center for Dance Medicine

CDMA Chain Drug Marketing Associates

CDR Clinical Dementia Rating

CDRH Center for Devices and Radiological Health (FDA)

CDS Christian Dental Society; Christian Doctors Sodality

CE   conjugated estrogens

CEA   carcinoembryonic antigen; Center for Early Adolescence; cost-effectiveness analysis

CEAP   Clinical Efficacy Assessment Project

CEASD   Conference of Educational Administrators Serving the Deaf

CEC   Cryogenic Engineering Conference

CEE   (unopposed) conjugated equine estrogen; Council on Electrolysis Education

CEO   chief executive officer

CEPH   Council on Education for Public Health

CEQ   Council on Environmental Quality

CERAD   Consortium to Establish a Registry for Alzheimer's Disease

CES-D   Centre for Epidemiologic Studies depression (scale)

CETS   Conseil d'Évaluation des Technologies de la Santé

CF   cystic fibrosis

CFCM   Committee for Freedom of Choice in Medicine

CFF   Cystic Fibrosis Foundation

CFH   Council on Family Health

CFMA   Council for Medical Affairs

CFO   chief financial officer

CFR   *Code of Federal Regulations*

CFS   chronic fatigue syndrome

CFSAN   Center for Food Safety and Applied Nutrition (FDA)

CGFNS   Commission on Graduates of Foreign Nursing Schools

CGSC   Cancer Genetics Study Consortium

CHA   Catholic Health Association of the United States

CHAMPUS   Civilian Health and Medical Program of the Uniformed Services

CHAMPVA   Civilian Health and Medical Program of the Veterans Administration

CHAP   Community Health Accreditation Program

CHC   Coalitions for Health Care; community health center

CHCS   community health care system

CHCT   Center for Health Care Technology

CHD   congenital heart disease; coronary heart disease

CHEM   Center for Healthcare Environmental Management

CHESS   Comprehensive Health Enhancement Support System™

CHF   Coalition for Health Funding; congestive heart failure

CHG   change

CHI   consumer health informatics

CHID   Center for Health Information Dissemination (AHCPR)

CHILD   Child Health Insurance and Lower Deficit (Act); Children's Healthcare Is a Legal Duty

CHIMIS   community health integrated management information system

CHIN   community health information network

CHIP   Children's Health Insurance Program; Community Health Intervention Partnership; Comprehensive Health Insurance Plan

CHIPS   Children's Health Insurance Provides Security (Act)

CHMR   Center for Hazardous Materials Research

CHN   community health network

CHO   carbohydrate

CHOICE   Center for Human Options in Childbirth Experiences

chol   cholesterol

CHP   comprehensive health planning

CHPA   comprehensive health planning agency

CHQC   Cleveland Health Quality Choice

CHSS   Cooperative Health Statistics System

CI   confidence interval; continuous improvement

CIC   Consumer Information Center

CICD   Center to Improve Care of the Dying

CICU   cardiac intensive care unit; coronary intensive care unit

CID   Choice in Dying

CIGS   cigarettes

CIH   Children in Hospitals

CIN   cervical intraepithelial neoplasia

CIO   chief information officer

cir, circ   circulation

CIR   Committee of Interns and Residents; Cosmetic Ingredient Review

CIS   Cancer Information Service; carcinoma in situ; Clinical Immunology Society; clinical information system

CIT   Center for Information Technology (AHCPR)

ck, CK   check

cl   clear

CL   center line; critical list

CLAO   Contact Lens Association of Ophthalmologists

CLAS   Clinical Ligand Assay Society; Congress of Lung Association Staff

Class A   (known human) carcinogen

CLC Child Life Council

CLD Council for Learning Disabilities

cldy cloudy

CLEAR Council on Licensure, Enforcement and Regulation

CLIA '67 Clinical Laboratory Improvement Act of 1967

CLIA '88 Clinical Laboratory Improvement Amendments of 1988

CLL chronic lymphatic leukemia

cl liq clear liquid diet

CLMA Clinical Laboratory Management Association; Contact Lens Manufacturers Association

CLSA Contact Lens Society of America

cm centimeter

CMA California Medical Association; Canadian Medical Association; certified medical assistant

CMC Center for Medical Consumers and Health Care Information

CMDS Christian Medical and Dental Society

CME continuing medical education; Council on Medical Education

CMH community mental health

CMHC community mental health center; comprehensive mental health center

CMHS Center for Mental Health Services

CMI chronically mentally ill

CMIS Computerized Medical Imaging Society

CMMB Catholic Medical Mission Board

CMMIS case-mix management information system

CMP competitive medical plan

CMPDL Commission on Mental and Physical Disability Law

CMRI Certified Medical Representative Institute

CMSA consolidated metropolitan statistical area

CMSS Council of Medical Specialty Societies

CMV cytomegalovirus

CNA certified nurse assistant

CNF Child Nutrition Forum

CNHI Committee for National Health Insurance

CNHS Coalition for a National Health System

CNI Community Nutrition Institute

CNM certified nurse-midwife

CNPA Central Neuropsychiatric Association

CNRHSPP Council for the National Register of Health Service Providers in Psychology

CNS central nervous system; Child Neurology Society; clinical nurse specialist

CO carbon monoxide

c/o, C/O complained of; complains of

CO₂ carbon dioxide

COA Commissioned Officers Association; Commission on Opticianry Accreditation; Council on Accreditation of Services for Families and Children

coag coagulation

COAP Cyclophosphamide, Oncovine, Ara-C and Prednisone

COB coordination of benefits

COBRA Consolidated Omnibus Budget Reconciliation Act of 1985

COC College of Chaplains

CODS Center for Organization and Delivery Studies (AHCPR)

COE Council on Optometric Education

COER Center for Outcomes and Effectiveness Research (AHCPR)

COFS Center for Cost and Financing Studies (AHCPR)

COHE College of Osteopathic Healthcare Executives

COI certificate of insurance

COLA Commission on Office Laboratory Assessment; cost-of-living adjustment

comp compound

COMPLX complication

CON certificate of need

conc concentrated

cond, COND condition

cont continued

CONQUEST Computerized Needs-Oriented Quality Measurement Evaluation System

CONSENSUS II Cooperative New Scandinavian Enalapril Survival Study II

CONSORT Consolidated Standards of Reporting Trials

COO chief operating officer

COOP Dartmouth Cooperative Primary Care Research Network (COOP)

COP conditions of participation; Cyclophosphamide, Oncovine, Prednisone

COPCORD Community Oriented Program for the Control of Rheumatic Diseases

COPD chronic obstructive pulmonary disease

COPE Conference of Podiatry Executives

COPHL Conference of Public Health Laboratorians

COQ cost of quality

CORE   Center for Outcomes Research and Education

COS   Clinical Orthopaedic Society

COSSMHO   National Coalition of Hispanic Health and Human Services Organizations

COTH   Council of Teaching Hospitals

COTRANS   Coordinated Transfer Application System

COVD   College of Optometrists in Vision Development

CP   cerebral palsy

CPA   certified public accountant

CPAM   certified patient account manager

CPBE   certified professional bureau executive

CPC   clinical pathologic conference

CPCRA   Community Programs for Clinical Research on AIDS

CPE   cytopathogenic effects

CPEM   Council on Precision Electromagnetic Measurements

CPEX   cardiopulmonary exercise testing

CPG   clinical practice guideline

CPHA   Commission on Professional and Hospital Activities

CPI   consumer price index

CPK   creatine phosphokinase

CPM   Cesarean Prevention Movement; continuous passive motion; counts per minute

CPME   Council on Podiatric Medical Education

CPOU   chest pain observation unit

CPP   cerebral perfusion pressure

CPQA   certified professional in quality assurance

CPR   cardiopulmonary resuscitation; computer-based patient record

CPRI   Computer-Based Patient Record Institute

CPSC   Consumer Product Safety Commission

CPT   current procedural terminology

CPT   *Physicians' Current Procedural Terminology*

CPT-4   *Physicians' Current Procedural Terminology - Fourth Edition*

CQI   continuous quality improvement

CQMI   Center for Quality Measurement and Improvement

CRAHCA   Center for Research in Ambulatory Health Care Administration

CRCPD   Conference of Radiation Control Program Directors

CPCR   Center for Primary Care Research (AHCPR)

CREOG   Council on Resident Education in Obstetrics and Gynecology

CRG   Council for Responsible Genetics

CRI   catheter-related infection

CRIS   Calcium Antagonist Reinfarction Italian Study

CRISP   Consortium Research on Indicators of System Performance

CRIT   criteria

CRN   Council for Responsible Nutrition

CRNA   certified registered nurse anesthetist

CRNA   certified registered nurse anesthesiologist

CRS   Council of Rehabilitation Specialists

CRT   cathode ray tube

CRTI   Center for the Rights of the Terminally Ill

CRTO   Coalition of Rehabilitation Therapy Organizations

CS   central service; cesarean section; customer service

C&S   culture and sensitivity

CSA   Center for the Study of Aging; Cryogenic Society of America

CSAP   Center for Substance Abuse Prevention

CSAT   Center for Substance Abuse Treatment

CSAVR   Council of State Administrators of Vocational Rehabilitation

CSB   Controlled Substance Board

CS&CC   culture, sensitivity and colony count

CSCR   Central Society for Clinical Research

CSD   Coalition on Sexuality and Disability

C-SECT   cesarean section

C-section   cesarean section

CSF   cerebrospinal fluid

CSH   Coalition on Smoking or Health

CSI   computerized severity index

CSICOP   Committee for the Scientific Investigation of Claims of the Paranormal

CSIE   Council for Sex Information and Education

CSII   continuous subcutaneous insulin infusion

CSP   certified safety professional

CSPI   Center for Science in the Public Interest

C-spine   cervical spine

CSPTE   Center for the Study of Pharmacy and Therapeutics for the Elderly

CSQ   Client Satisfaction Questionnaire

CSS   Cognitive Science Society

CSTE   Council of State and Territorial Epidemiologists

CSU   clearing and staging unit

CSWE   Council on Social Work Education

CT   computed tomography; contaminated

CTR   carpal tunnel release

CUFT   Center for the Utilization of Federal Technology

CUS   compression ultrasonography

CUSH   Computer Users in Speech and Hearing

CV   cardiovascular; coefficient of variation

CVA   cerebral vascular accident; cerebrovascular accident

CVC   central venous catheter

CVO   credentialing verification organization; credentials verification organization

CVP   central venous pressure

CVS   chorionic villus sampling

CW   Congress Watch

CWBHP   Center for the Well-Being of Health Professionals

CWI   Child Welfare Institute

CWLA   Child Welfare League of America

CWW   clinic without walls

Cx   cervix

CXR   chest x-ray

Dd

d   day; deviation

3 x d   three times daily

DA   delayed action

DAEEP   Division of Applied Experimental and Engineering Psychologists

DANA   Drug and Alcohol Nursing Association

DANB   Dental Assisting National Board

DAST   Drug Abuse Screening Test

DAT   dementia of the Alzheimer type

DATTA   Diagnostic and Therapeutic Technology Assessment

DAVIT   Danish Verapamil Infarction Trial

DBA   Doctor of Business Administration

DBCT   deep breath, cough, and turn

DC   discontinue; Doctor of Chiropractic

D/C   discontinue

D&C   dilation and curettage

DCBE   double-contrast barium enema

DCCT   Diabetes Control and Complications Trial

DCG   diagnostic cost group

DCIS   ductal carcinoma in situ

DD   differential diagnosis; directed donation; directed donor

DDA   Dental Dealers of America

DDNC   Digestive Disease National Coalition

DDP   Doctors for Disaster Preparedness

DDPA   Delta Dental Plans Association

DDS   Doctor of Dental Surgery

D&E   dilatation and evacuation; dilation and evacuation

DEA   Drug Enforcement Administration

DEC   decrease

def   defecation (bowel movement)

DEMPAQ   Develop and Evaluate Methods for Promoting Ambulatory Care Quality

DES   diethylstilbestrol

DETP   Department of Environmental and Toxicologic Pathology

DEXA   dual-energy x-ray absorptiometry

df   degree of freedom

DGI   Dental Gold Institute

DGMA   Dental Group Management Association

DHHS   Department of Health and Human Services

DHI   Digestive Health Initiative

DIA   Drug Information Association

DIAB   diabetic

diff   differential blood count

DIFF   difficulty

dil   dilute

DIS   Diagnostic Interview Schedule

disc, DISC   discontinue

dischg   discharge

disl   dislocation

DITC   Disability Insurance Training Council

DJD   degenerative joint disease

dk   dark

DKA   diabetic ketoacidosis

DKB   deep knee bends

DM   diabetes mellitus

DMA   Dental Manufacturers of America; Dietary Managers Association

DMAT   disaster medical assistance team

DMD   Doctor of Dental Medicine

DME   disposable medical equipment; durable medical equipment

DMFO   Defense Medical Facilities Office

DMPA depot medroxyprogesterone acetate (depō-Provera)

DMSA Defense Medical Support Activity

DMSSC Defense Medical Systems Support Center

DNA deoxyribonucleic acid; Dermatology Nurses' Association

DNR do not resuscitate

DO Doctor of Osteopathy

D&O directors and officers

DOA dead on arrival

DOB date of birth

DOC Department of Commerce

DOD Department of Defense

DOE Department of Energy; dyspnea on exertion

DOI date of injury

DOJ Department of Justice

DOL Department of Labor

DON director of nursing

DOT Department of Transportation;directly observed therapy

DPA direct provider agreement; Doctor of Public Administration; dual photon absorptiometry

DPH Doctor of Public Health

DPM Doctor of Podiatric Medicine

DPMA Data Processing Management Association

DPO director provider agreement

DPT diphtheria, pertussis, tetanus

DR delivery room

DRE digital rectal examination

DRG diagnosis-related group

DRI Dietary Reference Intake

drng drainage

DrPH Doctor of Public Health

drsg dressing

DS dosage schedule

DSG discharge

DSH disproportionate share hospital

DSM *Diagnostic and Statistical Manual of Mental Disorders*; disease state management

DSM-III *Diagnostic and Statistical Manual of Mental Disorders, Third Edition*

DSM-III-R *Diagnostic and Statistical Manual of Mental Disorders, Third Edition—Revised*

DSM-IV *Diagnostic and Statistical Manual of Mental Disorders, Fourth Edition*

DSM-IV-PC *Diagnostic and Statistical Manual of Mental Disorders, Fourth Edition—Primary Care*

D-spine dorsal spine

DSS decision support software; decision support system

DT delirium tremens; diphtheria and tetanus (vaccine)

D/T due to

DTP diphtheria, tetanus, and pertussis (vaccine)

DTs delirium tremens

DUE drug usage evaluation

DUHP Duke–UNC Health Profile

DUR drug utilization review

DVA Department of Veterans Affairs

DVT deep vein thrombosis

DW distilled water

DWI driving while intoxicated

dx, Dx diagnosis

D&X dilation and extraction

E enema

EACH essential access community hospital

EAFT European Atrial Fibrillation Trial

EAHCA Education for All Handicapped Children Act

EAI Emphysema Anonymous, Inc

EAP employee assistance program; evoked acoustic potential

EBAA Eye Bank Association of America

EBL estimated blood loss

EBRT electron beam radiation therapy; external beam radiation therapy

EBSR Eye-Bank for Sight Restoration

EBV Epstein-Barr virus

ECA Epidemiologic Catchment Area (study)

ECCE extracapsular cataract extraction

ECF extended care facility

ECFMG Educational Commission for Foreign Medical Graduates

ECG electrocardiogram; electrocardiography

ECMA Embalming Chemical Manufacturers Association

ECMHP East Coast Migrant Health Project

ECMO extracorporeal membrane oxygenation; extracorporeal membrane oxygenator

E coli   *Escherichia coli*

ECP   emergency contraceptive pill

ECRI   (formerly) Emergency Care Research Institute

ECT   electroconvulsive therapy

ED   (U.S.) Department of Education; emergency department

EDC   expected date of confinement

EdD   Doctor of Education

EDI   electronic data interchange

EDP   electronic data processing

EEG   electroencephalogram; electroencephalography

EENT   eye, ear, nose, and throat

EEOC   Equal Employment Opportunity Commission

EF   ejection fraction

EFA   essential fatty acid

eg   for example

EIB   exercise-induced bronchospasm

EIN   Emerging Infections Network

EIS   Environmental Impact Statement

EKG   electrocardiogram

ELISA   enzyme-linked immunosorbent assay

ELSI   Ethical, Legal, and Social Implications (branch of Human Genome Project)

EMA   Electronic Mail Association; Environmental Management Association; Environmental Mutagen Society

EMBS   Engineering in Medicine and Biology Society

EMCRO   experimental medical care review organization

EMG   electromyogram

EMIT   enzyme multiplied immunoassay technique

EMR   electronic medical record; emergency medical responder

EMRA   Emergency Medicine Residents' Association

EMS   emergency medical services

EMSS   emergency medical services system

EMT   emergency medical technician

EMTALA   Emergency Medical Treatment and Active Labor Act

EMT-P   emergency medical technician-paramedic

ENA   Emergency Nurses Association

ENACT   Effective National Action to Control Tobacco

ENC   Enteral Nutrition Council

ENT   ear, nose, throat

EOA   examination, opinion, and advice

EOAE   evoked otacoustic emission

EOB   explanation of benefits

EOC   episode of care

EOE   evoked otacoustic emission

EOM   extraocular movements

EOMB   Explanation of Medicare Benefits

EP   evoked potentials

EPA   Environmental Protection Agency

EPC   Evidence-Based Practice Center

EPO   Epidemiology Program Office (CDC); exclusive provider organization

EPSDT   Early and Periodic Screening Diagnosis and Treatment Program

eq   equivalent

ER   emergency room

ERISA   Employee Retirement Income Security Act

ERS   Evaluation Ranking Scale

ERT   estrogen replacement therapy

ERTA   Economic Recovery Tax Act of 1981

ES   Endocrine Society

ESA   Employment Standards Administration; Exer-Safety Association

ESO   early survey option

ESP   Economic Stabilization Program; erythrocyte sedimentation rate; extrasensory perception

ESPR   electronic surrogate patient record

ESRD   end stage renal disease

ess   essential

ESWL   extracorporeal shock wave lithotripsy

ETS   environmental tobacco smoke

Ex   example; exercise

exam   examination

exc   except

expir   expiration

expt   expectorant

F   Fahrenheit (degree or scale); female; fibrinogen

FAAFP   Fellow of the American Academy of Family Physicians

FAAN   Fellow of the American Academy of Nursing

FAANaOS   Fellow of the American Academy of Neurological and Orthopaedic Surgeons

FAAO–HNS   Fellow of the American Academy of Otolaryngology–Head and Neck Surgery

FAAOS   Fellow of the American Academy of Orthopaedic Surgeons

FAAP   Fellow of the American Academy of Pediatrics

FACA   Fellow of the American College of Angiology

FACC   Fellow of the American College of Cardiology

FACCP   Fellow of the American College of Chest Physicians

FACCT   Foundation for Accountability

FACD   Fellow of the American College of Dentists

FACEP   Fellow of the American College of Emergency Physicians

FACFS   Fellow of the American College of Foot Surgeons

FACHE   Fellow of the American College of Healthcare Executives

FACMGA   Fellow of the American College of Medical Group Administrators

FACOG   Fellow of the American College of Obstetricians and Gynecologists

FACP   Fellow of the American College of Physicians

FACPE   Fellow of the American College of Physician Executives

FACPM   Fellow of the American College of Preventive Medicine

FACR   Fellow of the American College of Radiology

FACS   Fellow of the American College of Surgeons

FACSM   Fellow of the American College of Sports Medicine

FAD   Family Assessment Device

FADE   focus, analyze, develop, and execute

FAF   Financial Accounting Foundation

FAHS   Federation of American Health Systems

FANEL   Federation for Accessible Nursing Education and Licensure

FAOTA   Fellow of the American Occupational Therapy Association

FAPA   Fellow of the American Psychiatric Association; Fellow of the American Psychological Association

FAPHA   Fellow of the American Public Health Association

FAQ   frequently asked questions; Functional Assessment Questionnaire

FARB   Federation of Associations of Regulatory Boards

FAS   Federation of American Scientists; fetal alcohol syndrome

FASA   Federated Ambulatory Surgery Association

FASB   Financial Accounting Standards Board

FASEB   Federation of American Societies for Experimental Biology

FAST   Functional Assessment Staging (scale)

FB   foreign bodies

FBA   Federal Bar Association

FBPCS   Federation of Behavioral, Psychological and Cognitive Sciences

FBS   fasting blood sugar

FCAP   Fellow of the College of American Pathologists

F cath   Foley catheter

FCIM   Federated Council for Internal Medicine

FCS   Food and Consumer Service (USDA)

FDA   Food and Drug Administration

fdg   feeding

FD&C   food, drug, and cosmetic

FDLI   Food and Drug Law Institute

fe   female

Fe   iron

FEC   freestanding emergency center

FEDRIP   Federal Research in Progress (database)

FEF   forced expiratory flow

FEHBP   Federal Employees Health Benefits Program

FEMA   Federal Emergency Management Agency

FEP   Federal Employees Health Benefits Program

FEV   forced expiratory volume

FEV1, FEV1   forced expiratory volume in one second

FFA   Federal Financial Assistance

FFP   fresh frozen plasma

FFS   fee for service

FFWHC   Federation of Feminist Women's Health Centers

F&G   Faulkner & Gray, Inc

FH   familial hypercholesterolemia; family history; floating hospital

FHCE   Foundation for Health Care Evaluation

FHCQ   Foundation for Health Care Quality

FHIP   Federal Health Insurance Plan

FHSR   Foundation for Health Services Research

FI   fiscal intermediary

FICA   Federal Insurance Contribution Act

FIC-SIT   Frailty and Injuries: Cooperative Studies of Intervention Techniques

FIGO   Federation of Gynecology and Obstetrics

FIM   Functional Independence Measure

FISH   fluorescence in situ hybridization

fl, fld   fluid

FLEX   Federation Licensing Examination

FLP   Functional Limitations Profile

FMC   Foundation for Medical Care

FMG   foreign medical graduate

FNAB   fine-needle aspiration biopsy

FNB   Food and Nutrition Board (IOM)

FNHP   Federation of Nurses and Health Professionals

FOBT   fecal occult blood test

FOIA   Freedom of Information Act

FORUM   Forum for Medical Affairs

FP   family physician; family planning; family practice; family practitioner

FPA   Federal Physicians Association

FPG   fasting plasma glucose

FPGEC   Foreign Pharmacy Graduate Examination Committee

FPMB   Federation of Podiatric Medical Boards

FPO   Federation of Prosthodontic Organizations

FREIDA   Fellowship and Residency Electronic Interactive Data Access

freq   frequency

FSCO   Federation of Straight Chiropractic Organizations

FSGH   Federated Societies of Gastroenterology and Hepatology

FSI   Functional Status Index

FSIS   Food Safety and Inspection Service

FSMB   Federation of State Medical Boards

FSQ   Functional Status Questionnaire

ft   foot

FT   Foundation of Thanatology

FTC   Federal Trade Commission

FTE   full-time equivalent

FTN   Family Therapy Network

FU, F/U   follow-up

FUO   fever of undetermined origin

FVC   forced vital capacity

FWB   full weight bearing

Fx   fracture

FY   fiscal year

g   gram

gal   gallon

GAO   (U.S.) General Accounting Office

GAP   Group for the Advancement of Psychiatry; Guidelines Appraisal Project

GAPP   General Administrative Policies and Procedures

GAPS   Goals-Assessment Planning Starting Approach; Guidelines for Adolescent Preventive Services

GASP   Group Against Smokers' Pollution

GB   gallbladder; governing body

GBS   group B streptococcal; group B *Streptococcus*

GCS   Glasgow Coma Scale

GDM   gestational diabetes mellitus

GDS   Geriatric Depression Scale; (Reisberg) Global Deterioration Scale

GED   general education degree

GERD   gastroesophageal reflux disease; gastroesophageal reflux disorder

GG   gamma globulin

GGT   gamma-glutamyl transpeptidase

GH   growth hormone

GHAA   Group Health Association of America

GHC   (formerly) Group Health Cooperative of Puget Sound

GHPM   general health policy model

GHQ   General Health Questionnaire

GHRF   growth hormone releasing factor

GI   gastrointestinal

GIFT   gamete intrafallopian transfer

GIMS   Graduates of Italian Medical Schools

GIPS   Gastrointestinal Pathology Society

GISSI-3   Third Gruppo Italiano per lo Studio della Sopravvivenza nell'Infarto Miocardico

GLMA   Gay and Lesbian Medical Association

GLU   glucose

gm, GM   gram

GME   graduate medical education

GMHC   Gay Men's Health Crisis

GMP   good manufacturing practice

GN   graduate nurse

GND   gross national debt

GNP   gross national product

GOG   Gynecologic Oncology Group

GP   general practice; general practitioner

GPIA   Generic Pharmaceutical Industry Association

GPIN   Group Practice Improvement Network

GPO   Government Printing Office

GPWW   group practice without walls

GRAE   generally recognized as effective

GRAS   generally recognized as safe

grav   pregnancy

GRD   gastroesophageal reflux disorder

GSA   General Services Administration; Genetics Society of America; Gerontological Society of America

GSPECT   gated single photon emission computed tomography

gtt   drops

G tube   gastrostomy tube

GUSTO   Global Utilization of Streptokinase and Tissue Plasminogen Activator for Occluded Coronary Arteries

GVH   graft versus host (reaction)

GVHD   graft-versus-host disease

GYN   gynecology

Hh

h   hour

H   heroin; hypodermic

HA   headache; Health Academy

HAA   Hospice Association of America

HACCP   Hazard Analysis and Critical Control Points (system)

HANES   Health and Nutrition Examination Survey

HAP   (Joint Commission) Hospital Accreditation Program

HAQ   health assessment questionnaire

HAS   *Hospital Accreditation Standards*

HAV   hepatitis A virus

Hb   hemoglobin

HbA   hemoglobin A

HbA1c   hemoglobin A1c (test)

HBAg   hepatitis B antigen

HbC   hemoglobin C

HBc   hepatitis B core antigen

HBC   Human Biology Council

HBcAG   hepatitis B core antigen

Hbg   hemoglobin

H2 blockers   histamine blockers

HBOC   hereditary breast-ovarian cancer

HBP   high blood pressure

HBs   hepatitis B surface antigen

HBsAg   hepatitis B surface antigen

HBSNF   hospital-based skilled nursing facility

HBV   hepatitis B virus

HC   Hastings Center

HCA   Haitian Coalition on AIDS

HCEA   Healthcare Convention and Exhibitors Association

HCFA   Health Care Financing Administration

HCG   human chorionic gonadotropin

HCHP   Harvard Community Health Plan

HCMMS   Health Care Material Management Society

HCN   health care network

HCPCS   HCFA Common Procedure Coding System

HCQA   Health Care Quality Alliance

HCQIA   Health Care Quality Improvement Act

HCQIP   Health Care Quality Improvement Program (HCFA)

Hct   hematocrit

HCV   hepatitis C virus

HCW   health care worker

HD   hemodialysis; Huntington's disease

HDA   Holistic Dental Association

HDL   high-density lipoprotein

HDL-C   high-density lipoprotein cholesterol

HDS   hospital discharge survey; human development service

HDSA   Huntington's Disease Society of America

HEDIS   Health Plan Employer Data and Information Set

HEENT   head, eye, ear, nose, and throat

HEI   Health and Energy Institute; Hospice Education Institute

HERO   Health Education Resource Organization

HSCA   Health Sciences Communications Association

HEV   hepatitis E virus

HEW   Department of Health, Education, and Welfare

HFHS   Henry Ford Health System

HFMA   Healthcare Financial Management Association

HFS   Human Factors Society

HFSG   Healthcare Financing Study Group

Hg   hectogram; hemoglobin; mercury

Hgb   hemoglobin

HGH   human growth hormone

HGP   Human Genome Project

HH   hereditary hemochromatosis

HHA   home health agency

HHS   health and human services

HHSSA   Home Health Services and Staffing Association

HI   Hospital Insurance Program Medicare, Part A

HIA   Hearing Industries Association

HIAA   Health Insurance Association of America

HIBAC   Health Insurance Benefits Advisory Council

HIBCC   Health Industry Business Communications Council

HIBR   Huxley Institute for Biosocial Research

HIC   Health Information Council

HICN   health insurance claim number

HIDA   Health Industry Distributors Association

HII   hepatic iron index

HIMA   Health Industry Manufacturers Association

HIMSS   Healthcare Information and Management Systems Society

HIP   Hospital Infections Program (CDC)

HIPC   health insurance purchasing cooperative

HIPE   hospital inpatient enquiry

HIRA   Health Industry Representatives Association

HIRE   Health Information Resource Executive (software)

HIS   Health Interview Survey; hospital information system

HIT   home infusion therapy

HIV   human immunodeficiency virus

HIV-1   human immunodeficiency virus type 1

HIV-ab   HIV antibody

HLA   histocompatibility leukocyte antigen; human leukocyte antigen

HLC   high lymph count

HMAC   Hazardous Materials Advisory Council

HMCRI   Hazardous Materials Control Resources Institute

HME   Health Media Education; home medical education

HMG   Healthcare Management Guidelines

HMO   health maintenance organization

HMU   Healthcare Management University

H&N   head and neck

HNA   Hospice Nurses Association

HNBA   Hispanic National Bar Association

HNPCC   hereditary nonpolyposis colorectal cancer

HO   house officer

H/O   history of

H₂O   water

HOH   hard of hearing

H&P   history and physical

HPC   high platelet count

HPI   history of present illness

HPQ   Health Perceptions Questionnaire

HPS   Health Physics Society

HPV   human papillomavirus

H pylori   *Helicobacter pylori*

hr   hour

HR   heart rate; hour

HRA   Health Resources Administration; health risk appraisal

HRET   Hospital Research and Educational Trust

HRQOL   health-related quality of life

HRSA   Health Resources and Services Administration

HRT   hormone replacement therapy

HS   Harvey Society; Hemlock Society; Histochemical Society; hour of sleep (bedtime)

HSA   Health Security Act; health service area; health systems agency; human serum albumin

HSAC   Health Security Action Council

HSC   Health Sciences Consortium

HSQ-12   Health Status Questionnaire 12

HSQB   Health Standards and Quality Bureau

HSR   health services research

HSR Proj   health services research projects (database)

HSRI   Human Services Research Institute

HSS   Health Screening Survey

HSUS   Health Services Utilization Study

HSV-1   herpes simplex virus type 1

HSV-2   herpes simplex virus type 2

5-HT   5-hydroxytryptamine

ht   height

Ht   hematocrit

HT   hypertension

HTA   health technology assessment

HTLV   human T lymphotropic virus

HTN   hypertension

HUAM   home uterine activity monitoring

HVWP   Hospitalized Veterans Writing Project

HWB   high white blood cell count; hot water bottle

Hx   history

Hyper   hypertension

HYST   hysterectomy

I   iodine

IADL   instrumental activities of daily living

IAETF   International Anti-Euthanasia Task Force

IAHB   Institute for the Advancement of Human Behavior

IAHCM   International Academy of Health Care Management

IAPSRS   International Association of Psychosocial Rehabilitation Services

IAR   Institute for Aerobics Research

IARASM   Institute for Advanced Research in Asian Science and Medicine

IASA   Insurance Accounting and Systems Association

IBD   inflammatory bowel disease

IBR   Institutes for Behavior Resources

IBS   irritable bowel syndrome

IC   intracutaneous

ICC   Injury Control Center

ICCP   Institute for Certification of Computer Professionals

ICCS   *International Classification of Clinical Services*

ICD   *International Classification of Diseases*

ICD-9-CM   *International Classification of Diseases, Ninth Revision, Clinical Modification*

ICD-10   *International Statistical Classification of Diseases and Related Health Problems*

ICF   intermediate care facility

ICF/MR   intermediate care facility specializing in care for the mentally retarded

ICLRN   Interagency Council on Library Resources for Nursing

ICP   intracranial pressure

ICPBC   Institute of Certified Professional Business Consultants

ICPI   Intersociety Committee on Pathology Information

ICPS   Interamerican College of Physicians and Surgeons

ICSI   Institute for Clinical Systems Integration

ICU   intensive care unit

id   *in diem* (during the day); intradermal

ID   infectious disease; intradermal

I&D   incision and drainage

IDA   Indian Dental Association

IDCNAA   Intra-Departmental Council on Native American Affairs

IDD   Inventory to Diagnose Depression

IDDM   insulin-dependent diabetes mellitus

IDL   intermediate-density lipoprotein

IDS   integrated delivery system; Inventory of Drinking Situations

IDSA   Infectious Diseases Society of America

I:E   inspiration to expiration

IEE   Institute of Electrology Educators

IEEE   Institute of Electrical and Electronics Engineers

IFA   immunofluorescence antibody

IFC   Infant Formula Council

IFG   impaired fasting glucose

Ig   immunoglobulin

IG   inspector general

Igs   immune globulins

IGSP   Institute for Gravitational Strain Pathology

IGT   impaired glucose tolerance

IH   infectious hepatitis

IHC   InterMountain Health Care

IHCA   individual health care account

IHCNE   Institute for Hospital Clinical Nursing Education

IHCP   Institute on Hospital and Community Psychiatry

IHI   Institute for Healthcare Improvement

IHPO   International Health Program Office (CDC)

IHPP   Intergovernmental Health Policy Project

IHS   Indian Health Service

IHWU   Independent Hospital Workers Union

IIA   Impotence Institute of America; Information Industry Association; Intelligence Industries Association

IICU   infectious intensive care unit

ILAR   Institute of Laboratory Animal Resources; International League Against Rheumatism; International League of Associations for Rheumatology

ILSM   interim life safety measures

IM   implementation monitoring; intramuscular

IMA   Islamic Medical Association

IMCARE   Internal Medicine Center to Advance Research and Education

IMD   institution for mental disease

IMDA   Independent Medical Distributors Association

IMDC   International Medical Device Codes

IMS   indicator measurement system; Institute of Mathematical Statistics

incr   increased; increasing

IND   investigational new drug

inf   infection

INH   isoniazid

inj   injection

INMED   Indians Into Medicine

inpt   inpatient

INR   international normalized ratio

INS   Intravenous Nurses Society

int   internal

in vitro   within a test tube

in vivo   within a living body

I&O   intake and ouput

IOCT   Information-Orientation-Concentration Test

IOL   intraocular lens

IOM   Institute of Medicine

IOP   intraocular pressure

IP   intraperitoneal

IPA   individual practice association; independent practice association

IPG   impedance plethysmography

IPMANA   Interstate Postgraduate Medical Association of North America

IPP   Impaired Physician Program

IQ   intelligence quotient

IR   infrared spectrometry

IRA   individual retirement account

IRB   institutional review board

IRDS   information resource dictionary system

IRET   Institute for Rational-Emotive Therapy

IRH   Institute for Reproductive Health

IRHP   Institute for Research in Hypnosis and Psychotherapy

irreg   irregular

irrig   irrigate

IRT   Institute for Reality Therapy

ISH   isolated systolic hypertension

ISIS   International Study of Infarct Survival

ISMP   Institute for Safe Medication Practices

ISQA   International Society for Quality Assurance

ISS   Injury Severity Score

It   immunotherapy

IT   inhalation therapy

Ith   intrathecal

ITP   idiopathic thrombocytopenic purpura

IU   international unit

IUCD   intrauterine contraceptive device

IUD   intrauterine device

IV   intravascular; intravenous

IVF   in vitro fertilization

IVPB   intravenous piggyback

IVT   Institute for Victims of Trauma; intravenous transfusion

Jj

JACC   *Journal of the American College of Cardiology*

JAMA   *Journal of the American Medical Association*

jc   juice

JCAHO   Joint Commission on Accreditation of Healthcare Organizations

JCAHPO   Joint Commission on Allied Health Personnel in Ophthalmology

JCAI   Joint Council of Allergy and Immunology

JCI   Joint Commission International

JCIH   Joint Committee on Infant Hearing

JCSMS   Joint Commission on Sports Medicine and Science

JDC   Joslin Diabetes Center

JIT   just in time

JNCI   *Journal of the National Cancer Institute*

JNC-V   The Fifth Report of the Joint National Committee on Detection, Evaluation, and Treatment of High Blood Pressure

JODM   juvenile onset diabetes mellitus

JPSA   Jewish Pharmaceutical Society of America

JRCDMS   Joint Review Committee on Education in Diagnostic Medical Sonography

JRCEMT-P   Joint Review Committee on Educational Programs for the EMT-Paramedic

JRCERT   Joint Review Committee on Education in Radiologic Technology

JRCOMP   Joint Review Committee for Ophthalmic Medical Personnel

JRCRTE   Joint Review Committee for Respiratory Therapy Education

JSDF   Jin Shin Do Foundation for Bodymind Acupressure

JUA   joint underwriting association

Kk

K   potassium

kg   kilogram

KHC   Karen Horney Clinic

KIPS   key items, probes, and scoring guidelines

KJ   knee jerk

KMAA   Korean Medical Association of America

KO   keep open

KPS   Karvofsky Performance Status

KQC   key quality characteristic

KRS   Kerato-Refractive Society

KS   Kaposi's sarcoma

KUB   kidney, ureter, and bladder

KVO   keep vein open

L   left; liter

L1–L5   lumbar vertebrae

L&A   light and accommodation

lab, LAB   laboratory

lac   laceration

LAMA   Laboratory Animal Management Association

LAN   local area network

lap   laparotomy

laser   light amplification by stimulated emission of radiation

lat   lateral

lb   pound

LB   low back

LBBB   left bundle branch block

LBP   low back pain

LBW   low birth weight

LCAO   Leadership Council of Aging Organizations

LCGME   Liaison Committee on Graduate Medical Education

LCIS   lobular carcinoma in situ

LCL   lower control limit

LCME   Liaison Committee on Medical Education

LCSW   Licensed clinical social worker

L&D   labor and delivery

LDL   low-density lipoprotein

LDL-C   low-density lipoprotein cholesterol

L-dopa   levodopamine

LED   light emitting diode

LEMA   Laser and Electro-Optics Manufacturers' Association

LEO   Lifelong Education for the Ophthalmologist

LEOS   Lasers and Electro-Optics Society

LGBPM   Lesbian, Gay and Bisexual People in Medicine

LGCPHW   Lesbian and Gay Caucus of Public Health Workers

LGHCS   Lutheran General Health Care System

LHA   Lutheran Hospital Association of America

LHEP   Lung Health Education Program

LHHS   Lutheran Hospitals and Homes Society

LHS   Lung Health Study

Li   lithium

LI   Lifegain Institute

LIA   Laser Institute of America

lig   ligament

LIMIT-2   Leicester Intravenous Magnesium Intervention Trial

LIP   licensed independent practitioner

liq   liquid

LKS   liver, kidney, and spleen

LLE   left lower extremity

LMD   local medical doctor

LMP   last menstrual period

LMW   low molecular weight

LMWH   low-molecular-weight heparin

LOC   level of consciousness; loss of consciousness

LOCM   low osmolality contrast medium

LOD   line of duty

LOM   limitation of motion

LOS   length of stay

LP   lumbar puncture

LPC   low platelet count

LPM   liter per minute

LPN   licensed practical nurse

LR   labor room

LSC   *Life Safety Code*®

LSD   lysergic acid diethylamide

LSi   Life Satisfaction Index

LSM   life safety management

L-spine   lumbar spine

LT   laughter therapy

LTC   long term care

LTCC   Long Term Care Campaign

LTCF   long term care facility

LUE   left upper extremity

LV left ventricular

LVN licensed vocational nurse

LVRS lung volume reduction surgery

L&W living and well

lytes electrolytes

M male; married; meter; murmur

MA mental age

MAC maximum allowable concentration; *Mycobacterium avium* complex

MADRS Montgomery-Asberg depression rating scale

MANA Midwives Alliance of North America

MAO monoamine oxidase (inhibitor)

MAODP Medic Alert Organ Donor Program

MAST medical antishock trousers; Michigan Alcoholism Screening Test; military antishock trousers

MAST-G Michigan Alcoholism Screening Test-Geriatric Version

MATCH Matching Alcohol Treatment to Client Heterogeneity (Project Match)

MATP Microhemagglutination assay for *Treponeina pallidum*

MB megabyte

MBA management by accountability; Master of Business Administration

MBC maximal breathing capacity

MBD minimal brain damage

MBO management by objectives

Mc, mC millicurie

MCA Maternity Center Association

MCAT Medical College Admission Test

MCF Medical Cybernetics Foundation

mcg microgram

MCH maternal and child health; mean corpuscular hemoglobulin

MCHB Maternal and Child Health Bureau

MCHC mean corpuscular hemoglobulin concentration

MCO managed care organization

MCPI medical consumer price index

MCV mean corpuscular volume; measles-containing vaccine

MD Doctor of Medicine; medical doctor; muscular dystrophy

MDA Mission Doctors Association

MDC major diagnostic category

MDD major depressive disorder; mean daily dosage

MDHBA Medical-Dental-Hospital Bureaus of America

MDI metered dose inhaler; multiple daily injections

MDiv Master of Divinity

MDPIT Multicenter Diltiazem Postinfarction Trial

MDR multidrug resistant; multiple drug resistance

MDR-TB multidrug-resistant tuberculosis

MDS Minimum Data Set

MDS+ Minimum Data Set Plus

MDV multiple dose vial

ME medical examiner

M&E monitoring and evaluation

MEC minimum effective concentration

med median; medication; medicine

MED mean effective dose; medication; medicine

medevac medical evacuation

Medi-Cal California's Medicaid (program)

MedisGroups Medical Illness Severity Grouping System

MEDISGRPS Medical Illness Severity Grouping System

MEDLARS Medical Literature Analysis and Retrieval System

MEDLINE MEDLARS online

MedPAC Medicare Payment Advisory Commission

MEDPAR Medicare Provider Analysis and Review

MEDTEP Medical Treatment Effectiveness Program

MEFR maximum expiratory flow rate

MEGO my eyes glaze over

mEq milliequivalent

mEq/L milliequivalent per liter

MES maximum electroshock seizure

MeSH Medical Subject Headings

MET metabolic equivalent of task

MF myocardial fibrosis

MFAQ Multidimensional Functional Assessment Questionnaire

MFI Master Facility Inventory of Hospitals and Institutions

mg milligram

Mg magnesium

MGMA Medical Group Management Association

MHA   Maryland Hospital Association; Master of Health Administration; Master of Hospital Administration; Mennonite Health Association

MHCA   Managed Health Care Association

MHI   Mental Health Inventory

MHIFM   Milton Helpern Institute of Forensic Medicine

MHIQ   McMaster Health Index Questionnaire

MHLP   Mental Health Law Project

MH/MR   mental health/mental retardation

MHS   multihospital system

MHSA   Master of Health Services Administration

MHSIP   Mental Health Statistics Improvement Program

MHSS   Military Health Services System

MI   myocardial infarction

MIAMI   Metoprolol in Acute Myocardial Infarction

MIB   Medical Impairment Bureau

MIC   minimum inhibitory concentration

MICU   medical intensive care unit; mobile intensive care unit

min, MIN   minute

MIND   Multidisciplinary Institute for Neuropsychological Development

MIPI   Medicine in the Public Interest

MIS   management information system

misc   miscellaneous

MISS   Medical Interview Satisfaction Scale

MITI   Myocardial Infarction Triage and Intervention

MIWHR   Melpomene Institute for Women's Health Research

MKSAP   Medical Knowledge Self-Assessment Program

ml, mL   milliliter

MLA   Medical Library Association

MLC   minimum lethal dosage

mm   millimeter

mM   millimole

MM   mucous membrane

MMA   Mercy Medical Airlift

MMAF   Maine Medical Assessment Foundation

MMLDP   Maine Medical Liability Demonstration Project

MMPI   Minnesota Multiphasic Personality Inventory

MMR   measles, mumps, rubella

MMSA   Medical Mycological Society of the Americas

MMSE   Mini-Mental State Examination

MMWR   *Morbidity and Mortality Weekly Report*

MNMC   Medical Network for Missing Children

MO   modus operandi

MOD   maturity onset diabetes

MODS   multiple organ dysfunction syndrome

MOM   milk of magnesia

MONO   mononucleosis

mos   months

MOS   Medical Outcomes Study

MOT   Medical Outcomes Trust

MPA   Master of Public Administration; medroxyprogesterone acetate

MPH   Master of Public Health

MPQ   McGill Pain Questionnaire

MQSA   Mammography Quality Standards Act

MR   may repeat; measles and rubella (vaccine); mental retardation

M&R   Milliman & Robertson

MRA   medical record administrator

MRAA   Mental Retardation Association of America

MR/DD   mental retardation/developmental disability

MRI   magnetic resonance imaging; medical record index (number); Medical Records Institute; Mental Research Institute

MRMC   Medical Research Modernization Committee

MRT   medical record technician

MS   multiple sclerosis

MSA   medical savings account

MSMIA   Medical and Sports Music Institute of America

MSN   Master of Science in Nursing

MSO   management service organization

MSP   modified survey process

MSSD   Model Secondary School for the Deaf

MSUSM   Medical Society of the United States and Mexico

MSW   Master of Social Work; medical/hospital social worker

MT   medical technologist

MTC   maximum toxic concentration

MUMPS   Massachusetts General Hospital Utility Multiprogramming System

MV   minute volume

MVP   mitral valve prolapse

MVR   mitral valve replacement

N normal

Na sodium

NA not accredited

N/A not applicable

NAAAA National Association of Area Agencies on Aging

NAACLS National Accrediting Agency for Clinical Laboratory Sciences

NAADAC National Association of Alcoholism and Drug Abuse Counselors

NAAHP National Association of Advisors for the Health Professions

NAAMM North American Academy of Musculoskeletal Medicine

NAANGHT National Association of Air National Guard Health Technicians

NAAP National Association of Activity Professionals; National Association of Apnea Professionals

NAAPABAC National Association for the Advancement of Psychoanalysis and the American Boards for Accreditation and Certification

NAATP National Association of Addiction Treatment Providers

NAB National Association of Boards of Examiners for Nursing Home Administrators

NABCO National Alliance of Breast Cancer Organizations

NABP National Association of Boards of Pharmacy

NABR National Association for Biomedical Research

NABSW National Association of Black Social Workers

NABWA National Association of Black Women Attorneys

NAC National AIDS Clearinghouse

NACA National Association of Childbirth Assistants

NACC National Association of Childbearing Centers; National Association of Counsel for Children

NACDS National Association of Chain Drug Stores

NACEHSP National Accreditation Council for Environmental Health Science and Protection

NACFT National Academy of Counselors and Family Therapists

NACHC National Association of Community Health Centers

NACHFA National Association of County Health Facility Administrators

NACHO National Association of County Health Officials

NACHRI National Association of Children's Hospitals and Related Institutions

NAD National Association of the Deaf; no acute distress

NADA National Association of Dental Assistants

NADAP National Association on Drug Abuse Problems

NADDC National Association of Developmental Disabilities Councils

NADE National Association of Disability Examiners

NADEP National Association of Disability Evaluating Professionals

NADL National Association of Dental Laboratories

NADONA/LTC National Association of Directors of Nursing Administration in Long Term Care

NADT National Association for Drama Therapy

NAEHCA National Association of Employers on Health Care Action

NAEMSP National Association of Emergency Medical Service Physicians

NAEMT National Association of Emergency Medical Technicians

NAEPP National Asthma Education and Prevention Program

NAER National Association of Executive Recruiters

NAF National Abortion Federation

NAFAC National Association for Ambulatory Care

NAFAR National Association of First Responders

NAHAM National Association of Healthcare Access Management

NAHC National Association for Home Care

NAHCR National Association for Healthcare Recruitment

NAHCS National Association of Health Career Schools

NAHDO National Association of Health Data Organizations

NAHHH National Association of Hospital Hospitality Houses

NAHMOR National Association of HMO Regulators

NAHN National Association of Hispanic Nurses

NAHQ National Association for Healthcare Quality

NAHSC National Association of Homes and Services for Children

NAHSE National Association of Health Services Executives

NAHU National Association of Health Underwriters

NAHUC National Association of Health Unit Coordinators

NALGAP   National Association of Lesbian/Gay Alcoholism Professionals

NAMCP   National Association of Managed Care Physicians

NAMDRC   National Association for Medical Direction of Respiratory Care

NAME   National Association of Medical Examiners

NAMES   National Association of Medical Equipment Suppliers

NAMI   National Alliance for the Mentally Ill

NAMO   National Association of Manufacturing Opticians

NAMP   National Association of Meal Programs

NAMS   North American Membrane Society; North American Menopause Society

NAMSIC   National Arthritis and Musculoskeletal and Skin Diseases Information Clearinghouse

NAMSS   National Association Medical Staff Services

NAMT   National Association for Music Therapy

NAN   National Academy of Neuropsychology

NANASP   National Association of Nutrition and Aging Services Programs

NANDA   North American Nursing Diagnosis Association

NANN   National Association of Neonatal Nurses

NANPRH   National Association of Nurse Practitioners in Reproductive Health

NANR   National Association for Nursing Research

NAO   National Academy of Opticianry

NAON   National Association of Orthopaedic Nurses

NAOO   National Association of Optometrists and Opticians

NAOSW   National Association of Oncology Social Workers

NAOT   National Association of Orthopaedic Technologists

NAPARE   National Association for Perinatal Addiction Research and Education

NAPC   National Assault Prevention Center

NAPCRG   North American Primary Care Research Group

NAPCWA   National Association of Public Child Welfare Administrators

NAPD   no apparent pulmonary disease

NAPGCM   National Association of Private Geriatric Care Managers

NAPH   National Association of Public Hospitals

NAPHS   National Association of Psychiatric Health Systems

NAPM   National Association of Pharmaceutical Manufacturers

NAPN   National Association of Physician Nurses

NAPNAP   National Association of Pediatric Nurse Associates and Practitioners

NAPNES   National Association for Practical Nurse Education and Service

NAPPH   National Association of Private Psychiatric Hospitals

NAPR   National Association of Physician Recruiters

NAPRR   National Association of Private Residential Resources

NAPT   National Association for Poetry Therapy

NAPTCC   National Association of Psychiatric Treatment Centers for Children

NAQAP   National Association of QA Professionals

NARF   National Association of Rehabilitation Facilities

NARI   National Association of Rehabilitation Instructors; National Association of Residents and Interns

NARIC   National Rehabilitation Information Center

NARMH   National Association for Rural Mental Health

NARN   National Association of Registered Nurses

NARO   National Association of Reimbursement Officers

NARPPS   National Association of Rehabilitation Professionals in the Private Sector

NARS   National Association of Rehabilitation Secretaries

NAS   National Academy of Sciences; no added salt

NASADAD   National Association of State Alcohol and Drug Abuse Directors

NASAHOE   National Association of Supervisors and Administrators of Health Occupations Education

NASAR   National Association for Search and Rescue

NASCD   National Association for Sickle Cell Disease

NASDAD   National Association of Seventh-Day Adventist Dentists

NASDT   North American Society for Dialysis and Transplantation

NASEMSD   National Association of State EMS Directors

NASLI   National Association for Senior Living Industries

NASMHPD   National Association of State Mental Health Program Directors

NASMRPD   National Association of State Mental Retardation Program Directors

NASN   National Association of School Nurses

NASP   National Association of School Psychologists

NASPE   North American Society of Pacing and Electro-physiology

NASPGN   North American Society for Pediatric Gastroenterology and Nutrition

NASPSPA   North American Society for the Psychology of Sport and Physical Activity

NASS   North American Spine Society

NASUA   National Association of State Units on Aging

NASW   National Association of Social Workers

NATA   National Athletic Trainers Association

NATCO   North American Transplant Coordinators Organization

NAVAP   National Association of VA Physicians and Dentists

NAVP   National Association of Vision Professionals

NAWL   National Association of Women Lawyers

NB   newborn

NBA   National Bar Association

NBAC   National Black Alcoholism Council

NBC   National Board for Certification in Dental Technology

NBCC   National Board for Certified Counselors

NBCOT   National Board for Certification of Orthopaedic Technologists

NBEO   National Board of Examiners in Optometry

NBIE   National Burn Information Exchange

NBME   National Board of Medical Examiners

NBNA   National Black Nurses Association

NBOME   National Board of Osteopathic Medical Examiners

NBPME   National Board of Podiatric Medical Examiners

NBRC   National Board for Respiratory Care

NBTA   National Board of Trial Advocacy

NBWHP   National Black Women's Health Project

Nc   neurologic check

NCA   National Certification Agency for Medical Lab Personnel;   National Council on Aging; Nurse Consultants Association

NCABHP   National Center for the Advancement of Blacks in the Health Professions

NCADD   National Council on Alcoholism and Drug Dependence

NCADV   National Coalition Against Domestic Violence

NCAHCP   National Council on Alternative Health Care Policy

NCAHF   National Council Against Health Fraud

NCAI   National Coalition for Adult Immunization

NCAPA   National Coalition for Alcoholism Program Accreditation

NCASA   National Coalition Against Sexual Assault

NCASC   National Council of Acupuncture Schools and Colleges

NCATA   National Coalition of Arts Therapy Associations

NCBL   National Conference of Black Lawyers

NCBLRDC   National Coalition of Black Lung and Respiratory Disease Clinics

NCBPNP/N   National Certification Board of Pediatric Nurse Practitioners and Nurses

NCCA   National Catholic Council on Alcoholism and Related Drug Problems; National Commission for the Certification of Acupuncturists

NCCAFV   National Council on Child Abuse and Family Violence

NCCC   National Center for Cost Containment

NCCDN   National Consortium of Chemical Dependency Nurses

NCCDPHP   National Center for Chronic Disease Prevention and Health Promotion

NCCEM   National Coordinating Council on Emergency Management

NCCH   National Council of Community Hospitals

NCCHC   National Commission on Correctional Health Care

NCCLS   National Committee for Clinical Laboratory Standards

NCCMHC   National Council of Community Mental Health Centers

NCCMHS   National Consortium for Child Mental Health Services

NCCNHR   National Citizens Coalition for Nursing Home Reform

NCCPA   National Commission on Certification of Physician Assistants

NCCR   National Coalition for Cancer Research

NCEC   National Commission for Electrologist Certification

NCEH   National Center for Environmental Health (CDC)

NCEMCH   National Center for Education in Maternal and Child Health

NCEP   National Cholesterol Education Program

NCFR   National Council on Family Relations

NCFS   National College of Foot Surgeons

NCH   National Center for Homeopathy; National Council on the Handicapped

NCHE   National Center for Health Education

NCHGR   National Center for Human Genome Research

NCHLS   National Council on Health Laboratory Services

NCHS   National Center for Health Statistics

NCHSTP   National Center for HIV, ST [sexually transmitted disease], and TB [tuberculosis] Prevention

NCI   National Cancer Institute

NCIC   Non-Circumcision Information Center

NCID   National Center for Infectious Diseases (CDC)

NCIPC   National Center for Injury Prevention and Control (CDC)

NCISD   National Coalition on Immune System Disorders

NCL   National Consumers League

NCLE   National Contact Lens Examiners

NCLEHA   National Conference of Local Environmental Health Administrators

NCLEX   National Council Licensure Examinations

NCME   Network for Continuing Medical Education

NCOA   National Council on the Aging

NCOMDR   National Clearinghouse on Marital and Date Rape

NCPAMT   National Coalition of Psychiatrists Against Motorcoach Therapy

NCPCA   National Committee for Prevention of Child Abuse

NCPDP   National Council for Prescription Drug Programs

NCPG   National Catholic Pharmacists Guild

NCPIE   National Council on Patient Information and Education

NCPOA   National Chronic Pain Outreach Association

NCQA   National Committee on Quality Assurance

NCQHC   National Committee for Quality Health Care

NCR   National Coalition for Research in Neurological Disorders

NCRA   National Center on Rural Aging

NCRC/AODA   National Certification Reciprocity Consortium/Alcoholism and Other Drug Abuse

NCRE   National Council on Rehabilitation Education

NCRPM   National Council on Radiation Protection and Measurements

NCRV   National Committee for Radiation Victims

NCSBCS   National Conference of States on Building Codes and Standards

NCSBN   National Council of State Boards of Nursing

NCSC   National Child Safety Council

NCSE   Neurobehavioral Cognitive Status Examination

NCSEMSTC   National Council of State Emergency Medical Services Training Coordinators

NCSL   National Conference of Standards Laboratories

NCSPAE   National Council of State Pharmacy Association Executives

NCTIP   National Committee on the Treatment of Intractable Pain

NCTR   National Center for Toxicological Research (FDA)

NCTRC   National Council for Therapeutic Recreation Certification

ND   Doctor of Naturopathy

NDA   National Dental Association; National Denturist Association; new-drug application

NDAA   National Dental Assistants Association

NDC   National Drug Code

NDDG   National Diabetes Data Group

NDDIC   National Digestive Diseases Information Clearinghouse

NDMA   Nonprescription Drug Manufacturers Association

NDTA   Neurodevelopmental Treatment Association

NDTC   National Drug Trade Conference

Nd/YAG   neodymium/yttrium aluminum garnet (laser)

NEA   Nutrition Education Association

neb   nebulizer

NECAD   National Episcopal Coalition on Alcohol and Drugs

neg, NEG   negative

NEHA   National Environmental Health Association

NEI   National Eye Institute

NEJM   New England Journal of Medicine

NEMA   National Emergency Management Association; National Emergency Medicine Association

NEMSPA   National EMS Pilots Association

NEP   needle exchange program

NESS   National Easter Seal Society

NEU   neurology

NF   National Formulary

NFA   Natural Food Associates

NFC   not for component

NFCPG   National Federation of Catholic Physicians Guilds

NFHO   National Federation of Housestaff Organizations

NFLPN   National Federation of Licensed Practical Nurses

NFNA   National Flight Nurses Association

NFNID   National Foundation for Non-Invasive Diagnostics

NFPA   National Fire Protection Association; National Flight Paramedics Association

NFPRHA   National Family Planning and Reproductive Health Association

NFSCSW   National Federation of Societies for Clinical Social Work

NFSNO   National Federation of Specialty Nursing Organizations

NFT neurofibrillary tangles

ng   nanogram

NG   nasogastric

NGS   National Geriatrics Society

NHA   National Hypertension Association

NHANES National Health and Nutrition Examination Survey

NHAS   National Hearing Aid Society

NHCA   National Health Club Association; National Hearing Conservation Association

NHCAA   National Health Care Anti-Fraud Association

NHGRI   National Human Genome Research Institute (NIH)

NHeLP   National Health Law Program

NHF   National Health Federation

NHGRI   National Human Genome Research Institute

NHI   national health insurance

NHIA   National Home Infusion Association

NHIF   National Head Injury Foundation (now BIA)

NHIS   Nursing Home Information Service

NHL   non-Hodgkin's lymphoma

NHLA   National Health Lawyers Association (now NHLA/AAHA)

NHLA/AAHA   National Health Lawyers Association/ American Academy of Healthcare Attorneys

NHLBI   National Heart, Lung, and Blood Institute

NHLI   National Library of Healthcare Indicators

NHO   National Hospice Organization

NHP   Nottingham Health Profile

NHPF   National Health Policy Forum

NHPP   National Hormone and Pituitary Program

NHR   National Heart Research

NHS   normal human serum

NHSA   National Heart Savers Association

NHSC   National Health Service Corps

NIA   National Institute on Aging

NIAAA   National Institute of Alcohol Abuse and Alcoholism

NIAD   National Institute on Adult Daycare

NIAID   National Institute of Allergy and Infectious Diseases (now NIAAID)

NIAMS   National Institute of Arthritis and Musculoskeletal and Skin Diseases

NIBM   National Institute for Burn Medicine

NICD   National Information Center on Deafness

NICHCY   National Information Center for Children and Youth with Disabilities

NICHD   National Institute of Child Health and Human Development

NICLC   National Institute on Community-Based Long-Term Care

NICO   National Insurance Consumer Organization

NICU   neonatal intensive care unit

NIDA   National Institute on Drug Abuse

NIDCD   National Institute on Deafness and Other Communication Disorders

NIDDK   National Institute of Diabetes and Digestive and Kidney Diseases

NIDDM   non–insulin-dependent diabetes mellitus

NIDR   National Institute of Dental Research

NIDSEC   Nursing Information and Data Set Evaluation Center

NIEHS   National Institute of Environmental Health Sciences

NIEI   National Institute of Electromedical Information

NIF   National Institute for the Family

NIGMS   National Institute of General Medical Sciences

NIH   National Institutes of Health

NIHB   National Indian Health Board

NIJ   National Institute of Justice

NIJH   National Institute for Jewish Hospice

NIMH National Institute of Mental Health

NINCDS-ADRDA   National Institute of Neurological and Communicative Disorders and Stroke- Alzheimer's Disease and Related Disorders Association (criteria)

NINDS   National Institute of Neurological Disorders and Stroke

NINR   National Institute of Nursing Research

NIOSH   National Institute for Occupational Safety and Health

NIP   National Immunization Program (CDC)

NIRE   National Institute for Rehabilitation Engineering

NIST   National Institute of Standards and Technology

NIT   Nurses in Transition

NITA   National Institute for Trial Advocacy

NKA   no known allergies

NKUDIC   National Kidney and Urologic Diseases Information Clearinghouse

NLCMDD   National Legal Center for the Medically Dependent and Disabled

NLCOA   National Leadership Coalition on AIDS

NLHC   National League for Health Care

NLM   National Library of Medicine

NLN   National League for Nursing

NLP   natural language processing

NMA   National Medical Association

NMAC   National Minority AIDS Council

NMCHC   National Maternal and Child Health Clearinghouse

NMCS   National Medic-Card Systems

NMDA   National Medical and Dental Association

NMDP   National Marrow Donor Program

NMF   National Medical Fellowships

NMHA   National Mental Health Association; National Minority Health Association

NMR   nuclear magnetic resonance

NMTCB   Nuclear Medicine Technology Certification Board

NNBA   National Nurses in Business Association

NNIS   National Nosocomial Infections Surveillance (system)

NNMC   National Naval Medical Center

NNSA   National Nurses Society on Addictions

NNV   nocturnal nasal ventilation

no   number

NOA   National Optometric Association

NOADN   National Organization for Associate Degree Nursing

NOAPP   National Organization of Adolescent Pregnancy and Parenting

noc   nocturnal (night)

NOCA   National Organization for Competency Assurance

NOCIRC   National Organization of Circumcision Information Resource Centers

NOD   National Organization on Disability

NOGLSTP   National Organization of Gay and Lesbian Scientists and Technical Professionals

NOHA   Nutrition for Optimal Health Association

NOTA   National Organ Transplant Act of 1984

NOVA   Nurses Organization of Veterans Affairs

NOWPA   National Osteopathic Women Physician's Association

NP   nurse practitioner

NPA   National Pediculosis Association; National Perinatal Association; National Phlebotomy Association

NPAP   National Psychological Association for Psychoanalysis

NPC   National Pharmaceutical Council

NPDB   National Practitioner Data Bank

NPDR   nonproliferative diabetic retinopathy

NPhA   National Pharmaceutical Association

NPI   no present illness

NPMA   National Podiatric Medical Association

NPN   National Prevention Network

npo   *nil per os* (nothing by mouth)

NPPV   noninvasive positive pressure ventilation

NPSF   National Patient Safety Foundation

NPT   normal pressure and temperature

NR   no refill

NRA   National Rehabilitation Association

NRAA   National Renal Administrators Association

NRBC   National Rare Blood Club

NRC   National Research Council;Nuclear Regulatory Commission

NRCA   National Rehabilitation Counseling Association

NRCC   National Registry of Clinical Chemistry

NRCHMI   National Resource Center on Homelessness and Mental Illness

NREM   non–rapid eye movement

NREMT   National Registry of Emergency Medical Technicians

NRHA   National Rural Health Association

NRLC   National Right to Life Committee

NRMP   National Residency Matching Program

NRWA   National Rural Water Association

ns   not significant

NS   neurosurgery; normal saline; nursing student

NSA   Neurosurgical Society of America

NSABP   National Surgical Adjuvant Breast Project

NSAID   nonsteroidal anti-inflammatory drug

NSC   National Safety Council

NSCT/NSPT   National Society for Cardiovascular Technology/National Society for Pulmonary Technology

NSD   normal spontaneous delivery

NSE   neuron-specific enolase

NSEA   National Standards Educators Association

NSF   National Sanitation Foundation

NSFTD   normal spontaneous full term delivery

nsg   nursing

NSGC   National Society of Genetic Counselors

NSH   National Society for Histotechnology

NSIDSC   National Sudden Infant Death Syndrome Clearinghouse

NSMS   National Safety Management Society

NSPRCA   National Society of Patient Representation and Consumer Affairs

NSPS   National Society of Professional Sanitarians

NSPST   National Society of Pharmaceutical Sales Trainers

NSSQ   Norbeck Social Support Questionnaire

NST   non-stress test

NSVD   normal spontaneous vaginal delivery

N/T   numbness and tingling

N&T   nose and throat

NTD   neural tube defect

NTID   National Technical Institute for the Deaf

NTIS   National Technical Information Service

NTRA   National Tumor Registrars Association

NTRS   National Therapeutic Recreation Society

NUBC   National Uniform Billing Committee

N/V   nausea and vomiting

N&V   nausea and vomiting

NVAC   National Vaccine Advisory Committee

NVHA   National Voluntary Health Agencies

NWA   National Wellness Association

NWB   non-weight bearing

NWDA   National Wholesale Druggists' Association

NWHN   National Women's Health Network

NWHRC   National Women's Health Resource Center

NWI   National Wellness Institute

NYHA   New York Heart Association

NYHAFC   New York Heart Association Functional Class (for angina severity)

o   hours

O   oral

O₂   oxygen

ō   without

OA   osteoarthritis

OAA   Opticians Association of America

OAG   open-angle glaucoma

OAM   Office of Alternative Medicine (NIH)

OAR   Office of AIDS Research (NIH)

OASDHI   Old Age, Survivors, Disability and Health Insurance (Program)

OASDI   Old Age, Survivors, and Disability Insurance (Program)

OB   obstetrician; obstetrics

OB-GYN   obstetrics and gynecology

OBRA   Omnibus Budget Reconciliation Act

OBSSR   Office of Behavioral and Social Sciences Research (NIH)

OC   oral contraceptive

occ   occasional

OCHAMPUS   Office of Civilian Health and Medical Program of the Uniformed Services

OCOO   Osteopathic College of Ophthalmology and Otorhinolaryngology

od   *omni die* (every day); overdose

OD   Doctor of Optometry; right eye

ODH   Office of Disability and Health

ODPHP   Office of Disease Prevention and Health Promotion

OEA   Optometric Editors Association

OEPF   Optometric Extension Program Foundation

OGTT   oral glucose tolerance test

oh   *omni hora* (every hour)

OHS   open heart surgery; Optometric Historical Society

OHTA   Office of Health Technology Assessment

OI   opportunistic infection

OIG   Office of the Inspector General

oj, OJ   orange juice

OJJDP   Office of Juvenile Justice and Delinquency Prevention

OJP   Office of Justice Programs

OJT   on-the-job training

OLA   Optical Laboratories Association

OMAR   Office of Medical Applications of Research

OMB   Office of Management and Budget

OMC   Office of Managed Care; Outcomes Management Consortia

OME   otitis media with effusion

OMSAP   Occupational Medicine Self-Assessment Program

OMT   osteopathic manipulative treatment

Onc   oncology

ONHIC   ODPHP National Health Information Center

ONS   Oncology Nursing Society

OOB   out of bed

OOSS   Outpatient Ophthalmic Surgery Society

OP   outpatient; operation

OPA   organ procurement agency

OPD   outpatient department

OPEC   Office of Prevention, Education, and Control (NIH)

OPHS   Office of Public Health and Science (AHCPR)

OPO   Organ Procurement Organization

OPRR   Office for Protection from Research Risks (NIH)

OPS   Ophthalmic Photographers' Society

OPTN   Organ Procurement Transplantation Network

OPV   oral polio vaccine

OR   operating room

ORI   Office of Research Integrity (NIH); Ophthalmic Research Institute

orient x 3   oriented to time, place, and person

ORS   Orthopedic Research Society

ORT   operating room technician

ORWH   Office of Research on Women's Health (NIH)

os   mouth

OS   left eye

OSA   Optical Society of America

OSHA   Occupational Safety and Health Administration

OSHRC   Occupational Safety and Health Review Commission

OSMA   Orthopedic Surgical Manufacturers Association

OSPD   Ordinal Scales of Psychological Development

OSPD-M   Ordinal Scales of Psychological Development-Modified

OSTP   Office of Science and Technology Policy

OT   occupational therapist; occupational therapy

OTA   Office of Technology Assessment

OTC   over the counter

OTR   registered occupational therapist

ou   *oculi unitas* (both eyes); *oculus uterque* (each eye)

OVC   Office for Victims of Crime

OWA   other weird arrangement

OWH   Office of Women's Health (NIH)

oz   ounce

Pp

p   probability

p̄   after

P   pulse

Pa   Pascal (unit of pressure)

PA   Parapsychological Association; physician assistant; professional association

P&A   percussion and auscultation

PAAO   Pan-American Association of Ophthalmology

PAAS   Pan American Allergy Society

PAC   Pediatric AIDS Coalition; political action committee; preadmission certification; premature atrial contraction; products of ambulatory care

PACE   Physician-based Assessment and Counseling for Exercise; Program of All-Inclusive Care for the Elderly

PaCO$_2$ arterial carbon-dioxide pressure (tension)

PADD   Protection and Advocacy for Persons with Developmental Disabilities

PAHO   Pan American Health Organization

PAMA   Pan American Medical Association

PAMI   Primary Angioplasty in Myocardial Infarction (trial)

PANLAR   Pan American League Against Rheumatism

PaO$_2$ arterial oxygen pressure (tension)

Pap   Papanicolaou (smear)

PAP   positive airway pressure

PAR   postanesthesia recovery room

para   paraplegic

Para I   having borne one child (subsequent births are II, III, etc)

PAR-Q   Physical Activity Readiness Questionnaire

PAS   preadmission screening; professional activity study

PASG   pneumatic antishock garment

PATA   Professional Aeromedical Transport Association

PB   paraffin bath

PBL   problem-based learning

pc   *post cibum* (after meals)

PC   personal computer; present complaint; professional corporation

PCA   patient-controlled analgesia

PCB   polychlorinated biphenyl; printed circuit board

PCCM   primary care case manager

PCE   potentially compensable event

PCHRG   Public Citizen Health Research Group

PCLG   Public Citizen Litigation Group

PCN   penicillin

PCO   posterior capsular opacification

PCP   phencyclidine hydrochloride; *Pneumocystis carinii* pneumonia; primary care physician

PCR   polymerase chain reaction (analysis)

PCRM   Physicians Committee for Responsible Medicine

PCRS   Precision Chiropractic Research Society

PD   personality disorder

PDA   Parenteral Drug Association

PDCA   plan-do-check-act (improvement cycle)

PDPC   process decision program chart

PDQ   Physician's Data Query (NIH)

PDR   *Physicians' Desk Reference*; proliferative diabetic retinopathy

PDSA   plan-do-study-act (improvement cycle)

PE   phacoemulsification; physical examination; probable error; pulmonary edema; pulmonary embolism

Ped   pediatrics

PEF   peak expiratory flow

PEFM   peak expiratory flow meter

PEFR   peak expiratory flow rate

PEN   Physicians Education Network

PEP   postexposure prophylaxis

PEPI   Postmenopausal Estrogen/Progestin Interventions (Trial)

per   by; from; according to

PERLA   pupils equal, react to light and accommodation

PERMS   Performance Measures for Managed Behavioral Healthcare Programs

PERT   Program Evaluation and Review Technique

PF   Physicians Forum

PFT   pulmonary function tests

PG   prostaglandin (A, E, or F)

PGH   pituitary growth hormone

PGY-1   postgraduate year 1 (subsequent years are PGY-2, PGY-3, etc.)

PH   past history; public health

PHA   Peruvian Heart Association

PharD   Doctor of Pharmacy

PharM   Master of Pharmacy

PharmB   Bachelor of Pharmacy

PharmD   Doctor of Pharmacy

PhD   Doctor of Philosophy

PHEWA   Presbyterian Health, Education and Welfare Association

PHHSA   Protestant Health and Human Services Assembly

PHLEB   phlebotomist; phlebotomy

PHN   public health nurse

PHO   physician hospital organization

PHPP   Public Health Practice Program (CDC)

PHR   Physicians for Human Rights

PHS   Public Health Service

PHSA   Public Health Service Act

PhysPRC   Physician Payment Review Commission

PI   performance improvement; present illness; protease inhibitor

P&I   pneumonia and influenza

PICA   Porch Index of Communicative Ability

PID   pelvic inflammatory disease

PIH   pregnancy-induced hypertension

PIOP   Pharmacists in Ophthalmic Practice

PIP   peak inspiratory pressure

PIVOT   Prostate Cancer Intervention Versus Observation Trial

PL   Public Law (or federal statute)

PLA   person living with AIDS

PLCO   Prostate, Lung, Colon, Ovarian (cancer screening project)

PLT   platelet

PLWA   person living with AIDS

PM   afternoon (noon until before midnight)

PMA   Pharmaceutical Manufacturers Association; Precision Measurements Association

PMDD   premenstrual dysphoric disorder

PM-DRG   pediatric-modified diagnosis-related group

PMH   past medical history

PM&R   physical medicine and rehabilitation

PMR   polymyalgia rheumatica

PMRS   Parachute Medical Rescue Service

PMS   People's Medical Society; premenstrual syndrome

PMSA   primary metropolitan statistical area

PN   pneumonia; practical nurse

PNP   pediatric nurse practitioner

PNS   peripheral nervous system

po   *per os* (by mouth)

pO$_2$, PO$_2$, PO$_2$ partial pressure of oxygen

POA   pancreatic oncofetal antigen

POAG   primary open-angle glaucoma

POC   plan of care; product of conception

POD   post-operative day

POMR   problem-oriented medical record

PORT   Patient Outcomes Research Team

POS   point of service; positive

POSNA   Pediatric Orthopaedic Society of North America

post   post mortem examination

post-op   post-operative

PP   postpartum; practice parameter

P&Ps   policies and procedures

PPA   Pathology Practice Association

PPC   progressive patient care

PPD   purified protein derivative

PPI   proton pump inhibitor

PPO   preferred provider option; preferred provider organization

PPP   platelet-poor plasma; Preferred Practice Pattern; Prevention Practice Project

PPPF   Positive Pregnancy and Parenting Fitness

PPRC   Physician Payment Review Commission

PPS   Private Practice Section (APTA); prospective payment system; prospective pricing system

Ppt   precipitate

PPV   percent of predicted normal value; positive pressure ventilation

pQCT   peripheral quantitative computed tomography

pr   per rectum

PR   public relations

P&R   pulse and respiration

PRC   Park Ridge Center

PRCLR   PR Committee for Licensing and Registration

PRE   progressive resistance exercise

pre-op   pre-operative

prep   prepare for

PRF   permanent renal failure

PRICE   Physicians for Research in Cost-Effectiveness

PRIM&R   Public Responsibility in Medicine and Research

PRIME-MD   Primary Care Evaluation of Mental Disorders

prn   *pro re na'ta* (as / if needed)

PRO   peer review organization; Peer Review Organization (HCFA)

prog   prognosis

PROM   passive range of motion; programmable read-only memory

ProMED   Program for Monitoring Emerging Diseases

ProPAC   Prospective Payment Assessment Commission

PROS   Pediatric Research in Office Settings

Pro-X   prothrombin time

PRSA   Public Relations Society of America

PS   Psychology Society; Psychometric Society; Psychonomic Society

PSA   prostate-specific antigen

PSC   Program Support Center

PSDA   Patient Self-Determination Act

psi   per square inch

PSI   Parapsychological Services Institute

PSN   provider service network; provider sponsored network

PSO   provider sponsored organization

PSQ   Patient Satisfaction Questionnaire

PSR   Physicians for Social Responsibility

PSRC   Plastic Surgery Research Council

PSRCA   Professional Standards Review Council of America

PSRO   professional standards review organization; professional services review organization

PSS   Patient Satisfaction Scale; Physical Status Scale

PSW   psychiatric social worker

PsyD   Doctor of Psychology

pt   patient

PT   patient; physical therapist; physical therapy; prothrombin time

P&T   pharmacy and therapeutics

PTA   prior to admission

PTAC   (Joint Commission) Professional and Technical Advisory Committee

PTC   plasma thromboplastin component

PTCA   percutaneous transluminal coronary angioplasty

PTH   parathyroid hormone; pathology; posttraumatic headache

PTS   post-traumatic seizures

PTSD   posttraumatic stress disorder

PTSM   plant, technology, and safety management

PTT   partial thromboplastin time

pulv   pulverized (powder)

PVC   premature ventricular contraction

PVD   peripheral vascular disease

PVFHP   Public Voice for Food and Health Policy

PVP   peripheral venous pressure

PVS   persistent vegetative state

PVT   proximal vein thrombosis

PWA   Person with AIDS

PWB   partial weight bearing

PWBA   Pension and Welfare Benefits Administration (VA)

PWC   Physicians Who Care

PYLL   potential years of life lost

Qq

q, Q   *quaque* (each/every); quart

QA   quality assurance

QALY   quality-adjusted life year

QAM   *quaque ante meridiem* (every morning)

QAP   quality assurance program

QC   quality control

QCT   quantitative computed tomography

qd   *quaque die* (every day)

qds   *quater die sumendum* (to be taken four times daily)

QFD   quality function deployment

qh   *quaque hora* (every hour)

QHR   Quality Healthcare Resources

qhs   *quaque hora somni* (every hour of sleep)

QI   quality improvement

QIC   quality improvement council

qid   *quarter in die* (four times a day)

QIP   quality improvement project

QIT   quality improvement team

ql   *quantum libet* (as much as desired)

qm   *quaque mane* (every morning)

QM   quality management

QMNET   Quality Measurement Network

qn   *quaque nocte* (every night)

QNS   quantity not sufficient

qod   *quaque altera die* (every other day)

qoh   *quaque altera hora* (every other hour)

QOL   quality of life

qPM   every night

QPMA   Quality and Productivity Management Association

QRB   *Quality Review Bulletin* (now *The Joint Commission Journal on Quality Improvement*)

qs   quantity sufficient

qt   quart

quad   quadriplegic

quant   quantitative; quantity

QUART   quadrantectomy, axillary dissection, and comprehensive breast irradiation

QWB   quality of well-being

Rr

R   range; respiration; right; roentgen

R̄   average range

Ra, RA   rheumatoid arthritis

RAC   Recombinant DNA Advisory Committee (NIH)

RAD   right axis deviation

RADIUS   Routine Antenatal Diagnostic Imaging Ultrasound Study

RAI   Resident Assessment Instrument (HCFA)

RAIU   radioactive iodine uptake

RAM   random access memory

RAMI   risk-adjusted mortality index

RANCA   Retired Army Nurse Corps Association

RAND   (formerly) Research and Development

RAPS   Regulatory Affairs Professionals Society

RAST   radioallergosorbent test

ray   x-ray

RBBB   right bundle branch block

RBC   red blood cell

RBF   renal blood flow

RBMA   Radiology Business Management Association

RBNI   reported but not incurred

RBRV   resource-based relative value

RBRVS   resource-based relative-value scale

RCC   ratio of cost to charge

RCPS   Royal College of Physicians and Surgeons of the United States of America

RCT   randomized clinical trial; randomized controlled trial

RD   registered dietitian; retinal detachment

R&D   research and development

RDA   recommended daily allowance; recommended dietary allowance

RDI   recommended dietary intake

RDS   respiratory distress syndrome

RDT regular dialysis treatment

RE regarding

REAL Revised European-American Lymphoma (Classification)

REG regular

rehab rehabilitation

REM rapid eye movement

RF rheumatic fever

Rh rhesus (blood factor)

RHC respiration has ceased

RIA radioimmunoassay

RID Registry of Interpreters for the Deaf

RIF reduction in force

RJS Ruth Jackson Orthopaedic Society

RLE right lower extremity

RMAAMT Registered Medical Assistants of American Medical Technologists

RMI relaxation/mental imagery

RN registered nurse

RNA ribonucleic acid

R/O rule out

ROM range of motion; read-only memory

ROS review of systems

RPA Renal Physicians Association

RPR rapid plasma reagin (syphilis test)

RPS Retired Persons Services

RPT registered physical therapist

RQ respiratory quotient

RR recovery room; respiratory rate

R&R rest and relaxation

RRA registered record administrator

RRC Residency Review Committee

RRCEM Residency Review Committee for Emergency Medicine

RRE round, regular, and equal

RRR regular rate and rhythm

RRS Radiation Research Society

RRT registered respiratory therapist

RRTT registered radiation technology therapist

RS Raphael Society

RSA Rehabilitation Services Administration; Research Society on Alcoholism

RSMA Radiological Systems Microfilm Associates

RSMF Royal Society of Medicine Foundation

RSNA Radiological Society of North America

RSRI relative serotonin reuptake inhibitor

RSVP Retired Senior Volunteer Program

RT respiratory therapy

RTC return to clinic

RTI Research Triangle Institute

RTOG Radiation Therapy Oncology Group

rt-PA accelerated recombinant tissue-type plasminogen activator

RTS revised trauma score

RTT registered technology therapist

RU-486 Mifepristone

RUE right upper extremity

RUG Resource Utilization Group

RV right ventricle

RVH right ventricular hypertrophy

RVS relative value scale

RVU relative value unit

RWJF Robert Wood Johnson Foundation

Rx *recipe* (take); prescription; treatment

Ss

s standard deviation

S second; single

$\bar{s}$ without

s^2 sample variance

$s_{\bar{x}}$ standard error

S1–S5 sacral vertebrae

SA single access; surgeon assistant

SAAC Society for the Advancement of Ambulatory Care

SAAST self-administered alcoholism screening test

SAC *Standards for Ambulatory Care*

SAD seasonal affective disorder

SADD Short Alcohol Dependence Data

SAEM Society for Academic Emergency Medicine

SAFP Society of Air Force Physicians

SAGES Society of American Gastrointestinal Endoscopic Surgeons

SAM Society for Adolescent Medicine; Society for Advancement of Management

SAMHSA Substance Abuse and Mental Health Services Administration

SaO$_2$ oxygen saturation

SART   Society for Assisted Reproductive Technology

SASP   Society for the Advancement of Social Psychology

sat   saturate

SAVE   Survival and Ventricular Enlargement (trial)

SB   stillborn

SBBT   specialist in blood bank technology

SBET   Society of Biomedical Equipment Technicians

SBHC   *Standards for Behavioral Health Care*

SBM   Society of Behavioral Medicine

SBO   small bowel obstruction

SBP   Society for Behavioral Pediatrics; systolic blood pressure

SC   Society for Cryobiology; subcutaneous

SCA   Society of Cardiovascular Anesthesiologists

SCA&I   Society for Cardiac Angiography and Interventions

SCASA   Straight Chiropractic Academic Standards Association

SCCM   Society of Critical Care Medicine

ScD   Doctor of Science

SCEH   Society for Clinical and Experimental Hypnosis

SCIA   Smart Card Industry Association

SCID   severe combined immunodeficiencies

SCM   Society for Cardiovascular Management (now ASCP/SCM)

SCME   Society of Clinical and Medical Electrologists

SCORE   Spinal Surgery Outcomes Consortium Research

SCP   specialty care physician

SCT   Society for Clinical Trials

SCVIR   Society of Cardiovascular and Interventional Radiology

SD   standard deviation

SDADA   Seventh-Day Adventist Dietetic Association

SDB   Society for Developmental Biology

SDD   sterile dry dressing

SDFS   Safe and Drug-Free Schools

SDMS   Society of Diagnostic Medical Sonographers

SDP   Shared Decisionmaking Program

sed   sedimentation

SEE   Self-Education and Evaluation (Program)

SEER   Surveillance, Epidemiology, and End Results

segs   segmented white cells

SEIU   Service Employees International Union

SENIC   Study on the Efficacy of Nosocomial Infection Control

sep   separate

SESAP   Surgical Education and Self-Assessment Program

SEXA   single-energy x-ray absorptiometry

SF   salt free; serum ferritin

SF-12   12-Item Short Form General Health Survey

SF-20   20-Item Short Form General Health Survey

SF-36   36-Item Short Form General Health Survey

SFPE   Society of Fire Protection Engineers

SGA   small for gestational age

SGDS   Short Geriatric Depression Scale

SGI   Society for Gynecologic Investigation

SGIM   Society for General Internal Medicine

SGNA   Society of Gastroenterology Nurses and Associates

SGO   Society of Gynecologic Oncologists

SH   social history; Society for Hematopathology

S&H   speech and hearing

SHC   *Standards for Home Care*

SHCN   *Standards for Health Care Networks*

SHFCC   Shriners Hospitals for Crippled Children

SHHV   Society for Health and Human Values

SHL   sensorineural hearing loss

SHMO   social health maintenance organization

SHNS   Society of Head and Neck Surgeons

SHOT   Society for the History of Technology

SHPM   Society for Healthcare Planning and Marketing

SHRM   Society for Human Resource Management

SHSWD   Society for Hospital Social Work Directors

SI   Le Système International d'Unités (International System of Units)

sib   sibling

SICU   surgical intensive care unit

SID   Society for Investigative Dermatology

SIDS   sudden infant death syndrome

SIECUS   Sex Information and Education Council of the United States

sig   significant

SIGBIO   Special Interest Group on Biomedical Computing

SIL   soluble interleuken; squamous intraepithelial lesion

SIM   Society for Information Management

SIP   Sickness Impact Profile

SIRS   systemic inflammatory response syndrome

SIS   Surgical Infection Society

SI units   Système International units

sl   slight

SLE   systemic lupus erythematosus

SLHR   Society for Life History Research

SLR   straight leg raising

sm   small

S&M   sadomasochism; sensory and motor

SMA   Sequential Multiple Analyzer; smooth muscle antibody; Society for Medical Anthropology

SMAST   Short Michigan Alcoholism Screening Test

SMAST-AID   SMAST Adapted to Include Drugs

SMCAF   Society of Medical Consultants to the Armed Forces

SMCR   Society for Menstrual Cycle Research

SMDA   State Medicaid Directors Association

SMFW   Society of Medical Friends of Wine

SMG   specialty medical group

SMH   Section for Metropolitan Hospitals

SMJ   Society of Medical Jurisprudence

SMMSE   Standardized Mini-Mental Status Examination

SMO   Society of Military Ophthalmologists

SMO-HNS   Society of Military Otolaryngologists-Head and Neck Surgeons

SMOS   Society of Military Orthopaedic Surgeons

SMR   standardized mortality rate

SMRI   Society for Magnetic Resonance Imaging

SN   Society for Neuroscience

SNACC   Society of Neurosurgical Anesthesia and Critical Care

SNE   Society for Nutrition Education

SNF   skilled nursing facility

SNM   Society of Nuclear Medicine

SNU   skilled nursing unit

SO   significant other

SOA   Society of Actuaries

SOAP   Society for Obstetric Anesthesia and Perinatology; subjective, objective, assessment, and plan

SOB   shortness of breath

SOC   Statement of Conditions; statement of construction

SOCA   suffuse osmotic chemisorb asphyxiation

SOEH   Society for Occupational and Environmental Health

SOF   Study of Osteoporotic Fractures

SOFT   Society of Forensic Toxicologists

SOHNN   Society of Otorhinolaryngology and Head/Neck Nurses

sol   solution

SOP   standard operating procedures

SOPHE   Society for Public Health Education

sos   *si opus sit* (if necessary)

SOT   Society of Toxicology

SOW   scope of work

S/P   status post

SPA   Single-photon absorptiometry; Society for Personality Assessment

SPAB   Society of Psychologists in Addictive Behaviors

SPAF   Stroke Prevention in Atrial Fibrillation (study)

SPBC   Society of Professional Business Consultants

SPC   statistical process control

SPCAP   Society of Professors of Child and Adolescent Psychiatry

SPCLS   *Standards for Pathology and Clinical Laboratory Services*

SPCS   Statistical Process Control Society

SPD   Society for Pediatric Dermatology

SPDC   Sensible-Problem Drinking Classification

spec   specimen

SPECT   single-photon emission computed tomography

sp fl   spinal fluid

sp gr   specific gravity

SPINAF   Stroke Prevention in Nonrheumatic Atrial Fibrillation (study)

SPIP   Standards for Pediatric Immunization Practices

SPM   Society of Prospective Medicine

SPN   Senior Plan Network

SPO   status post-operative

spon   spontaneous

SPP   Society for Pediatric Psychology

SPR   Society for Pediatric Radiology; Society for Pediatric Research; Society for Psychophysiological Research

SPRINT I, II   Secondary Prevention Reinfarction Israeli Nifedipine Trial

SPSLGI   Society for the Psychological Study of Lesbian and Gay Issues

SPSSI   Society for Psychological Study of Social Issues

SPU   Society for Pediatric Urology

SQ   subcutaneous

SQC   statistical quality control

SR   systems review

SRCD   Society for Research in Child Development

SRDRG   severity-refined diagnosis-related group

SRE   Society of Reproductive Endocrinologists

SRF   survey report form

SRHP   Section for Rehabilitation Hospitals and Programs

SROA   Society for Radiation Oncology Administrators

SRS   Scoliosis Research Society; Sleep Research Society; Social Relationship Scale; Society for Reproductive Surgeons

s̄s̄   one half

SS   social service; sum of squares

S&S   signs and symptoms

SSA   Social Security Administration

SSAT   Society for Surgery of the Alimentary Tract

SSB   Society for the Study of Blood

SSBD   Society for the Study of Breast Disease

SSI   Social Security insurance; Supplemental Security Income; surgical site infection

SSMPP   Society for the Study of Male Psychology and Physiology

SSO   Society of Surgical Oncology

SSP   (Joint Commission) Standards and Survey Procedures (Committee)

SSR   Society for the Study of Reproduction

SSRH   General Constituency Section for Small or Rural Hospitals

SSRI   selective serotonin reuptake inhibitor

SSSB   Society for the Study of Social Biology

SSSS   Society for the Scientific Study of Sex

SSTAR   Society for Sex Therapy and Research

ST   speech therapist

stat   immediately

STAT   Stop Teen-Age Addiction to Tobacco

STD   sexually transmissible disease; sexually transmitted disease

STF   special tube feeding

STFM   Society of Teachers of Family Medicine

STMS   Short Test of Mental Status

STOMACH   Study of Management and Costs of *Helicobacter pylori* Infection

STP   situation, target, proposal (brainstorming technique); Society of Toxicologic Pathologists

STQ   Safe Times Questionnaire (mnemonic for sexuality, affect/abuse, family, examination, timing, immunizations, minerals, education/employment, safety)

STR   Society of Thoracic Radiology

STS   Skinner's Trauma Scale; Society of Thoracic Surgeons

subq   subcutaneous

SUO-HNS   Society of University Otolaryngologists-Head and Neck Surgeons

supp   suppository

SUPPORT   Study to Understand Prognoses and Preferences for Outcomes and Risks of Treatment (prognostic model)

SUS   Society of University Surgeons

SUU   Society of University Urologists

SVN   Society for Vascular Nursing

SVS   Society for Vascular Surgery

SVT   Society of Vascular Technology

SW   social work; social worker

SWORD   Survival with Oral *d*-Sotalol

Sx   symptom

sympt   symptom

syr   syrup

Tt

t   teaspoon

T   occupancy factor

T   tablespoon; temperature

T1–T12   thoracic vertebrae

TA   technology assessment

T&A   tonsillectomy and adenoidectomy

TAANA   The American Association of Nurse Attorneys

tab   tablet

TABS   tablets

T-ACE   tolerance, annoyed by criticism, cut down on drinking, eye opener

TANK   Floatation Tank Association

TAP   The Angel Planes

TAPA   Turkish American Physicians Association

TAT   thematic apperception test; turnaround time

TB   tuberculosis

TBI   traumatic brain injury

tbsp   tablespoon

TBW   total body water

TC   throat culture

3TC   lamivudine

T&C   type and crossmatch

TCA   Tissue Culture Association; tricyclic antidepressant

TCC   The College of Chaplains

TC&DB   turn, cough, and deep breath

TCN   tetracycline

TCSG   The Center for Social Gerontology

TD   transverse diameter

TEC   Technology Evaluation Center

TEE   transesophageal echocardiography

TEFRA   Tax Equity and Fiscal Responsibility Act

temp, TEMP   temperature

TENS   transcutaneous electric nerve stimulation

TG   triglyceride

THF   The Healthcare Forum

THR   total hip replacement

TIA   transient ischemic attack

tid   *ter in die* (three times a day)

TID   time interval difference (imaging)

TIE   The Information Exchange on Young Adult Chronic Patients

TIME   Toolkit of Instruments to Measure End of life care

TIMI   Thrombolysis in Myocardial Infarction (trial)

tinc   tincture

TIUP   term intrauterine pregnancy

TKR   total knee replacement

TL   tubal ligation

TLB   The Living Bank

TM   transcendental meditation; tympanic membrane

TMD   temporomandibular disorder

TMJ   temporomandibular joint

TMP/SMX   trimethoprim-sulfamethoxazole

TNM   Tumor-Node-Metastasis (System)

TNS   transcutaneous nerve simulation

TOC   test of cure

tomo   tomogram

TP   total protein

tPA   tissue plasminogen activator; tissue-type plasminogen activator

t-PA   tissue plasminogen activator; tissue-type plasminogen activator

TPA   third-party administrator; tissue plasminogen activator

TPL   third party liability

TPLA   The Product Liability Alliance

TPN   total parenteral nutrition

TP&P   time, place, and person

TPR   temperature, pulse, and respiration

TQM   total quality management

Tr   trace

TRACE   Trandolapril Cardiac Evaluation

TRISS   Trauma and Injury Severity Score

TRUS   transrectal ultrasound

TS   Teratology Society; transferrin saturation; Transplantation Society; Trauma Score

TSD   Tay-Sachs disease

T-set   tracheotomy set

TSH   thyroid-stimulating hormone; thyrotropin

tsp   teaspoon

T-spine   thoracic spine

TSS   toxic shock syndrome

TSSNM   Technologist Section of the Society of Nuclear Medicine

TST   tuberculin skin test

TTE   transthoracic echocardiography

TTO   time trade-off

TU   tuberculin unit

TUR   transurethral resection

TURP   transurethral prostatectomy; transurethral resection of prostate

TWEAK   tolerance, worry, eye-openers, anger, cutting down (mnemonic for alcoholism test)

Tx   transplantation; treatment

T&X   type and crossmatch

Uu

U   unit

UA, U/A   urinalysis

UAPD   Union of American Physicians and Dentists

UAREP   Universities Associated for Research and Education in Pathology

UB-92   Uniform Bill of 1992

UBS   United Blood Service

U&C   urethral and cervical

UCC   United Cancer Council

UCDS   Uniform Clinical Data Set

UCI   urethral catheter in

UCL   upper control limit

UCO   urethral catheter out

UCPA   United Cerebral Palsy Association

UCR   usual, customary, and reasonable (charge)

ud   *ud dictum* (as directed)

UD   unit dose

UGI   upper gastrointestinal

UGME   undergraduate medical education

UHC   University HealthSystem Consortium

UHDDS   Uniform Hospital Discharge Data Set

UHMS   Undersea and Hyperbaric Medical Society

UI   urinary incontinence

UL   Underwriters Laboratories

UMANA   Ukrainian Medical Association of North America

UM-CIDI   University of Michigan Composite International Diagnostic Interview

UMDNS   Universal Medical Device Nomenclature System

UNESCO   United Nations Educational, Scientific and Cultural Organization

ung   *unguentum* (ointment)

unk   unknown

UNOCCAP   Use, Need, Outcomes, and Costs in Child and Adolescent Populations (study)

UNOS   United Network for Organ Sharing

UPDRS   Unified Parkinson's Disease Rating Scale

UR   utilization review

URAC   Utilization Review Accreditation Commission

URI   upper respiratory infection

URT   upper respiratory tract

US   ultrasound

USAFP   Uniformed Services Academy of Family Physicians

USAID   United States Agency for International Development

USAN   United States Adopted Names

USC   United States Code

USCLHO   United States Conference of Local Health Officers

USDA   United States Department of Agriculture

USFCC   United States Federation for Culture Collections

USFMG   United States foreign medical graduate

USI   urinary stress incontinence

USMBHA   United States-Mexico Border Health Association

USMG   United States medical graduate

USP   *United States Pharmacopeia; United States Pharmacopeil Convention*

USPC   United States Pharmacopeial Convention

USPSTF   U.S. Preventive Services Task Force

UTI   urinary tract infection

UTV   ultrasound transmission velocity

UV   ultraviolet

UVR   ultraviolet radiation

Vv

v   degree of freedom

V   volume

VA   Department of Veterans Affairs; Veterans Administration; visual acuity

VAcc   visual acuity with correction

vag, VAG   vaginal

VAMC   VA Medical Center; Veterans Affairs Medical Center

VAph   visual acuity with pinhole

VAsc   visual acuity without correction

VBA   Veterans Benefits Administration

VBAC   vaginal birth after cesarean section

VC   vital capacity

VCT   venous clotting time

VD   venereal disease

VDRL   Venereal Disease Research Laboratories (syphilis test)

VF   ventricular fibrillation

VHA   Veterans Health Administration; Voluntary Hospitals of America

VHD   valvular heart disease

VHS   Value Health Sciences

VI   volume index

VICA   Vision Council of America

vit   vitamin

VLBW   very low birth weight

VLDL   very-low-density lipoprotein

VNA   visiting nurse association

VNAA   Visiting Nurse Associations of America

VNS   visiting nurse service

VO, V/O   verbal order

VOCA   Victims of Crime Act of 1984

vol   volume

VP   venous pressure

VPI   Virginia Polytechnic Institute (anaerobic culture)

VPMS   Virchow-Pirquet Medical Society

VQ   ventilation quotient

VS   vital signs

VSS   vital signs stable

VT   ventricular tachycardia

VTE   venous thromboembolism

W   widowed; white

WA   Wellness Associates

WAN   wide area network

WB   Western blot; whole blood

WBC   white blood cell; white blood count; white blood cell count

WBGH   Washington Business Group on Health

wc, W/c   wheelchair

WC   workers' compensation

wd   well developed

WE   Women's Caucus of the Endocrine Society

WEHAC   Wills Eye Hospital Annual Conference

WF   Working Formulation of Non-Hodgkin's Lymphomas for Clinical Usage

WFL   within functional limits

WHAN   Wellness and Health Activation Networks

WHI   Women's Health Initiative (NIH)

WHO   World Health Organization

WHO–ILAR COPCORD   World Health Organization–International League of Associations for Rheumatology Community Oriented Program for the Control of Rheumatic Diseases

WHR   Women and Health Roundtable

WIC   Women, Infants, and Children's (supplemental food program)

wk, WK   week

WMA   World Medical Assembly

WMC   warm moist compress

WMS   Wilderness Medical Society

wn   well nourished

WNL   within normal limits

WOMAC   Western Ontario and McMaster Universities Osteoarthritis Index

WP   word processing

WPB   whirlpool bath

WPR   written progress report

wt, WT   weight

W/U   work-up

$\bar{x}$ except

X   multiply by; times; value

YAG   yttrium aluminum garnet (laser)

yo   years old

yr, YR   year

ZDV   zidovudine

ZEBRA   Zero Balanced Reimbursement Account

zig   zoster immune globulin